THE HIDDEN EUROPE

WHAT EASTERN EUROPEANS CAN TEACH US

FRANCIS TAPON

This book's buzz

"Francis Tapon is a modern incarnate of the spirit of Solon or Pericles: he travels to foreign countries to watch things, for the sake of contemplation. And he does it with an extremely sharp eye and lot of wit. *The Hidden Europe: What Eastern Europeans Can Teach Us* is not only the book of the year; it also sets the twenty-first century's standard for travelogues." — **Flórián Farkas, Editor-in-Chief of the *Journal of Eurasian Studies***

"*The Hidden Europe* is a brilliant and insightful book. Francis Tapon travels for years visiting every Eastern European at least twice. What emerges is a travelogue on steroids. It's profound, but has a light tone. You'll learn much and laugh often." — **Amar Bhidé, Professor at the Fletcher School of Law and Diplomacy at Tufts University**

"Francis Tapon is the master of taking highly complex issues about Eastern Europe and making them easy to understand and enjoyable to read. *The Hidden Europe* is a competition between profound insights and devilish humor. Either way, the reader wins." — **Marco Iansiti, Harvard Business School professor**

"This is the indispensable book for understanding Eastern Europe today as the area is on the verge of integrating into and perhaps overtaking Western Europe. With wit and perception, Francis Tapon takes you on a wonderful journey." — **Peter Stansky, Professor of History, Stanford University**

"In an age where travel books are increasingly about the latest homogenized fads, Francis Tapon reminds us of the stark differences between mere tourism and real travel. Combining sharp wit with casual style, he has produced a charming and insightful portrait of a swath of Europe still defining itself, and brings to life the large identities of small places." — **Parag Khanna, author of *How to Run the World***

"*The Hidden Europe* reveals a side of Europe that few know well. The book is entertaining and instructive. You may think you know Europe, but this book will change your perspective forever." — **Neven Borak, Adviser to the Governor of the Bank of Slovenia and author of *How the Yugoslav Economy Worked and How It Collapsed***

"When I last visited Eastern Europe in 1969, I failed in my goal of exploring its mountains. Luckily Francis Tapon's thrilling book has given me a you-are-there, vicarious sense of what I missed all those years ago. This new book is another triumph for our Great World Traveler, Francis Tapon." — **Ron Strickland, Author of *Pathfinder***

THE HIDDEN EUROPE
www.FrancisTapon.com
WEDEN
FINLAND
HELSINKI
OCKHOLM
TALLINN
ESTONIA
"The Ural Mountains"
RUSSIA
RIGA
LATVIA
MOSCOW
LITHUANIA
VILNIUS
KALININGRAD
MINSK
OLAND
BELARUS
WARSAW
KYIV
LIC
UKRAINE
SLOVAKIA
RATISLAVA
BUDAPEST
MOLDOVA
CHISINAU
NGARY
ROMANIA
IA
BELGRADE
ND
OVINA
BUCHAREST
SERBIA
BLACK SEA
KOSOVO
ENEGRO
PRISHTINA
SOFIA
BULGARIA
GORICA
SKOPJE
BANIA
MACEDONIA
TIRANA
ANKARA
GREECE
TURKEY

"Francis Tapon is the next Bill Bryson! Tapon's WanderLearn Series should be called the LaughLearn Series: it's funny and educational." **— Lawrence J. Leigh, Visiting Professor at the University of Belgrade**

"*The Hidden Europe* combines insightful analysis with a fascinating travelogue. It serves as a supplementary travel book for the serious tourist and it makes the reader think. It is a good read." **— Neil Mitchell, Senior Lawyer for the Center for International Legal Studies in Salzburg, Austria**

"*The Hidden Europe* is the kind of book you wish you had in school—it presents facts in a fun and unforgettable way. Learning has never been so entertaining!" **— Bruce Ward, President, ChooseOutdoors.org**

"Whereas some consider a three-week vacation long, Francis travels for three years! *The Hidden Europe* cleverly shares the inevitable wisdom and insights that comes with a long voyage." **— Laurie Bagley, Author of *Summit!***

"Francis Tapon is a rare person. He's an adventurer who has visited much of the world, a student of history and culture who learns through first-hand experience, and a teacher who finds life lessons everywhere he goes. The countries of Eastern Europe, which I visited in the 1990s, aren't among the more glamorous travel destinations, but are absolutely fascinating. Francis has brilliantly captured their essence in this highly readable, illuminating, and entertaining book. I enthusiastically recommend it." **— Hal Urban, Author of *Life's Greatest Lessons***

"*The Hidden Europe* is an insightful look into Eastern Europe that weaves your mind in and out of the region and encourages your imagination to physically take you there." **— Anil Polat, Travel Blogger, FoXnoMad.com**

"Francis Tapon found a unique, unexpected approach to present Eastern Europe. His accounts stem from his open curiosity accompanied by sound reasoning. His work, which includes a meticulous study on the history of the region, is most outstanding. As an amateur historian, I can also recommend his work as the clearest and most objective recent account on Hungarian history. Francis Tapon created an overview on this delicate subject with such clarity, focus, yet lightness, which I thought was impossible. I recommend his work not only to American readers, who will find it refreshing and exciting, but to every Eastern European reader as well. This book has a true potential to change the air of lingering suspicion among Eastern European nations to that of heartfelt friendship." **— Dr. Janos Molnar, Hungarian cell and molecular biologist**

Dedicated to a special mouse

and

René Tapon, my French father, who introduced me to Europe

Cover design by Yasmin Rahmani

Printed using soy ink because it's much more eco-friendly than traditional ink. Printed on acid free, 100% recycled paper (70% post-consumer content) because we love trees. All this makes the book more expensive which means we'll sell fewer copies, but we figure this planet is worth it.

1.0 Edition

First Printing 2012

Library of Congress Cataloging-in-Publication Data

Tapon, Francis

The hidden Europe: what Eastern Europeans can teach us / Francis Tapon

ISBN 978-0-9765812-2-2

TRAVEL / Europe / Eastern

Preassigned Control Number

Visit FrancisTapon.com

Printed and bound at Thomson Press (India) Ltd.

Contents

Introduction—stepping Into the Hidden Europe

"This would be a pretty lousy way to die," I thought.

I was locked in an outhouse with no way out. Outhouses sometimes have two latches—one on the outside and one on the inside. The outside latch keeps the door shut to prevent rodents and other creatures who like hanging out in crap from coming in. Somehow that outside latch accidentally closed, thereby locking me in this smelly toilet. I was wearing just a thin rain jacket and the temperature was rapidly dropping.

"This stinks," I mumbled. It was midnight, I was above the Arctic Circle, and the temperatures at night would be just above freezing. There was no one around for kilometers. If I didn't get out, I could freeze to death in this tiny, smelly, fly-infested shithole.

My mom would kill me if I died so disgracefully. She would observe that when Elvis died next to a toilet, he was in Graceland. I, on the other hand, was in Finland, not far from Santa Claus. This Nordic country was my warm up before setting out to visit all 25 countries in Eastern Europe over five months.

The fool wonders. The wise man wanders. — Susan Rea

I had started my hike at 5:30 p.m. and planned to hike all night. It was June 21 and the sun doesn't set when you're above the Arctic Circle on the summer solstice. So it really doesn't matter when you hike. At 11:00 p.m. I ate some food in a deserted cabin and then went to use the outhouse. I tried all sorts of clever ways of getting out and they all failed. Then I thought, "Wait a sec. I am an American. Therefore, I must love violence and be a brute. Hell, Arnold Schwarzenegger was my governor. What would he do?"

I decided that the old fashioned, just-bang-the-door-down method was best. I gave the door a swift kick. BLAM!

Nothing.

"Okay. . ." I took a deep breath of the foul air and then let out the hardest kick my legs could deliver. BING! BAM! BOOM! The door stubbornly stared at me.

I sat on the toilet to think. Finland has one of the most sophisticated telecommunications infrastructures in the world, far better than America. I may be in the middle of some remote forest around the Arctic Circle, but I wouldn't be surprised if those crafty Finns had a cellular phone tower nearby. Checking my phone, I had a solid reception.

"Gotta love the Finns," I smiled to myself. So as my California friends were getting ready for lunch, I punched out a text message to describe my predicament: *"Funny, but scary: I am trapped in an outhouse. The outside lock flipped when I went in. Nobody here. Getting cold. Trying 2 bang out."*

Most were busy eating a tofu burger so they didn't get back to me. One friend, though, suggested "CALL 911!"

"Good idea," I thought. But then I remembered that dialing 911 in another country usually doesn't get you the emergency services. However, it might get you a pizza delivery service, which would be nice.

On the other hand, even if I got an emergency service, I was so deep in the Arctic wilderness they wouldn't get here until morning at the earliest. By then I would be a frozen Popsicle. So I went back to kicking. Then I threw my measly body into the door a few times. I cursed, "I knew I should have eaten more cheeseburgers before I left!" I slammed my shoulder into the door so many times that I was nearly breaking a sweat in the frigid temperatures. "Damn it, Hollywood makes this look so easy!"

I screamed and lunged at the door with vigor. The door put me back in my place: on the toilet seat. I panted in the putrid air wondering what else I could do. I started to shiver as my sweat cooled my body. I couldn't tip over the outhouse. I couldn't break open the roof. Finally, I had one last idea: Matrix-like, Keanu Reeves rapid-fire kicks. I may not be The One, but I was the only one around, so I better kick some ass.

I lay down so that my back rested on the toilet seat while I looked at the ceiling. My legs were cocked close to my chest, ready to repeatedly slam the obstinate door into submission. I took a few deep breaths and then let out a fury of kung fu kicks that would make Bruce Lee proud. After 20 kicks (and nearly falling into the toilet), the tenacious door flew open.

I'm not as manly as you might think: I didn't even break the lock. The vibrations from the continuous kicks just made it unlatch. Nevertheless, I breathed a sigh of relief (and some fresh air), and hiked the rest of the night.

> *I had always wanted to live an adventurous life. It took a long time to realize that I was the only one who was going to make an adventurous life happen to me. — Richard Bach*

It was June 2004, exactly three years after I set off on my Appalachian Trail thru-hike. I craved another adventure. Once again, I wanted to wander and learn. I had visited Prague and Budapest in 1992, and Russia and Ukraine in 1999. However, the rest of Eastern Europe was still a mystery to me.

Therefore, in 2004, I set a simple goal: visit every country in Eastern Europe in six months and see what I could learn. I wanted the Eastern Europeans to teach me about their cuisine, history, languages, sites, innovations, economy, religion, and drinking habits. Then after five years, in 2009, I would return to spend two and half years there to see what's changed. By 2011, I had spent three years collecting the wisdom of the Hidden Europe.

This book is organized by country, which means that it's not in chronological order since I visited each country at least twice over a seven-year period. I mention dates for clarity and for the sake of any detective who wants to reconstruct the sequence of events. So get ready to hop back and forth in time.

Reopening the American mind

I am a first generation American. My mom was born and raised in Santiago, Chile. Her dad was laid off from his factory job when she was 16 years old, so she quit high school to work to help support the family. When she was 25, she emptied her retirement fund so that she could have enough money to buy a one-way ticket to America. She arrived in the United States with only $300 in her pocket—too little to buy a flight back to Chile. It was far easier to immigrate to America in 1964 than it is today. She barely spoke any English when she arrived alone in San Francisco. Within two weeks, however, she landed a job that didn't require speaking much English—being a clerk at Bank of America. My father was born and raised in France. He grew up with the Great Depression, the Nazi occupation, and World War II (WWII). Yes, my dad had issues, and not just because he's French.

By 1947, France's military was getting involved in Vietnam and Algeria. My grandfather didn't want to lose his only son after having lost his brother in World War I (WWI). Therefore, he put my 17-year-old dad on a one-way boat voyage to Buenos Aires, Argentina. He lived there for seven years under the rule of Juan and Evita Peron. He witnessed how their populist policies destroyed the economy, and so, at the age of 25, he immigrated to Philadelphia. After two years there, he crisscrossed the United States in his car and parked it in San Francisco. He started working there and several years later, he met my mom. They started a small business that imported goods from Latin America. In short, they achieved the American Dream.

My parents didn't just bring their bodies and hard work ethic to America. They brought their ideas. It's that fresh input of ideas that has kept America competitive and strong since its founding. America's open mind and flexibility helped it become the most powerful nation in the world. However, the fear of terrorism and xenophobic worries has made it incredibly difficult to immigrate here. Millions of brilliant minds lie outside our borders yearning to get in. If we don't get them, another country will. Our competitive advantage will decrease and the American Era will end.

Therefore, the purpose of this book isn't to just share Eastern European insights. Its purpose is also to stir curiosity in you. I hope to inspire you to wander and learn. I want America to open its borders and brains not just to the brightest minds of Eastern Europe, but to the brightest minds of the world.

When it's OK to stereotype

This book may offend you. You will read sweeping statements like "Slovenians are polyglots," or "Latvians like to dress up," or "Americans are idiots." Some people hate such stereotyping and generalizing, especially when it's negative. Nobody will complain if I say "Ukrainian women are beautiful," but they will say I'm a closed-minded, superficial American if I say "Polish women are fat slobs." Politically correct folks tell us that we should never stereotype. "Generalizations are always bad," they declare, not realizing the contradiction in their statement.

If our ancestors didn't stereotype, we'd be dead. Let's say cavemen with blue dots on their cheeks are responsible for killing half of your tribe. What would happen to your idealistic neighbor if she refused to generalize those with the blue dot? Let's just say she would produce few descendants. Hence, the human brain is wired to look for patterns and to categorize everything. We can't suppress that. It's part of being human. That's why when we're looking for potential suicide bombers, we instinctively look for young Arab men and not old ladies from Sweden.

You think you don't stereotype? Sure you do. You avoid dark alleys with disheveled humans, because you know that you're more likely to be assaulted there than in an office building. You stereotype office workers as peaceful creatures and gun totting gangsters in alleyways as high risk. Of course, these generalizations are sometimes wrong: office workers go on shooting sprees and gangsters can help you to a hospital. However, you continue to depend on stereotypes to get you through the day.

Stereotypes simply summarize the tendencies of a group of people. I've tried to document Eastern European tendencies, while recognizing that there are no absolutes and that there are plenty of exceptions. Therefore, when I say, "Albanians are friendly," obviously there are plenty who are assholes. Pointing out all the exceptions gets tedious after a while, especially for the intelligent reader who realizes that a generalization is not an absolute statement.

Admittedly, stereotyping gets tricky when you have few data points. Although I spent three years in Eastern Europe, sometimes I only stayed two weeks in a particular country. I would have loved to spend months (or years) in each country, but with 25 Eastern European countries, I had to keep moving. Therefore, a few of my observations are based on just a brief glimpse of a country. If I was unlucky to meet the only four jerks who live in Lithuania (and met no one else), it was hard not to walk away concluding that Lithuanians are jerks. I did my best to get around these limitations. For instance, I would ask neighboring countries, "Are all Lithuanians really jerks?"

They would usually reply, "No, but Americans are."

By asking the locals about how their life is really like, I could make up for my lack of data points. On the other hand, locals also make mistakes and spread false stereotypes. Bulgarians told me that most Romanians are thieves, which is obviously wrong, since Bulgarians are so poor that there is nothing to steal! (Relax, Bulgarians, I'm kidding.)

A great way to avoid the pitfalls of anecdotal evidence is to consider polls that survey thousands of people. Thus, we'll consider what reputable international pollsters, such the Pew Research Center and Gallup, reveal about Eastern Europeans, while recognizing that surveys have their own shortcomings. By combining extensive personal travel experiences with statistics and surveys, we should be able to paint a fair and accurate description of each country. You'll finally understand how an Albanian differs from a Kosovar.

Why not avoid stereotyping completely? "Please don't!" cry the Baltic states. Estonians, Latvians, and Lithuanians hate that the world thinks they are all the same. They each want their own identity. In short, they want their own unique stereotype. Slovaks, Belarusians, Slovenians, Croatians, Macedonians, Bosnians, and Ukrainians created their countries partly because they were tired of being lumped together with some other nationality and identity. Each region has a distinct personality. To claim that Germans and Italians, for example, have the same character is idiotic. It's cute and idealistic to believe that we should just avoid labels altogether and simply call ourselves *Homo sapiens,* but humans demand more granularity than that. Lastly, if we simply say, "There are all types of people everywhere," we miss an interesting opportunity to understand the traditional values, beliefs, and characteristics of a people.

Hence, the solution isn't to avoid generalizing—that's impossible. Instead, the solution is to have flexible stereotypes and to be open to exceptions. *More importantly, if you see enough exceptions, consider changing the stereotype.* For example, let's say you believe that most Arab men are suicidal, religious maniacs. However, after visiting an Arabic country, you quickly notice that most young men aren't blowing themselves up. Now you can create a new stereotype: *young Arab men are friendly, peaceful, and have fewer weapons than the average American.* In short, you still have a stereotype (because your brain demands it), but you've adjusted it to the new information you learned.

> *Travel is fatal to prejudice, bigotry, and narrow-mindedness. . . . Broad, wholesome, charitable views of men and things cannot be acquired by vegetating in one little corner of the earth all one's lifetime. — Mark Twain*

To avoid making inaccurate stereotypes, I sought to experience the country from the ground level—where the "real people" live. Unlike most tourists, I avoided hotels, fancy restaurants, taxis, and rented cars. I rode crowded buses, ate sketchy food from street vendors, shopped at farmers' markets, hitchhiked, and stayed with locals whenever possible. In short, I did my best to detect the subtle differences among Eastern European countries, while trying not to impose stereotypes or invent differences that don't exist. Of course, everything is extremely nuanced, especially a country's history.

Learning history from the locals

Even before this book went to press, it was already pissing off some people. When I shared early versions of it with Eastern Europeans, they would occasionally say, "I loved it! You're so accurate at depicting the people and places in Eastern Europe. However, what you said about *my* country is completely inaccurate and unfair. You're just like every other American: arrogant and stupid."

For example, some Albanians thought I depicted every country in the Balkans well except for Albania. Meanwhile, some Macedonians thought I depicted every country in the Balkans well except for Macedonia. In addition, some Eastern Europeans disagreed with how I summarized their country's history. As one Serbian put it in an e-mail to me, "U R so full of incompetence and not up to this story. But that's only my opinion and don't let me discourage U. Keep up the good work."

> *Pay no attention to what the critics say; there has never been set up a statue in honor of a critic.*
> *— Jean Sibelius, a Finnish composer*

Although I wanted to learn everything about each country from its locals, this methodology has its flaws. First, locals often lack accurate knowledge beyond their small region. Second, their impression of their neighboring countries frequently has no empirical evidence, just hearsay. Third, their recollection of history is highly selective. People remember and forget different events. They emphasize certain events while overlooking others. Every country does this. Throughout my travels in Eastern Europe, people would vividly recount how their country came to be and the root cause of their country's problems. I would travel 100 kilometers to another region and listen to others describe, with equal passion and zeal, the same events in a completely different way.

> *One of the things important about history is to remember the true history. — George W. Bush*

Not exactly, George. I had always believed that there was only one true, objective version of history. In theory, that might be true, but in practice it isn't. First, even if all history books in the world said the same thing, what really matters is what people believe, because that is what they will teach the next generation. It is said that "victors write history." That's true, but the losers don't necessarily read or believe it. Instead, they tell their children "what really happened."

Although I've thoroughly researched Eastern Europe's history, retelling history is a thankless task because it's impossible to please everyone. Moreover, I'm not a scholarly historian, so some snooty PhD might tell me that my facts are slightly off. Still, there's often no consensus even among professional historians, who love to gather in conferences and deliver astonishingly dull speeches meant to cure anyone of insomnia.

> *History is a set of lies agreed upon. — Napoleon Bonaparte*

If you dig deep enough, perhaps you can uncover the truth, but it is often a murky and tricky affair. However, in some ways the truth doesn't really matter to me. *I'm not a historian. I'm an explorer.* For me, perception is reality; the people's version of history is, for this book, the history that matters. I wanted to hear the history parents tell their children.

Even when I knew the locals were wrong, I had little hope (and even less interest) in changing their minds. My goal was to understand them, their reasoning, their beliefs, and their world view. This book compares their view of history with "what really happened," while recognizing that my sources (as objective as I hope they are) have their own biases. If all this ends up making you more confused than ever, wonderful. Welcome to Eastern Europe.

A not-so-stupid question: where is Eastern Europe?

Asking, "Where is Eastern Europe?" seems as stupid as asking, "Who is buried in Grant's tomb?" Obviously, Eastern Europe is in the eastern part of Europe. However, where to draw that line is extremely controversial. Indeed, it's hard to find two people who agree on which countries are in Eastern Europe.

Back in the good old Cold War days, defining Eastern Europe was easy: it was made up of all those losers who were on the wrong side of the Iron Curtain. Eastern Europe had those backward, communist countries which were frozen in the Stone Age.

Because the world had such a low opinion of Eastern Europe, nowadays nobody wants to admit that they live there. For example, let's just look at the Baltic countries. I've met Estonians who assert that they are in Northern Europe, Latvians who proclaim that they are in Central Europe, and Lithuanians who argue that they are in *Western* Europe!

If you were to believe everyone you talked to, you would conclude that Eastern Europe just doesn't exist! When pressed, Eastern Europeans admit that Eastern Europe exists, but they all believe that the region starts just east of whatever country they happen to live in. I like this definition. My father was French, so Eastern Europe, for me, starts in Germany. Sorry, Germans.

If you're European, it's time to review Geography 101. Any territory can be divided in a number of ways. For instance, you can divide it east-west and/or north-south. If you like, you can create a *central* region. To have even more granularity, you can create a northeast region, a southeast region, and so on. However, sometimes people don't want all those options. *They just want a simple binary division* (thereby eliminating the concept of a central region). For example, if you want to divide the US with a north-south split, you would probably use the old Civil War dividing lines. If you want a simple east-west split, you would use the Mississippi River, even though it's an imperfect split. Chicago boys may dislike being called an Eastern American just as a Hungarian might dislike being called an Eastern European. They both would yell, "We're *Central*, not Eastern!" Similarly, someone from Montana might say, "I'm not in the Western US, I'm in the *Northern* US!" They would all have a good point. However, if *central* and *northern* are not options (and they are not, when you divide a territory with a simple east-west split), then you must choose a side. You might not like east-west splits, but there's nothing evil about dividing any region that way. So get over it.

However, we still have the challenge of deciding where that east-west line should be. Let's be scientific about it. Geologists agree that Eastern Europe ends at the Ural Mountains, which lie hundreds of kilometers east of Moscow. It's 5,200 kilometers (3,250 miles) from Lisbon, Portugal to Perm, Russia (a city next to the Urals). The halfway point is Wrocław, a Polish city near the German border. If you extend a north-south line through Wrocław, it would cross the Czech Republic, Austria, and western Croatia. Only Slovenia would find itself on the west side of that dividing line (you can hear the Slovenians cheering now). In short, this 50/50 geographical split results in an east-west border that is quite close to the Cold War dividing line.

Another way to solve this tedious question is to learn where experts say is Europe's geographic center. Wherever that point is, we could project a north-south line across it, thereby clearly marking Europe's east-west division. Unfortunately, geographers can't agree on all the edges of Europe, so they can't agree on its exact center. Geographers have placed Europe's center as far west as Dresden (Germany), as far east as Rakhiv (Ukraine), and as far north as Estonia's island of Saaremaa.

> *War is God's way of teaching Americans geography.*
> *— Ambrose Bierce*

Before we invest too much time finding the perfect 50/50 split, let's remember that many east-west (or north-south) divisions are asymmetrical. For example, about two-thirds of America rests on one side of the Mississippi River. Russia's east-west line is the Ural Mountains, even though that results in a 75/25 split. Cities often have artificial and arbitrary east-west divisions that are hardly symmetrical. They might be based on a railway line or a river. Therefore, even if you play with a world map to "prove" that Europe's perfect 50/50 east-west split lies east of Romania, it doesn't mean that's where the division should be.

There's another good reason to use the old Cold War dividing line. History shapes who we are. Whether Eastern Europeans like it or not, the communist experience is still in their collective memory. Those who are under 30 years old might yell, "But I don't remember those days! I grew up with Western values!" However, their parents and teachers drilled their local history and values into their children's brains. It's part of who they are. The legacy of slavery can still be felt in the southern regions of the US, even though slavery ended 150 years ago. Communism, in contrast, ended less than 25 years ago. Communism may have left Eastern Europe, but its long shadow is still there.

Finally, there's one more thing that Eastern European countries have in common: they're still relatively hidden. Of course, businesses and tourists have poured into the region ever since the Wall came down in 1989. However, the world is still far more familiar with Western Europe than Eastern Europe. Most people can explain the difference between Italy and Ireland; however, they'll give you a blank look if you ask them to compare Slovenia and Slovakia.

In conclusion, for geological, historical, and even touristy reasons, I have defined Eastern Europe quite broadly. This book puts 25 countries in Eastern Europe. It includes western Russia, Germany's eastern half, and the ex-Yugoslav countries. It also includes three countries that few consider part of traditional Eastern Europe: Finland, Greece, and Turkey. Finland is east of Poland (and north of the Baltic), so geographically it certainly is in Eastern Europe. Greece is also geographically in Eastern Europe (it's south of the Balkans). However, we will only examine the part of Greece that is most tied to the rest of Eastern Europe: Greece's northern portion. Like Russia, most of Turkey is in Asia, so we will just look at its western side. In sum, I spent three years in 25 countries nearly 25 years after the Berlin Wall came down.

Americans may wonder why I'm taking so much time to define Eastern Europe. "What's the big deal, anyway?" you may ask. "So you're in Eastern Europe. So what? Who cares?" Trust me. It's a *really big deal* in this region. It's a highly charged and emotional topic that sparks endless and explosive debates. If you want to make Eastern Europeans twitch and squirm, just tell them that they are from Eastern Europe. The only people who don't seem to care are the Moldovans. They're just happy that anyone knows that Moldova exists.

About the lessons

Each chapter focuses on one Eastern European country, and ends with a brief summary of what that country can teach you. Although it's tempting to just read the summaries and skip the rest, that might make you jump to erroneous conclusions. I can already hear the proud Russian who skips right to the summary of the Russian chapter and then yells at me, "All you have learned from the biggest country in the world is how great it is to drink vodka?!"

Therefore, before you read the summaries, remember that:

- **These aren't the only things you can learn.** Just because there are only two ideas in a summary, doesn't mean that those are the only two things you can learn from a country. First, you can learn many more things within the chapter itself, which is packed with information about each country's culture. Second, the summaries mainly focus on practical ideas that you can implement in your everyday life. Third, there are plenty of things to learn about each country that I have missed.
- **Other countries may be able to teach you the same lesson.** Just because one good idea is in the summary, doesn't mean that you can't learn that same concept elsewhere. For instance, if five countries can all teach you the same concept, only one country will get credit so that you don't have to read about the concept five times.
- **Other countries may have been the pioneers.** Just because I give credit to one country for doing something clever, doesn't mean it invented the idea.
- **Other countries may do it better.** Just because I give credit to one country for something useful, doesn't mean they are the best at practicing it.

Therefore, to answer the patriotic Russian, "Yes, there's much more to Russia than drinking vodka; Belarus is also great at drinking vodka; Russia invented vodka; and nobody drinks more vodka per capita than Moldova. Now are you all happy?"

"No," says the Russian, "because Moldova doesn't drink the most vodka. Estonia does!"

"Yeah, you're right. See, I told you that Russia has a lot to teach you about drinking vodka."

Lastly, the main purpose of this book is positive—to learn the best things about Eastern Europeans; nevertheless, we'll also learn about the stupid and idiotic things in Eastern Europe. Indeed, sometimes the most effective Eastern European lessons are the ones where they show us what *not* to do. I fell in love with Eastern Europe, warts and all. Perhaps you will too.

> *Before the development of tourism, travel was conceived to be like study, and its fruits were considered to be the adornment of the mind and the formation of the judgment.*
> *— Paul Fussel*

I began my voyage in Finland. During the Soviet Era, Finland was a quasi-Eastern European country. It was neither in the North Atlantic Treaty Organization (NATO), nor in the Warsaw Pact. Therefore, it would be a good place to start the adventure. So we'll start there too, using it as a useful stepping-stone into the Hidden Europe.

1

FINLAND—OR CALL IT SUOMI

FINLAND IS NEARLY A PERFECT society. Everything works. Cities are clean. There is no crime. People are nice. It's just that the winters suck.

Finland is big and empty. It is 80 percent of the size of California, yet has 14 percent of the population. Most of the five million Finns live in the south, around Helsinki, to enjoy the country's best weather, which is horrible most of the year. According to a worldwide 2010 Gallup poll, only five percent of Finns thought global warming was a threat to them—that was the lowest rate on Earth.

Few Americans know exactly where Finland is. The answer is simple: it's where Santa Claus lives. Really. Rovaniemi is a quaint town on the edge of Lapland, the northernmost region in Finland, and is Santa's global headquarters. However, St. Nick was officially born in Korvatunturi (meaning "Ear Mountain"), which is even farther north. Santa Claus thought that Korvatunturi was a bit too chilly, so he set up shop a bit south of there in Rovaniemi. That's like moving from Houston to Dallas to escape the heat.

Although most of the world agrees that Finland is where Santa Claus lives, not everyone believes that Finland is part of Scandinavia. Looking at a map, it seems like Finland is in Scandinavia, along with Sweden and Norway. However, Finns told me that Scandinavia has little to do with geography and more to do with the historical, cultural, and linguistic heritage that Sweden, Norway, Denmark, and Iceland share. They said that if you must slap a label on Norway, Sweden, and Finland, then call them *Nordic* countries. Telling a Finn that he's from Scandinavia won't insult him, but telling him that he's from Eastern Europe will.

Still, maps don't lie—Finland is directly north of the Baltic states. Given that the Baltic states are solidly in Eastern Europe, that means Finland is in Eastern Europe. Of course, like all Eastern European countries, Finland will vehemently deny that they are in Eastern Europe. Finns will cry that they are in *Northern* Europe, and that Eastern Europe is a "political concept" that only includes countries that used to be in the Warsaw Pact. Despite their denials, I figured that two weeks in Finland would be a nice warm up for the "real" Eastern Europe. It's ironic that my "warm up" almost froze me to death.

Hiking all "night" at the Arctic Circle on the summer solstice

I celebrated the longest day of the year by going way north to the Hautajärvi Nature Center and hiking the 80-kilometer (50-mile)

Karhunkierros Trail. If you can say the name of that trail, you deserve a trip to Finland. It means "The Bear's Trail." The path starts at a place called Hautajärvi, which means "Grave Lake." With such cheerful names, I wondered if it was smart hiking this trail alone.

The rangers told me most people take four to six days to hike it. I had only two days of food and there were no stores nearby. I figured I'd move fast with a light backpack, so I went for it. However, after just five hours of steady hiking, a self-locking outhouse stopped me cold. Fortunately, I escaped and kept hiking throughout the night. At 2:00 a.m. the sun hid behind a mountain and 30 minutes later, it started rising again. The Karhunkierros Trail features ravines, primeval forests, and suspension bridges over whitewater rivers. The civilized Finns have built *pitkospuu* (narrow wooden paths) to preserve the vulnerable vegetation and to make you an easy target for the gangs of mosquitoes.

After hiking all night, I stopped at the Jussinkämppä cabin at 6:30 a.m. to sleep for four hours. After 13 hours of hiking, I had covered 45 kilometers (30 miles). Most of the trail, like most of Finland, is pretty flat, with some rolling hills. After my nap, I walked the last 35 kilometers, finished by midnight, and stayed in an adorable one-person hut at the trail's highest point, Valtavaara, which rises a modest 491 meters (1,600 feet). I was surprised that nobody was in the hut given the perfect conditions and the 360-degree views. Maybe it's because it's an emergency shelter and not meant for camping. Or perhaps it's just because there simply aren't that many Finns in Finland.

The rangers were shocked that I returned so quickly. What was my secret for covering 80 kilometers in 30 hours? Endless sun and some fine friends pushing me along: hordes of bugs. Only seeing the occasional reindeer would make me stop. And seeing Santa Claus too.

Hitchhiking towards Oulu

The next bus to Kuusamo was leaving in five hours. Hitchhiking would be faster. After 30 minutes, a small blue car pulled up. The muscular driver seemed bigger than the car he was driving. Not knowing if he understood English, I said, "Kuusamo?"

"Yes, come in," the dark-haired man replied with a unique accent. It's rare to see dark hair and olive skin in Lapland. When it's freezing nine months a year, you don't have much of a chance to get a tan. The driver was a 36-year-old Turkish man who had been living in Lapland for 17 years after marrying (and divorcing) a Finnish wife he originally met on a French beach. This former bodybuilder had biceps that could crush my skull like a nut.

He asked me, "So you're from America?"

"Yes," I sheepishly answered, knowing that this Turk could hate America. I quickly added, "But my mom is from Chile and my dad is from France." I figured that telling him this would make it more likely that he would just shoot me and not behead me.

He asked me, "So what do you think of Bush and the war in Iraq?"

I sighed. It was the summer of 2004 and the Iraq War was in progress and was unpopular throughout the world (except America). I said, "I think Bush should have been more patient and tried to get more countries to agree with him before going into Iraq. . . ."

"I think he did the right thing," he interrupted, "You know, Saddam was a really bad man. People in Iraq suffered. Yeah, Bush might have done some things better, but it's good that America went into Iraq. I like Bush."

A pro-Bush Turk? No wonder he was living in Finland! After about an hour of chatting, he dropped me off in Kuusamo. I caught a bus to the quaint port city of Oulu. While I was hanging out on the dock, I met a Finnish woman named Outi Joensuu. She invited me to join her and some of her friends for drinks by the wharf. Before bidding farewell, they taught me about Finland.

> *I like looking like the president of a country, even if it is a woman. — Conan O'Brien, TV comedian who is popular in Finland partly because he looks like Tarja Halonen, the first female President of Finland*

Finland might be the country that is least likely to start World War III. Finns are peaceful. Almost . . . too peaceful. Nobody hates the Finns. Still, some nations have invaded Finland anyway. First, the imperialist Swedes came in the 1100s. The Swedes conquered the Finns and ruled them for 700 years. The Swedes dominated the Finns so tightly that it wasn't until 1863 when the poor Finns finally convinced the Russians (who were ruling them at the time) to let Finnish have equal status as Swedish. Notice that the Finns didn't request to have their language be more important than Swedish, just equal. And it took over 700 years to reach that milestone.

> *Finland's rivalry with Sweden goes way, way back when we were under Sweden's rule. We always think they are better than us. We played against them so often for so many years. Every country has one opponent they want to beat and for us, it's Sweden. — Saku Koivu, former captain of Finland's national ice hockey team*

Ahvenanmaa—Swedish Islands in Finland

To fully understand how much the Swedes are still milking their 700 years of domination, consider the Ahvenanmaa archipelago (Åland in Swedish) in the southwest corner of Finland. It has approximately 6,500 islands (about 80 are inhabited). Ahvenanmaa is roughly between the Swedish mainland and the Finnish mainland, but it officially belongs to Finland. Swedes have made it an exclusive Swedish-speaking enclave. That's right, Finnish-speaking Finns are discouraged to live on an island in their own country because it's effectively reserved for Swedish-speaking Finns.

> Lentokonesuihkuturbiinimoottoriapumekaanikkoaliupseerioppilas — *The longest Finnish word, which means,* Airplane jet turbine engine auxiliary mechanic non-commissioned officer student *(with words like that, I might prefer Swedish too)*

Let's see how far the Swedes have imposed their way. In 1921, the League of Nations (the precursor to the United Nations) said that Ahvenanmaa belongs to Finland, but it doesn't seem that way. Unlike any other province in Finland, this island province has its own internal parliament, which shares the power with the governor. The Finnish government can't amend the Ahvenanmaa Autonomy Act without the approval of the island's parliament. Ahvenanmaa is a demilitarized and neutral territory. Even the Finnish Navy can't park their boats on these Finnish islands!

They collect their own taxes, spend it all on their 28,000 inhabitants, and have few financial ties with the rest of Finland. To own property, vote, and conduct business on Ahvenanmaa you have to obtain the Right of Domicile. To get that, you have to live on this Finnish island for five years and speak excellent *Swedish*. Any international treaty entered into by Finland requires the consent of the Parliament of Ahvenanmaa to become valid also in Ahvenanmaa. The archipelago has its own postage stamps and flag. Websites use the .ax suffix instead of the .fi Finnish suffix. While Finland has two official languages (Finnish and Swedish), Ahvenanmaa has only one official language: Swedish! The poor Finnish government has to translate all documents it sends there into Swedish if they want the local parliament to read it. It's amazing they don't use the Swedish currency and carry Swedish passports!

How did the Ahvenanmaa natives get away with all this? To find the answer you have to turn back the clock 200 years. The reason they're part of Finland and not Sweden is that Russia kicked Sweden's butt in the war of 1808–09. To end the war, the Swedes agreed to hand Finland over to Russia. Russia said that wasn't enough, so Sweden tossed them a bone, or, in this case, an archipelago—Ahvenanmaa.

Russia called all their newly acquired territory (including Ahvenanmaa) the Grand Duchy of Finland. Therefore, when Finland declared its independence from Russia in 1919, the Finns thought it was only fair to keep Ahvenanmaa. After all, for the last 110 years it was all part of the same duchy and Sweden lost that territory fair and square. However, the Ahvenanmaa populace preferred rejoining their Swedish motherland. The Finns, tired of fighting, agreed to a compromise that gave them all the autonomy that they enjoy today.

Many impartial observers believe Ahvenanmaa is an exemplary solution to a minority conflict. Ahvenanmaa is special not just because nobody died fighting for its autonomy, but also because it's been demilitarized for many years. Ahvenanmaa's relationship with the Finnish government is fascinating because Finns and Swedes basically get along well. As we'll soon see, Eastern Europeans get hysterical over much more trivial issues.

The Finnish Culture

Finnish culture discourages violence and emotional outbursts (unless you're drunk, which happens every weekend). On the other hand, just because they're peaceful doesn't mean they're wimps. They've defended themselves against the Russians many times and live in one of the coldest regions of the planet. They even think it's fun to jump in frozen lakes.

Still, when it comes to most disputes with the Swedes, they are like the husband who would rather not argue with his nagging wife. "Yes, dear," Finland says to Sweden. In the tranquil Finnish minds, it's just not worth getting upset about minor issues that hardly matter. In short, Finns have learned the Swedish language instead of telling Swedes the same thing Germans told the French: "Listen, you assholes, if you want to talk to me, you talk to me in English!"

It was 1:47 a.m. in Helsinki and I was desperately looking for someone who could speak English. That night I would learn something more about the Finnish character—they are unusually trustworthy and generous.

An odd night in Helsinki

The youth hostel where I was staying had a 2:00 a.m. curfew. After 2:00 a.m. there was absolutely no way to enter the building and it wouldn't reopen until 6:00 a.m. Unfortunately, with 13 minutes before closing, I was lost.

How did I get into this predicament? Earlier that evening I met an odd couple: a petite bubbly blond and a sour, chubby Goth girl. They had invited me to come with them to a nightclub. The hyperactive blond girl was named Aila—she was dressed in pink. Her best friend, Marketta, wore black clothes and seemed to use mascara and eyeliner by the liter. The nightclub played ear-splitting metal ~~music~~ noise. The bouncy blond did most of the talking while her Anti-Christ friend lurked in the shadows.

To overcome the screeching noise, Aila would yell at me like I was a 95-year-old without a hearing aid. Toward the end of the evening, she surprised me by inviting me to join her and her boyfriend at her family's summer cottage. I had met Aila just a few hours before, yet she was inviting me to her home. Those who hike long distance trails in America call such unexpected generosity from strangers *trail magic.*

Unfortunately, going to Aila's summer house would require staying in Finland longer than I had planned. I was eager to enter the "real" Eastern Europe. I thanked her profusely for her trail magic and then left the nightclub at 1:30 a.m. with my ears ringing. It sounded like Lapland's mosquitoes were still chasing me. Suddenly I remembered my hostel's 2:00 a.m. curfew. I needed a quick, cheap way to return home. Fortunately, Helsinki had a way to do it—free bikes.

Biking to an unexpected shelter

Helsinki is bike heaven. Bike lanes are on pink pavement located between the sidewalk and the street, so it's easy to avoid pedestrians and cars. They even have special traffic lights and signs for bikes. When I visited in 2004, the city also had free bikes. I spotted a colorful parked city bike and unlocked it by depositing a two-euro coin in it. I would get my coin back whenever I parked it at a designated bike station. Unfortunately, in 2010, Helsinki canceled this system because a few people would wreck the bikes or check them out indefinitely. It's just another tragedy of the commons.

I raced towards my hostel, but by 1:47 a.m. I was lost. The street was deserted. Then, in the distance, a lone woman was walking my way. She was a slender blond wearing pink pants. A few wrinkles in her face indicated that she was probably 40 years old. It was remarkable that she was walking alone in such a deserted area—it was either a testament to Finland's safety or to her stupidity. I pointed to my map and said to her, "I need to get to *here* in the next 12 minutes."

"You'll never get there," she said. "It's at least 30 minutes away. And you won't find a taxi around here either."

I had left all my camping gear in the hostel, so I couldn't camp out. I had only two options. I could get another room in a hotel, but that would be expensive and I would feel stupid renting a second room when I'm already paying for one. The other option would be to party all night. It was near late June, so the nights hardly got dark and Finns party until 6:00 a.m. While I contemplated my undesirable options, the lady stunned me when she said, "Well, if you want, you can sleep on my couch."

I couldn't believe my luck. This lady, named Lea, had spent just a few minutes talking with me and trusted me enough to invite me to her house! What's more stunning is that Lea had four children; mothers are usually cautious about bringing a stranger home. Finns obviously trust their fellow humans, or at least the ones riding free bikes.

Her apartment was small, clean, and modern. She offered some food. A *perinneruoka* is a traditional Finnish dish, which is traditionally not eaten. That's right; Finns only eat a *perinneruoka* if it's a holiday or if they're old farts. Instead, most Finns favor *kotiruoka* (home-made food). Even though it was the middle of the night, Lea offered *ruisleipä* (dark sour bread), *juusto* (cheese), and *lihapullat* (Finnish meatballs). After finishing our snack, things began to heat up.

The Finnish temple: the sauna

There was something unexpected in Lea's bathroom: a sauna. Finns value a sauna like Americans value a home theater—it's hard to be truly happy without one. As we finished our *kotiruoka,* Lea said, "Do you want to try the sauna with me?"

I hesitated. In America, getting into a sauna at 2:30 a.m. would be risqué. However, doing it in Finland might be just as innocent as watching a movie in an American's home theater. I agreed. "OK, then get in," she said, "And I'll go change my clothes."

I got naked, wrapped a towel around my waist, and walked into the hot sauna. Lea shocked me when she walked in: she was completely naked—not even a skimpy towel. She giggled when she saw me sitting meekly in a corner with a towel around me. She laughed, "You're obviously not Finnish! You don't wear towels in saunas! Give it to me," she said with a smile.

This was one of those travel moments when I was glad to be a man.

I wasn't in Rome, but I thought, "Do as the Romans do." I stood up and humbly took my towel off. I sat down again and looked at my penis. What was I supposed to do with it? Just let it lie there in plain view? Or should I cross my legs and tuck my unit in between my legs so that only my pubic hair is visible? Or does doing that make me gay?

Lea sat next to me and was saying something, but I wasn't listening. I was thinking about my penis and what to do with it. Then I observed her naked figure and thought: for a 40-year-old mother, she certainly has an amazing body. Uh oh. I am thinking too much. No, not with that head; my other head. Suddenly I lost control of my unit. He started to get bigger. *Oh no! Stop! Please!* Of course, the more I thought about not thinking, the more I couldn't help but think about what I was thinking.

It expanded more. Is she noticing? What is she chattering about anyway? *Who cares!* Just get that boy down! Maybe I should tuck it in! But if I tuck it in now, I'll draw her attention there. Just ignore it! *No!* It's getting engorged with blood. Is it hot in here or is it me?

Finally, I thought of the ultimate libido killer: Michael Moore. I repeated in my head, "Michael Moore. Michael Moore. Michael Moore . . . ." I imagined the fat, hairy Michael Moore next to me, naked. Instantly, I began to deflate. *Whew!*

I finally started listening to her and then interrupted, "Hey, where are your kids anyway?" I had seen their photos in the apartment and there were a few closed doors that surely led to their rooms.

"They're away for the weekend with their father," she said.

"Oh, that's nice," I said. Awkward silence.

Lea said quietly, "Would you like a Finnish massage?"

Oh no. Not again. My blood was leaving my brain again and heading south. How should I answer her question? Her delicate hands grazed my back. *Francis, behave. Michael Moore! Michael fucking Moore!!! Damn it! It's not working! I know, I'll lie on my stomach! That will hide everything!*

"Sure, I'd like to try a Finnish massage," I said while quickly flipping onto my stomach. Lea's soft hands caressed my back. Thinking of Michael Moore wasn't helping. I imagined Michael's hands rubbing my legs, but it was useless: Lea's hands were too small and she just wasn't a fat film director.

Lea's wet hands went up and down my body. Her soothing voice was as soft as her hands. I was in Finnish heaven. She eventually massaged my butt and that's when I blurted out, "You're, er, I mean, *it's* really hot," I stammered. "Can I take a shower?"

"Yes," she whispered. "It's just right there," she pointed to the nearby shower. I rose with my back to her so that she couldn't tell what else had risen. Of course, she knew something was up. She was grinning mischievously.

While I took an ice cold shower, little did I know that I would have two more interesting sauna experiences in Eastern Europe. Around 3:00 a.m. the sky was brightening as the sun started to rise. That's exactly when I went to sleep. As I lost consciousness, I realized that I was falling madly in love with Finland.

> *Software is like sex: it is better when it's free.*
> *— Linus Torvalds, the Finn who invented Linux*

When I woke up, Lea offered open sandwiches caked with margarine. Finns have been eating rye and whole grain bread long before the rest of world realized how healthy it is. For toppings, there was hard cheese and cold cuts. Lea also offered *viili* (sour yogurt) with muesli and jam. Lea was more lively than typical Finns, who are so calm that it's almost creepy. Germans are almost as stoic, but at least they get mad every once in a while and start a world war.

Finns admit that they are horribly shy (unless they are drunk). Still, Finns are friendly and helpful once you start talking with them. My experience with Lea is a perfect example of how safe, trusting, and generous Finns are. They also produce smart kids. When Lea bragged about how smart her kids were, I thought she was just another deluded parent. I was wrong.

The smartest kids in the world

In 2009, the Organization for Economic Cooperation and Development tested hundreds of thousands of teenagers in 57 countries. Finns were the best in science, and the second best in math and reading. International observers flew in from all over to learn the Finnish secrets. What they discovered surprised them.

The typical Finnish high-school doesn't have a school uniform, gets only 30 minutes of homework per night, has no honor roll or valedictorian status to strive for, has no tardy bell to hear, and hardly stresses about going to college. Teachers aggressively help struggling students. Meanwhile, a gifted student isn't sent to an elite school; instead, he becomes a teacher's assistant. Unfortunately, the young geniuses can be impolite. For example, when someone asks a stupid question, Finnish kids sometimes bark out, "KVG!" That stands for *kato vittu Googlesta* (Google it, you cunt)! You gotta wonder what it says about the future of the human race when the smartest kids on the planet are calling each other cunts.

So what is the secret to the Finnish success? While I waited for Helsinki's Museum of Modern Art to open, I observed Finnish teenagers to see if I could see the answer. They were smoking, had dyed hair, and sang Bob Dylan's "Knocking on Heaven's Door." They were similar to American teenagers, yet American students got a C in the global competition despite spending 20 percent more per student than Finland.

The main reason for Finland's educational success is that teachers are highly valued and have substantial autonomy. Although teachers in Finland are paid about the same amount as American teachers (and they have similar costs of living), the job is highly coveted—nine out of ten applicants are rejected. Unlike the US, all teachers get performance evaluations. Most importantly, teachers in Finland are entrepreneurs—they customize each class depending on the needs and abilities of the students, instead of having to strictly follow a national curriculum.

We don't need to copy everything in the Finnish educational model. A common mistake when people look at the best of the best is to conclude that we should copy everything. We forget that they may be the best *despite* a methodology, not *because* of it. Nevertheless, we ought wander to Finland and learn its habits.

Do you know what Finns call their country?

Understanding what the Finns call their country tells a lot about their non-confrontational nature. Before we learn what the Finns call their country, let's see what other countries call Finland: *Finlande* (French); *Finnland* (German); *Finland* (Swedish, Dutch, and Portuguese); Φινλανδία (Greek – it sounds like "Finladia"); *Finlandia* (Spanish and Italian); 핀란드 (Korean—sounds like "Peen-lan-duh"); Финляндия (Russian—sounds like "Finlyandiya"); フィンランド (Japanese—sounds like "Finrando"; and 芬蘭 (Chinese— sounds like "Fenlan"); *Ufini* (Swahili); *Finnország* (Hungarian); *Finnland* (Icelandic). Therefore, it's safe to say that most countries in the world call the country where the Finns live something that sounds like "Finland."

What do Finns call their country? *Suomi.* Huh? How did this happen? Simple. A few thousand years ago, the Finns introduced themselves to their neighbors. The exchange went something like this: "Welcome Stranger, what land do you hail from?"

"*Suomi*," replied the Finn.

"Oh really? Hey honey, this guy says he's from a place called Finland!"

"No," the Finn said, "It's not called Finland, my country is called *SUOMI!*"

"Yeah, whatever. You're from *Finland,* bucko!"

Languages do funny things with names. For example, Chileans named Francis are sometimes called Paco. In America, folks called Robert are also called Bob, and every Richard is obviously a Dick. Still, when naming a foreign land, we should try to pronounce it like the locals. For example, it's disgraceful that we call the capital of the Czech Republic *Prague,* when the Czechs call it *Praha*. Come on, how hard is it to say *Praha*? Why do we call the capital of Portugal (*Lisboa*) *Lisbon*? Saying *Lisboa* is hardly a tongue twister. Nevertheless, at least Lisbon and Prague aren't completely off the phonetic mark.

Bigger alterations are harder to forgive, like Greeks calling Switzerland *Elvitia* or English speakers calling *Deutschland* Germany. At least these are isolated cases. Most of the time countries pronounce foreign countries in the same phonetic ballpark of what the locals call it. However, the world has failed to call Finland by its proper phonetic name of *Suomi*. What's crazy is that nobody knows why this happened.

Why don't Finns launch a global campaign to get everyone to call them *Suomi*? Myanmar, a far poorer country than Finland, led an expensive global crusade to force everyone to stop calling their country Burma. Even cities have forced geographers throughout the world to redo their maps. Mongolia's Ulan Bator became Ulaanbaatar. Bombay now wants to be called Mumbai. Peking must be called Beijing. St. Petersburg has been a real pain in the ass for cartographers because it's changed its name three times in the last 100 years (Petrograd; Leningrad; St. Petersburg). If we can make the change for Myanmar, we can do it for *Suomi*.

It says a lot about the Finnish character that they don't force the world to change. Finns are relaxed, peaceful, and calm. Why fuss over such a petty issue? It's just a name. Thus, Finns quietly accept reality, just as they accept that Swedish is their official second language and that Swedes have taken over Ahvenanmaa. On the other hand, why don't Finns just call their country something that sounds like *Finland*? After all, if everyone calls you Ralph, then maybe you should just call yourself Ralph, even though your real name is John.

The reason Finns continue to call their country *Suomi* is also quite telling. Finns are tough and proud in their own subtle way. They're quietly intense. You may not realize how much they care about something until you push them over the brink. Finns are *not* like the stubborn child who will yell "NO!" and throw a tantrum; instead, they are more like the child who just shakes her head firmly and pouts without saying a word. With the kid who throws a tantrum, you have a chance of persuading him, but with the stubborn, quiet head shaker, you don't stand a chance. Therefore, next time you watch the World Cup or the Olympics and you see an athlete with jersey that says SUOMI, think about the meaning behind this amazing country's name.

Finlandization

After visiting pristine Lapland, I returned to Helsinki and visited the medieval town of Porvoo. Later, I saw Turko, the former capital of Finland, and the southernmost point of Finland, Hanko. They're all fascinating places to check out. Finland's complex history, filled with Russian and Swedish occupation, gives visitors a taste of Finland's dynamic past. Finland is idyllic and spacious. It's filled with shy, honest, and good-hearted people. I loved it. Then again, Finns told me that if I came in the winter time I might have a different impression.

Like Switzerland, Finland was neutral during the Cold War. However, just like Switzerland leaned more toward the West, Finland leaned more toward the East. This wasn't because Finns wanted to get cozy with Russia. On the contrary, Finns preferred the West. It still has an uneasy relationship with Russia. In the Cold War, Finland's efforts to appease the Russian bear became known as *Finlandization*. We could all use some Finlandization in our lives.

What Finland Can Teach Us

- **Ride a bike.** Lobby your local government for bike lanes and support a private company that creates a Finnish-like rent-a-bike program. Helsinki's weather is rougher than most of America's, yet Finns bike everywhere. Quit making excuses. When I lived near rainy Seattle, I had no car and I biked everywhere. Wear a raincoat, rain pants, a cap, and laugh in the rain! When I lived in San Francisco, I carried a backpack full of groceries and biked over fearsome hills. You'll lose weight and you'll never fight for a parking spot.
- **Be quick to trust people.** Don't worry so much about giving strangers a ride, inviting them to your house, or loaning them something you value. When you become more trusting, others will open up and trust you more. You create a virtuous cycle: mutual generosity and happiness soars. Being cynical and suspicious leads to mutual caution and misery. Obviously, women should be a bit more cautious than men, but life is boring if you selfishly shut yourself off from the world. Learn from Finns and assume that most people are good and honest.
- **Learn patience by having a broad perspective.** Finns keep events and their lives in a wide perspective so that few things bug them. Whenever you find yourself losing patience, take steps back and examine the situation from a broader point of view. Why get irritated when someone calls you Liz instead of Elizabeth? Why get angry if traffic is worse than you expected? Why fight when someone offends you? Why get offended in the first place? Finns aren't saints, but they're amazingly calm when most people boil and raise their voices.
- **How to run a school.** Finns have mastered the art of creating responsible kids and well-trained teachers. Instead of blindly dumping more money into our schools, let's pull out some cheap lessons from Finland's school playbook—like empowering teachers to become entrepreneurs.
- **Remember the meaning behind Suomi.** Don't always fight to be "right." You can be true to yourself, and you don't have to change others to be happy with your own life.

Places I saw and recommend in Finland: Helsinki; Lapland; Porvoo; Turko; and any of their southern islands.

Travel deals and info: http://ftapon.com/finland

Now, let's truly start the adventure in Eastern Europe. We're going to take a boat across the Gulf of Finland and enter one of the key gateways into Eastern Europe. We'll begin in a port city that used be called Reval. Today, it is known as Tallinn. It is the capital of an unusual country called Estonia.

2
Estonia—Revenge of the Nerds

Let's start with the basics: does Estonia even exist or is it just some made-up country? Like Albania, Estonia just doesn't sound real. Have you ever met someone from those two countries? Do you ever see those countries mentioned in the news? I didn't think so.

Estonia? Where's that?

Estonia is unknown. An Estonian named Triin Tammaru told me of a real conversation she had when she lived several months in Florida:

"Where are you from?" asked the American man.

"I'm from Estonia," Triin replied.

"Where's that?"

"Next to Finland."

"Where's Finland?"

"Next to Sweden."

The brilliant American exclaimed with all the confidence of a *Jeopardy* champion, "Oh, so you're *Swedish*!"

From then on, the American introduced Triin to his friends as "the Swedish girl." She didn't want to tell Americans that Estonia was next to Russia because then they might classify her as "the Russian girl," or "the communist girl."

Americans are so geographically challenged that it's amazing we can find our way home every evening. Triin estimated that one in twenty Americans she met during her four months in America had heard about Estonia. About one in a hundred knew exactly where it was. Triin met an American girl who thought Europe was just the name of *one big city* on the other side of the Atlantic Ocean. She also met a man who thought Europe was made up of one country: Germany. And no, that guy's name wasn't Adolph.

Before Europeans chuckle too much about ignorant Americans, it's clear that Western Europeans aren't geographic geniuses either. When one of my Lithuanian friends introduced herself to a Dutch man, he thought that Lithuania was in Moscow. Irina, a Russian friend of mine who lives in Spain, said that a Spaniard asked her, "What language do they speak in Russia?" Here's another gem: when Irina told a Western European that she's from Moscow, he got excited and said, "Really? I have another friend who is also from *Sweden!*" Obviously, Americans aren't the only people who need to be slapped around with a giant world map.

Learning facts and fiction

Estonia sounds so unreal that Scott Adams, the creator of the Dilbert comic strip, made up a bizarre country called *Elbonia*. It's no coincidence that Elbonia sounds like Estonia. According to the comic strip, Elbonia is a Fourth-World country where the national bird is the Frisbee. All Elbonians have beards (including women and babies), use cans attached to strings as telephones, and fly Elbonia Air (a massive slingshot that launches passengers so that they land far away in the waist-deep mud that covers the entire country). After overthrowing communism, Elbonia is fighting a civil war between left- and right-handed Elbonians. In an effort to increase tourism, Elbonia's dictator not only made gambling and prostitution legal, but he also made them *mandatory*.

Given this background, I was skeptical when I bought a boat ticket to Estonia. Was this just a hoax to squeeze money out of gullible tourists? On June 30, 2004, I sat in a waiting room in Helsinki. Soon we would board the Nordic Jet Line, which was not a jet going north, but rather a catamaran going south. The crew assured me that the vessel was going to Estonia and not Elbonia.

I relaxed my doubts by reading a few facts about Estonia in my guidebook. Estonia is slightly smaller than the combined size of New Hampshire and Vermont, yet it feels big because only 1.3 million folks live there. That makes it one of the least dense countries in Europe, with just 32 Estonians per square kilometer. Their mountains are really hills—Suur Munamägi, at 318 meters (1,043 ft), is the tallest point in the country. Estonia's flatness makes it a great place for cross-country skiing. Estonians drink liquor like water. That was still true in 2011: Estonia was the world's second highest per capita consumer of alcoholic spirits (after South Korea).[1]

Meeting Maiu Reismann

It was 3:00 p.m. and we would board the vessel soon. I had no lodging reservation in Tallinn, Estonia's capital. I would arrive at 5:00 p.m., homeless. I didn't panic because this was my normal routine—I rarely make reservations anywhere I travel. Instead, I carry a tarp and a sleeping bag wherever I go. This eliminates the pressure to find a place to stay. In the worst case, I can happily sleep in a park. Having spent many months sleeping in the mountains every day, I find it easy to spontaneously camp anywhere. Although I was prepared to camp in a random park near Tallinn, I wanted to consider other options. While I flipped through my guidebook, a young lady sat near me. Although guidebooks are great, local advice is sometimes better, so I asked, "Excuse me, are you from Estonia?"

"Yes," she replied with a soft, sweet voice. "I live in Tallinn," she said with a bit of an accent.

"Do you know of any cheap places to stay in town?" I asked.

"Yes. In fact, I have a degree in hotel management and I work in tourism."

And so began a 90-minute conversation on the turbulent catamaran with a 24-year-old named Maiu Reismann. She was petite and had sparkling hazel eyes that reflected her gentleness. She wore her dark brown hair in a ponytail as if to advertise her simplicity. She nearly threw up on me because she thought I was so revolting, but she claimed that it was the boat ride that was making her seasick.

Maiu was returning home after dropping off her American boyfriend at the Helsinki airport. They had been dating three years. She offered to walk me to a nearby hotel. It was pouring rain when our boat arrived. We leaned into the horizontal rain and splashed through puddles. When we arrived at the hotel, dripping wet, we learned that the price was exorbitant. Maiu sighed calmly, demonstrating her patience. She said softly, "There is another hotel I can take you to, but it's kind of far."

"That's no problem," I said. I've walked and camped in torrential rain for days, so spending a few minutes in a downpour would be trivial. However, the weather was bothering Maiu, even though her stoic attitude hid it well.

"On second thought," she said, "If you want, you can just stay with me. I am not sure what my brother will say, but we have a sofa that you can sleep on if you want."

On the one hand, I was thrilled. This would be a great glimpse into the lives of a local Estonian and I might save a couple of bucks. On the other hand, she could be a scam artist who will rob me during the night and have her big brother toss me in a dumpster. I accepted her generous offer. I figured I had nothing to lose except for my camcorder, a few hundred bucks, and my life.

Estonian has no sex and no future

Fortunately, Maiu and her brother were not ax murderers. When the rain stopped, Maiu took me to Tallinn, which was named the 2011 European Capital of Culture. As we walked into the medieval old town, I felt I should have brought chain mail, a steel helmet, and a sword. Tallinn's Old Town feels like a Hollywood set for *The Lord of the Rings.* A tall, thick stone wall encircles the old town, just as ready to receive a catapult projectile today as it was 500 years ago. A few burning torches make the town irresistibly romantic. Charming cobblestoned streets lead you through inviting alleyways and narrow passages. Cars rarely use the bumpy streets, so pedestrians rule the old town. All you hear are soft footsteps, classical music, and the occasional drunk Finn.

While Maiu and I dined at a medieval restaurant in Tallinn's Old Town, she taught me that the Estonian language has no sex and no future. Estonian has no sex because it lacks grammatical gender (just like in English). Thus, a *table* is not female and a *car* is not male. Also, Estonian has no future. Or better said, it has no future tense. To express a future event, Estonians use the present tense and then specify when it will happen. For instance, instead of saying *I will go home*, Estonians might say *ma lähen kahe nädala pärast koju* (I go home in two weeks).

In addition to not having to learn a future tense, there are some other aspects about Estonian that make it easy to learn. Unlike English, for example, every letter is pronounced the same way every time. Furthermore, Estonian has no articles. You can also use the same pronoun to refer to a man, woman, or a thing. Moreover, word order is not fixed. For instance, you can say *koer* (the dog) *hammustas* (bit) *poissi* (the boy). But if you change the word order, the sentence is still grammatically correct. Hence, you can also say *koer poissi hammustas* or *poissi hammustas koer*. Maiu was proud that Estonian has a vowel that few languages have: õ. It sounds like the sound you might make when you realize that you just stepped on a piece of shit: *eeww*.

Unless you live there, it's tough to get motivated to learn Estonian because only one in 10,000 humans speak it. Nevertheless, if you visit, it's good to know these words: *tere* (hello); *tänan* (thanks); *jaa* (yes); *ei* (no); *vabandust* (sorry/excuse me); and *head aega* (goodbye). If you're good, try saying *ma ei räägi eesti keelt* (I don't speak Estonian). When you consider Estonia's history, it's unbelievable that their language still exists today.

Want to run a country? Come to Estonia

It seems that everyone has had a chance to run Estonia. In the last 800 years Sweden, Poland, Denmark, Germany, and Russia have all called the shots in this territory. The habit of invading Estonia started in 1208, when crusaders wanted to convert Europe's last remaining pagans. Crusaders ordered Estonian pagans to become good Christians or die. (By the way, *pagan* in Estonian has two meanings: the first is the same as the one in English; the second means *damn!* It's funny hearing an Estonian who hits his finger with a hammer yell out, "*Pagan!*")

By 1219, the Danes controlled Tallinn. Three years later, the Estonians revolted and tasted freedom for *two short years*. That's when a Germanic people called the Teutonic Knights of the Livonian Order bought Estonia from the Danes. Unfortunately, the Teutonic Knights weren't so knightly. They limited Estonians to menial jobs and forced thousands to become Christians. On the other hand, the Livonian Order (being Germanic) was quite orderly. For example, they protected merchant trade routes and built beautiful buildings that still stand today, like Tallinn's Town Hall. After those two years of independence, Estonia wouldn't taste freedom again for another 700 years.

> *History is more interesting than politics.*
> *— Lennart Meri, 1929–2006, President of Estonia*

In the 1500s, Estonians nearly went extinct when over 70 percent of the Estonian population died during the Livonian War. After 25 years of bloodshed, Russia retreated and only 25,000 Estonians survived. Estonia was split between Sweden, Poland, and Denmark. It's remarkable that these traumatic events didn't permanently kill Estonia's language and culture. Estonians are tough.

With Russia out of the picture, Poles and Swedes looked at each other and said, "Hey, are you tired of fighting for the last quarter of a century? Cuz I'm sure not! Bring it on!" They went on killing each other for another 46 years! Swedes finally won and did nice things like starting schools, ending the famine, reducing the nobility's power, and importing some hot blonds. Even today, Estonians still call that era "the good old Swedish time."

Russia grew tired of all the peace and quiet, so in 1700 they started a 21-year war, which killed half of the Estonian population. This time Russia won. They kindly abolished serfdom and let German remain Estonia's official language, although locals continued speaking Estonian among themselves. Unfortunately, plague and famine killed 200,000 Estonians during the 200 years of Russian rule. Hence, Estonians still think of this period as "the bad old Russian time."

The Soviet and Nazi sandwich

In 1918, while Russia was busy with its civil war, Estonia declared independence, hoping that Russia wouldn't notice. It worked. After a couple of years of being sandwiched between Germans and Russians during WWI, Estonia finally became independent in 1920. This was the first time Estonians were free since that brief two-year period 700 years before.

This time, their freedom lasted 19 years. In 1939, the Union of Soviet Socialist Republics (USSR) told Estonia that they would "protect" them by placing 25,000 Russian troops in Estonia. Estonia's army numbered 16,000; it gave in. In 1940, about 10,000 Estonians, including Maiu's grandfather, were deported to Siberia. The seesaw battle for Estonia restarted when Germany reconquered Estonia in 1941. In 1944, the Russians grabbed it back and then the fun communist era started.

During the Soviet era, private property was abolished and Estonia's best food was shipped to Russia. Meanwhile, tens of thousands of Estonians were deported to Siberia, while tens of thousands of Russians poured into Estonia to replace them. If the other Russian period was called "the bad old Russian time," this was probably called "the really shitty Russian time." Fast forward to 1991, the USSR imploded and Estonia became free again. An Estonian named Yuliya Trutko observed, "We moved from one union to another—from the Soviet Union to the European Union." Finally, in 2011, Estonia celebrated its new record for being independent: 20 years.

Russophones in Estonia

Although the Soviets are out of Estonia, Russians are still in it. Over a quarter of Estonians are Russophones (people who prefer to speak Russian). In 2006, during my second trip to Estonia, I took a bus to Lasnamäe, a neighborhood on the outskirts of Tallinn filled with blocky, gray, dull high-rises. Over 85 percent of Lasnamäe's 160,000 residents are Russophones. Most moved in when the Soviets encouraged Russian migration to Estonia. On the bus ride a young blond with a round head sat next to me. I asked her what she thought of Tallinn. She said bitterly, "Tallinn is *boring*."

"Why?" I asked.

She answered with a strong Russian accent, "It's just a bunch of casinos, tourists, and restaurants."

"Sounds like Vegas," I mumbled. Although she had the gentleness of the Incredible Hulk, I continued, "So what do you think of Estonians?"

"Estonians are just a bunch of liars. They all lie. They pretend to be nice, but then when you turn your back, they do or say something else. You can't trust them. Russians are honest, they will tell you what they think, we are friendly and warm," she said in an angry tone.

I asked, "Do you think Russians should learn to speak Estonian?"

"No! Why should we? Russians are the majority of the population in Estonia!"

This is false. Russians are 25 percent of Estonia's population. There are two reasons she might have believed that Russophones are the majority. First, Russophones often live in enclaves that feel like you're in Russia: Russian signs are everywhere and everyone speaks Russian. Russophones often have no Estonian friends, only watch Russian TV, and shop exclusively at Russian markets. Therefore, it's easy for them to overestimate the Russophone population. Second, Russians are cynical about governments. You would be too if you were under communism for 70 years. The popular belief was: the truth is the opposite of whatever the government says.

Why Russians don't want to learn Estonian

Estonians view Russians as unwelcome immigrants, while Russians believe that they've been in Estonia "forever." So who's right? They both are. Russians have been in Estonia as long as there's been history to record it. In fact, Russophones dominate many Estonian border towns because they've lived there for countless generations. Victor, an Estonian Russophone, told me he could trace his Russian lineage over seven generations—all come from the same town in Estonia.

On the other hand, the USSR encouraged tens of thousands of Russians to move to Estonia. In 1932, Russians made up only 8.2 percent of Estonia; by 1989, they were over 30 percent. In short, some of the Russophones who live in Estonia today are the descendants of families who have lived in Estonia for 1,000 years. Others moved in last week.

Russophones who have a long history of living in Estonia feel no need to learn Estonian. Maiu's mom believes that there's another factor. She said, "Russians think that since they liberated us from the Nazis, we should be grateful. They don't think that they were occupying us; they were supposedly 'helping us.' Russians don't want to learn Estonian because they feel that we owe them one."

Meanwhile, Russophones are furious that their government is now treating them like second-class citizens. After transferring buses on my way to Lasnamäe, a Russian mother told me, "Estonians are fascists."

"Why?" I asked.

"Estonians want Russians out. They are closing down Russian schools. They won't even give us a passport," she said as she rose to leave with her five-year-old daughter.

"Why not?" I asked.

"They're *fascists!*" she yelled as she got off the bus.

I left my seat and approached three tall 20-year-olds who were standing at the back of the bus. They were all born and raised in Estonia, but they have no citizenship, and they "hate the Estonian language."

Later, Yuliya Trutko, a Russophone who grew up in Estonia, would tell me, "Russians are still separate, because that's their choice. They don't want to integrate. It's hard for them. I think it's even impossible for them."

Want a headache? Try to get an Estonian passport

After Estonia declared independence, it was stingy with giving away passports. People not only had to prove that they had been living in Estonia for years, but also that they were proficient in Estonian. At first, the language exam was hard. After years of Russian protests it became easier. In 2008, Alissa Avrutina, a Russophone polyglot, had to retake the exam because the government had changed the requirements again. "I've taken this exam four times!" she told me. "I've paid

$300 to take courses to help me pass the exam. I must take it again because some employers prefer that I pass the latest exam. It's frustrating."

Alina Lind, an Estonian Russophone, observed that Estonia's passport requirements are tougher than those in the West. In 2011, after eight years of hassle, she finally got a passport. Those who don't get a passport get a *Välismaalase Pass* (Alien's Passport). Russia invited those with the Alien's Passport to visit Russia without a visa. This angered the Estonian government, because it decreased the incentive for its ethnic Russians to learn Estonian. In 2008, Lev Jefremtsev, a 22-year-old Russophone, told me he didn't need Estonian citizenship, "If I get an Estonian passport, then I must pay $100 visa every time I visit my relatives in Russia. With my Alien passport, I can enter Russia for free."

I said, "But isn't there some benefit to having an Estonian passport?"

He said, "The only benefit is that you get to vote and travel outside of the European Union more easily. And I don't care about that."

Pursuing the Nobel Peace Prize in McDonald's

To meet English-speaking locals, I visited the McDonald's in Lasnamäe and asked a young Russophone couple if I could ruin their romantic meal. Dimitri spoke English, but Tatiana could only speak Russian and German. When I asked Dmitri what he thought of Estonians, he said, "There are good Estonians and bad ones, just like there are good Russians and bad ones. So when I meet an Estonian, I have an open mind."

I asked him, "Do Russians feel like second-class citizens here?"

"Russians feel at home in the Baltic. We have lived here for centuries. And as the Baltic becomes more international, life will improve."

Then I had a flash of brilliance and said, "What if Russians didn't have to learn Estonian as a second language, but had to learn English instead, and that Estonians had to do the same. This way you could each keep your native tongue and your common language would be English! What do you think?"

"This would be great!" he said.

Feeling like the Nobel Peace Prize was within my grasp, I shuffled over to a table where an Estonian couple was chatting. I made the same language proposal to them. Their response shattered my Nobel dreams: "Absolutely not! Then we'll lose our language! We'll use English to communicate with Russians and then we'll eventually use it to communicate between Estonians. We would lose our culture and identity. No way."

These Estonians were named Ronnie and Liis. It's rare to find Estonians who live in Lasnamäe, so I asked Ronnie what he thought about the Russophones. He said, "I'd just like to see all Russians go back to their country."

I asked, "What do you have against them?"

"They're loud and aggressive. The older generation expects you to speak Russian. Although things are getting better, most Russians refuse to learn anything about Estonian culture."

"But Russians say they can't get an Estonian passport," I said.

Ronnie sighed, "All they have to do is to take a really basic language test. It's so easy. But they're lazy or they just don't care. *It's about attitude.*"

Liis said, "Yes, the Russians just have such a bad attitude about it. If they just tried a little, we would understand, but they are so inflexible."

I asked, "Do you think Russia will invade Estonia in this century?"

Ronnie said, "No way. They wouldn't dare. We're part of NATO now. If they attacked Estonia, Europe and America would immediately defend us."

Although a foreign country has manhandled Estonia for 95 percent of its existence, "This time is different," people said. I talked with Ronnie and Liis in 2006. Back then, the situation *really did feel different*. NATO dismissed the question of what it should do if a Baltic country were attacked. It was a preposterous idea. However, in 2008, after Russia took action into South Ossetia, Georgia, things changed. Russia could justify invading Estonia by using the same excuse it used to enter Georgia: to defend ethnic Russians from an abusive local government.

In 2008, during my third visit to Estonia, the mood was different. I asked Herki, Maiu's brother, if he thought Russia could reoccupy Estonia in the next 50 years. He said, "Sure, why not? Look at our history. We're usually occupied." He said it with a casualness that people usually have when they ask you to pass the salt.

Estonia's arrogance towards Russia has deflated in the last five years, but they're still a bit cocky. Now that they're in NATO, they're like the nerd in the schoolyard who finally has a bodyguard to fend off the bully. However, it's remarkable that despite NATO's presence and despite being independent for 20 years, Estonia still has trouble moving a simple statue.

Estonians fight over a statue

In 2006, I touched Eastern Europe's most controversial statue, the Bronze Soldier. At that time, it was located near Tallinn's center. It depicts a common Russian soldier who is solemnly looking at the ground. It's about as tall as an NBA basketball player. Every May 9, Russians would gather around the statue to commemorate Victory Day—the end of WWII. This all seems rather innocent, but this simple statue set off an international crisis.

To understand why, we need some background. After winning WWII, the Soviets blew up the monument dedicated to Estonian independence. With "liberators" like these, who needs enemies? The Soviets erected a wooden pyramid in its place and dedicated it to their soldiers. Two courageous teenage Estonian girls burned down the new pyramid. They were eventually caught and sent to a Gulag coal mine for many years. In 1998, both girls, who were now in their late 60s, became the only Estonian women to be awarded their nation's highest medal. The key point is that the Soviets replaced the burned down pyramid with the Bronze Soldier.

For many Estonians the Bronze Soldier represents 48 years of Soviet oppression. Meanwhile, Russians believe that the statue represents the triumph over the Nazis. A few months before I returned to Estonia in 2006, an Estonian nationalist threatened to blow up the statue if it weren't removed. The police began to guard the statue nonstop. Urban legends spread. The Estonian Prime Minister (PM) said that some believed that what was really buried there was: (a) patients from a nearby hospital; (b) executed looters; (c) drunken USSR soldiers who had been run over by their own tank.

> *There are a terrible lot of lies going about the world, and the worst of it is that half of them are true.*
> — *Winston Churchill*

The PM's statement became so twisted that Russians told me that the PM said that what was really buried under the statue was a drunken prostitute! The PM never said that, nor did he say that he believed any of the rumors. He simply said that those were the rumors and that he wanted to excavate the site to end the speculation. The situation climaxed in an event called the Bronze Night.

The Bronze Night

In April 2007, the Estonian government voted to remove the statue within 30 days. Russophones rallied around the statue. The Estonian parliament gathered for an emergency session at 3:40 a.m. No, that's not a typo. They asked parliamentarians to roll out of bed, drive to the parliament building, and vote on a statue. And you think that the US Congress has strange priorities.

The groggy Estonian leaders voted to remove the statue immediately. Three hours later, the statue disappeared. Chaos erupted. For the next few days there was widespread rioting, looting, and vandalism. A prominent Russian leader demanded that the Estonian government resign.

Russians vandalized Estonia's embassy in Moscow. The Russian government said that the "zealots of Nazism" are behind the dismantling of the statue and "these admirers of Nazism" have made a "mockery of the remains of the fallen soldiers [which] is just more evidence of the vengeful policy toward Russians living in Estonia and toward Russia."

Estonians told me that they were scared. The government advised everyone to stay at home. People started whispering the word "war." Russia practically boycotted all Estonian commerce. Russian leader Vladimir Putin said that removing the statue "sows discord and mistrust." One restaurant in Russia was more blunt. It put up a sign stating: "ESTONIANS AND DOGS MAY NOT ENTER."

Reflecting on the Bronze Night

When the dust settled, 12 bodies were exhumed from the original site. Four were WWII Russian military officers. Their remains were returned to their families. The rest were unidentifiable and were reburied in Tallinn's Military Cemetery, where the Bronze Soldier now stands. In 2008, during my third visit to Estonia, I visited the statue after a snowfall.[2] The statue looked the same, but Estonia had changed. I asked locals to reflect on the issue.

Igor Kuzmitshov, a thoughtful Russophone, thought that the statue should have been left alone. He understood the Estonian perspective on the Bronze Soldier, but he said, "What Estonians don't understand is that Russians also suffered in communism. The average Russian was just as much of a victim of the totalitarian state as the average Estonian. Sure, a few Russians benefited from communism, but so did a few Estonians. Estonians forget that many Russians also had family members deported to Siberia, had property stolen by the state, and were scared of criticizing the government. *Everyone* suffered under communism, not just Estonians. Sometimes Estonians forget that."

Artur Kuldmaa, a computer administrator in Tallinn, has an Estonian father and a Russian mother, so he was objective. He looked at me intensely through his geeky glasses. I asked him what he thought should been done with the statue. In a typically calm Estonian manner, he said, "We should have left it where it was."

"So you think Russia was right?" I asked.

"No. Russia shouldn't have gotten involved in Estonian affairs. This is our problem. We, as a country, should decide what to do with the statue. It's none of Russia's business."

"So should Estonia have left the statues of Lenin and Marx behind too?" I asked.

"No, it was right to take those down. Those were political figures. This statue is of a common soldier. It is neutral."

"Now that everything has settled down a bit, what do Russians think of Estonians?"

"They think Estonians are fascists!" he smiled. "I went to a soccer match in Russia and a Russian asked me, in all seriousness, if it's true that Estonians walk through the street with Nazi swastikas on their clothes! I couldn't believe that some people actually believe that!"

Not only was Artur not wearing his regular Nazi outfit, but he also argued that Russophones must integrate in the Estonian culture. He said, "Russians living in Estonia should know who the most famous Estonian writers and singers are. They should know how to speak Estonian."

Although he and his wife, Nastya, both believe their child should learn Estonia's language and culture, they are sending their seven-year-old boy to a Russian school—a mediocre place to learn about Estonian language and culture. Nastya, who went to a Russian school in Estonia, said that Estonia's Tartu University was hard because she had to quickly learn Estonian, despite years of classes before college. I asked, "Given your beliefs about integration, why are you guys sending your son to a Russian school?"

Nastya replied, "When Estonians find out that a kid has Russian parents, they mumble, 'Ah, that explains everything.' In other words, Estonians often attribute any character flaw to your Russian heritage. Russian kids are picked on in Estonian schools. We hope our son learns Estonian language and culture later."

Future mothers may not have that option because Russian schools are disappearing. For example, Artur's mom teaches Russian in Tartu, and she says that five years ago there were five Russian schools; now there are only two.

The Bronze Night highlights the biggest issue in Estonia's future: not alienating its large Russophone population. That night proved to all Estonians just how fragile their independence is. A few more sloppy steps and Russia might have crushed Estonia just as it crushed Georgia in 2008. Estonia's future depends on making peace and co-existing with its large Russian population.

Estonia is calmer than the media leads you to believe

For the seven people on the planet who are curious about what's going on in Estonia, it may seem that its citizens are always embroiled with some Russian controversy. However, let's not exaggerate this perspective. Igor told me, "Our society is too politicized, mostly due to the brainwashing by nationalist politicians, and the two communities are separated indeed, but I hope you see that the picture is much more bright and relaxed."

He told me that he is "not against learning the Estonian language," but that he "hopes that people could be more reasonable." For instance, there's no sense in forcing people who live in Narva (an Estonian city next to the Russian border) to learn Estonian. Nearly everyone in Narva is a Russophone. Igor said, "They not only can survive without Estonian, but they actually have no practical use for it there."

He concluded, "I wish we could talk more about cinema, literature and travel—these are some of the things that really fill everyday life to much greater extent than external political issues. I hope you do not see people in Estonia from the perspective of national confrontation only. We actually live quite normally here."

I lived in Estonia throughout the winter of 2008–2009 and I agree with Igor. Few discuss the Russian-Estonian relations. Most just want to hang out in saunas, sing, and go canoeing.

Chaos on a canoe trip

The Maldives and the Netherlands may be the flattest countries on earth, but Estonia isn't far behind. Thus, when Maiu invited me to canoe the *Ahja Jõgi* (Ahja River) during my 2004 trip, I figured it would be just as easy as canoeing in a swimming pool. I was right: it was incredibly easy. Unfortunately, I underestimated how incompetent I can be.

The *Ahja Jõgi* is a shallow, lazy river that cuts through Estonia's Otepää region. Given how unassuming this river was, I laughed when we were given life jacket. I filmed the pleasant pastoral landscapes from the canoe as Maiu paddled. After an hour, Maiu noticed a part of the river that dipped a tiny bit, thereby creating whitewater that might scare someone without arms or legs.

I confidently shouted to Maiu, "Don't worry, I can navigate our way through this with my eyes closed!" I put my camcorder in my pocket and calmly prepared for the little dip. The canoe approached the dip at an angle, which was somewhat troubling. Suddenly we saw several metal protrusions right on the dip. We tried to avoid them, but the canoe slammed into the protrusions and flipped us into the river. Maiu fell gracefully into the water, but sharp rocks sliced my feet and bruised my lower back. On the other hand, the water was refreshing and I learned that life jackets really do work.

There was some good news and bad news about overturning the canoe. The bad news is that my camcorder got wet and began malfunctioning. Whenever I tried to turn it off, it would eject the tape. This irritating behavior would haunt me for the rest of my 2004 trip in Eastern Europe. To get around that problem, I would have to pop out the battery whenever I needed to turn it off. The good news was that Maiu stripped down to her underwear to dry off her wet clothes. I thought sacrificing my camcorder to see her petite body nearly naked was a fair trade.

Backpacking without mountains

Figuring that I should stick with what I know, we left the river behind and backpacked Estonia's gentle hills. I proposed a two-day 50-kilometer (35-mile) trip. Maiu thought that was insane, but she agreed to go as long as I carried her. She had never camped under a tarp and was surprised that we stayed dry during a rainstorm. She could have never imagined that two years after our first backpacking trip, she would spend four months living under a tarp. That happened when we backpacked 4,240 kilometers (2,650 miles) on America's Pacific Crest Trail.[3]

The day after the rainstorm, a family invited us into their house after they saw us lost in their backyard. Soon they served us *rosolje,* a classic Estonian dish that has *peet* (beet), *liha* (meat), and *heeringas* (Baltic herring, Estonia's national fish). Everyone also ate *leib* (black rye bread). Lastly, they offered Estonia's signature food: *kama.* Although Finns also eat *kama* (they call it *talkkuna*), it's hard to find anywhere else. *Kama* is a finely milled powder made of roasted barley, oats, peas, and rye. Imagine bread crumbs put through a coffee grinder—that's similar to *kama.* We swirled it in kefir. It's not sweet, although some mix it with sugar. During the five months I lived in Estonia, I ate *kama* almost every day.

Estonian cuisine is heavy. Russian and Germanic influences pervade in the Estonian kitchen. This translates into a meat and potato diet. Most of the Estonian population lives near the Baltic Sea, where herring, anchovies, and salmon are also popular. Estonian food won't win many culinary awards, but it tastes great when you're hungry.

An empty belly is the best cook. — Estonian Proverb

I assumed that since this nice family lived in the woods, they had no Internet connection. They not only proved me wrong, but they also demonstrated that Estonians make Americans look like the Flintstones.

E-stonia

Estonia is sometimes called *E-stonia,* because it is one of the most wired countries in the world. Many people assume that Estonia is behind the times, like most of Eastern Europe. However, in many ways Estonia is ahead of the US. For example, when Florida was debating the merits of punch cards and chads in the 2001 election, Estonians were voting in their pajamas. Estonians have a smart card that lets them vote from anywhere.

Estonia gets its tech culture from its Nordic neighbors. In 2011, Nordic countries had the highest percentage of households with high-speed Internet connections. Surveys show that Estonia is more wired than Germany, Spain, or France. Meanwhile, Southern European countries, like Italy and Greece, are in the Internet Stone Age.

Americans think we're tech savvy if we use PayPal, but Estonians make us look like we're still using the barter system. In 2008, Estonians were already paying each other through their mobile phones. Their phones act like a mini-bank. If you need to send someone money, just compose a text message (SMS) from your phone. Combine Estonia's smart ID card with your phone or computer and you can authenticate yourself for almost any transaction. Goodbye cash.

Next time you're lugging a bowling ball's weight in coins to get 10 minutes at the parking meter, think of Estonia. In 2006, Estonians were already paying for parking via SMS. Just SMS your license plate number to the number indicated on the parking lot's sign. When you leave, call them, and an automated system answers and sends an SMS with your parking bill. The amount is added to your phone bill. Although you won't save much money, at least you don't have to carry around a bunch of coins.

Finally, next time you Skype someone, thank the four Estonians who developed it. Also, Skype employees should thank Microsoft, which bought Skype for $8 billion in 2011. Now those four Estonians can finally afford to buy a legal copy of Microsoft Word instead of pirating it.

By the time you read this, you may think, "We do all these things in America now. What's the big deal?" The point is Estonia was doing it years before us. If you want to see the future, go to E-stonia.

The freest country on Earth

America calls itself "The Land of the Free." However, according to The State of the World Liberty Project, the US was number eight on the list of the freest countries. The project generated a composite score based on three factors: (1) economic freedom; (2) individual freedom; (3) government involvement and tax burden. The 2006 survey looked at 140 countries. The results: the least free country in the world was North Korea; the freest was Estonia.

Let's look at the three components to understand why. First, Estonia's *economic freedom* is high because its citizens have a high degree of personal choice, are free to exchange goods based on market prices, can compete in markets, and have excellent property rights. The second component, *individual freedom*, soared with the dissolution of the USSR. Estonians travel freely and can scream, "Bring Lenin back! The press is not free!" and nobody will care.

The third component, *government involvement and tax policy,* is where Estonia truly stands out. Estonia transformed itself from a totalitarian society into a libertarian one. Starting a business in Estonia takes less than seven days on average. Only Singapore offers a more efficient bureaucracy. Estonia soared up the World Bank's Ease of Doing Business survey—in 2011 it ranked 17th in the world, above Germany and Japan. Their finances are cleaner than a microprocessor plant. In 2011, while most eurozone economies weren't complying with their euro standards, Estonia was and joined the club. In 2010, Estonia's debt as a percentage of GDP was just 7.7 percent—that makes it one of the top 10 countries with the lowest debt burden.

Estonia's income tax is so simple that it's almost a pleasure to pay it. In 2011, all income exceeding the basic exemption is taxed at 20 percent. To make it insanely simple, the government totals up all your income sources and calculates your taxes for you on their secure website. All you have to do is log on and click "Approve." Payments or rebates get settled electronically. Even corporations pay the same 20 percent flat tax, so they don't have to hire an army of tax lawyers and accountants to understand the system. I couldn't find an Estonian who took more than 10 minutes to do his taxes.

In sum, there are five types of taxes: income, payroll, VAT, and excise taxes. That's it. No other sneaky taxes. Your parents die? No inheritance or estate taxes. You sold stock or real estate at a profit? Congratulations, no capital gains taxes for you. You want to reinvest your company's profits? No tax on that either. Move to another part of the country? No special local or regional taxes to pay anywhere. You just bought a car? No car or road tax for you. You own a home? Starting in 2013 there will be no property tax. There is no tax on many other things, including education, cultural events, and, most importantly, sauna services.

It's not surprising that because the tax code is so disarmingly simple, tax evasion is one of the lowest in the region. As a percent of GDP, taxes make up 31 percent of their economy. Although that's a bit higher than the US tax burden, it's lower than most European countries. The point is that the cost of tax compliance is super low because even a child can understand Estonia's tax regulations. The other remarkable point is that Estonia was able to transform itself from a totalitarian state to a libertarian one in less than 20 years. They did it in a peaceful and orderly fashion. We can all learn from that.

The sound of 300,000 people singing

To see one of the world's largest choirs, you must go to one of the world's smallest countries. Once every five years Tallinn hosts the *Laulupidu* (Estonian Song Festival). The climax is when nearly 30,000 singers stand on an enormous stage and chant Estonian folk tunes. I was lucky to be in Tallinn for the event in 2004. Hearing 30,000 singers gives you shivers and your heart soars. Although I didn't understand the lyrics, I understood the emotion. These were the songs that were banned under the Soviet regime. They were also the songs that helped bring down the USSR.

On September 11, 1988, *a quarter of the Estonian population,* 300,000 citizens, crammed into Tallinn and chanted banned national hymns. Maiu's entire family (including her grandmother) was there. The Soviets knew how to handle 300,000 Germans charging at them with rifles, but they weren't trained to deal with 300,000 Estonians singing at them armed only with their voices.

Maiu explained what life was like before the Singing Revolution. When she was a little girl, it was normal to see tanks in the streets. Few had cars back then, so tanks owned the road. "Seeing a tank was like seeing a car today," she said. "Whenever it would roll by our apartment, the earth would shake and the windows would vibrate."

Now imagine singing while a Soviet tank is pointing straight at your face. That's exactly what brave Estonians did when the Soviets tried to shut down their radio and TV stations. Estonians held hands, encircled the TV tower, and sang hymns as tears ran down their cheeks. Such bravery gave Estonia's leaders the courage to declare their independence on August 20, 1991. In short, Estonians regained their freedom by singing their hearts out. No blood was ever spilled. Estonia's Baltic neighbors, Latvia and Lithuania, were not so lucky.

Sauna experience part II

After the 2004 Song Festival, Maiu invited me to go to her summer house, which is in Lahemaa National Park. Founded in 1971, it was the USSR's first national park. Although Lahemaa is great for hiking and biking, Estonians see it as a hunting ground for berries and mushrooms. We followed the Viru Bog Nature Trail, which has a long boardwalk traversing the wetlands. From a wooden tower, we overlooked the park, admired the Baltic Sea, and snapped a photo of ourselves. Lahemaa is a paradise if you like bogs and swamps. While the rest of the world fights to get rid of their mosquitoes, Estonia is protecting a few trillion of them.

Maiu's summer residence had a large unfinished house, a primitive cottage, and a stream in the backyard. Although the kitchen had piped water, the only toilet was an outhouse. For a shower, they stored water in a large barrel. Like a true Estonian, the first room that Maiu's father built was the wood-powered sauna. Like Finns, Estonians are obsessed with saunas. Maiu's father would boil himself in the sauna and then jump in the frigid stream. He'd repeat this cycle until dawn.

He lived a good life, but he died of cancer when he was 55 years old. After telling me about her father, Maiu asked in her childlike voice, "Do you want to use the sauna?"

I immediately thought of my Finnish sauna experience that I had had the previous week. At this point, Maiu and I had spent several days together traveling throughout Estonia. Our relationship was platonic, although I was hopelessly attracted to her. *She has a boyfriend,* I reminded myself every hour. Going into a sauna with her would be torture, but I told myself what people like to tell themselves when they're masochists: *it builds character.*

This time I felt like a sauna veteran: I confidently entered the baking sauna naked. I told Maiu that she need not be self-conscious because without my glasses I can't see the big "E" at the eye doctor. Her towel dropped to the floor. Despite being nearly blind, I could see enough to admire Maiu's skinny, yet toned body. By now, I had learned a lot about her American boyfriend. They had spent most of the last three years apart. Maiu was no longer sure about whether she wanted to marry him. In fact, several years ago many Estonians began to question the very institution of marriage.

In 1996, Estonia had the highest divorce rate in Europe: it was twice the European average and four times higher than Poland's. Interestingly, Estonia's marriage rate that year was also the lowest in Europe. In other words, in 1996 few wanted to get married and the fools that did got divorced. So why did Estonians have such a high divorce rate?

The least religious country on the planet

One reason couples stay together despite a crappy marriage is that they are religious. For example, Greece, Ireland, and Poland are some of the most religious European countries and they also have some of Europe's lowest divorce rates. Estonia, on the other hand, is the least religious country on the planet—76 percent of Estonians said they have "no religion." Compare that to the 15 percent of Americans who are irreligious. In 2009, only 17 percent of Estonians told Gallup that religion was an important part of their daily life (only China and Sweden had lower rates). Meanwhile, just 12 percent of Estonians had attended a religious service in the previous week (only Vietnam was lower). Atheists rule Estonia.

By 2011, perhaps due to a decade of prosperity, the Estonian divorce rate diminished 30 percent. Although it's still above the European average, if you're a guy who is considering marrying an Estonian, then relax—Estonia's divorce rate is still lower than America's. Besides, Estonian women are incredibly hot, so go for it.

Speaking of hot Estonian women, while I was in the sauna with Maiu, I wasn't thinking about divorce rates and I certainly wasn't thinking about religion. As sweat dripped down Maiu's body, our bodies touched, she smiled, and I flooded my brain with: *she has a boyfriend!* She pressed up her warm, wet body against mine and looked at me flirtatiously. Overcoming near-death experiences in the wilderness had given me more willpower than the average naked dude in a sauna.

Officially, nothing happened in that sauna, but it was certainly hot in there. I explained to Maiu that I respected her relationship with her boyfriend. If she wanted to kiss, she would have to initiate it. If she wanted to break up with her boyfriend, she had to make that choice. We rinsed off using the water in the barrel. Later that evening, Maiu said she had made her decision. We embraced.

Part of me wanted to just settle down in Estonia and be with Maiu. On the other hand, I had promised myself to see every country in Eastern Europe and it was crazy to quit my journey after seeing just one country. Maiu understood this and eventually took me to the *bussijaam* (the bus station). I bought a ticket to the second of the three Baltic countries—Latvia. We hugged. I looked her in the eyes and said, *"Kohtumiseni."*

She replied, "I hope to see you soon too."

I put my backpack on, boarded the bus, and headed south to Latvia.

An old lady predicts Estonia's future

As the bus crossed the Estonia-Latvian border, I looked back and remembered a conversation I had had with an old lady on an Estonian bus a few days before. She was holding a transparent plastic bag that allowed me to spot an English children's book in it. It's hard to find old Eastern Europeans who speak English, so I asked her about what life was like now. She spoke excellent English. She said, "It's getting better. The young kids are more interested in learning the Estonian language and preserving the culture."

"What about the Russian population?" I asked.

"They are still separate. The integration is just starting. It will take time. This is only the beginning. Sorry, but this is my stop." She smiled and left. It was a perfect, succinct summary of Estonia's promising future and the obstacles it faces on that path.

What Estonia Can Teach Us

- **Adopt libertarian principles.** Estonia is Eastern Europe's economic star. Few have improved more in the last 20 years. Many are copying Estonia. For example, half of Eastern

Europe has a flat tax system, including Russia. Estonia has followed other libertarian habits like privatizing most industries, protecting personal freedoms, ending corporate subsidies, and abolishing tariffs to make goods cheaper for poor people. Estonia is no utopia, but it's doing remarkably well, especially when one considers where it started from and how few resources it has.

- **Bring voting to the twenty-first century.** Let's hope that by America's 2012 election, everyone will be able to vote over the Internet. Only half of eligible American voters exercise their right. One big reason for such low turnout is that we're lazy. If voting were as easy as visiting Facebook, then we'd have high participation.
- **Aim for low population density.** In 2011, Estonians had 31 inhabitants per square kilometer, which is the lowest population density in Europe. The average in Europe is 111 inhabitants per square kilometer. (The UK has 256 and the Netherlands is tightly packed at 491.) Although Estonians have government incentives to reproduce, it's nice that they have more elbow room than any other European.
- **Turn cell phones into banks.** Estonians pay each other by just sending a text command via their cell phone. They pay for parking via their cell phone. In short, their cell phones behave like mini-banks ever since 2004. In 2013, check out what Estonia is doing so we don't take another eight years to catch up.
- **Sing!** Estonia is called the Singing Nation for good reason. Let's follow their tune. Singing releases endorphins, works out your lungs, floods your body with oxygen, strengthens your abdomen, improves your posture, and stimulates your circulation. Most importantly, singing encourages socialization and bonding with others. And, every once in a while, it can even topple an empire.

Places I saw and recommend in Estonia: Tallinn's Old Town. If you have extra time, visit Lahemaa National Park, Tartu, and Saaremaa.

Travel info and deals: http://ftapon.com/estonia

Although I loved Estonia, I stayed there far longer than I had planned. As my bus pulled into Rīga, the capital of Latvia, I couldn't wait to step outside and explore.

3
Latvia—the Baltic core

Upon Arriving in Latvia's capital, Rīga, I went straight to the red light district. Even though it was the afternoon, there were already a couple of whores working the streets. However, I wasn't seeking their services, I was just looking for a cheap hotel. I found the one mentioned in my guidebook. I didn't have a reservation, but they had vacancy and a great price: $22 per night.

The room was minimalist. The wallpaper was peeling off, the bed was squeaky, and the bathroom needed a makeover. However, it was clean and its lack of luxury encouraged me to get out and explore Rīga. I was excited to explore Latvia because it brought back childhood memories.

Latveria vs. Latvia

Like Estonia, Latvia sounds like a place where a comic book villain would be based. In fact, it is. Dilbert has Elbonia, but Marvel Comics has *Latveria*. When I was a boy, I knew all about Latveria—it is an Eastern European country run by the brilliant and sinister Doctor Doom. His Romanian gypsy sorceress mother named him Victor von Doom. After getting his PhD, he got his cuddly nickname: Dr. Doom. He reigns over Latveria with an iron fist, literally. Like Darth Vader, Dr. Doom is a human underneath an armored suit. To prevent a potential *coup d'état,* Dr. Doom built a look-a-like Doombot to stand in for him while he's off subduing other countries. Before he took power, Latveria's capital was called Hassenstadt, which in German means "Hatetown." Dr. Doom changed it to a more cheerful, touristy name: Doomstadt.

Although Latveria is mentioned several times in the *Fantastic Four* movies, there's one fact that's omitted. It's that Latveria has a special holiday that can happen whenever Dr. Doom feels like his nation needs a break. He calls it Doom's Day. He hates when people confuse it with doomsday. Lastly, Dr. Doom's three main goals in life are modest: prove his superiority to Reed Richards of the Fantastic Four, venture to the underworld to recover his dead mother, and conquer the world.

Therefore, unlike most ignorant Americans, I knew exactly what Latvia was about. It was obvious to me that Latveria was simply modeled after Latvia and that the honest folks at Marvel Comics had just changed the name slightly for legal reasons. However, as I walked through the streets of Rīga and failed to see Dr. Doom's castle high on a mountaintop, I started questioning my preparation for this country.

Latvian cuisine will make a vegetarian cry

I entered a random restaurant to have a meal and get organized. I ordered a typical Latvian starter, the *aukstā zupa.* This beet and kefir soup is often topped with sour cream and is quite delicious. I asked the waitress to bring an entrée with lots of veggies, so she brought me an entrée with lots of ham.

It's hard for Latvians to imagine a meal without meat. They're afraid that if they don't get meat at every meal, they might not survive the winter. When they do feature vegetables, they often like to cook them to death. Latvians also avoid seasoning their veggies for fear that you might like them and become a vegetarian.

While I ate bland potatoes, cooked cabbage, and overcooked peas, I tried to learn the Latvian language. Latvian has little in common with Lithuanian and nothing in common with Estonian. It uses a turbo-charged version of the Latin alphabet with 33 letters. Letters with diacritics can change a word's meaning. For example, *pile* means *drop,* but *pīle* means *duck.* In addition, the verbal pitch can alter the meaning of a word. For example, if you say *loks* with a level tone, it means *green onion;* say *loks* with a falling tone, it means *arch* or *bow.*

> *Šis žagaru saišķis ir mans žagaru saišķis.*
> *— Latvian tongue twister meaning, "This bundle of sticks is my bundle of sticks."*

Among Latvia's 2.2 million citizens, only 60 percent consider Latvian their mother tongue. Most of the rest speak Russian. Still, it's useful to learn *sveiki* (hello), *paldies* (thanks), *jā* (yes), *nē* (no), *lūdzu* (please), *piedod* (sorry), and *cik?* (how much?). Saying *goodbye* is a tongue twister: *uz redzēšanos.* This is guarantees that you'll never say goodbye to a Latvian. If you must say *bye,* then say the informal version: *atā.* Lastly, in emergency situations, these two phrases are helpful: *kur ir tualete?* (where is the toilet?) and *es tevi mīlu* (I love you).

After you master Latvia's basic phrases, graduate to swearwords. The good news is that you already know them. Latvians think their swearwords lack the punch of English swearwords. Therefore, when you eavesdrop on young Latvians, you'll occasionally hear them say, in their Latvian accent, *fucked up, shit,* and *fucking asshole.*

A few Latvians have spiced up their swearing repertoire with Russian swearwords. The most popular is *bljin.* It's a derivation of brutally rude Russian word of *bljadj,* which few Latvians dare to utter because it's so strong (Russians use it like Americans use *fuck*). Therefore, Latvians toned *bljadj* down to *bljin,* which sounds better to their sensitive ears. I think they've toned it down a bit too much: *bljin* means *pancake.* When I accidentally hit my finger with a hammer, I need to scream something that has a bit more sting than *pancake!*

History etched in Rīga's buildings

Rīga is one of those towns that give you a sore neck. It's hard not to spend the whole time craning your neck to scrutinize every intricately sculptured church. In fact, every building is a work of art. If you know where to look, you'll see Rīga's famous whimsical *melnais kaķis* (black cat) on the top of an elegant yellow building. Inviting alleys, cobblestoned streets, and quaint cafés are everywhere. Rīga prides itself as being the jewel of the Baltic. In 2014, it will serve as The European Capital of Culture—a perfect choice.

There's something to learn from every building. For example, from the mighty Daugava River you can see three steeples dominating the Rīga's skyline. Built in 1211, the *Doma Baznīca* (Dome Basilica) is still the biggest cathedral in the Baltic. It had the largest pipe organ in the world in 1884. UNESCO recognized Rīga's new town (which isn't that new) as showing off some of the finest examples of Art Nouveau. Gargoyles, goblins, and ghouls seem to watch you wherever you go. St. Peter's Church is an 800-year-old Gothic masterpiece. The *Rātslaukums* (Town Hall Square) has the colorful House of the Blackheads, which was built in 1344 and recently had a fresh makeover. It's seems like an important building, but it's just where the Blackheads, a guild of unmarried foreign merchants, hooked up with chicks hundreds of years ago.

The Blackheads had another good tradition a few centuries ago that, unfortunately, has gone away. When a Latvian joined a guild, they started out as a tradesman. After spending three to five years as an apprentice, Latvians would travel for three to four years. After those years of wandering, they returned to make a masterpiece in their area of expertise. If the masterpiece was noteworthy, then the apprentice would be accepted into the guild. It's a pity we don't do this today. Our educational system underestimates how much young people learn by traveling.

The last 800 years have been rough for Latvia

Having the most desirable location in the Baltic isn't always a good thing, especially when you live between two strong and rich men: Germany and Russia.

> *Never wrestle with a strong man, nor bring a rich man to court. — Latvian proverb*

In the last 800 years Latvia has been beaten more heavily than a rented mule. If they can devote an entire museum to all the times someone has occupied their land, you know they've had some rough times. When I entered Latvia's Museum of Occupation, I learned that the first person to pummel Latvia was the Pope. In 1198, the curiously named Pope Innocent III declared war on Latvia. However, God wasn't on his side that year and he lost to the pagans. A couple of years later, the Pope tried again, but now armed with even more brutal German soldiers. This time the Christians managed to slaughter the Latvians and convince the survivors that their God was good.

For centuries, the fates of Estonia and Latvia were intertwined as they were considered one territory: Livonia. As a result, their histories are similar. It's an endless story of one country manhandling Latvia after another: first Germany, then Poland, then Sweden, then Russia, then Germany, then Russia. The Baltic states are like that little nerdy guy at school who always got beat up for his lunch money.

Consider their history since 1935. The Soviets gave Latvia just six hours to elect a pro-Soviet government. The Estonians and Latvians gave flowers to the Nazis because they liberated them from the Russian bear. However, the Nazis showed their true colors and killed almost 500,000 Baltic folks in concentration camps. They also imposed their ugly language and did all those nasty things that Nazis do. The Soviets forced Latvians to fight for the USSR; meanwhile, Nazis rounded up Latvians and threatened to kill them unless they joined the "Latvian SS *Volunteer* Legion." As a result, Latvians were shooting each other in WWII. After WWII, Joseph Stalin picked up where Adolf Hitler left off: he deported 250,000 Baltic citizens to Siberia.

Americans may often feel frustrated that we have to choose between a Democrat and a Republican. However, think of the Latvians: they had the pleasure of choosing between Stalin and Hitler. Wouldn't that make you want to stay home on election day? In 1989, however, the citizens of the Baltic did not stay home. They stepped outside and did something extraordinary.

The Baltic Way—the longest human chain ever

The Molotov-Ribbentrop Pact was a secret agreement between the Soviets and the Nazis right before WWII. In it, Stalin and Hitler agreed to split up Eastern Europe between themselves. For 49 years, the USSR denied that the pact had existed and they would punish anyone who mentioned it. However, in 1989, one week before the pact's 50th anniversary, the USSR admitted that the pact was real, although they claimed that the three Baltic states joined the USSR "voluntarily." On the 50th anniversary, the Baltic states performed what is arguably the most amazing collective act in human history.

On August 23, 1989 at 7:00 p.m., two million demonstrators formed a human chain that spanned 600 kilometers (373 miles). They held hands for 15 minutes. It started from the capital of Estonia (Tallinn), went through the capital of Latvia (Rīga), and finished in the capital of Lithuania (Vilnius). There were eight million people in those three states; therefore, one in four was in the chain. It was one of the longest unbroken human chains in history.

Maiu was nine years old during the Baltic Way protest. She held hands with her twin sister and her aunt. They were in the countryside while Maiu's parents were in Tallinn, participating in the protest there. It's impressive that even though Maiu and her twin sister were hundreds of kilometers away from their parents, for 15 minutes they were connected to them via a two-million person chain.

Jana Ladusāne, a Latvian that I met in Rīga, was also in the middle of the countryside during the Baltic Way demonstration. Her family drove to where people were stretching their arms far to stay connected. Although she was only 11 years old at the time, Jana recalled the event, "Many people had transistor radios to hear the live news. It was great feeling, and when I recently saw a movie about the Baltic Way, it gave me shivers to remember. I was kind of proud that I was there. This feeling of unity—that was really something."

Before the Baltic Way even happened, the communist leaders of East Germany and Romania both offered to help the USSR break up the demonstrations. Hey, what are friends for anyway? However, Soviet leader Mikhail Gorbachev let the protest happen. Perhaps he figured, "How could a couple of million unarmed people holding hands harm the mighty USSR?"

Less than three months after the Baltic Way, the Berlin Wall came crashing down. A month later, Gorbachev condemned the secret Molotov-Ribbentrop Pact. About three months after that, the Baltic states declared their independence. In January 1991, Latvians erected barricades in and around Rīga to fight for independence. They ultimately succeeded, although about five people died in the process. I had come to the end of the Museum of Occupation. It inspired me to go to the symbol of Latvia's freedom.

Russians in Latvia

Unveiled in 1935, Rīga's Freedom Monument is a tall obelisk with a copper woman holding three gilded stars. These stars represented Latvia's three constitutional districts. Starting in the late 1940s, the devious Soviets taught schoolchildren that the copper woman was Mother Russia, who was three stars represented her three grateful Baltic republics: Estonia, Latvia, and Lithuania. Despite the Orwellian attempts to rewrite history, the true history was quietly kept alive in every Latvian home.

Soon after their independence, Latvians would gather around the Freedom Monument once a year to honor Latvians who fought against the Soviets in WWII. That sounds reasonable, but Russians argue that Latvians are effectively honoring Nazi sympathizers, since those Latvians fought alongside Germany. Just like Russia said that the "zealots of Nazism" moved the Bronze Soldier in Estonia, Russians said that Latvian parties around their Freedom Monument is a glorification of Nazism. It's the standard Russian tactic: if there's any group you don't like, call them Nazi fascists.

Latvia's Russophone situation parallels Estonia's. About 100 years ago, Russophones made up about 10 percent of Latvia's population; by 2011, they made up a third. Latvia's new government was slow to offer Russophones citizenship and gave most of them Alien Passports. I asked Edite Lucava, a Latvian I met in Belarus, how Latvian-Russian were relations today. She said, "It's a very political and also an everyday problem. For example, Rīga is 40 percent Russian, and in some cities close to the Russian border it's over 60 percent Russian! Our relationship is easy in everyday life, but difficult in politics. Some Russians are isolated in their own societies. They can't talk in Latvian, but some are brave and integrate very well!"

I asked her, "Do you have Russian friends?"

"Yes, I have some nice, wonderful Russian friends, but they understand that Latvia is an independent country and not part of *Russia*! The problem is that the elder generation still doesn't accept that communism is over and they will never learn our language, they will never get citizenship and somehow they are isolated. Sad, but true!"

Boom, bust, but better than before

Visiting Latvia in 2004 was fun because it seemed like everyone was high on drugs. The economy was booming and Latvia had joined the EU and NATO. People were proud. When I returned to Latvia in 2006, it had become the fastest growing economy in Europe. Latvians acted like they had just won the lottery, or at least moved away from their mother-in-law.

I approached a professionally dressed banker who was eating alone at a café in Rīga. Her name was Maria. She was young, plump, and friendly. I asked her how things were in the banking industry. "Oh, it's crazy," she said with a smile. "Everyone is buying homes and apartments. Before you couldn't get a mortgage. Now it's so easy. Prices have doubled in nearly a year. People now have credit cards and car loans. It's out of control."

"When will it end?" I asked.

"I don't know," she admitted, looking at her coffee.

The following two years Latvia's economy continued surging 10 percent per year. Latvia experienced nearly a decade of explosive growth as it tried to catch up to Western Europe. Japanese call the 1990s the "Lost Decade" because, economically, they went nowhere for those 10 years. Latvians (as well as most Eastern Europeans) could call their lousy period the "Lost Century." They feel that they wasted the last century either in violent wars or under oppressive communism. There is a palpable sensation among Latvians that they want to make up for their Lost Century. They're tired of being in the Hidden Europe.

Latvia's small size makes its vulnerable to boom-bust cycles. Geographically, Latvia is about the same size as Ireland or West Virginia. Economically, it is smaller than North Dakota and accounts for just 0.15% of the EU's GDP. Thus, it quickly soared after communism, but then crashed hard during the Great Recession. It went from the fastest growing economy in the EU to the weakest economy. By 2011, its economy shrank 20% and housing prices dropped 66% from their peak. During the Great Recession, only 5% of Lithuanians and 6% of Latvians said that their "standard of living was getting better." Those were the lowest rates in the world, although 10 out of 12 of worst countries were from Eastern Europe.

Many blame the excesses on unregulated capitalism. They forget that communism also experienced booms and busts. We often underestimate the role that human psychology plays in economic cycles. In 2011, a Latvian told me, "What we call an 'economic crisis' today was our everyday existence during the Soviet period. Yes, poor people today are hurting more than they were under communism, but look at the average Latvian: they're driving modern cars, wearing nice clothes, shopping at well-stocked grocery stores, and watching satellite TV. Under communism, we would have loved to have such a 'crisis.'"

Maiu told me, "During the Soviet period, a popular gift was toilet paper."

"Why is that?" I asked.

"Because back then, everyone used newspapers to wipe their asses."

That's worth remembering next time anyone romanticizes about the government's ability to do anything well. If governments can't even make toilet paper well, what can they do well?

Finding Dr. Doom's castle

In November 2006, I found Dr. Doom's Latveria. Maiu and I visited Sigulda, which is located in Gauja National Park. Our timing was good, because in a few months, Sigulda would celebrate its 800th birthday, so the town looked like it had put on its best makeup.

The region has several castles set in dramatic places. For example, on one cliff, the red brick medieval Turaida Castle overlooks the valley below. Nearby there is the Dainu Hill Song Garden, which features a collection of enormous stone sculptures that look surreal in the grassy landscape. With the fog enveloping their stony faces and partially hiding the castle, I felt I was in Dr. Doom's Latveria. Further evidence lay on the other side of the Gauja River, where I saw the remains of Sigulda Medieval Castle. Clearly, the Doombots had blasted the rival castle with their missiles.

It's fascinating how graffiti becomes art after a few hundred years. For example, archaeologists celebrate prehistoric cave paintings without mentioning that cavemen may have scolded their teenagers for making those paintings on their living room walls. Similarly, just southwest of Sigulda Castle, along the Gauja River, old graffiti is preserved behind glass as if it were the Mona Lisa. The graffiti was done on the special sandstone near the caves of the Big Devil and Little Devil. The sandstone is soft enough to carve into, but strong enough to withstand Latvia's rough weather. Although the date and names are different, what's written is effectively "John wuz here 1723."

A tale of two cities that are one: Valga-Valka

When I returned to Latvia in February 2009, I entered via the border town of Valga (Valka in Estonia). I met Ainārs, a young man living on the Latvian side of the town. He claimed that before WWI, Valga was mostly Latvian. During WWI, Estonia helped Latvia fight off the Germans and Russians, who both wanted to take over the area. After the Baltic team won, Ainārs said that Estonians demanded the town as "payment" for their help. A British colonel split the town along a small creek, so that 80 percent of the town went to Estonia. During the USSR, this split didn't matter since Estonia and Latvia were both Soviet republics. After the USSR broke up, the town had an annoying border through it.

Today, the most interesting part of Valga-Valka is their hidden border. I took a bus from Tartu (Estonia's adorable university town) to the northern edge of Valga, Estonia. When Germans ruled the town, they called it *Walk*. So I walked through Walk. I passed a reddish church, an outdoor market, a pleasant Estonian museum, stately buildings, a gray church, and a grassy square with yet another church. When I bought a cheese-filled pastry, the vendor surprised me by talking in Latvian. She disapproved of the Estonian money I was offering her (this was before Estonia adopted the euro). I was confused. "Am I in Latvia now?" I wondered. I looked behind me. Where had I crossed the border?

I retraced my steps and I couldn't find any sign that announced that I had just left Estonia and entered Latvia. It's effectively one town with an invisible border. There are faint clues that show where the border checkpoint used to be. Once Estonia and Latvia joined the EU, they dismantled their border checkpoints. If Latvia adopts the euro as planned in 2015, then the only way you'll know where you are is by noticing how the store signs transition from one incomprehensible language to another incomprehensible language.

Dungeons and Dragons fantasies in Latvia's Vidzeme region

Like Sigulda, Cēsis is a quaint town located on the Gauja River. Although Sigulda has more castles, Cēsis has romantic cobblestoned streets and plenty of picturesque buildings that look lovely in the snow. Throw in some nice places to ski (or hike in the summer) and you'll understand why this part of the Vidzeme region is so popular. My favorite part was exploring the medieval castle in Cēsis in the snow. It's Latvia's best preserved castle. On the castle grounds I found something unexpected: a statue of Lenin lying in a coffin. I brushed off the snow that had collected on Lenin's cold, dark face. For a moment, I felt sorry for the guy. All that effort, all that hope, all those deaths for one grand failed experiment. Lenin meant well, but, in the end, his idea was pretty stupid.

I left Lenin in his cold coffin and carefully stepped through the snow-covered ice. On the castle's self-guided tour you're given a lantern with a real candle in it. The lantern helped fulfill my Dungeons and Dragons fantasies of delving into a ruined castle. It made me realize that it's incredibly easy for an orc to surprise a cleric. The candle sheds little light and your footsteps echo. Any dumb orc can hear you as soon as you enter the dungeon. In the darkness, you'll never know what hit you. I also learned that I have a low Dexterity score, as I slipped and fell hard on the ice a couple of times. It's good that I wasn't carrying a sword in my other hand.

As the sun set, the temperature was dropping, the snow was falling, and I had no idea where I was going to sleep that night. I was carrying the same sleeping bag that kept me warm during the snowy nights on the Continental Divide Trail. Nevertheless, it's a challenge to camp when it's snowing. Luckily, I found a covered and hidden place in town that was perfect, right next to the main church. Normally I wouldn't risk camping in such a central location, but the snowstorm guaranteed that no thieves would be trolling around at night. Although it was only 7:00 p.m., I was exhausted from having traveled hard for the previous three days. I wore all my clothes to increase my warmth, I watched the snow fall, and within five minutes I was unconscious.

Even though I was a little cold when I woke up at 6:00 a.m., I was well-rested and excited to trudge through the fresh powder to the bus stop. The streets were deserted and the sun wouldn't rise until 9:00 a.m.

The Baltic is a cold, dark place in the winter. It's a stark contrast with the summer, when the daylight never completely fades from the sky, even in the middle of the night. I boarded the bus to Rīga. I had been to Latvia in the summer and fall. When I returned to Rīga for the third time, I would use Couchsurfing.

Couchsurfing.org

One of the remarkable aspects of the Internet is how it brings together people with odd beliefs and philosophies. You might believe you're the only who likes to pour hot chocolate syrup over broccoli, but there's probably a website that unites you healthy chocoholics.

Similarly, there are odd people who love to sleep in the house of a complete stranger. What's more bizarre is that there are people who like complete strangers to come into their home, take a shower, and sleep on their couch. Both the guest and the host love meeting random people in an adventurous and spontaneous way. Servas.org and HospitalityClub.org pioneered this matchmaking, but latecomer Couchsurfing.org captured the biggest market share—by 2011 it had three million members and was adding about 20,000 members per week.

Participating in Couchsurfing is easy. You join for free and fill out a profile, which potential guests/hosts look at before deciding to meet you. Although you don't pay the host, a proper guest should always bring a gift and be generous. After meeting the couchsurfer, you write a reference, summarizing your experience as *positive, neutral,* or *negative*. Like eBay, you build a reputation based on your references. And just like eBay has remarkably few thieves, Couchsurfing has remarkably few date-raping-ax-murdering-psychopaths.

For example, on one random week in 2011, there were 38,448 positive real-life couchsurfing introductions and only 66 were negative. Among 3.2 million couchsurfing encounters, 99.6 percent of the users said it was a "positive" meeting. The 0.4 percent who rated the experience "neutral" or "negative" nearly always had relatively minor complaints that result in poor communication (like someone being late or inconsiderate). Stealing and sexual assaults are practically unheard of. Only one rape has happened (when a Moroccan raped a Chinese tourist in England in 2009), and he was sentenced to 10 years in prison. One rape in 3.2 million sleepovers indicates that couchsurfing with a stranger is safer than going out on a date with someone you know.

Although I had used Couchsurfing a few times, I had never tried it in Eastern Europe. By 2009, the Eastern European Couchsurfing community had grown significantly. My first Eastern European couchsurfing experience was when an Estonian lady named Anni Oja sent me an email asking to join her for a coffee in Tallinn. Anni is yet another unappreciated breathtaking blond who lives in Estonia.

Estonia is littered with so many beautiful women that you feel like you're walking through one big *Maxim Magazine* party.

Latvia also has plenty of babes. It helps that for every 100 Latvian men, there are 117 women. Estonia and Lithuania have similar ratios. No other European country comes close to this ratio. However, before you men pack your bags, consider that the main reason for the disparity is that Baltic men die relatively young. Latvia's male death rate is nearly twice as the European average. Clearly, Latvian men die young because all the hotties give them early heart attacks. Who cares? It's worth it.

Anni had just returned from visiting her boyfriend in Mexico and she wanted to practice her Spanish with me. I chatted with Anni and her cute five-year-old daughter while sipping tea in Pierre Chocolaterie, a cozy café in Tallinn's Old Town. I invited them to have dinner with Maiu and me. The four of us had such a good time that Anni and her daughter spontaneously crashed on Maiu's couch. A week later, Anni returned the favor and invited me to sleep on her couch in Tartu. Anni, a Couchsurfing City Ambassador, was a perfect introduction to couchsurfing in Eastern Europe. Ultimately, I would sleep on dozens of couches throughout the Hidden Europe.

My first true Couchsurfing experience in Eastern Europe was with Jana Ladusāne in Rīga. I asked her if I could stay two nights. She said she could only host me for one night since the second night was Valentine's Day and she had a hot date. Her job was marketing chocolates. Her day often started with a stack of new chocolates she had to test out. Yeah, I felt sorry for her too. She had blue eyes, brown hair, a great body, and was socially awkward—all typical Baltic features.

She took me to her apartment, which didn't have a couch yet, so I wouldn't be couchsurfing—I would be floorsurfing on her inflatable mattress. After dropping off my backpack, she drove me to a snowy park and beach so that I could see parts of Rīga that are hard to get to without a car. Along the way, we talked about one of the most popular Baltic pastimes.

Mushrooming

Jana told me that Baltic people love to go mushrooming. I imagined them doing psychedelic drugs. After all, what else could she mean by *mushrooming* anyway? It's not like they go out in the forest collecting mushrooms, right? Strangely, everyone in the Baltic does this. Yup, mushrooming has nothing to do with hallucinogenics, but rather it's bizarre pastime where people flock to the woods to collect fungi.

As Jana drove to the outskirts of Rīga, she explained why mushrooming is so popular. First, it's an ancient tradition. With a short growing season, food was always scarce in the Baltic. This forced the locals to harvest all possible food sources. The Baltic's cool, soggy weather is a mushroom's paradise, so you'll find them everywhere. Ancient Latvians naturally became mushroom connoisseurs. Why do Latvians continue this tradition? In typical Latvian style, Jana's answer was brief: "Communism."

Soviet grocery stores had a meager selection and quantity of food. The black market was an expensive and risky alternative, so Latvians delved into the woods to find mushrooms and berries to supplement their diets. In other words, one of the side effects of communism is that it extended the life of a tradition that had largely died 100 years ago in the West.

Mushrooming is as competitive as the Olympics. Baltic people calmly walk around their cities and villages with somber and expressionless faces. However, if you put them in a forest with a basket and a knife to collect mushrooms, their faces suddenly burst with life. As they're driving to the forest, the normally quiet and distant Baltic people become chatty and friendly. However, once they enter the forest, they morph into something far more evil and sinister. Their eyes squint as they scan the forest for a camouflaged mushroom. They hunch over like Frankenstein's servant, Igor, so they can be low to the ground and snatch a mushroom before anyone else. When they find a treasure trove of mushrooms, they never announce it to their friends. Instead, their eyes dart around to see if anyone spies them. Then, stepping quietly, they pull out their blade and slice the fungus with all the precision and stealth of James Bond.

As snow fell during our walk in the park, Jana explained that competitive Latvians believe it's always important to get up early to go mushrooming because "someone might get the mushrooms before you."

That confused me. "I know mushrooms grow quickly, but it's not like the mushroom grows overnight. Why don't you show up in the afternoon one day earlier?"

She gave me a blank stare as if this idea had never crossed her (or any other Latvian) mind. She stumbled, trying to explain why it's important to show up early, but then she realized that there really is no good reason to be an early bird. Indeed, you can show up a few *weeks* after your rivals and there will still be mushrooms somewhere in the forest. You just might have to walk a bit deeper into the forest. "Still," she insisted, "You should get up early when you go mushrooming."

Russian tensions even when mushrooming

Just like any competitive sport, Baltic people insult their mushrooming rivals. For example, when Maiu and I were mushrooming in Estonia, she taught me the proper technique: "You don't yank the mushroom out of the ground. You carefully cut it right near the base, leaving enough of the stem behind so it can grow again in the next season. I hate it when people just pull them out. Russians always pull them out," she said while shaking her head.

A few weeks later I went mushrooming with some Estonian Russophones to find out if this is true. As we set off into the forest, I asked Olga, a Russophone with an explosive temper, if it was OK to just pull the mushroom out. *"Nyet!"* she screamed. "You must leave enough of the stem behind or it will not grow back!"

I asked her, "Do you know anyone who does pull them out?"

"*Nyet!* Nobody does this! That's *stupid*!"

Yuliya, another Russophone who was mushrooming, added, "I have never met anyone who does this."

Although I'm not sure who is yanking the poor mushrooms out of the ground, I am sure that Baltic people have a love-hate relationship with Russians. Maiu's jab at the Russians not only shows the competitive nature of mushrooming, but it also illustrates how most Baltic people have deep issues with Russians. On the one hand, they respect Russians—complimenting their passion and rich cultural history. On the other hand, they still hold a grudge against them for having occupied the Baltic lands. This grudge shows itself in both subtle and overt ways. Jana, who speaks Russian fluently, confessed that there's a little part of her that gets bothered when she hears the Russian language in Latvia; hearing any other foreign language doesn't produce the same negative feeling. In short, it's fascinating how Russian-Baltic tensions are visible even in the benign pastime of mushrooming.

There's one more odd thing I learned while mushrooming. A favorite Latvian insult is, "Why don't you just go mushrooming?" That's their way of saying, "Why don't you just jump in a lake?" Both insults are a polite way of saying "fuck off," but they're odd because each of those activities are fun. Baltic people *love* mushrooming, just like Americans love jumping in lakes. So why would you tell someone who is annoying you, to go do something fun? Shouldn't you say, "Why don't you just go pick poisoned mushrooms?" Or "Why don't you just jump into a boiling cauldron?" Alas, insults are not always logical.

I was skeptical at first, but I learned to love mushrooming. What makes mushrooming great isn't the delight of cooking up fresh, organic mushrooms (or choking to death when you accidentally consume a poisonous one). Instead, it's the pleasure of being in the forest and partaking in a primal activity—hunting for fruit and fungi. It sure beats wasting hours on Facebook. On the other hand, mushrooming in the Baltic isn't as fun as mushrooming in Amsterdam.

Blue cows and Latvian traits

Jana ended her Rīga tour at a dark, deserted, freezing cold beach. We stayed just long enough to touch the frigid Baltic Sea. Chilled, we returned to her warm, modern apartment. Jana was a classic Latvian: she was a bit distant at first, but after a few hours, she warmed up and talked more freely. In the end, she was a great host. After some hot tea, I crashed on her floor.

The next day, as Jana got ready for her Valentine's Day date, she told me about Latvia's blue cows. Seth Godin, a marketing guru, instructs that when you market a product, you should make your product out to be a purple cow. Brown, black, and spotted cows are boring, but a purple cow is remarkable. Although Latvia has no purple cows, its Kurzeme region has blue cows. Clearly, having blue cows would be Godin's wet dream—a marketing slam dunk. However, Latvia has done an abysmal job marketing its blue cows—few know about them. The legend says that a mermaid, who fell in love with a Latvian farmer, brought the cows from the sea. Today, only 200 remain. They are not as blue as you might imagine (they're a bluish-gray), but they're still cool. One day I hope to return to Latvia and milk one of their blue cows.

I spent Valentine's Day in Jelgava, which is less than hour from Rīga. Jelgava is surprisingly pleasant, even in the middle of winter. Its immense palace looks like a poor man's Versailles. It's run down, but it's still quite elegant and regal. While I was admiring the reddish structure, a beautiful Latvian bride and groom jumped out of a limo to pose for a few quick photos. The bridesmaids shivered in their dresses that weren't designed for minus 10-degree weather. It may be romantic to get married on Valentine's Day, but I'd rather do it in Hawaii than in Latvia.

When I entered the grand palace, I wondered how this frozen wasteland got the money to build all these architectural marvels. Two sources were key: trade and amber. Rīga is located on the Baltic's most important river artery, which made it a natural trading post for centuries. Its massive bay and river attracted wealthy merchants. Moreover, Latvia had amber like Saudi Arabia has oil. Until the Middle Ages, amber was more precious than gold. These twin fortunes allowed Latvians to construct spacious buildings that had really high heating bills.

I was alone on Valentine's Day. Two weeks before, I had broken up with Maiu. As the gray sky darkened at 3:00 p.m., I jealously watched an amorous couple play ice hockey on a frozen creek. The ice looked thin, but the couple didn't seem bothered. I imagined the ice swallowing up the guy, while I would gallantly dash in to save the blond damsel from suffering the same fate. She would weep on my shoulder as her loser boyfriend froze to death. (The guy was much bigger than me, so this was the only way I could imagine getting the girl.)

I shuffled through the snow toward the center of Jelgava. Although I didn't have a romantic evening, I enjoyed chilling out with eight Latvians in a small art gallery. The most outgoing Latvians were either the ones who were well traveled or tipsy. Later, I asked my Latvian friend, Edite Lucava, if Latvians were as shy and introverted as I thought.

She said, "Yes, I totally agree with your opinion about Latvians. We have this characteristic feature. Generally we live very solitary from each other, but when something important happens, we can do great things together. You can see this Latvian phenomenon in the song festival, when thousands of people sing together! It's so great! Also, sometimes we act like small dogs! When somebody touches our country or says some bad words, we bark very loud because we are small and we can't do anything else, but we have big courage! And don't believe Latvians who say that they are not patriots. Deep in heart they are, and they will do their best for the country if there will be a need for that! Sometimes I just wonder how we managed to keep our traditions and language after all our terrible history!"

When I asked Edite what Americans can learn from Latvia, she wrote back: "It's hard to teach some big country who rules the world. And they will never understand the differences between the Baltic countries, somehow I don't feel the need to change that!"

However, I do.

What Latvia Can Teach Us

- **Hold hands.** When you want change, don't hold a weapon; instead, hold a hand. The Baltic Way protest showed what can happen when a quarter of the population holds hands across three countries. It helped topple the USSR.
- **Become an apprentice and travel.** Although it's a dying tradition, Latvians once were apprentices who travel widely before creating a masterpiece. The lesson is that we should explore our interests through travel. When you return home, your skills will improve faster than if you had never left.
- **Go mushrooming.** It's a great way to eat more organic vegetables, but most of all, it's a wonderful way to enjoy a forest and get out of the house.
- **Consider voting for a female politician.** Latvians became the first former USSR state to elect a female president. Some believe that if women ran the world, there would be no wars. While that's naive, there probably would be fewer wars. Unfortunately women would pass a law that demands that we all make our beds in the morning and put the toilet seat down.

Places I saw and recommend in Latvia: Rīga, Cēsis, Gauja National Park, Turaida Museum Reserve, and the secluded beaches near Liepaja.

Travel deals and info: http://ftapon.com/latvia

Whenever there are three of a kind and you've tried two, you must try the third. Having explored Estonia and Latvia, I had to see Lithuania. Would Lithuania be more similar to Estonia or Latvia? Or would it be in its own unique category? There was only one way to find out. I boarded the bus to Lithuania.

4

Lithuania—The Remnants of a Great Empire

In Finland, I met a Lithuanian in a hostel. It was 2004 and I still hadn't been to the Baltic, so I was curious about its people. I asked her what Latvians and Lithuanians thought of each other. She said that Latvians have a saying, "You're as dumb as a Lithuanian."

Demonstrating their profound originality, Lithuanians have their own saying, "You're as dumb as a Latvian."

Sensing I had found someone pretty dumb, I asked the Lithuanian what she thought about Finland. She said with disdain, "There are a lot of black people in Finland."

Really? Later, I ran to talk to the one black guy I saw walking through Helsinki. He was from Washington, DC and had been living in Finland for eight years. His mother had asked him, "So are there any other brothers in Finland?"

He told his mom, "Yeah, there's another one. We're good friends."

Clearly, that Lithuanian woman was a lousy source of information. Therefore, when I got to Estonia, I asked Maiu what she thought of Lithuania. As usual, she didn't blurt out an answer. No matter how simple the question, Maiu likes to take a few seconds to search for the answer in the ceiling. She always gives well-thought-out answers. If she doesn't see the answer on the ceiling after spending a while searching, then she'll say, "I don't know." All this deep thinking guarantees that Maiu will never give a wrong answer. This technique is so successful that she even applies it to trivial questions. Just for fun, I asked her, "Hey Maiu, what's your twin sister's name?"

She'll give me the look as if I have a booger hanging from my nose. Then her eyes will calmly look to the sky as she debates whether this is one of my trick questions. After a long pause, she'll finally answer, "Kristi."

Therefore, when I asked her what she thought of Lithuania, it didn't surprise me to see her eyes dart up and scan around. I expected a profound, thoughtful answer. Perhaps she'll mention the quality of Lithuania's music, their unique character, or their cultural capital. She sighed as if she were wondering where she should begin, given all there was to say about Lithuania. However, in the end, all she said was, "They have nice roads."

Nice roads!? Lithuania has been near Estonia for centuries, they've suffered through Soviet domination together, they've gone through the Singing

Revolution hand-in-hand, they perform at each other's festivals, and all Maiu had to say about them is that they have nice freakin' roads?!

Instead of saying that, I kept a straight face while Maiu elaborated, "During the Soviet time, all the roads were really shitty. Few had cars anyway, so it didn't really matter. At some point, the Soviets wanted to see what kind of difference there would be if they improved the roads. They chose Lithuania as the place to try it out. So they got really nice roads."

"I see," I said, trying to sound interested. "That's, um, fascinating, Maiu."

This was an example of what I call Baltic Blindness: that Baltic countries know surprisingly little about each other. Baltic people are more likely to have visited France or Thailand than to visit their neighboring countries. Most people in Latvia and Estonia gave me the impression that Lithuania was the ugly sister in the Baltic trinity. I couldn't trust what Latvians and Estonians had to say about Lithuania. I needed to go to the hidden country for myself.

Vilnius: Lithuania's picture-perfect capital

When I finally arrived in Vilnius, the capital of Lithuania, I was blown away by its beauty, history, and elegance. The streets are enchanting and its architecture is spectacular. Founded on Gediminas Hill (which has a thirteenth-century castle on it), Vilnius's Old Town is a maze of adorable streets with baroque churches everywhere you look. It was built on a swamp and some of the buildings are below street level. The *Aušros Vartai* (Gates of Dawn) is the only surviving gate of the original nine that encircled the city. The only reason that particular gate is still standing is that it has a Virgin Mary icon embedded in it. Russians feared destroying the gate, believing that God would punish them. Of course, God punished them anyway when He let communism happen.

After straying a bit from the main tourist spots in Vilnius, I accidentally entered another country. Few tourists know that there is a separate republic in a bohemian district of Vilnius. It is neither as well known as the Vatican, nor as serious. In fact, it's a complete joke. A few years ago the people of Vilnus's Užupis district declared independence, forming the Užupis Republic. Its people elected a President, wrote an anthem, and designed four flags (one each season). They have a not-so-grand palace, an army of 17, and a national holiday (April 1). On April Fools Day, comical guards protect the bridge and stamp everyone's passport.

Most importantly, the Užupis Republic has engraved its constitution on mirrors on Paupio Street. Among the 41 constitutional rights:

everyone has the right to live by the River Vilnelė, while the River Vilnelė has the right to flow by everyone; a dog has the right to be a dog; a cat is not obliged to love its master, but it must help him in difficult times; everyone has the right to die, but it is not a duty; everyone has the right to have no rights.

The Užupis Republic is amusing, but after the chuckles fade away, a Baltic mystery begins to be revealed. The big Baltic mystery is: *what is the difference between these three tiny countries?* I visited the Baltic countries to understand why they are separate countries, how they are different from each other, and what we can learn from them. If the Baltic people were homogeneous, they wouldn't have created independent countries. They would have just made one big country and called it *Balticstan*. As the Baltic mist parted, one of their many differences began to emerge.

Lithuania's confidence

The Užupis Republic demonstrates a Lithuanian trait that its two northern neighbors somewhat lack: confidence. Making silly jokes like the Užupis Republic takes confidence. The pranksters need a bit confidence to make such a declaration; meanwhile, the government must have enough confidence to ignore it. Try to make the same joke under Soviet or Chinese communism. Their insecure governments would have been party poopers.

Compared to the other two Baltic states, Lithuania also shows more confidence in dealing with Russia. While Russophones make up 25 to 30 percent of Estonia's and Latvia's population, they are less than five percent of Lithuania's population. Why do Estonia and Latvia have a Russian ratio that is nearly six times greater than Lithuania's? Some Lithuanians gave me a surprisingly answer: "We asked the Russians not to come."

Although it wasn't that easy, there is some truth to that. Within the Baltic nations, Lithuanians are known for being expert negotiators. During the Soviet period, Lithuanians had both the confidence and skill to stand up to Russia and win minor political fights. One of those fights was limiting the influx of Russophones. For example, when the Soviets set up factories in Estonia and Latvia, they imported Russians to run them. Lithuanians, on the other hand, convinced Russians to let Lithuanians study in Russia and return to Lithuania to run the factories themselves. The Soviets agreed, which is one reason why relatively few Russians live in Lithuania today.

At a Vilnius hostel I met Silvia Cardini, a 32-year-old Italian who was living in Germany. She was the classic Italian lady: dark hair, dark eyes, tan skin, and a contagious laugh. She was also traveling alone through Lithuania, but she knew a local named Virgis who was planning to drive across the country for a business meeting. She invited me to join them. The night before our road trip, we all went out to dinner. That night I would not only learn more examples about Lithuania's confidence, but I would also learn the source of that confidence. But first, I was eager to sample Lithuania's grub.

Lithuanian cuisine

The centerpiece of the Lithuanian diet is bread. Lithuanians link many beliefs and magic with bread. For example, in the cornerstone of a new house, Lithuanians often place a piece of bread to protect the home. The lady of the house has the honorable duty of baking bread. This duty is passed on to the eldest daughter in a special ceremony. In fact, Lithuanians use the feminine gender to refer to bread. One Lithuanian told me, "My grandmother used to say that the bread is holy and we should respect it. I still do what my grandmother taught me: if the bread falls to the ground, I pick it up with reverence, kiss it, and eat it. It's a Lithuanian ritual. We do this so that the home will never be without bread."

The most popular bread is *juoda ruginė duona* (black rye bread). You'll find it on every Lithuanian dinner table. Although refined flour (white bread) is becoming popular in the Baltic, the primary bread remains the healthier dark bread. There are two kinds of bread styles: plain fermented and scalded. Although Lithuanians learned to bake scalded bread in the twentieth century, the tradition of baking plain fermented bread has existed for thousands of years. Plain bread ferments overnight but must be kneaded for a long time, while scalded bread fermentation takes almost three days. As one Lithuanian grandmother told me, "Bread tastes delicious because it is hard to make."

> Be duonos sotus nebūsi.
> — *Lithuanian proverb, meaning "No bread, no bellyful."*

While bread and potatoes provide the starch, meat and sour cream seem to satisfy all the other Lithuanian dietary needs. Lithuanians eat meat for breakfast. When they wake up they might eat a sandwich with sausage, roast, or smoked meat. Other times they forget the sandwich part and just eat boiled sausages. It's common to eat these delights for lunch and dinner too. It seems that a Lithuanian's life quest is to die of a heart attack.

Later, I would talk with a Frenchman, Cédric Henriot, who had a surprising opinion about Lithuanian cuisine. He lives in Lithuania and is married to a local. Instead of having a condescending French attitude about Lithuanian food, he said, "Oh, I love Lithuanian cuisine! A lot of the cuisine comes from potatoes and pork. And they have a lot of fat in their cuisine. It's big and it fills you. You eat one portion and you're full. When it's the winter and you eat it, you feel good. You don't feel weak and you don't feel cold anymore." We were speaking over the phone, so I couldn't verify if his Lithuanian wife was standing over him with a rolling pin in her hand.

Virgis, Silvia, and I went to a traditional Lithuanian restaurant. The menu revealed the importance of potatoes in the Lithuanian diet. I couldn't decide whether to order the *bulvių plokštainis* (a potato pudding that's also called a *kugelis*), the *cepelinai* (big grated potato dumplings filled with meat or curd), the *bulviniai blynai* (potato pancakes), or the irresistible *vėdarai* (potato sausage stuffed with pork intestine).

Instead, I started my meal with *šaltibarščiai*, a tasty cold red beet root soup, which is popular in the summer. The soup includes beets, cucumbers, a boiled egg, sour cream, sour milk, scallions, and dill. For my entrée, I ordered the national dish: cepelinai. Although Lithuanians love it, they rarely make it at home because it takes forever to cook. You need several hours to make the potato dough, stuff it with grybai (mushrooms), mesa (meat), varškė (cheese), and then create the heavy sauce using sour cream, butter, bacon bits, and onions. By the time you finish making all that, you'll be starving and the dish will taste delicious.

Silvia ordered *bulvių plokštainis*, while Virgis picked *koldūnai* (ravioli stuffed with meat). For an appetizer and side dish, we ordered *virtiniai* (dumplings) and *kepta duona* (deep-fried black bread with garlic). When the plates arrived, it was clear that Lithuanians like pouring sour cream on everything.

When Silvia and Virgis ordered alus (beer), the waiter brought the most popular brand: the Švyturys Extra. I joked that they should have a potato-based beverage. Virgis said that Lithuanians brew one at home—degtinė (an alcoholic drink made with potatoes). If that doesn't tempt you, maybe the crazy flavors of Lithuanian vodka will. They offer vodka made with berries, herbs, rye, honey, pepper, and holy grass. Holy grass? Clearly, God approves of this kind of vodka. Once the alcohol started flowing, I asked Virgis why Lithuanians have more confidence than their Baltic neighbors. He summed it up in one word, "History."

Lithuania was once a superpower

At first, I wasn't that interested in learning about Lithuania's history. After discovering the parallel histories of Estonia and Latvia, I expected that Lithuania would just be another long, sad tale about big bullies smacking them around for 800 years. However, Lithuania's history is different. Instead of being a punching bag, Lithuania, for a few hundred years, was doing the punching. In fact, at its pinnacle, its kingdom stretched from the Baltic Sea to the Black Sea. It's true: Lithuania was once a superpower.

To understand the rise and fall of Lithuania, we'll start at its founding 1,000 years ago. Lithuania was the last pagan country in Europe. It had boldly resisted all efforts to Christianize it, but it finally gave in. Lithuania's rise truly started in 1253, when Lithuanians united to form the Grand Duchy of Lithuania. In 1386, Lithuania allied itself with Poland, and that ultimately led them to their golden era. Lithuanians and Poles swapped leadership of the Grand Duchy every generation. They controlled all of present-day Belarus and most of Ukraine. In short, the Grand Duchy of Lithuania and Poland ruled from the Baltic to the Black Sea.

Every young Lithuanian learns this rich history and is proud of it. Knowing that it once was a superpower gives Lithuanians that confidence that Estonians and Latvians lack. If Lithuania was once a peer with Russia and other Europeans, then why not act like one today? This glorious period is the source of Lithuania's confidence.

Unfortunately, Lithuanians and Poles bickered in the 1700s, which led to their mutual demise. (Sadly, their petty fights continue today.) They began to focus more and more on their differences, rather than on their common bonds. The empires of Russia, Prussia (Germany), and Austria smelled the weakness of the Lithuanian-Polish alliance. After a series of wars, Poland and Lithuania ceased to be—their conquerors assimilated the Grand Duchy into their empires. Thus, by 1796, Poland and Lithuania were wiped off the world map.

A few years later, Napoleon charged through Lithuania. The Frenchman called Vilnius "the Jerusalem of the North," because Jews made up half of its population. In 1785, William Coxe, a 31-year-old Englishman who traveled from Poland to Russia, wrote, "In our route through Lithuania we could not avoid being struck with the swarms of Jews. . . . If you ask for an interpreter, they bring you a Jew; if you come to an inn, the landlord is a Jew; if you want post-horses, a Jew procures them, and a Jew drives them."[1] Prior to WWII, Vilnius had 100,000 Jews; today, there are just 400. The Nazis (and their Lithuanian accomplices) managed to slaughter nearly 300,000 Jews throughout Lithuania.

When the Soviet reinstalled themselves in 1945, they picked up where they left off. During their 1940 occupation, they killed or deported 40,000 Lithuanians. When they returned in 1945, the Soviets deported or murdered another 250,000 Lithuanians. It wasn't good to be a Lithuanian in the 1940s.

We shared a dessert called *tinginys,* which means *lazy.* It is an easy dessert for lazy chefs that involves butter, cocoa, sugar, solidified milk, and biscuits. While drinking some honey vodka, Virgis told a joke about Russian intrusions: *A Lithuanian border guard notices that a Russian hasn't filled out the form completely. The guard doesn't know the*

Russian's job or occupation because the Russian left the line blank. So the guard asks, "Occupation?"

The Russian answers, "No, just visiting."

First to declare independence

Lithuania's inner confidence made it the Baltic domino that pushed Latvia and Estonia (and many other Soviet Republics) to obtain their independence. It started in 1988 when, after a series of protests, Lithuanians were able to replace the Soviet flag and anthem with their own. On March 11, 1990 they declared their independence, a year before Estonia and Latvia would have the courage to do the same.

On January 13, 1991, unarmed Lithuanians encircled their TV tower. Tanks ran over a human chain. Soviet troops shot protestors, while live TV broadcast the horror. The last thing Latvians saw was a soldier walking up to the camera and pulling the plug. When the dust settled, 700 were wounded and 14 were dead. The Soviets finally recognized Lithuania's independence on September 6, 1991. It was the first Soviet republic to receive such recognition. Eventually, 13 other Soviet Republics would follow Lithuania's leadership—resulting in the dissolution of the USSR.

> Kas nerizikuoja, tas negeria šampano.
> — *Lithuanian proverb meaning "He who doesn't take risks, doesn't taste the champagne."*

Unlike Latvia and Estonia, Lithuania was slow to tear down its Soviet statues. Perhaps they felt their freedom was secure. Still, they discarded many, but then the Mushroom King resurrected them. Lithuanians call Viliumas Malinauskas the Mushroom King because he made his fortune selling mushrooms and berries—the ultimate Lithuanian dream. He used that fortune to acquire 86 Soviet statues and create a sculpture park called *Grūtas,* or Stalin World. The waitresses in the café dress like Soviet pioneers (similar to girl scouts) and serve classic Soviet dishes. For those who missed out on the joys of totalitarianism, Stalin World is a great place to check out Soviet memorabilia, listen to communist propaganda blaring from speakers, and admire statues of Lenin, Stalin, and other winners.

After fighting so hard to throw the Soviets out, Lithuanians did something odd in their first democratic election in 1992: they voted to give the ex-communist party control of the government. They were the first ex-communist country to vote former communists back into power. These clever politicians re-branded themselves as "social democrats." Although they dismantled the communist system, they didn't last. In 2004, Lithuania joined the EU and NATO. They hope to adopt the euro by 2015. Lastly, it ratified the EU Constitution before any other EU country had the confidence to do so.

After the dinner, we returned to our hostel. Silvia and I bunked in the same room with a couple of other travelers. The vodka made Silvia a bit flirtatious, but I behaved. She teased me for being "boring." She's right, but I was happy to lie in bed with a smile on my face, thinking about my Nordic saunas experiences.

Lithuania's sand dunes

The next day Virgis, Silvia, and I drove across Lithuania twice. We left Vilnius in the morning, passing monotonous flat, grassy farmland for several hours. During long road trips it always helps to have an Italian in the car to keep everyone entertained. Silvia didn't disappoint.

We eventually arrived at the cute seaside town of Klaipėda, which has a long history of being under German rule. Attractive Germanic wooden houses still stand. While Virgis went to his business meeting, Silvia and I went to the beach to enjoy the warm July weather. We walked down the Curonian Spit—nature's fragile Baltic Sea breakwater. We got far enough to see the Russian border along the beach. The other half of the Curonian Spit is part of the little-known Russian territory called Kaliningrad. I would have never guessed that five years later, I would be in the middle of Kaliningrad's Curonian Spit lagoon, ice fishing with Russians while looking at Lithuania in the distance. We'll discuss that experience near the end of this book.

We ran up and down the sand dunes, which are surprisingly tall and steep. It makes you feel like you're in the Sahara Desert—except that most of the year here you'd freeze your ass off. We rejoined Virgis, who had another Lithuanian with him for the return to Vilnius. With two Lithuanians in the car, it was time to learn the basics of the Lithuanian language.

The Lithuanian language

The Lithuanian language might not exist today if it weren't for some smugglers. In 1864, in order to crush an uprising, the Russian Empire instituted the *spaudos draudimas* (Lithuanian press ban). This banned all Lithuanian language publications printed in the Latin alphabet (using the Cyrillic alphabet was acceptable). Students were not allowed to speak Lithuanian among themselves. Russian authorities conducted searches, inspections, and spying to enforce the ban.

The ban backfired. It encouraged the opposition to Russian rule and culture. *Knygnešiai* (book carriers) smuggled illegal books and periodicals. Parents withdrew their children from schools and home-schooled them. In exile, Lithuanian linguists agreed on a standardized written version. Russia eventually gave up. When I first visited in 2004, Lithuanians were celebrating the 100-year anniversary of the ban's end.

Although Lithuanian is hard to learn, the basics are easy. It has changed less than any other Indo-European language. In fact, Lithuanians can understand many Sanskrit words, which is a proto-language for Indo-European. My favorite Lithuanian phrase is saying *thank you*. Just pretend you're sneezing, say "ah-choo!" Spelling it looks a bit weird: *ačiū*. After you say *ačiū*, Lithuanians will say *prašau*. *Prašau* is another useful word to learn because its other meaning is *please*.

The other key phrases are also easy: *labas* (hi), *sudie* (goodbye), *taip* (yes), *ne* (no), *atsiprašau* (excuse me), *kur?* (where?), and *kiek?* (how much?). Once you've mastered that, try: *kur yra autobusų stotis?* (where is the bus station?) or *ar kalbate angliškai?* (do you speak English?). When you meet the one friendly bus ticket agent in the country, try saying *tu esi graži* (you are beautiful). Finally, if you've got all that down, try this:

> Geri vyrai geroj girioj gerą girą gerdami gyrė.
> *— Lithuanian tongue twister meaning, "Good guys in the good forest drank good kvass while praising it."*

Wacky names

At the end of the road trip, I asked Virgis (whose full name was Virginijus) something that had been bugging me since I met him. I told him, "Does Virginijus comes from the word *virgin*? If so, does such a name help you or hurt you with the ladies?"

Virgis laughed and said, "No, it has nothing to do with being a virgin! But many Lithuanians have interesting names."

He wasn't kidding. Consider the following common Lithuanian names: Gintaras, Vėjas, Linas, Ąžuolas, and Eglė. They sound pretty exotic and unpronounceable, but consider their literal meaning: Amber, Wind, Linen, Oak, and Fir. Imagine you're in a business meeting and your boss says, "I'd like Linen to update us on his marketing efforts. Oak and Fir will elaborate. Later, Wind will present their sales strategy that is more than just hot air."

Curiously, Estonians and Latvians also have unusual names. Some Latvians, for example, are called Jautrīte (Funny) or Gudrīte (Smarty). Meanwhile, Estonians can call their children: Säde (Sparkle), Mari (Berry), Veli (Brother), Aare (Treasure), Arved (Invoices), Aita (Help), Hilja (Late), Hele (Light), Helin (Ringtone), Sale (Slim), Ustav (Faithful), Vapper (Brave), Õie (Blossom's), Valve (Surveillance).[2]

This also makes for fun imaginary conversations in Estonian: "No, Brother is not my brother, Brother is my husband." Or "I can't believe Late is late again," or confusingly, "Late is early," or this stupid sounding question, "Is Late early or late?" Some might say, "Isn't Slim getting fat?" How about, "I can't believe Faithful cheated on his wife."

Finally, "Hey Invoices, I want you to look over these invoices with Surveillance looking over your shoulder. Also, make sure Brave is brave enough to deal that unhelpful Help gal."

What's remarkable is that people named Smarty aren't the child of drugged-out hippie parents. They're normal, everyday people. In fact, Estonian last names can be equally whimsical. This tradition started early in the 1800s, when Russians let liberated Baltic serfs have a last name. Many Estonians adopted "natural" last names like *Talvoja* (Winterbrook) and *Naarits* (Mink); unlucky ones got branded by the church with last names like *Patune* (Sinner) or *Koll* (Monster). Imagine going to a job interview or meeting your future mother-in-law and introducing yourself as Ustav Koll (Faithful Monster). Before we Americans giggle too much about these names, consider what Helen Uustalu, an Estonian, said to me, "At least we're not so cruel like Americans who call their baby *Dick*."

We had one last meal together before parting ways. Silvia returned to Berlin, where she earned a degree in behavioral-cognition therapy. In 2011, she was a private psychotherapist and also worked with prison inmates.

Šiauliai's Hill of Crosses

In 2009, I returned to Lithuania to see places that I had missed on my first trip. It was Valentine's Day and I had just finished exploring Jelgava. The next day I left Latvia and to visit Lithuania's fourth largest city, Šiauliai. In one week, the city would celebrate *Užgavėnės,* their version of Halloween. Children go trick-or-treating while adults wear carnival outfits and scary masks that are meant to chase the winter away. It never works, because March is always butt-freezing cold.

As soon as I arrived in Šiauliai, I met my 23-year-old couchsurfing host, Gediminas Rapalis. He greeted me and invited me to join a poker game that had just started at his friend's house. I still hadn't exchanged any *litas* (Lithuanian money), so he loaned me some litas to lose. Although half of his friends did not speak English well, we communicated well enough to agree that I had lost all the money I had bet.

Unless you're lucky enough to be invited to a poker game, there's no reason to spend any time in Šiauliai. It's a rather dull and gray city that still hasn't shaken its Soviet vibe. However, 12 kilometers north you'll find something worth seeing: *Kryžių kalnas* (the Hill of Crosses). As the name suggests, it's a hill with an insane number of crosses. Thousands of crosses of every size cover the mound, which takes just five minutes to climb. Although the hill is overflowing with crosses, there are a few paths that allow you to walk among the densely packed religious icons. Most crosses are personalized: they might indicate their country of origin, quote a Biblical verse, or ask God for cash. The hill has a surreal feel since it's in the middle of nowhere. It makes you wonder if the same aliens who made crop circles came here to plant a bunch of crosses.

The real story behind the Hill of Crosses doesn't involve aliens. In the 1300s, some guy planted the first cross. Thousands of crosses followed. Then the Soviets ruined the cross planting party by bulldozing them all. However, the night after the bulldozing, Lithuanians sneaked pass the guards and barbed wire to replant a few new crosses. Eventually there were enough new crosses that the Soviets bulldozed the hill again. Lithuanians would return to plant more crosses, which attracted more bulldozers, and the cycle would repeat until Lithuanians found a new religion.

Lithuania's religion: basketball

If you asked most Lithuanians what's more important, Christianity or basketball, most would say Christianity. However, they would be lying. In Lithuania, it's tough to choose between Jesus and Jordan. Michael Jordan inspired Lithuanians to devote their lives to throwing a ball through a hoop (or at least watching people do it on TV). Lithuania has received three Olympic bronze medals in a row in basketball. It's amazing that Lithuania destroys their Russian neighbors on the basketball court, even though Russia's population is 50 times bigger than Lithuania's. In 2003, Lithuania did much more—it won the European Championship. One year later, during the Olympics, Lithuania beat the USA.

After an hour of shuffling on the snow-covered Hill of Crosses, I couldn't find a cross with a basketball on it or a statue of Jesus dribbling. Nevertheless, if the Lithuanians ever win the gold medal in basketball, you can be sure they will rush to this hill to thank God for the miracle. I hitchhiked back to Šiauliai with two Japanese brothers. They were heading to Rīga, but generously took me 20 minutes out of their way. I was especially grateful because they were short on time—their 10-day European itinerary was packed more tightly than a Japanese microprocessor.

From Šiauliai, I took a bus that eventually went along Lithuania's second biggest river: the Neris. It merged with the legendary Nemunas River, the "father of all rivers." Almost every Lithuanian has memorized this famous passage, which is an anthem:

> Kur bėga Šešupė, kur Nemunas teka / Tai mūsų tėvynė, graži Lietuva. — *Maironis, Lithuanian poet. Translation: "Where the Šešupė runs, where the Nemunas flows / That's our homeland, beautiful Lithuania."*

The Nemunas and Neris rivers meet in Lithuania's second biggest city: Kaunas. Newlyweds love going to *Santakos Parkas* (Confluence Park) because it overlooks the confluence of the Neris and Nemunas. In the Lithuanian language, the Neris is a feminine noun and the Nemunas is a male noun. Therefore, this romantic site symbolizes marriage: it's where the male and female rivers join and then never split up. (Few mention that after merging, the river's toxicity increases as you go downstream.)

Kaunas: the city that just won't die

Founded in the thirteenth century, Kaunas has been reduced to ashes an amazing 14 times. Why don't the residents just give up on their idea of having a town at that location? Obviously, this city is just not meant to be. Curious to learn more about this immortal city, I visited Kaunas on February 16, 2009. I hoped to understand why this city just can't be wiped off the face of the Earth.

> Visur gerai, namie geriausia.
> — *Lithuanian proverb, often said by grandparents, meaning, "Everywhere is good (to live), but home is the best."*

I concluded there are five reasons for why Lithuanians love Kaunas and keep rebuilding it. First, it's at the confluence of the mighty Nemunas and Neris rivers, so the strategic location necessitates a settlement there. In fact, Lithuania's first brick castle, Kaunas Castle, was built at Confluence Park. I jumped around it in the snow and it's clearly here to stay.

Second, the *senamiestis* (old town) is quaint with its cobblestoned streets, inspiring churches, and romantic cafés. Beautiful merchant buildings encircle the *Rotušės Aikštė* (Central Square). The pure white Marriage Palace (the old city hall) looks like a church, but the 450-year-old structure has never served any religious purpose. That job goes to its neighbor: the St. Francis Xavier Church and Jesuit's Monastery. Also, on one corner of the square is the statue-filled St. Peter's and Paul's Cathedral Basilica, which just turned 600 years old. All these architectural masterpieces and old world charm make Kaunas photogenic.

A third reason to love Kaunas is that it is the second most pedestrian-friendly city in Europe (after Venice). *Laivės Alėja* (Liberty Avenue) is the longest pedestrian zone in Eastern Europe—1.6 kilometers long. This zone starts with a somber memorial to Romas Kalanta, a student who burned himself to death in 1972 to protest communism's oppressive regime. From that monument you can see, at just over a mile away, the end of the pedestrian zone—the grandiose St. Michael the Archangel Church, located on *Nepriklausomybės Aikštė* (Independence

Square). If you count the old town's foot-friendly areas (where cars are rare), then the total pedestrian distance is over three kilometers (two miles).

Fourth, unlike most Baltic cities, Kaunas has decent hills. Growing up in San Francisco, I like hilly cities. Although most Baltic towns are as flat as Nebraska, Kaunas has hills that are steep enough to warrant two of Europe's oldest funiculars.

Fifth, although Kaunas has many churches, the most impressive is the Memorial Christ Resurrection Church. It seems as if it were built for a bigger city than Kaunas. In a way, it was. When Lithuania became independent in 1922, Kaunas (not Vilnius) was the capital. To celebrate, Kaunas built this gigantic church, whose main tower rises 70 meters (about a 23-story building). However, the atheist communists converted the church into a radio factory. Today, it's a church again with a minimalist white interior. I knelt at a pew and asked God to introduce me to a hot babe. God answered my prayer.

Although it was snowing when I entered the local tourist office, I nearly melted when I saw the Tourism Supervisor, Inga Pažereckaitė. I have a weakness for thin brunettes with blue eyes, and Inga had this rare triple combo. My original plan to demand, "What's your problem? Why do you guys insist of rebuilding Kaunas each time it's destroyed? Give it up, you fools!"

Instead, I was enthralled with her beauty and just babbled, "Er, hi, I'm, er, looking for . . . . Does it normally snow in February? Sorry. Dumb question. I mean, um, a map? Do you have one? A map, I mean."

Inga tilted her head and looked at me curiously with her big crystal blue eyes. "I'm sorry, but may I help you?"

I explained that the reason I was stumbling was that I'm half-French and half-Chilean, and that English is really my third language. Fortunately, Inga deals with idiotic tourists every day, so she ignored my stupid excuses and handed me a map with a smile.

How some Lithuanians see foreigners

I asked Inga her impression of foreigners. She said, "Polish and French people always want to speak their languages. When I say, 'Sorry, I do not speak your language,' they become unhappy and upset. Sometimes they just leave the office with a twisted smile on their faces.

"Is there any troublesome nationality?"

"I do not like Italian men. They feel that they are very cute and nice, so they think and they behave like they can get any girl they want. They think that all girls are crazy about them. It's really funny!"

Lithuanians have a mediocre relationship with Poles and Russians. Andrius Gegužinskas grew up in Marijampolė, which is near the Polish border. His father is Lithuanian and his mother is Belarusian. He estimated that up to 15 percent of the population around Marijampolė is Polish and that most of them speak Lithuanian. Still, he confessed that "Lithuanians dislike Polish people. It's stupid, because we are the same people. But there is tension."

In 2011, Lithuanians and Poles were fighting like babies over whether Poles can spell their names on government documents using Polish spelling or if they must convert it into a Lithuanian-sounding name. This childish debate has reached the highest levels of government because apparently they have nothing better to do.

The source of their tension, as usual, comes from history. Dalia Vasite, a Lithuanian born of a Russian mother, who lives in San Francisco, summed it up, "Every time I travel and meet Polish people, they say 'Vilnius belongs to us.' Wow. It's in the middle of a country and you think it's yours. Wow."

Nevertheless, the Poles have a point. A few times in history Poland controlled Vilnius. Although Poles and Russians each only make up roughly six percent of Lithuania, they are a huge minority in the capital. That's why Vilnius doesn't feel very Lithuanian: I heard Polish, Russian, or English spoken on the streets as often as Lithuanian. (For a more "pure" Lithuanian city, go to Kaunas.) Lithuanians still have annoying tendency of blaming all their problems on the Russians or the Poles (or the rest of the world). Although they don't blame Estonians for their problems, they enjoy making fun of them.

Estonians get the last laugh

Estonians are the butt of most Baltic jokes. The theme is that Estonians are slow and dim-witted. The jokes below are in the original language, so you can get an idea at how impossible it is to decode it (and, if you know Russian, you'll see how none of Baltic tongues resemble Russian). Let's start with a few Lithuanian jokes about the slow Estonians:

> Estijoje labai brangiai superkamos sraigės, kadangi Estijoje labai mažai žmonių jas sugeba pagauti.
> *— You can make a lot of money selling snails in Estonia, because few Estonians can catch them.*

> "Kas ten stovi?" Klausia Latvį sutikęs lietuvis. "Ten estas bėga." — *"Who is standing there?" a Lithuanian asks a Latvian. "That's an Estonian running."*

Latvians also enjoy poking fun at the slow Estonians:

> Zīme Igaunijā: "Braukt pa apli." Papildplāksnīte: "Ne vairāk kā trīs reizes." — *Road sign in Estonia: "Roundabout." Extra sign added: "No more than three times."*
>
> Ir atminēts lodes no filmas Matrik lidojuma noslēpums. Atklājās, ka uz katras no šīm lodēm ir mikroskopisks uzraksts: "Made in Estonia." — *The secret of bullets in the Matrix movie is solved. It turns out that on each of those bullets is a tiny caption: "Made in Estonia."*
>
> Īstam igaunim dzīvē jāizdara 3 lietas. Ja paspēj. — *An Estonian should do 3 things in his life. If he can.*

Jokes about Estonians are funny, but inaccurate. Estonians have had the last laugh because they have the highest standard of living in the Baltic. Estonia's per capita GDP zoomed 20 percent higher than Latvia and Lithuania after 1995, and has kept that lead every since. Estonia's government finances are rarely in deficit, while Latvia and Lithuania act like teenagers with a credit card. What's most ironic is that Estonians told me that they're often frustrated doing business with Latvians and Lithuanians, "They are so slow!" one complained, "They take forever to get shit done."

During the Great Recession, Estonia left its Baltic neighbors in the economic dust. Estonia met the stringent fiscal requirements to adopt the euro, while Latvia and Lithuania may join the eurozone in 2015—but only if they learn how to move faster. Estonia's lightning-quick government slashed spending hard and fast at the first signs of a global economic slowdown. It raced through EU financed modernization projects, stimulating its economy and lessening the recession's impact. Nowadays Latvia and Lithuania can only comfort themselves with one joke: *Why are Estonians so rich? Because they spend their money s-l-o-w-l-y.*

10 things Baltic nations have in common

I spent half a year living in the Baltic in order to understand how Estonia, Latvia, and Lithuania are different. Foreigners view them as one unit—like a *Balticstan* state. However, Baltic people hate it when foreigners assume they're all the same. Before we summarize their differences, let's consider their similarities. As Jared Diamond argues in *Guns, Germs, and Steel,* much of what shapes a nation is its geography. By that measure, the three Baltic states are quite similar. They all have:

- Flat terrain (the highest Baltic mountain is in Estonia—it's just 318 meters).
- Access to the Baltic Sea.
- A similar latitude (so they get similar weather).

- Similar crops and cuisine (their geography limits their food choices).
- A border with Russia (which has influenced them throughout the centuries).

One would expect that people who have such similar geography would also share many characteristics. They do. Let's observe 10 common traits.

1. Baltic people are human squirrels

As winter approaches, Baltic people become human squirrels. Every autumn, Estonians, Latvians, and Lithuanians instinctively collect glass containers, sanitize them, and spend endless hours cooking fruits and vegetables in large pots. Their kitchens become mini-factories, pumping out dozens of preserves. They repeat this ritual every year for good reason: they wouldn't be here if they didn't.

The Baltic is well north of any state in America (except Alaska), so their winters are brutal and dark. The only way they could survive the winters was by filling shelves with preserves. Communist stores were poorly stocked, so preserves were a vital nutritional supplement. Although nowadays (thanks to global trade) you can buy mangoes and strawberries during the winter, most Baltic homes are still packed with glass bottles filled with homemade jams, mushrooms, and pickles.

"It's really not popular to buy jam from the shopping center," Inga explained. "Lithuanians take the view that homemade food is healthy, so lots of food is made at home. Many Lithuanians (or their relatives) have gardens, and its fruits and vegetables are always preserved for the winter. Every Lithuanian family has its own signature jam, depending on what it has access to. For example, this autumn I made some plum jam," she said with a smile.

Preserving food is only half the fun. The other half is collecting it in the first place. Like their Baltic neighbors, Lithuanians love picking berries, but are absolutely *crazy* about collecting mushrooms. Armed with knives and baskets, Lithuanians march like mad into forests to pick mushrooms. The most treasured mushroom is the *Boletus*. The frenzy reaches a high point in October during the Mushroom Hunting Olympics in Dzūkija, Lithuania's best mushroom forest. After the race, an award ceremony and festival honor the most successful mushroom picker.

All these mushrooms and berries would rot if it weren't for dedicated Baltic women preserving them (men participate in collecting the plants, but rarely help preserve them). Nowadays loving mothers still give their grown children preserves each time they return home for a visit. It's remarkable that the new generation seems to be continuing this tradition. It's a habit and skill that we could all learn from.

2. Poetic gifts

Another great Baltic tradition happens during Christmas. In America, when someone gives you a gift, you take it and say, "Thanks." That's not acceptable in the Baltic.

When a Lithuanian, for example, offers you a gift, you must recite a poem before receiving it. This rule is particularly true for children. During humbler times, when Lithuanian children weren't showered with a dozen presents, this tradition encouraged children to cherish each gift. Imagine if spoiled American children had to recite a poem each time they got a gift. Since poetry is a dying art form, many Americans wouldn't even know what to say. And if they did, then the unwrapping ceremony would take so long that exasperated parents might, in the future, give fewer gifts.

Although abundance is entering into Baltic society, Christmas is still not a holiday where people try to bury their friends and family with gifts. Therefore, you'll still see children and adults stand up and chant a simple poem in front of a gathering before receiving a gift. This powerful tradition not only keeps poetry alive, but it also shows a deeper gratitude than just saying "thank you very much."

3. Dodging the Eastern Europe label

Baltic people hate being called *Eastern European*. For example, in an American library I saw a woman who looked Eastern European. I looked at her two blond children at her side and thought she might be Russian. I was curious if I was right and so I said, "Excuse me, are you from Eastern Europe?"

She thought for several seconds and finally said, "No, I'm from Latvia."

"Cool!" I exclaimed, thankful that I hadn't told her that I thought she was from Russia. "But isn't Latvia in Eastern Europe?"

"No," she said firmly.

"Oh. So where would you say Latvia is?"

"We're in *Central* Europe," she said with confidence.

"Really? So does that mean that 'Eastern Europe' is Russia?"

She struggled with that question, realizing that the only thing east of Latvia was Russia, and then tentatively said, "I suppose. I'm not sure."

"OK," I nodded. "What about Ukraine? Is that in Eastern Europe too? Or is that Central Europe?"

Overwhelmed with these deep philosophical questions, she was flustered and said, "I'm not sure. I don't know."

I told her that I had visited Latvia and so she quickly felt comfortable enough to confess that she didn't like Russians. She struggled with how to classify Ukraine. On the one hand, Ukraine was like Latvia—just another Soviet satellite state dominated by Russia. On the other hand, Ukrainians look, talk, and smell more or less like Russians. Just don't tell that to the Ukrainians, especially western Ukrainians, as we'll learn later.

Therefore, this woman was torn between placing Ukraine in the same undesirable category of *Eastern Europe* as Russia was in, or keeping Ukraine affiliated with the "better" *Central Europe* category. However, she also didn't like classifying Russia as Eastern Europe. In her mind, Russia isn't part of Europe. Because only cool people are in Europe and Russia is definitely not cool. In her ideal world, Lithuania was Central Europe and Eastern Europe just didn't exist.

Unfortunately for her, maps just don't work that way. For instance, Lonely Planet has a guidebook called *Central Europe,* which covers Austria, Czech Republic, Germany, Hungary, Liechtenstein, Poland, Slovakia, Slovenia, and Switzerland. Alas, none of the Baltic countries made the cut; you can find them in the Lonely Planet guidebook called *Eastern Europe.*

Estonians and Lithuanians also resist the *Eastern Europe* label. For instance, when I posted a YouTube video about the Bronze Soldier entitled "The Most Controversial Statue in Eastern Europe," a few Estonians posted comments saying that Estonia wasn't part of Eastern Europe. "It's in Northern Europe," they wrote. Meanwhile, when I interviewed Dalia Vasite for my WanderLearn Podcast, she stubbornly tried to convince me that Lithuania was in *Western* Europe!

Instead of performing mental gymnastics to avoid the *Eastern Europe* label, Eastern Europeans should re-brand themselves. Make Eastern Europe the wild frontier where the cool and adventurous people go. Old stodgy people stay in Western Europe; the young, hip pioneers head to Eastern Europe. This is already happening as tourists tire of Western Europe and want to see something more edgy and exotic, so they go to Eastern Europe. Perhaps in a few years Eastern Europe will have such a cool image that the French will claim that they're in Eastern Europe too. OK, perhaps not.

4. The Social Retards

Baltic people are socially retarded. Yes, it's an outrageous statement, but nowhere do I find it harder to socialize than in the Baltic. To sum up social interactions in one word it would be: *awkward.* At first, I thought it was me. I realize I must smell bad, look funny, and say stupid things. However, I found other people who were the opposite of me struggled too. Kike Garcia, a Spaniard traveling through the Baltic with his buddy, told me, "We just couldn't connect with those people. They're so cold and distant."

Locals admit that they're socially awkward. Kati Loite, an Estonian studying in Virginia, admitted, "Estonians talk a lot less than Americans. An average Estonian is a cold person, who needs time to warm up."

I invited an Australian guy to join Maiu and two other Estonian women for drinks at a bar in Tallinn. Later Maiu and her friend Liis agreed, "We had much more fun with that Australian than if we were just with Estonians. Estonians just don't know how to have a good conversation. They just sit there and don't say anything." When I was living in Estonia, I always felt the pressure to initiate a discussion; otherwise, the conversation would be flat, dull, or nonexistent.

Russophones, by the way, are completely different. Russians aren't shy about chatting or laughing about anything. Conversations with Russians are fluid and dynamic. Maiu prefers the Russians in her office job because they're easier to talk with than her Estonian colleagues. "Russian people are warmer and more passionate than Estonians," she said.

Edite Lucava, a Latvian, said, "Our mentality is very closed. We don't make a lot friends. We don't live in villages like Russians, who live very close to each other. Our villages are spread out. Our mentality is different: we keep a distance. And that's why I feel very Nordic, for example, when I go to the Southern countries, where everything is very loud and together. I feel like I'm not very used to this."

Inga told me, "We Lithuanians are considered to be a reserved and grave people." When she described *Naujieji Metai* (New Year's), she said, "Once a year Lithuanians, who normally do not care too much to communicate with their neighbors, become very friendly and communicative. At midnight on the New Year's night they start kissing their family, relatives and even strangers around them like dearest friends."

When I spent New Year's Eve in Parnu, Estonia, intoxicated Estonians were hugging and kissing me on the cheek. The next day, however, several acted like they didn't even know me. When I tried to chat with them, several just mumbled responses and then slid away. Another example: Facebook has a page called "You know you've been living in Lithuania too long when . . ." and one of the entries is: ". . . you see someone smiling in public, you think: well, a bloody foreigner."

Dalia Vasite said, "Even though Estonians are considered Baltic, we Lithuanians don't assimilate with them. Whenever I met Latvians, they didn't really want to talk with us. Russians are more open to you. Lithuanians are more cold, in general. I wish we could be more open to others. I feel Lithuanians are very close-minded and can be cold. They are so stubborn. I feel a lot of anger from them."

I wondered about Lithuanians living in America. Dalia said, "American Lithuanians: it's day and night. These people wish you the best and want the best for you. They are so joyful and happy. But people from my country are not. I think part of the reason is the Soviet Union. We were equal. We had just enough to live and that was it. When they opened the market and people started to be different, that's when a lot of jealousy came. A lot of people are grumpy. You walk around in the stores, and you don't see the happiness. I smile, with my American smile, and they look at me and think 'She's suspicious.'"

After traveling in Italy, Jana Ladusāne got depressed when she returned to her home in Latvia. She told me that she began to realize that Latvians are "social retards." She had never really thought about it until she started traveling to other countries and seeing how people treated each other. In *Men Are From Mars and Women Are From Venus,* John Gray shows how men throughout the world like to retreat to their "cave" from time to time. Baltic men, however, seem to live in their caves . . . permanently.

Baltic social awkwardness is so high that you might begin to wonder how they ever reproduce. If men are incapable of charming a lady, how do they ever marry and have kids? Jana told me the answer, "We get drunk."

It's true: Baltic people must have alcohol to socially lubricate themselves. Without vodka, beer, and wine, there would be as much conversation in a bar as there is in a funeral home. Thanks to alcohol, Baltic people are not extinct.

5. Baltic people are envious

Whenever I asked Baltic people to describe themselves, they often said, "We're an envious people." This trait became obvious in Estonia when I read a government booklet written by Estonians describing Estonians. The book covered many issues, including how Estonians are full of envy. When I asked Maiu's mother to describe a typical Estonian trait, she said, "Envy."

What's curious is that when I asked Latvians to explain how they're different than Estonians, some Latvians said, "We're envious people." I struggled to keep a straight face, knowing that Estonians had just said the same thing when describing themselves.

I figured Lithuania would be different, but then Andrius Geguzinskas told me this popular Lithuanian joke: *In Hell, the Devil shows his minions a pot full of Russians. He says, "Don't worry about them, because if they escape from the pot, they'll just buy some vodka and then jump back in the pot." When he passes a pot full of Jews, the Devil says, "Make sure none of them gets out, because once one of them gets out, he will help all the others to get out too." Finally, the Devil passes a pot full of Lithuanians and says, "Don't worry about them. If one gets out, the others will drag him back in."*

Dalia alluded to this joke when she told me, "Lithuanians are jealous. With Jewish people, if you're doing well, they say 'I'm happy for you, and I will help you.' They have a community and they help each other. In Lithuania everyone does separate things, and nobody really wants to help you, and nobody really wants you to be successful, and if you're successful, we really don't want you to be successful. There is a lot of jealousy. They look down on you. If you're doing well, they're not going to be happy. 'I wish that person wouldn't be doing so well,' Lithuanians think."

It's remarkable that people from all three Baltic countries told me, without my prompting, that they are full of jealousy, that people don't help each other out, and they would rather pull someone down than celebrate their successes. It's also fascinating that each Baltic country sees *envy* as a unique trait that they have. Estonians never said that Latvians or Lithuanians are envious people. Or vice versa. When it came to *envy,* Baltic people were only self-critical.

However, what's really bizarre is that I didn't feel that Baltic people were any more envious than the typical American, Asian, or European. Since I'm not fluent in any Baltic tongue, it's hard for me to catch subtleties, but I didn't perceive an unusual amount of envy in the Baltic. I can only share what Baltic people told me about themselves. Their message was loud and clear: *we're an envious people.* OK, if you say so.

6. Supermodels on the streets

Yet another common Baltic trait is that the people are extremely fashion conscious. Women dress well and are incredibly feminine. They have long hair, often wear skirts, and always wear high heels. Even during the icy winter, it's almost impossible to find a woman who doesn't have boots with heels. Need to take your baby on a walk in a stroller through the park? Baltic mothers advise doing it in stilettos and a short skirt.

I'm a complete fashion moron, but it seems that everyone in the Baltic wears the fashion label *du jour*. Women flashed Prada and Gucci labels on their belts and clothes. Meanwhile, their stylish sunglasses showed off Armani, Versace, or a bling-bling D&G label. Some of the most decked out, over-the-top fashion nuts are Russians. As Patricia, a young Finn who had been living five months in a regional forest in Lithuania, told me, "Compared to Finns, Lithuanians are much more girlie-girls."

Men, she added, are also fashionable. Men wear whatever jeans are currently in vogue. They usually have nice shoes. They rarely wear sneakers, and when they do, they're never white, which screams, "Fashion police! Over here! A clueless American is committing a fashion *faux pas!*"

With their well-styled hair and perfect outfits, most Baltic men are a strange species of *macho metrosexuals*—they are fastidious about their image, but have a somewhat hard edge in their attitude. Patricia also observed that Lithuanian men "tend to spend more of their income on flashy phones and cars. They seem to care more about such things than most westerners." All these Lithuanian fashion comments apply to Latvia and Estonia too.

The Baltic fashion mantra seems to be: *it's more important to look good than to feel good.* For example, despite the wild temperature swings, Baltic men dress the same all year round. Whether it's a warm summer day or a snowy winter night, you'll find guys wearing well-fitting jeans, a shirt, and a light jacket or sweater. Fat bulky jackets must stay in the closet unless it gets to be minus 40 degrees, at which point you should stay home anyway, so that nobody sees you wearing that ridiculous poofy jacket.

Most importantly, Baltic *fashionistas* don't wear hats in the winter. That's totally uncool. A few men wear hoods, because that's hip. However, only wimps wear hats. Women don't wear hats either, for that might mess up their perfect hair. A woman's pride and honor is her long beautiful mane, so you want to show that off, especially if you're blond (and about half of the women are natural blonds). Although young people leave their hats at home, everyone has a scarf in the winter. It seems that conventional wisdom says that a scarf is all you need to survive a blizzard. A T-shirt is all you have this Baltic winter? No problem, as long as you have a scarf!

Perhaps the biggest Baltic mystery is: how do the Baltic people afford all the clothes, makeup, jewelry, and perfume they are wearing? Baltic salaries are less than half of what Western Europeans or Americans make. Furthermore, fancy clothes are nearly twice as expensive as in America. How do the Baltic babes do it?

Fake labels help bridge some of the economic gap. Idiots like me can't tell a counterfeit Yves St. Laurent purse from a genuine one. I'm not sure how pervasive knock-offs are in the Baltic, but it must be over 95 percent. Although fake labels drop the costs dramatically, they don't explain everything. In fact, many Baltic people avoid the pretentious labels altogether, and are still dressed in stylish, elegant clothes. Indeed, it's hard to find a slob in the Baltic. If there is one, he's a tourist.

There are two things that the high-heeled Baltic women do to stretch their fashion budget: (1) they live with their parents and spend most of their measly income on their image; (2) they skimp on food, which has an added benefit of making you skinny enough to squeeze into those sexy pants you just spent a fortune on.

However, let's be clear: Baltic women may be high maintenance, but they're not prima-donnas. Baltic babes are the ultimate male fantasy, because they're supermodels without the supermodel attitude. There are so many beautiful and well-dressed women walking around that the Megan Fox look-a-likes behave like the girl-next-door. Competition is so fierce that men will ignore the bitchy ones, focusing on those who have a good heart . . . and a nice ass. In conclusion, Baltic people will make your head turn, but rest assured, they are pretty normal people underneath the makeup and brand labels. Still, there is a dark side to all this obsession with fashion.

7. Materialism pervades

Materialism is a disease that has hit Eastern Europe hard ever since the Berlin Wall came down in 1989. In the Baltic, materialism reaches epic proportions. When the veil of communism lifted, Baltic nations heard a gunshot announcing the start of a race to catch up to the standard of living of West. During the 1990s, Western investment poured into the Baltic, flooding the region with jobs and cash. Baltic people acquired everything they weren't able to have under communism: clothes, mobile phones, laptops, meals at fancy restaurants, satellite TV, and books about what we can learn from Eastern Europeans.

Then the dawn of the twenty-first century brought a period of absurdly easy credit. This kicked off the second acquisition wave across the Baltic. People bought big ticket items: cars, homes, furniture, and expensive vacations. Debt soared, but since everyone was doing it, it seemed normal. Besides, it felt great! In just 20 years, the Baltic had caught up to Western standards. At least, so it seemed. Then, another veil lifted—the veil that hid reality.

Today, Baltic people still struggle to accept reality. Throughout the Baltic prices for many things are 50 to 100 percent more expensive than in the United States. Housing and energy are slightly cheaper, but food is often more expensive. Yet, people earn peanuts. Any financial adviser would say that it's time for the Baltic people to tighten their Gucci belt.

However, after 20 years of living beyond their means, Baltic people still have an insatiable hunger to buy more stuff. For example, Baltic people often have more than one mobile phone and SIM card. They say it's because they're trying to secure the best rate, but part of the reason is they just love to have more toys.

The materialism stretches beyond objects. Patricia, a Finn living in Lithuania, told me that both men and women often look at each other as trophies. For men, it's "look at my beautiful supermodel girlfriend."

For women, it's "look at my rich boyfriend with the nice car," she said. She concluded, "Baltic people are more materialistic than Finns."

Baltic people may be even more materialistic than the most materialistic people in the world: Americans. Although Americans consume more than anyone else, many have quit the acquisition game. They observe that at the end of rat race, you're still a rat.

The novelty of capitalism has yet to fade in the Baltic. However, as capitalism matures in the Baltic, many of its people will tire of spending their lives chasing toys. They're not there yet. For example, knowing that Baltic people are obsessed with cars, I told them that many urban Americans think that people who don't have cars are the coolest. Taking a bike to work is cool. Being stuck in traffic with all the other idiots is not cool, even if you have a Porsche. They found this concept hard to understand.

Let's hope that the young Baltic people reconnect with their grandparents, who lived through Stalin's tyranny and the Spartan communist way of life. That elderly generation knows what really matters in life and has much to teach its descendants.

> Šypsena nieko nekainuoja — *Ancient Lithuanian proverb meaning, "A smile costs nothing."*

8. Disliking Russia

By now it should be obvious that Baltic people share a common dislike for Russia. This feeling runs deep in the Baltic veins: they dislike Russia's language, culture, and people. Stephanie Carnell, who has deep Lithuanian roots, told me, "Lithuanians definitely wish the Russians would all just leave. Even the ones who have assimilated, who can pass for Lithuanians, the Lithuanians still believe that they should just get out."

Of course, the source of most of the Baltic animosity for Russians is the Soviet occupation. What Baltic people often forget is that when they were Soviet Republics, their leadership was often made up of local Baltic people, not Russians. Sure, Russians ran the show behind the scenes, but Estonians, Latvians, and Lithuanians held high political positions throughout the Soviet period. Nevertheless, the Baltic people view the Soviet period as an unfair and immoral occupation. Moreover, for them, *Russian* and *Soviet* are synonymous.

Baltic dislike for Russians is killing the prevalence of the Russian language. In the last century everyone in the Baltic spoke Russian. Now, less than half do, and it's dropping fast. Children who aren't going to Russian schools learn English as their second language, not Russian. Those who were taught Russian often didn't like learning it. Maiu and her twin sister were born in 1980 and had to learn Russian for eight years. Today, they speak only basic Russian because they made so little effort to learn it. Learning the language of your occupier can be degrading. Maiu regrets not having learned Russian well (she's fluent in German, English, Finnish, and Estonian). Nevertheless, her mediocre Russian skills don't hurt her much because she works in an Estonian company where all the Russophones speak English.

On the other hand, Russian will never die in the Baltic. Russophones have enough critical mass in the Baltic (up to 30 percent of the population) that many jobs require trilingual skills (the local Baltic language, English, and Russian). Moreover, Russians are horrible at learning other languages, so the Baltic people will continue to conform to the Russophones. Russians are trying to learn English. Perhaps by speaking a neutral third language (English), Russophones and Baltic people have a new hope of communicating between each other. With communication, comes understanding.

> *Before we can forgive one another, we have to understand one another. — Emma Goldman, a Lithuanian*

9. Celebrating the summer solstice

Countries at lower latitudes than the Baltic usually ignore the summer solstice. Some people don't know when it is and a few don't even know *what* it is! However, in the Baltic, the fabled White Nights is one of the most important celebrations of the year.

Usually falling around June 22, the summer solstice celebration has pagan roots. Lithuanians attempt to give the festival a Christian flavor by calling it *Joninės* (St. John's Day), and adorning those named Jonas and Jenina with oak-tree wreaths. Nevertheless, pagan rituals abound. They sing and dance until the sun sets. Then they race to find a magic fern blossom by midnight. Whoever finds it will secure happiness and wealth forever. Jana told me that Latvians also look for the fern blossom, but added, "Actually, that's the only time when Latvians are really looking for sex. The expression 'looking for the fern blossom' means 'trying to get sex.'"

If that doesn't work out, then they spend the rest of the year's shortest night jumping over bonfires. The smoky bonfire serves three purposes. It helps you to: (1) secure happiness and wealth; (2) get rid of all the witches and bad spirits flying around that night; and (3) protect you from mosquitoes. Estonians will have "singing fights" where two crowds try to out-sing each other. The ritual ends when they greet the rising midsummer sun and they wash their faces with the morning dew.

10. A Baltic woman's love for flowers

If Baltic women had to choose between men and flowers, most would take one nanosecond to pick flowers. OK, perhaps all women in the world would also agree with them, but it's clear that Baltic women have a special fondness for flowers. Enter any room with a Baltic lady and she'll zero in on the flowers, carefully evaluating their type, condition, and meaning. I might spend a month in a room before realizing that there's a flower in it.

Does the date March 8 mean anything to you? Probably not. However, in the Baltic it's as significant as January 1, February 14, and December 25. March 8 is International Women's Day. "It's a day that all men celebrate," said Inga of Lithuania. "It is often referred to as the Day of Tulips—almost every man buys at least one tulip for his wife, girlfriend, colleague, or mother- in-law." When was the last time an American bought a flower for his mother-in-law?

> *I'd rather have roses on my table than diamonds on my neck.*
> *— Emma Goldman, a Lithuanian*

Flowers carry profound meaning in the Baltic. When I first met Maiu's mom, I brought her purple flowers, and she ended up talking about them for two weeks, citing the significance of the species I picked. On the other hand, if you pick the wrong flower, you'll get in trouble. While I spent a few months in Estonia, I would bring Maiu flowers from time to time. Whenever she received them, her face brightened and a smile would spring across her calm face. However, one day, her face drooped.

"What's wrong?" I asked, extending the flowers to her.

"You brought me *Russian* flowers," she said with a mild scowl on her face.

I brought the flowers closer to me, examining them. They looked pretty to me. They smelled nice too. I had no clue that there was even such a thing as a "Russian flower." Flowers are flowers. Just different shapes, colors, and smells. Isn't it the thought that counts? Apparently not in the Baltic. Here's a handy tip, fellas: stick with tulips. I'm not sure what color, but tulips usually work.

10 ways the Baltic nations are different from each other

A funny thing would happen whenever I tried to learn how the three Baltic nations differ from each other. I would say to a Baltic person, "Do you know that the few Americans who have heard of the Baltic think that your three countries are roughly the same?"

"But we're not!" they would cry in desperation.

"How are you different?" I would ask.

"So many ways!"

"Great. Name something besides your different languages."

Suddenly, their contorted facial expressions collapsed. Their eyes would shift around, scrambling for an answer. They would stall and babble like a eight-year-old who is trying to lie to his parents.

Occasionally, I would get lucky and get an insightful answer. I compiled these answers and added a few of my own observations. Here are 10 reasons why *Balticstan* doesn't exist:

1. Although their languages are related, a Latvian can't communicate with a Lithuanian beyond Tarzan-speak. The Estonian language is so bizarre and unrelated that the only means of communication with the other two countries are by using hand gestures and grunts.
2. Estonia's standard of living has consistently been stronger than its Baltic brothers.
3. Poland influences Lithuania, Finland influences Estonia, and Russia influences everybody.
4. Out of 106 countries surveyed, Lithuania leads the world in suicides per capita. Latvia is 11th and Estonia is 17th (USA is #39; UK is #49).
5. Religious Estonians and Latvians are Protestants, whereas religious Lithuanians are Catholics. However, the vast majority of Baltic people are not religious at all.
6. Estonia drinks more alcohol per capita than Latvia or Lithuania. However, that statistic is deceptive because millions of Finns visit Estonia just to get hammered. On average, each Baltic citizen consumes about 11 liters of alcohol per year (that's 30 percent more than the average American).
7. About 83 percent of Lithuanians prefer to speak the national language, whereas in Estonia it's 69 percent and in Latvia it's just 60 percent.
8. Russophones are about 28 percent of Estonia's and Latvia's population, but only six percent of Lithuania's.
9. Russophones sometimes change their name just to get better jobs and opportunities in Estonia. They rarely do that in Latvia or Lithuania.
10. Latvia has more wolves in their woods than Estonia and Lithuania put together; Lithuania has more storks than the other two combined; and Estonia has the greatest number of mosquitoes.

Although we'll never adequately explain how Baltic people are different, you now have a head start. Baltic people will want to add to this simple list. In fact, some Lithuanians may scream, *"Manau šis skyrius apie Lietuvą erzinantis!"* ("I think this chapter on Lithuania sucks!")

However, one reason that it's hard to summarize the differences among Estonians, Latvians, and Lithuanians is that there are too many factors involved (e.g., who you talk to, where you go, what you ask, random chance, etc.). Perhaps the trickiest factor is that the Baltic people are constantly evolving. This brings us to the final mystery—their future.

The Baltic Future

As much as the three Baltic nations try to assert their individual identities, for the last 300 years, their fortunes have risen and fallen together. They have been rising since their 1991 independence, but whether they continue this trajectory depends on how well they do the following three actions.

First, they should overcome their deep-seated dislike for Russia. Too often Baltic people have a negative, emotional knee-jerk reaction to anything Russian. Although it's great that they've been looking to the West ever since their independence, it's stupid that they've been ignoring the biggest country in the world, which is sitting right next to them. If the Baltic nations play their cards right, Russia can become a fantastic partner and ally that helps the Baltic region prosper. Moreover, the Baltic can become the bridge, the peacemakers, between the EU-NATO and Russia. Let's hope the new generation, which is free of Soviet scars, works with Russia in a mature way that benefits all. The big Baltic fear is that Russia re-occupies them again; however, the best way to prevent that is by making Russia your friend and not treating the Baltic Russophones like second-class citizens. The Baltic nations have miraculously maintained their identity after hundreds of years of occupation. That alone should give them confidence to approach Russia as a friend and not be hampered by typical Baltic insecurity.

> Kas bus, kas nebus, bet lietuvis nepražus.
> *— Lithuanian proverb meaning, "Whatever happens, the Lithuanian will not perish."*

Second, they should discover their Baltic neighbors. Although few Baltic people say, "You're as dumb as a Lithuanian/Latvian," it's clear that Baltic Blindness is still common. It's great that the Baltic trinity is now in the EU and will adopt the euro. Baltic governments and businesses are also interacting more than before. Still, what's most important is that the people themselves go to their neighboring Baltic countries and meet each other. People need to attend each other's universities, work in each other's countries, and even marry across the Baltic. Although I met many Russian/Baltic couples (which is encouraging), I never met a mixed Baltic couple. I'm sure they exist, but the more there are, the better the chances of tighter integration and superior cross-cultural understanding.

Third, they should maintain their culture. Fortunately, the Baltic people are extraordinary at doing this, even after hundreds of years of occupation, so there is little risk of their culture disappearing. On the other hand, their insatiable materialism, along with their efforts to copycat the West, is diluting their unique cultures.

In many ways, the third action is the counterbalance of the first two actions. Because the Baltic has proven it can do the third, its main challenge will be doing the first two. Doing the first two will be hard because, as we saw, socializing is not their strength. However, the Internet and global media is loosening them up, as they learn how the rest of the world interacts. Indeed, compared to its parents, the youngest generation is already socially adept. Whatever happens, the Baltic will continue being a fascinating place.

What Lithuania Can Teach Us

- **Eat nutritious and delicious bread.** Many Eastern Europeans are proud of their bread; however, I couldn't find any that was as nutritious and delicious as the bread in the Baltic. Lithuanians (and their Baltic brothers) bake delicious dark bread that is rich in rye, fiber, and whole grains.
- **Recite a poem to receive a gift.** This Lithuanian tradition has three benefits: (1) It forces everyone to learn some poetry; (2) it shows a deeper level of gratitude than simply saying "thanks"; (3) It encourages people to buy fewer gifts during the holidays and to better appreciate the few ones they do receive.
- **Preserve your own food.** After collecting berries, mushrooms, and other foods, Lithuanians preserve them in glass jars. Some practice drying the food too. Partake in this old tradition to become more connected with your food.
- **Celebrate the summer solstice.** Electricity and modern conveniences have disconnected us from nature's cycles. Reconnect with the seasons and celebrate the longest day of the year with the same level of enthusiasm as the Lithuanians!
- **Encourage pedestrian zones.** It's almost impossible to find an urban area in America that can only be accessed by foot. Wherever people can go, cars can go too. It seems that the only outdoor pedestrian zone is in Disneyland. City governments and store owners must show more courage and believe that if you build a pedestrian zone, people will walk it. Americans hunger for a place without cars. Encourage your area to move beyond malls.

- **Have the courage and confidence to lead.** Lithuania was a tiny Soviet republic, but it played a key leadership role in getting more rights and, ultimately, complete independence. The Lithuanian leaders couldn't have done it with the bravery and support of their people. What movement are you leading?

Places I saw and recommend in Lithuania: Vilnius and Kaunas. If you have extra time, visit the Curonian Spit and the Hill of Crosses.

Travel deals and info: http://ftapon.com/lithuania

I wanted to spend more time in the Baltic, but if I did, I would never see the rest of Eastern Europe. It made me sad, because I wanted to do it all.

> *Life is much shorter than I imagined it to be.*
> *— Abraham Cahan, a Lithuanian*

Belarus is our next stop. Belarus is the hardest European country to get into. So it's gotta be good, right?

Little did I know that in Belarus I would fall in love with their kitchens, get a nice dose of radiation poisoning, watch porn with a Belarusian family, and be whipped while lying alone and naked in a sauna.

5

Belarus—Europe's Last Communist Country

With a hostile and negative tone, the Belarusian travel agent asked me, "Why would you want to go to Belarus?" Notice she didn't say, "Why *do* you want to go?," but rather, "Why *would* you want to go?" I was waiting for her to add, "Are you nuts? Why not just go to Iraq while you're at it."

It was August 2004 and I was sitting in a drab office in Tallinn, Estonia, trying to apply for a visa to Belarus, Europe's last communist country. The belligerent travel agent lived and worked in Estonia, but she spoke little Estonian or English, so helping non-Russophones irritated her. She treated me like dirt, but her attitude was so extreme that it was comical.

I handed her $50, two mug shots, my life story, and a signed document that promised that I would *never, ever* overstay my visa. Clearly, Belarus was having a tough time handling the armies of tourists who are trying to sneak into this Eastern European paradise. The Belarusian travel agent mumbled that the embassy would process my visa request "eventually."

Eventually, they did give me the visa, which helped me survive the border crossing ordeal. I left Vilnius in a bus packed mostly with old, fat Belarusians. The summer's heat and humidity made the bus feel like a wet sauna, minus the babes. I was sitting next to an obese man who insisted on showing me his hairy, deodorant-free armpit. I couldn't believe how long he could hold onto the rail above him. He was like a rock climber whose arms never tire of clinging onto a rock. Unfortunately for me, he was wearing his wife-beater tank-top and his bacteria-infested armpit was nearly buried in my nose.

We stopped at the border and a couple of folks tried to get off the bus to escape the heat (and the stench). The bus driver barked at them to stay on board. With no breeze flowing the non-air-conditioned bus, the temperature rose to oppressive heights. Finally, 30-hellish minutes later, the border guard collected our passports. After another 30 minutes, we drove up to another spot, where everyone got off to get our passports stamped. After half an hour, we all got stamped a few times and everyone was happy. Except the border guards. They're never happy.

Foreshadowing the inefficiency to come, we spent 90 minutes dicking around at the border. As we drove into Belarus, we passed an endless line of big rigs waiting to leave the country. The Belarusian sign said, "Сардэчна запрашаем у Беларусь" ("Welcome to Belarus").

Defining Belarus

Belarus is sometimes called White Russia because in East Slavic languages *bela* means *white,* and *rus* refers to *Russia* (or the *Rus* people). It's not any more snowy or white than the rest of Russia, but the name stuck. Although there are two ways to refer to Belarus, there are nine ways to call its citizens: Belarusian, Belarusan, Belarussian, Byelarussian, Byelorussian, Belorussian, Bielorussian, White Russian, and White Ruthenian. It was so much easier during Cold War; we just called them all *commies.*

Before exploring into Belarus, let's consider a few facts about this medium-sized, flat, and sparsely populated country. Belarus is slightly smaller than the UK or Kansas. Although it's easy to see that Belarus is in Eastern Europe, some tried to convince me that Belarus is in Central Europe. Like its Baltic neighbors, Belarus is on the Northern European Plain, and its highest point is only 346 meters (*Dzyarzhynskaya Hara* mountain). With only 9.5 million citizens, Belarus is one of Europe's most uncrowded countries. It's becoming even less dense, because 40 percent more Belarusians die than are born, so the population is declining 0.36 percent annually. Although the government is concerned that its fertility rate (1.26) is the ninth lowest in the world, so far it has done little to change that. Before WWII, about 10 percent of the population was Jewish. After the war, just a fraction of one percent were left. All this doesn't make Belarus sound particularly interesting, but once you dig deeper, you learn that it is.

Belarus is Europe's lungs

Belarus's flatness makes it a geographic bore, but its vast forests, wetlands, and swamps re-oxygenate Europe's air. The Pripet Marshes, for example, are Europe's largest marsh zone. Those marshes suck in our waste products and pump out oxygen. Another reason Belarus acts as Europe's lungs is that woodlands cover 40 percent of Belarus's land. Its most celebrated forest is the Belavezhskaja Pushcha National Park, a UNESCO World Heritage Site. Some learned about it because that's where the USSR formally dissolved in December 1991. It's Europe's largest primeval forest; it's what's left of the forest that covered Northern Europe 800 years ago. The park features 300-year-old pine trees and 600-year-old oak trees. It is also the oldest wildlife refuge in Europe, protecting otters, beavers, minks, badgers, elks, wild horses, wolves, boars, lynx, deer, and odd creatures named ermines.

However, the real stars of the park are the 800 remaining wisent (European bison, sometimes called a zoobr). A wisent is smaller than an American bison, but it's the largest land animal on the European continent. It's a miracle that wisents are still with us. Like its American cousin, the European bison was hunted to near extinction. Once it was everywhere in Europe, but by 1919, there was only one wild wisent left. The creature was in the woods looking for a nonexistent mate when a hunter thought it would be a bright idea to shoot it dead. So he did.

Fortunately, 52 wisents remained in the zoos. Biologists bred them back to life. Now there are over 3,000 wisents in the world, mostly in zoos. Although my bus crossed western Belarus, I didn't see any wisents running around.

Hotel Sputnik

As the bus bumped and jostled its way to Minsk, Belarus's capital, I wondered where I should sleep. My guidebook mentioned the Hotel Sputnik. I liked the idea of staying in a hotel named after mankind's first satellite. The USSR stunned the USA when it took the lead in the space race in 1957. The Soviet accomplishment inspired Americans to land on the moon, a feat that the Soviets could never reproduce. As I imagined the slow and delicate movements in space, the bus jerked to a stop at the terminal.

As the Belarusians shoved their way out of the bus sauna, I asked random people, *"Gde Hotel Sputnik?"* By observing their hand gestures and listening for the words *naprava* (to the right), *nalieva* (to the left), and *priama* (straight), I eventually found the uninspiring Hotel Sputnik. I hoped there would be a replica of the smooth, spherical Sputnik satellite nearby, but instead I found only an old blocky, gray building.

When I stepped into the hotel lobby, the receptionist ignored me. I walked up to her desk and stood next to her. She continued ignoring me. I said, *"Dobrey den."* Wishing her a *good day* made her raise an eyebrow and glance at me for a moment. And then she went on ignoring me. I said, *"Vi gavorite pa Angliski?"* Without looking at me, she just shook her head, indicating she didn't speak English. It was remarkable that in a decent hotel in the capital of Belarus, the receptionist didn't speak English. I asked her for *odin nomer* (one room). She exhaled as if I had just asked her to clean my filthy toilet. Then she checked her circa 1988 computer.

In 2004, Belarus's per capita GDP was one-sixth of America's and the average Belarusian made $100 a month (in 2011 it's one-ninth). You would think that hotels would be dirt cheap. Wrong. Welcome to communism, the land of frivolous price controls. The receptionist said the room's price, but I couldn't understand such a big number. My Russian is so pitiful that I can barely keep up with a Russian toddler. I peered over to see her computer screen. She pointed to the amount: *87,000 rubles*. Although that was just over $40, there were two numbers under the 87,000 one. One had a price of 42,000 and the other was just 26,000. I wanted to know more about those numbers, so I said, *"Shto eta?"* ("What is this?")

She explained that the 42,000 ruble price was for people from the former USSR. The 26,000 ruble price was for Belarusians. Because I was a foreigner, I had to pay four times more than a local for the exact same crappy room. "But maybe it isn't crappy," I thought. I wanted to see it, so I said, *"Ya hachu pasmatri eta nomer."* It was Tarzan Russian, but she understood and told me to go to the third floor. The elevator was broken, so I took the stairs and then met the floor guard, a chubby middle-aged woman who didn't look that happy either. The room she showed me was clean and had not been remodeled since the 1950s. It was certainly worth the Belarusian price of $12 per night, but $40 was ridiculous. Besides, I can't stand paying four times more than another person for the same thing. I left saying,*"Nyet, spasiba"* (no, thanks).

Exactly 10 years before, Belarus said *"Nyet, spasiba"* to capitalism. Indeed, what makes Belarus remarkable is that it's the only ex-communist country in the world who gave capitalism a shot, and then reversed its course. The story of this flip-flop begins when it plunged into capitalism in 1991. It did what most Eastern European countries had done: privatize state enterprises, accept foreign investment, and let prices float freely. Transitioning to capitalism was rough on all Eastern Europeans. Although it was tempting to return to communism, people had faith that the draconian economic reforms would eventually lead to a higher standard of living for all. However, just three years into the transition, Belarus lost its patience and pulled the plug on the capitalist experiment.

Aborting capitalism

The road back to communism began when Belarus elected President Alexander Lukashenko, who assumed power in 1994. He promised to conquer inflation, which was clearly the fault of evil capitalism. To crush inflation, he pulled a classic communist move: he just ordered it to stop. He dictated that prices couldn't go up more than two percent per month (or 27 percent per year). What a fool. If only taming inflation were so easy. Any economist would tell you that if you expand the money supply (print money) and you devalue your currency, then you will get high inflation, no matter what law you pass. Unfortunately, most politicians don't take Economics 101.

While inflation ignored Lukashenko's orders, he re-nationalized many private companies. At first, nationalizing something sounds like a good idea—you declare that the people now own something that was private before. It's good to stick it to those evil corporations anyway, right? However, when nationalization happens to you, it no longer seems so great. It feels more like a robbery. Imagine you took a huge risk and started chocolate factory. One day, a government official walks into your office and says, "Your company now belongs to the state. You shall work for the state; we will set the salaries, policies, prices, and procedures. If you disagree, you will go to prison."

> *An authoritarian style of rule is characteristic of me, and I have always admitted it. You need to control the country, and the main thing is not to ruin people's lives.*
> *— Alexander Lukashenko*

Under communism, people who had invested their life savings in owning a piece of a company, farm, or property, saw it vanish. Communists can even nationalize your home. For example, when I was staying with a family in Trinidad, Cuba, the owners told me what happened to their house when Fidel Castro took over. Their family had worked hard and saved money to buy a one-story house. The government decided it was too big for one family. So they literally drew a line down the middle and said, "Everything to left of this line is now government property. Don't worry, we will pay you a fixed rate to the father of the family." Unfortunately, this rate was non-transferable and would not adjust for inflation. In Cuba, getting a $10 rent check every month might have been acceptable 50 years ago, but a few short years of high inflation made that rental income worthless. What's more insulting is that once the father died, the family stopped getting those $10 checks. That's because when the father died, the state inherited half of his house and no longer had to "rent" it. Belarus copied Cuba by nationalizing private property that the government felt was "too big."

I wanted to rent a private apartment in Minsk since the state hotels were such a rip-off. After much searching, I found a studio apartment in Minsk's epicenter. For a week's stay, I gave the owner $150 in hard US currency. The apartment was on Praspekt Nezalezhnasti, in between Lenina and Kamsamolskaja streets. It was nice being near Lenin's street, and that just one block away was another attractive street called Karla Marxa.

Falling in love with a brilliant kitchen invention

In America, those who don't use a dishwasher perform a stupid ritual. I never realized just how stupid and inefficient it is until I came to Belarus. In the US, after washing a dish, we place it on a dish rack. After the dishes air dry, we put them away in the cabinet. Any Belarusian communist will tell you that this is highly inefficient.

The Belarusian solution is brilliantly simple and effective: the kitchen cabinet, which is placed over the sink, has dish racks embedded into the cabinet itself. Moreover, the cabinet has no bottom—it's open underneath. Therefore, you can place the freshly washed (and dripping) dish directly into the cabinet. Water drips through the opening on the bottom and lands in the sink (or the metal, waterproof countertop). Later during my Belarus trip, I would find some designs that had a removable tray that rests under the cabinet racks to catch the dripping water, in case you don't want it to drip through the cabinet's bottom. The open bottom allows enough airflow for dishes to air dry in the cabinet. Not only do Belarusians skip a step when dish washing, but they also gain extra counter space since they don't need a separate bulky dish rack. Genius!

I'm not sure who invented this brilliant design, but it's the kind of thing a Belarusian would make: it's not pretty, but it works. Since the cabinet's bottom is below eye level, its unattractive open bottom is out of sight. Belarusians are the masters of jerry-rigging things. Communism limits imports, so it's often hard (or prohibitively expensive) to obtain things you want. Instead of finding a new fuel pump for your car or a pipe for your plumbing, a Belarusian will spend hours repairing it with simple tools, lots of creativity, and liberal use of duct tape. The resulting solution won't win any beauty contests, but it will work. In this way, Belarusians are the opposite of Italians, who are obsessed about aesthetics and sometimes make things that have little purpose other than to look good. Belarusians care little about aesthetics, and instead just focus on if the damn thing works.

Pulse dial lives in Belarus

The smelly bus ride reminded me that I needed to do laundry. I figured the guy who rented me the apartment might know where I could find a laundromat. When I started dialing his number, I heard a sound I hadn't heard since I was a child: pulse dial. If you don't know what pulse dial is, that's my point—it's that old.

If you ever wondered how telecommunications was ages ago, come to Belarus. Pulse dial is what we used before we had touch tones. Belarus is the only European country that still uses it. The one benefit of having pulse dial is that you don't have to deal with, "If you want to check your account, press 1; if you want to murder the person who invented this automated system, press 2; if you wish you had pulse dial, press 3 and move to Belarus."

Beltelcom, Belarus's telecommunications monopoly, is in charge of mismanaging all the landlines and long-distance communications. In 2011, only two-thirds of the switching equipment is digital, so pulse dial still lives. Talking on a Belarusian landline is like talking on a phone half a century ago: static-filled connections and dropped calls are common. Like many of their jerry-rigged solutions, the damn phone works, barely.

On the other hand, all Belarusians have a mobile phone. It helps that there are three GSM providers competing for their business. I didn't have a cell phone, so after listening to the machine gun rattle of pulse dial, my contact picked up the line and I asked, *"Dobrey den,* where can I find a laundromat?"

"Laundromats don't exist in Belarus," he said. "The government doesn't think they're necessary," he added. Most tourists stay with relatives (who usually have a washing machine) or in a hotel (which will do your laundry). I considered hand washing everything, but my contact offered to do my laundry for a fee. They did a fine job, although they lost one of my socks.

The first thing you will notice about Minsk is how clean and safe it is. It's one of the benefits of living in a police state. There are more cops per capita in Belarus than in any other European country. Getting caught by a Belarusian policeman is about as much fun as going on a date with the Spanish Inquisition.

Nevertheless, a few try to meekly challenge the police. For example, at 8:00 p.m. on the sixteenth day of every month some Belarusians turn off their apartment lights and put a candle on the window. It's a symbolic protest against the disappeared political opponents. Some even show up with candles on Kastrychnitskaja Ploshcha Square, but the police quickly break up this silent protest.

Minsk takes a cultural vacation

I searched for a cultural event around Oktyabrskaya Square. Eastern European cultural events are a bargain. In 1999, for example, I saw a ballet in the Bolshoi Theater in Moscow for $9 and one in Ukraine's best theater for $6. Unfortunately, such events are 10 times more expensive today, but if you go to smaller cities, you can still find deals. Therefore, I was excited when my guidebook mentioned that, "Minsk has quite a lively cultural life." However, when I visited in the July 2004, I discovered that the circus was closed until August, the ballet was closed until September, dance performances were suspended until November, and the Philharmonic Hall was undergoing reconstruction. In short, this city of two million (22 percent of Belarus's population) had nothing going on.

One Russian said that the reason Minsk is quiet during the summer months is that most people go to the countryside. Fine, let's see what's so great about the countryside. For the next two days, I communicated with grumpy bus drivers in order to visit three towns in the countryside: Dudutki, Mir, and Njasvizh. They were nice, each one showing off a few dilapidated 500-year-old buildings. The sixteenth-century Mir Castle, a UNESCO site, was memorable. Located 85 kilometers from Minsk, the red brick castle has an archaeological museum. On the other hand, if you never see these places, you're not missing much. Moreover, I didn't see the hordes of Belarusians who supposedly had escaped from the culturally dead Minsk.

This wasn't the first time Minsk was nearly dead. Like Lithuania's Kaunas, Minsk has come back from the dead several times since it was born in 1067. Several fires burned Minsk to the ground throughout the centuries, Crimean Tatars sacked it in 1505, Napoleon ruined it in 1812, the Germans pounded it in 1918, and then the Poles came in to finish the job in 1919–20. Still, it was WWII that delivered Minsk's most brutal spanking: the city was leveled and half of its population perished, including nearly all of its 50,000 Jews. With this dismal history, how do real estate agents convince anyone to buy a home in Minsk?

The Great Patriotic War

Imagine if the US fought a war where a third of Americans died. That puts into perspective the importance of WWII for Belarus. Perhaps that's why Russians don't call it WWII, but rather The Great Patriotic War. For the Soviets it was symbolically equal to (Pearl Harbor + September 11) x 100.

When you enter the Museum for the Great Patriotic War, they ought to give you a barf bag—it's that graphic. There are photos of people (including women and children) getting hung and shot. Mutilated bodies are everywhere. It's gruesome to see photos of soldiers with blown-off heads, body parts strewn about, and close-ups of young dead faces. On the other hand, everyone should see such horrors. If more people saw just how ugly war is, we might think twice before getting involved in one.

Later in my trip, I would visit the border town of Brest, which has the best Soviet WWII memorial in the world. The Brest Fortress defends the confluence of the Buh and Mukhavets Rivers. For one cruel month in 1941, Soviet soldiers fought to the death against the Nazis. The relentless German siege consumed Soviet supplies and energy. Although the Soviets lost that battle, it cost the Germans dearly. In honor of those who fought so valiantly, a gigantic soldier's head, carved from a single rock, dominates the center of the memorial. The sculpture's name is *Valor*. Next to it, an obelisk pierces the sky, an enormous eternal flame burns, and violin-filled music that sounds like "Adagio for Strings" plays in the background. If this memorial doesn't move you, none will.

WWII was a big deal throughout Eastern Europe because they bore the brunt of the war's devastation. They had most of the concentration camps. They had to deal with the Nazis storming in, the Soviets pushing them back out, and then overstaying their welcome. They saw their Jewish population vanish. In some cities, Jews were up to 75 percent of the population. (One reason for this was that during the 1800s Russians forced its Jews to settle in Belarus.) Today, thanks to Hitler, Jews are only 0.3 percent of the population. WWII not only annihilated the Jews, it also killed 2.5 million Belarusians.

So many Belarusians died that they're still unearthing the bodies. In 1988, for example, an archaeologist digging near Minsk made a mysterious and gruesome discovery. He dusted off a 50-year-old human skull. Within minutes, he found another, then another. Eventually he estimated that the mass grave in Kurapaty contained the remains of over 200,000 corpses. It ended up being the third largest concentration camp in WWII. This should give you an idea of just how many people died in Belarus, when you realize that someone could sweep that many human remains under the carpet, right outside of Minsk, and nobody discovered it until 44 years later!

These Belarusians had been executed between 1937 and 1941. The question remained: who done it? The two usual suspects were rounded up: the Soviets and the Nazis. Belarusian nationalists concluded that the Soviets were to blame. They believed that the USSR was trying to wipe out Belarus's culture and language. As Soviet leader Nikita Khrushchev once said, "The sooner we all start speaking Russian, the faster we shall build communism." On the other hand, the Nazis had this thing for killing lots of people and making mass graves. Most objective historians conclude Stalin's regime is to blame.

What if the US suffered like Belarus did in WWII?

To understand how Belarus was nearly obliterated in WWII, try to digest these numbers. The fighting destroyed half of its economic resources, 72 percent of its cities, and 85 percent of its industry. Minsk looked like Hiroshima after the atomic bomb. Nearly a third of the country died—many were executed in over 200 concentration camps.

Let's compare what Belarus sustained in WWII with what America suffered in its deadliest war: the American Civil War. In our conflict, most our resources and infrastructure were untouched. Approximately 625,000 Americans died, which was about *two percent* of our prewar 1860 population. Compare that to *33 percent* of Belarus's population dying in WWII.

Let's imagine that what happened to Belarus in WWII happened to America. Imagine 100 million Americans dead—that every third person you know is dead. Imagine most of our industry in Michigan, Ohio, Illinois, and Silicon Valley obliterated. Imagine nearly three-fourths of our cities in ruin, including New York, Chicago, Miami, Los Angeles, Dallas, San Francisco, Seattle, and Atlanta. Imagine half of our farmland and forests burned, most of our lakes and rivers contaminated, and 85 percent of our schools and universities destroyed. Imagine Washington, DC completely flattened: the Washington Monument toppled, the US Capitol building without a stone standing, the Lincoln Memorial a pile of rubble, and the White House a charred and burning mess.

Now try to imagine what kind of psychological trauma that would have on the generation that had to rebuild. And then imagine trying to rebuild with the oppressive, totalitarian government with Stalin breathing down your neck. Perhaps only now you can begin to imagine the incredible hardiness of the Belarusian people. They've put up with a lot of shit.

If you are going through hell, keep going.
— Winston Churchill

After the Museum of the Great Patriotic War, my head was spinning one way and my stomach was spinning another. I had to go for a walk. Minsk is neither charming nor beautiful, but it's not bad. The architecture in the center of town is a mix between pleasant classic architecture and ugly, blocky concrete buildings. One nice building is the Church of St. Alexander Nevsky, built in 1898. It was closed during much of the atheistic Soviet era. Minsk also has a fake old town called *Traetskae Pradmestse*. It's fake because the real old town was pulverized. The Soviets rebuilt part of the old town to show what Belarusian architecture was like before they constructed the ugly Soviet buildings.

The balcony of my apartment overlooked Lenin's boulevard, which had just received a face-lift in 2004. Its wide sidewalk has elegant, warm, old-school lamps next to modern fountain jets that fire streams of water through the air at regular intervals. People of all ages stroll down the wide boulevard, enjoying the water-jet performance. I introduced myself to four young Belarusians who were sitting on a bench. After a few minutes of chatting, I invited them to my apartment for tea. They looked at each other, exchanged a few words in Russian amongst themselves, and concluded that I probably wasn't a CIA agent who would torture them with the Guantanamo Bay Special.

The government encourages students to fail exams

We ended up talking about our countries until 1:30 a.m. It was a great cultural exchange that Lukashenko wouldn't want to hear. They asked me not to reveal their names (for fear of getting in trouble with the authorities). There were two men and two women. Only one guy didn't speak English, he voiced his opinion through translation. I didn't have enough chairs, so some of us sat on the carpet, sipping tea. Their main criticism against Americans is that our friendliness is sometimes fake. I've heard this comment many times: we're all smiles, but we don't mean it. Hence, fellow Americans, work on your frown.

The students said that the government effectively encourages them to fail. If you pass your final college exams, the government won't let you go abroad. The purpose of this policy is to prevent brain drain, but it's not working. One student knew of 20 fellow classmates who were working in the USA (and who were doing their best to stay there). They had all failed their final exams.

Five years after meeting these four students, in 2009, I met another Belarusian student, who told me another revealing tale about Belarus's educational system. I was couchsurfing with a Flemish family in Brugges, Belgium. They were hosting Valentina Martman, a plump 18-year-old Belarusian, who had been staying with them every summer as part of a cultural exchange. Valentina explained that you have two options in the university: (1) you pay your own way and then you can do what you want afterward, or (2) you let the government foot the bill and for the next several years you have to work wherever the government wants you to work, to pay back your debt. They often send you to undesirable places. It's a form of indentured servitude. On the other hand, paying your own way so you can have freedom doesn't always pay off either: Valentina spoke about a dentist who had been unemployed for six years.

Valentina also said that Belarus is not a true communist country, because it allows some private industry and ownership. However, she admits that most Belarusians dislike the system. Lukashenko labels his particular communist-capitalist blend as "market socialism." Valentina jokingly called it "communism with a cappuccino." I call it "idiotic."

Take food, for example. Lukashenko (who was in charge of the collective farms before he became the dictator) claimed that if the state controlled the farms and food-processing industry, Belarus would no longer need to import any food. Fat chance. Within three years of nationalizing the food industry, the agricultural industry's share of the GDP nosedived from 24 percent to 14 percent. Here's another way to illustrate just how lousy a government can be at feeding you: state and collective Belarusian farms own 83 percent of the agricultural land and get most of the state subsidies; however, privately run farms (which use only 17 percent of the land) produce over 40 percent of the national output. Belarus is importing more food than ever.

In 2005, Belarus nationalized even more companies, including banks, so that by 2011 about 80 percent of all Belarusian industry is in the state's hands. There are price controls, currency controls, and the government manhandles the private sector. The communists change regulations randomly, conduct frequent strict inspections, impose new regulations retroactively, and throw businessmen they don't like in jail.

In Belarus, freedom doesn't just take a backseat to state control, freedom is put in a body bag and thrown in the trunk. Lukashenko limits the press, religion, free speech, and peaceful assembly. Although people can vote, it's a joke. Lukashenko has effectively castrated the parliament and taken over the government. The Belarusian Constitution limits a President to two five-year terms. Using phony "referendums," Lukashenko got rid of term limits. Thanks to his complete media monopoly and totalitarian control, his political opponents have no chance to dethrone him. In the last election, Lukashenko not only won 83 percent of vote, but also pro-Lukashenko candidates swept all 110 seats in the Legislature. If you believe those election results, I've got a Belarusian potato farm to sell you.

I often wondered why Lee Harvey Oswald shot John F. Kennedy. But then I learned he lived in Minsk. Living under this system of government would drive me to shoot someone too. Earlier that day, I had checked out Oswald's apartment. It's a great location, by the Svislach River and near the Victory Obelisk. While everyone was trying to defect from the USSR to the USA, Oswald was defecting the other way. Oswald left the US Marines and arrived in Minsk in January 1960. He spent his early 20s in Minsk, getting a job in a radio factory, marrying a local, having a baby, and changing his name to Alek. Eventually the KGB said, "We need you to return to America. We have a job for you. . . ." At least that's what one conspiracy theory believes.

The future of Belarus

Let's return to the four Belarusian university students who were hanging out in my Minsk studio. I asked them about Belarus's future. Two believed that Lukashenko and his totalitarian government would stay until he dies (around 2030). The other two believed Lukashenko would get kicked out by 2015. It seems that Lukashenko is standing on thin ice.

"Belarus's economy is a fantasy," said one student. It's true. The biggest delusion since he took power came from Russia, which sold oil to Belarus at well below market prices. Belarus would refine the oil and export it at normal market prices. It was a great deal for Belarus. Even a moron running an inefficient, bureaucratic business can make money when they get to buy products at a heavily discounted rate.

Belarus's dream is getting a wake-up call. In 2007, Russia required that Belarus give nearly all the duties that Belarus collects on exported Russian oil. In 2011, Russia sold gas to Belarus at world price levels, which caused severe inflation in Belarus. When Belarus didn't make debt payments, Russia stopped supplying electricity. Belarus, like a drowning swimmer, is fighting to stay afloat. They're improving energy efficiency, diversifying exports, selling off state assets, and tightening their fiscal and monetary belt. Nevertheless, they're still sinking. They're plugging the holes with borrowed money from Russia.

Ironically, this is exactly what brought down the USSR. As the price of oil dropped during the 1980s, the Soviets borrowed money like crazy. By 1991, the USSR was bankrupt. Russia is setting Belarus up for the same fate. Once Belarus is down on its knees, Russia's leader will make a Darth Vader-like offer: "Join me, my son, and together we shall rule the galaxy!"

It would be an offer that Belarus could not refuse. By merging with Russia, Belarus would just become another state within Russia and, therefore, would receive the internally subsidized energy prices. (Russia, like many oil-rich countries, sells its oil domestically at dirt cheap prices.) Like a heroin addict getting his fix after a long break, Belarus would breathe a deep sigh of relief and life would return to normal.

"But if Russia and Belarus merged," I asked the students, "Would Lukashenko remain in power? Would his totalitarian regime remain an island within the more free Russian country?"

"*Nyet*," said one woman. "I'm sure Russia will protect Lukashenko, give him a nice *dacha* and lots of money, but eventually Belarus would have to open up."

In 1999, Belarus signed a two-state union treaty with Russia, promising closer ties. Over a decade later, they had made no progress, mostly because Lukashenko prefers autonomy. However, don't expect Belarus's independence to last. Belarus has always been under a greater power, and this time it looks like it will be going under Russia's wing again.

It was 1:00 a.m., and given all the questions I was asking them, the students were beginning to wonder if I really was working for the CIA. Having heard their opinion on Lukashenko and the future of Belarus, there was one final puzzle to solve: the Belarusian language.

The elusive Belarusian language

Haven't heard any Belarusian? Don't worry, neither have the Belarusians. Although I had heard that Belarus has its own language, Russian is all I could see and hear on the streets of Minsk. The students assured me the language exists, but they weren't very convincing. I asked them, "So, do you speak Belarusian when you go buy something?"

"No."

"How about when you talk to the government?"

"No."

"When you're hanging out at your house with your friends?"

"No."

"In business?"

"No."

"So when do you speak it?"

"In some classes in school."

"That's it?"

"Yeah."

Dumbfounded, I later re-confirmed this fact several times. It seemed that nobody in the world speaks Belarusian, not even the Belarusians. What's Belarusian really like? One student told me that Belarusian is similar to Ukrainian. That meant little to me, so another described it as a blend of Polish and Russian. This is logical, since Belarus shares borders with Poland, Ukraine, and Russia. It's also makes sense because in the 1921 Treaty of Rīga, Poland and Russia split Belarus in two, and each tried to impose its language on the Belarusians. A few sample phrases back this up: *dobry dzyen* (good day) and *privitane* (hi) is similar to Russian's *dobrey den* and *privet; dzyahkooee* (thanks) is similar to Ukrainian's *dzyahkooyu,* which seems related to Poland's *dziękuję;* also, *kalee laska* (please) is similar to Ukrainian's *bud laska.* Of the three languages, Belarusian is most similar to Ukrainian. One Belarusian told me that he can "understand almost every single word" in Ukrainian. Russians, in contrast, struggle to understand the Belarusian and Ukrainian languages. However, none of this explains why Belarusians don't speak Belarusian.

To further confuse you, Belarus's official government website says that 37 percent of Belarusians spoke Belarusian at home (most of the rest spoke Russian). By asking enough people, I finally solved this mystery: Belarusian is spoken in villages. While Poland and Russia tried to erase Belarusian, peasants kept the language alive.

Yarik Kryvoi, a Harvard Law School graduate, spent half of his life in Belarus, and he told me, "People in rural areas speak Belarusian naturally, because they can't speak any other language. But you wouldn't hear much Belarusian in Minsk, unless you come across some young people or some old ladies who come from a village. For the young people, it's also a form of protest against the current political regime, because they sort of repress the Belarusian language, which is an interesting thing that the government of Belarus oppresses the Belarusian language. It does not want to support it. It's not really welcomed by the government. Speaking Belarusian is the way Belarusians show their position and what they think of the situation in the country. Lukashenko has decided to follow more anti-Belarusian language policies." It's ironic that after Poland and Russia attempted to erase the language, the Belarusian government is now trying to finish the job.

To hear the language and meet the "real Belarusians," I would have to go deep into Belarus. I wanted to visit a place so ridiculously remote that it would make the moon seem like a tourist Mecca. Scanning the Belarus map, my eye stopped in the southeast. It's a place that nearly everyone has heard of, but few have visited: Chernobyl.

On April 26, 1986, the world learned about a remote Soviet town called Chernobyl (Chornobyl in Ukrainian). On that day, the Chernobyl nuclear reactor melted down and ruined Belarus's day. Imagine a nuclear plant blowing up in the UK, dropping radioactive fallout on 25 percent of Britain's land, and poisoning the territory for decades. That's exactly what happened to Belarus (Belarus and the UK are a similar size). Even though the nuclear plant was in Ukraine, the winds blew about 70 percent of the radioactive isotopes on Belarus's southeast. Today, 250,000 hectares are still contaminated. The worst part is the Chernobyl Exclusion Zone, although areas around it aren't exactly the Garden of Eden. I wasn't sure if the few people who live there spoke Belarusian, but I was sure that they glowed and had three arms.

As my excitement of visiting this radioactive wasteland grew, I got the advice of a husky Minsk policewoman. We spoke for 45 minutes and she told me that her father had gone to Chernobyl immediately after the disaster. The government told everyone that alcohol protects you from the effects of radiation. Later, I would learn that most Belarusians still believe this. The cop told me how the government forced her father to drink liquor. She believes it's because they didn't want him to remember anything. It worked: he doesn't remember much. This creates a funny scene. Imagine a cop, who can barely stand, slurring, "Don't worry, *hic*! I'm heeeere to save you from the, errruumm, radiation! *Hic!*"

Off to Radiation Land

Everyone discouraged me from going to Belarus's southeast. A few Minsk citizens are still afraid of the radiation, even though they live far from Chernobyl and the event happened 25 years ago. For example, while it was raining at a bus stop, I met a hypochondriac who was afraid of the "radioactive" rain and eating the "contaminated" food in Minsk. Such people thought it was suicidal to visit the southeast. Even my guidebook was discouraging. It practically said, "DO NOT GO TO THE SOUTHEAST OF BELARUS UNLESS YOU ARE A COMPLETE FOOL. THERE IS NOTHING TO SEE AND YOU WILL GET AN UNHEALTHY DOSE OF RADIATION. YOU STUPID IDIOT."

So the next day I boarded a train to Gomel, in the southeast of Belarus. During the six-hour train ride to Gomel, I met a guy named Yuri. Despite his broken English, we talked for most of the way. I asked him, "So if I want to go to a really remote town in Belarus, near the Chernobyl Exclusion Zone, where would you recommend?"

"The town I live in: Dobrush," he answered. "Oh, but one thing: the government shuts off the hot water for one month to save money. They do that every summer. So your hotel won't have hot water."

"Perfect! Has an American ever visited your town?"

Yuri laughed, "No, I think you will be the first!"

Yuri's dad picked us up at Gomel and took us on the 30-minute drive to Dobrush. He dropped me off at the town's only *gastinitsa* (hotel) and wished me good luck. Yuri would be leaving for Moscow the next morning, so I needed a lot of luck. The streets of Dobrush were deserted, so once Yuri and his dad drove away, I felt quite alone in this little corner of Belarus.

Bizarre Belarusian priorities

The hotel receptionist was a bit surprised to find an American in Dobrush. In fact, she seemed surprised to see anyone—the hotel was empty. So much for Belarusians rushing to the countryside. She led me down a long, dark hallway; they kept lights off to keep the energy bill down. After she showed me the room, I said, *"Spasiba."* She smiled and welcomed me by saying, *"Pazhalusta."*

The hotel had bizarre priorities: the room had a TV and a refrigerator, but no hot water and no toilet paper. Granted, the TV received only two fuzzy channels and the temperature inside the refrigerator was nearly room temperature—obviously those appliances weren't huge priorities either. Nevertheless, for $20 a night, you would think they could spring for a roll of toilet paper.

Here's another example of Belarus's strange priorities. The government sells goods to the local state-owned enterprises. The government allows these monopolies to mark up everything from zero to 30 percent. Being a good little monopoly, the state-owned enterprise marks up everything to the maximum 30 percent. However, the government has a few exceptions which can only be marked up a small amount because they are "essential" products. The short list includes bread, bottled water, milk, and vodka. Now you know the Belarus's priorities: vodka is more important than toilet paper.

An alien in an alien land

It was time to hear the Belarusian language and to meet the radioactive people of Dobrush. Everywhere I went, I introduced myself to the locals. Most people looked at me like *I* was the radioactive one! *The nerve!* I never liked that the American government calls foreigners *aliens*. However, when I was in Dobrush, I felt like a Martian. Although I didn't see any locals in Dobrush with three arms, they would all twist their heads 180 degrees whenever I spoke in stores or public places. Showing how fast gossip spreads, some knew about me before I met them, "You're that American," a few said. Kids stared at me with their mouths open. Even Lenin's statue in Dobrush's main square seemed to look me over.

In the end, I met nearly 100 people, but only one person spoke English well enough to have a decent conversation. Her name was Irina Kurochkina. She was a simply dressed 23-year-old. She had shoulder-length brown hair and a curvy body. Her most stunning feature were her haunting crystal blue eyes. They were so big and intense that it almost hurt to look at them. She was shy, but she was excited to practice English. Over the next few days, she would show me a side of Belarus that few aliens have ever seen.

Irina invited me to have a meal with her family and friends. Upon entering her modest apartment, her large mom greeted me with a jovial, *"Zdravstvuite!"* She guided me to the kitchen's dining area, pointed to a chair, and said with a smile, *"Sadites, pazhalusta!"* So I sat down. I also met Irina's father, her shy little brother Denis, and three other visitors in the apartment. Everyone was eager to talk, but nobody spoke English and my Russian was too poor to have a meaningful conversation. Therefore, Irina was interpreting nonstop among all of us. Her English skills were good, but the mental strain was tiring her out. Luckily, she got a break when her mother brought out the food.

Belarusian cuisine

In the USSR, neighboring Soviet Republics disparagingly called Belarusians *bulbashi* (potato-eaters). This is odd because everyone in a 1,000 kilometer radius of Belarus also consumes an absurd amount of potatoes. Still, it's true that potatoes play a big role Belarusian cuisine. Irina's mom brought out stuffed *draniki* (potato pancakes) and *khalodnik* (beet soup with boiled potatoes and sour cream). Belarusians also love their dumplings, like *kolduni* (meat-filled potato dumplings) and *kletsky* (mushroom-filled dumplings). I was secretly happy Irina's mom did not offer the Belarusian finger-stuffed sausage (raw pig's intestine stuffed with minced meat) or *kravianka* (sausage made of buckwheat grain and pig's blood).

Belarus gets the same cold, wet climate that pervades in the Baltic, so they grow similar crops. For instance, rye outperforms wheat in soggy cold lands, so Belarusians use rye to make everything from bread to vodka. Because of their limited selection of vegetables, Belarusians hardly knew what a fresh salad was 70 years ago. Even today their idea of a fresh salad is something that has cooked cabbage or boiled beets. Otherwise, there's a potato salad, which often has cucumbers and dill drowned in sour cream or mayonnaise. Since communism limits the import of spices, their cuisine is often a bit bland. Nevertheless, those who grow up on the Belarusian diet adore it—for them, it's comfort food.

Irina's mom asked me what I thought about the Belarusian standard of living and how it compares to the rest of the world. I said that

Belarus is a five out of 10 on the global scale. She was surprised, thinking they were much lower, like a two. "If you're a two, then what are the African countries?" I said. That question made her recalibrate her scale. Like many Eastern Europeans, Belarusians compare themselves with Western Europeans and then feel poor. They forget that they're better off than Cambodians, Nigerians, and Nicaraguans.

Yarik Kryvoi would later tell me, "The most important characteristics of Belarusians is that they are not really proud that they are Belarusians. This is a good thing, because there are almost no ethnic or nationalistic conflicts in Belarus. On the other hand, because of that, they have no formulated identity, which makes it easier for other countries, like Russia, to influence Belarus and its political processes, and to impose guys like Lukashenko so that he rules Belarus."

A common human trait is that no matter where we are, we believe we're the center of the universe. That's not the case in Dobrush. The humble locals acknowledge that they live on a forgotten fringe of this planet. They know that if their part of the world disappeared, nobody would notice. That's ironic, because in 1986, they nearly did vanish, yet the world certainly did notice.

1984 in 1986

George Orwell's *1984* describes a totalitarian government that covers up the truth. In 1986, the government of Belarus (with orders from Moscow) waited several days before admitting that they had a little problem. However, they couldn't hide reality from those who were in the middle of the Chernobyl disaster area. After all, things were a bit freaky that day.

The old Belarusians in Irina's home described that April day as scorching hot. The temperature was ridiculously hot for spring. The sky was an eerie dark color. As they marveled at the bizarre weather, nobody had any clue that they were being doused with radiation. Nine tons of radioactive material was filling the sky. That's 400 times the Hiroshima atomic bomb. Over five million people had the distinct pleasure of having radioactive fallout land on their heads.

Irina was five years old when she witnessed the cataclysm. She said, "I remember a violent, horrible wind, unlike any I've ever felt. I knew something was wrong, but I didn't understand what was happening." Neither did the adults. The Soviets were atheists, but as doom descended on Dobrush, some believed that the end was at hand.

There are two things that are counterintuitive about the Chernobyl horror. The first has to do with who suffered the most. Everyone I met knew several people who had died of cancer or other ailments a few years after radiation rained on them; however, it's surprising who the victims were. You would probably predict that a five-year-old *dievushka* (girl) like Irina and a 70-year-old *babushka* (grandmother) would be the most likely to die five years after the radiation poisoning. However, according to the locals, the middle-aged folks fared the worst; those under 30 and over 60 fared better. Although it's good to question such anecdotal evidence, with the secretive Belarusian government, such stories may be the best source of information.

The second counterintuitive aspect about the Chernobyl aftermath is that its effects weren't as bad as you might imagine. The worst news: 50 direct deaths, up to 4,000 indirect deaths over many years, and a 12-fold increase in the rates of thyroid cancers among Belarusian women.[1] Although that's tragic, you might have expected worse news given that the explosion released 400 times the radiation dose of the Hiroshima atomic bomb. Indeed, the land around Dobrush looked surprisingly normal. The fact that girls like Irina survived without health problems seems miraculous.

Nevertheless, nowadays Dobrush locals blame nearly all their ailments on Chernobyl. Most Belarusians over 50 are fat, but they claim that Chernobyl is the reason that they have bad joints and high blood pressure. Unfortunately, since the government represses most of the little information it gathers, we may never know the full long-term effects of Chernobyl. All these mysteries only increased my curiosity. There was only one way to learn more: I had to go into the Chernobyl Exclusion Zone. But first, I had to go to Hell.

Sauna Experience Part III

The next day, Irina drove me to the outskirts of Dobrush (that sounds funny—it's like saying you're going to the outskirts of no-man's land). In a small farm house, Irina introduced me to three of her close friends: Dimitri, his fiancée Alla, and a crazy girl named Sveta. None of them spoke English, although the hyperactive, skinny, blond Sveta certainly tried. We barbecued some pork together and ate outside overlooking the surrounding farmland. We joked and laughed often, despite (or perhaps because of) our language differences. It's amazing how much one can communicate when two people really want to communicate.

As our meal winded down, Dimitri and I watched the girls go off into the potato fields to have their "girl talk." I rested my chin on my palm, admiring the beautiful girls as they walked into the summer's sunset. Just as I began fantasizing about having a sauna with them, Dimitri invited me to join him in a "*Russkaya banya.*" Although I understood the words (*Russian bath*), I didn't know what it really meant. "Maybe it's like a Jacuzzi," I thought. Nevertheless, I love jumping blindly into the unknown, so I agreed. Little did I know that I was jumping blindly into Dante's Inferno.

Dimitri led me to a small house. When I entered inside, I started sweating. It was hot like a sauna. Dimitri told me to strip. I did. Then he told me to follow him into another room. "But I thought we were in the sauna . . ." I mumbled as I followed him into the second room.

As I walked into the next room, hot air enveloped my skin. Sweat began dripping down my forehead, stinging my eyes. The naked Dimitri fiddled with a variety of things while I just closed my eyes and tried to breathe normally. As sweat poured down my back, Dimitri opened yet another door and then, like Satan, motioned me to follow him into Hell.

I am not sure what was the temperature in that third room, but I'm sure that even the Devil would get a heat stroke. The steam-filled air burned my throat. My head was spinning. Dimitri told me to lay my naked body on the bench. I laid on my stomach. I winced as the burning bench scorched my chest and legs. Sweat rolled down my brow as if I were running a marathon in the Amazon jungle.

In the fog of my mind, I saw Dimitri bring out a big, bushy plant. *What the hell is he going to do with that thing?* He started running it all over my body. It didn't feel good: it just felt like a big, bushy plant running up and down my wet, naked back—not exactly a dream sensation. Occasionally he shocked me by whipping me with it. *Whack! Whack! Whack!* I bit my lip and clenched my fists each time, not because it hurt, but because I was wondering what in heaven's name I had done to deserve all this.

After what felt like a lifetime, Dimitri told me that we could take a break from Hades. We cooled off outside for a couple of minutes, admiring the Milky Way. However, before my body could cool down to a boiling temperature, he said it was time to return to the inferno. I gave him a fake American smile and followed him back in.

He told me to lie down again. I did. Then with hand gestures and a semi-stern voice, he ordered that I flip over, on my back. Suddenly, saunas lost all their sex appeal. I thought of my sauna experiences in Finland and Estonia, but my smile vanished when Dimitri reminded me to roll over.

I did. Now, my penis was out in the open, feeling extremely vulnerable. Then Dimitri brought out that hell-spawned plant again. My penis shrieked. My wiener just wanted to run for cover in between my legs. But it was too late, Dmitri had us right where he wanted us.

Dimitri stood next to me, completely naked. He looked down on me with that big bushy plant in his sweaty hand. He had a malevolent stare, but that could have simply been an illusion in my heat-stroked state. The harsh sound of steam filling my ears only made the hellfire feel more hopeless. I closed my eyes and started asking the Lord Jesus for forgiveness. I asked for Muhammad's help too. And the Buddha.

He ran the plant all over my front side. Then he raised his arm high. I closed my eyes muttering, "Sweet Jesus, save me now." *Whack!* He gave me several good whacks. *Whack! WHACK! W-H-A-C-K!!!* Fortunately, not there.

After an eternity, Dimitri stopped battering me and I emerged from Hell. I felt like falling to my knees and singing *hallelujah!* Clearly, I was now a better man. Like a good Catholic, I had atoned for my sins. So now it was time to sin again.

Watching porn with a Belarusian family

After the Russian bath, I joined Dimitri's family and the girls for a small snack at 2:00 a.m. The TV was on in the background. Suddenly, I heard English! I was so excited that I turned to watch the TV. A sexy woman was walking across in a movie that looked like *Mad Max,* except Mel Gibson wasn't there. From the narrator's voice, I could tell this wasn't just some B movie. This was an X-rated movie. I warned my hosts that we were about to see some porn. They shrugged. Soon the movie "got into it."

This made for another bizarre scene. There I was, enjoying a fine meal in the outskirts of Dobrush, listening to everyone speak Belarusian, and glancing at some hardcore pornography in the background. Dimitri's mom probably didn't understand what the girls on TV meant when they screamed, "Oh yeah, that's it, fuck me *harder!*"

After 10 minutes of nonstop moaning and screaming, Dimitri's mom grew tired of the distraction and switched to the Russian version of "Who Wants to be a Millionaire?" It's the same show, except that the grand prize is a million *rubles,* not dollars. In 2004, that worked out to about $25,000. But with monthly wages averaging $100 per month, you would feel like a millionaire if you got that.

At 3:00 a.m., we went to bed. As I replayed the day's events in my mind, I realized that some may never believe that all this really happened. Even I couldn't believe it. Yet that was how I spent a warm summer day in Dobrush, Belarus.

Entering the Chernobyl Exclusion Zone

My Belarusian friends knew that I wanted to inhale radioactive air. Therefore, the next day Mikhail, Dimitri's father, offered to drive Irina and me into the Chernobyl Exclusion Zone. Although the Chernobyl reactor was in Ukraine, it was just 16 kilometers (10 miles) from the Belarus border. Since most of the radioactive plume blew onto Belarus, most of the contaminated Zone is in Belarus. The military was guarding all the entrances. Nobody could enter unless you had family ties in the zone. In 2004, it was illegal for any foreigner to enter the zone

(Ukraine opened their side of the zone to tourists in 2011). Therefore, Mikhail was taking a big risk in trying to sneak me in.

As we approached the checkpoint, Mikhail told me not to open my mouth. He will tell the guard that we're visiting relatives. Since he lives just 40 kilometers from the zone, it's a believable story. The guard examined Mikhail's documents. Then he looked at me. I stopped breathing.

The guard barked out a question in Russian. I had no clue what he was asking. My lips began to part, as I thought about something to say in Russian.

Just in time, Mikhail answered the question. The guard relaxed, raised the gate, and waved us through. I exhaled and took a deep breath of radioactive air. We were entering what was the most radioactively and chemically contaminated area in the world.

What's strange is that the zone didn't look so bad: it looked more like a ghost town than a wasteland. I expected a gray, desolate, and lifeless area. Instead, plants flourish everywhere. Abandoned buildings have trees and vines growing out of broken windows. Everywhere we drove, the streets were empty, but nature had taken over. Rusted heaps of metal lay off the road, as if they were quickly abandoned. All the man-made elements of the zone were dying, but life was springing forth in every corner. It was green everywhere you looked on that August day. The zone was a glimpse of what would happen if humans suddenly vanished from the earth.

We parked at the dilapidated house of Mikhail's father. The wooden structure was decaying; moss grew in the dark, wet places. Dust-covered tools and random objects lay on the floor, forgotten. There was a small farm in the back. Entropy ruled: you could see the remnants of an organized vegetable plot, but it was fading fast. Mikhail told me that scientists discovered mutated plants in the zone. Still, apple trees were bearing things that looked like fruit. I plucked an apple and examined it. It looked normal. I bit into it. Radioactivity never tasted so good! Finnish authorities warn against eating mushrooms and fish around Chernobyl because their levels of radioactive cesium-137 still exceeds the EU standards. Hey, they didn't mention apples, so I ate the whole thing! Who needs GMO apples when you can have yummy radioactive ones?

It's hard to believe, but a few loonies live permanently in the zone. We drove by two *babushkas* sitting outside their shacks. It's hard to imagine how these grandmothers live here. They have no electricity, police, stores, or government services. These Chernobyl survivors cling to their homes, because that is all they have. Probably only a few dozen live in the zone, but two million Belarusians still live in the hardest hit areas. They don't move because the state-controlled labor market is rigid. The government employs most people and helps with housing. If you move, good luck finding a job and a house. Besides, who are you going to sell your radioactive house to?

Mikhail said the government relocated 75,000 people "just for show." They were probably the folks who were glowing in the dark. Most had to stay put. The government didn't want to relocate two million people and abandon the vital industries in the southeast. In fact, just three months after the accident, the Soviets forced the surviving Chernobyl plant workers to return to their offices, which were located just a five-minute walk from the blown up reactor. They had to restart the remaining three reactors to make sure that people had power during the winter. Many Chernobyl workers died from prolonged radiation poisoning. Today, the government downplays the dangers of living in these areas. They are encouraging resettlement and are cutting benefits to those who suffered from the accident.

Leaving Belarus

Although the radiation therapy felt great, we didn't want to overdose on it. We left behind the verdant Chernobyl Exclusion Zone and came home to peaceful Dobrush. I took one last cold shower in my hotel that had no toilet paper. The next day, I gave long hugs to Irina, her family, and her friends. Yeah, I even hugged Dimitri.

Dobrush comes from the Russian word meaning *good* or *kind.* Irina and all the people I met there were truly good and kind to me. I'll never forget their generosity and warmth. I waved goodbye to them (and Lenin) as the minibus left the main square in Dobrush.

Seven years after visiting Dobrush, in 2011, Irina found me on Facebook. She was now 32 years old and living in Moscow. I was a bit sad when I looked at her photos. Although her beautiful haunting blue eyes remained, much had changed. She had dyed her hair blond and wore fancy clothes with heels. Gone was the simple girl that I met in Dobrush. She even sounded different. She wrote (excuse her imperfect English):

I am really thankful to Moscow for the changes of myself and what the city could do with me, my temper, character, and personality. I changed, I know, and feel it myself. I may say I became much stronger, a bit violent and much less sentimental. I changed my mind on a lot of different things, life events, principles and people too. I'm happy and now I don't want to change anything in my life.

In fashion, I prefer the classic style. In addition, here there are rules of office etiquette. On weekends, I wear modern, cheerful clothes for clubs and other city entertainment places.

Remember Sveta and Alla?! Both became mothers last year. And both of them have sons, Nikolay and Konstantin, my godsons. This year my brother Denis went to the Economical University, he's a student now, he lives in Gomel. I urged him to go to Moscow University, but he's a patriot of Belarus and decided to stay there, though he likes Moscow and visited me several times. That is my news.

Irina

Moscow had transformed the simple village girl I met in Dobrush. Nevertheless, I hoped that deep underneath her mesmerizing crystal eyes, there was still a part of her that hadn't forgotten the lessons she had learned while growing up in Belarus.

What Belarus Can Teach Us

- **Do a Belarusian kitchen remodel.** If you frequently hand wash your dishes, you will love doing what Belarusians do—put the wet, dripping dish directly into the cabinet. Belarusians don't use separate dish racks, because their cabinets have holes on the bottom to let the water drip out onto the waterproof counter (or onto a removable tray). Although this efficient design saves time, it still doesn't make dish washing fun.
- **Jerry-rig something.** When something breaks, Americans usually buy a new one. If we fix it, we hire a professional. Next time, do what Belarusians do: fix it yourself. Your solution may be a pathetic jerry-rigged solution, but you will have learned how something works, become a bit more self-sufficient, and saved a few bucks.
- **Suck it up.** Compared to Belarusians, most people are wimps. We've gotten soft with our many comforts, so that today we complain when the slightest thing is not perfect. Next time you're feeling whiny, think about what the Belarusians had to deal with after WWII. Then shut up and deal.

Places I saw and recommend in Belarus: Minsk, Brest, and the Chernobyl Exclusion Zone.

Travel deals and info: http://ftapon.com/belarus

When I was in southeastern Belarus, I was tempted to cross into Russia or Ukraine, but I had visited both of those countries in 1999, and I had never been to Poland. Besides, I knew I would return to those ex-USSR countries one day, so we will discuss them at the end of this book. I was a bit sad to leave Belarus. Its resilient people were good to me, even if they didn't always smile at first.

Now we shall go to Poland and re-enter the world of capitalism and tourists. To get you in the mood, here's a Polish joke:

An American is walking down the street when he sees a Pole with a long piece of wood and a tape measure. He's standing the wood on its end, while stretching and jumping to reach the top of it with his tape measure. Seeing the Pole's struggle, the American grabs the wood, lays it on the sidewalk, measures it with the tape measure, and says, "There! Two meters long!"

The Pole shouts, "You stupid American! I don't care how long *it is! I want to know how* high *it is!"*

6

Poland—More Than Just a Source of Polish Jokes

Two Polish guys rent a boat to go fishing in a lake. They catch so many fish that one says to the other, "We'll gotta come back here tomorrow!"

The other asks, "But how will we remember where this spot is?"

The first guy spray paints an X on the bottom of the boat, and says, "We'll just look for this X tomorrow!"

The other Polish guy says, "You stupid idiot! How do you know we'll get the same boat?!"

Unlike the Baltic countries, the typical American has *heard* of Poland, but besides that, it's one big mystery. The French, Italians, Spaniards, and British usually don't know much either, except that Poles are "stealing our jobs." In my case, all I knew were a bunch of silly Polish jokes. All this is rather embarrassing considering that Poland has 38 million people and is Europe's ninth biggest country (it's a bit smaller than New Mexico). We all ought to know a bit more about the land of the Poles. As my train creaked to a stop into Warsaw, Poland's capital, I wasn't sure what to expect.

Coming from Belarus, there were two obvious differences. First, people were in a hurry. Capitalism values time more than communism, so things moved quickly. People were walking and talking fast, making me feel like I was going to Warsaw's Old Town in slow motion. Second, when I arrived in the old town, I was overwhelmed by something I hadn't seen since Helsinki: tourists. It was August 2004, just four months after Poland joined the EU, and EU citizens were taking advantage of the new border-free area. Unlike many tourists, seeing hordes of tourists doesn't bother me. When exploring a place, it always feels hypocritical to complain about "all the damn tourists!"

Europe's "old buildings" myth

Warsaw's Old Town is impressive and lovely. The *Plac Zamkowy* (Castle Square) has intricate details on every building. Adorning their structures are painted facades, carved statues, and a multitude of colors. Everything looks so perfect. Too perfect. It made me suspicious. It all smelled too new. After a bit of investigation, Europe's biggest scam became clear.

To notice the scam you have to remember that WWII utterly leveled Warsaw. Warsaw got nailed three times during WWII. Germany started WWII on September 1, 1939 by attacking Poland. They took just one week to get within 40 kilometers (25 miles) from Warsaw, and then gave it its first pounding. Five years later, the *Armia Krajowa* (Polish Home Army) led the Warsaw Uprising, which damaged the city again. Although the Poles initially controlled two-thirds of the city, the ferocious Nazi response forced the rebels to retreat into the sewers, where the Germans systematically hunted them down. Half of its residents, about 700,000 people, died during WWII, and many of those perished in the final titanic battle between the Red Army and the Germans, who destroyed the remaining buildings out of spite. Over 85 percent of Warsaw lay in ruins. Looking at the photos of Warsaw in 1945, you might think an atomic bomb had been dropped there.

This leads us to Europe's biggest scam: its "old towns" aren't that old. *All the "old" buildings in Warsaw are younger than Disneyland!* Warsaw's Old Town didn't just get a face-lift, it was rebuilt from scratch, starting with the cornerstone. The "thirteenth-century" Royal Castle that overlooks the old town was rebuilt from the ground up just a few decades ago. What a rip-off!

Yes, the Poles were meticulous at reproducing the old buildings and they recycled some of the original material, but most of it is brand new. It's hard to tell nowadays, but just 65 years ago most European cities (except Paris, Prague, Rome, Venice, and a few others) were blown to smithereens. Nevertheless, Europeans have created this myth that they've got old buildings. American tourists dutifully stare with their mouths open, believing that they're looking deep into European history, but what they're really looking at is something that is *younger* than many American homes. Meanwhile, Europeans come to America, look at our buildings and sniff, "You Americans have no history."

When Europeans build phony old buildings, we gush at how beautiful and marvelous they are. Even UNESCO named Warsaw's Old Town a World Heritage Site. However, when Americans build fake old buildings, we criticize it as kitschy bad taste. Las Vegas has reproduced some of the famous buildings of Venice, Paris, and Rome. (OK, the talking robotic Zeus fountain in the Roman Forum isn't very authentic, but hey, it's Vegas.) Vegas's Venetian hotel, for example, has gigantic paintings that can make you think they were ripped straight off of the Louvre's walls. Sneak those same paintings into Versailles or the Vatican and few tourists would think that they were out of place. But no, only Europeans are allowed to scam the public into thinking they have old stuff.

In fairness, Warsaw is a fine city. It has Europe's largest square: Parade Square. The capital is clean and attractive. Nevertheless, the "historical buildings" scam bothered me. I posed for a few cheesy photos next to Warsaw's newest-old-looking buildings while flashing my phony American smile. And then I stormed out of Warsaw in disgust faster than a retreating German.

One of the few places to see some authentically old Polish buildings is in Poland's most enchanting city: Kraków. Kraków is the crown jewel of the Małopolska region. Małopolska literally means "Lesser Poland," but most tourists consider it the greatest part of Poland. Like Warsaw, Kraków lies on the *Wisła* (Vistula) River. Until 1596, Kraków was Poland's capital. Today, it's Poland's intellectual capital, being home to *Uniwersytet Jagielloński*. Founded in 1364, it's Eastern Europe's second-oldest university (the Czech Republic's Charles University is older). WWII hardly touched Kraków's marvelous buildings. Its Wawel Cathedral and Castle, soaring over the old town, beckons you to visit them. In the old town's core is the immense *Rynek Główny* (Main Market Square), which is Europe's largest medieval square. At the square's epicenter is the Cloth Hall, which is doesn't sell cloth, but rather souvenirs. Encircling the square is the marvelous St. Mary's Church and the fifteenth-century Town Hall Tower. It's fun to lose yourself in the various side streets, and it's even more fun to just let yourself fall in love with Kraków and its truly old buildings.

Wieliczka Salt Mine

Head 15 kilometers southeast of Kraków and you'll run into the Wieliczka (vyeh-*leech*-kah) Salt Mine. This UNESCO site is one of Eastern Europe's most original places. It began 900 years ago when Poles tunneled into the earth to extract salt. Over time, bored miners carved religious altars and statues for fun. Eventually, they became more creative, making whimsical gnomes and hardy dwarfs who seem to lead you into the underworld. It's an out-of-this-world experience.

For two hours, you can explore a subterranean world of labyrinthine passages, giant caverns, and underground lakes. An eerie light and its mysterious echoing chambers make it a fantasy lover's dream. Haunting figures stare at you in the semi-darkness. What's remarkable is that everything you see is made all out of salt! Lick things to confirm.

The most unforgettable room is the Chapel of Saint Kinga. The Poles started excavating this salt-filled room in 1895. More than 30 years later (and 20,000 tons of salt), the Poles finished and ended with a vast cavern. Dangling from its 12-meter-high (40 ft) ceiling is an ornate salt chandelier, whose light casts a magical glow on all the religious artifacts. All the richly ornamented sculptures are made of crystalline salt. One well-traveled eighteenth-century Frenchman observed that Krakow's Wieliczka Salt Mine was no less magnificent than Egypt's pyramids. But what the hell do the French know anyway? See it for yourself.

From utter whimsy and fun, I headed to the most infamous, depressing place in the world: Oświęcim. If Oświęcim (Osh-*fyen*-cheem) doesn't ring a bell, perhaps its German name will: Auschwitz.

The ultimate human death factory

Hitler had a problem. He believed Europe, especially Eastern Europe, had too many *untermenschen* (sub-humans). The *untermenschen* weren't just Jews, but were also Slavs and Roma (gypsies). Given that most Eastern Europeans were either Slavs, Roma, or Jews, this meant that Hitler had a *really big* problem. For example, when Hitler took over Germany, it had about 500,000 Jews, while Poland had nearly three million. He wondered what to do with them. Fortunately, about half of them fled abroad. Hitler resolved to put the remaining Jews in ghettos, which acted as a type of prison. However, once the war got started, managing these ghettos became a nuisance. Hitler toyed with the idea of sending the Jews to Madagascar. Imagine if he had done that: assuming that some would have stayed there after the war, today there would be perhaps a million Jews living side by side with the Africans of Madagascar. However, because Germany didn't have control of the sea passage to Madagascar, he abandoned that idea.

Instead, by the end of 1941, Hitler decided to solve the "Jewish question" with the *Endlösung* (The Final Solution). To do this, he established the *Einsatzgruppe,* a security police in charge of exterminating "sub-humans" in the occupied territories. Leading the way would be Hitler's *Schützstaffel,* an elite arm of the Nazi Party, which cruelly punished any resistance; the *Schützstaffel* became known as the *SS.* In the end, the SS and the *Einsatzgruppe* managed to find and kill almost all of Poland's three million Jews. Today, even after two generations of reproducing, Poland has only about 20,000 Jews. The story of how the Nazis committed this genocide is best told in Auschwitz.

> *Those who can make you believe absurdities can make you commit atrocities. — Voltaire, 1759*

Germans are *über*-efficient. This is great when they're making cars, dishwashers, and beer, but not so good when they're killing Jews. The Auschwitz complex was the most horrible concentration camp the Nazis ever made. German efficiency comes out in this ghastly killing machine. A train-load of tightly packed Jews (and other victims) pulled directly into the Auschwitz camp. The Nazis quickly selected the fittest 25 percent to work to death for 11 hours a day on 1,500 calories. The average man lasted about three months before dying from starvation, exposure, or weakness.

Meanwhile, the weakest 75 percent (including all the elderly, women, and children) were immediately executed. Firing squads were too slow and consumed valuable ammunition. The efficient Germans devised a faster way to kill them. Victims were led to a chamber, told to undress, remove all jewelry, shave, and take a shower for disinfection. The chambers had fake shower fixtures. The Nazis locked the doors and pumped in gas to exterminate 2,000 Jews in a few minutes. In most concentration camps, that gas was carbon monoxide. At Auschwitz, however, the Germans used the lethal pesticide agent Zyklon-B. Then, as if it were a Mercedes Benz assembly line, an electric lift would raise the entire chamber to a vast crematorium.

While the 2,000 bodies were being cremated, the Nazis would process their belongings. Clothes, eyeglasses, shoes, suitcases, and even hair would all be used towards the Nazi war effort. Jewish men would have to quickly clean out the grizzly remains of their fellow cremated Jews, while the Nazis would bring in the next batch of 2,000 victims. On September 11, 2001, about 3,000 innocent Americans died. Imagine September 11 happening several times per day. Then imagine waking up the next day and having September 11 repeat again, and again, and again.

It is hard to grasp the sheer size of the Auschwitz complex. Today, most visitors spend their time in the sprawling Auschwitz I, but the biggest death factory was Auschwitz II, just three kilometers away. The Nazis called it Birkenau and it's simply enormous. Imagine a small city, with over 300 prison barracks, capable of holding up to 200,000 inmates at a time. Its four gas chambers (capable of holding 2,000 persons each) were constantly busy. The Germans murdered hundreds of thousands of Roma and up to a million Jews in Auschwitz alone. Monowitz, a few kilometers to the west, also processed innocents. When these three death factories were in operation, they extinguished 1.5 million souls (about 90 percent were Jews). The Germans were expanding the death camps when the Red Army finally arrived.

It's hard enough to imagine the Germans killing 5.7 million Jews, but the Nazis also killed nearly nine million non-Jews in an equally cruel and systematic way. Germans murdered three million non-Jewish Poles, one million Serbs, hundreds of thousands of Roma, hundreds of thousands of slave laborers, and over 100,000 "mentally ill or physically retarded" Germans and Poles. Moreover, Germans killed up to four million Soviet prisoners of war, some in Auschwitz, but many locked in field camps without medical care or food. In sum, Germany murdered nearly 15 million people in their camps.[1]

The Nazi concentration camps changed Poland's demographics. For centuries, Poland had been a melting pot of ethnicities. Germans, Jews, Roma, Ukrainians, Belarusians, and Poles all lived together. After WWII, Germans who had been living for generations in Poland fled to Germany to avoid violent Polish retributions. Today, ethnic Germans make up less than 0.5 percent of Poland. Similarly, Ukrainians and Belarusians retreated to the USSR. As a result, today Poland is homogeneous: 97 percent are Polish. It's obvious on the streets. For instance, before WWII, 30 percent of Kraków was Jewish; today, good luck finding a Jew outside the historical Jewish ghetto. Although Auschwitz is emotionally draining and depressing, it's a tragic part of human history that we should never forget.

> *What good fortune for those in power that people do not think. — Adolf Hitler*

It was mid-August 2004 and I would leave Poland and enter Slovakia. I had only five months to see all 25 Eastern European countries and I had spent two months seeing just five. So I had to boogie. Kraków is near Zakopane, which is the gateway to Poland's magnificent High Tatras mountain range that form a natural border with Slovakia. I wanted to stand on Poland's tallest mountain, Mt. Rysy, to be 2,500 meters (8,200 ft) above sea level; however, I would climb the High Tatras from the Slovakian side later. Although I regretted rushing through Poland in 2004, I knew I would return five years later. In 2009, I would see other parts of Poland, but more importantly, I would do what I love most about traveling—meeting the locals.

Poland revisited: Gdańsk

It was February 19, 2009 and I was freezing my ass off. It was 10:00 p.m. in the Gdańsk train station and I was scanning all the bundled people trying to recognize my 24-year-old couchsurfing host, Emilia Łoś. I had seen her smiling photo on her couchsurfing profile, but people don't always look like their photos, especially when they're wearing 17 layers.

Suddenly, Emilia appeared with a big, warm smile and she gave me a hug. I'm not sure if she hugged me because she felt comfortable with me or because she was also freezing. Despite all her clothes, it was obvious that she was skinny, so it's probably because she was cold. Emilia exuded simplicity: her clothes were plain, her soft brown eyes had no makeup, and her straight brown hair was short enough to be manageable, yet feminine. She had a gray birthmark on her right cheek that was easy to get accustomed to. Her most obvious feature, however, was her positive spirit. She giggled and bounced around in a pleasant and endearing way. By the time we arrived to her apartment, I had already concluded, "It's impossible not to love Emilia."

She shared her Gdańsk apartment with two other students. I would be sleeping in the living room on the couch that converts into a bed. From the moment we met, our interaction felt like I was catching up with a long friend that I hadn't seen for a few years. Although it was late, we ended up chatting until 2:00 a.m. We hugged each other goodnight, and then I crashed on the couch and fell asleep in seconds.

The next morning, Emilia, who was getting a masters degree in biotechnology, had a lab session in Gdańsk's Old Town. She suggested we walk there together via a scenic route. She led me across the snow-filled *Góra Gradowa* (Hail Mountain), by the Fort Grodzisko, along an old defensive wall that now has open-air history exhibits. We climbed up to a hilltop, where we could look down on the old town and the famous Gdańsk shipyards.

The mustached hero

I was 10 years old when I first heard about the Gdańsk shipyards. The newscasters were often reporting about some Polish guy with a bushy mustache leading strikes in the Gdańsk shipyards. The video clips showed protesting Poles carrying a white banner with red scripted letters that said "*Solidarność,*" which I assumed meant "Solidarity" since the newscaster kept saying that word. I was too young to have any idea what this all meant, but I remember it clearly. I just knew that such protests didn't normally happen in those backward communist countries, so this mustached man must have had some serious balls.

That mustached man was Lech Wałęsa. He's an interesting guy. He was born in a poor family in Popowo, Poland in 1943—not one of Poland's better years. He didn't like how workers were treated at the Lenin Shipyards of Gdańsk, so he organized several strikes, which didn't go over too well with the communists. The last time the Poles tried to protest, the communists sprayed them with machine guns, killing dozens and injuring over 1,000. This time, however, they just threw Wałęsa in jail and enforced martial law. Being a good Roman Catholic, Wałęsa had faith that it would soon all work out. He was right: Time Magazine named him "Man of the Year," he won the Nobel Peace Prize, he overthrew the communists, and he still managed to find the time to father eight children.

What's remarkable is that he did not receive his 1983 Nobel Prize in person because he feared the Polish government wouldn't let him back in. That's right, he preferred to stay in crappy communist Poland than move his family to the free world where he could reap the benefits of his Nobel award. A true patriot. In 1990, the Poles elected him as President. Suddenly, after 20 years of complaining about the system, he had to fix it.

> *It's easy to turn an aquarium into a fish soup.*
> *— Lech Wałęsa, Poland's first freely elected post-war President, meant that it's easy to destroy an economy, but hard to build one.*

Unfortunately, Lech Wałęsa was no George Washington. Wałęsa was brilliant at leading the revolution, but he didn't know how to govern. He liberalized parts of the economy, but he maintained wage controls. That's like someone telling you to cook a fish soup with one arm tied behind your back. Inflation exploded and Poland's currency, the złoty, became worthless. Wałęsa's governing style was chaotic, often sacking political leaders just one year into their job. As a result, when he ran for re-election in 1995, he lost. When he tried again in the following election (2000), he got one percent of the vote. At least Gdańsk still loves him. In 2004, it renamed its airport the Gdańsk Lech Wałęsa Airport.

Exploring Gdańsk's Old Town

After admiring the shipyards and the old town from above, Emilia shouted with smile, "C'mon! Let's go!" She joyfully bounded downhill through the deep powdery snow like a deer. I tried to keep up with her. We eventually arrived in the old town, stomped the snow off our shoes, and walked under the Golden Gate. Being from San Francisco, it's clear that Gdańsk's Golden Gate is a bit different from the Golden Gate I grew up with. Their version is a medieval gate a few meters wide that leads you into the walled city. On the other hand, there's one thing the two gates have in common: neither is golden.

Emilia suggested visiting the three other city gates: the Green Gate, the Upland Gate, and St. Mary's Gate. Walking to each one makes you crisscross the town so that you see it all. We agreed to meet under the Golden Gate in two hours when her lab would be over. After Emilia left, I spun 360 degrees to look around. There is no doubt, Gdańsk's Old Town is simply magical.

Like Warsaw, Gdańsk was bombed into the Stone Age. However, at least they're honest about it. Right at the Golden Gate's entrance, there are two large black-and-white aerial photographs of Gdańsk in 1945. It looked like a city-sized elephant sat on the old town, flattening it out. It's nice that they put these two photos right up front—it's honest. It's their way of saying, "What you are about to see in the 'Old Town' was all built after 1945. Have a nice day."

I strolled down the wide pedestrian street, arching my neck to see an enormous cathedral stretch to the heavens. Adorable shops and cozy cafés lined the street. One of the most beautiful sites is Neptune's Fountain. Originally built in 1633, this ornate fountain is surrounded by colorful buildings with paintings and drawings on the exterior of the buildings—every house is a work of art. It's easy to see how Europeans get snobby: their old towns are far more beautiful than the typical American town. When I eventually reunited with Emilia, I told her, "Wow! You Polish people really know how to make a marvelous and aesthetically pleasing town! It's absolutely incredible!"

She laughed and said, "Thanks, but we didn't build it! The Germans built it!"

"Huh? What were they doing way out here?"

Then Emilia explained Gdańsk's deep German roots. She said that a few times in history Germany stretched across most or all of what is now Northern Poland. Poland often had just a thin corridor to the Baltic Sea, but sometimes it was completely cut off. I had forgotten about the period when the Germans wrapped around the entire Baltic coast, all the way to Tallinn (and built that charming old town too, by the way).

Following Gdańsk's history is like following a yo-yo. First, the Poles settled around Gdańsk because it's at the delta of their beloved Vistula River (which flows by Warsaw and Kraków). Then the Teutonic Knights (who were basically Germans) grabbed Gdańsk in 1308 and controlled it for about 150 years, until the Poles grabbed it back. Next, the Prussians (who were also basically Germans) snagged it back in 1793. They made it a special region of Prussia, kind of like a big tax-free store that you see at airports. It became even more special when it became the Free City of Danzig—an autonomous city like the Vatican. And just like Hong Kong become a vast commercial hub thanks to its special status in the twentieth century, Danzig (Gdańsk) flourished during its German period. Then Poland got it back after WWI. Finally, the Nazis (who were, yes, you guessed it, basically Germans) snatched it again, until a bunch of fighting left their masterpiece of a town in a heap of rubble.

> *After every war someone has to tidy up.*
> *— Wislawa Szymborska, Polish poet*

Emilia and I walked back to her flat to have a late *obiad* (lunch). She cooked up a classic Polish dish: *gołąbki* (cabbage leaves stuffed with rice and minced meat). It was Friday and she would be going to Olsztyn (*Ol*-shtin), her hometown, to stay with her parents over the weekend. She wanted to catch the next train, so she could make it in time for *kolacja* (dinner). She invited me to come along and stay there. I had planned to stay a night in Poznań, but the chance to stay with a Polish family was irresistible. We packed up our stuff and raced to the train station.

As the train rumbled to Olsztyn, we passed many streams in the flat landscape. Emilia described some of her camping trips at the nearby Great Masurian Lakes, which are the remains of ancient glaciers. Unfortunately, we didn't have time to go and it was a bit cold anyway. Then suddenly, in the distance, loomed an enormous structure. I said, "Holy shit! What the hell is that thing!?"

"Oh, that's Malbork Castle," Emilia said. "It's the largest Gothic castle in Europe."

"No kidding. It's huge! It sure looks dramatic in the sunset." We passed right next to it. Its monumental towers, high stone walls, long parapets, and wide moat made it a picture-perfect castle. I half expected to see Gandalf riding his white horse on the ramparts.

"Oh, and the Germans built that too!" Emilia giggled.

I mumbled, "Ah yes . . . those industrious little Germans . . . "

"And they destroyed it too!" she laughed. She's basically right, the Teutonic Knights built it over 700 years ago and a Nazi-Soviet battle blew it to pieces in WWII.

The Łoś family in Olsztyn

We hopped on a bus to Emilia's parents' house. When her parents opened the door, they embraced Emilia as if they hadn't seen her for a year, even though they saw each other last week. Her parents, Janusz and Elżbieta, were exactly like I imagined Polish parents to be: medium-sized, simple, unpretentious, humble, and generous. I shook their hands and said, "*Cześć,*" which is a bit too informal of a salutation to use with parents, but they smiled and seemed happy to meet an American who knew one Polish word.

The apartment had three compact bedrooms and everything was simple, yet functional. In one of the bedrooms was Emilia's 19-year-old sister, Paulina, who was hanging out with her friend, Karolina Bróździak. The girls were friendly, but shy when they spoke English, even though they spoke it well. In fact, Karolina also spoke excellent Spanish, but when I started talking with her in Spanish, she turned bright red and giggled nervously. We all laughed and then I left them to join Emilia and her parents at the kitchen table. Since I had to take an early train the next day, Emilia suggested we eat a snack and skip dinner so we could see Olsztyn's center before it got too late. I agreed, but first I wanted to talk to her parents because I knew they would have some interesting stories.

Elżbieta offered some food to snack on. There was the choice of meat, meat, or meat. Oh, there was some bread and cheese too. If you like heavy, meaty food, Poland is paradise. You can sample such culinary delights such as a *żurek* (sour soup with eggs and sausage), schab pieczony (roasted pork loin with herbs and prunes), and golonka (pig's knuckle with horseradish). Elżbieta saw that I was barely picking at the meat, so she opened her fridge, and pulled out jellied herring.

Now don't think that people who live near the Baltic Sea don't know what a vegetable is. Although at times it may seem that way, it's better than before. In 1518, for instance, Poles hardly knew any veggies beyond a beet. Who saved the day? Europe's culinary maestros: the Italians. After King Sigismund I of Poland married his second wife, the Italian queen Bona Sforza, she screamed to him, "*Bastardo! Voglio la cucina Italiana per favore! Basta* with your crappy food!"

The Italian queen imported an army of Italian chefs to Poland, who had to make do with what they could grow in Poland. The Italians introduced many Poles to lettuce, leeks, celery, carrots, and cabbage. Today, Poles call these veggies *włoszczyzna,* in honor of *Włochy,* the Polish name for Italy. I asked Elżbieta, "Has Polish food changed much since the communist days?"

She struggled with English and had a nervous look in her eyes when she spoke. She said that home food hadn't changed much, but restaurants had. The communists nationalized all the restaurants, set the prices at levels well above what the common person could afford, and eventually closed most of them down. The only affordable place to eat out were the lunch rooms or milk bars, which served cheap soups, noodle dishes, and *pierogi* (dumplings stuffed with mushrooms and cabbage). Today, Poland's restaurants offer many more choices, and if you look hard enough, you can even find a few establishments that offer something other than meat, pork, and sausage.

Our conversation touched many subjects, but eventually the mother and daughter got up to have their girl-talk, while Emilia's dad and I sat behind to talk about manly stuff like wars, history, and politics.

The Polish accordion

Poles know European history better than most Europeans. Janusz was no exception. Books covered nearly all the walls of their compact apartment. He pulled out one thick tome, dropped it on the table with a thud, and flipped through the pages until he found a series of maps depicting Poland over the centuries. Over time, all European countries are like accordions, expanding and contracting constantly as they conquer and get conquered. No European country is a wilder accordion than Poland. It helps that Poland is centrally located in Europe and that 95 percent of its lands are as flat as a Polish pancake. This makes it tempting for anyone with an army to roll right through it. And so, many have.

The first to roll into it after the Roman Empire collapsed were the Polanie, a Slavic tribe, which settled in the low plains between the Oder and Vistula rivers. Today, this region is still Poland's heart and soul. Hundreds of years later, in 966, the Polanie would give up their pagan ways, adopt Christianity, and create a nation called *Polska.* When the Germans shoved their way into Poland in 1038, Poles moved the capital from Poznań to Kraków. In the 1200s, invaders rolled in from both sides. The Tatars attacked from the south, while Germans squeezed in from the west. Although the Polish accordion contracted, soon it would expand to its greatest size.

The Jagiełłonian Dynasty was the beginning of Poland's golden age. It led to the Union of Lublin and the birth of the *Rzeczpospolita,* the Lithuanian-Polish Commonwealth, which we learned about in the Lithuania chapter. When Poland and Lithuania united in 1569, they moved the capital from Kraków to Warsaw, where they ruled what would become Europe's largest country, stretching to the Black Sea. Janusz wanted to talk all night about this fabulous period, but I was more interested in how the whole accordion collapsed again.

He grunted, flipped a few pages, and pointed out three maps, each showing the three partitions of Poland, and then told the short story behind each one. By the 1700s, the Lithuanian-Polish alliance had soured. While Catherine the Great of Russia used covert and overt means to chip away at Poland, the Germanic people worried about her expanding empire. So did the Germans stop Russia by helping the Poles? Not exactly. Instead, Austria and Prussia whispered to Catherine, "Listen Cathy, whaddaya say 'bout the idea that we each grab a piece of Poland, eh?" Catherine agreed and bribed several Polish politicians to seal the deal. In 1772, a quarter of Poland was doled out to Austria, Prussia, and Russia. That was the first of three partitions.

The next two were ugly. Patriotic Poles worked with Prussians to secure more rights, while Catherine worked with not-so-patriotic Poles to undo those rights. You can guess what happened next—war. Prussia abandoned the Poles and occupied western Poland, while Russia held eastern Poland. This was the second partition—Poland was shrinking fast.

Then in 1794, Tadeusz Kościuszko, who fought alongside Americans during the American Revolutionary War, figured he could repeat the same victory in his motherland. Although he started strong, Russia is a lot closer to Poland than Britain is to the United States. And it didn't help that Prussia and Austria teamed up with Russia to beat the last bit of life out of Poland. Hence, by 1797, Poland suffered its third and final partition—Poland ceased to exist. The accordion had vanished.

Poland's painful rebirth

For the next 123 years, Poland's story is tragically simple: Russia tried to convert Poles into Russians, Germanic people tried to convert Poles into Germans, and Poles tried to resist them all. In 1812, Napoleon gave the Poles a bit of hope when he promised he would reestablish Poland if the Poles would join his crusade against Russia. The Poles enthusiastically joined his doomed campaign and died for nothing.

Russian emperor Alexander I tried to play nice and give Poles a bit of wiggle room. However, by 1830, the dissatisfied Poles wanted more and screamed the refrain, "Give me liberty or give me death!" Like Darth Vader, Russia's Emperor replied, "As you wish," and gave them death. Russia shredded the Polish constitution, abolished the Polish government, crushed the Polish army, robbed Polish art and literary treasures, repealed their civil liberties, hampered their Roman Catholic Church, and forced them to learn Russian. Meanwhile, on the German side of Poland, things weren't much better. The Germans twisted Polish arms, screaming into their ear, "You're going to speak German, you're going to act German, and you're going to like it!"

Janusz raised his voice as he recounted this tragic part of Polish history, gesticulating like an Italian who had just spilled his pasta sauce. His exclamations attracted Emilia's attention—she stuck her head in the room, raised an eyebrow, and gave us a look that said, "Are you boys finished?"

"Just give us two more minutes," I begged. "And then we'll go to Olsztyn. I promise."

Emilia nodded and went away. I turned to her father with my notepad in hand and asked him what happened next. He took a deep breath, looked at his maps, and said softly, "Then it became very ugly."

He said that although Poland would return to the world map in the twentieth century, that period would be Poland's darkest hour. After WWI, Poland crawled back on European maps in the shape of a tattered accordion. Much Polish blood had been spilled to fight Russia and win back Vilnius (now the capital of Lithuania) and Lviv (now in Ukraine). At the dawn of WWII, Russia and Germany became the vise that would once again conspire to squeeze Poland's fragile accordion.

> *I belong to a nation which over the past centuries has experienced many hardships and reverses. The world reacted with silence or with mere sympathy when Polish frontiers were crossed by invading armies and the sovereign state had to succumb to brutal force. — Lech Wałęsa*

After conquering Poland in less than one month, Hitler gave the Poles three choices: be Germanized, be enslaved, or be eradicated. Jews only had the eradication option. Germany wanted to erase everything Polish from this planet. Nazis shut down Polish cabarets, cinemas, theaters, radio, newspapers, and schools. They burned Polish-language books. They gave Polish intellectuals a one-way ticket to a concentration camp. They destroyed nearly half of the educational infrastructure and scientific institutions. They fired Polish teachers, both figuratively and literally. As Nazi leader Heinrich Himmler wrote, "The sole purpose of this schooling is to teach them simple arithmetic, nothing above the number 500; how to write one's name; and the doctrine that it is divine law to obey the Germans. . . . I do not regard a knowledge of reading as desirable." When asked how Eastern Europeans should be educated, Hitler replied, "Instruction in geography can be restricted to a single sentence: *the capital of the Reich is Berlin.*"

> *I married a German. Every night I dress up as Poland and he invades me. — Bette Midler*

To be *über*-efficient, the Nazis pitted different ethnicities within Poland against each other, hoping that they would kill each other. For example, they forced Jews to destroy the statue of a Polish hero, filmed the act, and then released the video to the public. Later, the Germans burned a Jewish synagogue, filming Polish bystanders, and released the footage with the caption, "The Vengeful Mob!"

When the Nazis tried to put forth a good face, it came out crooked. For example, the only Polish cultural activities that Germany allowed were "primitive" ones that were crude or pornographic. That way they could not only show the world that they were letting Poles express themselves, but they could also "prove" that Poles were *untermenschen* (sub-human), who are only capable of producing vile art. They even invited neutral countries to see "Polish" performances that were either vulgar sex acts or deliberately boring. At the end, the Nazi propaganda official would turn to his guest and say, "Zee, zis is Polish culture! Horrible, no? Zis is exactly vat ve are saying: ze Polish people are *untermenschen!*"

> *In every tragedy, an element of comedy is preserved. Comedy is just tragedy reversed.*
> *— Wislawa Szymborska, Polish poet*

Life in the Soviet-occupied part of Poland was also no fun. Imagine being in the Polish army, sandwiched between Stalin's Red Army and Hitler's Nazi Army. Who would you surrender to? Poles chose the Germans, figuring that the Soviets would be even more brutal. Their instincts may have been right. The Soviets deported over one million Poles to Gulag concentration camps in Siberia. In the Katyn Forest near Smolensk, Russia, the Soviets massacred about 22,000 Polish military officers. In 2010, many of Poland's highest leaders, who were coming to Russia to commemorate the 60th anniversary of the massacre, perished in a plane crash near the mass grave. The bitter irony of that accident was impossible to ignore.

Like the Nazis, the Soviets also imposed their language on the Poles. When WWII started, many Jews initially fled east (into the Soviet-occupied zone), but after a few months of Soviet hospitality, they concluded, "Shit, this sucks even more! I'd rather be in the Nazi-occupied Poland!"

If you lived in Poland in 1939, one in six people you knew were dead just six years later. Indeed, Poland lost over 16 percent of its population during WWII—that's more than any other nation (Belarus lost 33 percent, but it was part of the USSR at the time, which lost 14 percent of its overall population). In all, six million Poles (half of whom were Jews) died. Those who survived were traumatized. And you thought you had a tough life.

The war-is-good-for-economy myth

It's time for a quick aside. There's a widespread belief that war is all about money and that war is good for business. Many argue that America attacked Iraq only to get access to cheap oil, even though the US was already buying Iraq's oil before the war and it became more expensive to buy that same oil after the war. America attacked Panama for the money received from controlling the Panama Canal, which, come to think of it, the US was already getting (and would give up a few years later, as promised). America went into Somalia because, well, we're not sure why, maybe sand is valuable. America attacked the tiny Caribbean island of Grenada because, well, there must be some vast economic interest there too.

The point is that nations go to war for many reasons. Money usually *is* a major reason, but it's often not the only reason or even the main reason. Sometimes we go to war for moral reasons (to stop a genocide or some other grave injustice), but there are many other factors too, such as religion, ethnic hatred, language issues, settling an ancient score, having a disproportionate number of unemployed young men in a society (i.e., a youth bulge), the "he-hit-me-first" excuse, getting back territory "that was historically ours," and, of course, having politicians with big egos and small penises.

"Never mind!" cry the cynics! "War is still good for business!" Really? Great! So let's drop a few atomic bombs on Spain to help their economy. Let's help out France by carpet bombing them. Oh, wait, they say it's great only for the *winner's* economy? Oh, OK. Poland and Belarus were victorious in WWII. By the end, they were mostly rubble and up to a third of their people were killed. France also won the war, but lost nearly half of its national wealth. The victorious USSR saw 1,700 towns and 70,000 villages utterly destroyed. Sounds like that really helped those winners out, doesn't it?

Oh, wait, they say it's just good for the *victor's economy who is untouched by war*. America was spending 90 percent of its federal budget on its war effort and going massively in debt during WWII (compared to 20 percent today). What do you think would have been a better use of that money: building things that go *boom* and then disappear after one use, or building something that lasts and can be used for many years? A war is an extremely inefficient way to stimulate an economy. If wars helped economies, then Africa would have most of the world's leading economies.

The truth is that wars do *not* help the economy: they devastate economies. That's why the stock market collapses when there are signs of war. That's why investments halt. That's why people stop spending money and start stuffing money and gold under their mattresses. That's why businesses lay off employees and stop giving raises. All this kills the economy and business.

Yes, there is one little sector of the economy, the defense industry, which is better off during war—their stock prices go up. Some may say, "The US spent $685 billion on the military in 2010! How the hell is that a 'little sector'?" Just put that $0.68 trillion into the perspective of America's $15 trillion GDP and you'll see that military spending is just *4.5 percent of the US economy—hardly a dominant sector*.

Therefore, given that the vast majority of lobbyists and campaign donors are *not* involved with the military, politicians would be fools to embark on a war, since most politicians are usually re-elected only if the economy is going well. Franklin Roosevelt knew this, which is one reason he wanted to stay neutral during WWII. War is the worst way to energize an economy. It's far better to sell stuff to the idiots who are killing each other than to be one of the idiots in the fight. That's why Argentina, during WWII, became one of the richest countries in the world: it sold goods to the countries that were spending their national wealth to kill people.

Therefore, next time someone tells you that "war is good for business and helps the economy," slap him with this book and say, "No, you dimwit, (1) wars hurt economies, (2) we don't fight wars just for money, (3) wars only benefit a small minority who are making weapons, and (4) the biggest beneficiaries are countries that are not in the war, but are supplying the warring nations."

> *Stupidity is also a gift of God, but one mustn't misuse it.*
> *— Pope John Paul II*

Ogling Olsztyn

Emilia was leaning against the door and yawning. "Yes, Emilia, we're going to Olsztyn's right now!" I put on my winter jacket. Although I was curious to see Olsztyn, I wasn't *that* excited about it. How good could it be anyway? Who the hell has ever heard of Olsztyn?

As usual, I was wrong. We walked through Olsztyn's High Gate, which used to be connected to the town's fourteenth-century walls, and stepped into a medieval fantasyland. Often Europe's old towns look better at night than during the day, because the lighting is so perfect. The warm golden lamps reflect off the snow-covered cobblestones and the high medieval walls, creating a cozy, romantic atmosphere. We strolled to the *Rynek* (Market Square) and gazed at the red-brick Cathedral of Św. Jakuba Większego in all its Gothic majesty. In my revelry, I said, "This town is spectacular, Emilia! Let me guess: the Germans built it."

She burst out laughing and said, "Yup!"

"And destroyed it?"

"Of course!" We giggled like mischievous school children.

I walked over to a statue next to the cathedral. I like checking out statues, even though I almost never recognize the guy. It's usually some dude who was important back in his day, but who today is virtually unknown. It's a nice way to remember that fame is fleeting. This statue was different, however. The guy was sitting down (which is unusual) and holding a globe in his hand (instead of a war instrument). Then I read his name. "Oh my God! This guy is my hero!" I shouted.

His name is Nicolaus Copernicus. He revolutionized the world by talking about revolutions; not political ones, but astronomical ones. He discovered that the earth revolved around the sun, not the other way around. That may not seem like such a big deal, but in 1543 saying that was heresy, and it could get you burned at the stake. That's why Copernicus waited until his health was failing to announce his discovery. On his deathbed, he received the first printing of his masterpiece. What I didn't know was that he was Polish. Nor did I know that he was the administrator of the Warmia region, where Olsztyn is located. So he was like a superhero: during day, he shuffled papers at his boring desk job, but at night, he would sneak up to his rooftop with his telescope and measure the universe.

Emilia took of photo of me sitting on Copernicus's lap while I tried to rip the globe out of his bronze hands. Then we climbed up a small hill to walk along the train tracks so we could have a view of the old town and the sixteenth-century castle above it. "Cute, pretty, and adorable," I said. Emilia smiled and we went home.

What Poles think of Russians and Germans

After saying *dobranoc* (goodnight) to Emilia's parents, we joined Paulina and Karolina, who were still busy "studying." I was curious, given Poland's rough history, what Poles born after 1989 thought of their neighbors today. Paulina's answer surprised me by showing just how profound Poland's scars are. She said, "I think it's somewhere deep inside in our society's mind that we should beware of Germans. My best friend, for example, hates everything German—it's not important what it is: the language, music, culture, people, anything. I guess people my age and older are too close to the years of 1939–45 to forget about it. But, of course, if somebody's younger, the process of forgetting about it is more in progress."

I looked over to Karolina, who said, "I dunno. I would say people my parents' age (about 50–60) still have a grudge against Germans. They still keep saying: 'Oh, the Germans came, took everything of value, they broke everything what was important for us, and left. And now they do just the same thing! They come, set up their companies and buy up our Polish corporations, they want to have a say in our government, and they want to get back the land that they originally took away from us during WWII! Bastards!'"

"What about you guys?" I asked Karolina.

"Many young people don't have such feelings," she said. "I don't think it's as negative as Paulina says. Young people assume that Germans do great work for the EU (and also for Poland), that they give us a chance to get a job by setting up those companies, and that current German society has nothing in common with those people from 1939–45, which is obvious," and then mumbled, "but not to everyone."

She took a deep breath, "So. The aversion to Germans will disappear slowly," she said, and then looked at Paulina and added, "OK, *very slowly*." We all laughed.

"But," Karolina continued, "I think that we (Poles, not me personally) dislike Russians more, and it's the same rule as in the German case—the older the person, the bigger the dislike."

> *Every man is responsible only for his own acts. The sons do not inherit the sins of the fathers.*
> *— Aleksander Kwasniewski, President of Poland*

Karolina's comment about Russians reminded me of a conversation I had a few days before with a 52-year-old woman who was born and raised in Ufa, Russia, but had been living in Poland for the last 22 years. Since she had a foot in both worlds, I asked her to compare Russians with Poles. She said, "What I love about Russians is that they are an open people. What you see is what you get with them. Poles are more closed. Also, Russians read more than Poles."

"What do you prefer about Poland?" I asked her.

"Although I'm not Catholic," she said, "I like that Poles are Catholic. They're disciplined. They have law and order. I dislike the crime and violence that is prevalent in Russia. I appreciate the Polish work ethic and their moral code. Also, Poles are highly cultured, especially with music and the arts."

I have always been and will be an enemy of communism, but I love all people. — Lech Wałęsa

It was midnight, so Karolina had to go back home. We hugged. I had to a 6:00 a.m. train to catch and I was utterly exhausted, but I didn't want to sleep. I talked with the two sisters until my brain finally shut down at 3:00 a.m. A couple of hours later, I woke up like a zombie and packed. Emilia offered a simple *śniadanie* (breakfast). Right before I left, Paulina stumbled out in her pajamas to say goodbye. She insisted on being woken up just so she could bid me farewell—very sweet. I gave her a tight hug and a kiss. "Now go back to bed," I said.

"Oh, I will!" she said with eagerness in her eyes.

Emilia drove me to train station. We stood on the platform as the train was about to leave. We looked into each other's eyes and smiled. When you travel, there are rare moments when you meet someone who is so special that you feel like you've known them forever. Communication flows effortlessly and there is a level of mutual empathy that normally takes years to develop. Such connections are as rare as the aligning of the planets. Copernicus could predict when such alignments happen, but we can't. Nevertheless, he would advise us to treasure such moments.

Emilia and I hugged for a long time. I climbed onto the train, and as it began to move, I waved goodbye. I lamented that I didn't have more time, but I treasured the moment.

Life lasts but a few scratches of the claw in the sand.
— Wislawa Szymborska, Polish poet

Poznań: Poland's birthplace

I was a zombie when I arrived in Poznań, but the cold February air slapped me awake. Poznań is for Poles what Philadelphia is for Americans: the nation's birthplace and first capital. And just like America moved its capital south to Washington, DC, Poland moved its capital south to Kraków (and then north again to Warsaw). Today, Poznań is the capital of the *Wielkopolska* (Greater Poland) region and it's yet another lovely Polish city.

Its pleasant pedestrian streets culminate in the *Stary Rynek* (Old Market Square). The square has plenty of museums, but I preferred gawking at the pastel-colored buildings, which looked particularly marvelous with the white cumulus clouds and snow. At the heart of the square is the elegant sixteenth-century Town Hall, which the Germans ran for centuries. Poznań flourished because it is strategically located between Warsaw and Berlin—a perfect pit stop for a merchant. In my case, it was a useful pit stop on my way to Gorzów

Wielkopolski, where I would stay with a Polish brother and sister. I wandered around Poznań for a few more hours and then boarded a train heading west. After seeing the marvelous towns of Kraków, Gdańsk, Poznań, Olsztyn, and even Warsaw, a nagging question started popping in my head.

Why are there so many Polish jokes?

As kids growing up in California, we would crack Polish jokes even though none of us had ever met a Pole. Indeed, we knew nothing about Poland and its people; we were just juveniles who thought the jokes were funny.

How do you sink the Polish Navy? Put it in water.

However, the jokes must have started for a reason. I couldn't figure it out. Poland was once one of the biggest and most powerful countries of the world. Today, it still has beautiful cities and a rich cultural history. Its people are kind, attractive, and intelligent. Therefore, it seems a bit odd that there are so many Polish jokes. Who started it? Should we blame the Germans as usual? Or how about those pesky Russians? Neither. This time the blame lands squarely on the Americans and the French.

When Polish immigrants poured into America (many settling around Chicago), the locals laughed at the funny things immigrants do. For example, one Iranian immigrant told me that for a long time she thought that the big mailboxes on American cities streets were garbage cans. She would regularly throw her unfinished drinks in them.

Think about when you first arrive in a strange, foreign land. You speak like a retarded three-year-old and you often have trouble with the simplest of things, such as how to: buy a train ticket, pay for fruit with bizarre-looking coins, find the center of town, obey the traffic laws, and even flush the toilet. Locals watch you, shake their heads, and conclude you're a moron.

How do you get a one-armed Polish guy out of a tree?
Wave to him.

Nevertheless, the Americans and French looked down on Poles long before any immigration wave. For instance, over 200 years ago, John Ledyard, a Puritan from America, wrote that the Polish-Russian frontier was "solely inhabited by Jews who are ever nuisances." Nevertheless, the hypocrite stayed in a Jewish home, which he described as "a large dirty house filled with dirt & noise & children." He was stunned by "not only the poorest Peasantry but the poorest men I ever saw." They were "wretched diminutive and ill formed, ill fed, ill clothed & ill looked."[2] He added that "there is a rude, unfinished, capricious fantastic Taste that divides both Poland & Russia from the Genius of Europe."[3] Ledyard "gladly" left Eastern Europe "for the Godlike Regions of the West." He was surprised that his tour proved "the inferiority of the Eastern to the Western World & that so vast a difference could be found in the qualities of the Hearts & even the Minds of men."[4] Ledyard concluded, "I cannot find any thing that interests me among the Poles; perhaps it is because I am stupid or inattentive, & I wish as good an apology in their Favour might exist, but in my Soul I doubt it."[5] So now we know the origin of the term *stupid American*.

As bad as Americans can be, when it comes to looking down on other countries, nobody tops the French. Louis de Jaucourt wrote the article about Poland in an eighteenth-century edition of the encyclopedia. The Frenchman starts the article off with minor jabs, saying that Poland is "the paradise of the Jews" and it has been "barbarous longer than Spain, France, England, and Germany." In describing Poland, he observes that "Europe has no poorer people" who have an "exaggerated devotion to the decrees of Rome" and a "superstitious fear." And then comes *le coup de grâce*—just like the French look down on America's lack of "culture," Monsieur Jaucourt sums up the lack of culture in Poland: "It has no school of painting, no theater; Architecture is in its infancy; History is treated there without taste; Mathematics little cultivated; south Philosophy almost unknown." At least he threw the Poles a bone when he concluded, "Time matures everything; perhaps one day Poland will achieve that which has been perfected in other climates."[6]

Another eighteenth-century French person, Mademoiselle Geoffrin, had this to say about Poland: "Everything that I have seen since I left [Paris] makes me thank God to be born French and a private citizen!" Of course, the big lesson from these two authors is very clear: the French haven't changed.

Regarding Poland, even French diplomats weren't diplomatic. Jean-Jacques Rousseau, the famous French political philosopher, warned the Warsaw court, "Let no Pole dare to appear at court dressed French style." *Pourquoi?* Because, *bien sûr*, it would denigrate the French heritage. In Rousseau's French brain, *enlightened* Europeans were clearly superior to the Poles: "A Frenchman, an Englishman, a Spaniard, an Italian, a Russian are all virtually the same man," but a Pole "must be a Pole."

Lastly, my favorite one. A 1780 French pamphlet that had the amusing title, "The Orangutan of Europe, or the Pole such as he is." Trying to appear scientific, the pamphlet claimed that it was based on research that "won a prize for natural history." It declared that Poles were "the worse, the most contemptible, the vilest, the most hateful, the most dishonorable, the dumbest, the filthiest, the falsest, the most cowardly creation among all the apes."[7] Wow. Sure sounds scientific to me. Makes me wonder what the non-scientific French pamphlets said. So now we know the origin of the term *French snob*.

Perhaps it's unfair to blame all Polish jokes on stupid Americans and French snobs. Germans and Russians certainly contributed. Nevertheless, it's clear that the habit of looking down on Poles started long ago and built up during the waves of Polish immigration.

> *And you have to remember that I came to America as an immigrant. You know, on a ship, through the Statue of Liberty. And I saw that skyline, not just as a representation of steel and concrete and glass, but as really the substance of the American Dream.*
> *— Daniel Libeskind, Polish architect who designed the new World Trade Center in New York City*

Finally, Neil Mitchell, who visited Poland in 1967, told me, "When the whole world has Polish jokes, the Poles have Russian jokes. The Soviet Union gave Warsaw a building modeled after the Seven Sisters in Moscow. I think it was called the Friendship Tower. It was imposing and ugly. The joke in Warsaw in 1967 was, 'Where is the most appealing view of Warsaw? On top of the Friendship Tower, because that way you cannot see the Tower.'"

Poland's four big Cs

Couchsurfing hosts often just give you directions on how to get to their place. Some hosts receive many guests and understandably can't afford to pick each guest up. Others are just busy. In Poland, however, my hosts always waited for me at the train station, demonstrating gracious Polish hospitality. Anna Szczodrowska-Rożek and her brother, Kuba, greeted me as I walked out of the train station in Gorzów Wielkopolski. They were in their late 20s and looked like siblings, sharing light brown hair and normal body proportions. We walked a few minutes to their 11-story apartment building. Upon arriving, Anna served me hot pasta, saying, "You must be hungry."

"*Dziękuję!*" I said. "It looks and smells delicious! What is it?"

"It's vegetarian," she said. *Vegetarian food in Poland?* Perhaps there is hope after all.

While I enjoyed the tasty bowl of pasta, Kuba asked me about life in America. I told him the things the CIA tells me to say, and then asked him about Polish heroes. After hearing Poland's rough history, I wanted to know who their bright beacons were.

Kuba began to name Poland's heroes. I call them the four big Cs: Copernicus, Chopin, Curie, and the Cardinal. Above the four big Cs is the biggest C of all: Christ. Although Jesus probably wasn't Polish, over 90 percent of Poles are Roman Catholic. It's hard to walk ten minutes in a Polish city and not bump into a church. Over 40 percent of Poles attend church every Sunday, and about 72 percent of Poles are not opposed to religious instruction in public schools. In 2010, Poland had Europe's highest score on Gallup's Religiosity Index, which is based on various surveys about the role of religion (Estonia and Sweden represented the other extreme). As usual, young people are less religious than old people, but the Polish youth practice their faith far more overtly than the typical European. Neil Mitchell, an American professor who has taught in Poland, said, "The Poles were always more Catholic than communist even at the height of the Soviet Union."

On the other hand, Poles aren't saints. For example, the World Health Organization estimated that among 15-year-old Poles, 21 percent of the boys and 9.2 percent of the girls were *not* virgins.[8] Although that's on the low-end of the European scale, it's similar to Estonia, which is the least religious country on the planet. One Polish poll showed that among 18-year-old Poles, the percentage rises to 50 percent for both genders.[9] Finally, my terribly unscientific survey estimates that about 10 percent of Poles are virgins when they get married. Although measuring premarital sex behavior is only one way to determine how religious a society is, it's clear that Poles are not too obsessed about the "decrees of Rome."

We already discussed Copernicus, so let's glance at the other three Cs. About 200 years ago, Fryderyk Chopin was born in Poland, but spent most of his life in France. Given what French opinion of Poles was back then, Chopin quickly changed his name to *Frédéric* Chopin. Polish folk music and dances, such as the polonaise and the mazurka, inspired Chopin's compositions. Imagine how talented and persistent this Polish composer and pianist had to be to overcome the extreme prejudices of that period. And to do it all before he turned 40. Like Mozart, Chopin died young.

> *I have a sweet tooth for song and music. This is my Polish sin. — Pope John Paul II*

Overcoming French prejudice against Poles was tough enough for a man, but imagine trying to do it as a woman; or worse, a woman *scientist*. This is exactly what Maria Skłodowska did. Like Chopin, she changed her name, which helped her be accepted in French society (she married a French scientist, Pierre Curie). Marie Curie discovered radioactivity and played with radioactive rocks most of her life. Today, her lab notes (and even her cookbook) are highly radioactive. Marie Curie's genius was rewarded when she won the Nobel Prize, *twice*. At first, people thought such an energetic substance must be good for you, so companies put radioactive elements in products like toothpaste. Unfortunately, when Curie learned radioactivity was dangerous, it was too late for her. She died of cancer.

> *Be less curious about people and more curious about ideas.*
> *— Marie Curie*

Finally, we arrive to the fourth big C: the Cardinal, yet another Pole who changed his name. In 1978, Cardinal Karol Józef Wojtyła, the archbishop of Kraków, became known to the world as Pope John Paul II. He is Poland's greatest hero and was responsible for strengthening the Catholic faith in Poland and beyond. Today, you'll see his face everywhere in Poland—only Jesus is more popular. Not only was he the only Polish pope in history (and the first non-Italian Pope since the 1520s), but he was instrumental in bringing down communism. He used his powerful position (and ability to speak 12 languages) to visit 129 countries and highlight the immorality of communism.

> *The collapse of the Iron Curtain would have been impossible without John Paul II. — Mikhail Gorbachev, the last General Secretary of the USSR*

Lastly, there's one fallen Polish hero: Polish film director Roman Polański. His first big movie hit was *Rosemary's Baby.* Although the Academy Awards nominated him for Best Director for *Chinatown,* he didn't win the award until he directed *The Pianist.* However, this Polish star has been tainted ever since he admitted to raping a 13-year-old California girl in 1977. He's evaded the US justice system, which angers most Poles. Polański wouldn't want Polish justice. In 2009, Poland instituted a new punishment for anyone convicted of having sex with children: mandatory chemical castration. At least it would be better than his mother's fate: she was murdered in Auschwitz. In 1943, when he was 10 years old, he escaped the Kraków Ghetto and survived by changing his name to Romek Wilk.

The lesson from all these well-known Polish people is obvious: if you're Polish and you want to be famous, change your name.

> *We value foreign things, but we don't value our own.*
> *— Polish proverb*

Drinking vodka in Gorzów Wielkopolski

I joined Anna and Kuba for a night out on the town of Gorzów Wielkopolski. We passed the Warta River, which links this industrial town with Germany. Gorzów isn't as pretty as the other Polish towns I saw, but it wasn't bad. It's also nice sometimes to see a place that typical tourists don't see. As we passed the city's medieval Gothic cathedral and the sixteenth-century fortifications, I had to ask, "So did Germans establish this city?"

"No," Kuba said calmly. "It started with a Slavic fortress in the eleventh century."

"Oh. But the Germans must have come at some point, right?"

"Of course. They built many of these historical structures. Even today Germans call this town Landsberg. They still think it's theirs. C'mon, let's have a drink in this bar."

It was Saturday night, but the bar was relatively quiet. I couldn't stop Kuba from ordering the first round of drinks. Sometimes Poles can be annoyingly hospitable. Kuba came back with some drinks and a grin, saying, "You should try this drink that the Polish people invented." He slid the shot glass across the table and said, "It's called *wódka.*"

"Really? You guys invented vodka? I would have bet that the Russians were behind it," I said.

"Well, they would probably think that too, but there's good evidence that we were the first," he said and then raised his glass saying, *"Na zdrowie!"*

I don't drink alcohol mainly because I don't like the taste. Still, I took a sip out of politeness and reconfirmed that I prefer drinking motor oil. "Damn, that's strong! What flavor is that?"

"Holy Grass!" he said as he slammed the empty shot glass to the table.

"No shit? I had heard about that flavor in Lithuania. I thought it was a joke. What is it? The Pope's secret recipe for making vodka with marijuana?"

"Nie, it's made with Bison grass from our Białowieża Forest, which is next to Belarus."

"How are relations with Belarus anyway? You guys used to have Brest . . ."

"And Vilnius, and Lviv, and a whole lot more. Yeah, we got screwed after World War II. Ah, it doesn't matter. It's the past. But if you want to know, I'll tell you."

It's a rather simple story of musical chairs. After WWII, Poland got some German land, but had to give nearly twice as much land to the USSR. Stalin argued that only a third of the 12.5 million people in that "Soviet" land were Polish, so he ought to get it, especially since the Red Army was the main reason Germany lost. The Allies gave Poland a piece of Germany to partly make up for the loss. Nearly 79 percent of the 8.9 million people in that territory were German. What happened next was a massive game of musical chairs. The Soviets kicked millions of Poles out of the new USSR land. The Poles kicked millions of

Germans out of the new Polish land. And millions of Germans kicked themselves in the ass for having started the damn war to begin with.

I asked Anna, "Given Poland's current borders, how do Poles divide Poland? Do they split it more by an east-west axis or a north-south axis? For example, Italy usually thinks of Northern Italy versus Southern Italy, whereas Germany usually thinks of East versus West Germany."

"Polish people think east-west," Anna said. "We use the Vistula River as the dividing line. East of the river, people are more religious, conservative, and agrarian, whereas people in the west are more technologically advanced and more liberal."

"That's true," Kuba said, "But one thing good about us Poles is that when times are tough, we come together. We may fight each other and be envious of each other, but when bad things happen to the country, we always come together."

I ordered the next round of drinks and we spent the rest of the evening solving all the world's problems. Unfortunately, I don't remember the solutions. The next morning, I thanked them for their superb hospitality, and they dropped me off at the train station.

Learning the Polish alphabet on the way to Wrocław

When I told the train ticket vendor that I wanted to go to "War-*claw*," she looked at me as if I had just asked her if she was a virgin. So I scribbled "Wroclaw" on a piece of paper and then slid it under the ticket window. She said, "Ah! *Vrots*-wahvf!" Huh? I re-examined the piece of paper to make sure I hadn't showed it to her upside down. Poles like to fake out English speakers with their city names. Warsaw isn't "War-saw," but rather "varh-*shah*-vah." Well then why don't we write *Varshava*?

Although it's great that the Poles use the Latin alphabet, it's annoying that they play around with the pronunciation of some of its letters. For instance, the letter *c* is pronounced like a *k*. That's easy, since English can't make up its mind how to pronounce the letter *c*—we often say it like a *k*. For example, *cat* in English sounds just like *kat*. (By the way, *kat* in Polish means *executioner*). Although Polish has several accented letters in its alphabet, they don't use the letters *q* and *x*. Therefore, in religious Poland, prior to marriage, people don't have *sex*. Instead, they have *seks*.

It gets tricky with w, which Poles pronounce like a v. Why? Perhaps because they've reserved the letter v for some other sound? No. They don't even have the damn letter v in their alphabet! They could have easily used it, but no, they use w instead, and then tell you to pronounce it like a v. It gets worse. Do you want to guess how their funny *ł* letter is pronounced? You're not going to like the answer. It sounds like a w. Thus, łindoł sounds like window. To summarize, the ł is a w, the w is a v, and the v doesn't exist. This all makes me want to find whoever invented the language and strangle his little Polish neck.

I asked Karolina, who is studying languages, why Polish is the way it is. She replied, "I really don't know why someone added *ł, ź, ć, ą, ę, ż, ź,* and other crazy letters to our alphabet. This is our Polish psyche—we like making our lives harder and harder."

They've succeeded—Polish is very hard indeed. For example, it uses the Old Slavic case system. We haven't discussed cases, even though most Eastern European languages use them. The main reason I've dodged the issue is that cases make me cry. They're complicated. I hate them. However, I'll quit being a baby and attempt to explain them in a simple enough way so that you won't strangle my little American neck.

Why grammatical cases will drive you insane

Imagine prepositions and articles were against the law. Now imagine that the law had a loophole—we could add suffixes to words. English would evolve, so that instead of saying the illegal phrase *Jane went into the store,* you might say *Jane went storeo.* The *-o* suffix would indicate going *into* something. If you said *Jane went storei,* the *-i* suffix would signify *out of* something. So that last sentence would mean *Jane went out of the store.* (I'm just making up these suffixes and their meanings to illustrate the concept.) OK, you got all that? Congratulations, you've just learned the idea of a grammatical case! Those were examples of two cases. See, that wasn't so bad.

Unfortunately, it is bad. Life gets complicated as you add cases. Polish has seven cases. That means each noun can have seven different suffixes. Hence, in everyday life, you might hear or read *storeo, storei, storewa, storeja, storeha, storepu,* and *storeya.* You would have to be clever enough to realize that *storeja* is not some other noun or verb, but that it's simply the root noun *(store)* being inflected (changed) with the case ending of *-ja,* which, let's say, means *on top of.* Such a transformation can happen with any noun. So *dog* could appear as *dogo, dogi, dogwa, dogja, dogha, dogpu,* and *dogya.* Which of the seven versions of the dog word you use depends on the situation. Saying *John dogja* would mean, *John is on top of the dog.*

Polish will torture you with its plurals too, especially when you're referring to *men.* The male human plural is special in Polish. For example, Poles say *to dziecko* (this child), *ta dziewczyna* (this girl), and *ten chłopak* (this boy). However, in plural they become: *te dzieci* (those children), *te dziewczyny* (those girls), and *ci chłopcy* (those boys). Notice that the plural versions of the feminine and neuter genders have the same *te* pronoun, but that the male plural pronoun becomes *ci.* Moreover, it's reserved only for men, not for other male things like *dogs: ten pies* (this dog) becomes *te psy* (those dogs) whether the dogs are male, female, or neuter. Hence, the *te* to *ci* transformation only happens when you're talking about human males.

At this point, the old German and Russian idea of stamping out the Polish language doesn't seem so evil anymore, now does it? Unfortunately, those imperialists wanted to replace it with their languages whose absurd grammar will also make your head explode.

It may surprise you, but English used to have cases too, because it sprang from Latin, a case-using language. However, the Romance languages and English wised up and did away with cases, using prepositions instead. You might think that since English replaced the complexity of cases and with complexity of prepositions and articles, it all cancels out, right? Wrong. Although Polish doesn't use articles, it still uses prepositions. Therefore, to learn Polish you have to deal with cases, prepositions, gender changes, and multiple verb conjugations. To learn English, you just have to watch MTV. It's unfair to say that languages that use the case system are more complicated than English, but I don't mind being unfair, so *yes, they are definitely more complicated*. Besides, bilingual English-Polish speakers agree: Polish is harder than English. By the way, if you really want to shoot yourself, try learning Hungarian: it has 18 cases.

Admittedly, English is not suffix-free. For example, it has one case: the possessive case. Instead of saying *the car belongs to John,* we can transform the *John* word by adding the *-'s* suffix: *John's car*. Moreover, English has several suffixes that we use all the time to transform words. Think of *laughable, doable,* or *singable*. We have many other suffixes besides the *-able* suffix. Here are a few suffixes we like to tag on words: -er, -ful, -ic, -ism, -ist, -ity, -ive, -ness, -ous, -age, -ate, -ion, -ish, -ize, -ly, and -ment. This allows us to easily create millions of words without having to memorize all the possibilities. We just recognize the root word and the suffix, and then we easily figure out the meaning. Many languages do this too, so budding English speakers quickly figure these things out. What make Slavic languages a pain for English-speakers is that we're not used to inflecting words so vigorously. We just know how to add an *-'s* and that's about as much noun-inflecting that we're willing to do. If you want us to do more, you better speak English.

If you understood 10 percent of this section, then congratulations—this means you understand cases about as well as anyone can. Fortunately, the basics of Polish aren't too bad. Here are a few survival phrases: *cześć* (hi), *dzień dobry* (good day), *dziękuję* (thank you), *proszę* (please), *gdzie jest . . . ?* (Where is . . . ?), *przepraszam* (excuse me), *nie* (no), and my favorite, *tak* (yes). Instead of learning all that, I spent most of the train ride to Wrocław just repeating its city name like a mantra.

By the time I arrived, Poles were impressed with my pronunciation. Little did they know that that's all I could say.

Wrocław is a dream

Ask Poles about any random city in Poland and you'll get a ho-hum response. Ask them about Wrocław, however, and they will gush about it as if they were reminiscing about their first love. They will recline, stare at the sky, and say with a smile, "Oh Wrocław! What a place!" Its Gothic and baroque buildings, its vibrant student population, and its precious old town add up to make it a special place in the Polish heart. You too would enjoy watching the mighty Odra River wrap around Piasek Island. From there, you would cross another bridge to reach the idyllic *Ostrów Tumski* (Cathedral Island), which lives up to its name. Finally, recross the bridges, admire the immense Centennial Town Hall and go to *Plac Solny* (Salt Square), where they sell flowers, not salt.

As you can guess by now, Wrocław wasn't always Polish. In the 1740s, Prussia took over the city (calling it Breslau) and made it a textile center. Germans did what they do best: clean things up, make things, get organized, be productive, make beautiful buildings, and, when they're done with all that, have a tasty beer. And if someone pisses them off while they're enjoying their beer, they start a world war.

It took nearly 200 years to build the Centennial Town Hall, and just a few seconds of WWII bombing to seriously damage it. At the end of WWII, 70 percent of Wrocław fell to pieces. Although Poles aren't afraid to admit that Germans built many of Poland's historical monuments, don't underestimate the Poles. They not only made their own monuments, but also deserve credit for preserving the buildings and rebuilding them from scratch.

Poland's future

Later in 2009, I would travel a couple of days in Albania with Jakub Pilch, a 26-year-old from Pamiątkowo, Poland. He studied international relations (specializing in former Soviet countries) and lived a few months in California. It was great to spend hours with him discussing Poland because he is a walking encyclopedia. When I asked him what we could learn from Poland, he paused to reflect, and then said, "How to be good friend. Poland has been a good loyal friend to America: whatever you ask, we do. But America has sometimes let us down."

As usual, when I asked Jakub for examples, detailed facts poured out of his mouth like an out-of-control fire hose: "(1) Poles, unlike most other Central Europeans, still need expensive visas to visit the US. (2) Despite having the fourth largest army in Iraq, Polish companies were not given any significant Iraqi contracts. (3) Most Poles wanted America's anti-missile defense system in Poland, but Obama ironically canceled it on the 70th anniversary of the Soviet invasion of Poland. (4) Poland bought American military gear in exchange for American investment into Polish enterprises, but hardly any investment came. (5) The US sold used military equipment to Poland, but it was mostly rusting junk—Poles felt treated like suckers. (6) Obama's attempts to reconcile with Russia were not well-received in Poland, where the public is wary of Russia's increasingly assertive role; Poles have the impression that America is doing nothing to challenge Russia and is just accepting the rebirth of Russia's sphere of influence. OK, I'll stop now."

While I was taking notes of what Jakub was saying, a timid Albanian street dog approached us cautiously. It made me think that sometimes Poland seems like an abused puppy. The puppy's former masters have beaten it, starved it, and tried to make it into a German Shepherd or a Russian Husky, instead of just loving it and accepting it as a Polish Poodle. The mental and physical abuse it has suffered has traumatized it, but like most dogs, it never stops hoping. Every time a new person approaches it, the puppy wags its tail enthusiastically, saying, "Are you going to be my friend? C'mon! Let's be friends! I'm loyal. I'm hard working. I won't let you down! I'll always be there for you! Hey, I'm Polish after all!"

Poland seeks strong friends because for the last three centuries it hasn't had any, and it's suffered greatly as a result. The Nordic countries above Poland and the southern countries below it are not strong enough to protect Poland, which has been caught in a German-Russian love sandwich. As Jakub said, "Poles are pro-American, fearing Russians, and seeing the US as the only country that can guarantee our freedom. We don't trust other Europeans in security matters. We had security guarantees from the UK and France in 1939, but they didn't help us. Poles rely on America as the only country that can save Poland from Russia."

Although Poland's confidence is rising, it's still uncertain about its future. The title of their national anthem, *"Mazurek Dąbrowskiego,"* is revealing. It means "Poland Is Not Yet Lost." Notice the "Yet" word—it's as if they knew, subconsciously, that someday Poland would once again be overrun by invaders.

Poland just wants to eat its *pierogi* in peace. That's why it's being such a good friend to the EU and America. Poland has enthusiastically adopted western capitalism. It eagerly joined NATO in 1999 and has been one of its fiercest hawks, as Jakub demonstrates. It joined the EU in 2004 and threw its heart and soul behind the union. In 2015, it plans to rip up its currency and adopt the euro.

It's a courageous transformation considering that during the Soviet era Poland was relatively more important than it is today. In terms of size and importance in the Soviet sphere, Poland was second only to the USSR. Now in the EU, it's number 10. Although some Poles reminisce about the communist days, few want to go back. However, to go forward, Poland needs to approach an old enemy.

Just like the Baltic states need to kiss and make up with Russia, Poland must also revitalize its relationship with Russia. It's hard because, according to a 2010 Pew Global Survey, 59 percent of Poles believe Russia has a bad influence on Poland. Changing this perception starts with getting over the past, which also means realizing that Poland hasn't always been a saint either. Kasper, a young Pole I met in the Wrocław train station, understood this and said, "Many people in Poland don't like Russians. But we weren't better than the Russians. In the past, we did the same things to the Russians. When we were fighting Russians in 1920, we captured many Russian soldiers, and we didn't give them food, so they starved to death."

The same is true with how the Poles treated innocent German families after WWII—it wasn't pretty either. Poland has mostly reconciled with Germany. Now it needs to do the same with Russia. Fortunately, Poles are better than most Eastern Europeans at knowing their history, but not letting it rule their lives. It was refreshing to hear Poles laugh about their history instead of becoming furious like so many other Eastern Europeans I have met. Polish hospitality demonstrates how Poles are great friends on an individual level. Let's hope that Poland takes that same warmth and has the courage to extend a hand of friendship to Russia.

When I first arrived in Poland, I knew nothing except a few silly Polish jokes. Although I wasn't an expert when I left and I may never learn their crazy language, Poland is no longer such a mystery. I was impressed by its beauty and its people. We have much to learn from them. Lastly, for Poles who think this chapter sucked, remember what the great Polish poet, Wislawa Szymborska, said, "Even the worst book can give us something to think about."

What Poland Can Teach Us

- **Learn history, but don't take it too seriously.** Like most Eastern Europeans, Poles know European history well. However, unlike most Eastern Europeans, Poles aren't so emotional about it. They can laugh about, shrug it off, and focus on the present, while not completely forgetting the past. So study history and learn from it, but don't obsess about it.
- **When things go bad, come together.** When things get bad, Poles put aside their trivial jealousies and focus on the good

of the nation. The fact that Poland has survived its rough history shows the power of helping your neighbor.

- **Be a good friend.** Poles are loyal friends. According to Gallup, 94 percent of Poles said they can count on their friends and relatives whenever they need them. Only three countries in the world had higher rates of confidence (Ireland, UK, and Iceland). Cultivate Polish-like relationships.

Places I saw and recommend in Poland: Kraków (including side trips to Oświęcim-Auschwitz and the Wieliczka Salt Mine), Gdańsk, Poznań, Wrocław, and the High Tatras Mountain Range.

Travel deals and info: http://ftapon.com/poland

Those who do not move, do not notice their chains.
— Rosa Luxemburg, Polish Activist, 1870–1919

It was time to move again. After hearing so much about Germans sticking their nose into Eastern Europe, it was obvious that I should go to Germany, especially eastern Germany, to hear their side of the story. While waiting 20 minutes for a train to go to Słubice, I chatted with Mikołaj, an 18-year-old Pole who lives near the German border. He has German friends and says that relations between the two countries are good. Nevertheless, he said, "Sometimes East Germans have an arrogant attitude and think they're superior to us. But we don't take them too seriously."

"Why not?" I asked as the train pulled up.

He said, "East Germans are poorer and less organized than other Germans." He crushed his cigarette and added, "East Germans aren't real Germans."

"We'll see about that," I mumbled as I boarded the train that was going to the German border. Let's end with one last Polish joke:

A Pole wanted to learn how to skydive. The instructor jumped a few seconds after the Pole. The Pole pulled the rip cord and his parachute opened up successfully. The instructor's parachute, however, failed to open, so he flew by the Pole. The Pole undid the straps to his parachute, and yelled out to his instructor, "Oh, so you wanna race, eh!?"

7

Eastern Germany—Nearly 25 Years After the Wall

Słubice is a Polish town that will make you ask yourself, "What the hell am I doing here?" There were snow flurries and the town was as vibrant as a morgue. Fortunately, in less than 10 minutes, you can walk across the whole town and get to the bridge that spans the Oder River. On the other side of the river lies *Deutschland*. I took a deep breath and started marching across the bridge to East Germany.

Just as I started moving, a fast-walking blond lady, dragging a small suitcase with wheels, started passing me. It was surprising to see anyone walking this bridge in such sleety weather. Figuring that misery loves company, I asked her if she spoke English. She shook her head and continued walking. So I tried communicating in incomprehensible German and Polish. Perhaps feeling sorry for my efforts, she admitted, "OK, I speak some English. I just hate this language."

"Why?" I asked.

"I don't know. We just had to learn it in my Polish school."

"And you like the German language?"

"Yes! I want to live in Germany. I like it there."

I got the feeling that if she hadn't been stuck walking across a bridge with me, she would have done a better job at ignoring me. So I asked her one last question: "I want to interview some regular people for my book. Where do you suggest I go on this lovely Sunday?"

"McDonald's," she pointed it out as we were nearly across the bridge. "It's the only place that's open. But you might have trouble finding anyone to speak with you. Germans are not very open and friendly."

Unlike you, Ms. Polish Ice Queen, I thought. But instead I said, "And yet you want to live there?"

"Yes, there are better opportunities there. Life is better there than in Poland. Good luck."

Once we got across the bridge, she picked up her pace and I happily slowed down. I was now in a small town called Frankfurt an der Oder, which means Frankfurt on the Oder (River). Germans gave it this long name so that you don't confuse it with the "real" Frankfurt in Germany. I paused at McDonald's glass door, mentally replacing the few Polish words and phrases I knew with the German ones. I opened the door while saying to myself, "Alrighty, let's meet some Germans."

Meeting the easternmost Germans

The upstairs dining area had a few customers, but unfortunately nobody was alone. I calmly approached a German couple whose children were busy goofing off in the McDonald's playroom, and asked the man, "*Entschuldigung, sprechen sie Englisch*?"

The man raised an eyebrow and said quietly, "A little."

"*Sehr gut.* I'm an author," I said while showing him the cover of *Hike Your Own Hike,* "I'm now writing a book on Eastern Europe. I would like to ask you some questions about living here in Frankfurt."

He paused and looked at his wife skeptically. Then, as if the answer lay there, he looked down at his McDonald's Happy Meal. He finally broke his silence and said, "OK."

His name was Tomas and he was a taxi driver who was born and raised in East Germany. Knowing that Germans prize efficiency, I got straight to the point: "How is life different now compared to 25 years ago under communism?"

He looked around to see if the KGB or CIA were listening. Then he said, "Ze gut zing now is ve have more better health insurance. More freedom."

"What was better before?"

"Everyone vorked. Ve all had jobs. Now, 15 percent have no jobs. Zis is bad. But ze government is gut at giving zem money."

"What do Germans think of Polish people?"

He rolled his eyes and pushed back from the table for a second. He shifted around. This taxi driver was struggling to be diplomatic. Finally, he said, "Ve have some problems vit the Polish people. Zey vork heer vitout proper papers. Zo zey get paid under ze table, you understand? No tax. Zen other Polish come and steal our cars. Zis is a problem."

> *Visit Poland, your car is there.*
> *— East German saying referring to car thefts*

Tomas explained that this problem is diminishing now that all Polish cars must be registered in the EU database. Before this, it was hard for authorities to track down stolen cars. We talked for about 10 minutes, but his kids needed attention, so I thanked him for his time, and searched for my next victim.

A lone, thin, tall man was wolfing down a Big Mac as if the meat were still alive. I approached him cautiously and, while trying to suppress my American smile, asked him if I could interview him for a few minutes. He stopped chewing for a second and looked at me as if I had just asked him to polish my shoes. Then, with the sternness of an SS soldier he held up five fingers and said, "*Fünf minuten.*"

"Danke," I said, carefully sitting down next to his Coke and French fries. It was clear that if I had tried to speak with him for more than five minutes, he would have tossed me into the nearby Neo-Nazi concentration camp. Little did I know what kind of man I was about to talk to. He would end up surprising me in so many ways.

Before the Wall

Before we learn about this East German, let's understand the world he was born into. Although we were talking in one of Germany's easternmost points, Frankfurt an der Oder used to be in *Mitteldeutschland* (Middle Germany). That's because several times in history "East Germany" was well east of the Oder and Neisse rivers—it was firmly established all along what is now Northern Poland, Kaliningrad, and Western Lithuania. However, as we saw with Poland, nations are like accordions that expand and contract regularly. In Germany's case, after WWII, its accordion not only contracted, but then it also split in two.

The US and USSR planted the seeds of the split when they agreed to have their invading armies to meet at the Elbe River, which slices across Germany. Once Admiral Dönitz, who led Germany after Hitler's suicide, learned of those plans, he continued resisting the Russian invasion to slow them down, while negotiating with the Americans and British to create a safe passage for the millions of retreating Germans. He knew that Germans would be treated better in the west, safe from the inevitable revenge that would happen in the east. He was right: what would happen next was the biggest ethnic cleansing in history.

In the movie *Terminator,* Arnold Schwarzenegger delivered his famous quip with his thick Austrian accent, "Get out, asshole." After WWII, that's exactly what Eastern Europeans said to Germans who were living in their country. The vast majority of those who had to move were simple, innocent German families who happened to be living outside of Germany's new post-WWII borders. Eastern Europeans were barbaric with Germans who tried to stay in their homes (even if they had been there for generations). Vengeful Poles, Hungarians, Czechs, Romanians, and many others didn't care if you were a good German who had been living and working there for decades and helping the community. You were German, "So you must leave now or we'll burn your house down!" *Ethnic cleansing isn't just about killing people, it also includes forcefully moving them.* From 1944 to 1948, about 15 million Germans in Eastern Europe were brutally given *das* boot. Up to three million Germans died in the largest eviction ever. It's ironic that most people think the biggest ethnic cleansing in history was done by the Germans, when it was, in fact, done *to* the Germans.

The Soviets were also licking their lips with vengeance on their mind. They shipped a third of East Germany's industrial equipment to the USSR, which is like taking the medicine away from a dying woman. And then it's as if the Soviets had slashed one of her wrists when they forced East Germany to give them $10 billion (an astronomical sum back then) of free products over the years as payback. East Germany's coal mines and its best port (Stettin-Szczecin) were now in Poland. East Germany lay in ruins. They had nothing.

Meanwhile, the Soviets didn't want a democratic election so they put communists in power, who came up with an ironic name for the new country: *Deutsche Demokratische Republik* (German Democratic Republic). (Both DDR and GDR are its popular acronyms, but we'll just use GDR.) At that point many East Germans said *auf wiedersehen* (goodbye). The exodus to the west crushed hopes of a quick post-war recovery as East Germany's finest drained away.

Because communism is so wonderful, the communists didn't want anyone to leave the party and miss out on all the fun. By the mid-1950s, the communists had sealed off most of East Germany's border with the West, but there was still one escape hatch open: Berlin. After WWII, the Soviets logically argued that all of Berlin should be under the Soviet Occupation Zone, given that everything around Berlin was in the Soviet sphere. That was the reasonable and sensible thing to do. However, Americans proposed this wild-ass idea of making an exception for Berlin by splitting the city into *four* zones: American, British, French, and Soviet. Americans felt that Berlin, having been the capital of the Third Reich, should be unnecessarily complicated.

The Soviets caved in. Thus, it became easy for East Germans to go into the Soviet part of Berlin and then dash across a street into one of the three western zones. Once there, they could hitch a ride into Western Europe. Therefore, while it was easy to stop East Germans from crossing the borders in the countryside, it became a nightmare stopping them within Berlin. Voting with their feet, East Germans went to Berlin just to flee to the West. In August 1961, to prevent more people from leaving the totalitarian fiesta, the communists built the Berlin Wall.

That was also the year this Big-Mac-devouring East German that I was talking with was born. His name was Veit and he was born in the East German town of Lebus. After breaking the ice for two minutes and 47 seconds, I asked Veit what he remembered of the GDR and its communism regime. He looked at me so intensely that it felt like I was the one being interviewed. He said, "It's strange, but I only have gut memories of the GDR. I know things ver bad, but I don't seem to remember zose memories. Ve seemed to have everything ve needed. Food. Clothes. Home. School. Vork. It vas gut."

"Yes, that is an important observation," I said. "Some people don't know that communism made sure everyone had the basic necessities. You say you had good memories, but was there anything you remember *not* liking?"

He reached for his fries while keeping one suspicious eye on me, and then said, "*Ja.* Every May 1st, ve vere forced to participate in ze May Day parade to celebrate communism. I hated that. It vas a vaste of time."

Time! Shit! I quickly looked at my watch: four minutes and 23 seconds had elapsed. *Whew!* There's just enough seconds left to wrap up. "Veit, I see our five minutes is almost up, so I want to thank you very much for taking the time to speak with me . . ."

"It's OK. We can talk longer if you vant."

"But you said '*fünf minuten.*'"

"*Ja,* I know. It's OK. Ve can talk a little longer."

"*Wunderbar,*" I said and got a bit more comfortable in my seat. I decided to push my luck and ask him what he thought of Poles. His eyes widened and he gave me that funny look again. *Uh oh. Have I pissed him off?*

While studying me, he took a sip of his super size Coca-Cola and then said, "If Poland had the same money as Germany, Polish people would be like Germans."

Trying to determine if I was talking with a little Adolph, I asked him, "What do you mean?"

"Ze only real difference between ze two countries, except for language, is money. Ve are ze same people. Ve have same values, ve both vork hard, ve are ze same. Ve just have more money zan Poland. Zis is ze main difference."

"So are you optimistic or pessimistic about Poland's future and your relations with it?"

"Optimistic. *Ja.* Zey are in EU now and zey vil get more money. Zings vil be better."

An unexpected tour

We continued talking for about 20 minutes. He admitted that Polish people learn German, but Germans don't learn Polish. He said Poles buy stuff in Germany because it's cheaper than Poland, although Germans buy cheap Polish gasoline and cigarettes. Furthermore, only five percent of the couples he knows are German-Polish marriages, indicating that the two populations are still far from integrating. After our conversation, I thanked Veit and stepped away to pack my things. However, before I could leave the McDonald's, he approached me and said, "Bad veather today. I show you around. I have car. Come."

What a transformation! He had started so cold and unfriendly, now he's offering to take me on a tour of the town! When we got into his car, I noticed it was an Opel. That's a General Motors brand. "You're German and you're driving an American car?" I blurted out before being able to censor my thoughts.

"*Ja,* but zis is a joint venture between GM and Germany," he said, as if that excused him of his transgression.

We drove one minute to the center of town, while the freezing drizzle continued. It was indeed more comfortable to see the town from his warm car. Besides, the town was bleak and felt a bit abandoned. Veit explained that when the Wall came down in 1989, Frankfurt an der Oder's population was 90,000, but today it's just 65,000. Another East German town, Hoyerswerda, saw its population decline from 70,000 to 40,000 over the same period. East Germans closed the town's inefficient communist factories and businesses, so thousands moved west to find jobs. Moreover, East Germany has the lowest fertility rate in the world: the average woman produces only one child. As a result, many East German towns are dying. He methodically pointed out the key sites, "Zis is ze Mayor's house. And over heer is the River Oder." He continued until he parked at St. Mary's Church, the most impressive structure in town. "Vould you like to zee it inside?"

I still couldn't believe my luck and said, *"Ja, sehr gut! Danke!"* ("Yes, very good! Thanks!")

It seemed like a regular church from the outside, but the inside is stupendous. The church had no pews, so its vaulted ceilings take you to the heavens. The medieval ecclesiastic architecture dominates the 800-year-old church. Several times Veit pointed out proof of the building's age, "Look zere, you zee zis tombstone is over 600 years old."

Like most things in Germany, the church was destroyed in WWII. The GDR was an atheist country, so the church was still in ruins in 1981. Eventually, the Germans, methodical as they are, repaired it over decades. As we walked around, the sound of a hammer or drill would interrupt the echoes of our footsteps. The brochure points out, with classic German precision, all the key statistics: the chancel's height is 39.5 meters, there are 111 stained-glass windows, a special large 12-meter scaffolding helped the Germans rebuild the arches, and 89,000 visitors came in 2008. The free brochure even has a simplified blueprint with the exact measurements and color combinations. You gotta love the Germans.

Besides giving away the brochure, the church's office sold a few items that reminded me of East Germany's most famous man: Johann Sebastian Bach. His birthplace in Eisenach is now a Bach museum, which includes over 300 of his instruments. Although he's famous for being the king of the Baroque musical style, most don't know that he was an orphan at 10 years old. He remained in East Germany, spending much of his life in Leipzig, where he died, according to a 1750 newspaper, "from the unhappy consequences of the very unsuccessful eye operation."

When Veit and I returned to his car, I asked him if he knew where Poland's nearest train station was. He wasn't sure, but he started driving into Poland. He never said he would take me there, but in his own quiet way, he ended up taking the most efficient route to the station. After driving 10 minutes, he stopped by a humble train station. He walked out in the storm to confirm with a parked Polish policeman that this was the correct station. Veit and I shook hands and I thanked him profusely.

This simple, working-class German had undergone a complete transformation. He had started as a cold, suspicious man, offering me only five minutes of conversation. But in the end, he spent 93 minutes with me, drove me all around the town, and went completely out of his way (and into another country) to drop me off at the train station. It is often said that Eastern Europeans are cautious at first, but once they like you, they will go to the ends of the earth for you. Although Poland wasn't the end of the earth, for a German, it is.

Santa Claus really existed in East Germany

There's a reason East Germans are a bit cold and suspicious at first. They grew up with Santa Claus watching them. Their Santa knew when you had been naughty and nice, but mostly cared about when you were naughty. The GDR called Santa *Staatssicherheit.* Kids just called him *Stasi.* It stood for Ministry for State Security and it was about as cuddly as the Soviet KGB.

The Stasi was Big Brother incarnate. Paranoid people who think the government is watching their every move would have loved living in the GDR: everyone would finally believe your paranoia was justified. By 1989, the Stasi employed a whopping 91,000 people to look over 16.4 million citizens. However, the reality was worse: anyone could be an informant. Neighbors would snitch on each other to get favors from the government, like the right to travel abroad. Therefore, when some stranger says, "Hi, I'd like to ask you some questions about life in East Germany," how are you going to behave? For decades East Germans were suspicious of everyone and everything around them. It will take more time for that habit to fade.

Neil Mitchell, who took a special bus trip from Brussels to Moscow in 1967, recalled a funny story of crossing into communist Germany. He told me, "East German communists were still human. When we entered East Germany, *all* of our luggage was carefully inspected.

They were looking for any Western publications as they could contain propaganda from the evil West. Our inspector was a big *buxom* German woman. She carefully went through all the luggage. It took two or three hours at the border. Ah ha! She found a magazine. She studied intently one particular page. My fellow passengers were getting nervous. Would they ever let us in? She was standing right by my seat and I am rather tall, so I could see what she was studying. It was an advertisement for bras! It was hard not to laugh. She confiscated the magazine. Maybe she used mail order."

The smell chair and other spy gadgets

James Bond would need his best gadgets to defeat Evil Santa. It's extraordinary that 25 to 50 years ago, the Stasi had sexy spy toys that are still hard to find today. Ashtrays had hidden recording devices. Cameras were hidden in pens, statues, and bras. Remember this was the disco era: such gadgets were science fiction. The best gadget was the Stasi *smell chair*. This chair had a special cloth that looked like a normal cushion. After sitting on it, evil Santa would put the cloth into an airtight jar. The scent was a pheromonal fingerprint that Santa could later use to identify you next time you sit down. It's not clear why Santa really needed the smell chair. However, East Germans, in an effort to confuse Evil Santa, would sometimes fart on whatever chair they sat on. "Honey, I'm sorry for the stink bomb, but I was just trying to elude the Stasi!"

Evil Santa had 4,000 elves whose only job was to snoop on other people and acquire blackmail fodder. The Stasi, being *über*-efficient Germans, built a machine that used steam to open 600 letters per hour and another machine to reseal them twice as fast—all in the effort to leave no trace of their spying. One of the most spied-on women, Ulrike Poppe, inspired the excellent movie The Lives of Others. She founded Women for Peace and had the pleasure of being arrested 14 times and tossed in jail for treason. The Stasi terrorized her. They would steal her baby stroller and deflate her bike tires. They put video cameras across her apartment, opened her letters, and bugged her friends' bedrooms. Although the widespread espionage may have nipped budding resistance movements within the GDR, its oppressiveness also fueled the desire for such a revolution. Hence, the Stasi's efforts gave the communists no net gain. In fact, the guy in charge of spying on Poppe committed suicide. As the winds of revolution swept through Eastern Europe in 1989, Evil Santa had to cover his reindeer tracks.[1]

As the Berlin Wall came crashing down, the Stasi themselves were the ones who became paranoid: "What will people do once they find out what we've been up to all these years?" Just like the Nazis tried to cover their tracks by destroying the concentration camps as they fled, the Stasi tried to destroy their paperwork as they bailed. There was one problem: they had a lot of paper. If you were to put all the Stasi paperwork on one shelf, it would have been over 160 kilometers (100 miles) long. That didn't stop the stubborn Germans. Evil Santa unleashed the *papierwolfs und reisswolfs* (paper-wolves and rip-wolves). These people ran shredders day and night until they broke. Then they started ripping the documents up by hand. However, time ran out. About three months after the Berlin Wall collapsed, Germans stormed into the Stasi office as soon as they heard about the shred-fest. The *papierwolfs und reisswolfs* had managed to tear up 45 million documents into 640 million scraps of paper. It was an extraordinary effort that only the Germans could pull off. However, try to grasp this: that was only about five percent of the files.[2]

Need to recover 45 million shredded documents? Call Germany

Today, East Germans are demanding that the government reveals all, including the five percent that was shredded. Recover 45 million shredded documents? Are you kidding? Believe it or not, that's exactly what headstrong Germans are doing. They've started with the *reisswolf* shredded documents, because it's easier to reassemble hand-ripped paper than machine-shredded paper. There are 16,327 bags of such manually ripped paper. Each bag has 40,000 fragments. In 13 years, 25 patient Germans have reassembled 620,500 pages. That's one bag per worker, per year. They've done 327 bags and have 16,000 to go. At this pace, they'll be done in 700 years.

You think that would discourage a German? On the contrary, it only encourages them to invent ways to do it better! Creative Germans have devised a way to automate this process. They've combined scanners and clever software to automatically reassemble the fragments. Meanwhile, 1.7 million Germans have asked what the Stasi knew about them. It's part of what Germans call *Vergangenheitsbewältigung,* which means "coming to terms with the past," or "dude, what was *that* all about?" The German parliament spent $9 million to test out the new automated scanning system by processing 400 bags and producing 22 terabytes of data. To ramp up production (so that they take much less than 700 years) will cost $300 million. That's a lot of Mercedes Benzes.

The point of recounting all this is not just to show what life was like in the GDR, but also because there is no better way to illustrate why there are *homo sapiens* and then there are *Germans.* They're two different species. Only Germans could invent space-age gadgets while the rest of the world was dancing to the Bee Gees and smoking pot. Only Germans could produce such a volume of surveillance data. Only Germans could shred so much paper in so little time. Only Germans could dare to reassemble the 640 million of fragments. And only Germans could pull it off.

Every other nation on this planet would have said, "Oh well, we only lost eight kilometers of the original 160 kilometers of paper. Let's just forget about it and enjoy reading the 152 kilometers of paper that are intact." Only Germany would say, "No, that's not acceptable. We can do better." The only other nation that could possibly keep up with Germany is Japan. So that's the lesson: there are Germans and Japanese, and then there are the rest of us mere mortals.

The day the Iron Curtain melted away

Shortly after the 20th anniversary of the Berlin Wall's collapse in 2009, I reunited with a childhood friend, Jyll Tsouo, who had lived in Berlin from 1985 to 2005. We were having dinner in Aix-de-Provence, when she said, "Living in Berlin before the Wall came down was like living in an island. It was super safe. I could walk around alone in the middle of the night without any problem. Berlin felt like a village. There was no traffic. It was so nice!"

"But didn't you feel like a prisoner?" I asked. "Wasn't it hard to leave Berlin?"

"A little. We would often fly, which was easy because the airport was right next to the city. Driving was a pain. After crossing Checkpoint Charlie, the Germans would give us a set amount of time, say, two hours, to get to the West German border. If we were a few minutes too early, that meant we were speeding, so we were fined. If we were a few minutes too late, that meant we must have stopped along the way and interacted with an East German, possibly collaborating against the communist regime. So we were fined. They were so strict and precise."

The GDR were smart to build the Berlin Wall to plug a hole in the Iron Curtain. The farsighted communists feared that if they didn't, all of Eastern Europe would pour through it. They were right, because in the summer of 1989, Hungary poked a hole in the Iron Curtain. It opened its borders with the West, allowing anyone to exit. Over 200,000 East Germans raced to Hungary and drained out of the hole. The Czechoslovakia copied Hungary, so now there were two big holes. People were gushing out of the dam's two holes and cracks were spreading. Time was running out. The GDR considered closing its borders with its communist neighbors, but riots and protests were erupting everywhere. The moment the GDR Propaganda Minister mumbled that everyone can travel freely, people smashed across the Wall. Helmut Kohl, the West German Chancellor, didn't see it coming: he wasn't even in the country. Suddenly, the cozy little town of Berlin became a chaotic mess.

"I got a call in the middle of the night," Jyll remembered. "I started hearing sounds of celebration in the streets. It was surreal."

East Germans had no hard currency, so the West German government gave each East German 100 German marks to spend in the west. Jyll laughed, "I knew a couple of people who got their 300 marks by going through the line three times."

> *I love Germany so dearly that I hope there will always be two of them. — Francois Mauriac, French novelist, 1885–1970*

It's not clear what's more surprising: how fast the Wall crashed or how fast Germany united afterward. Many people were against the union. Many West Germans were against it, knowing that it would cost them extra taxes to integrate the poorer East Germans. They also worried that East Germans would "steal their jobs." The USSR was against the union too. Gorbachev only agreed to let it happen when NATO promised that it would not expand east of Germany. (NATO lied: within a few years, various Eastern European states joined NATO.) Even East Germans (who supported the union overall) worried the mass exodus would hurt those left behind. Despite all the doubters, Helmut Kohl rammed East Germany down West Germany's throat. It was a courageous step and it was amazing that he pulled it off. On October 3, 1990, less than one year after the Wall tumbled, Germany was together again.

According to a 2009 Pew Research Center's survey, 81 percent of East Germans and 77 percent of West Germans say that the unification was either "very positive" or "somewhat positive." Fully 63 percent of Germans believe their lives are better as a result of unification, up from 48 percent in 1991.

When rats experimented on humans

Although humans like to experiment with rats, there was a time when rats experimented with humans. The rats took a bunch of humans who spoke the same language, shared the same history, and looked the same (at least to a rat's eyes). The rats split these nearly identical humans in two groups. The rats were only interested in measuring the impact of one key variable, so they left one group of humans alone as their control group. The rats, however, injected the second group with something called *communism*. Once the effects set in, the rats left the lab, turned out the lights, and would not return for over 40 years.

The results of the rat experiment were remarkable. After just one human generation, the two groups of humans hardly recognized each other. The first group had not changed: they were still competitive, creative, and hard-working. The communism-infected group, however, was nearly the opposite. In that group, state-owned enterprises earned 97 percent of the total net national income. The few non-state businesses were taxed up to 90 percent. The state bore 80 percent of the costs of basic supplies, from bread to housing. The state was everything.

All this altered people's behavior. They got married early because it took less time to get a state apartment if you were married. They also tended to have children at a young age because the state guaranteed childcare and employment. Their lives were steady and predictable, which was comforting, but communism also sapped their motivation and drive. There were often shortages. For instance, they had to wait 13 years to get a Wartburg, a crappy commie car. The industrious, innovative spirit diminished. Paranoia grew. Moreover, the most promising, talented humans usually escaped out of the communist rat labyrinth. The rat scientists spent years studying the data. In the end, they summarized their findings in their lab book. On the last page, they scribbled their conclusion: "Communism sucks."

Women often forget the pain of childbirth and only remember the joy; similarly, today some people reminisce about the "good old communist days." Throughout Eastern Europe, people shared with me their nostalgia for that period. Whenever I heard such romanticizing of the past, I always asked, "If it was so great, then why doesn't your country go back? Who's stopping you? Go ahead. Would you like to go back to those days?"

As if I gave them an electric shock, they would wake up and say, "Oh no! I prefer it now. Most people do. Maybe only some of the senior citizens would be willing to go back." However, I found it hard to even find old people who were willing to go back. The few people who would want to go back are those who are lazy (because they like not having to work hard to have their basic needs covered), those who are extremely risk averse (because they like the stability and predictability of communism), or those who value economic equality above all else (because they are willing to sacrifice nearly anything just so that everyone ends up economically equal). Such people are a minority on this planet, which explains why communism has few fans.

In Europe, the rat scientists may have ended their experiment of taking twin regions and separating them at birth, but they have one other similar experiment still going on today. It's been running now for nearly 70 years. In this experiment, the nearly identical people weren't split east-west, but rather north-south. The place is called Korea. Although the results are not yet in, it's probable that the rat scientists will reach the same conclusion.

Although these experiments on twin human societies are the most powerful evidence against communism, there are plenty of other examples. Communism has been tried in big countries (Russia and

China), small ones (North Korea and Cambodia), cold countries (Mongolia), warm ones (Cuba), Caucasian countries (Ukraine), Asian ones (Vietnam), Hispanic ones (Nicaragua), and Black ones (Angola). Prior to China's move toward capitalism, there was a vast disparity of living conditions between Hong Kong and Chinese cities just a few kilometers away (another fascinating twin experiment). The communist countries that still survive today are hanging by a thread, forced to adopt a quasi market-based economy. As we've seen, Belarus is a Soviet time capsule that continues only because Russia is keeping it on life support.

No matter where humans have tried communism, the results have been lousy. Neighboring capitalist countries always enjoy a higher standard of living. If you disagree, then ask yourself why capitalist citizens are not sneaking into communist countries. Why are the walls and barbed wire designed to keep the communist people trapped in as prisoners, and not to keep the neighboring people from moving into their utopia? If life there is so great, why do they have to force people to stay? When capitalist countries build walls (like America's silly wall on the Mexican border), it's not to keep people from rushing *out*, but rather to keep them from rushing *in*. In conclusion, people vote with their feet.

Today, it's not fashionable to celebrate the benefits of capitalism. Humans enjoy complaining, so capitalism is an easy target, especially since nowadays nearly every country practices it to some degree. As a result, the grass-is-greener-on-the-other-side syndrome takes over, nostalgia distorts our memories, and it's easy to forget Eastern Europe's most profound lesson. Indeed, the downside of free markets winning so decisively over controlled ones is that today we have almost no more failing experiments to point out to young people. The shocking results of a poll showed that only half of German 18-year-olds agreed that the GDR was a dictatorship and 66 percent didn't know who built the Berlin Wall. Let's not forget the time when the rats experimented with humans.

Lastly, there's absolutely no doubt that capitalism is often brutal, inhumane, and cruel. In fact, it's even fair to say that it also sucks. However, compared to heavy government control, it sucks less.

Desperate memories in Dresden

When I was in Berlin in 2005, I told three different groups of young locals that I wanted to visit Dresden. The conversation usually went like this:

"Oh my god!" they would say, "Why would you want to go there? That's, like, *East* Germany."

Each time I would resist the urge to pull out a map to show them that Berlin was also in East Germany. Instead, I would ask, "But have you been to Dresden?"

They shook their heads. It was surprising how little Berliners knew about East Germany. It's as if the Wall were still up.

Thanks to Pink Floyd, I knew more about Dresden than some Berliners. In my all-time favorite album, *The Final Cut*, the song "The Hero's Return" has these lyrics: "And even now part of me flies / Over Dresden at Angels One-Five / Though they'll never fathom it, behind my / Sarcasm desperate memories lie." I was 13 years old when this song came out. Being an obsessive teenager, I wanted to understand every lyric. "Angels One-Five" is aviator-speak, referring to an altitude of 15,000 feet (4,573 meters). Now what were these "desperate memories"?

The answer lies near the end of WWII, when Dresden was the only major German city that was still mostly undamaged. It was an important transportation hub with military facilities in its outskirts, which the Allies used as an excuse to bomb Dresden into oblivion. If you lived in Dresden in 1945, your Valentine's Day was full of hate, not love. Hate rained from the sky as 1,300 low-flying heavy bombers dropped 3,900 tons of bombs onto Dresden. The Allies first dropped the bombs to break water mains and create air pockets, then dropped 650,000 incendiary bombs, which created a massive firestorm. People were swept off their feet and sucked into a raging firestorm that was hungry for oxygen. "Desperate memories" haunted some pilots who believed, along with many impartial observers, that the bombing of Dresden was so unethical that it was a war crime. Although the Allies destroyed 90 percent of Dresden's city center, many military facilities were largely untouched. Most of the 25,000 people who died were civilians. The bombing of Dresden remains one of the most controversial Allied military actions in WWII.

In 1985, Dresden's symbol, the *Frauenkirche* ("Church of Our Lady") was still in ruins. That year, Vladimir Putin, Russia's future President, was beginning a six-year assignment in Dresden for his employer, the KGB. After the communists left, the Germans continued rebuilding Dresden. They restored the stunning *Semperoper* (the Saxony state opera house) and the Zwinger Palace. I was fortunate to visit the *Frauenkirche* at its grand reopening in 2005. In 2006, Dresden celebrated its 800-year anniversary. Today, it's one of the most beautiful cities in Europe.

Dresden's other lesson

There's a profound, often overlooked, lesson in Dresden. The moral that most people draw from Dresden is that the Allies were also cruel during WWII. However, Dresden's other lesson, indeed, the lesson of all of post-war Germany, is what a remarkable people the Germans are. Imagine that in 1945 you could have one of these five territories that were untouched by WWII: Montana, Spain, Argentina, Saudi Arabia, or Congo. Or you could pick Germany. What kind of fool would have picked Germany in 1945? Its resources were depleted or confiscated. Its cities and infrastructure were ash and rubble. Its people were demoralized and broken. Meanwhile, the other five territorial options had plenty of resources, decent infrastructure, and upbeat people. Germany had nothing. Only an idiot would bet on Germany over those other options. And yet, that idiot would be a genius. In less than 40 years, Germany (the size of Montana) would rise from the ashes and not only blow past all those other territories, but would also become one of the five most powerful economies in the world. In 2009, Germany was the largest exporter in the world! They exported over $1 trillion of stuff to the world, which was more than China or America, countries that are vastly larger than Germany. In 2010, China finally became the world's top exporter, but Germany still exported more than the USA.

We Americans like to pat ourselves on the back by saying that Germany bounced back thanks to our Marshall Plan. We flatter ourselves. The Marshall Plan is overrated. It cost $13 billion over four years. Thanks to inflation, one dollar was worth about 10 times more in 1948 than 2011. Therefore, $13 billion in 1948 equals about $130 billion in 2011. Although that's a decent amount of money, we forget that it was spread out over 17 countries. Italy received roughly the same aid as Germany, France got 58 percent more, and the UK got well over twice as much assistance. Of the $13 billion, Germany received less than $1.5 billion—that's only $15 billion in today's dollars. Nowadays America routinely gives $15 billion to any country with a bank account. In fact, after German unification, West Germany was giving East Germany $100 billion in aid *annually,* making the Marshall Plan seem like peanuts.

We also forget that instead of helping West Germany immediately after WWII, the Allies kicked Germany while it was down, trying to send it back to Bronze Age. The Allies initially wanted to turn Germany in a pastoral, agricultural state. After WWII, the Allies destroyed 1,500 German manufacturing plants so that Germany's heavy industry would drop to half of its 1938 levels. In 1946, the Allies capped German steel production to 25 percent of the prewar production level and dismantled the "redundant" plants. German car production could not exceed 10 percent of its 1938 level. Germany, the Allies believed, should be reduced to a standard of living equal to 1932—at the low point of the Great Depression. As a result, after WWII, many Germans were without money to heat their house or to eat, froze and starved to death.

East Germany had an even steeper hill to climb: it got the anti-Marshall Plan. It had to give its best agricultural lands and best port to Poland, and was encumbered with $10 billion in debt to the USSR; that's practically the value of the entire Marshall Plan! That's like saddling Maine (which is a similar size as the GDR) with $100 billion in debt today. It's as if the Soviets had said to East Germany, "Instead of *getting* a Marshall Plan from us, you're going to *give* us a Marshall Plan. Oh, and please do that with just the ash that you have. Don't worry, our brilliant communist economic system will help out. Thanks."

The pugnacious East Germans said, "OK, if these are the cards we're dealt, let's make the most of it." Within 40 years, East Germany had a higher standard of living than all the communist countries in the world. Appropriately, the GDR's anthem was "*Auferstanden aus Ruinen*" ("Risen from Ruins"). It's as if there had been a marathon and East Germany was told to start one hour after everyone else and was forced to run it with its hands tied behind its back. Despite those handicaps, East Germany still managed to come from behind and win the race.

Some might say, "Yeah, but Germany has a great position being in the center of Europe." OK, let's imagine if Germany and Russia had to swap territories. Is there any doubt that Germans would transform the Russian land and make it by far the most powerful country in the world? Russian writer, Fyodor Dostoyevsky, didn't mention the Germans, but he should have when he wrote, "If only Englishmen or Americans lived in Russia instead of us! . . . Oh, they would have opened up everything: the metal ores and minerals, the countless deposits of coal."[3]

Geography doesn't explain everything

Imagine shipping everyone from Congo (which is the size of Western Europe and has plenty of resources) and moving them to Germany while making the Germans move into Congo. How would the Germans utilize Congo's rich land? In a few years, Germans would be pumping out more cars than ever, harvesting the sun's energy with solar panels, and curing cancer thanks to some exotic plant they find in Congo's forests. Imagine if they had Argentina, or Saudi Arabia, or Spain. Those countries would be top five global economies. And what if Germans took over Canada? Or the USA? They would work the land and within decades build the mightiest nation the world has ever seen. Transplant any other people onto German lands and they could not equal the output of the Germans.

Some continue to insist, "C'mon, you can't make such arguments. Germany is the way it is because of its geography. If you moved Germans to another continent, they wouldn't be the same people." True, geography molds people, but it is only one factor; otherwise, France, Germany, and Poland would all be nearly identical (since they have similar geographies). However, even though Germany was light-years behind France in 1946, it managed to outperform France in just a few decades. In 1948, the USSR thanked Poland for rejecting the Marshall

Plan by giving it nearly half a billion dollars, valuable factories, a lucrative five-year trade agreement, and 200,000 tons of grain. Despite Poland's huge head start, tiny East Germany passed them too. The point is that Germans were able to make something out of nothing. In fact, they had less than nothing when you consider their debt burdens and all the anti-German feelings after WWII. All Germans really had after WWII were their hands and brains.

The Germans can do this because they have their shit together. They make the rest of us look like bumbling buffoons. Of course, saying such things is terribly taboo, because (gasp!) you might be a Neo-Nazi fascist! Can we be a bit more mature in the twenty-first century, please? Let's give credit where credit is due and stop censoring people who applaud and admire Germans. Nobody would argue with you if you observed that 4,000 years ago the Egyptians were light-years ahead of everyone else. If you transplanted the Pharaohs and their people to some other part of the world, they would also be capable of making the most out of the situation because their culture was disciplined, organized, and hard-working. Italians like to think they're descendants of the Romans, but if you consider the extreme organization and industriousness of the Romans, you'd conclude that they had more in common with today's Germans than today's Italians. Imagine challenging today's Italians and Germans to rebuild Rome's Colosseum from scratch. How long would each take? The Germans would be cutting the ribbon while the Italians would still be in the pizzeria negotiating the design with the mafia.

Countries (and people) are full of excuses as to why they're so retarded. They'll blame colonialism, a communist hangover, a heavy debt burden, a lack of resources, a poor geographic location, a tough history, or a crappy childhood. We could all learn from Germany's attitude: they take whatever conditions they are dealt and make the most out of them. Of course, Germans whine and complain just like anyone, but immediately afterward, they roll up their sleeves and get to work. Other societies roll back into bed and feel sorry for themselves. Moreover, although Germans can be ridiculously stubborn, they also know when to be flexible. That balance is one of the secrets to their success. Germans, who usually look down on East Germans and are a bit sexist, showed their flexibility in 2005 when they elected Angela Merkel, an East German woman, as their leader.

> *It is nonsense to say that Germans are unable to change.*
> *— Angela Merkel, Chancellor of Germany, raised in East Germany*

When Veit left me at the Polish train station in Subice, I asked him what he thought Germans do best. He said, "Germans are gut at managing money and their economy." I smiled. That's the understatement of the century.

What Eastern Germany Can Teach Us

- **How to rebuild a country.** No other country in history (except perhaps Japan) has bounced back so fast after being so utterly destroyed and handicapped. The Germans did it by putting the past aside, focusing on the present and future, ignoring their petty differences, and working toward the good of the nation. Use the same technique to rebuild your life.
- **How to reintegrate.** West Germans still grumble about the cost of reintegration and a minority of East Germans still reminisce about the communist days. However, they've shown the world how two societies, separated by a rat experiment, can unite in one generation.
- **Play the hand you're dealt as best as you can.** After WWII, Germany had all the excuses in the world to become a screwed-up, backward country. Instead, they said, "No excuses, let's rebuild." So many people say they can't do A, B, and C because of X, Y, and Z. Next time you're feeling sorry for yourself, remember Germany. After complaining, shut up, then roll up your sleeves and get to work.
- **Have the courage to apologize.** Every nation has sinned, yet few have Germany's courage to not only admit their sins, but to seek atonement for them. Instead, most countries continue either denying their evil deeds, justifying them, or whitewashing over them. Ask yourself: "What sins has my country committed?" If you can't think of any, something is probably wrong. Talk to others and objectively reanalyze your nation's history. And then do the same with your personal life.

Places I saw and recommend in eastern Germany: Berlin and Dresden.

Travel deals and info: http://ftapon.com/germany

As much as I admire and respect the Germans, listening to their language hurts my ears. Indeed, in my ignorant opinion, German is the ugliest language in the solar system. The most I ever stayed in Germany was one month—that's when hearing their awful-sounding language starts to drive me insane. So let's move on to Eastern Europe's prettiest country, which happens to have long (and not always pleasant) history with Germany: the Czech Republic.

8

Czech Republic—Eastern Europe's Most Civilized Country

My first visit to Eastern Europe was in 1992, when I had just graduated from college. For Americans, doing a European tour after college is a rite of passage. Just three years after the Iron Curtain came down, those 22-year-olds who craved some edginess stuck a toe in Eastern Europe. In my case, my best friend and I visited Prague and Budapest. Although nowadays Czechs and Hungarians will tell you 10 times per day that they are in *Central* Europe, not *Eastern* Europe, in 1992 they were only saying it about twice a day.

Prague—Eastern Europe's most beautiful city

In my opinion, Prague is not only Eastern Europe's most beautiful city, it is one of the five most beautiful cities in the world. Venice and Paris are the only two major European cities that top Prague in the City Beauty Contest. In 1992, Prague was like a supermodel who had just finished a five-day muddy backpacking trip: you could still tell that underneath all the dirt and grime, there was a hottie.

Today, Prague has not only taken a shower, but she has put on some makeup and a glamorous dress. Tourists have showered the city with money, enabling her to restore herself to her glory days when she was the capital of the Holy Roman Empire and, later, the capital of the Habsburg Empire. Even the worst flood in 200 years barely slowed down renovations—nearly $4 billion poured in to help Prague bounce back. When I returned in 2004, just two years after a major flood, I couldn't see any damage and was once again enamored with the city's beauty. Today, this city of 1.3 million is a gem on the world stage. It seamlessly blends 900 years of architecture (Romanesque, Gothic, Renaissance, Baroque, Art Nouveau, Cubism, and Modern) into one tight package. It is not only an incredibly romantic city, but nearly every architectural marvel has a story behind it.

Take the saint's tomb in St. Vitus Cathedral, for example. The Czechs started building this Gothic cathedral in 1344 and finished it almost 600 years later. While it was being built, King Wenceslas IV was suspicious of his queen, so he demanded that John of Nepomuk, the priest who heard her confessions, reveal what she had confessed. John refused, saying that it's against church code to do so, even if the king demands it. The enraged king had John suited up in heavy armor, and tossed to his death in the Vltava River. For his loyalty to his priestly oath, he was canonized a saint and rests in a Baroque tomb made with two tons of silver.

New York has Brooklyn Bridge, San Francisco has the Golden Gate Bridge, but Prague has the *Karlův Most*—the Charles Bridge. Its 30 unique statues can inspire you on a sunny day or frighten you on a foggy night. It's hard to pick Prague's prettiest part, but this breathtaking bridge is my favorite. Built in 1357, it was Prague's only bridge until 1841. It was so well built that it survived the catastrophic 2002 flood. The bridge's best story was in 1648, when unlikely heroes (armed students and Jews) stopped an unlikely invader (Sweden) from crossing the bridge, thereby ending a 30-year war.

The Czech way to start a war

Even Czech windows have stories. In 1419, someone in the *Novoměstská radnice* (New Town Hall) threw a stone at marching Christian reformers, who, in a vengeful fury, broke into the building and threw a dozen Catholic councilors and a judge out the window. If the fall didn't kill them, the mob did. This event, which sparked a 17-year war, is called the *Defenestration of Prague. Defenestration* comes from Latin, meaning *out of the window*. About 200 years later, the locals would start an even bigger war by throwing some other Catholics out of a different window.

That famous window grabbed the headlines in 1618, when the Protestants did what they do best: protest. After convicting two Habsburg Catholic governors of violating the freedom of religion, Protestant nobles ignobly chucked them (along with their scribe) out of the upper window of the Prague Castle. This act is naturally called the *Second Defenestration of Prague.* What history books usually neglect to mention is that the Catholic guys fell 30 meters (100 feet) in a dung-filled moat and were barely hurt. However, they bruised their egos enough to declare war on the Protestants. For the next 30 years, Christians killed each other in a fight that would have an unimaginative name: the Thirty Years' War (1618–1648). The Protestant Czechs lost the war, a quarter of the Bohemian population died, and much of Central Europe lay in ruins. For the next 300 years the Germans would beat the Czechs into submission, forcing them to learn German, become Catholic, build baroque buildings, and make tasty beer.

The Wallenstein Palace is another amazing building in Prague with a story of divine justice behind it. Albrecht von Wallenstein was a Protestant until he realized that the Catholics would win the Thirty Years' War. Therefore, like Bulgarians, Italians, Romanians, and Slovaks in WWII, he switched to the winning side. Then he stole all the money from his former Protestant buddies to build himself a sweet palace. When the Catholic emperor found out that Wallenstein was going to switch sides again and rejoin the Protestants, he had Wallenstein assassinated.

After the Thirty Years' War, the triumphant Catholic clerics built the ornate *Malá Strana* (Little Quarter). They emphasized the ostentatious Baroque style throughout the district (and especially in the St. Nicolas Church) because that's exactly what the Protestants hated. Another nice Prague neighborhood is the Hradčany district, where you'll find the Prague's largest monastic library, the Strahov Library. Next to model ships, there's the most unusual exhibit you'll ever find in a monastery: a couple of whale penises.

What makes Prague special is that it's one of the few European cities that wasn't damaged during WWII. That's because the Czech Resistance made a deal with the Nazis: leave freely, just don't destroy any of the buildings on your way out. The Germans honored the deal and surrendered to the Red Army a few days later. Nevertheless, the Nazis did leave a trace.

Prague was once home to 120,000 Jews; today, about 4,000 remain *in the whole country*. For centuries, Jews had cycled between prosperity and persecution. The Vatican was the first to order the construction of a walled Jewish ghetto in the 1200s, because it felt Jews and Christians shouldn't mingle. Prague holds Europe's oldest still-open synagogue, which was built during that era. Over the centuries, the Jewish population grew, but then the Nazis nearly killed them all. The three sisters of the most famous Czech writer, Franz Kafka, were murdered during the Holocaust. The Nazis had plans to exhibit Jewish artifacts in The Museum of An Extinct Race.

Older than the Jewish Synagogue is Prague's *Staré Město* (Old Town), which is so beautiful that it can bring tears to your eyes. The highlight is the *Pražský Hrad* (Prague Castle): the world's largest ancient castle, covering seven football fields. A story-filled astronomical clock animates on the hour. Lose yourself in the street maze and you might end up in *Nové Město* (New Town), which isn't exactly new—it was founded in 1348. Today, its St. Wenceslas statue is famous for being the epicenter of many Czech protests. For example, one Czech student made the ultimate protest there—he burned himself alive. To understand why, we have to go back to the spring of 1968.

Prague Spring

In April 1968, the Czechoslovak communists instituted policies that resembled the *glasnost* and *perestroika* policies that the USSR would introduce 17 years later. They released political prisoners, relaxed the heavy economic intervention, stopped censorship, reduced travel restrictions, and encouraged democracy. It's everything that Gorbachev would do 17 years later, but in 1968 the Soviets weren't ready for such radical reforms. Moscow demanded that the Czechoslovaks reverse their policies. The Czechoslovaks called the event the

Pražské Jaro (Prague Spring), because it represented "socialism with a human face."

The Prague Spring lasted through the summer, until August 21, when Soviet tanks rolled through Czechoslovakia along with 200,000 Warsaw Pact soldiers. That's more soldiers than the US sent to Iraq to topple Saddam Hussein. The Soviets expelled 14,000 Communists Party functionaries and fired 500,000 communist members. Over 300,000 fled the country. The USSR imprisoned rebels and sent educated professionals to labor camps or to become street cleaners. The Soviets sent Czechoslovakia's President to work for Slovakia's forestry department.

A few months after the Warsaw Pact killed the Prague Spring, a student protested the action by burning himself alive. As his flesh burned, he staggered down the steps of the *Národní Muzeum* (National Museum), and then collapsed. A cross-shaped monument marks the place where he fell. What's tragic is that he wasn't dead. It took him four agonizing days to finally die. The next day, 200,000 Czechs gathered in the square in his honor.

When a young Gorbachev visited Prague soon after that student's self-immolation, he saw anti-USSR graffiti and encountered workers who didn't want to talk with any Russian visitors. That trip was an epiphany that made him realize what every Eastern European already knew: that communism was unjust and unsustainable. The Prague Spring planted the seed of *perestroika* into Gorbachev's brain. Nearly 20 years later, when he finally had the power to usher in a Prague Spring all over Eastern Europe, he did.

Discovering the rest of Czechia

Many countries have long, flamboyant names. One the worst offenders is The United States of America. What a mouthful! Fortunately, we have shorter versions (USA or America). Other countries with long-winded names have a short alternative: The People's Republic of China (China or PRC), The Russian Federation (Russia), and The Republic of Moldova (Moldova). Unfortunately, the Czech Republic hasn't popularized a catchy word to call itself. In an effort to promote one, we'll use the best candidate: *Czechia*. That way, when someone asks, "Where are you going?" or "What country makes the best beer?" you can say, *Czechia*, instead of *the Czech Republic*. Now let's explore the rest of Czechia.

Whenever I told Americans that I was going to spend a couple of years traveling in Eastern Europe, they would usually say, "So you're going to Prague?" For many Americans, Prague is Eastern Europe. This is ironic for two reasons. First, the Czechs hate it when you say they're from Eastern Europe. Second, Prague is the least Eastern European city in Eastern Europe. It might as well be in France. The only difference is that the Czechs are polite.

Czechia is split into two major areas: Bohemia (west) and Moravia (east). Bohemia, which is two-thirds of Czechia, got its name from a Celtic tribe called *Boii*. The French popularized the term *bohemian* because they erroneously believed that Roma (gypsies) came from Bohemia. Puccini's opera, *La Bohème,* solidified the idea that bohemians are artists who live an unorthodox way of life. Still, if you visit Bohemia, you'll discover that artists are rare, although it's cool that the Czechs elected a playwright as their first President. Moravia got its name from the Germans who called its main river Moravia, which means *marsh water*. In 2004, I visited Brno, the capital of Moravia and Czechia's second biggest city. I only spent two days there because I was racing to meet Maiu in Prague.

Several Czechs told me that Brno is nothing special. They're right, as long as you believe that seeing another perfectly beautiful old town is nothing special. Like Prague, Brno pays attention to architectural details and is filled with attractive streets. Brno's main square, *Nám Svobody,* is more like a triangle with pedestrian streets jutting out from every angle. Brno's second square, *Zelný Trh* (Cabbage Market), has a symbolic fountain in its center. Three female figures on the statue represent the three old empires: Babylon, Persia, and Greece. On top of them all is a snobby chick, who represents Europe. I asked the mayor to put another girl at the very top and say that it's America, but he didn't like the idea.

A better idea than putting an American girl at the top of the fountain would be to put Brno's most famous resident there. He was a nineteenth-century superhero: monk by day; scientist by night. His favorite pastime: playing with peas and bees. His name was Gregor Mendel and he's called the Father of Genetics, which is an odd title since he had never heard of *genes* or *DNA*. Nevertheless, Brno has dedicated a museum about his studies of plant and insect reproduction, which lay the foundation of modern genetics. Be polite when visiting Brno and try not remind proud Czechs that Mendel was, in fact, an ethnic German.

The next day Maiu would be flying into Prague from Estonia, so I would only have one night in Brno. I hadn't seen her since we first met and I was thrilled to see her again. We would spend a week exploring Czechia. That night, to save a little money, I looked for a camping spot. The best spots are in the hills, where few venture. High on Petrov Hill is the enormous Cathedral of Saints Peter and Paul. That was a good place to start searching. However, I was way down below, next to the Church of St. James. In 1473, a disgruntled mason, who didn't get to work on the prestigious Peter and Paul Church, carved on the Church of St. James the image of a man mooning Petrov Hill.

Despite all the churches, Czechia is the second least religious country in the world (after Estonia). According to a 2005 Eurobarometer poll, about 19 percent of Czechs believe in God (versus Estonia's 16 percent), 50 percent "believe there is some sort of spirit or life force" and 30 percent "do not believe there is any sort of spirit, God, or life force." Another survey showed that nearly 60 percent of Czechs are irreligious (75 percent of Estonians feel the same way). Similarly, Gallup's Religiosity Index (which uses a variety of surveys to produce an aggregate score) ranks Estonia as the least religious country in the world, followed by Czechia.

As I waited for my irreligious Estonian girlfriend to arrive, I found a decent place to camp in a park on Petrov Hill. To avoid potential thieves, I would always set up camp at dusk and leave at dawn. I wouldn't put up my tarp unless it was raining to keep a low profile. After sleeping well, I took a train to the Prague Airport to meet Maiu. We greeted each other with a long hug. After exploring romantic Prague for a couple of days, we went to the picturesque Bohemian town that the Germans called Budweis.

Beer: Czechia's holy water

Budweis, now called České Budějovice, is a quintessential Czech town with one of the largest European squares: *Nám Přemysla Otakara II*. At the center of the colorful square is the eighteenth-century Samson Fountain. Surrounding it is the Baroque town hall and the ominous Black Tower. When the American founders of Anheuser-Busch were brainstorming for a brand name for their beer, they stole it from this town, which calls its beer *Budweiser*. In Czechia, every town has its signature beer, which is often named after the town itself. That's why Pilsner-style beer was born in the Czech town of Plzeň and why Budweis makes Budweiser beer. After visiting Budweis, the Anheuser-Busch founders couldn't find a better beer, so they named their awful beer after the best beer in the world.

> *Milk is for babies. When you grow up, you have to drink beer. — Arnold Schwarzenegger*

According to the World Health Organization, *Czechs drink more beer per capita than anyone else on Earth*. Nobody is even close: the average Slovak drinks less than half as much beer as his Czech neighbor. The Czechs even swallow 21 percent more beer than the Irish.[1] Who can blame the Czechs, anyway? Many beer connoisseurs believe that Czech beer is the best.

When you drink more beer than anyone else, you could use a Czech invention: *a sobering-up station*. After getting thoroughly sloshed, stumble to a sobering-up station, where you can spend one night, under medical attention, until you overcome your wicked hangover. At their peak, Czechia had 63 sobering-up stations, which treated over one million drunks. Poland and Russia copied the idea. With the collapse of communism, Czechs cut back on such state-funded operations. However, they kept on drinking. Since you probably won't find a sobering-up station in Czechia, there are only two Czech words you need to know: *pivo* (beer) and *nazdraví* (cheers)!

After spending all day roaming the enchanting České Budějovice, Maiu and I went to Český Krumlov. This town of just 15,000 residents is like a mini-Prague, which is why it another UNESCO World Heritage Site. We climbed up a hill to visit the picture-perfect castle, Czechia's second largest. Down below, practically encircling the *Vnitřní Městro* (the Inner Town), is the Vltava River, making it clear why the richest family in Bohemia put their pad here: the river acts as a natural moat and is a highway to Prague to boot. Buildings with Renaissance and Baroque facades surround the town square. We strolled along the romantic, narrow cobblestoned streets enjoying the warm August sunset. Our strategy was to alternate between camping and staying in a hotel, so that we would save money and not get too smelly. That evening we camped in a nearby forest. We were exhausted from being tourists all day, so we slept soundly.

Wear the "tourist" badge with pride

It's a pity that the word *tourist* has a negative connotation. It should be a compliment and something to aspire to. Instead, people make statements like: "I hate going there, it's so touristy," or "Tourists are so annoying," or "I'm not a *tourist*, I'm a *traveler*."

It's time we transform the negative *tourist* connotation into a positive one. First, things are touristy for good reason—they're often amazing in some way. There's a reason why the Louvre is so touristy and the museum in Lyon is not. It's because the Louvre is better. The Golden Gate Bridge is touristy because it's more breathtaking than the bridge in Harrisburg. Similarly, the Grand Canyon attracts more tourists than the Great Divide Basin because the Grand Canyon is far more spectacular. We can have pedantic debates about beauty being in the eye of the beholder, but I hope you will understand the point. Tourists are smart and well-informed and so they spend their time, money, and energy going to extraordinary places. They would be stupid to do otherwise, so let's stop saying that tourists are stupid and that touristy places are lame.

Second, tourists are more alive than a local resident. When a tourist visits Prague, she walks around like a child, observing every building, every sign, and every scent. The local, on the other hand, walks with tunnel vision, oblivious to the world around him. He's a zombie in his own city. Ask the local about a building, a statue, or the city's history, and you often get a shrug and "I dunno." Ask the tourist, and she has the answer because she read it in her guidebook. Or at least, she'll be curious to know the answer.

Most locals know surprisingly little about their towns. They know how to get to their job, their three favorite restaurants, a few major streets and stores. That's it. Meanwhile, the tourist fastidiously explores every nook and cranny of a foreign city, absorbing it like a sponge. Tourists study maps while the local often doesn't even own one because he knows enough to get around and isn't curious to explore unknown parts of his city. Ask a local about his town, and it's amazing how ignorant they are. One day, for example, I asked a guy in San Mateo, California if he knew where the Kinko's store was. He didn't. I asked where he lived. He was a local. Before he left, I told him that he was standing right underneath the sign for Kinko's.

I didn't realize how little I knew about San Francisco until I began traveling. When I returned to my hometown, I looked at it with brand new eyes, with the eyes of a tourist. Suddenly I noticed and appreciated its Victorian architecture. I understood why Haight Street is special, why our steep hills are outrageous, and why our gay neighborhoods are unusual.

Third, locals who live in a "touristy" town should love tourists, because without tourists the locals might not be able to live there. Every year tourists pour billions of dollars in regions throughout the world. Without tourists, Venice would already have sunk into its lagoon. Without tourists, San Francisco's cable cars would have stopped long ago, its Golden Gate Bridge would not be so golden, and Alcatraz would be a crumbling ruin. Even if your job doesn't directly depend on tourism, many of the services you enjoy exist because tourists contribute billions into the local economy through the taxes they pay. Furthermore, you wouldn't have such a great selection of restaurants, stores, and events if tourists weren't there to use them.

So why do tourists have such a bad reputation? They sometimes do stupid things like walk into the middle of street to take a photo of a cable car in San Francisco, they drive on the wrong side of the road in England, and they enter a mosque in shorts. However, locals do plenty of stupid things too, like jaywalking across a busy street, running stop signs, and defacing a mosque. In short, humans do stupid things. And it's easier to forgive a tourist for making mistakes than forgiving a local. Instead of getting angry at a tourist who does something stupid, give her credit for getting out of the house and exploring. Remind yourself that we're all locals on this planet.

Finally, before you claim that you're not a tourist, think of whatever city you traveled to. When you went to Paris, did you not gaze at the

Eiffel Tower? In conclusion, next time someone bitches about tourists, defend the tourist. Educate others that tourists are noble creatures that we should all aspire to be.

Germany's influence on Czechia

During our last day in Český Krumlov, Maiu and I were lazy tourists. We sampled Czech cuisine, which is heavier than an elephant. It's like German food without the fish option (Czechia is a landlocked country). I struggled between eating the unappealing *knedlíky* (dumplings) and the less-appealing *svíčková* (roast beef with sour-cream and spices). I ended up going with the classic Czech dish, *vepřo-knedlo-zelo* (roast pork, bread dumplings, and sauerkraut). It's not my kind of meal, but when in Czechia, order like a Czech. Maiu got a *cesneková* (garlic soup) and we split a *ovocné knedlíky* (fruit dumplings). After a week of eating Czechia's pork sausages, frankfurters, and bratwursts, I understood why so many Czechs just skip the meal and drink beer.

Cuisine isn't the only way that Germany has influenced Czechia. Germans dominated the Czechs for 300 years (and a few hundred more, depending on how you count). In fact, when Czechoslovakia was born in 1918, it had three million Germans living in the new country, especially in the Sudetenland region. That's because after WWI, the winners punished the losers by giving some of their territory away, but without ethnically cleansing that land. As a result, after WWI, millions of Germans woke up to learn that they were now living in Poland or Czechoslovakia. Hitler didn't like that. Thus, in 1939, he reacquired those lost German lands. Czechs didn't like that. Thus, in 1942, Czech paratroopers assassinated a cruel Nazi governor near Prague. Friendly tip: it's not good to piss off Nazis. As payback, Nazis razed the villages of Lidice and Ležáky, shot every male, and deported all the women and children to concentration camps. After WWII, Czechs ethnically cleansed Sudetenland, viciously deporting 2.7 million Germans and murdering thousands. At that moment, the world had little compassion for the Germans and did nothing to stop Czechs from being cruel hypocrites.

Throughout the communist era, Germans grumbled about the injustice that millions of innocent Germans suffered, while Czechs said their actions were morally justified given what the Nazis did to them. However, in 1990, after the *Sametová Revoluce* (Velvet Revolution), the wise Czech President Václav Havel had the guts to formally apologize to the Germans. In 1997, the top German and Czech politicians signed a mutual apology, where both nations basically said, "Sorry about that. We fucked up."

As the summer of 2004 came to an end, so did my romantic holiday with Maiu. She had to return to Estonia for work, whereas I had to continue exploring the Hidden Europe. We went to the bus station, where she would return to Prague to catch her flight home. It was so easy to travel with her: she was always calm, positive, and flexible. I was so attracted to her gentle spirit, her utter simplicity, and her child-like innocence. Our special time in Czechia strengthened our bond, which would help us endure months of being apart. With sadness in my heart, I kissed Maiu goodbye.

Czechia: a world leader in income equality

A clever Italian, Corrado Gini, devised the Gini coefficient, which is a number between zero and one that measures the distribution of income or wealth. When applied to income, a score of *one* means that one lucky guy earns 100 percent of the nation's income—it's good to be the king. A score of *zero* means that the nation's income is equally distributed, meaning that everyone from the janitor to the president earns exactly the same paycheck—it's communism's wet dream.

If we multiply the Gini coefficient by 100, the score for the whole world is about 60. In the late 1960s, the US had its lowest recorded Gini score: 39. Now it's 45. If we reach 50, then that will imply that 25 percent of the people earn 75 percent of the nation's income. It's remarkable that despite all the cries of income inequality, compared to the world average, the US isn't so unequal. Doubting Americans should visit the places with the highest income disparities: Latin America and especially Africa.

Still, relative to Europe, the US has more income inequality: EU countries score around 31. Czechia is the fifth lowest in the world with a score of 25.7 (average of the CIA and UN surveys). According to the CIA, the Gini global extremes are Sweden (23) and Namibia (71). However, if you're a communist, don't move to Sweden just because it has the lowest *income* Gini coefficient. You might also want to check out its *wealth* Gini coefficient (which measures the distribution of a country's net worth). In Sweden, the richest five percent have 77 percent of the wealth.

Perhaps the real world leader in income equality is Japan, followed closely by Czechia. Why? Because the Gini isn't the only way to measure income inequality. Another method is to compare what the bottom 10 percent earns versus the top 10 percent. In three global studies that used this method, Japan won the gold while Czechia took home the silver.[2] Some may argue that income equality is a mark of a civilized society. If so, few societies are as civilized as Czechia.

Igniting a civilized, but passionate debate in Olomouc

On February 25, 2009, I returned to a snowy Czechia. My goal: find an ugly Czech town. However, as my train came to a grinding halt in

Olomouc (pronounced *Olla-moats*), I realized that I would need to keep looking. When a train station is ugly, the town may still be great; however, when a train station is pretty, the town is always great.

My mission was to find a certain *hospoda* (a pub that serves basic food) in a square named *Václvské Nám.* There I would find my couchsurfing host, Petra Šarhanová, a PhD student in biology. She had invited a couple of her friends to join us at the *hospoda* so that they could offer input for my book. The cold winter darkness enveloped the town, but there were enough warm lights that hinted at the town's hidden beauty. The streets were quiet, which is remarkable for a town of 100,000, but winter has a way of making people stay inside. I listened to the crunch of my footsteps on the frozen snow as I walked past the magnificent UNESCO-protected *Sousoší Nejsvětější Trjice* (Holy Trinity Column). With time to kill, I strolled by the Gothic monstrosity, the St. Moritz Cathedral, which took over 100 years to build. Finally, I arrived at *Václvské Nám.* It's a charming square that has the oldest building in town, the St. Wenceslas Cathedral, which was first consecrated in 1131. The *hospoda* was empty, so I sat inside on a long wooden bench until Petra arrived.

Within a few minutes Petra burst in with an energetic smile. She shed her coat, revealing her strong, athletic body which comes from her passion for Irish dancing. Between writing her doctoral dissertation in biology, she competes in Irish dance contests. Multidimensional people like Petra are what makes Couchsurfing so much fun. Two of her friends would soon join us: Teresa (a Czech plant biologist) and Serge (a Serbian academic journal editor). After the usual pleasantries and debates about whether Czechia is in Eastern Europe, I asked them, "What have Czechs ever done for the world?"

Teresa said, "We've given you Antonín Dvořák, the composer."

Petra said, "Two Czech chemists invented contact lenses."

Serge said, "There's also the most famous Czech writer, Franz Kafka. Ironically, even though he was born and raised in Prague, he never wrote books in Czech. He was a Jew who wrote in German."

My favorite Czech writer is Karel Čapek, who wrote the play "R.U.R. (Rossum's Universal Robots)." It's significant because that's where Čapek coined the word *robot.* In Czech, *robota* means *forced labor,* and *rab* means *slave.* The play describes a world where robots, who do the dirty work, revolt against their masters. It was written after WWI, during a time when communism was spreading, and the idea of the proletariat rebelling against their capitalist masters was popular. Robots fascinate me, so Čapek's linguistic contribution is unforgettable.

A book must be the ax for the frozen sea within us.
— Franz Kafka

I told them, "I'm writing a book that's meant to crack open the frozen American mind, so that we learn more about the world around us and learn from other countries and cultures. With that in mind, what can Eastern Europe teach us?"

Teresa blurted out the easy answer, "Czechs can teach you how to make beer!"

After taking a sip from her gigantic beer glass, Petra said, "One thing you can learn from the Czechs is that we fix things ourselves. That comes from communism. When something breaks in America, you call someone to fix it. Here, people usually fix it themselves."

As you may recall, we learned this lesson from the Belarusians, who are the Kings of Jerry-rigging. I looked over to Serge, who was clasping his beer with both hands. He said, "The best thing you can learn from us Serbians is what *not* to do!"

We all laughed. Serge added, "OK, seriously, what you can learn from Serbia: food and music. Czech food is terrible. They have few fresh fruits and vegetables. There's not enough flavor and spices. Serbians know how to cook."

Petra objected, "Hey, but we have some of the best bread around. I'm really proud of our bread."

Many Eastern Europeans are proud of their bread. Later, I would try bread from the bakery that Petra recommended, but I was not impressed. It was too white, fluffy, and plain. I prefer dense bread, made with nuts and whole wheat. Baltic bread is best. Petra disagreed with me. Bread is like language: there's nothing like our own.

Next, I asked them why Czechoslovakia broke up in 1992, thereby creating Czechia and Slovakia. Teresa said, "It was a stupid political decision. There was no referendum. Just a few politicians made the decision for the two regions. The Slovak leader at the time was very popular. He convinced people that it was a good decision for the Slovaks. But I think most Slovaks weren't really for it, if they stopped and thought about it."

Petra nodded and said, "Slovaks are our brothers. I still feel like we're one nation. When I visit Slovakia, I don't feel like I'm going to another country, like in Germany or Poland. I feel like I'm in the same country."

"What do Czechs think about the Poles anyway?" I asked.

"Czechs don't like the Poles," Petra said. "They have a different mentality. They try to take the easiest way to make a lot of money. They are too religious, too close-minded, too everywhere."

Teresa said, "When we see Poles in the Tatra Mountains, they are easy to spot. They are very loud. Also, many times Poles are not very well prepared. They underestimate the toughness of the mountains."

I said, "Petra said that Poles have a 'different mentality.' What do you think of their mentality, Teresa?"

"They have a primitive mentality," Teresa said. "It comes from their language. A long time ago, Poles and Czechs shared the same language. However, a few hundred years ago, the Czech language started evolving, becoming more sophisticated. Meanwhile, the Polish language stayed the same. The primitive nature of their language, the fact that it didn't evolve, shows the problem they have. The Polish didn't improve their language . . . "

"Hold on," Serge interrupted. "What you're saying is totally wrong. It's the opposite. Polish is a richer language than Czech. What is Czech anyway? It's just a destroyed Slavic language. The average language in the world has about 500,000 words. The most widespread and sophisticated languages are English and Chinese. They each have over two million words. Czech has fewer than 250,000 words. More than most languages, Czech uses homonyms everywhere. It's a poor language."

As you can imagine, the conversation erupted into all sorts of directions. I don't know enough about Czech to declare that it's a "poor language," but I do know enough about it to say that it would be a rich language in *The Wheel of Fortune.*

No need to buy a vowel in the Czech Wheel of Fortune

In case you're a Czech and you've never heard of it, *The Wheel of Fortune* is an American TV game show where contestants try to guess a phrase by spinning a wheel with consonants. When the wheel lands on a consonant, you get cash for the number of times that consonant appears in the phrase. You can use the cash you win to buy vowels. At any point, you can try to guess the phrase to win mega-bucks. In Czechia, contestants would end up with much more money than most languages because they would never need to buy a vowel! Therefore, from *The Wheel of Fortune* perspective, Czech is a rich language. Consider these Czech words: *trh* (market), *zmrzl* (frozen solid), *ztvrdl* (hardened), *scvrkl* (shrunk), *čtvrthrst* (quarter-handful), *blb* (fool), and *smrt* (death).

The Czech language is the anti-thesis of the Estonian language, especially if you observe their use of vowels. Estonians love vowels; Czechs abhor them. Estonians didn't think the standard five vowels were enough, so they added four more: ä, õ, ö, and ü. What's fascinating is that two vowels in Estonian can have a meaning, like *öö* means *night*. Estonians enjoy stringing vowels together to form tongue twisters like *hauaööõudused*, which, of course, means *horrors of the night in the grave*. And if you ever need to say *a moon researcher's work-night at the edge of the ice*, then you would just have to say *kuuuurijate tööööjääärel.*

A Czech uttering so many vowels would be shot. Czechs view vowels as evil letters that must be destroyed. For example, try saying this: *prd krt skrz drn, zprv zhlt hrst zrn.* It's worth taking the time to learn this useful phrase, because you never know when you might have to say *a mole farted through grass, having swallowed a handful of grains.*

Perhaps you're looking for a shorter and more useful phrase. Try to say this famous Czech insult: *strč prst skrz krk.* The Czechs assured me that it is not hard, because it's pronounced exactly how it is spelled. I'm not kidding. They really told me this with complete seriousness. I told them, with far less seriousness, "Thanks for the helpful tip."

What does this insult mean anyway? *Stick your finger through your neck.* That's a fine insult, but I prefer *motherfucker.* When I was in Belarus, I learned that a few years after the Wall came down, Belarusians started using *motherfucker* as an insult. Before that, no one said it. So now we have three great exports to Belarus: McDonald's, Coke, and Motherfucker.

Before we return to the *hospoda* in Olomouc, let's learn some phrases that are more useful than *motherfucker.* Learn *dobrý den* (hello), *na shledanou* (goodbye), *děkuji* (thank you), *promiňtě* (excuse me), *ano* (yes), *ne* (no), *prosím* (please), *kolik to stoji?* (how much is it?), *jak se máte?* (how are you?), *kde je . . . ?* (where is . . . ?), and *kdy?* (when?).

> Třistatřicetři stříbrných stříkaček stříkalo přes třistatřicet tři stříbrných střech.
> — *Czech tongue twister, meaning "Three-hundred-and-thirty-three silver fire-engines were spraying over three-hundred-and-thirty-three silver roofs."*

When the great language debate was over, I asked about the Czech-German relationship. Petra's boyfriend worked with German clients in his job and they often frustrate him. She said, "Germans think they are the kings. My boyfriend has to often tell them that something is not possible, because they make ridiculous demands. They always look down on us Czechs."

"When you speak to Germans, do you use English?"

"Yes."

I said, "All of you speak English well. I feel like 20 percent of Czechs are fluent in English, which is about double of what I saw in Poland, which is 10 times better than Belarus. About one percent of Belarusians could speak English well."

"That's so true!" said Serge, who is fluent in five languages. "I often had to call Russia for my job. When I would ask if anyone could speak English, they would usually just put down the phone. Not hang up. Just put it down and never pick it up again. Other times they didn't even bother answering the question. Whenever we got close to making a sale, we would have to talk to the executives. The CEO of one of Russia's biggest companies, cannot speak English. Think about that! Russians are the worst at learning a foreign language."

"So, Serge," I said, "I'm going south after this, eventually visiting your country, Serbia. Any thoughts?"

"As you move south, you'll see that food and music gets better. Also, people become more emotional and irrational—that's a fact."

On that promising note, I raised my glass and said, "To Eastern Europe!" We all raised our glasses and said in unison, "*Nazdraví!*"

What the Czech Republic Can Teach Us

- **How to avoid wars.** Although not as clever as Switzerland, Czechia has done a remarkable job at avoiding wars. After throwing people out of windows became an unfashionable way to start a war, Czechs calmed down. WWII could have started in Czechoslovakia, but Czechs resisted firing the first shot. Instead of starting a war after Soviets crushed the Prague Spring, the Czechs stewed for 17 years until they had the peaceful Velvet Revolution. Even when Czechoslovakia split, there was no civil war—simply a Velvet Divorce. In 2011, it was fifth out of 153 countries in the Global Peace Index. By resolving conflicts peacefully through discussion and non-violent protests, Czechia proves it is one of the most civilized countries in the world. Think about them whenever you're tempted to support a violent solution to a problem.
- **Beautify your town.** Czechia is one of the prettiest countries in the world partly because Czechs think about the outside of their buildings as much as the inside. It's a pleasure to walk in a beautiful town, so pay attention to the details. Participate in cleanups, plant flowers, and give your home and neighborhood a face-lift.
- **How to make a tasty beer.** One reason the Czechs drink more beer than anyone else in the world is that their beer is arguably the best in the world. Go to Czechia and try their beer before you decide who makes the best pint.

Places I saw and recommend in Czech Republic: Prague, České Budějovice, Český Krumlov, Olomouc, and Brno.

Travel deals and info: http://ftapon.com/czechia

In the summer of 2009, I returned to Czechia for a fourth time, still hoping to find an ugly town. This time I poked in the southwest corner of the country, which guidebooks rarely talk about. If there's an ugly town in Czechia, perhaps that's where they're hiding it. But no, I just saw more quaint villages and pretty towns. Therefore, my dear Czech Republic, you win: you're beautiful through and through.

Although Petra's friends shared their thoughts about Czechoslovakia's divorce, there were many unanswered questions about Czechia's neighboring country, Slovakia. What do Slovaks have to say about Czechoslovakia's split? How are the Slovaks different from the Czechs? And does the Slovak language have more vowels than the Czech one?

9

SLOVAKIA—FOR THE MOUNTAIN LOVERS

I WOKE UP IN my sleeping bag in a tiny, cold, wet cave that was completely off-trail, high in Slovakia's mountains. Little did I know how much misfortune would happen to me that misty morning. The day before, I had asked a ranger if I could go off-trail and traverse the *Vysoké Tatry* (High Tatras). He said, "Not without a guide. You'll never make it."

I pointed out, "But have you considered the fact that I have no boots, no map, no compass, and I'm sporting all-cotton clothing?"

The ranger smirked. I burned the topographical map into my visual memory, scribbled some notes, and thanked the ranger, who shook his head as if he expected to see me later in a body bag. The ranger was right to warn me: once I was off-trail, I was spending about 20 percent of my time using my hands to get around. After 12 hours of scrambling, I climbed up a steep mountain and camped in a tiny, cold, wet cave because it was getting dark.

After remembering the previous day, I groaned out of the sleeping bag. Sleeping on uneven rock left me with slightly sore back. Still, the view was thrilling: swirling clouds hugging sharp, craggy mountains with no trees in sight. A small lake below completed the alpine scenery. While leaning against a big rock, I looked down the mountain face I had climbed the day before. "Boy, I'm glad I don't have to climb *down* that," I thought while I pulled out my camcorder from my pocket to film the surroundings. Somehow the camcorder took on a life of its own and jumped out of my hands as I stood over the steep drop. In slow motion, I said, "Nooooooooo . . ."

The camcorder didn't listen. It crashed on the first rock, bounced high, and then fell down to the next rock, and the next, and the next. I watched it do somersaults, back flips, and half twists down the mountain. I cringed at every impact, as if, with each blow, someone were kicking me in the balls.

I couldn't see where it came to a rest. Like a rubbernecker who gets a perverse pleasure from seeing the carnage of a car accident, I wanted to see the final state of my poor camcorder. I climbed down until I found it. Surprisingly, it was in one piece. Demonstrating an irrational level of optimism, I flicked the power switch. My eyes widened. The damn thing turned on! Although the video camera was no longer working, it could still take digital stills like a camera. This was the same faithful camcorder that had somehow semi-survived a dunking into an

Estonian river when I overturned a canoe. I kissed it and thanked its brilliant Japanese engineers.

> *For myself, I am an optimist—it does not seem to be much use being anything else.*
> *— Winston Churchill*

After stuffing my sleeping bag, I thought, "OK, I gotta put this in a secure place because everything around here is at such a steep angle. This looks like a nice spot . . ." It stayed there . . . for about two seconds. And then it also took a life of its own. And it rolled away, way, way down the mountain. I yelled again, "Nooooooooooooo . . ."

Because of its loft, the stuffed sleeping bag bounced *much* farther than the camcorder. It fell so far that it took me 20 minutes to retrieve it and come back. Miraculously, despite the sharp rocks and the long fall, the stuff sack only got a minor tear. I couldn't decide if I was incredibly lucky or unlucky. With two unnecessary trips down the mountain to retrieve my crap, I was no longer a happy camper. Finally, as I was putting away my glass jar of peanut butter, it suddenly leaped out of my hands, "Noooooooooo!!!!!"

Fortunately, it didn't roll down the mountain, but when it hit the rock at my feet, it shattered. I cursed my butterfingers and picked up the broken peanut butter jar as if it were a priceless framed family photo. Finding peanut butter in Eastern Europe is like finding the Holy Grail. Therefore, despite the broken glass everywhere, I decided to finish it off. Besides, tossing food during a backpacking trip is sacrilege. As I began eating it, I thought that maybe this wasn't one of my brightest ideas. There could be micro-shards of glass in the peanut butter. I paused, examining it for a few seconds, and then sighed, "Whatever." I worked around the glass shards and spread it on some bread. I was chomping away when suddenly I heard a *CRUNCH!*

I froze. That wasn't the sound of a peanut being crushed in my mouth. That was the sound of me chewing glass. I spit what I thought was the bad portion and swallowed the rest. Hey, I was hungry. I felt minor pain for about five minutes afterward. Maybe it was psychological. Otherwise, I had no internal bleeding. The glass tasted yummy! Just like peanut butter!

Later, I would have one last minor misfortune: I would lose my phone's belt clip. Although it wasn't a big deal, just for fun, I screamed, "Noooooooo!!!"

Fortunately, a few days later when a store didn't have just a belt clip, the clerk gave me a complete holster for free. He said, "It's a gift from Slovakia."

One of Eastern Europe's finest backpacking

Despite my misfortunes, I fell in love with the High Tatras, which offer some of the best backpacking in Eastern Europe. Compared to America, the Tatras combine the majesty of the Grand Tetons, the jagged peaks of the Ansel Adams Wilderness, the alpine views of the Wind River Range, the cozy huts of the White Mountains of New Hampshire, and the diabolical trails of Maine.

I spent the second day scrambling over rocks, drinking from pure mountain springs, and sometimes standing on a ridge, with one foot in Poland and one in Slovakia. I walked by Slovakia's highest peak, Gerlachovský Štít, which touches 2,655 meters (8,711 ft). As the sky darkened, I was once again stuck above the tree line. With storm clouds gathering fast, I needed to find a place to pitch my tarp. Like a Belarusian, I jerry-rigged the tarp up by securing its guy-lines on top of two enormous boulders by using heavy rocks. Just as I crawled under the tarp, the sky lit up and thunder roared. How poetic it was, considering that Slovakia's national anthem is called *"Nad Tatrou sa blýska"* ("Lightning over the Tatras"). I curled up in my sleeping bag as the sky boomed. It would be another lonely night sleeping next to sinister-looking mountains. The dramatic lightning storm just made it extra spooky.

Although I was often off-trail, even some of the marked trails are insane. Slovaks blur the line between hiking and rock climbing. Some trails require you to cling onto a long metal chain to move up or down the mountain. These trails are so treacherous that they are one-way routes—the park prohibits going against the designated direction to minimize traffic jams and accidents. At the exit-point of one of these crazy trails, the sign forbade me from going further. It was 6:00 p.m., so most hikers had retired to the huts and the trails were deserted. Therefore, I went ahead.

Within a few minutes, as I looked down the near vertical grade, I imagined someone losing their grip here—they would resemble my camcorder bouncing down the rocks. Every year about a dozen hikers die in the Tatras. If you don't bring gloves, the cold metal chain quickly numbs your hands. This is a pity, since your life depends on your grip, which weakens when your hands are cold. I was dangling off a chain hoping my bare, frozen hands wouldn't fail me. Temperatures were dropping fast as the sun set behind the formidable mountains. As I probed for a foothold, I mumbled, "It's moments like this when I'm glad my mom is not watching me." She would probably agree.

After making it through that tricky trail, it was a relief to camp under warm trees. The next day, I stuck to the designated trails. I asked a Slovak why there was so much toilet paper on the trails. She blamed "tourists." I said to her, "Honey, this is a national park—we're all tourists. So can you be more specific? Why don't people pack it out?"

She said that "90 percent of the hikers in the Tatras are from the Czech Republic, not Slovakia." Although Czechia has twice the population of Slovakia, it takes Czechs several hours to reach the Tatras. Later, an 18-year-old man admitted that Slovaks bear much of the responsibility. Having visited Slovakia's less touristy parks and seeing toilet paper everywhere there too, it seems that leaving your trace with toilet paper is a Slovak tradition. In fact, there was one outhouse that did not contain the human waste at all—anything that went down the poop-hole just landed in the steep gully. With a little rain, all the toilet paper and shit would roll down the mountain into the pristine sources below. Brilliant.

Ignoring these minor annoyances, the Tatras are perfect. You might see a fox, rabbit, weasel, muskrat, bear, wild boar, or a *vlk* (wolf). Slovaks keep improving the park's conditions, so after 2011 the park will be cleaner than ever. People call the Tatras "the biggest-little mountains in Europe" because they're only about 2,500 meters high (8,200 feet), but they look and feel much higher. Therefore, do what the Slovaks do: head to the High Tatras and *ist'na prechadsku* (go for a walk).

As always happens after backpacking for a few days, I was ravenous. I took the enjoyable cog railway to descend to civilization and ordered the Slovak national dish, the *bryndzové halušky* (potato dumplings with cheese made from sheep's milk with a bit of bacon). Maybe it's because I was famished, but it was absolutely delicious. After ordering another *bryndzové halušky*, I started feeling guilty that I really didn't know much about Slovakia. The only thing I knew about it is that it's about twice the size of New Hampshire. It was time to see some civilization and to answer the number one question on my mind.

Why did Czechoslovakia break up?

Obviously, the main reason Czechoslovakia broke up is that its name was too hard to spell. However, perhaps there was another reason. Although the Czechs had given me their opinion, I wanted to hear the Slovak side. I took a train to Trenčín, a pleasant town of 57,000 that's near Slovakia's capital, Bratislava. A picturesque castle overlooks Trenčín and reminds you of its medieval history. It was 2004, just 12 years after Czechoslovakia broke up, so people must be knowledgeable and passionate about the breakup story. It's fun learning a nation's history from the locals, so I asked a young Slovak why Czechoslovakia broke up. He said, "I don't know."

That wasn't exactly the answer I was expecting. I shuffled over to another local and asked him the same question. He took a drag from his cigarette, exhaled, and then said, "Politics."

Fascinating. Thanks. I couldn't believe how little Slovaks had to say about the breakup of their country. Imagine it's 1877, just 12 years after the end of the American Civil War. Imagine the Confederates won and the US had split into two countries. Then imagine asking someone, just 12 years after the breakup, to explain why it happened. You'd think everyone would be bursting with things to say. Strangely, it was hard to find a Slovak who had much to say about Czechoslovakia's breakup. I kept asking around.

> *Blessed are the curious for they shall have adventures.*
> *— Lovelle Drachman*

I finally found Slovaks who were capable of saying more than three words about their country's breakup. Some Slovaks said they wanted independence because Czechs were "too dominant." Slovaks were "tired that most of Czechoslovakia's government functions were on the Czech side," not the Slovak side. They wanted "respect." Other Slovaks said that Czechs wanted to break up because the Slovaks were "dragging them down," just like East Germany was dragging West Germany down after they united. They also said that some Czechs felt that having Slovakia was "hurting their chances to get in the EU." Many Slovaks I met thought the breakup was "stupid" and they were against it; however, "over-sized political egos" made it happen. This random sampling was revealing, but I went to Bratislava to learn more.

Bratislava is the best border town in the world. That's not saying much, since most border towns are as attractive as a fat, hairy man in a Speedo. However, Bratislava is grand—it's one of the four elegant European capitals on the Danube River (the others are Vienna, Budapest, and Belgrade). From its outskirts, you can easily bike to Austria or Hungary. Slovakia is such a mountainous country that Bratislava feels out of place, resting on a large, flat plain. Moreover, its rich, sophisticated architecture contrasts sharply with Slovakia's rustic mountain towns. Founded in 907, Bratislava boomed under Austrian rule, and today it has about half a million residents. After strolling through the pedestrian zone and admiring the *Hodžovo nám* (Center Square), you can check out the *Bratislavký Hrad* (Bratislava's castle) on the west side of the Danube. However, I went to the university library to learn why Czechoslovakia broke up.

You'll never believe where Czechoslovakia was born: Pittsburgh, Pennsylvania, USA. In 1917, as WWI neared its end, future Czechoslovaks signed the Pittsburgh Agreement, which promised a common country made of two equal parts: Czech and Slovakia. Later, Czechoslovakia's first President argued for a stronger union. Czechoslovakia worked fairly well until Hitler gobbled up a bit of Czechoslovakia.

At that point, Slovaks had two fabulous options: (a) be completely under Nazi Germany or (b) be a puppet regime under Nazi Germany. They declared independence from Czechoslovakia, thereby choosing option b.

After WWII, Czechoslovakia reunited and Slovaks hung their former president for his Nazi collaboration. Communists ran Czechoslovakia until the 1989 Velvet Revolution overthrew them. Czechoslovakia would do the strangest things to stay united. For example, during their hour-long newscasts, the news anchor would, at precisely 30 minutes, switch from speaking Czech to Slovak. The anchor sometimes did it in the middle of a story. The Czech-Slovak marriage seemed healthy, when it unexpectedly ended in the Velvet Divorce.

Sometimes velvet can feel like sandpaper

The root cause of the Velvet Divorce was a clash of political egos and a temporary surge of nationalism. In the 1992 elections, the new Czech leader, Václav Klaus, and the new Slovak leader, Vladimír Mečiar, fought like babies over whether Czechoslovakia's government should be more or less centralized. It's a similar debate American politicians have between federal versus state control. Mečiar, who also wanted to slow down the libertarian reforms, stirred up enough nationalism within his Slovak politicians to vote for complete independence. Neither Mečiar nor Klaus were willing to budge, so they agreed to split Czechoslovakia in two. Czechoslovakia's President, the playwright Václav Havel, was so disgusted with the decision that he resigned in protest. He was in touch with the public, because just two months after Slovakia's declaration of independence, polls showed that only 36 percent of Czechs and 37 percent of Slovaks favored the breakup. In November 1992, the federal parliament ignored public opinion and voted to dissolve the country.

It's as if Czechoslovakia were a couple who had been married for years, but then got drunk one night, had a fight over how to squeeze the toothpaste, and then yelled at each other, "Fine! That's the way you want it? OK then, this marriage is over! I want to divorce! Tonight! Call the lawyer! Now!" The next morning they both woke up with a hangover, wondering, "What the hell did we just do?"

Without a parallel universe, we'll never know for sure if the divorce was a wise or not. However, most people I talked with either regretted the move or were indifferent. Some Czechs thought they would soar economically without the "poor Slovaks holding them back." Meanwhile, some Slovaks thought they would blast off economically now that they were "free of Czech domination." Although both countries prospered from 1993 to 2008, so did nearly all European countries during that period. Although we'll never know, it's probable that Czechs and Slovaks would have done at least as well had they stayed together. After all, they wouldn't have incurred the costs of a divorce.

As any divorced couple will tell you, even a velvet divorce is a bureaucratic mess. The two governments spent endless hours separating their assets (e.g., military equipment, rail and airline assets) using a 2:1 ratio, because there were twice as many Czechs as Slovaks. They each created new currencies to confuse everyone. They each applied to the UN as new nations, doled out new passports, built new border checkpoints between themselves, set up new relations with other countries, created new telephone country codes, designed new flags, wrote new anthems, and printed new letterhead.

After this expensive and time-consuming process, what did they do? They both joined NATO, so they effectively reunited their military. They both joined the EU on the same day: May 1, 2004. This meant they had to once again synchronize their laws (to match the EU standards); their separate passports were now meaningless since Czech and Slovaks were now free to travel, live, and work in each other's countries; and they had to tear down their border checkpoints before the paint had dried. In 2009, Slovaks replaced their short-lived currency with the euro; if the Czechs do the same, then they will have the same currency. In conclusion, although they didn't remarry after their divorce, they're now domestic partners. It's similar to what the East Germans and West Germans did: they woke up one day, looked at each other, and said, "Hey, why are we sleeping in separate beds anyway?"

The utter foolishness of the divorce explains why so many Slovaks have a difficulty explaining why it happened. It's as if they're embarrassed to admit the futility of the Velvet Divorce. A 2009 Pew Research Center survey revealed that less than half of Slovaks believe the divorce was a good idea and that most Czechs say it was a bad idea. The only reason Czechs and Slovaks don't reunite completely is that they feel a bit silly making Czechoslovakia letterhead again after having just burned up the original ones. It's simply inertia that's still keeping them apart, rather than a deep dividing difference between them. Indeed, even their languages are practically identical.

The Slovak language

Eric Wiltsher is an Englishman who has been to over 40 countries and worked at NPR, Voice of America, and the BBC. He's been living in Poprad, Slovakia for over six years, working for Radio Tatra International. He told me, "Czechoslovakia was kind of like Scotland and England. They were together, but they weren't."

"But aren't their languages pretty different?" I asked.

"No! That's like saying that someone in Ohio has a different accent than somebody from downtown New York. Yes, there are some parts of Czech language, where it is slightly different in the enunciation and the letter sounds are different, but if you have a film on TV from the Czech Republic, a Slovak person would understand 99.999 percent of that movie. They would be able to converse equally as well. Now I struggle a little bit if my boss goes into Czech (cuz he's actually a Czech guy) far more than somebody in Slovak because there are differences, but for the most part, you'll find that a Czech and a Slovak citizen will communicate, quite amusingly, one in Slovak and one Czech, and they get along famously well. So there isn't so much of a problem in terms of language as most people would suggest."

A Hungarian told me, "If a Czech nose is congested, you'll hear more difference there than between the Czech and Slovak languages."

To verify these claims, let's compare how Czechs and Slovaks count to ten. One, two, and three are identical, but then things change slightly: 4 = *čtyři* vs. *štyri,* 5 = *pět* vs. *päť,* 6 = *šest* vs. *šesť,* 7 = *sedm* vs. *sedem,* 8 = *osm* vs. *osem,* 9 = *devět* vs. *deväť,* 10 = *deset* vs. *desať.* By the way, 100 and 1,000 are pronounced the same way. The word for *arrival* is *přjiezdy* vs. *príchod* and *departure* is *odjezdy* vs. *odchod.* Neither of them like vowels: *prst* (finger) and *krk* (neck). Saying something like *where is the bus stop?* is identical in both languages: *kde je autobusová zastávka?*

In short, although there are a few words that are completely different, many words are only slightly different and quite a few are identical. Hence, there's more difference than a simply congested nose, and a better analogy than Ohio vs. New York would be British English vs. American English. The biggest difference is between eastern Slovak dialects and Czech, but they still can understand each other. Moreover, Slovaks tend to understand Czechs more than Czechs understand Slovaks. That's because Slovaks are more often exposed to Czech media than Czechs are to Slovak media. Therefore, if you're going to travel between Czechia and Slovakia, make the effort to learn these Slovak phrases, because the Czech ones are often the same: *dovidenia* (goodbye), *d'akujem* (thank you), *kolko to stoji?* (how much is it?), *áno* (yes), *nie* (no), *prosím* (please), *trh* (the market). My favorite is *hello,* because you get to sound like a sailor: *ahoj!*

A Brit describes Slovaks

I asked Eric to describe Slovaks. He said, "Slovaks and English have a lot of traits that are similar. They can both be positively negative! Unbelievable! And equally, I think Slovaks are a nation of shopkeepers, rather like the English: they often sit there and wait for the order to arrive."

Slovakia is more agrarian than Czechia. Moreover, Eastern Slovakia, where Eric lived, is especially traditional. Eric confirmed this when he said, "Slovakia is like being in England 30 years ago because there is still a great deal of respect for people. You haven't got to the stage of people throwing waste out the window when they're driving down the road in the car. And the notion that a teenager could stand in front of a policeman and the policeman would say, 'If you don't behave yourself, I'll tell your parents.' That kind of strikes fear into people. Which is probably a very good thing. So it's kind of like a time-warp in many ways. Having said that, on the other side of it, it's so far advanced, whereby my mobile phone will work down a big hole, whereas my mobile phone didn't work in the middle of London. You get this crazy young country that has a new infrastructure, new aims and ambitions. The younger Slovaks are so fabulous: they have drive, energy, and passion, which is great. You'll find that tourists who come here won't go home!"

With mountains surrounding them, Slovaks are natural environmentalists. Eric confessed his London habits, "We were terrible. You walk in at night, you turn on 20 light bulbs, on would go the TV, everything else, you could see the national grid melting as people went into the house. In Slovakia, they'll put *one* light on rather than five. Here, they'll put the rubbish in the bin. The notion of recycling is normal. . . . Slovaks care, almost too passionately, about the environment, and about the implications of what is eco-friendly and what isn't. In fact, the Slovak tourist board and the government are spending millions of euros making sure the environment doesn't get damaged. And that is a trait of Slovakia that is not necessarily a trait of other European countries."

Eric is mostly correct, although Slovakia environmental policy isn't perfect. Its coal-burning plants create air pollution and acid rain; similarly, some of its rivers are so polluted that they barely support aquatic life. On the other hand, Slovaks have high environmental standards, which may explain why, in 2010, only 43 percent of Slovaks told Gallup that they were satisfied with their country's efforts to preserve the environment. That same year, Slovakia's Environmental Performance Index score was the highest in Eastern Europe (unless you count Finland, which barely edges it out). Slovakia ranked number 13 in the world, just above the UK (Iceland was number one and the USA was 61 out of 163 countries surveyed).[1]

When I asked Eric to compare Czechs and Slovaks, he said, "The Slovak people tend to be more generous than the Czechs. They'll take more abuse. They'll roll with the punches more before they get upset about that. It's kind of like saying, 'Alright, you won that little battle, but I'll win the war later.' And so you can almost be horrible to a Slovak person and get away with it, because they'll take more. They're more forgiving. They have a lot more family orientation than other countries. And I think that just makes it a nicer place to be."

Europe's business hub

Eric final thoughts were, "Slovakia is an incredibly good place to base a business. The great rail network is amazing. And it even works in the winter when there is a foot of snow. It doesn't slow down, nobody cares, it just carries on. The young Slovaks are very driven to make their country fabulous in the world. There's some amazing talent and business here which you can plug into."

Businesses agree with Eric. In 1997, after Slovakia introduced a 19-percent flat tax and other liberalizing measures, foreign investors poured in. For example, Volkswagen, Peugeot-Citroen, and Kia opened car plants each worth more than $1 billion. This not only created thousands of jobs, but also attracted parts suppliers, which created even more jobs. By 2007, Slovakia was pumping out 570,000 cars a year. In 2013, it expects to produce about 850,000 cars per year. They produce more cars per capita than any other country in the world.

Slovakia's central location in Europe makes it an attractive business hub. A Spanish businessman that I met on a train cited Slovakia's strategic location as one reason he moved to Bratislava. When I asked him if he liked living there, he said, "If I didn't, I would go back to Spain."

I asked him in Spanish (so that nobody in the train would overhear us), "What's the main difference between Spaniards and Slovaks?"

He glanced around and said, "Slovaks are very serious."

Slovakia is serious about catching up to the rest of the EU. Although Slovakia still lags behind Czechia economically, it's closing the gap. When I visited Košice, it was obvious that Slovakia had come a long way in a few years. Košice was dressing-up for its 2013 party, when it will be the European Capital of Culture. Pretty pastel-colored buildings surround the pedestrian zone, which features a colorful, musical fountain. At the city-center stands the Cathedral of St. Elizabeth, a Gothic masterpiece. If it were placed in the High Tatras, it would look like Dracula's evil, brooding castle. I approached Slovaks who were hanging out by the musical fountain to learn what was new. They talked about a thorn on Slovakia's side: Hungary.

Why Slovaks and Hungarians don't get along

Hungarians and Slovaks have been having some problems recently. And by "recently," I mean for the last 140 years. Whenever I asked Hungarians to rank their seven neighboring countries in order of a positive relationship, Slovakia was always dead-last. Slovaks aren't too fond of Hungarians either. Ján Slota, chairman of a major Slovak government party, summed up the sentiments of Slovak extremists when he said, "Hungarians are a tumor on the body of the Slovak nation that needs to be removed without delay."

How did these neighbors get into such a mess? History explains it all. We'll examine Hungary's history more closely later, but for now it's only important to understand that for about 1,000 years, Hungarians ruled (among other places) what is now called Slovakia. Depending on who you ask, life under Hungarian rule was either fabulous, crappy, or somewhere in between. One thing is fairly clear: for most of those 1,000 years, Hungarians let the Slovaks (and other non-Hungarian ethnicities) keep their language and culture.

However, that loose grip began to tighten 140 years ago, when Hungary started to *Hungarianize* its citizens. For example, Hungary forced Slovaks to speak Hungarian in official business, converted about 70 percent of the Slovak elementary schools into Hungarian ones, closed nearly all Slovak secondary schools, gave the right to vote to only the top 5.9 percent of the population (effectively silencing the Slovak political voice), and encouraged Slovaks to change their names into Hungarian-sounding ones. As one Encyclopedia states, "Under Hungarian rule, Slovaks were pressured to give up their language and cultural identity and become Hungarian. Mainly rural, landless peasants, the Slovaks had little economic status and virtually no role in the political life of Hungary."[2] Therefore, by the time Hungary lost WWI, Slovaks were happy to end 1,000 years of Hungarian rule.

After you manage a territory for 1,000 years, it's hard to let it go. Therefore, when Hitler offered Hungary one-third of Slovakia's land, Hungary couldn't resist, especially since it was land where the majority of the inhabitants were ethnically Hungarian. To thank Hitler for returning Hungary some of its former territory, the Hungarian Army fought side by side with the Nazis as far east as Stalingrad and sent hundreds of thousands of Jews to their deaths.

When Hungarians lost WWII, they had to face the furious Slovaks, who viewed the Hungarians as Nazi collaborators. This accusation was wildly hypocritical, since the Slovak government and military were also allied with the Nazis! Slovaks may argue that Hitler forced Slovakia to join the Axis, but they forget that Hitler twisted Hungary's arm too. Consider that when German troops began crossing Hungary to attack Yugoslavia, Hungary's Prime Minister committed suicide. He wrote on his suicide note, "I have allowed our nation's honor to be lost. The Yugoslav nation was our friend. . . . But now, out of cowardice, we have allied ourselves with scoundrels."

Slovaks are right to say that, under Hitler, Hungary got a better deal than Slovakia: Hungary's territory increased, whereas Slovakia's decreased. One reason Hitler favored Hungary is that, in his warped mind, Hungarians were better than Slovaks because they weren't Slavic. Nevertheless, Slovakia sent thousands of Jews to their deaths and its army fought alongside the Nazis until it was clear that Germany would lose the war, which is when the Slovaks finally mounted an effective uprising. Although Slovakia had an anti-Nazi government in exile, plenty of Hungarians were also against the fascists. In conclusion, although Hungary was a stronger and more passionate Nazi supporter than Slovakia, Slovakia was hardly anti-Nazi.

When WWII ended, Slovaks conveniently forgot these details. They just remembered Hungary conspiring with Hitler to take one-third of Slovakia's land. Edvard Beneš, Czechoslovakia's President after WWII, summed up Slovakia's sentiments when he said, "After punishing all the delinquents who committed crimes against the state, the overwhelming majority of the Germans and Hungarians must leave Czechoslovakia. . . . Our people cannot live with the Germans and Hungarians in our fatherland."

Thus, Hungarians (and Germans) living in Czechoslovakia were slapped with the Beneš Decrees, which allowed Slovaks to confiscate Hungarian property and force Hungarian families to move. Czechoslovakia deported 90 percent of its Germans, but the Allies told them that they had to treat Hungarians differently. To kick a Hungarian out, Czechoslovakia had to let Hungary kick a Czechoslovak out. About 73,000 Hungarians and Slovaks, many who had lived for many generations in their homes, were forced to move. Zsuzsa Rodgers, a Hungarian, told me, "Very large numbers of Hungarians were murdered, and others, luckier ones, like my grandparents, were relocated to Hungary, but their lands and wealth confiscated, and all connections to relatives severed."

What Hungarians often forget is that Hungarians deported and mistreated many Slovaks (and Germans) in Hungary. Hungarians will say that they didn't *want* to kick the Slovaks out—they were just doing it because the Allies told them to do the population exchange. Besides, compared to the Slovaks, the Hungarians are convinced that they were far nicer when it came to confiscating property and deporting people.

Adults acting like children

In 2007, Slovakia's parliament reconfirmed the Beneš Decrees, using the stupid excuse that if they didn't, then would be admitting guilt and would have to compensate the victims. Meanwhile, Hungarians are equally ridiculous about the Beneš Decrees, acting like they are still being enforced. This is absurd because Hungarians in Slovakia aren't being deported or having their property stolen. The right thing to do would be for the Slovaks to repeal the Beneš Decrees and for the Hungarians to ignore them if they don't.

Instead, both sides continue to argue like brats. In 2009, Pál Csáky, the leader of the Hungarian political party in Slovakia's Parliament, said that Ján Slota (the Slovakia National Party leader) and the Beneš Decrees are "Slovakia's shame." Slota replied, "If I am considered to be the shame for Slovakia, then he is a vomit, a rotten piece of shit."[3]

Slota's beliefs are so extreme, it's comical. He said, "If the Slovak National Party is extremist, then Hungarians are radioactive extremists—they radiate more than Chernobyl. The best solution would be back-fill them with concrete." His solution with dealing with the Roma (gypsies) is "a long whip and a small yard." He drew a connection between the Hungarian Minister of Foreign Affairs and Hitler when he compared her to "that little mustached person in a Munich cellar. He had the same rhetoric as this woman. Perhaps her mustache is also starting to grow." In addition, he's called the Hungarian Turul (the mythical Hungarian falcon) an "ugly parrot" and Saint Stephen, the first King of Hungary, "a clown on a horse."[4]

Although Slota's fiery tongue represents the lunatic fringe of Slovakia, the fact that many Slovaks voted for his nationalist party worries Hungarians. It's just one more indication of just how lousy Hungary-Slovakia relations are. Indeed, Hungarians and Slovaks will bicker about almost anything. For example, in 1977, their communist governments (Slovakia was part of Czechoslovakia at the time) agreed to build the Gabčíkovo-Nagymaros Dam next to the Danube River. Hungary illegally canceled the agreement, citing environmental concerns. Meanwhile, Czechoslovakia illegally went ahead with the river diversion without Hungary's approval. In 1997, the International Court in the Hague found both Hungary and Slovakia at fault and ordered them to compensate each other—they still haven't.

Elsewhere, a Hungarian student alleged Slovaks assaulted her, writing anti-Hungarian insults on her clothing. The Slovak police said she was lying and accused her of perjury. In another incident, Slovak police beat up Hungarians during a soccer game, even though the Hungarians were allegedly not doing anything that warranted an assault. Meanwhile, in Hungary's capital, two Molotov cocktails landed (but didn't detonate) next to the Slovak embassy.

Slovakia's Language Law

In 2010, the latest idiotic fight was over Slovakia's Language Law. The law gives Slovak priority over other languages in road signs, ads, and government affairs (such as contracts, postal services, police, and fire departments). The law does not apply in communities where minority language speakers (like Hungarians) make up over 20 percent of the population. For instance, if you live somewhere where only 10 percent of the population is Hungarian, then you must speak Slovak in the post office, unless, of course, you don't know any Slovak. On the street, in restaurants, and bars you're free to talk in Hungarian, Japanese, or Swahili.

The law seems pretty harmless, except that after a written warning, violators could be fined up to 5,000 euros ($7,500 dollars). Although Slovaks aren't enforcing the law (nobody has been fined), Hungarians are so hysterical over it that they're distorting reality. For example, several Hungarians (who don't live in Slovakia) assured me that "in Slovakia, it's illegal to speak Hungarian in public. Slovaks will beat you up if they hear you speaking it." Hoping to start a fight when I was roaming the streets of Slovakia, I merrily yelled out *"köszönöm"* ("thank you" in Hungarian), but nobody cared.

Hungarians are right that Slovakia's Language Law is asinine. Slovaks should re-write the law to match the standard language laws that several EU countries have. Thanks to EU pressure, Slovakia's Prime Minister took the teeth out of the law when he promised that "no individual will be fined in Slovakia for using their own language."[5] It's a pity that Slovaks are so insecure about their language that they feel they even need such a law. If their language could survive 1,000 years of Hungarian rule, it will do just fine in their independent country without any silly Language Law. In fact, it should be even easier now to keep their language since there are fewer Hungarians than ever. In 1910, the Kingdom of Hungary estimated that about 30 percent of those who live in what is now Slovakia were Hungarian. Over the last 100 years, that number has eroded to less than 10 percent today.

Krisztina Szirmai, a well-traveled Hungarian, told me that "to introduce a fair and inclusive language and minority policy, you need to be confident in yourself, your history and so on. It's not enough to have a language, traditions, and folk songs that are 1,000 years old, you must have a stable state, a long-existing constitution, a long history of literature and others. Slovakia lacks these things. It's quite usual that when a new country is being born, having nothing to hold into, can only find itself in abusing other nationalities, especially the ones that previously had control over it."

Yet another immature fight broke out in 2010, when Hungary offered citizenship to all Hungarians, even if they live in other countries. Slovakia saw the move as a jab and promptly made dual citizenship illegal for its citizens. These two EU countries continue their race to the bottom for the grand prize of who is the biggest baby.

What's the root cause behind these petty fights?

Part of the Slovak's anti-Hungarian mentality is rooted in vengeance. During the communist era, Hungary banned the Slovak and German languages. Before that, as we saw, Hungary was trying to

Hungarianize Slovaks. Therefore, for Slovaks, it's payback time, especially since there are a few diehard Hungarians who believe that Slovakia belongs under Hungary. They refuse to call it *Szlovákia,* and instead use the name it had under the Kingdom of Hungary: *Felvidék* (Upper Hungary).

Indeed, these passionate Hungarians feel that everything about Slovakia is artificial. László Marácz called Czechoslovakia a "completely artificial creation."[6] One Hungarian woman wrote to me, "The Beneš Decrees were created to exterminate Hungarian and German populations in the newly born, artificial country of Slovakia." Another Hungarian, who also wished to go unnamed, expressed a similar idea when he wrote to me, "Slovak is an artificial language to give identity to a never-existed country, Slovakia. It was during the nineteenth century that the *tót* (that's their real name) identity (*Slovakia* and the word *Slovak* appeared, to my knowledge, only after 1920) strengthened, along with their wonderful buildings and richness built by Hungarians."

Imagine you're a Slovak and you hear Hungarians saying your country and language are "artificial" and that even the name of your nationality is wrong ("Dude, you're not a *Slovak,* you're a *Tót*!"). At some point, you too might support an ultra-nationalist like Ján Slota who once promised that if Hungarians keep trying to teach Slovaks the Lord's Prayer in Hungarian, he would send tanks to "flatten Budapest."

Hungary and Slovakia ought to copy Czechia and Germany by issuing a joint apology for past misdeeds. However, in 2009, instead of saying *mea culpa,* Hungary's President tried to unveil a statue of Saint Stephen, Hungary's first king, *in Slovakia*. That's not exactly a good way to kiss and make up. Slovakia responded by not letting him in the country—which raised eyebrows in the EU since EU citizens are allowed to travel across borders freely. To apologize, you need courage and an ability to not take yourself too seriously. Hungary and Slovakia aren't there yet.

> *Anyone who takes himself too seriously always runs the risk of looking ridiculous; anyone who can consistently laugh at himself does not. — Václav Havel*

There's hope

There's a happy ending to this Hungary-Slovakia debacle: it's not as bad as it seems. Talk to the average Slovak (or ethnic Hungarian living in Slovakia) and they probably won't bring up the issue, because it's really not that big of a deal. I only learned about it at the end of my third trip to Slovakia in 2011. And the only reason I discovered it was that I love asking provocative questions; otherwise, I would be oblivious to the tension. In fact, for many years in America, my doubles volleyball partner was a Slovak, yet he never once mentioned anything about Hungarians. Zuzana Sedlackova, a Slovak, summed it up well in an email:

Politicians make it sound like it's the worst relationship on earth, just to build up some reputation and dramatize the situation. Let's face it, people love dramatic situations and they rather read horrible news than good ones.

I don't think relationship between those two countries is dramatic; on the contrary, I think people in general really do not care and live their life together without any issues (look at the history of Slovaks, have we ever been aggressive nation?). According to the news (if we can trust them) there has been one attack on some Hungarian girl in Slovakia—and it became international issue.

Of course in every country (including Slovakia or Hungary) you have many "ultra-nationalists" who are out of their minds, but I think you can find them more in Germany or even UK . . . and they don't make it such an issue out of it.

Now there is an issue about Hungarian language to be used as an official language in Slovakia. What an issue and lovely game for politicians AGAIN! I believe that people should speak Slovak in Slovak bureaucracy; however, I don't see a reason why Hungarians could not speak Hungarian to the person if the clerk speaks Hungarian as well. Just like when an English person comes to our offices and speaks in English—if you speak the language, you explain it in his language to make it easier and understandable for him. As Slovakia is in the EU, we should have all official documents available in all EU languages. What's important is that if you are Slovak in Slovakia you should not have problem with your mother-tongue in your own country.

I deeply believe it is only a political issue. They are just playing dirty games and do not communicate on professional political level. Unfortunately it is our (Slovaks and also Hungarians) problem that we have voted those people to be in the government.

In short, Hungarians and Slovaks coexist everyday with no more trouble than you might find anywhere else. There's even a Facebook group called "Slovakia + Hungary = Peace, Love & Empathy" that has over 16,000 members—far more than all the anti-Hungary or anti-Slovak Facebook groups combined. In 2010, Ján Slota's radical political party lost over half their seats in parliament as Slovaks rejected his abrasive tactics. In conclusion, a few politicians and their followers create most of drama because it's more fun for them to stir up trouble than to do any real work.

What Slovakia Can Teach Us

- **Play outside.** Slovaks are outdoor-freaks who take advantage of their spectacular mountains and parks. Follow their example and ist'na prechadsku (go for a walk). Go jog, raft, ski, snowshoe, hike, and bike in your surroundings, even if they're not as pretty as Slovakia's.
- **Improve your environment.** One comprehensive survey rated Slovakia as the twelfth most environmentally conscious country in the world and the cleanest in Eastern Europe (after Finland). Follow Slovakia's example by reducing your consumption, reusing things, and recycling. Live a low impact life by driving an eco-friendly car (or don't use a car at all), as well as reducing your energy use and waste. Buy local food and ecological products.

Places I saw and recommend in Slovakia: High Tatras, Bratislava, and Košice.

Travel deals and info: http://ftapon.com/slovakia

With all this talk about Hungary, it's natural to make it our next stop. Compared to Slovakia, Hungary's landscape is flat and boring. However, it makes up for it with a rich and complex history, language, and culture. Let's hope I've whetted your appetite for Hungary.

10

HUNGARY—A SHADOW OF ITS FORMER SELF

One viral YouTube video that spread through Hungary was of an American game-show where the contestant was asked, "Budapest is the capital of what European country?" When a fifth-grader gave the correct answer, the shocked blond bimbo said, "Hungry? That's a country? I've heard of Turkey, but Hungry? Never heard of it."

While Hungarians (and many others) say this is a perfect example of American ignorance, they overlook a few points. First, some don't know that the dumb blond contestant was the American Idol singer Kellie Pickler, who enjoys emphasizing that she's just a simple country singer from North Carolina, and who admits to not being the sharpest tool in the shed. Second, many miss the other message of that TV game show, which is called "Are You Smarter Than a 5th Grader?" It proves that some of America's fifth graders are pretty smart. Indeed, how many Hungarian fifth-graders (or adults) would know the answer to "La Paz is the capital of what country?"

Most Hungarians wouldn't know the answer, even though when compared with Hungary, Bolivia has just as many people (10 million) and 10 times more land. Vientiane is the capital of what country? Hint: It's a country that's geographically twice the size as Hungary. Answer: Laos. Or closer to Hungary: Chişinău is the capital of what European country? It's less than 1,000 kilometers from Hungary (half-day drive): Moldova. Hungarians (and other Europeans) might say, "OK, so I didn't know the answers, but these are small, not-so-well-known countries." Exactly. Just like Hungary. Challenge random people outside of Europe to find Hungary on a map and they might also point to starving Ethiopia.

Although Americans are embarrassingly ignorant, Europeans are not far behind. Answer this: *how long does the earth take to go around the sun?* According to a Eurobarometer poll, nearly one in five British people answered, "One month." Over 20 percent of the people in Ireland, Spain, Denmark, and Austria agreed with those British geniuses. I suppose these Einsteins believe the earth goes around the sun 12 times to make a year. Unfortunately, this question wasn't asked to the American audience, but I'm confident that we Americans would be just as stupid as Austrians. Why? Assuming that Austrians and Germans are similar (a fact that everyone on this planet would agree on, except Austrians and Germans), consider that 79 percent of Americans know that the earth revolves around the sun, whereas only 74 percent of Germans and 67 percent of Brits know that. The rest either believe that the sun revolves around the earth or they don't know. By the way, don't blame religion for these beliefs, since no religion teaches that the sun orbits the earth. Let's face it: Americans don't have a monopoly on ignorance.[1]

I was ignorant of Hungary until my college volleyball teammate, Steve Rodgers, introduced me to his new girlfriend: a Hungarian named Zsuzsa (pronounced *Jewja*). She was a skinny girl with pale skin and raven-black hair. Like most Hungarians I would meet over the next 20 years, she loved intellectual discussions and had a verbose opinion on everything. She would cheer for us at every volleyball match, including our away-games. I'm convinced her support made us win the only volleyball championship in Amherst College's history. To thank Zsuzsa for supporting our team, Steve married her and had three children. He claims there were other, more important reasons for creating a family with her, but guys are supposed to say stuff like that.

> *Getting divorced just because you don't love a man is almost as silly as getting married just because you do.*
> *— Zsa Zsa Gabor, a Hungarian actress*

Budapest: two cities for the price of one

Zsuzsa encouraged me to visit Budapest, so the next summer I did. It was 1992, just three years after Hungary had shed its communist coat. Budapest was the hip new European city to discover. Lonely Planet had ranked Budapest the number one place to see in Eastern Europe, even above Prague. The first thing I learned when I arrived was that there are two cities in Budapest: Buda and Pest.

Buda is posher than Pest. Buda has the impressive Castle Hill, luxurious housing, and grand buildings. It was the seat of royalty and the site of an ancient fortress. Today, tourists go there to enjoy the breathtaking view of the Danube River's many bridges, the sharp spires of the Parliament, and the city lights of Pest. Although not as regal as Buda, Pest is where most of the action is. To get there, walk down the medieval cobblestones and cross Eastern Europe's most beautiful bridge: *Széchenyi Lánchíd* (Chain Bridge). Or ride Europe's second oldest underground subway. Walk down Andrássy Avenue and make sure you see *Hősök tere* (Heroes' Square) during the day and night—you'll feel like you're in Paris.

My favorite place in Budapest is the *Széchenyi Fürdő* (Széchenyi Medicinal Bath). Built in 1908, it's the largest medicinal bath in Europe and is fed by the world's largest thermal water-cave system. You'll feel like royalty in its saunas and baths. The best way to enjoy the grand outdoor pool is to go there on a snowy winter night, relax in its hot spring waters, and admire the surrounding statues and architecture. It's like bathing in the fountains of Versailles.

Hungary's ocean: Lake Balaton

I may know the only Hawaiian in history who has a summer home in Hungary. *Just the concept of a Hawaiian having a summer home is a bit odd.* The fact that it's on the other side of the planet makes it especially wacky. These are the strange things that can happen when a Hawaiian marries a Hungarian. Steve (my college volleyball buddy) was born and raised in Hawaii; thus, after he married Zsuzsa, they settled in Hawaii, which, they thought, was a slightly better place to live than Hungary.

Although Zsuzsa loved her new island home, she kept her family's summerhouse at Balatonkenese, a village on the shores of Lake Balaton. Landlocked countries like Hungary attach mythic importance to their biggest lake. Given that Lake Balaton is Europe's largest freshwater lake outside of Scandinavia, Hungary's affection for it is fanatically high. Sometimes it seems that Hungarians value their lakeshore more than Hawaiians value their seashore. When I visited Lake Balaton in 2004, Steve and Zsuzsa invited me to stay with them. They opened my eyes to a Hungary that I had never seen when I was staying in hostels 12 years before. It started with them teaching me some Hungarian.

Proof that UFOs exist: the Hungarian language

UFO believers would be far more convincing if they just used the Hungarian language as proof that Earth has had extraterrestrial visitors. When you travel through Europe, it's easy to see how languages are connected to each other. They usually fall into one of these categories: Slavic, Germanic, Scandinavian, Baltic, or Italic (Romance). There are obvious connections between German and Dutch, French and Italian, Spanish and Portuguese, Polish and Russian. One can see how these Indo-European languages evolved from a common source and slowly morphed into the languages we know today. They're all related. And then, there's Hungarian.

> Öt török öt görögöt dögönyöz örökös örömök között.
> *— Hungarian tongue twister, meaning "Five Turks are massaging five Greeks amid everlasting delights."*

Hungarian doesn't seem European, but instead has a distinctly Martian flavor: *igen* (yes), *nem* (no), *kérem* (please), *köszönöm* (thank you), *elnézést* (excuse me), *a nevem . . .* (my name is . . .), *hol van . . . ?* (where is . . . ?), *mennyi?* (how much?), *szeretlek* (I love you). The only weakness in my Hungarian-Martian hypothesis is that Hungarians clearly stole *goodbye* from colloquial English: they say *szia* (sounds like *see ya*). Confusingly, Hungarians also use *szia* to say *hello.*

More Martian evidence: Hungarian is one of the few languages in our solar system that agglutinates, which means it often *glues* root words together to create new words. For example, in English, *unwholesomeness* glues *un-whole-some-ness*. English speakers sometimes agglutinate, but Hungarians carry an endless supply of Krazy Glue. As one Martian explained to me, "Hungarian is not based on words. It is based on roots: there are less than 100 basic roots. This small number of basic roots are expanded to around 600 to 800 roots. By combining the roots together, or modifying the roots with additives, you get the Hungarian vocabulary. The beauty is that you need not memorize each word, you need to understand the roots, and thus you can understand words, even those you have never before heard."

An American polyglot told me that Hungarian is mind-bending, "Hungarian is so damned difficult to learn for outsiders. I learned from a teach-yourself book at the beginning. It used the root-based system to teach. I rebelled against it, trying to make Hungarian fit my linguistic logic. I soon learned that this was futile." After years of effort, he speaks Hungarian fluently. To show how agglutination works, you can glue words around *mond* (say) to create *legel**mond**hatatlanabbul* (in the most unspeakable manner). Glue other words onto *mond* to make more tongue twisters like *el**mond**hatatlanabbul, ki**mond**hatatlanabbul, legel**mond**hatatlanabb,* and *legeslegel**mond**hatatlanabb* (all these words have something to do with *unspeakable*).

Hungarian pronouns are out of this world. For example, whereas most European languages have just a formal and informal way of saying *you*, Hungarian has four ways. Which one you use depends on the level of respect you want to give, although the informal way (*tegeződés*) is gaining popularity.[2] They may have four ways of saying *you*, but they have no way to say *he* or *she*. They just have *ő*, which can mean either *he* or *she*. One Hungarian told me that this helps them tell white lies; it may also explain their high divorce rate.

Hungarian has even more oddities that prove its Martian origins. For instance, its alphabet not only can throw accents on vowels, it also has nine digraphs (*cs, dz, ly, ny, ty, zs, gy, sz*) and one trigraph (*dzs*). These are independent "letters," just like *ll* has its own section in a Spanish dictionary. Hungarian has 18 cases, more than any other European tongue. Their name order is "backwards." For instance, it's *Marx Károly* (Karl Marx), *Luther Márton* (Martin Luther), and I'm Tapon Francis. Hungarians even have special words to indicate the relative age of a family member. For instance, an *older sister* is a *nővér* and a *younger sister* is a *húg*—which you shouldn't confuse with *húgy* (urine).

You might believe that I'm offending Hungarians by saying that their language comes from Mars. You're right. Hungarians would be offended because Mars is not strange enough! They'd prefer that you say it's related to languages emanating from the Sirius star system, 8.6 light years away. Seriously, Hungarians are incredibly proud of having such an unusual language in the middle of Europe. They delight in the confusion it causes. They adore that they can speak in other countries and be confident that nobody will eavesdrop. They love that Hungarian is a bizarre linguistic island in Europe. As one Hungarian told me, "Although every language has some degree of difference in their logic, Hungarian stands out like something from a different planet." Indeed, where their language comes from is a mystery.

Although linguists haven't classified Hungarian in the Martian language family, their proposals aren't much better. The conventional theory is that Hungarian is part of the Finno-Ugric language group. That means that Finnish and Estonian are related to Hungarian. However, Estonians and Hungarians don't feel they have much in common linguistically, just like English and German speakers fail to see a connection between their languages (even though technically there is one). A few linguists argue that Hungarian evolved from the Turkish language, but that's a stretch. Some pot-smoking linguists (who aren't so bold to support my Martian-origin theory) claim that Hungarian evolved from Sumerian. Given that Sumerian was spoken in Mesopotamia (around Iraq) 5,000 years ago, the Hungarian ties to it are as weak as a spider's thread. Those who cling to this theory believe it's cool to say that Hungarian is a direct descendant of one of the world's oldest written languages. However, depending on how you define "related," you can "prove" that Hungarian and Sumerian are related to African-American jive talk.[3]

A bizarre linguistic connection

With such feeble explanations for the origin of the Hungarian language, my Hungarian-Martian theory is starting to sound plausible. Fortunately, there's one more clue to consider: the Khanty and Mansi people speak languages that are eerily similar to Hungarian. What's strange is where Khanty and Mansi speakers live: western Siberia, Russia.

Yeah, that's not exactly where I was expecting to find them either. Normally, speakers of tightly related languages are neighbors. Although the Khanty and Mansi people are neighbors, their Hungarian linguistic brothers are over 5,000 kilometers (3,125 miles) away. That's like having an obscure language in Arizona and finding its linguistic sister in Alaska (strangely, this is true for the Native American Athabaskan languages). This raises the obvious question: how could this have happened?

This is where UFOs come in. A long time ago, Hungarian-speaking aliens mixed their DNA with Siberian locals and then flew a bunch of them in their flying saucers to Finland and Hungary. *Voilà!* Mystery solved!

On the other hand, perhaps our pot-smoking linguist friends have a better idea. Let's suppose some Sumerians migrated out of Mesopotamia, goofed around for a long time in Scythia (Kazakhstan), and that their descendants finally settled east of the Urals in Siberia. Once settled, their language evolved into something like the Khanty-Mansi languages (let's call it proto-Ugric). Many years later, some Ugric-speaking people got bored with Siberia and Kazakhstan, hopped on their horses, and rode either northwest to Finland and southwest to . . . Hungary.

Why did the tribes split? Hungarians joke that when their ancestors left the eastern Urals, they found a sign indicating "To civilization." Illiterate ones went northwest and became Finns. Those who could read it, went southwest and became Hungarians. (Finns reverse the joke.)

Distance distorts language. Hence, it seems that such a migration would be too far to preserve any kind of linguistic heritage. However, there's only one major mountain range between Kazakhstan and Hungary (the Carpathians), so the journey would be relatively flat and easy. After crossing a Carpathian mountain pass, the nomads saw the flat Danube Basin as paradise. Perhaps it reminded them of their ancestral home in Western Kazakhstan/Siberia: endless plains. It was a perfect place for reproducing their traditional way of life. Or perhaps they just found a bunch of hot single women there.

Although the migration was far less painful than if it had been over endless mountain ranges, the nomads still racked up plenty of frequent walker miles. That's why the Hungarian language, even when compared to its nearest relative (Mansi/Khanty), is quite unique. The few thousand remaining Mansi and Khanty speakers can't understand Hungarian TV.

This grand unifying theory solves many mysteries. It explains (1) why there's a vague Sumerian-Hungarian connection, (2) why Scythians may also be one of Hungary's ancestors, (3) why today there are Hungarian-like speakers east of the Urals, (4) why there are linguistic similarities between Hungarian and Finnish-Estonian, (5) why Hungarians thrived in the flat Danube Basin, and (6) why we're all clueless when Hungarians communicate.

There are two problems with this grand theory. First, we don't know when these migrations occurred or how long they took. Some Hungarians claim that their ancestors made the journey to Europe over 4,500 years ago. Most non-Hungarian historians say the main migration happened *much* later. The second problem is that I'm not an expert in linguistics, so don't take my opinion as gospel. In fact, be skeptical about *anyone* who claims to know the origins of Hungarians and their language. There are many loony theories out there. My reasoning (which I don't claim is original) simply merges what seem to be the most credible explanations. However, this theory could be more wrong than my original Hungarian-Martian hypothesis.

More evidence that Hungarians are Martians

Do you believe that intelligent alien beings are abundant in the universe? If so, physicist Enrico Fermi would ask you to explain one paradox: why is there no evidence of these creatures? Leó Szilárd, a Hungarian physicist, answered Fermi's Paradox easily, "They are already here among us; they just call themselves Hungarians."

It's a funny joke until you realize how true it is. Throughout the first half of the twentieth century, many gifted Hungarians immigrated to America. They would eventually invent the ballpoint pen, holography, the BASIC programming language, and artificial blood. Joseph Pulitzer, a Hungarian publisher, established his famous prize for journalism and writing. Other Hungarians played key roles during the early stages of Hollywood. For example, when the Hungarian government nationalized its film industry in 1919, Michael Curtiz went to Hollywood and went on to direct over 100 movies, including *Casablanca* and *Yankee Doodle Dandy*. Another Hungarian, Adolph Zukor, founded Paramount Pictures. The Hungarian Harry Houdini got out of puzzles, while Ernő Rubik created one—the Cube that bears his name. Andrew Grove co-founded Intel, while George Soros's financial wizardry made him a billionaire.

> *Well, you know, I was a human being before I became a businessman. — George Soros (Soros should have added, "And before I became a human being, I was a Martian.")*

Although these contributions are impressive, the field where Hungarians truly showed their Martian origins was nuclear physics. They invented nuclear reactors. Indeed, so many Hungarians were involved in developing the atomic bomb that it's said that when the Italian Enrico Fermi left a meeting, he said, "Gentlemen, feel free to speak Hungarian." One German Nobel Laureate wondered if John von Neumann, a Hungarian prodigy who excelled in various scientific fields, was proof of a new superior species. Similarly, Isaac Asimov observed that there are two intelligent species on earth: humans and Hungarians. When nobody could explain how a small country with an odd language could produce so many intellectual Supermen, the joke about Martians having visited Hungary became only a half-joke. Hungarian geniuses cheerfully supported the theory. In fact, György Marx wrote a book whose subtitle was "Hungarian Scientists Who Shaped the History of the Twentieth Century in the West." The book's main title is more revealing: *A Marslakók Érkezése*, which means *Arrival of the Martians*.

> *Discovery consists of seeing what everybody has seen, and thinking what nobody has thought. — Albert Szent-Györgyi, Nobel Prize winning Hungarian scientist*

Even if you disbelieve the Hungarian-Martian hypothesis, it's still hard to find consensus over where Hungarians come from. Early theories said that Hungarians came from the empire of Attila the Hun, which would explain the term *Hun*garian. That seems like a much more reasonable explanation than saying they got their name because they were hungry.

Still, most historians today believe that the word *Hungarian* didn't come from the Huns, but rather from the Turks who referred to them as *Onogur* (meaning *ten tribes/arrows*). On the other hand, this is somewhat irrelevant since Hungarians call themselves *Magyar*. Their nation isn't *Hungary*, but rather *Magyarország*. Magyars got their name from the confederation of Magyar tribes, led by Prince Árpád, who entered Hungary in 895 AD. Árpád is Hungary's Napoleon: a dude who kicked ass all over Europe.

Unfortunately, a few Hungarians dislike this migration story because humans often want to be native pure-breeds. Some people believe that someone who is 100 percent English, or French, or Hungarian is better than those who aren't. Moreover, many Europeans treat immigrants as second-class citizens, so it's best to claim that you and your descendants have "always" lived where you live. That's why a few Hungarians reject the idea that they showed up in Hungary in 895 AD; they prefer to argue that they've been there for over 40,000 years.

The genetic reality is that we're all mutts and immigrants. There's no such thing as a "pure-breed" of any nationality since our genes are a complex cocktail of endless mixing. Similarly, nobody is a true "native" since our ancestors all emigrated from Africa. The passionate fights over Hungarian origins probably mean that there is a bit of truth in all the theories. Hungarian DNA has traces from the Celts, Romans, Huns, Turks, Sumerians, Scythians, Avars, Urgics, Slavs, Austrians, Germans, and your uncle Harry. Although that's not the clean answer that some Hungarians crave, it's the closest to the truth. Over the centuries, Hungary has conquered and been conquered. It's spread its DNA and had other DNA injected into its gene pool. Their language has also been pushed and pulled along the way, which explains its uniqueness.

Hungarians and their language are like a tree that was born in Asia and transplanted to Europe. Over generations, the tree's descendants adapted to the new environment so that it no longer had much in common with its Asian roots; however, it didn't adapt too many European features either. Thus, Hungarian seems alien to both its Asian ancestors and its European neighbors. My friend Mimi Wallace recalled her visit to Hungary in 1967 and 2000 saying, "I sort of felt like I was stepping back into time to some degree. The people are highly sophisticated, yet have this history of always seeming to belong to another world."

Although the Hungarian language is bizarre, you can learn it. Steve, for example, learned Hungarian from Zsuzsa and speaks it fluently today. Whether I hung out with them in Hawaii or Lake Balaton, I heard them speaking to their three children in Hungarian most of the time. We relaxed by Lake Balaton playing the Settlers of Catan board game for hours. Zsuzsa beat us all every time, reminding us of her superior Martian genes.

Alex Kuli in Budapest

It's fascinating how Facebook can reconnect you with old classmates whom you barely knew when you attended school together, and yet after many years you end up talking with them more than you ever did in school! This is exactly what happened when I reconnected with Alex Kuli, who was in the class above me in college. After reconnecting on Facebook, he invited me to crash a few days at his Budapest apartment. It was a snowy March in 2009, five years after I had met with Steve and Zsuzsa. Alex would reveal another side of Hungary. I never knew just how politically incorrect and brutally honest Alex was until we met again. He'll never be a diplomat. He's refreshingly funny, because he rules his life by one simple rule: absolutely no bullshit.

When I asked him about his family background, he said, "My old man was born in Hungary in the city of Szombathely in February 1945. He and his family escaped to Germany (mostly because that's where the US army was). After the war ended, my grandmother came back to the family home of Mezőcsát in Eastern Hungary with my dad. My grandfather stayed in Germany because he found out the Russians wanted to execute him."

"When did they immigrate to America?" I asked.

"My grandmother and father stayed in Hungary until 1947, when a policeman friend advised my grandmother that it would be a *really* good idea for her to get the hell out. She then claims she walked with my father from Mezőcsát to Nürnberg, where they reunited with my grandfather. (My grandmother sometimes exaggerates, but I'm sure she walked a good deal of the way.) The family came to America around 1952."

Later, in the summer of 1969, Alex was born in Buffalo, New York, and then grew up in Belgium. Although we didn't know it at the time, Alex and I were both making our first visit to Hungary in 1992. After graduating from college, he settled in Budapest. Although he left Hungary for a few years to get a master's degree in journalism, he spent over 11 years living in Hungary. He was a news reporter and political analyst, which gave him deep insight in the country. He said, "It was basically an accident that I ended up staying in Hungary."

I asked, "How much longer do you plan to stay?"

"When does the next train leave?"

Hungarians are in love and depressed

Alex's funny quip illustrates the first thing he told me about Hungarians: "They are a very pessimistic people. They're constantly complaining about something. They feel bad if they are not complaining about something."

A worldwide Gallup poll supports this: Hungary is by far the most depressed country in Europe. In 2010, Hungarians were asked, "Did you experience depression yesterday?" A stunning 30 percent of said *yes*. This makes them more depressed than people in Afghanistan.

On the other hand, in May 2007, when asked "Did you experience love yesterday?", an impressive 88 percent of Hungarians answered *yes*. That puts Hungary fourth from the top of the world. (Belarus was fifth from the bottom with just 39 percent saying they experienced love the previous day.) When Zsuzsa first told me that "Hungarians bring their children up with love," I discounted her statement figuring that every nation could say that about themselves. However, it seems that Hungarian water is spiked with a potent love potion. Thus, Hungarians are in love . . . and depressed. How can we explain this paradox? Clearly, love makes you depressed.

When I asked Krisztina Szirmai, a Hungarian, what she disliked about her country, she echoed what Alex said, "I hope you are prepared for a long rant on my part here. Yeah, I'm no different from other Hungarians in that I like to complain. Of course I could complain about how much Hungarians complain in general."

"So how is life in Hungary different than America?" I asked.

She wrote, "Americans often say Hungarians are often looking depressed or indifferent while we are on the streets. Yes, this is true. But I think it's all about the different attitude we possess. We simply want to show our emotions to the people we care about and not to everyone. Most of the time we don't care what the wide world thinks of us. Someone once said that 'in America everyone is happy, everyone is doing his best and once a month he goes to see his psychiatrist.' So seeing a Hungarian with an indifferent face on public transportation does not mean his life is f--ked up. And yes, a foreigner smiling at us will most probably confuse us."

Everything sucks: the politicians, the economy, the EU, my life

Although Hungarians are complaining and depressed about many things, their favorite topics to bitch about are politics and the economy. Of course, every nation loves to whine about these two issues, but Hungarians take it to a new level. Alex asked the girl who sat next to him at work what she thought Americans could learn from Hungarians. Her reply was, "Ummm, I dunno. Food. And corruption."

We'll get to tasty Hungarian food later, but first let's look at corruption. We'll examine the survey results from the Pew Research Center's Global Attitudes Project along with Gallup's polls. In 2009, Hungarians ranked the three biggest problems facing their country as corruption, crime, and pollution. Hungarians are "overwhelmingly" dissatisfied with how their democracy is functioning, with three-quarters saying political corruption is a major problem. Within Europe, they were the least satisfied with the way democracy is working for them (77% "not satisfied"). It's not that they don't believe in democracy; on the contrary, polls show that they support democratic ideals and institutions more than all other Eastern Europeans. It's just that they're failing to achieve their democratic aspirations. The researchers concluded that "even in a region [like Eastern Europe] where disillusionment is common, Hungarians stand out."

When Hungarians are not depressed about their corrupt politicians, they're depressed about their economy. In 2009, only three percent of Hungarians said the economy was "good." Only Lebanon and Zimbabwe were more downcast. Moreover, less than half of Hungarians approved of moving toward capitalism. That's sharply down from 1991, when 80 percent supported the move. A depressing 72 percent of Hungarians believe that they are now economically worse off than they were under communism. That's far higher than any other Eastern European country; only Ukraine and Bulgaria have over 50 percent feeling similarly.

"All of this is total bullshit," said Alex. "All you need to do is look at newsreels from 1989, and even these bitchy people will begin to realize how bad it was back then. The point of this is, that the people who think their situation hasn't changed at all, or has gotten worse, generally belong to the boo-hoo gang (although I have no scientific proof). You could hand them a kilo of gold, and they would still find a way to consider it an insult, and find a way to blame it on the Romanians/Jews/Gypsies."

In 2010, Gallup surveyed 151 countries with the question, "Do you have confidence in the quality and integrity of the media?" Americans, who have a reputation of being naive people who believe whatever their media feeds them, scored surprisingly low: only 30 percent had confidence in the media. That was lower than all Europeans except Estonia (27%), Greece (16%), and Hungary (14%). Hungary had the most cynical rate on Earth.

I told Alex that one Hungarian said to me, "On average, Hungary is not doing bad, but Hungarians are faring extremely badly."

Alex said, "This is a rather typical whiny Hungarian thing to say: Hungary as a nation is different from the Hungarian people. So, even though the economic indicators are OK, everything still sucks."

Hungarians are also negative about the EU. In 2010, only one in five Hungarians think the EU is good for Hungary and 71 percent think European integration has hurt Hungary's economy. (By the way, 63 percent of Bulgarians also think that the EU dragged them into the economic toilet.) Part of this negativity is based on reality, but part is mistaking *correlation* with *causation*. Just a few years after Hungary (and Bulgaria) joined the EU, the world experienced the Great Recession of 2008–2010. Hungarians (like most people on the planet) suffered economically during that period. Hungary would have gone down the economic tubes whether it was in the EU or not (Switzerland and Norway aren't EU members, but they suffered economically along with the rest of Europe during that global downturn). Unfortunately, it seems that Hungarians (and Bulgarians) foolishly correlated the two events, believing that their EU membership *caused* their economic woes. One Hungarian told me, "Every since Hungary joined the EU, Hungarians have no say regarding their own fate as a nation."

"Baloney," says Alex. "Hungarians voted in favor of joining the EU, and they can vote to leave it, too. Some Hungarians even say that, because of EU laws, you need a one-year degree in supermarkets in order to work behind the cheese counter. Baloney again."

Finally, when Hungarians aren't depressed about the economy, they're depressed about their lives. In 2009, only 15% of Hungarians rated their lives a 7 or more on a 1 to 10 scale. It was even worse in 1991, when only 8% rated their lives so highly. *That 7-point improvement is the lowest improvement on that question among Eastern Europeans, and also puts Hungary at the bottom of Europe.* The oldest Hungarians are the grumpiest. In 1991, 7% of those over 65 years old showed high satisfaction with their lives. By 2009, only 9% were in that category. All other Eastern Europeans showed far greater improvement over that 18-year period. Are things really that bad in Hungary? Or does Hungary simply have a bunch of jerks who like to whine and complain?

> *The number of jerks per capita in Hungary is two.*
> *— Géza Hofi, Hungarian comedian*

The negativity can overwhelm visitors. Alex recalled meeting a Greek tourist in an elevator. She came to Hungary to visit some friends, but she couldn't wait to go home. When Alex asked her why, she said with a heavy accent, "I don't like Hungary. I like life!"

It's ironic that Hungarians, who resist the *Eastern Europe* label more fiercely than most, conform so nicely with the negative stereotypes of an Eastern European: they're depressed, grumpy, corrupt, and prefer the communist economy. Krisztina said a better description of Hungary might be that it is "an Eastern European country that desperately wants to be Central European." Hungarians are so negative that they don't debate whether the glass is half empty or half full, but rather if the glass is even there!

All this raises three questions. Are Hungarians really as depressed as these polls show? If so, what are the deep underlying issues in the Hungarian psyche that make them feel this way? Does Hungary truly suck as much as Hungarians say it does?

Let's tackle these questions in order. First, the polls don't lie: there is indeed a high level of negativity in Hungary. Remember: the polls aren't saying that *all* Hungarians are negative; there is no poll where 100 percent of Hungarians agree on anything. The polls simply indicate that, compared to Europe (or the world), Hungarians tend to perceive their lives more negatively. My anecdotal evidence agrees: Hungarians I met tended to be highly critical of their world, and they said (without my coaxing) that their fellow citizens were often pessimistic too. Zsuzsa told me, "You are right about our national psyche, we are not an optimistic nation."

Why is that? What's up with Hungary's collective psyche? The answer is neither easy nor obvious. To answer this well we must examine Hungary's 1,000-year history, travel extensively, and meet lots of Hungarians. Let's do that now so that by the end of this chapter, we'll have our answer. Along the way, we'll also learn if life in Hungary truly sucks as much as Hungarians say it does.

Middle Ages were Hungary's good ages

The Middle Ages were a shitty time for Europe. After making so much progress under the Greek and Roman Empires, Europeans went backwards during the Middle Ages. There was the devastating Black Death, an oppressive and corrupt church, brutal serfdom, constant wars, ugly art, no democracy, few scientific advancements, and they didn't even have the cool wizards that they have in *The Hobbit*.

Despite the downsides of the Middle Ages, Hungarians glorify that period because back then Hungary was the big man on the European campus. Their golden age begins with Hungary's unforgettable birthday: December 25, 1000 AD. That's when King Stephen I became the first ruler of the Kingdom of Hungary, which controlled far more land than Hungary controls today. It was bigger than France and it was Europe's third most populous nation.

To understand how Hungary became so big, we must remember that a long time ago geographic features (such as seas, rivers, and mountains) created natural borders between tribes. Modern transportation makes us oblivious to these geographic barriers, but they were major obstacles 1,000 years ago. Tribes would usually expand until they hit a natural barrier. Adventurous ones and rebels would cross the barrier and start a new tribe on the other side. Over time, their languages and culture would evolve in different directions and perhaps become rivals. After many generations, the tribes would become as different as Austrians are to neighboring Italians.

Now look at a topographic map of Europe.[4] Hungary sits on a huge plain called the Carpathian Basin (or the Pannonian Basin). This area extends beyond Hungary's current borders and crosses into Slovakia, Romania, Serbia, Croatia, and Slovenia. That basin was Hungary's domain because a millennium ago Hungarians didn't just come to a random point in the plain and say, "Alright fellas, that's far enough. Let's let some other tribe take the land beyond there."

Instead, they would keep expanding until they hit a natural barrier like a mountain range, which is exactly what they did. They thrived in the plains and pushed into all the crevices they could, including the western slopes of the Carpathian mountain range. The natural southern border with the Slavs was the mighty Danube River and the nearby mountains. As Yves de Daruvar put it, "The physical map of Central Europe alone demonstrates more convincingly than words could do that essential unity of the ancient kingdom of Hungary which hits the eye at first glance."[5]

To teach me some medieval Hungarian history, Zsuzsa introduced me to her friend, János Molnár. He was born and lived 23 years in Hungary, but also lived in Algeria, Brazil, and Hawaii. He's a molecular biologist and electrical engineer with a passionate interest in Hungary's history, especially during the Middle Ages. János said, "What happened between 1100 to 950 years ago in the age from Árpád to King Saint Stephen is what defines us Hungarians. Every single Hungarian intellectual realized that the national identity of Hungarians and their desires, and morale is based on King Saint Stephen. Modify his memory, and you'll change the entire nation."

Although János may be overly dramatic, he's right that Hungarians are more nostalgic about the Middle Ages than most Europeans. When I asked János to describe what the world can learn from Hungarians, he spoke of their golden age, "Hungarians have given lots of things to the world. They were born from Hungarian culture, on Hungarian soil, with Hungarian religion: 1. Freedom of religion. 2. Freedom of rights. 3. Rights to foreign nationalities. 4. Legislation based on representation, the basis of modern democracies. What the modern world holds as most dear values: freedom and the workings of democracy were born from Hungarian culture."

I asked Alex, "Is that accurate?"

Alex replied, "Of course it is. We also invented water, porn, and Cheetos."

If you read enough history books, you'll learn that many people claim that their country created the innovations that János mentions. The reality is that democracy, capitalism, and freedom are as old as humans. Democracy started when a bunch of cavemen voted on whether to hunt for a mammoth or a deer. Capitalism started when one caveman offered two stone hammers for one lion carcass (and another offered to do the trade for just one hammer). Freedom and toleration started when a caveman leader said, "I don't give a shit who you are, what you do, or how you worship. Just don't poop in the cave and pay my monthly tax by giving me a rabbit."

Nevertheless, there is some truth in János's hyperbole: the Kingdom of Hungary was more socially liberal than its medieval neighbors. Hungary was unusually tolerant during an intolerant age.

The Renaissance was the rebirth of bad news

The Renaissance was perhaps the best period for Europeans. Minds were opening, free speech was tolerated, science advanced, plagues diminished, arts exploded, the monarchy loosened its tyrannical grip, and a few sailors discovered a New World. For the Hungarians, however, the Renaissance was the beginning of their slow decline. Beginning in the 1400s, Hungary's vast empire started weakening. By 1541, the Turkish army drove into Hungary like a dagger, stabbing its heart (Budapest), and breaking the kingdom into three pieces. For 150 years, Turks would rule much of Hungary.

Hungary had a glimmer of hope when the Turkish winning streak ended at the gates of Vienna in 1683. A multinational force, led by the Austrians, routed the Turks. These victories helped Hungarians become cocky again. In 1799, Charles-Marie, the Marquis de Salaberry, traveled to Istanbul via Hungary. He observed that it was easy to spot Hungarians because they have an "extreme prejudice in favor of their country which is, according to them, the first country of the world." That's funny coming from a Frenchman. He concluded, "If you hear men or women speaking thus, young people or old, these are Hungarians."[6]

The French people appear to have outstripped the rest of the human race by 2,000 years.

— Maximilien "the Incorruptible" Robespierre, who, in 1794, was guillotined by his fellow French people

Hungarian haughtiness diminished when they began to feel like Iraqis after the Iraq War: as the euphoria of kicking out the oppressive dictator faded, they grew tired of their new occupier. After helping to liberate Hungary, Austria overstayed its welcome. By 1848, Hungarians revolted and demanded independence. Although the revolution failed, 20 years later it would bear fruit in the Austria-Hungary Compromise. This Dual Monarchy was one of history's oddest couples.

Perhaps an even odder couple is Austria and Germany. They are so similar in so many ways, yet over the last 1,000 years they've rarely been united. They're a like a boy and a girl that everybody thinks should marry each other, but instead bicker like brats. Austria and Germany almost tied the knot in the mid-eighteenth century, but decided to kill each other instead. Austria had the possibility (for centuries) of hooking up with a perfectly compatible mate, one that spoke the same language and had a similar culture, but what did Austria do? It united with Hungary, a country with an alien language and culture. That's like the United States choosing to unite with Mexico instead of Canada. Austria, the rebellious lady, didn't want to marry the rich man who grew up next door. Instead, she chose the bad boy from the wrong side of the tracks. The marriage with Hungary lasted only 51 years. In geopolitical terms, that's about as long as a marriage with Zsa Zsa Gabor.

You never really know a man until you have divorced him.
— Zsa Zsa Gabor, Hungarian actress who married nine times

The Austria-Hungary Empire was huge: if it existed today, it would have 70 million citizens (versus 18 million if you combined today's Austria and Hungary). However, the empire was linguistically fragmented: only 24 percent preferred to speak German and 20 percent preferred Hungarian; the rest preferred speaking one of the other 10 official languages. The fragile union couldn't contain the rising nationalism, which culminated when a Serb murdered Austrian Archduke Ferdinand in Bosnia and Herzegovina, a territory within the empire. That assassination started WWI, which would ultimately ruin Hungary.

A brother-in-law named Austria

Hungary flourished during the Austria-Hungary Empire. Alex explains that era: "Everyone in Europe considered Hungarians a bunch of ignorant peasants with weird-ass Asiatic ancestry. Beginning in the mid-1800s, Hungarians began to build a society that sought to be every bit as good as Austria or France. They did it through the dint of their own hard work. They turned Kolozsvár into a major center of learning. Most of Budapest was built around 1900 (my own building turns 100 this year). Timişoara (which was Hungarian at that point) was the first city in Europe to have electric street lighting. Budapest had Europe's second underground metro system. They did a hell of a lot in a very short period of time. And that is to their credit."

"What were others doing?" I asked.

"The other ignorant peasants of the region, the Serbs, Croats, Romanians, Bulgarians, Slovaks, and Czechs also have accomplishments that they are very proud of. But speaking as objectively as possible, I don't think any of them managed to pull off what the Hungarians did between 1850 and 1920."

When evaluating the Austria-Hungary Empire, some Hungarians have a double standard: they give little credit to Austria for the positive side of their partnership, but they blame Austria for anything negative (especially the oppression of minorities and getting involved in WWI). Austria was Hungary's big brother for hundreds of years, including during the Dual Monarchy, which was never an equal partnership. Krisztina told me, "We actually call Austrians our 'brother-in-laws,' which seems to be quite accurate in a way that we regard them at least as interfering as a brother-in-law can be. Moreover, long ago it was about as hard to get rid of the Austrians as to get rid of your brother-in-law."

It's wrong to blame everything on Austria and it's also wrong to not give Austria some credit for Hungary's progress. For 235 years Austria had substantial control over Hungary's affairs. They weren't as dominant as the Turks were for 150 years, but they had the upper hand. However, they weren't all-powerful; Hungary usually chose to follow Austria's lead. Hungary could have resisted Austria's idea of getting involved in WWI just like they resisted Austria in 1848. János was right when he told me that Hungarians weren't thrilled about WWI. A popular Hungarian saying right before WWI was, "If Germany loses, we lose too. If Germany wins though, we're lost." In the end, Hungary decided to be a team player and went along with Austria. It would pay dearly for that mistake. As we will now see, Hungary would become but a shadow of its former self.

Hungary's defining moment: The Treaty of Trianon of 1920

It's impossible to understand Hungary's negative national psyche without understanding a treaty you've probably never heard of. László Marácz wrote that the treaty was a "millennial crime" and "one of the most violent peace treaties of recent history."[7] János told me, "It was the most anti-humanitarian treaty in the twentieth century ever forced upon a country." Zsuzsa said, "It is truly one of the saddest chapters in modern European history." She added, it "was the greatest injustice and something that millions still suffer from." George Roux said that it "was punishment the like of which has rarely been meted out to a nation in the course of history." Yves de Daruvar wrote that "the Treaty of Trianon is probably one of the most terribly cruel treaties of history."[8] Yikes. Sounds rough. What the hell was it?

The Grand Trianon is a beautiful baroque palace in Versailles, France. For Hungarians, however, it's the site of an evil crime. It was there, on June 4, 1920, that Hungary signed a treaty that would cut it to pieces. With a pen stroke, *Hungary lost a whopping 72 percent of its territory.* As a result, it lost: (1) 64 percent of its inhabitants, (2) half of its 10 biggest cities, (3) its sea access, (4) two-thirds of the banking institutions, (5) over 84 percent of its timber and iron, and (6) all its precious metal mines. It was a bad day for Hungary.

Where did all those resources go? Most of it got split between Czechoslovakia, Romania, and Yugoslavia, while smaller parts went to Austria, Poland, and Italy. By losing nearly three-fourths of their land, the number of Hungarian citizens collapsed from 21 million to 7.6 million overnight. More importantly, about a third of the ethnic Hungarians didn't just wake up on the wrong side of the bed, they woke up in another country.

Over 400,000 Hungarian refugees fled from their new countries to find shelter in what was left of their shrunken motherland. János wrote to me, "Here's what happened after Trianon: many Hungarians in the lost territories were deported. Some survived deportation (like my great-grandparents) and some not. They would stop trains next to marshes and shoot tens of thousands—including women and children. My great-grandparents were very wealthy with a huge farm in Slovakia, and everything was taken away. They had half an hour to say goodbye to relatives and pack up. All they could carry was some food and clothes."

To put the scale of Hungary's humiliation into my Californian brain, Zsuzsa said, "Imagine if they proclaimed that California is to be a part of Mexico and the Mexican government forbids the use of English, forcefully relocates English speakers to all-Mexican areas so they would assimilate, flood entire villages to eradicate them, close English-speaking schools and jail anyone who would dare speak English aloud. It's just a taste of what millions of Hungarians had to suffer after Trianon."

In his book, *Hungarian Revival,* László Marácz says that Trianon was a tragedy that hurt everyone: "For Hungarians Trianon was traumatic because it led to humiliation and to the 'fragmentation' of their country. For other peoples Trianon constitutes a psychosis because they . . .

are plagued by the fear that one day the Hungarians will band together and claim the right to self-determination. . . ."[9]

The new borders severed industries and transportation links. Trade collapsed to five percent of its prewar level. Endless refugees strained an already broken economy. The treaty limited Hungary's army to 35,000 men, which wasn't enough to help maintain law and order. Daruvar describes Hungary's butchering: "It is thus that today the Hungarian lowlands, artificially separated from their mountain perimeter and the Transylvanian highlands survive as but a shapeless torso whose limbs have been severed . . . those limbs separated at Trianon from Hungary's millenary body have also cruelly suffered ever since from that monstrous dissection."[10]

Why did Trianon happen?

Were the guys at Trianon smoking some strange weed? Probably, but one reason for Trianon's outcome was that WWI peace treaties were designed to punish the losers (Germany, Austria-Hungary, Bulgaria, and the Turkish Empire). That meant taking away some of their territory and slapping them with heavy war reparations. The concept was: cripple them so they don't get any bright ideas about starting another world war. (Hey, it sounded like a good idea at the time.) As a result, after WWI, Germany lost 13 percent of its territory and Bulgaria lost 10 percent. But why did Hungary get the 72 percent deal? Alex bluntly points out the iniquity: "WWI did not have good guys and bad guys, like WWII did. It only had side A and side B, both of whom were equally fucked up. The Trianon Treaty wasn't just punitive, it also lacked any sense of justice. No country—not even Germany—lost proportionally so much territory as Hungary."

However, punishing Hungary wasn't the only reason for Trianon's outcome; another reason was that the Allies had to fulfill a promise. When France and Britain were getting their butts kicked during WWI, they begged Romania to join their team. In exchange, they promised to give Romania the land they coveted. Romania signed up and got nailed: nine percent of Romania (748,000 souls) died in WWI. Only Serbia (16%) and the Turkish Empire (14%) lost a higher percentage of their population during WWI. (Austria-Hungary lost 3%.) Romania's sacrifice, plus the Allies' failure to support Romania during the war as they had promised, added to a sense of guilt that "we owe them one."

The Allies had promised Romania all of Hungary's land east of the Tisza River (which today is well inside Hungary). It was unrealistic to give them that much land, so they tried to compromise. While the Trianon Treaty was being drafted, Romania sent a strong message that it didn't want to be shortchanged: it drove its army all the way into Budapest. They only backed down when the Allies assured them that they would get a big chunk of Hungary called Transylvania. It was less than what Romania had been promised, but it was still horrible for Hungary: Transylvania was home to two million Hungarians whose ancestors first settled there over 1,000 years ago. Under Romanian rule, these Hungarians became abused, second-class citizens.

Alex brings up another point: "There's no question that the Allies promised Romania Transylvania and eastern Hungary. But did they have to fork over southern Slovakia and the northern tip of Serbia too? And why on earth did they give Burgenland to *Austria*—an enemy power allied with Germany?"

The theory behind those giveaways was that Trianon was trying to fulfill the objectives outlined in US President Woodrow Wilson's 14 Points, which proclaimed that post-WWI borders ought to follow ethnic lines. Slavs lived in Hungary, so they should get their piece of the Hungarian pie. Burgenland had many Austrians, so Austria got it. However, given that 3.4 million Hungarians found themselves outside their country, it seems that Trianon did a lousy job at following Wilson's principle of self-determination.

Finally, there was the communist threat. In the post-WWI turmoil, a commie named Béla Kun took control of Hungary. France saw him as a regional threat. Thus, Kun's rise gave one more reason for Trianon's harsh judgment: crush Hungary to crush communism. János told me, "Without the communist agent Béla Kun (who clearly had nothing to do with the Hungarian nation), the Treaty of Trianon would have no grounds for dividing the country into five parts."

Alex said, "I'm not sure if János is trying to disqualify Kun as a Hungarian because he was a Jew, or because he was an ally of Lenin. Kun was a Hungarian. He fought for Hungary in WWI and got taken as a prisoner of war by the Russians. They managed to turn him into a communist. He was able to seize power after the war because every single other political leader cut and ran. Like every communist, he was a disaster. In fact, Kun's lack of foreskin gave a major boost to the silly Jewish-Bolshevist conspiracy theory."

János explains, "I meant that he did not stand for Hungarian values, nor tradition. He was a communist—which ideology is extremely removed from the Hungarian culture and nation. He spoke Hungarian? Well, there are loads of people who speak several languages well enough. His Hungarian was not perfect, sounded as if he learned it as a second language. There is a big difference of being a president of a nation and being one of the nation."

Krisztina said, "I don't like how some people 'reserve' Hungarianness for themselves, saying that everyone who disagrees with him is communist, Jewish and above all, the enemy of the nation. There are good Hungarians, heroic Hungarians, great Hungarians—and there are Hungarians who make bad things, commit crimes and use their powers to cause misery to people. These are all Hungarians and if there is such thing as 'collective responsibility' then we do have to accept this. One of the great poets of the Hungarian nation, Miklós Radnóti, wrote in his very beautiful patriotic poem *"Nem tudhatom"* ("I Cannot Know"): *'Hisz bűnösök vagyunk mi, akár a többi nép / s tudjuk miben vétkeztünk, mikor, hol és mikép'* ('For we are guilty too, as others are / knowing full-well when and how and why we've sinned so far.')."

Alex said, "Around 20 years ago, I used to be amused by blacks who declared that Clarence Thomas was not really black. Hungary has got the same deal going on—whenever they disagree someone, they seek to disqualify him as Hungarian. Kun was an idiot and his policies were disastrous, short-lived though they were. What I do know is: no matter which way you slice the pie, he was Hungarian."

Eventually, a Hungarian navy admiral kicked Kun out, but it was too late. The Trianon authors had already determined Hungary's fate. By June 1920, there was little the admiral could do except sign on the dotted line. As Hungarians say: for the next 24 years, Hungary would be a kingdom without a king, ruled by an admiral without a fleet, in a country without a coastline.

Why all the fuss over Trianon today?

The Trianon trauma humiliated Hungary. However, I couldn't understand why so many Hungarians were still passionately talking about it today, nearly a century later. It's as if it had happened yesterday. Hungarians admit they're obsessed: a Facebook group called "You know you're Hungarian . . ." includes this entry: ". . . when any foreigner's passing mention of Transylvania will set off a 20-minute rant about the Treaty of Trianon." That's not accurate: it's more like a 60-minute rant.

After listening to a few rants, I did my best to avoid talking about history, but Hungarians would bring Trianon up anyway. For example, when I asked a Hungarian named Kálmán for advice about visiting Bosnia, he mentioned that "Bosnians don't like Hungarians because we used to rule them. But that was before Trianon." When I mentioned to Zsuzsa that I was going to Romania in a month, Zsuzsa said, "Yeah, much of Romania used to be part of Hungary."

This was weird. Europeans might talk about WWII, but they bring up WWI as often as they bring up their admiration for American culture. As usual, we have to ask: why are Hungarians different? Many countries get downsized after wars. While Hungary's chopping was unusual, it's also unusual that the issue is still such a hot topic after a nearly century.

One reason why Hungarians bring up the nearly 100-year-old news of Trianon every five minutes is that it's somewhat fresh news for them. During the communist era, Hungarians weren't taught about it. Zsuzsa said, "There was maybe one sentence in our school history books about how come Hungary is a fraction of its former size. We knew nothing. You grow up and realize, much you have been taught is a lie."

In the lovely Hungarian town of Szeged, I couchsurfed with Gyöngyi Tóth. She was unusual because she never brought up Trianon during the two days I spent at her place. Later, I asked her why. She said, "With foreigners it's not the topic I generally start a conversation with. Among Hungarians it's a more frequent thing to talk about."

Since Gyöngyi was born in 1986, I asked her to ask her parents if communists had brushed Trianon under the carpet. She said, "My parents told me that in schools really little was taught about Trianon, and in the family it wasn't a common thing to talk about. It was more a painful fact. This is a really interesting cultural phenomena that affects today's Hungarians. More and more books have been written about it since the change of regime in 1989. My grandparents told me that after Trianon, Hungary had a saying to keep the memory of Trianon alive."

> Csonka Magyarország nem ország, egész Magyarország mennyország
> — *Hungarian saying meaning, "Truncated Hungary is not a country, greater Hungary is heaven."*

According to the Encyclopedia Britannica, communists "forbade even mentioning this question during the three decades following World War II." Therefore, after so many years of whispering about Trianon, Hungarians exploded with discussions after 1989 and haven't shut up since.

Although there are positive aspects of discussing Trianon *ad infinitum,* the nationwide obsession has been detrimental to Hungary's soul. It's a big reason behind their frustrated self-esteem as well as their depressed and melancholy outlook. Imagine if your country were downsized in a similar way. You'd feel negativity in the air too. However, whenever people discuss an issue like Trianon mainly amongst themselves, myths develop. These myths exaggerate the Trianon trauma and make Hungarians even more depressed than they need to be. Therefore, if you're ever at a cocktail party stuck with a Hungarian who is blabbing endlessly about Trianon, it's best to be armed with several myth-busting facts.

The top 18 myths of Trianon and Greater Hungary

I wish we could ignore Trianon, but it plays such an important role in the collective Hungarian psyche that we must understand it well if we wish to understand Hungarians. It explains much of why Hungary is the most depressed and bitter nation in Europe. Moreover, *Trianon also holds the key to liberating Hungary from its depressive burden. Once Hungarians debunk their myths, then Hungary can rise again.*

Some of these myths are widely believed, while others have only a small (but significant) following. Although I quote my Hungarian friends often, you'll hear similar views from Hungarians everywhere, from the coffee shop to the Internet. Deep down inside, Hungarians often know that something is just a myth, but they perpetuate it by only telling you (or themselves) half the story. Like many myths, there's a bit of truth in them. Let's separate fact from fiction in the 18 myths.

Myth #1: Hungary basically controlled Greater Hungary for the last 1,000 years. Assuming that Hungary was effectively an Austrian puppet (which is what Hungarians usually argue when they explain why they got involved in WWI and oppressed their minorities), then Hungarians haven't really controlled Greater Hungary for the last 500 years. János confirmed this when he told me that "Hungary has been occupied since 1541, living under foreign rule for five centuries. Compared to the Tatar, the Turkish, Habsburg terror, the current hardships are but a bite of a fly. Hungarians had ample practice how to survive such things in the last 500 years."

Given that Hungary hasn't controlled the Trianon lands for 500 years, it's tough to argue that it's "theirs." Hungarians wouldn't like it if Poland, Lithuania, and Turkey were claiming large tracts of European lands as "theirs" just because they ruled them for a few centuries hundreds of years ago.

Myth #2: Medieval Hungary is tightly related to today's Hungary. It's tempting to look at political maps of 1100 or 1400 and believe that Hungary's Kingdom was a united nation just like Hungary is today. However, the kingdoms during the Middle Ages didn't work that way. For example, there was no common language: Hungarian nobles spoke Latin or a Germanic tongue, while their peasants spoke one of the many Hungarian, Slavic, or Romanian dialects. Think of medieval Hungary like the EU is today: a variety of languages and cultures mixed together in a loose confederation, highly decentralized, but with a common currency. If Hungary today is the United States, then Hungary in the Middle Ages is the EU. This was true for most kingdoms in the Middle Ages—for instance, probably the only common word in medieval Italy was *pizza.*

Without linguistic unity, there was hardly any political or national unity like we know today. Instead, the kingdoms were just a collection of fiefdoms. People had more solidarity with their village and their ruling nobles than with their kingdom. There was no national consciousness, which didn't start until the 1800s when technology let each nation standardize their language and mass communication began. Today's nationalists love to draw a direct connection from ancient times to the present, but such a connection is far feebler than most people imagine.

Hungarians resist this fact because it weakens their Greater Hungary claims further: if Hungary didn't control Greater Hungary for the last 500 years, and if the time before that is largely irrelevant because it was a different world, then how credible are their Trianon claims today?

Myth #3: Trianon was an unprecedented treaty. As we saw earlier, Hungarians wail about Trianon's cruel and unusual punishment. Zsuzsa rhetorically asked me, "Did Germany, Italy or Japan lose two-thirds of their territory? Germany did lose parts, but not nearly the scope of what Hungary did."

For all of human history, the standard procedure after you lose a war is to fork over some or all your territory to the winner(s). If you're unwilling to do that, then don't lay down your weapons, and keep fighting to the death. However, eventually countries prefer to trade land for lives. It's War 101. Back in the good old empire-building days, taking only two-thirds of an enemy's land would be wildly generous. When Julius Caesar, Alexander the Great, or US President James Monroe conquered your nation, you lost 100 percent of your land. You became just another state in a vast empire. It's a cruel question, but why aren't Hungarians grateful that the Allies didn't swallow their entire country?

Hungarians need to talk to Poles about the late 1700s. As we saw, Poland was dismembered in three phases, disappearing completely in the last. Talk to all of the nations throughout the world that have lost 100 percent of their territory when empire builders swallowed them whole. Or chat with Mexico, which lost 55 percent of its land to the US in 1848. "Yeah, but those were other times!" cry Hungarians. Really?

After WWI, Hungary lost 72 percent of its land and 63 percent of its people. Was it alone? At the same time Austria lost 73 percent of its territory and 78 percent of its population; the Turkish Empire lost 62 percent and 40 percent, respectively. Hungarians sometimes act like they were the only country that was substantially downsized after WWI. That's a myth.

Hungarians will quickly argue that Austrians and Turks lost *occupied* land, whereas Hungarians lost *their* land—land that they weren't "occupying." We'll examine this claim later, but let's remember that Austrians and Turks were occupying those lands for centuries. How many years does one have to occupy a land before one can claim it's "theirs?" If the US suddenly lost 73 percent of its land to the Native American nations, would Hungarians say that it doesn't compare to Hungary's loss? Perhaps some Hungarians would say, "That was never really America's land anyway, because you guys were occupying Native American land for only a few hundred years."

Alex addressed a related Hungarian claim, "Was the Treaty of Trianon illegal? Today, you might be able to make the argument, but I'm not sure international law really existed to that extent in 1921. The League of Nations had only just started. There were certain articles of international law, but it was all very weak and nobody paid much attention to it."

Finally, for those who believe that the brutal downsizing of a country is a war custom of a bygone era, talk to the 14 ex-Soviet republics. Estonia, Latvia, Lithuania and other nations lost 100 percent of their lands when the USSR swallowed them whole after WWII. Although some of those nations don't have as long of a history as Hungary, calling Trianon "unprecedented" or "uniquely cruel" is a hyperbole. This doesn't mean Trianon was fair, but it certainly wasn't the worst treaty ever.

Myth #4: Austria didn't lose much land after WWI. Zsuzsa told me, "It is true that Hungary had no say in entering the war because it was under Austrian rule. As the result of the war, Austria did not lose much." János concurred, "The real culprit got away: Austria even gained territories at the end of WWI, even though it was the starter of the WWI!"

Alex responded, "Huh? First of all, there never was a nation of Austria before World War I, per se. It was only the Habsburg lands. They stretched from Liechtenstein to what is now Ukraine. How the fuck is that not losing territory?"

Most Hungarians don't believe that Austria gained more land than it lost, but they are bitter that Austria gained Burgenland at Hungary's expense. However, that Trianon decree wasn't as crazy as it seems: Burgenland was 75 percent Austrian and only nine percent Hungarian. Given the post-WWI goal of self-determination, it wasn't completely illogical to give Austria Burgenland.

In short, the myth that Austria gained land only tells half the story. Yes, it did gain Burgenland from Hungary, a land heavily dominated by Austrians. However, Austria lost just as much land as Hungary overall. The Treaty of Saint-Germain-en-Laye doled out 73 percent of Austrian land to Czechoslovakia, Italy, Poland, Romania, and Yugoslavia.[11]

Myth #5: Hungary lost two-thirds of their people after Trianon. Yes, they lost two-thirds of their *population*, but over half of those people were not ethnic Hungarians. They were mostly Slavs and Romanians who generally didn't feel Hungarian or want to remain in the country. The reality is that about *one-third* of Hungarians found themselves outside their country. A third is still a lot, but it's *half* of the often-cited and misleading two-thirds figure.

Myth #6: Trianon hurt everyone, not just Hungarians. A few Hungarians will whip out this argument when they sense that you're getting tired of their self-centered viewpoint. The idea is: "It's not all about us! Trianon screwed everyone!" For example, János told me that the treaty is "a major act of crime against all of Central Europe."

If Trianon was such a bad deal for non-Hungarians, then why didn't they reverse it? They certainly would have Hungarians supporting that decision. If life in Romania, for example, was so much better under Hungary, then why didn't the Romanians join with the local Hungarians to undo Trianon? They could reverse it tomorrow if non-Hungarians were also bitter about it.

Here's the cold reality: life under Hungary was better in some ways, but worse in others. The economies were better under Hungary, but the local self-esteem was lower. An objective Romanian might be like a Mexican today; tell a Mexican, "You know, you'd be better off if you became part of the USA. Americans would run your economy and government more efficiently and you could enjoy all the civil rights you have today, schools, languages, you name it."

The Mexican would reply, "*Señor Gringo,* you're right, but I'd rather be under my dysfunctional, corrupt government and our incompetent economic bureaucrats than be under the flag of non-Mexicans. My country may have problems, but at least it's *my* country!"

As bad as things have been, Romanians would have said something similar to Hungarians in the last 100 years: "Thanks, but no thanks."

Myth #7: Hungary lost 90 percent of its resources. János wrote to me that, "The 1910 map shows somewhat that 40 percent of Hungarian ethnicities were cut off from their motherland. However, what does not show on the map is that approximately 90 percent of Hungary's natural resources were taken away. This equals the destruction of economy and industry in every area: 60 percent of the Hungarian population left with 10 percent of the economy after Trianon! (For the mainland Hungarians this was the real tragedy.)"

Not exactly. First, 33% of Hungarians were cut off, not 40%. Second, when you lose 72% of your land, you will (assuming an evenly spread distribution) lose 72% of your resources. Although Hungary lost 84% of its timber and iron and 100% of its precious metal mines, by most other economic measures its losses were *less* than 72%. That's because, as you might expect, the best parts of Hungary's economy were in its core. Hence, it lost "only" 10% of its engineering and printing industry, 50% of its 10 biggest cities, 55% of its industrial plants, 61% of its arable land, and about 64% of its railroads and hard surface roads. All these loses, while devastating, were disproportionally in Hungary's favor and far from the 90% figure sometimes claimed. In conclusion, it was the Trianon lands, not Hungary, that got less than their "fair share."[12]

That 90% number comes from what I call *hysteria inflation*. Some Hungarian screams, "We lost 75% of our resources!" Later another says, "Did you know we lost 80% of resources!?" With enough time, gossip, and myth-building, we get to 90%. Fortunately, there's no idiot claiming that they lost 100% of their resources.

Myth #8: Trianon killed the economies of Hungary and its neighbors. János asserted, "*All of Central Europe suffered* a damage that destroyed at least a century of development and education." Although "a century" is an exaggeration, János is right that Central Europe suffered after Trianon. But was that Trianon's fault?

In a related issue, Gyöngyi told me that Trianon was "a big economical crush. For example, in my town the mill industry was important. The grains came from Vojvodina (northern Serbia), which was a big agricultural center. Obviously now the mills are just trash there, not used for ages. But this is just one tiny bit, Trianon is also the reason why the train system of the country now is so fucked. That's why from Novi Sad to Szeged you can hardly arrive in five hours, when it is the same distance between Szeged and Budapest. Or why when you go from Pécs to Szeged, you must go through Budapest, which is nonsense. It's because the infrastructure was completely smashed."

Hungary's seemingly illogical and inefficient railway links aren't all Trianon's fault. Just buy a plane ticket from Florida to Texas; your plane may make a stop in Chicago. Railway links throughout the world also work on a hub system that may result in a circuitous journey. Transportation companies do this because it's economically efficient for them. Trianon didn't block a straight, flat route between Pécs and Szeged, but it's more fun to blame Trianon.

Gyöngyi is right that going between Novi Sad (Serbia) and Szeged takes forever. Is that Trianon's fault? Let's find out. Back when Hungary was big, the transportation infrastructure was designed for the empire. Suddenly, after Trianon, railway lines and roads went into foreign countries with border checkpoints (or closed borders), thereby disrupting commerce that used to go unimpeded. After WWI, a shocking 95 percent of commerce vanished. On the other hand, in war-ravaged countries, postwar commerce always lags behind its prewar commerce. War screws up everything and it takes time to get back in gear.

Nevertheless, here's the important question—who should get the blame for the diminished trade: the architects of the Treaty of Trianon or the xenophobic, nationalistic politicians who ran the Central European countries after the war? These politicians could have said, "Although we now have borders between us, let's create a free-trade zone, so commerce can flow as easily as it did during the Austria-Hungary Empire." Instead, they became protectionists. It's the country leaders who shot themselves in the foot, not the writers of the treaty.

Borders don't destroy economies. There are borders around the small countries of Lichtenstein, Switzerland, and Luxembourg, but on a per capita basis, they're all among the top 10 richest nations in the world. They wouldn't be so rich if their economies were closed like North Korea.

Therefore, the real mistake that the Trianon authors made wasn't so much the new borders, but rather that they didn't mandate a free-trade zone between the new entities. It's a pity because it was point number three in Wilson's 14 Points: "The removal, so far as possible, of all economic barriers and the establishment of an equality of trade conditions among all the nations consenting to the peace and associating themselves for its maintenance."

Still, it's wrong to place all the blame for the lack of free trade on the Trianon authors. *There was nothing stopping Hungarian, Austrian, Romanian, and Slavic politicians from forming a free-trade zone themselves.* Their own moronic protectionist leaders bear much of the blame for their countries' economic woes. Their stupid fantasy of being self-sufficient and "protecting the jobs at home" hurt everyone, including themselves. Had they encouraged free trade and passport-free travel, businesses would have quickly revived and flourished beyond their prewar levels. Trains would go from Szeged and Novi Sad as fast as they did in Greater Hungary. The only real new burden would be having to exchange money to trade with the new Trianon areas. Consider the US: after America's Revolutionary War, commerce between England and America quickly picked up again; former enemies did business once more. Hungary and its Trianon orphans could have done the same thing, but they didn't and that's mostly their own fault.

Myth #9: Hungary treated its minorities well. Yves de Daruvar's book, *The Tragic Fate of Hungary: A Country Carved-up Alive at Trianon,* sums up this belief: "The oppression suffered by the minorities in the old Kingdom of Hungary is no more than a myth. On the contrary, the Hungarians became eventually the victims of a perhaps excessive liberalism shown in treating their national minorities throughout the centuries."[13]

The myth that Hungarians treated its minorities well has some truth to it. No matter what period of time you examine, Hungary has usually been better than its neighbors at dealing with minorities. However, given some of Hungary's neighbors, that's not saying much. The truth is that Hungary didn't always treat their minorities well and that they were at their worst in the 50 years leading up to Trianon.

László Marácz, who usually argues the pro-Hungarian perspective, admits, "It is true that after 1870 dualist Hungary had embarked on an ambitious policy of Magyarization [Hungarization]."[14] For example, Hungary had a Nationalities Law that supposedly protected other languages, but Hungarian leaders ignored it. Instead, they made Hungarian the sole language for administration and justice (similar to the Slovak Language Law that Hungarians are complaining about today). Aside from the low-level businesses and social events, everything had to be in Hungarian.

Let's look at schools. After 1900, Hungarians withdrew the autonomy of minority church schools. Primary schools were disproportionately Hungarian. From 1880 to 1913, Hungary closed half of the minority language schools and doubled the Hungarian-only schools. In 1913, about half of Hungary was ethnically Hungarian, yet 80 percent of the primary schools were Hungarian. The remaining primary schools were not proportional to the populations (e.g., less than two percent of primary schools were Slovak and Serbian, which was totally out of line with their demographics). Secondary schools were worse: *all secondary education was in Hungarian*. Therefore, about half of Greater Hungary had to send their kids to secondary schools in their non-native tongue, even though they had been living in their areas for many generations.

In the 50 years before Trianon, only the wealthiest six percent could vote. Since nearly all the rich at that time were either Hungarians, Germans, or Jews, that meant other minorities could not vote. Despite all their ethnicities, minority members held only six of the 386 seats in Parliament. Imagine you're a Slav in Hungary in 1910 and your Slavic neighbors are saying, "Dude, why do you let those Hungarians rule you? You can't even vote! Join us Slavs!"

Yves de Daruvar stupidly defends Hungary by saying, "If Hungary had really oppressed its minorities, they would have disappeared long ago." Imagine the Turks saying: "If we had really oppressed the Hungarians, they would have disappeared long ago."

By not giving their minorities the autonomy and respect they desired, Hungary sowed the seeds of Trianon. Frustrated minorities not only wanted independence from Hungarians, but also vengeance against them. We can't fault the Hungarians who don't see this. Hungarians don't spend much time learning about how their ancestors were jerks to the minorities among them for the same reason we Americans don't spend much time learning how we were assholes to the Native Americans: people don't like to remember that their great-grandparents were bastards.

Myth #10: Hungarians make up the majority of Transylvania. Hungarians believe this myth because it justifies their Transylvanian claim. However, this myth has not been true for hundreds of years.

But don't take my word for it, let's look at the censuses that Hungary itself conducted. According to Hungary's 1869 Transylvania census, *only a quarter of the population was Hungarian* while six in 10 were Romanians. By 1910, Hungarization helped shift the numbers to 31.7 percent Hungarian and 55 percent Romanian. *Bottom line: between 1869 and 2011, Hungarians were usually in the 20 to 32 percent range in Transylvania.* Before 1869, there's no good evidence that Hungarians were the majority there. Perhaps they were five centuries ago, but that's not only hard to prove, it's so long ago that it hardly matters.

Hungarians love to repeat László Marácz's observation that after Trianon "over three million Hungarians found themselves living in successor states. Seven out of every twenty ethnic Magyars [i.e., Hungarians] ended up in one or other of the successor states where they were subject to foreign rule."[15] That's unfortunate, but why was the pre-Trianon border any better? Under Greater Hungary, nearly seven in 20 Romanians and nearly all Slovaks felt under foreign rule. Was that better? A Hungarian may say, "Yes, it's fairer to leave it the way it's always been." Meanwhile, a Romanian or Slovak may say, "No, the border favored Hungary for 1,000 years, now it's our turn. Let's have the border favor us for the next 1,000 years."

In conclusion, according to Hungary's own statistics (not Romanian propaganda), Romanians have been the majority in Transylvania for the last few hundred years.[16] Given that, Trianon's dictate to give Transylvania to Romania doesn't seem that absurd or immoral.

Not surprisingly, this myth has some truth in it: Hungarians *are* the majority in a large area in Transylvania called *Székelyföld* (Székely Land). According to the 2002 census, 612,043 Hungarians live there, making up 75% of the population. Hungarians love to cite higher numbers, so they cherry-pick towns with high Hungarian presence. I'll mislead you by doing the same. The Székely Land town names are tongue twisters whether they are in Romanian (or Hungarian). Hungarians are 75% of Sfântu Gheorghe (Sepsiszentgyörgy), 81% of Miercurea-Ciuc (Csíkszereda), 88% of Gheorgheni (Gyergyószentmiklós), 95% of Cristuru Secuiesc (Székelykeresztúr), and 96% of Odorheiu Secuiesc (Székelyudvarhely). I propose a simple solution to dealing with the Székely Land: whoever comes up with easier-to-pronounce town names gets to keep the land.

Focusing on Székely Land doesn't change the reality that Transylvania hasn't had a Hungarian majority for centuries, nor does it prove that Trianon was wildly wrong to give Transylvania to Romania.

Myth #11: Hungarians in Transylvania are just like regular Hungarians. The best example of a high concentration of Hungarians living outside of Hungary are the ones who live in the middle of Romania. What's fascinating is that some of these Hungarians don't even consider themselves Hungarian. They prefer the label *Székely*.

Alex explains, "Székelys have a distinct dialect of Hungarian and a distinct culture. In fact, up until WWI, Székelys were usually classified as a separate ethnic group. They are a sort of 'proto-Hungarian,' which is one reason why the Hungarians consider Transylvania to be the cradle of their civilization. Székelys are responsible for most of the art and lacework that is today considered 'Hungarian.'"

Hungarians admire the Székely. Zsuzsa gushed, "I am pretty much in awe of Transylvanian Hungarians. Actually kinda make me feel inferior, as their national identity seems to come from a much deeper place."

János said, "The Székely of Csík are renowned to be the toughest of the Hungarians. Many say that their Hungarian souls burn with the strongest flame. They are the most Hungarians of all Hungarians, they still have Hungarian traditions alive, while Hungarians in Hungary are but shadows of Hungarians, who have forgotten almost everything—they are Hungarians only in their language."

Krisztina echoed the reverence many Hungarians have for the Székely when she said, "If you ask any Hungarian about his thoughts on Slovakia, Romania, or Serbia, the answer will most probably be negative. I'm sure you have heard of the Treaty of Trianon, which is still a sore point for most Hungarians. Reactions on it may be anything between 'we want everything back' to 'these countries must change their discriminative minority policy.' What is sure—those towns and castles over there [in Transylvania] were all built under the Kingdom of Hungary and often, Hungarians from there are more faithful keeping their hundreds of years old traditions than us from present day Hungary."

I asked Krisztina, "What do you think Romanians think of Transylvania?"

She said, "Of course, Romanians have a totally opposite opinion on this subject than we do. For example, they think that Transylvania is an ancient Romanian land. In this case, like many other cases, the answer might be somewhere between the two extremes and I suppose neither of our history books are 100 percent right on the issue."

Amen. *So are the Hungarians in Transylvania just like regular Hungarians or is that a myth?* Although it's not really a myth, it's clear that the Székely are in a class by themselves. They've always been somewhat independent of Hungary's core. Because of this, how much claim does Hungary have over them? *Was it really so evil that Trianon separated the Székely from Hungary given that their connection was never super strong?* Perhaps. Székelys would certainly prefer being under Hungary than Romania; however, what's perhaps even more important to them is *autonomy*. Therefore, given that Transylvania was mostly Romanian,

Trianon's real mistake wasn't giving that land to Romania, but not guaranteeing Székely autonomy within it.

We'll examine the Székely more in the Romania chapter, but it is not surprising that Székelys have a special Hungarian accent. After centuries of being surrounded by Romanians, they not only speak Romanian, but they picked up a Romanian habit of pronouncing long Hungarian vowels in a short way. Doing this in Hungarian can change the meaning of the word. Still, most Hungarians understand them. Let's end with a Székely joke:

> *An old Székely man goes to a language school to learn Aramaic. The teacher asks him, "But at your age, why do you want to learn Aramaic?"*
>
> *"Because if I go to heaven, I could talk to Jesus Christ."*
>
> *"But what happens if you go to hell?"*
>
> *"That's no problem," he answers. "I already speak Romanian."*

Myth #12: Hungarians were definitely in Transylvania before Romanians. Alex addresses this myth: "These records are disputed—what is 100 percent clear is that the Székelys were in Transylvania long before the Magyars arrived, long before Saint Stephen began proselytizing in 1000 AD. Were Romanians in Transylvania before the Magyars arrived? Clearly. Were they there before the Székelys arrived? Almost definitely. The question is, who was a majority, when? Did the Romanians ever form a majority in Transylvania before the Turks? There is some evidence saying they did, there is some evidence saying they didn't."

I said, "Many of your countrymen would burn your Hungarian passport for saying that Romanians were in Transylvania before Hungarians. Let's say you're wrong. Does any of this even matter?"

"No. This whole 'who's on first' argument is shit. If it were legitimate, then the Delaware Indians would have the right to Manhattan. The Bulgarians would have the right to Albania. The Greeks would have the right to northern Egypt. And heterosexuals would have the right to San Francisco."

Myth #13: Hungarians were the majority in Greater Hungary. When I looked at maps as a boy, I assumed that each country's borders neatly corresponded with the ethnic and linguistic makeup of the region and that every country was homogeneous. I imagined that once you crossed the border from Italy to Austria, for example, the people and languages would instantly change, with no sloppy transition. In my little brain, China was made up only of Chinese, Iran was 99 percent Iranian, and the UK was comprised exclusively of polite English gentlemen.

The breakup of the USSR taught me reality. When it broke up, it's as if someone had lifted the Soviet skirt and revealed the dirty details that were hidden underneath. What seemed like one homogeneous, united country was actually a patchwork of ethnicities, nations, religions, and languages. This is true of many countries—you don't learn this about the UK until you tell a Scottish man that he's English.

Nationalistic Hungarians make the same mistake I made as a boy when they look at maps of Greater Hungary. A guy in Budapest will assume that because the borders encompassed large parts of Slovakia, Serbia, Romania, and other places, that the people within those borders must have been mostly Hungarian. More open-minded Hungarians intellectually realize that there were many minorities within Hungary, but they'll sometimes imply that Hungarians were basically the majority nearly everywhere. The fact that there still are regions today with a majority of Hungarians (e.g., southern Slovakia and parts of Romania) "proves" to them that they were once dominant everywhere. They believe these Hungarians are the remnants of a Hungarian majority that was everywhere. If Hungarians are no longer the majority in their lost lands, then that also "proves" that Hungarians were victims of ethnic cleansing. Let's tackle this headache.

First, a quick demographic summary. Prior to the Turks, *in the 1400s, Hungarians made up roughly 75 percent of the Kingdom of Hungary*. After a massive Turkish ethnic cleansing, *in 1720, Hungarians were just 35 percent of Hungary*, according to the Encyclopedia Britannica.[17] It hovered around that percentage until 1900 when the Hungarization programs finally helped Hungarians break the magical 50-percent barrier. They peaked at 54.3 percent in Hungary's controversial 1910 census. However, that figure doesn't include Hungary's autonomous province of Croatia-Slavonia, which is included in every Greater Hungary map. With that province the percentage drops to just 48 percent. In conclusion, *for at least 300 years before Trianon, Hungarians were never the majority in Greater Hungary*.

Moreover, the percentages represent the *average* for all of Greater Hungary; in most Trianon areas, Hungarians have been 10 to 35 percent of the population for hundreds of years. For example, even in 1910, at the peak of the Hungarian demographic expansion, the percentage of Hungarians in Prekmurje, Slovenia (15%), Burgenland, Austria (9%), and Croatia (3.5%) was quite low.

Alex said, "It's simply idiotic to say that Transylvania was Hungarian for 1,000 years, or that the pre-1500s map of Hungary should be considered 'regular.' Even at that time there were tons of ethnic minorities living in Hungary's territory. Two of the most popular Hungarian last names today are Tóth, which means *Slovak*, and Horváth, which means *Croatian*. So, if everybody was Hungarian, how did that happen?"

It's remarkable that some Hungarians are still furious that Trianon gave a region called Banat to Serbia and Romania. In 1774, Hungarians made up *less than one percent* of the Banat. Most were Romanians, Serbs, and Germans. Even a Hungary-biased book reports that the 1857 Banat census put Hungarians at only 15 percent of the population.[18] The 1910 census reported a similar percentage. Most of the time, the percentage was lower: in 1880 it was five percent, which is lower than the percentage of the Hungarians living there today. Hungary conducted the Banat census from 1800 to 1920; therefore, if the numbers are wrong, then it's much more likely that they are *overestimating* the Hungarian population, not *underestimating* it.

Similarly, a few Hungarians believe that before Trianon they dominated Serbia's Vojvodina province and its capital, Novi Sad. László Marácz argues, "Vojvodina is no natural region but an artificially constructed region that was created at the end of the First World War after a series of violent conquests that had been carried out in an ethnically homogeneous area almost completely inhabited by Hungarians."[19] However, according to Hungary's own 1910 census, Hungarians made up just 28 percent of the region. Reality: for the last few hundred years, Slavs have dominated that land. There were (and still are) *districts* within Novi Sad (and Vojvodina) with a heavy Hungarian presence, but overall it's been Slav dominated for centuries. It's similar to the Transylvania myth: Hungarians focus on the pockets of a territory that they dominate, forgetting that they are a minority overall.

Trianon areas were overwhelmingly covered with Romanians and Slavs, which is why Hungary was initially reluctant about starting WWI. If they won, they would have gotten even more minorities. Prior to WWI, Hungarian Count Andrassy was referring to Slavs when he said, "Hungary's boat is already carrying too much cargo; a little more will make it capsize."

Myth #14: The map of Greater Hungary tells the whole story. The favorite map of Hungarians illustrates the outline of Greater Hungary. Gyöngyi said that Hungarians "should never forget about our history, where we are coming from and Trianon. Nowadays there is hardly a home where you can't find something remembering the Big Hungary map: it's on fridge magnets, stuff on the car's window, etc. I have it too on my fridge and a giant map." Indeed, you can see the Greater Hungary map on bumper stickers, T-shirts, flags, posters, and underwear. It symbolizes not only Hungary's former greatness, but also reminds them of the Trianon trauma and perpetuates its myths.

It would be better if the Hungarians would wave around an *ethnographic map of Greater Hungary*. In the last 150 years, all those maps show the same pattern. Let's use the 1890 census as an example (see map below).[20] It shows the concentration of Hungarians within

Greater Hungary. Aside from the concentration of Hungarians in the empire's easternmost point (eastern Transylvania), *the vast majority of Hungarians were already living within the post-Trianon borders long before the Treaty.* Wikipedia has many ethnographic maps based on censuses Hungary conducted over the last 150 years.[21] The story is always the same: except for Hungary's eastern flock (the Székelys), the bulk of Hungarians were living within the present-day borders of Hungary.

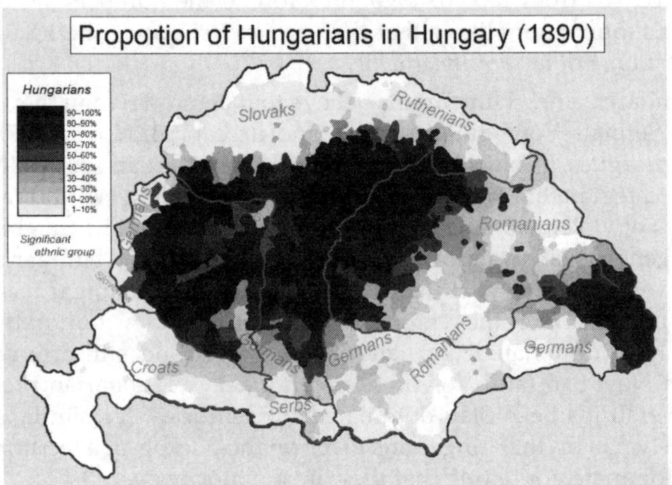

Now imagine that you're at the Trianon Peace Conference looking at this ethnographic map. You're given a pen and a mandate: draw new borders that correspond to the ethnic lines. Can you draw simple borders that follow ethnic lines? You can't! That pocket of Hungarians in the east makes a clean ethnic map impossible. So what do you do?

You can: (a) give Romania all the eastern lands, thereby separating the Székelys from their homeland; (b) unite the eastern Hungarians with Hungary's core by creating a corridor to connect them, thereby leaving millions of furious Romanians within Hungary; (c) give the east to Romania, but guarantee autonomy to the Hungarians living there. A dispassionate alien would choose (c). However, because Hungary lost WWI and anti-Hungary passions were running high, they got the worst deal: (a). *This was Trianon's first injustice.*

Trianon's second injustice was that it drew the border about 40 kilometers (25 miles) too tight. The WWI winners decided that Greater Hungary was like a sheep that had to be trimmed. However, instead of cutting the wool down to the sheep's skin, the French barber cut off part of the skin too! In other words, the intent of Trianon was to trim Hungary to its ethnic size, but the barbers went too far. They didn't go as radically far as Hungarians may lead you to believe, but they did overdo it. They drew the new border about 40 kilometers too tight. That doesn't sound like much, but because it's a long border, it ended up putting about one million Hungarians on the wrong side of the border. The US President Wilson argued for a more ethnically accurate border, but he caved in to the political pressure of his allies.

It's important to note these two injustices in Trianon, but it's also important to recognize the lesson of the ethnographic map of Greater Hungary. It reveals crucial information that the popular Greater Hungary map hides. It also shows that the post-Trianon borders were not insanely wrong.

Myth #15: All of Hitler's ideas were evil and bad. Although Hitler isn't known for his fairness or bright ideas, he did have two reasonable thoughts: the two Vienna Awards. He recognized that Trianon was flawed. To gain Hungary's support for his diabolical plans, Hitler awarded Hungary some of the lost Trianon lands, including a wide corridor into the middle of Romania.[22] That region is called Northern Transylvania. After Hitler's Vienna Awards, Romania's map looked like it had a Hungarian dagger piercing into its core.[23]

The results of the 1930, 1940, and 1941 censuses of Northern Transylvania depended on who you asked. Predictably, Romania's censuses consistently claimed that Northern Transylvania had a slight Romanian majority, while Hungary's censuses said there was a slight Hungarian majority. Nevertheless, one thing everyone agreed on: there was a sizable minority of Hungarians in Romania's core. It was a tough call, but this will probably be the only time where you'll catch me saying that one of Hitler's solutions was reasonable.

Still, it wasn't a perfect solution either: Northern Transylvania had millions of Romanians. It ended up exchanging one headache/injustice for another. When Hungary lost WWII, the Allies reversed the Vienna Awards. Even though the logic behind the Vienna Awards was sound, it would be illogical for the Allies to reward any of Hitler's actions. And after WWII, Hungary was in no position to negotiate.

Myth #16: Ethno-genocide was the main reason Hungarians left Trianon lands. To eliminate the risk of something like a Vienna Award down the road, Romania brutally forced Hungarians to leave and tried to convert those who stayed into Romanians. Czechoslovakia and Yugoslavia instituted similar savage programs. As evil as those programs were, Hungarians often ignore a more important reason for why a fifth of Hungarians left the Trianon lands.

To understand that, let's imagine that California becomes part of Mexico. Isn't it natural to expect that Mexico would promote the Spanish language throughout California? English-speaking Californians would revolt against "the oppression of their culture" just like

Hungarians did in Trianon lands. However, even if Mexico didn't create a single evil anti-American law, what do you think at least a fifth of the Americans living there would do? Get the hell out and move to the motherland. Who would want to stick around and live under a "foreign" Spanish-speaking government, especially when that government and its educational system are more poorly run than the American one?

> *Romanian schools produce idiots.*
> *— Traian Băsescu, President of Romania, 2010*

Compared to Slovakia, Serbia, and Romania, Hungary's government and economy has usually been better run. Therefore, you'd expect a natural exodus to Hungary. What's remarkable is that so many Hungarians stayed behind![24] This suggests that the evil programs weren't as pervasive (or as severe) as some Hungarians imply. Although Romanians brutally forced thousands of Hungarians to leave, the majority left because Romanians don't know how how to run a government and an economy as well as Hungarians.

> *What's the difference between a Hungarian and a Romanian? Both of them would sell their grandmother to make a fast buck, but at least with the Hungarian you know he'd deliver. — Serbian joke*

Myth #17: Hungarians are still being persecuted in the Trianon lands. Hungarians who have spent little time in the Trianon territories sometimes believe that ethnic Hungarians are getting regularly abused there. Like any good myth, it mixes fact with fiction. The fact is that Slavs and Romanians oppressed Hungarians for decades after WWI and WWII (when pent-up anti-Hungarian feelings were released). However, by the early 1990s, the abuse stopped everywhere except Yugoslavia and Romania, which were both suffering from widespread chaos and turmoil. Under such conditions, *everybody* was getting abused, not just Hungarians.

Unfortunately, Hungarians like Bishop László Tőkés misjudged the situation and wrote in the mid-1990s, "The [Trianon] repercussions are being felt especially by the Hungarians who have been artificially separated from each other and by Hungarian national communities that have fallen prey to strange nationalistic oppressors. . . . Hence the reason that we have to keep on talking about Trianon until the catastrophic consequences of it for our people and our region finally come to an end."[25]

Bad news travels faster than good news. With this issue, the good news is traveling at glacial speeds. Hungarians in Hungary (and those living in the US/UK) still believe that life for Hungarians in the Trianon areas is unjustly rough. They haven't gotten the memo that tension, violence, and oppression evaporated over a decade ago. This has led to out-of-control myth-building which is so hysterical that it's comical.

In 2011, Miklós, a Hungarian engineer, wrote to me, "When Hungarians fight each other over an issue it is a *one-to-one fight* with some swearing, cursing, few punches, and all is forgotten by next day. When Serbians beat you up: *one Hungarian is attacked by 10+ Serbians*. Intensive care guaranteed, and you won't get out of the bed for a couple months at least. Pray that the local police does not arrive, or does not get information about it, because then you're target for regular beatings."

Miklós emphasized that being Hungarian today in Trianon lands "means living *constantly in fear* that you are *not safe* on the streets, because you *will* get *beaten up* sooner or later just because *you are Hungarian*."

"I've traveled throughout the Trianon lands," I said, "and I've never heard of any such problems. Let me guess, Romania is bad too?"

Miklós said, "In Romania, the Hungarian beatings were infamous. Now they still happen, but they are not nearly as bad, they happen only on the streets, while during Nicolae Ceauşescu times (and before) it was the job of police. In Transylvania, Hungarians suffered tremendous brutality after Trianon, mostly the women. Gang rapes and rape using a horse was common."

When I discuss this issue with some Hungarians, it reminds me of what Alex told me about Hungary: "Everything is seen as a personal affront. People take themselves and everything too seriously. Hungarians often speak from emotion. They are not logical."

When I asked Miklós for proof, he scoffed, "Who do you ask this proof from? Get real! That kind of stuff does not get recorded anywhere, except the group psyche."

Alas, Hungary's group psyche has been taken over by the Great Trianon Myth Making Machine. You can't really blame Hungarians who fall for the propaganda since few can wander through the Trianon lands for months, talking with random people to learn what life is really like there. During one of my many travels in northern Serbia, I met Helena Kolar, a Hungarian who grew up in Subotica, Serbia. I asked her if Serbians abuse Hungarians in any way. The normally cheery and chatty Helena rolled her eyes and gave me a curt reply, "No."

I asked Norbert Šabić, an ethnic Hungarian who lives in Vojvodina, Serbia, if he felt discrimination. He said, "No. I don't think that I am oppressed in any way. On the contrary, in Serbia, Hungarian organizations get more money than Serbian ones because both the Hungarian and Serbian governments fund them! As individuals, we might have disadvantages if we don't speak Serbian properly, but we might also have an advantage because we speak Hungarian. For example,

I work in a college where you can't get a job if you don't speak basic Hungarian too."

I told Norbert, "I read in one Hungarian book that the Hungarian language was banned in Vojvodina and that the Latin script was abolished, forcing everyone to use the Cyrillic alphabet."

He said, "I don't think that the Latin script has ever been abolished. Also, Hungarian is one of the official languages of Vojvodina, and in every town where more that 15 percent of the population is Hungarian. Elementary and secondary education is completely in Hungarian in several towns. Only higher education is partly covered in Hungarian. I wrote a very good research paper about minority education in Vojvodina, so trust me, Vojvodina has a quite good education for minority groups."

"How much Hungarian-targeted abuse is going on today?"

"I would say none at all. Sometimes the Hungarian media reports about some individual cases where two drunk young people get into a fight, so they portray it as aggression against the Hungarians. But honestly, I believe they were fighting more because of a woman than because of ethnic origin. And of course there are nationalists on both sides who make incidents from time to time. Serbia has today one of (if not the) most advanced minority protection laws in Europe! Of course, it's hard to top Switzerland."

Unfortunately, myths are hard to kill. Zsuzsa wrote, "The problem with Trianon is that there are still hundreds of thousands of Hungarians suffering every day for it. We just want to be able to live and speak our language, and not be beaten up for doing so."

"Horseshit," Alex said. "Ain't nobody gets beaten up for speaking Hungarian, but they do sometimes get beat up because they run into the wrong gang of skinheads. I got beat up once for speaking English. According to the *Magyar Hirlap* newspaper, a bunch of gypsies recently beat up some guy for being Hungarian—in Hungary!"

Myth #18: Western Europe owes Hungary something. Zsuzsa feels that Western Europe betrayed Hungary with Trianon given that Hungarians "fought the Turks valiantly, thus sparing the rest of Europe from pillage." *The Tragic Fate of Hungary* says that the country's "historic role and mission may well be qualified as invaluable for Western Christianity," that it's been "playing that role and fulfilling that mission successfully" as "the living bulwark of the West," and that it has "shouldered the noble mission."[26] The subtle implication is that since Hungary had helped defend Western Europe, it owed Hungary gratitude instead of slamming it with an unfair treaty.

Reality: Turkish and Asian invaders came to Hungary. Hungarians didn't volunteer for their "noble mission." Their backs were against the wall. They weren't doing it to protect Western civilization. They were just doing it to save their own asses. It's similar to your neighbor saying that you owe him one because his house was in front of your house during a tornado, sparing you the direct hit. You never told your neighbor to have his house there just like nobody ever told Hungarians to settle on the path of Asian invaders.

More importantly, put yourself in 1918: WWI is over and you're burying all your countrymen that the Hungarian Army just killed. At that point, you're not exactly thinking about what Hungarians did for you hundreds of years ago. That's like you catching me stealing from you and then I say, "Hey don't punish me! Don't forget that my great-grandfather helped build your great-grandfather's barn!"

Indulging in Hungary's ultimate fantasy

Before we wrap up this tedious Trianon discussion, let's dive into Hungary's ultimate fantasy: let's imagine that Trianon never happened. Zsuzsa said that "without France's leadership, there would have been no Treaty of Trianon and Hungary might still be intact." The Hungarian author of *A Concise History of Hungary* argues that the French leaders behind Trianon "created an unstable region, new centers ripe for ethnic conflict, not to mention frustration among the main victims of this unfortunate and unjust peace deal—the Hungarians."[27] Did Trianon create instability? Would Hungary be intact without Trianon? Or are these just more myths? To find out, let's fantasize that after WWI, the Austria-Hungary Empire was split, but that Hungary was able to retain its borders. What would have happened to Greater Hungary?

Let's recall that WWI had killed 661,000 of Hungary's people and depleted its economy. Its currency and agriculture output had dropped in half by the end of the war. Its national spirit was defeated. In short, *it was the war that created instability, not Trianon*. Had Trianon not happened, there would have been *more* instability as furious minorities revolted. In fact, that started to happen in 1919 when Romanian troops took over Budapest. If Trianon hadn't happen peacefully, Romanians would have made Trianon happen by force. That uprising would have encouraged the Slavs to fight a similar fight. Hungary couldn't stop Romania, so it certainly couldn't have taken them all on. In short, Trianon helped Hungary avoid an ugly, destabilizing civil war.

It's fun to blame the French (I certainly do at every opportunity), but in this case, the French (and their allies) spared Hungary from a bloodbath. Hungary would have been crushed from all sides and possibly carved up completely. Ferocious invaders, with lips dripping with vengeance, wouldn't want to just dismember Hungary, but to annihilate it. The Székely, surrounded by furious Romanians, would have been an easy target for mobs to liquidate. Such a massacre would have made Ceauşescu's despicable anti-Hungarian acts seem harmless by comparison. Instead of crying over a peace treaty, Hungarians would be mourning a massacre of genocidal proportions.

Nevertheless, diehard Hungarians cling to what I call *Hungary's Switzerland Pipe Dream*. They believe that if Trianon hadn't happened, then Hungary would have graciously granted broad autonomy to its minorities, reversed the Hungarization programs, and appeased the masses. Such wishful thinking fails to understand the post-WWI situation—Hungary was too weak to hold itself together and its minorities were too eager to leave. For example, even though Croatia-Slavonia had enjoyed vast autonomy for 50 years, the Slavs there still demanded complete independence. Moreover, Hungarians seem to forget that their WWI army was killing Slavs and Romanians. Why the hell would those people want to stay in Hungary? Trianon or no Trianon, Hungary was going to be downsized.

My confession

When I first approached the Trianon topic, I was biased. I've been friends with Zsuzsa for over 20 years and care for her and her family dearly. I naturally wanted to support her arguments and perspective, like any good friend would. The same goes for János, since he's Zsuzsa's friend, and also my generous Hungarian Couchsurfing hosts. I figured that since their opinion about Trianon was similar to the ones I had heard in Hungary's cafés and media, it must be right. I was eager to conclude that Trianon was a supremely unjust and horrible treaty, and then move on to other topics.

Unfortunately, my annoying habit of considering all sides of a story derailed me. The more I traveled, read, and debated, the harder I found it to support many of the arguments that my Hungarian friends made. At that point, it was tempting to simply ignore Trianon and not stir up any trouble, but Hungarians mentioned it so often that I had to discuss it.

> *It is one of the maladies of our age to profess a frenzied allegiance to truth in unimportant matters, to refuse consistently to face her where graver issues are at stake.*
> *— János Arany, Hungarian journalist, writer, and poet who was born in Bihar county, Hungary, which is now in Romania, 1817–1882*

Since Alex was a political analyst and journalist in Hungary, I asked him to fact-check many of the positions that my friends had about Trianon. After sending him a long list of their arguments, he replied, "I feel like a mosquito at a nudist camp: I don't know where to begin. Your friends are apparently people who still believe all the nationalist myths with which my Hungarian grandparents tried to brainwash me. I only got over it when I tried to write papers about the Greater Hungary issue at Amherst College, and I couldn't find a single reliable source to support their allegations. This is part of the problem: Hungarians, Romanians, and Slovaks are all myth-makers. All these myths have the grain of truth in them. However, these are subject to wild exaggeration and selective interpretation. This is what leads to modern-day ethnic conflicts—when one side or the other feels cheated."

When will Hungarians approach Trianon like their Nobel Prize winning scientists would? Can they analyze the issue like a true alien, one who has no agenda or preconceived ideas? I confess I was a lousy scientist. I began with a bias: I wanted to prove that my Hungarian friends were right. In the end, however, that was hard to do.

The fair solution to Trianon

If Trianon could be magically revised, what would you do? Alex answered, "First off, everyone with a brain knows that if they restored the pre-1920 borders, Hungarians would be a minority in their own country. Not even Hungary's ultra right-wing Jobbik party advocates restoration of those borders. Also, if the land were restored, what would people have to whine about?"

I said, "I'm confident that they'll think of something."

Alex continued, "Some Hungarians—myself included—think it might be a good idea to reattach the southern part of Slovakia. But trust me, there is not a single Hungarian who would be willing to shed a drop of blood for those lands, unless he is a football hooligan or a demented geezer in a nursing home. What *is* deep in the psyche is, 'We were cheated! Woe is us!' Nobody gives a toss about the land itself."

In 1927, Lord Rothermere of England proposed a brilliant solution. His plan would have arranged plebiscites in all the disputed areas. Assuming that people would vote along linguistic lines, then a narrow strip of land along Hungary's border would go to Hungary. In the 1920s, that 40-kilometer strip of land had 1.9 million inhabitants, of which 85 percent were Hungarian. That relatively small border shift would slash the number of Hungarians being cut off from their motherland by more than half. This would have silenced many of the Hungarian cries (or at least made us feel less guilty about ignoring them).

On the other hand, Alex says, "Eastern Europe is a hodgepodge of nationalities. No matter how you draw or redraw the borders, there are going to be minorities. These people should be allowed to maintain their minority status, and should be supported in this endeavor. I think history shows what happens when you try to forcibly deprive a people of their identity."

Trianon's only other major error was regarding the Transylvanian Hungarians. The best solution would be to give them autonomy. Although Romania tried that for many years, it took it away and is unwilling to try again. Nevertheless, the Székely issue is largely irrelevant today since Hungary and Romania are both in the EU, which guarantees basic human rights. As Alex said, "Almost all the Hungarians are now united in the EU. You can work, own property, set up a company, run around naked as you please."

Hungary's pity party

Hungary has been having a pity party for too long. Hungarians are frustrated that many people don't know Hungary exists, and if they do know about it, they don't think much of it—it's just another ex-communist country that is struggling to catch up. They want to be taken seriously. Hungary could paraphrase Norma Desmond in *Sunset Boulevard*, "I *am* big! It's *my country* that got small!"

I'll sum up Hungary's rant: "Take us seriously, please! Look at our fabulous history! Our rich culture! We were huge! And important! We invented lots of stuff! We're *European!* In fact, we're in the *center* of Europe! Our language is special! We're special! Don't you see? We're not like those other backward Eastern European countries! In fact, we used to rule their asses! Our peer group used to be France, Britain, and Germany, not those screwed-up losers out in the east! We were *equals* to the big boys like the Austrians (except when they started wars, of course, cuz that's when we were *forced* to do naughty deeds, it wasn't our idea, really). And when we lost wars, we always got more screwed than the Austrians and Germans who started it to begin with. Do you know that we unjustly lost two-thirds of our territory after WWI? (Oh, I've already told you this 57 times? OK, well here's 58.) And then after WWII, we got screwed again! Austria and West Germany (the assholes who dragged us into another war) lucked out again at the end of the war by not ending up under Soviet domination. Meanwhile, we innocent Hungarians got it up the butt from those damn Russians. So now we're playing catch-up, but we only have one-third of our original land, so how can we possibly recover our former glory? C'mon! We lost over two-thirds of our land after WWI! *Two-thirds!* And now we're in the EU and we thought that would help out, but we're getting shafted there too! The fucking rich EU countries are just using us to have another nice market to sell their crap to and we don't get shit in return! We just have to pay big fees to be an EU member, but they don't do anything for us! *We're screwed again!* We had hoped that by joining the EU we would play a big role in Europe and be taken seriously again, but it's hard to really make an impact when two-thirds of your land has been unjustly stolen from you. Did you know that after WWI *we lost two-thirds of our land*?"

Hungary, get over it

After unraveling Trianon's myths, we see that its injustices are neither as many nor as great as many Hungarians claim. Trianon's two biggest flaws (the overly tight border and the lack of guaranteed Székely autonomy) were unfair. Unfortunately, nations write peace treaties during emotional and unstable times, so they are often flawed. Has there ever been a peace treaty that all parties were 100 percent happy with?

Why have we analyzed Trianon so closely? Why does Trianon matter today? László Marácz explains: "The marginalization of the Hungarians has enormously affected the mental-moral atmosphere in the country. Hungary is an inward looking and socially unstable country. The pessimistic mood has penetrated deep into Hungarian culture. Artists expressing feelings of loneliness and losers have been given a prominent place in Hungarian culture. The Hungarian culture is full of metaphors for 'desolation', 'sorrow' and 'loneliness' and the country has numerous statues and other depictions of fallen revolutionaries. The post-communist system cultivated this 'Hungarian sorrow' sentiment and the image of 'Hungarians as losers'."[28]

In other words, Trianon matters because it's psychologically keeping Hungary down. One Hungarian, Norbert Šabić, lamented, "Honestly, I am sick of this Hungarian self-pity."

Speaking of self-pity, János wrote to me, "The Trianon wound is bleeding and is wide open, millennial old Hungarian regions are gone forever, marking Hungary forever a small country, the death sentence of a world power lasting a millennium. Hungary never regained her power status, and has no hope to step out from the list of backwards nations of Europe."

Can Hungary blossom or are its hands tied without its Trianon lands? Let's see how countries smaller than Hungary are doing. Hungary is nearly five times bigger than Israel and has 40 percent more people, yet Israel's GDP is 30 percent higher than Hungary's and its per capita GDP is nearly twice as high as Hungary's. Israel is in a desert and isn't blessed with the natural sources that Hungary has. Compared to Singapore, Hungary has twice as many people and 133 times more land, but Singapore's GDP is higher than Hungary's! Need a landlocked country example? Try Switzerland: its GDP is 3.8 times bigger than Hungary's despite having half the land and fewer people.

Hungary has no excuse, but if the toilet isn't flushing, it's definitely Trianon's fault. Alex said, "While I do agree that Trianon was a historic tragedy, I do not have any sympathy for Hungarians who invoke Trianon as the source of their problems today, 90 years later."

However, instead of getting over it, Hungary opened the Trianon Museum in Varpalota. You'll find Trianon memorials in the towns of Békéscsaba, Csátalja, Kiskunhalas, Kőszeg, and in every living room. These totems impede Hungary's ability to get over Trianon and move on. Hungarians lose countless hours discussing Trianon *ad nauseam*. When referring to injustices, people often say "never forget," but there's another saying that is usually better for everyone: "Forgive and forget." Sadly, Hungary's mantra is more like, "Never forgive and definitely never forget!"

The 24-year-old Gyöngyi shows that Trianon isn't fading away for the new generation either. She said, "Now I think it is our task to teach our children about Trianon and this is why I'm really glad that the new government made the Trianon Memory Day recently: 4th of June!"

Great. One more reason to recall old news and keep old myths alive. Imagine if the British lowered their flags on the 4th of July to mourn the loss of their American colonies. Or if Germans were still furious that its former lands and people are now in many other countries. Hungary cheered when Belarus, Estonia, Latvia, Lithuania, and Moldova broke away from the USSR. Oppressed minorities in those Soviet republics overthrew the government just like Hungary's minorities would have done if Trianon hadn't happened. However, few Hungarians had sympathy for the millions of Russians who, having lived for countless generations on those lands, were now separated from their motherland. Even though it happened just 20 years ago, Russia has moved on. Meanwhile, Hungary has not. Get over it.

I've visited Austria many times and *never* has an Austrian observed that they lost 73 percent of their lands after WWI. In Hungary, it's hard to ask for extra paprika without the waiter reminding you about Trianon. Austrians focused on turning their country, which is smaller than Hungary, into a country whose GDP per capita is in the world's top 15. And sorry, the "but we were under communism" excuse is getting old. Estonia and Slovenia had their communist ordeal too, but they've used the last two decades productively while Hungary has distracted itself with century-old news. Get over it.

Hungarians need to emulate the Germans again. Germany got over the first half of the twentieth century quickly. They buried their grandiose fantasies, destroyed their myths, apologized for their sins, forgave others for their crimes against millions of innocent Germans, and focused on the future. As we saw in the Eastern Germany chapter, Germany bounces back from bad news instead of swimming in it. Get over it.

Krisztina wrote, "We Hungarians don't like to admit we are wrong. And when something is going wrong, it's usually the fault of everyone else, not us. In socialism, the state did everything instead of us. With democracy, we got freedom, but we didn't learn how to be *responsible* citizens. If a person from a Western European country has an old bench in front of his yard that looks pretty miserable, he will probably get a bucket of paint and paint it in his free Sunday afternoon. In Hungary, we are more likely to complain aloud how the local community doesn't do anything to renovate or remove this bench and how unlucky we are that we *have* to stare at it every time we leave home. And even if there is a man, one in a thousand, who still decides to renovate it on his own—he can be sure that it will be vandalized and covered in graffiti in less than one month."

"Really?"

"Yes. People like to blame the state for weeds appearing in every possible place—instead of pulling out one single weed. They like to blame everyone else for littered streets and congested roads, instead of thinking about throwing their litter in the bin and choosing public transportation or cycling instead of contributing to traffic jams themselves. They don't pay taxes, because 'it will be stolen by the politicians anyway.' So the ones who are honest, who want to make a difference will be the ones who will suck big time and who will probably be laughed at. It seems that we forgot our old saying: *Segíts magadon, az Isten is megsegít* (Help yourself and God will help you, too)."

Alex said, "The thing Yanks can learn from Hungarians is: why it's a bad idea to allow self-pity to become the main motivating factor in your life. The Hungarian saying I hate most is, 'Ez *van, ezt kell szeretni*.' It loosely translates as, 'That's the way it is, you gotta live with it.' I hear that too many times a day. The good news is that Hungarians don't waste time trying to change things they can't—the trouble is, almost everything qualifies as unchangeable in the Hungarian mind. Not too many Don Quixotes in Hungary, I guarantee you."

A Gallup poll supports this. Hungarians are the least willing within the EU to take risks (43% saying they generally take risks vs. the EU average of 65% and the USA's 82%). Also, only 4 in 10 like competitive situations (vs. 55% in EU and 77% in USA), putting Hungary at the bottom of the EU again. *Indeed, when Americans say, "What can we do?" it signals the beginning of a discussion; in Hungary, it signals the end of the discussion.*

In 2020, Hungary will mark the 100-year anniversary of Trianon. If Hungarian leaders are wise, the theme of the celebration should be: *Get Over It*. Instead, it seems like the theme will be: *Get Into It*. Or perhaps it'll be: *Let's Bang Our Hungarian Heads on the Trianon Wall for Another 100 Years.*

It's time Hungary puts Trianon behind it, shatters its 18 myths, stops blaming others for it, realizes it would have happened anyway, quits blaming the EU or its neighbors for its woes, shut up with all the excuses, and make Hungary great again. *Get over it and move on!*

The 12 things I love about Hungary

Thankfully, there are plenty of Hungarians who don't give a shit about the Treaty of Trianon. What's great is that their numbers are growing. In their honor, let's finally focus on what's great about Hungary.

1. **Hungarians are not boring or bored.** Hungarians are the fourth least bored people in world. Only one in ten Hungarians were bored the previous day when Gallup surveyed them in 2007. Why they're not bored has something to do with the next point.
2. **Rich and engaging discussions.** I've talked with thousands of Eastern Europeans during my three years of travel. No other country comes close to Hungary in jumping into profound discussions about anything. Hungarians would write me the longest (and most thoughtful) emails by far. Conversations were intellectually stimulating. No topic was taboo. Debates are civil and entertaining.
3. **Freedom.** Alex said, "The best thing is that Hungarians have the leave-me-the-hell-alone attitude. It's a redneck's dream." For instance, he has old neighbors who don't call the police if he has a loud party.
4. **Urban renewal.** Compared to my 1992 visit, Budapest has made great progress. They got rid of squatters, upgraded the transportation network, and cleaned up the city. Today, all Hungarian cities have lovely centers.
5. **Courage.** Hungarians led three of the most important and momentous anti-communist events. First, in 1956, when other Eastern Bloc accepted their communist oppressors, Hungary staged a massive protest. Thousands died, but it eventually led to reforms. Second, on September 20, 1989, it had the courage to open its border, which then led to opening of the Berlin Wall several weeks later. Third, a Hungarian priest in Romania led the protest that would eventually bring down communism there.
6. **One napkin.** Hungarian restaurants are stingy with their thin napkins. You only get one unless you ask for another. It's a good habit.
7. **Celebrating science and engineering.** Whereas other cultures focus on musicians, athletes, and actors, Hungary's heroes and role models are its scientific and engineering geniuses.
8. **Easy to break into social circles.** Geoffroy Chiocca, a Frenchman who worked for seven months in Hungary, told me at a

party that he loves that "the social cliques are not so strong" and that "foreigners are welcomed."

9. **Hungarians derive their value on how much they help others.** Alex said, "Hungarians view themselves as *segítőkész* (ready to help) and *vendégszerető* (guest-loving). If you ever go to a Hungarian's house in the countryside, you will be plied with food and alcohol until you can't walk. Hungarians will always greet everyone upon entering an elevator, workplace or the changing room at the gym." While such friendless may not always be sincere, it's better than the standard Eastern European grunt.
10. **Hungarians keep their traditions.** Krisztina wrote, "On Easter Monday it's a popular activity of boys to go to sprinkle girls so they won't wilt. In cities it's usually done with a bottle of cologne, but in the countryside young men prefer the traditional way: a bucket of cold water. You can even call the Fire Department for this purpose. Girls then give some chocolate, alcohol, painted eggs or money. Boys and men accompany this ritual with locsolóvers (a small poem)."
11. **Lake Balaton gatherings.** Hungarians use a bogrács (cauldron) and cook something delicious (usually goulash soup or potatoes with paprika) in it. They accompany it all with a heavy dose of alcohol. It's not my thing, but some participate in a disznóvágás (slaughtering of a pig and tasting everything that is made of it after).
12. **Swearing.** Hungarians have some real zingers.

One Hungarian told me, "We have a wide vocabulary in swearing. Maybe it's only Russians who do it better than us. It's actually not only swearing, but a way you can show off your innovative self and the literature expert in yourself."

Alex, who is fluent in three languages, said, "Can't vouch for the Russians. But the Hungarians certainly outclass any other swearing culture with which I am acquainted." By now it probably won't surprise you that Alex was happy to share swearwords with some real punch. Try: *bedugok egy esernyőt a seggedbe és kinyitom* (I'm going to stick an umbrella up your ass and open it), *menj az anyád picsájába* (get back into your mother's cunt), or my favorite, *bassza meg a kurva isten* (the whore god should fuck it).

Turkish trails left in Szentendre, Pécs, and Eger

It's fascinating to search for remnants of the Turkish Empire in Hungary. Zsuzsa said that the "150 years of occupation seeps into the culture in many ways, like children's songs about bad Turkish deeds.

The funny thing is that when I went to Turkey, those guys look fondly upon their time spent in our land, calling it a 'visit'—for a century and a half! And calling us 'Hungarian brothers.' I found this really funny."

Since Hungary was at the edge of the Turkish Empire, it never established that firm of a foothold there compared to the Balkans (where the Turks ruled for 500 years). However, in southern Hungary, near the Balkans, you'll find the best traces near Pécs (pronounced *paich*). For example, in the center of the town is the curious *Mecset Templom* (Mosque Church). The Turks built the mosque on top of stones of a former church. However, after they fled, Hungarians removed the Islamic traits, slapped on a few crosses, and *voila,* instant church! What's more impressive is the Szent Péter Bazilika with its four towers and its eleventh-century crypt. For even older stuff, walk to the fourth-century *Ókeresztény Mauzóleum* (Christian Mausoleum) which the Romans built. In 2010, the year after I visited it, Pécs was named the European Capital of Culture.

Sometimes the Turkish trail is extremely faint. For example, Serb refugees, who fled from the Turks, established a huge presence in Szentendre, a town that is 30 minutes from Budapest. Today, few Serb remnants remain. Szentendre's main square, the Fő Tér, is filled with colorful eighteenth-century buildings and pedestrian streets leading in every direction. On the highest point is the Szent János Plébánia Templom, a church that was rebuilt in 1710 and has great views of the Danube and the town. Today, the most obvious Turkish legacy in Szentendre is that street vendors try to hustle Turkish spices alongside Hungary's cocaine: paprika.

The Turkish legacy is visible in one of Hungary's most lovely cities, Eger (pronounced *egg-air*). Its baroque buildings, its castle on the hill, its breathtaking churches, and its pedestrian walkways all make it absolutely irresistible. Eger's claim to fame is that it put a temporary halt to the Turkish advance through Europe in an amusing way. In 1552, Hungary's military commander, desperate to pump up his demoralized soldiers, gave them bottles of Eger's famous red wine. The soldiers drank so much that their beards had a reddish color when they launched their drunken attack. Seeing the red beards, the Turks concluded that the Hungarians had become supermen by drinking bull's blood. The terrified Turks fled. At least, that's what the legend says. Today, Hungary's best red wine is *Egri Bikavér* (Eger Bull's Blood).

The Turks regrouped 44 years later and conquered Eger's Castle because the Hungarians weren't drunk. However, less than 100 years later, Hungary kicked the Turks out for good. Today, the northernmost European remnant of the Turkish Empire is still in Eger: a lonely 40-meter minaret.

In Eger I stayed with the kind brother and sister team of Szabi and Zsófia Énekes. They showed me buildings that you can only find in Central Europe—a unique architectural style that blends late baroque and neoclassicism. The Egri Bazilika, built in 1836, has a warm color on the outside and greets you when you first enter the town. At the Dózsa Tér, Szabi left to meet some other friends. Zsófia and I walked up the hill into the *Egri Vár* (Eger Castle), admiring the fortress that stood up to the Mongols and the Turks. Afterwards, Zsófia wanted to walk me to the Szépasszony völgy. She said, "It's a valley where there are lots of wine cellars. It's super popular and quite pretty."

When I told her that I don't drink alcohol, we agreed that it wasn't worth it to walk there. I asked her, "What does Szépasszony völgy mean anyway?"

"The Valley of the Beautiful Women," she said with a beautiful smile. I guess all women become beautiful after a few bottles of wine.

> *I never hated a man enough to give him diamonds back.*
> *— Zsa Zsa Gabor*

Zsófia and I met back up with her brother for the tram ride home. I met their warm mother, Gabriella, who served us a tasty *székelygulyás* dish (goulash stew with meat) seasoned with paprika. In Hungarian cooking, paprika is more important than salt, pepper, or water. There's the *pörkölt* (paprika-flavored stew), *paprikás csirke* (chicken stew with a cream-tomato-paprika sauce), *töltött káposzta* (cabbage rolls stuffed with paprika favored rice and meat topped with sour cream), *halászlé* (pouched fish with paprika, green peppers, and tomatoes), and *gulyás* (goulash with beef, tomatoes, onions, and a dash of paprika). I love Hungarian food more than most Eastern European food because they use spices liberally. They're convinced that everything tastes better if it has a healthy dose of paprika and a heaping scoop of sour cream.

At dinner, their playful father, József, pointed to the Greater Hungary map on the wall. Don't worry, I'll spare you that long discussion. However, during his monologue, he casually said that "Jews created communism." I asked him to expand on that idea. Zsófia rolled her eyes and shook her head with that here-we-go-again look. She was already getting embarrassed by what her father was about to say.

Hungary's love-hate relationship with its Jews

Few things are ever simple in Hungary. Perhaps that's why *magyaráz* means *to explain,* but also implies *to Hungarian.* In other words, Hungarians like to explain—perhaps because many things there are complicated. Hungary's view of Jews is complex and nuanced. There are three basic viewpoints: love, hate, and reality.

In one way, Hungarians **love** their Jews, or at least their accomplishments. For hundreds of years Hungary was a safe place for Jews so that by 1914 there were almost one million Jews in Budapest, which earned the nickname *Jewapest*. Some Hungarian Jews were extremely successful; for example, all the Hungarian-Martian Nobel Prize winning scientists that we discussed at the beginning of this chapter were Jewish. Hungarians rarely mention that nearly all their scientific geniuses were Jewish and that most emigrated to America before they won their prizes. Why they omit those facts isn't clear, but Hungarians definitely love to celebrate their successful Jews.

Successful Jewish scientists aren't unique to Hungary. Although Jews are only 0.2 percent of the world's population, they've won a quarter of all the science-related Nobel Prizes. I asked Alex if he knew why Jews excelled in science and math. He said, "Peter Tordai, former head of the main Jewish organization in Hungary (Mazsihisz), explained it to me: it's a part of Jewish culture for the parents to force their kids to learn as much as possible. Parents sometimes force their kids to study until they're in their early 30s, and they support them financially all the way. That's why Jewish kids were especially good at math and science. That's why they won Nobel prizes. And that's why most of them left Hungary."

> *A mathematician is a device for turning coffee into theorems. — Paul Erdős, Jewish Hungarian mathematician and vagabond who published more papers than any other mathematician in history*

Jewish scientists weren't the only ones to leave Hungary and become successful elsewhere. Jewish film industry leaders, actors, inventors, and entrepreneurs all left Hungary behind. Yet Hungary still loves them. For instance, one state-sponsored commercial highlights the accomplishments of 13 Hungarian superstars to prove that Hungary produces winners. Alex pointed out that "only four of them actually lived and worked in Hungary. The rest of them were born in Hungary, and got the hell out of Dodge, usually because some bald guys in brown shirts wanted to shove a bayonet up their circumcised asses."

Which brings us to the **hate** viewpoint. In 1939, Hungary passed an Anti-Jewish Law which decreed that Jews can only hold five percent of the government and commercial jobs. In 1941, Hungary prohibited Jews to marry or have sex with non-Jews. Despite those laws, in 1943, Hungary still had over 800,000 Jews, far higher than any other Eastern European country. Hitler pressured Hungary's leader to send the Jews to concentration camps, but he sent "only" 10,000 to appease Hitler. By 1944, Hitler lost his patience, took control of Hungary, and, with the help of many Hungarians, started sending 12,000 Jews a day to death camps, reaching a total of 437,000 Jews. A third of those who died in Auschwitz were Hungarian Jews. Incredibly, 124,000 Jews were still alive in Budapest when the Soviets took over Hungary thanks to heroic Hungarians who protected them.

In 2010, the Pew Research Center revealed that 29 percent of Hungarians had an "unfavorable" view of Jews; Lithuania (37%), Poland (29%), and Slovakia (27%) also have roughly a third of their people who dislike Jews. In comparison, seven percent of Americans have an unfavorable view of Jews. There's an amusing poll that revealed how some Hungarians dislike people who are different from them. Pollsters asked Hungarians if they would restrict the immigration of the following people: Arabs (87% said yes), Chinese (81%), and Piréz (68%). Here's what's funny: there's no such thing as the Piréz people—they don't exist!

> *If I'd known how old I was going to be, I'd have taken better care of myself. — Adolph Zukor, Jewish Hungarian founder of Paramount Pictures, who died at 103 years old*

We have seen evidence that Hungarians love and hate their Jews, now for the complicated **reality.** Alex, who has investigated this issue thoroughly for his job, provides outstanding insight: "Why are Hungarians anti-Jewish today? One reason is traditional hatred, the kind that is totally indefensible; the other is resentment toward the communist elite. These people were unprincipled opportunists who continued to confer privilege upon themselves after communism collapsed. When Hungarians rail against Jews today, chances are it has nothing to do with religion or ethnicity, but resentment against a rich person who steals your money and robs you of your rights (this rich person may or may not actually exist). By the same token, when they call someone a 'stinking Jew,' there's a good chance he has nothing to do with Judaism and has no Jewish ancestry."

"Give me an example," I said.

"One-time communist secret services chief László Rajk is constantly denounced as a Jew. Rajk has nothing to do with the Jewish religion or the ethnic group. In fact, Rajk's brother was one of the higher-ups in the Nazi-affiliated Arrow Cross. Another interesting point: when I was covering the 2006 riots, one thug marching down Budapest's Grand Boulevard told me that Hungarian Prime Minister Ferenc Gyurcsány was a 'stinking Jew.' Gyurcsány has no religion except his own personal accumulation of power and, as far as I know, his foreskin remains intact. For Hungarians, the term 'Jewish' is associated not with religion, but with unprincipled accumulation of wealth and privilege. Plenty of non-Jewish Hungarians did the exact same thing, but you don't get people calling Gyurcsány a 'dirty Christian.'"

"Alex, you're a professional political analyst in Hungary. How many politicians there are really Jewish?"

"Very difficult to say. There are very few 'real Jews' in politics. I can think of only about a dozen off the top of my head. If you tell that to a Hungarian, they'll say it's because they're pulling the strings behind the scenes."

"How do Hungarians communicate their anti-Jewish feelings?"

"Anti-Jewish comments take place in whispers. In public, anti-Jewish Hungarians use a number of well-known metaphors to denounce Jews: they rail against 'bankers' or 'the people behind globalization' or 'the people who use capitalism to destroy the common folk.' They say things such as 'liberal intellectuals control the media' or, in more daring moments, they may say things like 'we don't want Hungary to suffer the same fate as Palestine.'"

"That's funny."

"At the same time, there are no physical attacks against Jews or synagogues. Even Jews in Hasidic garb can walk around in total safety. Bored teenagers in a village might go out at night and spray-paint swastikas on Jewish gravestones, but according to the former head of the main Jewish group in Hungary, this is normally just because they want to create a national scandal, not because they hate Jews. It's exciting when police and TV cameras come out to your piece-of-shit village."

At dinner, József told me that Jews were behind many of the problems in Hungary. I said that it was hard to believe, given that Jews are less than 0.5 percent of Hungary—a tenth of their pre-WWII proportion. He assured me that they were in charge and that Jews work in mysterious ways.

Months later, Alex would conclude, "The gist of anti-Jewishness is this: *there are evil, foreign forces living among us that want to destroy us.* The overwhelming majority of Hungarians don't buy it. But low-level prejudice does exist. The main danger is that low-level prejudice can become inflamed into something much uglier."

Kecskemét, Szeged, and Sopron

From Eger, I traveled to Szeged via Budapest and Kecskemét. This meant traversing Hungary's *Nagyalföld* (Great Plain), which is where much of Hungarian mythology takes place. Those legendary stories are undoubtedly more stimulating than the flat scenery. However, Kecskemét makes up for it. Its main square, Szabadság Tér, is a handsome open area with Art Nouveau buildings surrounding it. After a few hours of wandering, I took the train to an even more spectacular town, Szeged (pronounced *seh*-ged).

At the Szeged train station, I met my friendly, energetic, and pretty Couchsurfing host, Gyöngyi Tóth. She lent me her extra bike so we could ride along the wide Tisza River. We crossed the *Belvárosi Híd* (Inner Town Bridge) until we arrived at the neoclassical Móra Ferenc Múzeum, one of the town's prettiest buildings. Szeged is one of Hungary's finest gems. It's especially vibrant thanks to its large university. In the evening we walked our bikes through a busy carnival and gorged on *véres hurka* (black sausage) and *kabanos* (more sausage). Like many Hungarians, Gyöngyi wasn't afraid to discuss hard topics, including how she was struggling with her boyfriend who went to Central America for several months "to find himself." Weeks later, she told him to get lost.

> *I want a man who's kind and understanding. Is that too much to ask of a millionaire? — Zsa Zsa Gabor*

In 2011, I returned to Hungary to reunite once again with Zsuzsa and Steve Rodgers in their summerhouse in Balatonkenese. We goofed off in Lake Balaton. Later, I followed Zsuzsa's advice and visited the nearby Trianon Museum. It opened in 1999 and features over 100 Greater Hungary maps, yet only three tell the full ethnographic story. I also stayed again with Alex Kuli in Budapest. He was moving to Brussels because he was tired of the corruption in the Hungarian media. On my way out of Hungary, I visited Sopron, a magnificent city with the impressive Fertőd palace nearby.

Hungary's future

Hungary doesn't suck like some Hungarians say it does. On the contrary, by most measures, it's far ahead of all eastern and southern European nations. Most countries in the world wish they were blessed with Hungary's strengths: the Danube River, Lake Balaton, an educated population, elegant cities, a unique culture, a central location in Europe, and fertile land everywhere.

The only thing that does suck in Hungary is the current national psychology. While some Hungarians deny it, much of their self-pity, frustration, negativity, and defeatism is ultimately tied to their Trianon myths. *Let's be clear: the vast majority of Hungarians rarely discuss Trianon among their friends and family, because beating a dead horse in front of the same crowd gets boring after a while.* Still, either consciously or subconsciously, many Hungarians don't believe that they can create a greater Hungary without Greater Hungary's borders.

There are ways for Hungary to become Eastern Europe's leader. Sell Hungary as Europe's central hub. Have global investors take advantage of Hungary's educated citizens. Hungary has geography on its side as all the mountains descend into the huge basin. It can use this strategic position to be the connector between countries. Having

Hungarians in every neighboring country is an advantage, not a disadvantage. Because Hungary has a foot in all its neighbors, it has power and influence on regional matters. In addition, Hungary should use its ancient Asian roots as a way to reach into Asia and cultivate ties there too. Once Hungary changes its perception of its history and its current position, its bright future will become the present.

The blond bimbo from North Carolina at the start of this chapter didn't know anything about Hungary. Her state is bigger than Hungary, which is the size of Indiana. Hungarians probably don't know much about North Carolina or Indiana either, but people from those states who have read this chapter now know more than just the capital of Hungary.

What Hungary Can Teach Us

- **Appreciate a thermal spring.** Hungarians value their water sources (the Danube, Balaton, and their hot springs) more than many countries with sea access. Soak in one of Hungary's 100 public thermal baths. Protect your waters by thinking twice about what goes down your drains.
- **Avoid boredom.** Hungarians are the fourth least bored people in the world. One reason for that is that they have dynamic discussions about profound topics. Avoid "safe" subjects and don't write trite emails. Dig deeper, read voraciously, and debate vigorously. Stir rich discussions and you'll never be bored.
- **Idolize scientists and engineers.** With America gaga over Lady Gaga, it's nice to see a country that celebrates its science and engineering stars more than its movie and athletic stars. What scientist is your role model? Which engineer do you idolize? Tell the world and help us refocus our values.

Places I saw and recommend in Hungary: Budapest (especially the Széchenyi Medicinal Bath), Eger, Szeged, Fertőd, Sopron and Kecskemét.

Travel deals and info: http://ftapon.com/hungary

Hungary is like America in one aspect: we're both useless at learning foreign languages. The EU surveyed 28 European countries and concluded that the worst at speaking a foreign language is Britain. However, right behind it is another monolingual state: Hungary. Only 29 percent of Hungarians say they can have a conversation in a foreign language. The UK is tad better than the US, where only 25 percent are fluent in a foreign language.

In 1990, Hungarians celebrated that they no longer had to learn Russian. However, instead of replacing that useful language with some other language, they seem to have decided not to learn any other language. Eva Balogh, a Hungarian who taught Eastern European history at Yale, said, "The teaching of foreign languages in Hungarian schools is bad. Very, very bad. As far back as I can remember it was bad."

Some argue that it's hard for Hungarians to learn a foreign language since most other languages are so vastly different from their alien tongue. However, Finns also have a bizarre language and yet they usually speak several languages.

Hungarians should visit their southwest neighbor and learn from Europe's polyglots: the Slovenians. We'll head there now and learn how and why Slovenians speak so many languages. You'll also learn why Slovenia has Europe's most dangerous backpacking, why Slovenians are workaholics, what makes the ex-Yugoslav countries so damn complicated, and how my six months in Slovenia changed my life.

11
Slovenia—Land of the Industrious Polyglots

I SLIPPED, BUT MANAGED to cling desperately to a snow-covered rock. There was a 100-meter drop below me—there is no way I could survive such a fall. I craned my neck up; the nearly vertical wall continued on many more meters. My blood was dripping on the snow from my fingers that were sliced by the sharp rocks I gripped. I didn't feel like dying on the tallest mountain of Slovenia. "How and why did I get myself into such a position?" I wondered.

We'll get to that soon, but first let's take a step back and learn a bit about Slovenia, a dinky country between Italy, Austria, Hungary, and Croatia. Of course that means nothing to us geographically ignorant Americans, so all you must know is that it's somewhere in Europe.

On the other hand, Americans who know that Slovenia is in Europe are a bit smarter than a French guy I met in Aix-en-Provence, in the southeast corner of France. When he handed me a paper promoting a bus transportation company, I asked him, "Do your buses go to Slovenia?"

He answered, "No, they only go to countries in Europe."

I smiled, "But Slovenia *is* in Europe. In fact, it's right next to Italy, 1,000 kilometers away, just a seven-hour drive from here."

"Oh. Well, then we go there."

You gotta wonder what continent this Frenchman thought Slovenia might be in. If it wasn't in Europe, did he think a country called *Slovenia* would be in Africa? Let's see . . . Sudan, Congo, Senegal . . . Slovenia! See, it fits right in! Does *Slovenia* sound like an Asian country? South American? More importantly, if Slovenia were on those other continents, does the dumbass really think I would want to take a bus that far?

In Italy, I met another geographical genius. This Italian was getting a PhD in history and asked me where I was going. I said, "One of your neighboring countries." He started guessing: France? Austria? Switzerland? Malta? He gave up. When I told him "Slovenia," he looked at me as if I had said "Burkina Faso."

Then he processed the concept and said, "Oh! *Yugoslavia!*"

"No, Yugoslavia hasn't existed for 20 years," I said. If an Italian PhD student doesn't know about Slovenia, what hope does the rest of the world have? Surely political leaders know, right?

Slovenia, Slovakia, Slavonia, Slobbovia

When a reporter asked George W. Bush if he would make Slovakia a priority, Bush replied, "The only thing I know about Slovakia is what I learned first-hand from your foreign minister, who came to Texas, and I had a great visit with him. It's an exciting country. It's a country that's flourishing, and it's a country that's doing very well."[1] Here's what's funny: Bush never met Slovakia's foreign minister; he met the Prime Minister of *Slovenia.*

Poor George at least had a decent excuse: he lives in America, far away from Slovenia and Slovakia. It's tough to remember every detail about the 193 countries of the world. Do you think that political leaders from Slovenia and Slovakia might get confused between Paraguay and Uruguay? Mauritius and Mauritania? Niger and Nigeria? Guinea and Guinea-Bissau?

At least European political leaders who share a border with Slovenia know all about it, right? Europeans lecture Americans for being geographically ignorant, so surely their leaders wouldn't make the same error as "stupid George Bush," right? Italy shares a border with Slovenia, so let's hear how Italian Prime Minister Silvio Berlusconi introduced the Prime Minister of *Slovenia:* "I'm very happy to be here today with the Prime Minister of Slovakia."

On the other hand, let's give Bush and Berlusconi credit: at least they didn't call it *Slobbovia.* Like Elbonia and Latveria, Slobbovia is yet another imaginary country invented by an American cartoonist. Hollywood has invented many others too. For example, there's Freedonia, Klopstokia, Vulgaria, Ignoramia, Moronica, and the twin states of Tomainia and Bacteria. All these countries were invented at a time when Eastern Europe was a mystery to most of the western world, which means they were invented last week.

Although we won't explore all these imaginary countries, it's worth checking out Slobbovia. Like Slovenia, Slobbovia is an interesting place. Slobbovians constantly live in waist-deep snow, speak with a strange Russian sounding accent, have icicles hanging from their frost-bitten noses, and are ruled by King Stubbornovsky The Last. The national dish of the famished Slobbovians is raw polar bear. Polar bears also fancy raw Slobbovians. Lastly, one Rasbucknik, the Slobbovian currency, is worthless, and a million Rasbuckniks is worth even less.

When Eastern Europeans were hiding behind the Iron Curtain, it was fun to invent stories about them. Today, they want us to take them seriously and learn their identity. However, they don't always make it easy for us. For example, Slovenia and Slovakia not only have similar names, but their flags are so similar that during an Olympic ceremony, organizers raised the wrong flag. What's worse is that there's also a large region called *Slavonia,* which is near Slovenia and Slovakia, but located in northeastern Croatia—wherever the hell that is.

A German who read the first chapters of my book said, "It's obviously written for Americans because you assume your reader doesn't know where Latvia is or anything about it." I challenged him to walk through the streets of Germany with a map of Europe that shows only the country borders and ask random Germans to find Latvia on the map. I promised him that far less than half could place it correctly. He never replied.

Later, when I told my German friend who lives near Munich that I was in Slovenia, he said, "Where's that?" He lives only 500 kilometers from Slovenia. That's like someone from Vermont not having any idea where New Jersey is. (By the way, Slovenia is smaller than New Jersey and Germany is smaller than Montana.) This wasn't some insular German farmer who is missing his two front teeth. My friend has traveled to 25 countries and driven from Munich to Estonia. I conclusion, Bush, Berlusconi, Italian PhDs, and well-traveled Germans aren't the only ones who are ignorant of Slovenia (and the rest of Eastern Europe). Let's discover this hidden part of Europe.

Surviving Slovenia's tallest mountain: Triglav

The first place I visited in Slovenia is a town called Bled. The hostels were full, so I slept with some dead roommates in a cemetery. It was drizzling, but I found a covered spot under the gardener's shed. Perhaps sleeping in a graveyard was a bad omen. Two days later, I would face Death.

Bled is one of the top fairy-tale locations in Europe. A romantic castle clings to the edge of a dramatic cliff, which overlooks a pristine lake. You can ride a gondola to visit the lake's small island that has a picture-perfect church on it. Couples love to marry in this enchanting setting. The enchantment fades for the groom when he must follow tradition and carry his bride up the church's 99 steps.

Besides being an idyllic place to wed, Bled is also a gateway to Eastern Europe's most dangerous mountains: the Julian Alps. My guidebook offered two warnings: (1) "Never *ever* try to trek alone." (2) "Above 1,500 meters you can encounter winter conditions anytime." I planned to hike to 2,864 meters (9,394 ft) alone. I shrugged, "What the hell do stupid travel writers know anyway?"

As I hiked up the mountain in the cold August rain, it was snowing on the peaks. Instead of staying in a mountain hut (which costs $30 per night), I camped outside with a tarp despite the freezing temperatures. As I fell asleep, I admired tomorrow's goal: the snow-covered summit of Mt. Triglav, Slovenia's highest peak.

At 5:00 a.m. I shook off the morning frost from the tarp and warmed up by hiking uphill vigorously. I didn't have a map because I've got this unfulfilled fantasy of having a helicopter rescue me from my own stupidity. Besides, how hard can it be to find your way to the summit of the tallest mountain in Slovenia? Just keep hiking up the well-marked trails until you're the tallest thing around, right?

Unfortunately, the brilliance of my logic quickly faded once the fresh snow obscured the trail. I stumbled through the snow, occasionally spotting a half-buried trail marker. After hours of breaking through virgin snow, I came to an apparent dead end. Everywhere I looked was a near vertical rock wall. Right before I turned around to retrace my steps to see where I had gotten lost, I spotted a blaze high on the rock face. That's when I learned that Slovenians have a loose definition of a "trail."

The steep 100-meter (328-ft) wall had a few metal handholds, a couple of meters of cable, and a dicey mix of fresh snow and ice. The handholds and cables were sometimes spaced far apart, leaving you to grip the sharp rock with your bare hands. This would be challenging in snow-free conditions, but without gloves my hands were so cold that they burned in pain. My sneakers were lousy at keeping my feet warm and gripping the icy rock. While kicking the snow off to find a foothold, I saw a trail of blood behind me. My adrenaline had made me ignore my sliced and bloody hands. If I slipped now, it would be a bumpy and disagreeable ride down. If you don't count my previous night in the cemetery, I'd never been so close to death.

Suddenly I heard a helicopter. "Oh good, they're coming to save me," I thought hopefully while hugging the rock. Instead the helicopter landed next to a hut far below, probably to drop off supplies and pick up the bodies of yesterday's failed hikers.

I eventually made it up the wall and ran into a pair of hikers at the pass who had taken an easier trail. They couldn't believe I was wearing sneakers. After celebrating at the top, I took the easiest way down, which wasn't super easy. Along the way, I found my favorite Slovenian. He had a rock climbing helmet, sturdy boots, gloves, a winter parka, and a twisted look on his face. He shouted something to me in Slovenian. I smiled and told him that I didn't understand. So he pointed at the white powder around us and yelled, "*Snow*!" Next, he vigorously pointed at my snow-covered sneakers and screamed, "*Shoes*!!" Then he formed his complex sentence: "*You IDIOT!!!*"

Ljubljana: the lovely capital of Slovenia

Ljubljana (pronounced lyoo-*blyah*-nah) doesn't feel like a European capital. With only 272,000 residents, it's one of Europe's smallest capitals. Its downtown center is so compact that after walking a few blocks you're done. Although it's tiny compared to other capitals, the lovely Ljubljana lives up to its name. In Slovenian, *ljubljena* means *beloved*. Slovenians promote a similar play on words in English as they often write their country's name as S**love**nia.

If Slovenia's core is Ljubljana, and Ljubljana's core is *Prešernov Trg* (Prešeren Square), then the core of Prešeren Square is truly the heart of the nation. So what's at the core of Prešeren Square, symbolizing the very soul of Slovenia? A statue of an alcoholic.

Prešeren Square gets its name from Slovenia's most famous drunk, who also wrote some profound poetry. Prešeren's larger-than-life greenish statue looks longingly across the beautiful square at the home of the rich girl he wanted to hook up with. After years of trying to win her, he gave up, married another girl, had three children, had several affairs, drank like a fish, tried to commit suicide twice, and died confessing his unfulfilled love—he was 48. Decades after he died of liver disease, Slovenians dusted off his poems and said, "Hey, that loser actually wrote some pretty good shit!"

Today, Prešeren is Slovenia's greatest poet. The Prešeren Award is Slovenia's highest reward for artistic achievement. He's on their two-euro coin. The day he died is a national holiday. His clever and epic poems united Slovenians after centuries of foreign rule. Most Slovenians can recite parts of his poems, especially "*Zdravljica*" ("Toast"), which the Austria-Hungary Empire banned. Today, it's Slovenia's national anthem.

Springing forth from Prešeren Square is the iconic and pedestrian-only *Tromostovje* (Triple Bridge), which spans the Ljubljanica River. The medieval *Ljubljanski Grad* (Ljubljana Castle) overlooks the city on a forested hill. As pleasant as Ljubljana is, it's more bewitching to visit Slovenia's underworld.

Three otherworldly Slovenian caves

Imagine if the Grand Canyon were underground—that should give you an idea of what to expect when you enter the *Škocjanske Jame* (Škocjan Caves). Lonely Planet listed them as one of the top 10 attractions in Eastern Europe. They're also on the UNESCO World Heritage list and get 100,000 visitors a year. They live up to their reputation by being one of the largest underground canyons in the world with the Reka river still carving through it. At 60 meters wide and 140 meters deep, this canyon is a fraction of the Grand Canyon's size, but the fact that it's all underground makes it feel bigger. When you cross the canyon via the narrow Hanke Canal Bridge, you'll see the roaring river far below. You'll realize that you could fit a fat 45-story skyscraper in this subterranean world.

The Škocjan underworld is so enormous that a unique ecosystem has evolved here—it's home to strange blind creatures that have never seen sunlight. The most bizarre one is the proteus. Slovenians informally call it the *človeška ribica* (human fish). This alien vertebrate is as long as your forearm, has a long tail for swimming, gills, four legs, pigment-free skin, a highly sensitive nose, a sensor for detecting weak electrical fields in the water, and a pair of atrophied lungs and eyes that don't really work. They're a weird amphibian that lives almost exclusively in water. Their life cycle is mystifying: they live almost as long as humans, they become sexually mature as teenagers, they have never been seen reproducing in the wild, their babies hatch out of eggs, and they can live up to 10 years without food. It's one of the most hidden creatures in the Hidden Europe.

About 30 minutes away from the Škocjan Caves is the Postojna Cave, which features perhaps the most thrilling underground train ride on Earth. To help you explore part of the 21-kilometer cave system, an open-air train whisks you through cavern after cavern in what feels like a Disneyland ride. The difference is that everything you see is real! As you zip under narrow openings, you'll sometimes feel like you need to duck to avoid hitting a stalactite. The ride feels like it's straight out of Jules Verne's *Journey to the Center of the Earth*. The train eventually stops and the one-hour walking tour begins. The tour's climax is a subterranean chamber called the Concert Hall, which holds music events that can accommodate an audience of 10,000.

Slovenia's third amazing cave has a gaping mouth so enormous that a castle is embedded in it! The invincible and surreal Predjama Castle is straight out of one of Tolkien's visions. A medieval Robin Hood, Erazem Lueger, used this fantasy fortress as his hideout. When Austrian soldiers laid siege for months, he tossed fresh cherries and flowers on them to prove that he had a secret magical portal that let him come and go at will. His fun ended when he was sitting on the toilet and an Austrian cannonball landed on him.

Dušan Trušnovec in Slap Ob Idrijci

Although Slovenia is tiny, I returned five years later because I felt I hadn't seen enough of it. It was the final stop of my second tour through every country in Eastern Europe. Keeping with the theme of my 2008–2011 tour, I focused on villages and lesser-known parts of each country. A hamlet with the bizarre name of Slap Ob Idrijci seemed like a perfect place to start. It's there that, thanks to Couchsurfing, I would meet a man who would change my life.

At first glance, Dušan Trušnovec seems like a typical Slovenian. He's a robust 53-year-old man with a wife, three dogs, two children, and a small farm with potatoes, kiwis, persimmons, and horses. He's constantly busy doing something. It's usually something productive, but even if it's not, that doesn't matter to most Slovenians—at least he's doing *something*. Also, like most ex-Yugoslavs, he believes many of the region's fables. And, in his more creative moments, he invents a few new ones.

On the other hand, Dušan seems like from another planet. He's a vegetarian who is involved in Sri Sri Ravi Shankar's Art of Living Organization. Dušan meditates and often travels around with his huge didgeridoo. He's built several yurts on his property to host people and events for free, surviving on donations alone. He's a fanatical believer in *laisser faire* to the point that he truly lets his children do whatever the hell they want—which has produced two radically different kids. His kids call him "Dušan," not "Dad," because Dušan wants to be their friend, not their authority figure. Whereas most Slovenians will shake your hand, he'll insist on hugging you. He believes love is the answer to any problem. He's a hippie with practically no hair.

Before I met Dušan, I thought that Slap Ob Idrijci got its name because the bad Mr. Idrijci slapped people around there. Instead, in Slovenian, *slap* means *waterfall* and *ob* means *by,* so the village's name translates to *Waterfall by the Idrijca (River).* It's false advertising since there's no longer a waterfall there. Still, steep mountains soar around this green and enchanting valley near Tolmin. Deep in the soil of this idyllic wonderland is the blood of a million people killed there in WWI. Ernest Hemingway was injured there while driving an ambulance during the brutal fighting; he wrote about it in *A Farewell to Arms.* WWI was arguably more dramatic and important for Slovenia than WWII. Slovenia will have many ceremonies commemorating the 100-year anniversary of WWI in 2014. Dušan showed me some of its haunting remnants. He also drove me on obscure dirt roads that took us to forgotten mountain villages where the locals make tasty cheese. Later, we drove by the quaint villages along the turquoise Soča River, which is Europe's most beautiful river.

After staying a few days in Dušan's three-story house, he took me to his sea house in Crveni Vrh, Croatia. The simple house was built during the Yugoslav period, which means that it has a certain quirky, piecemeal randomness to it. For example, it's not watertight, the outdoor drains are secured with a cord, parts of the floor are uneven, the staircase is irregular, and the kitchen and one bathroom is outside. On the other hand, it has a world-class view that overlooks the Adriatic Sea, the old Venetian town of Piran, and the snowy Julian Alps.

After chilling out there for a couple of days, I bid Dušan and Eastern Europe farewell. I was going to spend a few months goofing off in 10 Western European countries, climbing solo up Mont Blanc in trail runners, and hiking across Spain twice (first traversing the Pyrenees and then trekking El Camino Santiago). While I was in Spain, Dušan made me an offer that I couldn't refuse. He invited me to return to Slovenia and write my book at his sea house. His family spends little time there in the winter, so I would be alone. I had originally planned to write my book in Montenegro and Moldova, but Dušan's generous offer made me change my mind. That decision would set in motion a chain of events that changed my life.

Meeting Anamarija Mišmaš

December 10, 2009 was a rainy day in Koper, a port city that has had many names through the ages. Ancient Greeks called it *Aegida,* back when Koper was an island that had a canal separating it from the mainland. The Romans raised goats there and called it *Capris*. The Byzantines named it *Justinopolis*. In the 1200s, it got the name *Caput Histriae,* meaning "Capital of Istria," which Italians morphed into *Capodistria*. After the Venetians built their architectural masterpieces, the Slavs kicked them out and changed the town's name again. None of this mattered as I waited in the drizzle for my couchsurfing host to pick me up from the Koper bus station. Dušan was busy with one of his many mysterious tasks, so he couldn't meet me in Koper for a while. Therefore, I had to find a host for a few days.

Some spend hours looking for the perfect couchsurfing host, but I have a simple method. When I search for a host, I sort the results by "newest accounts" first and contact the first 10 of those. There are four reasons I do this. First, new couchsurfing accounts are eager to get their first reference so they can easily couchsurf when they travel too. Second, because I have over 100 positive references (and no negative ones), it gives new hosts confidence that I won't steal their computer, rape them, or blow their house up. After a positive first experience, they participate more in the couchsurfing community, thereby expanding it and taking some pressure away from other hosts. Third, new hosts are enthusiastic, whereas veteran hosts can be jaded. Fourth, if they don't reply to me, that makes their "couchsurfing response rate" drop from 100 percent to zero (assuming I'm the only guy who has written to them); this helps weed out the deadbeats. I often stay with hosts who have neither a photo nor a complete profile. Despite this Russian Roulette method, I've only had great experiences.

I didn't know much about Anamarija Mišmaš, my Koper couchsurfing host, before I met her. Ana's couchsurfing profile showed that she had just signed up two weeks before I wrote to her and that she was a 20-year-old nursing student who loves books, languages, and nature. Her only photo on her profile was a fuzzy one of her hopping on a seaside rock in her winter clothes. When I first saw Ana, she was walking toward me with a carefree, I'm-just-happy-to-be-alive stride. We had exchanged several emails before we met, so we felt familiar enough to hug in the rain. She was much more beautiful than I expected.

Ana gave me a tour of Koper and helped me refresh my basic Slovenian. Koper is like most of Slovenia: clean, attractive, and efficient. In less than an hour you can walk everywhere in the old town. Its narrow pedestrian-only streets and attractive Venetian architecture show off Italy's fingerprint. We stopped to have a tea, a sweet snack, and review the basics of Slovenian: *dober dan* (good day), *prosim* (please/you're welcome), *hvala* (thank you), *oprostite* (excuse me), *adijo* (goodbye), *ja* (yes), *ne* (no), *kje je . . . ?* (where is . . . ?), *kako ste*? (how are you?), and I love the sound of *koliko*? (how much?). Although the basics are easy, mastering the language is not.

Slovenians think a pair is significant

Since I would be living a year either in or near Slovenia, I decided to learn the difficult Slovenian language. Andreja Nastasja Terbos, a Slovenian with a master's degree in English and Italian Translation, believes I'm wrong to characterize Slovenian as "difficult." She said, "There's no such thing as easy or difficult languages." We're friends who enjoy sending combative emails to each other, so if she sounds angry, don't worry, she's (probably) not. She has many buttons to push, which makes it hard for me to resist pushing them. For example, I had to ridicule her prediction that Chinese will be the world's *lingua franca* by 2050. Later, I mischievously pressed another of her buttons when I said, "If linguists were to rank languages in order of difficulty, English would be classified as easier than Slovenian. To believe that the ease of language has little connection with its popularity is stupid."

Andreja Nastasja wrote, "There's no such concept as 'easiness' in linguistics, Francis, as I've told you many times. That's a laical way of looking at languages so *no* linguist would tell you that you can do such a thing as *ranking* languages the way you want them to. They'd say (myself included) that *that's* stupid."

Let's see how stupid that is by examining Slovenian closely. Let's start with the fact that Slovenians think a pair is significant enough to merit special conjugation—it's called the *dvojina (*the dual). Most languages have verbs in singular and plural forms; for example, *on teče* (he runs—singular) and *mi tečemo* (we run—plural). But in Slovenian, if something involves two males or a male and a female, then you would say *midva tečeva.* But if you're a girl and you're with another girl (dual-feminine), then it's *midve tečeva* (both of us girls run). In some ways, the dual is easy since *midva* simply combines *mi-* (we) with *-dva* (two), meaning *we-two*. However, there are six dual pronouns, each requiring a unique conjugation—this will leave your head spinning and wondering what's the point.

Andreja Nastasja insists there are benefits to the dual, "What it really expresses and creates is the intimacy between two persons." Many Slovenians agree that the dual, especially between a man and a woman, has a romantic, cozy ring to it. Dušan's son, Nejc, told me, "My grammar teacher once told us that because of the dual, Slovenian is a language of love." However, when you're learning it, it feels more like the language of torture.

A Slovenian biology teacher, Tamara Čelhar, told me the dual is "practical because you avoid having to ask how many you were or who you were with." She also agrees that the dual "can conjure a sort of intimacy." However, because of that, Slovenians will sometimes trick you by not using the dual, especially when they're referring to someone they're not romantically involved with. They'll incorrectly use the plural, even though only two people are involved. This deceitful tactic has saved countless Slovenian relationships.

Sometimes the dual leads to more questions, not fewer. For example, Andreja Nastasja's roommate, Željka, is talking about her day with her boyfriend and says, *"Šli smo v trgovino"* ("We went to the store"). Because Željka used the plural and not the dual (*"Šla sva v trgovino"*), Andreja Nastasja imagines that there are at least three people going to the store. This makes her ask who the other person was. Željka must clarify that there were only two of them. (She's from the only part of Slovenia that doesn't religiously use the dual.) Time to push another button, so I said, "Andreja Nastasja, only a fool can't see that the dual adds an extra layer of complexity."

She shot back, "I challenge you to think if Slovenian grammar really is complicating things. My opinion is that it's not. It may be time-consuming for you but kids here learn it with no effort. *Besides*, what are we really arguing about regarding the dual here? It's two fucking endings! And to complicate things even further, they are painfully similar to the plural! It's *-(s)va* and *-(s)ta*. *Midva hodiva* (we two walk), *vidva hodita* (you two walk), *onadva hodita* (they two walk). Now if that's too big of a deal for people to learn, then they may as well not learn Slovenian at all and live in their ultra-simplified ignorant-adapted worlds."

Let's consider how our beautifully ultra-simplified ignorant English world conjugates the verb *to cook*: I cook, you cook, we cook. The only change we make is for the third person singular, where we add a single letter—he/she cook*s*. In Slovenian, verbs change depending on: if it's singular, dual, plural (3 or more), if the person is male or female, if you're being formal or informal, and on the position of Venus. This results in: *jaz kuham* (I cook), *ti kuhaš* (you cook), *on/ona kuha* (he/she cooks), *midva/midve kuhava* (us two cook—dual), *vidva/vidve kuhata* (you two cook—dual, formal), *onadva/onidve kuhata* (the two of them cook—dual, informal), *mi kuhamo* (we cook—informal), *vi/ve kuhate (you cook*—formal), *oni/one kuhajo* (they cook). Easy, right?

The dual also complicates simple concepts like *naš* (ours), *njihov* (theirs), and *tvoj* (yours). To be merciful, let's just examine *tvoj*. If you're referring to a female noun, you say *tvoja;* however, if you're being respectful, you'd say *vaš* (male noun) or *vaša* (female noun). Although that's more complex than English, many languages play such games. However, the demonic dual transforms *yours* into: *vajin* (dual—male nouns), *vajina* (dual—female nouns) *vajino* (dual—neuter nouns). That's six unique ways to say *yours.* If you count grammatical case variations, then add *vaši, vaše, vašo, vašim, vaših, vašega, vašem,* and *vašemu*. That's 14 ways to say *yours.* At this point, you'll want to tell a Slovenian, "Up *yours*."

The dual is evil and must be destroyed. Do you think that I'm a close-minded, stupid English speaker for saying that? Of course I am. Still, all Slavs (except Slovenians) happen to agree with me. Hundreds of years ago, the Polish, Slovak, Czech, Serbian, Croatian, Russian, and Bulgarian languages all used the dual. In fact, Arabic, Hebrew, Tagalog, Hungarian, Finnish, Estonian, Greenlandic, Greek, German, and even Old English had the dual! Lithuania was last seen using the dual in the 1920s. In short, over the centuries, nearly the whole planet wised up and got rid of the dual because they thought it was a pain in the ass. *Earth to Slovenia: give it up, dude!*

Andreja Nastasja didn't budge, "I'm proud of the Slovenian dual and so are most of us. If I have children, I hope they use it after I help them realize it's nice that there exists an absolute form for just 'me and somebody else,' just the two of us, in *one* word. And hopefully they will be proud of it, too. It builds character to stick to something after so many have given up on it."

Thanks, but I'd rather be characterless. If you think the dual is a royal headache, then get ready, it all gets much worse.

Singular, dual, plural, and large plural

Slovenians complicate the simplest of things. In English, if there's more than one noun, we generally just add an *-s*. In Slovenian, nouns can be changed in four ways depending on if the noun is singular, dual, plural (three or four), or large plural (five or more). Among Slavic languages, only Slovenian is so complicated. For example, whereas we say *one condom, two condoms, three condoms, four condoms,* and *five condoms,* Slovenians say *en kondom, dva kondoma, trije kondomi, štirje kondomi,* and *pet kondomov.* Notice that *three* and *four* condoms share the same ending, but that the ending changes one last time when you get to five or more. It all makes you want to only buy *en kondom.*

What's worse is that the plural endings will change depending on the sex of the object. Let's say you want to say, *one table, two tables, three tables, five tables; one chair, two chairs, three chairs, five chairs; one town, two towns, three towns, five towns.* Since the gender of these objects is obvious (just examine them to see if they have a penis), you'd say: *ena miza, dve mizi, tri mize, pet miz; en stol, dva stola, trije stoli, pet stolov; eno mesto, dve mesti, tri mesta, pet mest.* Did you notice how nearly every word changes? Do you know how badly I want to find the jerk who invented this language and beat him over the head with five chairs and two tables?

Some languages do fun things with plurals. For example, in two African languages (Gworok and Ngiti) the plural is indicated by tone alone. Imagine saying *one dog* and *10 dog* (but *dog* here is said with a different tone to indicate the plural). North America's Kiowa people have a plural marker that means *of unexpected number*. Let's say that plural marker is *x*, then you could say *he walked on his legx* (which means he has either *one* or *more than two legs*—an unexpected number). Or *the basketball team playerx went onto the court* (since the standard basketball team has five players, this means that there were not five players—an unexpected number). The Japanese are super simple: they have no plural! Indeed, why don't we just say *there are 52 table and many chair*? How the Ngiti, Kiowa, and Japanese people deal with the plural is fun; how the Slovenians do it is not.

Whenever Slovenians argue that the dual or the large plural is no big deal, tell them to imagine if English not only had the dual, but the triplet—so whenever you refer to three people, there is yet another way of declining the noun. Furthermore, imagine if English didn't just have a special suffix for the dual, plural, and large plural, but also a different one for the extra-large plural (for 5–6 things), the XX-large plural (for 7–9 things), and the XXX-large plural (for 10 or more things or anything pornographic). The Slovenian would cry, "But that's an extreme and unnecessary complication!" Exactly. Just like the dual and the large plural.

Tough dilemma: learn Slovenian or commit suicide

Slovenian not only assigns gender to every object, but that gender also infects their numbers. For example, the number *pet* (five) becomes *peti november* because a *month* is masculine, but you must say *peta lekcija* because obviously a *lesson* is feminine and *pet lekcija* might be too easy. Fortunately, most feminine words end with *-a*, so they're easy to spot. However, *dva* is the masculine version of the number *two*; hence, if it's two female thingies, then it's not the feminine-sounding *dva*, but the masculine-sounding *dve.* In sum, numbers are either masculine, feminine or neuter, at least until you get to the number five. That's when the bastard who invented Slovenian got bored with giving each stupid number a different gender and decided that all numbers over five won't have any gender. It's just a pity he didn't come to that brilliant conclusion a bit earlier, say, at the number *one.* Speaking of *one,* Slovenian has four ways to say that lonely number: *en, ena, eno,* or *eden.* Which one you use depends on what phase the moon is in.

Unlike other Slavs, Slovenians don't even know how to count. To say 23, Slovenians say *three-and-twenty.* Or 79 is *nine-and-seventy.* Of course, they don't read all their numbers from right to left, because that might be consistent and logical. Instead, 154 is *one hundred four-and-fifty,* and 24,893 is *twenty-four thousand eight-hundred three-and-ninety.* This makes it tough for a Slovenian novice to write down phone numbers, since they rattle off phone numbers by using big numbers and not individual numbers like English speakers do. Thus, 485-8426 is *four hundred five-and-eighty, eight thousand four hundred six-and-twenty.* The same goes for years. So 1952 is *one thousand nine hundred two-and-fifty.* That's hard to follow in English; now try decoding it in Slovenian: *tisoč devetsto dvainpetdeset.*

A cultural relativist would accuse me of using English linguistic logic when judging Slovenian. To see if there is such a thing as universal logic, I asked Slovenians what they thought when they first learned how people count in English. Aprila Cotič summed up what most told me, "My first reaction was, 'Of course! Why don't we do this way? Duh!'"

Slovenians picked up this illogical way of counting numbers from the world's most logical people: the Germans. Clearly, Slovenia's proximity to Austria made them adopt this bad habit, whereas all the other Slavs didn't follow the German example. Interestingly, over 100 years ago English, being a Germanic language, counted like the Germans and Slovenians. In fact, remnants of this logic appear in our "teen" numbers (e.g., *sixteen,* instead *teen-six*). Fortunately, the English wised up and unfortunately the Germans and the Slovenians did not. Nevertheless, I suppose we should all be grateful that Slovenians don't count like the French, who say 73 as *sixty-thirteen* and 95 as *four-twenty-fifteen* (the "logic" there is that 95 is four times twenty plus fifteen).

Before English speakers get too smug about our superior way of counting, our numbering system needs simplification. Since we say *ninety, eighty, seventy, sixty,* and *forty,* shouldn't we say *fivety* for 50, *threety* for 30, and *twoty* for 20? We should also change the spelling of *four* to *for,* so that it's consistent with *forty.* While we're at it, we could count down like so: nineteen, eighteen, seventeen, sixteen, *fiveteen,* fourteen, *threeteen, twoteen,* and *oneteen.* Or even better: *teen-nine, teen-eight, teen-seven . . . .*

Another way that Slovenian is illogical is that it uses double-negatives. I often correct Ana, who sometimes uses double-negatives in

English, because that's normal in Slovenian. Three examples: *nihče ni tukaj* (literally, *nobody is not here,* meaning *nobody is here);* or *on ni nikoli utrujen* (literally, *he is not never tired,* meaning *he is never tired*); or *jaz ne grem nikoli nikamor peš* (literally, *I don't walk never anywhere,* meaning *I never walk anywhere).* Shakespeare used double-negatives, but modern English made them illegal because they're inherently contradictory and illogical, but that obviously doesn't bother Slovenians.

If none of this drives you to commit suicide, this will: Slovenian has 52 dialects (divided into eight major groups). After months of studying, you'll be able to say *šli smo domov in se spet imeli lepo* (we went home and had a good time again); then some jerk who lives a couple of hours away from Ljubljana will say the same sentence this way: *šli smo domou in se palik meli fajn.* Although Slovenia may be smaller than New Jersey, the differences in its dialects are greater than the different ways of speaking English in Australia, America, England, Wales, and Scotland. Compare the last line of the Lord's Prayer: *temveč reši nas hudega* (official Slovenian), *nego odslobodi nas od hüdoga* (Prekmurje dialect) and *nek nas zbavi od sekih hudobah* (Medžimurje-Kaikavian dialect). Also, Slovenian movies often don't use proper Slovenian, so if that's all you know, you'll be confused. The fact that most Slovenians *can* speak official Slovenian doesn't help you when they lapse into their dialect, which they do often. If you want to follow what they're saying, then you'll have to learn their jive talk that makes English slang seem pompous.

It's politically correct to gush about the beauty of every language, to admire their alphabets, the sound of their words, and their unique grammar. Often people who engage in such revelry aren't learning many languages. They admire them from afar, just like we might admire an Eskimo—they're fascinating, but few would want to live like they do. Similarly, Slovenian is cool if you're just passing through, but once you have to learn the damn language, you realize what a pain in the ass it is.

300 hairy bears

Learning Slovenian is as much fun as repeatedly hitting your finger with a hammer. Therefore, you'll soon want to learn a few swearwords. Unfortunately, the story here is disappointing too. Slovenians are fucking pussies—they don't even know how to swear properly.

I was helping Dušan repair the roof of his sea house. Occasionally, he would mutter, "Shit" or "Fuck!" I asked him, "Dušan, are you swearing in English just because I'm around or do you normally swear in English?"

Dušan said, "Usually I swear in English, but sometimes I swear in Croatian."

"So when do you swear in Slovenian?"

"Almost never," he said. "Our swearwords aren't very good."

Hence, Slovenians have something in common with Latvians: they use foreign swearwords because their native words lack sufficient punch. If you recall, Latvians borrow swearwords from Russian and English. Meanwhile, Slovenians borrow their bad words from Croatian and English. How weak are the Slovenian naughty words? Try: *pojdite se solit!* (go salt yourself!), *križana gora!* (crucified hill!), *jebela cesta!* (white road!), and the earth-shattering *tristo kosmatih medvedov* (three hundred hairy bears).

Dumbfounded, I begged Dušan to think hard of the most potent insult a Slovenian could muster. After working on the roof for another hour, he finally figured it out, "*Kurc te gleda.*"

"Great!" I said. "What does that mean?"

"A dick is watching you."

Unless you're the world's biggest homophobe, that's about as insulting as *a bitch is watching you*. I couldn't take it anymore, so I begged Dušan to share what real Slovenian men say when they're furious. If they don't use English swearwords, then Slovenians use Croatian zingers like *jebem ti mater* (I fuck your mother) or *u pičku materinu* (into the cunt of mother). Nevertheless, even some Croatian insults are a bit puzzling: *ko te jebe* (who fucks you) and *jebem ti sunce, ti jebem* (I fuck your sun, I fuck).

Slovenian is slowly simplifying

As a language spreads, it tends to simplify. English used to have several past tenses; now we generally just add *-ed*. Nearly half of 177 irregular Old English verbs are now regular and predictable.[2] English continues to simplify: few care about split infinitives, the subjunctive case, and the once-common words *shall* and *whom*. Because Slovenian hasn't spread as far as other Slavic tongues, it's been slower to simplify. Nevertheless, there are three bits of evidence that show that even Slovenian may be simplifying. First, Slovenians in Slovenian Littoral are not using the dual consistently. They credit the Italian influence and the laid-back coastal Slovenians who can't be bothered with the tedious dual.

Second, in the Julian Alps, a few mountain women conjugate words like men. Normally you change words if you're a woman so that *sem pozen* (I'm late) becomes *sem pozna* if you're a woman. In Slovenia's Upper Carniola, women just say *sem pozen* and only the out-of-towners giggle. As any English speaker knows, you can survive without gender distinctions and some feminists would say that it's less sexist to have a gender-neutral language.

Third, the informal nature of the Internet and text messages is encouraging a few Slovenians to use *ti* (the informal way of saying *you*) nearly exclusively. Dušan likes that English doesn't have a formal and informal way of saying *you* "because we're all human beings." He likes that English doesn't have hierarchy and status embedded in the language—it's intrinsically egalitarian. However, given that Slovenia is a somewhat formal society, it's unlikely that this simplification will catch on.

Slovenian is also doing what most languages of the world are doing: borrowing English words. For example, instead of saying *denar* (money), young Slovenians often say *keš* (which sounds like "cash"); hipsters also say *frend* instead of *prijatelj* (friend). However, such straightforward borrowing is a bit too simple for Slovenians, who prefer to complicate their language as much as possible. Therefore, instead of directly borrowing an English word, they'll bastardize it. For instance, *gremo* means *let's go* or *let's start*, but nowadays Slovenians may say *startamo.*

One English bastardization you'll hear every five minutes in Slovenia is the word *full.* A few years ago, a bored Slovenian teenager decided that *zelo* isn't a cool way of saying *very.* However, he didn't think that *very* sounded very cool either. Yet for some unknown reason he felt that the English word *full* was a hip way of saying *very* or *zelo,* probably because *full* has something to do with *to the max.* What's funny is that because of their accent, Slovenians pronounce *full* so that it sounds like *fool.* Don't get me wrong, I love Slovenia; its language is the only thing about this country that is not *full cool.*

The Slovenian blessing and curse: writing it

Before I finish bashing the poor, innocent Slovenian language that never meant to hurt anybody (except all the foolish foreigners who try to learn it), let's briefly bash English. I could write a book documenting all the reasons why English sucks. However, since we're staying focused on Eastern Europe, let's just examine one aspect of English that I hate: its spelling system. Slovenians can't believe that in English *no* and *know* have the same sound. Same for *cot* and *caught,* or *to, too,* and *two,* or *their, there* and *they're,* or *right, write,* and *rite,* or *knight, night,* and *nite,* or *where, wear,* and *ware.* That's not the only way that our spelling is boneheaded. Some words are spelled the same way, but have different pronunciations, as in *the dove dove in the bushes.* Each of these words has two possible pronunciations: *wound, produce, read, refuse, present, sow, subject, intimate, object,* and *sewer*. Say this sentence aloud to see how maddening English can be: *the soldier decided to desert his dessert in the desert*. This kind of linguistic bullshit would never happen in Slovenian!

When I was a child, my mom would piss me off whenever I asked her how to spell something in English. She would always tell me to "look it up in the dictionary." Often I didn't even know which letter to start with! *Cacophony* might be *kakofony* or *kakofoni*. Or I'd be looking up *faro* instead of *pharaoh*. What hope do you have of finding *schizophrenic* in a dictionary if you logically believe that it's spelled *skitsofrenik*? Whenever I asked Ana how to spell a Slovenian word, she said, "You foreigners are funny. Slovenians never ask how to spell something. Every letter is pronounced just one simple way, so there is only one obvious way of writing anything."

I would love it if English had the simple, logical Slovenian writing system, but there are three dirty secrets that Slovenians don't tell you. First, they sometimes don't pronounce letters; for example, *pes* (dog) is pronounced *ps*, *megla* (fog) is pronounced *mgla*, and *čmrlj* (bumble bee) is pronounced *čmru*. Second, sometimes *l* or *v* are pronounced like a *u*, like in *rjav* (brown), *včeraj* (yesterday), *potolči* (beat), and *Triglav*. Many languages that have logical phonetic spelling systems also have a few minor exceptions like this, so it's easy to forgive. However, the third secret is the big ugly green monster.

Slovenia's blessed writing mechanic comes with a curse. *In Slovenian, you write like a word sounds, but you don't write like you talk.* Slovenian books don't sound like people talk. They write everything with the same awkward, wordy, and formal manner that you might find in a boring English academic textbook. The difference is that Slovenians don't reserve that style for textbooks—they use it in anything that's written. Compare the written way, *ne moreš se tako pogovarjati*, with the spoken way, *ne morš se tko pogovarjat*. They both mean *you cannot talk this way*, but if you only know the official spoken way, you will write it incorrectly. If you say it like it's written, then everyone will laugh at you for being a dork. This complicates life for the fool who dreams of reading and writing in Slovenian. It also detracts from their glorious phonetic writing system. Fortunately, many young Slovenians are rebelling and using spoken Slovenian in their e-mails and text messages. Let's hope that the new generation also ignores the dual and stops counting like morons.

Perspective check on Slovenian

We're not good at analyzing our native language. For example, while Tamara and I were walking, she denied that Slovenian grammar has a large plural concept, "We only have the dual," she assured me. I pointed to a car and asked her to count five cars. She rolled her eyes, but just to prove the ignorant American wrong she started counting, "*En avto, dva avta, trije avti, štirje avti, pet avtov . . .*" Suddenly, she looked like she had just learned that her parents are really Albanian.

I hate that most French words aren't spelled how they sound. When I said that to a French lady who teaches English (you'd think a language teacher would be self-aware of her native language), she said that I was wrong. We opened a random book. As I pointed to nearly every word, her eyes became as wide as an owl's, and she whispered, "My God, you're right. . ." Likewise, English speakers are oblivious that we have an overwhelming number of synonyms, an excessive number of verb tenses, and an annoying habit of using cryptic idioms every ten minutes. Has all this been driving you bananas?

The reason languages feel like they're designed by a committee is that they are! Languages are the work of a committee of millions. That's why languages are like the outcomes of many committees: they're inefficient, illogical, and idiotic. The easiest, most logical language wasn't made by a committee, at least not a very large committee. It's called Esperanto and one guy designed most of it. As a result, it's logical and incredibly simple. After a few centuries, languages, like most committees, will admit that their output stinks and they will begin to simplify things. This is especially true if vast numbers of adults (who are less patient and less accepting of senseless rules than infants) must learn the language.

For example, Old English had many declinations, inflections, and cases. It had informal and formal pronouns (*you* vs. *thou*). Even more twisted: in Old English, the simple article *the* could morph into a variety of forms, including masculine, feminine, or neuter; it also had five different forms as a singular and four forms as a plural! As English spread, more people said, "This is retarded, let's simplify this." Because Slovenian is not as widespread as English, it has been slow to simplify.[3]

If it's true that "*no* linguist" would say that one language is more complicated than another, then all linguists should be shot. Even though a Slav invented Esperanto, it doesn't use cases because he felt they're too complicated. Esperanto's intuitive rules, easy spelling system, and lack of irregular logic allows people from all countries to learn it in record time. A Croatian, Daria Dzaja, told me, "If I wanted to confuse the CIA's wiretapping spies, I would create a code language that uses cases."

Fortunately, there's at least two linguists who should not be shot. University of Wisconsin Professor Gary Lupyan grew up in Belarus and has published statistical research that shows how languages tend to simplify as they spread. He wrote to me, "It is indeed true that most linguists believe all languages to be equally complex. This is based on dogma, not facts." UC Berkeley's Professor John McWhorter has shown how not all languages are equally complex by proving how English has simplified far more than its many Germanic sister languages.[4] Professor

Lupyan told me, "There is absolutely no data backing up the claim to which many linguists are attached that all languages are equally difficult or easy to learn. There is no invisible hand that somehow equalizes the difficulty of all languages."

Finally, a joint US-Slovenian study showed that American and Slovenian infants reach an equal level of language competency at 1.5 and 3 years, respectively. This either proves that Slovenian is more complicated than English or that Slovenian babies are stupid. We Americans will not tolerate some puny, insignificant nation trying to claim that it's stupider than us. We've worked hard to earn the reputation of being the stupidest country in the world, so I'd rather conclude that some languages are indeed more complicated than others.

As much as I love to critique languages (including English), I end up learning more phrases than the average tourist who might scold me for saying the awful things I say about a foreign language. It's horrible that many tourists never even bother to learn how to say *thank you* in whatever foreign country they are traveling in. As punishment, they should be forced to spend three months learning Slovenian. Therefore, let yourself be shocked at the folly of every language, but do your best to learn it anyway.

Nation of polyglots

The complexity of *slovenščina* (the Slovenian language) isn't the main reason few try to learn it; the real reason nobody tries to learn it is that Slovenians usually speak your native language. Within Europe, Slovenians come in third in speaking a foreign language. Europeans proclaim they're all polyglots, but 44 percent of EU citizens can only speak one language. In contrast, it's nearly impossible to find a monolingual person in Slovenia. While 28 percent of Europeans speak at least three languages, a whopping 71 percent of Slovenians are at least trilingual. Only the Netherlands (75%) and Luxembourg (92%) have higher percentages.

In Eastern Europe, I often had to ask 10 random people to find one good English speaker. In Slovenia, I had to ask 10 people to find one person who did *not* speak English. They also normally spoke either Croatian, Italian, or German (and many spoke all three of them). Several Slovenians I met also understood Spanish, thanks to the *telenovelas.* Sanela Kadić, a Slovenian who is fluent in six languages, told me, "Slovenians always make the effort to learn other people's languages, so nobody bothers to learn Slovenian." That's the price you pay for being a nation of just two million surrounded by much larger linguistic regions (Italy, Germany, South Slavic). Nevertheless, Slovenians are rightfully frustrated that some immigrants live in Slovenia for years and never learn Slovenian properly. Since Slovenians are the masters of learning many languages, they can teach the world how they do it.

How to learn a language quickly

With seven in 10 Slovenians being trilingual, they know all the tricks to learn any language fast. They shared their tips with me. First, it's a myth that kids are better at learning languages than adults. If an adult spends as much time as a child does to learn Latvian, he'll know it just as well as a child. The only reason children seem to learn faster than adults is that they spend more time studying. Still, a child does have one advantage over an adult: pronunciation. Although an eight-year-old can't learn Bulgarian any faster than a 40-year-old, the child will be better at speaking it without an accent. Before 14 years old, humans are able to mimic the correct sounds of any language. However, after 14, we begin to lose that ability. That's why some American immigrants use words that only a Scrabble nut would know, but say with an accent.

Now that you know you can learn any language, let's see how Slovenians do it quickly. Andreja Nastasja, who is fluent in three languages and proficient in three more, offered great advice: do what children do. Watch cartoons (which is easy with YouTube), read children's books and comic books. They all use core vocabulary, basic grammar, and helpful pictures. Don't feel stupid reading *Little Red Riding Hood* in Hungarian. When you read books, don't discourage yourself by trying to understand everything. Favor small dictionaries because they're easy to carry and have the essential words. Improve your vocabulary by associating it with experience—you're more likely to remember what a *mešalnik* is if you use one (it's a blender). Listen to music in your desired language, decode the lyrics, and sing along. Many children aren't afraid to make mistakes—neither should you.

If you lack discipline, hire a young tutor. They're cheap and are unlikely to teach you the traditional (not commonly used) way of saying something. Favor solo learning over group learning. Groups often don't focus on your needs and your weaknesses. Online courses and resources can help. Listen to audio courses during your commute and while you exercise. Finally, remember that the material is more important than the teacher.

The Slovenian wife of a Belgian man explained how she helped him become fluent in Slovenian. Write text messages: since you're limited to 140 characters, it's good for simple sentences. It's also good to receive a text message because decoding them is like a mini exercise. Skype and instant messaging are also good ways to handle a language in bit-sized chunks. Improve your skills by writing emails. Talk to yourself to see when you're missing a word, then look it up. Watch foreign TV programs over the Internet.

Dušan is fluent in five languages and advises that if several languages interest you, start with the easiest one. Some believe, "I'm going to learn Japanese, because if I can learn that, I can learn anything." Yes, that's true, but you might commit *harakiri* first. Pick something that helps you make quick progress. Once you have one or two languages in the bag, learning a fourth or fifth language becomes easier, even if they're weird ones. That's how Pope John Paul II learned over a dozen languages. This strategy works because sometimes seemingly unrelated languages have some random thing in common. For example, in Russian, *mokri* means *wet*. Since I speak Spanish, *mokri* reminds me of the Spanish word *mojado*, which also means *wet*. The connections continue: thanks to my basic Russian, it was easy for me to learn the Slovenian word for *wet—moker*.

A Slovenian language teacher advised me, "Learn verbs first. Verbs are the core of any sentence. Without them, a sentence collapses." Another strategy is to learn the most common words first. The 100 most commonly spoken words in English are: a/an, after, again, all, almost, also, always, and, because, before, big, but, can (verb), come, either/or, find, first, for, friend, from, go, good, goodbye, happy, have, he, hello, here, how, I, am, if, in, it, know, last, like, little, love, make, many, more, most, much, my, new, no, not, now, of, often, on, one, only, or, other, our, out, over, people, place, please, same, see, she, so, some, sometimes, still, such, tell, thank you, that, the, their, them, then, there is, they, thing, think, this, time, to, under, up, us, use, very, we, what, when, where, which, who, why, with, yes, you, your.

Although every language has its own list of common words, use this list as a starting point, and translate these hundred words into the language you want to learn. The best way to learn them is through association. Use the way the word is written or the way it sounds to associate it with something. For example, in Slovenian I recall *ljudje* (people) by thinking of a bunch of *lewd people;* or to remember the action *iti dol* (go down) I visualize an *E.T. doll* going down.

Ana, who understands five languages, helped me by taping a piece of paper on every object in the house and writing what it was. That way, you'll learn that you enter through the *vrata* (door) using a *ključ* (key), then look at yourself in the *ogledalo* (mirror), put your jacket in the *omara* (closet), open the *hladilnik* (fridge) to get a six-pack of *pivo* (beer) and get drunk on the *kavč* (couch). Say the words aloud when you see them and eventually add verbs to describe how you interact with the object.

Moreover, figure out what you will be doing with the language. If you only learn what the books tell you to learn, you may lose interest. Therefore, if you mainly plan to meet people, then learn phrases of introduction. If you will mostly be reading texts, then focus on reading words, not how to pronounce them. If you will be surfing, then learn how to say *water, waves, surfboard, beach, sand, rocks, sunset, undertow,* and *wipe out.*

Everyone knows that the best way to learn a language is to live in a country that speaks it, but many who get that chance don't fully immerse themselves. Instead, they hang out with people who prefer speaking in English. Advice: greet English speakers with a smile, then run away. However, what if you live in Kentucky and you want to learn Romanian? Thanks to the Internet, it's easy to find speakers of any language in your community. Believe it or not, there are about 150 Slovenians in North Dakota.

Ana gave great advice: destroy the dubbing industry. Spain, France, Germany, Italy, Poland, Russia, and Hungary spend millions of dollars trying to teach their children English in school and have miserable results. They could achieve that goal far more cheaply by simply firing those involved in dubbing and replacing them with people who make subtitles. It saves money too: dubbing is three times more expensive than subtitling. It's easy to predict which countries have lots of English speakers—it has nothing to do with their educational system; it's all about whether they dub or not. Slovenians never dub over a foreign language, whether it's the Discovery Channel or a foreign politician speaking on the news. In Poland, dubbing is so bad that they use one voice for all the actors. Imagine seeing the final romantic scene of *Casablanca* and hearing one Polish male voice speaking for Humphrey Bogart *and* Ingrid Bergman.

Although you can't destroy TV dubbing, you can destroy movie dubbing: *always watch foreign movies with subtitles; if you watch enough of them, you'll start to understand the language.* When you're good enough, watch them with subtitles of the language you're trying to learn—you'll learn writing and listening simultaneously. Dubbing doesn't seem like a big deal, but since the average guy spends thousands of hours watching TV and movies every year, subtitling can passively teach us another language.

Although these are all excellent shortcuts to learning a language, ultimately you'll need to invest several hundred hours to become proficient. There is no magic formula that will let you become fluent in a week. Put in those hours by letting a language infiltrate every part of your life. Then, just like a child, within several months you'll be speaking some weird language.

A hot winter night in Izola

After Ana and I finished our tea and snack in Koper, she drove me to her nearby home in Izola. The inside of Slovenian homes are similar to American ones, except that the older ones have that clunky (though functional) communist vibe. Her house was pleasant, as were her four housemates. The rain had stopped, so Ana and I went for an evening run. We ran along the cold Adriatic Sea until we got to Izola's precious old town. I had started that day in Venice (just two hours away) and was now ending it at another romantic Venetian town. We slowed down to admire Izola's architecture and the lapping of the waves. Ana's mesmerizing blue eyes smiled at me.

We ran home, took a shower, and cooked dinner. Slovenian cuisine is an eclectic mix of Balkan, Italian, Hungarian, and Austrian food. Slovenians often eat *mlinci* (corn pancakes), *dunajski zrezek* (Vienna steak), *rižota* (risotto), *golaž* (goulash), (pasta filled with chives and cheese), and every Sunday they must eat *goveja juha z rezanci* (beef soup with thin noodles). Ana feels that the classic Slovenian dessert is a *potica* (nut roll), which they serve on festive days. She said that another typical pastry is the *prekmurska gibanica* (layered cake) from Slovenia's northeast region. Although you don't pay your couchsurfing hosts, I give back by buying food and cooking them a meal. Since Slovenians will eat anything (as long as it's not too spicy), we made pasta with pesto, fresh sliced tomatoes, and grated Parmesan cheese.

Although it was getting late, her roommates were still in the living room watching Slovenian TV on the couch that was meant to be my bed. To not bother them, Ana suggested we watch a movie, *The Stepford Wives*. There was only one chair in her room and the roommates were using the living room, so I wasn't sure where we would watch it. She lay her sexy body down on the bed, resting on her stomach, with her computer in front of her. To encourage me to join her, she tapped the spot next to her as if I were a dog.

Stepford Wives is a story about a town whose ravishing wives are too good to be true; at this point, I felt similarly about the situation I was in. I told myself: *stay cool, don't over-analyze, she's just being friendly, she has no interest in a man who is 20 years older than her, and just because she looks and acts like a Stepford wife, doesn't mean she is one.*

I smiled and gently laid down next to her. Around the part of the movie where the protagonist starts realizing what's really going on, our feet touched. This reminds me of a useful diagram that I studied when I was a teenager. On one page was a simple, scientific drawing of a naked woman standing, while on the other facing page was one of a naked man. The title was "Erogenous Zones of a Man and Woman." Both drawings had about 50 arrows pointing to these pleasure zones. In the female diagram, the arrows pointed to nearly every part of her body, including her hip, calf, and elbow. In the male diagram, all 50 arrows pointed to one spot.

I mention this because while I didn't think much of my feet touching Ana's feet, it seemed to transform her. She let out a soft moan. Soon, her feet began to wiggle and caress my feet. As the movie played on, our legs became intertwined. *"Stop it, Francis," an Angel said.*

"But why?" said the Devil. "He deserves some fun. He's been single for almost a year!"

"That doesn't matter," said the Angel. "Francis, remember your rule: never make a pass at a couchsurfing girl who hosts you! C'mon! It's couchsurfing, not slut-surfing!"

The Devil whispered in my ear, "Don't worry about it. Ana made the first move. So you're covered, buddy. Listen to how she's breathing deeply now! It's a big green light, man! Go for it!"

The Angel shouted, "Don't you dare! Stop and consider the situation! You sad, pathetic, dirty old man! Francis, for heaven's sake, she could be your daughter!"

"Hell no! She's too good-looking to be his daughter."

Suddenly, Ana rolled off her stomach, clumsily threw herself into my arms, and kissed me.

The next day, Ana greeted me with a huge smile. Because of our age difference, my relationship with Ana wasn't certain at first. However, as the months passed, our feelings for each other deepened. Because of Dušan, I met Ana. And because of Ana, my life would change forever.

The most dangerous backpacking in Europe

In July 2010, I suggested that Ana prove she's Slovenian. To do so, she must complete the Slovenian rite of passage: climbing to the summit of Mt. Triglav. Slovenians half-jokingly say that you're not a true Slovenian until you make it to the top of Slovenia's tallest mountain, which was also the tallest mountain in Yugoslavia. It has such mythical importance that it's on the Slovenian euro coin and on the national flag.

Triglav isn't that tall (2,864 m / 9,394 ft), but as my first experience on it showed, it can be quite challenging if you take a tough route and/or climb under rough conditions (Triglav's latitude is similar to Mt. Rainier in US). Dušan joined us and he suggested we avoid the easy (and crowded) way up the mountain. We woke at 3:00 a.m. in Dušan's home in Slap Ob Idrijci so that we could get a predawn start at the base of Triglav. This three-day trip taught me that Slovenia has the most dangerous backpacking in Europe.

In the spirit of communism, Yugoslav leaders wanted everyone to have equal access to the mountains, so that mountaineering wouldn't only be a sport for the elite. However, instead of making a standard one-meter wide trail everywhere, the trail designers put a network of handholds and cables throughout the Julian Alps. In these sections, the trail is usually only as wide as your forearm, so that you're practically dangling over a long drop while holding onto the cables. Other times they've constructed primitive metal ladders; if you slip off those, don't worry, Death will catch you. You're supposed to bring a harness and safety equipment, but we didn't know that. I've backpacked 20,000 kilometers (12,500 miles) and I've never found such difficult and dangerous "trails."

There's another challenging element: the Julian Alps are made of Swiss cheese. Although they may look like the solid mountains that most backpackers experience in the US, these limestone mountains are as porous as Swiss cheese. A Serbian, Jovan Cvijić, popularized the geological term *karst* after the nearby Dinaric Krast region, which is made mostly of soluble bedrock. The first karst region in the world that was seriously studied was in Slovenia, perhaps because nearly half of the country is made out of this hollow rock. The problem with karst is that despite all the snow on the mountains, the snow-melt disappears into the rock, so backpackers are effectively hiking in a mountainous desert. The benefit of karst is that it carves cool caves that would even make Batman envious.

Because there's hardly any fresh water (except in the mountain huts, which price it like gold), you have to carry five liters. Most hikers either do a day-hike or stay in the mountain huts, so the water burden isn't so bad. However, we were also carrying a tarp, sleeping bag, and food for three days. Climbing the treacherous ladders is a bit more difficult with a full-loaded backpack. After reaching the summit of Triglav, we descended to camp at one of the rare mountain lakes. The next day, we traversed a diabolical trail that had an extremely narrow pebble-filled trail, a steep drop, and no cable to hold onto. It seemed suicidal. Ana's hands were shaking with fear. After crossing it, she got down on her knees and cried.

Dušan and I helped Ana gather herself. She toughed-up because she knew that the next few hours of backpacking would be filled with sketchy situations. Even though it was a perfect July day, the only hikers we met during that long section were a French couple who were covered in scrapes and bruises. The Frenchman pointed to his bleeding leg and advised us to turn back, "There is no trail here! It's crazy!" We ignored him, made it through, and eventually returned to Dušan's car in the late afternoon. As planned, Dušan dropped Ana and I off at Vršič Pass, which has the best view in Slovenia that you can drive to. Dušan returned home to work, while Ana and I loaded up on water and camped nearby.

The next day was thrilling as we went through the *Veliko Okno* (Big Window), which felt like going through Mordor's All-Seeing-Eye in *The Lord of Rings*. We labored to the summit of Mt. Prisojnik and then followed the fiendish trails to the *Malo Okno* (Small Window), where we had to descend a vertigo-inducing ladder that made me question my sanity. The transverse to Mt. Razor was sadistic, but we eventually descended to Ana's car by sunset. We originally planned to drive all the way back to the coast, but despite guzzling caffeine, Ana could barely stay awake. So instead, we stayed at Dušan's nearby home. Our exhausted bodies were asleep before our head hit the pillow.

Slovenian extreme athletes

Compared to many Slovenians, we were wimps. Slovenia is filled with athletic nuts. It helps that Slovenia is a big playground: although it's smaller than New Jersey, it has 7,000 kilometers (4,375 miles) of trails and 165 mountain huts. Igor Božeglav, a physical education instructor, told me that Croatians have a saying, "If you see someone talking loudly, he's Italian; if he has a beer in his hand, he's German; and if he has ski gear in his hand, he's Slovenian."

The quantity and quality of Slovenian extreme athletes is remarkable given there are only two million Slovenians. In the Olympics, Slovenia is usually in the top 10, when one ranks countries by the more meaningful *medals per capita* metric. For instance, one Slovenian gymnast, Leon Štukelj, won six Olympic medals. They perform superhuman feats elsewhere too. Martin Strel swam the length of the Danube, Mississippi, Yangtze, and Amazon rivers. Dejan Zavec was recently the International Boxing Federation's welterweight champion. The first married couple to climb Mt. Everest was from Slovenia. Davo Karničar was the first man to ski down from the summit of Mt. Everest.

Sometimes pushing the extremes leads to tragedy. While an American (Lance Armstrong) won the Tour de France seven times, a Slovenian (Jure Robič) won the Race Across America an unprecedented five times. Robič set a world record by covering 828 kilometers (519 miles) in 24 hours. He biked 4,800 kilometers (3,000 miles) across America in less than a week. However, Robič's winning streak ended in 2010 when he was zooming down a rarely used, narrow dirt road in Slovenia while an old man in a car was driving up it. A bike contest organizer once said, "[Robič] can die on the bike and keep going."[5] That day, however, Robič stopped going.

Another tragedy happened to Tomaž Humar, a Slovenian who pioneered several first ascents in the Himalayas. Reinhold Messner, the best mountaineer ever, said that Slovenian climbers "are the best in the world" and called Humar "one of the most intriguing and enigmatic high altitude performers of today."[6] In 2009, Humar would fall down a Himalayan mountain and break his ribs, leg, and spine. He was alone. He had enough energy to radio for help, but not enough energy to survive a cold night at high altitude in that condition.

> *We are only really free when we don't care and when we are not attached to anything. — Tomaž Humar*

Igor, a physical education teacher, said there are three reasons why Slovenia produces extraordinary athletes. First, it's a continuation of a Yugoslav tradition. Second, Slovenia's first Olympic medal (in 1992, one year after it became an independent) spurred enthusiasm for a repeat. Three, talented athletes get special status in school. I think there are two other factors: their inviting landscape and their rigorous work ethic.

A nation of busy bees

About 90 percent of the houses in Croatia's Crveni Vrh village are Slovenian summer homes. Dušan and I were there cutting wood at his sea house when I told him that the only time I saw one of his Slovenian neighbors was when they came to mow the lawn and clean the yard. He said, "Yeah, they always do that. Every few months they just come for a day or two. They work the whole time and then go back to Ljubljana. I've never seen them relaxing and enjoying their home. They're crazy." He shook his head. Then he wiped the sweat off his forehead and said, "Pass me another log to cut."

Slovenians can't sit still—they always have something productive to do. It can be annoying. I've lived in three Slovenian houses and my neighbors were always working on something. It didn't matter if it was early on a Sunday morning, my neighbors would be drilling something, banging in a nail, painting a wall, mowing the lawn, clipping their trees, picking their fruit, soldering metal, cutting wood with a chainsaw, watering the plants, or building a staircase to heaven.

In Novo Mesto, the capital of Slovenia's *Dolenjska* (Lower Carniola) region, I would learn more about the Slovenia's workaholic ways. In 1365, Duke Rudolph IV of Habsburg founded a town on a horseshoe bend of the Krka River and called it Rudolfswerth. Luckily the locals thought that was an ugly, unpronounceable name and immediately changed it to a far more agreeable *Novo Mesto*, which means *New Town*. Its *Glavni Trg* (Main Square), like most of the town, is cute. From the *Kandijski Most* (Kandija Bridge) you can see how the town used to have a wall encircling it, but that once medieval siege warfare was no longer the fashionable way of killing each other, the locals replaced the walls with houses. After a month in Bosnia and Serbia, I stopped in Novo Mesto for a few days before returning to Slovenia's coast. A few experiences in Novo Mesto reminded me about Slovenia's legendary work ethic.

Suzana Hočevar had generously agreed to host me over Easter. Suzana is a kind lady in her 30s who works for Slovenia's largest pharmaceutical company, Krka. On Saturday she introduced me to Nina, Zdravko, Angelina, Miran, and Bojan, who were all spending Easter "relaxing" by their recreational vehicles. After the initial introductions and chatting for 15 minutes, four out of five of them began to read magazines and books. As we'll soon see, Slovenia's Slavic brothers in Serbia or Bosnia would never exhibit such anti-social behavior. It's as if the Slovenian DNA instructs them to do something productive at every moment.

I spent an enjoyable Easter Sunday lunch with Suzana's family in Cerov Log, a village with 300 people near the Croatian border. Suzana's hospitable parents showed me their small vineyard. Mini-vineyards are a national obsession. Slovenians have wine cellars and produce their family wine that they often put in recycled plastic bottles. A vineyard or small piece of farmland is a perfect way to keep yourself busy in case your day job isn't enough.

> *Plant your garden for yourself and adorn your soul, instead of waiting for someone else to bring you flowers.*
> *— Tomaž Humar, Slovenian mountaineer*

On Sunday evening, Suzana and I visited Vesna and Borut, a couple renovating a massive historical home near Kostanjevica. Borut is a busy architect who is happy that he can use his mansion as a lifelong project that will fill any possible idle time that he may ever have. In Borut's eyes, I could see that same workaholic spirit that drives Slovenian athletes to stretch themselves to unexplored extremes.

Slovenia is like a really big beehive. This nation just doesn't stop and rest. People run around back and forth nonstop. Like bees, they're rarely hysterical about it. They're just deliberate and purposeful. They often have reasonable work hours at their job, but when they come home, they immediately engage in some other project. The rarest sight in Slovenia is seeing someone who is staring out into space and doing absolutely nothing. While other ex-communist countries were busy picking their noses, Slovenia's work ethic catapulted them to the highest per capita GDP in Eastern Europe. It's the most Western country in Eastern Europe not just geographically, but also economically and socially. One common Slovenian word sums them up: *priden.* It means *diligent, good, well-behaved,* and *hardworking.* From an early age, Slovenians are told to be a *priden otrok* (diligent child). Clearly, they've never stopped being *priden.*

Three Americans living in Slovenia

During Easter, I met Gary Carlson in Novo Mesto. He's an American priest who has been living in Slovenia for a couple of years. I asked him to compare life in Slovenia with life in America. He said, "Slovenians don't have the hyper-individualism that we have back in America. You don't get that 'me, me, and just me' attitude. Slovenians have a sense of community. They are about consensus, about leveling the playing field, and giving people equal health care and opportunities. They live a healthy life. They are surprisingly clean and organized. They are open-minded to the rest of the world, but they are fixed to their land."

"What can we learn from them?" I asked him.

"Modesty: not to show off."

"Give me one more thing that's different in Slovenia compared to America."

"They are into their families, but they are not 'huggy-huggy' types."

That reminded me of what Aprila told me when I asked her to compare Slovenians to Serbians. "We Slovenians are colder people," she said. "We have calmer parties and colder men. Serbians have more passion." Nejc added, "Slovenians need some alcohol to open up." Aprila also echoed Gary's modesty point. When I asked her what Slovenians can teach the world, she said, "I only learned the answer to that after living abroad. Three things: we're humble, hard-working, and not super nationalistic."

Another American, Donald Reindl, is an Assistant Professor of English Translation in Slovenia. He told me, "Americans could learn better eating habits, recreational habits, and healthcare (especially preventive healthcare) practice from the Slovenians, as well as workplace equality between men and women. None of these aspects of life are perfect in Slovenia—the traditional diet contains too much fat, for example, and womens' pay is 'only' 93 percent that of men. However, these compare favorably to US practices. The independence of Slovenian children at the primary level and the confidence that they gain outside the family circle is also commendable here."

"Don, can you give me an example of preventative healthcare that Slovenians have?"

"Primary schools have resident dentists that regularly inspect the children's teeth. This helps prevents more serious problems later on. Sick days off from work require a doctor's note, which entails seeing the doctor and being routinely looked at for things like blood pressure, etc. This can catch problems before they become bigger."

"What about this idea of young Slovenian children having independence?"

"Children almost all start preschool by age two (many by age one). During preschool they take class trips that involve up to three nights away from home without parents starting at age four. This pattern continues into primary school, with class trips and scouting trips (without parents) often lasting a week even for the youngest schoolchildren."

The third American I interviewed was Mary Ann, a 71-year-old who has been living at the foothills of the Julian Alps for six years. First, she loved the country's safety. She said, "They're a law-abiding people. There's also strict gun control." Like Don, she praised the medical care and said, "You can do your own medical tests, without the approval of a doctor. It's a cheap, pay-as-you-go system." Lastly, she said, "People are helpful and accessible, but not intrusive." However, not everyone agrees that Slovenians are not intrusive.

Slovenia is a big village

Everybody is famous in Slovenia. I made about 20 friends while living in Slovenia. Whenever I needed anything, at least one of my 20 friends knew someone-who-knew-someone who could help me. They're all inter-related. I lived a few months on a hill in Koper where, among the four houses there, everyone was a blood relative. This hyper-connectivity makes Slovenia feel like a big village, where everyone knows everyone—and knows what they're doing too. In America, social media websites (YouTube, Facebook, Twitter) have created the micro-celebrity. Slovenia is way ahead of us. Since the dawn of time, everyone in Slovenia is a micro-celebrity.

> V majhnih cerkvah so majhni svetniki veliki.
> *— Slovenian proverb meaning, "In small churches, small saints are big."*

The British call the people of Slovenia *Slovenes,* but I prefer the term *Slovenian* for two reasons. First, *Slovenian* just rolls off the tongue more naturally than *Slovene.* Second, *Slovene* conjures the image of a *sloven* person, which certainly doesn't describe the Slovenians. Although they don't dress fancy, they're always clean and proper. This is related to their village mentality. Slovenians always seem to worry, *"Kaj si bodo sosedje mislili?"* ("What will the neighbors think?")

Despite all their modernity and having the nicest cars in Eastern Europe, if you look deep inside the Slovenian soul, you'll probably find a *kmet* (peasant). Their eyes sparkle when they see a fruit growing on a tree. Even an urban snob from Ljubljana can do what most Americans can't: identify a potato plant in a field. Like farmers, Slovenians are practical and peaceful people. They quietly thrive in their little country, which is surrounded by bigger countries that have often bullied them around. Slovenians are adaptive: they will learn any language and never make a fuss if you don't speak Slovenian. They humbly realize that their culture and language are insignificant on the European stage. It's as if they know that their country only exists because greater powers let them exist and not because they are too hard to conquer. Aprila summed them up, "Slovenians are calm, organized, and safe." To consider how little has changed in the last 70 years, read what one traveler observed while traveling through Yugoslavia in the 1930s:

> *The [Slovenians] are a sensible and unexcitable people who [have] had better opportunities than their compatriots to live in peace.*
> — *Rebecca West,* Black Lamb and Grey Falcon, *1942*

Of course, Slovenians also have that hardy East European attitude—a stubbornness that refuses to give into a foreign power. They will learn foreign languages and even borrow some of their words, they will happily trade with whoever wants to buy and sell goods with them, and they will bend to the will of the big boys when they must. Still, whenever they surrender, they do it knowing that it is just a temporary defeat. Slovenians, like those stubborn Baltic people, always come back. They hibernate for centuries while strong powers run all over them, prohibit their language, and crush their spirit. However, when the time is right, they crawl back from the dead and say, "See, I'm still here!"

Slovenia's income equality paradox

Although Czechia is the world's number two leader in income equality (see page 180), Hungary, Finland, Slovakia, and Slovenia also have some of the highest levels of income equality in the world. According to UN and CIA data, Slovenia's richest 10 percent earn six times more income than the poorest 10 percent (in the USA, that difference is 16 times). When comparing the top 20 percent with the bottom 20 percent, the ratio is 4:1 (the USA ratio is about 8:1). *These results put Slovenia in seventh and sixth place in the world.*

Here's the paradox: whenever I asked Slovenians why there is such income equality in Slovenia, they nearly all said, "That's a lie." This was strange since to my eyes it seemed that all Slovenians had a similar standard of living. While I was traveling to Kranjska Gora, I met Svitlana, an experienced accountant. To uncover the paradox, I asked her to explain why Slovenia is sixth in the world for income equality. She immediately said, "Impossible! There are so many rich people here with nice houses and cars. I don't believe it."

Like most Eastern Europeans (especially ex-Yugoslavs), whenever Slovenians encounter something that doesn't smell right, they immediately say it's a conspiracy and a lie. They rarely consider that such a fact may, perhaps, be true and that it's worth making a tiny effort to try to understand why. I persisted and asked the accountant about Slovenia's tax code. She said, "We have about a 45-percent tax. It's a complicated system."

It's not just complicated, it's as burdensome as a mother-in-law. According to KPMG's annual global survey of effective tax rates, if you made $100,000 in May 2009, nobody would tax you more than Slovenia. Sweden may tax that $100,000 income more than anyone else in the world (37.5%), but employee social security brings their effective up to just 41 percent. Meanwhile, in Slovenia, those two combined taxes deliver the world's highest effective tax rate: 54 percent (the USA is less than half that). This crushing tax rate increases the more money you make. This decreases the incentive to pay someone 20 times more than another person since the government will swallow most of it. Thus, in Slovenia the percentage difference between the janitor's and President's pay is far lower than in most countries.

Another reason for Slovenia's income equality is its socialist policies for the last 70 years. Today, many countries with relatively high income equality are former communist countries, proving that communism lived up to its promise of redistributing wealth and income. Still, communism died 20 years ago, so why did Slovenia maintain its income equality while other communist countries became far less equal? In fact, the only remaining communist country in Europe, Belarus, has seen its rich-poor income gap increase during the last two decades, while Slovenia has stayed more equal than Belarus. What's Slovenia's secret?

Matej Akrapović answered half of that puzzle when I had dinner with him. He was the first Slovenian I met who didn't instinctively reject Slovenia's income equality as government propaganda. He explained, "The difference between the top 20 percent and the bottom 20 percent is low because when our government enterprises privatized, everyone got a fair, proportional share. How much you got was based on your age. For example, my parents got $5,200 worth of shares. I was just 12 at the time, so I got $650 of shares. After getting the distribution, lots of people sold their stocks immediately, but I held onto it."

"How did you do?" I asked.

Matej said, "I invested my $650 in the pharmaceutical company Lek, which was bought by Novatis, a Swiss company. I sold my shares a few years later for $5,200."

The way the Slovenians sold off their nationalized industries was quite different than other post-communist countries. Russia, for example, privatized its national firms unequally, which resulted in billionaire oligarchs. Russia's unequal redistribution effectively flushed away 70 years of communist progress. Today, Russia's income inequality is almost the same as America's. The popular Croatian term *privatizacijska pljačka* (privatization robbery) sums up the crooked privatization efforts in Slovenia's neighbor.

So why are Slovenians in such denial about their income equality? Because they don't know how to calibrate their scale. Like a villager, they just know that Mr. Tuš has a plane and can afford to buy three scoops of gelato every Saturday afternoon. Still, the presence of a few rich people doesn't necessarily mean that the government is monkeying around with the data. To rank high, what matters is how you are *relative to other countries.* While Slovenians might feel that it's unfair that their richest 20 percent makes 3.9 more than their poorest 20 percent, that's the sixth lowest ratio in the world because other countries are much more unequal. Japan (3.4) has the world's lowest ratio, but compare Slovenia with the multiples of some other countries: Austria (4.4), Belarus (4.5), Canada (5.5), the UK (7.2), Russia (7.6) US (8.4), and, 50 countries later, Namibia (56) and Sierra Leone (57). If Slovenians learned about the even greater inequality that exists everywhere else on this planet, then they might abandon their conspiracy theory.

Although Matej explained why Slovenia didn't quickly lose their wealth equality after communism, he didn't explain the second half of the puzzle—why Slovenia was able to hold onto it for the last 20 years. To answer that question, I went to interview Slovenia's greatest economic historian.

A Yugoslavia poster child becomes an economic historian

Neven Borak is a fascinating man. He's a living embodiment of Yugoslavia. His father is a Croatian Serb and his mother is a Slovenian. He was born in Slovenia and raised in Macedonia until the age of seven, and then lived in Šibenik, Croatia until he was 18. In short, he was the poster child for Yugoslavia—a perfect blend of its many regions. He's also the author of *Ekonomski vidiki delovanja in razpada Jugoslavije* (*How the Yugoslav Economy Worked and How It Collapsed*). Today, he's the Adviser to the Governor of the Bank of Slovenia. I dropped by his Ljubljana office on a Friday afternoon and we talked well past closing time. He finally provided the final piece to solve the income equality puzzle.

Neven said, "Although you probably know about our highly progressive tax code, the other factor is that there are collective agreements everywhere in Slovenia. These are social contracts between the people, government, and businesses. Wages and budgets are put out in the open. The three groups must approve. It's a long, complicated process, but it has kept the rich-poor gap from spreading."

Of course, for Neven, solving this mystery is child's play. So we turned to a far more challenging puzzle: why did Yugoslavia break up? This simple question is so thorny and complex that it will take the next 10 chapters to properly answer it. Don't worry, we'll discuss many other things too, but this topic will pop up from time to time. Neven's balanced and unemotional perspective will appear often over the next few chapters because, as we shall see, many ex-Yugoslavs are highly irrational and biased about this issue. Neven's calm, level-headed, and fact-based reasoning is refreshing when you're surrounded by one-sided lunatics.

Among the ex-Yugoslavs, Slovenians are the calmest and the least prone to wild conspiracy theories and fairy tales. Nevertheless, they're not completely objective either. Before we consider the minor myths they believe, let's summarize Yugoslavia's history super simply. After WWI, Yugoslavia was born out of one of the war's losers: Austria-Hungary. After a bumpy start, Yugoslavia settled on six republics (similar to how the USA has 50 states). We'll examine Yugoslavia's history more closely in the next chapter. For now, all that matters is that Slovenia was one of those six republics and that it became independent in 1991.

Why Slovenia wanted out of Yugoslavia

The most commonly cited reason why Slovenians wanted independence from Yugoslavia is that they were tired of sending so much money to Belgrade (Yugoslavia's capital; now Serbia's capital) and getting so little in return. They felt that slothful Yugoslavs in the other republics were sucking away much of Slovenia's output. Indeed, communism's idea of redistributing wealth sounds fantastic until they take your hard-earned money and give it to lazy bums.

To understand how serious this problem was, I asked every Slovenian I met to quantify the disparity: what was the ratio of money sent away to the value received? Most people would think a one-to-one ratio (1:1) is fair: your region pays $1 million in taxes, you want your government to spend $1 million on your region in the form of roads, schools, social security, etc. What's shocking is that not one Slovenian could answer the question! Everyone told me that it was a "huge and important problem," but nobody knew any facts about it! They just knew that they sent away "a lot" of money and got "little" in return, or that the ratio was "very bad." A few daring Slovenians guessed that it was a 5:1 to 10:1 ratio, but they admitted they had no data to back it up. In short, the most commonly given reason for leaving Yugoslavia had zero hard evidence behind it. For all they knew, the reality could be close to 1:1 or even 1:2 in their favor, thereby making their argument completely groundless. It felt like I was talking with children asking them why they believe in Santa Claus: "I don't know, I can't prove he exists, but I just know he does."

Despite the complete lack of strong evidence, I wasn't worried. I would just get the answer from Slovenia's most knowledgeable economic historian, Neven Borak. It was the first thing I asked him when I sat down in his office. His response was jaw-dropping.

"I don't know," Neven said softly. "Nobody does."

At this point, I felt like jumping on his office table, pulling his pretty tie, and screaming into his face, "Are you kidding me?! How the hell can you not know this?! Every damn Slovenian says this is one of the biggest reasons for ditching Yugoslavia! And you're telling me that nobody in this entire fucking country has ever bothered to see if it was even true? *What is wrong with you people!?"*

Instead, I raised an eyebrow and in a calm, almost bored tone, I said, "Oh really? Fascinating."

Perhaps Neven saw the steam coming out of my ears, so he explained as much as he knew. First, Yugoslavia had "para-budgets." These off-the-books, parallel budgets were a massive pool of cash for all the undocumented transactions to dip into. Neven estimates that this covert budgets were roughly three-quarters of the size of the official budget. Most of it was a wealth transfer from the rich regions to the poor ones. Furthermore, "the central bank redistributed wealth through credits and loans at negative real interest rates." The whole system was "a matter of huge discontent because it was not transparent and accountable." Even high-ranking economists couldn't track the majority of the money flows. It was such an opaque fiscal system that even Yugoslavia's top politicians probably weren't sure how money was being spent. Neven said, "Francis, your simple and clear questions have no clear answers because accountability and transparency were not high on Yugoslavia's agenda."

I waved Neven's book around and said, "Neven, you have over 100 data-rich graphs and tables in your book. Can't you infer an answer from them?" Like two swordsmen, we danced around this issue. Every time I tried to corner him, he cleverly got away. He finally gave in when I resorted to pathetic begging. He shrewdly emphasized that he was simply guessing, and humbly added that it wasn't even an educated guess. He guesstimated that Slovenia's ratio of taxes paid to money spent was "around 2:1."

One more thing Slovenia has in common with New Jersey

After listening to Slovenians whine about how their republic was getting shortchanged, Americans might wonder if something similar is going on in the USA. Despite living three decades in America and having traveled to 47 states, I've never heard of anyone complain about this issue. Was that because the ratio for every state was 1:1? Or does nobody care?

According to the Tax Foundation, a non-profit tax watchdog, 30 US states get more federal spending than they pay in taxes, while 20 get less than they put in. In general, rich states (on a per capita basis) contribute more than they get. Hence, states like Connecticut, New Hampshire, New York, California, Florida, and Minnesota pay more in taxes than they receive. Meanwhile, relatively poor states, like Mississippi, Louisiana, West Virginia, Alabama, Kentucky, and the Dakotas get more than they put in. The biggest winner is New Mexico: it receives over $2 for every $1 it pays. The biggest loser gets just $0.61 in federal spending for every $1.00 it contributes in taxes. That state is the one that has nearly the same geographic size as Slovenia: New Jersey.

Despite this, Americans aren't complaining about it. Of course, probably on our Annual Tax Day a couple of New Jersey newspapers grumble about being shortchanged, while the New Mexico media stays quiet, hoping that nobody will notice. I've never heard about the issue, even though I grew up in California, a state that pays about 10 percent more in federal taxes than it receives in spending.

So why did the issue drive Slovenians to arms? First, even though nobody could prove it, their ratio was worse than New Jersey's ratio (although probably not much worse). Second, because the government didn't share the information, it encouraged the conspiracy-prone Slovenian minds to spread rumors of absurd ratios that they heard from the one drunk guy at a bar.

Yugoslavia's workhorse

Although the exact inflow-outflow ratio will remain a mystery, what is certain is that Slovenia was always Yugoslavia's economic and industrial powerhouse. For example, by 1938, Slovenia had 3 times more people than Montenegro, but had 41 times more factories (912 vs. 22). Along with the nearby lands of Croatia and Vojvodina, Slovenia had 85% of the banking capital and two-thirds of the industry and agriculture after WWI. Slovenia had a budget surplus in 70 out of the 72 years it spent in Yugoslavia, while the other republics struggled to balance their checkbooks. Towards the end of Yugoslavia, *Slovenia was just 8% of Yugoslavia's 24 million population, but was delivering over 20% of Yugoslavia's tax revenues and producing 32% of the hard-currency exports.* Slovenian factories were 3.3 times more productive than the Bosnian ones, 7 times more than the Macedonian ones, and 8 times more productive than the Montenegrin ones.[7] Like the little battery that powers your watch, tiny Slovenia was Yugoslavia's mighty economic engine.

This turbo-powered motor increased the disparity between the standard of living of Slovenia and the other republics. In 1971, depending on the issue, Yugoslavia's regions were five to 40 years apart in development.[8] Although Slovenia increased the gap between all the republics, the most obvious was with Kosovo. In 1950, Slovenia's per capita income was three times more than Kosovo; by 1960, it was five times more. When Yugoslavia broke up (1991), it was nine times more. (In 2011, it was over 10 times more.) Such disparities were embarrassing for the communists who ran the country—they were supposed to be increasing equality, not disparity. However, the more they monkeyed with the market, the more inefficient Yugoslavia became, which just made the industrious Slovenians work harder, thereby increasing the living standards even more.

Still, as much as the Slovenians labored, the very nature of communism made them far less efficient than the West. Thanks to their proximity to Austria and Italy, Slovenians saw how Western Europeans were outperforming them. In 1950, Italy's and Austria's GDP per capita was about 2.2 times greater than Yugoslavia's. By 1986, Italy was 3.7 times ahead of Yugoslavia, while Austria was 4.3 times.[9] Slovenians knew something was wrong with their economic system when even the Italians could outperform them.

Neven critiques Slovenia

One of the hardest things to find among the ex-Yugoslavs is someone who is willing to criticize his own country or ethnic group. Everybody is a whiny victim and it's always the other guy's fault. The rare times I found someone with a gram of objectivity were usually people with mixed heritages. Therefore, it's no surprise that Neven, with his highly diverse background, was able to criticize his fellow Slovenians as easily as he could the other former republics. I asked him what he thought about Slovenians who argue that Yugoslavia was effectively exploiting them and draining them of their wealth.

"Such arguments weaken when faced with other facts," Neven said. "In Yugoslavia, Slovenia benefited from having captive markets to buy raw materials at artificially low prices and also having captive markets to sell finished products to." He explained that although Yugoslavia was more open than the rest of Eastern Europe, its communist economy was still largely closed to competitors, prices were highly regulated, and asset allocation was relatively centralized. As a result, Slovenia would buy raw materials at below-market prices from the other republics and employ their cheap labor to make a mediocre product that millions had to buy. In a true free market, the other republics would either buy from China to get the same quality for a cheaper price, or from Germany to get better quality at the same price as Slovenia. Instead, Yugoslavia's republics had to buy Slovenia's communist vacuum cleaner that doesn't suck enough.

Within Yugoslavia, Slovenia enjoyed a massive internal trade surplus. The value of Slovenian internal exports was up to 67 percent higher than its internal imports. Slovenia was the only Yugoslav region that consistently had such a positive ratio. Kosovo, as usual, was the laggard, sometimes buying nearly twice as much stuff as it sold to other regions.[10] While workaholic Slovenians love to focus on all the taxes Yugoslavia collected from them, they forget how much Yugoslavia's market tampering benefited them. Neven ironically observed, "Slovenia had the highest economic growth in their history during dictatorships (Austria's Empire, the Kingdom of Yugoslavia, and Tito's Yugoslavia)."

The Ten-Day War

With all the ugly fighting that happened in the 1990s in Croatia, Serbia, Bosnia and Herzegovina, and Kosovo, it's easy to forget that the sneaky Slovenians pioneered the way out of Yugoslavia. In the 1980s, Slovenians demanded the same things Americans asked for in the 1770s: free speech, right to assembly, democracy, and more control over the taxing and spending. They made two mistakes on their way to independence. First, in November 1989, Slovenia prohibited Serbs and Montenegrins from coming to Ljubljana to protest against Slovenia's constitutional changes. This hypocritically contradicted their demand for free speech and free assembly. Before, a Yugoslav passport could take you anywhere in the world, now it couldn't even take you to another Yugoslav republic!

Their second mistake was firing a gun. In 1991, Slovenia's declaration of independence led to a ten-day civil war with Yugoslavia. It's hard to find a Slovenian who will admit, "We didn't win the war; the Serbs and the Yugoslav National Army (JNA) let us win it." Here's the Ten-Day War summary: you're carrying a grenade launcher and you're fighting a seven-year-old Slovenian boy with a water pistol. "Bang! Bang! You're dead!" the boy screams. You fall to the ground, pretending to be dead, and the boy declares victory.

A day before the JNA deployed troops to Slovenia's border, they told the Slovenians exactly what they would do: they would take control of the border-crossings, the main airport and seaport. They even explained how and when they would do it. Armies do this when they know that it's not a fair fight. Imagine Eisenhower calling Hitler to tell him when, where, and how D-Day would happen. Although the JNA was enormous, it sent only 2,000 men—hardly a threatening force, even for a puny country like Slovenia. The JNA started moving to the Slovenian border in the middle of the night. Slovenia's President hysterically called the JNA's Deputy Commander, who then told the President, "Why are you so annoyed? The troops that have left the barracks aren't even armed. Calm down and go back to sleep."[11]

Slovenians, in preparation for a dramatic war, had put up barricades with big agricultural and transport vehicles. The JNA used their armored vehicles to push the barricades aside as if they were plastic toy trucks. The most thrilling part of the ten-day "war" was when Slovenia shot down a JNA helicopter. Its cargo? Bread. The pilot and the mechanic died. They had no weapons. Several foreign truck drivers, oblivious to the conflict, died, caught in random crossfire. Given that "only" 66 people died in the ten-day civil war, it was quite "civil." After slapping Slovenia's wrist for leaving Yugoslavia, the JNA left and Slovenia became an independent country for the first time in history. On June 25, 2011, Ana and I celebrated Slovenia's first 20th birthday party.

Given the outcome, why was it a mistake? Because it set a bad precedent: it taught the other republics that violence works. The US Secretary of State James Baker observed that the Helsinki Accords state that violence is not a legitimate way to gain independence. Nevertheless, Germany (and eventually other governments) rewarded Slovenia's violent behavior by recognizing Slovenia's independence. It would have been far wiser if Slovenia had copied Martin Luther King's non-violent protests. Let the world watch JNA tanks rumble around while Slovenians carry flowers. Recall that during that period Eastern Europeans were having casualty-free revolutions everywhere. World sympathy and diplomatic pressure would have eventually led to Slovenia's independence and it would have taught their trigger-happy Balkan brothers that violence isn't the answer.

On the other hand, the other ex-Yugoslavs sometimes take this criticism too far and behave like children in a playground: they love to blame Slovenia for "starting it." Although it was the first official war, it wasn't the first violent event. Several other bloody incidents between Serbs and Croatians happened before Slovenia fired a shot. For example, two months before, in Borovo Selo, about 20 Croatians and Serbs died in a skirmish. That's about a third of the causalities of Slovenia's Ten-Day War. In short, Slovenia's ten-day conflict did *not* "condemn the rest of Yugoslavia to war," as Warren Zimmerman, the last US Ambassador to Yugoslavia, tried to argue.[12] Such a conclusion ignores the accelerating violence elsewhere and assumes that the Balkan Yugoslavs are robots. They didn't have to copy Slovenia by choosing the violent path to independence. There was a peaceful path available, as Macedonia ultimately proved to all. In short, Slovenia set a poor example, but the other Yugoslavs didn't have to follow it. They could have been wiser, but they weren't.

Slovenian imperialism

We'll return to Neven's insights in the upcoming chapters, but for now we'll end with his observations about Slovenia's economy today. Thanks to their workaholic nature, in just 20 years Slovenians have nearly closed the gap with Western Europe. For example, Italy's per capita GDP is no longer 3.7 times ahead of Slovenia, but just 0.4 times larger. Still, Neven thinks they can work smarter. He said, "We don't know how to rule differently than we did in the past. Slovenian émigrés don't know how to build world-class companies. We don't know how to compete on the world stage. We hate to admit it, but we still have some bad communist habits."

I asked, "So what happened after Yugoslavia's protectionist barriers disappeared?"

"We had to turn south, to the Balkans, because we couldn't compete with Northern Europe. Unfortunately Slovenians have gone into the ex-Yugoslav countries with an arrogant sense of superiority. They're setting up companies everywhere. It's a type of Slovenian imperialism."

"Now that's a funny oxymoron: *Slovenian imperialism*."

Neven smiled and concluded, "We have much to learn. Slovenia, like the EU, has a good, educated labor force, but we don't want to move. We're not as willing as Americans are to move from the area we were born in. This inflexibility will haunt us."

What others think of Slovenians

Slovenians are innocuous: they harmlessly go about their business, not bothering anyone. Nearly all its neighbors agree: Hungarians have excellent relations with Slovenians; Austrians also like their peaceful neighbor, often crossing the border to hike in the Julian Alps and enjoy the seaside; and Italians generally don't know Slovenia exists, so they have nothing bad to say. Indeed, the only Italians who have a chance of finding Slovenia on a map are the ones that live about an hour from the border or who have to drive through it to get to their real destination: Croatia.

However, Slovenia's only other neighbor, Croatia, thinks Slovenia is inhabited by assholes. According to a 2010 Gallup poll, only 18 percent of Croatians think of Slovenia as "friendly." Although a quarter thinks Slovenia is "neutral," 44 percent believe it's "hostile." Croatians would be shocked that the 2011 Global Peace Index put Slovenia in the top 10 most peaceful nations in the world (Croatia was #37 and the USA #82 out of 153 countries). The index is a composite score based on 23 indicators, which Croatians will probably accuse of being corrupted.

> *When you open an umbrella in Ljubljana, you will poke the eye of a guy in Maribor.*
> *— Croatian joke that makes fun of Slovenia's small size (Maribor is a city near the edge of Slovenia)*

Anecdotal evidence confirms Gallup's results. Andreja Nastasja met a Croatian at an international seminar who was unfriendly to her. In the end, the Croatian girl hugged all the non-Slovenian girls at the seminar, but just shook Andreja's hand. Damjana Tomšič, a Slovenian, told me, "When I go to Croatia's coast and speak Italian, they politely tell me the menu selections and smile. But if they hear me speak Slovenian, they'll just toss me the menu and walk away." A Dutch lady who worked in Croatia told me, "Croatians say that Slovenians are 'animals' and other negative things. But whenever I go to Slovenia, I see cleaner streets, more organized people, and a higher standard of living than in Croatia. So I'm unconvinced." Nejc had friends who have gone to Zagreb, Croatia and had their tires slashed because of their Slovenian license plates. He suspects young unemployed Croatians "have an inferiority complex. They're frustrated and jealous that the Slovenians have a better economy."

Although Croatian envy over Slovenia's success is one factor behind the animosity, a bigger reason is that for the last 20 years the two nations have been bickering over their border. We won't analyze this long, tedious discussion here. I'll simply say that I believe that Slovenia is being the bigger baby in this argument.[13] Fortunately, in May 2011, the two nations registered their border arbitration with the UN. They expect to resolve the border dispute by 2015. At that point, Croatia will have been in the EU for two years, which means that the border will effectively vanish no matter where they finally draw it. Let's hope that the negative feelings between the people vanish along with it.

Slovenia's popularity within the Balkans increases the further you move away from it. The percentage of people who think Slovenia is "friendly" varies: Serbia (24%), Bosnia and Herzegovina (33%), Montenegro (43%), Kosovo (46%), and the furthest away, Macedonia (68%). The 2010 results are better than they seem: a small percentage of those nations said Slovenia was "hostile," often choosing "neutral" instead. It's really just Croatia that has a negative opinion of Slovenia. To find out more, we're heading to all these countries next.

Every country believes it is at the center of the universe. Slovenia truly is at a fascinating crossroads between Eastern and Western Europe, the Balkans and Italy, Austria and the Adriatic Sea. The Slovenian paradox is that it can argue that it's at the center of the cosmos better than most countries, yet nobody knows it exists. Now you do.

What Slovenia Can Teach Us

- **Speak many languages.** Slovenia has the third highest concentration of polyglots in Europe—they are the masters of foreign languages. Review the tips Slovenians gave us in this chapter and, with some effort, you'll be able to speak another language fast.
- **Think in a different perspective.** Slovenians absorb many perspectives and take the best they find. Read different newspapers or channels to broaden your mind.
- **Be *priden* (hardworking).** Slovenians are busy bodies. They sometimes overdo it, but there's a healthy societal benefit. They are not talkers; they are doers. They always ask themselves, "What productive activity can I do now?" If you're lazy, ask yourself that more often.

- **Be humble.** Slovenians were Yugoslavia's economic engine and had its highest standard of living. Today, it continues way ahead. Still, the vast majority of Slovenians just do what they do best, work hard and don't brag about it. Remember there's always someone better than you.

Places I saw and recommend in Slovenia: The Julian Alps (Triglav), the Soča River, its two best caves (Škocjan and Postojna), Ljubljana, Maribor, Ptuj, and the seaside (Piran/Izola/Koper).

Travel deals and info: http://ftapon.com/slovenia

Ana always wanted to visit the Balkans, so we packed up her car to visit Croatia and Bosnia. We spontaneously extended our trip to include Montenegro. And we accidentally went to Serbia, too. It's a journey that all young ex-Yugoslavs should do, because when you wander, you learn how wrong you are about so many things. Aprila lamented, "The new generation of Slovenians and Croatians don't understand each other, because we don't speak the same language anymore." Now that we understand the Slovenians (at least somewhat), let's turn to the Croatians.

WARNING: *Confusion ahead—we're heading to the Balkans. We will spend the next 10 chapters traveling through Europe's most perplexing, inscrutable, and headache-producing regions: the Balkans. Fasten your seat belts, it's going to be a bumpy ride.*

12

Croatia—Honey, Are We Still in Eastern Europe?

When I first entered Croatia in September 2004, I had no idea that one day I would return to live there for over a year. Instead, I was happily lost in the pretty streets of Zagreb, Croatia's capital. After passing elegant restaurants and shops, I stumbled onto the lively Dolac vegetable market near *Trg Bana Jelačića* (Ban Jelačić Square). I soon fell in love with the colorful checkerboard roof of St. Mark's Church—it's the coolest church roof I've ever seen. Although Zagreb is a worthwhile city to visit, even the most proud Zagreb native will admit that Croatia's finest sites are along its enchanting Dalmatian coast.

Fast forward six years later: Ana and I were driving down Croatia's Dalmatian coastline looking for a place to camp at dusk. "There! Turn right!" I said while pointing to a dirt road. Ana slammed on the brakes and turned sharply onto the dirt path. We found a secluded spot to park the car next to a vineyard. We set up a campsite nearby. We were tired. We had left Slovenia at 4:00 a.m. to maximize our daylight hours along Croatia's coast. We stopped often on our way to Šibenik. The best stop was Paklenica National Park, a rock-climbing paradise overlooking the Adriatic. We also spent several hours touring Zadar, a precious Venetian-styled town with a grid street pattern. After a sunset walk around Šibenik, we drove away from coast to find a hidden place to camp. The next morning we planned to leave at dawn to avoid anyone who may ask us why we're camping there and also to enjoy the full day. We intended to continue down the coast toward Dubrovnik. However, before getting into that story, we need to orient ourselves.

Croatia isn't where everyone says it is

Some people confuse geographical facts with geographical connotations. As we've seen many times, Eastern Europeans dislike being told that they're in Eastern Europe, even though half of Europe *must* be in Eastern Europe (when you do a simple east-west split). They resist it because they dislike the negative connotation of Eastern Europe. As an American living in Croatia told me, "Croatia is not in Eastern Europe, we're in *Central* Europe." Yeah, you and every other Eastern European nation.

We find a similar habit regarding the Balkans, which is a geographic region in Europe's southeast. It got its name from the Balkan Mountains that are mostly in Bulgaria. According to conventional geography, mainland Greece is the southern Balkan boundary, while the east-west Balkan edges are the Adriatic and Black Sea. The Danube River and Sava River create the northern Balkan limit. This puts less than half of Slovenia and a tiny part of Romania in the Balkans, so it's reasonable to leave them out of the Balkans. However, most of Croatia's land is south of the Sava River, so it's fair to say that Croatia is in the Balkans. Just don't say that to a Croatian—when a 2010 Balkan Monitor survey asked Croatians if they identify with the Balkans, 72 percent said either "only a little" or "not at all."

That's because many Croatians believe that the Balkans, like Eastern Europe, has a crappy image. In *Balkan as Metaphor,* a Bulgarian author acknowledged the "undeniable facts" about the Balkans: "bloody Balkan wars, political intrigues and irrationality, nationalist hysteria, senseless fragmentation into weak small states, governmental chaos, poverty, economic, and intellectual backwardness." The Balkans is a "contaminated kingdom of repressed European demons: cruelty, machismo, hysterical passion, murderous barbarism, ignorance, arrogance, undisciplined eroticism. . . ."[1] Oh, he forgot to mention that they have great food and pretty girls too.

Because of the negative Balkan stereotype, Croatians play the same amusing games that Eastern Europeans play to resist the icky *Eastern Europe* label. Franjo Tuđman, a Croatian politician, won his presidential campaign with the slogan "Tuđman, not the Balkans."[2] That's like saying, "Obama, not North America." After returning from Washington, Tuđman proudly said, "We have been assured by the unreserved support of the United States that Croatia belongs to Central Europe and not to the Balkan region." I wonder if America also assured Panama that it's not in Central America. We'll debate whether the metaphor is accurate and if it applies to Croatia, but we won't debate the geographical fact—most of Croatia *is* in the Balkans.

What's weird is that in 2010 only nine percent of Croatians said that they "extremely strongly" or "very strongly" identify themselves with "Europe." That was the lowest rate in the Western Balkans. Furthermore, only 57 percent identified strongly with their own nation—that's also lower than any other Western Balkan country (except Bosnia and Herzegovina with 54 percent). Less than half of Croatians strongly identify with their religion—that's the second lowest rate in the Western Balkans (after Albania). In conclusion, Croatians don't identify strongly with much of anything. Perhaps that is why seven in 10 Croatians believe "cultural differences" are either an "important obstacle" or "some obstacle" to more Balkan cooperation.

Here are a few more facts and terms to orient us. Croatia has 4.5 million people, which is the same as it had in 1968. It has the same population as Louisiana in a territory the size of West Virginia at the latitude of Oregon. Furthermore, we'll sometimes refer to the *Western Balkans*—it's all the Balkan countries except Bulgaria and Greece. Although some call a person from Croatia a *Croat,* we'll use *Croatian* because it's intuitive and sounds right, whereas the other term sounds too much like *croak* (to die).

Finally, we'll define a new term: *Balkanian*—someone from the Balkans. *Balkanian* is a neutral term based on geography and fits with similar terms, as in *the house is North American, she is Scandinavian, and he is Balkanian.* Although it technically includes people from Albania, Bulgaria, Greece, Kosovo, and Macedonia, we'll use it mainly to refer to the people from Bosnia, Croatia, Montenegro, and Serbia. The reason for this is that, besides living in a common geographical area, the people from those four countries share a common language.

Four countries, one language

A Croatian told me a common trick they do in America when looking for a job. On their resume, they say they're fluent in four languages: Bosnian, Croatian, Montenegrin, and Serbian. The ignorant American is impressed and says, "Wow! You're Einstein! You're hired!" What the stupid American doesn't know is that it's like saying that you're fluent in English, Australian, Canadian, and American.

The eternal debate among linguists is: what's the difference between a language and a dialect? In theory, differences between languages should be greater than differences between dialects. However, there are more differences between two dialects of Slovenian than there are between the Norwegian and Danish languages. Linguists can't agree on a standard definition, so here's my common sense one: *if two people can communicate with 100 percent comprehension, then they're speaking the same language or dialect; if the comprehension rate is between 90 to 99 percent, then they're speaking dialects of one language; below 90 percent, they're using different languages.* We can debate the exact thresholds or if it should include the written language too, but the overall concept is intuitive and logical. For example, it would mean that the many flavors of English are all dialects of one language and that a few exotic Slovenian dialects are separate languages. It's not a perfect system since there are few black-and-white issues in languages, but it's better than the inconsistent and illogical way we do it now.[3]

Similarly, Bosnian, Croatian, Montenegrin, and Serbian are all dialects of one language, which has been called Serbo-Croatian. After speaking with hundreds of Balkanians, they confirmed that they can understand 99 percent of what someone from one of the other three regions says. Of course, like most languages, they have several dialects. *Čakavian* is popular in Dalmatia, *Kajkavian* is the default in northern Croatia, and *Štokavian* is the main dialect everywhere else (these three dialects get their names from how they say the word *what—Ča, Kaj,* and *Što).* There are also sub-dialects whose pronunciation differences can change how you spell a word since Balkanians write words like they sound. Thus, *belo* (white) may become *bijelo,* and *mleko* (milk) can morph to *mliko* or *mlijeko.* There are vocabulary differences too. Compare Serbian vs. Croatian words: *šargarepa* vs. *mrkva* (carrot), *šlem* vs. *kaciga* (helmet), *avion* vs. *zrakoplov* (airplane, literally meaning *air flier*), and *helikopter* vs. *zravomlat* (helicopter, literally *air mover*).

Nevertheless, there are plenty of differences between British and American English too, but we don't call them different languages. Brits write *colour, programme,* and *theatre* and pronounce many words so differently that some Americans can't understand them. Similarly, a Texan might be misunderstood in London (or even Chicago). Brits use the words *bloody, knackered,* and *rubbish* far more than Americans, but we understand each other. If we wrote words like we pronounce them, then we'd have completely different dictionaries! Regardless, our vocabulary is sometimes different. Brits ride up a *lift,* not an *elevator;* they push babies in a *pram,* not a *stroller;* they wear *trousers,* not *pants;* they have *hoardings* on the side of the road, not *billboards;* and they fill up their *lorry* with *petrol*, rather than filling up their *truck* with *gas*. Despite these (and many other) differences, we both claim to speak English.

The most obvious difference between the South Slavic languages is their two alphabets. Serbs traditionally prefer the Cyrillic alphabet, while everyone else prefers the Latin alphabet. At first glance, that fact alone seems to justify categorizing them as separate languages. Compare *Kraljevina Srba, Hrvata i Slovenaca* with Краљевина Срба, Хрвата и Словенаца. Because the characters are so different, it's tempting to conclude that they're different languages. However, not only do they have precisely the same meaning ("Kingdom of Serbs, Croatians and Slovenians"), but they also have the same pronunciation and same number of characters. That's because both alphabets have 30 characters with a phonetic twin in the other alphabet. Hence, the Latin letter *c* is absolutely identical in sound as the Cyrillic letter ц. Thus, if a Croatian spends a few hours memorizing the 30 Cyrillic characters, he will be able to write in Serbian as well as a native Serb. Likewise, that Croatian could pick up any Serbian book and understand it as easily as if it were written in Latin characters. Meanwhile, although Serbs may prefer Cyrillic, they can all read and write in Latin characters and the popularity of Cyrillic is slowly fading. Globalization has encouraged about half of the Serbs, especially the new generation, to use Latin characters. In short, while the two alphabets appear to create a vast difference, it's just an illusion.

A fun example of this was when Ana and I accidentally drove to Serbia later in our trip. Whenever we saw a sign written in Cyrillic,

I would read it aloud because I know how to read Cyrillic and she doesn't. However, I wouldn't know what the words meant (I can just make the correct sound), but Ana would understand perfectly since she speaks Croatian. Ana just hasn't made the simple effort of learning the Cyrillic alphabet. It was an odd situation: an American reading Serbian Cyrillic words aloud, having no idea what he was saying, but a Slovenian understanding it because she can also speak Croatian.

Fortunately, only the most brainwashed nationalist will claim that there's any real difference between Bosnian, Croatian, Montenegrin, and Serbian. Unfortunately, most of the Balkanian intellectuals, politicians, and linguists who could agree to give their common language one name are brainwashed nationalists. Croatian linguists are the most guilty of dusting off old books and trying to forcibly introduce old Croatian words into the modern vocabulary. They're trying to reverse Serbia's historic influence over the language instead of being grateful that at least one other country can understand what the hell they're saying.

Similarly, Serb chauvinists want Serbia to use Cyrillic exclusively and trash the Latin alphabet. Bosnian language crackpots are making a big deal about a few "Turkisms" that they have, while Montenegrins have added two characters to their alphabet (*ś* and *ź*) to make a big deal of a difference that hardly exists. None of these extremists are making much progress on their agendas because they're fighting the rising tide of globalization, which creates common ground, not differences. One encyclopedia concludes, "The differences between the pronunciations of British and American English are much greater than those between the varieties of Serbo-Croatian."[4]

The Balkanian language

One final problem: coming up with a good name for the common language spoken in Bosnia, Croatia, Serbia, and Montenegro. Most linguists will say it's *Serbo-Croatian,* but this is a poor name since it leaves out Bosnia and Montenegro. They should have called the language *Yugoslav,* but it's too late now. Another option would be calling it *South Slavic*—but that's too long and boring. Some have used BCS (Bosnian-Croatian-Serbian), but that leaves out the fun Montenegrins. Still, BCMS isn't sexy either.

In an effort to give it some sex appeal, I thought *Bocromos* (BoCroMoS) would be good. However, there are two problems with that name. First, *Bocromos* sounds like a forgotten Greek dialect, not a Slavic tongue. Second, Bocromos will be obsolete the moment the Balkan political landscape changes again (and it will). For example, if Vojvodina were to declare its independence from Serbia (highly unlikely), it would lobby to change Bocromos to *Bocromosev* (the *se* comes from

*Se*rbia and the *v* comes from *V*ojvodina). And if tomorrow they all unite under one Bosnian Empire, their language would become just *Bo*. So that's no good.

How about calling the language after something the linguistic region shares in common? They all eat *ćevapčići* (sausages), so why not call the language *Ćevapčian* (or *Chevapchian*)? Or how about *Burekian*, after the delicious *burek* (pastry pie filled with cheese, meat, or spinach) that is everywhere in the Balkans? Unfortunately, *Ćevapčićian* and *Burekian* have problems too, especially that proud nationalists who take everything too seriously would object to it just like flag-waving Americans wouldn't want our language to be called *Hamburgerian, Coca-Colian,* or *McEnglish.*

So that leaves only one good option: *Balkanian*. The name won't change if their diet changes. Whether they reunite or break up into 37 countries, the language can remain Balkanian. Just like *Russian* and *Lithuanian* refers to both a people and a language, *Balkanian* can do the same. Therefore, just like we used the term *Czechia* instead of *the Czech Republic,* we will no longer be referring to the Bosnian, Croatian, Montenegrin, and Serbian languages. It's just Balkanian, which has four national dialects, each with their own sub-dialects. Hyper-nationalistic Balkanians who are having a heart-attack right now should visit Latin America or any English speaking country. People don't speak Argentinian, Ecuadorian, or Nicaraguan, they speak *Spanish*. People don't speak Australian or Canadian—they speak *English*. Can we please take a break from rabid, knee-jerk nationalism on this issue? Let's stop waving our flags for five minutes and be rational.

Slavs don't know what a hand is

Ana and I left our stealthy campsite at dawn and got to Krka National Park before it opened. The long, thin park celebrates the glorious Krka River. At the south entrance, we followed a dirt trail that went down to the river. You can hear the river's roar long before you see it. There's a series of wide waterfalls, some with big drops, others with staircase-like cascades. Fat, twisted trees grow out of their watery roots. Wooden walkways traverse the river in several directions, allowing you to closely examine the fascinating ecosystem. As we promenaded through the empty paths, Ana looked at me romantically and said, "Give me your arm."

Ana says this because she's not used to using a special word for *hand*. Slovenians just call that thing you write with a *roka* (arm). Balkanians also have just one word for *hand* or *arm: ruka*. This is insane. I can understand that a language doesn't create a word for a *defibrillator* or a *catalytic converter,* but a freaking *hand*? Wouldn't you think that when you're inventing a language, that's one of the first five things you'd want to name? *Food, water, home, fire,* and *HAND*. Instead, Balkanians invented about 500,000 other words first.

Tatiana, a Serbian alternative medicine practitioner, said I'm wrong. She insisted that Balkanian has a word for *hand*—it's *shaka*. I told her that she just knows that because she's into palm reading. To prove me wrong, she suggested I test her friends. So I went to one and pointed to my arm and said, "What do you call this?"

"*Ruka*," he said.

"And this?" I asked while pointing to my hand.

He paused, glanced nervously at Tatiana, and then, with a bit less confidence, said, "*Ruka*."

"No!" Tatiana screamed. "It's *shaka*! C'mon you know that!"

"OK, I guess so," he said, "But we usually don't call it that. That's kind of a medical term."

Imagine Balkanians getting shocked that Americans don't use the word *frontal lobe* everyday. They would say, "Can you believe it? Those Americans just say *brain!* They don't even bother to distinguish between the two! They say 'Think with your *brain*!' and not 'Think with your *frontal lobe*!' Crazy Americans!"

Here's what's far more crazy: Balkanians aren't alone. There are over 200 languages that don't make a hand-arm distinction! Who are these freaks?! How is this possible? Are they even human? If you need evidence that aliens live among us, this is it!

A study of 620 languages shows that these scary mutants tend to live near the equator and that their numbers decrease as you move towards the poles. For instance, among the 292 languages that are spoken relatively far from the equator, nearly 80 percent have a name for that thing you punch people with. That's an eerily low percentage. Still, what's truly hair-raising is that the *majority* of the 328 languages near the equator don't have a special name for that five-fingered thing you use to masturbate with.[5]

This is so demented that it seems like half the world has gotten a frontal lobotomy. Nevertheless, there are two theories to explain this. One is that a fleet of flying saucers landed in areas near the equator. The other theory is that people who live far from the equator tend to have colder climates that require gloves, which draws attention to that body part, thereby encouraging people to give it a unique name. Although this is a reasonable theory, all Slavs (except Poles) don't know what a hand is! And of course, Slavs have always used gloves since they generally live in places that can get butt-freezing cold.

I'm stupefied. This whole issue may be the world's greatest mystery that nobody talks about. At least this explains why there can never be peace in the Balkans. All their peace treaties are based on armshake agreements. (Sorry.)

See Split, then split

Ana and I hiked out of Krka National Park and debated whether to hike up Dinara, Croatia's tallest mountain (1,831 m / 6,000 ft). The mountain's base was only one hour away, but it would take most of the day to hike up and down. Instead, we went by Šibenik again to follow the coastal road to Trogir. Driving by Šibenik brought back good memories of the previous day. This Venetian-styled town is my second favorite Croatian town (after Dubrovnik). It's a fabulous seaside maze to explore. Unlike Zadar, Šibenik is built on hilly terrain. Its multiple levels, along with its quiet, pedestrian-only streets that overlook the Adriatic Sea, make the town a romantic dream. Ana and I especially enjoyed the sunset over the Adriatic from the top of the city's ancient fortress.

While driving to the UNESCO-protected town of Trogir, the cute hamlet of Primošten seduced us. Along the Dalmatian coast you'll occasionally find tiny towns like Primošten. They're adorable towns that Venetians and Croatians built on easily defended parts of land that jut out into the Adriatic Sea. It generally takes less than 30 minutes to walk across these endearing hamlets. Trogir is larger than Primošten and even more captivating. It was my second visit to Trogir, but I still got lost in its narrow streets. Ana and I admired Trogir's impressive defensive wall from the nearby bridge. After a gelato, we split to go to Split.

Although Split isn't as famous as Dubrovnik, it's Croatia's second biggest city after Zagreb. The Roman Emperor Diocletian put Split on the map when he built his retirement home there. The Palace of Diocletian is the best preserved Roman palace in the world. Its tall walls are about two football fields long. Even though the basement halls are completely bare, they're useful for helping you imagine the original (and now vanished) rooms upstairs. That's because the basement was a mirror image of the Palace's layout upstairs. It's obvious that the retired Roman Emperor enjoyed his final years here, reminiscing about all the innocent Christians he gleefully slaughtered and executed.

A Frisbee becomes a boomerang

To understand a people, you must understand their history—that includes what objective historians say, as well as what the people on the street say. In the Balkans, that's as easy to do as pulling a tooth out of an alligator. Nevertheless, as promised, we'll examine Yugoslavia's history. But first, we'll zip through 1,100 years of Croatian history.

After the Roman Empire split, Slavs started showing up in the Balkans. Croatia's glory days were 925 to 1102 AD. Like Hungary has nostalgia for its medieval heyday, Croatians celebrate the only time when their nation was shaped like a Frisbee—it controlled about half of what is now Bosnia and Herzegovina. Croatia would go under Hungary's wing for a few centuries until the Turks thrust into Croatia (then part of Hungary's kingdom). That thrust left a permanent scar: it carved Croatia into the shape of a boomerang. It's stayed that way ever since.

A year before I visited Split with Ana, I was taking a bus from Trogir to Split when I met Dario, a 29-year-old Croatian. He was wearing his team's soccer uniform and had just finished a game. I hoped he would be a stereotypical soccer hooligan who would say all sorts of stupid shit.

I asked Dario to tell me about Croatia's history. He surprised me by starting a few centuries before Christ, saying, "The Illyrians were here first." You know history is a big deal in a region when even a sweaty soccer player will start a history lecture with an obscure ancient civilization. He was the first person to explain to me why Croatia has a boomerang shape. He also said that some Croatians don't like the people of Dubrovnik. When I asked him why, he said, "The wealthy merchants of Dubrovnik paid the Turks a bunch of gold for peace instead of fighting them like the rest of the Slavs. The people of Dubrovnik just sat there while the rest of the nation died to save Europe."

"Hold on," I said. "You're saying that today's Croatians are pissed at today's Dubrovnik residents because of what Dubrovnik residents did 500 years ago?"

"Yeah. I'm not saying everybody feels this way, but some do. Listen, people are crazy here. Croatian children are taught to hate Serbs. They see a Serb and think, 'Hey, you killed my father!' They're stupid. I tell them, 'No, *he* didn't kill your father. Someone else pulled the trigger.' And even if that was the person who pulled the trigger, that was what he was supposed to do. He was probably dragged into that stupid war and forced to fight against people he didn't want to fight."

"What about Bosnians?"

"The Bosnians were good and happy before the war. You could go there and people were so multicultural that everyone would accept everyone. You would arrive and they would say, 'You're a stranger? So are we. Come in and join the party.'"

"Do you understand Bosnians when they speak?"

"Yeah, we understand everyone except Slovenians and Macedonians—they're different. But even though we're just 4.5 million Croatians, there are big language differences between us. The people on the coast use many Italian words, while the northern Croatians use more Hungarian and Slavic words. In Dalmatia, the language teachers teach proper Croatian, but they'll speak incorrect Croatian in the other classes and outside of school. So that's why sometimes it's hard for other Croatians to understand us here in Dalmatia."

Before we got to Split, I asked him, "Are Croatians excited to join the EU?"

"They're worried. Many Western Europeans come to buy homes and set up lives here, but once they see the bureaucracy, they're turned off and go home. That bureaucracy helps us Croatians because we know how to navigate through it. But it's not that easy for us either. Once Croatia joins the EU, that bureaucracy must go away because of common EU laws. Then a flood of rich Europeans will come, making it impossible for Croatians who live here to own a house."

I was impressed with Dario's English speaking skills and disappointed by his lack of immature hooligan behavior.

From kingdom to communism

For 888 years Croatia was not an independent country. Like Estonians, Latvians, Belarusians, and Slovaks, Croatians have nearly always been a region within another country or kingdom until it finally gained independence two decades ago. Before it became independent, however, it went through the grand experiment called Yugoslavia. *Jug* (sounds like *Yug*) means *south* in Balkanian; hence, *Jugoslavia* (Yugoslavia) means *Land of the Southern Slavs*. Its original name was *Kingdom of the Serbs, Croats, and Slovenes*, which didn't mention the Albanians, Bosnians, Macedonians, Montenegrins, even though they were in the country. Still, it didn't matter, because from the beginning to the end, Yugoslavia was mostly a wrestling match between the Croatians and Serbians. The other guys just had front row seats.

The drama begins in 1892 in the humble Croatian village of Kumrovec, where a Slovenian woman was in labor. Of the 15 babies she would produce, this one was number seven. Her husband, a Croatian peasant, named the baby Josip Broz. In Josip's late 20s, the Russians captured him during WWI. It seemed meaningless at the time—Josip was just one of thousands of prisoners. Nevertheless, it would change him and Yugoslavia forever. When Josip escaped from prison, he didn't run back home. Instead, he stayed in Russia, married a 14-year-old Russian girl, and fell in love with a hip, untested economic system based on fairness and equality—it was called communism.

After five years in Russia, Josip returned to Yugoslavia and was frustrated by the seesaw battle between the Serbs who wanted centralization and the Croatians who wanted decentralization. Standardizing the national language was also a nightmare fight. The Balkan passion was so high that a Serb politician killed five Croatian politicians in parliament.

The Serbian King declared a dictatorship, but was later assassinated. During these turbulent times, Josip (now in his 30s) promoted communism as the solution. For that, he went to jail for six years. In his early 40s, he got out and went to Moscow for two years of commie training. When he returned to Yugoslavia in 1936, Stalin had Yugoslav's Communist Party leader assassinated and put Josip in his place. When Yugoslavs asked Josip for his name, he now said that it was "Tito."

Tito criticized Serbians, who were 45 percent of the population, for being too dominant over the other Yugoslav minorities (Croatians were the second most populous with 24 percent). This belief would guide Tito's political philosophy for the rest of his life. He believed that Yugoslavia could only function if Serbs shared the power evenly; otherwise, the other Yugoslavs would revolt. Since Serbs were dominant before WWII, Tito advocated breaking Yugoslavia up. Ironically, once he took power, he would ruthlessly crush anyone else who tried to break it up.

The Ustaše—Croatia's Nazis

When WWII exploded, Tito retreated to the safety of the Balkan mountains while the Nazis and the Ustaše, Croatian fascists, took over Yugoslavia. Tito established a rebel group called the Communist Partisans. At first they could do little against the powerful Ustaše, who unfurled Croatia's 1,000-year-old checkered flag and were as adorable as the Nazis. The Ustaše built death camps like Americans build malls. The estimates for the number of Jews, Serbs, Croatians, Bosnians, and Roma that the Ustaše killed in Yugoslavia's biggest concentration camp (Jasenovac) vary from the tens of thousands to the hundreds of thousands. The Ustaše wanted revenge against the Serbs for having dominated the Croatians during the previous years. By banning Cyrillic, labeling the Serbian Orthodox religion a "Greek Eastern faith," and executing thousands of innocent Serbs, the Ustaše burned an idea into the Serb brain: Croatians want to murder us.[6]

While some Croatians were immorally slaughtering thousands, other Croatians were busy creating the first Yugoslav military unit *against* the Croatian Ustaše—the First Sisak Partisan Detachment. In fact, the movement that ultimately defeated the Ustaše and Nazis was not led by a Serb, but by a Croatian: Tito. Although Serbs also created their own anti-Ustaše group (the Četniks), in typical Balkan fashion, they were unwilling to join forces with Tito's Partisans to fight the common enemy. Instead, using Balkan "logic," Serb Četniks eventually switched sides and allied themselves with the Serb-killing Ustaše and Nazis, partly just to spite the Partisans.

Thus, toward the end of WWII, Tito's Communist Partisans now had three enemies: Nazis, Ustaše, and Četniks. Despite the Croatian-led team defeating the Croatians fascists and Četnik Serbs supporting the Croatian fascists, the memory that was seared into the Serb psyche was *Croatians want to murder us, especially those who wave that 1,000-year-old checkered flag*.

Serbs sometimes make a big deal about the fact that the Ustaše killed more Serbs than anyone else and that far more Serbs died in WWII than other Yugoslav group. However, it would be strange if that didn't happen: Serbs were nearly half of Yugoslavia's prewar population with the next highest (the Croatians) being less than a quarter. Assuming proportional deaths, you'd expect about twice as many Serbs to die than Croatians since there were nearly twice as many Serbs to start with.

Furthermore, Jozo Tomasevich points out in *War and Revolution in Yugoslavia, 1941-1945* that Germans and other occupiers didn't kill most of the Yugoslavs—the Yugoslavs largely killed themselves. For instance, Serbs murdered thousands of Bosnians and Croatians in revenge for the Ustaše killings. If Yugoslavs didn't kill someone because their ethnicity and religion was different, they'll shoot them for having the wrong political beliefs. Hence, Četnik Serbs killed plenty of Partisan Serbs and Partisan Croatians killed plenty of Ustaše Croatians. Welcome to the Balkans.[7]

Croatian fascists certainly targeted Serbs, although not as efficiently as they targeted Jews. The Ustaše-Nazis killed "only" 67,000 Jews, but that was over 90 percent of Yugoslavia's Jewish population. One Serb told me, "Serbia was nearly wiped of the face of the planet." Not quite: 6.7 percent of all of Yugoslavs died in WWII, which is a lower percentage than that of Belarus, Germany, Greece, Latvia, Lithuania, Poland, and Russia. Serbs suffered higher than the Yugoslav average, but not dramatically higher.[8] It's important to consider the percentage of a people killed, not just the gross number. Serbs wouldn't like it if America made a big deal that it suffered just as much military loses as Yugoslavia did in WWII, even though it did (both countries lost about 425,000 soldiers). Serbs would say that America's military loses were less meaningful than Serbia's since those 425,000 men were "only" 0.32 percent of America's prewar population. Serbs should remember that logic when they make a big deal about their WWII loses compared to other Yugoslavs. In sum, thanks to the Ustaše, Serbs suffered proportionately more (though not dramatically more) than other Yugoslav ethnic groups, while Yugoslavia suffered a higher than average nationwide casualty rate (though it was not in Europe's top seven).

Seven reasons why Tito was the most loved dictator ever

Dictators are usually dicks. Therefore, I was shocked when nearly all ex-Yugoslavs that I met showered Tito's 35-year dictatorship with praise. Whenever I asked people to rate him on a one to 10 scale, in most cases they would say, "10." Some even said, "11!" It didn't matter who or where I asked, the answer was nearly always high. Of course, I eventually found a few oddball detractors. Still, if you ask enough people, you'll find people who hate Lincoln, Washington, Jefferson, and even Gandhi. It's impossible to be universally loved (especially as a politician), but Tito was close to perfection. It raises the obvious question: *why?*

1. Tito won the war and focused the country on forgiving, forgetting, and moving on. Although he punished the worst war criminals and expelled innocent Germans (like most countries did), he generally took a forgiving approach so that Yugoslavia wouldn't dwell on the past. He never visited Jasenovac (their worst death camp) because this might stir up horrible memories and he wanted people to focus on the future.

2. Tito kept Yugoslavia independent. He not only won the war, but he did it with little Allied assistance. That allowed Yugoslavia to not fall into either side of the Cold War. Although Tito started cozy with Stalin, three years after WWII he broke off his ties and declared his neutrality. This infuriated Stalin, who tried to assassinate Tito many times.

> *Stop sending people to kill me. We've already captured five of them, one of them with a bomb and another with a rifle. . . . If you don't stop sending killers, I'll send one to Moscow, and I won't have to send a second.*
> *— Tito, in a letter to Stalin*

3. Tito was a diplomatic genius. After breaking with Stalin, Tito turned to the West for help, but not so much that he would be in their pocket. Instead of falling into one of the Cold War camps, the brilliant mastermind created a third camp: the Non-Aligned Movement. Countries as diverse as India, Egypt, and Saudi Arabia joined this neutral organization. This put Yugoslavia on the world stage. Tito cleverly extracted money and favors from both the USA and the USSR. It turned Yugoslavia into a big communist version of Switzerland.

4. Tito blended Yugoslavia's many factions. He realized that Yugoslavia's Achilles' heel was its various linguistic and religious blocs. He knew that the only way to create a united Yugoslavia was to mix people up and turn up the heat of the melting pot so that everyone blends together evenly. He led by example: his fourth (and longest lasting) marriage was with a Serbian. That symbolically united the country—Tito was half Croatian, half Slovenian and was married to a Serbian. He made everyone learn Balkanian and encouraged many to move within Yugoslavia. For example, a Slovenian living near the

Italian border told me, "Tito invited Yugoslavs from far away, offered them a job and a nice house here in Istria. Istrians had an identity, but so many came from all over that we've lost that identity." Not only was military serve mandatory, but soldiers had to serve in one of the other five republics. This cracked open provincial Balkan brains. It taught close-minded Yugoslavs that Serbs, Croatians, and Bosnians aren't demons who eat their children.

5. Tito crushed all forms of nationalism. Serbs cry that Tito castrated them by drawing internal borders that didn't follow ethnic lines and put two autonomous provinces within it to dilute their power. They're right, he did. Croatians whine that Tito ruthlessly rained on the Croatian Spring uprising where they demanded more autonomy. They're right, he did. Slovenians bitch about Tito stealing their wealth to give it to other republics. They're right, he did. Albanians, Bosnians, Montenegrins, and Macedonians all have their petty grievances against Tito too. They're right, he did. Tito beat down any nail that was sticking out. His justice was sometime brutal, but compared to the acts of other communist leaders, Tito was gentle. Most importantly, he never consistently favored one national group over the other. That was Tito's talent.

6. Tito let people travel freely. Unlike other communists, Tito let people come and go. Thanks to their neutrality, a Yugoslav passport let you travel anywhere on the planet without a visa. Although ex-Yugoslavs make a big deal about this, they never mention that they didn't get such freedom until 1967—that's 22 years after Tito was in power. So for half of Yugoslavia's post-WWII existence, Yugoslavs were just as stuck as the other Eastern Europeans. Still, Tito changed this policy and it became a source of pride for the Yugoslavs. As *The New York Times* reported in 1980, "Yugoslavia gradually became a bright spot amid the general grayness of Eastern Europe."

7. Tito was flexible. Although Tito believed in the communist ideology, he wasn't married to it. For instance, he relaxed trade restrictions. Michael Edwards, an American with a Macedonian wife, told me, "One thing that caught my eye when visiting Yugoslavia in 1976 was that you could find Soviet, Chinese, and American products sitting on the same shelf in the government-run department stores. That was a rare sight only found in very, very few countries at the time." Tito also loosened free-speech and private ownership laws. In short, Tito practiced *glasnost* and *perestroika* before Gorbachev knew how to spell it.

Tito's mistakes

Tito made fewer mistakes in his 35-year dictatorship than a typical American President makes during his four years in office. Anyone who disagrees should try leading Yugoslavia for a few years to see how easy it is. Perhaps Tito's greatest error was not doing a better job at preparing Yugoslavia to live without him. Tito either had to find another balanced and enlightened despot like himself (which is hard to do in a land filled with myopic politicians) or create a system that would impose that balance naturally. Although Tito didn't groom a successor, he rewrote the Constitution every decade, trying to find the perfect formula to contain a country with too many nationalistic hotheads. What might have helped even more was leaving Yugoslavia with an economic system that didn't suck.

Yugoslavia, like many African countries, depended on economic assistance to keep the lights on. Slovenian economic historian Neven Borak told me, "Starting in 1960, the money flows from the West were more important than the money from the USSR. Western banks invested in Yugoslavia in the 1970s to help us extract commodities, whose prices were rising rapidly at the time. However, those loans had a variable interest rate, which started to skyrocket in the late 1970s. Meanwhile, starting in the early 80s, the value of commodities started to drop. Our inefficient industries could not produce goods fast enough to pay off debts. All these factors killed us economically."

Consider the numbers. In 1970, Yugoslavia had $2.35 billion in debt. By 1981, it had ballooned to $20.6 billion. Tito tried the standard trick of printing more currency to pay off the debt, but that predictably led to 14 percent inflation and devalued the currency. Suddenly, imported goods and trips abroad were too expensive. Unemployment and inflation continued to soar after Tito's death. By 1988, Yugoslavia's inflation was a back-breaking 250 percent. The Yugoslav finger-pointing party began.

Tito's fatal mistake was building an economic system that depended on the Cold War lasting forever. He should have abandoned it and copied a sustainable economic system from a neutral country like Austria, Switzerland, Sweden, or Finland. Instead, like an African economy that lives off donations and delivers little economic value, Yugoslavia became worthless to the West once it was clear that the USSR was going to fall. The money stopped flowing in and Yugoslavia's economic house of cards crumbled.

Tito died in 1980, three days before his 89th birthday. When the news hit, professional soccer players in the middle of a televised game collapsed on the field in tears. Yugoslavs everywhere did the same. Mahmut Bakalli, an ethnic Albanian, said, "We all cried, but we did not know we were also burying Yugoslavia." One Bosnian told me, "Tito was a real politician, who really cared about the people, not just about himself." But it wasn't just Yugoslavs who loved Tito. During his life, he received 119 major awards from 60 diverse countries. Many ex-Yugoslavs proudly reminded me that high-level diplomats from 128 countries attended Tito's funeral. Based on the number of participating nations, it was the largest state funeral in world history. When I asked Neven to rate Tito, without any hesitation, he said, "10."

> *Why did 128 countries come to Tito's funeral? Because he owed them all money. — Yugoslav joke*

Croatia's great escape: its islands

Tito had 32 homes, but perhaps his favorite was on one of Croatia's northernmost islands: Brijuni National Park. It's a paradise, but not the only one in Croatia. In 2011, Ana and I visited the nearby islands of Krk, Cres, and Lošinj—each has cute towns, tough green vegetation, and endless aquatic opportunities. They're hard to leave.

I first fell in love with Croatia's islands in 2004. After camping in Ploče, a coastal town, I took a 5:00 a.m. ferry to a long, skinny peninsula called Pelješac. By 2016, instead of a ferry, there may be a $400 million bridge. Its main purpose is to bypass an annoying Bosnian checkpoint, which will disappear if Bosnia joins the EU—that's Balkan logic for you. On Pelješac I hitchhiked to Orebić with a bread delivery guy. I bought some bread off him to thank him, even though he wanted to give it to me for free. A ferry from Orebić took me to the biggest island in a 48-island archipelago: Korčula (pronounced Core-chu-la).

The Venetians ran Korčula for 400 years and left their lovely mark with their tight, convoluted streets that are meant to kill the brisk wind that often plagues the island. Throw in a few churches, plazas, and blue waters all around, you end up with another resplendent town. As pretty as it is, it must get boring after a while. That explains why nearly 750 years ago Marco Polo, the archetypal world traveler and one of my heroes, left his Korčula birthplace and began a 24-year journey across the Silk Road to Asia. Although Polo is known as a traveler, many don't realize that he parked it in China for 20 years. Polo's Korčula home still stands, but it's in poor condition—he was obviously a lousy housekeeper.

After crossing Korčula Island by bus I grabbed a ferry from the cute town of Vela Luka to another island paradise: Hvar. Hvar's turquoise waters make it as irresistible as a gelato. It's yet another place where the artistic Venetians left their perfect mark. Everywhere you look stone buildings have been cut and crafted into works of art that you can live in. The 500-year-old Venetian Fortress looms over this Shangri-la. Unfortunately, the Fortress couldn't stop the Turks from conquering the town just 20 years after it was built. I camped under Hvar's pine trees and the next day I took a crowded bus to the precious port of Stari Grad, which shows off its Venetian heritage. I really want the

Venetians to invade and take over America. When the Venetian Empire spread down Dalmatia, they beautified every city they touched. If they conquered America, we'd finally have some truly graceful cities in the USA. And we'd get some good pizza and pasta too.

An irredentist: far worse than an evil dentist

When you wander through these old Venetian-styled towns, you may eventually wonder, "Where are all the Italians?" The locals speak Balkanian, although they sprinkle Italian words over their Slavic tongue. Imagine if the Oregon coastline were covered with Chinese architecture and that the locals spoke English with random Chinese words tossed in. What would you think happened there?

That story starts when the Venetian Republic bought the Dalmatian Coast in 1409. Venetians were classy and civilized. Why fight if you can pay each other off? Instead of starting a messy fight with the Kingdom of Hungary, they just bought the land. Instead of a bloody battle with the Turks, the Dubrovnik people just slipped them some "protection money." What if, during the 1990s, the Yugoslavs had settled their differences that way? How much death, pain, and suffering would have been avoided?

For nearly four centuries, the Venetians built the jewels in Dalmatia. Sadly, the Venetian Republic fell in 1797, but luckily the architecture stood. Even though the Republic disappeared, the Italians didn't. In the early 1800s, about a quarter of Dalmatia was Italian, according to independent surveys done over several years by Italians, French, and Austrians. Croatians would later claim that only seven percent were Italians. In 1857, the Austrians (who were controlling Dalmatia at the time) took another census that showed 17 percent Italians along the coast. Austria's 1910 census showed that Italians were 38 percent of Istria. Most Italians were concentrated in the cities, while Slavs dominated the countryside. For example, in 1910, about two-thirds of Rijeka and Zadar (both in Croatia) were Italian. In 1945, 96 percent of Piran, Slovenia was ethnically Italian. Just 11 years later, only 15 percent of Piran would be Italian. Today, all these places are Italian ghost-towns.

This created the irredentist, a term which got its name when some Italians cried about *"Italia irredenta"* (unredeemed Italy). Thus, an *irredentista* (irredentist) advocates acquiring a foreign region because it was once (or still is) somehow tied with one's nation. A perfect example of irredentism is the Greater Hungary fantasy that we analyzed extensively. Irredentism is a disease that plagues Eastern Europe because nearly every nation was, at some point, bigger than it is today. Hence, it's easy to find bitter people who "want land back that was historically ours!" Like Hungary's irredentists, their claims have some truth behind them, but they're usually built on myths.

Such fantasies are dangerous, as Hitler showed with his *Groß-deutschland* (Greater Germany) irredentist arguments. You'll find irredentism in nearly every country in the world except one: the United States. America is immune to this disease because to get infected you need to have lost some land during your history. Since its founding, America has only expanded. The day we lose Alaska, Hawaii, Texas, or Florida, the first American irredentist will be born.

Irredentists love ethnic cleansing

When an irredentist finally gets back "his unredeemed land," he often finds that people living there aren't like him. That's when he gets lots of soap for some deep *čišćenje terena* (cleansing of the territory). Although the Balkanian term *etničko čišćenje* (ethnic cleansing) became popular during the Yugoslav Wars, the practice is as old as Adam and Eve. Indeed, God ethnically cleansed the Garden of Eden when he booted Adam and Eve out.

If kicking out the dirty ones doesn't leave it clean enough, then force them to assimilate or kill them. Today, Slovenians will bring out the violin when they tell you about the cruel Italians who forced the coastal Slavs to speak Italian. Slovenians will speak of Italy's WWII Rab and Gonars concentration camps (where over 2,000 Slavs and Jews died) and Trieste's Risiera di San Sabba camp (which killed 3,000). They'll share how Italy's government never prosecuted or extradited 1,200 Italians accused of war crimes. However, Slovenians won't tell you that Slavs cruelly forced Italians who lived in Istria and Dalmatia to give up the Italian language or leave. Nor will they bring up the Foibe killings, where Slavs executed thousands of Italians during and after WWII. In 2007, Italy's President commemorated the Foibe massacres, calling them "*un disegno annessionistico slavo*" ("a Slavic-designed annexation").

That's partly why Tito tacitly agreed not to make a big deal about Italy's war crimes as long as Italy didn't make a fuss about Yugoslavia's war crimes. Meanwhile, Italians who had been living in Dalmatia and Istria for generations were, overnight, no longer in Italy, but in a strange new communist country called Yugoslavia. Soon after WWII, Yugoslavia confiscated large property, prohibited travel, and oppressed anyone who disagreed with them. Italians, stuck in this unappealing land, had a mass exodus: about 250,000 went to Italy. Yugoslavia said, "Don't worry, we'll pay you $110 million for all the Italian homes we took over." By Yugoslavia's breakup, Italy had only received $18 million. At least the Croatians have kept the old Venetian towns looking pretty.

Hitchhiking off Mljet Island with an irredentist

In March 2009, I was stranded on Croatia's Mljet Island. I went to enjoy the empty island for an overnight trip. However, after the boat left the postage-stamp sized village of Šobra, I learned that it wasn't coming back for several days because the winter storm was intensifying. If I had to be marooned on the forested island for several days, I preferred being in the national park on Mljet's western edge. Luckily, one man was driving across the island, so I offered him gas money to get me to Polače, in the middle of the national park. The stormy weather motivated me to get a hotel with a balcony overlooking a small bay—the $30 winter rate was attractive. Over the next few days, I explored the island's many trails with a rain jacket. One of its two saltwater lakes, Veliko Jezero, has a quaint island with a mini-monastery and restaurant. With no boat going there during the winter, I would have to swim. No thanks, I was wet enough.

I've hitchhiked hundreds of times, but I've never hitchhiked off an island. First, I had to hitchhike to Mljet's port. I got lucky because my driver (and his father) were not just going to the port, but were also taking their car onto the ferry, and, once on the mainland, they were driving to Dubrovnik—which is where I wanted to go. I gave them $10 for their kindness and their irredentist stories.

Although the son, Danny, was calm and healthy, his father had a bad case of irredentism disease. He erupted with fiery passion as he explained how Croatia was picked apart by many powers. "Croatia was better 1,000 years after Christ!" he declared. Using broken English and wild hand gestures, he communicated that he wasn't pleased about losing bits of Croatia to Serbia, to Slovenia, to Italy, to Bosnia, to Hungary, and to Montenegro. I was glad that his relaxed son was driving. He ranted about Herceg Novi and Kotor, two Montenegrin towns that are somewhat near Croatia's coastal border. "Herceg Novi!" he exclaimed. "This not Montenegrin name! It Croatian name! Listen! *Herceg No-vi:* comes from Croatian word! No Montenegro! And Kotor also! Where does name *Kotor* come from? *Ko-tor*: Croatian! No Montenegro! *This was ours!*"

I looked at my watch. It was 10:30 a.m. I thought, "Yeah, it was about time for my daily dose of a kooky nationalist madman from the Balkans. I wonder who my 2:00 p.m. appointment will be?"

Playing sex games with objects

About a year later, I looked at my watch: 1:58 p.m. Ana and I had left Split and were driving south toward Omiš. As we drove, Ana told me that Balkanians and Slovenians have difficulty communicating since their languages are fairly different. In the past, that wasn't a problem since all Slovenians could speak Balkanian. Ana said, "My parents learned Balkanian in school and the TV channels were in Balkanian with Slovenian subtitles."

"And now?" I asked.

"Now Slovenians don't watch Balkanian channels; we prefer Slovenian or American shows. And we don't learn Balkanian in school. Young Slovenians now learn English, Italian, or German. Croatians never learned Slovenian since we all spoke Balkanian. At least they're learning English. I guess English is now our common language."

I asked Ana, "Is Balkanian like Slovenian in that it assigns every object a gender?"

She said, "Yes, of course."

"That's so fucking stupid," I said. "I don't give a shit if over half the world does that—it's totally retarded. I could understand saying that a *table* is feminine and that a *knife* is masculine if there were a remote possibility that the knife could have sex with a table and produce a child! But sadly, even a fuckin' *drill* can't have offspring no matter how many things it screws! And that's why a *drill*, and all other non-living objects in the universe, shouldn't have dumb-ass gender!"

Ana looked at me like a madman saying, "Hey relax, it's not such . . ."

"Furthermore, I would grudgingly accept giving inanimate objects a gender if everyone on this damn planet could agree on what each object's gender was! But we don't! That's because inanimate objects don't have reproductive organs! The fuckers who invented these stupid languages were arbitrarily pulling these genders out of their asses! Sure, the Germans, Spaniards, French, Slovenians, and Croatians all agree that a *house* is feminine—that's wonderful. But Spaniards and Slovenians think a *bed* is feminine while the fuckin' French and Croatians think it's masculine! However, no matter how you stack Slovenian and Croatian beds on top of each other, they'll never ever get pregnant and produce a *fuckin' baby-sized bed*!!!"

Ana said, "Francis, calm down. You're sounding like a complete lunatic! You're like some crazy American nationalist who thinks English is the best language ever. Hey, what time is it anyway?"

I looked at my watch: 2:01 p.m. "That's funny," I mumbled, "Right on time . . ."

> *The main difference between men and women is that men are lunatics and women are idiots. — Rebecca West*

The road to Dubrovnik

The surreal town of Omiš was one of my favorite stops that Ana and I made on our way to Dubrovnik. It takes only 10 minutes to walk most of Omiš, but the setting is out-of-this-world. Omiš is squeezed between the Adriatic Sea and a near vertical mountain range. What's dramatic is that it seems like God cut a narrow slice off the mountain range to let a river sneak through. When you ride along the river and peek on the other side of the mountain wall, you'll see that the mountains plunge into a valley. In short, the mountain range is thin, but tall, and has a narrow gap to go through it. It's marvelous.

We continued driving down the coast until I said, "Hey, look! There's Jesus!" A lone man was walking along the narrow two-lane highway. He had sandals, a trench-coat, a staff, and a Santa-Claus-like beard. OK, so he was older than Jesus, but he looked like a religious pilgrim (or a hobo). We pulled up next to him so I could ask him in my horrible Balkanian if he needed a lift. He stunned me when he said, "Sorry, I only speak English."

His name was Bob and he grew up in Tallahassee, Florida. He had started his pilgrimage in Trieste, Italy and he was walking to "Major Glory." That's actually *Međugorje,* which sounds somewhat like he pronounced it. Međugorje is a sacred site in Bosnia and Herzegovina where six kids claimed that they saw the Virgin Mary in 1981 and that they could communicate with her regularly. They allegedly saw miraculous visual effects around the sun. In 2010, the Holy See created a commission to investigate their claims. Meanwhile, for the last 20 years a million pilgrims visit it annually, and a few of them ruin their eyes in their vain attempts to see the same apparitions in the sun.

This was Bob's second pilgrimage to the site. His rule: never stick your thumb out for a ride, but if someone offers, accept. He told us of his screwed-up childhood, his odd jobs, his two failed marriages, his alcoholism, and how Christianity saved him from all of it. Like him, we would also be camping that night under the stars, but we wanted privacy, so we let him off at sunset in Makarska while we found a perfect camping spot off of a dirt road nearby. The next day, we left at dawn and found Bob pugnaciously continuing his pilgrimage. Once again we stopped and welcomed him into our car for another lift. We finally dropped him off where the road breaks away to enter Bosnia and Herzegovina. We continued going to Dubrovnik.

About a year earlier, I was on a bus going from Dubrovnik when I met two ethnic Croatian women who live in Dubrovnik. Ružica was born in Bosnia, grew up in Switzerland, and married a Swiss man. Gabriela grew up east of Zagreb and married an American man. They all live in Dubrovnik. Given their marriages, I asked them to compare Croatia with the West. Gabriela said, "Easterners focus on the internal in life, while Westerners focus on the external. But it's complicated, because we dream of the West. For Croatians, the West is still a goal to reach for."

I said, "Ružica, what do you think is the biggest difference between Balkanians and the West?"

Ružica said, "Some Balkan people think that they are more important than others because of their history. Here people are still looking behind. People need to start looking forward. Even young people, trained by their parents, spend too much time thinking about the past. People are stuck in the past."

Gabriela interrupted, "I agree that Croatians don't think of the future as much as Western people, but perhaps we also live more for the moment than the West does."

Is the Croatian man marriage material?

I asked the two ladies why they had not married a Croatian man. Ružica had an easy excuse—she grew up in Switzerland. Gabriela diplomatically said, "I just fell in love with an American guy." A year later, I would ask two Westerners what they thought about Croatian men; both of these women were living in Istria.

For some Croatians, Istria is like what Alaska is for Americans—it's over there somewhere. "I'll visit it someday," we tell ourselves. Istria looks like a downward pointing arrowhead, sticking out like a tumor in Croatia's northwest. It was my home for most of 2010 and 2011, where I wrote much of this book. I lived on the edge of this hinterland, in a coastal village called Crveni Vrh, near Umag. When I moved there in December 2009, I didn't have enough wood to heat the house, so the inside temperature was around five degrees Celsius (41 F). Hence, if there are typos in this book, it's because my hands were cold. Throughout the winter the village's 70 summer homes were as lively as a graveyard. At 8:00 p.m. you would be lucky to see three lights on in the whole village. And usually those three lights were coming from my house.

Despite the isolation, just a 15-minute walk away, near Savudrija, was a five-star resort. The $400 million facility was the newest addition to the German Kempinski luxury brand. In the lobby is a wall of falling water, while outside are a couple of pools and an elevator that takes you to an intimate pebble beach. The resort is dead during the winter, but I appreciated its wireless Internet—my only connection to outside world. I was surprised when the first receptionist that I met at the hotel was a pretty lady from Seattle. Her name was Kendra and I wondered how she ended up in this forgotten corner of Croatia. "I just married a Croatian!" she said.

"Cool! So how is it marrying a Croatian man?" I asked.

"The Croatian generosity for a wedding is incredible," she said. "We had 131 people at the Croatian wedding and 174 at the Seattle one, yet we had *four times* more gifts in Croatia! Remember, Americans make nearly four times more money than Croatians. In America, a random wedding guest may give you $50, but in Croatia they'll give you $300. Given how little they make, it's a super high level of generosity."

Later, I became friends with Karin Jongman, the hotel's Rooms Division Manager. She's a tall Dutch lady who speaks six languages, but not Balkanian, because after taking a few classes, she concluded "it was too hard." Besides, very few hotel guests were Balkanians and she would be going to China in a year for another assignment. She said about two-thirds of the clients came from Germany or Austria. Americans don't come because, "For Americans, Croatia is only Dubrovnik."

I said, "If you want to learn Balkanian, you should copy Kendra and find yourself a Croatian man."

"No way," she said.

"Why not? Are they not tall enough?" Dutch people are the tallest people in the world and Karin lived up to that stereotype.

"That's one problem," she said, "But mainly it's because they're not liberal enough. I'm a Dutch woman. Croatian men are too old-fashioned and traditional. That wouldn't work for me."

"It works for Kendra."

"Her husband is not a typical Croatian. He was educated in Switzerland, so c'mon, right there that says a lot. And also, his family is well-off, so they're more worldly and open-minded than the typical Croatian."

Several months later, Ana and I had dinner with Kendra and her husband, Jadran Jergović. I asked Jadran, who had spent half a year in America, how American women are different than Croatian women. He laughed, "I've had to learn how to do the dishes."

Kendra said, "Croatian men are much better than American men about being a gentleman. They open doors, bring flowers, protect the woman, and treat her like a lady. The flip side is that they have expectations of you. Once I called my Croatian friend and asked her where her husband was. She said, 'He's out with his buddies.' And do you know what she was doing? Ironing! Her husband's out having fun and she's home ironing! Crazy!"

I asked, "What else is different about life in Croatia compared to America?"

Jadran said, "In Croatia, the family really takes care of you. For example, my dad built three houses: one for him, one for my brother, and one for me. They pay for your university, travel, car, everything. They keep taking care of you even when you're in your twenties. In America, after 18 years old, kids are on their own."

"That's true," Kendra said, "But there's a price for the Croatian philosophy. Croatian parents have an expectation that you will take care of them when they get old."

Ana said, "Yeah, the worst thing you can do to Slovenians is put them in a home for old people!"

Kendra said, "Yeah, but that's weird to me. When I'm old, I'd love to be in a home for elderly people! You get to socialize and have activities with others. But here in Croatia, you gotta take care of your aging parents."

Corrupt, but not thieves

Although interacting with the locals is a fun way to get to know a people, it's a highly unscientific process. Surveys have their own flaws, but they provide another insightful angle to understand a culture. In most cases, I've found that surveys and my personal experiences agree. A prime example is how Balkanians view corruption. According to a 2010 Gallup poll, a whopping 92 percent of Croatians and 91 percent of Serbians believe corruption in business is widespread, making them slightly better than the world's worst country, Sierra Leone. Alex Kuli, a journalist in Hungary, told me that throughout Eastern Europe "there's a belief that everyone who is rich got that way illegally."

Consider Gallup's Corruption Index, which aggregates a variety of surveys that measure the perceived level of corruption. A low score (like Singapore's 3.3) indicates low corruption, while a high score (like Croatia's 91.2) indicates high corruption. Croatia has the third highest score in the world, but it's not alone in Eastern Europe, which is far more corrupt than Western Europe. Except for Portugal (83.5) and Italy (76.4), all Western Europeans score *less* than 70, whereas all of Eastern Europe's countries (except Finland, Estonia, and Belarus) score *more* than 70. Given Belarus's widespread and well-known corruption, it seems that someone has corrupted Belarus's low score (40.3) as a practical joke.

It's logical to assume that a corrupt culture would also have a high theft rate. For example, when asked if anyone in their household had something stolen from them in the past year, nearly half of those in Sierra Leone said *yes*—that was the world's worse theft rate, according to Gallup's 2011 results. On the other extreme was Croatia: only four percent of Croatians said *yes*. That's the best score in Europe (tied with Montenegro). Croatians are basically saying, "We may be as corrupt as Sierra Leone, but we'll never steal your bike."

The diamond of Dubrovnik

After dropping Bob off on his pilgrimage to Međugorje, Ana and I continued to Dubrovnik. Riding down the Dalmatian coast made me ask Ana, "Honey, are we still in Eastern Europe?" It's one of the most beautiful coastlines in the world—it's Eastern Europe's Riviera. It's far from the stereotypical grayness and blocky Soviet architecture that still pervades in many places. Because of Dalmatia's beauty, it's natural that it's the first place in the Hidden Europe that is no longer so hidden. Nevertheless, it's remarkable how many people have still not explored it.

It's fun to read old travelogues to see how little has changed. In the mid-1930s, Rebecca West was "cramped" in a Yugoslav train compartment with "unhappy-looking German tourists" who were taking a break from Nazi-land. The Germans had a sense of "German superiority to all non-German barbarity." So Rebecca had to ask, "But why are you going to Yugoslavia if you think it is all so terrible?"

The Germans replied, "We are going to the Adriatic coast where there are many German tourists and for that reason the hotels are good."[9] Today, German tourists still flock to Dalmatia, and a few still carry that same attitude of 80 years ago.

If the Dalmatian Coast is the crown of Croatia, then Dubrovnik is the finest jewel on that crown. Lord Byron called Dubrovnik "the pearl of the Adriatic." Founded 1,300 years ago, Dubrovnik fell to the Venetian Empire in 1205. In 1358, Hungary defeated the Venetians, but in 1382 Dubrovnik bought its freedom from Hungary and become an independent and wealthy republic. It did well until Napoleon crashed the party in 1808. I've arrived in Dubrovnik by taking a seven-hour ferry from Hvar, a bus ride from Split, and a hitchhike from Mljet, but this time, I rode in Ana's car. No matter how you come to Dubrovnik, you won't want to leave.

Dubrovnik is Venice's ugly sister, but Venice is such a supermodel that Dubrovnik is still incredibly beautiful. Unlike Venice, Dubrovnik is like a grid in a bowl. Because the edges of the town curve up, it adds a cool dimension, although people who hate stairs will avoid the town's edges. After entering through the Pile Gate, you walk down the Placa, the main promenade, until you reach the clock tower. Everywhere you look is a work of art. Dubrovnik was built like a fort. You can walk on top of its impressive walls. They're two kilometers (1.25 miles) long and up to 25 meters (yards) high with 16 towers. Dubrovnik is the poor man's Venice and that's still pretty darn good.

Ana and I considered the meal options. Most of Croatia prefers heavy food like stews, *štrukli* (boiled cheesecake), *manistra od bobića* (beans and corn soup), and turkey with *mlinci* (baked noodles). However, Dalmatian cooking has Italy's influence. We went for a minor adventure and picked the *crni rižot* (cuttlefish risotto) and the *salata od hobotnice* (octopus salad).

While we ate, I told Ana of my two minor adventures during my first trip to Dubrovnik. The first was when I swam to Lokrum Island, which is half a kilometer away from Dubrovnik. It looked pretty close, but after 15 minutes of swimming I realized that it's not. Luckily no motor boats ran me over and my muscles only started cramping at the end. Unfortunately, I didn't bring sandals and walking barefoot on that island is more challenging than swimming there. Besides enjoying a nice view of Dubrovnik, you can explore old buildings and a fort. The best reason to swim to the island: the people operating the ferry don't ask for tickets on the way back to Dubrovnik, so you'll save $10.

The second minor adventure was climbing to the hill above Dubrovnik. The view is spectacular and I found some remnants of the Montenegrin military that was stationed there in 1992. They held Dubrovnik under siege for seven months. Dubrovnik had no military value, but the Montenegrins wanted to annex Croatia's southernmost point. They shelled the UNESCO World Heritage Site, damaging 68 percent of the buildings and killing 43 civilians. The International Court at the Hague sentenced two of the military leaders to seven years of jail for the war crime. In 2000, Montenegro's President apologized to Croatia for the siege. The Dubrovnik siege distracted the world from a far bigger and uglier battle that was raging in Vukovar, Croatia.

The boomerang goes boom

On August 25, 1991, about six weeks before Montenegrins started attacking Dubrovnik, the Croatian War officially began in Vukovar. Although Slovenia's Ten-Day War had symbolically started the Yugoslav Wars, Vukovar was the first serious battle. Unlike Slovenia, Croatia had areas (like Vukovar) where there was a heavy Serb presence. These Croatian Serbs didn't support Croatia's independence movement; they preferred to stay in Yugoslavia or join Serbia. That disagreement led to the battle that would echo throughout Yugoslavia.

To learn more, I traveled to Vukovar in April 2010 and couchsurfed with a 26-year-old Croatian Serb named Slaviša Andrić. He promised to give a "fair and unbiased" view of the Yugoslav Wars. I was skeptical. An *objective Balkanian* is an oxymoron. Nevertheless, Slaviša's self-description was surprisingly accurate.

Slaviša picked me up at the bus station and drove me to his two-story house on the edge of Vukovar. Although the war happened nearly two decades ago, some of the houses on his street still had bullet holes. His parents, Etelka and Ostoja, live a couple of houses away from him. We walked there and his mother served us a humble, but tasty meal of soup, veggies, and potatoes. She couldn't speak English, but when she learned that I was writing a book about Eastern Europe, she proudly showed off her coffee table book about Tito. She had good memories of that era. We returned to Slaviša's home, where I met his older brother, Milovan. They're both carpenters who share a passion for biking, having the lean bodies to prove it. When Milovan was putting on dirty work clothes, I asked Slaviša if Milovan was going to work, he replied, "No. He always wears those clothes during the week, even if he's not officially working. Just habit. He always finds things to do."

I said, "He acts like a Slovenian."

Slaviša laughed and said, "Yeah. Bastards."

We laughed. We had fun pretending to be ridiculous nationalists. When we went for a bike ride around Vukovar, we passed a massive factory that was in ruins. Slaviša explained that before the war, it employed thousands—that explains Vukovar's 40 percent unemployment rate. Now all the factory has are two pro-Serb graffiti messages on the wall. The first was written in Cyrillic. It said something like, "Never abandon Cyrillic." A few meters away was the second message, "Kosovo is Serbia." Since both messages were written with the same red spray paint, it was amusing that the second message was written in English instead of Cyrillic.

Balkanians are obsessed with symbols. The vandal drew an outline of a human holding up three fingers. Slaviša explained that this is the universal sign of being a Serb, "Because Orthodox Serbs believe in the Holy Trinity. Sometimes Serbs will arrogantly wave at Croatians by showing three fingers." Slaviša posed for a photo next to the image pretending to be a Croatian nationalist holding up just two fingers. I asked Slaviša what symbol agitates Serbs. He said, "The *šahovnica.* It's Croatia's checkered flag. It's similar to the flag that the Ustaše used in WWII. When Croatia declared independence, they waved that flag around and Serbs got nervous, thinking, 'Oh shit, here we go again.'"

Although Croatians had good reasons for using their checkered design, given the tense situation, it was a tactless and provocative move given WWII's history. On the one hand, resurrecting the checkered design was natural since it's symbolized Croatia for the last 1,000 years. In fact, it's even on the flag of the Kingdom of Serbia! On the other hand, Croatian politicians should have known that with the jittery situation, bringing out that flag would only increase the tension since Serbs associated it with the fascist Ustaše. If the southern states in the US declared independence today, they'd probably dust off the Confederate flag. However, that would conjure up images of slavery, which would immediately stress out the large black population that lives there. Instead of minimizing the flag's importance, Franjo Tuđman, Croatia's President, kissed the checkered flag. Serbian TV played this image over and over again, sometimes ominously juxtaposing it with images of the Ustaše.

Thank God my wife is neither a Serb nor a Jew.
— Franjo Tuđman, Croatia's President

Slaviša and I biked to Vukuvar's center. Nearly half the buildings still had war scars. One new item was a statue of Tuđman's head. I asked Slaviša if Tuđman was still popular. He said, "Croatians have mixed feelings. Tuđman's supporters in Zagreb tried to rename Roosevelt Square or Tito Square after Tuđman, but Croatians rejected those proposals. There are three statues of him in Croatia and it's ironic that one of them is here in Vukovar because he sacrificed this city."

"What do you mean?" I asked.

"He wanted to gain Western sympathy for Croatia's struggle for independence. He needed a sacrificial lamb for Serbs to slaughter that would force NATO to act. Some say that even when it was clear that the war was going to start, Tuđman ordered a bus full of children that was heading to the seaside to return to Vukovar, just to make an even bigger sacrifice for the media to capture."

The media took the bait. They filmed the Serb paramilitaries and JNA cooperating to lay siege to Vukovar for nearly three months. Although the Serbs won, it was costly victory in many ways. First, over 3,000 people died, compared to the 66 deaths in Slovenia's Ten-Day War. Second, it proved that the JNA was weak and divided—it struggled to take just one small city. Third, Croatia won the world media battle. The Western news reported the standard tragedies of war (innocent civilians killed and prisoners massacred) as well as miraculous tales: a wounded man in a hospital heard something ripping through the floors above him and then felt a sharp pain on his foot. He was shocked to see what had hit his foot—a bomb that failed to explode. Slaviša was also lucky. He was seven years old when the war started and one day a grenade landed near him, but failed to detonate.

Vukovar today

When we came to an Orthodox church, Slaviša explained that only one church in Vukovar was completely destroyed. It was one of the Catholic churches where the Croatians were allegedly distributing weapons. Then we came to Vukovar's water tower, which was still heavily damaged. Slaviša said, "It's funny, but when I was seven, I kind of enjoyed the war because we wouldn't have to go to school and we would go into the buildings to play war games. We'd take chairs up the water tower and drop them to see them crash."

I asked Slaviša, "What was the ethnic makeup of Vukovar before and after the war?"

He smiled ironically and said, "It didn't really change. In 1991, it was 37 percent Serb and 44 percent Croatian. Today, it's 33 percent

Serb, so not a big change. There are still Serb schools in Vukovar that teach primarily in Cyrillic. What did change was that over half of the town's population left. There are a lot of empty houses."

Although Slaviša is right about Vukovar, overall Serb presence in Croatia has declined over the last 60 years. In 1948, Serbs represented 14.8 percent of Croatia. By 1981, they were 11.5 percent. Today, it's just 4.5 percent. A similar story happened with Croatians in Serbia. Today, Croatians make up less than one percent of Serbia.

Given that Slaviša's dad is a Serb, his mom is a Rusyn, and he was born in Croatia, I asked him what he considers himself. He said, "I really don't care about nationality any more in my life. When people ask me about nationality, I say that I don't know. I prefer to be without nationality. I am sick of nationalities. I'm not religious either. You can see in Vukovar how religions and nationalities can divide people."

After staying with Slaviša for three days, I was impressed that he could discuss the Balkan issues without passion or prejudice. He participates in the Coalition for Recom, a neutral Balkanian humanitarian organization that works with all nationalities to undercover the truth. That explains why he is so well-informed. Unfortunately, not all young Balkanians are so wise. For example, Slaviša told me that when he goes to bar, he often says, *zdravo* (hi) when he meets a girl. He says half of the Croatian girls will immediately look down on him because he used the Serb salutation and not the Croatian one (*bok*). It illustrates how some young people are continuing their parents' bad habits. Despite all their similarities, many Croatians and Serbs refuse to date each other. Slaviša has dated Croatians, but said, "*Bok* just doesn't sounds as nice as *zdravo* to my ears." Although I agreed with him, I gave him a handy tip: if the Croatian girl is super hot, just say *bok.*

Croatia's future

The Balkans is stumbling into the future. According to a 2010 Gallup poll, about 86 percent of Croatians, Bosnians, and Serbians believe that "historic animosities" are either an "important obstacle" or "some obstacle" to more Balkan cooperation. The difference between 20 years ago and today is that now more Balkan politicians are focusing on common ground rather than differences. For instance, in November 2010, Croatia's and Serbia's Presidents met in Vukovar for the first time since the war. Their purpose: to make peace.

Croatia is blessed. Although we've focused on Dalmatia, there are many other incredible places of Croatia. One of my favorite spots is Plitvice Lakes National Park. Ana and I discretely camped in this UNESCO World Heritage Site, marveling at the countless waterfalls that spill into turquoise-colored lakes, which then produce more waterfalls that go into more lakes, and so on. Istria is incredible too. One can still feel Opatija's glamour from its heyday as an Austrian aristocratic hangout. Pula has one of the world's best preserved Roman amphitheaters. And I have a great memory of coming in third place in a 12-kilometer race in Premantura—it's truly on Croatia's edge. (Don't ask how many other runners there were in that race.)

In 2011, after living in Croatia for a year, it was clear that it had made great progress since 2004. After years of skepticism, in July 2011, Croatian opinion finally tipped in the EU's favor— 56 percent were in favor of joining the EU. Thus, in 2013, Croatia will join the EU. Croatians can be overly pessimistic, but deep in their hearts they love their country. When Gallup them if they would like to move to another country temporarily or permanently, only 13 percent said *yes*. Indeed, who would want to leave such an enchanting place?

What Croatia Can Teach Us

- **Preserve your historic monuments.** Without a single building, the Croatian coast would still be majestic. Croatians have made it truly precious by carefully restoring and maintaining the precious architecture that covers their coast. Do the same in your local area.
- **Mix wine with water.** Croatians call that drink bevanda. Croatians drink more wine per capita than any other Eastern European, but when money is tight, they water it down. So if you're on a tight budget or trying to diminish your alcohol consumption, have a bevanda instead.
- **Be generous at weddings.** If Croatians can give four times more than Americans at weddings, perhaps we need to give a bit more.

Places I saw and recommend in Croatia: Dubrovnik, Plitvice National Park, Šibenik, Hvar, Korčula, Split, and Zadar.

Travel deals and info: http://ftapon.com/croatia

One can never understand Croatia without understanding Serbia. And vice versa. Croatia and Serbia are like Cain and Abel: two brothers that can love each other at times, but can murder each other at other times. The Biblical analogy isn't perfect because in the case of Croatia and Serbia, there's no blameless Abel or guilty Cain. In the Balkan case, they both have innocent blood on their hands. As Larry Leigh, an American professor who lectured at the University of Belgrade, told me, "It would be interesting to compare Croatia with Serbia because of the two should be really one nation if it wasn't for the hotheads." To understand these Slavic brothers, we must cross the Danube that flows next to Vukovar, and go into Serbia.

13
SERBIA—EUROPE'S MOST MISUNDERSTOOD COUNTRY

IT'S GOTTA SUCK TO lose four wars in eight years. Talk about a losing streak. Imagine what that does to a nation's psyche. Now imagine trying to understand it. It's no surprise that Serbia is Europe's most misunderstood country. In fact, it's so misunderstood that even Serbians often don't understand it.

I confess that I completely ignored the Yugoslav crisis in the 1990s. I was in my 20s, and although I normally followed current events, the Yugoslav conflict was as incomprehensible as a woman. This is what the news sounded like to my ears: ". . . Croatians . . . Balkans . . . Serbians . . . Kosovo . . . ethnic cleansing . . . Sarajevo siege . . . Herzegovina . . . Albanians . . . Slobodan Milošević . . . refugees . . . Croatian Serb . . . Bosnian Croats . . . Bosnian Serbs . . . Muslims . . . Srebrenica . . . Dayton Accords . . . blah blah blah . . ."

I always mumbled, "Whatever," and changed the channel. It was just way too complicated for my little brain. I prefer following conflicts where it's easy to identify the good guys and the bad guys: Nazis (bad guys) vs. Allies (good guys); USSR (evil empire) vs. USA (good empire); Saddam Hussein (asshole) vs. George W. Bush (er, well, maybe sometimes it's not that black and white). Nevertheless, with Yugoslavia, it seemed you needed a PhD in Balkan history to understand 10 percent of what was going on. So I ignored it completely.

Thus, when I bought a night train ticket to Belgrade (Serbia's capital) in September 2004, I had no idea what to expect. In the train compartment I met Helena Kolař, an ethnic Hungarian who lived in Subotica, Serbia and studied in Budapest. While we were chatting, a guy came into our compartment and sat down. After hearing us speaking English, he asked me where I was from. I said, "The United States. How about you?"

"I am from Novi Sad," he said, "and you guys destroyed the three main bridges in my city."

Well that's a great way to start a relationship, I thought. *Where the hell is Novi Sad anyway? Is that in Serbia?* Helena was looking at the ground. I had no idea what this guy was talking about, so I asked, "Why did we do that?"

"I don't know," he said. "You didn't bomb Belgrade's bridges. But you hit several military targets in the city and you also bombed the Chinese Embassy."

Since he hadn't explained why and when we did it, I thought: *maybe the CIA decided that the Chinese and Serbians were behind September 11.* I didn't know what else to say except for a clumsy, "Sorry about that."

The Serbian was surprisingly calm and friendly given that I came from a country that had bombed him. I felt bad about bombing Belgrade, at least until I found out that it has been destroyed and rebuilt over 40 times in its 2,300 year history. What's one more sacking between friends? The man continued, "I wish Yugoslavia could be like America. In America, everybody feels like they're an American, regardless of their race, religion, or language. In Yugoslavia, nobody really identified strongly with Yugoslavia. They felt they were Croatians first and Yugoslav second, for example. Or Bosnians first and Yugoslavs second."

I had no clue what this guy was talking about. He sounded like one of those newscasters that I ignored throughout the 1990s. Clearly it was time to do a bit of research on this country I was traveling in.

Poor marketing

Serbia is misunderstood because of poor marketing and there's two reasons for that. First, Serbia was living in a bubble and underestimated our interconnectedness. It made little effort to work with the Western media, while Croatia and Slovenia eagerly contacted them, gave interviews, and even hired American public relations companies. When Serbia's academic elite wrote an important and controversial Memorandum in 1986, it took them nearly a decade to translate it into English. This allowed the clueless Western media to invent lots of myths around that infamous document. Second, Serbia didn't try to market itself because it figured Russia could help them, but they didn't anticipate that Russia would also be falling apart in the early 1990s.

Because of this poor marketing, Western media has done a terrible job at portraying Yugoslavia's breakup fairly and objectively. The Western pundits have demonized Serbs instead of trying to understand them. Therefore, as tricky as it is, we will try to examine Serbia in an unbiased way. Our conclusions will disappoint extremists on all sides, but let's hope that it's closer to the truth than what the mainstream Western media and the Serb chauvinists have fed us.

> *We are not angels. Nor are we the devils you have made us out to be. — Slobodan Milošević, former President of Serbia*

The big boys of Belgrade

When the train jolted to a stop, I woke up in Belgrade. Surveying the city map, I was surprised to see that Belgrade didn't rename its Kennedy Boulevard after the US bombed the city. That's remarkable, considering that Croatia quickly changed several key street names after its independence. Maybe Serbians aren't as nationalistic as some think.

Starting from the *Trg Republike* (Republic Square), I walked down *Knez Mihailova* (Prince Michael), a pedestrian street filled with fancy stores, big men, and beautiful women whose legs never seem to end. Although Belgrade has many splendid buildings, what's even more impressive is the number of giants walking around. Serbian men are enormous, which explains why they produce an army of world-class athletes. Meanwhile, watching Serbian women is like observing a ballet of supermodels. I hadn't seen so many high heels and head-turning babes since the Baltic.

The pedestrian zone ends at the Kalemegdan Citadel, the site of 115 battles over the last 2,300 years. Score: 71 home-team wins and 44 losses. Its strategic location at the confluence of the Danube and Sava Rivers makes it a tempting target. The last battle in Belgrade wasn't a traditional fight. No foreign troops stormed the city. Instead, NATO informed Serbia where and when it would drop their laser-guided bombs. A few smart bombs stupidly hit the wrong target, including a hospital. Serbians got lucky and shot down one "invisible" F-117 Nighthawk stealth fighter plane. When Serbians celebrated, Vladimir Ivosević, a Serbian friend of mine, told his buddies, "Don't get too excited fellas. I think they have a few more of those." It's true, the US had another 53 in the hanger.

If you go to Belgrade's War Museum, you'll see a piece of that F-117 and you'll also get a Serbian viewpoint on the war in the late 1990s. The exhibit begins with a Balkan map that shows arrows from all directions pointing toward Serbia, indicating that it was an unfair fight of Serbia versus the Planet Earth. Tables summarize the NATO's extreme military advantage over Serbia. There's no mention of Bosnians or ethnic Albanians in Kosovo; instead, there are pictures of innocent Serbs that NATO killed. The exhibit says that NATO used internationally banned weapons and it implies that NATO attacked Serbia for no good reason. Although the exhibit reeked of bias, it's worth making an effort to understand Serbia's point of view during Yugoslavia's breakup.

America and Yugoslavia faced a similar problem

The eternal theme among Balkanians is that Serbs wanted proportional representation (one person gets one vote), whereas others wanted proportional representation of the nations (e.g., the Serb nation gets one vote and the Croatian nation gets one vote). It's similar to the argument that the fragile USA had at its founding. America's solution was to create a House of Representatives (that was based on the population) and a Senate (that gave each state two senators regardless of the population). It's also the reason why we have our now-outdated Electoral College election system. These solutions were all designed to prevent populous states from overly dominating small states. In 1776, the original 13 US states had far more defined personalities, religions, dialects, and cultures than they have now; in short, they were similar to the Balkans today. We overcame those differences by creating a government that protected small states from being overrun by the big ones.

Yugoslavia faced a similar challenge. However, its Founding Fathers in 1918 were less wise than the ones in the US in 1776, and in 1945 they only had one Founding Father (Tito) who was such a genius that he nearly single-handedly reproduced what all the US Founding Fathers did. Unfortunately, the struggle of balancing the power is not a one-time job—it's an evolving process. For example, today's US federal government and executive branch are far more powerful than they were at the founding. That's because, as the US became more united, the fanatical arguments for state rights diminished and the people preferred having centralized and consistent laws, rights, and customs. Yugoslavia never got to that point because once Tito's 35-year tightrope walk was over, Yugoslavia fell.

The Yugoslav Wars for dummies

Let's sum up the Yugoslav Wars in a nutshell. Although the six Yugoslav republics had their own national identity, there was mixing in all of them. It's similar to how some Californians live in Nevada and how some New Yorkers spill over into New Jersey. When Yugoslavia's economy suffered throughout the 1980s, the majority of Yugoslavs concluded in 1991 that breaking up their union would magically solve their problems. Meanwhile, other Eastern European countries, which were also in the economic toilet, focused on the real cause of their problems: communism. They concentrated on moving from communism to capitalism, while Yugoslavs focused from moving from union to disunion.

Whenever a country wants to split up, it faces a headache: where to draw the border. The standard way is to use the preexisting internal borders. Hence, if California declares its independence, the new country would probably use the existing borders between it and its neighboring states. However, what if nearly everyone who lives around Lake Tahoe (which is split between California and Nevada) prefers going with the newly independent country of California? What if those who live on the Nevada side of the lake chant, "We're Californians!"? Should we let the principle of self-determination prevail? If so, we'd have to draw a new border (which would piss off Nevada). Or should we respect the preexisting internal border despite the wishes of the locals?

This thorny dilemma is largely what most of the Yugoslav Wars were about. Redrawing the borders based on plebiscites would open a titanic can of worms. On the other hand, if a large group didn't want to remain part of a new country, shouldn't we respect their vote? Isn't that what democracy and the principle of self-determination is all about?

Serbia's side of the story

Serbs generally wanted to redraw the borders based on self-determination, while everyone else mostly desired to leave the original borders unchanged. One major exception was Kosovo, Serbia's autonomous province. Over 85 percent of the people in Kosovo didn't want to stay in Serbia, but Serbs argued to keep the preexisting borders. Serbs felt that in the Kosovo case the principle of self-determination wasn't such a hot idea.

Croatians were also hypocritical. They consistently argued to leave the original borders unchanged, except in Bosnia, where they wanted the law of self-determination to rule. Aside from the Kosovo double standard, the general Serb argument was, "We should follow the will of the locals." It was a reasonable demand—the USA used the same argument to gain its independence from the British in 1776.

There's another sensible Serb point of view that Americans (and Britons) may identify with: they wanted to preserve the union. While Slovenia, Croatia, Bosnia, and Macedonia were eager to secede, Serbia wanted to keep Yugoslavia together. They faced the same challenge Britain faced with Northern Ireland and that the US faced 150 years ago. Just like the Northern US was willing to fight the Confederate South to preserve the union, Serbia was willing to fight the separatist republics to keep Yugoslavia together. What's wrong with that?

In short, what the incompetent Serbian marketing team had trouble communicating was that Serbs wanted to preserve the union and, failing that, they generally wanted self-determination. These are noble goals that most nations can identify with. So why did the Westerners not support them? Even worse: why did we demonize Serbs? And why the hell did we bomb them?

> *We have no quarrel with America. We all know NATO is the strongest military machine in the world. We simply want them to stop being so busy with our country and worry about their own problems. — Slobodan Milošević*

To learn more, I met with my friend Vladimir, whose bombing stories were surprising. He was an 18-year-old in Belgrade during the 78-day NATO bombing campaign in 1999. I expected Vlad to be huddled in a bomb shelter and praying nonstop. Instead, he was on the roof of his apartment building, reclining on a lawn chair with his friends and family, drinking beer and watching the spectacle just like Americans watched the "shock and awe" bombing campaign in Baghdad. The difference is that Vlad wasn't watching a TV screen—the bombs were falling nearby. He wasn't scared because he had confidence that NATO would only use laser-guided bombs on military targets and not on a civilian apartment building. It's a dramatic difference from the carpet bombing campaigns of WWII.

Although twenty-first century warfare is far more "clean" and "humane" than last century's warfare, it's not perfect. Between 500 to 1,200 civilians died during the NATO bombing. Nevertheless, considering there were 1,000 NATO planes dropping thousands of bombs, even the 1,200 figure (which the Yugoslavs estimated) is remarkably low. About the same number of civilians died in just one battle between Serbs and Croatians (in Vukovar). Imagine Serbia dropping thousands of precision bombs on America—civilians would certainly die, no matter what the precautions. NATO reasoned that targeted bombing would help avoid the Kosovo violence from escalating into another Bosnian War, where roughly 150,000 people died. Without a parallel universe, we'll never know if the NATO bombing saved more lives than it killed.

I asked Vlad, who was eight years old in 1991 when the war erupted, to describe what it was like. He said, "I didn't know about the war initially. Then the war mentality came. They start teaching you to hate Croatians—Croatians are bad. But when you grow up a little, you meet some Croatians during a vacation, you talk with them and see that they're not devils. Then I learned that much of what people had told me that I hadn't checked was based on stereotypes and media manipulation."

Hungarians in Serbia

Not satisfied with my knowledge, I returned to Serbia five years later, in 2009, by taking the cheapest train ride in Eastern Europe. It runs between Szeged, Hungary and Subotica, Serbia. Calling the vehicle a "train" is a bit generous. It's more like a bus on tracks. One guy operates this one-car train. We moved so slowly that it seemed like turtles were passing us. Nevertheless, the one-hour journey covered 60 kilometers (37 miles) and cost just $2.

Subotica's exquisite town hall, built in 1910, seems too big for the size of the city. Art Nouveau buildings spill out around it. My couchsurfing host in Subotica was Norbert Šabić, an ethnic Hungarian who grew up there. While Norbert and I were eating outside in a pizzeria, a woman yelled, "Francis!" I turned around and couldn't believe my eyes: it was Helena, the woman I met five years before on my first train ride into Serbia! We had only talked an hour and we both remembered each other. It's one of those stunning travel coincidences. They invited a few friends along and we all hung out for a couple of days. They were all ethnic Hungarians, so I was curious how life in Serbia was like for them.

I remembered Miklós (whom we met on page 241) telling me that "even today, the ex-Yugoslav region is the center of the most brutal Hungarian beatings. The police is an accomplice: Hungarians are beaten at the police station and no record is preserved of the incident. Recently a Hungarian from Hungary was beaten up by a gang of Serbs for no better reason than speaking Hungarian. They called the police, who then also beat them up! This is not an isolated incident. It happens all the time."

All the ethnic Hungarians I hung out with said that was false. Norbert said, "On the contrary, many times being Hungarian is an advantage and not a disadvantage. Hungarians are at least bilingual, which gives them an advantage in the labor market. Now there's a law that grants absolute autonomy for all minorities in Serbia to manage their cultural, educational, and media rights by themselves. Even though I consider myself part of the Hungarian minority in Serbia, I hate those Hungarians who always complain how bad it is for them, and don't really do anything to make their lives easier."

In 2010, I was in the studio audience of *Kosmos*, a Serbian TV show, where the featured guest was a Hungarian named Gabor Macanko. He was born and raised in Serbia. During the break, Serbians told me he had an accent when he spoke, but nobody showed any prejudice. Gabor and I had dinner after the show and he assured me that nearly all Serbians are accepting and welcoming of Hungarians.

How do Serbians handle ethnic and racial minorities?

In 2010, 75 percent of Serbians told Gallup that their area is a "good place" for ethnic and racial minorities. That's far higher than their Balkan neighbors who had rates around 55 percent (although Montenegro had 70 percent). Consider Gallup's Diversity Index, which measures how well a community accepts different racial, ethnic, and cultural groups. It aggregates a variety of global surveys. The 2010 results show a clear east-west divide in Europe: all Western Europeans (except Italians) scored above 53 (on a 100-point scale) and all Eastern Europeans scored below 53, with two exceptions, Finland and Serbia. Therefore, according to these results, Serbians are the most accepting Eastern Europeans (assuming you don't consider Finns as being Eastern European).

An alien examining this evidence might come to one of three conclusions: (1) it's likely that close-minded Croatians, Bosnians, and Albanians ignited the Yugoslav Wars by not welcoming Serbs in their communities; (2) perhaps non-Serbs were just as accepting as Serbians, but by the time the survey was taken, that trusting attitude had eroded (if so, then why did it not erode as much in Serbia?); (3) since the index is based on each community's responses, perhaps Serbians just like to think of themselves as being more accepting than they really are (and/ or non-Serbs are more self-critical than Serbs). So what's the right answer?

Like most things in the Balkans: there is no obvious answer. First, it's foolish to base one's entire analysis on one index, even if it does merge several surveys based on thousands of participants. Second, although the index shows a meaningful difference between Serbs and non-Serbs, it's not *that* big of a difference. Third, the Serbian results only consider Serbs in Serbia, not Serbs elsewhere. In other words, Gallup would file the opinion of Serbs who live in Croatia, Bosnia, and Kosovo under those countries, not Serbia. Therefore, if Serbs in Kosovo, for example, are extremely close-minded toward others, they would drag down the Kosovo index, not the Serbian index.

Conclude what you want, but these results should at least cast reasonable doubt on the standard Western media image of Serbians being intolerant devils. It should make everyone question that stereotype and consider that perhaps Croatians, Bosnians, and Kosovars bear more responsibility for all the fighting than many Western analysts originally argued.

Gay Serbia

Homosexuals are testing Serbia's tolerance. In the 1930s, Rebecca West observed three Balkan men and remarked, "It is heartrending, to stray into a world where men are still men and women still women."[1] Maria Todorava observes that in literature the "standard Balkan male" is usually "uncivilized, primitive, crude, cruel, and, without exception, disheveled."[2] In short, Serbian men are macho, and not the Village People type of Macho Man either.

In 1978, homosexual male sex was against the law in Serbia, except in Vojvodina, which used its autonomous status to make it legal (and then lost it in 1990). However, in 1994, Serbian politicians, in the middle of the war, found the time to pass a law legalizing homosexuality. In 2003, they made anti-gay speech illegal. In 2006, they lowered the age of consent to 14. In 2010, gays could serve in the military. At this point, you might think that Serbia is as gay-friendly as San Francisco.

Nevertheless, if you're gay, don't bring your fabulous pink shorts to Serbia just yet. In 2001, Belgrade held its first-ever gay parade and hooligans beat up the demonstrators. The police soon arrived and joined in the fight—beating up the gay people too. In 2010, in protest of a second gay parade, about 6,000 thugs attacked police, cars, shops, buses, and set fire to ruling political party's headquarters.

According to a 2010 Balkan Monitor survey, over 70 percent of Serbians "strongly agree" that "homosexual relations are always wrong." Only 16 percent of Croatians felt the same way. When asked, "Is the area where you live good place for gays and lesbians to live?" only 22 percent of Serbians said *yes* in 2010. That's higher than Moldova, which had Europe's lowest percentage—seven percent. In fact, all Eastern Europeans (except Czechs and Finns) had response rates of under 40 percent. In contrast, all Western Europeans had rates of 40 percent or higher. The Iron Curtain is now the Gay Curtain.

When I was in a Belgrade bar in 2010, I asked some big Serb guys why homophobic Serbs are so stupid. "If I were you," I told them, "I would be cheering those gay guys and handing out pamphlets that celebrate all the benefits of being gay, hoping to convert lots of heterosexual men." They looked down on me strangely, as if they were trying to decide which of my bones they were going to break first. And then I added, "If I had to kick somebody's ass, *I would beat up pretty lesbians!*"

At that point, the joke entered their thick skulls and they broke a smile. Earlier that evening I had a drink with two pretty lesbian partners, Sanja and Jelena, who were frustrated with Serbia's homophobia. They want to move to San Francisco together. Sanja had lived in Tyler, Texas for seven months where the father of her host family was an alcoholic and the mother was a hypochondriac. They eventually threw Sanja out of the house, so her exchange program helped her find a new host in a small town. When I asked her what she thought Serbians could teach Americans, she said, "Three things: how to make something from nothing; how to survive with just $400 per month; and how to get out of shopping malls."

I looked to Jelena and asked, "Are you optimistic about Serbia's future?"

Jelena, who works as a photo editor, said, "No. Communism taught us to not work. It taught people to live with their parents forever and avoid work."

Serbians have little motivation to work hard. Gallup asked 153 countries, "Can people in your country get ahead by working hard?" Serbia was the bottom of the planet, with just a quarter saying *yes.* Serbians may be the most downbeat about being rewarded for one's efforts, but it's a common feeling throughout Eastern Europe. Indeed, 22 out of the 29 countries on the bottom of the list were all from Eastern Europe. In contrast, Western Europe is the opposite—only Portugal doesn't have a majority believing that hard work is rewarded. Higher than all European countries (except Norway) were Canada (91%) and the US (88%) whose citizens believe they live in a meritocracy.

Did Serbia get Western postwar aid?

Sanja said, "The only solution would be if a Japanese leader came and took over. I would vote for him. A Japanese could fix our messed up system. Nobody from here can do it. Greece and everyone in the Balkans is like us: they are not used to working. For the Balkans to work, we will need to become like the Japanese. Serbia received all sorts of aid after the wars, but there are no results. There's too much corruption and inefficiency."

That was the opposite of what a Serbian-American named Andre wrote to me, "Now, 11 years after the bombing, we have not seen any aid to Serbia. Instead, the West wants to chop Serbia up even more. Sure, Germany's postwar suffering was massive, but it was short-lived, as opposed to the Serbian plight, which is much longer. There is no recovery, aid, or support in sight."

So who's right? The EU has set aside $4.4 billion in aid for Serbia. US Aid gave hundreds of millions. Between 2000 and 2006, the US also gave $773 million in military aid to Serbia. Thus, total aid to Serbia was $6 billion (EU $4.4b + USA $1b + $0.6b from other nations).[3] In today's dollars, Germany got $15 billion from the Marshall Plan. Therefore, Serbia got over a third of what Germany got. However, Germany has 11 times more people than Serbia. Thus, on a per capita, inflation-adjusted basis, Serbia has gotten nearly 4 times more aid than post-WWII Germany. Sanja is right and Andre is wrong. Serbia has squandered much of the aid. I asked Sanja, "How do you imagine Serbia will be in 20 years?"

Sanja said, "I don't care what will happen in 20 years. I don't want to live here. I'm 30. I've lived here nearly all my life. I lived through the war. We were hungry during that period. I've given this country everything to make it better. But nothing has changed. So I'm leaving."

Sanja's not alone. In 2010, nearly two-thirds of Serbians were also pessimistic about Serbia's future, according to the Balkan Monitor. Serbians not only led the Balkans with that gloomy statistic, but also with the percentage who were struggling to get by: 78 percent. In fact, 22 percent of Serbians said that at times they didn't have enough money to buy food. Lastly, Serbians are the world's biggest worrywarts: 61 percent said they were worried the previous day; that's a higher rate than any other country, although all ex-Yugoslav countries were near the top of the worrywart list.

Marija and Dijana in Novi Sad

Years after I met that guy who mentioned Novi Sad's bombed-out bridges, I spent several weeks in his city in 2010. After the bombing, Novi Sad organized the Exit Music Festival to help the society *exit* from that negative period. The festival is set in the Petrovaradin Citadel's natural amphitheater. Today, it's Eastern Europe's premier annual music event.

My Novi Sad couchsurfing host was Marija Krgović, a funny blond translator, and her laid-back roommate, Dijana Pavlović. I asked them if life was hard. Marija said, "Serbians love to complain about how hard things are, but look at us. It's 2:00 p.m. on a Thursday and we're just relaxing. I should be translating some documents, but there's no rush. Dijana hasn't been to work all week because she claims she's 'sick.' We eat well. Our apartment is not fancy, but it's fine. Our standard of living is pretty normal for Serbs in cities. Sure, Germans and Americans have nicer things, but they also work harder than we do."

That reminded me of when Mariana Primorac of Subotica told me, "Serbians somehow always find a way to take it easy, enjoy life, and make fun of the bad things."

When I asked Dijana about the war, she said, "I was born in Croatia, but I didn't know I was Serbian until the war broke out. Overnight, people started making a big deal about whether you were Serbian or Croatian. I was too young to understand it."

I said, "But during the NATO bombing in 1999, you were a teenager. How was that?"

Dijana laughed, "We were drunk everyday, all the time! Nobody worked. We just drank! We went to the bridges everyday wearing T-shirts with big red targets on them that said, 'Bomb me!' Looking back, we were kinda stupid, but we were teenagers. People would camp on the bridges."

I asked, "So did a lot of people die when NATO bombed the three bridges that cross the Danube?"

"No. People were there nonstop for weeks, but in the middle of one night, the Serbian police ordered all the demonstrators to get off the bridges. A few hours later, NATO's bombs destroyed the bridges. I think NATO had told Serbia that they would bomb those bridges that night and to make sure nobody was on them."

Marija started laughing and said, "My mom and grandmother were so funny during the bombing. At night they would say, 'Turn off all the lights! You'll give away our position!' We were laughing so hard. I said, 'Mom, this isn't WWII! There are no troops outside to shoot at us. It's just planes. All the street lights are on, so turning off one light-bulb in our apartment won't help hide our city from the planes!"

Despite the classic Serb black humor, the 1990s was hard. The economy shrank in half. Inflation was so bad that you could use money as toilet paper. A Serb on the train told me that when he collected his father's pension, he had to run to the market to use it to buy 25 eggs.

If he waited until the next morning, he could only buy *one* egg with the same money. On average, prices would double every 1.4 days—it was the third worst hyperinflation in history. Money was so worthless that the government printed on only one side of the bill to save ink. You needed just one bill to be a billionaire: the 50-billion dinar note. A week after it came out, the government introduced the 500-billion-dinar note. With just two of those bills you were a trillionaire, except that you didn't feel like one.

Cyrillic is ill

Since Marija is a linguist, I asked her how Cyrillic is doing in Serbia. She said, "Until 1950, Serbia just used the Cyrillic alphabet. From 1970, the Latin alphabet started being used more and more. Since 2000, the Latin alphabet has become more popular among young people—it is a symbol of being modern and more 'European.' Also, Cyrillic is more popular in South Serbia and less popular in north Serbia, Vojvodina. I don't think that we have any precise statistics, I believe that now in Serbia (especially in Vojvodina) the Latin letter is used more."

In 2010, during a train ride from Novi Sad to Belgrade, I asked Ana Sinik, a 21-year-old passenger who was sitting next to me, to write down the name of places to see in southern Serbia, which was my next destination. She started writing in Cyrillic. Given that we were speaking English, I asked her why she wrote in Cyrillic. She said, "Instinct. It's natural. For Serbians, it's the first alphabet you learn. You don't learn the Latin alphabet until you're seven or eight years old."

I said, "That makes it surprising that the Latin alphabet is so popular in Serbia, especially in cities. So when your friends write on your Facebook wall or send you emails, what percentage use Cyrillic?"

She observed Vojvodina's flat countryside as it rolled by and then said, "Less than 15 percent. I have 170 Facebook friends, but only five of them prefer using Cyrillic."

It's too early to proclaim that Cyrillic is on its deathbed, but it is ill. The government, church, street signs, and villages are the only places that consistently use Cyrillic. Nevertheless, that may be enough to keep Cyrillic alive despite the growing EU influence. Also, there are enough passionate Cyrillic fans, like the Orthodox Church, to make sure that it stays on life-support.

Although the Orthodox Church plays an important role in Serbia, some overestimate its influence. Bojan Hočevar, a Slovenian man, told me a common belief, "Yugoslavia broke up because of religious differences." Some believe religion was one of the biggest reasons for the breakup. That's right and wrong: religion was behind it, but it was neither Christianity nor Islam.

The real Balkan religion: Victimism

Everyone in the ex-Yugoslavia is always the victim, never the oppressor. Balkanians are convinced that whatever misfortune they've suffered is someone else's fault, never their side's fault. Their people are blameless and faultless. Although some deliberately and knowingly spread such lies, the majority have honestly deceived themselves into believing the Victimism dogma. Even educated people, who can normally analyze another conflict zone in another part of the world with a high degree of objectivity and balance, suddenly lose all such faculties when examining their own world. Gray becomes either black or white.

Related to the Victimism religion is the Balkanian love for portraying themselves as the underdog. For example, Slovenians were the working slaves for the other republics; Croatians were the underdog against the Serbs, who twisted them into accepting their language; Bosnians were the mistreated Muslims; Serbians were the underdog against the Croatians and Slovenians who controlled all the wealth and resources. In short, they're all victims. Let's see some examples.

In 1986, the Serbian Academy of Arts and Sciences was writing a document that became known as the Memorandum. Before it was finished, it was leaked to the press. Because it's an unfinished document, it's not worth taking too seriously, even though many did. On the other hand, given everything that's said about it, I read it to find out the real story. Some say the Memorandum was a political plan. No, it was a call for a political plan. Some say it encouraged nationalism. Not really, it warned about the danger of it and noted that it was rising.[4] Others say it advocated a Greater Serbia. No, at least not directly. So if it was none of those, then what was it?

Here's a summary: "Whine, whine, whine, boo-hoo, I'm a victim, it's all their fault, I've done nothing wrong, I'm persecuted, whine, whine, whine, I'm a saint, I don't deserve bad treatment, we've been victims for centuries, the world is against us, boo-hoo, whine, whine, whine." When you talk to other ex-Yugoslavs, the lyrics will change, but they'll sing the same tune. They seem to have a competition for who has the biggest violin.

Let's listen to the Memorandum's melody, which the believers of Victimism still chant today: "The cultural achievements of the Serbian nation have become alienated, usurped or denigrated, ignored and left to decay; the language is being suppressed, and the Cyrillic script is progressively disappearing. . . . No other Yugoslav nation has had its cultural and spiritual integrity so brutally trampled upon as the Serbian nation. No one else's literary and artistic heritage has been so despoiled and ravaged as the Serbian heritage. . . . Serbian culture has more writers and intellectuals who are out of favor, proscribed, ignored, or deemed undesirable than any other national culture in Yugoslavia; to make matters worse, many of them have been completely wiped out of literary memory." Furthermore, "the Serbian nation has had to bear trials and tribulations that are too severe not to leave deep scars in their psyche . . . ."

At Andre's pity party, he told me, "If you look at history, the Serbs were enslaved by Muslims for 600 years and were almost wiped of the face of the planet in WWI and WWII. It is quite obvious that the Serbs are the prey and not the predator. Even in this latest war it was the Serbs that paid the highest price hands down."

Even though the Republic of Serbia was the biggest state in Yugoslavia, the Memorandum dramatically claimed, "After four decades in the new Yugoslavia, [Serbs] alone are not allowed to have their own state. A worse historical defeat in peacetime cannot be imagined." It repeats this hyperbolic mantra when it says, "But the worst misfortune of all is the fact that the Serbian people do not have their own state, as do all the other nations." Huh? Did these guys look at a map of Yugoslavia?

Finally, it says, "Admittedly, the first article of the Constitution of the Socialist Republic of Serbia contains a clause declaring that Serbia is a state, but the question must be asked what kind of a state is denied jurisdiction over its own territory or does not have the means at its disposal to establish law and order in one of its sections, or ensure the personal safety and security of property of its citizens, or put a stop to the genocide in Kosovo and halt the exodus of Serbs from their ancestral homes."[5] Conclusion: we have a state, but it doesn't count, so feel sorry for us, please.

Western analysts blame the 1986 Memorandum for starting nationalism, but that's wrong. The Memorandum simply said aloud what Serbs had been saying to each other in whispers. *Nationalism was brewing in every Yugoslav coffee shop and bar long before the Memorandum came out.* The Victimism-filled Croatian Spring uprising happened 15 years before the Memorandum. In 1968, in the middle of Titoism and 18 years before the Memorandum, a Slovenian booklet wrote, "It is clear that, economically speaking, to the Slovenian people Yugoslavia is constant loss of funds and an obstacle to a normal economic development. . . . [Yugoslavia] does not allow us to independently manage resources to obtain the standard of living the Slovenian economy makes possible, the standard of living we could have if our development was not held back, the development the nation deserves for working hard and could have already reached if a large part of its resources had not been alienated from it against its will. . . . Yugoslav economic integration is not very highly valued by Slovenians and is even considered a great economic loss."[6] Clearly, Serbs weren't the founding members of the Church of Victimism.

The Balkan sport: Hyperboling

Balkanians act like children in a playground, each of them inventing a bigger, more exaggerated story to stir the biggest reaction they can get from you. Balkanians try to convince you that they've suffered the most and you should feel sorry for them. For instance, Balkan historians seem to have a competition between themselves as to who can claim more lives lost in a war. The one-upmanship feels like an auction, "I hear 100,000 dead! Anyone wants to claim 200,000? 200,000! And the man with the Croatian hat says 500,000 dead! But the guy eating a burek claims 700,000! The gentleman waving a Serb flag says one million! Do I hear two million!? Mujo and Haso claim 60 million!"

Then one day a few objective Russian and Western historians visit Yugoslavia and say, "Are you guys nuts? There's no evidence for these absurd numbers." For example, to get the 1.7 million WWII deaths that Balkanian "historians" were claiming, they ignored the 660,000 who emigrated out of Yugoslavia and they took into account 335,000 births that *would have* happened had it not been for the war (these weren't abortions—the estimate assumes that if all those people had not died, they would have produced 335,000 children, so let's add that to the "death toll.") Jozo Tomasevich's *War and Revolution in Yugoslavia, 1941-1945* documents how every side in Yugoslavia exaggerated its WWII loses. They did it to get more war reparations, to make more people feel sorry for them, to justify oppressing the other group as "payback," and to gain respect. Tomasevich calls it "syndrome of being victimized."[7]

It continues today. For example, Andre, a Serb-American, told me that *half* of Serbia's population died in WWI. Reality: 16 percent of the Kingdom of Serbia died in WWI. That death rate was higher than other countries involved in WWI (the Turks were second with 13.7%), but that's not good enough when you're competing in the Hyperbole Olympics.

Aleksandar Svetozarević, a young Serbian who was couchsurfing at my place in Slovenia, made an accurate estimate, but put a hyperbolic twist: he said that WWI killed 30 percent of Serb men. That's true, but citing the male-death percentage usually doubles the standard percentage since most people who die in wars are men. This cleverly doubles the pity factor. It also implies that there's a type of genocide going on—that evil people are targeting virile Serb men for extermination and stealing their women and children. It's all part of The World's Grand Plan to bring down the Serb man.

Speaking of genocide, the Memorandum decried the "genocide" that was going on in Kosovo prior to 1986. Yes, between 1946 and 1986, Albanians killed several Serbs. Still, calling that "genocide" is hyperbole. It's like Americans calling the Boston Massacre (where British troops killed five Americans) a "genocide." Even the attacks of September 11 weren't genocide. In both cases, it was *mass murder*.

Similarly, when Germans bombed civilians in London, it was *war*, not genocide. However, what Americans did to some Native American tribes *was* genocide.

If we refer to every mass murder as genocide, it dilutes the meaning of *genocide*. *Genocide* is a loaded, emotional word that some people use just to get attention. On the other hand, I disagree with radical Jews who like to reserve the word just for their holocaust and complain when anyone else uses it. In the Kosovo chapter we'll discuss if and when there was genocide there, but for now what is clear is that between 1946 and 1986 there was no genocide in Kosovo—that's just another example of Balkan hyperbole.

Hyperboling in the Yugoslav Wars

When describing the Yugoslav Wars, a Bosnian told me that among his friends "a third stayed, a third left, and a third died." That echoed Mile Budak, the Ustaše leader who suggested eliminating Serbs from Croatia by "killing one third, expelling the other third, and assimilating the remaining third." Or Hermann Neubacher, who said during WWII, "A third must become Catholic, a third must leave the country, and a third must die!" These spectacular sayings are for drama queens. The reality is that "only" about four percent of Bosnians died in the Yugoslav Wars. That's grim, but not a Belarus grim (where a third really did perish in WWII).

Croatians and Bosnians claimed that Serbs raped over 100,000 women—another hyperbolic lie. The danger with hysteria inflation is that when the UN finally offers a more objective estimate, people trivialize the reality: "Oh, *only* 12,000 women were raped?"[8] Even America played the Hyperbole Game. The Clinton administration claimed that 100,000 ethnic Albanians were "missing" and used that as an excuse to bomb Serbia. Later, "only" about 2,000 Albanians were confirmed dead. The "Oh, that's all?" reaction creates another cycle of self-pity as Balkanians say, "Now they belittle our suffering. Nobody cares about our plight."

There are three motivations for victimism. First, some people love being the underdog—if they triumph, their victory is that much sweeter. Second, it brings sympathy from others. Third, it justifies any of your future selfish (or even evil) acts. If you tell yourself that Serbs have always persecuted your people, then you'll feel justified to persecute the Serbs. Of course, people throughout the world (including Americans) play the I'm-the-biggest-victim-ever game. Still, in the Balkans you'll find it reaching acute (and annoying) levels.

On the other hand, perhaps we should be grateful that Victimism is the Balkan religion and not the opposite—Victorism. These people don't drown in self-pity, but instead bathe in their victories. If you follow the dogma of Victorism, then you have an unrealistically grand view of your history, culture, and nation. You're always the best, you've always won, nobody is better. Gee, sounds like the French. Given the two options, perhaps it's best to listen to whiny victims rather than vainglorious boasters. Obviously, the best is for nations to have a realistic and balanced view of themselves, but that's hard to do when we look at ourselves in the mirror.

Where the Memorandum was right

Although the Memorandum wastes too much time preaching the Gospel of Victimism, it makes some excellent points in between sermons. For example, before reading the Memorandum, I believed that Tito did the right thing decentralizing Yugoslavia in 1974. Each republic was demanding more and more autonomy and the centralized communist command-and-control apparatus was inefficient and bureaucratic. The Memorandum makes an intelligent counterpoint: decentralization created redundant bureaucracy and increased differences among the republics. This led to an "us-versus-them" mentality rather than "brotherhood and unity."

When Croatia and Slovenia proposed evolving Yugoslavia into a confederacy in 1990, Serbia said, "Huh? First of all, we're practically a confederacy already—that's what the 1974 Constitution was all about, remember? It decentralized everything. Besides, we've been arguing that it's that decentralization that got us into this mess, so what we really need is centralization!" On the other hand, given the loud demands for autonomy in the early 1970s, it was unrealistic for Tito to ignore them forever; otherwise, Yugoslavia might have broken up in 1981 instead of 1991.

The centralization-decentralization debate and the ethnic issues were a distraction from the biggest problem: communism. The Memorandum correctly identified the rotten system: "The conditions prevailing within the underground communist movement left deep traces: conspiratorial methods, internal hierarchy, the participation of only a handful of individuals in decision-making, insistence on ideological unanimity and unquestioning acceptance and carrying out of assignments, and harsh epithets ('factionalist,' or 'enemy') for anyone who disagreed with or criticized the adopted political line."

Furthermore, the Memorandum revealed how communism had corrupted the work ethic: "There is virtually no appreciation in society of what it means to do an honest day's work. . . . The salaries paid out in enterprises often depend less on performance and more on someone's agility in fighting for higher prices or lower taxes. The systematic practice of covering the losses of some firms with the earnings of others kills incentive for both sides."

Many countries that have ethnic and linguistic challenges (e.g., Belgium, Spain, Canada) would splinter if their economies were as dysfunctional as a communist one. Yugoslavia's fatal error was letting petty issues distract them from fixing their number-one problem: communism. Indeed, the only time Yugoslavia was truly united was from 1953 to 1965. Why? The West and East were pouring money in because Tito was two-timing the superpowers. Money makes people shut up. Everyone complains less and their neighbor doesn't seem like such an asshole anymore. Perhaps he still is one, but I'm not going to make a big deal about it because I'm fat and happy. That's why Belgium, Spain, and Canada are still in one piece and Yugoslavia is not.

The other Memorandum

It's good to read the 1986 Memorandum to understand what Serbian intellectuals would have told you after a couple of beers.[9] Nevertheless, because the Memorandum was just a draft, it's unfair to take it too seriously. There's a lesser known memorandum that came out in 1995 that the Serbian Academy of Arts and Sciences did finish and sign. The 92-pager is called "Answers to Criticisms" to the Memorandum. It rebuts a decade's worth of criticism and myths around the original Memorandum. Although it's fun to listen to wild villagers, it's also useful to hear what Serbia's top academics have to say.

They recycle some of the Memorandum's original points: "In 1991 . . . 25% [of all Serbs] lived in other republics . . . 16% of all Serbs . . . lived in [Vojvodina and Kosovo], often under difficult circumstances, as was the case in [Kosovo]."[10] That's misleading: only 2.3% of Serbs were living in Kosovo; the other part of that 16% were in Vojvodina, hardly a "difficult" place to live. On the contrary, it's probably the best place for a Serb to be.

Moreover, if Yugoslavia were to still exist today, 27% of Serbs would be living outside of Serbia (assuming that Serbs in Kosovo are outside of Serbia). So despite all the ethnic cleansing, the number has barely budged. If you include the whole world, about 40% of Serbs live outside of Serbia. *By saying these facts are unjust, the Academy implicitly believes that every ethnic group should live in one state and not outside of it.* If you buy that, then cry over these statistics: 16% of Croatians live elsewhere in the ex-Yugoslavia lands; in addition, if you consider the whole planet, half of Croatians live outside of Croatia, which is "worse" than Serbia. By focusing on these facts, Serbs distract you from their better argument: that Serbs ought to have basic human rights no matter where they live.

The Academy complains that all the factories and investments were going to Slovenia and Croatia. At first glance, this argument is weak. If you're going to open a manufacturing plant in the USA, you'd probably pick somewhere in America's Manufacturing Belt—the Midwest. There's plenty of existing expertise there, which makes it easy to find trained workers. Putting your factory in Mississippi (a state with a weak manufacturing tradition) is a poor allocation of resources. On the other hand, communism was all about a poor allocation of resources! It put equality in front of efficiency. Therefore, if there are far more factories per capita in one republic (like Slovenia), then a communist should spread the wealth and make future factories in undeveloped places (like Kosovo), even if those new factories would be five times more efficient in Slovenia.

The Academy argues that "Serbia was economically underdeveloped and Slovenia and Croatia enjoyed accelerated growth thanks to their political and economic dominance."[11] The reality is that those two nations did better for the same reason they have always done better economically than the southern Balkans—they work harder. Having spent 18 months traveling throughout ex-Yugoslavia, it's clear that the further south you go, the more laid back people get. Slovenians are uptight workaholics and Macedonians are relaxed we'll-do-it-tomorrow people. In between are the transition people; thus, southern Serbians are less industrious than northern Serbians, while Montenegrins are lazier than Croatians. In short, southern Balkanians are more fun than Croatians, Slovenians, and Vojvodinians, but if you need to get shit done, you give it to the northern guys.

> *If we have to, we'll fight. I hope they don't be so crazy as to fight against us. Because if we don't know how to work and do business, at least we know how to fight.*
> *— Slobodan Milošević*

If it's true that Slovenia and Croatia were economically ahead of the other republics mainly because Tito's cronies gave them unfair advantages, then Serbia and the rest of the southern Balkans ought to catch up to Slovenia and Croatia any day now. If a lazy work ethic, corruption, and disorganization had little to do with their backwardness, then soon we should see economic equality among the former republics. Of course, we won't, and another bunch of excuses will come: "the EU is not letting us in, the war hurt us more than others, and our sexy women distract us." Although these are good excuses, in 30 years the story will be the same. The reason Serbia will probably never equal Slovenia's per capita economic output is that they're not Germans. Slovenians aren't Germans either, but they're a decent substitute. On the other hand, who would you rather socialize with? I'll take the Serbs any day.

Lastly, the Western media claims that Serbs "dominated" Yugoslavia. That's debatable. It's true: Serbs were 41 percent of the population, but had most of the government jobs, including about 75 percent of the police and army positions.[12] The head of the military was a Serb. The Academy claims all this was because Croatians and Slovenians had much better economies and better pay and didn't want to lower themselves to the crappy federal government jobs. Perhaps, but a better explanation is geography: the capital of Yugoslavia was in the middle of Serbia, so most of the federal government jobs were there. On the other hand, Tito and Edvard Kardelj, the two top dogs during most of Yugoslavia, were not Serbs. In fact, it's possible that this duo made up the infamous saying, "A weak Serbia ensures a strong Yugoslavia." Although I don't buy that Tito was truly anti-Serb, he certainly wasn't pro-Serb either. What is quite clear is that Serbs did not disproportionately rule Yugoslavia for most of its existence.

Visiting "the real Serbia"

Just like Americans call the middle of the US "the real America," Serbians call southern Serbia "the real Serbia." Most of the tourist and business action happens in Vojvodina and Belgrade, but Serbia's heartland is south of Belgrade. In 2010, I couldn't find a Serbian couchsurfing host in Belgrade, so I stayed with Jasmin, a 28-year-old German accountant who was working on behalf of the EU. She had to go to Niš, the main city in southern Serbia, for a business meeting. Her company was providing a ride and she invited me to hitch along. To maximize our time in southern Serbia, we spent the weekend before her Monday meeting couchsurfing with a Serbian family in Sokobanja, a town about 40 minutes north of Niš. Traveling with an unknown person is somewhat risky if your personalities don't match. Jasmin was very German, but I liked her anyway.

We stayed with the family of Žika Dinic, a 25-year-old man who is a fanatical host. Hospitality is a universal human custom, but in some parts of the world it reaches epic proportions. Southern Serbia is one of those places. If it would make his guests happy, Žika would try to move the moon. What's remarkable about his generosity is he was welcoming to a German and an American—citizens from countries that bombed his country. He held no prejudice. Instead, he rolled out the red carpet.

When we arrived at his three-story house, he showed us our rooms and then offered to show us the town and surroundings. Sokobanja is a simple, but popular town. Its main attractions are its six hot springs, especially the Turkish bath in the main park. Next to the bath they advertise a "natural inhaltor which contains large amount of gas radon." They claim that "it is proven that radon has a positive effect on the human organism." While Americans pay money to get radon out of their house, some Serbians pay money to inhale it! They believe radon cures breathing problems like emphysema. Some also believe that, depending on the type of hot spring you soak into, you can help cure or alleviate diabetes, stomach problems, and "lighter forms of Parkinson's disease."

We stopped at the tourist office, where Žika insisted on buying two Sokobanja guidebooks for Jasmin and me. After walking along the Moravica River, we visited Sokograd and Vrmdza, which have a nearby ruined medieval fortress that was built on a Roman stronghold. Later, Žika took us to the Ripaljka Waterfall, whose 40-meter (132 ft) drop is one of Serbia's highest. We eventually returned home, where Žika's mom, Snežana, cooked a royal feast.

Serbian cuisine

Because each country in the Balkans is relatively small and their cultural exchange is relatively large, it's hard for any Balkan country to argue that their national dish started there. Momo Kapor, a famous Serbian writer, wrote, "The food they call Serbian is from all other countries." Nevertheless, the iconic Serbian dish is *ćevapčići* (grilled mixed meat). Other popular meals are *ražnjići* (pork or veal kebabs) and the *pljeskavica* (spicy hamburger), which any real American would love.

There are two reasons Serbian cuisine is tastier than Northern European food. First, they use lots of fresh vegetables. Veggie options include *zeljanica* (cheese pie with spinach), *pasulj prebranac* (spicy beans), and *gibanica* (cheese pie). Second, unlike Northern Europeans, Serbians know what a spice is and use it liberally.

My favorite Serbian condiment is *ajvar* (pronounced *i-var*). It's a red bell pepper relish that has a dash of garlic, eggplant, and chili. It has different levels of spiciness. You put it on bread, salad, or any dish that needs more flavor. Although you can buy it in stores, most Balkanians make it at home. In the fall, Balkanians harvest red peppers, then they roast them, peel them, mash them, toss them in a bucket of spices, cook them for hours in large cauldron, and finally store the orange mush in glass jars so they can enjoy them throughout the winter and beyond. This Serbian ritual is performed all over the Balkans today.

Snežana started the dinner off with the hearty *čorba od ječma i sočiva* (barley and lentil soup). Then she brought out *đuveč* (grilled pork with spicy peppers, tomatoes, and rice) along with a *srpska salata* (Serbian salad, with onions, tomatoes, peppers, oil and vinegar). I hadn't enjoyed such delicious cooking for many months. Since her husband wasn't home, I asked her (through Žika's translation) how life really is like for Serbian women.

A woman's role in Serbia

Snežana looked at me with her big blue eyes and sincerely said, "Serbian women cook and do house things, but we do it because we love our family and our kids. Nobody is forcing us. We do it out of love, because we want to."

I asked, "But is that true for the new generation of Serbian women? How about your daughter, for example?"

She laughed and said, "Let me tell you a story. Žika's sister, who is 26, told me many times, 'Mom, I'm never going to cook!' Recently she moved in with her boyfriend. Soon she was calling me for recipes. She asked me, 'Mom, how can I make a tasty sandwich for my boyfriend's lunch?' She even calls me from the grocery store for advice while she's shopping for food."

> *Family is the house and women are the pillars.*
> *— Serbian proverb*

Months earlier, I observed to Igor, a Slovenian man, that Serbian women are more sexy and feminine than Slovenian women. Igor said, "True, but that's because Slovenian women are more liberated than Serbian women. In Serbia, the woman is part of a man. Serbian women must attract a man to sponsor her."

A few weeks before, on my train ride to Belgrade, I asked a young Serbian named Ana Sinik if that was true. She said, "It depends on the generation. My generation is less traditional than the older generation. For example, my grandmother always says, 'Don't tell me about your grades or what you're doing in school. Just tell me if you're married. And if you're not, tell me *when* you are going to get married. That's all that matters.'"

I asked her, "So who controls the relationship?"

"In general, the man. Men pay the bills. Men will drive, even when they are drunk. And women always cook."

That's not totally true. In a barbeque, for example, men cook. Moreover, in Novi Sad, in all four homes that I visited, the man was the chef. This illustrates the cultural differences between Serbia's north and south, as well as the difference between urban and rural societies. Nevertheless, Serbian women are generally more traditional than American women. And they certainly dress better. When we went out to a bar that night, Jasmin confessed her difficulty of "keeping up with Serbian women" who dress like male magnets.

The Tito doppelganger conspiracy theory

In 2004, I was attracted like a magnet to a pregnant Serbian woman eating at a vegetarian restaurant in Belgrade. It's not that she was sexy, but she was the only person who was eating alone and I wanted to meet locals on my first day in Serbia. She let me join her. The most memorable part of our conversation was when I asked her where Tito was from. She looked around to see if anyone was listening and then whispered, "Nobody knows."

This seemed strange. At that time, I didn't know anything about this Tito guy except that he had been Yugoslavia's dictator for a long time. You'd think people would know his origins. Didn't anyone bother to ask him? Did he just refuse to answer? I said to her, "C'mon, really? Don't people know if he was Serbian, Croatian, or something else?"

"No," she said. "Nobody knows for sure. He had a strange accent. It's mysterious."

Later, I found out that Tito was born in Croatia, near the Slovenia border, from a Croatian father and a Slovenian mother. The pregnant Serbian wasn't the only Balkanian who doesn't accept this standard story. Back in Sokobanja, Žika's father, Miliša, joined us for some of his wife's tasty *vešalica* (grilled strips of pork loin meat). That's when he told us about the Tito doppelganger theory. Miliša explained, "Tito wasn't from Yugoslavia. He was either a British or Russian imposter. Probably British. This explains why he had a strange way of talking—he sounded like a foreigner, because he was a foreigner."

Jasmin raised an eyebrow in disbelief, but I played along. "Really?" I said. "How did that happen?"

While serving himself rosemary-scented potatoes, Miliša said, "After Tito came back from Russia, he wasn't the same man. He was replaced with a British agent who looked like him and had learned our language. When Tito's mother saw him, she said, 'I don't recognize him anymore. He's not my son.'"

When I looked at others at the table skeptically, Snežana gravely assured me, "Yes, Tito's *own* mother said, 'This is not my son. He has changed.'"

When I asked why this had happened, Miliša replied matter-of-factly, "Because the big powers wanted to control Yugoslavia. After WWII, this British secret agent easily convinced America to give Yugoslavia lots of money, so we could industrialize quickly and prosper. When Tito died, their agent was gone, and so they let Yugoslavia die. It's true. Even his own mother didn't know him."

At the time, I figured this doppelganger conspiracy theory was simply misinterpreting what Tito's mother—she was probably saying it figuratively, not literally. Tito undoubtedly came back changed—that's what a few years in the Soviet Union will do to anyone. Just ask Lee Harvey Oswald.[13] Still, here's the funny thing: about a week later, I was back in Novi Sad and retold the story to Marija, who then burst out laughing. She said, "But that's impossible! When Tito came back from Russia, Tito's mother was already dead!"

It's true: when Tito returned from his two years of Russian commie training in 1936, his mom had been dead for 18 years. She died on January 14, 1918, during Tito's first trip to Russia (when he was a prisoner of war). She never saw him return. She was 54 years old when she died. His father died early too.

There's two things that are worrisome about this fable. First, Žika believes it and will probably keep the myth alive for the next generation. Second, Miliša isn't the stereotypical uneducated Balkanian farmer who dreams up tall tales when he's bored. On the contrary, Miliša was Sokobanja's former mayor.

Although Miliša didn't mention it, one possible origin for Tito being an English imposter is that Tito (whose real name was Josip) had two code names in the USSR: Tito and Walter. Although he eventually settled on Tito, in Russia, he was often called Walter. *Walter* ain't Slavic. Probably a lazy conspiracy theorist drew an imaginary connection: Walter was British.

The Balkan explanation for everything: conspiracy theories

This Tito myth was just one of the many conspiracy theories that Miliša shared with me. Miliša wasn't odd. On the contrary, most Balkanians are overflowing with cloak-and-dagger fantasies and half-baked explanations for everything. It doesn't matter if they're an illiterate villager from Bosnia, an ex-Mayor from Serbia, or an academic from Croatia—Balkanians are suckers for screwball conspiracy theories.

For example, Miliša not only believed that Tito was a free-mason, but also that Jews control the planet. He said, "Did you know that Stalin was from Georgia and that he was part Jewish? His nickname was 'Little Jew.' It's a fact: Jews control 80 percent of the world and 90 percent of the media."

Poor Jasmin tried to hide her shock. Since WWII, Germans have learned to crush the slightest hint of anti-Jewishness. Proclaiming Hitler-like beliefs nowadays in Germany gives you a good chance of ending up in a modern-day German concentration camp. Miliša, being a clever politician, added, "I'm not anti-Jewish. I just ask questions. Who do you think caused this current world economic crisis? What about the worldwide Great Depression of 1930, which started in America? The Jews took out all their money right before the Depression. Then they bought everything for cheap. And who was the US President at that time? What's his name? *Abraham* Lincoln."

At that time I didn't know anything about Tito to debate the doppelganger theory, but I am one of those rare Americans who knows something about our history. So I said, "Hold on. First of all, the US President at the beginning of the Great Depression wasn't Lincoln, it was Herbert Hoover. Lincoln was the President during the 1860s, not the 1930s. Second, are you suggesting that just because Lincoln has a 'Jewish' name like *Abraham* that he was Jewish?"

Miliša said, "I am only asking questions." He was clearly unmoved by my points.

I said, "In the 2008 US presidential election, Mitt Romney struggled to get nominated because he was Mormon. About 50 years before that, John F. Kennedy nearly lost the race because he was *Catholic*. Do you think that 150 years ago there was any chance of a *Jew* being elected President? We can barely elect a Catholic today! We're more likely to elect a communist-lesbian-African-American atheist than a Jew!"

Miliša shrugged. Jews are a useful all-purpose scapegoat. In the mid-1300s, many Europeans blamed Jews for the Black Death. They believed Jews were poisoning the wells. Near today's French-German border, thousands of Jews were liquidated with the hope that the bubonic plague would disappear if the Jews disappeared. I said, "Miliša, you've been a mayor, so you must know politics. You're suggesting that Jews control Serbia. Can you name me a single Jewish politician in Serbia?"

He thought, then finally shook his head slightly and said, "No."

"OK," I continued, "How about a single prominent Jewish businessman in Serbia?"

"I don't know any."

"Alright. Do you personally know *any* Jew in Serbia, anywhere?"

"Yes, I knew one. But she was killed."

"So let me get this straight: Jews are all-powerful and control Serbia, but they have no politicians or leading businessmen, and the one Jew you knew apparently wasn't powerful enough to stop herself from getting killed."

Miliša chewed his pork and seemed unaffected. He's certainly not the only one who subscribes to the Jewish Conspiracy Theory.

> *America is totally under control of the Jews, you know. I mean, look what they're doing in Yugoslavia. — Bobby Fischer (1943–2008), American world chess champion, said this on the radio on May 24, 1999. His mother was Jewish.*

The America-Conspired-To-Destroy-Yugoslavia theory

With a masochistic curiosity, I asked Miliša why Yugoslavia broke up. I suspected he would offer another amusing conspiracy theory. He did, but it wasn't original. It's the same one I had heard many times from Slovenia to Macedonia. The theory is simple: it's all America's fault. Miliša summed it up, "Yugoslavia had a successful communist system. People could travel. We lived well. We showed that communism could work. America didn't like that. So they wanted to destroy Yugoslavia."

Dušan (from Slovenia) repeated a related conspiracy theory (that will remind you of the Tito doppelganger theory): Serbian leader Slobodan Milošević went to New York many times, supposedly to work with some banks, but his real purpose was to secretly meet with the CIA. The CIA taught Milošević how to ignite ethnic tensions and ruin Yugoslavia. After his clandestine CIA training, Milošević returned to Yugoslavia and executed this sinister plan.

A third related conspiracy that I heard many times was that the US wanted to demolish the JNA, which supposedly was "the fourth largest army in Europe." On March 12, 1991, JNA chief Veljko Kadijević asked the government to declare a state of war, ominously alluding to a conspiracy: "An insidious plan has been drawn up to destroy Yugoslavia. Stage One is civil war. Stage Two is foreign intervention. Then puppet regimes will be set up throughout Yugoslavia."

Although I'm just a brainwashed American who only spent 18 months in the puppet regimes of ex-Yugoslavia, let's try to examine how much truth there is behind these conspiratorial ideas. Let's start with the last one. Although the JNA was the fourth largest army in Europe in 1950, it didn't last. Most peacetime economies spend between one and five percent of their GDP on the military. Because Western European capitalist economies zoomed past Yugoslavia's GDP, Yugoslavia's gross military spending (and so its overall military might) weakened relative to others. By the early 1980s, Yugoslavia's depressed and debt-heavy economy forced so many military cutbacks that the JNA was hardly a threat. The demoralized army couldn't conquer one of the smallest countries in Europe, Slovenia. Or a better example: one poorly equipped infantry brigade fought off the mighty JNA for months in Vukovar. In short, the Pentagon wasn't losing any sleep over Yugoslavia's military.

Now let's determine how often Americans were thinking about Yugoslavia. Serbs routinely told me that when they visited America and told random people that they were from Serbia, a common response would be, "Where again? Siberia?" Andre said, "Most people in America don't know who or what Serbia is. My former boss once told me, 'They were talking about Bosnia on TV the other day. Isn't that in Africa?" Nenad Stojanović, a Serbian from Niš, told me that when he was in Italy, an Italian wondered where Serbia was, "Is that in Asia?"

Of course, these are common, ignorant people. Surely America's clever and conspiring politicians have deep interest in Yugoslavia.

They probably even know where Sokobanja is. In 1991, US Secretary of State James Baker was busy with the Middle East, the collapsing Soviet Union, the emerging Eastern European countries, and his golf swing. Nevertheless, he attempted to save Yugoslavia from collapse, saying, "Knowing full well that we had very little chance of succeeding, we went and made the effort."

If America was behind Yugoslavia's breakup, then Baker would certainly know about it. Montenegro's President, Momir Bulatović, asked Baker, "What do you want from me?" Baker gave him a dumb look, then he shuffled through his briefing book and turned to the page about Montenegro. Bulatović later said, "I look into it to see what it said about Montenegro. I peeked into it and there were just two lines: (1) the smallest republic in Yugoslavia (2) a possible fifth vote for Mesić." Mesić should have been Yugoslavia's President (they rotated among eight presidents), but the government structure broke down six weeks before and Baker incorrectly believed that just putting Mesić in power would defuse the crisis. Even at the height of the crisis, Baker was clueless. Baker basically said, "Can you guys settle down and behave nicely to each other?" It was wise advice, but hardly demonstrating the level of sophistication that a cunning, conspiring superpower ought to have.

Conspiracy theorists should love the Contact Group, an organization created by five powerful nations to solve the Yugoslav Wars. It fits the fable—five powers working in unison to carve up and control Yugoslavia according to the nefarious Grand Plan. Let's watch these brilliant masterminds at work. A Bosnian government official, Ejup Ganić, was examining a map with the Contact Group members. He said, "Some of them were trying to find Banja Luka in Romania [it's actually in Bosnia]. They had started from scratch and did not know anything. They did not know who lived where."[14]

Here's my favorite story. Brent Scowcroft, US National Security Adviser, was concerned about Yugoslavia, but he said, "President [George H. Bush] and Baker were furthest on the other side. Baker would say 'We don't have a dog in this fight.' The President would say to me once a week, 'Tell me again what this is all about.'"[15] Obviously, this is proof that Yugoslavia was a vital piece in America's clandestine and wicked plot for global domination.

When Clinton bombed Serbia, one Montenegrin general was so upset that he fired a missile at the USA. Days passed and no response. He fired another missile. No response. A third one. Still nothing. The general called Clinton to say that Montenegro had fired three missiles at America and he wanted to know why they had not responded.

Clinton said, "We will fight back as soon as we figure out where Montenegro is located!" — Balkan joke

When the evidence isn't pointing to America's apathy or ignorance toward Yugoslavia, it points to America's support. In the 1950s, 72 percent of Yugoslavia's economic assistance came from the US. After Tito's death in 1981, the US created the "Friends of Yugoslavia" consortium, which encouraged Western governments to give more aid to Yugoslavia.[16] If the US wanted Yugoslavia to die, why offer it economic assistance?

When Germany wanted to recognize the independence of Slovenia and Croatia, the US recommended against it. On October 1, 1990, President Bush told Yugoslavia that it had the full US support. While conspiracy theorists would say, "Of course, he would say that on the surface, but behind the scenes he was doing the opposite." That's unlikely, because Bush (and President Reagan before him) acted quite differently with most of the other Eastern Europeans countries. The US Presidents made it clear that they wanted the other Eastern European countries to break away from the Soviet sphere. If the US policy was so overt with those countries, why would it be covert with Yugoslavia?

The ego-busting reality

The truth is that the US hoped Yugoslavia would follow the example of other Eastern European countries: transition to a free-market, democratic system, *but in a peaceful and united way to avoid destabilizing the region.* By the late 1980s, Yugoslavia was already moving toward democracy and capitalism, but what worried the West was that they would do it violently. Neven Borak, a Slovenian economic historian, told me, "The US didn't want Yugoslavia to collapse. On the contrary, Secretary of State James Baker made a special trip to Belgrade to show his support for the country. America wanted Yugoslavia to continue to be stable and friendly to the US. And I don't believe that the USSR wanted Yugoslavia to collapse either."

Several Balkanians told me, "But the CIA predicted Yugoslavia's breakup!" It's true. On November 28, 1990, *The New York Times* reported that the CIA predicted that Yugoslavia would collapse and that war would break out within 18 months.[17] They were right: war started in seven months. However, Balkanians confuse *prediction* with *causality:* a Bosnian told me, "the CIA predicted that breakup, so it happened." But just because the CIA accurately predicts the weather, doesn't mean it caused the weather. Many analysts also predicted Yugoslavia's collapse. It wasn't rocket science: by November 1990, Yugoslavia was one of the only Eastern European countries that had *not* overthrown its government. The CIA's forecast was like predicting that the last domino in a long chain would fall.

Even if the CIA wanted to destroy Yugoslavia, could it do it? Although it did have a few successful covert operations, it failed miserably in Cuba, a country that, compared to Yugoslavia, was far weaker, practiced a more closed version of communism, and was next to the US. These differences would make the CIA much more motivated to act decisively than in Yugoslavia. If the CIA couldn't topple Cuba, then what hope did it have in Yugoslavia? Besides, US-Yugoslav relations were good—why overthrow a friend? Yugoslavia fell on its own because it was based on an unsustainable system.

In conclusion, here's the ego-busting pill for ex-Yugoslavs to swallow: most of the world doesn't give a rat's ass about the Balkans. The Yugoslav population is just 0.3 percent of the world population. Its share of the world GDP and landmass is less than 0.5 percent. And no, its share of the population and the GDP hasn't changed much since Tito's glory days. It's never been more than one percent of the world. Geographically, Yugoslavia was smaller than Nevada: it was 2.6 percent the size of the US or 1.5 percent of Russia. Its GDP was about equal to Kansas and Nebraska put together (two states most Americans think about once every 13 years).

Furthermore, its republics were even more forgettable. Consider Serbia, Yugoslavia's biggest republic: it was smaller than South Carolina. If South Carolina disappeared, the only people on the planet who would give a shit are those in North Carolina. And the only reason they would care is that now they could just call their state *Carolina.*

In short, Yugoslavia wasn't so much a toy that the Great Powers like to play with, but rather a toy that's in their closet and they hardly know it's there. It's fun to blame the US government for everything crappy thing in our lives, but in this case Yugoslavia not only crumbled all by itself, but did so despite America's efforts to keep it together.

A Megan Fox joke explains why conspiracy theories are usually wrong

A guy is stuck on a deserted island with Megan Fox. Realizing no help will ever come, they eventually have sex. After several weeks of wild sex, the guy tells Megan to put on a fake mustache and beard, and then to walk in one direction around the island, while he walks in the opposite direction. When they finally cross paths on the other side of the island, the guy approaches the male-looking Megan and says, "Dude! You'll never believe who I am sleeping with! I'm fucking Megan Fox!"

This joke is a perfect illustration of human nature: when we have a juicy story, we have to share it, at least with our closest friends. If you never share it, it's as if it never happened, and that's no fun. People often don't want to die with juicy secrets. For example, the famous

1933 Loch Ness monster photo was really a toy submarine in a bathtub. The photographer revealed the truth when he felt he was near death. Similarly, at 91 years old, Mark Felt couldn't resist telling the world that he was the Deep Throat who exposed the Watergate conspiracy. Copernicus waited to the end of his life to share his knowledge about the orbits of the planets. Newton created calculus and solved countless problems without bothering to tell anyone about it for years, yet even he eventually spilled the beans.

This doesn't mean that all conspiracies are discovered. You and I can conspire to rob our employer. And we can get away with it, perhaps forever. However, if we involve dozens or hundreds in our conspiracy, then it will eventually be discovered because people can't shut forever when they have a good secret. It's impossible to consistently suppress the human tendency to gossip no matter how large the incentive is to stay quiet. If 10 people know about flying saucers in Area 51, there's a good chance that at least one of them will tell his wife or best friend about it, who will tell another close friend, and so on until the secret is blown with real evidence, not just rumors. To pull off a massive conspiracy (like dismantling Yugoslavia, a country of 22 million people), too many people must get involved, which makes it inevitable that someone will blow the whistle and reveal hard, damning evidence.

This doesn't mean that big conspiracies never happen. They do. For example, at the end of the 1700s, Russia, Austria, and Prussia successfully conspired to rip Poland apart. In 1915, Italy made a secret agreement in London to switch sides in WWI. Hitler and Stalin conspired to divide Eastern Europe. Milošević and Tuđman (Croatia's President) denied conspiring to divide Bosnia, but a bunch of their former aides testified that they had. Therefore, large, complex conspiracies happen, but are also quickly discovered.

Can a massive, evil conspiracy be hidden for more than a generation? No, unless you believe that not one among hundreds of people who have access to hard, incriminating evidence will have a conscience to share it. Consider these intricate conspiracies (and approximately how long it took before conclusive evidence emerged to expose them): Project MKULTRA (20 years), COINTELPRO (15 years), the Dreyfus Affair (12 years), Operation Mockingbird (10 years), Watergate (2 years), the California Water Rights Conspiracy (10 years), the 1919 Black Sox Scandal (1 year), the GM streetcar conspiracy (5 years), Bay of Pigs (2 years), the Secret Bombing of Cambodia (2 months), Operation INFEKTION (5 years), the Iran–Contra affair (2 years), the Lavon Affair (1 year), the Niger uranium forgeries (1 year), the Abramoff Indian lobbying conspiracy (9 years), the Enron and Arthur Andersen conspiracy (3 years), the Las Vegas Venetian Rigged Drawing (2 years), the CIA's secret prisons (2 years), the DRAM price fixing (2 years), the Bernard Ebbers conspiracy (2 years), the Bernard Madoff pyramid scheme conspiracy (2 years), and the Karađorđevo agreement between Milošević and Tuđman (5 years).

Given all the large, evil conspiracies we've uncovered, why haven't historians uncovered major, malevolent conspiracies that were hidden for more than a generation? In the rare cases that a historian discovers an old conspiracy, it either involved few people (e.g., Julius Caesar's assassination) or was not diabolical (e.g., the Underground Railroad in the early 1800s) or both (e.g., burial site of Genghis Khan). When have they ever found a conspiracy that is big, fiendish, and stayed hidden for over a generation? Finding that triple combo is elusive, implying that it doesn't occur.

Thus, is it possible that the pharmaceutical industry is colluding to create diseases just so they can make billions selling drugs? Sure, but as more people get involved in that top secret plot, it becomes exponentially more difficult to stop the truth from leaking out. Given the complexity of that conspiracy, it's effectively impossible to stay hidden for long.

Americans can certainly whip up crackpot conspiracies theories as fast as Balkanians, but there are two important differences. First, Balkanians use conspiracy theories far more often than Americans. In the Balkans, there's a conspiracy behind everything, whether it's the elections or your toaster. Second, conspiracy theorists are on America's fringe, whereas they're the mainstream in the Balkans.

Why Balkanians are suckers for conspiracy theories

The main reason Balkanians are so quick to believe conspiracy theories is that they've lived through communism and war. Eastern Europeans are prone to conspiracy theories because communism restricted the information flow. An entire generation grew up with the belief that *anything that the media and the government tells you is a lie*. They had good reason to believe that—communist governments notoriously spread propaganda and obstructed information flow. For example, the West obtained hard evidence for the secret Molotov–Ribbentrop Pact immediately after WWII (just six years after the fact). The official confirmation quickly spread throughout Eastern Europe via word-of-mouth, but the communists denied it for 50 years, until Gorbachev publicly admitted it. Such experiences reinforced the Eastern European habit of distrusting the media and government.

Furthermore, unlike other Eastern Europeans, Balkanians had a double-whammy: the post-communist era was replaced with a wartime situation. Governments always tightly control the media during times of war, causing people to doubt it. Even governments with long traditions of free press and free speech clamp down on their media during intense wars. Thus, until the twenty-first century, Balkanians have always lived a society of misinformation.

> *News should be checked not twice, but three times.*
> *— Balkan proverb*

The problem is that now that communism and the wars are over, Balkanian beliefs haven't adjusted. They've kept the habit of doubting everything and having more confidence in whatever their drunken buddy dreamed up at the barbeque. Vlad told me, "The Balkans is the perfect ground for prejudices because accurate information doesn't travel well. Mexicans and Americans know each other much better than Serbians and its neighbors. Our information infrastructure is bad. The people in villages just know stories. Although that's true everywhere, it's a bigger difference in the Balkans than in Western societies."

Balkanians are suspicious of everybody. In 2010, Gallup asked, "Generally speaking, would you say (a) most people can be trusted, or (b) you have to be careful in dealing with people." Only about 15% of Balkanians picked (a). Macedonia was the least trusting (9%) and Croatia was the most trusting (22%). The Balkans had Europe's lowest rates. Germany, Spain, and Italy all score in the low 30s. The UK and USA around 40%. The European countries that have the most trust in their fellow human were Scandinavian ones, all scoring 66% to 75% (in the Finland chapter we noted the Finnish trustworthiness). Part of the Balkan distrust again comes from the war mentality that still lingers. If, for a decade, you hear stories of neighbors betraying and killing other neighbors, you might also question everyone's sincerity.

In addition to communism and war, there are two more reasons why conspiracy theories are popular. First, they're great for cognitively lazy people. They confuse the probability that a series of events would happen *if* they were a conspiracy with the probability that a conspiracy exists *if* a series of events occurred. Furthermore, when trouble erupts in the Balkans and your daughter asks you to explain it, it's much easier to say that the boogeyman is behind everything. Such mental shortcuts help you avoid the tedious task of analyzing a complex situation. Second, conspiracy theories make us feel like clever, independent thinkers. We smugly conclude, "I'm not naive. I'm smart and see through all the media bullshit. I know what's *really* going on."

For example, Andre told me, "I think people who use the term 'conspiracy theory' are rather naive, because if we wanna be realistic and we talk about governments and countries and world powers, one would be rather naive to think that things can just happen randomly. Since people are inclined to be naive, a vast number of people are led to believe that somehow this guy 'George Bush' came to power in a rather strange way, and somehow it's idiocy, and not extreme cunning, that leads America into Iraq. The funny thing is people actually buy that. So the world's most powerful government is linked to powerful businesses like the *Three Stooges* with slapstick humor and idiotic mistakes that lead to Iraq, Afghanistan, and all their foreign policy. Is that what I am supposed to believe in order to be a non-conspiracy theorist? To believe that these political events that include whole countries and massive amounts of money just randomly happen? When you are talking about trillions and trillions of dollars, I am sure they make sure that nothing happens that has not been thoroughly planned out."

Rich and powerful people aren't as smart and as united as you think

Unless you're a freak, you'll agree that humans (and not aliens) run governments and businesses. Therefore, they make the same stupid mistakes that humans do. Just putting a bunch of smart, rich people in a room won't produce brilliant decisions. Most people who disagree have never been in a room full of rich and smart people.

> *We shall not commit the same errors again. I am sure we'll make others. — Winston Churchill*

Hitler, for example, spent a year meticulously planning Operation Barbarossa (Germany's surprise invasion of the USSR). It was not a random event. There were billions of dollars of value at stake, such as the Caucasus oil fields and perhaps the very fate of the world. Still, many historians believe this was Germany's biggest blunder in WWII. The Nazis weren't as funny as the Three Stooges, but their strategy was just as foolish. There are countless examples, but the point is that rich and powerful countries, companies, and people sometimes make big bets and lose. Even seemingly invincible empires miscalculate due to hubris and other factors, and then slip and fall. What's clever about the conspiracy theorists is that they say, "That's because the puppet-masters shifted their allegiance."

This raises the second issue: the elite aren't united. They'll collude at times (like OPEC), but such alliances are fragile and fleeting. Industry and political titans spend more time competing with their rivals than conspiring with them in a Jacuzzi.

How to be a Balkan conspiracy theorist in 10 easy steps!

Balkanians have mastered the art of dreaming up conspiracy theories, so let's learn how to copy them in 10 simple steps:

1. Pick a big, negative event or situation where you have to trust an official source to understand why it happened.
2. Claim that the officials didn't arrive to their conclusions based

on evidence, but rather on collusion. Reject whatever evidence they offer by declaring that it was fabricated.

3. Find something in the official story that seems odd, and build a preposterous theory around it. A classic tactic is to find whoever benefits from the event and say that they were secretly behind it. For example, if lots of people died, argue that companies that make coffins were behind the event.
4. Use the reverse scientific method: decide your conclusion first and then look for facts to prove it.
5. Practice confirmation bias: celebrate facts that support your point and toss the rest!
6. Build your case on an emotional example like, "My sister got cancer after visiting Kosovo; therefore, depleted uranium in Kosovo is giving everyone cancer." Make sure your random "fact" overrides the mountain of evidence against you. Hope that nobody notices how horrible you are at logic and statistics.
7. Make stupid analogies like, "Croatians were allied with the Nazis; therefore, today's Croatians are Nazis."
8. Enlist a pseudo-expert to support your theory. Ideally this charlatan should have a PhD so he can con gullible people into believing his half-baked ideas, which seem to make sense as long as you don't think too much about it.
9. Set absurd standards for your opponents like, "If you want me to believe that the US wasn't behind Yugoslavia's destruction, then you must give me a letter from a US President that says so." If your opponent fulfills your request, raise the bar.
10. Most importantly, proclaim that the satanic, all-powerful, all-knowing elite are constantly lying to the innocent masses. Profess that these shadowy figures are united in their pursuit of one sinister plan, which includes establishing a corporate global government, mind control, and atheism.

The danger of conspiracy theories

Although it's fun to laugh off conspiracy theories, they have a dark side. One downside of conspiracy theories is that it's impossible to have a calm, rational debate. How can one debate the causes of the Srebrenica massacre with a Serb who refuses to believe it even happened? How can you discuss the economic situation in Yugoslavia with a Croatian who claims all the economic data is fake? *When a Balkanian wants to believe something, he requires hardly any proof or evidence; when he doesn't want to believe something, no amount of proof or evidence will change his mind.*

Researchers conducted four experiments where the subjects read phony news articles (such as, "American military was behind the fall of Yugoslavia"). Then they were shown the next issue, where the newspaper apologizes for making an error and that the story is false. Researchers learned that those who were politically leaning a particular way beforehand, didn't change their opinion. In some cases, the correction paradoxically *strengthened* their beliefs.[18] When sticky bias pervades, voters make ill-informed decisions.

Ignoring conspiracy theories can be dangerous. For instance, soon after WWI, a few Germans started mumbling the *Dolchstoßlegende* theory (the *stab-in-the-back* legend). It's a myth that Bolsheviks, Jews, and socialists conspired together to sabotage the German WWI effort. If it were not for this "betrayal," then Germany would have won WWI. Hitler latched onto this conspiracy theory, along with his belief that the satirical *Protocols of the Elders of Zion* was legitimate. The terrorist Timothy McVeigh killed 168 in the Oklahoma City bombing because he was sure that the government was conspiring all sorts of slimy deeds. Naively believing phantom conspiracies can be dangerous, but healthy skepticism can help us catch real conspiracies. How can we strike the right balance?

A guide on spotting phony conspiracy theories

Take three steps. Getting to the truth, requires at least three steps, but conspiracy chumps only take two. First, evaluate the official story. Second, consider alternative views, which point out apparent flaws in the official story and present another explanation (sometimes with dubious evidence to back it up). *Third, listen to the counter-arguments to the alternate view.* It is in this crucial third step where most conspiracy theorists go wrong. Those who believe the 9/11 attacks were staged, that Oswald didn't kill JFK, or that FDR had foreknowledge about the Pearl Harbor attacks rarely spend any time investigating what others say to dispute the conspiratorial arguments. They spend all their time memorizing the conspiracy theory and no time considering those who debunk it. When in doubt, visit Wikipedia.org and Snopes.com, which often provide counter-arguments to conspiracy theories.

> *We tend not to be especially critical when presented with evidence that seems to confirm our prejudices. — Carl Sagan*

Don't confuse rumors with reality. Usually right before a real conspiracy gets exposed, rumors proliferate. Hence, it's tempting to conclude that all rumors are signs that the truth is trying to leak out. However, gossip is often inaccurate. To prove a conspiracy, you need hard evidence, not hearsay and hypotheses. Therefore, until someone produces concrete documentation that five short Jewish guys at the Pentagon control the planet, it's wiser to assume it's just an urban legend.

Remember the Megan Fox joke. People love to share juicy secrets. As the number of people involved in an immoral conspiracy increases, it becomes exponentially more difficult to keep everyone's mouth shut. The bigger the ambition, the more people must get involved. Thus, it's effectively impossible to pursue a big, unethical objective without damning evidence leaking out within a generation.

Conspiracies are harder than ever to pull off. In this century, hiding any conspiracy, especially a large one, is unfeasible. It's too easy for whistle-blowers to record evidence with their mobile phone, upload it to YouTube, and put it on Facebook. Now that most documentation is digital, it's also easy to make copies and send them around the world; it's also hard to permanently destroy digital files. Just ask Wikileaks. As CNN's National Security Analyst said, "The dirty little secret of the intelligence world is that much of what you really need to know isn't exactly a secret anyway."[19]

The flip-side is that now it's easier than ever to spread urban legends and myths. Any fruitcake can spread his half-backed theory on the Internet. Therefore, don't be naive and believe conspiracy theories just because they sound good, except for this one: there is profound and deep meaning that Serbia is chapter 13 in this book. It's a signal for the unholy alliance of those who seek to destroy Serbia. In fact, if you take the first letter of every page, you'll spell a message that only the Illuminati (and the monsters in your closet) can decode.

Leaving Sokobanja

During my last night in Sokobanja, I spoke with Nemanja Petković, a calm physical trainer, at a loud bar in Sokobanja. He had spent half a year in Boston. He said, "What surprised me most about America is that after you live there for one month, you're an American. That's different than Europe." Or as Serbian director Srdjan Dragojević put it, "Americans don't care about your origin, but just about your ability to make money."

It reminded me of a conversation I had with Mile Zukić in Slovenia. He said, "I was born in Slovenia, lived here all my life, speak perfect Slovenian, but some people don't consider me a Slovenian just because my mom is a Serb who was born in Vukovar. They call me a *čefur*, a Balkan immigrant. A professor of mine told me that he wouldn't consider anyone a Slovenian unless his parents, grandparents, and great-grandparents were all Slovenian. Because of this, I'm sometimes treated as a second-class citizen in my own country."

When I asked Miliša what he thought was the difference between Serbs and Americans, he said, "Serbs look at their roots." Nemanja echoed that, but pointed out the downside, "Our problem is that we spend too much time thinking about history. We either live in the moment or live in the past. But we don't think about the future."

Nevertheless, I asked Miliša to think ahead and share his concerns. He said, "In Yugoslavia, people shared property. We said, 'this is ours,' not 'this is mine.' I'm afraid we are losing this now. I'm also afraid that we will live to work, and not work to live. And I'm afraid that we will desire things that we don't need."

Unemployed and broke in Niš? Have fun anyway

At the bus station, Žika and Nemanja gave Jasmin and me a warm farewell. We were going to Niš to stay with Nikola Trifunović, our 27-year-old couchsurfing host. Nikola's well-traveled friend, Nenad Stojanović, picked us up. He told us that Nikola would join us 11:00 p.m. at a bar. Even though it was Sunday night, the bar was packed. Nenad yelled in my ear, "It's because Serbia's unemployment rate is 40 percent! In Niš, it's 70 percent! And with young people, it's close to 90 percent!"

By 1:00 a.m., Nikola still hadn't arrived. Nenad laughed and said, "He's on Serbian time!" By 2:00 a.m., we gave up and went to Nikola's apartment, where Nenad let us in. Nikola came home around 4:00 a.m., but I didn't hear him, since I was sleeping. On Monday, the unemployed and groggy Nenad came at around 10:00 a.m. He introduced me to Paola, a 20-year-old Croatian who was couchsurfing with him on her way to work on a Bulgarian farm. After some potent coffee, Nenad showed us around Niš, which is a fine city, but nothing glorious. Its highlight is the Skull Tower, which Turks built centuries ago using Serb heads.

Nikola woke up in the afternoon and joined us. Soon, 10 of his friends showed up. We were a Serbian tribe, walking along the Morava River, and drinking coffee in the park. Sometimes it seems that the loyalty and commitment between Serb friends runs deeper than blood. When their friends are in need of any help, Serbs will drop everything (including the baby they're holding) to rush to help. Although valuing friendship is a universal human trait, Serbs take it to unusually high levels. Mirjana, an English teacher from Niš, who has a Greek husband, told me, "Compared to the Greeks, Serbians are more connected to friends than family."

The angry Serb

Despite my 18 months in the Balkans, I've never met the stereotypical "angry Serb." All the Serbs I met in the Balkans were friendly,

Clockwise from top:

1. Tallinn's Old Town in Estonia.

2. Maiu Reismann and Francis in Estonia's Lahemma National Park.

3. Maiu and Kristi Reismann, the Estonian twins. (Photo by Diana Unt).

4. Orthodox church in Latvia with Francis.

All photos were taken by Francis Tapon, unless otherwise mentioned.

Hill of Crosses in Šiauliai, Lithuania.

The Soviets bulldozed this site several times, but Lithuanians kept returning to put more crosses.

Today it's a pilgrimage site. People keep bringing crosses from all over the world.

Right: *Laisvės Alėja* (Liberty Avenue), in Kaunas, Lithuania. Lined with linden trees, it is Eastern Europe's longest pedestrian street.

Bottom right: Belarusian friends. Left to right meet Sveta, Alla, and Irina Kurochkina.

Bottom: Dainu Hill Song Garden in Latvia.

Emilia Łoś on the train ride from Gdańsk to Olsztyn, Poland. She was getting a master's degree in biotechnology. She and her family hosted Francis in February. They taught him what a grammatical case is and why you should fear it.

Left: Steve and Zsuzsa Rodgers in their summer home on Lake Balaton, Hungary. Two of their three bilingual kids. They all live in Hawaii, so they dress like this all year round. Unlike most Hungarians.

Below: Helena Kolar and Francis randomly reunited in Subotica, Serbia.

Top: On the far right is Norbert Šabić, Francis's couchsurfing host in Subotica, Serbia. Helena Kolar brought some of her ethnic Hungarian friends along. They all live in Serbia and they love it.

Right: Bled, Slovenia in the wintertime. The Bled Castle, high on a cliff, overlooks the glacial lake. Slovenia is one of Eastern Europe's smallest countries, but it is one of the most beautiful too.

Opposite page:

Top: View from the Croatian sea house where Francis wrote most of this book. Slovenia's old town of Piran sticks out. In the horizon are the snowcapped Julian Alps. Mt. Triglav is the tallest one.

Left: Francis, Ana Mišmaš, and Dušan Trušnovec on Triglav's summit.

Below: Francis celebrates on Mt. Triglav. You would jump like this too if you made it up this hard mountain.

Slaviša Andrić, an ethnic Serb in Vukovar, Croatia. He was a level-headed Serb posing next to a classic slogan. A factory destroyed by Yugoslavia's civil war is behind him.

Francis and Ana Mišmaš in the magical Plitvice Lakes National Park, Croatia.

Francis entering Dubrovnik, Croatia.

Predrag Borojević overlooking the Vrbas River by the Fortress Kastel in Banja Luka, Bosnia.

Francis and the Mostar Bridge, Bosnia. Courageous ones jump off the bridge.

Serbians in Novi Sad, Serbia. Daniel, Dijana Pavlović, Francis, and Marija Krgović.

Up: Francis in Dubrovnik, Croatia.

Right: The Mehmed Pasha Sokolović Bridge over the Drina River in Višegrad, Bosnia and Herzegovina.

Below: Ana and Nedžad Osmanlić in Otoka, Bosnia.

Ana in Piran, Slovenia with three funny Serbians from Niš: Nikola Trifunović (waving), Nenad Stojanović (wearing hat), and Branislav Srđanović.

Ana and Francis on Mt. Lovćen, Montenegro.

Francis at Njegoš mausoleum, Montenegro. It feels like the pearly gates of heaven.

Overlooking Kotor Bay, Montenegro. Kotor's Old Town is just out of sight below.

Aleksandar Dragojević (right) and Ilija Popović are two Montenegrins playing with a gun in Njeguši. Alex helped Francis often in Montenegro.

Son of the owner of this ferry that goes down the Drin River in Albania.

From the Rozafa Fortress, which overlooks Shkodër, Albania.

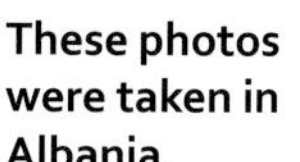

These photos were taken in Albania.

1. Nevrus Lame and Francis toasting.
2. A white hat!
3. Helpful kids in Tirana.

Above: Afrim Gerbeti and his sister in Shkodër.

Right: Dhërmi beach. View from the abandoned hotel. A 4-star campsite! It beats sleeping in the pillbox bunker.

Left: Shpejtim Morina and his friendly family in Prizren, Kosovo. Portrait of Skanderbeg is behind them.

Below: Backyard of the Francis's pot-smoking host in Strumica in Macedonia.

Across: Destroyed Orthodox Church in Prishtina, Kosovo.

Right: Elly Roupcheva in Turkincha, Bulgaria.

Below: Francis backpacking through Bulgaria's Rhodope Mountains in early April.

Crazy hosts in Thessaloniki, Greece. Left to right: Irini, Maria, Anna, and Niki Tsonidou. They had just returned from the police station after their party was shut down.

Left to right: Martin Marinov, Lidiya, Rumi Doncheva, and Francis. Walking through the park in Varna, Bulgaria.

Bozin Kostadinov's family enjoying an Easter lunch near Nesebar, Bulgaria. Bozin is the man with glasses on the far left, sitting across from Francis. Notice the big beer bottle.

Sulina's deserted beach at the end of the Danube Delta, Romania. This international group had explored the delta that day. The Black Sea is behind everyone.

The *Arcul de Triumf* (Triumphal Arch) in Bucharest, Romania. It looks like Paris, although Romania's flag says otherwise.

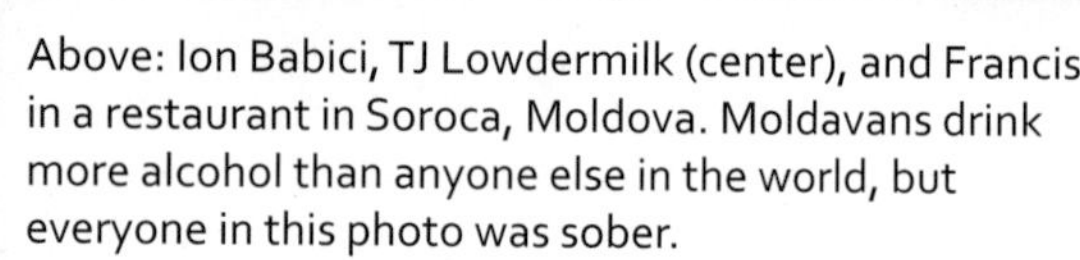

Above: Ion Babici, TJ Lowdermilk (center), and Francis in a restaurant in Soroca, Moldova. Moldavans drink more alcohol than anyone else in the world, but everyone in this photo was sober.

Left: Francis under a WWII monument in Rîbnița. This was in the breakaway republic of Transnistria in Moldova.

Clockwise from top:

1. Corina Nicolae and Dragoş by the Endless Column in Târgu Jiu, Romania.
2. Silviu with his Rom wife, Bianka in Craiova, Romania.
3. Romantic setting for a wedding in Tiraspol, Moldova.
4. Vladislav Fukalov with Francis in Kaliningrad, Russia.

Left: An ice fisherman on the Curonian Lagoon in Kaliningrad, Russia. His portable barrier protected him from the cold wind.

Right: Francis, Vadim Zangliger, and his son Artyom in Koenig, Kaliningrad.

Bottom: Qolşärif mosque in Kazan, Russia. The Tatar culture is widespread around Kazan.

Above: Zelenogradsk, Kaliningrad. Baltic Sea in February.

Left: Zoya Panteleeva and Valentina Ushakova (sitting) in Zoya's home in Polonoye, Russia.

welcoming, and, most of all, *funny*. They have a wicked sense of humor, where few things are sacred—least of all, themselves.

> *Why is Turkey such an underdeveloped country? Because they spent 500 years in Serbia. — Serbian joke*

What's remarkable is that they never changed their attitude once they discovered I was from America. If anything, they seemed to become friendlier. The only times that I met an angry Serb was in America. One example was Andre, whom we've already heard from. Another was Ivan Sokolov, who first wrote me an email in 2006 which began, "I was born in Belgrade and moved to Houghton, Michigan at age 10 in 1988. I hated every moment living there. Being a Serb in America, especially in a small town, was not an easy thing. Propaganda did a good job. Clinton and the rest of his white trash cronies did the rest."

He wailed against the West: "Let's start with the bloody English. The English are by far historically the most evil people of the world. From the atrocities they committed against the Irish and Scots, to the atrocities they committed to the people in India and it never ends. . . . I have never met an English person who has ever admitted their thousand-year history of wrong doings. So, my question for you Francis, why the hell should Serbs admit theirs? Especially considering the fact that every single atrocity that Serbs committed during the 1990s was because somebody did that to them first at some point. England does not have that excuse. Neither do the French. Or the Dutch for that matter with their atrocities in the West Indies, Surinam, and South Africa."

He read my web page where I mentioned that everyone was super friendly in Turkey. So he wrote, "I don't like the Turks. I don't care that they were nice to you. And it is important to note that Turks, much like Albanians, are very unpopular all over Europe. If you are curious to know why I hate the Turks, I will tell you. First of all, they enslaved the people of the Balkans for close to 600 years. Knowing you Francis, you will tell me that, 'Hey Ivan, that was a long time ago. The Turkish rule of the Balkans has been over for more than a hundred years.' And I will tell you then, that 'The atrocities lasted for more than 600 years before that.'"

I'm not sure what he meant by that, but he continued his diatribe, "What I find the most sicking about all this, is that the Turks don't even show any kind of moral obligation for this entire Balkan mess. It is truly sad and disgusting that the Turks, the people who created Albanians and infected the Balkans with Islam, are now used as the peacemakers. Truly sickening. But, of course, Francis, we should all forgive and forget. Well I am waiting for the Turkish apology first, not just for the past, but also for the present."

He ended his tirade with crazy myth, "Francis, also please don't forget one of the key things in the Koran. One of its key statements is that anybody who is Christian or Jew should be put to death. Is it just me or is the whole Islamic faith based on hate?"

We had a few email debates, and then, four years later, when we reconnected, I couldn't recognize Ivan. In 2010, he wrote, "Emir Kusturica was a person who always interested me. If some day I am able to understand his anger and his choices, then perhaps then I would also be able to understand my own. Then again, the old crazy emotional Ivan is slowly dying and the newly reformed calm version of myself is slowly forming. Who would have thought? :) Francis, thanks for always looking in for the good in people."

Emir Kusturica is Yugoslavia's Steven Spielberg. He wasn't born Emir, but Murat. He got his Muslim name because he was born in a secular Muslim family in Sarajevo, Bosnia. When he was nearly 50, he was baptized in a Serbian Orthodox Church to reflect his staunch pro-Serb beliefs.

Perhaps the anger in Emir, Andre, and Ivan comes from constantly hearing what the Western world is saying about your motherland and knowing that it's not the whole story. This compels you to passionately argue the polar opposite point of view, even when you know that the truth is somewhere in the middle. As a result, you come off sounding like a close-minded nationalist. If you do that enough, you'll begin to believe your one-sided story and become yet another fist-pumping chauvinist. I felt this frustration when Europeans, who have spent little or no time in America, say that Americans are fat and stupid. It angers me that they don't realize that we're also ugly.

The Western donkey is telling the Serb rabbit that it has big ears

In 2004, angry Ivan explained another reason why some Serbs are furious. He said, "I find this really funny that all these Western countries that did so many bad things throughout history and were never punished, but now all of the sudden, they are trying to be moral and trying to portray the Serbs as evil villains. In my opinion, that's bullshit. I honestly believe that the rest of the world should shut up and leave the Serbs alone. If they want the Serbs to come clean and admit their sins, then I only have one thing to say to the English, French, Dutch, and especially the Turks. And that is, 'You admit your sins first!'"

Andre agrees, "The world only recognizes the injustices committed by the Serbs. Serbia had been more than fair in taking its share of the blame. All other participants have not. Telling Serbia to admit its wrong doing is like a donkey telling a rabbit that he has big ears."

We are indeed hypocrites. We intervened in Yugoslavia to stop the ethnic cleansing Serbs were doing, but did little to stop the ethnic cleansing against the Serbs. For example, during Operation Storm, Croatian forces pushed Serb forces out of Croatia and pushed out over 150,000 Serb civilians in the process. The EU's Special Envoy called it "the most efficient ethnic cleansing we've seen in the Balkans." Half of those Serbs never returned to their homes. Similar Serb ethnic cleansing happened in Kosovo and Bosnia. NATO did little to stop such atrocities. For that, Serbs are justifiably upset and that is showing up on people's faces.

Grumpy Eastern Europe

Fake smiles are prohibited in Eastern Europe. If Eastern Europeans don't know a person and they're not drunk, then they have a serious look, often a frown. Workers in shops, supermarkets, buses, and especially the government are usually grumpy. Customers are grouchy too. If you smile, it's a sign of weakness or stupidity. Just for fun, sometimes I would smile to an Eastern European on the street—that would confuse them for three days.

In 2010, Gallup asked the world, "Did you smile and laugh a lot yesterday?" There was a clear east-west European divide. All those in Western Europe (except Italy) had at least 70% of their population answering *yes*. All those in Eastern Europe (except Finland, Poland, and Kosovo) had smile/laugh rates under 70%. The worst in Europe, and second worst in the world, was Serbia (40%). Only Togo (36%) smiled and laughed less than Serbia.

It's remarkable that most of the next 15 spots after Serbia were taken by Eastern European countries. Sprinkled among them were countries that seem to have much better reasons to be crabby: Haiti, Ethiopia, and Congo. To illustrate how economic well-being is only loosely correlated to smiling and laughing, consider the top four in the survey: Costa Rica, Panama, Namibia, and Nigeria. Most people from those four countries live more modestly than Serbians (and many other people on the planet), but that didn't stop nine out of 10 of them from smiling and laughing a lot. Given the widespread Eastern European grouchiness, you can't blame everything on the Yugoslav Wars. It's probably something in the water.

Is half justice better than no justice?

The International Criminal Tribunal at the Hague has given Serbs yet another reason to not smile or laugh: about 75 percent of the Yugoslav War indictments were against Serbs. Andre ranted, "If Serbian war criminals go to EU courts, does that mean that EU war criminals will be judged by Serbian courts? The Hague should not be run by participants of the war, but rather by Jamaica, or India, or Swaziland, or some other country which had nothing to do with the issue and has nothing to gain with the outcome."

I said, "Funny you should mention Jamaica. The President of the Tribunal and the presiding Judge of the Appeals Chamber is from Jamaica."

Andre said, "That harvested Jamaican judge is a weak attempt at being fair. He was still chosen by a participant country."

I said, "First you demand a Jamaican judge. Not only do you get two of those, but the Yugoslav Tribunal also has judges from Guyana, Malta, China, Senegal, South Korea, Sweden, Switzerland, Congo, Pakistan, and Bulgaria. Instead of shutting up and being impressed, you brush it all off saying, 'Baahh! They're all crooks anyway! The whole system sucks! The evil UN is controlling everything anyway!'"

Despite the Tribunal's efforts to be objective, it doesn't get away from the fact that Serbs are disproportionately accused. On the other hand, did the British commit roughly the same number of war crimes as the Nazis in WWII? In the early 1800s, who committed more war crimes: Americans or Native Americans? During wars, crimes happen on both sides, but sometimes one side behaves significantly worse than the other. I suspect that war crimes are usually 50/50, but in the aftermath of a war, it's almost impossible to prove that because the winners run the courts.

In other words, although it is possible that Serbs committed far more crimes than their enemies, the real reason they've been punished more than others is that they lost. After WWII, Germany was punished far more than the Allies, even though Soviets and Americans committed many war crimes too. Was Stalin ever punished? If Hitler had won, Stalin (and many Russians) would have been executed (and few, if any, Germans would be punished). Welcome to War Justice 101: winners don't get punished nearly as much as losers. It's unfair, but that's how it goes.

This raises a moral question. Let's say a Serb kills an innocent Croatian lady and a Croatian kills an innocent Serb, yet only the Croatian is punished. Would it have been better if nobody were punished? Is half justice better than no justice?

Finally, Serbians should read this book's chapters on eastern Germany and Hungary to learn how each of those countries' postwar attitude produced different results. Serbs are in danger of developing myths and excuses as deep and debilitating as Hungary did over the Treaty of Trianon. Such extreme self-pity will paralyze Serbia from getting out of its rut and onto a ridge. In 2014, the Tribunal will hear the final appeals for its verdicts against war criminals in the former

Yugoslavia, including Bosnian Serb leaders Radovan Karadžić and Ratko Mladić. Let's hope that Serbia does what Germany did after the Nuremberg Trials: forgive, forget, focus on the future, and make the most out of what you have.

Couchsurfing with a future Orthodox priest in Vladičin Han

Sokobanja and Niš are good places to get a feel of southern Serbia, but Jasmin and I wanted more. I wrote to Nemanja Milosavljević, a 26-year-old couchsurfing host with no experience. He had a degree in architecture, but was also studying to become a priest. He lived in Vladičin Han, which is close to the Kosovo border. I was excited to meet him. I figured he'd be bitter man, who would rant for hours about the Albanians stealing Kosovo, with its magnificent Orthodox monasteries. As usual, I was wrong.

When Nemanja picked us up at the bus station, the first thing I noticed was his large black beard—the classic Orthodox priest look. He also had long black hair, which he carried in an orderly ponytail. His black leather biker jacket made him look like a member of Hell's Angels, but given his occupation, more on the angel side. His voice was soft, calm, and almost hypnotic. We walked five minutes to his home. Vladičin Han isn't a ghost town, but time clearly moves in slow motion. There were few cars or people outside. On the street level of his house was his family's restaurant, which was empty. "Business has been slow for many years," Nemanja said quietly.

We walked upstairs, where we met his mom, Zlatica. She was petite, spoke no English, but gave us a warm greeting that instantly made us feel at home. She smiled, invited us to sit, and brought out *čaj* (tea) and cookies. Given the level of hospitality they were showing to a German and an American, I thought that, despite their proximity to Kosovo, perhaps they weren't that affected by the 78-day NATO bombing. I asked Nemanja about it. He pointed to a bridge that was over 100 meters (yards) away and said, "See that bridge? A NATO bomb struck it and the force of blast shattered all our windows and blew our roof off."

In such moments, it feels useless to say "sorry," but I said it anyway and asked if anyone had been hurt. "Not in my family, but during the bombing, shrapnel hit a young girl and her little brother on the street. Even though the boy suffered far more injuries, the girl died of sadness from seeing her brother hurt badly. He survived. She didn't."

Zlatica probably thought we were talking about the weather because she smiled and asked us if we'd like to have dinner at their restaurant. We went downstairs and the waiter served us soup, salad, grilled steak, and polenta. The restaurant was empty, except for two guys who were smoking and having a beer in a corner. While we ate the tasty food, I asked Nemanja to help me solve a paradox: given the universal Serb warmth and humor that I had seen, why has there been so much fighting in the Balkans? Nemanja smiled slightly and said, "The Balkan mentality is that we love people who come from afar, but we can't love our own brother."

"Give me an example," I asked.

"People fight over property with their relatives all the time. I know cases where the grandmother is only allowed to walk around in one part of the house because of some long lasting family dispute."

"That's crazy," I said. "But I've heard similar tales throughout the Balkans. It seems that you're all pretty similar."

"We are!" he said. "We're like brothers. The family analogy is right. We're brothers who love each other, yet hate each other. We break up, but then we always come back together. We don't agree on anything for long. That's the Balkan mentality."

Two Serbs, three political parties. — Serbian proverb

After dinner, we walked around Vladičin Han with two of Nemanja's buddies. They were all unemployed, although they did odd jobs when they could. They were in late 20s and the economy has been horrible ever since they were born. They told me the dating scene was also pretty hard in the small town of Vladičin Han, since most people know each other. When I suggested they go over the border and date Albanian women in Kosovo, they laughed. But then Nemanja said, "Actually, some Serbs go to Shkodër in Albania to look for wives. It happens."

I asked the gang to tell me a uniquely Serbian trait. One blurted out, "*Inat*!" *Inat* means to do something out of spite. Many Eastern Europeans told me (especially in the Baltic) that there's a saying that if your cow dies, you want your neighbor's cow to die too, so you're still equals. Nemanja said, "But in Serbia, after your neighbor's cow dies, you want yours to die too."

"Why?"

"So you don't have to sell your neighbor your cow's milk."

"But that's crazy," I said.

"Yeah, but that's *inat*."

15 things you must do to be a Serb

Talking about *inat* reminded me of Momo Kapor's book, *A Guide to the Serbian Mentality*. He wrote a long list of all the things you need to do to be a Serb. Of course, there are plenty of exceptions, but it's amusing to see how one celebrated Serbian writer depicts his fellow Serbs. I've adapted the list below, picking some of my favorites:

(1) Eat lots of meat. (2) Live in the tavern. (3) Do things out of spite.

(4) Drink *rakia* like water. (5) Only listen to folk music. (6) Go out at night only after 11:00 p.m. (7) Live with your parents for at least 30 years. (8) Fight with your neighbors. (9) See more soccer games and less theater. (10) Save money all year to go to the sea during the summer. (11) Spend more than you make. (12) Sleep late. (13) Help your friends to the death. (14) Be an expert about the police. (15) Swear often.

Serb kindness, including to those who bombed them

The next day, Nemanja drove us to the enormous Vlasina Lake, which is in the mountains near the Bulgarian border. It was March 28 and there was plenty of snow everywhere, although the lake was not frozen. The beautiful mountain scenery in southern Serbia is more attractive than the boring plains of Vojvodina. With all of Nemanja's driving, Jasmin and I tried desperately to pay for his gas, but he refused. We weren't even able to pay for our meals at his family's restaurant, no matter how much we insisted. Serbians were warm and generous everywhere I went. Marija's brother gifted me his jacket because it was snowing in March and I was underdressed. Nikola and Žika invited me into their homes. Even a Serbian dentist cleaned my teeth for free.

A 2011 Balkan Monitor report showed that only 12 percent of Serbians approved of America's leadership and only nine percent thought NATO was friendly. Nevertheless, Larry Leigh, an American Law School professor who taught in Belgrade, told me, "Everyone was friendly to me, even though I was an American and thus associated with the country that led the NATO bombing in 1999."

I asked Larry what he thought Americans can learn from Serbians. He wrote, "How to make do with less wealth and still have a high quality of life. . . . The Serbs are quite a physically attractive people. If you walk the streets of Belgrade, you will find a relatively fit and trim urban population. Frankly, they just look better at all ages on the average than Americans when it comes to fitness and general health."

Serbia's ego is bruised, but sometimes getting humiliated helps a country. America ate humble pie after Vietnam and Iraq, and the country healed. In the previous decade, Serbians learned that living in the past gets you nowhere. You can't buy food with slogans and rhetoric. In 2010, Serbia applied to join the EU, with the majority of Serbians supporting the move, although it probably join before 2018. It's hard to predict what Serbia will be like in 2037, but I bet it will no longer be Europe's pariah.

> *It will no more occur to a normal person to mate with a person eugenically unfit than to marry a habitual criminal. — Nikola Tesla, Serb inventor (1856–1943), predicting life in 2037. He never married or had children.*

Drinking hard liquor with a nun in southern Serbia

Before we left Vladičin Han, Nemanja took us to Mrtvica, a village whose hill has the monastery *Uspenje Presvete Bogorodice* (Assumption of Mary). Nemanja's four-wheel drive jeep struggled up the hopelessly muddy road. When we entered, I felt I was in a convent: there was one young guy and 10 women. The oldest nun, Makrina, dressed in her traditional garb, greeted us warmly and told us to sit on the long bench next to the table. The other women soon brought tea and, surprisingly, *rakija*—Serbia's national drink. It's a fruit brandy that is usually homebrewed. It comes in many fruity flavors, but the most popular is *šljivovica* (plum brandy). You'll find it at births, weddings, and funerals. Given the high percentage of alcohol, it's hard to understand how Serbs can distinguish between the different flavors.

Although the nun couldn't speak English, Nemanja translated between us. Traditionally, young people aren't into religion as much as the older generation and I asked Makrina if that's also true in Serbia. She smiled and said, "Not really. More young people are interested in religion than before. There is more democracy now and more freedom of religion. This is good. On the other hand, this passion for religion is not very deep. Many go to church. But how many practice the true Orthodox faith? Not many."

By now, a dozen of ladies had gathered around the table or sat on the benches to listen to the head nun talking with the curious American. I asked her, "Do you think there's a difference between Serbia and the West?"

"Yes, I think there is deeper spirituality in Serbia than in the West. Serbians live with more emotion. They are less rational than Westerners. But we are spiritual. God lives in southern Serbia."

"How did the war affect you and your beliefs?"

"We learned from the war. The war came from God. God gave us this war to teach us, so we could learn. It was God's will."

Finally, with the room quiet, I came to the theme of this book, the question I asked everyone I have met, "What can you learn from Serbians?"

Without hesitation, the nun held up her glass and yelled out, "How to make *rakija*!"

The room erupted in laughter.

What Serbia Can Teach Us

- **Have a two-hour coffee with your friends.** It helps to have a 20 percent unemployment rate, but even if it were two percent, Serbians would make time to socialize for hours in cafés. Sometimes it seems that Serbians put friendship before family, they'll have a coffee with anyone.
- **Take care of yourself.** It's not necessarily about how you dress, although Serbians pay a lot of attention to that. What's more important is to maintain a healthy fitness level. Serbians are more athletic and trim than the average American.
- **Eat food in season.** Serbians don't buy tomatoes in the winter. Although it's changing, they're still old school and favor fresh fruits and vegetables.
- **Don't judge a citizen the same way you judge his government.** Throughout Serbia I didn't hide behind my French and Chilean nationality. Instead, I boldly introduced myself as an American to see what kind of reaction I would get. I came from a country that had bombed Serbia just a few years before. Nevertheless, Serbians never flinched or gave me a suspicious look when they learned I was American. Their knee-jerk reaction was positive, friendly, and welcoming. It wasn't fake kindness either—they welcomed me to their homes and rolled out the red carpet. Some of them had negative feelings about the US, but they never let those feelings get confused with an individual American. We should all separate our feelings for a nation with our feelings for individuals from that nation.
- **Laugh at your own misfortune.** Despite their victimism, Serbians keep their sense of humor. It's a unique, biting, dark sense of humor, but it's a healthy sign that most Serbs know not to take life too seriously.
- **Earn $500 a month (the average Serb wage in 2011) and live like you have $1,000.** And they do it without credit cards or debt. How they do this is still somewhat of a mystery.

Places I saw and recommend in Serbia: Belgrade, along with the villages and countryside in the south.

Travel deals and info: http://ftapon.com/serbia

Having examined Croatia and Serbia, we are somewhat prepared to step into a far more complex country: Bosnia-Herzegovina. When I was leaving Slaviša, my Serb couchsurfing host in Vukovar, I told him that I would eventually be going to Bosnia. He gave me a hug and then said, "Good luck. Bosnia is a crazy country. Nobody can understand it."

14

Bosnia and Herzegovina—As Complicated as Its Name

Bosnia and Herzegovina is Europe's most complicated country. That's ironic, because it's filled with Europe's simplest people.

Just how complicated is it? Try to understand this: Bosnia and Herzegovina is a bit smaller than West Virginia, but has three religions, three ethnic groups, yet one language (some claim that there are three languages). However, the country is not divided in three regions, but in two. Yet the exact definition of those two regions depends on what you're talking about. The two-way split can either be between the Bosnia region and the Herzegovina region or between the Republika Srpska and the Federation of Bosnia and Herzegovina. Oh, but then there's the tiny autonomous Brčko District, which you might call a third region. The three ethnic groups elect a President for a four-year term; each President controls the country for an eight-month period before handing power over to one of the other two Presidents. They rotate among themselves six times. On the other hand, none of that matters because there's this third guy, a foreigner called the High Representative, who has king-like powers.

> *Nothing is simple in the Balkans. — David Owen, author of two failed peace attempts during the Bosnian War*

To make this chapter simple, let's begin with some definitions. Bosnia and Herzegovina adopted its long name in 1326, when Bosnia conquered Herzegovina. Although it's unclear where Bosnia got its name, Herzegovina got its name from *Herceg* (Duke) Stjepan Vukčić. He humbly named his territory after himself, so that Herzegovina means *Dukeland*. Today, Herzegovina, which is in the country's mountainous southern corner, is a quarter of the size of Bosnia. Therefore, for simplicity, we'll just call the country *Bosnia*.

Next, let's define some demographic terms. Just like there are *Mexican Americans* (Americans with Mexican ethnicity), there are *Bosnian Serbs*. However, the Balkans reverses the way Americans use the term. The first word indicates where the passport comes from and the second word indicates the ethnicity. Hence, a *Bosnian Serb* is an ethnic Serb with Bosnian citizenship and a *Bosnian Croatian* is ethnic Croatian with Bosnian citizenship. Remember these terms or else you'll get confused. What's the difference between a Bosnian Serb and a Bosnian Croatian? Practically nothing, but don't tell them that.

The three main groups in Bosnia are often said to be Serb, Croatian, and Muslim. However, that classification lacks parallelism. The last term is a religious identification, whereas the first two are not. So instead of *Muslim*, we'll call the third group *Bosniak.* Thus, the four million Bosnians come in three flavors: Bosniak (48% of the population), Serb (37%), and Croatian (14%). Genetically, they're basically identical.[1]

Since these three groups look the same, talk the same, and smell the same, the only notable difference between them is their religious affiliation. Generally speaking, Bosniaks are Muslims, Serbs are Orthodox Christians, and Croatians are Catholics. However, as we'll soon see, few Bosnians are truly religious, which is why they're effectively one people. It's just that in the last 20 years they've been pretending that they're not.

The overnight bus from Belgrade to Sarajevo

In 2004, during my first visit to Bosnia, it was clear that even a decade after a war, Bosnia was still dysfunctional. In Belgrade, a bus ticket agent accidentally sold me a ticket for the 10:00 a.m. bus, not the 10:00 p.m. overnight bus that I wanted. I didn't notice the mistake until I handed the ticket to the bus driver. He told me to refund the ticket (so I could get 90% of the value) and then give him the cash. He pocketed the cash and let me board the overbooked bus. That's a little bit of Balkan bribery for you.

The dysfunctional situation became clear when the bus's final stop was in Sarajevo's outskirts, not the city center. That's because Serbs and Bosniaks were still bickering so much that they couldn't even share a bus station. As a result, the Serb bus dropped us off on the edge of the Republika Srpska (RS)—the Serb Republic, which controls 49 percent of Bosnia (the Federation controls the other 51%).

The bus driver told us that we just had to catch an intercity bus that crosses the RS border and takes us downtown. That seemed easy, so Marco Pettinari (an Italian), Maria Högbacke (a Swede), and I spontaneously joined forces to find that bus. However, none of us had any Bosnian money, the Konvertible Mark (KM), to pay for the bus fare. No problem, we'll just go to a bank cash machine and get some KMs. Unfortunately, the banks still hadn't re-integrated with the international community, so they rejected our Italian, Swedish, or American plastic cards. We finally found an enterprising taxi driver who would accept our euros as long as he could financially rape us.

Sarajevo is unlike any other European capital. In a few blocks, you might run into a mosque, a synagogue, or a church. The architecture shows influence from the Turkish, Austria-Hungary, and Byzantine Empires that all ruled there. The Romans ruled the Balkans from the third century BC until 395 AD, when their empire split in two. The Romans made the split right along a river that still divides Bosnia and Serbia today. Marco, the Italian, couldn't believe the Romans had ruled the Balkans for 700 years. As he looked up to several enormous Balkanians who dwarfed him, he whispered, "I can't believe we beat these guys."

Turkish shadows

The next people to beat up "these guys" were the Turks, who ruled Bosnia for 400 years. Serbs love to recount the horrors of the Turkish occupation, which lasted from 1463 to 1878. Turks crushed Slavic national identities, seeded the Balkans with Turkish colonists, cajoled Christians to become Muslims, made those who didn't convert become serfs, enforced laws based on the *şeriat* (the laws of the Koran), and forced everyone to drink Turkish coffee.

Furthermore, during the Turkish time, non-Muslims had to pay the *cizye*—a special Islamic tax. Turks also added the *haraç,* a land-tax. Still, these combined taxes were sometimes lower than what previous Christian rulers were taxing the population. Also, before you conclude that being a Muslim was a great tax haven, Muslims had to pay a *zekat*, an alms tax. It's unclear what was most important to the Turks: converting Christians to Muslims or just raising tax revenues.

Turks were also interested in raising the world's second biggest army. The *devşirme* system took promising Christian boys to Istanbul, the center of the Turkish Empire, and raised them to be future leaders, military troops, and bodyguards. The best of these so-called *Janissaries* became grand viziers, powerful sultan allies. The recruitment of Janissaries is still controversial. Nobel Laureate Ivo Andrić begins *The Bridge on the Drina* with the image that Serbs have of the *devşirme*: dark shrouded men riding black horses, sweeping through Slavic towns, abducting young boys, and riding off into oblivion while the mothers helplessly wail.

This image made sense to me until I talked with Armin Šuvalić, a Bosniak, whom I met on a bus going from Doboj to Tuzla. He said, "But that's not how it was. On the contrary, it was an honor to have your child selected to go to Istanbul. It was like sending your kid to Harvard or an elite boarding school. The Turks only picked the most promising kids. Only one in 40 households was selected. When they returned, these Janissaries had leadership positions and gave back to the community. It was an honor to be chosen."

Perhaps. Still, what is clear is that the Janissaries became quite powerful. In fact, to keep their loyalty, the sultans had to pay the Janissaries more, as well as let them marry and live outside the barracks. Eventually, the sultans grew tired of the lazy, spoiled Janissaries, and attempted to create a modern army to replace them. The Janissaries rebelled and lost. The Turks abolished the Janissary system in 1826. Armin concluded, "We Muslims don't see the Turkish period as bad. On the contrary, Turks brought big improvements in education, infrastructure, and organization."

Still, Serbs have issues with that period. When I was having coffee with Ana Milovanović in Niš, she told me, "If I ask for 'Turkish coffee,' the waiter might frown. So, to be safe, I always use the euphemism 'domestic coffee.'"

Trading one occupier for another

Sometimes Hungarians and Balkanians proclaim that they "saved Europe from the Turks," implying that the rest of Europe owes them for their "sacrifice." For example, Slobodan Milošević proclaimed in a speech, "Six centuries ago, Serbia heroically defended itself in the field of Kosovo, but it also defended Europe. Serbia was at that time the bastion that defended the European culture, religion, and European society in general." The crowd chanted, "Europe, don't forget that we defended you!"

First of all, anyone alive today deserves absolutely zero credit (or blame) for anything that happened anywhere more than 80 years ago. None of us picked our ancestors or had any control over them. Second, the reality is that Hungarians and Balkanians slowed down the Turks. The people who truly "saved" Western Europe were the Austrians and Poles. *For the Turkish Empire, Hungary and the Balkans were a speed bump; Austria was a road block.* Nevertheless, Austria certainly depended on valiant Hungarians and Slavs to help rout the Turks. Moreover, Russians helped deliver the final death blow to the Turks in 1878.

When Turks moved out of Bosnia, the Austrians and Hungarians moved in. They modernized Bosnia by building railroads, developing mines, and even installing street lighting before Vienna. Ivo Andrić summed up that era in his Nobel Prize winning book, "Not that the new existence was in any way less subject to conditions or less restricted than in Turkish times, but it was easier and more humane, and those conditions and restrictions were now far away and skillfully enforced, so that the individual did not feel them directly. Therefore it seemed to everyone as if the life around him had suddenly grown wider and clearer, more varied and fuller. The new state, with its good administrative apparatus, had succeeded, in a painless manner, without brutality or commotion, to extract taxes and contributions from the local people which the Turkish authorities had extracted by crude and irrational methods or by simple plunder; and, moreover, it got as much or more, even more swiftly and surely."[2] Nevertheless, when Austria-Hungary annexed Bosnia in 1908, it was clear that the foreigners were here to stay. Over the next six years, the Balkan powder keg would expand until a 19-year-old lit a match.

As Marco, Maria, and I toured Sarajevo together, we noticed the traces of the Austria-Hungary period. Buildings from that period still stand, alongside the ones from the Turkish period. Trams calmly weave through the relaxed capital. For lunch, we went to the Baščaršija in the city center and ate the Bosnian specialty, the *burek*. This greasy pastry can be filled with *sir* (cheese), *meso* (meat), *pecurke* (mushroom), or *krompiruša* (potato). After licking our oily fingers, we walked to a bridge that I've always wanted to see.

The Bosnian who changed the world

On the morning of June 28, 1914, Gavrilo Princip, a 19-year-old Bosnian Serb, was determined to sacrifice his life to change world history. He and five wanna-be assassins conspired to kill the Austria-Hungary heir, Archduke Franz Ferdinand, during his Sarajevo visit. Ferdinand had promised that once he took power, he would grant equal rights for all Slavs and improve the legal system. "That's not good enough," thought Princip as he loaded his pistol.

Princip's co-conspirator tossed a grenade at Ferdinand's car. The timing was off and the explosion injured the wrong people. The would-be assassin took a cyanide pill and jumped into the river. However, the pill had expired (it just made him sick) and the river was too shallow, so he was easily caught. Meanwhile, five other co-conspirators (including Princip) were stuck in the crowds while Ferdinand's car sped away to a short diplomatic meeting.

Half an hour later, Princip couldn't believe his luck. Right in front of him, on Sarajevo's Latin Bridge, Ferdinand's driver took a wrong turn, slammed on the brakes, put it in reverse, and the car suddenly stalled. Princip pounced. He pulled out his pistol, butted a pedestrian, and at point-blank range shot Ferdinand in the neck. Ferdinand's wife instinctively covered her husband's body as Princip fired another shot, striking her stomach. Then Princip tried to commit suicide with his gun, but failed. He swallowed a cyanide pill, but, like his co-conspirator, vomited the expired tablet. The police captured him, but Princip had accomplished his mission: the Archduke and Duchess were dead.

Animal lovers might see some poetic justice in Ferdinand's death. He was a zealous hunter. Over 100,000 stuffed creatures adorned his palace. According to his log books, he killed over 300,000 animals. After having been the predator all his life, he ended up being the prey.

Marco, Maria, and I walked across the Latin Bridge to stand on the epicenter of a world changing event. There used to be a plaque that showed the footprints of Princip. However, Bosnians removed it either because they didn't want to commemorate the actions of an ethnic Serb or they felt bad celebrating an event that led to the death of nearly 100 million people.

Indeed, the assassination set off an unfortunate chain of events. First, the furious Austrians declared war on Serbia. That's logical: if one Bosnian kills your leader, punish everyone in Serbia. It's kind of like America's reaction to September 11. We found out that 15 out of the 19 hijackers were from Saudi Arabia, so we attacked Afghanistan.

When the Austrians attacked the Serbs, Russia lent a hand to its Slavic brother. That makes sense. Americans would do the same if some country attacked Canada, since Americans feel a certain brotherhood with Canadians. The problem is that Germans felt a brotherhood with the Austrians. So when Russia stepped in, Germany felt it needed to step in and lend a hand too. That also makes sense. Meanwhile, France had secretly promised to help Russia if ever the need arose, so France had to fulfill that obligation. That makes sense too. Although all these individual decisions make sense, the result was senseless: World War I. Because WWI's aftermath was irresolute, it led to WWII. In short, one Bosnian Serb ignited the two deadliest wars in history.

Of course, without a parallel universe, we'll never know just how important Princip's action was. Princip knew even less. Being a month shy of his twentieth birthday, he couldn't be executed, so he was sentenced to 20 years in a shoddy prison. From his cell, he lived through most of WWI. His diseased arm had to be amputated. Nearly four years after killing the Archduke, he died of tuberculosis, weighing just 40 kilograms (88 pounds).

By the end of the day, Marco and Maria walked me to the train station in Sarajevo to say goodbye. I knew I'd return to Sarajevo in five years, but I never thought I'd see Marco again. However, a week later, we randomly bumped into each other in Dubrovnik and then traveled together for several days in Montenegro. But that story will come in the next chapter.

Eastern Europe's prettiest bridge

In 2009, five years after my first visit to Bosnia, I returned to visit Mostar, a beautiful city that still had 15-year-old war wounds. Some houses were still in ruins. Many inhabited homes had grenade scars and bullet holes. From my simple hotel on the east side of the Neretva River, I walked to Eastern Europe's prettiest bridge.

Mostar's *Stari Most* (Old Bridge) is a captivating UNESCO World Heritage Site. The pedestrian-only stone bridge arches over the swiftly moving river far below. The Islamic architectural influence is evident. Walking over it transports you out of Europe and into another age.

After it was built in 1556, guards stood by the bridge's stone towers. However, they were not there to protect it in 1993 when Croatians bombed the bridge to pieces. It was rebuilt in 2004, two months before my first visit to Bosnia. The significance of the bridge is embedded in the city's name: *Mostar* means *keeper of the bridge*. Today, thrill-seekers jump off the 20-meter (66-foot) high bridge. Unlucky ones perish. Just south of the *Stari Most* is the *Lučki Most*. It seems you'd have better odds of surviving on the *Lučki Most*.

Restaurants with superb views are on one side of the bridge, while the other side, the Ottoman Quarter, is filled with cafés, artistic shops, and Turkish houses. The old town has an intimate, cozy feel with its narrow, cobblestoned streets. Nearby is one of the front lines of the Bosnian War. Shattered buildings testify that Croatians and Bosniaks fought each other vigorously. You can also visit a Croatian-built concrete Catholic Church. Its campanile is outrageously tall, as if to say to the nearby mosque minarets, "Screw you, we're taller."

Eating Bosnian brains

Ex-Yugoslavs may argue about many things, but nearly all agree that Bosnians are fun, simple, easy-going people who cook better than anyone else. Bosnian cuisine is lighter than most Eastern European food. It's a perfect blend of all their former occupiers (Turkey, Austria, and Hungary). During their snowy winters, heavy cabbage-filled stews warm you up. They often eat lamb, veal, pork, or beef. Although I normally eat vegetarian cuisine, when I'm in an exotic place, I sometimes order exotic food. When I saw cow brain on a Mostar menu, I had to try it. I won't try it again.

Later, I spoke with Šime, a Croatian medical school student who was going to school in Mostar because he didn't have good enough grades to get into a Croatian one. About 70 percent of his school were Bosniaks and 30 percent were Croatian. He said they mixed well. He confirmed that they share the same Balkanian language: *zdravo* (hello), *hvala* (thanks), *molim* (please), *doviđenja* (goodbye), *da* (yes), *ne* (no), *nema na čemu* (you're welcome), *oprostite* (excuse me), and *koliko košta* (how much is it?). I asked, "So if language differences weren't the problem, what was?"

He sighed, "It's a long story."

Bosnia's elusive identity

To understand twenty-first century Bosnia, we have to understand twentieth century Bosnia. We saw that although the Austria-Hungary period was somewhat better than the 400-year Turkish period, it wasn't that great, which explains WWI. After WWI, Bosnia joined the Kingdom of the Serbs, Croats, and Slovenes. Notice that the word *Bosnia* isn't in that Kingdom's name, even though there were more Bosnians than Slovenes (i.e., Slovenians). That's because Serbs and Croatians didn't want to admit that a Bosniak (a Slavic Muslim) existed; instead, they believed such people were simply Serbs or Croatians who were confused or brainwashed. This belief remained popular until it ripped Yugoslavia apart.

It's always been hard to pinpoint Bosnia's identity. During WWII, Bosniaks committed savage crimes against Serbs, but many others fought alongside Serbs. Alas, the Balkans is messy. Stevan Pavlowitch said of Yugoslavia in 1944: "Whatever the Yugoslav government represented, it was not unity."[3] Tito vowed to give each Yugoslav ethnic group its own republic. However, he forced Bosnians to identify themselves as either Catholic or Orthodox. It wasn't until 1971 that he created a third category: Muslim.

Censuses are revealing. A census in the 1860s showed that 33% of Bosnians were Serbs (which is similar to today). Later, during the Austria-Hungary time, Bosnia was 32% Bosniak and 68% Serb/Croatian. The 1971 Yugoslav census indicated that only 27% were Bosniaks. By 1991, Bosniaks were 44%. Thus, in Yugoslavia's final 30 years, Bosniaks had become Bosnia's biggest force. Why?

First, in the 1960s, Serbs and Croatians left Bosnia not because of ethnic tensions, but rather for economic opportunities: Belgrade, Novi Sad, Vukovar, and Zagreb offered better job opportunities than any Bosnian town. Second, Bosniaks also had a slightly higher reproductive rate than the other Slavs. Third, the increased religious freedom gave them courage to identify themselves as Muslims (Bosniaks) whereas before they might not have openly admitted it.

Yugoslavia failed to copy America

A few Bosnians didn't call themselves Serb, Croatian, or Bosniak—they called themselves *Yugoslavs*. Yeah, what a concept. In Yugoslavia's 1961 census, only 2% were self-identified Yugoslavs. The Bosnian Republic had the highest percentage of people calling themselves Yugoslav, but few Bosnian regions topped 10%. The highest percentage of self-described Yugoslavs was in Sarajevo: 20%, in 1981. It's remarkable that never in Yugoslavia's history did more than 8.4% of the people call themselves Yugoslavs first.[4]

This is hard for an American to understand. If you ask a guy from California to either label himself a *Californian* or an *American,* he would choose American. Even immigrants will pick *American* over their motherland identity, especially after one generation. Many Balkanians told me, "I wish we could have copied that part of America. We never truly saw ourselves as Yugoslavs first, always second."

With all its immigrants, America could have been Balkanized. In 1915, President Theodore Roosevelt told the Irish Catholic Knights, "There is no room in this country for hyphenated Americanism. . . . The one absolutely certain way of bringing this nation to ruin . . . would be to permit it to become a tangle of squabbling nationalities, an intricate knot of German-Americans, Irish-Americans, English-Americans, French-Americans, Scandinavian-Americans or Italian-Americans, each preserving its separate nationality, each at heart feeling more sympathy with Europeans of that nationality, than with the other citizens of the American Republic. . . There is no such thing as a hyphenated American who is a good American. The only man who is a good American is the man who is an American and nothing else." Five years later, President Woodrow Wilson agreed, "Any man who carries a hyphen about with him carries a dagger that he is ready to plunge into the vitals of this Republic whenever he gets ready."

In short, America and Yugoslavia both struggled to unify their populations under one identity. The US should learn why Yugoslavia failed, because history predicts that American unity will be tested again.

What were ethnic relations really like during Yugoslavia?

Did Bosniaks, Serbs, and Croatians party together often in Yugoslavia? Did conflict erupt out of nowhere? Or were there always ethnic tensions? I asked every Bosnian I met these questions. They gave conflicting answers.

Some said that ethnic relations were fabulous under Yugoslavia. They gave two pieces of evidence. First, prior to the Bosnian War, Bosnia's ethnographic map shows a perfect melting pot—ethnic clusters were randomly distributed all over Bosnia. For that to function, there had to be significant inter-ethnic cooperation. Second, as we saw, Bosnia had the highest percentage of people who identified themselves as Yugoslavs. Bosnia personified the Yugoslav slogan of "Brotherhood and Unity."

Armin argued that the conflict was artificial. He wrote to me, "The outsiders wanted to divide the country and rule it; they worked at dividing and turning its population against each other. It is all the media presentation where the people were presented on the opposing sides, but only people of this country know how many of them never bothered with the fact that his neighbor is Bosnian Serb or Bosnian Croatian. It is all the outside politics that created an image of the war within one country, but the truth was much different."

On the other hand, there's evidence the ethnic harmony was an illusion. The fact that nearly all Yugoslavs preferred identifying themselves by their ethnic group proves that the seeds of "us versus them" always existed. When Yugoslavs spoke of "their nation," they meant their ethnic group, not Yugoslavia. In 1970, Yves de Daruvar wrote a brilliant prediction, "Czechoslovakia and Yugoslavia obviously remain structures incapable of unbuttressed survival, for only naked force keeps together Czechs and Slovaks, Serbs and Croats respectively. To this day they cannot stand one another—their divorce, sure to materialize sooner or later, is written in the stars."[5] If a foreigner who doesn't speak Balkanian can notice the negativity, then obviously the situation wasn't as rosy as some Balkanians say it was.

The reality is that Yugoslavs put aside their ethnic tensions when the economy was booming. Once the economy sank, the finger-pointing fiesta began. It's wrong to blame outsiders: a foreign power can try to make people from Nebraska hate people from Kansas, but it will only work if there's already a preexisting rivalry. Otherwise, the propaganda will fall on deaf ears. Ultimately, Yugoslavs paid lip service to Yugoslav unity, but few truly believed it. Yugoslavia failed to pass the key test: to stay together when economic times are hard.

A bus ride to Banja Luka

In 2010, during my third trip to Bosnia, I took a bus from Zagreb to Banja Luka. The small bus had five old people on it, but none of them spoke English. As we got closer to Bosnia, the ride poked along through windy single-lane roads. Half-built houses and farmland lined the road, which had occasional potholes. The pitch of the bus's motor increased as it began its struggle up the hills. Seeing the hills made me smile: that meant we were about to enter Bosnia, a land of endless mountains.

Before crossing the border, a 20-year-old girl climbed on the bus and sat in front me. She was dressed in tight-fitting jeans, a pink sweater that matched her long pink nails, and a black jacket with fake fur on it. We started chatting. She was a Bosnian Serb named Olja. I asked Olja what it was like to live in Bosnia's Republika Srpska. She said, "I hate being in Bosnia. I'm not Bosnian. I'm Serbian."

I said, "When you go to Belgrade, do people notice that you have an accent?"

"Yes."

"How about Bosnians? Do each of the three ethnic groups have a unique accent?"

"No, not really. We all talk the same."

It's ironic that she felt so Serbian, even though, linguistically, she had more in common with Bosniaks. She unwrapped a sandwich in aluminum foil and started eating. Then, demonstrating Bosnian Serb hospitality, handed me one of her sandwiches. Upon crossing the border and entering Gradiška, about 20 college students packed tightly into the bus. I asked Olja how Serb-Bosniak relations were. She said, "Not good. We still fight all the time."

Suddenly a woman's voice behind us said, "That's not true."

Olja and I turned around and greeted Mirsada, an attractive Bosniak student with dark hair and dark eyes. Mirsada continued, "It's not true that relations with Serbs are bad. I'm a Muslim and I have plenty of Serb friends. I don't feel discriminated."

Olja stared straight ahead and rolled her eyes. Mirsada added, "Bosnians look the same. We make a big deal about our differences, but the differences are rather small. I lived in Germany for many years. The difference between the Turks and Germans is much bigger than the Bosniaks and Serbians, but Germans treat Turks more fairly and evenly than Bosniaks and Serbians treat each other."

Eventually, Olja and Mirsada expressed their points of view and Olja warmed up to Mirsada, at least superficially. They were both studying law. Perhaps someday they will find each other on opposite sides of a courtroom and they'll have a real fight.

Narcissism of minor differences

Mirsada's comment reminded me of what Sigmund Freud said in *Civilization and its Discontents.* He wrote that there are "communities with adjoining territories, and related to each other in other ways as well, who are engaged in constant feuds and in ridiculing each other—like the Spaniards and Portuguese, for instance, Germans and South Germans, the English and the Scotch, and so on. I gave this phenomenon the name of 'the narcissism of minor differences.'"

Although Freud didn't name Balkanians, their "narcissism of minor differences" is more extreme than in the communities that Freud mentions. As Vlad told me, "We're the same people. We're just making excuses to fight each other."

For example, some Serbs would lecture me about the significant difference between the *č* and *ć* letters, as in the word *ćevapčići.* To most humans, both letters sound like *ch.* Thanks to Marija, a Serbian language teacher in Novi Sad, I managed to produce the two sounds correctly. She said that while it's a uniquely Serbian linguistic trait, some Serbian regions don't bother making an audible distinction between the two letters. She laughs that Serbs make a big deal about this nearly unnoticeable feature. She said, "In the Balkans, we live under a magnifying glass. Every little thing, we blow out of proportion. We examine it and make a big deal about things that most of the world would never notice or care about."

Balkanians are like twin brothers who endlessly debate who is the oldest. Indeed, nationalism is a form of group narcissism. In the

Balkans, nationalism reaches preposterous heights. As Karl Popper said, "Communism has been replaced by this ridiculous nationalism. I say ridiculous, because it sets against each other peoples who are virtually all Slav."[6]

After seeing the Balkan narcissism, you can understand why Tito has such a god-like status among ex-Yugoslavs. Only a god could bring these people together and keep them together for over 40 years.

Couchsurfing with Bosnian Serbs in Banja Luka

A cold March air entered our bus when it opened its doors in Banja Luka. It was dark and there were patches of snow on the ground. I eventually found the apartment of my 25-year-old couchsurfing host, Predrag Borojević. Most couchsurfing hosts have a bit of hippie philosophy in them: give freely and good things will happen to you. Predrag not only had this attitude, but had an enormous mass of hippie-like curly hair to go along with it. Predrag was skinny despite his best efforts to eat as much food as possible. His roommate, Rajko Stijaković, was a friendly, tall volleyball player. His Croatian girlfriend, Jelena Bucalo, was also visiting. We talked for hours and their basic message was, "We're tired of all the political bullshit. We hold no prejudice against anyone. We just want to get along and move along."

Predrag and his friends represent the hopeful side of the Balkans. Youth likes to rebel, and they demonstrate that spirit by rejecting their parents' petty nationalism and obsession with the past. These young Balkanians, who exist in every ethnic group, are fed up with the old, small-minded generation that harbors grudges and wants to settle old scores. This new generation looks forward and wants to focus on the future. Predrag says, "Yeah, I'm a Serb, but I don't like labels. I'm not Orthodox. I'm agnostic. I don't care about religion."

However, within Predrag's generation, there are others that I've met who recycle their parents' beliefs and myths. Like parrots, they make the same shortsighted points that cranky old Balkanian farts argue. The future of the Balkans will be a tug-of-war between these two tribes.

The we-fought-because-of-religion myth

Predrag and I talked about what role the three Balkan religions played in the Yugoslav Wars. He agreed that many blame religious differences for causing the trouble. That sounds like a reasonable conclusion because, as we noted, there is no other obvious difference between the three groups. So religions must be guilty, right?

Wrong. After WWII, religion in Yugoslavia became less important. In 1964, for example, belief in a religion sank to 70%. By 1984, it was just 25%. The most religious republic was Croatia, but just a third were religious. After Yugoslavia broke up, Slovenia was the only republic that blamed religion or ethnic differences for the rise of nationalism. Instead, most blamed the lack of modernization.[7] Most Balkanians don't care about your religious practices. When asked if their area is a good place for religious minorities to live, 78% of Serbians (and Macedonians) said *yes*. In fact, everywhere in the ex-Yugoslavia was above 70%, except for Slovenia (56%).

This doesn't mean religions are irrelevant. Professor Neil Mitchell told me, "We were in Serbia when the patriarch of the Serbian Orthodox Church died. Hundreds of thousands lined the Belgrade streets for the funeral procession. The city came to a halt. Although few go to church regularly, the Serbian Orthodox Church is in the soul of Serbia. It embodies the nationalism that is both a curse and a benefit to Serbia."

A Croatian agnostic, Toni Bralić, told me, "In Croatia, when we have sexual education, they call priests. Religion is taught in school. The media will often invite the Catholic church in TV debates."

Meanwhile, Armin, a young Muslim, believed that 40 percent of Bosniaks pray five times per day, as the Koran instructs. He also guessed that about 15 percent are virgins before they get married. Other Bosniaks felt these estimates were way too high. Armin emphasized that the mujahedin's way of practicing Islam is "quite the opposite way of our way of practicing Islam. They are converting people, growing big beards, and have six to 10 children." In short, most Balkanians may claim to be religious, but few practice it or profoundly care about it.

Balkanians claim that religion is important, but they act differently. When asked if "religion plays an important part in your daily life," here are the percentage of people saying *yes* in each country: Kosovo 89%, Macedonia 76%, Croatia 68%, Montenegro and Bosnia 60%, Serbia 53%, and Albania 43%. However, when asked if they "had attended a place of worship or a religious service in the past week," only about a third of Balkanians said *yes*. They're all talk, no action.[8]

People in the Balkans are much more likely to partake in religious rituals when they're in the ethnic minority. For example, only 20% of Serbians attended a religious service in the previous week, but in Kosovo (where Serbs are about 10% of the population) 45% of Serbs said they had. Similarly, in Bosnia (where Serbs are a minority) 40% of Bosnians Serbs went to church regularly. Likewise, in Albanian minority areas in Macedonia 52% went to a religious service, but in Albania only 17% went. In short, in areas where people are a minority, they seem to use religious services as a way to band together and keep their communities strong. If Balkanians feel secure (because they're in the majority), then their religious attendance plummets.

In conclusion, Balkanians mostly treat religion like a social club, a flag, or a symbol, but not as a code for behavior. It's just their way of asking, "Are you with us or with them?" During the Yugoslav Wars, religions served as a useful mascot. Vlad summarized the Balkan war mentality, "If nationalism doesn't work, we'll use religion. Religion makes it easy to recruit. We say, 'Hey, they're Catholics. Let's fight them.'"

Mirjana, a Serbian who teaches English in Niš and is married to a Greek man, told me, "Greeks are more connected to the church than Serbians. Niš has four churches. The same sized city in Greece would have 25 churches. Also, Greeks go to church every Sunday. Serbs don't."

Čedomil Mijatović, a respected Serbian historian and diplomat, wrote in 1911 something that is still perfectly true 100 years later not just for Serbians, but for all Balkanians: "The religious sentiment of the Serbians is neither deep nor warm. Their churches are generally empty, except on very great Church festivals, and on political festivals. The Serbians of our day consider the Church as a political institution, in some mysterious manner connected with the existence of the nation. They do not allow anyone to attack her, nor to compromise her, although, when she is not attacked, they neglect her."[9]

The seven reasons why Yugoslavia broke up

Ever since the Slovenia chapter, we've been trying to understand why Yugoslavia broke up. Along the way, we've proven that some theories are unconvincing. For example, we've shown how Slovenia's all-the-money-was-going-to-Belgrade excuse is weak. We've debunked the America-did-it theory in the Serbia chapter. And we just saw that religion played only a minor role. Should we blame the Balkan media? No way, say most ex-Yugoslavs. According to Gallup, only Bosnia and Macedonia had majorities who blamed the media for fueling their desire to kick their neighbor's ass. The five other Balkan countries overwhelmingly disagreed with this idea.

> *We will never be able to agree on what caused the war.*
> *— Drago Kovačević*[10]

When you ask people why Yugoslavia broke up, they often give you just one reason. A Croatian may blame Milošević. A Serb may blame Tuđman. A Bosnian may blame the unequal distribution of wealth. Americans may blame Germany for recognizing Slovenia's and Croatia's independence too quickly. Neven Borak, Slovenia's foremost economic historian, told me, "Perhaps the strongest factor of the breakup was the disintegration of the USSR." That's true, but that doesn't explain why Yugoslavia broke up violently while other multi-ethnic communist countries stayed together or, in the case of Czechoslovakia, broke up peacefully.

In my opinion, there are seven factors that caused Yugoslavia's violent demise (in order of importance):

1. **Failure to quickly abandon communism.** It's the economy, stupid. When Yugoslavia's economy was doing well, the country was united and ethnic tensions were minimal. However, in 1989, when the rest of Eastern Europe was ditching communism, Yugoslavia focused on silly issues (see #3). Had they concentrated on quickly transitioning their economy, they would have survived like other multi-ethnic countries did (e.g., Romania, Estonia, and Latvia). Thanks to Yugoslavia's more open version of communism, they had a head-start over other Eastern Europeans. The tragedy is that they blew their lead and went backwards.
2. **The collapse of communism throughout Europe.** Once the USSR and Eastern Bloc disintegrated, Yugoslavia's strategic raison d'être was gone. Its dual income stream evaporated. The senseless communist system was exposed.
3. **Narcissism of minor differences.** Many Eastern European countries have ethnic minorities that have greater differences than those in Yugoslavia. However, Yugoslavs emphasized and exaggerated the few differences that existed between themselves. Had they not done that, they would not have broken up.
4. **Passionate, violent, and nationalistic minorities on all sides.** When things go wrong, people love to blame their leaders, not themselves. However, a chauvinistic and belligerent leader won't rise to power if he doesn't have a nationalistic population to support him. Every country has baby Hitlers spouting xenophobic and evil ideas all the time. You can find plenty on YouTube. To actually take power, these budding Hitlers need at least a strong minority of the population behind him and, in order to rise high enough, the majority of the population. Yugoslavia had that critical mass of nutters. Yugoslavs must bear some responsibility for their country's downfall.
5. **Inflexible leaders.** Milošević, Tuđman, Alija Izetbegović (Bosnia's leader), and many other Balkan leaders were stupidly stubborn. If they had been more flexible and more willing to compromise, Yugoslavia would still be united today.
6. **Victimism.** Balkanians are obsessed with historical myths. They remind themselves of all the (real and imagined) injustices that their people have suffered over the ages. This provides the moral justification to seek violent revenge.
7. **Religion.** Although we shouldn't overestimate the role of religions,

they did provide a useful rallying cry. Religions weaved victimism-filled stories along with images of martyrdom to motivate the masses.

When a Kosovo TV interviewer asked Serbian peacemaker Ivan Vejvoda why Yugoslavia broke up, Vejvoda summarized the first two reasons well, "Yugoslavia had a privileged position, but then [after the fall of the USSR] it didn't. It was an in-between country and suddenly was not an in-between country. Its main flaw was that it was a communist country. No political freedoms. There was no freedom of speech. No freedom of association. And that is what broke the back of that country."

The numbers are revealing. In the 1950s, most of Yugoslavia's trade was with Western countries. By 1980, it accounted for less than half their trade. Meanwhile, trade with the USSR went from practically no trade in 1950s to over 20% of their exports in 1980.[11] That exposure stung when the USSR collapsed. Before that, debt doubled in just four years (1968–1972). Debt doubled again in the next four years. Real income dropped 25% from 1983 to 1988. About 60% who were under 25 years old were unemployed. That didn't let them trim the fat that many mismanaged monopolies had. Strikes didn't help productivity either. Still, all Eastern European economies suffered similar meltdowns. What made Yugoslavia tip towards violence were the last five reasons. We can debate the order of importance of the seven reasons, but they explain, once and for all, why Yugoslavia blew up.

Dražen in the tourist office of Banja Luka

I walked around Banja Luka, which is the Republika Srpska capital and has 300,000 inhabitants. The main pedestrian drag, *Gospodska ulica,* is a standard European people-friendly street. A bit more interesting is the Fortress Kastel, which is a five-minute walk from the center. Although the Fortress is dead during the winter, the summertime sees plenty of concerts and events. Imagine how surprised medieval rulers would be if they knew how we use their military forts today.

Bosnia isn't a top European tourist destination, so I went into Banja Luka's tourist office to hear if they think it should be. Dražen, a Serb who spoke excellent English, gave me a welcoming smile when he learned that I was from America. He invited me to sit down on the couch and have some tea—it's classic Bosnian hospitality, he explained. Although Sarajevo and Mostar are special, he said that many tourists miss out on Bosnia's natural wonders. For example, you can kayak or canoe down the Vrbas River, which runs right through Banja Luka. You can ride horses near the Lisina mountain, or across the pastures and meadows near Rogatica. Or visit Jahorina, the site of the 1984 Winter Olympics. Soak in Banja Vrućica, Bosnia's biggest hot spring, in Teslić. Its spa complex has 1,000 beds, a bowling alley, saunas, and a variety of courts for most sports. Because it hasn't had a major renovation for decades, the prices are reasonable and it's a great way to return to the 1970s.

Bosnians believe hot springs have magical healing properties. For example, in Kiseljak, where there are nine springs, a grandmother named Dunja maintains the grounds. According to her, the nine springs each have a specific healing property: this one for high blood pressure, that one for diabetes, this one for the heart, that one for the nervous system, and so on. Dražen said that some have reported that after spending six days drinking the water from the *Banja Dvorovi* (Dvorovi Bath/Spa), their kidney stones vanished. Never mind that kidney stones often go away on their own without a magic potion.

After talking for 30 minutes, I asked Dražen how relations were between Serbs and the other Bosnians. Dražen said, "They're OK. It's strange to visit Sarajevo now. Serbs are gone. The Serb heart isn't behind this country. In sport matches, Bosnian Serbs always cheer for Serbia's team, even when they're playing against Bosnia."

Who started the war?

It's the most popular and futile question in the Balkans. I never found any consensus. A funny scene in the film *No Man's Land* sums it up. A Bosnian Serb points his gun at his Bosniak prisoner and demands, "Who started the war?" The Bosniak insincerely says that the Bosniaks started the war. Later, after a scuffle, the Bosniak gets the gun and asks the Serb the same question, "Who started the war?!" Now the humble Serb mumbles, "We did."

Trying to determine who fired the first shot in the Yugoslav Wars is like trying to answer, "Who was the first person killed in the Arab-Israel conflict?" Some shrug it off saying that it's all about "ancient hatreds." Richard Holbrooke, who led the Balkans to the Dayton Peace Accords, admitted that the term "ancient hatreds" was a "vague but useful term for history too complicated (or trivial) for outsiders to master" making it "impossible (or pointless) for anyone outside the region to try and prevent the conflict."

What is clear is that Milošević and Tuđman, the leaders of Yugoslavia's two biggest tribes, conspired to divide Bosnia between themselves. A year later, Serb forces controlled 70 percent of Bosnia. Today, Serbs control 49 percent. How that happened is the story of the Bosnian War.

The Bosnian War in two minutes

Before the war, Bosnia was an ethnic mess—and that's why it was lovely. Bosniaks, Serbs, and Croatians lived side by side throughout the land. It was rare that an ethnic group dominated an area, and when they did, it was a relatively small area. Bosnia was the perfect melting pot.

When Slovenia and Croatia declared independence, Bosnians had to decide what to do: declare independence, go with Croatia, or go with a Serb-dominated Yugoslavia. Without Croatia and Slovenia, Yugoslavia's demographics shifted from roughly 40 percent Serb to nearly 70 percent Serb. Bosnians Serbs naturally preferred sticking with the Serb-led Yugoslavia. However, Bosniaks didn't feel comfortable in that situation and wanted complete independence. Meanwhile, Bosnian Croatians didn't like either option and preferred joining Croatia. Suddenly, the lovely ethnic mess became an ugly ethnic mess. The Balkanian saying *ko će kome pomoci ako ne svoj svome* (who else can you help but your own) became *ko će kome uvalit ako ne svoj svome* (who else would screw you but your own).

For the next three-and-a-half years, the three ethnic groups fought to conquer as much land as possible. This involved ethnic cleansing: harassing the groups you don't like, raping them, forcing them to flee, burning their houses, and, if none of that worked, killing them. All three ethnic groups did this to each other. They all succeeded. That's why Bosnia's ethnographic map now looks "clean": Serbs in the Republika Srpska, Croatians in south, and Bosniaks everywhere else. The other result: about 150,000 dead and a dysfunctional state where everyone says that life was better before the war.

> *As has so often happened in the history of man, permission was tacitly granted for acts of violence and plunder, even for murder, if they were carried out in the name of higher interests, according to established rules, and against a limited number of a particular type and belief.*
> — *Ivo Andrić,* The Bridge on the Drina[12]

Ethnically clean, but a politically messy

After a country-wide game of musical chairs and a severe NATO bombing campaign, the three hotheaded adolescents were ready to behave like adults. They went to Dayton, Ohio for 17 days to negotiate a peace agreement. The best moment was when US Ambassador Holbrooke was negotiating with Milošević and Momir Bulatović (Montenegro's President) on how to split up Bosnia's territory. Using a tool that resembles the satellite images you see on Google Maps (10 years before the rest of the world could use it for free), Holbrooke remarked after zooming in on a large piece of land, "There is nothing there. Just mountains. There are no houses, no villages."

To reassure Holbrooke that he was using the right maps, Bulatović said, "That's right, but that is Bosnia."

Holbrooke put his head in his hands and said, "This is going to ruin my marriage, ruin my life. Look at what you're fighting for. There's nothing there."[13]

And that, folks, is your summary of the Bosnian War. Indeed, only eight percent of Bosnia is below 150 meters (500 ft), so there are hills and mountains everywhere you look. Green rivers slice through the mountains in all directions, although most merge with the Sava River to the north, a Danube tributary. It's a pretty, but sparsely populated country. And it's remarkable how many died for it.

> *Ask a Bosnian about politics and he will reply, "I am in three minds about that." — Bosnian joke*

The Dayton Accords produced a puzzling political system. It would have been cleaner to simply sell the Republika Srpska (RS) portion to the nation of Serbia for a reasonable price. If the Bosnian Serbs don't want to be part of Bosnia, why force them? Another clean solution would have been to not create the RS and just say, "Sorry, but Bosnia is just one nation and you guys will just have to learn how to get along. You've done it for hundreds of years, so dust off your history books and figure out how your ancestors used to do it."

Instead, Bosnia's redundant and bureaucratic government makes the Soviet government seem more efficient than a Swiss train. Government expenditures are nearly half the GDP. What's worse is that all those layers of government are irrelevant because the Office of High Representative (OHR) has near absolute power. The EU appoints the High Representative to make sure Bosnia's politicians behave.

> *The Dayton constitution is not perfect; it was written in three weeks in an airport.*
> *— Valentin Inzko, High Representative for Bosnia*

On the one hand, the OHR seems necessary: according to Gallup's 2010 poll, nine out of 10 Bosnians believe their national politicians are either "some obstacle" or an "important obstacle" to more regional cooperation. On the other hand, only 15 percent of Bosnians Serbs and 55 percent of those in the Federation believe Bosnia needs the OHR for the country to function. Serbs want more autonomy, while Bosniaks want more centralization and unity. Of course, nothing will happen until the OHR (and the EU) believes that Bosnians can behave without adult supervision.

Going from Banja Luka to Doboj

It was special staying with Predrag for three days because I got to meet his roommates and friends. All the Bosnian Serbs I met were supremely friendly and welcoming. Now I wanted to see the Bosniak point of view. Predrag suggested going to Doboj and then to Tuzla. We said our goodbyes and I took off to Doboj.

Doboj's highlight is the Gradin, a thirteenth-century fortress that's loaded with medieval weapons and overlooks the Bosna River. Doboj is on the Republika Srpska border, yet has the Selimija Mosque and the *Bejt Šalom,* a Jewish house. It's a simple town and I was eager to get to Tuzla, so I took the only seat available on the next bus. Luckily, my neighbor was a 20-year-old guy who was getting a degree in English. His name was Armin Šuvalić and he was going to the University of Tuzla. He was reading W. Du Bois and a variety of English literature that I ignored as a teenager. Just for fun, I asked him who started the war. He said, "Probably a third of Bosniaks believe that America started the war."

"Of course we did," I said with a wry smile. I continued, "You were about five years old when the war broke out. What do you remember?"

He said, "When the Serbs invaded, I was playing outside. Suddenly, I sensed something was wrong. I could see the troops moving in. We ran across the field and I actually saw a bullet fly by. I saw it! When we got into the house, I felt safer, but a bullet flew through the window and hit a wall."

"Did anyone in your family die?"

"No, but in one of my classes during middle school, the teacher asked the kids to raise their hand if they had lost at least one family member during the war. One in five kids raised their hands."

"Speaking of school, do you have a national history book?"

He chuckled, "About 10 years ago, the government tried to make one national history book, but it was impossible. Nobody could agree on one truth. So each ethnic group has its own history book."

A 2010 Balkan Monitor survey showed that nearly two-thirds of Bosniaks believe that a common history book is worth doing to help "preserve peace and facilitate development." Only about one-third of other Balkanians agreed. History repeats itself. In the 1950s, Yugoslav historians started writing an ambitious four-volume book, *A History of the Nations of Yugoslavia.* Things went fine until they got to the third and fourth volumes, which dealt with the nineteenth and twentieth centuries. It was impossible for the historians to agree on what really happened. Those volumes were never written. Sadly, each ethnic group is incapable of objectively examining its history. It's the Balkan curse.

Listening to Bosniak students in Tuzla

When we arrived in Tuzla, Armin invited me to attend his English class and to meet his professor from Minnesota. The American Corner funds a cross-cultural operation and the university is happy to offer their students American teachers. The professor kindly gave me 20 minutes to interact with her 25 students, most of whom were Bosniaks. Tuzla (and Brčko) are ethnic bright spots in Bosnia, where ethnic groups get along like in the old days. I said to the students, "Even though you haven't been to America, what do you think Bosnians can teach Americans?"

"Hospitality," said one.

Another added, "Yeah, we are welcoming people. Also, when we have a barbeque, it can last for 12 hours! People here spend a lot of time with their friends. But definitely hospitality is our greatest strength."

Suddenly, a student walked into the class late. She had not heard anything and took the only available seat, which was right next to me. Before she could get settled, I asked her, "So what do you think Bosnians can teach Americans?"

She looked at me as if I had commented on her bra. Then she blurted out, "Hospitality."

The class laughed. It's not that Bosnians think that Americans are not hospitable; it's just that they think that Bosnians excel in hospitality. When I asked Rajko what Bosnia's advantage was, he said, "We're social and friendly." Bosnians are indeed quite warm and welcoming. At the same time, this is a common trait throughout the Balkans. Thus, I'm not sure if I'd put Bosnia far above Serbia, Montenegro, Albania, and Macedonia on that issue. What's obvious to me is that the Southern Balkans is Europe's most hospitable and friendliest corner.

The reverse sign-on bonus

Tuzla is a pleasant town with a cute pedestrian-only district. Along the way I met Huseljić Mirza, a young man who spoke English well and was happy to chat. I asked him what life was really like in Bosnia. He said, "We have a corrupted society. Even our schools are corrupt."

"How so?" I asked.

"Professors advise you to buy the books that they wrote. They make money from the sales."

"What if you don't buy their book?"

"Then you won't get a good grade."

"Are the books any good?"

"No, they're usually shitty."

"How about life outside of school?"

"It's worse. During a job interview, people will ask you irrelevant questions. For example, they will ask you what soccer teams you like and what kind of food you like to eat. The people who get the job are the ones who are willing to pay $3,000 for it."

"What? You have to *pay* someone to get a job?"

"Sure. All the time. Look at me. I'm getting a degree in psychology, but there is almost no chance that I get a job without paying at least $8,000 for it."

"That's insane! In America, some employers give you an $8,000 sign-on bonus. Here, it's the reverse! Who gets to keep the money?"

"Usually your future boss, but sometimes it goes to someone higher than him. It's hard because the unemployment rate is 40 percent. We have a saying, 'I've got a PhD, an MBA, a JD, and an MD, but I ain't got a J-O-B.'"

Unfortunately, this perverse practice happens throughout the Southern Balkans. For example, in Serbia, I learned that about half of the Serbians pay $5,000 to $15,000 for a job. This habit is most pervasive in southern Serbia. In 2011, $10 per hour is a good wage, so you'll have to pay $10,000 to get such a job. To be a doctor, you have to pay up to $15,000. If you get laid off because of a bad economy, you'll never get your money back.

These bribes are enormous given the pay level. It's hard enough to survive on $5 per hour in Bosnia. Few Bosnians have thousands of dollars in the bank, so they must get a loan to pay the bribe. While they pay back the loan with their meager salary, they hope that they have enough to pay for food and shelter too. This explains why most kids live with their parents until they're old enough to charge the next generation bribes.

Bribes thrive

It's not clear why some Bosnians don't use that bribe money to start up a business. Some suggested that starting a business often involves more bribes. Others simply blamed the lack of entrepreneurial spirit in Bosnia. Rajko told me, "Communism screwed us. People don't think. They look to the government to solve all their problems, instead of doing it themselves."

Some say the bribe culture became popular after Yugoslavia's demise, as desperate people were looking for ways to make money. In Niš, Ana Milovanović teaches middle school, works three hours per day, 180 days a year, and makes $500 per week. That's good money in Niš. To get this kind of job, she said, you would have had to pay about $7,500. She didn't because she had a connection. That reminds me of the 1986 Serbian Memorandum, which said, "Nepotism is universal, and the favoring of relatives when hiring is done has virtually gained the force of customary law."

Thus, it seems that the bribing habit is old. Ana Sinik, a Serbian, told me, "You still have to bribe doctors around $200 to get good treatment. It's expected. If you don't do it, then you don't know how well they will treat you or if you will get the drugs you need. The police is also corrupt. One policeman pulled me over and said, "The fine is $75. Isn't $75 too much for you?"

In 2010, most Bosnians told the Balkan Monitor that organized crime affects them either "occasionally" or "every day," while 90 percent agreed that "organized crime is widespread." This explains why only 36 percent of Bosnians were satisfied with their "freedom to choose what they did with their lives." All these responses were the most worst in Europe.

The outsider's perspective

Andrej Hrabar, a 33-year-old Slovenian, was working in a processing pellet production plant in Nova Bila, near Travnik. In 2010, he told me, "Nobody cares about Bosnia. It's always been ruled by the outside, even today. The government is too big, too hungry for cash, and too dependent on outside help. We have a factory, but basically there is no industry."

"Are there still ethnic tensions?"

"Yes. The Balkans is highly flammable. Nobody can understand the people and the culture. When I was interviewing Croatians for a job, they said to me, 'I'd rather not have a job than work for a Muslim.'"

Andrej said that some might even make a big deal about the three slightly different ways to say *coffee*: *kahva* (Bosnian); *kafa* (Serbian); *kava* (Croatian). Over 99 percent of words are identical in all the Bosnian dialects. The industrious Slovenian concluded, "Bosnians know everything, everyone, but when you want them to *do* something, they won't *do* anything."

When I visited Belgrade, I met Raquel Caquillos, a 30-year-old Spanish teacher. When she was an adventurous 23-year-old, she moved to Lake Bikal in Siberia to teach Spanish, even though she didn't speak any Russian. After four long, cold winters, she spent two years teaching in Moscow. Finally, she moved to Belgrade. By now her parents are used to having their daughter go to "strange Slavic places."

When I asked her what Balkanians are like and what we can learn from them, she said, "People here are the way they are because they are at that stage of economic development. They don't get married early and don't have kids because they're Serbs, but because economically they are where Spain was 20 years ago. In Spain, 20 years ago, we didn't care about seat belts, or obsess about the dangers of foods, or care where our kids played outside, or believe in defending the rights of minorities, women, or gays. The Balkans is the way it is not because they are intrinsically that way, but because that's where they in their level of economic development. As their economy matures, their beliefs and values will change and be more like ours."

I said, "So is there nothing they can teach us?"

"Yes, there are," she said, "But they are lessons from our past. Balkanians live life today the way the West used to live over 20 years ago. They are good lessons, but I'm not sure if we can really follow them without going backwards in other ways. A society's values and behavior are too tightly linked with their economic development. It's hard to separate the two."

I mention this conversation because it's related to a conversation I had with a 28-year-old Bosniak named Dino. He was sitting at the back of a nearly empty bus that was going from Tuzla to Bijeljina. Usually the most fun and social people are at the back of the bus, so I asked him what percentage of Bosniak women are virgins. This question is one way to measure how strictly a society adheres to its religious beliefs (since most religions prohibit premarital sex). He said, "About 60 percent of women are virgins in their early 20s, but by the time they get married, perhaps only 30 percent are virgins."

I suspect that you'd have to go back to the America of the 1950s to find a similar percentage. That's a bit more than 20 years ago, but Raquel did say "over 20 years ago." I asked Dino, "So how does it work for a single guy like you?"

He said, "It's tough when you're trying to, you know, get sex. Once you realize that you're dating a girl who is saving her virginity till marriage, then you just gotta tell her, 'Sorry, but I gotta go elsewhere for what I need.'"

A Srebrenica denier

After following the Drina River for nearly an hour, our bus arrived in Bijeljina. With little to do there, I bought my ticket out of Bosnia. I was going to Novi Sad, Serbia. I planned to return to Bosnia in six months to complete my final two wishes: visit Bosnia's northwest corner (Bihać) and stay with a Muslim family. But first, let's meet an interesting Bosnian Serb whom I met on my bus out of Bosnia.

His name was Degan. He was a 30-year-old who was wearing casual clothes with a baseball cap. He sat across from me, so I asked him if he spoke English. He said "yes," but not with the typical Bosnian friendly smile. He was a bit cold and distant. He was born and raised in Sarajevo, but now lives in Novi Sad. When I told him that I was born in San Francisco, but was half-French and half-Chilean, he snorted, "Oh. A typical American."

Degan slowly relaxed his guard. He was a painter. He showed me photos of his artwork on his laptop. Some of his commissioned paintings included the face of a Serbian military hero and an Orthodox priest. He was disappointed that I didn't recognize their faces. He closed his laptop, looked me sharply and said, "Tell me, in all honesty, what did you think of Serbians before you came here? Didn't you think we were villains or bad people? C'mon, be honest."

I said, "To be totally honest, I had absolutely no opinion of Serbians before I came to Serbia. Although I had heard about the Yugoslav Wars, I had no idea who the 'good guys' were and who the 'bad guys' were. So I came here with a blank mind, just listening to everyone's stories and opinions. It's funny. A few Serbs have asked me that same question. The reality is that most of the world doesn't know Serbia exists. So the bad news is that Serbia isn't as important as you think. The good news is that Serbs are not burdened with a negative image since most Americans have no opinion at all."

He looked at me skeptically, so finally I said, "OK, who were the good guys and the bad guys between the Hutus and Tutsis? First of all, most Serbs couldn't place those two African tribes on a map. Those who can probably can't remember who was more at fault (if anyone) in that conflict."

At last he seemed to believe me. So I asked him what it was like to be a teenager growing up in Sarajevo when the war started. He said, "I remember when my Muslim neighbor told my family to leave our home. 'Fuck you,' I thought. Leave our home? Listen, I was born here in Sarajevo. This is my home. You can't tell me I don't belong here.'"

"So did you stay?"

"No. The pressure was too strong on my parents. We had to leave. So we left my home. *My* home," he said with his voice cracking.

I said, "How was it visiting Sarajevo today?"

"I hate Sarajevo," he said. "It's not my city anymore. Have you been there? Have you seen all the mujahedin people walking everywhere, with their beards and traditional clothes? Have you seen the women, all covered up? We didn't have any of that when I was growing up there. They've changed the city. I don't feel comfortable there anymore. They took it and they can have it. I don't care. I'm in Novi Sad now. Go ahead, ruin Sarajevo. I don't give a shit about the land." He looked at me intensely and said, "Remember, *honor* is more important than the *land*."

While the bus went over Fruška Gora, Serbia's beautiful mountain range, we somehow started talking about Srebrenica. It's a town whose main attraction is the Banja Guber, which has four hot springs. You can guess what three of the magical springs supposedly do for you just by knowing their names: *Očna Voda* (Eye Water), *Sinusna Voda* (Sinus Water) and *Voda Ljepotica* (Beauty Water). The most famous spring is the *Crni Guber* (Black Guber), which has a high level of bivalent iron. This supposedly heals anemia, sclerosis, rheumatism, and other hard-to-spell words.

However, Degan and I didn't talk about the town, but about the massacre that happened there. According to most objective observers, it was the largest mass murder in Europe since WWII. Bosnian Serb forces executed about 8,000 men and boys in an event that the International Criminal Tribunal (and later the International Court of Justice) labeled a genocide. Degan said with a stone-cold face, "There was *no* killing or genocide. That's a complete lie and propaganda. Those people 'disappeared' because they *moved*, not because they were *killed*. Those are the facts."

"Where did they go?"

Degan's painter's hands were shaking with emotion, but he kept a level tone when he said, "They went to Tuzla, to Sarajevo, to Mostar, to villages. There were no killings. *That* is the truth."

A month after this conversation, Nataša Kandić, a leader of the Humanitarian Law Center in Belgrade, said, "War crimes denial is still present in Serbia. We have to do something, we have to insist on the establishment of facts, and once they are established we have to urge institutions to accept them and that will create a significant pressure on the government of Serbia to stop denying war crimes."[14]

A year later, in March 2010, Serbia's parliament narrowly passed a resolution condemning the Srebrenica massacre and regretting that Serbia didn't do more to prevent it. Today, few Serbs deny that there was mass murder in Srebrenica. Still, some reject labeling it "genocide," unless some of the mass killings of innocent Serbs is also called a genocide. As we got off the bus in Novi Sad, Degan said, "Remember this: people in the Balkans may have put down their weapons, but they did not put down their anger."

Ex-Yugoslav voices

Degan isn't the only one angry about the war's outcome. After Novi Sad, I eventually went to Višnjan, an Istrian village in Croatia. I was visiting a married couple, Zoran and Snežana, who were building their retirement home and cultivating olives, potatoes, and kiwis. They're also cultivating a distorted view of the Bosnian War.

Zoran, an agnostic Bosniak, grew up in Zenica, Bosnia. He and his best friend, a Serb, forged documents to escape the Bosnian War. The Serb pretended to be a Bosniak, while Zoran pretended to be a Croatian. To complicate matters, Zoran's 12-year-old daughter was with them. At the various checkpoints, they showed phony papers that claimed that they were organizing an important art exhibit in Slovenia. The hoax worked. Eventually, he met and married Snežana, a Slovenian. Snežana subscribed to the conspiratorial belief that "the elite is behind everything. That's why I don't read newspapers. There is no truth in them." Usually such an attitude is a guise to make one's cognitive laziness seem shrewd.

She complained that the "US stayed out of the war for three years, and then they come in near the end of the war, stopped it from finishing, and then imposed the stupid Dayton Accords."

I said, "But if the US had stayed out, wouldn't things have turn out poorly for Croatia and Bosnia?"

"No," she said, "Croatians were pushing back the Serbs before the US got involved. We were winning without NATO. We didn't need their help."

I said, "But most of Yugoslavia's weapons and military production was in Serbia. Where were the Croatians getting their weapons? From the trees?"

She struggled with that question, realizing that NATO was supplying the Croatian army and that without that support the Serbs could have crushed Croatia. Operation Storm, the successful 1995 Croatian offensive that forced the Serbs to retreat, wouldn't have happened without NATO support. Meanwhile, Serbs were begging Russia for help, but the timing was horrible: the USSR was imploding. Serbia was like a drowning man begging someone in a sinking ship for help.

Later, in Croatia, I met Stanka, a 60-year-old Serb, who lived all over Yugoslavia. She was married to a Bosnian Serb and they had a big house in Bosnia that was burned down during an ethnic cleansing operation. She wasn't angry, but she was frustrated. She hopes one day to go back, but feels that it's still too early to return. She said, "Relations are still bad even 15 years later."

Divided over the Hague

There are mixed feelings about the International Court Tribunal's impact on the region. Those who believe that it "does not serve the interest of the region and just keeps past conflicts alive" include Serbians (81%), Bosnian-Serbs (71%), Croatians and Montenegrins (57%). On the other hand, Muslims (Bosniaks and Kosovars) generally believe that the international court "helps the reconciliation and strengthens peace." Similarly, the opinion of the proceedings and verdicts is also split along the same lines with most Serbs believing that the court is a sham, while Muslims believe it's open and impartial. The same goes for Balkanians' opinion of the UN, EU, and NATO.

What's interesting is that even though Croatians won the war, they're not nearly as supportive of international organizations as are the Muslims (Bosniaks, Albanians, and Kosovars). Part of this stems from believing that the international community didn't let the Croatians have a "complete" victory—we stopped them soon after the military tide was turning. The other reason they're not so thrilled about the international community is that they've had several of their war heroes get sentenced. Just imagine that after winning WWII, Eisenhower and Churchill had to spend 30 years in prison for war crimes in Dresden.

Crossing the bridge on the Drina

On my fourth visit to Bosnia, I went with Ana Mišmaš, the Slovenian you've met in the Slovenia and Croatia chapters. We were in Montenegro and we wanted to drive cross Bosnia and finish in Bihać. The trip got off to a funny start: instead of driving to Bosnia, we accidentally drove to Serbia. The Serbian border guard laughed when we told him that we thought that we were entering Bosnia. We shrugged and camped off a dirt road near Priboj. The next day, we took advantage of our boneheaded move and visited a bridge that I had always wanted to see.

Whenever anyone gets a Nobel Prize, every group wants to claim that the winner is from their group. When Ivo Andrić won the Nobel Prize for his book *The Bridge on the Drina*, Bosnians said he's a Bosnian, because he was born in Travnik, Bosnia. "But his family was Catholic, so he's a Croatian!" say the Croatians. "Perhaps," say the Serbians, "But he lived most of his life in Belgrade and a couple of times he identified himself as a Serb."

Whatever Andrić was, he wrote an excellent book. The novel is about the birth and life of a bridge in Višegrad, as well as all the events that happened around it. The story begins when a Slav, Mehmed Pasha Sokolović, is taken to Istanbul as a boy. He returns to his hometown, Višegrad, to build a bridge with nine pillars. The story covers 500 years of history, with the bridge being the only constant. I got goose bumps when I first saw the bridge.

The Mehmed Pasha Sokolović bridge is simple, solid, and beautiful. In the center of the pedestrian bridge is the famous stone *kapia* (couch). Ana and I sat on it and I thought of what Andrić wrote: "Every human generation has its own illusions with regard to civilization; some believe that they are taking part in its upsurge, others that they are witness of its extinction. In fact, it is always both flames up and smoulders and is extinguished, according to the place and the angle of view. This generation which was now discussing philosophy, social and political questions on the *kapia* under the stars, above the waters, was richer only in illusions; in every other way it was similar to any other."[15]

Traversing Bosnia

Ever since Degan told me that Sarajevo had changed, I wanted to revisit it to see if it really had become overrun by Muslim fundamentalists. It was Ana's first visit to Sarajevo and my second after a six-year break. We spent the day watching people while eating three *bureks* each. My favorite was the spinach *burek*, while Ana's favorite was the meat-filled *burek* that's covered with sour cream. There were a few women with a shawl covering their head, but you'll find more of them in Paris or London. There was one big bearded, mujahedin-looking guy next to a mosque, but otherwise Sarajevo did not feel like Mecca.

When we left Sarajevo, Ana blasted the radio which was playing the Bosnian music that you'll hear everywhere in ex-Yugoslavia. Bosnian music is like Turkish music with lyrics from an Argentinean tango (tragic heart-breaking love songs about unrequited love). The energetic rhythm annoys me after an hour, but Bosnians love listening to it all their lives.

Bosnia's roads curve up and down the hills, occasionally following a river in a valley, before climbing over the next hill. At dusk, near Jajce, we did what we had done often on our trip: turn onto a dirt road in the middle of nowhere, park the car, and camp in the nearby woods. Nobody would bother us or our car during the night since we were on a quiet dirt road. We would leave at dawn as invisibly as the deer around us.

Staying with a Muslim family in Otoka

The next day, we drove to Otoka to spend four days with Nedžad Osmanlić, a 24-year-old Bosniak couchsurfing host. But first, we went to Bihać, a pleasant, functional city. When Ana asked a policeman for directions, he helped us and then said, "Enjoy Bosnia's clean and fresh air!" And then he added, laughing, "It's clean because all the factories are closed and nobody works!"

Like Bihać, Otoka is in Bosnia's northwest corner, near the Croatian border, on the Una River, and is dominated by Bosniaks. Nedžad's couchsurfing profile said that he was a practicing Muslim, which is one reason I wanted to stay with his family. Staying with families is ideal because you get to meet several people across different generations, thereby giving you greater insight into a culture. In Eastern Europe, people over 50 rarely speak English. It's a great way to hear their stories through the translation of their children. The older the person, the more interesting their tales.

Nedžad had square glasses, somewhat shaggy sandy blond hair, and an athletic body. His favorite hobby is parkour, which involves acrobatically jumping around in urban settings until someday you either ruin your knees or break an ankle. Nedžad introduced us to his robust father, Hasan, his warm mother, Mediha, and his pretty younger sister, Emina. The family supplements Hasan's modest military pension by raising chickens. He sells them via word-of-mouth for a premium price because people feel these homegrown chickens are healthier. I'm no farmer, but their current batch of 50 chicks didn't seem to be living the good life. They were fed a corn mix and lived in one room all their lives. Through a window, they could see an outside world that they would never walk in.

After Nedžad's third prayer of the day, we explored Otoka. We walked down to the hill, admiring the soft mountains and the spires of the town's two mosques. We went to an island that's on the Una River. We paid a guy $1 to take us to the tranquil island via a hand-cranked raft that travels along a metal cord. Once it started drizzling, we walked back home and I asked Nedžad to show us his mosque, which was a two-minute walk from his house. Otoka's imam entrusts the mosque's key to Nedžad, so that he can pray there whenever he wants. Nedžad explained that Allah values prayer done in a mosque slightly more than prayer done elsewhere. He showed me his 100-prayer beads and demonstrated how he uses them: mumbling an Arabic prayer before moving onto the next bead and repeating the process 33 times, plus one bonus incantation. He admitted that while many locals come to Friday evening services, few take Islam seriously.

The next day we went whitewater rafting on the Una. It was a class-five rapid with a 20-meter (60-foot) waterfall that we avoided by walking around it (and letting the raft fall down by itself). There was one four-meter (13-foot) drop that the guide and I did while the others waited downstream to pick up our dead bodies. The rest of the ride had a few thrilling moments, especially when we stopped to jump off two 20-meter cliffs.

A Bosniak soldier's perspective on the war

Nedžad's family invited us for dinner, where I asked them about life before and during the war. Although he's an imposing man, he has a gentle, humble attitude. He said life during Yugoslavia was simple, but good. He said, "Nobody had TV. So we had to be nice to the one guy who had one, even though it only received one channel."

I asked, "Is your son's generation better off than your generation under Yugoslavia?"

He said, "Life is better for this generation."

When I asked him who started the war, he didn't blame the usual suspects (Serbia, Croatia, or the USA). Instead, he said, "Slovenia started it. They wanted independence and were the first to really fight for it. It was easy for them because they were homogeneous."

The Bosnian War was especially complex and dangerous for Bosniaks who lived around Otoka and Bihać. Their zone was called a "Muslim pocket" because enemies surrounded them. On one side were Serbs, who hoped to swallow this Bosnian corner. On the other side were Croatians, who wanted to annex 30 percent of Bosnia, including the area around Bihać. I asked Hasan, "What was the low point of the war?"

He said, "It was when Fikret Abdic, a popular Bosnian leader near Bihać, betrayed us. The traitor agreed to join the Serbs in exchange for being the governor of this region. He committed treason because he was frustrated that he wasn't elected as Bosnia's President and he had some business interests that he felt the Bosnian government threatened. That was the low point—we had three enemies. Bosniaks were killing Bosniaks."

I asked Mediha how the war touched her. She said the hardest part was when she was walking into her house and a sniper shot her. The bullet sliced part of her neck off. She showed me where she collapsed next to the entrance to her house. Her young children and her husband ran to help her.

Hasan also brushed with death. He was the army captain in charge of clearing mines. Of the 30 men in his company, two died and several were injured by mines. After one mine clearing operation, his men told him that the path was clear. Displaying confidence in his men, he was the first to walk down it. He barely heard the *click* sound when he stepped on a mine. He was lucky to have only stepped on the edge of the mine, so that only a small part of his foot was blown off.

Although Nedžad's parents aren't serious Muslims, Hasan encouraged his son to study Islam. He's delighted that Nedžad is devoted to the religion. I asked Nedžad if he could marry a non-Muslim. He said, "No. Islam is too important in my life. It's hard to find the right girl. Many Bosnians say they're Muslims, but only 10 percent of them are serious."

Emina is one of the 90 percent who is Muslim only in name. She would not want to date a serious Muslim. She also said that she had nothing against Croatians and Serbians. So I asked her if she could ever marry a Serb. "Oh no," she said. "I could never do that to my dad."

The next morning we hugged everyone goodbye, except Nedžad. He would be coming with us to Croatia's Plitvice National Park. He had never been there and had no camping experience. Using satellite maps, I determined a backdoor entrance into the park. We would just have to walk 10 kilometers (6.2 miles). We got to enjoy the magical park after closing time. I gave Nedžad my sleeping bag; Ana and I shared her sleeping bag by opening it completely and using it like a blanket.

After sunset, Nedžad found a private place in the woods to pray. He said that when a Muslim travels, you have an option to use an express version of the ritualistic prayers. At dawn, he prayed again, and then we spent the rest of the day exploring the magnificent park. We drove him to the Bosnia border, where we had to turn around and go back to Slovenia. He would be hitchhiking the rest of the way home. Nedžad had been the perfect host. With sadness, we waved goodbye to him and to Bosnia.

Bosnia's future

When I stayed with Predrag and Rajko in Banja Luka, I asked them if they were optimistic about Bosnia's future. Predrag said, "A little. I just wish we could bring a more professional attitude in Bosnia. To take pride in being punctual, organized, and clean. Everything is always such a disorganized mess here. Customer service is terrible."

I told him, "Be careful what you wish for. When I visited Chile as a child, it was a laid-back society like Bosnia is today. However, once they adopted free-market policies and capitalist spirit, they became more professional, but they also became less fun and easy-going."

Rajko laughed and said, "I'd rather be poor, but happy."

Bosnia's future is uncertain. In 2011, Bosnians were happy that they could now travel to the EU without a visa. Fortunately, only one in 10 thought that "armed conflict" would erupt before 2015. If all goes well, Bosnia will join the EU in this decade. On the other hand, a 2010 poll indicated that four in 10 Bosnians believed their country would fall apart.

Part of the gloom comes from loose ends. The Balkan Humanitarian Law Center noted, "Even 14 years after the armed conflicts in Croatia and Bosnia and Herzegovina and ten years since the end of the conflict in Kosovo, victims have not yet been named and recognized, and only a small number of the perpetrators have faced justice."[16] Although the quest for justice is important, it also stalls progress. Indeed, the Balkanian obsession with history imprisons them.

> *Rule Number One: no history lectures, no bullshit.*
> *— US Ambassador Richard Holbrooke told Milošević at the start of the Dayton Peace Conference*

Bosnia is one of the most fascinating countries in Eastern Europe. It's a place of hope because it's where Catholics, Orthodox Christians, Muslims, and Jews all peacefully co-existed for centuries. It's also a place of horror because it has shown what happens when people focus on their differences rather than on their commonalities. Had I written this book 30 years ago, I would have said that Bosnia can teach us how to co-exist with a diverse peoples. They were an exemplary multi-ethnic state. However, in 2009, Sudbin Music, a member of the Association of Prijedor concentration camp prisoners, said, "Unfortunately, Bosnia and Herzegovina is still very deeply divided."[17] Joining EU will accelerate the healing. When faced with the vast differences among EU countries, the petty Balkan narcissism will fade.

How Americans and Bosnians are different

When I asked Jasminka, a Bosniak in Tuzla, how Americans are different from Bosnians, she wrote back, "First, Bosnians have a more laid-back attitude towards life, this might look as if Bosnians are too relaxed, but it is something that Americans might learn to be. Second, the attitude towards food is very much different, due to the fact that Bosnians are not that interested in the quantity of food they consume and they are not as calorie conscious as Americans, which probably results in the fact that the percent of obese people in Bosnia is lower than in America. Third, Bosnians are less self-centered and they always worry about other people's problems; this is also something that the Americans might learn from the Bosnians."

I challenged Armin Šuvalić to write me an email that summarizes what he thinks Bosnains can teach Americans. He proved his command over the English language when he replied, "Americans need to see the spirit of enjoying the simple things, and seeing the world with different eyes. . . . Something that Bosnians can be proud of is this blend of different cultures, different religions, and different ethnicities. It is the trinity of everything in the country, starting from the three Presidents to the lowest levels. Three different cultures share the same place, and live with each other without being burdened because his neighbor is different. . . . The truth is that no matter how small, and no matter how far and unimportant the country is from the European and world integration unions, people of this country will always know how to enjoy their lives. They will know how to share the last penny to make others comfortable, and to make them their guests. They will always know how to make their atmosphere positive, and how to make themselves to enjoy the time spent together. They will always know how to help one another, and finally no matter how painful or how bad situation is these people will always know how to smile. These things are something that Americans should take as something that Bosnians have, and something that is incorporated into their identity, and as such it can only be a positive marker of the nation, but also to serve others as an example how to behave and how to enjoy their lives."

What Bosnia and Herzegovina Can Teach Us

- **Hospitality.** Bosnians have humble means, but they have abundant hearts. Open your house to strangers, invite strangers to parties, and roll out the red carpet for your guests.
- **Being joyful no matter what.** By nearly all economic measures, Slovenia, Croatia, and Serbia are doing better than Bosnia. And yet when you ask ex-Yugoslavs who is happiest, most would say the Bosnians. Train yourself to enjoy the simple things in life and to derive happiness from it.

Places I saw and recommend in Bosnia and Herzegovina: Sarajevo, southern mountains around Herzegovina.

Travel deals and info: http://ftapon.com/bosnia

Congratulations. You've graduated. If you've managed to understand 10 percent of the last three chapters (Croatia, Serbia, and Bosnia), then you can understand plasma physics. In addition, you'll find the rest of this book less confusing. For those who skipped to here and just want a five-word summary, then it would be: Bosnia is a simple enigma.

> *The trouble about man is twofold. He cannot learn truths which are too complicated; he forgets truths which are too simple.*
> *— Rebecca West, who traveled throughout Yugoslavia in the 1930s*

Whenever anyone asks me, "If you could live anywhere in Eastern Europe, where would you live?"

I always answer, "Montenegro."

Let's find out why.

15
MONTENEGRO—THE SMALL COUNTRY THAT HAS IT ALL

THE HIGHEST COMPLIMENT YOU can give a place is to say, "I want to buy a house here." It's more meaningful than saying "I want to live here," because buying a house is a deeper commitment than renting. These were my thoughts as I walked through the romantic streets of Kotor, Montenegro.

Montenegro is smaller than Connecticut, but it has Alpine scenery, deep canyons, coastal fjords, old Venetian-style towns, and a sparsely vegetated, limestone mountain range that plummets into the azure Adriatic Sea. Montenegro has it all. But it was Kotor, a town which lies in the largest fjord in southern Europe, that stole my heart.

The highlight of Eastern Europe

In 2004, I randomly bumped into Marco in Dubrovnik. We had originally met in Belgrade and then traveled to Sarajevo together. We were happy to see each other again and we agreed to explore Montenegro together. Less than a decade had passed since Croatia and Montenegro were at war, so there were still no nonstop buses between the countries. The bus let us off at the border, where we walked across the border with our backpacks, and then boarded a Montenegrin bus that would take us to Herceg Novi, an attractive seaside town. Palm trees, a good sandy beach, and a quaint old town make Herceg Novi a worthwhile stop. After a few hours of wandering, we bought a bus ticket to Kotor. And that's when the magic really began.

My heart rate increased as we approached Kotor. The bus followed a twisty road that hugs the coastline. Soon, we passed the mouth of Kotor Bay. My jaw dropped. Glorious, steep mountains soar out of the sea, inspiring you to climb them, or at least admire them. Like a child, I pressed my face and hands onto the bus window, marveling at the two adorable islands in the sparkling bay, each with a picturesque church on it. It's as if we were entering a hidden kingdom, guarded by a narrow bay opening and vertical mountains. I told Marco, "This place is a fantasy."

After the bus arrived at the Kotor terminal, we walked to the old town. It quickly became clear why it's a UNESCO World Heritage Site. We entered the walled city through the main gate, admired the great clock in the *Trg Oktobarske Revolucije* (October Revolution Square), and started looking for *sobe* (rooms) to rent for a couple of days. Cars and bikes are prohibited in the old town, so it's peaceful. We enjoyed getting lost in the narrow streets, which inevitably open up into beautiful squares. We found a nice lady who was renting her rooms for $15 per night. We left our backpacks and decided to see how far we could hike up the mountain.

Climbing Montenegro's mountains with Marco

One of Kotor's most captivating features is that there's a fortress high above the town. A medieval stone wall zigzags up the steep mountain culminating in a solid stronghold. Marco and I wanted to check it out. After 137 steps, we got to the beginning of the wall. At the wall's entrance, a house caught my eye. It wasn't a pretty house. On the contrary, it needed work. Because it was the highest house in the town, it had an impressive view. We could see the rooftops of the old town, including its two main churches, the blue water of Kotor Bay, and the fjords rising behind it. It was the perfect view. Marco was eager to start climbing, so I noted the house, and we started walking up.

In less than 10 minutes, we reached the Church of Our Lady of Health. Through its gated opening, Orthodox icons stared back at us. We absorbed the glittering Kotor Bay and then continued ascending for another 15 minutes to get to the fortress. We explored the ruins like children, peeking through every opening and climbing every step. We spotted a hidden chapel behind the fortress. It's impossible to see the chapel from Kotor. We wanted to explore it and then find a way further up the mountain.

We exited through a window that must have been a secret back-door entrance to the fortress. In five minutes, we were at the humble, open chapel. We eventually found a path that continued up. It was a weak trail, but we followed it for a few hours under the hot September sun. At times we had to use our hands to keep climbing. It felt like we were trekking up a rarely explored mountain, but then suddenly we ran into a paved road. It's always a bit of a letdown to work your way up a mountain only to find fat tourists admiring the same view from their cars.

We asked a fat Austrian couple if we could ride with their car back down to Kotor. They refused. After 20 minutes of trying to hitchhike, a 45-year-old Montenegrin agreed to take us. His name was Aleksandar Dragojević, but he went by Alex. When the Yugoslav Wars broke out, he went to England to "escape the bullshit in Yugoslavia."

I asked how long Montenegro had been using the euro. Alex said, "The first day it became available! We were tired of Serbia screwing us with their damn dinar. There was crazy inflation under Milošević, so we just said, 'Fuck you, we're going to use the German deutchmark.' When the euro came out, we switched to that. No more bullshit."

I asked him how much his Jeep SUV cost to see the price difference with the US. He laughed, "It was cheap because it was probably stolen. That's how Montenegrins get their nice cars."

My dream home

I told him that I was interested in buying the house that I saw at the top of Kotor's Old Town. I hoped he could help me. He struggled up the 137 steps (Alex is a big man) and then rang the doorbell. An old, wiry lady opened the door. She said she had been thinking about selling the house so that she could use the money to buy an apartment for each of her three granddaughters. She invited us in.

It was an odd house. There were two bedrooms, a large attic, and an itty-bitty "kitchen" that could only hold one person. Because the house was so high, it wasn't connected to the town's water supply. Translation: no plumbing. The old lady hauled water from her well in her overgrown garden. There was an outhouse and she would take showers outside, even during the cold winters.

She lived her whole life in the mountains and hated "city life." When her daughters demanded that she move to Kotor, she only agreed to do it when they found this particular house. She loved that it was disconnected from the old town. Climbing up 137 steps and the lack of plumbing helps.

Despite the oddities, I fell in love with it. I imagined writing my book there, admiring the mountains, the bay, and the old town with a clear view of the St. Tryphon Cathedral and the St. Nicholas Church. It was a dream spot for a writer. I figured that when I traveled, I could rent it out to tourists. Sure, it needed work, but historic houses always do. Besides, Montenegro's real estate would surely boom once the memory of the Yugoslav Wars faded completely. I was sold.

Several weeks later, Alex revisited the old lady to negotiate a price for me. He emailed me her price: 120,000 euros (in 2004, that was about $140,000). I had no clue if that was a fair price. I figured Balkanians must haggle, so I offered 100,000 euros. She countered: 120,000. Huh? The stubborn old lady didn't budge. Fine, grandma. I offered 110,000. A few days later, I got her answer: 120,000. Damn, she's hardcore. Alex explained that a typical apartment costs 40,000 euros, so to buy three for each of her granddaughters, she needed 120,000. Offering 115,000 would be a waste of time. I either had to buy it for 120,000 or walk.

I started to consider reality. Remodeling the house would cost $50,000. However, since I'm an American, Montenegrins would overcharge for everything, including the kitchen sink. Contractors could justify the surcharge based on the 137 steps. It's hard to blame them.

Imagine lugging a refrigerator up there. You can't even drive to the base of the steps since no cars are allowed in the old town. What about the nightmare of getting building permits for a UNESCO-protected home? Also, I'd need to hire a trustworthy property manager to collect the rent while I'm traveling in Africa for three years. Could I realistically rent it to tourists? Who would want to carry their luggage up 137 steps? Only young people, but they'd rather stay in a $15 per night in a hostel. Then there's a headache of getting in and out of Kotor. Dubrovnik is the closest decent airport, but it's two hours away by bus, budget airlines don't serve it, and it's in another country (two chances for custom duties to nail you). I'd also have to learn the Balkanian language. Kotor is adorable, but in one hour you can walk down every street. Would I be bored after one month? What if war broke out again and the new government confiscates foreign-owned property or anti-Americanism erupts? Given that I'm traveling most of the time, how much time would I realistically spend in the house? Was I just buying the biggest headache my brain has ever known?

I walked. Six years later, in 2010, I revisited the house. I'll share that story later.

A doomed man and a doomed business

Alex, Marco, and I thanked the old lady and we strolled through the town. Alex showed us the town's biggest tree, which is so large that it seems to have been growing since the sixth century, when the town was first built. The tree fills a plaza with shade. While we walked, Alex said that once the Yugoslavs Wars were over, he returned to Montenegro and invested the money he made in England into a restaurant for tourists. Busloads of Austrians pass his mountain village on their way to Njeguši and the Njegoš mausoleum. Hungry Austrians would buy as many sausages as he could make. At that time, Alex had no idea that his business was doomed.

Later, Alex introduced Marco and I to a doomed man. We went for a drink at one of the Café Moka in the main square. After seeing my interest in buying property in Kotor, Alex asked me if I'd like to learn about a hotel-casino project that he knew about. I said, "Sure." Alex made a phone call and within 20 minutes Dragan "Fric" Dudić showed up. Fric (pronounced *Fritz*) needed to raise $2 million to finish his hotel-casino project called Maximus. He was looking for investors. The project was 70 percent complete when the Yugoslav Wars froze the project for over a decade. Perhaps I had Harvard classmates who would be interested, he suggested. Or maybe I knew Donald Trump, he joked. What's funny is that my classmate, Pam Day, was a contestant on *The Apprentice* TV show. Thus, I knew someone who had met Trump. Unfortunately, Pam got eliminated about halfway through that season, so I would probably have more luck at asking my Slovenian friends if anyone knew Trump's Slovenian wife.

I told Fric that I can't promise anything, but I'd be happy to take a closer look at his Maximus project. Soon a middle-aged man wearing a dark red polo shirt and sunglasses showed up. He looked like a reject from *The Sopranos.* He was Branko Nedović, the former President of Kotor's Parliament. Branko would be giving Alex, Marco, and I a tour of the facilities. When we got up to leave, Fric waved the waiter away. Fric owned the café and covered our tab. We thanked Fric, shook hands, and entered Maximus. No one could imagine that six years later, Fric would die on the chair he was sitting on.

Developing the Kotor Fantasy

Maximus had a perfect location in Kotor's northwest corner. We walked through the half-finished hotel and it was clear that it would be a five-star facility. We spun the roulette wheel in the small, but elegant casino. We explored the discotheque's empty shell. The designers wisely kept the original medieval stone walls and arches. With proper lighting and a fashionable bar, it was clear that it would become the coolest place in Kotor Bay. Finally, we went to a rooftop, which had an outdoor bar and could have a gondola car ride that would take lazy tourists to the top of the fortress. The Maximus project was well named.

Although I didn't have $2 million to invest, my Kotor Fantasy was seductive. I imagined remodeling the old lady's house into a pimped-out pad. For a job, I'd write my book and raise money for Maximus. I'd be a minority shareholder, but for once in my life I would be able to enter a nightclub through the VIP entrance. I'd have a reserved booth in the lounge area with the name tag "RESERVED for the American Stud Muffin." Once I sat down, a flock of Montenegrin girls in miniskirts and high heels would crowd around me. I'd bob my head slightly to the thumping music, but not too much to look uncool. While wearing my Versace sunglasses, I'd order drinks for all the babes. The waiter would never bring me the bill. Every night, I'd invite the hottest chick (and maybe a couple of her slutty friends) to join me in my outdoor Jacuzzi at my house. The gossip rags would call me "the Hugh Hefner of the Adriatic."

Weeks later, reality splashed water on my satisfied smile. Those drunk, high-heel-wearing-gold-diggers would turn around after the 50th step to my house. The bitches would whine, "Don't you have an elevator?" Besides, I don't even like discos: the smoky atmosphere and ear-drum-splitting music is as much fun as getting your teeth worked on by a blind dentist. And guys who wear sunglasses in dark places look stupid.

On our last day in Kotor, Marco and I had breakfast, then he returned to Italy while I continued south toward Albania. Along the way, I spent a night in Budva, Montenegro's top beach resort. Like Kotor, it is a walled town that was rebuilt after two earthquakes in 1979. The difference was that Budva had substantial remodeling done, while Kotor still needed work. Moreover, Budva had a nice beach, while Kotor had a polluted bay. On the other hand, Budva lacks Kotor's fjords and its inexplicable charm. Seeing Budva confirmed that investing in Kotor was a no-brainer. Next to Kotor were two cities that had a recent facelift: to the north was Dubrovnik, to the south was Budva. Both cities were clearly booming with tourism and wealth. Kotor was not, but savvy investors would discover it soon. Money would pour into Maximus, which would start a growth cycle. On the other hand, Montenegro had its skeptics.

A Montenegrin is . . .

Ask an ex-Yugoslav for one word to describe the people of one of Yugoslavia's former republics and you'll get different answers for every republic, except Montenegro. In Montenegro's case, all ex-Yugoslavs (including Montenegrins themselves) will say that Montenegrins are lazy.

> *Why do Montenegrins have a chair near their bed? To rest after they get up. — Balkan joke*

It's not clear when Montenegrins got this reputation for indolence, but in 1780, Carlo Gozzi, an Italian traveler, noted it his book, *Memorie Inutili* (Useless Memoirs). The book's title may explain why it took him 17 years to convince someone to publish his *Useless Memoirs.* In one of the most useless parts of his *Useless Memoirs,* he writes about the Morlacchi, a people who lived in the Dalmatian mountains, including Bosnia and Montenegro. Gozzi observed 230 years ago, "I asked the most civilized persons of those lands the reason for the general rural lazy indolence of Dalmatia. People replied to me that it was impossible, without risk of one's life, to oblige the Morlacchi to do more than they do, or to introduce the smallest innovation to reform their labors in the fields. . . . [They said] that many Dalmatian gentlemen had tried to bring industrious peasants from Italy, and that a few days after their arrival they were found killed across the country, without anyone able to get to those guilty of their deaths. . . I marveled that these gentlemen laughed instead of weeping when they gave me this information."[1]

The Morlacchi have vanished after assimilating throughout the Balkans, but their reputation for being lazy shepherds seems to have stuck only on Montenegrins. Alex confirmed the stereotype. When I asked him why Montenegrins are lazy, he said, "Montenegro's mountains are not good for cultivating plants. So Montenegrins just raise animals, like sheep and goats. People who grow plants have to work every day, but a shepherd can just sit on his ass all day."

> *Where do Montenegrin women put their money? Behind a shovel, because her lazy husband will never pick it up.*
> *— Balkan joke*

Which is the laziest country in the Western Balkans?

Throughout my 18 months of travel in the Balkans, Montenegrins didn't seem remarkably lazy. The only discernible pattern is that people from the south (southern Serbia, Bosnia, Montenegro, Kosovo, and Macedonia) are generally more slothful and relaxed than those in the north (Slovenia, Croatia, and Vojvodina). Still, that's just my opinion based on personal observation and interviews. Let's use a somewhat more scientific method to find the kings of sloth.

In 2010, the Balkan Monitor asked Western Balkanians, "If you were offered a job by an employer that required you to work 30 hours per week or more, and if it was the kind of work you wanted to do, would you take the job?" Only 63 percent of Montenegrins said *yes*, which was the worst rate among ex-Yugoslavs, but not significantly lower than other Balkanians.

Bosnia is a candidate for the Lazy Award. First consider that for the last 10 years Bosnia's unemployment rate has been around 43 percent. Yet when the Balkan Monitor surveyed Bosnia in 2010, only 12.5 percent said they were actively looking for a job—that was the lowest rate in the Western Balkans. What the hell are these people doing?

First, the CIA estimates that Bosnia's large underground economy means that Bosnia's *real* unemployment rate is roughly 28 percent, not 43 percent. Second, after spending years looking for a job and finding nothing, even the most diligent person might quit looking. Among the jobless, 90 percent of Bosnians told the Balkan Monitor that the last time that they had a regular job was either "more than a year ago" or "I've never had one."

These are good excuses, but let's face it: Bosnians like to chill out. They're rarely hurrying anywhere and they're usually smiling. The Balkan Monitor asked, "Would you have been able to begin work had you been offered a job within the last four weeks?" Only 13 percent of Bosnians answered *yes*—that was the lowest rate in the Western Balkans. Given their unemployment rate, such a response suggests that they may be even lazier than the Montenegrins.

Perhaps one reason Bosnians aren't so hungry for work is that then they'd have to pay taxes. About half of Bosnians feel that "the money

I pay as taxes is lost," while the other half feels they are contributing to "services I need such as education, health services, and transport." Only a quarter of Montenegrins agree with the disgruntled Bosnians, making Montenegrins the least cynical Western Balkanians on this issue. In conclusion, when Balkanians make jokes about the lazy Montenegrins, maybe they should poke fun of the Bosnians instead. On the other hand, few work harder in Slovenia, Croatia, and Serbia than Bosnian immigrants—they do all the dirty, back-breaking jobs.

> *A Montenegrin wants to be a snake: just lie down all day long and not have to walk. — Balkan joke*

Montenegrins are known to be lazy, but perhaps they should be known for their anger. In 2010, when Gallup asked Montenegrins, "Did you experience anger yesterday?" 42 percent said *yes*. That's the fourth highest rate in the world (under Pakistan, Bahrain, and Iraq). Amy Lane, an American who lives in Montenegro, thinks the results are misleading. She told me, "I don't think Montenegrins are angrier than others by any means—but I know that if you want them to do what you ask, you must yell—it seems this is the only way they notice that you are serious about getting a job done. So, I think the yelling bit isn't really anger—just how they present themselves as being serious."

A man-made island, built over 500 years

Ever since I left Montenegro, I dreamed of returning, especially to Kotor, a place that makes my soul sing. Although I've been to 75 countries so far, I've only fallen madly in love with three towns: San Francisco (my hometown, so I'm biased), Venice, and Kotor. Because I only spent three days in Kotor, I wasn't sure how deep my love was. Kotor was like a beautiful girl that you meet briefly and become passionately attracted to. You want to see her again so you can verify that she is still as enchanting as you remember. Was it true love or did the stars just randomly align when you met? Would the magic still be there? I had to find out.

Once again, I entered Montenegro via a bus from Dubrovnik. As the bus entered Kotor Bay and the fjords surrounded us, I couldn't stop smiling. I felt like Odysseus reuniting with Penelope. And just like Odysseus didn't blindly race into Penelope's arms when he arrived, I delayed returning to Kotor. I stopped 18 kilometers short of Kotor and visited Perast, a small, elegant waterside village. It's the best place to view Kotor Bay's two islands. One is natural, the other is man-made. How they built it is remarkable.

The locals created the Lady of the Rock island by dropping stones on the site every July 22. Eventually someone observed that this was sure a slow way to build an island. Therefore, a few hundred years ago, the locals loaded 87 captured ships with rocks and then purposefully sank them onto the site. That certainly helped their progress. It took 550 years, but there it is, and a man-made island built before earth moving equipment.

A Serbian-Montenegrin couple in Perast

On March 9, 2009, I met an attractive couple, Predrag Begović and Tijana Tajić, in Perast. After they asked me to take a photo of them, I asked them if we could have a drink together. They agreed. Predrag was a trade adviser from Podgorica, Montenegro's capital. Tijana was a graphic designer from Serbia. The well-dressed Montenegrin-Serbian couple was spending a romantic weekend in Perast. I asked them why their countries broke up. After the Yugoslav Wars, Serbia and Montenegro remained connected until 2006, when 55 percent of Montenegrins voted to separate from Serbia. Predrag said, "I'm Montenegrin, but I didn't want to separate. Serbs are like family. We should be together. But many Montenegrins were in a hurry to transform Montenegro into Monte Carlo."

Tijana said, "Yeah, Montenegro felt Serbia was holding them back. The war crimes trials would slow down Montenegro's ability to join the EU by 2015. The main reason most people want to join the EU is so that they can travel freely."

I asked, "What can Montenegrins teach Americans?"

Predrag said, "We don't work as much as Americans. We have a good balance of life and play."

Predrag and Tijana were driving back to Kotor before going home, so they offered me a ride. We took a photo together, said goodbye, and I walked into Kotor with a big smile on my face.

A dream turns into a nightmare

Revisiting the Kotor's streets after five years felt like I was revisiting my hometown. I couldn't believe how clearly I remembered how to get around. Everything felt so familiar. The biggest change was that the Maximus hotel-casino was now open. I walked inside like a proud parent, thrilled to see the well done interior design. I ordered a drink, but the harem of Montenegrins in miniskirts failed to materialize.

I was excited to fulfill a dream: camp above Kotor in the fortress. At 9:00 p.m., I walked up the steps in the dark with the confidence of someone who has done it 1,000 times. I set up camp in a roofless building. I didn't have my tarp (I had forgotten it in Estonia and would pick it up in Romania). I was concerned with the gathering clouds, but I fell asleep anyway. At midnight, thunder woke me up.

Although it wasn't raining yet, I quickly packed up and walked up the mountain to execute Plan B: camp under the semi-protective cover of the Church of Our Lady of Health, high above Kotor. After 10 minutes of going uphill, I arrived at the church's porch. I put my sleeping bag on the stone floor. The wind began to howl. That was bad news because the roof overhang wouldn't be protective enough against diagonal rain. I was too lazy to continue climbing to find a better spot, so I stayed put and prayed for the best. The worst came. A vicious downpour and nearly horizontal rain hammered at me. My down sleeping bag started getting wet. I packed up as fast as the lightning that was streaking across the sky.

Plan C: camp in one of the ancient guard stations along the way. These stone structures were effectively caves. After 10 minutes of climbing in the storm, I found a suitable guard station. The rocky ground was uneven, but it was fully enclosed, so horizontal rain couldn't touch me. I lay out my groundsheet and sleeping bag in a damp corner and tried to sleep. Incredibly, I heard raindrops hitting my sleeping bag. How? Limestone leaks. Limestone is everywhere in Montenegro. If I didn't move, in one hour my sleeping bag would be soaked. It was 1:15 a.m. I repacked again and kept climbing up in the storm.

Plan D: camp in the fortress itself. Once I got there, it was clear that the fortress leaked more than the crappiest hostel I've ever stayed in.

Time for Plan E: camp in the hidden chapel that Marco and I discovered five years before. Would it be open at 2:00 a.m.? I stumbled in the dark and in the rain, struggling to find the obscure portal that leads to the chapel. Finally, I found it. I thanked God that the chapel was open, and, most importantly, that it was watertight. I fell asleep feeling safe, secure, dry, and happy.

Birthday present: a day in Kotor

The next day, March 10, was my birthday. I slept in until 7:00 a.m. knowing that it was unlikely that someone would walk 40 minutes uphill on a Tuesday morning to pray in this chapel. Still, I packed up, left no trace, and walked back to Kotor's Old Town. I went to Maximus to check my email. Alex had responded with his new cell phone number. Although we spent only one day together five years ago, we greeted each other like old friends. He had put on a little weight and I had lost some more hair.

I asked him about my dream home. He said, "Last year someone tried to buy it from that old lady for 500,000 euros and she refused! Real estate is now so fucking expensive! You should have bought it five years ago for 120,000 euros, my friend."

"Yeah, no kidding. But 500,000 seems too high for a small place with 137 steps and no plumbing. What's the story behind that?"

"The old lady still wanted to buy three apartments for her granddaughters. But an apartment doesn't cost 40,000 euros anymore. It costs 200,000 euros. So she had to raise her price."

Alex drove me to a place where he had never been to: the fjord that is directly across from Kotor. It was a military zone during Yugoslavia, so he never visited it. It offered panoramic views of the entire bay. Later, we drove to learn about Montenegro's George Washington.

Exploring the birthplace of Montenegro's greatest ruler

The road from Kotor to Njeguši is breathtaking. It has about 30 hairpin turns as it climbs to the heavens. Alex said, "The Austrians built this road when they ruled us. Let me show you two other things they made."

Once the road leveled off, he parked and we walked to a cliff. He pointed at the remains of a cable gondola system. Austrians built it to efficiently transport materials up and down the mountain. They dismantled it after they built the road. Then we drove to the second Austrian invention. Alex exclaimed that despite all the snow in the mountains, Montenegro has water shortages because most of the water drains through the limestone. We toured the ruins of the water catchment facility that the Austrians built in the 1930s. Alex said, "It worked perfectly, but after WWII, angry Montenegrins got rid of all the Austrians and Germans. They also destroyed this water system, just because the Austrians built it. So stupid! Now, 65 years later, we're finally rebuilding this Austrian invention."

Alex shared the story of Montenegro's founding father: Petar II Petrović-Njegoš. He was born in 1813 in Njegoši. Today, his birthplace is a museum. He wrote many poems, plays, and books that defined Montenegro's culture. Although he was an Orthodox priest, he transformed Montenegro from a theocracy to a secular state. He died of tuberculosis when he was 38 years old. Alex pointed to the snowy summit of Mt. Lovćen and said, "He's buried there. C'mon, let's go see his mausoleum."

Although I was excited to drive up Mt. Lovćen (1,749 m / 5,771 ft), the mountain was covered in snow and we were driving in a Yugo. The title of Jason Vuić's book says it all—*The Yugo: The Rise and Fall of the Worst Car in History*. Although it wasn't really the worst car in history, it gave other commie disasters on wheels some competition in their race to the bottom. The reason the Yugo is well-known is that Americans bought over 100,000 Yugos for under $4,000. They stopped buying them once they realized that it was a lemon. Other four-wheel

Eastern European catastrophes included the Dacia, Wartburg, Polonez e, and Volga. My favorite was the Soviet Zaporozhet car, whose engine was fire-prone and could barely power a bicycle.

When I asked Alex what happened to his four-wheel drive Jeep, he said, "I had to sell it after my restaurant burned down!"

"What happened?!" I said.

"A random fire. We rebuilt. But a couple of my neighbors opened their own restaurants. One slips money to the bus companies to make sure they park at his restaurant. So my business is shit. I need to find something else to do."

"That sucks," I said. "So why did you buy a Yugo? Why didn't you buy another stolen car?"

"We don't do that anymore, my friend. The government wants to get into the EU, so they're cooperating with the EU to find stolen cars. So that's why I drive this piece of shit."

Alex stepped on the gas as the road started to climb. It was March, we were at 1,000 meters, snow was everywhere, the road wasn't plowed, and we had another 749 meters (2,456 ft) to go up . . . in a Yugo. I looked at my altimeter on my watch as Alex drove with rose-colored sunglasses: 1,005 meters . . . 1,010 meters . . . 1,015 meters . . . then Alex yelled, "Fuck! Shit!"

We were stuck. On the other hand, we had gone up 15 vertical meters. Another 734 meters and we would have made it. For the next 40 minutes, Alex and I dug through snow, spun the wheels, and went nowhere. Finally, we found the right combination: I drove while he pushed. I turned the car around at a hairpin turn and we drove the poor, overworked Yugo back down the mountain.

Meeting a Montenegrin mountain man

Although Montenegro is tiny, there are really three Montenegros: coast, mountain, and valley. Real Montenegrins live in the mountains. Those who live around Podgorica (the valley) and Kotor are the wimpy Montenegrins. Montenegro's heart and its desire for independence have always been centered in the mountains. Just like you need to go to Nebraska to find a real American, you need to go to Montenegro's mountain villages to find a real Montenegrin. When our plan to visit the mausoleum failed, Alex drove me to Njeguši to visit a Montenegrin mountain man.

Ilija Popović was a robust 58-year-old man with a 50-year-old wife, Radmila, and a 10-year-old son, Marko. Their home was next to a small Orthodox church, which was nestled between Lovćen and another mountain. This sparsely populated village survives off their livestock. Ilija couldn't speak English, so he waved me inside. Radmila served us *rakija* (brandy) and *čaj* (tea). Ilija explained that there are about 100 tribes in Montenegro. You know the person's tribe by their last name. Each tribe gathers on their annual Tribe Day to celebrate. He said that families always protected men who were the only men of the family. For example, they might cut off the man's finger so that he couldn't serve in the military. Even if they did serve, they would not be sent on dangerous missions. The purpose was to preserve the tribe. Each tribe has a reputation. Pity those who are born in the Tribe-of-the-Imbeciles.

Montenegro is especially proud that it was the only Balkan nation that the Turkish Empire could not conquer. On the other hand, back then, Montenegro was the size of a postage stamp. Its "kingdom" centered around Cetinje and its mountain region. The Turks controlled everything else. Still, Montenegrins have a fierce, fanatical fighting spirit. Bozidar Jezenik's book, *Wild Europe,* describes how Montenegrins decapitated the heads of their enemies and kept them as a sign of valor. The more heads you had, the cooler you were. Even in the last century, people would still brag about the number of heads they had. I asked Ilija how many heads he had in the barn, but fortunately Alex didn't translate what I had said.

Ilija showed me his barn, where he stored many racks of dried pigs and cows. Later, he showed me his revolver and rifle—prized possessions of any mountain man. Not everyone in Montenegro shares this hardy, independent spirit. In 2006, Montenegro's referendum for independence passed by the narrowest of margins: just 2,300 votes. That's because only 43 percent of Montenegrins consider themselves ethnically Montenegrin; 32 percent are Serbs and 16 percent Muslim (Bosnians and Albanians). On the other hand, Montenegrins are as different from Serbians as Canadians are different from Americans. In other words, 99 percent of the planet (including Americans and Serbians) think the two similar groups are effectively identical. The only ones who disagree are some proud Montenegrins (and Canadians). When I asked how Serbians and Montenegrins are different, Ilija cited a Montenegrin saying, "Serbians say, 'Don't touch my money or my pig.' Montenegrins say, 'Don't touch my pride, my integrity, or my family.'"

Hanging out with a Russian and Chadian in Podgorica

Alex invited me to his home to celebrate my birthday with his wife and two young kids. They were fantastic hosts. Later, I slept on their couch. The next morning, Alex raced me to the bus station, where he illegally drove into the bus parking lot to flag down the Podgorica bus just as it was leaving. We waved goodbye as the bus took off to Montenegro's capital.

During the Yugoslav era, Podgorica was called Titograd, meaning "Tito's City." When Yugoslavia disintegrated, they reverted to their historic name, which means "under the small hill." Today, it has about 170,000 inhabitants, a third of Montenegro's total. You'd think that Montenegro's touristic coastline and mountains would generate most of the country's GNP, but the aluminum processing plants near Podgorica still capture the lion's share of the economy (about 40%). After reveling in Montenegro's coast and its spectacular mountains, Podgorica is a letdown. Its two main commercial streets, Slobode and Hercegovačka, are functional, but dull. Its Turkish clock tower, the *Sahat kula*, is nice, but the city lacks the charm and aesthetics that the rest of Montenegro has. It has a good excuse for being an ugly concrete jungle: it was bombed over 70 times in WWII and they built it back up in a hurry.

When I went to a café and saw a man in a business suit eating by himself, I asked if I could join him. His name was Yaroslav and he was a Russian from Vladivostok. He moved to Moscow, but he was doing business in Montenegro for a few weeks. I asked him what he liked about Montenegro when compared to Russia. He said, "I love Montenegro's clean air and water. In Moscow, we have gray or yellow snow. Montenegro's ski resorts have a beautiful clear, light blue snow. Also, there's no traffic problems like we have in Moscow."

I asked, "What do you dislike?"

He said, "The medical system seems bad. I can't find antibiotics, for example. But otherwise, it's a good country. Montenegrins in Podgorica are much more open and friendly than Russians in Moscow. Also, Russians feel very welcomed in Montenegro—there's that Slavic connection."

When I was considering living in Montenegro, some people said that "a lot" of Russians live there. According to the 2003 census, among Montenegro's population of 620,145 there are 240 Russians—that's 0.03 percent. Even if that number has tripled in the last decade, it's still insignificant. Nevertheless, Russians are buying large summer homes and making big investments that attract attention. In fact, in 2008, Montenegro received more foreign direct investment per capita than any other European country. After chatting with Yaroslav, I saw an unusual man.

When you spend three years traveling in Eastern Europe, you start acting like Eastern Europeans when they see a black person: you stare. Blacks are extremely rare compared to Western societies. In this case, this young guy was as black as coal. I had to get his story.

His name was Misdongarde and he was from Chad. We spoke in French. He had been living in Podgorica for three months as part of his one-year soccer contract. He was the center-forward and was traded after playing one year for the Belgrade team. In addition to his salary, the team paid for all his expenses. I asked him what it was like to live in Montenegro instead of Chad. He looked out the window on the cold, drizzly March day and said, "I miss Chad's weather. Yes, sometimes it gets too hot in Chad, but here it's too cold and wet. But I love Montenegro's beautiful beaches and mountains. It helps you forget your problems."

I said, "Do you experience racism?"

He said, "Not really. Sure, people look, but Serbia and Montenegro are much less racist than I expected. I've never had a problem. People here are good and friendly."

After talking for 20 minutes, we shook hands and I left to grab a bus to Kosovo. But that story will have to wait for the Kosovo chapter.

Going to Montenegro with Ana

In 2010, Ana was eager to see the town that I rave about: Kotor. Before you buy the next plane ticket to Kotor (Tivat is the nearest airport), realize that after you see it, you'll probably conclude, "Yeah, Kotor's nice, but it's not *that* great." You'll probably prefer Venice or Dubrovnik because they are much more grandiose than poor little Kotor. However, I treasure overlooked gems, and I'm a sucker for beautiful seaside towns that are set at the base of glorious mountains.

Ana and I left Dubrovnik, spend a few hours in Herceg Novi, and then we entered Kotor Bay. Ana drove slowly and pulled aside often to absorb the scenery. I pointed out how the snowy Lovćen massif looms over Kotor. I gave her a tour of Kotor as if I were a local. Ana admired the narrow sinuous streets, picturesque shops, antique monuments, and enchanting plazas. Kotor is a baby Venice. Although Kotor doesn't have canals, maybe global warming will change that.

We considered our meal options. Montenegro's cuisine is a mix of Slavic meat and potatoes with a Mediterranean blend of veggies, olive oil, and fruits. On the coast, fish, salad, and Italian cuisine are popular. Vegetarian dishes include *pasulj prebranac* (cooked dish of spicy beans), *zeljanica* (cheese and spinach pie), and *gibanica* (cheese pie). We settled on a pizzeria that had outdoor seating next to the Cathedral of Saint Tryphon, which was built in 1166. After hearing my story about the hidden chapel that saved me during a rainstorm, Ana wanted to sleep there too. Therefore, at 9:00 p.m., we worked off our pizzas by hiking up to the fortress, through the discrete portal, and then to the lonely chapel. Throughout that week, Ana had proved she had an adventurous spirit. I was falling in love with her.

Murder in Kotor

Exactly one month after Ana and I left Kotor, Fric (the man who had asked me to help him raise $2 million to invest in Maximus) was drinking his morning coffee at the Café Moka, where he and I said goodbye. While tourists and locals were walking by, Ivan Vracar whipped out a pistol and shot Fric dead. The assassin ran and Fric's bodyguards sprinted after him. The guards caught him outside the town's gate. While petrified tourists helplessly watched, the guards nearly beat the assassin to death.

The murderer's motive is unclear, but Fric's death illustrates the sleazy, mafia-like intrigues that occur behind Montenegro's pretty touristic face. Fric, who owned Maximus, was well-connected with the Montenegrin government. He was also buddies with Darko Sarić, a drug smuggler. Fric allegedly laundered money through his Marshall Island companies, two of which had suggestive names: Monteflowery and Maximus Shipping. It's not clear if his murder was for vengeance or to silence Fric's potential testimony against Sarić. Milka Tadić, a Balkan journalist, said that the murder says "all too much about the way Montenegro works. . . . What sort of a country have we got in which you can be both the partner of a drug dealer and elected authorities?"[2]

Alex was shocked. Fric was his friend. In 2011, I asked Alex what he planned to do now that his restaurant business had failed. He said, "I'm going to go into the diamond business. I'm leaving now to spend a few months training and building contacts in Togo and Congo."

Going to heaven

Ana and I left Kotor and we drove to the snowy summit of Mt. Lovćen, where Alex and I failed to go the year before. Ana and I had three advantages over my previous attempt: it was late spring, the road was plowed, and we didn't have a Yugo.

The Njegos mausoleum, which is at the summit of Lovćen, is deeply symbolic for Montenegrins. When Peter II died, Montenegrins buried him in a small chapel on Lovćen's summit. During WWII, Montenegrins fiercely defended the chapel despite Italy's constant bombardment. Imagine the effort Americans would make to defend Mount Rushmore from a foreign invader—that's what the Njegos mausoleum means to Montenegrins. Ironically, after fighting so hard to defend it, the communists demolished the chapel.

Yugoslavia's communists replaced the chapel with the secular mausoleum that you can visit today. We walked up the grand, monumental staircase that tunnels through the mountain's flesh. Although the tunnel is a clever way to avoid clearing snow, the opening at the top was buried in it, which makes for a slippery climb to the pinnacle. When we finally arrived, it felt we were at the pearly gates of heaven. A wide stone path leads to a glorious entrance, where two dark female statues, three times the size of a human, guard the entryway. Their heads seem to hold up the entire building. Peter II's actual tomb isn't as impressive as the viewpoint area, where it seems that all of

Montenegro lies at your feet. After enjoying our time in heaven, Ana and I returned to Earth.

Camping in Durmitor National Park

Although Kotor's fjords are mesmerizing, Alex said that Montenegro's real mountains were in Durmitor National Park. Ana and I aimed to get there by sunset. We descended Lovćen and casually explored Cetinje, Montenegro's original capital. It's on a high plateau, which helped Montenegrins keep the Turkish Empire away. Although Cetinje is mentioned in many epic poems, it's not an epic city today. We continued, picked up a hitchhiker in Podgorica, and dropped him off in Nikšić. Next, we learned that what looks like a shortcut on a map may not be one in real life. We spent over an hour navigating atrocious roads that seemed to have more potholes than paved parts. With one hour of daylight left, we arrived in a chilly Durmitor and camped.

We woke at 4:30 a.m., put our camping gear back in the car, and set off on an ambitious day hike. We started at *Crno Jezero* (Black Lake) and were soon hiking above Lovćen's altitude (1,749 m). We were poorly equipped for the snow-filled terrain. Although I had compass and altimeter, we didn't have boots or ice axes. According to my optimistic plan, we were supposed to go over one of the lowest mountain passes, Međed (2,287 m / 7,500 ft). However, once we got to 2,000 meters, we could see that the final ascent was devilishly steep and snowy. The other side of the pass might be even icier. It was 2:00 p.m. and we had no camping gear. If we had problems near the steep pass, it would be a bad place to run out of daylight. It was my first hike with Ana, so I did something I rarely do: be wise and back down. We hooted as we slid down the snowy slope on our butts. I looked back at Durmitor's majestic peaks and vowed that I would revisit them one day.

The big secret becomes a little secret

Montenegrins share the friendly southern Balkan spirit. For example, after our first meeting, Alex invited me to spend months writing my book in his home in Njegoš. Goranka Slavujević, a Serbian who was living in Italy, told me, "Montenegrins are generous. For instance, I met a man while going for a walk, and he invited me to have coffee with him and his family. Within 30 minutes, he offered me a spare room to stay in over the summer free of charge!"

Amy Lane, an American who lives in Montenegro, told me that "Americans could learn how to relax and slow down a bit more like Montenegrins. What I love the most is that it is not so heavily policed, although that is changing. Also, I have two little girls and I love how Montenegrins come and give love to your children. In America, people are afraid for strangers to hug and kiss their kids."

I asked Amy, "What was surprising? Or something you dislike?"

She said, "The most surprising fact was how tall and thin Montenegrins are! What I dislike is the way they disrespect the beauty of the country with trash. The whole place looks like a construction site!"

Fortunately, that's changing. Montenegro's government has bet their country's future on tourism. As a result, Montenegro was much cleaner in 2010 than it was in 2004. Taking care of the environment is a rich man's obsession. When you're poor, environmentalism is a luxury—you're too focused on survival. As Montenegro's tourism industry matures, its wealth expands and the country's environmentalism will improve. Montenegro has an 18-percent flat tax and strong incentives for foreigners to invest.

In 2004, my guidebook said, "Kotor is a big secret." It could have said that Montenegro was a big secret. Although Montenegro is no longer such a big secret, it holds some of Eastern Europe's most precious gems. Someday, I want to buy a house there.

What Montenegro Can Teach Us

- **Chill out.** Montenegrins aren't as lazy as their reputation implies. Or at least, they're not significantly lazier than others in the southern Balkans. Still, they know how to relax. When you drive through Montenegro, you'll see half-finished houses with people drinking rakia next to them. In Slovenia, they'll all be hammering in a nail. When you're not sure if you should work a bit more or relax, be a Montenegrin, and chill out.
- **Defend yourself.** Montenegrins were the only country in Southeastern Europe that didn't fall to the Turkish Empire. Despite their small size, they've kept and defended their identity.

Places I saw and recommend in Montenegro: Kotor, Budva, Perast, Lovćen's Mausoleum, and Durmitor National Park.

Travel deals and info: http://ftapon.com/montenegro

In 2004, my last stop in Montenegro was Ulcinj, which is the country's southernmost city. The *Stari Grad* (Old Town) of Ulcinj has twists and turns that make it charming and fun. Its *Mala Plaža* (Small Beach) and *Velika Plaža* (Great Beach) have sand that stretches all the way to Albania. Throughout the Balkans, you'll hear all sorts of horror stories about Albanians. I was extremely curious to see for myself what Albania is really like. What I learned was surprising.

16

ALBANIA—HOME TO EUROPE'S FRIENDLIEST PEOPLE

IN THE 1998 SATIRICAL movie, *Wag the Dog*, a Hollywood producer and a political spin-doctor helps the US President create a fictitious war to distract the public from a sex scandal. The conspirators have to pick the most obscure, hidden country for the phony war. One suggests Albania. "Why?" asks the other.

"Why not? What do you know about them? "

"Nothing."

"Precisely."

"They seem shifty, they seem standoffish. I mean, who knows from Albania? What do you know about Albania? Who trusts Albanians?"

Later in the movie, one conspirator says to the other, "Anybody know who's ever eaten in an Albanian restaurant?"

"Is there such a thing an Albanian restaurant?"

"Has to be. They have to eat."

"Is there a national dish?"

"No. Nobody would know. We can make it up."

They go on to make a phony news clip with an "Albanian" actress fleeing a digitally-generated burning village. Ironically, just one year after the movie came out, real Albanians were fleeing real burning villages. Although I had seen the movie, it didn't teach me anything about Albania, except that perhaps the country doesn't exist. Thus, in 2004, when I first headed to Albania, the only thing I knew about Albania was whatever the Balkanians had told me.

Albania's crappy reputation

Nearly all Balkanians dislike Albanians. Ivan from Serbia told me, "If you think that the hate in Bosnia was bad, multiply it by a billion, and that is the hate against the Albanians." Balkanians said that Albanians steal, stink, are dirty, have eight to 20 children per family, are ugly due to inbreeding, wear an odd white cap, are fanatical Muslims, only speak Albanian, follow a tome called the Kanun which advocates a medieval code, and murder or injure for trivial reasons. And that's just for starters. Over a beer they would really let the insults fly. Furthermore, it wasn't just Slavs making such slurs. Nearly every European has a low opinion of Albanians. It's hard to find Europeans agreeing on anything, but they agree that Albanians are less desirable than Donald Trump.

What's more impressive is that most of those who dished out such derogatory statements didn't qualify them by saying that "some Albanians are like this" or "most are like that." Instead, they emphasized that *all* Albanians are like this. It was nearly impossible to get anyone to concede that maybe one or two in this nation of three million could be different. Wow. I had to meet them. It's not every day that you get to meet a nation of assholes. Except France, of course.

I had heard that there were many Albanians causing trouble in Ulcinj, a Montenegrin border town. "Be careful," the Montenegrins advised. I clutched my wallet tightly as I walked through the streets of Ulcinj. In one hour, I would be taking a minibus to Albania. I looked around to try to spot an Albanian. Balkanians told me that Albanians have distinctive facial structures and all the men wore white caps. I walked to Ulcijn's beautiful beach, admiring the 500-year-old fortress overlooking the sea. Everyone looked normal. No white hats. I thought, *maybe the Albanians are hiding*.

Entering Albania

I sat next to two nuns in a *furgon* (minibus). One flirtatious Albanian nun taught me her language. So much for the first stereotype that they're all Muslims. None of the men on the *furgon* wore white hats. *Maybe they're not Albanians*, I thought. On the other hand, what else could they be? It's not like Montenegrins are banging down the doors to visit Albania.

After crossing the border near the Buna River, we stopped in Shkodër, where everyone got off. Everything I did irritated my brusque *furgon* driver, but when I said *"falem nderit"* (thank you), he broke out a wide smile. He helped me find the next *furgon* to Tirana, Albania's capital. I was about to board when I spotted an old man wearing a white cap. We had driven by hundreds of Albanians and I finally found one old guy with a white cap. I wanted to run to him, kiss him, and get his autograph, but I had to go.

My next driver had piercing blue eyes and sandy blond hair. I didn't expect such fair features this far south in latitude. When the *furgon* was full, he turned on the radio and started blasting . . . Arabic music? My driver didn't look like a Muslim. Meanwhile, a Christian cross jostled under his rear-view mirror. This was all quite confusing.

The roads to the capital were narrow and filled with potholes. Some of the main roads weren't even paved. This was understandable because 15 years before my visit it was effectively illegal for an Albanian to own a car. Only the communist elite could have a car. The good news is that you could ask the commies to grant an exception for you. The bad news is that during the entire 45 years of communist rule, only two non-government members received the permit to have a car. That's right, *two exceptions* in 45 years.

Thus, among the three million Albanians, who lived in a country the size of Maryland, there were only 2,000 cars. You needed a special permit to own a car, typewriter, or refrigerator. The upshot of the car-less society: Tirana was the cleanest city in Europe. Today, with over 500,000 cars, Tirana is the most polluted capital in Europe. Only 54 percent of Albanians are happy about their air quality, ranking them at the bottom of Europe and seventh from the bottom of the world.[1]

The *furgon* dropped us off near *Sheshi Skënderbej* (Skanderbeg Square), which is the heart of Tirana. It's easy to imagine how the square was 20 years ago without any cars. The city still hasn't bothered to paint car lanes on the wide street that encircles the bronze statue of the Skanderbeg, Albania's national hero. With no designated cross-walks or lanes, the square is a chaotic soup of buses, cars, and people that somehow works.

The atheist communist government had a habit of bulldozing mosques, but it kept Tirana's eighteenth century Et'hem Bey Mosque because it was especially graceful. The Muslim near the entrance graciously led me inside (after I took off my shoes) and softly explained the significance of the beautifully painted interior. There were a couple of guys in the mosque with white hats, but of the thousands of people milling about Tirana I rarely saw a white hat. Where are these white-hat guys hiding? Perhaps Albania's National History Museum had the answer.

Eastern Europe's obsession

Most Balkanians, like most Eastern Europeans, are eager to tell foreigners their country's history—they're obsessed. In Montenegro, a museum tour guide condescendingly told a group of English speakers, "For you Americans, history was yesterday, but we study thousands of years of history. And not just our history, but *world* history."

I told her, "You know, you're right. I can't even remember what I had for breakfast this morning."

The tour guide was right that Balkanians dwell on history much more than Americans, yet this is precisely what ignites Balkan conflicts. A Canadian, who was in the same tour group, said, "Folks in the Balkans spend so much time looking back. North Americans look forward."

A guy from New Zealand laughed, "And we look upside down."

Zsuzsa, a Hungarian, told me, "Eastern Europeans have a very strong sense of identity and somehow we tend to dwell more on our differences than on our similarities. Not to mention dwelling on historic grievances."

Andrew Harrod, my college classmate and a PhD from the Fletcher School of Law and Diplomacy, recalled what a French lady told him while they were interning at the Bundestag in Germany: "She commented that Americans do not have an *Erbfeindschaft* (hereditary hatred) like the French and Germans once did. As a nation of immigrants, successive generations of Americans intermingle with each other and direct their attention to the problems of the day, but do not have any societal basis for unquestioned obsession with long-ago disputes. New generations of immigrants come to America as a land of opportunity for tomorrow, not as a place to dwell on the past. Such a future-oriented country constantly welcoming new arrivals entails a certain degree of historical amnesia."

For Americans, history only appears in boring textbooks, and so soon we are left with just a vague recollection of a foggy past. A century ago, Ford Motor Company's founder summed up the way many Americans view history today:

> *I don't know much about history, and I wouldn't give a nickel for all the history in the world. History is more or less bunk. It's tradition. We don't want tradition. We want to live in the present and the only history that is worth a tinker's damn is the history we made today.*
> *— Henry Ford (1863–1947), Interview in the* Chicago Tribune, *May 25, 1916*

A Polish Nobel laureate, Czeslaw Milsz, remarked that the main difference between Eastern Europe and the West is "memory and lack of memory." A Serbian professor of Slavic and Comparative Literature remarked, "This lack of memory allows great powers to act with only their own present interest in mind, treating the past as a menace that causes pathetically small nations to seek identification with a power they don't possess."[2] This is why the Montenegrin tour guide puffed herself up by telling us that Montenegro had one of the world's first printing presses while American pilgrims were learning how to carve a Thanksgiving turkey.

> History, n. *An account mostly false, of events unimportant, which are brought about by rulers mostly knaves, and soldiers mostly fools.*
> *—Ambrose Bierce (1842–1914),* The Devil's Dictionary

Unfortunately, Eastern Europeans are selective about remembering their history. They love to go back far enough to recall their glory days. They tell themselves that they were the original natives and that they didn't ethnically cleanse any previous culture because it was "virgin land." By omitting the years before they peaked and glossing over their eventual fall from glory, they linger on that moment in history when they had a much larger chunk of territory than they control today. They either implicitly or explicitly say that they ought to have that territory back because it was once theirs. When you have at least eight countries in a small area all playing this game (like in the Balkans), you inevitably get endless wars because they're constantly feeling bitter that they're no longer the big bad asses they once were. Every Balkan nation is guilty of this, including Albania.

Meet the Illyrians

Upon entering Albania's National History Museum, you'll immediately notice a difference between Albania's historical emphasis and that of most Slavic historians. Slavs like to start the clock around the sixth century, just like Americans like to start our historical clock in 1492—because that's when our direct ancestors showed up and began kicking out (or assimilating) the natives.

Albanians go back much further: around 1,200 BC, because that's when the mysterious Illyrians showed up and dominated the Balkans. The Illyrian glory period ended in 167 BC, when the Romans conquered them. Illyrians are ideal ancestors because they're distant and vague, so it's easy to claim you're related to them and to build myths around them. Moreover, connecting with a large ancient civilization helps justify any modern territorial demands. Hence, Albanians embrace the Illyrians as their ancestors, even though the evidence supporting the relation is inconclusive.

The danger of encouraging such a connection is that people will superimpose ancient maps on modern maps and assume that nobody has moved. Thus, because Montenegrins live on "Illyrian land," an Albanian told me, "We do not have a big problem with Montenegrins, because, unlike the Serbs, they have Illyrian blood." Such a sloppy conclusion overlooks the fact that Illyrians occupied parts of modern Serbia and that Montenegrins came with the same Slav migration as the Serbs. Besides, the Albanian-Illyrian connection is flimsy; some scholars believe Albanians migrated from Romania or Eastern Serbia many centuries ago. The origin of Albanians is still an enigma.

> *All the ancient histories, as one of our wits say, are just fables that have been agreed upon. — Voltaire*

What Albanian has in common with Hungarian

The Albanian language has nothing to do with Hungarian. In fact, it has practically nothing to do with any other language, which is exactly what it has in common with Hungarian. Like Hungarian, the Albanian language is so unique that it seems to have fallen out of the sky.

At times you might hope that Albanian is related to some other language you might know. For example, *në ç'orë arrin autobusi?* (what time does the bus arrive?) sounds vaguely Italian. Also, if you count from one to ten, you sound like a drunken Slav (*një, dy, tre, katër, pesë, gjashtë, shtatë, tetë, nëntë, dhjetë*). Nevertheless, once you hear a complex phrase, you'll be completely lost and realize that Albanian has nothing to do with anything you know. For example, to say *does it include breakfast?* you have to say *a e përfshin edhe mëngjesin?* It makes you not want to care if the hotel's price includes breakfast.

> Pirdh o prift ne prill pirdh. — *Albanian tongue twister, meaning, "Fart, priest in April, fart."*

Albanian is alien. It has 36 characters, including double letters like *dh* and *ll*. Place names come in two forms: *bulevard* (a boulevard) and *bulevardi* (the boulevard). *Tirana* means *the Tirana,* but all the buses say *Tiranë* because that means *to Tirana*. Even the basics are odd. To say *hello,* you have to say a mouthful: *tungjatjeta*. Fortunately, Albanians don't say *hello* to each other. It's too formal. They're more likely to say *c'kemi?* It sounds like *sh-kemi* and it means *how are you?* Most people answer *mirë* (good). Other essential phrases: *ju lutem* (please), *ku është . . .* (where is . . .), *(nuk) kuptoj* (I (don't) understand), *më falni* (sorry), *sa kushton* (how much is it?), *si quheni ju lutem?* (what's your name?), *lamtumirë* (goodbye), *po* (yes), and my favorite, *yo* (no).

Just like the unique Basque language implies that the Basque people have been around long before their neighbors, Albanian supports the same argument. Unfortunately, we know little about the Illyrian language, so we can't prove that Albanian evolved from it. Still, whereas we know that Hungarians came to Europe *after* the Slavs, it's almost certain that Albanians came to the Balkans *before* the Slavs. That's because if the Albanians had come after the Slavs, then there would certainly be a record of their mass migration (just like there's a record of the Hungarian migration). Moreover, if Albanians were a spin-off from the Slavic, Greek, or Italian culture, then their language would share far more elements with them. Therefore, it's almost certain that Albanians evolved from either the Illyrians or the Dacians (a pre-Roman civilization centered around Eastern Serbia and Romania). What's strange is that we can't even prove where the name *Albanian* comes from.

What Albania and Finland have in common

There is a world of difference between Finland and Albania, but they both call their country something that doesn't sound like what the rest of the world calls them. As we saw in the chapter on Finland, Finns call their country *Suomi* (while nearly all other countries call it something that sounds like "Finland"). Albania has the same deal: the Italian, Indonesian, Norwegian, Polish, Portuguese, Romanian, and Spanish languages call the Albanian country *Albania*. Other languages have a similar phonetic sound: *Albanie* (French); албания "Albaniya" (Russian, Bulgarian); *Albània* (Catalan); "Aherbainieya" (Chinese); *Albanija* (Balkanian, Lithuanian, Slovenian); *Albánie* (Czech); *Albanien* (Danish, Swedish, German); Albanië (Dutch); *Albānija* (Latvian); *Albánsko* (Slovak); *αλβανία* (Greek); and *Albanya* (Filipino).

So what do Albanians call their country? *Shqipëria*. Yeah, I didn't expect that either. They call their language *Shqip*. Why did all that happen? Nobody knows. First, the origin of the *Albanian* term is an enigma. There are few clues: in the second century BC, Polybius mentioned the Arbon tribe. About 400 years later, Ptolemy marked the city of *Albanopolis* near modern-day Durrës in Albania. There are other ideas, but nothing conclusive.

Second, scholars can't agree on where *Shqipëria* comes from either. One theory is that it comes from the verb *shqipoj*, implying *one who understands*. The other theory is that *Shqipëria* comes from *shqipojnë* (eagle). Albanians have been using the double-headed eagle symbol for at least 600 years. The Albanian flag, one of the coolest ones in the world, has a red background and a black two-headed eagle on it. But why call yourself *Shqipëria* if everyone calls you and your land something that sounds like *Albania*? Imagine if Europeans, Africans, South Americans, and Asians didn't call us something that sounds like "Americans," but instead called us something that sounds like "Kertians." At some point, why not just give in to the peer pressure and call ourselves Kertians? We could change our country's name to the United States of Kertia.

Would stupid pride hold us back? Probably. Fine. Then why don't the Albanians (and the Finns, for that matter) promote their real name? *Shqipëria* is a tongue twister, but we can pronounce *Shiperia*. The people could be called *Shiperians* and their language *Shiperian*. There. Easy, no? Other languages could invent similar sounding words and we'd all be in sync. Problem solved.

Instead, Albanians are insulted when foreigners try to imitate their real name. For example, Balkanians call them *Šiptar* (sounds like *Shiptar*). That's close to *Shqip*. However, Albanians becomes furious when someone calls them a *Šiptar* instead of an *Albanac*. Somehow it's as derogatory as *negro* is to a black man. Thus, it seems that Albanians prefer to keep things unchanged. By the way, there's no mutual sympathy between those from *Shqipëria* and those from *Suomi:* Finns call the Albanian land *Albania* while Albanians call the land of the Finns *Finlandë*.

Riding down the Drin River

Six years after my first visit, I returned to Albania via a dramatic and hidden backdoor. I took a pre-dawn *furgon* from Đakovica, Kosovo and went over the snow-covered border near Prushi and Bajram

Curri. The Albanian Alps, which reach up to 2,751 meters (9,023 ft), form a natural border here—their icy towers have helped keep Albania isolated. The road descended to Fierza next to the Drin River, where cars loaded onto a small ferry boat that floated down a spectacular canyon for two hours. I spent most of the breathtaking journey talking in basic Italian with a young Albanian man who operated the ferry for his father. At one point he said, "You know that Albanians are very different than those guys in Kosovo."

"How?" I asked. I was curious because Balkanians never made a distinction between Albanians from Kosovo and those from Albania.

He said, "People in Kosovo are animals. They have lots of babies and have sex with their cousins."

"*Benisimo!* Sounds like my kind of people," I said. "So do most Albanians look down Kosovars?"

"Yeah. Of course, we're connected with our language, but they're not as civilized as we are. They're poorer. Less educated."

We continued to talk as the ferryboat glided downstream with vertical, snow-capped mountains surrounding us. It felt like we were entering a fantasyland filled with angels and demons. For thousands of years, the river had been slicing through these mountains so that today it is over 100 meters (328 feet) deep. The water looks pristine, but in 2010 only half the Albanians were satisfied with the quality of their water—that's the lowest rate in Europe. Eventually, we stopped near Lake Komani, where I boarded a waiting *furgon* that negotiated the worst dirt road I had seen in Eastern Europe. It felt like we were driving on top of a jackhammer.

After an hour, the road went from being a complete disaster to a regular disaster. At one stop, Albanians piled into the *furgon*. A young, tall Albanian with hip sunglasses sat next to me. His name was Afrim Gerbeti and he had served in Iraq for a non-profit. He was one of the rare Albanians that I met that had five siblings. He was surprised to find an American in this corner of Albania. I asked him about something Balkanians had warned me about: a set of laws called the Kanun.

The Kanun

Nothing is more misunderstood in Albanian culture than the Kanun. Its name comes from the Greek word that means *canon* (i.e., sacred scripture). Most consider the Kanun a brutal medieval code of ethics. True, but have you read Leviticus lately? Afrim said, "The Kanun is similar to many holy texts. It discusses our duties, our professions, how to assemble, how to judge and have a jury, and how to punish crimes. It's all about honor."

The Kanun started as an oral tradition and it was written down in the 1400s. Afrim explained that it's based on four pillars: *Nderi* (Honor), *Mikpritja* (Hospitality), *Sjellja* (Right Conduct), and *Fis* (Family Loyalty). It declares that all men have equal rights and that all women have their own equal rights (this sounds like an American document that was written three centuries later). You're free to act more or less as you like as long as you don't hurt others. It gives you tips on how to dishonor a man: call him a liar in public, insult his wife, denigrate his hospitality, and worst of all, take his weapons. Indeed, the right to bear arms was alive and well in Albania hundreds of years before Americans put it in the Bill of Rights. This all seems pretty tame. So what's the big deal?

There are two reasons that the Kanun raises eyebrows today. First, some believe that Albanians still follow the Kanun today. This wouldn't seem so bad if it wasn't for the second concern: that the Kanun permits blood feuds. A murdered man's relatives can rightfully "take their blood back." The Kanun also gives you the green light to burn down a criminal's house, kick out his family, and, of course, execute him (and his family). In the 1800s, there was a macabre case that started when one Albanian man accused another of promising merchandise and not delivering. That set off a chain of murders and retributions that left 132 men dead and 1,218 houses burned down.[3]

On the other hand, vengeance is common in many societies. Who is prone to seek revenge? After surveying 89,000 people in 53 countries, one study concluded that the most vengeful humans are women, the old, the poor, and people who live in high-crime areas. Also, most vengeful people tend to live in countries that have widespread poverty, an uneducated population, and weak rule of law. They're also common after wars and in linguistically fragmented populations.[4] The Kanun was simply recording the moral code that many societies have anyway. Afrim told me, "There are two myths about the Kanun. One is that there's just one Kanun. There's actually five versions, each one customized for an Albanian region."

I asked, "And the second myth?"

"That Albanians actually give a shit about it. Maybe a few old men in the Albanian Alps are still following the Kanun, but most people, especially young people, don't care about it all."

The stuffy *furgon* jerked to a stop in Shkodër and everyone was eager to get out. Afrim introduced me to his skinny sister, Esmeralda, who was waiting for him. She was wearing tight black jeans and a mini fur coat—not looking like the stereotypical Muslim at all. They showed me Shkodër's Catholic cathedral, which during the atheistic communist period was converted into a volleyball court. Before leaving, I asked Afrim, "What about the white hats? Serbs told me that all Albanians wore them."

He laughed, "That's as stupid as an Albanian saying that all Serbs wear a *šajkača,* the traditional Serb hat. It has a slightly different shape and is usually a dark color, but it's the same idea as the Albanian white hat. Serb military commanders during the Bosnian War wore a *šajkača.* Old villagers might still wear it. But Serbs mostly don't. It's like saying that all Americans wear a cowboy hat. Sure, a few do, but it's just fashion. There's no meaning behind it. I saw many Americans in Iraq wearing baseball hats. So what?"

I'm broke, but I can still afford cigarettes

Afrim helped me find a bus that goes to the Rozafa Fortress, which overlooks Shkodër. He wished me well on my plan to traverse Albania from north to south. Soon after getting on the bus, the fare collector came by. There was a guy smoking in the back of the bus and I expected him to tell him to stop smoking. Instead, he asked him for a cigarette and started smoking himself. Mothers with crying babies were nearby. I had taken off my shoes to air out my feet for a few minutes and the guy pinched his nose and pointed at my feet. I pinched my nose and pointed at his cigarette. He laughed and walked away.

Albanians pump out more smoke than a coal factory. You'll often see Albanians stacking cigarette boxes in eye-catching positions, selling them out of their cars. Most Albanians barely make $100 per week yet they choose about 10 percent of their income on cigarettes. Cafés and restaurants are filled with smoke, most of it coming from men. In 2009, Albania finally put a ban on smoking in public places, but the law is only loosely enforced. Unfortunately, cigarette butts and trash litter much of the country.

The Rozafa Fortress's strategic location over Lake Shkodër guaranteed its turbulent history. Around 500 BC, the Illyrians constructed the first fort. The Romans struggled to conquer it. So did the Byzantines, Slavs, Venetians, and Turks. In 1913, Montenegro tried to conquer Shkodër, but only came away with Ulcinj. Today, Montenegrins talk about Albanians "invading" Ulcinj. Their selective memories don't remember that Ulcinj was part of Albania for a long time. It's like Californians who complain that Hispanics are everywhere, forgetting that Hispanics were there before the American migrants. The open-air Rozafa fortress is covered with grass and has an invigorating view of the snowy Albanian Northern Alps. On my way back down, I passed a child taking four goats for a walk. Like the fortress, it seems that some things in Albania haven't changed much.

Most Albanians don't live in Albania

On my bus trip from Shkodër to Krujë, I talked about current events with Avni and Gazmir, two young English students. They spoke about the Albanian diaspora: there are 700,000 Albanians in Italy, 320,000 in Germany, 200,000 in Switzerland, and 200,000 in the USA. Add up the Albanians spread all over the Balkans and you'll find that less than 40 percent of the world's 7.5 million Albanians live in Albania.

The Albanian diaspora continues. Avni and Gazmir were part of the 38 percent of Albanians who want to leave Albania if circumstances allowed. According to another 2010 Gallup poll, 28 percent of Albanians have had a family member move to a foreign country during the last five years—that put it in the world's top 10. In 2010, 42 percent of Albanians would "would you like to move permanently to another country." That was the highest rate in the Balkan Monitor. When I asked Avni what life is like for Albanians abroad, he said, "When Albanians sneak into other countries or break laws abroad, the authorities just ship them back to Albania. However, Greeks and Serbs will just kill them. They both want to exterminate us."

That sounded like hyperbole, so we talked about Kosovo instead. Gazmir told me the opposite of what the ferryman had said. He said, "Kosovo is more civilized than Albania because it enjoyed the Yugoslavia's influence while Albania was closed to the world."

That seemed plausible. Clearly, we need to go to Kosovo next to see who's right. Then I asked them, "How's life for women?"

Gazmir started to say, "Albanians are fanatical about protecting their women..."

"...and culture," Avni interrupted. He added, "Women aren't as free as they are in America. Our culture is still conservative and traditional."

Before I got off the bus to go to Krujë, I asked them about their post-graduation job prospects. Avni said, "Not great. Our country's realistic unemployment rate is about 25 percent. The average salary is just $300 per month. Now you know why we want to leave our country."

Albania's paradoxical hero in Krujë

It's so easy to befriend Albanians that within seconds after jumping off the bus, a couple of young guys were happy to walk me to my next *furgon* stop. Along the way, they showed me a curious café. It had a picture of a pair of Albanian and American flags side by side. The name of the café was surprising: "Bar/Kafe George W. Bush." The Albanians told me that in 2007, Bush visited Albania and had a drink at this café. He was the first US President to visit post-communist Albania. After he left, the owner renamed the café in Bush's honor. Although Bush was the least popular US president in polling history, Albanians love him (and Clinton) because US policy favored Albania. In 2011, Gallup reported that 88 percent of Albanians approved of US leadership. Later,

I saw two Albanian postage stamps: one with the Statue of Liberty and the other with the Bush's smiling face. In July 2011, Krujë erected a tall statue of Bush.

The *furgon* snaked its way up a mountain and left me in front of a statue of another popular guy named George. Born in 1405, the youngest of nine children, George Kastrioti Skanderbeg is Albania's fascinating and paradoxical national hero. The Turkish Sultan Murad II took Skanderbeg away from his Albanian home at the age of 18. After 20 years of being a Muslim and serving the sultan in various military expeditions, Skanderbeg deserted him. He went to Krujë, rejected Islam, became a Christian, united various Albanian princes, raised an army of 12,500, and unveiled a red double-headed eagle flag for the first time.

Skanderbeg was a military genius. For 25 years, he consistently defeated the far stronger Turkish military. Sultan Murad II couldn't stop him after years of trying. After he died, his son tried too, and failed twice. Even the guy who conquered Istanbul couldn't take Krujë. Skanderbeg became a hero throughout Europe for resisting the "unstoppable" Turkish Empire. Armies couldn't kill him, but a mosquito did: at 62 years old, Skanderbeg died of malaria.

Although Murad II's son finally conquered Krujë 11 years after Skanderbeg died, Skanderbeg was immortalized. Voltaire praised him in his works. Three operas are named after him, including one by Antonio Vivaldi. You'll find statues of him in Geneva, Brussels, Italy, and even Michigan. His 25 years of rule were Albania's glory years. He became Albania's symbol of independence. Today, many Albanian homes have a painting of him. The Skanderbeg Museum celebrates his remarkable life. Nevertheless, after I left the museum and walked through Krujë's cobblestoned bazaar, I was scratching my head.

According to the CIA, about 70 percent of Albanians are Muslim and only 10 percent are Catholic. Mosques are common throughout Albania; churches are rare. Isn't it strange that Albanians idolize Skanderbeg, a man who made a living slicing and dicing Muslims? In fact, he kicked so much Islamic ass that the Pope had appointed Skanderbeg to Captain-General of the Holy See and gave him the title *Athleta Christi* (Champion of Christ). There's still a mansion in the Vatican City called *Palazzo Skanderbeg*. In 1735, George Lillo wrote a book about Skanderbeg called *The Christian Hero*. If Skanderbeg returned to Albania today, would he say, "Hey, thanks for all the statues, but if you love me so much, why aren't you guys Christian? Why did you give into the enemy and become Muslims?"

If George Washington had been a Muslim fighting the British-Christian infidels, would we still have him on the one-dollar bill? Albanians seem to have brushed Skanderbeg's Christian background under the carpet. Instead, they focus on him being the first Albanian to unite the nation, albeit for just 25 years and in just a section of Albania. Skanderbeg's deeds kept the dream of Albanian independence simmering during the centuries of Turkish occupation. Finally, in 1878, exactly 400 years after the fall of Krujë, Albanians revolted against the Turks. The rebellion was crushed like a nut. They kept trying until 1912, when they succeeded. Albanians call the period from 1878 to 1912 the *Rilindje Kombëtare* (National Renaissance). Still, they fell short of Skanderbeg's vision: about half of the Albanian population was not within Albania's borders. Most of those disconnected Albanians were now in Serbia, in a land called Kosovo.

Europe's friendliest people

I left Krujë to meet my Latvian couchsurfing host in Tirana. Her name was Sinty Jakane and she had two Albanian roommates. I figured she had moved from Latvia to enjoy the warmer weather, but I asked her if there was some other reason. She smiled and said, "Yes, the people! Latvians are cold, grumpy. When I first visited Albania, I fell in love with the friendliness and warmth of the people. Albanians smile and laugh often! Latvians frown too much. Albanians are happy and full of joy! I wanted to surround myself with such people, so I moved here."

It's true: Albanians are remarkably warm and outgoing. No matter how badly Albanians spoke English, they wanted to communicate. For example, while I was sitting on a bench counting white hats, two mothers and their teenage daughters started talking with me after I asked one mother a simple question. The mother knew probably 20 English words, but she cheerfully tried to communicate with me for almost 30 minutes. She laughed often and clearly enjoyed the interaction. What a difference between Albania and the Baltic, where people who could speak English were sometimes either reluctant or rude. Meanwhile, in Albania, locals will make heroic (and often humorous) attempts to speak English, Italian, or sign language.

Albanians are also touchy-feely. When I asked men for directions, they would sometimes grab my arm and pull me next to them to show the way. Women often walk together holding hands or locking arms. What's most surprising is that a few men would walk arm-in-arm and even kiss each other on the cheek. Although I'm used to seeing this in San Francisco, I suspected these men weren't gay. On the contrary, Albanians are homophobes. When asked, "Is the area where you live good place for gays and lesbians to live?" only one in 10 Albanians said *yes*.

On my second night in Tirana, I couldn't find my way back home. I was lost at 9:00 p.m. I didn't have Sinty's street address and she wasn't answering her phone. After 30 minutes of going in circles in the neighborhood, seven kids said they'd like to help. They were all between six and fourteen years old. Obviously Tirana is safe enough for children at night. The two oldest ones could speak enough English to translate to their young gang and passing adults. For 40 minutes my young, enthusiastic Albanian supporters went up and down streets with me, sometimes declaring, "Hey! I think I know where you live! Follow me!" They were always wrong, but their positive spirit was contagious. Eventually a student who spoke excellent English brought me to her father, and together we solved the mystery. The moral of this story is that Albania is a great place to get lost.

On the other hand, maybe I was just lucky. When Gallup asked the world if they had helped helped a stranger who needed help in the previous month, only 24 percent of Albanians said *yes*—that was the world's third lowest rate in 2011. In fact, all countries in the Balkans scored near the bottom. This is strange because whenever I asked for help in the Balkans, I usually got it. Perhaps Balkan people said *no* because no stranger had asked them for help in the previous month because it's not a common practice. (The USA had the world's second highest rate, 73 percent, after Liberia.)

When I finally found Sinty's place, she introduced me to her second couchsurfing guest, Jakub Pilch from Poland. Jakub and I got along well and we agreed that the next day we would explore Berat, a town that's about a two-hour bus ride south of Tirana. Jakub didn't have a sleeping bag, so Sinty invited him to share the bed with her. This rarely happens in Couchsurfing. Obviously both strangers must feel comfortable with each other. Before you conclude that the Albanian touchy-feely attitude transformed Sinty into a slut, I was sleeping in the same room at the foot of the bed in my sleeping bag. Jakub behaved like a gentleman and didn't even complain when Sinty stole most of the covers during that cold night.

The next morning, I hugged Sinty goodbye and went with Jakub to the bus station. Jakub is a great travel companion because his brain seems to have a direct link to Wikipedia. He will inform you that during WWI, the following countries had their turn occupying Albania: Greece, Serbia, France, Italy, and Austria-Hungary. That's a lot of flag changing. He observed that in April 1939, five months before WWII got started in earnest, Mussolini invaded Albania. Sometimes Jakub will cite obscure facts like how right before WWII Albania's ruler, King Zog (I'm not making up his name) stole lots of gold from the nation's treasury and rented out the floor at London's Ritz Hotel. Indeed, Albania's post-WWII history is crazy.

A wacky dictator

For over 40 years, Albania was run by Enver Hoxha, one of the wackiest dictators the world has ever seen. Hoxha (pronounced *Ho-ja*) founded Albania's Communist Party in the middle of WWII while he led the fascist resistance. Albania's surreal post-WWII history begins with the fact that it was the only European nation to end the war with more Jews than it started with. Only one Jewish family was deported and killed. It's fascinating that Europe's most Islamic nation was the one that did the best job at protecting its Jews. Perhaps it helped that Hoxha was an atheist.

It's hard to decide if Hoxha was an insecure paranoid psycho or just a paranoid psycho. Tito tried to suck Albania into his country as Yugoslavia's seventh republic, but Hoxha gave Tito the finger and cut off all relations with Yugoslavia. The USA and UK tried to overthrow Hoxha, but Hoxha dodged those efforts and cut off all relations with English speakers. In 1948, Albania became buddy-buddy with Stalin's USSR. Albania did the classic communist five-year bonehead plans along with the ugly commie architecture. Nevertheless, in 1961, Khrushchev demanded that Hoxha let the Soviets make a submarine base in Vlorë. Hoxha told him, "Dude, did you read the title on my business card? It says *Supreme Comrade*. Go back to Moscow, Ruski boy!"

A couple of years after cutting off all Soviet relations, Hoxha got cozy with Mao Zedong in China and brought Chinese communist culture to Albania. He collectivized agriculture, prohibited western literature, and banned all religions. Albania became the only officially atheist country on Earth. When the Soviets invaded Czechoslovakia in 1968, puny Albania left the Warsaw Pact and decided to defend themselves by building 750,000 igloo-shaped concrete bunkers all over the country. When Mao Zedong died in 1976, Hoxha didn't like the new Chinese leadership, so, you guessed it—he cut off all relations with China too. Who was left? Nobody. In 30 years, Albania had managed to reject Yugoslavia, the UK, the USA, the USSR, the Warsaw Pact, and China. Flyspeck Albania was all alone in the world. It traded with no one, had no friends, and soon had no money.

In 1985, Hoxha died. Albania was Europe's poorest country, and it soon became even poorer. The collective farmers stopped working because they weren't getting paid, so the city folk starved. Industries stopped paying their workers, so they stopped working. Spare parts ran out and the machines stopped moving. Like Ayn Rand's *Atlas Shrugged* predicted, the engine of their country simply stopped.

In 1990, thousands of Albanians burst into Western embassies hoping they would help free them from their country that had become a prison. Later, 20,000 Albanians jumped on pathetic rafts to sail to Italy. For decades a 10-meter-high (33 ft) gold statue of Enver Hoxha overlooked Tirana's central square. Just like a mob tore down Saddam Hussein's statue, Hoxha's statue was brought down in 1991. Hoxha also had a massive concrete pyramid mausoleum nearby, but after

1992 Albanians removed his body and tossed it in an ordinary grave in the city's outskirts. When I visited the former mausoleum, kids were skateboarding around it. In 2011, Albanians were thinking about leveling it and replacing it with a new parliament building.

When I asked Albanians what the best thing about the communist period was, most said something similar to what Avni told me, "Albania was super safe. A woman could walk alone in the middle of a night anywhere and not have a problem." That's the benefit of a police state. According to Tirana's National Historical Museum, political rebels suffered: 30,383 were exiled, 17,900 were jailed, and 5,157 were executed. Albania's communist period was similar to North Korea in 2011. They were frozen in time. Finally, in 1992, when the blinds were lifted, Albanians could find out what the rest of the world was doing.

The Wild West in Eastern Europe

After their totalitarian nightmare, Albania went to another extreme: the Wild West. In the 1990s, smuggling operations exploded, farms became marijuana plantations, and stolen Mercedes Benzes flooded the country. Without internal travel restrictions, the farmlands emptied out and the population of Tirana tripled.

Without financial controls, financial pyramid schemes took off. Albanians quit their jobs because they were earning more money just off the interest in their bank accounts. They celebrated as their savings went up 50 percent each month. Predictably, the Ponzi schemes collapsed. About 70 percent of Albanians lost all their savings. Chaos, riots, and mayhem erupted in the streets as the former communists learned their first hard lesson about capitalism: if it sounds too good to be true, it probably is.

> *Whenever you find yourself on the side of the majority, it is time to pause and reflect. — Mark Twain*

Albanians looted the few industries that still survived the communist period. Once they destroyed all the machines and factories, poverty expanded. Meanwhile, in 1999, nearly half a million Albanian refugees poured in from Kosovo. They were fleeing the war with the Serbs. The poorest country in Europe, who could barely take care of its own three million citizens, could hardly help half a million refugees. The last century was rough for Albania. Then again, the previous six centuries weren't much better.

So far, this century has been a bit more positive. Albania is no longer the poorest country in Europe. Compared to the rest of the world, its GDP per capita is average. In 2007, Albania instituted a flat tax of 10 percent on capital gains, personal, and corporate income. Albania's ranking on the World Bank's Ease of Doing Business Index improved from 138th place (in 2008) to 82nd place (in 2011). Nevertheless, it's not easy enough. For example, Sinty updated me two years after I couchsurfed with her. She had been doing graphic design for Albanian political parties and four Albanian magazines. She became frustrated with the "communist working habits that still haven't died." She said, "I found a Lithuanian woman who moved to Albania to help me. But after a while it was hard to work with the Albanians. She and I did most of the work. So after a year, it was time to leave."

Albania still has a big underground economy and a weak infrastructure. In 2010, only a quarter of Albanians had Internet at home—the lowest rate in Europe. They were also at the bottom of Europe in Gallup's Communications Index, which measures the digital connectedness of a country. At least it's no longer the Wild West.

Changing religions is easier than you think

Jakub and I arrived in Berat, the "Town of 1,000 Windows." The town got its nickname because from the river, you can see a hill covered with handsome white Turkish houses with red-tiled roofs. Some Albanians live within the fourteenth century fortress that overlooks the city. Jakub pointed out that the Illyrians, Romans, Byzantines, Serbs, Bulgarians, Turks, Italians, and Albanians have all controlled this town at some point. Thinking about that and the rest of their history helped me understand the Skanderbeg Paradox.

At first glance, it seems impossible to force people to switch religions. For example, when I asked Jakub to stop being a Catholic, he politely refused, even after I offered him a thick bar of chocolate. However, what if I did the Turkish thing and said, "Become a Muslim or I'll raise your taxes." After a couple of generations, enough people would convert. At first, they may be insincere devotees, but after a few generations of indoctrination in schools, a high percentage would become true believers. Thus, 200 years after Skanderbeg, most Albanians were no longer phony Muslims who just went through the motions to appease the authorities. They became sincere Muslims.

Then came Hoxha, who swept away Islam and replaced it with atheism. At first, devout Albanians resisted, but after a couple of generations, most Albanians stopped taking religion too seriously. The US State Department estimates that only about a third of Albanians actively participate in a religion. In 2010, a Gallup survey revealed that only 17 percent of Albanians had gone to a "place of worship or religious service in the previous week." Therefore, the Balkanian claim that all Albanians are Muslims is misleading. The reality is that most don't take Islam (or any religion) too seriously. As we saw, that's a similar attitude that Balkanians have, although Albanians are especially apathetic.

Along Tirana's tree-lined Bulevardi Dëshmorët e Kombit there's a statue of Mother Teresa. She was an ethnic Albanian, but a Christian, not a Muslim. All this helps explain the Skanderbeg Paradox. Albanians aren't deeply tied to a religion—they're tied to their language. As Hoxha said, "the only religion of Albania is Albanianism." Skanderbeg and Mother Teresa are Albanian heroes because of their language and ideals. With so many occupiers coming and going, Albanians have had to stay flexible in order to keep the core of their culture alive: their language. Many humans seem to switch religions more easily than they switch languages. Bosniaks gave up Christianity for Islam. Most Europeans gave up their pagan beliefs for Christianity. Ex-Soviet countries are far more atheistic than before. Albania teaches you that religions and languages are constantly evolving, but that language is more stubborn.

Jakub was returning to Tirana, while I was going to the coastal town of Vlorë. We grabbed a parting meal. In 2010, 88 percent of Albanians told the Balkan Monitor that they ate healthfully the previous day—that was a much higher percentage than ex-Yugoslavs. I had *tarator* (chilled yogurt and cucumber soup) and a *Fërgesë Tiranë* (meat, eggs, and tomatoes). Meanwhile, Jakub bought a *byrek* (same as the Balkanian *burek*). As he chewed, he observed, "A *burek* is the fast-food hamburger of the Balkans."

Riding along the Ionian Sea

When I arrived in Vlorë in the afternoon, the last bus heading south had already left, so I was stuck there for the night. Vlorë is Albania's Philadelphia—it's where Albania declared its independence in 1912. A monolithic communist statue commemorates this event. The city has a long palm-tree-lined boulevard that could make you feel like you're in a resort town if it weren't for the unimaginative blocky buildings that detract from the fantasy. It has nice beaches, but the ones further south are much better, so I went to a café instead. After watching nicely dressed young Albanians come and go, I hiked up a hill with my flashlight and camped under the stars.

The next morning, I took a small bus that wound its way over the 1,000 meter (3,280 ft) Llogaraja Pass. Reflecting the unhurried Balkan atmosphere, the bus stopped near the summit so that everyone could have a coffee or a snack for 15 minutes. As we crested the pass, the view opened up: the marvelous Ionian Sea stretched as far as we could see. Directly west of us was the Strait of Otranto, where Italy and Albania are just 72 kilometers (45 miles) apart and the Adriatic meets the Ionian. We descended to Dhërmi and I asked the bus driver to drop me off at the *plazhi* (beach).

Beach bunkers

At the beach, I saw something I've always wanted to explore: an Albanian bunker. Albania has 750,000 pillbox bunkers scattered along the country's borders; still, unless you know what to look for, you may not see them. They're made out of heavily reinforced concrete and are big enough to fit one or two armed men. There's a narrow opening to stick your machine gun through. The domed top gives them a retro space-aged look. The story behind these concrete igloo bunkers is humorous in retrospect.

Hoxha was tired of relying on undependable bigger powers for his country's defense. He crafted the ultimate self-defense: pillbox bunkers, lots of them. When Hoxha's Chief Engineer announced that he had constructed a bunker that could sustain a direct blast from a tank, Hoxha said, "Wow! That's awesome! Are you sure it's strong enough to survive a direct tank assault?"

"Yes," the Chief Engineer said confidently.

"Great. Get in it now. I'll send a tank over to blast you to see how strong it really is."

The Chief Engineer gulped, but everyone has to obey the Supreme Comrade. He crawled into the bunker as the tank moved into position. The tank fired its cannon, the Chief Engineer said his prayers as the projectile flew toward him. The blast erupted. The spectators watched nervously. The dust settled. Miraculously, the Chief Engineer emerged. His head was spinning and his ears were ringing, but he was alive. Hoxha said, "Excellent. Make 750,000 bunkers like that and put them throughout Albania."

The Chief Engineer nodded (or perhaps his head was still bobbing from the aftershock). Although I've altered the dialogue, the story is true. Thus, from 1950 to 1985, the five-ton bunkers were placed everywhere. Perhaps we should give Hoxha some credit: nobody attacked Albania ever since the first bunker was made. They're so hard to move that most remain, in varying states of decomposition. Creative Albanians have colorfully painted them. Nowadays, the bunkers are the best place for teenagers to lose their virginity.

I was interested in the bunkers not because I wanted to lose my virginity (although that would be nice), but because they are a perfect campsite. The ones on the beach have soft sandy ground and a nice view from the slit. More importantly, the shelter would protect me from the rain and tanks.

Camping in a luxury hotel by the beach

For backpackers, one of the best things about poor countries is that there are often a lot of half-built buildings everywhere. That's because limited cash flow forces people to take over five years to build a house or a sudden economic crash derails ambitious plans. These half-built structures are excellent shelters. The trick is to go into them at night and leave before 6:00 a.m. (while leaving no trace behind). Although I was happy with my bulletproof shelter, I explored a half-built hotel overlooking the beach. Given the *fleur-de-lys* symbols on the mosaic floors, it was meant to be a luxury hotel. The lack of construction materials implied that the project had been put on hold for years. The fourth floor corner room had a million-dollar view of the Ionian Sea. As much as I wanted to camp in an armored home, I couldn't pass up camping in this luxury suite that had no plumbing, doors, or glass windows.

With a luxurious camping spot picked, I spent the rest of the day eating and hanging out at the only open restaurant along the beach. The cool mid-March temperatures kept most tourists away, although you could already walk in the sun in a T-shirt. Dhërmi is a surreal beach because directly above it are snow-covered mountains. At the restaurant, I met Elton and Virma Çaushi, who worked in the travel industry and lived in Tirana. I asked Virma if things have changed in Albania for her in the last 10 years. She said, "When I was a teenager, men were more totalitarian. Back then, I didn't feel as independent or as equal as I do now. Even an old lady could not have her own car. It was hard to get permission to go out. Now there are more opportunities."

Residual effects of this controlling atmosphere remain. Only four in ten Albanians told Gallup that they were able to choose how they spent their time the previous day. That's the third lowest rate in the world, after Haiti and Azerbaijan. Virma added, "Women in the south are more liberal; in the north, it's more of a patriarchy."

I asked Elton if there was something he liked about communism. He said, "The communists developed a great education system. When Hoxha took over, most people were illiterate. He implemented a Russian educational system, built universities, and developed the arts. By the 1970s, everyone could read and write."

I asked, "How would you characterize Albanians?"

Elton reclined on his chair and said, "Albanians are more isolated than others in the Balkans. We're less open minded than others. We're more defensive. The mountains that surround us make us this way. But Albanians who live abroad are different. They don't want their capital to be Tirana, but Brussels."

"What's changing nowadays?" I asked.

"Now it's becoming cool to not smoke," he said as he lit a cigarette.

After they left, I shuffled over to a French couple who was exploring the Balkans. They had a tent and were planning to camp on the beach. I invited them to visit my suite on the fourth floor and offered to check them into one of the vacant rooms down the hall. Given the view and the price, they agreed to be my hall mates for the night.

Hitchhiking along Europe's least developed Mediterranean coastline

The next morning, without knowing the bus schedule, I went to the road and stuck out my thumb. Soon, a black sporty car unexpectedly pulled over. A somewhat overweight man with black sunglasses invited me in. He looked like he was a 35-year-old Albanian mafia hit man. Awesome. I got in.

We spoke English most of the way, but sometimes used Italian or French. The stereotype of Albanians only speaking Albanian seemed hard to prove. My driver was going to Sarandë, which was 90 minutes away. He was proud of the newly paved coastal road because it used to be dreadful. Traffic was light, although we had to slow down when 30 sheep needed to use the road. When I asked him what he did in Sarandë, he said, "I'm the Chief of Police."

He said that crimes were diminishing and that violent crime is quite rare in Albania. I didn't bring up the Balkan bribe culture. According to the Balkan Monitor, nine percent of those in Kosovo said they had to bribe someone in the previous year—that was the lowest rate in the Western Balkans. On the other extreme was Albania, where over *half* of the people had to bribe someone in 2010. Most Balkan bribes don't go to the police, but to doctors and medical workers. Besides, it's nice to know that Balkan bribes are the most "efficient" in Albania: 74 percent of the time the guy who gets the bribe delivers his end of the deal. Now that's service.

The drive along Albania's southern coast is one of the most scenic rides in Eastern Europe. We passed Drymades and Himara's beaches, along with several more intimate beaches. Cliffs drop steeply into the turquoise waters of the Ionian Sea. After an hour, we stopped for a coffee. Everyone knew the Chief. People would tap their horns to say hi to him. While having a drink, he told me that his wife and kids live in Vlorë. It would be too long of a commute, so he has an apartment in Sarandë for the four nights a week that he spends there. The other days he stays with his family in Vlorë. Why not move the family to Sarandë? With a slight smile, he said, "Things are good this way. I have my liberty."

When we got to Sarandë, he gave me his name and cell phone number and said, "If you have any problems while you're in Albania, call me."

I thanked him profusely for the ride and offered him several hundred *lekë* (Albania's currency) to pay for the gas. He refused my bribe.

Butrint: a microcosm of Mediterranean history

Although Sarandë has a nice boardwalk, it's not that pretty of a town. Still, it's on the water, has a nice view of the Greek island of Corfu, and experiences 290 sunny days per year. Although Sarandë is Albania's southernmost coastal city, it's worth going another 24 kilometers (15 miles) south to the Greek-Albania border. There lies one of Eastern Europe's greatest historical treasures: the UNESCO World Heritage Site of Butrint.

An aerial look explains why Butrint has a desirable location. It looks as if nature built a moat around a piece of land. Because a river snakes around it, it's practically an island with a narrow "bridge" to the mainland. It's easily defended and has access to the Ionian Sea. If you are looking for the dream location to live (or to build a fort), this is it.

Butrint is a microcosm of Mediterranean history. As you walk through it, you walk through layers of history. First came the Greeks in the sixth century BC. Virgil wrote that fleeing Trojans founded Butrint. The city's earliest building was a healing sanctuary to the god Asclepius. You can walk through the third century BC theater that the Greeks built, which held 2,500 spectators. The Romans expanded the theater and the city. The urban center struggled during the fifth century. After the Roman Empire split, the Byzantine rulers turned Butrint into an ecclesiastical center. In the sixth century, the Byzantines erected the Great Basilica. The Normans conquered Butrint in 1081. Then the Venetians bought it in 1386 and, for the next 400 years, did the wonderful things that the Venetians do. By the end of the 1800s, the Turkish Empire added some defenses to the fort. Then, Butrint returned to Greece. Finally, Albania got it. What makes Butrint so special is that there are multiple layers of history all in one small area. It's one of most interesting off-the-beaten-track places I visited in Eastern Europe.

A 66-year-old who can't speak English invites me to his home

The bus out of Butrint didn't go all the way to Sarandë. It dropped me off in the small town of Kasmil, where I needed to transfer to another bus. Instead, I explored the coastal town. While I was walking on a rocky and deserted bay, a thin 66-year-old man saw me and called out. I yelled back, "*Më falni, nuk kuptoj.* I don't speak Albanian."

That didn't discourage him. He smiled and said something else that I didn't understand. I pointed to myself and said, "Me. From San Francisco. California. America." He smiled, laughed, and said another incomprehensible phrase. I started walking slowly. Instead of waving goodbye, he walked next to me. We continued our gorilla-communication until we figured out that we both spoke ultra-basic Russian. He must have learned it in school when he was a boy in the 1950s during Albania's pro-Russian period. Given our poor Russian skills, we graduated to Tarzan-communication.

We walked together along the waterfront, occasionally exchanging a few words, but mostly enjoying our silent company. He asked me to call him Melo, but his real name was Nevrus Lame. With that last name, it's good that he didn't go to an English-speaking school. He pointed to a tiny hut and he said, "*Bar*!" He unlocked it. It was a small storage room for summer gear and his stash of alcohol. He poured me *raki* (homemade liquor), even though he understood that I don't drink alcohol. It was a tiny amount compared to his serving. We toasted, enjoyed the beach sunset, and then eventually continued walking. He led me to his house and invited me in for a "*kafe*." His 60-year-old wife greeted me and probably thought, "Why does my husband always have to invite strange Americans into our home?"

Later, an old lady showed up and we watched *Big Brother* on TV. Melo invited me to have dinner with them. I shared the bread that I was carrying and we had some pasta and salad. They explained that their son was living in Chicago. After dessert, they invited me to sleep on their couch. The next day, Melo walked me to the bus stop. We exchanged a warm goodbye. Albanians were hardly the demons that Balkanians made them out to be.

The Albanian population growth myth

Balkanians claimed that Albanians have eight to 20 children. That may have been true over 60 years ago when Albanian women who had an above-average amount of children got cash and were labeled *Nënë Heroinë* (Heroine Mother). Many Europeans had similar programs and high fertility rates back then. Nevertheless, Ivan Sokolov (a Serb) told me, "I honestly believe that full peace in the Balkans can only happen if the Albanian rapid population growth stops. If it doesn't, the problems with the Albanians will spread to other regions of Europe. Consider the fact that their population grew from 1.5 million in 1900 to close to five million by the year 2000. That says a lot in my opinion."

Actually, it doesn't. That's a growth rate of 3.3 times. America grew from 76 million to 281 million over the same period—growing 3.7 times. The reason why Balkanians believe Albanians are reproducing like rabbits is that Albanians have the fastest reproduction rate in the Balkans. Still, that's not saying much. Globally, Albania is well below average. According to the CIA's 2011 report, Albania has 1.48 children per woman. That's a wee bit less than the claimed 8 to 20 children. In fact, it's below the 2.1 replacement rate and puts them in 187th place in the world (Serbia ranks at 201 with a rate of 1.4). Although Albania's population growth rate is still slightly positive (0.27%), it will soon join the rest of the Balkans and have a negative growth rate.

Albania's massive emigration is accelerating Albania's population decline. Waves of Albanians have fled whenever Albania has had a crappy period. Unfortunately, they've had *many* crappy periods. These Albanian émigrés send home so much money that it accounts for nine percent of Albania's GDP. This emigration and a 1.48 fertility rate doom Albania to depopulation. Vladimir Ivosević summed up why Serbians (and other Balkanians) are deluded, "Few Serbians have been to Albania and so many think that Albanians are some form of gypsy."

Paradoxes

Usually stereotypes have at least some truth to them. Nevertheless, throughout the journey through Eastern Europe, we've found a few exceptions. Albania is the most extreme case of being disconnected from their stereotype. Consider the stereotypes versus what I found. Balkanians told me that they:

- **Steal:** Yet no one tried to rob me or short-change me. I left my bags with the hotel, in the back of furgons, and in a casino. Nothing was ever taken. A 2010 Gallup poll showed that 11 percent of Albanians had something stolen from them that year. Other countries that had an 11 percent theft rate included Cuba, Denmark, Ireland, Macedonia, Mali, the Philippines, the UK, and Vietnam. Canada and the USA had higher theft rates.
- **Stink:** Yet they certainly don't stink more than any other European.
- **Are dirty:** The poor were dirty, but that's usually the case anywhere you go; at night highly fashionable Albanians roamed the streets.
- **Have eight to 20 children per family:** The biggest family I met had six children. Almost every Albanian I talked with came from a two-child family. Moreover, they said that most people they knew had a similar sized family. The statistics confirm this.
- **All look the same and are ugly due to inbreeding:** Their looks were incredibly varied and there were tons of handsome men and hot women. Hardly any women were covered up.
- **Are all Muslims:** From 1967 to 1990 Albania was the only officially atheist state on the planet. The government banned public religious services and converted many churches into theaters or cinemas. Today, Albania is Earth's least serious Muslim nation.
- **All the men wear a white cap:** Yet only about one out of 100 men wore one and they were all senior citizens.

- **Only speak Albanian:** Yet many speak Italian and some speak English. If anything, there are more polyglots in Albania than in most Eastern European countries.
- **Follow the medieval and barbaric Kanun:** Yet Albanians scoffed when I asked about it, saying that only those in Albania's rural north pay any attention to the Kanun. Most couldn't even give me a couple of laws from the Kanun.
- **Murder or injure for trivial reasons:** Yet I purposely bumped into people and farted in public and no one shot me.

In short, I searched to confirm the stereotypes, but I came out finding the opposite. Instead, I learned that we can all learn something from Albania.

What Albania Can Teach Us

- **Be friendly and helpful.** We should send most of Eastern Europe to Albania to learn how to smile.
- **Touch others.** Although Americans don't value personal space as much as the Japanese, we could touch each other a bit more. Touching is a primal way of connecting with others. Albanians are never shy about gently touching each other or getting close to each other. Moreover, they don't have a homophobic response when a man touches another man.
- **Honk only if you're happy.** Americans are quick to honk whenever they're irritated. Albanians usually only honk when they're happy. They tap their car's horn whenever they want to say hi to anyone, for example. If they're on a collision course with someone or another driver is blocking traffic and being stupid, they simply take evasive action without honking their horn.

Places I saw and recommend in Albania: Drin River ride, Albanian Alps, Butrint, and the southern beaches.

Travel deals and info: http://ftapon.com/albania

I entered Albania confused and I left confused. Where were all these nasty Albanians? Maybe they're in Kosovo. Let's find out.

17

Kosovo—The Land of Myths and Legends

Kosovo is a bit bigger than tiny Delaware, but it's more complicated than America. Simply put, Kosovo is a story about two tribes, the Serbs and the Albanians. Each believes that Kosovo is rightfully theirs and that the other tribe has victimized them for a long time. Each group is heavily armed with facts and myths to support their passionate (and often illogical) beliefs. Each group is about as calm and rational as a baby who hasn't slept or eaten for 20 hours.

Trying to understand who is right is like finding a dead body with two guys standing over it holding bloody knives claiming that the other guy did it. Both suspects are incredibly persuasive, showering you with statistics while calling the other guy a liar. Who do you believe? They both seem honest, but your instincts tell you that they're not giving you the full story. Where does fact end and fable begin? It will take a mountain of facts to unequivocally shatter Kosovo's many myths and solve this perplexing whodunit.

Before we begin, let's define the people. A *Kosovar* is someone from Kosovo. In 2011, about 90 percent of Kosovars were ethnic Albanians and most of the rest were ethnic Serbs. There's effectively no linguistic or ethnic difference between an *Albanian Kosovar* and an *Albanian;* nor is there any meaningful difference between a *Serb Kosovar* and a *Serbian* (especially a southern Serbian). Therefore, instead of using cumbersome terms like *Albanian Kosovar* and *Serb Kosovar,* we'll just call them *Albanians* and *Serbs*. That's what they usually call themselves anyway.

Entering an unstable land

In April 2004, as my bus came to the Kosovo border, I knew only one thing about Kosovo: that five years beforehand there had been a war. I did *not* know that the war wasn't fully over: one month before I arrived, widespread unrest left 19 dead, 800 houses destroyed, and 35 Orthodox churches desecrated. I also did not know what locals thought of Americans. Most Europeans disliked George W. Bush (who was the US President at the time). For example, when I told a Croatian mother that I was from San Francisco, she said, "Oh. America. I hate Americans. And I hate your President too." Yeah, it was a pleasant conversation. I had no idea if Kosovars hated us even more. For all I knew, I could be like a clueless German tourist visiting Moscow in 1946.

At Kosovo's heavily fortified border, UN vehicles and personnel were everywhere. Despite all the security, the border guard just glanced at my American passport and immediately gave it back to me. *Maybe they like us,* I thought. Signs, billboards, and menus were often in English, apparently catering to the legions of relief workers and NATO soldiers. I felt like a tourist on the edge of a war zone. Not a minute would pass without a UN vehicle, a police SUV, a military vehicle, or an armed guard going by. When you see such tight security, it's hard to know if you should feel safe or insecure.

Upon arriving in Pristina, Kosovo's capital, I couldn't believe what I saw: a six-story-high photo of Bill Clinton smiling and waving. The caption said, "Welcome to Bill Clinton Boulevard!" I blinked a few times and took another look. The picture was still there. I checked my medications. Yup, the capital's most important road was named after Clinton. Nearby was the new Hotel Victory, which had a seven-meter (23-ft) replica of the Statue of Liberty. Is it possible that the Kosovars like us or is America imposing its icons on this Muslim region? The last time America invaded a Muslim country to drive out an unwanted regime, the local reaction was lukewarm at best.

I walked the streets to learn more and followed the sound of loud music and the smell of food coming from an outdoor gathering. Most of the party-goers were well dressed, so it would be hard to blend in with my dirty jeans, old T-shirt, and huge backpack. Nevertheless, I took a deep breath and entered the gathering as if it were my own house.

Crashing a Kosovo party

People looked at me curiously as I walked in. I tossed my backpack in a corner and went up to a random couple and said, "Hi! I'm visiting from America. What are we celebrating today?"

They were a bit surprised at my boldness, but the man told me that this was a party for employees of the Albanian Radio Television of Kosovo. I said, "Cool, so you're journalists! I don't know anything about Kosovo. So who do you consider your allies in the region? Your best friends?"

The woman said, "America!"

That surprised me, so I said, "Why?"

"Because they helped us."

"Why did we help you?" I asked, not knowing the answer to that question either.

"Because I think America understands what it means to be human. We love America and are very grateful."

This was intriguing. I said, "You're Muslim, right?"

She nodded. So I said, "Why do you think that Muslims here in

Kosovo love Americans so much and see us as liberators, but that many Muslims in Iraq hate us?"

A gnarled expression swept across her face. "What? Muslims don't hate America! Don't equate Muslims with those terrorists! We're not terrorists! Those terrorists in Iraq aren't Muslims!"

I calmed her down, afraid that she might blow herself up. She offered to introduce me to her boss, Fatmir Bajrami, the Cameraman Supervisor for the station. He was a 55-year-old ethnic Albanian with a French wife. While I waited for Fatmir, I guzzled orange soda and stuffed my face with hamburgers and sausages. Fatmir had tan skin, gray hair, and dark probing eyes. He had filmed Nixon, Reagan, Bush, and Clinton. He had traveled the world. Although he spoke English well, his French was a bit stronger so we spoke in French. I said, "Albanians have tensions in all their neighboring countries. Why? Why do Albanians not like to integrate with the country they are in?"

"You have to understand the history," he said.

Oh great, here we go again, I thought. At least he spared me from regurgitating the glorious Illyrian history. He drew a map of the Balkans. He showed how Albanians overflow into Macedonia and Montenegro. Those border towns are primarily made up of Albanians. Fatmir explained, "Albanians lived in all these regions. They wanted to unite, since they felt like one nation. But after the First Balkan War in 1912, parts of Albania were divided among the victors."

"So Albanians don't want to integrate because they feel like it's their land that's getting occupied?"

"Exactly."

I got here first

Eastern Europeans are obsessed with the idea of who-got-here-first. In fact, most humans care about this idea too. This belief is so widespread that we apply it to our everyday lives. For example, imagine walking into a café or movie theater and telling someone to move seats because you want to sit where he's sitting. Or telling a camper to move so you can camp in his spot. It's culturally unacceptable to make such requests because there's an unspoken law that whoever got to a territory first has slightly more rights than whoever comes later. We get this from animals. Lions spray a territory to tell other lions, "This is my land and I got here first, so don't mess with me." Humans and nations piss around their land and tell their neighbors, "Hey dude, anything that stinks like me is mine."

The problem is that, unlike most animals, humans like to transfer these privileges to their children. Thus, we inherit rights, land, property, whereas the offspring of most animals have to start from scratch.

Eastern Europeans (and many other humans) like to pursue this inheritance logic to the extreme. They not only draw connections with their grandparents, but also with faceless ancestors, even though the genetic and cultural connection is weak or nonexistent. By drawing a continuous line, you can walk into a café and tell someone, "Get off my seat. My great-great grandfather used to sit there."

> *We seem to crave privilege, merited not by our works, but by our birth. — Carl Sagan, astronomer*

As Elton Çaushi told me, "Albanians, like most people in the Balkans, are obsessed with who was here first. Greeks, Macedonians, Albanians, Serbs, and Croatians all care about this issue. Albanians want Greeks to compensate us for land that they took that was once ours. But they say that we have land that was once theirs!"

Kosovars bring up ancient history even when you don't expect it. For example, when I asked Fatmir what he thought of Serbs, instead of talking about modern-day Serbs, he said, "Well, they're descendents of slaves. They came out of Russia and are still trying to live on this land."

He made it sound like Serbs are recent Balkan immigrants, yet Serbs have been in the Balkans for 1,500 years. At what point are you a native and no longer an immigrant? And why should that matter anyway? Unfortunately, it matters in the Balkans, especially in Kosovo. Kosovars debate ancient history as if it happened yesterday. Few Eastern Europeans are as obsessed about old history as Kosovars. *Therefore, to understand Kosovo we have to study its history deeply, especially its demographic history, not because it truly matters, but because Kosovars think it does.*

Serb origins are clearer than Albanian origins. In 2006, *The Journal of Human Genetics* studied the DNA of 20 Slavic populations and placed "the earliest known homeland of Slavs in the middle Dnieper basin [in Ukraine]."[1] Slavs showed up in Balkans around 650 AD. As we saw in the previous chapter, it's not clear where Albanians came from, although it's probable that Albanians were roaming around the Balkans before Serbs. It's ironic that Europeans make such a big deal about their differences. Of all the continents, none is as genetically homogeneous as Europe.[2]

Is Kosovo Serbia?

The Serbian nationalist mantra is "Kosovo is Serbia!" If Latinos living in Florida declared their state's independence, then we'd probably have Americans shouting, "Florida is America!" Is Kosovo Serbia? All sane Serbs admit that for at least the last 20 years, Kosovo has been over 80 percent Albanian. Thus, the Serb claim over Kosovo is based on political and demographic history, not on recent ethnographic statistics.

The boldest Serbs will claim that (until recently) Kosovo has "always" been dominated by Serbs. Let's turn back the clock and see how true that assertion is.

Serbs often say that Kosovo is the "cradle of their civilization." This is a myth. The earliest Serbian state was born and developed north and northwest of Kosovo (in present-day southern Serbia and Montenegro) around the eleventh century. By the time Serbia moved its power center to Kosovo, it had been out of its cradle for over 300 years. This grown-up Serbia ruled its medieval kingdom from Kosovo for 250 glorious years. During that time, they left their mark by building numerous monasteries and churches. Therefore, while Kosovo is not the cradle of Serbia's civilization, it is (in the words of Serbian academic Predrag Simić) "an area that sublimes the collective identity of the Serbian people just as Jerusalem does, for instance, for the Jewish nation."[3]

Regardless of Serb feelings, the cold reality is that Serbs dominated Kosovo for only the last third of their first 800 years in the Balkans. Before the Serbs, Bulgarians also held Kosovo for about 250 years.[4] However, Bulgarians don't use their historical ties to Kosovo to make modern-day territorial claims. So why do Serbs insist that "Kosovo is Serbia"? To answer that, we need to run through the next six centuries.

The Battle of Kosovo in 1389

Believe it or not, Serbs put a lot of significance into a battle that happened over 600 years ago. The Battle of Kosovo in 1389 involved tens of thousands of Serbs and Turks. For Serbs, the Battle of Kosovo symbolizes three things. First, the honor of dying for your beliefs: "I'd rather be a Serb Christian martyr than become a Turkish Muslim." That patriotic theme echoes in today's Serbian nationalist rhetoric. Second, the battle also symbolizes what happens when Serbs are not united: they lose. The third symbol is that the battle marks Serbia's fall from glory. What's surprising is that the last two symbols are somewhat mythological.

The first myth is that the Turks decisively won the Battle of Kosovo. The battle was a tie: both armies lost their leaders and suffered heavy causalities. The difference is that the Serbian army was effectively depleted, whereas the Turks could eventually mount another army that ultimately did the Serbs in.

The second myth is that the Battle of Kosovo marks Serbia's fall from glory. If you had to pick the year when Serbia's empire ended, you might pick 1355 (Tsar Dušan's death, which led to the empire's fragmentation) or 1459 (when Serbia completely surrendered to the Turks). You wouldn't pick 1389, especially since the Battle of Kosovo was a tie. It was folklore that made the Battle of Kosovo a bigger deal than it was in reality.[5] Nevertheless, the Turks effectively conquered Kosovo soon after 1389 and would control it until 1912.

So let's look at the Kosovo scoreboard during the 1,000-year period from 912 to 1912. Bulgaria and Serbia each controlled Kosovo for about 250 years, while the Turkish Empire had it for about 500 years. Therefore, what's more correct: "Kosovo is Serbia" or "Kosovo is Turkey"? Sure, the Turks were occupiers, but how long does you have to occupy a land before it's considered "yours"? Americans have been "occupying" lots of Native American land for only about 200 years. Is it not ours? Should we say "Dalmatia is Croatia" or "Dalmatia is Italy"? How about "Vojvodina is Serbia" versus "Vojvodina is Hungary"?

Unraveling Kosovo's demographic history

Albanians have myths too. Some believe that Kosovo has been an autonomous entity since ancient times. Not exactly. Kosovo was a province within the Turkish Empire, but certainly not an autonomous one. In 1868, it became a *vilayet* (political district), but not an autonomous one. Moreover, some believe that Albanians have "always" been the majority in Kosovo. However, Noel Malcolm, British author of *Kosovo: A Short History*, argues that this is "simply not credible." If it were true, then most of Kosovo's town names would be Albanian, but they're not—they're mostly Slavic.[6] Sorry, Albanian dreamers, Serbs were the majority in Kosovo throughout the Middle Ages.

What happened after the Turks moved in is less clear. During the five centuries of Turkish rule, many Serbs in Kosovo did not want to (or could not) live under the Turkish Empire, so they migrated north. When these migrations happened and how great they were is disputed. Nevertheless, what is clear is that vast numbers of Serbs settled around Belgrade, Vojvodina, and Hungary during the Turkish period. By the time the Turks fled the Balkans in 1912, Serbia's cultural core was no longer in Kosovo, it was centered around Belgrade.

I asked most Serbians I met, "What percentage of Kosovars were Serbian a century ago?" Most Serbs, even those who had no chauvinism, guessed between 60 to 90 percent. That's a myth. For example, between 1877 and 1880, an English geographer, a French geographer, and a English-German geographer each independently drew ethnographic maps of Kosovo. They all agreed that Kosovo was mostly made up of Albanians and that Serbs only dominated the northern tip (which they still do today).[7] In the 1890s, Austrians concluded that the majority of Kosovars were Muslims.[8] In 1906, British journalist H. Brailsford estimated Kosovo was one-third Serb and two-thirds Albanian. German scholar Gustav Weigand found that Serb presence in Kosovo towns ranged from 10 to 40 percent (with Albanians making up the balance).

In fact, Serbia's own 1912 census estimated that only 25 percent of Kosovo was Serb Orthodox.

These facts are hard for Serbs to accept today because they've been taught that Serbs have always dominated Kosovo and that Albanians just showed up yesterday. The propaganda claims Serbs were the majority in Kosovo until 1945, when, in the post-WWII confusion, Albanians sneaked into Kosovo and reproduced like rabbits on Viagra.

Serb recolonization of Kosovo

Like Serbs today, Serbs in 1913 couldn't accept reality. Having been disconnected from Kosovo for 500 years, they imagined that it hadn't changed much demographically, but their own surveys disproved that. Therefore, they attacked Pristina in 1913 and, according to their revised survey, claimed that no Albanians lived there. Still, in 1915, a Russian journalist remarked that half of the town was Albanian. A year after that, a Bulgarian census found 11,486 Albanians in Pristina (over two-thirds of the city).[9]

Since denying reality didn't work, Serbians tried to colonize Kosovo. In 1914, the Serbian government offered at least 11 hectares (27 acres) plus many other benefits to each Serb family that would move to Kosovo. After WWI, more colonists participated thanks to additional incentives, such as free land, free one-way transportation to the land (including your livestock and building materials), agricultural subsidies, and interest-free loans.[10] About 70,000 colonists moved to Kosovo, accounting for 10 percent of the population. A Serb official celebrated the "success" because he reported that Serb demographics rose from 24 percent in 1919 to 38 percent a decade later.[11] Even if we believe this Serb official's figures, they're far less than the 60 to 90 percent figure that many Serbs believe.

Foreign surveyors and Yugoslavia itself documented that Albanians were the majority in Kosovo throughout the 1920s and 1930s. In 1921, Yugoslavia's first census said that two-thirds of Kosovo was Albanian.[12] A few years later, an Italian surveyor estimated 700,000 Albanians were in Yugoslavia and a Romanian geographer in 1931 said there were 800,000.[13] Therefore, assuming that at least half of these Yugoslav Albanians were in Kosovo (where else would they be?), then that indicates that most of Kosovo was Albanian in the 1920s. Yugoslavia's 1931 census said 60 percent of Kosovars were Albanian (and a third were Slav). In conclusion, all surveys, including Serbian-Yugoslav ones, estimate that in the first half of the twentieth century, Serbs were less than a third of Kosovars; most of the rest were Albanians. This is the opposite of what many Serbs believe today.

In the Serb fantasy, Serbs were Kosovo's majority from the Middle Ages until the 1940s. The fable claims that Croatians, Germans, and

Albanians combined to liquidate the Serbs, thereby bringing them down as a percentage of the population. It also claims that for some mysterious reason Tito discouraged Serbs from returning to Kosovo and encouraged Albanians to leave totalitarian Albania and fill in the Kosovo vacuum. Tens of thousands of Serbs certainly left Kosovo during the 1940s, mostly because of the war. Still, if such a population reversal happened in the 1940s, then Yugoslavia's 1948 and 1953 censuses certainly didn't reflect that. They both indicated that Kosovo was about 27 percent Serb/Montenegrin and 68 percent Albanian, which is similar to the figures we saw for the previous 50 years.[14]

The demographics finally began to tip toward Albanians in the 1970s. They grew from being 67% of the Kosovars to 77%, according to the 1981 Yugoslav census (Serbs shrank to 13.2%).[15] By the 1991 census, the estimated ratio was 82% Albanian and 11% Serb.[16] Today, Kosovo is about 90% Albanian.

So let's summarize the last 1,000 years of Kosovo's demographics. In the Middle Ages, Kosovo was mainly Serb. At some point during the Turkish period, Serbs became a minority. It's not clear when that happened. My best guess is that it happened in the 1800s because that's when different censuses start to contradict each other on who held the majority. What's clear is that by 1900, Serbs were definitely the minority in Kosovo, making up between 25 to 33 percent of the population. Moreover, they remained at roughly that level until the 1970s, when they began their decline to roughly 10 percent.[17] Now the obvious question is *why*?

Do Albanians have 11.5 children?

On the one hand, the reason Kosovo's demographics changed is simple: many Serbs left Kosovo and Albanians were having more babies than the Serbs who stayed behind. On the other hand, both of these facts have a not-so-simple story behind them.

For instance, the Albanian reproductive rate was (and still is) relatively high, but not as outrageously high as many Balkanians claim. In 1953, for every 1,000 people there were 38.5 live births in Kosovo. That compares to 35 in Macedonia and Bosnia, 28 in Montenegro, and about 23 in the remaining republics. By 1988, the rates had fallen nearly in half everywhere, except Kosovo, which only saw a 25 percent decline.[18] Why?

First, infant mortality rates were highest in Kosovo and Macedonia. While other republics lowered their infant mortality rates around 90 percent, Kosovo (and Macedonia) only lowered them by about 62 percent, partly because Kosovars had the fewest doctors per capita in Yugoslavia. In 1953, Macedonians had twice as many doctors per capita than Kosovo; the other republics had four to five times more. By 1988, nearly all the republics (including Macedonia) had at least twice as many doctors per inhabitant than Kosovo had.[19]

In Yugoslavia's planned economy, Kosovars blamed Belgrade for not allocating more doctors to their region. Moreover, Kosovo's economy was Yugoslavia's least developed and most rural. Thus, like most rural and undeveloped places, people have more babies than average. Today, Kosovo is still largely rural and poorly developed compared to its neighbors, which partly explains why its birthrate remains higher than average.

Balkanians become comically irrational when talking about Albanian reproductive feats. Consider Aleksandar Svetozarević, a proud young Serbian from Niš. On his Facebook page, he has photos of himself waving the Serbian flag in a soccer stadium, Moscow's Red Square, and Zagreb's main square. His father was a military officer. While I hosted him in Slovenia, I asked him to rate Tito and Milošević on a one to 10 scale. His answers were the opposite of what most Serbians said. He gave Tito a *three* and Milošević a *nine,* even though "Milošević was a spy for the US." When I asked him if he knew Kosovo's fertility rate (the average number of children a woman has), without hesitation and with supreme confidence, he said, "11.5."

This was in line with the eight-to-20 estimate that most Balkanians repeatedly claimed. At first I thought they were joking, but they usually weren't. As we saw, this figure is totally wrong about Albania, but does it apply to Kosovo? When I asked Aleksandar to prove the 11.5 figure, he spent 20 minutes surfing Serbian websites without any success, but he kept insisting that it was true. When I showed him UN and CIA data indicating that Niger was the only country in the world that had fertility in the rate over seven, he maintained that the average Albanian woman in Kosovo had 11.5 children. The fact that the world's average is less than 2.5 also didn't persuade him. When I asked him what was the largest Albanian family he had ever found in his trips to Kosovo, he said, "I once met a family with eight children!"

I said, "So you're saying that the *average* family has 11.5 children, yet the *largest* you've ever seen was not even close to that average."

He shrugged. When I showed American estimates that Kosovo had moderate fertility rates, he said that you "can't trust American statistics because they have an interest in the region." When I showed him UN estimates that were similar, he said, "But how can they know that? The Albanians boycotted the 1991 census and all the censuses after that. So there are no official numbers. No one can know."

I said, "Yet you seem to have no trouble believing the 11.5 figure that you found once and can't seem to find again. Think: Europeans don't reproduce anywhere close to that rate—not even Africans do."

He said, "Albanians are not Europeans, they're *Muslims*."

Of course. Anyway, I finally figured out where he got his 11.5 number. It's a low estimate for the number of births per 1,000 Kosovars. That statistic is often called the *birthrate*. It's easy to see how someone can confuse *birthrate* with *fertility rate* (which measures the average number of children a woman produces). What's ironic is that Kosovo's 2011 birthrate is probably much higher than 11.5—the Population Reference Bureau estimates that it's 21.

To put a birthrate of 21 into perspective, in 2011 Niger had the world's highest birthrate (50), Monaco had the lowest (7), and the 2011 world average was 17.5. Kosovo's birthrate was roughly equal to India and twice that of Serbia (9.2) and Albania (12.2). Kosovo's birthrate today is almost half of what it was in 1953 (as we saw above, it was 38.5 in Kosovo and 23 in Serbia proper). After pointing all this out and debating for one hour, Aleksandar finally conceded that "maybe" the average Albanian doesn't have 11.5 children, but he still assured me that "they definitely have a lot of babies."

How many kids do Albanians really have?

The allegedly "sky-high" Albanian reproduction rate is one of the best examples of widespread Balkan hyperbole. Still, there is a bit of truth to it: Albanians pump out babies faster than anyone in Europe. According to the US State Department, the average female Kosovar has 2.9 children. The Population Reference Bureau says 2.5 is a more accurate estimate. Either way, it's Europe's highest fertility and roughly twice Serbia's depopulating 1.39 rate.[20]

Whereas most Eastern European countries are depopulating, Albania and Kosovo (along with Greece and Macedonia) are still growing. In fact, Kosovo's net population growth rate is 1.4 percent, which is the highest in Europe and is similar to India's rate. Therefore, while Kosovo's growth rates are slightly above average on the global scale, because they're around twice as high as its depopulating neighbors, it seems like they're having 11.5 children.

Aleksandar later admitted, "Serbs in Kosovo have a lot more children than Serbs in Central Serbia and Vojvodina." This has also been true throughout the last century. In fact, in the 1950s, Serb Kosovars had a *higher* population growth rate than Albanians (2.7% vs. 2.1%) partly because Serb infant mortality was lower than the Albanian one. By 1981, the average Serb Kosovar had 3.4 children versus roughly 4.7 children that Albanian Kosovars had. There was also a big disparity between rural Albanians (6.7 children) and urban Albanians (2.7).[21] Finally, the Serb abortion rate was higher than the Albanian rate. In 1989, 68 percent of Serb pregnancies were aborted.[22] In 2011, it's 23 percent (which is the same as America's rate). Meanwhile, Bosnia and Kosovo, countries with heavy Muslim populations, have abortion rates of less than five percent.[23]

Kosovo's baby boom has made it Europe's youngest country—the average Kosovar is 26 years old. Only 23% of Kosovars are retired; in Croatia, 57% are. Their youth is evident in the streets; about 27% of Kosovars are under 15 years old. In conclusion, one reason why the Albanian population surged in Kosovo after 1970 was that they pumped out more babies than Serbs. Unfortunately, the Balkan tendency to hyperbole facts has made this issue a much bigger deal than it really is. Today, Kosovo's fertility rate continues to decline. Now let's move onto the second reason for why Kosovo went from 66% Albanian throughout most of the last century to 80% in 1991.

Why Serbs left Kosovo

In the preface of *The Migration of Serbs and Montenegrins from Kosovo and Metohija,* the Serbian authors reasonably estimate that between 1961 and 1987, about 100,000 Serbs left Kosovo. There are two reasons why they left. First, some Albanians were harassing them. Albanians often deny this and they may point to a survey done in the 1980s that showed that less than 0.1 percent of Serbs blamed Albanians for wanting to go out of Kosovo.[24] These results are laughable and reek of a pro-Albanian bias.

On the other hand, it's hard to find an objective poll on this issue. In the 1980s, the Serbian Academy of Sciences interviewed 500 Serb households to learn why they had left Kosovo. About 41 percent said that "indirect pressure" from Albanians was a reason, while 21 percent cited direct pressure (e.g., verbal abuse, material damage, and personal injury).[25] The truth probably lies somewhere between these two biased surveys. One indication that implies that ethnic tension existed is that two-thirds of Serb émigrés came from mixed areas in Kosovo; heterogeneous regions are more prone to ethnic tensions than homogeneous regions.[26] Still, most of the harassment were misdemeanors and petty crimes; official government statistics showed that rape and murder in Kosovo were below the Yugoslav average.[27]

The other reason for the Serb exodus was that Kosovo was stuck in the Stone Age. Throughout the last century, Kosovo was Yugoslavia's retarded child. All the other Yugoslav regions would donate money and resources to help Kosovo catch up. On a per capita basis, Kosovo received up to four times more aid than Bosnia, Montenegro, and Macedonia.[28] Despite that assistance, Kosovo was always light-years behind. For example, Slovenia has maintained a similar-sized population as Kosovo, but in 1988, Slovenia accounted for *18 times* more of Yugoslavia's output.[29] Kosovo's 1990 unemployment rate was four times higher than Croatia's and six times higher than Slovenia's.[30] In

1952, Slovenia's per capita GDP was three times higher than Kosovo, but today it's 14 times higher.[31] In 1953, only 2.4 percent of Slovenians were illiterate versus a staggering 62.5 percent of Kosovars. By 1988, 18 percent of Kosovars were still illiterate.[32] Perhaps by 2013, Kosovo's literacy rate will finally approach Slovenia's 1953 rate.

As TV spread in the 1970s, Kosovars realized just how backwards they were. Those who could go north, did. Making the cultural transition from Kosovo to Belgrade, Zagreb, and Novi Sad was easier for a Serb than for an Albanian. Thus, Serbs were more likely to leave Kosovo. To blame Albanian harassment as the main or only cause for the Serb exodus ignores the fact that Bosnia also saw a net outflow during the same period. Those migrating Bosnians also went to Yugoslavia's most prosperous regions. Kosovo had the highest percentage decrease in people because it had the weakest economy. In fact, from 1971 to 1981, 45,000 Albanians left Kosovo too. Everyone was leaving Kosovo because its economy stunk.

Some Serbs still insist that during the Tito era, Albanians committed "genocide" against the Serbs. So what's more likely and logical: (a) that Tito, whose all-seeing eye uncovered and crushed all types of nationalism and protests, somehow ignored Albanians kicking Serb ass and that Serbs didn't complain to Tito about it, and if they did, Tito ignored them, even though Serbs were a far more important political base than the Albanians; or (b) that Serbs left on their own because Kosovo's economy was horrendous. Another way to think about it: if Kosovo's economy had been similar to Vojvodina's economy, would all those Kosovars have left? If Kosovo was *better* than the rest of Yugoslavia, then Serbians (and even Slovenians) would have migrated *to* Kosovo.

Staying in an Albanian home

I thanked Fatmir for letting me crash his party, and then I left to catch a bus to Prizren, Kosovo's prettiest town. I told the bus driver before I bordered that I have no euros, only dollars. He patted me on the back and said, "No problem, my friend!"

"My friend?" No Eastern European bus driver has been that cheerful. The bus was one of the nicest in Eastern Europe. Your tax dollars at work. It had a TV that displayed a nearly naked woman dancing. No singing. Just gyrating. It's not exactly what you expect from a so-called "Islamic" country.

I asked the guy who sat in front of me if he spoke English. He did. I asked if I could sit next to him and talk. He enthusiastically agreed and said his name was Shpejtim Horina. He was well dressed in a loosely buttoned, white pressed long-sleeved shirt and fashionable jeans. When the ticket collector came by, I mentally prepared myself to explain in simple English why I didn't have any euros. But then Shpejtim said, "*Dy*," which is the Albanian word for *two*.

"Wait, wait. . ." I said, "Here, take $5. Don't pay for me." Shpejtim didn't even know that I had no euros. He paid for my three-euro ride (which isn't cheap for Kosovo) regardless of what I said. I asked him, "Why did you do that?"

Shpejtim said, "Because I will never, ever forget what you Americans did for us. I am very grateful. You saved us."

In 2004, this was strange to hear, because most countries, especially Muslim countries, hated the US. A few months later, I learned that a worldwide 2004 Gallup poll showed that Kosovo rated US foreign policy higher than any other country on Earth: an 88 percent approval (at that time, only 10 countries were over 50 percent).

When the war broke out, Shpejtim fled to Switzerland and was still working there. His generosity, friendliness, and good sense of humor were overwhelming. Because of that, I wasn't afraid to ask him a hard question, "When you immigrate to America, you must learn English. Forget about creating Spanish-only public schools, for example. English is our language and it's what helps keep us together. Why do Albanians insist on having Albanian schools in Montenegro for example?"

"Why not?" he said calmly. "When I am a minority in a country, like Switzerland, I learn the language. I speak German well. Nobody wants to have an Albanian school there. All Albanians who live there learn the local language, of course. But once we're over 50 percent of a region, why shouldn't we have our own schools, especially in areas where our representation tops 85 percent?"

We had a civil discussion the rest of the way. Before we got to Prizren he said invited me to stay with his family. He said, "I'll take you to my house, and if it's OK, then you stay. If you don't like, then you can go. No problem!"

I can't resist staying with a local when I get a chance. In Prizren, Shpejtim introduced me to his parents, his brother, and sister. They all greeted me warmly. His mom served us fresh tomatoes, goulash soup, and succulent dumplings. While we enjoyed the tasty dinner, the power went out. Within seconds, they brought out candles and electric lanterns. I asked, "How often does this happen?"

"A couple of times a day," they shrugged. Indeed, the cities of Kosovo were extremely loud because the stores had small gas-powered generators running on the sidewalk. Since they were one after another, the whining decibel level was quite high. Although the situation has improved recently, Kosovo has always been chronically short on power.

I talked for hours with Shpejtim and his family. They gave me hope for the Balkans. His ability to speak rationally and calmly about difficult subjects was refreshing. Moreover, he never condemned all the Slavs. He always emphasized that a minority causes most of the problems. Likewise, he admitted that Albanians aren't perfect either. If more people in the Balkans can learn Shpejtim's ability to forgive and move on, then there is hope. Before going to sleep, we talked about the year he was born, 1974.

How Serbia is similar to Oklahoma

In 1974, Serbia became like Oklahoma. Most Yugoslavs were not happy with the centralized economy and they thought decentralization would fix things. To avoid a revolt, Tito agreed to increase everyone's autonomy. Among the five republics, Serbia was the only one to have two autonomous provinces carved out of it: Vojvodina in the north and Kosovo in the south. Albanians were begging Tito for republic status, but Tito picked the compromise solution: autonomy. As a result, Serbia turned into Oklahoma.

Oklahoma, along with several other western US states, has large Native American reservations within it. Although the US has 50 states, there are about 310 autonomous Indian reservations within them. These autonomous regions are similar to Serbia's two autonomous provinces. Indian Tribes have their own government, their own laws, and a separate court system. They handle all Indian-on-Indian crimes, but if a non-Indian is involved, it usually goes to the federal courts. They are only subordinate to the US federal government, not to the state government. In other words, Oklahoma cannot tell a tribal land to do anything. Only the federal government has any authority—and that authority is minimal. The US Constitution specifically protects "Indian tribes" by saying that they are neither part of a state nor part of the federal government. The Federal government cannot tax the Native American regions; they collect their own taxes. The Tribal Lands have the power to expel non-Native Americans from their reservations. US states have often tried to control the tribes, but the US Supreme Court has always said that the tribes must work directly with the federal government and that the states have no power over the tribal lands.

Now imagine that the US were breaking apart into separate countries. Florida becomes a Spanish-speaking country. Texas becomes the Lone Star nation. Alaska and Hawaii declare independence and join the UN. California does the same. New England states join together to form one country, and so on. During such a disintegration, what would the Cherokee Tribe in Oklahoma do? Would they join the new country of Oklahoma? Or perhaps, would they say, "Sorry, we've always been autonomous, so we're declaring our own separate independence. We're now the Cherokee Nation." If so, then Oklahoma protesters might say, "*The Cherokee Territory is Oklahoma*. It's been part of

Oklahoma for the last 100 years. We refuse to recognize your independence and we'll go to war with you if you try to break away from us."

This is a similar situation that Yugoslavia set itself up for with its 1974 Constitution. Because it was a compromise, neither the Albanians nor the Serbs were happy with it. Serbs lamented being "butchered" into three pieces. Albanians disliked not having republic status. Albanians observed that there are over three times as many ethnic Albanians in Kosovo than there are ethnic Montenegrins in Montenegro, yet Montenegro was a republic and Kosovo was not. In fact, ethnic Montenegrins were only 40 percent of Montenegro, whereas Albanians had been over two-thirds of Kosovo for at least 100 years. "So why can't we be a Yugoslav republic?" Albanians cried.

On the other hand, the only real difference between an autonomous region and a republic was the name. As the 1986 Memorandum stated, "Autonomous provinces were put on an equal footing with the republics in all respects . . . ." After Tito's death, Kosovo's President served as one of Yugoslavia's eight rotating Presidents. Milošević referred to how much power Kosovo had when he complained about Kosovo's anti-Serb policies by saying, "The Albanians could do this because the province of Kosovo was virtually a republic. The local council had the power to implement what I'd call a truly Nazi policy."[33]

Given the minor difference between a republic and an autonomous province, why did Albanians make such a fuss about being upgraded to a republic? The main reason was about respect and symbolism. Kosovo had a strong identity just like similar sized (or smaller) republics like Slovenia, Macedonia, and Montenegro, so it should have the same status. A less obvious reason—but one that would become critical when Yugoslavia broke up—was that republics ultimately had the right to leave Yugoslavia, while autonomous provinces did not. It's not clear how important that argument was for Albanians in 1974, but it explains why Kosovo's road to independence was much harder than for the seven republics. They started down that road in 1981.

The 1986 Memorandum said, "In the spring of 1981, open and total war was declared on the Serbian people." That's pure hyperbole. What really happened was that thousands of Albanian demonstrators demanded they get republic status. The Presidency declared a state of emergency and when the dust settled, about 10 were dead. If that's "open and total war," then I'm not sure how they would describe WWII.

Recycling history

Winston Churchill said something that many ex-Yugoslavs would agree with: "I prefer the past to the present and the present to the future." Ex-Yugoslavs not only love to dwell on history, but they adore connecting themselves with it. Doing so gives meaning to random current events by placing them into a grand, epic story. Unfortunately, by recycling history, they doom themselves to repeat it.

For example, in 1985, Đorđe Martinović, a 56-year-old Serb, came to a Kosovo hospital with a broken bottle in his butt. He confessed to a JNA Colonel that he had put the bottle on a stick, masturbated while it was going in his ass, and then, lost his balance and sat on it. Much later, Martinović would take back his confession, claiming that the JNA Colonel (a Serb) forced him to say that in exchange for getting his son a job. It's not clear why a Serb Colonel would tell a Serb to make up such a lie, especially when Martinović's new story was that two Albanians attacked him in the field and shoved the beer bottle up his anus. Why would a Serb Colonel not want to blame Albanians, if that is what really happened? It seems more likely that to avoid embarrassment, Martinović made up this story. It's remarkable that Martinović (who died in 2000) never pursued the case, never filed charged against his alleged attackers, nor did any Serbian or Yugoslav entity follow up. Despite the lack of evidence or clear suspects, Serbia went into a frenzy. The Memorandum drew the historical connection: "The Martinović case is . . . reminiscent of the darkest days of the Turkish practice of impalement."

Even if we assume that two Albanians really committed such a perverted crime, is it really worth rallying an entire nation over it? In America, horrific crimes between blacks and whites happen, yet few will conclude that we're returning to the days of slavery. Stjepan Gabriel Meštrović observes that it's different in the Balkans. He said, "The Martinović affair presented an ideal opportunity for transforming the Albanians into 'Turks' in the group consciousness of the Serbian masses."[34]

Balkanians try to insert themselves into an imagined cosmic drama. In 1995, the Serbian Academy of Arts and Sciences said that giving Kosovo autonomy was like "a return to the time of the Ottoman Empire."[35] When Bosnian Serb military commander Ratko Mladić liquidated Srebrenica, he celebrated that he had liberated the town from the "Turks" instead of saying "Bosniaks" or "Muslims." Tuđman, Croatia's leader, played the same game when he said that Bosnia's leader was a "fundamentalist front man for Turkey" who would "flood Bosnia with 500,000 Turks." Andre, a Serb, wrote to me saying, "The only thing Serbia is guilty of is trying to undo the historical injustices by the Muslim invasion and by the Nazis."

> *People are trapped in history, and history is trapped in them. — James Baldwin*

In 1989, at the 600-year anniversary of the Battle of Kosovo, a Serbian academic wrote that Milošević tried to unify "history, memory and continuity," by creating "the illusion that the Serbs who fought against the Turks in Kosovo in 1389 are somehow the same as the Serbs fighting for Serbian national survival today."[36] Moreover, at that speech, Milošević romanticized the past by saying, "Serbs have never in the whole of their history conquered and exploited others." Obviously Serbia's greatest emperor, Tsar Dušan, conquered much of the Balkans not by exploiting and conquering others, but by using flowers.

Sometimes we glorify history and have nostalgia for an era we know little about. For example, Andre wrote, "Before, Serbs found the grave better than being a slave. Modern Serbs have changed unfortunately, because there has been a constant war on morals and principles. Serbs have been degraded, with nonstop materialistic blabber everywhere. We went from being a poor, war-weathered people whose only possession was pride and freedom to now being conditioned to be no different than any other country: a Serb is a self-serving materialist who only worries about his own ass. I am not saying that for the population as a whole, but the pride and martyrdom mentality has largely been traded for cell phones and name-brand obsessions, especially after this last failed attempt at some type of redemption of the 1990s."

Perusing prohibited places

After staying overnight at Shpejtim's house, I thanked his family for their outstanding hospitality. I waved them goodbye and went to explore Prizren. As in everywhere in Kosovo, new or half-built buildings were abundant. Therefore, it was surprising to see that Prizren's best location was destroyed. You'd think they would rebuild the central neighborhood that overlooks the river and its beautiful arched white-stoned bridge. Fire scars and collapsed roofs testified to a war's aftermath. At the neighborhood's edge, there was a big sign: "WARNING: KFOR Zone. Use of weapons permitted." KFOR stands for Kosovo FORce. It's the NATO peacekeeping force. The sign implied that you may be shot on sight. Excellent. So I went into the destroyed neighborhood.

As I slowly walked between ruined houses, it finally dawned on me why Albanians hadn't rebuilt this. It must have been a Serb neighborhood! *Duh!* As I walked through the narrow and once-quaint streets, I took pictures of the demolished kitchens, the broken windows, the overgrown gardens, and the dilapidated living rooms. I carefully stepped over shattered glass and fragments of metal and wood throughout the street. I wondered if Serbs or Albanians had planted mines to discourage what I was doing. I thought of the innocent Serb families who once lived here. How unfair that their homes were destroyed simply because they were Serbs. Suddenly, about five meters away, a man wearing camouflage appeared with a massive assault rifle in his arms. The gun seemed bigger than he was. I smiled, but felt quite vulnerable.

"Hallo," he said. "*Sprechen sie Deutsch*?"

I answered, "*Entschuldigung, ich spreche kein Deutsch*," which I think means, "I surrender, mighty Nazi!"

The man had the German flag on his KFOR uniform. He was pretty skinny and had dorky shaded glasses. He was a German geek with a really big gun. He didn't speak English, but he pointed to my camera and shook his head. Great, I could use my favorite German word, "*Das ist VERBOTEN*?"

"*Ja*," he nodded.

I showed him the pictures I took within the KFOR area and each time asked, "*Verboten*?" ("Forbidden?") He nodded and said "*Ja*" to each one. I deleted them all. He seemed happy, but still didn't smile. He escorted me up the hill to the Orthodox Church of Holy Salvation. There was a bunker made out of sandbags and barbed wire all around the church. The fourteenth-century church had broken stained-glass windows, a charred stone exterior, and a collapsed roof. Germans were standing guard carrying assault rifles. I asked to talk with a soldier who could speak English. A soldier whose belly indicated he had drunken a few too many German beers came over. Since he was German, I got straight to the point, "Who do you think should be blamed more for all the problems in Kosovo, Serbs or Albanians?"

He took a step back, looked at the horizon and said, "I would blame the Albanians."

"Why?" I asked.

"Look at this Serb neighborhood," he said while pointing to the ruined houses below. "That just happened last month because a few Serb kids supposedly chased three Albanian children into a river, where they drowned. As vengeance, they burned hundreds of Serb houses all over Kosovo. Look at this church. Albanians burned it. Other churches and monasteries have been completely destroyed. We didn't have enough men to stop them. You want to hear a crazy story? A bunch of Albanians broke into a Serbian doctor's house and made him watch as they murdered his wife and his three children. Today, that doctor is insane. He babbles and has completely lost his mind. It's sick."

I asked him, "How long have you been here?"

"Six months. And I'll be here for another six."

"How long will NATO and KFOR stay here?"

"Twenty years," he said with his thick German accent. "I'm serious. I think they want us to stay. We build roads and houses for them. And it's all free for them. We provide free security. But they're crazy."

"Why?"

He lit a cigarette and said, "We'll build five houses for the Serbs and a gang of Albanians will come and burn them down. Then we'll build five houses for the Albanians and a gang of Serbs will come and destroy those houses." He sighed, "I don't understand these people."

"What about this Serb neighborhood," I asked, "Are the Serbs going to try to live here again?"

"Yes, they will. I don't understand them. Their neighbors burned down their houses, but they say, 'It's my house and I want to live there.' You know, if I come to America and people say, 'Fuck you German,' then I'll leave and go somewhere else. But these Serbs insist on living here, even though they're surrounded by people who hate them. I just don't understand these people," he said while shaking his head.

His analogy wasn't perfect because most of the Prizren Serbs aren't recent immigrants—they were born there. Some are descendents from the 1920s colonists, but others come from Serbs who have lived in Kosovo for centuries. Thus, a better analogy would be if a German in parts of Lithuania, Poland, or Czechia had his house burned down. Those three countries have areas that were German for centuries. How would this German feel in *that* situation? That's the situation that millions of Germans found themselves in when they were kicked out of those three countries after WWII despite having had a long history of being there.

Most Kosovars aren't going anywhere. In 2011, the Balkan Monitor reported that only about 13 percent of Kosovars think it's "likely" that they will move in the next year—and most of those aren't moving out of the country. I asked the German, "Is it worth it to walk to the top of this hill?"

"Yeah, you will see an old fort and a good view. But if you come here at night, you'll see about 50 young Albanians marching up the hill to. . ." he thrust his hips forward.

"Ah, yes. Not very Muslim of them, is it?"

He smiled and smoked. I felt bad for these poor Germans. They're so orderly and civilized, but they're sent to live in this incomprehensible mess. I thanked him, shook his hand, and went up the hill to see if I could get lucky.

Religion in Kosovo

As I climbed up the hill and looked down at the burned-out church, I concluded that Kosovars are religious zealots. In some ways, I was right. Nine in 10 Kosovars told Gallup in 2010 that "religion was an important part of their daily life." That's the highest rate in Europe, and it's a stark contrast with Albania, which had the lowest rate in the Western Balkans (44%).

On the other hand, I was wrong. In 2010, only 32 percent of Kosovars had visited a place of worship in the previous week. That's hardly fanatical—Germans were more likely to go to church weekly. As we saw in the Bosnia chapter, ex-Yugoslavs partake in religious rituals when they live in a threatened community. Hence, Serb Kosovars are far more religious than the average Serbian. In the Balkans, religion is a social glue that keeps communities together rather than a strict set of rules to follow.

As I talked with more Kosovars, it became clear that they're not fundamentalists. For example, the Islamic political party gets less than two percent of the vote. Furthermore, few Albanians pray five times a day, most drink alcohol, and women are far more likely to wear a sexy skintight outfit than to cover themselves. Albanians have been this way for a long time.

> *The Greeks hardly regard them as Christians, or the Turks as Muslims, and in fact they are a mixture of both, and sometimes neither. — Lord Byron writing about Albanians nearly 200 years ago*

Just like the other Yugoslav wars weren't religious wars, the Kosovo War wasn't a religious war either, even though religious sites were often targeted. Albanians didn't attack Orthodox churches because they hate Christianity. They attacked them because they hate Serbs. Albanians didn't burn Catholic churches because most Catholic Kosovars are Albanians. So it wasn't Christianity versus Islam, but Albanian versus Serb.

If Serbs were Catholics, then the Catholic monasteries and churches would have been destroyed. If Albanians truly hated the Orthodox faith, then it's strange that 20 percent of Albania is Orthodox Christian and survives without problems. Therefore, Albanians targeted Orthodox sites not because they were against the Orthodox dogma, but because they wanted to hit Serbs where it hurts. Similarly, Serbs destroyed mosques throughout Serbia not because they're necessarily anti-Islam or religiously intolerant, but just to get revenge for whatever Serb sacred site got defiled in Kosovo. It's all part of a senseless cycle of violence.

An Albanian perspective on growing up in Kosovo

Seven years after Shpejtim Morina paid for my bus fare and invited me into his home, he told his former Albanian classmate, Lumnije Xhezairi, about me. She contacted me and agreed to share her experiences. She was born in Prizren in 1974 and spent her first 27 years there. She spoke excellent English and said, "I was a Muslim, but like most Albanians, we weren't really practicing. I had no idea what Islam was about and why I was a Muslim. My grandmother was conservative. She would tell me, 'Stop reading books. Books are for men, not for women. Put that down.' She was illiterate, like most people in her generation."

I asked Lumnije, "What was it like growing up in Kosovo?"

She said, "We had to learn Serbian since first grade. Nobody liked it. It was the language of the enemy. But I was best friends with Serbians. I'm sure that there are good people in Serbia."

"Any childhood memories that stand out?"

"It bothered me that we were not free and independent. Only two of my teachers were Serbs; all the others were Albanians. Yet they would make me stop talking if I asked a question about independence. They called my parents to say that I was putting the teacher at risk and that the teacher could go to prison. Once we were decorating the classroom and I put a star on top of Tito's picture. The Serbian principal shouted at me, 'Take that down! Nothing goes above Tito!'"

"How were your parents?"

"They struggled. I was the youngest of their five children. My mom never used contraceptives. Nobody in her generation had a real education. They had to quit their jobs to take care of the family. We had fun though. We watched movies together and went to concerts. I remember that nothing tasted better than Slovenian milk."

"What happened to your siblings?"

"My oldest brother is now a dentist. Another is studying technology and electronics in Mitrovica, Kosovo. Another is an English professor who does advertising and short movies. My sister is a nurse in Austria and I am a nurse working in Saudi Arabia."

"Did you marry an Albanian?"

"No. They have arranged marriages in Kosovo. Someone will knock on my dad's door and say, 'I know someone who lost his wife in the war and he needs a wife.' No thanks. I'm not going to be someone's slave. I got offered a nursing job in Saudi Arabia because they need nurses and their women don't work. I eventually met an American in the military compound here and we got married."

Yugoslavia's death began and ended with Kosovo

Let's look at Kosovo's final years in Yugoslavia from both sides. First, imagine you're Albanian. Your friends are blaming Serbs for the crappy situation, because until 1974, Serbs controlled Kosovo. So whatever is wrong in your life is obviously their fault, not yours. After 1974, however, your problems continue despite the increased autonomy.

This is because conditions throughout Yugoslavia are deteriorating, but instead you conclude that the real problem is that the 1974 reforms didn't go far enough. Kosovo needs to be a republic, because somehow that will fix everything. You partake in peaceful demonstrations, but they either get crushed or ignored. Since everything else you've tried hasn't worked, maybe violence is the answer.

Now imagine you're a Serb. You hear stories of a Serb being robbed or raped in Kosovo. Of course, in any population of 200,000 Serbs (or any nationality), there's going to be daily crime, especially if the economy is terrible. When over 80 percent of population is Albanian, then it's probable that Albanians will commit most of the crimes, whether they're crimes against other Albanians or against Serbs. Still, such logic doesn't enter into your mind when a hysterical TV reporter tells you that an Albanian stole from a Serb.

In 1987, the Serbian media was talking about the "widespread" rape going on in Kosovo, including the raping of Serbian nuns. Serb author Vesna Kesić wrote, "The emphasis was immediately placed on the ethnic dimension of these rapes; facts were neglected and numbers exaggerated. Although it was rather soon proved that Kosovo police had registered only one rape of a Serb woman by an Albanian man, and subsequent research showed that rapes in Kosovo basically did not cross ethnic lines, the allegations of inter-ethnic rape generated fear and helped form the basis of the future culture of terror."[37] The negativity gives you one more reason to leave and to support Milošević who promises to protect Serb rights in Kosovo.

In 1990, Milošević revoked Kosovo's autonomy—a serious step backward for Albanians who were demanding just the opposite. Milošević banned all Albanian media, expelled nearly all of the university students, and replaced the Albanian police with Serbs. When Kosovo's parliament declared that it was a republic, Milošević abolished the parliament. Albanians began losing confidence that a peaceful, democratic solution was possible. It was the beginning of the end. Still, Albanian leader Ibrahim Rugova urged peaceful resistance. During that time, the Slovenian, Croatian, and Bosnian Wars started and ended. Then all eyes turned to Kosovo.

It's at that point that a few Albanians defied Rugova and stepped up the violence. The newly formed Kosovo Liberation Army shot two Serb policemen in Mitrovica, detonated a bomb in Podujevo, and attacked Pristina University's Serb Rector. If this happened in your country, your government would call them terrorists. However, if you're feeling oppressed by that government, you'd call those terrorists "freedom fighters" or "patriots."

Guerrilla warfare ensued. Refugees from both sides flooded neighboring states. NATO didn't want another Bosnian War (where about

150,000 died), so they exaggerated the situation to justify a fierce 78-day bombing campaign that forced Milošević to let NATO and the UN take over Kosovo in June 1999. The non-partisan Humanitarian Law Center concluded that 9,260 Albanians and 2,488 Serbs died in the Kosovo War. With that, Yugoslavia was finished.

Trapped in Kosovo

I tried to leave Kosovo before sunset, but the bus never showed up. While I was waiting, I talked with an Albanian who was born and raised in Macedonia. He said, "It's terrible that the Macedonians don't make any effort to learn Albanian."

"Why should they?" I asked. "You're all living in Macedonia after all, not Albania."

"But we make up a large percentage of the region."

"OK," I told him, "Let's say a bunch of Kenyans move to your country and become a pretty significant part of the population in a region. What would you say if they tell you, 'Hey buddy, you should learn to speak some Kenyan!?'"

"But that's different," he said, "This isn't their native land. Albanians have lived in this region before it was Macedonia."

"Do you know who owned California before the Yankees? Mexicans. But no Mexican who comes to California today would tell an American that he should learn to speak Spanish. The Mexican knows that he is in the United States and it's his responsibility to learn English, not our responsibility to learn Spanish."

He was speechless and then said he was going to look into where the bus might be. I don't think he liked me because I never saw him again. Since I missed my bus, it was a perfect opportunity to join my fellow Americans and set up camp in Kosovo. I camped on the third floor of a half-built house thereby becoming the first person to sleep in it. Although I could have had nightmares about a lunatic Kosovar finding me there and ethnically cleansing me, I slept like a baby.

Kosovo in America

The next day, while on my bus out of Kosovo, I tried to imagine if Kosovo could happen in America. It's similar to something Andre told me. He wrote, "How would America act if Mexicans declared independence in Texas? Would America do nothing? What kind of country would do that? America would never allow that and they would surely react in the same way Serbia reacted. The only fault Serbia has is that it is not as strong as America."

He's right. America's deadliest war was its Civil War, which was about a group of states wanting to secede. In 1869, the US Supreme

Court ruled in *Texas v. White* that unilateral secession was unconstitutional, but added that if such a move were mutually agreed on, then it could happen. Little has changed since then. One recent poll revealed that only 22 percent of Americans believe that "any state or region has the right to peaceably secede and become an independent republic."

I wanted to talk to a Mexican living in the US and ask him if Mexicans could identify with the Albanians. However, Kosovo is a bit far the US, so I put off that dream for when I got back home. Then a stocky, tan skinned, 50-something-year-old man with slick black hair sat next to me on the bus. I asked him if he spoke English. He said he did, but with a Spanish accent. He was from south Texas and was born in Mexico. He had six children. We spoke in Spanish. He was working for the US military in Kosovo. He did not think the situation with Mexican Americans is similar to Kosovo because "there's just too much hate in Kosovo. The hate is so deep."

I asked him, "Do any of your Mexican friends wish that there were Spanish-only public schools in America?"

"No, we just want to come and work in America."

"The Mexican population in the US is exploding. If they get critical mass, do you think that they would ever want to separate from the US, like some Albanians in Macedonia, Serbia, and Montenegro want to do?"

"No, Mexicans have no interest in that." He continued, "I don't understand these Albanians. They don't learn from others and have no interest in assimilating. I'm looking forward to going home."

Could Kosovo happen in America? The Pew Research Center estimates that by 2050 Hispanics will be 29 percent of the US and Caucasians will be 47 percent. In cities and in schools, Caucasians will become a minority much sooner. Fatmir reminded me that Kosovo's problem isn't unique: England has its trouble with Northern Ireland, Spain has the separatists in its Basque and Catalan regions, Mexico has Chiapas revolutionaries, Russia has Chechen rebels, Iraq and Turkey have their Kurds, and China has Tibet. Having concentrated areas of minorities is tricky to manage. Just ask how Canadians feel about Quebec or how Belgians feel about the Flemish/French divide. Even the perfect Swiss struggle. The challenge is making sure that the majority doesn't make the minority feel like second-class citizens. Still, those in the majority have limits to how much flexibility they want to give to the minority. Serbs (and every other country) need to visit Ahvenanmaa in Finland to see just how much autonomy one can give a minority (see page 20).

You'd think that Serbs and Albanians would provide the world a perfect model on how to get along. Look at a Balkan ethnographic map and you'll see that Serbs and Albanians both spill over into other countries. Neither has political borders that correspond perfectly with their ethnic borders—they've both been "short-changed." Thousands of Serbs live in Croatian and Bosnian enclaves, while thousands of Albanians live in Macedonia, Montenegro, Greece, and Serbia. Therefore, you'd think that they would both have empathy for minorities within their own country and that they would treat them like they would like to be treated. However, neither has done a good job. Fortunately, that's changing. As Naser Lajqi said, "If we tell the Serbian people that they are all criminals, or if they tell us that we, Albanians, are all criminals, I think it will be an ideal breeding ground for hatred between the two ethnic communities."[38] In the last couple of years, Serbia and Kosovo have each dramatically improved minority rights.

Why Serbs are frustrated

When I talked with Vlad, he said that one reason the 1990s were so hard for Serbia is that "Serbs have a history of always being on the right side. We fight moral fights and we win in the end. In the 1990s, we lost and were labeled as evil. That was hard on our ego."

He summed up their string of military and moral victories. In 1878, Serbs were on the winning side that helped push the Turks out of most of Europe. In 1912, they won another "just war" when they threw the Turks completely out of the Balkans. In 1913, in the Second Balkan War, Serbia beat Bulgaria. In 1914, an ethnic Serb started WWI, to protest another unjust occupation (against the Austria-Hungary Empire). Serbs won WWI and created Yugoslavia. In WWII, Serbs ultimately triumphed against the despicable fascists. With such a string of successes (and victors always feel like they're doing the righteous thing), it crushed Serb pride to not only lose four wars in a eight years, but to be labeled as "evil" on top of it.

Serbs are also furious at the hypocrisy of those who condemned Serbia. For example, why did NATO bomb Serbia, but doesn't do anything about injustices elsewhere in the world? Although it's easy to criticize a country's selective intervention strategy, it's hard to come up with good alternatives. Invading everywhere or nowhere are not realistic solutions either.

Ivan Sokolov offered me another example of hypocrisy. He wrote, "The Dutch government was one of Serbia's harshest critics. That's very funny considering what their people did in South Africa, let alone what their people will do once the Arabs living in Holland rise up. I won't even get in to the Arab issue in France. It really seems that the whole world was in the business to cash in and make the Serbs look as bad as possible in order for the rest of the world to overlook and possibly forget their own sins."

Losing Kosovo was the ultimate slap on the Serb face. Moderate Serbs might admit that Serbia was stretching when it tried to grab pieces of Croatia and Bosnia for itself. However, they'll say that Kosovo wasn't a land grab—it was rightfully theirs. They believe it's always been theirs even when the Turks controlled it or after the Albanians took it over demographically. Given Serbia's history of triumphs, they will look for a way to redeem themselves. How they will do that this time is unclear.

Coffee with a Balkan mutt

In 2011, I had coffee with Mile Zukić, a 28-year-old who was writing a PhD about ethnocentrism and nationalism in Slovenia. He said that he was "a mixture of everything in the Balkans. My dad's father was Bosniak, my dad's mother was Croatian, but my dad was born in Slovenia. My mom is Serbian, I have a Macedonian girlfriend, I was born in Slovenia, and I have many Albanian friends."

When you meet such "mixed breeds," talk with them—they are usually more objective than the average guy. He shared the conclusions of a university paper he wrote about Kosovo. He said, "Kosovo is the most important myth in Serbian history. The Serbian perspective is, 'We gave Albanians everything and now they rebel against us.' They're like a disappointed parent."

"But didn't Yugoslavia give a lot to Albanians after 1974?"

"Yes. They had Albanian schools, an Albanian university, Albanian signs, their own police force, their own parliament, a national bank, and they even got to fly the Albanian flag. The other republics also showered Kosovo with financial aid."

"Man, what more do you need?"

"Unfortunately, many of these advances were reversed after Milošević. Kosovars had huge problems finding a job and living a life like Slovenians and Croatians. When you don't have your basic needs, then you start searching for enemies to blame. If you have propaganda and sick nationalist leaders on both sides, then you have troubles."

I said, "It seems that if Serbs wanted to keep Kosovo under their wing, they needed to make Kosovo's economy roar. But it never did. If Serbia 'gave everything' to Kosovo, where did it all that money go? The place is still dirt-poor."

"First of all," Mile said, "Corrupt bureaucrats ate up all the contributions from the other republics. Secondly, they didn't give enough. The thinking was, 'Why develop Kosovo if it was going to be 90 percent Albanian in a few years?'"

"You say Kosovo is a big myth for Serbs. Give me an example."

"Serbs 500 years ago were not Serbs. What I mean is that the culture 500 years ago was completely different than today's. History should not be looked as a contiguous vector. The concept of a nation didn't begin until the nineteenth century."

As we finished our drinks, I asked Mile, "What was the conclusion of your paper?"

He said, "That a 20-year-old Albanian has much more in common with a 20-year-old Serb than a 50-year-old Albanian. The young Albanian and Serb both have the same need for alcohol, dancing, and Facebook. Before their common language was Serbian. Now, it's English. In short, the big cultural gap in Kosovo is between generations, not ethnic groups. "

Why did Serbia get screwed?

Serb chauvinists were hypocritical. They wanted Serb minorities to have the right to break away from whatever territory they live in to join the Serbian state (like in the case of Croatia and Bosnia). Meanwhile, they denied the right of other ethnic majorities to break away from Serbia to create their own state (like in Kosovo). They wanted it both ways, which is contradictory. On the other hand, isn't the international community being hypocritical for not letting Serbia get one of those two options?

The logic (whether you like it or not) is based on the concept of preexisting political units. The parts of Croatia and Bosnia that had Serb majorities were never autonomous political units. They were simply an internal region like Northern California is in California. They had no special political status. On the other hand, Kosovo did. But it wasn't special enough. Had Kosovo been a republic within Yugoslavia, then its declaration of independence in 2008 would have been easy to legally justify. Instead, they were in a gray area, just like the Indian Territories in the US will find themselves in when the US Balkanizes.

The international community was more legally consistent than Serbs realize. Like Kosovo, Preševo and Bujanovac wanted independence from Serbia. They were municipalities with Albanian majorities, but they were never autonomous. They were just like Serbs in the Croatian or Bosnian regions who wanted to secede. The international community told the Albanians in Preševo and Bujanovcac the same thing they told the Serbs in Croatia and Bosnia: "Sorry, but your region doesn't have preexisting autonomy, so you must stay in Serbia even if the majority of the people in your region don't want to stay there."

The international community has maintained that logic when addressing North Kosovo, the biggest region in Kosovo that Serbs have consistently dominated for at least 100 years. This region is located in the Ibar River valley and is home to Kosovo's most divided town, Mitrovica. The river divides the town into Serb and Albanian neighborhoods. Despite the clear ethnic divide, the international community didn't allow North Kosovo to separate because it had no preexisting legal autonomy. Therefore, while the international community's decisions may at first seem hypocritical, there is a logic to it. Whether you agree with that logic, is another question.

Not surprisingly, 40 percent of Serbians believe that in the last 20 years, the international community has been either "harmful" or "extremely harmful" to Serbia. Among other Balkanians, a slim majority believed that the international community helped. It's only in Albania and Kosovo where there's a strong majority with pro-international-community feelings.

Political courtroom arguments will continue for many years. For example, Bosnia's Republika Srpska has legal autonomy. Bosnian Serbs use the Kosovo precedent to make a case for why they should be allowed to separate from Bosnia. That legal battle may be as inconclusive as the Battle of Kosovo in 1389. That's because, as of 2011, only 40 percent of the UN members recognize Kosovo's independence. The main reason why Kosovo is struggling to get accepted is that if countries with separatist movements (e.g., Spain, Slovakia, Romania, and Cyprus) recognize Kosovo, then it will be harder to stop their own separatist groups from spinning off. It seems that once again the Balkans has given the world a big headache. At least it's a courtroom battle this time, not a real one.

Serbia, talk to Hungary

Serbians who feel they've been screwed need to talk to Hungarians. Serbians dislike it when Hungarians act like Vojvodina is theirs by saying that it was historically Hungarian land. Yet it was, and Hungarians once outnumbered Serbs in Vojvodina, just like Serbs once outnumbered Albanians in Kosovo. Hungarians built many of Vojvodina's old buildings, just like Serbs built many of the old buildings in Kosovo. Nevertheless, over the last couple of centuries, the Hungarian presence diminished in Vojvodina just like the Serb presence diminished in Kosovo. Like Serbs, Hungarians left their lands to seek better economic conditions up north, but also to flee from conflict. Hungarians had three forceful migration waves out of Vojvodina: one was due to the Turks and two were due to the Yugoslavs (after WWI and WWII). With each forceful eviction, the Hungarian population dropped significantly to the point where today relatively few remain. In short, the Hungarian story in Vojvodina is quite similar to what happened to Serbs in Kosovo over the centuries.

Don't tell the Serbs that I said this, but in a perverse way, Serbs benefited from the Turkish invasion. If you had to choose between Vojvodina and Kosovo, any real estate agent would tell you that Vojvodina is a far more valuable land. It's closer to Europe's wealthy center, the Danube flows through it, and the land is extremely fertile. Kosovo is far less desirable. Before the Turks invaded, Hungarians were solidly in Vojvodina. The Turkish invasion forced people to shift north a few hundred kilometers. Thus, when the dust settled, Serbians lost Kosovo, but gained Vojvodina. Hungarians invited Serbs to settle in Vojvodina to help them defend the border against the advancing Turkish Empire. By the twentieth century, the descendents of these Serbs felt at home in Vojvodina, which is why they fought against Hungary in both world wars just to keep the land.

There's a similar story in Poland. In 1939, the USSR swallowed eastern Poland. After WWII, Poland was compensated for this loss by getting a comparatively smaller piece of Germany (what is now western Poland). Poles migrated from eastern Poland to German land (western Poland). Today, western Poland has few Germans, just like Vojvodina has relatively few Hungarians. Some radical Poles say, "We want our old eastern Poland back!" Today, pieces of it are in Lithuania, Belarus, and Ukraine. Few Poles live there anymore, just like relatively few Serbs live in Kosovo. If you told these Poles, "Fine, you can have your old eastern Poland back, just give western Poland back to Germany," or if you told Serbs, "Fine, take Kosovo back, just migrate all your Serbs out of Vojvodina and give it back to Hungary," then both Poles and Serbs would say, "No thanks. We'll keep things as they are." That's because Poles (like the Serbs) benefited from the land swap. Western Poland is full of metals, minerals, and industry, whereas bygone eastern Poland is mostly poor swampland. Similarly, Vojvodina is much more valuable than Kosovo. If there is anyone to pity, it might be the Germans and Hungarians, who both experienced a large net loss of valuable territory. Naturally, few Serbs consider any of this. Still, reflecting on these ideas might help them heal from the Kosovo trauma. However, what's more likely is that they'll send me hate mail.

While I'm offering controversial, sacrilegious thoughts to contemplate, here are four hard changes that Tito should have made after 1974 (leaders after Tito didn't have the courage, wisdom, or power to make them): (1) Revoke the autonomy status of Vojvodina, (2) put North Kosovo into the Serbian Republic, (3) elevate the rest of Kosovo to republic status, (4) provide stronger guarantees of protection of all minority rights in all republics. Those four moves might have prevented the Kosovo War or at least made the separation cleaner than it was.

Returning to Kosovo

In 2009, five years after my first visit, I returned to Pristina, Kosovo's capital. The ugliest building in the world, the *Biblioteka Kombëtare Dhe Universitare e Kosovës* (Kosovo's National University Library), is still there. When I first saw it, I thought it had unsightly metal bars all around it like an exoskeleton to protect it from potential war damage. Now I realize that it's just some guy's hideous architectural concept.

At the library's entrance, a US, EU, and Albanian flag flew next to the new Kosovo flag. There was no Serbian flag. The nearby Orthodox Church was still in ruins. Near the Skanderbeg's statue was Bill Clinton's new statue on Bil Klinton Bulevardi. Businesses were named after Clinton, while a bakery and a disco were named after Hillary. Graffiti in the city center said "Thank you America" and "I love USA." A 2010 Balkan Monitor survey showed that 95 percent of Kosovars see the US as "friendly," while 57 percent of Serbians view America as "hostile."

Near Peja (*Peć* in Balkanian), I visited two of Kosovo's best preserved Orthodox monasteries. Italian KFOR troops protected each monastery. They checked my passport, searched me, and then let me walk five minutes to get to the entrance. In the first monastery, the beautiful grounds have a stream rolling through it and snow-capped mountains above it. In fact, Kosovo's tallest mountain, Djeravica (2,656 m / 8,711 ft), is nearby. The Serb caretaker was rude and grumpy, but she finally let me enter the church. The colorful medieval paintings adorn every centimeter of the walls and ceiling. Next, I went to the protected Patrijaršija Monastery, which is two kilometers from Peja's center. It is also set in an idyllic location with architecture that reminds of the era when Serbs dominated Kosovo. Most of Kosovo's monasteries aren't as well preserved as these two. It's hard to imagine what priceless works of art were lost when Albanian mobs ransacked and destroyed dozens of Orthodox churches and monasteries.

In the afternoon, I watched Albanians in Peja, a city of 70,000. The streets were filled with teenagers who were let out of school. Like most people in the southern Balkans, Albanians usually have dark hair—only about 10 percent are blond. Moreover, just like people in Albania are physical, so are Albanian Kosovars. Kids (including boys) occasionally walk arm-in-arm. They'll grab each other's cheeks. In Gjakova (*Đakovica* in Balkanian), a waiter rubbed the backs of two of his customers who were eating their meals. Then he caressed the back of their heads. The macho men didn't flinch. Later, an old man came in and the waiter not only shook his hand, but then gently butted heads with him! These aren't gay men. Albanians are just touchy-feely people. Men would lean on me while sitting on a bus seat, even though they could avoid it. When they talk to you, they don't mind getting so close that you can feel their breath. Still, don't let their body language deceive you: declaring your homosexuality in Kosovo is about as bright as a man entering a random bar in Texas and squealing, "Hellloooo boys!!!"

Serb-Albanian relations today

Judging how well Kosovo's two tribes are getting along depends on who you ask. For example, in 2011, Slobodan Malić, who was born in Slovenia with Croatian Serb and Bosnian Serb parents, told me, "In Mitrovica, some Serbs are worried about crossing the bridge to the Albanian side. They say, 'Those Albanians will kill you!'"

Similarly, Andre told me, "Today, NATO troops are protecting the few Orthodox monasteries that remain in Kosovo. Meanwhile, busloads of Albanians visit Belgrade or Niš and they don't need anyone to protect them. Now I challenge you to go to Kosovo or Croatia without police protection and speak Serbian as you walk around the city. Be polite, of course, but just speak Serbian and see what happens to you. And then come to any city in Serbia and speak Albanian or Croatian and see the difference."

I cannot personally test his theory since I'm not fluent in Balkanian or Albanian, but Nenad, a Serbian world traveler who lives in Niš, told me, "I've never had a problem when I've been to Prishtina, even though my car has Serbian license plates. No matter where I've parked it in Kosovo, nobody vandalizes my car, and I've been there several times. I speak to Albanians in Serbian or English with no problems at all. Albanians would have more problems coming to Serbia than Serbs would have going to Albania."

Given the shortcomings of anecdotal evidence, let's look at some Balkan Monitor surveys. In 2010, half of the Albanians believe Kosovo's "Albanian leadership has to do everything to protect Serbs living in Kosovo." That's up from a third feeling that way in 2009—so things are improving. Another revelation: 70 percent of Albanians "think it will be possible to live together peacefully with the Serbs in an independent Kosovo," while only 2.6 percent of Serbs think peaceful coexistence is possible. I'd bet that far more Serbs would say that they could peacefully coexist with Albanians if the question hadn't said "in an independent Kosovo." From my experience, it seems like Albanians and Serbs continue to be like most neighboring ethnic groups in Europe: peacefully disliking each other.

The Heroin Bridge

Several Balkanians repeated what seemed to be a perverse nursery rhyme, "Albanians have at least 10 children: three to stay home and help the family, two to send to foreign countries to send money home, three to send to wars, and two to be criminals." Ilija Popović told me a variation, "Albanians have a minimum of seven children: four go to the mafia and three become prostitutes."

In some ways, Kosovo is like Sicily, minus the sea and oranges. In 2010, 22 percent of Kosovars say that organized crime affects them "daily," which is the highest rate in the Balkans. Kosovo's underground and illegal economy employs thousands of Kosovars. Still, things are changing at Europe's Heroin Bridge. It's a myth that Albanians are the drug leaders in the European cartels. For example, in 2006, only 6% of drug-related arrests in Italy were ethnic Albanians (while 65% were Italian and 19% were North African). In the chaotic 1990s, about 40% of Europe's heroin went through Kosovo. Today, it's down to 15%.

In 2010, 72 percent of Kosovars "have confidence in the local police," which is highest rate in the Western Balkans. The story is the same when the issue is about confidence in the EU institutions, NATO, UN, and Non-Governmental Organizations: Kosovo is far more positive than all the other Western Balkanians. Despite all this confidence and enthusiasm for these institutions, Kosovars are just as bad as Serbians are paying their taxes. Nearly six in 10 admit that tax evasion is "very widespread."

Kosovo is Europe's Mississippi

One popular Balkan myth is that America wanted to take Kosovo from Serbia to gain Kosovo's fabulous riches. On the contrary, for at least 150 years, Kosovo has been an economic nightmare for whatever sucker has had to manage it. three out 10 Kosovars live below the poverty line. According to the CIA, Kosovo's 2010 per capita GDP was $6,600—that's worse than Angola and Turkmenistan. The conspiracy-minded Balkanians then declare, "Yeah, but Kosovo is rich in resources like oil, gas, and mines that America and the EU want to extract! That's why NATO got involved!"

Dream on. For at least 50 years, Kosovo's oil and natural gas production has been zero. Although they have coal mines, they can't even extract enough of it to keep their own lights on. What little minerals and metals they do have (lignite is the only one they are abundant in) is hard for them to extract since their machinery hasn't been upgraded since Tito's time.

Wild Balkanian theories persist. Ilija Popović, a Montenegrin, whispered to me why Americans want to be in Kosovo so badly, "To extract all the uranium out of Kosovo." Huh? What uranium? Most of the uranium Kosovo has is from all the toxic depleted uranium that's left over from NATO's bombing campaign.

Everyone who romanticizes about the idea that we should return to an era where everyone grows their own food should visit Kosovo, because that's exactly what many Kosovars do. Their farming is inefficient and their yields are low. Their small plots can't justify tractors and there's little science behind their use of fertilizer, so they overuse it. Even though 24 percent of Kosovars work in agriculture (the highest rate in Europe), they don't grow enough food to feed themselves—they are a net importer of food.

Kosovo's economy doesn't produce squat: they import five times more products than they export. In fact, about 14% of their pathetic GDP doesn't even come from their country—it comes from Kosovars who work abroad and send money home. They work abroad because Kosovo's unemployment rate is 43%—among the world's worst. In 2010, 72% of Kosovars told the Balkan Monitor that they have "never had a regular job." Maybe that's why 79% of Kosovars felt "well-rested" when Gallup surveyed them in 2010; that makes them the most well-rested people in Europe. Ironically, they live next to the second *least* well-rested Europeans: Serbians.

It's tempting to blame the war for Kosovo's economic misery, but as we saw, Kosovo has been light-years behind everyone else since at least the 1950s. The last time it was an economic powerhouse was probably under Tsar Dušan in the 1340s. Thus, Kosovo is like America's poorest state: Mississippi. It takes more than it gives, it's an economic burden, and we'd all be financially better off without it. Contrary to Balkanian myth-makers, Kosovo is not an economic jewel—it's a great place to burn money.

Sometimes you have to wonder if some Serbs wanted to keep Kosovo out of *inat* (spite). If Milošević had been economically practical, then when Kosovo asked him for independence, he would have said, "Funny you mention it, because I've been looking for an excuse to get rid of your ass, because you're a total drag on our economy. Every time I give you two dinars, a couple of years later you give me back one dinar. It's been fun having you part of the gang, but guess what? We won't miss you. Goodbye!"

The Camp Bondsteel myth

After you dismiss the America-wanted-to-extract-Kosovo's-wealth theory, then Balkanians will bring up the America-wanted-to-establish-the-biggest-overseas-military-base-in-the-world theory. I heard this conspiracy theory nearly every time I asked Balkanians to explain why the Kosovo War happened. The conversation would usually go like the one I had with Aleksandar Svetozarević. He said, "America intervened in Kosovo because it's a very strategic place. They wanted to build the biggest American base outside of the USA. It's true! I've seen it on satellite photos on Google Maps. It's called Camp Bondsteel."

I yawned, and then I challenged him to prove it. I took a 20-minute nap while he searched English and Balkanian websites. Eventually he found an article on Croatia's Wikipedia that claimed that Bondsteel "is one of the biggest US bases in the world." I pointed out that the statement didn't reference the source. He kept trying, but eventually gave up.

What's the reality? First of all, Camp Bondsteel really does exist. It was named after US Medal of Honor recipient James Bondsteel. I've met Americans who work in Camp Bondsteel and I've even met Serbians who sell chickens to Camp Bondsteel. It's a big place. In fact, it's the biggest US base in the . . . Balkans. Yeah, not the *world* and not even *Europe*, just a little corner called the *Balkans*.

Let's put things in perspective. Camp Bondsteel can only house 7,000 men. The US base in the Kaiserslautern Military Community in Germany, which includes the Ramstein Air Base, holds 53,000 US military and civilians—that's *seven times bigger* than Camp Bondsteel. Ramstein has several elementary, middle, and high schools. It has American restaurants and feels like an American town in the middle of Germany. It's the largest US overseas community, but it's not the only one.

In 2011, outside the USA, there were 820 US military installations in over 135 countries. The US has 268 bases in Germany, 124 in Japan, 87 in South Korea, over 80 in Afghanistan, and about 100 in Iraq. As of 2011, there were 100,000 US military personnel in Iraq, 56,222 in Germany, 33,122 in Japan, 28,500 in South Korea, 31,100 in Afghanistan and approximately 9,700 in both Italy and the UK. GlobalSecurity.org lists the 75 *major* overseas US military bases and Camp Bondsteel is not on the list.

The US wasn't desperate for a base in the Balkans because it already had over 1,000 US troops in every Balkan country except Montenegro. Bulgaria, for example, gives the US the right to use two of its air bases as well as the Novo Selo training range for American troops. If there's trouble in the Balkans, the US can send a fleet of planes out of Italy's Aviano Air Base or Bulgaria's Bezmer Air Base and be anywhere in Southeastern Europe in less time than it takes to boil an egg.

Here's the funny thing: the US is hardly using Bondsteel's 7,000 men capacity. In 2011, there were only 1,400 Americans still in Kosovo. There were 5,000 NATO troops throughout Kosovo, but they're decreasing so that by 2015 there will be less than 2,300. At that point, Camp Bondsteel may close down permanently. Notice it's a "camp," not a "base." Americans are "camping" in Kosovo. They won't be there forever. For example, Camp Virginia in Kuwait had 15,000 soldiers (twice Bondsteel's size) until it shut down in 2010.

When Branislav Srđanović became the 23rd Balkanian to tell me the Bondsteel conspiracy theory, I showered him with reality and he suddenly became the most honest, self-aware Balkanian I've ever met. He said, "Oh, I'm sorry. It's just that we in the Balkans like to think that we're the *biggest* and *the most* whatever. I guess most people overestimate their country's importance."

This doesn't mean that having a military base in Kosovo wasn't one of the reasons America got involved there. It's likely that "Establishing a base" was one of the many bullet-points in the Pentagon's top-secret PowerPoint slide show on "The Benefits of Kicking Ass in Kosovo." Still, it wasn't the *only* reason, and probably not even the *main reason* either. It's like someone accusing you of going to your friend's barbeque just for the food. Perhaps you would have gone anyway, but free food sweetens the deal. Unfortunately, the Balkanian conspiracy theorists have a couple of more sinister (and fictitious) plots that we must debunk.

The pipeline myths

The creative conspiracy theorists say, "Fine. OK, so maybe America didn't go into Kosovo to rape it for its trivial resources. And maybe Camp Bondsteel isn't the biggest US military base in the world. But let me tell you the *real reason* for Camp Bondsteel: it's to guard the new AMBO oil pipeline that will cut across Kosovo! It's always about the oil, dude!"

Reality check: the AMBO pipeline does not go through Kosovo, which is why there's no "K" in the acronym. AMBO stands for *Albanian Macedonian Bulgarian Oil*. "Fine," say the conspiracy theorists, "Maybe I got my facts confused. Then it must be a *gas* pipeline going through Kosovo! It's about *gas!*"

There are three major gas pipelines going from Russia to Western Europe (Yamal, Brotherhood, and Soyuz). Russia is planning to make two new ones: the North Stream (which will go under the Gulf of Finland to Germany) and the South Stream (under the Black Sea and into Bulgaria, Greece, and beyond). *None of them will go through Kosovo.* And then there's the Nabucco gas pipeline that will come online in 2017, but it goes from Turkey to Bulgaria and Romania. It also bypasses Kosovo and Serbia. If for some reason the US wants to protect these pipelines, they already have thousands of troops in Bulgaria, Romania, Turkey, and Greece. A Kosovo presence is not needed.

Finally, the latest Balkan conspiracy theory is that Russians are building a secret military base near Niš, Serbia. The excited conspiracy believers think that Russia is putting that base to oversee the planned South Stream gas pipeline that will cross Serbia. Never mind that the Italians are co-developing the pipeline and would be well aware of the "secret" base. As we observed in the Serbia chapter, the Balkans is full of myths and legends; however, nowhere are they as plentiful (or as creative) as they are in Kosovo.

If Balkanians really want a juicy US-Kosovo conspiracy theory that has a bit logic to it and is moderately defensible, then they ought to say, "America got involved in Kosovo because Bill Clinton needed a way to distract the media away from his shenanigans with Monica Lewinsky."

Kosovo's time to shine

What's great about Kosovo's independence is that it eliminates one of the big excuses it had for being so economically retarded. While they were under Yugoslavia's and Serbia's thumb, they could always blame their problems on their "oppressor." Now they are in the driver's seat. Like any screwed-up nation, they have a pocketful of excuses to explain why they're still economically incompetent. It's unlikely that any of those excuses will be, "It's our fault." Instead they will point the fingers at phantoms who are somehow holding them back.

Re-read the chapter on eastern Germany to see how one nation that had far more problems than Kosovo and yet was able to become an economic superpower in less than 40 years. Or research Singapore, which was a screwed-up country in 1960 and today is a near-perfect society. To paraphrase Hungarian Count István Széchenyi, "When a country is screwed up for a few years, blame its leaders. When it's screwed up for many decades, blame its people." Kosovo has had the "luxury" of blaming its leaders. Ever since 2008 (when it declared independence), the clock has been ticking. Let's see how quickly it can get its act together.

As we've noted, Kosovo has few natural resources. Despite what the conspiracy theorists say, Kosovo's location is not strategic. It's rather lousy. On the other hand, its population is eager, friendly, and enthusiastic. What it needs to do is copy tiny landlocked economic superstars like Andorra, Lichtenstein, Luxembourg, and Switzerland. They're all richer than their neighboring countries. Like Kosovo, none of them had abundant natural resources. Their secret? They are free-trade meccas and they offer attractive banking laws. Kosovo must minimize all taxes and eliminate corporate taxes to make Kosovo a magnet for companies who will build businesses, create jobs, and employ taxpayers. If they pull that off, then Kosovo will become the cultural and financial center of the Balkans for the first time since the medieval Kingdom of Serbia.

The Greater Albania dream

Kosovo is to Albania like what Montenegro is to Serbia. Some say, "Kosovo is not a nation, they're Albanians, not Kosovars." That's like saying "Montenegro is not a nation, they're Serbs, not Montenegrins." In some ways, both of these statements are true. There's little difference between Kosovars and Albanians, just like there's hardly any difference between Montenegrins and Serbians. That's why Montenegro and Serbia have often been united under one flag. And that's why some Albanians want to unite Kosovo and Albania under one flag. It's the idea behind the Greater Albania.

Predrag Begović was born and raised in Montenegro, but considers himself a Serb. "We're one people," he told me. He added, "Kosovo is a painful subject. Albanians came to live there and now they take our land. Unfortunately, it is all part of their plan for a Greater Albania."

In the Skanderbeg museum in Krujë, Albania, you'll see many old ethnographic maps. The common theme is that Albanians have been living in the lands that they are living today for many centuries. The museum's message is: today, ethnic Albanians dominate Kosovo, Montenegro's southern tip, western Macedonia, and parts of Greece because they've always been there. The implied dream is to unite them all under one country. It's a story we've already heard in several other countries. When I first visited Kosovo, I asked Fatmir, "Do you think those regions in Montenegro and Macedonia that have a heavy Albanian presence will become independent or part of Albania?"

He said, "No . . . not yet. Maybe later."

Fatmir is not alone. A 2010 Balkan Monitor survey showed that support for a Greater Albania was significant in Macedonia (51%), Albania (63%), and Kosovo (81%). Still, those who think that "the creation of Greater Albania is likely in the near future" are less numerous: Albania (26%), Macedonia (42%), and Kosovo (49%). Given that Albania and Kosovo both support the idea, there seems little barrier to stop it from happening, assuming Serbia will recognize Kosovo this century. Breaking away from Macedonia will be trickier. In the next Balkan war, you can bet that the Greater Albania issue will be an important factor.

Kosovo's future

Nemanja Milosavljević, an Serb Orthodox priest in training who lives near the Kosovo border, told me, "We in the Balkans are more connected to the past than to the future." Let's try to look ahead anyway. One challenge is getting Serbia to accept Kosovo's independence so they can begin to trade efficiently again. According to the Balkan Monitor, only one in five Serbians think their country will recognize Kosovo's independence by 2020; two-thirds say it will "never" happen. Still, Serbia narrowly agrees that "part of a future solution" would be that Kosovo be "partitioned."

The logical solution would be to give North Kosovo to Serbia in exchange for Serbia's Preševo Valley, which is mostly Albanian. Unfortunately, both sides are too stubborn for that to happen. The danger of not recognizing Kosovo is that it could increase the chance of Albania annexing Kosovo. Such a move might let Kosovo inherit the benefits of an "established and recognized" country like Albania and would nearly complete the Greater Albania vision. At the same time, such an action could destabilize the region.

To avoid that, the EU could offer EU membership to Serbia and Kosovo simultaneously. Of course, Serbia is far more EU-ready than Kosovo, but if Serbia enters the EU first, then it could use its member status to block Kosovo's entry in classic *inat*-fashion (like Slovenia tried to do to Croatia). Another idea would be to simultaneously invite all the Balkans into the EU, including Albania. Having a border-less Balkans would, in a way, not just complete the Greater Albania vision, but also the Greater Serbia and Greater Croatia dreams (and any other nationalistic fantasies). Finally, everyone would be in one happy Balkan family. Don't laugh.

According to the Balkan Monitor's 2011 report, most people in the Balkans want to join the EU. Albanian Kosovars are the most enthusiastic, with 92 percent saying that they would vote to join. Serb Kosovars are polar opposites: 72% would vote *not* to join. The rest of the Balkans, including Serbia, have majorities who would vote for joining the EU. Although the EU is not enthusiastic about inviting the Balkans to join their club, it may want to do it in the name of Balkan stability.

Albanians are irrepressible optimists. Statistically, Albanians have the worst standard of living in the Balkans. Still, according to the Balkan Monitor, Albanians Kosovars were the only group in the Balkans where a majority was satisfied with their standard of living in 2010. Albanian Kosovars also show by far the lowest levels fear, sadness, or worry. Compared to everyone else in the Balkans, they're *far more* likely to agree with these statements: *I like what I do everyday; I have a lot of love in their life; my physical health is near perfect; I can't imagine living in a better community than the one I live in today; I have more that enough money to do what I want to do.* It's as if the whole nation is practicing positive affirmations.

As my bus zigzagged up Kosovo's mountains and the dawn light peeked over the Albanian Alps, I looked back to Kosovo. I also had optimism that Kosovo's future will be brighter than its past. Still, that's not saying much. The international community has been supplying most of Kosovo's money. What will happen when they close that artificial money faucet? It's hard to imagine the relaxed, fun-loving Kosovars working their asses off to become like Luxembourg.

And then there's Serbia's ghost. In 2011, Slaviša Andrić, a Croatian Serb, told me, "Today, Serb children are still singing songs about how Kosovo is the heart of Serbia."

What Kosovo Can Teach Us

- **Be grateful.** America hurts many countries. However, it helps many countries too. I've never been to a country that is as deeply thankful and grateful as Kosovo. Examine your life. What are you grateful for? Who are you grateful for? Tell him or her how much you appreciate them. And be grateful for whatever you have, even if it doesn't seem like much.
- **Be optimistic.** Albanian Kosovars are insanely optimistic. Norway and Sweden were the only European countries who scored higher than Kosovo in Gallup's 2010 Optimism Index. What's remarkable is that Kosovars are dirt-poor and their economy is atrocious, but they sincerely think life is great and that it's getting better every day. Wear rosy-colored sunglasses today. It's all in your mind.

Places I saw and recommend in Kosovo: Prizren and the mountains near the Albanian border.

Travel deals and info: http://ftapon.com/kosovo

There's one final piece to the ex-Yugoslavia and Albanian puzzle: Macedonia. But maybe we should say that we're going to FYROM.

"Huh? What's FYROM?" you say?

You'll be sorry you asked.

18

MACEDONIA—OR WHATEVER YOU CALL IT

THE YEAR IS 4512. Africans have ruled the world for the last 1,000 years, so things have changed a bit. Now blacks are the dominant population throughout Eastern Europe. The Black Eastern European Empire is made up of several republics, and one of its poorest is the Republic of Croatia, which has been populated by ethnic Kenyans for the last 14 centuries.

Meanwhile, Serbia is the only Eastern European country that kept its Slavic identity and independence over the ages—Croatians went extinct in the 2300s. Of course, the Serbians have changed: their language would be extremely hard for a Serbian from the twenty-first century to understand and they're no longer Orthodox—they believe in the Quantum Religion and gay rights. Still, there's a faint connection between the Serbian of 2012 and the one from 4512.

Moreover, Serbia's borders have also changed: in 4412, they conquered eastern Croatia, a territory that borders the Black Eastern European Empire's Republic of Croatia. To honor the extinct Croatian people, Serbians call the eastern Croatia region simply *Croatia*. In fact, Serbs who live there like to call themselves *Croatians* just as often as they call themselves *Serbian*.

Suddenly, in 4513, the Black Eastern European Empire breaks up because of another American-led conspiracy. Each republic within the Black Eastern European Empire declares independence, including the Republic of Croatia. The Kenyans who live there decide to call their new country *Croatia*.

At that point, Serbia erupts in fury, screaming, "Calling their country *Croatia* is an aggressive act! Those Kenyans are trying to make a claim on the Serbian territory of Croatia! Naming the country *Croatia* is a threat to Serbia's security and integrity!" This makes most of the solar system laugh because Serbia's robotic army is 10 times stronger than the tech-poor, pathetic Republic of Croatia.

Serbians are also furious because, "By calling themselves Croatians, these black Kenyans are stealing our heritage! Croatians and Serbians in the twenty-first century spoke the same language! We were *one* people back then! Same culture!" Finally, the Serbians go nuts when the Kenyans call their main spaceport the Petar Krešimir Spaceport. Serbians say, "Petar Krešimir IV was Croatia's greatest king in the Middle Ages. Under Petar, Croatia was bigger than it ever was in history! They're robbing us our cultural symbols! Now, those Kenyans are putting an enormous hologram of Petar in Zagreb! The horror! Petar is *ours*!"

Meanwhile, a few Kenyans who are taking Martian drugs claim that they are descendants of the ancient Croatians who lived in between the seventh and twenty-fourth centuries. Of course, Kenyans mixed their DNA with the locals when they migrated to the Balkans in the 3100s, so technically there is a faint genetic connection between the twenty-first century Croatians and the new Croatians, but it's such a weak link that it's not even worth mentioning. Still, a few Kenyan nationalists make the ridiculous historical link. Instead of laughing about it (like the rest of the galaxy), the Serbians go bonkers. Serbians scream at the Croatian Kenyans, "Damn it! You're not *Slav*! You're *Africans*! I don't care if you've been living in the Balkans for the last 1,400 years, you're not related to the ancient Croatians! So shut the hell up!"

To join the United Planetary Nations, Serbians force Kenyans to call their country *The Former Black Eastern European Empire's Republic of Croatia* or FBEEERC, instead of *Croatia*. Furious Kenyans tell Serbians, "But it's a lie that Croatians and Serbians were one people! They had separate languages and sometimes even fought each other in wars."

Serbians reply, "That's not totally true. The ancient text of *The Hidden Europe* says that Croatians and Serbians effectively spoke one language, Balkanian. That old book also says that Croatians and Serbians were like brothers who sometimes argued, but that they were basically one people! So by calling yourself Croatians, you're stealing our identity!"

"C'mon," say the Kenyans, "*The Hidden Europe* was a brainless book written by a twit! It's so full of garbage that it only sold 57 copies. Yet even that yellowed tome pointed out all the wars between the ancient Croatians and Serbians. They were rivals just as often as they were buddies! If we're guilty of exaggerating our connection with them, well then, so are you!"

"Shut up! And how dare you claim that you speak Croatian! You speak an African tongue, not a Slavic one! And remember, we have a region called Croatia too! You're falsifying history!"

They kept arguing about this issue for over 20 years. During that time, the rest of the Milky Way Galaxy would tell the Serbians and Kenyans, "Your debate is so fucking stupid! Who cares!? Grow up guys, and get a life!"

Defining Macedonia

If you're like most people on this planet, you know almost nothing about Macedonia. Therefore, you're probably wondering what the hell this futuristic story has to do with today's Macedonia. Believe it or not—everything. This story is a parallel tale about what is going on today in Macedonia. Incredibly, for over 20 years, Greece and Macedonia have been passionately and fanatically fighting each other over Macedonia's name. It sounds absurd (and it is), but it's true. Welcome to the Balkans.

When Yugoslavia broke up, it gave birth to seven new countries that were all boring when it came to naming themselves. They simply made their republic's name into their country name. For example, when Yugoslavia's Republic of Montenegro became an independent country, it called itself the *Republic of Montenegro*. Yugoslavia's Republic of Macedonia copied the republics and declared that their newly independent country would be called the *Republic of Macedonia.* That seemed reasonable, but when that happened, Greece became stormier than Poseidon in a hurricane.

Just like the US has 50 states, Greece is divided into several internal states, and its northernmost one is called Macedonia. Greece argued that when Yugoslavia's Macedonia called itself Macedonia, it was threatening Greece's Macedonia. They have never explained how Yugoslavia's poorest republic could threaten Greece, which is part of NATO. Macedonia is not part of NATO, so if they attacked Greece, they would be inviting all of NATO, including the US military, to come knocking on their door.

Nevertheless, enraged Greeks imposed an embargo against Macedonia, blocked Macedonia's entry into the UN, and said it would not stop until Macedonia changed its name. After a 20-month embargo, Macedonia agreed to call itself the *Former Yugoslav Republic of Macedonia,* or FYROM. Greece agreed to not block Macedonia from joining any international organization as long as it used the name FYROM. So now FYROM is in the UN. However, in 2008, Greece blocked Macedonia's application into NATO, even though Macedonia applied using the FYROM name. In 2011, Macedonia appealed the UN's highest court saying that Greece illegally vetoed Macedonia's NATO application, because it had no good reason to do so, other than to take a cheap shot at Macedonia. The quarrel gets more stupid.

When Macedonia renamed its main highway and airport after Alexander the Great and put a statue of him in Skopje, Greece had a dramatic heart-attack and gasped, "You're stealing our heritage!" The final death blow to the Macedonia-Greek relationship was when a few Macedonian "intellectuals" started trumpeting the theory that today's Slavic Macedonians are descendants of the ancient Macedonians. At that point, if Greece had nuclear weapons, it would have used them.

It's not just Greece's politicians and academics who are furious—the average Greek on the street is surprisingly passionate about this farcical issue. For example, after Macedonia's independence from Yugoslavia, about one million Greeks rallied in Thessaloniki to protest against Macedonia's name. Even 100,000 Greeks in Melbourne, Australia took to the streets over the name dispute. American Greeks took out two full-page ads in *The New York Times* to make the point. Today, any YouTube video, Facebook page, or news article about Macedonia's name will get an Everest-sized mountain of passionate (and often insulting) comments. A 2010 Gallup survey of Greeks showed that 82% thought that the problem was "completely" or "mostly" Macedonia's fault, 72% looked at Macedonia unfavorably, and 85% thought that if Macedonia doesn't change its name, then Greece should block Macedonia's entry into the EU. In addition, about 66% of Greeks thought this whole debate is "very important" and 29% thought there could be war in the region soon.

Since FYROM doesn't roll off the tongue, Greeks often call Macedonia by its capital city, *Skopje*. It's like telling all Americans that they should say, "I'm from Washington," and not, "I'm from the United States of America." An American told me that when she was crossing the border to Greece, the Greek guard asked her where she was coming from. She said, "Macedonia."

"No!" he shouted, "You're coming from *Skopje!* And *now* you're in Macedonia!"

When I visited Macedonia's National Museum in Skopje, I said to the museum's curator, "I realize Greece is being a big baby, but why not just make it easy for everyone and change your country's name. What's the big deal?"

He bristled and said, "But we can't. That's our name. It's who we are."

In fact, that's what 77 percent of Macedonians would say too. So I told the curator, "I got a better name for you: *Roman Empire*. Change it from *Macedonia* to the *Roman Empire*. After all, the Romans were here too."

He smiled, "But then we might get Italy angry at us."

"Well then, how about calling your country *Greece Sucks*?"

He laughed.

Macedonia's ancient history

It's tempting to ignore this controversy because it's so incredibly petty and infantile. I kept asking Greeks and Macedonians, "Don't you guys have anything better to do?" Given the 20 years that Macedonians and Greeks have wasted on this issue, we owe it to them to spend a few minutes analyzing it. That should help us determine if they're acting like nine-year-olds or five-year-olds.

First, let's cover 3,000 years of history in one paragraph. Nearly 3,000 years ago, Macedonians started to establish their civilization. Around 2,360 years ago, they attacked Athens, Thebes, and other Greek city-states. About that time, Alexander III of Macedon earned the name Alexander the Great because he briefly controlled much of the known world. He did it with the help of the Greeks, although his top generals were Macedonian. After he died, his kingdom Balkanized. About 2,180 years ago the Macedonians and the Greeks were assimilated into the Roman Empire. Things changed again about 1,300 years ago, when Slavs moved into the Balkans. The Bulgarian, Serbian, and Turkish Empires each controlled Macedonia for centuries. Finally, over 100 years ago, the Slavs and Greeks basically split what was once the core land of the ancient Macedonians. And that's how it remains today. Now let's look at the key points in the world's most tedious debate.

How Greek was Alex?

Greeks claim that ancient Macedonians were fundamentally Greek. That's debatable. On the one hand, the Greeks were Alexander the Great's most important ally. Alex spoke Greek and Aristotle was his personal tutor. Alex carried Aristotle's personally annotated version of *The Iliad* with him on his military campaigns. He idolized Greek heroes. Alex's mother claimed that he was the son of Zeus, a Greek god.

On the other hand, Macedonians were not Greeks. Let's start with an obvious (but often overlooked) point: they often called themselves *Macedonians* and not *Greeks*. They wouldn't do that if there wasn't a difference. When Alexander counted the men in his army, he categorized them by the number of Macedonians, Greeks, Thracians, Illyrians, and so on. If Greeks and Macedonians were identical, they wouldn't have two categories when accounting for the number of men in the army. Therefore, the question isn't *was there a difference*, but rather *how big of a difference was there*? In other words, were the ancient Macedonians substantially different than the Greeks or were they suffering from the Balkan narcissism of minor differences?

In the futuristic tale that opened this chapter, I used a Croatian-Serbian analogy to support the Greek argument that there was hardly any difference. However, a Slovenian-Serbian analogy would probably have been more accurate. Slovenians and Serbians are South Slavic, just like ancient Macedonians and Greeks were Hellenistic. Still, each group has a distinct culture. Educated Slovenians are fluent in Balkanian, just like educated Macedonians were fluent in Greek. Nevertheless, Slovenians have their own language that Serbians struggle to understand. Similarly, if an ancient Macedonian spoke his language in Athens, the Greeks would ask him to please speak Greek.

Because of modern transportation and communications, we forget just how far away Macedonia was from Greece. An Athenian would have to travel about 400 kilometers (250 miles) to get to Macedonia. Today, such a trip only takes about four hours in a car. However, in ancient times, when most people got around on foot, such a journey could take a month! Indeed, walking all day only gets you to the suburbs of Athens. Thus, even though Macedonia was Greece's neighbor, it was a world away.

To believe that Macedonia's culture was nearly identical to Greece's underestimates how distance alters language and culture. Even with the fast modern travel we have today, there are still cultural and linguistic differences between different Greek regions. In ancient times, those differences were far greater, which is why ancient Greece was a collection of city-states rather than one united nation. That's also why Macedonians attacked some Greek city-states (like Athens and Thebes) while they remained friendly with other Greek city-states. In conclusion, ancient Macedonians and ancient Greeks were similar, but not as similar as some Greeks think.

Are today's Macedonians related to the ancient Macedonians?

My Macedonian couchsurfing host in the town of Strumica is famous for growing marijuana. He's been interviewed on TV and the police visit his house regularly. When I stayed with him, he was often smoking grass and playing guitar. I stayed in one of the two psychedelic mini-cottages he had in his backyard. Eventually, he showed me his secret marijuana garden. What's interesting is that no matter how stoned he got, he would never claim that Macedonians are related to ancient Macedonians. Still, a few Macedonian academics have made such a claim, which clearly proves that they're smoking something much more powerful than marijuana.

Any historian with a brain will agree that Slavs migrated to the Balkans around the sixth century. That's about 1,000 years after Alexander the Great kicked butt. By the time the Slavs showed up, not only had the ancient Macedonian Empire vanished, but even the Roman Empire had come and gone. The Balkan power *du jour* was the Byzantine Empire. Over those 1,000 years, the local culture and language had changed dramatically. For a Slavic Macedonian to claim that he is a descendant of the ancient Macedonians is as absurd as a typical American claiming that he's a descendant of the Native Americans.

Of course, the Byzantine DNA must have had a bit of Roman and ancient Macedonian DNA residue. A few Slavic immigrants had babies with these Byzantines, just like a few European immigrants had babies with Native Americans. Nevertheless, lots of mixing has happened since then. In Macedonia's case, the Turks injected their DNA into the Balkan genetic soup. And don't forget the Albanians too. Thus, most modern Macedonians probably have at least some trace of ancient Macedonian, Roman, Byzantine, Greek, Turkish, and even Albanian DNA. Like all of us, they also have a bit of African DNA too. To disproportionately emphasize one genetic link is wildly deceptive.

Until now, linguists, archaeologists, and historians have drawn us an incomplete and uncertain map of where we all come from. Now a fourth expert has entered the room: the geneticist. In this century, we'll develop a clearer picture of where we all come from. We may discover that today's Iranians are more related to ancient Macedonians than today's Macedonians. Once geneticists closely examine the modern Macedonian and Greek DNA, it's likely that everyone will be disappointed. Neither will be as tightly connected to their ancient heroes as they would like to be. And everyone in the Balkans will probably have more Turkish DNA in them than they ever suspected.

Regardless, who the hell cares if you're a descendant of Alexander the Great? Sure, he established some towns (which he mostly named after himself), but he was kind of an asshole. He killed his cousin and several other potential rivals (because he feared they would threaten his throne). A few times, after conquering a city, he had all the city's military-aged men executed and the women and children sold to slavery. He not only put to death a conspirator, but killed his innocent father too. In a drunken argument, he personally killed a man who had once saved his life. When one of his closest friends died, he liquidated a nearby town to make a sacrifice for his friend's "ghost." He was Europe's version of Genghis Khan, ruthlessly hacking and slashing his way through a vast territory, stealing treasures, and causing widespread terror. Would you be proud to have that guy as an ancestor?

There are two hilarious aspects about this I'm-related-to-Alexander-and-you're-not debate. First, Alexander the Great died when he was 32 and had only one child, who was quickly killed. Therefore, *nobody* can claim to be Alex's descendent since he didn't produce any descendents. Second, today's Macedonians and Greeks are usually homophobic. Yet there's strong evidence that Alex was, like many of his contemporaries, bisexual. Therefore, I propose a simple test for Macedonians and Greeks to prove that they're related to the ancient Macedonians: whoever can demonstrate that his population is more gay than the other wins.

It's cool to be old

As immature as this Greek-Macedonian spat is, it reveals a profound lesson. Normally, youth defines coolness. However, in the Balkans it's cool to be old. Or at least to be tied to ancient stuff. Whereas powerful countries like Japan, Russia, and China have healthy egos that are linked to today's reality, the self-image of puny countries often depends on being attached to things of yesteryear. Chauvinists believe that being ancient legitimizes their territorial claims. When your country is the size of Alabama (like Greece) or Vermont (like Macedonia), you use the vague past to boost your self-esteem.

Ivaylo Ditchev, a professor at Sofia University, wrote, "The race toward ancientness, in the Balkans, was certainly launched by the Greek national movement, which captured the desire of romantic Europe and privatized the classic heritage of Antiquity. No Balkan country would resist the temptation to dig up some obscure ancestors that would be at least as ancient as the ancient Greeks—Ilyrians, Thracians, Dacians, et cetera. One of the paradoxes of community sentiment is that historical truth is of secondary importance. The symbolic war over ancestors itself makes nationals stick together, exclude traitors, and recognize who 'we' and 'the others' are. . . . Nevertheless, the effort to represent the Balkan nations as eternal substances encountered one major difficulty, which was the gap separating modern states from the supposed glory of their ancestors. Thus the major problem confronting identity builders was *continuity*."[1]

Therefore, Macedonian "intellectuals" tried to bridge the 1,000-year gap between the ancient Macedonians and the Slav arrival, as well as the other 1,000-year gap between the medieval Bulgarian King Samuel and 1945. Such cockeyed efforts to establish continuity makes everyone giggle except the Greeks, who pay attention to the babbling imbecile instead of ignoring him.

What's so fascinating about watching Eastern Europeans describe themselves is that they often pretend that they're more connected with their ancient history than with their recent history. They repress their embarrassing recent history (communism and periods of occupation) and then revel in a wispy and distant "golden age." It's amusing to hear modern humans acting like the ancients are as related to them as their great-grandfather. The reality is that you need 100 "greats" before the word "father" since there are about 100 generations separating you and the ancient Macedonians. Meanwhile, some of us can hardly believe we're related to our siblings or parents.

It's hard for Americans to understand this need to stretch the truth to connect yourself to ancient history, because Americans just don't bother. Given that Europeans showed up 500 years ago, the only way we could argue that we're connected with the ancients is to "prove" that we mixed with "the natives." Thus, our later generations would have blood mixed with "the ancients." Instead of trying to sell this fantasy, our practical historians simply focused on admitting the truth instead of inventing myths and fables about a connection that hardly exists.

Nevertheless, there are exceptions in the USA. Many Native Americans, for example, believe that they were created in North America and did not migrate across the Bering Strait 12,000 years ago. Some cling so tightly to this falsehood that they are fighting to participate in the National Geographic's Genographic Project, which is sampling the DNA of thousands of people to create a global migration map that illustrates our origins. Some Indian tribes are boycotting the project because they don't want to know the truth, preferring to keep their myths alive and avoid the not-so-romantic reality. The Chairman of the Massachusetts Commission on Indian Affairs admitted that he preferred sticking his head in the sand. He explained why his Mashpee Wampanoag tribe is boycotting the project, "What the scientists are trying to prove is that we're the same as the [European] pilgrims except we came over several thousand years before. Why should we give them that openly?"

Privatizing ancient history

In their attempts to construct mythic national identities, Balkan intellectuals are trying to privatize their national heritage: "It's ours and you can't use it unless we allow you to." This degrades into a competition, a land-grab of ancient history, where every Balkan nation tries to claim that some dead guy is "theirs" only. Hence, Croatians and Albanians both claim the Illyrian culture; Bulgaria, Greece, and Macedonia all believe the Saints Cyril and Methodius are "theirs"; and of course, Greece and Macedonia are wrestling each other over that bisexual guy.

An example of privatizing history is the Olympics. When Western countries wanted to create an international competition of many sports, they thought it would be nice to call the event the *Olympics*. Instead of being honored, the Greeks protested, saying that doing so would be "stealing Greek heritage." After much negotiation, the Greeks finally agreed to let the world use the word *Olympics* as long as the fire came from Olympus and Greek athletes always got to march in first at the major ceremonies.

As Ivaylo Ditchev put it, antiquity in the Balkans is like petroleum. First, Westerners discover it by excavating ancient sites. Second, locals who created their country last week claim that they're related to the ancient people who built it and nationalize the site. Third, the locals sell Westerners tickets to see the ancient places. In *Nationalism and Modernism,* Anthony D. Smith wrote, "We should not be misled by the paradox that nationalists claim their nations are rooted in antiquity and self-evidently natural, when they are in fact quite recent and novel constructs."[2]

Macedonia: the prankster

Whenever someone takes themselves too seriously, it's tempting to make fun of them. Macedonia behaves like a mischievous child who enjoys ridiculing Greece. You tell a child, "Don't stick your tongue out!" What does the child do? Sticks his tongue out. Yell the command, "Don't say 'Alexander the Great'!" The child will say, "Alexander, Alexander, Alexander, Alexander, Alexander, Alexander, Alexander, Alexander, Alexander, Alex . . . ."

Sometimes it seems as if the Macedonians say to themselves, "What can we do today to piss off those overly-sensitive Greeks? I know! Let's use a Greek symbol in our flag! Yeah! Oh, and let's also name our main arena and hospital after Philip II, the father of Alexander the Great! Yeah, that should rattle them!" Sure enough, the Greeks fall for it every time. If the Greeks just ignored their runty northern neighbor, the Macedonians would get bored with all their sophomoric pranks.

Are the tough Greeks really so insecure to believe that Macedonia (or anyone) will "steal the Greek heritage" and that the international community will fall for it? That's like Egypt losing sleep because they think that neighboring Sudan will steal ancient Egyptian history. Moreover, it would be easier to sympathize with the Greeks if the Macedonians were insulting the ancient Macedonians, like making a statue of Alex with a bronze dog peeing on it. Instead, they're celebrating and honoring the guy by putting him everywhere. There's a statue of US President Franklin Delano Roosevelt in Oslo, Norway. I was happy to see him there. There's a statue of Gandhi in Slovenj Gradec, Slovenia. Are Indians furious and boycotting Slovenian products and stopping them from getting in the UN? Perhaps they would if they only knew that Slovenia exists.

Listening to the Greek point of view

Later, I would debate this issue with a Greek woman. She screamed, "You think this is about the name? It's not about the name! It has nothing to do with the name! It's about FYROM stealing our heritage and claiming it as their own."

I said, "I understand. That's a legitimate point. So if Macedonia signed a statement agreeing that ancient Macedonia was Greek, that Slavs had nothing to with it, and that they are not the descendants of Alexander the Great, then would you let them name their country Macedonia?"

"No."

"Why not? You just told me that the name wasn't the issue."

"Because it's not right that they use that name!"

And now you know why they've been bickering for 20 years.

The Greek fury would also be easier to understand if the Greek Macedonians wanted to declare independence at some point in this century. In that case, they would also want to call their new country Macedonia. For example, let's imagine that North and South Korea are under Chinese rule for a long time and that they both become independent simultaneously. However, South Korea manages to submit its UN paperwork before North Korea and claims *Korea* as its name. In that case, the North Koreans would be understandably angry that the South Koreans hogged the name. Yet Greece's Macedonia has absolutely no interest in seceding from Greece, nor have they mentioned this scenario during their 20-year debate.

In 2011, as some Eastern Europeans learned that I was writing this book, I would sometimes get amusing emails. Eleftheria Paez sent the following email with the title "Macedonia is Greek." (I have not corrected the mistakes, so that you can join in on the fun.) She wrote, "If you lost and you have no clue were Macedonia is, go to Macedonia Greece in Pella, and other areas of Greece and you see the real Macedonia and Macedonians. You will fill Macedonia in your bones and in your blood, and you will not fill lost. Everything was written in Greek not Bulgaroslavophonic language. My Grand Mother was from FYOM and we were told that this language she was speaking was Bulgarian. Greek and Macedonian Geneology came from the Hiraclides not from TITTO THE COMMUNIST. You will see that this people have no connection to the Macedonian the Greek. 10% of the FYOM land belongs to Greece. Yugoslavia does not want them, neither the Greeks, because they are trablemakers. The Albanians are same. They still and kill the elderly people in Greece. If I was me in charge in Greece I could have deported those scums with in a second. They are bunch of jail birds, totally uneducated zoo."

Greeks need to visit Bolivia and Luxembourg

I like to ask Greeks, "Why aren't Venezuelans furious at the Bolivians?" After a blank stare, I inform them that Bolivia is named after Simón Bolívar, a heroic revolutionary who helped liberate much of South America. What's interesting is that Bolívar was not from Bolivia. He was from *Venezuela*. So why aren't Venezuelans demanding that Bolivia change their name? Why aren't Venezuelans accusing Bolivia of "stealing their heritage" and "monopolizing" Bolivar's name? Why aren't Venezuelans boycotting Bolivian products or demanding that Bolivia call itself *One of the Many Former Spanish Colonies in South America* or *OMFSCSA?*

Maybe Venezuelans aren't bothering Bolivia about this because they're honored that a country will name their country after a Venezuelan national hero. Or maybe it's because Venezuelans are relaxed, easy-going people (I lived there for four months, so I know). Or maybe Venezuelans believe that each country has a right to call itself by whatever name it wants. Or maybe it's because Venezuelans have a life.

Let's pick an example from Europe. Belgium's southern region is called Luxembourg. Walk south and you'll run into a country called Luxembourg, whose capital is also called Luxembourg! Why didn't Luxembourg and Belgium fight for decades over that? Why doesn't one country think that the other is "aggressively announcing its territorial ambitions" or "embezzling" the regional history? Maybe it's because they'd rather focus on building and improving their rich economies than squabbling over small-minded and childish issues.

The only good Greek argument

There is only one good argument Greece makes for why Macedonia should change its name: there's a geographic region called Macedonia and the Republic of Macedonia is just a piece of it. The geographic region of Macedonia is shared by Macedonia, Greece, and Bulgaria. Imagine if Norway called itself *Scandinavia* or if Vietnam called itself *The Republic of Asia*. It would be confusing and might annoy others in those respective geographic regions. Indeed, it would be fascinating to see what would happen if Macedonia changed its name to *The Balkan Republic*. What would the other Balkan Slavs say?

Thus, Macedonia is arguably monopolizing a geographical term. If Norway called itself *Scandinavia* and Norwegians were called *Scandinavians*, then saying, "I'm married to a Scandinavian" or "I visited Scandinavia" would become ambiguous. Still, ambiguous geographical terms are common. Just ask the people who live in Washington state in the US. When they say they live in Washington, they have to clarify that it's not DC. Those who live in Luxembourg have three possible options in a small area. There's also a town called *Macedonia* in Alabama, Georgia, Illinois, Indiana, Iowa, and Ohio. What about South Africa? Shouldn't all the countries in south Africa force South Africa to change its name? Instead, the relaxed Africans call their region Southern Africa, even though Africa's northern region is called North Africa. If Tunisia had more balls, it would call itself North Africa.

The worst offender of hijacking a geographical name is America. Indeed, *America* and *Americans* are geographical terms (as Central and South Americans love to remind US citizens). Ironically, Greece doesn't mind the ambiguity in this case, since it often uses the term Αμερική (America) to refer to the United States.

Therefore, the Macedonia-is-seizing-a-geographic-term argument isn't great, but it is the only argument that Greece should emphasize. All the other objections are irrelevant. To understand why, imagine if Macedonia calls itself *Vardar* (it's one of Greece's proposed alternative names and is based on the name of Macedonia's longest river). In that case, Vardarians could still claim to be descendants of the ancient Macedonians, still have territorial ambitions to take over Greece, still put statues of Alexander the Great in every village, and still erect temples for Zeus. In fact, Vardarians would be *more likely* to take such actions out of spite if Greece forced them to change their name. Therefore, changing the name doesn't solve any of those issues, so it's pointless to use those reasons as a justification for a name change.

As this book went to press in 2011, there is still no solution. I predict that sometime in the next 1,000 years Macedonia's final name will be either the *New Republic of Macedonia* or *The Republic of North Macedonia.* Today, about two-thirds of the world's countries recognize Macedonia by its desired name, *The Republic of Macedonia.*

Analyzing this annoying controversy produced one useful finding. Earlier we were unable to solve the mystery as to why Albanians and Finns call their country by a completely different sounding name than what the rest of the world calls them. Now we know. Long ago, they had a naming dispute with a bordering country. Albanians wanted to call their nation *Shqipëria* and Finns wanted to be called *Suomi*, but a neighboring bully forced them to change their name. The locals kept their original, desired name and everyone else used the name given by the bully. Let's hope that in 4512, when a Black Croatian reads this book, he'll learn why Vardarians call their country *Macedonia* and why everyone else calls it *Vardar*.

The most humble church in Eastern Europe

As my bus entered Skopje, the capital seemed unexciting. In 2004, Skopje was a collection of gray, blocky buildings that seemed like entries in the World's Most Atrocious Building Competition. At least they had a good excuse for it: in 1963, a massive earthquake leveled Skopje. They rushed to rebuild it and it shows. I hopped off the bus, put on my backpack, and explored.

One cool place to see is Eastern Europe's most humble church. The Church of Sveti Spas isn't a spa, but it has an interesting story. In the 1600s, the Turks had a law that no building could be taller than a mosque. Christians wanted a nice high vaulted ceiling, so they came up with an ingenious solution: put half the church underground! You have to take steps *down* to enter it. The steeple isn't high, so they didn't get in trouble with the ruling Turks, and the Christians were happy to have a high ceiling. It's ironic that today a massive cross, complete with bright lights, is perched on the summit of the mountain that overlooks Skopje (and all its mosques).

As I walked around, Skopje got more interesting. The *Čaršija* (Turkish bazaar) has cobblestoned streets and a vibe that will make you feel like you're in Turkey—minarets, mosques, and Muslims mingle in the streets. Nevertheless, the Slavic language, nearby Orthodox churches, and the occasional blond person remind you that the Turkish Empire has been gone for a century. Still, this historic Turkish quarter, with its bathhouses, shows off a side of Europe that is hard to find anywhere else. Nearby is a bronze statue of Mother Teresa, along with her birthplace, and a new memorial house. The beautiful fifteenth-century *Kamen Most* (Stone Bridge) takes you over the swift moving Vardar River and into *Ploštad Makedonija* (Macedonia Square). It's a fine square that needs work, which is exactly what the government is doing.

In 2014, Skopje plans to get a grandiose $300 million facelift. They plan to build 15 elegant governmental buildings and to litter the city with statues and monuments, including a triumphal arch. In July 2011, they mounted a $7.6 million, 22-meter (72-ft) tall statue of Alexander the Great, complete with a fountain. The city's makeover is controversial, and not just because of the statue. Whenever a city spends money to beautify itself, some residents complain that the money should be spent elsewhere (e.g., transportation, hospitals, education, etc.). Nevertheless, sometimes people underestimate what a pretty city can do for you: just ask Paris or Venice. If Skopje became the prettiest city in the Balkans, then the money would follow.

The Macedonian Question

In 2004, a San Francisco friend introduced me to Audrey Pitonak, a petite 30-year-old American who was the Assistant Head of Nova Schools, a private Macedonian-American high-school. She offered to host me for a few days and also invited me to teach three of her high-school classes. The first class was a writing class. I focused on how to do travel writing. I gave them a few hints, but told them that if they wanted some real tips, they should sign up for my $499 workshop in San Francisco. No takers. The next two classes were geography classes. They asked me questions about the countries I've visited. I told them that everybody in America is fat, everyone in Africa is hungry, and all the men in Albania wear white hats.

Ultimately, the teenagers taught me a few things, especially about Macedonia's geography and history. It became obvious that Macedonia has an identity crisis. The fight over the ancient Macedonians is just the tip of the iceberg. They explained that in the last 100 years there's been a more meaningful fight over Macedonia's real, current identity. That debate became known as the Macedonian Question.

Macedonia is like a seat that everyone's sat on and so when you ask who owns the seat, everyone raises their hand. The land is like a Balkan community recreation room: it's had multiple uses over the centuries. Greeks, Bulgarians, Turks, Serbians, and Albanians have all controlled part or all of Macedonia. Although such a multi-use territory is common throughout Europe, in Macedonia you can really see the headaches that such regions produce. Fundamentally, the Macedonian Question is *who are the Macedonians?* Loaded in that question is *what is their language and who should rule them?*

Obviously, there isn't a clear answer. If the answer were obvious (like should Kansas be part of the USA?), there would be little debate. However, the debate has raged for 100 years. The question popped up when Slavs and Greeks conspired to kick the Turkish Empire out of Europe in 1912. After liberating themselves, they needed to draw new borders. They agreed to draw them based on ethnic lines. Most of the Balkan ethnographic map was relatively straightforward, but Macedonia was a mess. It had thousands of Bulgarians, Serbians, Albanians, and Greeks. Oh, and then there were also some Slavs who called themselves Macedonians and argued that they were neither Serbian nor Bulgarian and that they are the rightful owners of Macedonia. The powerful Bulgarians and Serbians ignored these Macedonians. And Greece was happy to ignore them too.

The tug-of-war over Macedonia

For Bulgarians, a better name for Macedonia is *Western Bulgaria* or *Vtora Buganjo* (Second Bulgaria). The 1911 *Encyclopædia Britannica* (written on the eve of the First Balkan War that would kick the Turks out) summarized the ethnic composition of geographic Macedonia and seemed to agree with Bulgaria. It's funny how politically incorrect encyclopedias were back then: "The typical Greek, with his superior education, his love of politics and commerce, and his distaste for laborious occupations, has always been a dweller in cities. . . . In southern Macedonia the Hellenic element is strong; in the northern towns it is insignificant. . . . Almost all independent authorities, however, agree that the bulk of the Slavonic population of Macedonia is Bulgarian. The principal indication is furnished by the language, which, though resembling Serbian in some respects (e.g. the case-endings, which are occasionally retained), presents most of the characteristic features of Bulgarian."[3]

After the First Balkan War, the tug-of-war over Macedonia began. Bulgaria was angry that Serbia didn't honor its prewar promise, so they (and others) clashed in the Second Balkan War. Serbia won and kept Macedonia as its prize. A year later, WWI started and Yugoslavia came out of it with Macedonia falling into "southern Serbia." In the 1920s, Serbians closed Bulgarian and Greek schools, ejected non-Serbian priests and teachers, and demanded that locals transform their last names into something that sounded Serbian. In WWII, Macedonians were initially happy that Bulgarian troops liberated them, but then joined the Yugoslavs to oust the Bulgarians, especially after Tito promised them a republic and a unique identity. After WWII, last names changed again to adopt a Macedonian '-ski' ending to help the narcissists celebrate minor differences.

Macedonia may remind you of Bosnia. As we saw in the Bosnian War, Serbs and Croatians both believed that Bosnia was "theirs," and that the leaders from Serbia and Croatia (Milošević and Tuđman) secretly agreed to split between themselves. Yet Bosnia had a third group, the Bosniaks, who felt that they were the most native of all and that they truly defined Bosnia. Macedonia has a similar story. Just replace *Croatia* with *Bulgaria and Greece*, so that you have three "outsiders" claiming Macedonia (Bulgaria, Greece, and Serbia); meanwhile, you have the humble "locals" (the Macedonians) who feel like telling all the bigger boys, "Hey ya bullies, this place ain't yours. It's mine!"

Macedonian language

To answer the Macedonian Question, we must consider the Slavic Macedonian language. Macedonian is a perfect example of how languages don't sharply start and stop at a border, but rather transition along a smooth continuum. For example, most Serbians speak a language that has seven cases, whereas Macedonians and Bulgarians don't use cases at all. What's fascinating is that southern Serbians, who share a border with the Macedonians and Bulgarians, use only two cases. Thus, the Bulgarian decision to abandon cases spilled over into Macedonia and has influenced southern Serbia's dialect. As a result, when I asked Serbians in Belgrade or Novi Sad if they could understand Macedonians, they said it was hard. Serbians in south Serbia, however, said they could understand Macedonians and Bulgarians fairly well. Finally, Macedonians and Bulgarians (especially western Bulgarians) told me they could understand each other perfectly.

Indeed, Macedonian and Bulgarian (especially Bulgaria's western dialect) are extremely similar. They are the only Slavic languages that lack cases, that use definite articles, and that have an unusually high number of verb tenses. They both use a suffixed definite article; for example, *knigata* (the book), *knigava* (the book near me), and *knigana* (the book over there). In addition, their verbs also share witnessed and nonwitnessed forms. Given all these similarities and mutual intelligibility, wouldn't it be more logical to say that Macedonian is simply a Bulgarian dialect? Of course it would, but then Macedonian patriots would find it harder to justify their independent state. The logic being: if you speak Bulgarian, then you are Bulgarian, and if you are Bulgarian, then why doesn't your territory just join Bulgaria?

Therefore, ever since 1946, Macedonian intellectuals have raced to differentiate official Macedonian as much as possible from Bulgarian (and Balkanian too). The more unique their language, the more they can claim that they need their own state. It's similar to the games Balkanians play with their various dialects (Bosnian, Croatian, Montenegrin, and Serbian). When Yugoslavia broke up, Croatians quickly printed the *Dictionary of Differences* to help make a big deal over trivial divergences.

Bulgarians played them same game in 1879 when Bulgaria had to pick its official language. Among its many dialects, it based its official language on an eastern dialect because it was most differentiated from Balkanian. That dialect also had the least in common with Macedonian. Meanwhile, when Macedonia picked its official language in 1945, they based it on a western dialect because it was the most differentiated from Balkanian and Bulgarian. As a result, official Bulgarian and Macedonian are as different as they can be from each other, which is still not that much. Meanwhile, eastern Macedonians and western Bulgarians can understand each other as easily as a New Yorker can understand a Texan.

If you visit Macedonia, it's worth learning a few phrases because you'll be able to use them in Bulgaria and even south Serbia. Memorize *zdravo* (hello), *blagodaram* (thank you), *molam* (please/you're welcome), *do viduvanje* (goodbye), *kolku čini toa?* (how much is that?), *da* (yes), *ne* (no), *kade je. . . ?* (where is. . .?), and *jas ne sum nacionalist!* (I am not a nationalist!)

Who are the biggest nationalists in the Western Balkans?

In 2010, the Balkan Monitor asked, "How strongly do you identify with your nationality?" The results showed that Croatians had the weakest identification with their nationality; meanwhile, Kosovars and Macedonians were on the other extreme. Macedonians have been pushed that way. Imagine that for decades your annoying neighbors say, "You're Bulgarian!" "No! You're Serbian!" "Not exactly! Lots of you are Albanian!" "Shut up! You're all wrong! You're really Greek!!!"

At some point, you'll say what a guy named Goran told me at a coffee shop in Strumica. He said sternly, "Listen, I'm *Macedonian.* My father was Macedonian. I was born in Macedonia. I speak Macedonian. *I am Macedonian.*"

> *I am dying from the treatment of too many physicians.*
> *— Alexander the Great*

I said to Goran, "I understand, but it seems that in the last 100 years all your neighbors believe they deserve a piece of Macedonia for themselves: Albanians want the west, Serbs want the north, Bulgarians want the east, and Greeks want the south."

He put out his cigarette and said, "Listen, they're all wrong. It's not that other countries should get a piece of Macedonia. The truth is that Macedonia *should get a piece of other countries.*"

"Huh? What do you mean?"

"There are still Macedonians in Bulgaria and Greece. Each government denies it, but thousands live there, and we make up the majority in many regions. So the right thing is not to make Macedonia *smaller*, but to make it *bigger!* About half of our country is still in Greece and about 10 percent is in Bulgaria. Our country should be almost three times bigger than it is!"

Just when I thought I understood everything, folks in the Balkans confuse me again. Indeed, after talking with dozens of Macedonians, I finally found one who seems to believe in the United Macedonia dream, which is yet another player in the thrilling Balkan Irredentist Game.

Beyond Skopje

Skopje may have a quarter of Macedonia's population, but it's takes up just a fraction of the country's territory, so there's a lot more to see. Audrey invited me to join her 190 high-school students on a field trip to eastern Macedonia. We packed in four buses and did a trip through Veles, Štip, and Krupište. Most of Macedonia is on a rugged plateau that is roughly 750 meters (2,500 ft) in altitude. Mountains that reach up to 2,764 meters (9,396 ft) completely surround the country. Everywhere you look you'll see farmland with rivers that stream down into this large basin. We visited a few precious Byzantine churches and a waterfall. The highlight was tossing an American football with Audrey in a small town square. Macedonian girls marveled at seeing Audrey throw a perfect spiral. When we left, a group of boys followed me all the way to the bus. They couldn't believe a Californian was visiting their small town. I had to show them my California drivers license to prove it. Visit Macedonia while it's still hidden.

After the fun day-trip, I said goodbye to Audrey, the teachers, and the students. I grabbed a bus to Macedonia's southwest, where I visited Lake Ohrid, the deepest lake in the Balkans (294 m / 964 ft). It's also one of the prettiest. UNESCO has it on its World Heritage List because it's one of the world's oldest lakes and has unique fauna. The lake's European eel, for example, acts like salmon in reverse. After spending 10 years making a living in the lake's depths, it swims downstream to the middle of the Atlantic Ocean, where it reproduces and dies. Its offspring swim all the way back to Lake Ohrid to repeat the cycle.

When I visited Lake Ohrid, the graceful monastery of Saint Panteleimon had just been renovated. Nearby is the thirteenth-century

Sveti Jovan (Saint John) church at Kaneo. It's perched on the lake's edge, which makes it impossible to take a bad photograph. The old town of Ohrid is small, but splendid with its narrow, steep cobblestoned streets, and historic buildings. I rented a bike and almost got to the top of Galicica National Park, which overlooks the lake. I rode down to the lakeshore on an exhilarating dirt path. Along the way, I nearly destroyed the bike and my face.

The next day, I went to southern Macedonia to visit Bitola, which has the ancient Heraclea Lyncestis ruins. It's what's left of a city that Philip II, Alexander the Great's father, founded in the fourth century BC. The outdoor ruins include magnificent ancient mosaics, baths, basilicas, and a theater. It's the best preserved ancient Macedonian site in Macedonia. Having hung out with the ancients, it was now time to hang out with young people again.

Hanging out with teenagers in Kruševo

Audrey had referred me to Zlatka, a 16-year-old girl living in the hilly Macedonian town of Kruševo. Audrey said that Zlatka's family loves receiving visitors. They warmly invited me to stay with them a couple of days. To get to Kruševo, I first went to Prilep, a simple, functional town that has the inspiring Babuna peak as a backdrop. Zlatka met me with her friend, Kate. Zlatka had dark hair and eyes and was a bit chubby. Kate was a future supermodel. They both spoke English well, although Kate was painfully shy. We took the bus to Zlatka's home, where I met her friendly parents who unfortunately could not speak English. They served us *tavče gravče* (beans in a skillet), which is their tasty national dish and it's made with beans, onion, and dry red pepper. Radmila Petkovska, a Macedonian who immigrated to America 40 years ago but visits her homeland often, told me, "Macedonians complain that they are poor, but you will never know it because when you visit Macedonian house there is plenty to eat and drink."

Radmila's American husband, Michael Edwards, said, "Macedonian family ties are very strong and the elderly most often live with their children. My wife does not understand why there are so many nursing homes in America and why the young leave home so early. One of her cousins once told me that America is not such a good place because I have to drive 17 hours to see my son. He cannot imagine not seeing his children every day."

Family is obviously important in Kruševo, where horses and livestock are often walking down its cobblestoned streets. Most Macedonians still live in towns and villages, which encourage family bonding. Still, that doesn't mean that there aren't generational differences. For example, while we ate the savory *tavče gravče*, Zlatka said, "I'm a very picky girl."

"Yeah? Why?" I asked.

"Because I must take a shower every day."

I wondered if I misunderstood, so I said, "But that doesn't sound so unreasonable. Many people shower once per day."

"Not in the older generation," she said. "My parents and especially my grandparents will usually just shower once a week. Sunday is when you're supposed to clean everything: your body and your clothes. I hate that tradition. I must have my daily shower."

Feeling the Albanians

The next day, I went on a field trip with Zlatka's school and I learned about how young people feel about Albanians. When you're engrossed in the Bulgarian-Greek-Macedonian-Serb melodrama, it's easy to forget that 25 percent of Macedonia is Albanian. I assumed that most Macedonians, like most Balkanians, thought Albanians were poor and desperate. However, these teenagers argued the opposite. While eight of us were relaxing outside, one girl said, "They have nine children because they're rich." A guy added, "They have the best jobs in Macedonia and they favor other Albanians. They are buying all our land with all their money. They want to take part of Macedonia from us. And they all wear white hats."

I asked them, "Have any of you ever been to Albania?"

They looked down to the ground, indicating no. I told them, "I've been there recently. Trust me, Macedonians are richer than Albanians. You guys all need to go to Albania and learn a bit about their culture and country."

Like a chorus, they replied, "Oh no! But Albanians *hate* Macedonians! They would *kill* me there! I *never* ever want to go to Albania! I have absolutely *no interest*!"

In Macedonia's northwest, centered around Tetovo, is a huge Albanian enclave. Macedonians like to repeat the familiar Slavic fable that Albanians showed up yesterday and started reproducing like bacteria. However, various ethnographic maps and surveys indicate that they've been there for centuries. One thing we've learned from Eastern Europe's ethnic disputes is that despite the constant wars, it's surprisingly difficult to make one ethnic group displace another. Eastern Europeans are stubborn: if they grew up there, they want to stay there, no matter what. The only way to get them to disappear is to be ruthlessly efficient and evil. The best examples were when the Germans liquidated the Jews and when Eastern Europeans, in revenge, cleansed the Germans; and earlier, when the Turks forced the Slavs north and, centuries later, the Slavs forced the Turks back out. Otherwise, people stick around, even under crappy, discriminatory conditions.

In 1995, Albanians around Tetovo felt they were being discriminated because Macedonia didn't let them have an Albanian-speaking university. The constitution stated that Macedonian is the official language and that using tax dollars to create such a university is illegal. As a result, Albanians created the National Liberation Army, which started terrorizing Macedonians with random violence. An Albanian tried to assassinate Macedonia's President, but only managed to rip out the President's eye. In February 2001, a regional war erupted. A few months later, the Macedonian agreed to recognize the Albanian language and made other concessions. It was the only violence that Macedonia experienced since WWII. It was the only Yugoslav republic that peacefully seceded.

After a couple of wonderful days with Zlatka and her family, we gave each other warm goodbyes. Zlatka took me to the bus stop. While we were waiting, I saw a handsome young man with sandy blond hair and hypnotic blue eyes. Zlatka had told me she dreamed of finding her perfect husband. I thought I had found a good candidate, so I said, "There you go, Zlatka, there's the man of your dreams."

She choked. "He's Albanian," she said.

I was stunned. "How do you know?"

"He's done some work for my family. He's a carpenter."

"So if you didn't know that," I asked, "Would you have been able to tell that he was Albanian just by looking at him?"

"Oh yes, of course!"

"How?"

She looked at me intensely, "You can just *feel* them."

Really? I had to try. I closed my eyes. Relaxed my mind. Listened to my feelings. All I could feel was Zlatka's stubborn and senseless hate. Once again, the Balkan paradoxes sent my head spinning. How could such lovely, friendly, and intelligent teenagers hate so blindly and absolutely?

Audrey later told me that kids throughout the Balkans are taught to hate certain people from an early age. For example, Albanians are taught to blindly hate the Serbs and vice versa. Kids learn to hate from their parents and grandparents. They pass down the prejudices just like white Americans a hundred years ago taught their kids that blacks are scum. Tragically, the Balkans struggles to shake its vicious cycle of hate. They don't seem to understand that their collective future depends on each individual's ability to forgive and move on.

Remember upon the conduct of each depends the fate of all.
— Alexander the Great

Growing pains

While exploring a medieval fort next to Lake Ohrid, I met a wise, yet young Macedonian archeologist who had lived in England for a couple of years. He took a break from excavating history to chat. I asked him how life was in Macedonia compared to England. He said, "Since I've been back, I feel the ethnic tension. People are complaining about the Albanians."

I asked, "What do you think the Macedonian government should do about it?"

He said, "One politician offered a sensible solution of giving Albania areas of Macedonia that are over 80 percent Albanian, like Tetovo and Gostivar. In exchange, Albania would give us some of their land around Lake Ohrid that used to be part of Macedonia."

"That sounds like a pretty good deal, especially for Macedonia. So is it going to happen?"

He chuckled, "That politician's career is now over."

People in the Balkans are so entrenched in their views, their tolerance for difference is so low, their nationalism (and ethnic pride) is so high, their view of history so skewed, and their ability to forgive so pitiful that it's clear why they're always fighting each other. What's the solution? The archeologist told me, "What we need are jobs and a good economy. A third of us are unemployed and in poverty. When people are working and making money, they don't have time to think about the past. We'll start looking forward instead of backward."

Macedonia is trying. They have a 10-percent flat tax and they're taking full-page ads in magazines encouraging businesses to invest in Macedonia. Macedonia was in 38th place in the World Bank's Ease of Doing Business Survey—a vast improvement over a couple of years ago. Macedonia has also significantly decreased its public sector corruption, according to Transparency.org. On overall corruption, Macedonia scored a 4.1 out of 10, which ties it with Croatia and is much better than Greece (3.5). Nearly all Eastern Europeans countries are below five, while everyone in the West is above five.

Tragicomic border crossing story

Despite the improvements on corruption, habits don't change overnight. While my Serbian friend, Nenad Stojanović, was couchsurfing with me in Croatia, he told me a tragicomic story about when he was going from Albania to Macedonia in 2009. He said, "Two days before crossing the border, I put a €100 [$140] bill in my passport. I wasn't thinking about it when I did it. I just put it there to put it somewhere. I had forgotten about it by the time I got to the border checkpoint. While they were carefully inspecting my car, which normally takes 10 minutes, I gave the authorities my passport."

"Oh, no," I said. "What happened?"

He laughed. "Within seconds, the guard came back, gave my passport back to me, and told the other guards to '*immediately*' stop inspecting. And then he told me to 'Go! Go! Go!'" Nenad waved his arms as if he were encouraging a race-car driver in a pit-stop to take off.

"And so then what happened?" I asked.

"I drove away without understanding why the guard had changed his attitude so quickly. Then after a few minutes, I said, 'Oh shit!' I opened my passport and the €100 bill was gone. So I drove back to the border checkpoint. When I asked for my €100 back, the guards said, '€100? What €100?'"

Macedonia's future

I accuse the Balkans of being trapped in their history, but the West is also trapped in our perception of the Balkans. The few who know anything about the region pigeonhole it as a complicated place, full of problems with few solutions. In short, the Balkans is nowadays a metaphor for conflict and division. There's the Balkanization of the Internet, America, China, and toothpaste brands.

I confess that I'm somewhat guilty of spreading this stereotype. At the same time, there is a lot of truth to that stereotype. In fact, Balkanians are the first to admit that their land is incomprehensible—they don't fully understand it. They're the ones who told me that things are illogical and chaotic. Nevertheless, they also showed me their hospitality, their contagious joy, their delicious food, and their carefree we'll-do-it-tomorrow attitude.

When I first visited the Balkans in 2004, I wrote a gloomy prediction on my blog. Although I was positive about Balkan countries on the Adriatic Sea, I was pessimistic about the rest. I wrote, "Macedonia is waiting for its enemies to pick it apart. Albania will improve, but their poor reputation will hamper their growth for decades. Bosnia and Herzegovina has few resources to amount to anything. Serbia has a decent foundation thanks to the years of being the center of Yugoslavia, but a decade of civil wars has taken its toll and the country will struggle for a while. Kosovo is an economic deck of cards that will collapse as soon as NATO pulls out."

Now, as I write this in the Balkans in 2011, I'm more optimistic. After getting slammed with the Great Recession, the Balkans is moving forward. Governments now sometimes seem to have a competition with who can offer superior minority rights. Serbia, for example, has some of the most progressive ethnic protection laws in Eastern Europe.

Although attitudes are slower to change than the laws, they are catching up. The aging population helps too. Old people are less enthusiastic about picking up a gun just because people in the next village have a funny accent.

Chatting with the US Ambassador to Macedonia

When I was in Skopje, Audrey invited me to come to an event at the house of the US Ambassador to Macedonia, Larry Butler. Ambassador Butler's previous roles in the US Foreign Service included being the Director for European Affairs for the National Security Council, working on the Dayton Accords, and opening an office in Kosovo to report and mediate human rights complaints. He was also involved with Bulgaria. When he's not being a referee in the Balkans, he's an ice hockey referee. The event, which was held at his spacious house, was to promote Macedonian folk art. I was surprised by the lax security. They didn't check my bag for the grenades and Uzi I was carrying. They didn't ask for my passport or notice the bazooka on my back.

They served mouth-watering Macedonian appetizers. Macedonian love to *skara* (barbecue) meat, pork, and chicken during their cold winters . . . and the rest of the year too. I devoured enough food to equal my tax bill. Although Ambassador Butler was understandably busy, it didn't stop me from cornering him. (OK, so I had to knock down a few of his aides to get him, but it was worth it.) When I told him about the book I was writing, he looked at me with his crystal blue eyes and said, "You're right, there's a lot we can learn from Eastern Europeans."

"Like what?" I asked him.

"First, there's the importance of family. Macedonians, for example, always come back to their family. They don't understand when Americans go to college thousands of miles away and then don't return to their homes after they graduate."

"What else?"

"Macedonians are no more than one generation away from the farm. They all have relatives that are in rural areas that they visit during the holidays, for instance. This keeps their connection with the land and food. It's something we don't generally have in America."

"Are there any downsides to these values?"

"Sure. For example, the labor markets here aren't very liquid, because people are unwilling to move far from their family. This prolongs economic downturns. Also, I remember hearing about these two farmers who were unwilling to talk to each other because their *great-grandfathers* had an argument."

"Wow."

"Yeah. Nevertheless, Macedonians and Eastern Europeans can teach us many lessons."

What Macedonia Can Teach Us

- **Stay in touch with farmers.** As US Ambassador Butler said, Americans can be disconnected from their sources of food. Although we can't decide to have relatives in the farmland, we ought to spend more time visiting farms and learning how food is grown.
- **Obtain independence without bloodshed.** Like Estonia and Slovakia, Macedonia was able to get its independence in 1991 without a physical fight. What makes Macedonia's feat remarkable is that all the other ex-Yugoslavs chose the war path. When your political leaders want to solve a problem with bloodshed, make sure they thoroughly explore non-violent solutions.

Places I saw and recommend in Macedonia: Skopje and Lake Ohrid.

Travel deals and info: http://ftapon.com/macedonia

As we close this chapter on Macedonia, we're also closing the chapter on the seven ex-Yugoslav countries. Given all their paradoxes, passions, and history, it's stunning that Tito managed to keep them together for so long. At the same time, you can see the common South Slavic thread that runs through them. Like any dysfunctional family (and all families are dysfunctional), the ex-Yugoslavs will always be connected, no matter what. Without a doubt, the ex-Yugoslav countries are Eastern Europe's most fascinating and captivating collection of nations.

Now we're leaving Macedonia and going to . . . Macedonia. Yeah, Greece's Macedonia.

19

GREECE—DEFENDER OF ALL THINGS WESTERN IN EASTERN EUROPE

WHENEVER YOU THINK OF the founder of western civilization, you probably think of Greece. The Greeks gave us Homer's epic poems, the Corinthian columns that are everywhere, and an early version of democracy. Just the names of Greek places conjure up wondrous images: Athens, Thebes, Sparta, Crete, Rhodes, Mount Olympus, and the Aegean Sea. Western companies use the names of Greek gods and heroes: Zeus, Athena, Poseidon, Hermes, Apollo, Perseus, Hercules, and of course, Nike. Western literature and ideas were born out of text written in Greek such as *The Iliad, The Odyssey, Oedipus, Medea,* and the Bible's New Testament. Western heroes include Greeks like Plato, Socrates, Aristotle, Thucydides, Herodotus, Euripides, Archimedes, and countless others. Greeks built our foundation in mathematics, medicine, science, and philosophy. The astronomer Carl Sagan observed that if the repressive Middle Ages had not come and Europe had stayed on the technological path that the Greeks had started us on, then we would have colonized the Solar System by now.

Given that everyone associates Greece with western culture and civilization, it's ironic that Greece is in Eastern Europe. Americans don't like looking at maps, so it's easy to forget that Greece's northern borders touch the Eastern European countries of Albania, Macedonia, and Bulgaria. In fact, Greece is so far east in Europe that you only have to drive two hours east from the Greek border and you'll have left the European continent and entered Asia! Istanbul, the gateway to Asia, is short drive away. Hence, geographically, it's obvious that Greece is in Eastern Europe. Just don't tell the Greeks that, it will piss them off.

Greece symbolizing the west in the east

Why does it sound so strange to say that Greece is in Eastern Europe, even though it's obvious from a map that it's located there? It's because Greece has great marketing. Greece has been associated with the West for a long time. It started when the West tried desperately to associate itself with Greece. That's because over 2,000 years ago Greeks were light years ahead of the barbarians in Western Europe. The Roman Empire started the tradition of acknowledging the immense Greek contribution to civilization. Back then, Europeans were more likely to view Europe on a north-south continuum rather than an east-west one; the south had the civilized, technological advanced societies, whereas the north had the losers.

That way of looking at Europe shifted when the Roman Empire split in two. Greece suddenly was no longer associated with the West or the South—it became part of the Eastern Roman Empire, often called the Byzantine Empire. Later, when the Turkish Empire ruled Greece for over 400 years, Greece became even more Eastern. Fast forward to the 1800s, Greece finally rid itself of the Turks. By then, however, they had spent the last 1,500 years being associated with Eastern Europe. If you had asked a European 100 years ago if Greece was in Western Europe, he'd have laughed and said, "Dude, have you looked at a map? Those guys are practically in Turkey!"

After WWII, the West wanted Greece to rejoin the Western European club. As the Iron Curtain fell across Europe, Greece nearly fell in the Eastern Bloc. They had plenty of Greek communists begging Stalin to help make Greece communist. However, the Western Allies lobbied hard to keep Greece in their domain because Greece is strategically located on the Adriatic and has utopian beaches. Stalin relented and told the communist Greeks to back down on their revolutionary dreams. Greece joined the EU, NATO, and the eurozone. Because these organizations are linked with Western Europe, Greece re-associated itself with Western Europe after a 1,500-year break. Today, connotation distorts geography. Quick: what's more eastern, Bosnia or Greece? Most would instinctively say Bosnia, but that's wrong because all of Greece is east of Bosnia.

In conclusion, Greece is like Finland: a country that geographically is in Eastern Europe, but culturally is not. Therefore, this chapter will only focus on the part of Greece that is directly linked with the rest of Eastern Europe—Greece's Macedonia.

Meeting three Kiwis

In March 2009, while I was visiting Butrint and Sarandë in Albania, it was easy to see Greece's westernmost point: the island of Corfu. If you're strong enough, you can swim to Corfu from Albania—it's just three kilometers (two miles) away. Instead, I preferred staying dry and dealing with a troublesome Greek immigration officer who seemed to want a bribe. The ship left without me while we were haggling, but eventually turned back to pick me up.

On the ferry, I met a New Zealand couple, Olaf and Judy, and their five-year-old child, Oscar. These three Kiwis had been exploring the world for a couple of years in search for the perfect place to settle down. They wanted great weather, nice people, healthy food, an affordable cost of living, and a view of the water. That wish-list explains why they've been traveling so long—that's a hard combination to find. Nevertheless, they thought they had found it on Malta's Gozo Island in the Mediterranean Sea. Unfortunately, after living there for one year, they left because the winters were surprisingly windy and cold, plus the Maltese air exacerbated Judy's allergies.

After traveling around, they settled in Sarandë, Albania. It also seemed to match their wish-list. Their apartment had a breathtaking view of Corfu and the Ionian Sea, and everything else seemed perfect too. Nevertheless, after six months, they began to have doubts. Although Albanians were the cheerful, helpful, and friendly people that Olaf and Judy desired, they were almost too friendly—to the point of being nosy and smothering. Moreover, they questioned whether the Albanian school system would be good enough for Oscar. They concluded that while Albania is a promising country, they felt they were being a bit too pioneering. When I met them, they were thinking about moving to Corfu. Although it's just three kilometers away from Albania, it's a world of a difference.

They invited me to squeeze into their small car to hitch a ride to Corfu's north coast. I happily accepted. I wasn't sure how I would fit in the car given that Olaf seemed bigger than the car. Although Olaf grew up in New Zealand, he was born in Netherlands of Dutch parents. Like most Dutch people, he is a giant. Meanwhile, Judy is bubbly and enthusiastic with short blond hair and big blue eyes. They're a delightful couple: Judy is bouncing with energy, while Olaf is supremely calm and cool. Both have a wonderful sense of humor. They're also both professional photographers, specializing in portraits and wedding events. I wedged into the backseat with my backpack on my lap and Oscar in his child-seat on my right. We set off to explore Corfu.

Touring Corfu

Corfu is an odd place. It feels neither Greek nor Albanian. Instead, it's a mix of both, plus a dose of the Venetian Empire that ruled the island for four centuries, and the British Empire that controlled it during the 1800s. The British influence may explain why most of the locals speak English well. We went by the Palaio Frourio, a Venetian citadel, and then journeyed to the north coast. Corfu is covered with olive plantations. When they're not growing olives, they're growing grapes. The island is covered with soft hills, although its tallest peak, Mount Pantokrator, reaches 906 meters (2,972 ft). After exploring a few scenic promontories, we went to the small town where they had a hotel reservation by the beach. It started to rain. To save money, I preferred camping. I lucked out because next to the hotel was a house that was under construction. Therefore, I had a perfect shelter during the stormy night.

The next day it was still drizzling, so instead of leaving early and hitchhiking around the island, I hung out with the Kiwis, who had a relaxed pace. In the late morning, we hit the road again and slowly drove down Corfu's west coast. Corfu has 217 kilometers (135 miles) of pleasing coastline. We stopped often during the drizzly weather. As photographers, Olaf and Judy couldn't resist capturing the many sights. They were also curious about the housing market, since they were seriously considering moving there. At the end of the day, we went to their next hotel reservation, which was set in an oak tree forest. They generously invited me to shower in the hotel's bathroom. To avoid the rain, I luckily found another protective shelter.

On my final day with the Kiwis, we glimpsed the most rugged and spectacular part of Corfu: its southwest coastline. Using the steep topography to their advantage, the Venetians successfully thwarted multiple Turkish attacks between the 1537 and 1716, thereby becoming European heroes. We drove as far as the poor car could go and then they dropped me off at the island's southern port. We hugged each other and I boarded the ferry to mainland Greece.

Ultimately, Olaf and Judy didn't settle in Corfu. Nevertheless, they did settle on a Greek island: Santorini. A couple of years later, during their tour of the Balkans, they stayed with me at the Croatian sea house where I wrote most of this book. Today, they still do photography in Santorini, but they admit that their wanderlust may infect them again.

A bus driver's thoughts on Albanians

My ferry arrived in Igoumenitsa, a ho-hum port town, where I took a bus to Metéora. After we passed by Ioánina, I asked the middle-aged bus driver about Albania. He said, "Albania? *Hrumph!* Albania. I go one week vacation Albania. Bad food, bad hotel, bad place. Five days later, come back. Albania?! Crazy!"

As if on queue, when we were driving in the middle of nowhere over the Pindus Mountain range, two young guys were waiting by the side of road. The bus driver pointed to them as the bus stopped and said, "Albanians." The two skinny young men entered the bus and after they sat down, the driver said to me as he hunched over in a sneaky pose, "They come at night. Secretly cross border."

An hour later, some more young men climbed on board. Once again, the driver looked at me and said, "Albanians." He pinched his nose and then opened his window to let in cold fresh air. The men did smell bad. It was a combination of sweat and cigarettes. The bus driver shook his head and mumbled, "Albanians."

This bus driver has company: many Greeks dislike Albanians. Half the foreigners in Greece are Albanians. Like Mexicans in the US, Albanians do most of the dirty work. Greeks believe Albanians are responsible for much of Greece's crime. Yet crime statistics indicate that the average Albanian immigrant is not any more criminal than the average native Greek.

Xenophobia is more than just a Greek word

On the long bus ride, I met Vela, a calm, sweet Greek pediatrician. I asked her how Greeks feel about Albanians. She answered, "It's getting better. A few years ago, Greeks had a hard time accepting Albanians. But now many Albanians are well integrated: they speak Greek, and so Greeks have learned to live with them. I used to have prejudices about the Albanians too. Yet when I started helping them in a hospital, I learned that if I'm nice to them and they see that I care, they are good to me too."

I was curious about all Greece's neighbors, so I asked, "What about Macedonia?"

Her eyelashes fluttered while she said, "What do you mean, *Macedonia?"*

"I mean the country," I said casually, knowing that it's a sore subject, but pretending to be ignorant.

She took a deep breath and said, "Most Greeks have a problem with this country. We call it *Skopje."* I had hoped that she would make a point that I had not thought about or heard about. However, after talking for 20 minutes about it, she recited the same arguments that we discussed at length in the previous chapter. Therefore, let's move onto the next country. "How about Bulgaria?" I asked.

She sighed, "We have some problems with them too. It's about history. We've fought many times over the land. It's complicated."

"OK, how about the last one: Turkey."

"This is embarrassing," she said. "We don't like them either. They occupied us for centuries. They did many bad things. We still fight with them over Cyprus. It is bad."

"So basically, out of your four neighboring countries, you don't like any of them. Why is that?"

She looked out the window and thought. Finally, she said, "Maybe we have a bit of . . . do you have this word: xenophobia?"

"Yes, we do. You mean the fear of foreigners and foreign things."

"Yes, that's right," she said softly. "It's a Greek word. *Xenos* means *foreigner* and *phobos* means *fear*. Greeks are afraid of losing our identity, our culture, and our way of life. It's happened to us in the past. So we're suspicious of the countries next to us."

Unfortunately, xenophobia is common throughout Eastern Europe. Whether it's a Croatian who hates the Orthodox or Islamic faiths, or Serb hooligans who beat up gays, or Latvians intellectuals who invent a word for *marketing* out of fear that English will overtake their language—in every case, they're striving to protect their imagined ethnic or national purity. Even Americans, who tend to accept foreigners more easily than Europeans, sometimes suffer from xenophobia, especially regarding the "Mexican invasion."

Ivaylo Ditchev observed, "The Greek national revival set another trend that would be followed throughout the Balkans, which was the invention, in the nineteenth century, of an artificial language, purified of foreign imports and rather difficult to understand by the common man, that was supposed to prove the direct link between the prestigious antiquity and the poor modern Balkan nation."[1] By 1976, however, Greeks rejected the pure *katharevousa* Greek language in favor of the *demotiki* (popular) version. I asked Vela, "So is there anyone nearby that Greece likes?"

"Serbia," she said. "Greece is part of NATO, but we didn't bomb Serbia. Instead, we had concerts to raise money for them. We like them because they are Orthodox like us, and we have a history of cooperation. Sorry, but this is my stop."

Vela got off the bus at the town of Malakásion. That's a funny name for the Greeks because if there's one word that they seem to use in every sentence, it's *malakas.* Although *malakas* basically means *a jerk,* it's become an all-purpose word that Greeks use for nearly anything: *malakas* this, *malakas* that.

Europe's most amazing monasteries

If you were looking for evidence that Hades, the Greek god of the underworld, was trying to claw his way to our plane of existence, it's in Metéora. It seems as if his stony fingers are piercing through the earth's flesh and reaching toward Zeus in defiance. In Greek, *Metéora* means *suspended rocks.* About 60 million years ago (five million years after the dinosaurs went bye-bye), Metéora's sandstone pinnacles formed. Weather carved them into their shape today. They may remind you of Monument Valley in Utah. What makes Metéora truly special is that hundreds of years ago Greeks built celestial monasteries on top of these rocks. When you see them, you'll ask yourself, "How the hell did they build that there?"

Nearly 1,000 years ago, hermit monks who were seeking a perfect place to have an extended timeout moved into the natural cracks and caves of Metéora. Over the next several centuries, they built over 20 monasteries. Today, only six remain. Until the 1920s, the only way to visit them was to go up sketchy rope ladders or be hauled up in a net by a dodgy rope and pulley system.

Visiting them nowadays is much safer, but it can still be a minor workout. Instead of taking a taxi, I walked from the nearest town (Kalambaka) with my backpack and I visited five of the monasteries via little used paths. To enter many of the UNESCO-protected monasteries, you'll sometimes need to climb steep, narrow, and slippery sandstone steps. About 10 monks live in each monastery; one of them is for nuns. Given the surreal place, you'd think Hollywood would have filmed many movies here. However, the only major film to feature it is the 1981 James Bond movie *For Your Eyes Only*, which highlights the Monastery of the Holy Trinity. Regardless, Metéora is heavenly.

Me, help a stranger? You kidding?

Monasteries may teach people to be a good Samaritan, but the Greeks aren't listening. When Gallup asked Greeks if they had, during the past month, volunteered any time to an organization, only three percent said *yes*, ranking them last on Earth. In fact, Hungary, Romania, and all Southeastern European countries had volunteer rates of eight percent or less (except Kosovo, which had 16 percent).

Eastern Europeans have largely lost whatever sense of brotherhood that communism may have instilled in them. Gallup's Civic Engagement Index is based on polls about donating money, helping a stranger, and volunteering. The US topped the index with a score of 60.3. Among Eastern Europeans, only Finland, Kosovo, Poland, and Slovenia had scores of 30 or more. All Western Europeans had scores above 30 (except Italy and Portugal). Seven out of of the 11 lowest scoring countries in the world are from the Balkans, with Greece being third from the world's bottom (Burundi and Madagascar were the worst).

Balkan people might try to excuse their unwillingness to aid a stranger by saying, "We'd love to volunteer and help a stranger, but we're just too busy trying to survive! Only rich people have the time to volunteer." However, the top four countries in terms of volunteerism, in order of participation: Turkmenistan, Liberia, Sri Lanka, Cuba, and Tajikistan. That's not exactly a list of rich countries.

Stefan, a frustrated Greek

Had I known about these surveys, I would have never tried to hitchhike out of Metéora, because hitchhiking depends on the kindness of strangers. Being blissfully ignorant, I stuck out my thumb when the first lonely car approached. A Greek guy named Stefan picked me up. One data point doesn't disprove a mountain of survey data, but it reminds us the dangers of generalizing categorically.

On the way to Trikola, Stefan told me his life story. He was 32 and had been living in Germany for the last seven years. Now, he's returned to Greece, but, given his opinion of Greece, it wasn't clear why. He said, "The jobs in Greece are very bad. I'm a specialist with plumbing and they'll pay me $25 a day. In America, they would pay me $150 per day! $25! It's better to go fishing!"

"At least you have the Greek women . . ." I suggested hopefully.

"Ha! Greek women only care about money, money, money. If you don't drive a nice car or wear a smoking outfit, they're not interested. They're all prostitutes!"

"So what do you love about your country?"

"Nature. It's beautiful. We have some of the most beautiful places in the world. But the Greek government is bad, the Greek people are bad, the Greek economy is bad. Everything else is bad!"

"What about Germany?"

"Germany is good. They are so organized!" he gestured around his lips to pretend he had a little mustache and shouted, "*Heil!* They are all little Hitlers, those Germans. So organized!"

Greece's ego

It's hard to decide if Greece has a big strong ego or a little fragile ego. Many Greeks aren't like Stefan. On the contrary, they are almost comically proud of their country. If an alien interviewed humans from around the world and knew nothing else about the planet, it might conclude that Greece is the most powerful country in the world, after France, *bien sûr*.

This inflated ego comes from the Eastern European habit of reminiscing about the good old days when their country was an empire. Although Western Europeans do a little of this too, it's not nearly as common in Western Europe as it is in Eastern Europe. For example, the British, Spanish, Portuguese, and Dutch all had vast empires, but the locals don't waste much time talking your ear off about it. The Germans are the meekest of all about their past glories because they've been taught since WWII to keep their mouths shut about that kind of stuff. The only Western European country that shares the annoying Eastern European practice of reveling in their glory days is France. The French go one step further: they somehow think that their glory days haven't ended. Oh well, someday they will get the 200-year-old memo.

Meanwhile, Greece's ego is a paradox. From birth, Greeks are reminded that their ancestors founded all things western, that their land is the birthplace of the world's greatest philosophers as well as one of the earliest developed languages. They're right. If you want to show an alien where modern civilization really got going, you'd probably direct his flying saucer to Greece. Thus, you'd think that Greece would have the combined confidence of Achilles, John Wayne, and Yoda.

> *When we did this, you were climbing in the trees.*
> *— Greeks say this to remind everyone that they were the pioneers for everything*

And yet, Greece seems incredibly insecure. A self-confident, cocky country wouldn't even notice that Macedonia became independent, let alone make a fuss about their name. They wouldn't be insecure about the world using the word *Olympics.* They wouldn't try to artificially re-engineer their language to take out foreign words. These aren't actions of a country with a large ego, but a fragile, insecure one. What's going on?

Feeling like the son of Jesus

Imagine if your father were Einstein, Plato, Leonardo da Vinci, or, even worse, Jesus Christ. Everyone would come up to you and say, "Wow, your father was truly amazing. So, um, what have *you* done with your life?"

That's how Greeks must feel at times. You grow up reading nonstop about the extraordinary feats of the ancient Greeks, which makes your spirit soar sky-high, but then you read the morning newspaper and your spirit comes crashing down to Earth. Few countries show such a big difference between the past and present as you see in Greece. When the EU was an exclusively Western European club, Greece was usually at the bottom of the economic ladder. To keep up appearances, Greece spent money as if they had King Midas working in the treasury. According to the authors of *This Time Is Different,* Greece spent about half of the last 200 years in financial default. That ultimately threw the euro into a crisis, casting an embarrassing spotlight on Greece. For Greece to fiscally thrive, they would have to adapt to Spartan ways for several years. But that's the problem: today's Greeks aren't Spartans.

Such a disconnect between the ancient Greeks and the modern Greeks happens to tourists too. For example, Mark Twain "had thought modern Greeks a libel on the ancients." The English poet Byron was shocked when he came to Greece expecting to find the tall, blond, blue-eyed heroes of antiquity and was disappointed to find the opposite. When you visit Greek cities, you expect everything to look like the Parthenon. I imagined the sidewalks would be made of marble, that every building would have Corinthian columns, that Greeks would be dressed in togas, and that they would drive chariots instead of cars.

In short, Greece is a victim of its own brilliant marketing. It's sold us the illusion that it's an ancient country, when in fact for 90 percent of the last 2,000 years, Greece wasn't even on the world map. After the Romans inhaled Greece, it didn't return as an independent country until 1829. You gotta wonder if Greeks and Italians secretly get together for joint pity parties, where they cry on each other's shoulders, asking themselves, "Where did we go wrong?"

Couchsurfing with four Greek girls in Thessaloniki

Most couchsurfing profiles feature either one person or a couple, so when I saw four Thessaloniki girls sharing one profile, I figured there had to be good story there. Their names were Anna, Irini, Maria, and Niki. Not only did they accept me, but Niki Tsonidou asked me to email her my first book. We exchanged amusing and teasing emails. For example, a few days before I arrived, they said, "We forgot to tell you'll be sharing a bed with the German Basketball Team."

After they offered to pick me up at the train station, I wrote, "I will be the guy with a blue jacket, about 175 cm, and with a cute ass. I will have a big black backpack, maybe glasses, maybe, unshaven, and maybe with Brad Pitt. If I don't see you, then I will wait until 18:00. Then I will find your home. If I don't find it, I will cry and camp in the streets. Someone will find me when I'm sleeping, murder me, and you will feel bad for a day or two. But my mom will feel bad for one week."

They wrote back simply, "Hope your ass is really sweet. C U."

Maria and Niki picked me up at the train station. Maria was a 30-year-old brunette with a hoarse smoker's voice and a confident, sexy attitude. Niki was a gorgeous 24-year-old who had reddish long hair and seemed to talk faster than I could think. The three of us immediately got along. While I was going upstairs, Maria said to Niki in a voice that was purposefully loud enough for me to hear, "He does have a nice ass."

When we came to their apartment, I met Irini and Anna, who were both in their late 20s. Irini was a petite, energetic brunette, while Anna was a medium-sized blond accountant. Everyone was super positive and smoked like chimneys. Before taking a shower, they switched on the water heater. They did this smart habit to save money. It would take 20 minutes to get warm and then they would switch it off. We'd save significant amounts of energy if we all followed this practice. Niki had prepared two moussaka casseroles and a large Greek salad. She invited the five of us to sit down for a late lunch.

> *You are about to have your first experience with a Greek lunch. I will kill you if you pretend to like it. — Jacqueline Kennedy Onassis, who married a Greek man after JFK*

According to my tastes, Greece has the most delicious food in Eastern Europe. They energize their meals with fresh ingredients like tomatoes, eggplant, feta cheese, onions, olive oil, yogurt, zucchini, nuts, and honey. During the Byzantine and Turkish period, Greeks incorporated spices like oregano, dill, bay leaves, and mint. Today, popular dishes include *souvlaki* (anything marinated in olive oil, salt, pepper, oregano and then skewered), *dolmathes* (grapevine leaves stuffed with rice, veggies, and sometimes meat), and *tzatziki* (yoghurt with garlic and cucumber). Even their fast food is delicious: *gyros* (meat roasted on a vertically turning spit and served with sauce and garnishes on pita bread) will make you give up hamburgers. Finally, *baklava* (phyllo pastry layers filled with nuts and drenched in syrup or honey) is a decadent dessert to end any meal.

It's all Greek to me

Over dinner, the four Greek girls gave me a crash course on Greek. Niki was particularly instructive because she has a degree in the ancient Greek language. Basic phrases include *yashoo* (hello), *adio* (goodbye), *puinne. . .* (where is. . .), *posho kani?* (how much?), *tikanish?* (how are you?), *treno* (train), *pote* (when), *tikanish?* (how are you?), *poli kalo* (very good), *katalava* (understand), *signomi* (sorry), and, most importantly, *efharishto* (thank you).

About every 10 minutes Niki (whose name means *Victory*) loved to remind me that some English words I said were derived from Greek. She could have interrupted me more often: about 12 percent of the English vocabulary has an ancient Greek origin, including words like *mathematics, astronomy, democracy, philosophy, thespian, athletics, theater,* and *rhetoric*. Still, this doesn't mean Greek is easy for us. Most Greek verbs are irregular. They have four cases. They even have three ways to write their *sigma* character. The first is upper case (Σ), the second is lower case (σ), and the third is used only when the word ends with the sigma character (ς). Σo σentenceς would read juσt like thiς.

There are two other annoying things besides the Greek alphabet. First, while most European countries use a word that sounds like *bus* or *autobus,* the Greeks call that vehicle a *leoforio.* WTF? Second, to say *yes,* you have to say *neh,* which sounds like a negation in most European languages. So when I ask, "So the *leoforio* leaves today?" they'll nod and say, "*Neh!*" Meanwhile, to say *no,* you say *ohhi.* As William Shakespeare said, "For my part, it was Greek to me."

> *There is a misleading, unwritten rule that states if a quote giving advice comes from someone famous, very old, or Greek, then it must be good advice. — Bo Bennett*

After stuffing ourselves with Niki's divine cooking, the five of us talked for hours. Niki would be working most of the night at a bar, so she told me to sleep in her room. When she came home at 4:00 a.m. she would go sleep in Maria's room. The next day she promised to give me a tour of Thessaloniki.

Busted in Thessaloniki

The next morning, I woke up to what sounded like an air raid. Vendors in pickup trucks use megaphones to announce that they have potatoes or other items to sell. If you don't speak Greek, then these megaphone announcements sound like air-raid warnings. It was a relief that big, bad Macedonia wasn't finally launching their planned attack against the poor, defenseless Greece.

In the late morning, Niki woke up and soon got ready. To avoid a 40-minute walk to the center, we took a bus. She assured me that we didn't need to buy a bus ticket because nobody ever checks. Of course, two ticket checkers caught us. Clever Niki pretended to be a tourist from Norway and I was her "husband from America." The ticket checkers made us get off the bus and said, "You can either pay $150 later or pay $50 in cash right now."

Niki said, "We'll pay later."

She gave her address and they left. Then she said, "Don't worry. They will never, ever send us the bill. The Greek government is so disorganized. Even if they send it, you can ignore it and nothing will happen. But God, I can't believe what those guys were saying about us on the bus! After I said that we were foreigners, they started saying the rudest things you can possibly imagine in Greek. It was hard not to react! Be glad you didn't understand."

After that thrilling start, we walked everywhere and avoided buses. Thessaloniki is Greece's second largest city and the capital of Greece's Macedonia. The greater metropolitan area has nearly one million inhabitants. It was founded in 315 BC and was named after Thessalonike, the half-sister of Alexander the Great. By 1519, half the city became Jewish when the Muslim Turks invited Jews who were booted out of Spain to settle there. In 1913, they had about 61,000 Jews, about 40 percent of the population. In 1917, a massive fire destroyed the city and many Jews left. The Nazis took care of the remaining ones in the 1940s. Today, just 1,200 Jews remain, about 0.27 percent of the population.

Thessaloniki has nine UNESCO World Heritage Sites, which is more than any other Greek city. We saw several, including the huge Hagia Sophia Church. When we walked by the grand Aristotelous Square, Niki told me that in 1997, Thessaloniki was the Cultural Capital of Europe. Despite all the recognition, Thessaloniki (like Athens) isn't as gorgeous as you might expect. It's the ancient Greece marketing curse: Greece is overly hyped. In 2012, Thessaloniki is starting a massive 15-year renovation project, so that reality matches the marketing by 2027.

When Couchsurfing is like getting a lap dance

While Niki was giving me her Thessaloniki tour, she would sometimes get close to me. She would giggle in a flirtatious way. While we walked, she put her arm through my arm and, at one point, held my hand for a few minutes. I wasn't sure how to react. When you're in a strange land like Greece, you never know what the social norms of the native tribes are.

It was especially awkward for me because she was my couchsurfing host. It was tempting to escalate the tension because Niki was sexy and charming. More importantly, I had been single for months, so I was mentally weak. At that point, I hadn't met Ana (that would happen nearly two years later). Despite being single and having a throbbing libido, I was hesitant. What if I was misreading her? If so, our couchsurfing situation would become quite uncomfortable. I was supposed to be staying for two more nights. So instead, I played it cool, pretending that Californians also like to hold the hands of semi-random strangers.

Some men think it must be a dream to couchsurf with a hot girl. It's not. It's a nightmare. Couchsurfing with an attractive woman is like getting a lap dance. I've never understood why men pay for lap dances. Think about it: you pay lots of money for a Victoria's Secret model to dance and rub herself all over your body, but if you dare to lay a finger on her, a big bouncer named Tony will fling you out of the "gentlemen's club."

Just like a lap dance is torture, couchsurfing with a seductive, single woman is also agony. Sure, there are cases where romance erupts. In fact, while CS stands for *CouchSurfing,* a few couchsurfers joke that it really stands for Casual Sex. Naughty women call it Cock Surfing. Nevertheless, there's an unspoken rule that men must always honor: treat couchsurfing like a lap dance. That means, no monkey business. Therefore, while Niki tempted me like the Sirens tempted Odysseus, I tried to behave like a monk from Metéora.

Eventually, Maria and Irini joined us, which defused the sexual tension. Still, the girls had a raunchy sense of humor. They told me that they have a spreadsheet where they've rated every sexual partner they've ever had. Although they wouldn't show me the spreadsheet, they shared their average scores. They ranged from 4.7 to 6.7, with 10 being the maximum score. Apparently Anna was either the luckiest or the easiest to please.

The four of us walked along the waterfront by the iconic White Tower and the statue of Alexander the Great. Throughout the day I was people-watching. It seems that Thessaloniki Greeks are comfortably dressed, avoiding the fancy Baltic or Serbian fashion. The most striking image is how the widows dress. They show their respect for their husbands by dressing completely in black for the rest of their lives. I'm not sure why these Greek widows always are incredibly small ladies, but perhaps tall Greek women die before their husbands.

Getting lucky at a gay bar

That evening, the girls wanted to go to a gay bar and asked if I wanted to join in. Being from San Francisco, I had to agree. Besides, it's not every day that you get to go to a gay bar with four cute girls. Their drag queen friend, Xvanda, was having a performance that evening and they wanted to support him. Niki didn't believe me when I said that San Francisco was the Gay Capital of the world. However, after she introduced me as "Francis from the San Francisco," she believed me because every gay boy would squeal with delight.

That evening at the gay bar, I got lucky. We were all dancing for a couple of hours while waiting for Xvanda's singing performance. Instead of peanuts at the bar, they had bubble gum. Niki put some bubble gum in her mouth for a few seconds, walked up to me while I was dancing, and then, without warning, put the bubble gum in my mouth with her tongue. And then she just walked away with a wicked, devilish smile. I stood there as still as a Greek statue.

When we returned home, Niki said, "I'm really sorry about this, but Maria's boyfriend is going to stay with her tonight, so I can't sleep in her bed. I hope you don't mind if we sleep together in my bed."

I smiled and thought, "This is going beyond lap dancing."

Partying with a transvestite

My three-day stay turned into a week. During that time, the girls hosted a party with nearly 200 people. Their apartment was packed. The star of the evening was, once again, Xvanda. Don't conclude that all Greeks are tolerant of gays and drag queens. Like most couchsurfers, my Greek hosts (and their friends) are much more open-minded than most. In 2010, only a third of Greeks told Gallup that their area "is a good place for gays and lesbians."

Eventually, the police closed down the noisy party. They were happy to take all four dressed-up housemates to the station for "further questioning." While they were gone, I chatted with the Geoffroy, a Frenchman who worked near Athens. He said that there were two things he liked most about Greece. He said, "In a French café, people quickly drink their coffee and go. But in Greece, people take their time. The other thing that's great is that you can buy alcohol in a kiosk." The girls eventually returned and shut down the party.

Greece's future

In 2011, Gallup asked the world to predict their future. First, they were asked where their life was on a one to 10 scale (10 being ideal). Then they were asked where they thought their life would be in five years. Only two of the 27 EU countries predicted that their life would be worse in five years: Romania and Greece. Greeks rated their current life at 5.84, while their future life 5.28. Moreover, 43 percent predicted their life would be worse—the highest percentage saying that in the EU. In Gallup's Optimism Index, Greece had the world's second lowest score, just above Togo.

Greece now appears as dysfunctional as many of its Balkan neighbors. The rest of the Balkans, now free of communism and war, will close the standard of living gap with Greece. In 2010, Transparency International announced that Greece was the most corrupt country in the EU. In July 2011, in the middle of Greece's euro crisis, Niki told me a paradox, "We are feeling the downturn—we will all be poor in a while. But still, all the cafés and taverns are fucking full of smiley people."

Besides economics, there's another long-term issue that concerns Greeks: climate change. Global warming is one of the few issues where Europe isn't divided east-west, but rather north-south. Those in the south are far more concerned than those in the north. For example, only five percent of Finns believe global warming is a "very serious" threat, while 63 percent of Greeks feel that it is. That makes Greece the most concerned European country on this issue, according to a 2010 Gallup survey. After having spent a winter in Estonia, I can understand the northern European indifference to global warming.

Maria and Niki dropped me off at the Metropolitan Railway, which will get a facelift in 2012. As a parting gift, I gave them five-liters of olive oil. Given their consumption, it might have lasted them a week. We hugged each other goodbye, although Niki said she would see me a couple of weeks in Bulgaria. I blew them a kiss as I boarded the train to Macedonia (er, sorry, I mean FYROM).

When I was halfway done with this book, a high-school classmate learned about it and said, "Francis, you know what you're doing is an ethnographic study." I told him that I had never heard of that term. I also didn't know that *ethnography* comes from Greek: *ethnos* (folk/people) and *graphia* (writing). The Greeks, especially the ancient Greeks, have filled books with their lessons. Here are a couple of more.

What Greece Can Teach Us

- **Live a less structured life.** Go with the flow more. Although it's good to plan ahead, don't let those plans rule you.
- **Turn on the water heater only when you need it.** Nearly all Americans leave their water heater on nonstop. Most Eastern European bathrooms have a water heater switch next to their light switch. They just turn it on right before they need it. If also do that, you'll save money and energy, especially if your water heater is not well insulated.

Places I saw and recommend in Northern Greece: Metéora. I'm sure it's fun to climb Mt. Olympus, but I was too busy having fun in Thessaloniki.

Travel deals and info: http://ftapon.com/greece

Saints Cyril and Methodius were both born in Thessaloniki. We'll learn more about them in the chapter on Bulgaria. Mustafa Kemal Atatürk, the modern founder of Turkey, was also born in Thessaloniki. We'll learn about him next. In 2011, Greece contemplated building a wall between it and Turkey to discourage illegal immigration. Let's race across the border before it gets built.

20

Turkey—Europe's bridge to Asia

Turkey is one of only four countries that want to be associated with Eastern Europe (the other three are Belarus, Moldova, and Ukraine). While every other Eastern European country stubbornly resists the *Eastern Europe* label, Turkey embraces it. And yet, many Europeans don't want to give Turkey the "honor" of being in Eastern Europe, because they believe that Turkey isn't a part of Europe.

Geographically, Turkey has only a toe in Europe. About five percent of Turkey is in Eastern Europe; the rest is in Asia. Because of this lopsided ratio, it's tempting to exclude Turkey from this book. Still, just like eastern Germany is a legacy member of Eastern Europe, Turkey (due to the Turkish Empire's dominance in the Balkans for five centuries) is also a legacy member. Moreover, modern Turkey is part of NATO, has strong ties to the Balkans, and is a serious EU candidate. In addition, while only a small part of Turkey lies in Europe, about 10 million Turks live in that part—that's a bigger population than many European countries. Thus, we must consider Turkey. Nevertheless, we'll focus on Turkey's western side—the part that's most connected to Europe. I plan to analyze Turkey much more thoroughly in Book Four of the WanderLearn Series, which will cover the Middle East.

Before we take our short tour of Western Turkey, let's consider the country's name. Several Turks told me that they hate it when their country is called *Turkey* instead of *Türkiye* (sounds like *Tur-ki-yea*). Of course, they wouldn't have a problem with Turkey if the word didn't have three unflattering meanings: a winged animal, a *jerk*, and a *flop*. If *turkey* meant *awesome*, then no Turk would complain. Hungary faces a similar problem with its name. Hungarians call their country *Magyarország*. Like the Turks, Hungarians are tired of people cracking jokes about their country.

> *Ethiopia was disappointed with the World Cup draw. They were hoping to get Turkey, but got Hungary instead.*
> *— Bad joke*

Therefore, in this chapter, we will honor the Turks by encouraging a little movement (like we're doing with *Czechia*) and call their nation *Türkiye*.

Entering Türkiye via the Black Sea

In 2004, the first time I visited Türkiye, I entered via an unusual way. I took a three-day boat ride across the Black Sea from Sevastopol, Ukraine to Istanbul, Türkiye. It was November and winter was blowing into Eastern Europe. I was eager to flee cold Ukraine and enjoy a warmer climate. The $100 ticket incdluded a bed for two nights, primitive hot showers, two dinners and breakfasts, plus one lunch. The boat held about 50 passengers. I shared a cabin with a Russian salesman. I could speak with him as effectively as a two-year-old Russian boy. With five more years of practice, I hope to speak like a three-year-old.

On the morning of the third day, we saw Istanbul's minarets. After getting through immigration, I stepped into Türkiye. Within just a few hours of wandering, it was already obvious that Turks are extremely friendly and warm. It didn't matter who I talked with, everyone was happy to help. What's remarkable is that usually the biggest city of a country has the country's least friendly people. Istanbul has 13 million inhabitants. Therefore, if Turks in Istanbul were this friendly, what were the Turks deep in the country like?

When I asked a guy where the Hagia Sophia was, he said, "Let me take you there." He took me on a 10-minute walk around the center, chatting the whole way. He owned a clothing store and liked relaxing near the mosques when he had free time. I was sure he would ask me for money at the end of his little tour. He dropped me off in front of the museum and said, "OK, here you are. I'll wait for you here when you come out."

I said, "Um, that's OK. I'm fine. Thanks!"

"OK then! Bye bye!"

I felt bad that I was cold to him at the end. I thought he would want money, but he never even hinted at it. A cynic may say that he really did want my money, but after meeting dozens of helpful Turks, it's more likely that he was just a nice guy. Or maybe he was just bored out of his mind. That's quite possible, because Turks are the most bored people on Earth. Gallup surveyed 141 countries, asking people if they felt bored the previous day. Six in 10 Turks said *yes*, resulting in the highest level of boredom in the world.

Istanbul's sensory assault

After leaving my bored Turkish friend, I entered the awe-inspiring Hagia Sophia. For 1,000 years, it was the biggest cathedral in the world, but then Muslims converted it into a mosque. It's so much more civilized to convert a house of worship rather than destroying it. Today, it's not a religious building—it's a museum. Trying to describe the Hagia Sophia is like trying to describe the Vatican. Let's just say that it's big and awe-inspiring.

Other sites confirm why Istanbul was the European Cultural Capital in 2010. For example, next to the Hagia Sophia is the exalted Sultan Ahmed Mosque, which is often called the Blue Mosque because of its exquisite blue tiles. It flaunts its size and importance by having six minarets. I wandered into the Basilica Cistern, a grand, sixth-century water storage facility that still works. In 2004, Istanbul was my last stop on my five-month, 25-country Eastern European tour, so I searched for bargains and souvenirs in the Grand Bazaar, which is the oldest and one of the world's largest covered markets. Tempting aromas filled the air. When I was visiting, it was Ramadan—a period when Muslims fast, don't smoke, or have sex during the day. After sunset, there's probably an orgy of cigarettes and food in every home.

Istanbul assaults the senses. People touch and grab you when they're giving you directions, practically pulling you in the correct direction. The smell of *buğulama* (steam-cooked fish with lemon and parsley) must torture those who observe Ramadan. Every few steps, street vendors shout offers. Turkish and Byzantine architecture delights your eyes. The taste of Turkish spices takes your tongue to culinary places you'll never visit in most of Eastern Europe's comparatively bland cuisine.

Atatürk: the modern Turk

It's hard to understand Türkiye without knowing about Mustafa Kemal Atatürk, the nation's modern founder. In 1924, he made both sexes equal before the law. In 1928, he replaced the Arabic writing system with one that was based on a modified Latin alphabet. Unlike America, Atatürk didn't seek to separate church and state. He tried to put religion *under* the state. Atatürk created the *diyanet,* a government body that appoints the imams in the 77,000 mosques and dictates what they should preach—sometimes even writing their sermons for them. Imagine if the US Congress appointed the priests throughout the land and told them what to say.

Atatürk's struggle to westernize Turkey's culture continues today. For example, English is Türkiye's preferred second language and only religious schools teach Arabic. Nevertheless, everyone must take a religion class. Meanwhile, you cannot wear a headscarf in the Parliament, but most people on the streets are men because women are encouraged to stay at home. This tug-of-war comes from geography—Türkiye is where Europe's influence collides with the Middle East's.

A couple of years after visiting Türkiye, I interviewed Hakan Akgül and Denise, two Turks in their 20s who were born and raised in Istanbul. They immigrated to the US in the mid-1990s. They said that Atatürk is widely admired and respected in Türkiye. Turks aren't super serious about religion. Hakan and Denise estimated that about half of Turks are serious Muslims who pray five times a day; perhaps five percent are fanatical. A 2010 Gallup poll agrees: while 83% of Turks claim religion is "important in their daily life," only 42% went to a house of worship the previous week. That's less devoted than Italy (47%) and Poland (67%).

Hakan and Denise said that Türkiye's education system is strict and has a high standard. Denise said it's extremely competitive to get into universities. When you're a child, Hakan said that "you can get whupped for not doing your homework, and your parents will be happy about it. There's a saying when you take your kid to school, 'You take the meat; you give me the bones back.'"

Following legendary footsteps in Ephesus

After visiting Istanbul, I took an overnight bus trip to the ancient city of Ephesus. The Turkish bus was far more luxurious than the standard overnight buses in Eastern Europe. It had comfortable reclining chairs, trays, a movie (appropriately, *Troy*), headphones, tea, free snacks, and (the real shocker) friendly bus drivers.

A Greek legend says that Amazons, the mythical female warriors, founded Ephesus. Others say the founder was the Athenian Prince Androklos, although the story of how he chose the site is a bit fishy. Supposedly he consulted the Oracle at Delphi, who told him that a fish would show Androklos the place for a new colony and a boar would lead them to the future site of Ephesus. While preparing a fish dinner along the shore of the Aegean, the fish jumped out of the pan. The surprised cook caused a brush fire, which then scared a boar. Androklos followed the boar and eventually killed it. He decided to fulfill the prophecy and built Ephesus right where he killed the boar. The fact that there was a good harbor area, fertile land nearby, and a fresh water stream available might have also helped.

About 2,000 years ago, Ephesus was the second biggest city in the world, after Rome. During the first and second century, up to half a million people lived there. It was exciting to walk in the footsteps of the elite who walked its streets. For example, Alexander the Great conquered Ephesus and offered to help complete the Temple of Artemis. The builders turned down his funding because Alex wanted his name carved in big fat letters on the Temple in exchange for the cash. To avoid offending Alex, the Ephesians cleverly said that it was not fitting for one god to dedicate a temple to another.

Other elite visitors included Julius Caesar, who visited Ephesus while he was chasing Pompey the Great. Cleopatra's sister, Arsionoe, fled to Ephesus after losing a fight for the Egyptian throne. Cleopatra eventually convinced Mark Anthony, her lover, to kill her sister there. With family members like this, who needs enemies?

In 32 BC, Queen Cleopatra and Mark Anthony had a romantic rendezvous in Ephesus. Anthony was assembling his forces against Octavian. His troops disliked Cleopatra's presence and their morale plummeted. During the fight, Cleopatra fled faster than a French general, taking her sixty Egyptian ships with her. Anthony followed her in a single ship, leaving the rest of his fleet to be destroyed. With commanders like this, who needs enemies?

The Virgin Mary accompanied the Apostle Paul in Ephesus towards the end of her life. Paul almost caused a riot with Artemis souvenir vendors, who encouraged him to leave. After living there for two years, Paul left, but not before establishing a center for Christianity. St. John allegedly wrote his gospel on a hill in Ephesus. You can still visit St. John's Basilica and tomb. Finally, the glorious Roman Celcus Library teaches you that men haven't changed much. Next to the library was a brothel. An underground tunnel connected them. Thus, men could tell their wives that they were "going to library" to "pull an all-nighter."

Chasing the elusive Temple of Artemis

In 1863, the British Museum sent John Turtle Wood, an architect, to search for the lost Temple of Artemis, which was one of the seven wonders of the ancient world. Wood struggled. The region was infested with bandits. Workers were difficult to find. His budget was too small. Oh, and he also had no clue where the temple was located. He searched for the temple for six years. Each year the British Museum threatened to cut off his funding unless he found something significant, and each year he convinced them to fund him for just one more season. Wood probably told them that he had to conduct "more research" in the "library."

During his first season Wood broke his collar bone when his horse tossed him. Two years later, Wood was stabbed within a few centimeters of his heart. By his fifth year, he must have missed London's weather. Finally in 1869, at the bottom of a muddy seven-meter deep-test pit, his crew struck the base of the ancient temple. Wood excavated the foundation, removing tons of swamp and leaving a hole the size of a football field.

The best remains were shipped to the British Museum so that today there's not much to see at the original site, which makes local tour guides moan. Nevertheless, Ephesus is impressive because it is one of the largest Roman ruins in the world. Today, there is a body of water near it. However, 2,000 years ago the Aegean Sea filled the valley, allowing ships to dock at Ephesus. River silt ultimately dried out the harbor, which helped bring an end to the glory days. Today, Turks are digging a channel to the sea. Therefore, visitors may once again be able to park their boats on the shores of Ephesus.

Will Türkiye join the EU in 2023?

Although Ephesus is no longer the second biggest city in the world, Istanbul has practically taken its place. Istanbul went from a population of 2.7 million in 1980 to 13.2 million in 2010, thereby making it the third biggest city in the world. About 70 percent live on the city's European side. Türkiye has nearly 80 million inhabitants, more than any other European country. Türkiye also has NATO's second largest army (after the USA). It's the world's biggest cement exporter. It pumps out so many cars, shoes, furniture, and electronics that it's effectively Europe's China.

Because of Türkiye's size and influence, EU leaders have been debating whether to invite the Turks into their club. Absorbing a small Balkan country like Bosnia or Serbia won't have such a dramatic impact on the EU; however, Türkiye is 10 times bigger than Serbia and it would tip the scales. Türkiye has put on lipstick for the EU: they've abolished the death penalty, trimmed the army's powers, and given women more rights. They have visa-free travel and free trade for all EU members, including non-EU countries, like Serbia. They allow abortion, even though in 2008 Türkiye's Prime Minister said that he wants every woman to have "at least three children." Most of these moves are positioning Türkiye to join the EU in 2023, which would be the 100th anniversary of the Turkish Republic.

Despite Türkiye's efforts, it's unlikely that the EU will invite them. In 2011, after six years of negotiation, Türkiye had only completed one of the 35 steps required to become an EU member. Politicians in Austria, France, Germany, and the Netherlands snap up easy votes whenever they bash Turks. These EU snobs won't invite Türkiye to their community because they like white people with tans, but they don't like people with natural tans.

Another reason the EU won't admit Türkiye is the standard-of-living gap. For example, 27 percent of Turks told Gallup that in 2010 there were times when they didn't have enough money for shelter—that was the worst rate in Europe. Therefore, Western Europeans imagine a flood of poor, desperate Turkish immigrants invading their countries. It's been hard for the EU to digest Bulgaria and Romania. The EU will get a stomach ulcer trying to digest Türkiye. Moreover, because there would be so many Turkish immigrants, they would have the critical mass to establish ethnic enclaves, thereby destabilizing each country's culture. Europeans tolerate immigrants who quickly learn the local language and adopt local customs. However, if immigrants set up a parallel world and live in a separate bubble society, then Europeans go nuts. In addition, there's also Islamophobia.

Still, some cultural differences aren't as obvious as languages and religions. For example, Europe's east-west divide appears in recycling rates. In Western Europe, 77% of Germans recycle (which is the *lowest* rate it Western Europe in Gallup's 2008 survey). In Eastern Europe, on the other hand, all countries had recycling rates below 60%. Turkey was Europe's worst at just 6% (Russia and Ukraine were both around 10%).

The Türkiye-EU debate comes down to what the EU wants to be when it grows up. Some want it to be as big as possible so that it can compete with the US and China. Others prefer quality over quantity: they want an elite group that isn't dragged down by poor, needy countries. On the other hand, the EU may have to accept Türkiye in 2023. As Europe's population ages, they will need young immigrants to help support their generous welfare states or face radical cutbacks. Without youthful Türkiye, the aging EU will fade into irrelevance. Moreover, if the EU rejects Türkiye, the Turks will deepen its relationships with the Middle East. This could slow down Türkiye's Europeanization, which could be bad news for the EU. Nevertheless, European xenophobia is so high that it's hard to imagine that Türkiye will join the EU in 2023.

Perhaps the most likely scenario is that the EU will invent a quasi-EU category for Türkiye. This might include certain benefits (e.g., free trade and visa-free travel), but not others (e.g., the right to live and work in any EU country). Perhaps the EU could offer such a diluted membership to Ukraine, Belarus, Russia, and any other country that the EU wants to sleep with, but not marry.

The 2:00 a.m. tea

My 12-hour overnight bus trip from Ephesus back to Istanbul was not as nice as my first overnight trip. This time there was a shrieking child in the seat across from me. At midnight, when the child finally got bored with screaming his head off, the mother began talking loudly with the bus driver's assistant. You'd think she would be exhausted from her child's tantrums, but they kept talking for hours. I was bored with it all.

The most bizarre part of the bus ride happened at 2:00 a.m. They turned on the lights and started passing out caffeinated tea and crackers. Huh? I was surprised that nobody got furious for being rudely awakened. Instead, everyone happily accepted the handouts. Do all Turks set their alarm clocks for 2:00 a.m. so they can have tea and biscuits?

In 2010, according to the Pew Global Attitudes Project, 60 percent of Americans thought the US was generally disliked. That year, America and Türkiye were the only countries in the world whose people were more likely to say that their country was disliked rather than liked. Call me a contrarian, but I like the US and Türkiye.

What Türkiye Can Teach Us

- **Be helpful.** Unlike the average Eastern European on the street, most Turks are incredibly warm and helpful. What's remarkable is that people in big cities (like Istanbul) and extremely touristy areas (like Ephesus) generally have people who have little patience for tourists. Imagine how friendly Turks outside of these areas are like.

Places I saw and recommend in Türkiye: Istanbul and Ephesus. My visit (and this chapter) is short because I'm saving Türkiye for my book about the Middle East.

Travel deals and info: http://ftapon.com/turkey

After we have visited a key gateway into Eastern Europe, we now have five countries left: Bulgaria, Romania, Moldova, Ukraine, and Russia. Let's begin with the country which popularized the Cyrillic alphabet that you see in many Eastern European countries: Bulgaria.

21
Bulgaria—Defying Standards

In 1785, Alexandre-Maurice Blanc de Lanautte, count d'Hauterive, was 31 years old when he left the French Embassy in Istanbul to go to Moldavia. Like any self-respecting Frenchman, he looked down on the world around him, including Eastern Europe. He quickly concluded that Bulgarians were "always savages incapable of speaking reason about anything."[1] Give the Frenchy some credit: after a couple of weeks, he admitted that there were a few exceptions.

Eastern Europeans would usually warn me about their neighboring country, saying, "Be careful. There are a lot of thieves there. Hold onto your bags." Such warnings are as old as the countries. In 1786, for example, Lady Elizabeth Craven was in Istanbul and needed to return to Vienna. She considered going through Belgrade, but everyone told her that there were endless thieves on that road. Hence, she decided to go through Bulgaria, just like the Frenchy had done the year before. Still, some said that there were "much greater risks in taking this new route, for that I should find heads stuck up on poles at every mile, those countries being much more infested with robbers and murderers than the other." Lady Craven went anyway with the "two most excellent little English pistols I wear at my girdle."[2]

In the first of my three trips to Bulgaria, I didn't have any pistols at my girdle. However, I wish I had shock absorbers. I took an overnight bus from Skopje to Sofia (Bulgaria's capital). The rocky road made the bus ride feel like a nonstop two-hour earthquake. When we finally arrived in Sofia at dawn, my head was still bouncing.

I was a bit worried about Bulgaria. In Lonely Planet's 2004 *Eastern Europe* guidebook, they listed "The Bottom 10 Things in Eastern Europe." Number eight was "Most of Bulgaria." Ouch. The rest of the list consisted of specific places, not entire countries. It hurts when travel experts say that your whole country stinks.

> *These are big achievements for this country, and the people of Bulgaria ought to be proud of the achievements that they have achieved. — George W. Bush, 2007, in Sofia, Bulgaria*

Even though I felt like a zombie when I arrived in Sofia, the city of 1.3 million residents seemed nice. It's Europe's highest capital (545 m / 1,600 ft) and the inspiring snow-capped Mt. Vitosha looms nearby. The National Art Gallery is outstanding. One of Sofia's most impressive buildings is the Aleksander Nevski Church, which was built to honor the 200,000 Russians who died to liberate Bulgaria from the Turkish Empire. Although it's important to visit a country's capital, it's more eye-opening to explore beyond the capital.

From Rila to Veliko Tarnovo

After Sofia, I headed south to the tenth-century Rila Monastery, which is on UNESCO's World Heritage List. It's nestled in the magical and inviting Rila Mountains. Besides the 1,200 glorious murals, one of the treasures they have is the heart of Tsar Boris III, the Bulgarian leader who refused to give into Hitler's demands of deporting 50,000 Jews to Nazi concentration camps.

After visiting the Rila Monastery, I followed a trail into the mountains. I camped at the tree line and woke up with frost on my tarp. Normally, you can run into *hizhas* (huts) every few hours, but a sign said that the trail was treacherous and that the huts were closed. Nevertheless, I went ahead and discovered the magnificent Seven Lakes. I purposefully went off-trail, took a break, and accidentally left my tarp behind on a pile of snow. I've never owned a house, bed, chair, couch, table, or TV, so my tarp is one of my few valued possessions. That particular one had served me on the Appalachian Trail. Let's hope it's now serving a Bulgarian mountaineer.

After Rila's mountains, I went to Plovdiv, which is Bulgaria's second biggest city. I witnessed a well-dressed woman trying to pickpocket a tourist; 30 minutes later two 12-year old girls made another failed attempt. Aside from the pilfering females, Plovdiv is a nice town that is filled with historic homes. The Romans founded Plovdiv in the third century. They called it Philippopolis and the well-preserved Roman theater is remarkable. Having been founded by the Thracians, there's strong evidence that Plovdiv is the oldest city in Europe.

From Plovdiv, I went north to my favorite Bulgarian city, Veliko Tarnovo. The city was Bulgaria's capital for over 200 years. It's set on a horseshoe bend of the Yantra River, which carves a gorge and practically creates a rocky island. It's a perfect spot for the medieval Tsaravets Citadel. Given its strong defenses, it's remarkable that the Turks managed to sack it in 1393. Whoever lost that fight probably was probably taken to Execution Rock, which is a great place for a fatal dive into the Yantra River.

Above the Citadel's Royal Palace and the Patriarch's Complex is the rebuilt Church of the Blessed Savior. Its fantastic murals were redone in the 1980s. They have a dark fantasy theme that you'll never find in any other church in the world. In town, Stefan Stambolov Street offers superb views of the winding river. Attractive houses cling to the steep hill. In the city center is Asenovtsi Park, which has the State Art Museum, but also the enormous and dark Asenev Monument, which is dedicated to four Bulgarian kings. Finally, if you walk down by the river, you'll see a Byzantine church and an old stone bridge. Veliko Tarnovo is a dream.

A quick tour through Bulgarian history

The beauty and history embedded in Veliko Tarnovo motivated me to learn more about Bulgaria's history. Over 5,000 years ago, Thracians were the first major civilization to show up in Bulgaria. The Romans took over in the first century, establishing places like Plovdiv. In the seventh century, the Bulgars, who were descendants of people from Central Asia (near Iran), migrated to Bulgaria. They mixed with the locals and, in 681 AD, carved the first Bulgarian state out of a part of the Byzantine Empire. After a few hundred years, the Byzantines reconquered the land, but they felt the need to poke out the eyes of 15,000 Bulgarians first.

Eventually the Bulgarians started their second kingdom in 1185, placing the capital in Veliko Tarnovo. That lasted nearly 400 years, when the Turkish Empire crashed the party. For the next 500 years, Turks ruled Bulgaria. At that point, according to one melodramatic Bulgarian historian, "The brilliant medieval Christian culture of the Bulgarians fell into decay."[3] The Turkish legacy explains why one in ten Bulgarians today is an ethnic Turk. In 1878, the Russians and the Bulgarians booted the Turks out. After winning their first war in the twentieth century, Bulgaria lost the next three: the Second Balkan War, WWI, and WWII.

The WWII story is tragicomic. Bulgaria wanted to remain neutral during WWII, but both sides tried to seduce Bulgaria by offering it new territory. Hitler offered a better deal, so the Bulgarians reluctantly signed up. When the Germans were retreating in August 1944, the Bulgarians did something cute—they declared that they were now neutral. The Soviets grinned. The Bulgarians tried to keep a straight face and repeated, "Really. We're neutral now. Honest."

Three days later, thousands of Soviet tanks and troops poured into Bulgaria, unopposed. In one day, Bulgaria was conquered without a fight. After the war, Russia blessed Bulgaria with communism. Todor Zhivkov ruled Bulgaria from 1956 to 1989. Toward the end, he made some reforms like granting limited free speech, closing labor camps, stopping executions, and ending church persecution. It wasn't enough. After 1989, he was placed under house arrest until he died in 1998. After the fall of communism, Bulgaria looked to the west. Bulgaria joined NATO in 2004 and the EU in 2007. Nevertheless, Bulgaria has a positive relationship with Russia, largely thanks to the alphabet that unites them.

Кирилица

In the ninth century, Saints Cyril and Methodius, two Greek brothers who were born in Thessaloniki, wanted to spread Christianity to the Slavs who lived north of them. Since there was no standard way of writing Slavic languages, the brothers created an alphabet that was loosely based on the Greek alphabet and that eventually evolved into modern Cyrillic. It's not clear why the alphabet is named only after Cyril. Maybe Methodius was goofing off most of the time.

It's sacrilegious to criticize saints, but Кирилица (*Cyrillic* in Bulgarian) was a mistake. The brothers should have copied either the Greek or Latin alphabet instead of inventing a new alphabet. When they needed to modify sounds that don't exist in Greek, they could have simply redefined the sound of a letter or added an accent. Instead, Cyrillic borrows characters from Greek, Latin, and Hebrew, and also creates a few new characters. This innovation was as unnecessary as the idea of creating an additional power plug standard.

Russians thought they were improving Cyrillic when they adopted more Latin letters, but they complicated everything by changing many sounds. Let's see the confusion this can cause by matching Cyrillic letters with similar-sounding Latin letters in parenthesis: н (n), и (i), р (r), г (g), п (p), л (l), д (d) в (v), у (oo), с (s), я (ya), з (z), э (e), ш (sh), ц (ts), х (h).

Now decode these seemingly incomprehensible Russian words (the phonetic answer is in the parenthesis): спорт (sport), газ (gaz), супермаркет (soopermarket), ресторан (restoran), банк (bank), бар (bar), парк (park), такси (taxi), компьютер (computer), зоо (zoo), паспорт (passport), пресс (press), киоск (kiosk), and хот дог (hot dog). You might even find amusing-looking words: *royal,* as in the *royal burger* that Ukraine's McDonald's serves is transliterated роял.

> *Шест шишета се сушат на шест шосета от шест сешуара. (Transliteration: Shest shisheta se sushat na shest shoseta ot shest seshuara.)*
> *— Bulgarian tongue twister meaning, "Six bottles are being dried on six highways by six blow-driers."*

Some Bulgarians told me that they needed a unique alphabet because the Greek and Latin alphabet didn't have all the Slavic sounds. However, that didn't stop Slavs in Poland, Czechia, Slovakia, Slovenia, and Croatia from using the Latin alphabet. They simply redefined the sounds of a few letters and threw accents on others, like *ł, č, š, ż,* and *ž*. As a result, when you see Polish words, you can stumble through them: *szkoła* (school), *róża* (rose), and *sałatka* (salad).

A common alphabet lets us learn other languages more easily than if we have different alphabets. For example, guess what these Latvian words mean: *kalendārs, mandarīns, ģitāra, tomāts, krēms, pīpe, piramīda, magnēts, literatūra, mehāniķis, limuzīns, tramplīns, kostīms, mūzikls, mūzika, tīģeris, universitāte.* You could probably correctly guess most of them. Now let's transliterate this list into Cyrillic (i.e., reproduce this list using the phonetically equivalent letters in Cyrillic): календаарс, мандарииинс, гитаара, томаатс, креемс, пиипе, пирамиида, магнээтс, литератуура, мэхааникйс, лимузиинс, трамплиинс, костиимс, муузиклс, тиигйерис, университаате. Ask a Latvian who knows Cyrillic to read both lists aloud and you won't hear a difference. So why invent a new alphabet? Because we like the squiggly lines?

Still, it's wrong to completely blame Cyrillic. The jerk who invented Latin caused problems in the first place by taking Greek characters and assigning them completely different sounds. For example, here are Greek letters and their equivalent sounds in the Latin alphabet in parenthesis: Γ (g), Ρ (r), Υ (oo). The Greeks had a perfectly good-looking *P* (Π) that we could have used (which is what Cyrillic did). Instead, Latin ignored some Greek standards and now we're all confused.

I'm also not suggesting that the Latin alphabet is superior to Cyrillic. On the contrary, Cyrillic has the advantage of having little difference between uppercase and lowercase letters, whereas the Latin alphabet often has significant changes (e.g., A/a, B/b, D/d, E/e). CYRILLIC'S LOWERCASE IS LIKE SMALL CAPS IN ENGLISH, WHICH MAKES IT SIMPLE. Indeed, Cyrillic would be a great universal alphabet. Example: "Иф ю но зэ Сириллик алфабет, ридинг зис Инглиш сэнтэнс из изи." That sentence isn't written in the Bulgarian or Russian language. It's an English phrase, but using Cyrillic letters. It says, "If you know the Cyrillic alphabet, reading this English sentence is easy."

In short, the Cyrillic and Latin alphabets are unnecessary inventions. They both deviated significantly from their Greek mother. We could all be using the Greek alphabet (with a few minor modifications). Then we'd have one unified alphabet, thereby making it easier to learn new languages. Alas, the world is not so simple and logical.

Today, for better or for worse, the Latin alphabet is the most widely used alphabet in the world. In the 1920s, Turkey adopted the Latin alphabet. Bosnia, Montenegro, and Serbia are showing signs of abandoning Cyrillic. Nevertheless, the Greeks or Bulgarians may never abandon their respective alphabets since they're proud to be the first to use them.

Standards and a universal alphabet

Many, especially Cyrillic fans, say that I'm "missing the beauty and diversity of languages! Having different alphabets is great! It's part of the culture! It would be a boring planet if we had fewer alphabets!"

Fundamentally, we're debating the benefits of standards versus diversity. If you're a Bulgarian and you find my remarks about Cyrillic offensive, then fly to France and write me hate mail from a French keyboard. The French use the AZERTY keyboard, which moved the positions of the following keys: Q, W, Z, M, A, semi-colon, and colon. That's puzzling, but it gets worse. They've also inverted all the number/symbol keys. So if try to type *1234*, you will get *!@#$* unless you hold the shift-key. (To get symbols, you don't hold the shift-key; all numbers require holding the shift-key.) The most baffling and utterly French thing about their keyboard is that you have to press the shift-key to get a *period*! Even though 99 percent of sentences end with a period (and so it's a symbol that ought to be easy to access), the French force you to hit two keys to produce a period. The French made these changes so that they can paraphrase Louis XIV by saying, "Le Keyboard C'est Moi." In conclusion, before the angry Bulgarian can finish typing me a long hate mail, he will scream, throw the French keyboard out the window, and then see my point: standards are useful.

The French and Bulgarians aren't the only ones who like to defy standards. Russians have a non-standard train track width. The British and the Japanese drive on the left side of the road. The Swiss and the Italians have unconventional power plugs. And Americans not only call football *soccer*, but we're also the only idiots in the world (besides the folks in Myanmar) to not adopt the brilliant metric system.

Diversity is great when it's meaningful. However, there's nothing meaningful about writing decimals like 1.52 versus 1,52, or 9/22/2018 versus 22/9/2018, or PAL versus NTSC, or having the hot water on the left knob and the cold on the right. These are arbitrary decisions, just like deciding what the H symbol sounds like.

You want diversity? How about if Bulgaria said that one hour is made up of 80 units of time, not 60? Or if Hungary didn't have 12 months per year, but had four 91-day months instead (one for each season)? Or if each country had its own measurement system? Or if every province had its own power plug? Or if every city had its own alphabet? Globalization is about standardizing things. Some treat every step toward universality as a tragedy, but we shouldn't. A universal alphabet would be a net positive.

The idea of a universal alphabet sounds crazy, but we already do this with numbers. In most places in the world, if you write *438*, people will interpret those three squiggly symbols as *four hundred and thirty eight*. In some ways we already have a universal alphabet—it's the International Phonetic Alphabet. Still, like Esperanto, it's an artificial alphabet and won't be adopted because most people are emotional about alphabets and languages.

Languages are like guns

Some lament the loss of alphabets, dialects, and languages, arguing that it's a tragic casualty of globalization. However, why not celebrate such losses? Most conflicts throughout history are between groups who speak different languages. If civil war ever erupts in Spain, Belgium, and Canada, you can be sure that the battle lines will match the linguistic lines. Although nations with identical languages still attack each other, it's rare. Imagine if Latvians and Estonians only spoke Russian. Instead of looking at Russians as invaders, those Baltic people would look at them like Canadians look at Americans who move to Canada—a relatively harmless (and sometimes annoying) immigrant.

Moreover, those who lament the loss of languages often don't experience the challenge of being unable to communicate or read. Next time you're lost in a mountain village in Bulgaria during a snowstorm and nobody understands you and you can't read the signs, you'll wish there were a universal language or alphabet.

We attach deep, patriotic meaning to languages, instead of viewing them simply as tools to communicate. We sometimes forget that the message matters more than the medium. With alphabets, we're making a big deal about scribbling. Today, Bulgarians are more likely to defend the alphabet of Saints Cyrillic and Methodius than to defend the message they brought with it: the 2005 Eurobarometer survey indicated that only 40 percent of Bulgarians "believe there is a God."

One of the favorite phrases among gun lovers in America is, "Guns don't kill people. People kill people." In other words, banning weapons doesn't lower the homicide rate, because people will just find other ways to kill people. There's truth to that: although per capita firearm deaths are high in America, the homicide rate isn't that different compared with countries which have banned firearms. Similarly, languages don't cause wars, people cause wars. If we all spoke one language, we'll still have plenty of things to fight about. Still, we'd have one less excuse.

We inhabit a language rather than a country.
— Emile M. Cioran. Romanian philosopher

Although globalization is helping consolidate languages, don't expect us to have fewer than 100 world languages in the next century. Therefore, if you love having dozens of different languages out there to confuse you, don't worry, they'll be with us forever.

No means yes in Bulgaria

Bulgaria has defied a few standards. When Bulgaria became the first place to adopt Cyrillic, they supported an alphabet that defied the Greek standard. Later, they defied the Slavic standard of using grammatical cases. Like English, Bulgarian abandoned grammatical cases in favor of prepositions. I learned about their biggest defiance of standards when I asked a waitress in Veliko Tarnovo if I could see the menu. She shook her head from side to side, turned her back, and walked away. I stood motionless, dumbfounded by her rudeness. I started to leave, when she ran after to me and said, "Wait! I bring!"

I said, "I'm sorry, but you say no."

"I know! I understand. I meant *yes*!" she said. "I forget, you are not Bulgarian."

Just when you think globalization is everywhere, you discover that Bulgarians never got the memo that nodding is the universal signal for *yes* and that shaking your head means *no*. Bulgarians do the opposite. I couldn't find a Bulgarian who could explain why this is. This cultural oddity made me wonder if Bulgaria has more date-rape cases than the average country. After all, it's a country where *no* means *yes*.

Hitchhiking across Bulgaria

Bulgaria is slightly larger than Tennessee, but I had missed several places on my first visit. Therefore, I returned five years later, in 2009, to explore some more. I entered through its southwest corner. The Macedonian minibus took me near the Novo Selo-Zlatarevo border, which is surrounded by the snowy UNESCO-protected Pirin mountains. I walked across the border and hitchhiked to Petrich. From there, I visited Sandanski, Melnik, and the thirteenth-century Rozhen Monastery, which isn't as spectacular as the Rila Monastery. Then I wanted to somehow get to the Rhodope mountains to do some backpacking.

Instead of returning the way I came, I hiked on a dirt road behind the Rozhen Monastery. I wasn't sure if it would get me to Dospat, but my compass indicated that I was going in the right direction. After walking one hour, a lonely car approached. I stuck out my thumb. An ex-military officer invited me in. We chatted in basic Russian and he dropped me off on a paved road. I tried to hitchhike with some old folks who were traveling with horse-drawn carriages, but no luck.

Eventually, a friendly 21-year-old student in a sporty car picked me. He was driving to Gotse Delchev. We zipped over a mountain pass and then he invited me to have a drink with him in a pleasant town square. He said that buses to Dospat were infrequent, so it's best to hitchhike. He dropped me off at a good hitching location and within 20 minutes a middle-aged man picked me and took me 25 kilometers to a gas station. When two sexy young girls showed up at the gas station, he asked them if they would be willing to take me to Dospat. They agreed. I began liking Bulgaria more and more.

The seductive driver, Vania, and her best friend, Mimi, were on a joyride. They didn't need to go to Dospat, but they were happy to take me since they just wanted to drive and smoke pot at the same time. They offered me some marijuana, but I said, "No thanks, I prefer looking at the road."

When they dropped me off at Dospat, the sun was setting so I looked for a campsite. The nights were chilly and I had no tarp at the time. A half-destroyed home among a bunch of normal homes was perfect. I sneaked in through a broken window and camped among the rubble in the living room.

While I was trying to hitchhike the next day at 5:20 a.m., three policemen in a jeep stopped and asked me for my papers. I gave them my French passport. They couldn't speak English, so when they asked me where I slept last night, I just said, "Hotel." They wanted to know which hotel, but I just played dumb and said repeated, "Hotel." They asked me for more identification. I gave them my American passport. They were satisfied and left.

The police patrol Bulgaria's southern border tightly to catch Turks who sneak into Bulgaria. Most of Bulgaria's 750,000 Turks live in the south and the relations are poor. Bulgarian nationalists tried to ban the Turkish-language news. They also want Turkey to compensate Bulgaria for Turkey's 1913 deportations. Whenever that silly demand comes up, Turks remind Bulgaria that Bulgarians ethnically cleansed thousands of Turks in the 1970s and 1980s.

Backpacking in the Rhodope Mountains

I hitchhiked to the Devil's Throat (a cave) and eventually got to Trigrad, a small town nestled in the Rhodope mountains. I bought bread, cheese, tomatoes—enough food to help me traverse the mountains and get to a village. At 11:00 a.m., I followed a wide trail whose switchbacks took me to 1,500 meters (5,000 ft). It was April 2, and there were still patches of snow everywhere. I didn't have a shelter, so I needed to hurry to get to the village before sunset. My urgency picked up when it started drizzling. However, right as the rain started, I found an unexpected building—the Chairski Ezera Mountain Hostel. Because it was early in the season, it was closed. Luckily, one door had an open window. I climbed through it and had the huge hostel to myself. Instead of pressing on in the rain, I ended the day at 4:00 p.m., found a comfy bed with extra blankets, watched the rainstorm, and enjoyed the solitude.

The next morning I discovered just how lucky I was to find that shelter. The next two hours of backpacking were through nonstop snow, which made navigation tricky. When I finally arrived at the mountain village, there was no obvious shelter. Therefore, had I pressed on the previous day, I would have arrived in the dreary village tired and wet, and I'd have to camp in a leaky barn. It's nice to occasionally make the right decision.

I bought some more food at the only store in the rustic village. I ate while drying my wet feet next to the store's wood stove. I was wearing all my layers, but it was still cold. Snow patches littered the village, whose bleakness implied that little had changed in the last 50 years. After pigging out, I continued on the snow-covered trail to Shiroka Laka.

As the trail elevation approached 2,000 meters (6,560 ft), the snow was knee-deep. Fortunately, there were enough trail blazes that peeked out of the snow, which helped me navigate. Frozen waterfalls dripped enough fresh water to drink. Near a foggy mountain pass, a closed mountain chapel was half-buried under snow. With no place to camp, I slogged through the snow quickly before darkness fell. With two hours of daylight left, I got to the end of the trail.

Although Bulgaria's mountains are not very high (the tallest is Mt. Musala at 2,925 m / 9,594 ft), they are stunning. In fact, Bansko, which is between the Rila and Pirin Mountains, will probably try to host the 2018 Winter Olympics. Given that one-third of Bulgaria is covered with mountains, there's much to explore. I walked down the paved mountain road and two young men drove me the rest of the way down to the quaint town of Shiroka Laka. Next to its Roman bridge, a car picked me up and took me to the Pamporovo ski resort. From there, I caught the last bus to Plovdiv, where I arrived at midnight. After revisiting the city at night, I hung out in a hotel bar until I could grab the pre-dawn bus to Sofia.

The curious rocks of Belogradchik

After spending all day in Sofia, I went to Belogradchik, which is in Bulgaria's northwest corner. The town of 5,000 people is famous for its sandstone rocks that may remind you of Greece's Metéora. However, instead of building monasteries on them, the locals built the Kaleto Fortress around it. The Romans were here in the first century. Eventually, the Turks built the fort's defensive walls. Some say the reddish rock formations resemble people, but you need some serious drugs to see that.

After Belogradchik, I hitchhiked to Vidin, which is one of the only Bulgarian cities on the Danube. One driver invited me to his house for tea and to meet his wife. It's a great sign when it's easy to hitchhike in a country. It indicates that people are compassionate and trusting. Therefore, when I boarded the ferryboat that would go across the Danube to Romania, I was sad to leave Bulgaria. I planned to return later that year to spend a couple of weeks in a village and visit the Bulgaria's Black Sea coast.

The village of Turkincha

While I was traveling in Eastern Europe, my high-school friend, Sarah Spiridonov, made me an offer I couldn't refuse. I hadn't talked with Sarah since we were 18 years old, but thanks to Facebook, we reconnected. She was married to a Bulgarian and they had two boys. To help me with my book, she generously proposed that I stay a couple of weeks in her family's summer home in Turkincha, a tiny village about 20 kilometers (12.5 miles) from Veliko Tarnovo. I was extremely grateful for the opportunity to take a closer look at a rural Bulgarian setting. The experience ended up surprising me in numerous ways.

To get there, I revisited Ruse, Bulgaria's biggest city on the Danube. In 2009, it still was the only bridge between Bulgaria and Romania. The train rumbled across the mighty Danube and kept going to Veliko Tarnovo. Two friendly brothers named Vlado and Gosho, who were Sarah's Bulgarian relatives, picked me up. They took me to a superstore, where I loaded up on food to help me survive for a couple of weeks. I wouldn't have a car and there was no bus to the village. Turkincha had only 20 houses, several of which are empty most of the year. There were far more goats than people.

Sarah's family's two-story house was beautiful and in excellent condition. It had a large backyard with 20 fruit trees. The brothers handed me the keys, waved goodbye, and then the perfect silence of the village flooded my ears. I hooted a few times to make sure my ears were still working.

Meeting the unusual villagers

The next morning, I went for a 10-kilometer run through the countryside. Soft hills and farmland filled the tranquil scenery. There were far more dirt roads than paved roads. I met a shepherd with his goats and sheep, but otherwise no humans were around. The nearby village of Balvantsite was also quiet. Just when I concluded that this was a typical Eastern European village, things got strange.

While I was taking photos of Turkincha's abandoned community building, a woman that looked like she had just walked off the set of *Baywatch* came walking toward me with her German Shepherd. She had bleached blond hair, tan skin, a petite body, a cute yellow T-shirt, and blue jeans. The thing that seemed out of place in this fantasy vision was that she was wearing plastic purple Crocs shoes instead of high heels. I wasn't expecting to see any supermodels in a Bulgarian village. I took the blunt approach and said in English, "Excuse me, but you look out of place here. Who are you?"

Apparently, she understood English because she replied, "I'm Elitza Roupcheva, but you can call me Elly. I'm visiting my parents who live here. Where are you from?"

"San Francisco."

"Really? And so what are *you* doing here?"

We shared our stories while we walked her dog. Elly had finished her degree at Aalborg University in Denmark. She had lived in Perth, Australia for a year and still had an Australian boyfriend. She wasn't sure is she would return to Australia or if she should find work in Sofia. She wasn't that interested in raising sheep in Turkincha.

We ended up having tea in the backyard patio of Sarah's home. She told me a surprising fact: about a fifth of Turkincha's population was British. This innocent-looking Bulgarian village was becoming more and more freaky. The Brits retire to Turkincha to enjoy the low cost of living and the nice weather. Still, it's odd that they all ended up here. Elly said that she would return the next day and introduce me to a few locals. She left and I went to have lunch with my neighbors.

Meeting the Bulgarian villagers

Sarah told me to meet her trusted neighbor, *Baba Bobka* (Grandma Bobka). I knocked on Bobka's door and gave her ground coffee and several big bars of chocolate (knowing that she has a weakness for them). Bobka was a tiny 65-year-old woman with the vitality of a 20-year-old. She smiles freely and has the confidence of a matriarch. When five of her relatives (including her husband, Ivan Dyado) sat down for lunch, Bobka sat at the head of the table.

Bobka served us a creamy vegetable soup, lamb, mashed potatoes, and a pie soufflé made with eggs and ham. The only person who could speak English was Maya Pavlova, Bobka's pretty 28-year-old granddaughter. Maya lived in Ruse and helped organize boat tours down the Danube. Even though Turkincha looked like a ghost town, people were watching you. The proof that the villagers were observing was when Bobka asked me, "Who was that blond girl you were with today?"

The next afternoon, I met with that blond girl again. Elly wore a tight black shirt that said "New York," and a denim miniskirt—not the traditional farmer's daughter outfit. After chatting outside for two hours, we saw a farmer with his flock of sheep grazing in front of Sarah's house. Elly took photos of me trying to mount the farmer's donkey and the farmer laughing at my incompetence.

While we were goofing off, a fit grandmother named Stefani was walking by with her eight-year-old granddaughter. Elly knew them and the four of us walked to Stefani's house. Elly translated as Stefani shared her thoughts. Stefani grew up in Turkincha, but then left it when she was 20. In 2001, she returned to live out her last final years in the home of her birth. While Stefani gave me a tour of her flower and vegetable garden, she lamented that most Bulgarians had left the villages. She said there are over 200 empty villages in Bulgaria.

Stefani also said that Bulgaria has more corruption than during the communist time. It doesn't help that in the government fined a Bulgarian periodical €14,000 ($20,000) for publishing a reader's letter that accused a politician of corruption. Nor does it help that top police officials drive around in confiscated sports cars that they've adopted into the police fleet.

Although Stefani was friendly, she complained about Bulgaria. When Gallup asked people to rate their life on a one to 10 scale, Bulgarian and Macedonians averaged 4.2—the lowest in Europe. Serbia and Bosnia were next in line. Paola, a Croatian who worked on an eco-farm in Bulgaria, told me, "Older people in Bulgaria are really nice, but a bit annoying. Lots of them complained about everything—they don't have work, they don't have money, the government is fucked up. They complain about the dark, instead of turning a light on. You just can't escape the Balkan complaints."

Stefani had mixed feelings about the Brits who have moved into Turkincha. On the one hand, she was very happy that they were here because they've helped resurrect the dying village. They've renovated their houses and helped the economy. On the other hand, she didn't like that the Brits have made little effort to learn Bulgarian. Bulgarians would like to talk with them and be closer friends, but the Brits hang out with themselves or expect the Bulgarians to speak English. She also didn't like how Brits would have loud parties and throw trash on the street. "They wouldn't do that in England," she said. She suspects that Bulgaria has gotten the lower-class Brits. She believed that the wealthiest, most educated, and well-behaved Brits wouldn't move to Turkincha.

Meeting the Brits in Turkincha

After hearing so much about these Brits, I had to meet them. Stefani said that we could find them at the village store, which converts into a pub at night. Elly and I walked there and, sure enough, the pub had about five Brits around a table drinking Bulgarian beer. The Brits were in their 50s and 60s. They told me that they wanted to escape the rat race and the dismal British weather.

I sat next to Tony, a stately, plump Englishman in his 50s who had big blue eyes and a baritone voice. He had been living in Turkincha for three years. Later, he would invite me to his home, which was tastefully renovated. He was happy in this hidden Bulgarian village. I asked him what we can learn from Bulgarians. He said, "To avoid debt. The financial crisis didn't hurt Bulgarians as bad as it could have because most Bulgarians have relatively little debt."

Brett, another middle-aged Turkincha immigrant, added, "Bulgarians are more family-oriented than the British. Children are included in most events, whereas in England they are often put in a separate place."

I asked him, "How much Bulgarian do you speak?"

"Very little," he admitted. "You can get by with knowing just a few words."

"Have you learned any useful phrases?"

"Yes. *Oshte bira, molya.*"

"What does that mean?"

"*Another beer, please.*"

Elly's analysis

The next day, Elly came to say goodbye because she was returning to Sofia. I invited her to chat in the backyard patio. She gave me a parting gift: a copy of her 96-page college thesis that she wrote for Denmark's Aalborg University. It had an intriguing title: "To What Extent is the Development of a Country Dependent on its National Culture?" Elly said, "In the paper, I ask: is Bulgarian culture making the country unproductive and preventing further prosperity?"

It's an important question given how negative Bulgarians have been recently. In a 2009 Pew survey, 76% of Bulgarians said they were dissatisfied with the democratic system, 63% thought that free markets did not make people better-off and only 11% believed that ordinary Bulgarians had benefited from the post-communist changes. Elly said, "Bulgaria has a culture of stagnation. It's the opposite of modern cultures, which are characterized by movement and the search for opportunities in the future. Successful Bulgarians follow principles, values, and practices that are not typical for Bulgaria."

"So what should Bulgarians do?" I asked her.

She said, "First, we need to stop looking back at past glories. Second, we need to stop pointing fingers away from ourselves. We blame the 'Great Forces' for hurting us during the twentieth century. We blame our problems on our geography, which supposedly lacks natural resources. Also, Bulgarians who lived under communism sometimes believe that your status comes from your origin, education, connections and so on, and not from established abilities and actual achievements."

"That's not very entrepreneurial."

"No. Managers in Bulgaria prefer loyal employees than self-confident professionals with their own opinion. We should stop educating our children the way our grandfathers did. We should reform Bulgarian educational system, which makes children conformists and unable to think independently."

"How does Bulgaria's education system compare to your experience in Denmark?"

"Bulgarian schools emphasize memorizing information. Everything is centralized; the teacher is the center and the teacher imposes his truths. We look for 'right' answers and memorize absolute truths. Pupils almost fear their teachers. If you're an ambitious or assertive student, that's a negative."

"Is there corruption in Bulgarian schools?"

"Absolutely. Often the only way to pass an exam is to read the teacher's book. The teacher makes money off of every book sale. Also, many Bulgarians aren't interested in learning—they just want a diploma, even illegally. They'll buy it."

Our intellectual discussion was convincing me that there are brains behind Elly's beauty. Clearly, she's a fake blond.

Communism's long shadow

Elly rhetorically asked, "Why are Bulgarians often late for meetings? Why do cars not give way to pedestrians? Why are some western management techniques ineffective in Bulgaria? Or why is teamwork difficult in Bulgaria?"

I said, "I don't know. Why?"

"Because we believe there's a loser in every deal. One survey showed that 93 percent of Bulgarians believe that it is impossible to have a win-win situation when two parties participate in a deal. This shows the communist legacy and mentality, where everything was a state expense. Also, a large part of the Bulgarian population does not believe that honest and hard work pays off."

"Why not?"

"Because we're suspicious of others. We trust no one except our family and our closest friends. That's why Bulgarian firms are relatively small and why private firms are mostly family businesses. Another reason our companies are small is that we're intolerant of uncertainty and stress."

"Seems like this is just more evidence that the long shadow of communism still lingers in parts of Eastern Europe."

"Yes, Bulgaria still has a culture of collectivism, not individualism. Bulgarians care about what others think. It's a culture of shame. And we live in the past. We have nostalgia for socialism. A few years ago a British survey concluded that Bulgarians are one of the least motivated workforces in the world."

"But obviously not all Bulgarians are like that. Look at yourself."

"True. In my paper, I argue that there are three types of Bulgarians.

First, there are those like me, who are modern and believe in the market economy. Second, there are those who are nostalgic for the tranquility and security of the sham socialist welfare. Third, there are those who have basically returned to the nineteenth century—to self-sufficiency through agriculture, natural exchanges, and reciprocal services. Look at all carts in Turkincha. Notice that many fields are being plowed with horses or oxen. It's like we're going backwards. The world is changing fast but Bulgaria's culture is too conservative to keep up."

"I suppose there's not much transparency in Bulgarian society either."

"No, there's not. Bulgarians prefer to manage everything by pulling strings, through illegal ways. This shows up in how we manage business relations. Then Bulgarians have a negative attitude towards entrepreneurs, believing that no one gets rich in an honest way. We look for excuses for our uneasy life. We buy into conspiracy theories. It's a mess. We need a cultural revolution."

"How does Bulgaria do that?"

"Bulgaria must realize that real welfare is in future opportunities. The more we open ourselves to the world and to new things, the better we will make use of those opportunities. We should consider globalization as an opportunity, not as a threat. Only in this way can our culture and the nation prosper."

Academics on Bulgaria's culture

Elly produced academic sources to show that she's not on the lunatic fringe. Some Bulgarian researchers argue that instead of creating entrepreneurs and inventors, Bulgaria has produced treasure hunters who seek to game the system. Bulgarians, like many Eastern Europeans, want to skip the hard work that it takes to build a strong capitalist economy. They just want the Western European welfare system without making the effort to fund them.[4]

Another Bulgarian academic argues that Bulgarians put the collective before the individual. They are intolerant of people who dare to distinguish themselves. Bulgarians pass their collectivist and conformist mentality to the next generation thereby making people dependent on inaccessible leaders.[5] In *The Virtues of the Bulgarian Person,* the Bulgarian author argues that Bulgarians need rules and laws to feel safe and protected, but they dislike obeying them. They prefer illegal deals and cozy affairs. Over a century ago, German travelers noted: "We haven't seen another nation that creates so many laws and abides by them so little."[6]

Bulgarians are cynical business people. They expect the other side to lie and cheat in every economic action.[7] According to a 150-country

Gallup survey in 2010, no other country had less confidence in their judicial system than Bulgaria (Lithuania was the second worst). Davor Rostuhar, my couchsurfing host in Zagreb, told me that Eastern Europeans ultimately support the corruption. He made his point one day when he exploded in fury in a Croatian fruit market after two vendors tried to overcharge him. He screamed so that everyone could hear, "You all complain about rich and powerful people being corrupt, but you're just as corrupt! Corruption starts here in the fruit market! We may be poor, but our values are just as corrupted as the rich!"

In addition to corruption, Bulgaria struggles to shake off lazy communist habits. In 2011, the World Bank reported on real labor productivity among many Europeans countries. Western Europeans were generally two to ten times more productive than Eastern Europeans (with exception of Finland). Bulgaria was the least productive of all. This implies that inefficient, bureaucratic, and slothful communist habits still linger in Eastern Europe.[8]

Like most people, Bulgarians don't like to work. The difference is that Bulgarians show us how it's done. A worldwide survey added up holidays, vacation days, and sick leave off in various countries. Bulgarians have, on average, 55 days off—more than any other major country. They have over 50 percent more paid time off than Americans, Japanese, and Germans. This sounds fabulous, but Bulgarians shouldn't be surprised that the rest of the world is out-competing them, resulting in fewer jobs, investments, and lower pay than more industrious countries. This slothful work culture is a communist legacy. As Eastern Europeans used to say, "They pretend they pay us, and we pretend we work."

Pew Research asked Bulgarians what was more important: that the state lets everyone "pursue their life's goals" or "that the state play an active role to guarantee that nobody is in need." The 2010 results indicated that two-thirds of Bulgarians under 40 years old and 76 percent of Bulgarians over 40 prefer the active, paternalistic state. That was the highest rate in Europe.

Bulgarian intellectuals and Bulgarian on the street agree: the communist ghost is still in the nation's closet. Westerners notice this once they scratch beneath the surface. As a result, a Bulgarian professor in Sofia wrote, "With the end of the ideological era, the Balkans slipped back to what they had been before the war, that is, a periphery of Europe: at best, a virgin frontier land to civilize, at worst, a ghetto to contain unwanted populations from emigrating to the West."[9]

Elly's insights, along with the academic literature, reveal why Bulgarians have a grim view of their lives. Gallup's Suffering Index is a composite score based on various surveys that measure how individuals see their present and future life. In 2010, Burundi had the worst score in the world, and was followed by Bulgaria. It's a strong indication of how down Bulgaria is. It has some nearby company: the next three positions were Macedonia, Tanzania, and Serbia; Hungary was eighth from the bottom. In 2011, 40 percent of Bulgarians were classified as "suffering," which was the highest percentage in the 124-country Gallup survey.

It's been two decades since the Yugoslav Wars and much of the Balkans has improved. Croatia will join the EU in 2013. Serbia has visa-free travel. Albania and Kosovo are doing better than ever. Unfortunately, Bosnia is still murky and Bulgaria is struggling. Referring to the Balkan Wars 100 years ago, one Romanian scholar observed, "It is as though some unwritten law proclaims that the Balkan countries can be happy only by turns and never all at the same time."[10]

On the bright side

I asked Elly what she missed about Bulgaria while she was living in Australia. She said, "I missed that here we know our neighbors and we usually become friends with them! In Australia (and everywhere else I've been), no one cared about their neighbors. We had three young girls living next door, but they never invited us to their parties, and every time we invited them to do something with us, they never came. It is weird, because Aussies are friendly people, but they do not like to know the people living around them!"

I said, "But is that Bulgarian tradition of knowing your neighbors also true in a big city like Sofia?"

She said, "Yes! It is because we live in big apartment blocks and people 'live together' kind of. The men fix their cars or drink beer in front of the blocks together, the women gossip and drink coffee with their neighbor housewives, and the children play with the children of the neighbors. This is also how I grew up!"

Clearly there are benefits of having a collectivist culture. Another related habit is that Bulgarians keep gatherings simple. Often Americans would rather meet their friends in a bar or restaurant than have a humble gathering at home or in a park; there's sometimes pressure to put on a "show" if people come over. Bulgarians have no such obligation.

Another positive communist legacy is that Bulgarians often don't turn on lights unless they need to. In villages, for example, they often don't have lights on in shops if the natural light is sufficient. When I walked through the University of Sofia, the hallways were dark. If it wasn't for all the students walking around, you would think that it was closed for the season, but they are obviously saving energy. Although they do it for financial reasons, it does reduce pollution since most Eastern Europeans, like most Americans, get their power from coal plants.

When Bulgarians want to call someone dimwitted, they say that he's slow like "an Albanian radiator." That's because in Bulgarian "to heat up" also means "to grasp." Apparently, Albanian radiators are of poor quality and slow to heat up. Ironically, a Bulgarian newspaper noted in a headline, "Even in Albania they describe slow-wittedness as a 'Bulgarian radiator.'" Therefore, let's just say that Elly was brainy like a Japanese radiator.

After our long and fascinating discussions, Elly had to go back to Sofia. We hugged goodbye. As she walked away, I thought of the ongoing struggle in her soul. It's a similar dilemma that many bright Eastern Europeans face: should they invest their time and talents in their country or should they take the more comfortable journey and live in an advanced country? Elly would enjoy a higher standard of living in Australia. Why deal with the uphill struggle of reforming Bulgaria's culture? Why not just move to a place whose culture is more in line with your own? At the same time, Bulgaria needs people like Elly to prosper. In 2011, Elly made her decision: she stayed in Sofia because, "I want to be happy around the people I care for."

Niki returns

The day after Elly left, Niki arrived from Greece, and the Turkincha village gossip immediately followed. I ignored the curious looks and let the villagers have their fun. I felt like yelling, "Hey, you don't need to whisper! I can't understand you anyway!"

Niki had taken an overnight train from Thessaloniki. She thought it would be fun to chill out in a Bulgarian village for a week. We went to Veliko Tarnovo where she got a taste of Eastern European service. The American service industry is filled with fake smiles. I miss them in Eastern Europe, where you often get a scowl mixed with an occasional grunt. It's a communist legacy. Sometimes I had to practically beg people to take my money. For example, a Bulgarian waitress advised us that we should probably go have dinner somewhere else because "the kitchen is very busy." Only a third of the seats were taken. We found better service in Arbanasi, a nearby historical town. We had a drink while enjoying a panoramic view of Veliko Tarnovo.

After relaxing a few days in Turkincha, we took a long walk to the twelfth-century Dryanovo Monastery. It was nicely rebuilt in the 1700s, but after having seen so many monasteries, I was suffering from *monastery overdose*. After a while, monasteries, like churches, begin to look similar. Churches are usually in cities, so it's easy to quickly check them out. Monasteries, on the other hand, are often in the middle of nowhere. When you finally see it, you ask, "Is that it?" You might experience *monastery regret:* "Why did I go through so much trouble to see this?"

Nevertheless, the Dryanovo Monastery, like most monasteries, is set among beautiful nature. For centuries, monks maintained trails that you can enjoy today. After hiking around its hills and having a picnic, we hitchhiked back to Turkincha. In the village cemetery, we discovered a curious Bulgarian tradition: to leave beer bottles next to gravestones. Sometimes they have flowers in the bottles, but the idea is that if the dead ever get thirsty, they can have a sip of beer.

One night we invited Vlado, Gosho, and their wives for dinner. Niki made a delicious Greek feast. Sadly, and all too quickly, our week of merrymaking ended and we had to go our separate ways. After our romantic goodbye, Niki returned to Thessaloniki, while I went to the part of Bulgaria that I've always wanted to see—its Black Sea coast.

Burgas, Nesebar, and Sunny Beach

Burgas was the first Black Sea city I visited. It's an important port with 200,000 people, but it's not as attractive as Nesebar, which is 35 kilometers (22 miles) away. Bozin Kostadinov, a 40-year-old couchsurfing host with no experience, invited me to stay with him there. Our first meeting illustrates the extraordinary trust and hospitality you can find when couchsurfing. He picked me up in his car, drove five minutes, took me to the fourth floor of a building, showed me a big room with four single beds, kitchen, and bathroom. He said, "This is your room. Sleep in any bed you like. I don't live in this building, but my mom lives in the apartment downstairs. If you need anything else, call me. Here are the keys. I gotta go. Bye!"

It's remarkable that a total stranger lets you crash in their empty apartment. Nevertheless, Bozin wasn't blindly trusting me. When a couchsurfing member has over 50 positive references and no negative references, then you can be sure that he or she will respect you and your property. As a result, many hosts gave me a key. What made Bozin unusual is that he didn't live in the building and that he spent less than five minutes verifying that I wasn't a criminal.

At 11:00 p.m., Bozin picked me up and took me to Nesebar's main Orthodox church for the Easter midnight service. Nesebar's Old Town is a UNESCO World Heritage Site set on an enchanting rocky isthmus surrounded by the Black Sea. In one hour, you can stroll by several Byzantine churches. Bozin pointed out historic buildings with Greek architecture—the first floor is made of stone and a second story is made of wood. He said, "For centuries Greeks were the main population in Nesebar and many other towns along Bulgaria's Black Sea coast."

I asked, "So what happened to them?"

"We did a population exchange with Greece."

"A *what?*"

"Parts of Greece had many Bulgarians and parts of Bulgaria had many Greeks. So about a century ago, when both countries wanted ethnic purity, they did an orderly population exchange. It's like a peaceful ethnic cleansing," he said with an ironic smile.

On Saturday morning, Bozin lent me a bicycle so I could revisit the old town and then bike a few kilometers to Slanchev Bryag. It's hard to promote a huge tourist town with a name like Slanchev Bryag. Try to say that and you'll prefer to go somewhere else. Therefore, Bulgarians advertise its English name: Sunny Beach. During the communist period, there was a special section of Sunny Beach that was only open to Westerners—not even Bulgarians could go there. Russians and other Eastern Bloc vacationers came often, but most of the development occurred in the last 20 years.

Nowhere else in Eastern Europe will you find a better example of ugly over-development than Sunny Beach. This once-pristine beach is now full of ugly 15-story high-rises and hotels. When Bulgaria discovered capitalism, it indulged in an orgy of Western money. Instead of developing tasteful and elegant high-rises, they just built functional ones. As a result, Sunny Beach has neither charm nor elegance. Yes, it's warm and the sand is great, but that's it. Still, that's good enough for the thousands of Western Europeans and Russians who have bought cheap apartments to use as vacation homes. Sunny Beach can hold 30,000 sun worshipers, yet the hotels can house 100,000 people. And then there are thousands of condos. Do the math.

Easter lunch

Bozin invited me to join 11 of his relatives in the countryside for an Easter lunch. It was April 19 and it was warm enough to eat outside. All the generations were represented, from the five-year-old Bulgarian boy to the wrinkled, friendly grandmother. Most couldn't speak English, but they welcomed the American anyway.

Bulgarian cuisine is a refreshing relief from the standard heavy Eastern European food. Nearly every meal features a generous salad, like a *shopka salad*. In our case, we had a finely chopped spinach salad mixed with green onions. As a side dish, we had feta cheese and chopped hard-boiled eggs. The main dish had sticky rice with veggies and stewed pork. People were drinking juice and beer in two-liter bottles. The centerpiece of the meal were the many colorful Easter eggs. Other popular Bulgarian cuisine options include the *banitsa* (cheese pastry), *boza* (fermented soft drink), *rakiya* (brandy), *kebabche* (spicy sausages), and *kavarma* (stew). Bulgarians will grill anything, but pork is their prime target.

Before sunset, Bozin took me to the bus stop where I could catch a bus to Varna, Bulgaria's biggest city on the Black Sea. I thanked him immensely for his outstanding hospitality, climbed into the bus, and continued my journey north along the Black Sea. In Varna, I would have a unique couchsurfing experience.

Trusting hosts in Varna

It's not clear what the Thracians called their Black Sea settlement 6,000 years ago, but the Greeks called it *Odessos* in the six century BC. By the end of WWII, the Bulgarians, to honor the Soviet leader, changed the name of the city to *Stalin*. They were trying to kiss ass and make up for the fact that they were against the USSR for most of WWII. After they did their brown nosing, the Bulgarians changed the name back to its original name: *Varna*.

After writing to several couchsurfing hosts in Varna, Rumyana Doncheva accepted me. Rumi warned me that her studio didn't have a shower and the bathroom was in the hallway, shared with others on the floor. I told her that I'm used to camping, so such conditions were luxurious. She also told me that she wouldn't be able to pick me up at the bus station, but that Martin Marinov, one of her couchsurfing friends, would be able to meet me at the bus station. When Martin picked me up, we walked 30 minutes to Rumi's studio apartment and took the elevator to the top floor. Martin let me into the small studio, told me that Rumi wouldn't be staying in this apartment that night, gave me the keys, and left.

At this point, I started to wonder if Bulgarians have a tradition of giving random strangers keys to their homes and walking away. At least Bozin talked with me for five minutes before leaving me the keys to the kingdom, but Rumi gave them to me without even having met me! Of course, she must have checked my couchsurfing reputation before entrusting me, but it's still amazing. Westerners often think of Eastern Europe as a dangerous and barbaric land, but such examples prove the opposite is true.

That night, I went out with Orlin Dimitrov, another couchsurfing member. He was a web developer. He looked like a classic geek: a chubby guy wearing nerdy glasses. Like most geeks, he was smart and intellectually curious. After a long walk and a drink, I asked him what we can learn from Bulgarians. He said, "When there is a problem, we usually don't make such a fuss about it. On the other hand, maybe that's why we have so many problems!"

The next morning, Rumi, Martin, and Lidiya took me on a tour of Varna. We walked the pedestrian Knyaz Boris I Street and eventually turned toward Primorski Park, an eight-kilometer long park that adjoins the beach. The coolest part of the beach is that it has a couple of hot springs that pop out and flow into the sea. The best section has antiquated public pools where fat middle-aged Bulgarian men like to bathe in. We had an enjoyable tea by the sea and then we said goodbye—I would be going to Romania.

The world's fastest disappearing country

Back in 2009, I struck up a conversation with a 26-year-old Bulgarian who was walking his dog in a park in Sofia. I asked him if he had a girlfriend or children. He didn't, but he wanted a family. When I asked him how many children he wanted, he said, "I want at least four children! Bulgarians aren't having babies, so our population is going down. It's a crisis!"

Although Bulgaria doesn't need to outlaw condoms just yet, Bulgarians are an endangered species. According to the CIA, Bulgaria is depopulating faster than any other country on Earth. In 2011, it was shrinking at 0.78 percent per year. It's got company—Eastern Europe leads the world's depopulation boom. For example, right above Bulgaria are Montenegro, Estonia, Ukraine, Latvia, Russia, and Serbia. In fact, most of the 30 countries that have a negative population growth rate are from Eastern Europe. If this keeps up, I'll have to call the next edition of this book *The Hidden Europeans*.

Bulgaria is like a deflating balloon. In 1989, it had nine million people. In 2001, it had eight million. In 2021, it will have seven million. Still, when you visit, don't expect to see apartment buildings becoming vacant before your eyes. Unlike the Black Death or WWII, this depopulation is relatively slow. Nevertheless, the decline, according to the EU's predictions, will continue so that by 2060, Bulgaria's population will drop to 5.5 million.[11]

As Eastern Europe goes, so goes the world

For once, the world is following Eastern Europe's lead. Let's examine fertility rates, which indicate the average number of babies a woman produces. Today's worldwide fertility rate is 2.5. The Goldilocks fertility rate, where you have a stable population, is approximately 2.1 (because not all children make it to reproductive age). Fertility rates are dropping faster than ever. Britain went from having 5 children per woman to 2 in 130 years (1800–1930). It's taken South Korea just 20 years to do that (1965–1985). Meanwhile, Iran dropped from a fertility rate of 7 to 1.8 from 1984 to 2011. From 1950 to 2011, Europe's fertility rate dropped in half. In the 1970s, 24 countries had fertility rates of 2.1 or less; today, there are nearly 100 countries. In Germany, Italy, and Japan, about a quarter of women who are in their 40s are childless. Clearly, fertility rates are going down the tubes.

A country's *population growth rate* doesn't just depend on its fertility rate, but also on its death rate and immigration/emigration rate.

Eastern Europe scores below average on all these metrics. During the 1990s, for example, Russia became the first developed country to see its life expectancy decrease, which increased its death rate. Life expectancies throughout Eastern Europe declined in the 1990s and are still below their 1970 level. Moreover, once the Berlin Wall vanished, millions of Eastern Europeans emigrated west. Few came to fill the void. Thus, a low fertility rate, an increasing death rate, and a net emigration have created the perfect storm for Eastern Europeans to disappear in.

For example, consider Bulgaria's vanishing act. Yes, its fertility rate is relatively low (1.42 in 2011), but there are 18 European (mostly Eastern European) countries that have lower fertility rates. In fact, Bulgarian women bear children earlier than any other EU country (26.6 years old).[12] Therefore, one big reason Bulgaria has the world's fastest depopulation growth rate is that Bulgarians are running for the exits. To halt that exodus, Bulgaria needs to implement the cultural and economic reforms that Elly talked about. Otherwise, the brain (and body) drain will continue.

In 2012, we will cross two important population milestones. First, half the world's countries will have fertility rates of 2.1 or less. Second, we will have seven billion humans on Earth. In 2016, according the UN Population Division, the majority of the world will be below the replacement rate. By 2020, the entire planet will dip below the replacement rate for the first time in human history.

Of course, the world's population growth rate *must* slow down. That's because, according to the UN, *if the world fertility rates stayed exactly where they are today, in 2150 we'd have 244 billion people and by 2300 we'd have 134 trillion!*[13] At that point, sardines would start using the expression of being "packed like humans." Obviously, our current growth rate is unsustainable. Still, let's explore an outrageous question: can we (and will we) pack one trillion humans on the Earth?

Why the world population won't decline

When you live in Eastern Europe, it's tempting to conclude that humans are going the way of the dinosaurs. Nevertheless, over the next 38 years, we'll add 2.3 billion humans to the planet, so that we'll have roughly 9.3 billion in 2050. Unless a catastrophe happens, that forecast is certain. What happens after 2050, however, is debatable.

Many pundits believe that Eastern Europe is a preview of coming attractions for the rest of the world—that our global population will decline as wealth spreads (once a country's per capita GDP approaches $10,000, the fertility rate usually drops below 2.1). Thus, depopulationists forecast that we'll revisit five billion someday. Others predict that we'll find a happy equilibrium around 10 billion. They're both wrong.

To understand why, consider Bulgaria, which expects its 2060 population to be 40% less than it was in 1989. How will Bulgaria cope with that? Will 40% of its homes be vacant in 2050? Will 40% of schools and farms close? Will businesses sell 40% fewer goods? Will there be 40% more parking spots available? It depends. Bulgaria can easily deal with this change if it were the only one experiencing it. Their economy can grow with a declining population by exporting more and inviting immigrants to fill the labor shortage. Easy. Hong Kong has been doing this for a while.

However, what happens when all of Europe (or all of the world) experiences a similar decline? We would see deflation, GDPs dropping year after year, and ghost towns becoming ghost cities. Immigration could slow down the effects, but nationalists would cry that immigrants are "diluting" the country's culture. Nations with 1.3 fertility rates need to import immigrants equal to 1.5 percent of their population every year—that's five times America's current immigration rate and over 10 times the EU immigration rate. Europeans, who are more anti-immigrant than Americans, would revolt. Eastern Europeans can't attract Western European immigrants and they're too xenophobic to attract Asian, Middle Eastern, or African immigrants. So would they just watch their economy implode or start handing out Viagra for free?

Another challenge: aging and declining populations have little hope of paying off their national debt. Governments are used to growing their way of out of debt, but that strategy becomes difficult with widespread depopulation. For example, one rating agency predicts that Greece (with a meager population growth rate of 0.083%) will not regain its 2008 GDP level until 2017. If Greece (and most of the world) were seriously depopulating, it would never see its real 2008 GDP level again. The Greeks would have to declare bankruptcy, or sell the Acropolis.

Such a fate frightens Eastern European governments, which is why they're scrambling to stop the decline. Estonia's government, for example, started offering 10 months of maternity leave. The benefit was increased to 12 months in 2007 and then 18 months in 2008. That boosted their fertility rate by five percent. In 2011, Slovenia was depopulating by 0.16 percent per year, so the government reacted. If you have one child, Slovenians will get as little as $25 per month. However, if you have three or more children, Slovenians can get up to $150 *per child*, plus basic medical care and free education through the university level. The extra $450 per month for a three-child family (versus $25 for one child) is meaningful in Slovenia.

Russia is taking action too. In 1991, it had a population of 150 million. Today, it's 140 million. The UN estimates that if the immigration in Russia stops and if their 1.42 fertility rate doesn't increase, then by

2050 Russia's population may plummet by a third, resulting in a population of 92 million. In 2006, Vladimir Putin highlighted these issues in his 2006 state of union address and then doubled monthly support payments and gave $9,200 for every second child. In July 2011, Russia passed a law to restrict abortion (Russia had 1.3 million abortions in 2009). All these actions have helped Russia's depopulation rate slow down dramatically.

Western Europe is also taking action. In 1994, France's fertility rate had dropped to 1.6. The government panicked and began granting women four months of paid maternity leave, abundant part-time work, job protection, affordable childcare, and benefits that offset education, housing, and transportation expenses. As a result, France's fertility rates soared to 1.96 in 2011. Add some immigration and France's population is now growing by 0.5 percent annually. Nordic countries are also growing partly because mothers get generous financial benefits. Even Italy offered $1,400 one-time payment for the second child. Thus, most rich countries that dip below the 2.1 rate, drop to about 1.3, and then start going back up.

This pattern is also apparent when you compare the UN's Human Development Index (HDI) with fertility rates. The HDI measures life expectancy, average income per person, and education level. Fertility declines as the HDI increases, but countries with extremely high HDI scores usually see their fertility rates swing back up to nearly 2.1.[14] Part of the rise comes from immigrants, who tend to have more children than the locals. However, much of the rise comes from incentives to have unprotected shagging.[15]

Boosting babies

Europe has a history of encouraging babies. Mussolini wanted to increase the population by 20 million, so he taxed bachelors heavily and gave financial aid to large families. Italy had childbearing contests where the winners were paraded as national heroes, given medals, sent on tours, and celebrated in magazines. Abortion and contraception were criminalized. Nazi Germany and Spain took similar actions around the same time. German mothers got the Cross of Honor, while the father got cash awards. Tito supposedly promised to be the godfather of any woman's ninth child in Kosovo. If current depopulation trends continue, Bulgaria and others will revisit such policies.

That seems like an absurd idea, but it won't be once the full impact of depopulation hits Europe. In 1900, Europe represented 25 percent of the world's population; by 2060, it will be six percent (a third of those will be senior citizens). As proud Europe sinks into irrelevance, don't you think its leaders will sweeten the incentives to reproduce? When they do so, Europeans will start spending more time in the bedroom.

If the world population doesn't decrease, then won't it stabilize? No. Let's do the math. To achieve zero percent population growth, we'll need roughly half the world to have a positive growth rate and half the world to have a negative growth rate. In 2010, 16 percent of the countries had a negative growth rate, while 84 percent had a positive growth rate (only the Vatican was perfectly flat). Those who have a negative growth rate are offering big carrots to become positive again—many are succeeding. In conclusion, it's hard to imagine half of the world's countries being satisfied with a prolonged negative population growth rate, which means that a stable world population is a pipe dream.

Why the world population will boom beyond 100 billion

If you accept that nations will not tolerate a consistently declining population and that a stable population is unrealistic, then there is only one possible conclusion: the world population will continue rising until it hits a resource constraint. In his *Essay on the Principle of Population,* Thomas Malthus predicted that humans would outstrip the food supply in 1798. Ironically, over 200 years later, the biggest health problem we have is obesity. Furthermore, the percentage of our income spent on food is at an all-time low—indicating that food is cheaper than ever.

Although Malthus's timing was way off, his logic wasn't. How far can we stretch our resources before we hit a population wall? What's Earth carrying capacity? Answering that will take us off the main topic of this book, but it's worth briefly discussing because it has implications for the long-term future of Eastern Europe and the world.

There are two ways to halt (or reverse) our population growth. One is a cataclysm: a massive asteroid, a planet-wide synchronized eruption of volcanoes, out-of-control global warming, a glacial period, a planetary pandemic, or a global nuclear war. Don't overestimate pandemics and war. Aside from the bubonic plague in the mid-1300s (when Europe lost a third of its population), the world population hasn't declined from any pandemic (it didn't suffer a net decline during the 1919 Spanish flu). Even the deadliest war in human history could not stop our growth—the world's net population grew every year during WWII.

The only other way to stop population growth is if we run out of food and water. We're getting better at seeding clouds so that it rains where and when we want. We're improving ways to desalinate and purify water. Such innovations in this century will give us an oceanic water supply, which will allow us to transform coastal deserts into farmland. This water revolution could feed tens of billions.

We're not space-constrained either: at seven billion, humans occupy four percent of the planet's surface with only a fraction of humans living in space-efficient skyscrapers. We could theoretically put seven billion into Texas with room to spare. We could also build artificial island metropolises on the oceans. I'm not suggesting that living in a world with 100 billion people would be fun. Indeed, those who lived in Biblical times would probably dislike our current human density, although they would probably think that lethal injection is an improvement over crucifixion.

We won't run out of energy either. Solar and nuclear energy will be cheaper than fossil fuels long before we run out of fossil fuels. We're harvesting a fraction of one percent of the sun's energy today—we've got a long way to go before we've used up that power source. With power, food, and water, we can keep expanding. Assuming we continue growing our population at one percent per year, then in 2050 we'll have 10 billion, in 2100 we'll reach 16.8 billion, and in 2280 we'll hit 100 billion. But why stop? In 2441, we'd reach 500 billion, and in 2512 we'd hit *one trillion*.

These numbers seem absurd. However, if you had told Christopher Columbus that his world's population of 400 million would be 17 times bigger 500 years later, he would have said, "Oh, sure. And the world is flat." Similarly, envisioning a world population of 119 billion (that's 17 times bigger than today) seems ludicrous, but many underestimate technological progress. Had you told a caveman that one day there would be one million humans on the planet, he would have cried, "Impossible! There are not enough caves!"

Among the most revolutionary technological changes will be when *Homo sapiens* become— what I call—*Homo enhanced*. Ever since the industrial revolution, we've been adding one year to human life expectancy every four years. If that keeps up, then in 100 years, the average human will live to 100. In fact, by 2050, the average life expectancy in Japan will probably be 95 years. The Homo enhanced will tweak their genes to increase their longevity, even if it means they can't reproduce with *Homo sapiens*. The narcissistic Homo enhanced species will clone themselves, which will balloon the world population. Moreover, the Homo enhanced will extend their life by growing organs in labs and becoming cyborgs who may even run on electricity, not glucose. That will free them from food production and instead focus on harvesting nuclear or solar energy, which will allow us to get to one trillion Homo enhanced people, and a handful of *Homo sapiens* in zoos.

Paradoxically, extending human life so that we live for hundreds of years might stop human population growth. People who expect to live 500 years would vote to pass draconian laws that limit human reproduction. We can tolerate the population tripling in our lifetime, but knowing that it will go up 142 times in our 500-year lifespan will motivate us to tax children (instead of offering them tax credits as we do now). If that doesn't work, we'll send out the Castration Police.

These ideas probably sound as crazy as the concept of cultivating crops and raising livestock sounded to a caveman. My only hope is that someday, around the year 2512, some intergalactic archeologist dusts off this book and says, "This idiot predicted that our population would be one trillion! Ha! The foolish numbskull couldn't imagine that we actually reached 10 trillion!"

Sarah Spiridonov's reflections

Before we end this chapter, let's return to the year 2011, when our planet had fewer than seven billion humans. I was grateful for Sarah Spiridonov's family for letting me stay in their Turkincha home. I was curious about Sarah's perspective, since she's an American who is married to a Bulgarian, and visits Bulgaria every year. She said, "My greatest personal lesson from my Bulgarian friends and family has been to become much less materialistic, and instead to view life as a series of events that brings close friends and family together, and our possessions help us to do that. In my American life, I see lots of people idolizing their possessions and enjoying them individually, protecting them from others, instead of sharing them."

I asked her, "What surprised you most when you came to Turkincha?"

She said, "Our neighbors made us feel welcome. Every day they were calling for us over the fence to give us some plums, some eggs, some tomatoes, then maybe some more plums. Every day. Never mind that we had more plum trees than them. Other villagers brought us things too. For example, early one morning a kind lady came by to give me warm (just milked) goat milk. She instructed me to boil it and then serve it to my boys for breakfast so they could have some fresh goat milk—it was good for them, she said. The boys really weren't crazy about warm goat milk in a two-liter Fanta bottle—but I am sure if we lived there, they would have appreciated the generous offer much more!"

"Yeah, they would have asked for a refill."

"My relatives called this the 'village exchange.' Whenever you have something, you give some away. If you have goats, you give goat milk away, if you have plums, you give plums, if you have honey, you give honey, just because you have it. This stabilizes a living situation where you are basically relying on your own garden produce and the sometimes-rare visit by younger relatives to bring you something from town. It is a generous spirit between villagers who recognize that they need each other to live."

"How does that compare to America?"

"It's completely the opposite of how Americans live. I think we often pretend that we achieve our success on our own, and to some degree we don't need others to get on in life in the US, but in Bulgaria you are truly interdependent on a network of family, friends and contacts to get past personal barriers, bureaucracy, economic losses, and lack of fruit or vegetables in your garden!"

"It's the upside of the collective culture."

"Yes, I really do feel that people are much more important in Bulgaria to each other than they are in the US. I feel that people there are constantly in contact with each other, talking to each other, and appreciating each other. It's a common thing for Bulgarian immigrants in the US to feel lonely, and to feel a lack of human contact. My family also really enjoys the people that surround us when we are there. An American friend was asking me about shopping in Bulgaria, where to go, and what to buy. I wanted to shout that the moments that really should be enjoyed were the moments with people at the table, sharing warm conversation and jokes. What she should treasure are the warm hearts and generous spirit in Bulgaria, not souvenirs!"

What Bulgaria Can Teach Us

- **Consider defying standards.** Whether it's being the first to adopt the Cyrillic alphabet, abandon grammatical cases, or shaking your head to mean yes, Bulgarians have defied standards. Standards are usually useful, but every once in a while it's good to challenge them.
- **Dim or turn off the lights.** Bulgarians conserve energy by turning off any light that they are not using. For example, museums even turn off lights when there isn't anyone in the room. If you forget to turn things off, then use a timer. In America, bright lights flood the stores. In Bulgaria, many of the stores outside the big cities didn't have any lights on if natural lighting was sufficient. Yes, bright light is more convenient, but let's save money and pollute less.
- **Get to know your neighbors.** Whether they're in a village or in a high-rise, Bulgarians get to know their neighbors. They form a natural community and support group. Do the same and reach out to your neighbors.
- **Have more simple gatherings.** Often in America people don't want to invite people to their homes because many view it as a big production. Instead, many of Americans just stay home and watch TV. If they do meet friends, they do it at a bar or restaurant. However, this ends up costing the group more money. It's cheaper to do what Bulgarians do, host a humble get-together at your house, offer tea or snacks, and

keep things simple. The point is to turn off the TV and have friends over instead.

- **Opening your home to strangers.** Every culture in the world has a tradition of being hospitable to strangers. However, some countries do it better than others. Eastern Europeans are more guarded than most cultures, but Bulgarians, with their collectivist mindset, welcome strangers better than most Eastern Europeans.
- **Live with a low birth rate.** Bulgarians are disappearing faster than any other nation, but they are panicking less than other depopulating countries. Let's hope nations focus on the advantages of having more elbowroom and stop calling a declining population a "problem." The best way to solve all our environmental troubles is to accept and enjoy the benefits of a depopulating nation.

Places I saw and recommend in Bulgaria: Veliko Tarnovo, Rila Mountains, Rhodope Mountains, Nesebar, and Sofia.

Travel deals and info for Bulgaria: http://ftapon.com/bulgaria

By leaving Bulgaria, we're also finally leaving, after 10 chapters, the fascinating and enigmatic Balkans. I will miss it. It's home to Europe's friendliest and most passionate people. Its paradoxes and mysteries will send you on profound historical and ethnographic treasure hunts. Along the way, you'll enjoy extraordinary cuisine, pleasant weather, and an occasional war.

A few geographers have placed Romania in the Balkans. However, I agree with the majority of geographers who use the Danube River as the northern Balkan border, which would put nearly all of Romania outside the Balkans. Some Romanians want to exclude themselves based on the Balkan connotation. For example, in 1999, the Romanian writer, Alexandru George, wrote, "I think that is an insult to say Romania is situated in the Balkans. . . . This term (which is disgraceful, fabricated in the old times by the Chancellery of Vienna) should be excluded, under the penalty of law, from the vocabulary of the employees of the Ministry [of Foreign Affairs]. . . . Compared to Serbs' and Turks' cruelty. . . Bulgarians' dull earnestness, Greeks' craziness, and Russians' cruel fanaticism, we are a white spot on the map of Europe."[16]

Yeah. We'll see about that.

22
ROMANIA—THE LATIN OASIS

HALLELUJAH! THAT'S WHAT I shouted when I first entered Romania. It was September 2004 and I had spent the previous four months traveling in countries that spoke languages that were either Baltic, Slavic, or Martian (i.e., Hungarian and Albanian). For many moons I was hopelessly illiterate: my knowledge of Romance languages was useless and my ludicrously simple Russian was futile. Finally, I found an Eastern European language that felt familiar and easy. Sure, I only understood about 20 percent of it, but Romania felt like a Latin oasis in a Slavic desert.

The Romanian language brings up the tiresome defining-Eastern-Europe debate again. We've primarily used geography to define Eastern Europe, although we've also considered Eastern Europe's common historical connection to communism. Still, there's another way to draw Europe's east-west dividing line: using the Catholic-Orthodox borderline. In that case, Lithuania, Poland, Hungary, Slovakia, Croatia, and Slovenia would all fall on the Catholic side, while Russia, Belarus, Ukraine, Romania, and much of the Balkans would fall in the Orthodox camp. Such a division would be meaningful if Eastern Europeans took religion seriously. However, communism's atheistic tendencies diminished the importance of religion in most Eastern European countries (with the exception of Poland and Romania). In fact, Estonia, Latvia, and Czechia have more non-believers than believers. Thus, using religion as an Eastern European dividing line is inadequate.

Yet another way to draw the Eastern Europe border is by using the Slavic language. This would create a nice contiguous bloc if only Romania and Moldova were Slavic, but they're not. To illustrate just how important language is, notice how Russia generally has better relations with Slavic Eastern European countries than the non-Slavic ones (Baltic, Albania, Hungary, Romania, and Moldova). Therefore, Romania ruins the potential contiguous linguistic unity in Eastern Europe because it is a Latin island in a sea of Slavs.

Romanian language

Romanian sounds like a language that was invented by an Italian who grew up in Russia. For example, they say *da* (*yes*) and about 14% of their words have a Slavic origin. Some Romanians, like Nicolae Stanciu, a lecturer of Romanian Language and Civilization, prefer to minimize their Slavic ties. He told me that although 3,000 Romanian words have a Slavic origin, that's less than 2% of the vocabulary. That is hard to believe given that Romanians have lived next to and traded with Slavs for centuries; the 14% estimate seems more reasonable. Nicolae also told me that 60% of Romanian comes from French words. Other sources say that French/Italian words are only about 38%, although overall about 80% comes from Latin. Regardless, it's clear that Romania is far more Latin than Slavic.

For example, *la revedere* (goodbye) alludes to *arrivederci* or *au revoir*; *scuzati-mã* (excuse me) and *bunã seara* (good evening) sound like *mi scusi* and *buona sera* in Italian. If you know a Romance language, you could understand these Romanian phrases: *unde este un hotel* (where is a hotel?); *pot plãti în monedã localã?* (can I pay with local money?); *unde este biroul pentru bagaje de mânã?* (where is the left-luggage room?); *multi ani!* (happy birthday!); *nu înţeleg* (I don't understand); *cum se chema?* (what's it called?); *cît costâ?* (how much is it?); *bunǎ* (hello); and *ne* (no). The origin of some words is less obvious: *vǎ rog* (please) and *mulţumesc* (thank you).

> O babă bălană mănâncă o banană babană.
> — *Romanian tongue twister meaning, "A blond old lady eats a huge banana."*

Romance language speakers can easily learn the days of the week (starting with Monday): *luni, marţi, miercuri, joi, vineri, sîmbătă, duminică.* Counting from one to ten is elementary: *unu, doi, trei, patru, cinci, šase, šapte, opt, nuoǎ, zece.* Even transport vehicles sound familiar: *vaporul* (boat, like the Italian *vaporeto*), *autobusul, trenul, tramvaiul,* and *avionul.* Because words were familiar, I could guess the meaning of Romanian sentences, like this saying: *cea mai bunǎ legumǎ e carnea de pui şi cea mai buna carne de pui e carnea de porc* (the best vegetable is chicken meat and the best chicken meat is pork).

Where do Romanians come from?

Because Eastern Europeans are obsessed with who-got-there-first, they like to argue about the Romanian roots. We've heard such debates about the origins of Hungarians, Albanians, and Macedonians. One side tries to claim that they've been there "forever," while the other side tries to claim that that's a lie and that they showed up yesterday. In short, "I'm native and you're not." Because our language is our flag, we look to linguistic history to answer this childish debate.

Romanians say that they're products of the Roman colonization of Romania. By 106 AD, the Romans had conquered much of the Dacian Kingdom (which was basically where Romania is today). We know little about the Dacian language, but we know that the Romans imposed their Vulgar Latin language on the region when they colonized it. By 271 AD, the Roman Empire retreated from its Dacia Province. It's unclear if Latin-speaking locals stayed behind or left temporarily and returned hundreds of years later. Assuming European habits haven't changed much, I'd bet that they stuck around.

This leaves us with three mysteries. Why did a Latin language survive in Romania, but not in the Balkans, which the Romans had also colonized? Why did the Romans have such a long-term linguistic impact during their relatively short 165-year rule over Dacia, whereas they had hardly any such impact on the Balkans? Why did the Slavs (who showed up hundreds of years after the Roman colonization) fail to impose a Slavic language on Romania?

I couldn't find definitive answers, so here's my theory (which may be neither original nor correct). Dacia was rich in precious metals, so the Romans colonized it more intensely than the Balkans. As a result, when the Roman Empire eventually retreated, it left behind a critical mass of Latin-speaking people in the region to resist the Slavic takeover. Thus, the Roman descendents adopted Cyrillic and the Orthodox faith, but not the Slavic language.

Alternative origin theories

A few Slavic and Hungarian intellectuals try to argue that the Romanian language (and by implication, its speakers) is a relatively new arrival in Eastern Europe. For example, János Molnar told me that some Hungarians believe that Romanian evolved out of a Slavic tongue about 200 years ago. He wrote, "I heard this theory from the renowned Hungarian culture-historian Pap Gabor. He said that those were observations made by a Romanian linguist, who himself was flabbergasted by what he saw. I have never seen old or new Romanian texts, so I have no idea about its validity. However, Pap Gabor is an academic authority and would not say such a thing if it were not true."

When you consider both sides, ask yourself what is harder to believe: that Romans conquered and colonized what Romania is today and that Romanian is simply a descendent of the Vulgar Latin that Romans spoke, or that 200 years ago, Romanians, who were surrounded by Slavs, suddenly got the bright idea of ditching their 'Slavic language' and adopting a Latin-based language.

What most sane scholars will agree on is that about 200 years ago Romanians stopped writing their language in Cyrillic. At that time, Romanian intellectuals wanted to emphasize the Latin-Italian connection, so they adopted the Latin alphabet. As we saw in the previous chapter, we could write English using Cyrillic characters without changing the vocabulary, pronunciation, and grammar. It was easy to make such changes when most of the population was illiterate.

The poor man's Paris

After being instantly attracted to Romania's language, I was drawn into Romania's capital, Bucharest. It wasn't easy getting there, however. I arrived in Ruse, Bulgaria in the afternoon and there were no trains going across the Danube to Romania until 3:30 a.m. Therefore, I tried walking across the bridge, but that was impossible. I returned to the train station, pulled out my sleeping bag, and camped on a table next to a Jordanian gastroenterologist.

Bucharest feels like a poor man's Paris. Romanians would rather you call it *Little Paris,* or at least *The Paris of the Balkans*. Whatever you call it, it's lovely. In the late 1800s, French and French-trained architects completely remodeled Bucharest. As a result, it's filled with glorious *Belle Époque* buildings. They have their own *Arcul de Triumf* (Triumphal Arch), which is dedicated to the reunification of Romania after WWI. They even have a wide, tree-lined boulevard that is 3.2 kilometers long. To taunt the French, they made their boulevard six meters longer than Paris's Champs-Elysées.

Romania's adoption of French architecture is symbolic of their desire to associate themselves with the West and not with its neighbors. Romanian historian Adrian Cioroianu wrote in his article "The Impossible Escape: Romanians and the Balkans" that, "Should you intend to offend someone in Romania, tell him he behaves *like a Balkan,* and nine of ten chances, he will get angry."[1] That's ironic because being overly emotional and quick to anger is a stereotypical Balkan trait.

Romania kept looking west. After ditching the Cyrillic alphabet in favor of the Latin one, Romanians converted Slavic words from their Orthodox practices and replaced them with Latin ones in 1859. In the 1920s, Romanian hero Nicolae Iorga claimed that Slavic influences in Romanian were "superficial" and that you didn't need to use Slavic words to speak Romanian. That's funny, because the most basic of word in Romanian has a Slavic origin: *da* (yes). Nevertheless, Iorga insisted, "The Romanians are more neighbors to Paris than to Belgrade and Sofia."[2] Romanians encouraged the image by calling their country the *Belgium of the Orient.*

> *A country does not belong to the place where it lies, but to the target it looks at. — Nicolae Iorga, Romanian historian*

In short, Romanians feel like an alien among the "savage" Slavs. Like Hungarians, Romanians feel that they're special and feel that they should be part of the Western European club. Still, despite all the French architecture, the Latin language, and the self-aggrandizing visions, Romanians shouldn't completely deny their Eastern European DNA. As Romanian historian Adrian Cioroianu put it, "[Romanians] are concomitantly *inside* and *outside,* actors *in* and audience *at* a play; owing to this ambiguity, they neither perform nor watch very well."[3]

Traversing the Transylvanian Alps

After Bucharest, I went to Transylvania armed with a stake, cross, mirror, and garlic breath. I started by going to Sinaia, a Carpathian resort town that is home to the fairy-tale Peleş Castle. It's one of Eastern Europe's finest castles. It's quite humbling that it was only the "summer residence" of a Romanian king. Unfortunately, the tour only showed us the first floor, because the "second floor can't handle so many tourists." Why can't they use the admission fees to reinforce the floor? During the tour, an Oxford-educated man was surprised to discover that Romania was no longer a monarchy. (It hasn't been one since 1947.) See, Americans aren't the only ignorant ones!

From Sinaia, I wanted to see Bran, which is close if you're a bird. You'd just have to fly over the Transylvanian Alps. A sensible tourist would take a circuitous bus ride around the towering mountains. Instead, I acted like a flightless bird. I went to Busteni and climbed over Romania's second tallest mountain.

Whenever I backpacked in Eastern Europe, I would stash most of my gear in a locker so that I could travel fast and light. However, since I wasn't doing a loop this time, I had to take everything with me. I was grateful to have lost nearly half my gear during the previous months. Nevertheless, in 2004, I hadn't mastered ultralight tourism, so I had two backpacks (a big one and a small day-pack). I cursed my heavy gear as I lumbered up the Transylvanian Alps.

> *To see far is one thing, going there is another.*
> *— Constantin Brâncuşi, Romanian sculptor*

When I arrived at the summit of Mount Omul (*Omul* means *Human*), I met someone even more unexpected than Count Dracula—a beautiful, thin 28-year-old plastic surgeon. Her name was Corina Nicolae and she was with this fat, old guy. He didn't look like Dracula, so at first I didn't understand why she was with him. His name was Horia and he didn't speak much English. They were both plastic surgeons who were staying at the Mt. Omul Hut. The hut's kitchen served us a bean and sausage soup, which we enjoyed on an outdoor table overlooking the majestic Carpathian mountain range. Corina and I only talked for 30 minutes, but over the next five years we would occasionally chat over the Internet. In 2009, she invited me to stay at her apartment, but that story comes later.

Back in 2004, I wasn't thinking about the next five years—I was just worried about the next five hours, because that's how much daylight remained. Having lost my tarp in Bulgaria, I needed to hurry to get below the tree line and find a place to camp. Corina and Horia wished me luck while I hiked away with my cumbersome load. I dreamed of returning with a lighter load and thru-hiking the Carpathians, which form a backwards "C" across Romania. Such a month-long trek would surely be magical.

The spooky cabin

In case you're unsure, what follows is a true story. Daylight had nearly vanished when I got below the tree line and found a cabin that looked like the cabin at the end of the *Blair Witch Project* horror movie. It was dark and dusty. The wooden floors creaked loudly. A pitiful red LED was my only light source. This was creepy.

There were several openings on both levels for anything to enter. I hadn't seen anyone in hours. The cabin appeared empty, although a spider raced across the floor. As I went deeper into the cabin and walked under a collapsed portion of the second floor, a large owl flapped its wings and flew out of a window. I was in Transylvania. Dracula's Castle was just down the mountain. I lay down on the cold, dusty wooden floor and eventually fell asleep. Then something woke me up in the dead of the night.

It was the disturbing sound of something chewing either my sleeping pad or sleeping bag. It was as if it were making its way to my flesh. My food was on my left side. This thing was clawing on my right. Could it be a bat? Will it go for my neck? Is this a nightmare? Or am I already dead?

Not knowing the size of the creature, I swung my fist into the darkness. I pounded the ground. The chewing stopped.

It was so dark that I couldn't see my hand in front of my face. I fumbled for my red LED. I reached for my glasses. The air in the room was deathly cold. I finally turned on the blood-red light. I could see my breath in the chilling air. Disturbed dust floated in the air.

I scanned around. Nothing. Was it a rat? A bat? Or a vampire?

I'll never know.

The real Dracula

Dracula truly ran around Transylvania in the 1400s. His father's name was Vlad Dracul. In Romania, if your father is named Dracul, then you become the diminutive: Dracula. When the evil prince Dracula became an adult, he adopted a new name: Vlad Ţepeş. For Romanians, Ţepeş was a far more chilling name than Dracula because Ţepeş means *Impaler.* He became Mr. Impaler because he had a cruel habit of impaling his enemies. If you angered Dracula, he would carefully drive a wooden stake through your backbone without rupturing any of your vital nerves, so that you would suffer in agony for at least 48 hours before dying. The medieval period is misnamed. It should be called the fullyevil period.

When Bram Stroker, author of the famous 1897 *Dracula* novel, learned about Vlad "Dracula" Ţepeş, he modeled the novel's villain after the malevolent Romanian ruler. In the 1800s, the mysterious, hidden Eastern Europe was a convenient place for Western Europe's greatest fears and horror stories. Nowadays, it still is.

In the morning after my nightmare night, I touched my neck. It felt normal. I packed up and hurried out of the haunted cabin. Frost covered the grass. After several hours of hiking down the Transylvanian Alps, Dracula's Castle came into view. It's officially called Bran Castle. It was a cold and cloudy morning, but the castle didn't look that sinister. Maybe that's because it never was Dracula's real castle.

Not surprisingly, there are many myths about the real-world Dracula. One of them is that he lived in Dracula's Castle. The truth is that he only stayed in Bran Castle for a short while, if he stayed there at all. Instead, he spent most of his time in Poienari Castle, which is in ruins on a steep hill that few visit. Because Poienari Castle is modest and remote, vampire souvenir vendors like those in Dracula's Bazaar and the Skeleton's Tavern have promoted the grandiose Bran Castle as Dracula's former residence.

Another myth is that Dracula was evil and diabolical. For nearly 10 years, Vlad Ţepeş was the Prince of Wallachia, not Transylvania. Romanians see him as a heroic ruler who successfully resisted the Turks. Bucharest honors Dracula by having a statue of him in the Old Princely Court. A 2006 Romanian TV Series named him as one of the "100 Greatest Romanians." Although his torture methods were cruel, they were consistent with the standard European medieval torture techniques. Finally, Dracula was not a vampire who lived for centuries. During Dracula's final battle, a Turk sliced off his head. He was 45 years old. Several years after his death, the Turks conquered Wallachia and Transylvania.

Tempting vampires in Braşov and Sighişoara

Before sunset, I arrived in Braşov, a medieval Germanic town surrounded by verdant Transylvanian hills. Its *Piaţa Stafalui* is one of Eastern Europe's prettiest plazas. It's also where witches were once burned alive. Elegant baroque buildings and pedestrian walkways make the town of 284,000 people feel cozy. At night, I made an audacious and stealthy camp in a bush in the *Parcul Central*. Like a vampire who should never be caught sleeping outside after sunrise, I vanished from the campsite at dawn.

My next stop was Sighişoara, another quaint Germanic town with plenty of cobblestoned streets to trip on. It's full of perfectly preserved medieval buildings. Its mountaintop citadel is a UNESCO site that is over 800 years old. There's a great view from the *Turnul cu Ceas* (Clock

Tower). There's also a pleasant torture room inside. In the town's *Piaţa Cetăţii* (Central Plaza), people used to buy fruits and watch the executions. Now they just buy fruits. Within the medieval citadel, you'll find Dracula's birthplace. Vlad Ţepeş was born in 1431 and reputedly lived there until he was four years old. The site is now a bar and restaurant. Fresh blood is missing from the menu.

As the moon rose during the cold night, I challenged the vampires again. Next to the town's Gothic church, I climbed up a spooky, dark-covered staircase with 172 steps. Sighişoara lay below. Without a tarp, this location would provide adequate shelter from the frigid, damp air. The downside was that I would be trapped if a vampire came up the stairs. I lay in wait. I only heard the rustling of the leaves. Although Dracula didn't suck my blood or even stop by to say hi, I loved Sighişoara.

Cluj-Napoca and Székely Land

My next stop was Cluj-Napoca, which is next to Transylvania's Apuseni Mountains. A Roman Emperor founded the Napoca colony in 124 AD. About 40 years ago, Romanians added "Napoca" to the name in a vain effort to remind everyone of its Roman origins. Few mention Napoca, everyone just calls it Cluj (sounds like Kluge). The fourteenth-century St. Michael's Church overlooks the city's main plaza, Piaţa Unirii. Cluj's university fuels the city with life. It's not obvious to a casual tourist, but Cluj, Braşov, and Sighişoara are near the center of Romania's most controversial region—the Székely Land—which we discussed in the Hungary chapter (pp. 233–235). Ethnically, Romania looks like a doughnut, with ethnic Hungarians living in the center.

About 17 percent of Cluj County is Hungarian, but there are two nearby counties (Harghita and Covasna) where Hungarians are 74 to 85 percent of the population. That zone is the heart of Székely Land. Although Hungarian-Romanian tensions have always existed, some have a distorted view of history. For example, a Hungarian wrote to me, "Romanians killed Hungarians 'just for fun.' Have you heard about Bözödújfalu (or Bezidu Nou)? It was a small Hungarian village in Transylvania. But the Romanian government decided to build a reservoir. The village was in the way. They simply flooded it without compensating the families. They destroyed several villages like this."

Even though this is true, several villages that were ethnically Romanian suffered the same fate. Moreover, Hungarians sometimes act like thousands of Hungarians drowned when the village was flooded. Nobody died. People were displaced, which often happens whenever any reservoir is created. Just ask the Chinese who used to live near the Three Gorges Dam. Romanians didn't kill Hungarians "just for fun," nor were reservoirs built "just for fun."

Imaginary pains are by far the most real we suffer, since we feel a constant need for them and invent them because there is no way of doing without them.
— Emile M. Cioran, Romanian philosopher

Meanwhile, Romanians can also be highly irrational about Hungarians living in the heart of Romania. For example, Marius Eugen Ciurea, a Romanian medical doctor, assured me that Hungary has never ruled Transylvania. No matter how much I questioned his facts, he insisted that Transylvania has always been autonomous and was never directly under Hungarian rule.

Despite his graduate education, he didn't know that Hungarians made Cluj Transylvania's capital for about a century. Nor could he adequately explain why there's a statue of Hungary's King Ladislaus I in Oradea, Romania. In addition, Cluj's center has a statue of the fifteenth century Hungarian King Matthias Corvinus. Romanians don't have a habit of building monuments dedicated to Hungarians. That last statue was built in 1902, when the Hungary ruled Transylvania as part of the Austria-Hungary Empire. If a doctor denies such facts, you gotta wonder what Romanian villagers believe.

The fact is that when the Austria-Hungary Empire ruled Transylvania, Romanians were mistreated. Later, when Romanians controlled Transylvania, Hungarians were abused. Nevertheless, both sides are tremendously resilient. The Székely are especially tough as this joke illustrates:

China has conquered the whole world except the land of Székelys. The two armies stand against each other when the Chinese general asks the Székely general, "Aren't you afraid?"

The Székely says, "No. Why should I be?"

"Because our army has 200 million men and yours has only 40,000!"

The Székely leader is shocked and turns to his followers: "Székely! Where on Earth are we going to bury 200 million Chinese?"

Although the Székely have held strong for centuries, they've known defeat too. For example, Alex Kuli, an American in Hungary, told me, "The Székelys once dominated Transylvania. Then they got their jockstraps handed to them by the Turks, Romanians, and others. That's the way it was back in medieval times: kick ass or get yours kicked. There was no idle chit-chat about human rights, international law, or peace conferences."

"So how are things now?" I asked.

Alex said, "Now the Székelys live in a tenuous peace with their Romanian compatriots as members of the EU. They're talking about creating an autonomous zone for Székelys, which I think would be a good idea, but it will never happen as long as the Romanians have a nationalist knot in their collective underwear."

Although the knot is still there, in 1996, Romania and Hungary signed an agreement that improved their relations. There are bilingual signs throughout Székely Land. Nearly a third of Cluj's Babeş-Bolyai University courses are taught in Hungarian. Hungarians have their political party that is active and influential in Romania's government. Book stores sell Hungarian works and you can watch Hungarian TV in Romania. When Hungarians make up over 20 percent of the local population, they can use the Hungarian language in official government communication. And yes, you're free to speak Hungarian wherever you please. In conclusion, although Romanian-Hungarian tensions still exist, tragedies do not.

> *What would be left of our tragedies if an insect were to present us his? — Emile M. Cioran, Romanian philosopher*

Southern Bucovina's painted monasteries

From Cluj, I went to Suceava, which has four nearby painted monasteries that are on UNESCO's World Heritage List. The Southern Bucovina monasteries are covered with frescoes on the building's exteriors. The grandest painting is the Voroneţ monastery's *Last Judgment* fresco. It uses a blue pigment known as Voroneţ blue, which I failed to appreciate in the drizzle. Moldoviţa Monastery is fully enclosed as if it were a castle. The Suceviţa Monastery is the largest and was finished in 1601. The Humor Monastery has the best preserved interior frescoes, but none of them are funny.

The painted monasteries are noble, but I was disappointed. It didn't help that it was raining, so their famous colors were muted. Still, it seems they need a new paint job. Moreover, there's a disappointing pattern in many Eastern European monasteries: the monks are grumpy. It's sad that God's ambassadors are rude and unfriendly. Yes, tourists are annoying, but that's no excuse, Mr. Holy Man. Set a good example or go to hell.

Romanians say religion is important, but it's unclear how deep their commitment is. According to a 2010 Gallup poll, 75 percent of Romanians "have confidence in their religious organizations." That's the highest rate in Europe, even higher than Turkey. Eight in 10 Romanians said that "religion was an important part of their daily life," which was the third highest rate in Europe (after Kosovo and Turkey). On the other hand, only 36 percent said that they had gone to a church in the previous week. Nicolae Stanciu told me, "I believe that most of the Romanian religious interest is fake. It's ritualistic, not profound. It's hard to believe that people who, under communism, said that they were atheistic and then suddenly became religious."

We understand God by everything in ourselves that is fragmentary, incomplete, and inopportune.
— Emile M. Cioran, Romanian Philosopher

Returning to college in Iaşi

While I waited for a bus to the train station, two college students named Andrei invited me to join their classmates during night train ride to Iaşi (pronounced *Ya-shi*). We joked around on the train and by the end of the journey, one Andrei invited me to sleep on his dorm room floor. Like typical college scholars, we partied until 3:00 a.m.

Andrei, a chemistry major, skipped his morning class. I joined him for his 11:00 a.m. physics class. This would be my first college-level physics class, and my first class in Romanian. I doubt I would have understood anything even if it had been taught in English. The stern, corpulent, old Romanian teacher made it especially tough. Unlike American students, Romanian students don't talk. They just take notes nonstop. To blend in, I wrote and passed around a list of "The Top 10 Things This Teacher Says During Sex." It was sophomoric behavior, but I was, after all, hanging out with sophomores.

We had lunch and then they gave me a history lesson as we toured Romania's second largest city. They explained that in Middle Ages, there were three Romanian regions: Wallachia, Moldavia, and Transylvania. In some ways, they were like what Bosnia, Croatia, and Serbia are today: related, but different. Wallachia forms Romania's cultural core (Bucharest is the capital). As we've seen, Transylvania has a mixed heritage, with Romanians, Hungarians, Székelys, and Germans all influencing what it became; even the Turkish and Roman influence is still visible. Finally, there's the third region, Moldavia. Today, Moldavia is mostly split between Romania (where Iaşi is the capital) and Moldova, whose border is just 20 kilometers (13 miles) from Iaşi.

For centuries, Romanians pursued the *România Mare* (Greater Romania) dream, which seeks to unify these three Romanian regions. *Mihai Viteazul* (Michael the Brave) pulled off this miracle in 1600, but the union didn't even last a year. Soon the Turks came, then the Austrians and Hungarians. The only other time when Greater Romania existed was between WWI and WWII. Interesting, when I asked Professor Nicolae Stanciu when Romania's golden age was, he didn't mention either of the brief Greater Romania periods. He said, "Romania's best period was in the late 1800s, during the reign of Carol I. In just 50 years, he transformed the face of Romania."

Ironically, King Carol I was German, not Romanian. As usual, Germans know how to run a tight ship, even when they're handicapped. Adrian Cioroianu, a Romanian historian, noted, "Without knowing exactly where Romania was located on the map, and without ever getting a good command of the Romanian language, Carol I became the most efficient ruler Romania ever had, making important contributions to the modernization (i.e., *Westernization*) of the country." Indeed, 'under the rule of this icy man' who was 'never seen laughing heartily,' Romania became a kingdom in 1881."[4] He focused on developing Romania's strengths.

> *You cannot be anything if you want to be everything.*
> *— Solomon Schechter, Moldavian born Romanian Jewish Clergyman, 1847–1915*

The three Romanians students took me to Iaşi's main plaza, the *Piaţa Unirii*. Nearby is the *Biserica Sfinţilor Trei Ierarhi* (Church of the Three Hierarchs) that has a fabulously decorated exterior. Still, the real star building is the *Palatul Culturii* (Palace of Culture). Although it was completed in 1926, it looks old, thanks to its neo-Gothic style. It was hard to leave Iaşi. I was living one of my titillating fantasies: being a college student without any homework. Thus, with some sadness, I boarded the bus to Ungheni that continued onward to Moldova.

Raluca Guta and Romanian driving habits

That's how my 2004 trip through Romania went. Soon we'll see what happened when I returned to Romania five years later and visited places near the Danube and the Black Sea. But first, let's review the Romania's communist period. In the Hungary chapter, we thoroughly discussed Transylvania's history (pp. 232–242), which includes how Romania gained, lost, and regained Transylvania in WWI and WWII. At the start of each war, Romania tried to stay neutral. As Raluca Guta told me, "Romanians have never started a war. We're too disorganized to start a war."

Raluca and I met over email after Corina Nicolae digitally introduced us. Several years later, I finally met Raluca in person. She was living in Frankfurt with her German boyfriend, Ralf. I stayed with them for a few days. While we were overlooking the Main River from their balcony, Raluca shared stories from Romania's communist past. Her grandfather, Aurelian Guta, once criticized the communists, so the police picked him off the street and threw him in jail. His mother had no idea what had happened to him. When she questioned the police, they said they knew nothing. The pain of not knowing her son's fate was so hard that she needed closure to move on. She held a funeral and "buried" her son. You can imagine her reaction when, four years after his disappearance, he rang her doorbell.

Several years later, during one of Romania's tough traffic jams, Aurelian got out of his vehicle and screamed, "Why do we put up with this bullshit? This government should do better! We need a revolution!" The police threw him in jail for six years for this tirade. Ralf, who worked in Romania for a year, said with his calm German accent, "I've been to several countries, and I've never seen people become so crazy in a car like the Romanians."

Raluca interjected, "That's true. When you get in front of someone in traffic in Romania, they take it as a personal offense. They don't interpret your action like, 'Hi, I'm just trying to get home like everyone else and excuse me while I move into your lane.' No. They believe you are making a personal attack on them."

Ralf continued, "They will scream at each other and sometimes get out of their cars and start fighting. It's incredible. I've never seen anything like it."

I asked Ralf, "Name me another difference between Romanians and Germans."

He said, "Germans are more team-oriented than Romanians."

"You might be right about that," said Raluca, "But Romanians are more family-oriented than the Germans. For example, whenever I go back home, I'm always surprised that nearly all my friends are still in the same town. Nobody moves away from home. The home is important."

I said, "For centuries, Germans were living in Romania. Why didn't Romania keep some of that organized German spirit?"

Raluca said, "It's our own fault. It's who we are. It's a hard habit to break."

That was an unusual answer. Often Eastern Europeans act like they're toys that the Great Powers play with. This provides a convenient excuse to explain why things are screwed up and avoid taking responsibility. Nevertheless, there's a bit of truth over the common excuse. For example, over a drink and on a napkin, Churchill proposed to Stalin that the communists could get Romania if the West gets Greece. Churchill was fond of the Greek islands. It's slightly depressing to know your country's entire fate can be determined by some fat English guy scribbling on a napkin.

Romania's real-life vampire: Nicoloe Ceauşescu

After WWII, Romania had 13 miserable years of Soviet occupation followed by 30 wretched years of Nicoloe Ceauşescu's leadership. To be fair, this Romanian dictator wasn't a total loser. Like a baby-version of Tito or Hoxha, Ceauşescu challenged the Soviets. Romania was the only Warsaw Pact member to condemn the Soviet crushing of the 1968 Prague Spring and the Soviet invasion of Afghanistan. Ceauşescu established relations with the West and also campaigned to rid Eastern

Europe of nuclear weapons and foreign military bases. Queen Elizabeth II decorated him. He dreamed of winning the Nobel Peace Prize. His grand visions for Romania were his strength and his Achilles' heel. Because of those visions, Ceauşescu spent money faster than Ilie Nastase's wife.

> *I haven't reported my missing credit card to the police because whoever stole it is spending less than my wife.*
> *— Ilie Nastase, Romanian tennis player, ranked number one in 1973–1974*

Communism's numskull economics could never finance Ceauşescu's fantasies, but he tried anyway. He buried Romania under a mountain of debt as he pursued his lofty ideas. For example, he made a budget-busting canal to the Black Sea. He bulldozed priceless historical districts in Bucharest to build the second biggest building of the world (his office). In 1987, he wanted to move Romania beyond its antiquated agricultural economy, so he forced farmers to abandon their fields and move into concrete apartment blocks. He ordered the destruction of 8,000 villages. He abused ethnic Hungarians. If anyone really pissed him off, that rebel would get tortured with *radu*—low-level radiation doses that would induce cancer. Like a vampire, Ceauşescu sucked the life out of Romania.

By the late 1980s, Romania was drowning in debt. To save money, Ceauşescu cut off power supplies. Romanians started using candles. To pay off foreign debt, you have to make something useful to sell to other countries. However, communism is incompetent at producing valuable innovations. The only valuable thing Romania produced was food and it couldn't produce a surplus. Ceauşescu forced Romanians to ration their food and export the rest. As winter set in, Romanians were starving to death. He had already bulldozed dozens of villages when Romanians started rioting. He calmed the masses for several months, but then the Berlin Wall came down.

About a month later, an ethnic Hungarian priest condemned Ceauşescu's government in Timişoara, Romania. Protests spread. A few days later, on December 22, 1989, Ceauşescu climbed on his podium to showcase his support. The crowd booed him. Ceauşescu ordered tanks to run over the protestors. Ten demonstrators died. The next day, the megalomaniac reappeared on his balcony with his wife, who also held a high government position. Again, protesters outshouted his megaphone. Like a villain in a Hollywood movie, Ceauşescu escaped in a helicopter. Soon, his own military caught him. On December 25, Romania received their Christmas gift—they televised Ceauşescu and his wife standing before a firing squad. The world watched their execution.

The great irony is that by the time Ceauşescu died, Romania had paid off its foreign debt. The lesson is: austerity works, but it's not such a great idea if you're the guy who has to implement it.

> *For you who no longer possess it, freedom is everything, for us who do, it is merely an illusion.*
> *— Emile M. Cioran, Romanian philosopher*

Crossing the Danube

Only the Danube River separates Romania and Bulgaria, but the two countries act as if there's an ocean between them. Although the Danube is a wide river, it's straightforward to make a bridge across it. The Romans showed us how in 105 AD with Trajan's Bridge. Over the next 1,900 years, cities and countries would build many bridges over the Danube. For example, Novi Sad has three bridges across the Danube, Budapest has nine, and Vienna has 21. Yet during the last 19 centuries, Romania and Bulgaria, despite having a shared river border that's hundreds of kilometers long, have built just *one* bridge between them. And that's only because Stalin forced them to build the Friendship Bridge, which they just call the Danube Bridge.

I learned this because when I first saw a map that showed that the one-kilometer wide Danube was the only thing that separated the Bulgarian town of Vidin from the Romanian town of Calafat, I assumed that there would be a bridge between them. After all, these towns have been next to each other for centuries. However, when I arrived in Vidin in 2009, the only way to cross the Danube was to take a rusty, uncovered flatboat ferry. As we crossed, we could see that the Danube Bridge 2 was finally being built. It opens in 2012. The lack of bridges perfectly illustrates why Romania and Bulgaria are hidden from each other.

Reuniting with Corina

Five years after meeting Corina (the plastic surgeon on top of the Transylvanian Alps), I went to her place to pick up my tarp. In 2009, I had forgotten my tarp in Estonia and I had been traveling for two months without it. An ultralight tarp gives me the peace of mind that no matter what happens, I'll have shelter. For two months, I had that annoying pressure of "where will I sleep tonight?" Because I'm spontaneous when I travel, it was hard to predict where I would be in a couple of weeks or to have a trusted place to ship the tarp to. Corina was my best option and she invited me to stay with her for several days.

Although we just talked for 30 minutes on top of Mount Olmu, Corina and I had kept in touch through instant messages and emails a few times a year. During that time, she told me of the day she met Dragoş, who was walking a dog in the park. She said, "When I met him, I knew

I would marry him one day." She emailed me their wedding photos. A year later, she emailed me photos of their baby girl, Doreea. With no public transportation out of Calafat on a Sunday, I hitchhiked to Corina's town, Craiova. When I came, Dragoş picked me up. He doesn't look like the kind of guy who could get a hottie like Corina. He's somewhat short, balding, and slightly overweight. Thank God women are less superficial than men.

Dragoş and I drove to a distant picnic spot where Corina and her daughter were waiting, along with their friend Marius Ciurea, his wife Raluca, and their little boy. We enjoyed an afternoon picnic. The next day, the seven of us walked along to the Jui River, which is located in a spectacular canyon. It's a rock climbing paradise. Later, we went to Târgu Jiu to see the slender *Coloana Infinitului* (Endless Column) that seems infinite when you stand right under it.

They introduced me to Romanian cuisine when we had lunch at a traditional outdoor restaurant in the Târgu Jiu Park. If you know a Romance language, reading a Romanian menu can be easy. For example, you can recognize *vacă* (cow), *porc* (pork), and *salată asortată* (assorted salad). On the other hand, some items aren't so easy to figure out unless you know Romanian: *ficat* (liver), *cabanos prajit* (fried sausages), *piept de pui* (chicken breast), *clătite* (crepes), *ardei umpluţi* (stuffed bell pepper), and *plăcintă* (turnovers). I ordered a *ciorbă de legume* (vegetable soup). Romanians like to plop sour cream in their soups (and everywhere else too).

> Dragostea trece prin stomac. — *Romanian proverb meaning, "Love passes through the stomach"*

It's surprising that Romania's most popular dish comes from South America: *polenta* (corn meal). Romanians call is *mămăligă.* Romanians consider it a poor man's meal, saying, *"Nici o mămăligă pe masă."* ("He doesn't even have *mămăliga* on the table.") During Ceauşescu's winter of starvation, many Romanians didn't even have *mămăliga.*

Eastern Europe's challenge: the Roma

When we returned to Craiova, we discussed an ethnic group that has an enormous presence in their city: Roma. A few Hungarians and Slavs dislike that Romanians have named themselves after the Romans to reinforce a connection that they claim doesn't exist. Meanwhile, Romanians dislike what Roma have named themselves because it seems derived from *Romania.* In fact, *Roma* is the plural for *Rom* and comes from the Romani word for *men.* Regardless, many people call them *gypsies,* while Romanians and Slavs call them a derogatory term that sounds like *Tsigani.* Roma are unpopular. In 2009, a Pew Research survey showed that 33% of East Germans, 45% of Spaniards, 56% of

Bulgarians, 69% of Hungarians, 78% of Slovaks, 84% of Czechs and Italians have an unfavorable opinion of Roma.

Romanians blame their poor reputation in Europe on Roma. They believe that whenever a news report says that a "Romanian" committed a crime in an EU country, it's "always" a Rom who did it, not a "real Romanian." When I was hitchhiking near Barcelona, Torstem, a German truck driver, picked me up. He was driving tons of Spanish oranges to Germany. He said that when he was in Romania in 2009, he had 200 liters of diesel sucked out of his truck while he was sleeping. Torstem also said that there were also many carjackings before Romania joined the EU. If a Romanian overheard these stories, he would probably blame Roma for these crimes.

Eastern Europeans have issues with Roma. A 2006 Czech government report said that 80,000 Roma live in over 300 ghettos, 80 percent of which were created in the last decade. In 2010, a Slovak gunman burst into an apartment killing six Roma, and then killing another person on the street, injuring 14 random people, and finally shooting himself. Roma are picked on everywhere from Kosovo to Russia. In 2010, a few Hungarian politicians demanded that Roma be forced into internment camps. Slovak police arrested six Roma teenagers for allegedly stealing a purse. To punish them, the police forced them to strip naked, hit and kiss each other, while the police filmed the degradation.

Roma have problems. The Human Development Index for Romania's Roma is similar to Botswana's, even though Romania ranks almost 50 spots higher than Botswana. According to the UN, Roma infant mortality rates in Bulgaria are six times above the national average, while their income is a third.[5] Amnesty International reports that in Slovakia, Roma make up less than 10 percent of the regular school population, but 60 percent of the special (i.e., retarded) school population. Perhaps the only positive thing that Roma are known for is their musical talent.

> *It is impossible to imagine a more complete fusion with nature than that of the Gypsy.*
> *— Franz Liszt, a Hungarian composer*

Some Eastern Europeans act like Roma are recent invaders, but they're descendents of people who migrated from India to Europe in the 1300s. Romani words like *dand* (tooth), *mun* (mouth), *khel* (play), *lon* (salt), and *akha* (eyes) are identical with those in Punjabi, which is spoken in northwest India. Roma also sway their head from side to side in an ambivalent way just like Indians. Today, there are almost 10 million Roma in Eastern Europe. The Council on Europe estimates that Romania has the biggest population of Roma (1.9 million), but that Bulgaria has the highest concentration (about 12 percent of the population).

Just like Jews were an ethnic group without a country (until Israel was made in 1947), Roma have been treated like second-class citizens everywhere they go. Sometimes Europeans ignore them. Sometimes they try to liquidate them: Nazis killed hundreds of thousands of Roma—about a quarter of the Roma population. Other times they try to sterilize them: from 1973 to 2004 the Czechs forcefully sterilized many Roma. Nowadays Europeans are trying to integrate them. The World Bank estimated that it costs Bulgaria, Czechia, Romania, and Serbia $7.3 billion every year for failing to integrate the Roma. Therefore, Eastern Europe launched the "Decade of Roma Inclusion," which will end in 2015.

> *Gypsies are a litmus test not of democracy, but of a civil society. — Former Czech President Václav Havel*

The opening scene of *Borat* supposedly took place in Kazakhstan, but it was actually filmed in the Roma town of Glod, Romania. *Glod* in Romanian means *Mud*. The scene showed dirty villagers who rape, have casual incest, and easy abortions. The Glod Roma were angry because they were paid just $5 each and were misled about the film's true intentions. A couple of villagers sued the film's producers, but the lawsuit was thrown out because the charges were too vague. Romanians like that the film ridiculed the Roma. As the local vice-mayor Petre Buzea said, "They got paid so I am sure they are happy. These gypsies will even kill their own father for money."

Into the epicenter of the Roma

Ask Romanians where you should go to meet Roma, and they'll say Craiova. Ask Craiovans where to go, and they'll send you to Craiova's open-air market. So I went to the Roma epicenter. The bazaar was filled with hundreds of Roma. Women were covered with colorful headscarves and skirts. While I searched for a Roma who could speak English, a Romanian told me with disgust, "Everything here is stolen from other countries." There's no way I could prove that. Like any market that sells used goods, you have no clue how the seller acquired it. What's clear is that you can buy almost anything you could ever want in Craiova's flee market.

I eventually found Silviu Condoiu, a 25-year-old Romanian who was married to a Rom named Bianka. He was perfect because he had a foot in both worlds. I wanted to disprove the stereotype that Roma were money whores, but once Roma around Silviu learned that he would let me interview him, they started clamoring, "Ask him for money if he wants to interview you!"

Silviu tried to brush off the pesky Roma away, but they kept hounding him, wanting to know what he was saying. Exasperated, he led me away from the crowd so that we could talk in peace. Even though we were pretty isolated, his eyes rarely looked at me because he was too busy scanning the scene, seeing if someone he knew would see us talking. The first question I asked him was, "What is the biggest myth about Roma?"

"That they're all thieves. Most are very honest," Silviu said. "Romanians are hypocrites because they call Roma thieves, but all the big thefts are done by Romanian businessmen and politicians. Roma just do small crime. Romanians are smarter than Roma, so they do the bigger crimes."

"What's another myth?"

"That there's just one type of Roma. For example, the Huni are some of the richest and sometimes most criminal of Roma. The Costorari are the poor Roma. The Lâieti are the working-class Roma. The Bozgori are lazy Roma. The Tismanari are those who are mixed Roma and Romanian."

"So your four-year-old daughter is a Tismanari?" I asked.

"Yes." He had introduced me to her and his wife before we walked to our peaceful location on the edge of the market. "But," he added, "My wife's family is Huni, which is why it was hard to marry her."

Marrying a Roma girl

Silviu explained what it's like having Huni in-laws. Most Huni create an agreement with the groom that if he divorces his daughter, then the groom will pay a certain amount in gold. The amount depends on how prestigious the daughter is, but usually it's about $30,000. That explains the low divorce rate. At first, such an agreement might seem odd, but it's similar to what some Americans do: a prenuptial agreement.

In addition, the groom is also expected to give money to the girl's family. The amount depends on the wealth of the groom, but usually it's between $15,000 to $75,000, preferably paid in gold. Weddings can be huge. Sometimes 400 people are invited to an exotic location. However, these rules are flexible. For example, Silviu and Bianka eloped to Spain because her family was being difficult. They finally returned to Romania once Bianka's family agreed to accept Silviu. He didn't pay anything for his wife because her family realized that he has no money. His job pays $200 per month, which is similar to the average Roma. The family was hoping for a richer husband for their only daughter; she has five brothers. I asked him, "Do Roma follow traditional male and female roles?"

Silviu said, "Yes, women do all the housework. Men are the boss."

"What about the justice system within the Roma society?"

"They resolve disputes among themselves," he said. "They only use the Romanian court system when they can't solve the problem within their own justice system."

"Do Roma solve problems by killing each other?"

"Not anymore. They used to do that, but now it rarely happens."

Some of Eastern Europe's biggest, most ostentatious houses are Roma homes. Craiova has neighborhoods where you can see row after row of Roma mansions. They challenge the stereotype that Roma are dirt-poor. Romanians told me fanciful stories about these houses: that the houses only look good from the outside, but that they're empty and incomplete inside; that all the furniture is covered with plastic to make sure that nothing gets dirty since Roma are such materialists; that Roma keep their horses in the mansions, while the people live in the barn. Silviu laughed at these fabrications. He said that after visiting several of these mansions, he said, "The houses have nice, normal interiors and nobody keeps horses in them."

I thanked Silviu for his insights and started walking toward the exit with Corina when a fistfight broke out between several blubbery middle-aged Roma. They were screaming at each other in Romani, so I didn't understand what they were fighting about. One man shoved another while his wife was holding him back. After a bit of pushing and lots of yelling, they went their separate ways. Corina shook her head and gave me a look that said, "See what I mean?"

After three gratifying days, I thanked Corina and Dragoş for their hospitality and took a bus to Bucharest. In 2011, Corina told me that they had moved to Lupeni, which she prefers since there are mountains around. Meanwhile, Dragoş surprised everyone by going to medical school. It would be fun to reunite with them in five years to see what else has happened.

Falling in love with Eastern European toilets

My couchsurfing host in Bucharest was Simona Palade, a successful stage actress. She regularly performs in the big venues in Romania's capital. Normally, I arrive with a gift for my hosts, but I didn't have anything for Simona, so moments before we met, I bought her flowers from a street vendor. She happily received them and we walked to her modern apartment, where she introduced me to her one-year-old baby. Then I went to the bathroom and realized that I was falling in love.

Simona is an attractive blond 29-year-old, but at that point I was in love with her toilet. Unlike American toilets, most Eastern European toilets offer you a choice. You can either do a full flush or a half flush. Depending on how serious your business is, you press the appropriate button. It's a brilliant innovation for those of us who live in arid areas like California. I grew up with the rhyme, "If it's yellow, be mellow; if it's brown, flush it down."

Although the dual-flush toilet was invented in dry Australia, Eastern Europeans have bought more of them than Australians. It ends up saving the average household 67 percent of its normal water use. For a small family, this can translate into saving 32,000 liters of water per year. Not bad for a crapper.

The second biggest building in the world

Simona had never toured the second biggest building in the world, so I invited her to join me. The *Palatul Parlamentului* (Palace of the Parliament) is smaller than the US Pentagon, but it looks better from the ground. In 1984, Ceauşescu needed to make some space for his office. Therefore, he demolished a vast neighborhood, including 7,000 homes and 26 churches. He bulldozed glorious historic buildings modeled after French architecture and erected buildings modeled after North Korean architecture. Not a great trade.

While Simona and I were waiting for our tour to start, Barry Raw, a British sailor, overheard our conversation about couchsurfing and introduced himself. He was a blond dapper 35-year-old who was touring Bucharest. The three of us embarked on an hour-long tour, which only shows 10 percent of the 12-story palace. It took $5 billion, 700 architects, and 20,000 workers working three shifts over five years to complete the building that Ceauşescu euphemistically called, "The People's Palace." It has 330,000 square meters, 3,100 rooms, and looks like it was designed by a communist who wanted to copy Versailles on a tight budget.

After the tour, Simona had to go to her rehearsal, so Barry and I strolled around the city. When we visited the excellent Museum of the Romanian Peasant, we found statues of Lenin piled where they should be—in the basement. Later, we all reunited at Simona's apartment for dinner. While we ate, Simona observed that "Romanian villages are still like the Middle Ages; the church plays a huge role."

The next day, while I was on a bus to the train station, a lady named Floria told me something similar. She said, "Whatever happens, Romanians explain it via religion. For example, if something bad happens, it's because they didn't pray to Saint Mary. If something good happens, it's because they prayed to Saint John. We're also superstitious. If the bride drops the flowers at the wedding, the parents might freak out, seeing it as a bad omen."

Floria grew up in Bucharest, but studied music in Canada. She now lives in Cologne, Germany and is married to a German man. She said that Romanians are more streetwise and handy than Westerners. They're also more direct: "If they don't like you, it's obvious."

Floria admitted that customer service is still weak in Romania. "They treat you like shit. I feel like telling them, 'Hello? I'm a *customer*.'"

I asked her what other differences she saw between Romanians and Westerners. She said, "We have a different mentality. When Romanians have a picnic, you know it because of all the trash they leave behind. They have little respect for nature. That's different than Canadians and Germans. Of course, not all Romanians are like this; those who are educated respect nature. Also, it's basically impossible to make a lot of money in Romania and be honest. Corruption is everywhere."

Bulgarian twins studying in Romania Giurgiu-Ruse

As my train crossed the Danube Bridge and entered Bulgaria, I met Ani and Dimcko Gaydarova, Bulgarian twins who were studying in Cluj. Dimcko dominated the conversation and interrupted his twin sister often. She rolled her eyes and bit her tongue, which reflects the lingering machismo in Eastern Europe. I asked them how Romanians treat them. Dimcko said, "Pretty well, but in Eastern Europe, most people hate their neighboring countries."

I asked, "What do your nations have in common?"

He said, "Romanians and Bulgarians are patient. Greeks protest. We just accept and adapt."

"What's different about you?"

"Bulgarians are good to their children. In Romania, they treat them like animals."

Romanians told Gallup that there's some truth to that. In 2010, six out of 10 Bulgarians said that "children in their country are treated with respect and dignity." In Romania, only three in 10 agreed—that was the lowest rate in Eurasia.

When I asked Dimocko what he thought of the EU, he said, "It's good. Globalization has given us the opportunity to learn about other cultures. For example, we're Bulgarians studying in Romania. Also, people can find jobs in other countries."

"What about gypsies?"

He said, "Gypsies are like a disease."

Romania's Black Sea coast

On my third visit to Romania, I visited its Black Sea coastline and the *Delta Dunarii* (Danube Delta). Once again, illustrating the shocking disconnectedness between Romania and Bulgaria, there was no public transportation from Varna, Bulgaria to Constanța, Romania, even though they're both major cities along the Black Sea that are relatively near to each other. Eventually, I found a van that was going from Varna to Ukraine. The Ukrainian driver agreed to drop me off at Constanța along the way.

Constanța is a pretty city in a region called Northern Dobrogea, which has the best evidence of the Roman period. There are Roman ruins and in front of Constanța's graceful History and Archaeological Museum there's a statue of Ovid, who was exiled here in 8 AD. The city's Moscheia Mahmudiye Mosque testifies to the Turkish period. Constanța is compact, but delightful. The most beautiful building is the 1860 Genoese lighthouse that overlooks the Black Sea. Eventually, I went to Tulcea (sounds like Tool-*cha*), a city that the Dacians founded in the seventh century BC. It's where most go to begin exploring the Danube Delta labyrinth.

The Polluted Danube

Neil Mitchell, an American professor who taught environmental law in Serbia, wrote to me saying, "The Danube is not the 'Blue Danube,' it is the Brown Danube. Pollution has created an algae bloom that extends several kilometers into the Black Sea. Everyone likes to blame other countries for the pollution. Ex-Yugoslavs are happy to blame Romania for the one issue that they seem to agree on: that Romania is bad, retarded, poor, or whatever negative adjective one chooses."

"So who should we blame?" I asked.

He replied, "All of the countries that touch the Danube play a part in its pollution. Belgrade certainly does. According to my students, as of 2009, Belgrade did not have a functioning secondary treatment plant (STP). Can you imagine a city of two million without an STP!? I suppose that after primary treatment all the sewage goes to the Danube downstream from Belgrade. Alas, it is not fair to blame Romania for all the pollution of the Danube! Belgrade will get a STP if it joins the EU."

Despite the knee-jerk belief that "capitalism is bad for the environment," communism was worse overall. Communists didn't care about externalities (like pollution) anymore than capitalists because the communists were too busy trying to achieve their unrealistic five-year plans. The environment was the last thing on Ceaușescu's mind. Moreover, a corrupt system with little rule of law meant that environmental laws (if any) were ignored. Communism's main environmental advantage was that it forced people to live simple lives; it consumed fewer resources per capita than capitalist economies. On the other hand, communism's non-market-based pricing often encouraged waste. Because Soviet energy was heavily subsidized, for example, people consumed it recklessly. Based on most environmental metrics, communism was a disaster.

Ultimately, environmentalism is an obsession of the rich. When Gallup asked people if they "avoided using certain products that harm the environment," all countries in the West had at least 60 percent saying yes, while all Eastern European countries were below 60 percent. Similarly, the lowest ranking countries on Yale's Environmental Performance Index are mostly poor, while the highest ranking ones are mostly rich. That's because once you're well-paid, well-fed, and well-housed, you can worry about that crap you're throwing in the river.

When I made these points to Neil, he replied, "You are correct. There is one other factor worth mentioning. Communism usually creates a command-and-control economy and society. There is not much room for dissenting voices. There was not much room for non-governmental organizations (NGOs) in communist countries. NGOs play a significant role in environmental matters. They have standing both in the US common law system and in the EU civil law system. In the communist system there is no room for such feedback in administrative law. One does what one is told or allowed to do. That was the rule of law. One could not challenge the government."

Floating to the Danube's end

In Tulcea, I learned that the Danube Delta has three main branches to the Black Sea: Sfântu Gheorghe, Sulina, and Chilia. The shortest and most direct route to the Black Sea is the Sulina Branch, which is 64 kilometers (40 miles) long. An infrequent ferry goes from Tulcea to the town of Sulina, which lies where the Danube spills into the Black Sea. The ferry calmly floated down the wide, straight channel, making a few stops at small towns along the way. Trees and reeds grew all along the river banks. It felt as if we were leaving Eastern Europe behind.

After a couple of hours, we arrived at the final stop—the humble town of Sulina. As we got off, I met five people in their early 20s who were traveling together. They were an odd bunch: two French women, one French man, one Italian man, and one American woman. They were taking a short vacation from a Romanian school that they were assisting. They invited me to join them as they looked for a guide to take us around the delta's narrow channels. In the process, they also rented rooms in a house and the owner agreed to let me camp outside for free. I got to use the shower, so I was thrilled.

The next morning, the six of us put on lifejackets, squeezed into a small boat, and traveled down one of the many canals. The first hour was disappointing. I expected a twisty, narrow maze of canals going through tunnels of vegetation filled with animals. I imagined it would be Europe's Amazon jungle. Instead, it was extremely civilized. The canals were man-made: straight and with a consistent width. Nor was this Animal Planet TV—the most exciting wildlife we saw were a few horses, house cats, and a rare fisherman. Although reeds and grassland were everywhere, we weren't going through a tunnel of trees. It felt like we were driving down a road in Kansas, but in a boat.

Some in the group thought that the delta was dull. Our poor Romanian tour guide probably felt like an African safari tour guide who drives around for hours without seeing a damn giraffe. Despite the cold air and uncomfortable seats, two of the girls fell asleep. Fortunately, after lunch, our guide found a large lake that had what we were looking for.

At one end of the lake were an army of birds socializing on the water. As our guide accelerated the boat toward them, we could see swarms of swans, ducks, herons, egrets, and pelicans. Within the Danube Delta, there are over 300 bird species and 160 fish species. It is a bird watcher's paradise, where you might spot falcons and white-tailed eagles too. Because it's a bird sanctuary and home to one of the world's largest reed marshes, it's a UNESCO World Heritage Site. It's disgraceful that Ceauşescu wanted to drain the marshland and turn it into farmland. As we approached the flock of birds, they flew into the air, scattering in all directions. Hundreds, perhaps thousands of birds blanketed the sky. Our tour guide smiled.

Three Danube mysteries

There were three mysteries about the Danube River that I struggled to solve. First, why is there only one bridge across Romania and Bulgaria? We basically answered that mystery: vast language differences kept the two groups separate for centuries and the communists preferred functioning in closed economies.

Second, why hasn't Romania built any major city on the Danube? There are only three Romanian cities on the Danube with over 100,000 people: Galaţi, Brăila, Drobeta-Turnu Severin. None of them have populations of over 500,000. The Romanian towns on the Danube that I visited (Calafat, Giurgiu, and Tulcea) were small and forgettable. Why has Romania ignored the mighty Danube when it's one of the most important rivers in the world? It touches 10 countries. It's so strategic that Vienna, Bratislava, Budapest, Novi Sad, and Belgrade are all on it (that's four country capitals!). The Danube has always been a major trade route. Instead of developing another superb European city on the Danube, Romanians have spent centuries neglecting it.

Finally, there's the third and biggest mystery: why is Sulina such a pitifully small town and not a metropolis? Wherever a major river meets the sea, there's almost always a major town there. Here are a few cities that are located near the mouth of a river (with the river's name): New York (Hudson), Shanghai (Yangtze), Hamburg (Elbe), Gdańsk (Vistula), Le Havre (Seine), Marseille (Rhône), San Francisco

(Sacramento River), Rostov-on-Don (Don), Hanoi (Red River), Odessa (Dnieper), and Rīga (Daugava). Even rivers that end with complicated deltas usually have a major city: Alexandria (Nile), New Orleans (Mississippi), and Calcutta (Ganges). It's so logical to establish a city where a significant river meets the sea that it's strange when it is not done. Yet the population of the entire Danube Delta is only about 15,000. That's two humans per square kilometer—the least dense place in temperate Europe. In 1912, Sulina had a population of 7,347, but today it has less than 5,000, even if you count the cats.

Some say that there is a major city at the Danube's end: Constanța. Thanks to the Danube-Black Sea Canal, you can bypass the delta. For four years, prison labor (including many political prisoners) built the canal. Tens of thousands died in cruel conditions, which made the Canal earn the name *Canalul Morții* (Death Canal). The project was paused in 1953 and then Ceauşescu restarted it 23 years later. It is 64 kilometers long and has shaved off about 400 kilometers of navigation through the delta. Ships have to pay to go through the canal's two locks. The canal cost $2 billion and they hoped to pay it off in 50 years. However, given their recent revenues, it will take six more centuries to break even. Because the canal is a recent development, it doesn't explain why there wasn't already a metropolis at the Danube's natural end.

To solve this mystery, I asked most Romanians I met if they knew the answer. Most people had no clue and had never thought about it. Even journalists couldn't find the answer. One professor told me, "There's no money to build such a city." However, the international cities mentioned previously are older than money. They were built at the end of the river because it was a superb location. Another excuse: it's a fragile, swampy delta that's too tough to build on. Humans have never let that stop them before. St. Petersburg was built on a mosquito-infested wetland. New Orleans, Gdańsk, Alexandria, and Calcutta were all built on complex, swampy deltas.

A few Sulina locals told me that the reason there's no significant port at Danube's mouth is that it freezes in the winter. And St. Petersburg doesn't? Lots of rivers freeze, but that doesn't stop inventive humans from building on prime real estate. Romanians have icebreaking boats, which they use just a couple of times per month during the winter to help the trapped people at the end of the Danube. Locals stock up on supplies to survive the winter if the icebreakers don't come. If supplies are low, those in Sulina could easily take a boat and trade with the Ukrainians, Russians, Turks, and Bulgarians who are all busy living along the Black Sea during the winter. Instead, they claim they're trapped and isolated. Regardless, a freezing Danube is no excuse—ice-breakers work.

It's not clear what is more surprising: the fact that Sulina isn't an international destination or that few Romanians have ever thought about why it isn't. After asking an embarrassingly high number of Romanians and not getting a logical response, I finally found the answer in an obscure article written in 1954.[6] There are two reasons why Sulina is not a coastal metropolis. First, there's no great place to load and unload container ships. They could have created a deepwater port, which would have been cheaper than building the Danube-Black Sea Canal. However, they would still have the second problem: none of the three branches are good for navigation. The Chilia branch is deep, but has an unstable mouth. The Sulina branch is not deep enough for maritime ships and is disconnected from the rail lines. The Sfântu Gheorghe branch is too twisty and shallow.

There is one root cause behind both of these problems: a large amount of sand and silt that accumulates at the end of the Danube. This is a common issue at any river's end, especially when it ends in a major delta. Nevertheless, other major cities have solved this problem, so why hasn't Romania?

Blame Russia. For centuries, Russia controlled the delta and didn't want to develop a major port that might compete with its ports on the Black Sea, especially Odessa. Therefore, Russia neglected to maintain the delta, letting deposits and natural barriers to accumulate. To demonstrate how important it is to do maintenance, consider that during one eight-year period, the Sulina branch's depth decreased by almost half. The branches became too shallow for navigation and a proper port was never made. The Danube remained a blue highway without a fitting exit.

Still, it's unfair to blame Russia for everything. For long periods, Turks and Romanians also controlled the delta, and nothing was stopping them from making a navigable path and transforming Sulina into a metropolis. The winner of all this negligence is the wildlife that thrives in the delta today. Given how few Romanians think about the delta's strategic location, it's likely that it will remain a sleepy hidden corner of Europe.

Reflections at the end of the world

After our Danube Delta tour, the six of us walked to Sulina's sandy beach for the sunset. There was not a soul around. We felt like we were on the edge of the world. Nearby, the Danube gushes into Black Sea after its long run across Eastern Europe. The Danube is Europe's second longest river (after Russia's Volga). During the colorful sunset, I observed the pristine beach from the lifeguard tower and reflected about Romania.

The fact that Romania underutilizes the Danube implies that Romanians are insular. Countries that look outside themselves love to trade.

If Romanians were more outgoing, the Danube and the Black Sea coast would have Romania's economic centers. Instead, the biggest cities are Bucharest and Iaşi—both inland. There are a few major industrial areas and cities near the Hungarian border that the Hungarians developed and gave to Romania after the Treaty of Trianon. Perhaps Romania's inward-looking tendency may explain why the Romanian language has fewer Slavic words than you might expect. Had they interacted more with their Slavic neighbors, Romania's language would reflect that. Instead, most Romanians dislike their Slavic neighbors and keep the door closed. When Romania does look outside itself, it looks far away, to Western Europe. The day Romania develops the Danube River, the Danube Delta, and the Black Sea coast, is the day you'll know that Romania is coming out of its shell.

The next day, our guide took us down the Canali Cordon Litoral to the small town of Sfântu Gheorghe, where we took its circuitous branch back to Tulcea. At Tulcea's bus station, I left the group of five. I went to Galaţi, where I transferred to a minibus to Moldova.

Traveling to Timişoara

Many months later, while in Novi Sad, I was racing to get to Timişoara to catch a plane to Rome. I once again assumed that when two major cities are about 100 kilometers (63 miles) apart, there will be public transportation between them, even if they are in different countries. In Europe, that's always the case, except with Romania. There was no connection between Varna and Constanţa. Likewise, there was no bus between Novi Sad and Timişoara. Romanians truly act like they're living on a Latin island in an endless Slavic Sea.

I promised my Timişoara couchsurfing hosts that I would be there at 8:00 p.m. I was giving myself four hours to cover a measly 100 kilometers, yet it wasn't enough time. From Novi Sad, the closest you can get to Timişoara is a Serbian village three kilometers from the Romanian border. While I walked those three kilometers, I tried to hitchhike, but only five cars passed me in 40 minutes. The Serbian border guard was surprised that an American was walking across the border. He asked me to empty out my backpack and to show him my wallet. My gear didn't interest him, but he asked how I could be traveling entering a country with only $15. I told him about the magic of ATM cash machines. Perhaps he was disappointed that I didn't have lots of money for a potential bribe. He didn't know about my hidden money belt which had hundreds of dollars. He let me go.

The friendly Romanian border guards connected me with a trucker who was driving the final 50 kilometers to Timişoara. Then I learned that Romania's time zone is one hour ahead of Serbia, so I lost an hour—it was 9:00 p.m. The truck driver dropped me off on the outskirts. I took a tram to the center, raced to the Metropolitan Cathedral, and met my patient and forgiving couchsurfing hosts at 10:00 p.m.

The next day, I explored Timişoara, which may be Romania's best city. Locals call it *Primul Oraş Liber* (First Free Town), because Ceauşescu's overthrow started here. For a city of just 322,000, it's filled with plazas. *Piaţa Libertăţii* (Liberty Plaza) is where the 1989 revolution started. The *Piaţa Unirili* has two cathedrals (one Orthodox, the other Catholic) that were both built in 1754. The gracefully long *Piaţa Victorei* has the Metropolitan Cathedral on one end and the National Theater and Opera House on the other. There are three smaller plazas too. Near the center of town is the *Parcul Civic* (Civic Park). Meanwhile, the southern part of the town has six parks that are connected to one another. Credit Hungary for the brilliant design, since it ruled Timişoara (and the Banat region) for centuries until they lost it after WWI. After a full day, I went to Timişoara's airport and flew to Italy.

Romania's paradox

Imagine that you could wave a wand and that all the people of the world would disappear, but that everything else, including the buildings and infrastructure, would stay as they are. Now, you're walking around with a real estate agent trying to decide where to establish your new kingdom. You probably wouldn't pick Kosovo or Macedonia. However, you might pick Romania. It has the stunning Bucharest and Timişoara, castles like Bran and Peleş, charming towns like Braşov and Sighişoara, the majestic Carpathian mountains that make for great hiking and skiing, the abundant wheat, wine, and plums of the Banat region, the strategic Danube River, the precious metal and oil deposits, the Black Sea destinations like Constanţa, and the wilderness paradise of the Danube Delta. Romania has it all. It's truly blessed.

And yet, Romania is always fucked up. This is the paradox. Why is a country that has so much potential perpetually stuck in the mud? Romania's Minister of Foreign Affairs wrote that Romanians "seek historical alibis for their eternal lamentations."[7] It's tempting to blame the people, but under the proper leadership, Romania has flourished, as evidenced by the architectural marvels that have been built over the centuries. Before WWII, it was one of the world's largest food exporters. Under Ceauşescu, it starved. Today, it's not much better. In 2010, nearly half of Romanians told Gallup that in the previous year there were times when they didn't have enough money to buy food—that was the worst rate in Europe.

In 2010, only four percent of Romanians were "satisfied" with their country's "efforts to deal with the poor." That's the lowest rate in the world. Still, they have nearby company: of the 17 least satisfied countries, 12 were from Eastern Europe. In 2010, only nine percent of

Romanians had confidence in their government—that was the lowest rate on Earth (right above it were Latvia, Lithuania, and Haiti). Romania also had the world's worst score on Gallup's Corruption Index. Lastly, only 16 percent had confidence in the honesty of elections—the lowest rate in Europe and worse than Congo, Haiti, and Zimbabwe.

In 2011, Sinzina Demian, a Romanian reporter, wrote to me, "Romania is in a mess. There really aren't that many good things I could say about this place right now. Much seems to be going in the wrong direction: the education and health care systems are appalling, unemployment is rising fast, and the once-successful Romanian athletes (whose wins would always alleviate the general bitterness) are nowhere to be found anymore. Not to mention how bribing still holds first honors here, in pretty much every sector. So, overall, I am quite disillusioned and angry these days, that such a beautiful country with so much potential is still stuck so badly over 20 years after 1989."

Three Romanian students who were studying in Slovenia told me that all Romanians are to blame. The corrupted leadership is at fault for stealing as much as they can, but the people are at fault too. They said, "Compared to Romanians, Slovenians are fast. Slovenians wake up early in the morning and do everything. They have so much energy to do so many things. They move so fast on the streets. We prefer to sleep later. We move slow. We don't like to work."

Romanians are like Africans who can't seem to break out of their cycle of corruption, laziness, and disorganization. However, they're the opposite of the Africans: Romanians look at their "colonial times," when a foreign power dominated them, as periods of prosperity. Some say they were better off when German King Carol I was running the show. They even joke that if they get occupied again, it might be the best thing that happens to Romania.

Romania's crystal ball is grim. When Gallup asked the world to predict how their life would be like in five years (on a 1-10 scale), Romanians were the second most gloomy country on Earth (4.8). Only Burundi (4.7) was more despondent in 2010. Still, Romania had plenty of Eastern European company: Bulgaria (4.9), Macedonia (5.0), Serbia (5.1), Greece (5.3), Bosnia (5.4), Hungary (5.4), and Latvia (5.5) were all more pessimistic than Afghanistan (5.8).

Nevertheless, we can still learn from Romanians. When I asked Sinzina what she liked about Romania, she said, "Romanians make fun of the worst situations. Sometimes it's in bad taste, and I could see on many occasions that foreigners were taken aback, thinking they were the target of mean Romanians. We're often *very* politically incorrect, but once you get it, you can see the humor. Romanians really call things as they see them—no veils, no politeness. In certain contexts it's really terrible and very unprofessional, but somehow people get a kick out of it and perpetuate it. Cruel honesty rules here, with its good and bad parts."

There's evidence that Romanians have an entrepreneurial spirit that will help its future. When Gallup asked people everywhere what they would do if they suddenly inherited a significant amount of money, 42 percent of Romanians said they would start a business. In 2011, that was the highest rate in Europe (only 11 percent of Western Europeans said they'd be entrepreneurs). Now, if they can just inherit that money. . . .

What Romania Can Teach Us

- **Use a dual-flushing toilet.** Shop around and you'll find these water and money saving toilets. They're all over Eastern Europe and they should be all over America.
- **Close the door.** In the US, stores sometimes leave their doors wide open while the climate control systems work overtime. Money and energy pours out our shops' doors. In Romania, they have a simple solution that we rarely do anymore in the US: close the door and have a sign that says OPEN.
- **Reuse.** Romanians, like most Eastern Europeans, reuse whatever object they can. They make everything survive longer than you thought was possible. It's one of the positive environmental legacies of communism.
- **Be direct.** Romanians don't sugarcoat their words. Although they sometimes take it to an extreme, consider speaking your mind if you tend to use subtle communication methods.

Places I saw and recommend in Romania: Bucharest, Timişoara, any of its mountains, Sighişoara, Braşov, and the Danube Delta (but only if you're an avid bird watcher).

Travel deals and info: http://ftapon.com/romania

Four of the first five chapters of this book were about countries in the former USSR. We've come full circle—now the last three chapters of the book will be about countries that were also once republics in the USSR: Moldova, Ukraine, and Russia.

23

Moldova—Poor, Torn, and Drunk

"You must leave Moldova by October 14," the Moldovan consulate official told me in French.

"And if I don't?" I wondered aloud.

"You will have big problems," she assured me with a smile. That sounded like the standard impaling treatment. My $30 transit visa gave me three days to get through Moldova and into Ukraine. Given that Moldova is a bit bigger than Maryland, this wouldn't be hard to do.

Why is it that the less desirable the country, the more difficult it is to get in it? You'd think that elite countries would be highly selective about who visits and that undesirable countries would let any jackass in. Not so. In 2004, Belarus and Moldova were the most troublesome places to get into. Fortunately, you don't need a visa anymore to get into Moldova. Perhaps they realized that playing hard-to-get wasn't attracting the tourists.

What divides Romania and Moldova

My bus crossed the Prut River, which divides Romania and Moldova. It's basically the only thing that divides Romania and Moldova. Linguistically, they're identical. In 2002, the Moldovan Minister of Justice said that Romanian and Moldovan are the same language. Moldova's Education Minister and President agreed. Nevertheless, in 2003, a Moldovan-Romanian Dictionary was published, which is about as useful as having a New York-Texas Dictionary—a complete waste of paper.

Moldova is torn: among its population, three times more people claim to speak Moldovan than to speak Romanian. Since the only real difference between these languages is their name, this poll implies that Moldovans believe that there's more than just the Prut River that separates them from Romanians. A 2009 survey indicated that 47 percent of Moldovans believe that the Romanian and Moldovan identities are "different" or "entirely different," while only 26 percent felt they were "the same" or "very similar."

The Soviets encouraged the belief that Moldovans are different than Romanians by making Moldovans use the Cyrillic alphabet. This took Moldovans back over 200 years, when they (and the Romanians) used the Cyrillic alphabet. However, after gaining their independence from the USSR 20 years ago, Moldovans reverted to the Latin alphabet, thereby making their language indistinguishable from Romanian. Nevertheless, the notion that they are different remained. That partly explains why most Moldovans do not want to reunite with Romania.

Ethnically, 70 percent are Moldovan/Romanian and 20 percent are Russian/Ukrainian. Most Slavs live on Moldova's eastern edge, where they make up the majority. Lastly, four percent of Moldovans are ethnic Gagauz, who are Christians that speak a Turkish dialect. The reason this tiny country is so divided is that the region has traded among various rulers more times than a stock on the New York Stock Exchange.

Europe's poorest country

Our bus arrived in Moldova's capital, Chişinău (pronounced *KEE-shee-now*). The city has 664,325 people and has a flat, grid layout. People were mostly speaking in Romanian, but Russian signs and communication were common too. Aside from a few communist-styled buildings, there's little touristy stuff to see. Perhaps Chişinău's most remarkable attribute is that it seems like a normal Eastern European city. You might expect less when you're in Europe's poorest country.

Indeed, Moldova's 2010 per capita GDP was just $2,500, thereby placing it at Europe's economic bottom; the CIA ranked it equal to Nigeria. Among the 4.3 million Moldovans, over a quarter live in poverty. For those who prefer other ways of measuring wealth, consider the UN's 2010 Human Development Index. Moldova was easily the worst country in Europe, and was right below Botswana. Moldovans are struggling: according to Gallup's 2010 poll, Moldovans were once again the least well-rested people in Europe, and fourth from the world's bottom. Nevertheless, it's surprising that no matter how poor an economy is, there are always crowds buying stuff on the streets, yapping on cell phones, dyeing their gel-filled hair, frequenting cafés, and wasting money on cigarettes.

Another paradox is that the poorer the country, the more the budget traveler spends on lodging. Relatively expensive Eastern European countries like Slovenia and Czechia have a developed hostel network where it's easy to spend less than $20 per night. Meanwhile, the poorest countries, like Kosovo and Moldova, have few hostel options, which force you to pay hotel prices that are at least twice as expensive as a hostel. In controlled economies (like Belarus), tourists really get nailed. Moldovans seem to miss their controlled economy, because in 2010 the communist party won 40 percent the vote, thereby getting the most seats in parliament.

It's remarkable that Moldovans voted communists back into power given their Soviet experience. First, the USSR conspired with the Nazis to take Moldova away from Romania. They imposed the Cyrillic alphabet. Stalin deported tens of thousands and caused over 216,000 to starve to death. Leonid Brezhnev, leader of the Moldovan Communist Party (and future leader of the USSR), also deported tens of thousands. The Soviets relocated thousands of Slavs to replace the vanished Moldovans. Despite this atrocious track record, many Moldovans thought the 1990s were worse.

In 1992, Moldova had a mini-Bosnian War. After Moldova became independent in late 1991, two of its minorities (the Slavs and Gagauzes) wanted their own independence. It's similar to how ethnic Croatians and ethnic Serbs wanted to carve out pieces of Bosnia after Bosnia declared its independence. The difference is that Moldova's civil war lasted only five months and a few hundred lives—far less destructive than the Bosnian War. The aftermath was also different. The Gagauz compromised and got autonomy, while the Slavs got a quasi-state called Transnistria, which is one of the most bizarre places I visited in Eastern Europe.

Transnistria: a hidden, wacky part of Europe

When countries draw their internal borders, it's a pity that they rarely ask themselves what would happen if each region became independent. If they did, we would avoid many civil wars. Instead, most countries sloppily draw their internal borders. We saw the problem in Yugoslavia; it's the same issue in Moldova. For the last few centuries, the Dniester River divided Slavs from the Romanians (Moldovans). Slavs were mostly on east bank, while Romanians preferred the west bank. In fact, Romanians called the east bank *Transnistria* because it means *beyond the Dniester River*. That's because things begin to change when you cross the Dniester.

Instead of using this natural, historical border, the Soviets (due to some complicated "logic" that we won't go into) put a thin piece of the east bank into the Moldovian SSR. Thus, when the Moldovian SSR eventually declared its independence from the USSR and became Moldova, it wanted to keep the whole territory, including its piece on the east bank. The Slavs who lived there didn't like that idea. Thanks to Russian military support, they've created their own central bank, currency, postage stamps, police, justice system, and border checkpoints. They called their breakaway state *Transnistria*. For the last 20 years, Igor Smirnov has ruled Transnistria with an iron fist. Now in his 70s, he still vows not to step down until the international community recognizes Transnistria. However, no UN member, not even Ukraine or Russia, recognize the sovereignty, passports, or currency of Transnistria.

Transnistria illustrates how the Dniester River has been evolving from a soft border to a hard one. The percentage of Russians in Transnistria has more than doubled in the last 100 years, while Moldovans have dropped from nearly half of the population to a third. Ethnically, the half million Transnistrians are now divided into roughly equally sized groups: Russians, Ukrainians, and Moldovans. However, no ethnic Moldovans are members in the Transnistrian council of ministers. Russian is the default language. You can write in Moldovan, but only using the Cyrillic alphabet. Although most Transnistrians are still Moldovan citizens, many hold Russian or Ukrainian passports. In 2006, Russia issued 80,000 passports to Transnistrians and continues to hand them out liberally.

In 2004, I was the only foreigner on the minibus to Tiraspol, Transnistria's capital. Although I was used to being a lonely tourist in Eastern Europe, Transnistria's sketchy state made me wonder if I was being stupid this time. The Dniester River border was heavily policed. The Russian border guards asked for $10 for a one-day visa and told me to register with the military in two different places. I was in.

The official Moldovan currency is not accepted within Transnistria, so I converted some dollars into the Transnistrian ruble, which appeared in 1994 and quickly became worthless. In January 2001, the government declared that the new ruble was worth the same as one million old rubles. Even today, it's impossible to find anyone outside of Transnistria, including Moldova proper, who will value the Transnistrian ruble more than toilet paper.

Transnistria wanted to restore communism, but after several disastrous years of trying, they reverted to capitalism. Still, Soviet symbols are everywhere in Tiraspol. You can walk down Lenin Street, through the dilapidated Kirov Park, and then down Karl Marx Street. The city's prettiest building is the white *Dom Sovetovul* (The House of the Soviets), where Lenin's white face overlooks traffic. On the main boulevard, there's a Soviet tank on a pedestal. Nearby is the Tomb of the Unknown Soldier with an eternal flame honoring fallen soldiers in the 1992 civil war. I wanted to translate the inscription, so I approached the only two people walking around on that chilly October afternoon.

Meeting the Transnistrians

Russophones usually have one of two extreme reactions when I ask them if they speak English. Either they are thrilled to meet an American, or they act like I just told them that their mother is a whore. For example, when I first arrived in Tiraspol, I asked two young Transnistrians if they could speak English. They frowned, squinted their eyes, and walked away without saying a word. They're so rude it's comical.

Fortunately, the two women by the war memorial were the friendly type, although neither spoke English well. They wanted to learn about what a Californian was doing in Tiraspol and I wanted to know how life is really like there. Despite our difficulty communicating, they suggested that we go to a warm café. The women, Katia and Vita, were in their mid-20s and were studying economics. Both had blond hair and switched between English and Russian when they spoke. Katia was married and Vita was not. When they asked me where I was staying, I told them that I still didn't know—it was 3:00 p.m. and I often didn't make such decisions until the last second. Katia said that I was welcome to stay in her family's apartment. Given the lack of hostel options, I happily agreed. They had to leave, so Katia gave me her address and invited me to come by that night, which would give me more time to explore Tiraspol. Little did I know what would happen that night.

I stayed out later than expected and got lost trying to find Katia's place, but I finally arrived at her eighth-floor apartment at 9:30 p.m. Katia didn't mind that I was late. In the living room, she introduced me to a Russian couple who had a baby. In the kitchen, Katia ordered me to sit down and then served a delicious potato soup. Katia spoke to me in Russian like she would speak to her three-year-old son, but I understood less than he would.

After eating, she showed me the bathroom. They had no hot water, but they had gas. So Katia boiled a pot of water, mixed it with a bigger bowl of cold water, and I enjoyed an overdue sponge bath. While I bathed, I was curious why I hadn't met Katia's husband and two boys. Maybe their kids were already sleeping and her husband was out late. I shrugged. When I finished washing up, it was already 11:00 p.m. I was exhausted. Being a tourist in a land where you don't speak the language is draining. Katia showed me my room saying, "*Tam spat. Spakoinoi nochi.*" ("Sleep there. Goodnight.")

As I got into the bed and reflected on my situation, something seemed odd. Why was I sleeping in a bed? I expected to sleep on a couch in the living room. Maybe it's because Katia's friends with the baby were still there. In fact, they looked like they might sleep there. If so, where would Katia and her husband sleep? And her kids? Obviously, this apartment must be bigger than it appears to be. Doors that I thought led to closets probably led to other rooms. Whatever. Such thoughts were too complex for my worn-out mind. I quickly fell asleep.

Suddenly, in the middle of the night, I woke up. My door was opening. A shadowy person was entering my dark room.

Torture in Tiraspol

As my foggy mind woke up, I saw that it was Katia. She was wearing skimpy lingerie. She stood over me, motioned me to scoot over, and then said with a stern voice, "Do *not* touch me. Must not touch. If touch, I *kill* you!"

I said, "OK, OK: No problem! Don't worry."

I acted like Katia had the plague. I moved as far I could to the opposite end of the bed. I was on the edge, pressed against the wall. She seemed satisfied with the amount of space I was giving her. She pulled back the sheets and slipped into the bed. I prefer sleeping on my back, but I slept on my side with my back against the wall to give her the most space possible and to make sure we didn't touch. After my adrenaline wore off, I fell back to sleep.

A few minutes later, I woke up because Katia was pressing her back against my chest. Then she pushed her butt into my groin. She wiggled her ass a bit as if to find just the right spot. Finally, she found it—right against my penis.

I was frozen. We weren't saying anything. I didn't know what to do. We both acted like nothing had happened. I tried to behave like a statue, yet only one part of me was getting hard.

I tried to concentrate and relax. I breathed slowly. Finally, she grabbed my right arm and put it around her body. We were spooning—the back of her body pressed against the front of my body. After she wrapped my arm around her, she twisted her head and whispered in my ear, "No more. If you do more, I kill you. Understand?"

"Yes, yes, I understand," I said. I understand that I am sleeping with a psychopath. Never mind. This was somewhat comfortable anyway. It was nice to snuggle after so many months of no action. This was October 2004 and the last time I had gotten naked with someone was in July 2004 in Dobrush, Belarus. That's when a naked Belarusian man whipped me hard in a sauna.

This was a much better experience. Katia had a sexy body. So I drifted off to sleep while holding her. Within a few minutes, however, she started "adjusting" her butt again. Her thin lingerie barely covered her ass, which she began slowly grinding into my crotch, waking it up again. Meanwhile, she took my hand and delicately placed it on her juicy breasts. I could feel the thin lace of her lingerie that covered her nipples, which became aroused once my hand rested on them. She continued firmly rubbing her body into mine. The more she pressed against me, the harder it was to behave like Jesus. I instinctively and lightly squeezed her breasts. Then suddenly she turned around and whispered loudly, "*Stop!* I told you, no touch!"

Ugh. I concluded that I'm sleeping with the Tiraspol Torturer. For the next couple of hours, she toyed with me. She would run her nails up my leg, then grab my penis and squeeze it firmly a few times. After turning me on, she would remind me of our "don't touch" deal. She teased me until 4:00 a.m., when a bit of dry humping seemed to satisfy her. We finally went to sleep.

When I woke up at 9:00 a.m., Katia was gone. As I went to the bathroom, Katia's friends were leaving. We said goodbye and I went back to sleep. While I was sleeping, my Transnistrian Teaser climbed back into bed. She employed the same arousing tactics, but this time, she escalated our Russian-American relations. Let's just say that I won't be detailing the events in the international policy magazine *Foreign Affairs*.

Hell's highway

At noon, I thanked Katia for her unique "hospitality" and left. Her story continues later. With my visa soon set to expire, I set off to Ukraine on Moldova's hellish highway. The two outer lanes went in opposite directions, but the middle lane was a free for all. Nobody had the right-of-way. It was a constant game of chicken. When you're blasting down the middle lane, there's nothing stopping anyone from going in the opposite direction to challenge your position. It's times like these that I just sit in the back of the bus and find God.

Crappy roads are common in Eastern Europe. Cars were prohibitively expensive under communist regimes, so Eastern Europe is struggling to catch up to Western standards. According to a 2010 Gallup poll, at least 60 percent of Western Europeans (except the British and Italians) were satisfied with their roads, whereas all Eastern European countries (except Finland, Croatia, and Turkey) had satisfaction rates under 60 percent. The most dissatisfied Europeans were Moldovans (15%), who ranked sixth from the world's bottom.

While we bumped along hell's highway, the minibus blasted a song that I heard in every Eastern European country in 2004: O-Zone's tune "*Dragostea din tei,*" which most of the world knows as "Numa Numa." It hit number one on the charts throughout Europe and was number three in the UK. YouTube amateur lip-synching video versions of the song have gotten over one billion views. Their other hit song, "*Despre tine,*" also came from the same *DiscO-Zone* album. Eastern Europeans consistently told me that they were a Romanian pop group. However, they originated out of Moldova. Sadly, Moldova rarely gets credit for the most famous song it ever produced.

Who drinks the most alcohol in the world?

Wherever I went in Eastern Europe, people told me that their country drank more than anyone else. I was so tired of hearing such claims that I had to find out: *who are the heaviest drinkers in the world?* The answer is in the World Health Organization's comprehensive 2011 survey.[1] The results show that Czechia is the second highest per capita beer consumer in the world (after Palau). However, beer has relatively low alcohol content. You don't need to be Russian to know that drinking one liter of beer ain't the same as drinking one liter of vodka.

Therefore, to find the definitive answer, we need to measure the *per capita consumption of pure alcohol*. Measured in liters, here are the results of several countries: Turkey 2.9, Albania 6.7, Macedonia 8.5, USA 9.4, Bosnia 9.6, Canada 9.7, Serbia 11.1, Poland 13.3, and the UK 13.4. And now, for the world's top 10 alcohol consumers (notice that they're all from Eastern Europe): Lithuania 15.0, Croatia 15.11, Belarus 15.13, Slovenia 15.19, Romania 15.3, Estonia 15.5, Ukraine 15.6, Russia 15.8, Hungary 16.3, Czechia 16.5, and Moldova 18.2. Andorra, a tiny country between Spain and France, had 15.5 liters. However, Andorra's results are misleading, since many tourists visit the dinky country to get wasted, thereby skewing the per capita results (which divides liters of alcohol by the number of permanent residents). The Drunk Award goes to Moldova.

At first, you might think that Moldovans are getting drunk on their world-famous wine. Indeed, Moldova's Mileştii Mici has the world's largest wine cellars. It's a staggering 250 kilometers (160 miles) long, holds two million bottles, but has a capacity to store four million. About 70 percent are *negru* or *roşu* (two types of red wine), 20 percent are *vin alb* (white wine), and 10 percent are dessert wines. Don't forget to specify if you want *sec* (dry), *dulce* (sweet), or *spumos* (sparkling). The most expensive bottles were made in 1973 and cost $700 each.

Despite Moldova's extraordinary wine, it only accounts for about one-third of Moldova's alcohol consumption. About one-third comes from beer and the other third comes from spirits, like vodka. Moreover, only 8.2 liters comes from "recorded consumption," while 10 liters of alcohol is "unrecorded," which includes sketchy home-brewed liquor. The consequence is severe. Moldova's road traffic accident rates are usually high. Furthermore, in 2005, for every 100,000 people, 132 men and 109 women died of liver cirrhosis. *This is off the charts*—no other country comes close to have such an epidemic of damaged livers.

An American who worked in Moldova told me, "The alcohol problem is very apparent. Drinking goes on regularly at the work place. Basically, any excuse is a reason to buy a bottle of vodka or cognac and do shots. If an American college fraternity is a drinking sprint, Moldova is a drinking marathon. My host family, albeit very social, made 2,500 liters of wine one year. They started drinking it in October and it was gone by the end of June."

Hitchhiking halfway across Moldova

Five years after my first visit to Moldova, I returned for another adventure. My 2009 trip started when I took a bus from Galaţi, Romania to the small town of Oancea, which is on the Moldova border. The last bus to Moldova had already left, so I walked to the border. I told the border guards that I wanted to hitchhike to Moldova. Within five minutes, they found a middle-aged man who agreed to take me. He already had two passengers: a man in his early 20s and a woman in her early 30s. It wasn't until he dropped us all off at a gas station on the outskirts of Cahul that I learned that the driver's two passengers were also hitchhikers.

After he dropped the three of us off, we realized that we were in a worrisome situation. Actually, I was not worried, but my two Moldovan hitchhiking partners were. They wanted to cross nearly half of Moldova and get to Chişinău, but the sun was setting in one hour and there were three of us. It would be hard to find a ride that would accept three hitchhikers. Trying to cover hundreds of kilometers made our goal even more unlikely. I was relaxed because I had a tarp and sleeping bag, so I could easily camp in the fields near the gas station. However, they would be stranded. They couldn't afford a taxi or hotel. They were desperate.

After one hour of failing to get a ride and the sunlight vanishing, the young man called his friend and asked him for an enormous favor: drive a couple of hours to pick us up. His friend eventually showed up. My female hitchhiking partner said, "You want to learn what Moldovans can teach Americans? This is it. See what we are willing to do for our friends."

She also showed remarkable team spirit by inviting the three of us men to crash at her Chişinău apartment. We arrived at midnight, so we all went straight to sleep. I slept on her couch. In the morning, while having tea, I asked them how Moldovan-Russian relations were. They said they co-exist fine, but it's not perfect. They told me a joke that illustrates how some Moldovans feel.

An American, a Frenchman, a Russian, and a Moldovan are on a rescue boat after their vessel sank. The rescue boat is too heavy and water is coming in, so the American throws bags of dollars overboard. The others say, "Are you crazy?"

"Don't worry," the American replies, "There are plenty of dollars at every street corner in the USA."

Still, the boat is too heavy, so the Frenchman throws cases of fine wine overboard. The others say, "Are you demented?"

"Don't worry," the Frenchman says, "There is plenty of great wine on every street corner in France."

But the boat still doesn't recover. Suddenly, the Moldovan throws the Russian overboard. The others say, "Have you gone bonkers?"

The Moldovan says, "Don't worry, there are plenty of Russians on every street corner in Moldova."

Revisiting the Russians in Transnistria

In the winter after my sexually charged visit to Moldova in 2004, Katia sent me an email with a few typos. She wrote, "Forgive my troubling you. I decided to bother you. We've had a jolly time. We only went to sleep at four in the morning. You are very kind. It was a real pleasure for me to do this. Don't be angry. Write to me, please. I am looking forward to your letter. Every day. In the Transnistria very cold. It is 9-17 below zero. What nasty weather! Very cold. I wont a warm weather and a hot man. I wont see you. Very wont. I'm grateful to you for all you've done for me. Write to me. I'm waiting."

Clearly, Transnistria's Temptress is effective over email too. Vita, her friend, later told me that Katia was ill at the hospital and in her delirium she supposedly cried my name. Who knows what was true. Perhaps Katia was married, but separated. Or she was divorced. Or she had never been married, and that she just claimed to be married to fulfill her fantasy of having a lustful affair. Regardless, about once a year, we would exchange emails. When she learned that I was returning to Moldova, she invited me to visit her again in Transnistria. It wasn't clear if I would meet her phantom husband and kids this time. I was too curious to refuse her invitation.

I know nothing about sex, because I was always married.
— Zsa Zsa Gabor

Katia had moved from Tiraspol to Rîbniţa. After WWII, the Soviets invested heavily in Moldova, but mostly in the thin sliver of Transnistria. By 1990, 40% of Moldova's GDP and 90% of its electricity came from Transnistria, even though they only had 17% of the population. The biggest company was Moldova Steel Works in Rîbniţa, which accounted for about 60% of Transnistria's budget revenue. The Soviets also invested in textiles, so that today Transnistria has one of Europe's largest textile companies. Moldova doesn't feel dense, but it was the USSR's most densely populated republic. Paradoxically, Moldova is also the least urbanized country in Europe.

When I took the bus from Chişinău to Transnistria, a 21-year-old student named Inesse sat next to me. I told her that my guidebook warned that tourists should expect to pay a $30 bribe to get in a visa, which was more than the $10 one-day visa that I paid in 2004. She agreed to help me translate and negotiate with the Russian-speaking border guards. At the border, everyone got off the minibus to complete immigration forms. Ironically, Inesse, who lives in Transnistria, had to pay a $2 fee, but the guards let me in for free. Later, a Westerner who entered Transnistria by car, told me that he had to pay a $30 bribe. It's a common border theme: foreigners with cars must pay more bribes than foreigners in buses (although sometimes there is a legitimate road tax).

Right before I knocked on Katia's door in Rîbniţa, a horrible vision flashed in my mind. Moldova is a famous source for human trafficking. Most victims are females who are sold to European and Middle Eastern men who sexually exploit them. Children are also stolen and used as beggars. Even Moldovan men are trafficked—usually as slave labor. In 2008, the CIA reported that over 25,000 Moldovans were sold as forced laborers. I hardly knew Katia. Maybe she was just setting me up. Maybe Katia's husband will open the door and five Russian thugs will sneak up from behind, tackle me, and tie me up. Then they'll sell me for $999 to a Saudi Prince who will force me to write a book about Eastern Europe.

Moldova's lifeblood: remittances from abroad

I rang the doorbell anyway. Katia answered with a devilish smile. No hooligans attacked me. In the last five years, her English hadn't improved, nor had my Russian. She said that her husband had moved to St. Petersburg and that she will move there too in a few months. He was probably sending her money for their two boys. This is common in Moldova. Over 30 percent of Moldova's GDP comes from Moldovans working abroad who send money home—that's one of the world's highest remittance rates.

Gallup's 2010 survey of 13,200 people from the former USSR had more insights. Extrapolating from the results, we can estimate that 70 million people in the former USSR (25% of its population) would migrate temporarily for work and 35 million would leave permanently. Over half of Moldovans would like to move for temporary work—that's higher than any other former USSR country. And 36% of Moldovans would like to permanently move to another country, which is the second highest in the former USSR. Perhaps that's because 54% of Moldovans (more than any ex-USSR country) "have contacts in other countries that they can count on for help" and 24% of them "received some kind of financial help in the past year." One Westerner who lived in Moldova for a couple of years told me, "Moldova's lack of prospects is pretty depressing. I told my Moldovan friends that if I were them, I would be trying to emigrate to anyplace where there are more opportunities for a better life."

Indeed, what Moldovans will do to escape their country is almost funny. You've probably never heard of underwater hockey, but Moldova's underwater hockey team is famous. It's not that the team dominates the sport, but rather that their teams have unusual tactics. In 2000, Moldova's men's team puzzled Australian referees when they needed help putting on their flippers. Moldovans looked at the flippers like it was the first time they had seen them. During the matches, every competitor destroyed them. Nobody could figure out why Moldovans had traveled halfway around the world to get their underwater ass kicked. However, their true purpose became clear when they filed for refugee status with the Australian government.

Two years later, Moldovan women demonstrated an even better way of doing it. The Tiraspol-based Moldovan Underwater Hockey Federation begged the Canadian embassy to give their women a visa so they could compete in the Underwater Hockey World Championship in Calgary. The Canadians issued the visas. When the rarely heard Moldovan national anthem started playing at the opening of the games, the Moldovan team didn't show up. Why? The clever ladies were 1,000 kilometers away, in Toronto, filing for refugee status. Each woman had paid $1,200 to be on the underwater hockey team—a sweet deal for the chance to move from Moldova to Canada. And best of all, unlike the men, the women didn't have to get their butts kicked underwater.

The Transnistrian Temptress revisited

Katia showed me around Rîbniţa. First, she had to register me with the Transnistria state authorities. We had to run around for an hour photocopying my passport and filling out forms. Doing useless paperwork is a hard commie habit to break. Rîbniţa has classic communist design. It's filled with gray, unimaginative high-rise apartment blocks with poorly maintained playground areas. There's an occasional stern, monolithic Soviet monument and a few attractive Orthodox churches. Communist cities were functional, but they lacked charm and beauty—it's the exact opposite of Italian cities.

Katia introduced me to her five-year-old and eight-year-old sons. So they did exist. Still, it was still not clear if Katia was truly married. She seemed to indicate that they have an "open relationship" when they're not together. She still indulged in her perverted, torturous fantasy of simultaneously tempting and resisting me. I'm not sure about Moldova's law on adultery. Moldova's sex laws have changed dramatically in the last 20 years. Before 1995, for example, it was a crime to perform homosexual acts. Less than 10 years later, Moldova made a complete change—now it's legal to have sex with anyone as long as you're over 14 years old. Chişinău has an annual Gay Pride march. Thus, Moldova went from being a sexual prude to as liberal as a San Francisco transvestite.

Months after I left, Katia wrote to me from St. Petersburg. She invited me to write my book in her apartment in Moldova while she was gone for months. She promised, "You will have a free and empty apartment. Also, I will find you a sexy girlfriend." Ah yes, she truly is the Transnistrian Temptress.

Hitchhiking around Northern Moldova

Happy that Katia didn't enslave me, I eventually left Rîbniţa to explore Northern Moldova. I started with Saharna, which has a pretty 500-year-old blue monastery set under steep hills. After busing it to Trebujeni, I got tired of waiting for the next bus, so I hitchhiked in a van that I hoped would take me near the *Complexul Muzeistic Orheiul Vechi* (Orheiul Vechi Monastery Complex). They dropped me off 15 kilometers (9 miles) short of the monastery. While waiting for another ride, two women appeared across the street from me, attempting to hitchhike in the opposite direction. The Moldovan road was quiet, with one car passing every five minutes. The women could tell I wasn't a local. Finally, one yelled out, "Where are you from?"

"San Francisco!" I yelled back.

"What the hell are you doing here?"

"I was asking myself that same question!"

They laughed. We had a nice chat, shouting across the street. I got a ride before they did. A gruff, fat man in a tiny car eyed me suspiciously. I told him in Russian that I don't speak Romanian (or much Russian for that matter), but he agreed to drive me a few kilometers. He became less grumpy after I gave him 20 lei (about $2). I thanked him for getting me closer to the monastery, and tried hitchhiking again. After 20 minutes, a couple driving a yellow VW Beetle pulled up. The driver, Emil Bojescu, spoke excellent English because he had lived in the UK for a few years. Fortunately, they were also going to the monastery.

The *Mănăstire in Peşteră* (Cave Monastery) is set among limestone cliffs with dramatic views of the river that carved them. For 500 years monks lived in this superb setting, but they abandoned it in the 1700s. In 1996, monks dusted off the cobwebs and reopened this religious masterpiece. There's a church above ground, built in 1905, which the Soviets closed in 1944. It's now renovated. After touring the grounds, Emil dropped me off next to a highway heading to Bălţi. The sun was setting and I was prepared to camp nearby, but instead, I brazenly stood on the highway's shoulder. That was probably illegal, but Moldova inspired me to take risks.

A man in a van picked me up and gave me a great experience. First, he just happened to be going to the exact town I wanted to go to: Soroca, which is next to the Ukrainian border. He had a taxi business and picked up a few other hitchhikers along the way. I offered him $10 for the 90-minute trip. Along the way, he let me use his phone to call my couchsurfing host, TJ Lowdermilk, to get his street address. We arrived in Soroca at 9:00 p.m. and TJ still hadn't picked up his phone. I told my driver to just drop me off anywhere in town because I would find a place to camp. He said that I was crazy and took me to his apartment.

He invited me to sleep there. He introduced me to his wife, who served me seasoned potatoes and tea. I had unpacked my backpack and spent about 30 minutes at their place when TJ finally called back. I repacked and my taxi driver drove me to TJ's apartment for free. It's remarkable that a taxi driver went out of his way to take care of me, even though we could hardly communicate.

Couchsurfing with a Peace Corps volunteer

TJ was a tall 28-year-old American Peace Corps volunteer who was helping Moldovan entrepreneurs get started. He looked like a thoughtful, sensitive American activist: he had thin brown hair, glasses, and a goatee. He lived in a minimalist studio—I would be sleeping on the hardwood floor that night, which is firmer than the typical camping spot. His building didn't have hot water. He said that the next day we could visit his girlfriend's place and take a hot shower there. I was in no hurry—at one point while I was backpacking the Continental Divide Trail for seven months, I went 45 days without a shower.

Although the Soroca Fortress is the humble town's star attraction, walking through the Roma neighborhood is more interesting. The town has Moldova's highest concentration of Roma. Just like there were Roma mansions in Calafat, Romania, there are ostentatious mini-palaces in Soroca. Some people might say that Roma build their houses backwards: several half-finished homes had all the flashy exterior details completed, but they hadn't started on the interior. For example, some houses had elaborate Corinthian columns, detailed stone carvings, or bronze statues of horses mounted on the rooftop. Meanwhile, the home was still an empty shell. Most people would wait until the end to add decorative elements. Indeed, many Balkanians live in half-finished homes, where the exterior is far from complete. It seems that Roma believe that if they can't have their flashy details, then there's no point moving in.

While TJ guided me through the Roma neighborhood, I asked him what we can learn from Moldovans. He said, "With food, they always ask, 'Is it fresh?' Unlike Americans, Moldovans are obsessed with freshness. Much of their food comes from their gardens. They always eat things in season. They also preserve their own food for the winter. Another difference is that in America everyone has their own beer bottle, but in Eastern Europe they have two-liter beer bottles. I like that because it encourages sharing and drinking only what you need."

"Or it encourages drinking like a Moldovan. Why do they drink so much anyway?"

"Moldova has outstanding soil that produces huge amounts of high-quality fruit. It's like the grandfather in *The Grapes of Wrath* who talks about going to California to escape the drought, stuffing fruit in his pants, and dying happy. You can do that in Moldova. You can just walk down a street and pick apples, apricots, cherries, or whatever is in season. No one really cares because there is no way that they'll all be eaten. This explains why Moldovans produce so much homemade alcohol. It's like obesity in America. In the US, food is abundant and cheap, so we overeat; in Moldova grapes are abundant and cheap, so Moldovans overdrink."

To switch subjects, I said, "So you're getting kinda serious with your Moldovan girlfriend. Do they have any different marriage traditions?"

"Yeah, given their small income, they give huge gifts at weddings. Also, they announce how much they are giving at the wedding. How's that for peer pressure? They also have a great marriage tradition: instead of just having a best man and maid of honor, newlyweds pick a couple that will advise them throughout the marriage. They are like the godparent, but for the relationship. They teach you how to resolve conflicts and improve your marriage."

I said, "I know an ethnic Russian in Transnistria who might have benefited from that tradition. What other habits do they have that we don't?"

"Guests randomly come over. They often don't announce that they're coming. Also, Moldovans are very direct. For instance, when you gain weight, people will say, 'Hey, you look fat.'"

Lunch with the Dacia Youth Resource Center Director

TJ introduced me to his boss, Ion Babici, who was the Executive Director at Soroca's Dacia Youth Resource Center. Ion was a husky middle-aged man who spoke English well. Ion had worked with children all his life. According to the CIA, 9.6 percent of Moldova's 2009 GDP was spent on education—that was the world's seventh highest ratio. No other European country was higher (the US and UK were at 5.5 percent).

The three of us enjoyed a typical Moldovan lunch at a restaurant. I ate sliced cabbage salad, cornmeal, a heap of sour cream, eggs, and a bit of pork. While we ate, Ion said that one of the problems Moldovans have is that they "don't have their own story, their own identity." He said that a politician once said that because Moldova is neither Russian nor Romanian, it's a "hermaphrodite."

When I asked Ion how has life changed in Moldova ever since the USSR collapsed, he said, "Life was better in Moldova during the Soviet times. After Moldova became independent, the standard of living declined. That's because during the USSR, Moldova received more help and investment than it produced. In some ways, that continues today in Transnistria. Russians keep giving economic assistance to that region."

"Was there any way Moldova could have prevented Transnistria from breaking away?"

"Maybe," Ion said. "The big problem was that after Moldova declared independence, they made Moldovan the only official state language. Some nationalists wanted to encourage Russians to speak Moldovan. That made the Russians angry and encouraged their independence movement."

Our lunch was tasty, although a bit fatty and heavy like most Eastern European food. Whenever I asked Eastern Europeans what they can teach Americans, a common answer was, "How to make good food." After Ion said this, TJ said, "I totally agree with Ion. The food in Moldova is much better than the food in the US. Even organic vegetables from farmer's markets in America don't come close to how good the vegetables are anywhere you go in Moldova."

They're right, but because few Eastern Europeans have visited America, they assume that we only eat at McDonald's. They believe that we just eat "artificial" food. They have no idea about the millions of Americans who are obsessed about healthy food, buying only organic produce and free-range, hormone-free meat. If Eastern Europeans knew about our vegetarian, vegan, and raw-food restaurants, they might wonder how people can survive by only killing plants.

Furthermore, nearly every nationality is proud of their food and thinks it tastes delicious. Eastern Europeans rave about their food, but if it's so great, then it should be as common as finding cuisine from Thailand, Italy, China, France, India, Turkey, France, Japan, or Mexico. However, it's hard to find Eastern Europe cuisine outside of Eastern Europe. Still, they're convinced that it's stupendous. In short, humans love whatever food we grew up with. A 2007 Gallup poll proved this: 63 percent of Moldovans told Gallup that they had eaten some "good-tasting food" the previous day. What's fascinating is that Moldova had the *lowest* rate in Europe (tied with Albania). Portugal and Canada had the world's highest rate, with 94 percent adoring their food.

Interviewing a Moldovan museum director

After lunch, TJ introduced me to Nicolae Bulot, who was the Director of Soroca's Museum of History of Ethnography. He was born in 1952, so he spent most of his life in the USSR. Since he specializes in examining cultures, I asked him to compare the cultures of Moldova and Romania. He said, "Because of communists and nationalists, we have a generation that believes that Moldova is unique and shouldn't be part of Romania. They are brainwashed just like the people of Transnistria."

"What's the solution for Transnistria?" I asked.

Nicolae said, "It's difficult. Russia wants a foot in this strategic land. That's why they're making it easy for Transnistrians to become Russian citizens. Over 20 percent already have Russian passports. The best solution would be to give Transnistria to Ukraine, but that will be hard. Russia and Moldova want it more. Moldova wants it because it has most of Moldova's heavy industry."

"Why do so many Moldovans vote for communists?"

"Communists convinced the village police, the tree cutter, and the postman that they will lose their job if a communist is not be elected. People believe it."

"What's a cultural difference between Moldovans and Americans?"

"The expression of the Moldovan face is open and honest. We wear our feelings on our face. Americans don't. Americans are more closed. They smile when they are not really happy."

"What about life for Moldovan women?"

"We're still a traditional society. A girl who is not married is called a *fata mare* (fat girl). It's sad that we still have an expression that says, 'An unbeaten wife is like an unswept floor.'"

Before I left, I asked if he thought Moldova would ever join the EU. He said, "Yes, but not soon. Sometime before 2035. We need the EU's stricter laws, but we need to reform our culture ourselves. Moldova has too much corruption. You can't fish in murky water."

TJ helped me find the minibus that went to the nearby Ukrainian border. I thanked him for revealing a side of Moldova that few see. On the other hand, few people see any side of Moldova. It's truly hidden. People are more likely to know about the humorous book *Molvanîa: a Land Untouched by Modern Dentistry*. It's not based on Moldova, but is a parody of Eastern European countries. The book says that the Molvanîan language is so complicated that it takes 16 years to learn. To understand something, you need to hear the tone *and pitch*. Which article you use depends on whether a noun is masculine, feminine, neuter, or a cheese. Let's hope you've learned more about the real Moldova.

What Moldova Can Teach Us

- **Invest in education.** Moldova is one of the world's top 10 countries based on education spending as a percentage of GDP. You don't always need to spend money to educate yourself and your children, but you must invest time. Read and travel more: it's the best form of education.
- **Use the metric system.** Although Americans are the main audience for this book, I've used the metric system as the default

way to describe measurements because it's better than the maladroit American-Imperial system. The only foolish countries that are not using the metric system are Myanmar and the US. Even the slow-to-change British, who gave us our graceless measurement system, are adopting the metric system. The American scientific community already uses the metric system because they're smart—they use the most logical system available. The beverage industry has taught us what a liter is, so it's not that hard for gas stations to give up gallons. Medication doses are often given in milligrams. Runners (and the US military) already know what a 10K is, so adopting kilometers isn't rocket science. Moving to Celsius and kilograms will be tougher, but anyone can adapt with a few minutes of practice. Once we do that, the world (and the next generation of Americans) will be forever grateful. Therefore, learn and use the metric system in your everyday life. Teach your friends how easy it is. Go the extra kilometer.

- **Before you get married (or even after), pick a couple you admire to advise you.** Moldovans have this tradition, which can save relationships and is cheaper than hiring a marriage counselor. Moreover, they can focus on preventing problems before they become so big that you need a professional marriage counselor (or a divorce lawyer).

Places I saw and recommend in Moldova: Tiraspol.

Travel deals and info: http://ftapon.com/moldova

We're nearing the end of the journey. Europe's two biggest countries remain: Ukraine and Russia.

24

Ukraine—Stumbling Forward

One Ukrainian tourist website proclaims: "Ukraine is the geographical center of Europe!" And then, confusingly, the first sentence after that title is, "Ukraine is one of the mightiest countries in Eastern Europe."[1] One of those proclamations is true: Ukraine is the biggest country that is wholly in Europe. Russia's European piece is bigger than Ukraine, while Denmark is bigger than Ukraine if you count its Greenland territory. However, if you ignore these two cases, then Ukraine is the biggest. In fact, it's almost as big as Texas. Starting in 1999, I visited Ukraine every five years. Each time I returned, Ukraine seemed to have taken three steps forward and two steps backward.

Traces of communism

In 1999, I flew into Ukraine's capital, which is often called Kiev, but we will use its official name: Kyiv (pronounced *Kee-v*). I stayed in the Mir Hotel. I learned that *mir* is a cool Eastern Slavic word that has two meanings: *world* and *peace.* Although communism had officially disappeared nearly a decade before, its remnants were everywhere. For example, every floor of the hotel had a middle-aged, overweight female gatekeeper who was in charge of the floor. Besides having the thrilling task of policing the floor, this stern woman would also hold your keys, which clearly the receptionist in the lobby was incapable of doing. Similarly, at the bottom of every subway escalator, there was a guard whose stimulating job was to verify that life around the escalator was OK. Communism's goal was to give everyone a job, so it invented millions of useless jobs. Many of these pointless jobs remain.

Another example of a communist leftover was the controlling and corrupt police force. When I saw Kyiv's colossal titanium Mother Motherland statue from far away, I used my camera's zoom to take a photo. While snapping the picture, a policeman ran up and ordered me to stop. He thought I was taking a photo of a nearby military building that was in the line of sight of the distant statue. I showed him the photos so that he could believe me when I said that I wasn't a spy.

Although I never faced corruption during any of my visits, in 2010, travel blogger Justin Klein got "shaken down" by police officers on five separate occasions during a short trip. He offered tips on how to avoid such encounters: keep quiet when the police are around (so they don't overhear you speaking English). If they ask you for a bribe, reinforce that you're just a poor traveler who is staying in cheap hostels and traveling on second-class trains. Say that you've already had to pay other officers "fees" for minor "violations." Carry little cash in your wallet (or at least the wallet you show them); they're unlikely to walk you to a bank to get more money, so you might get away with a small bribe. Finally, pretend you don't understand them and hope they get bored. Justin nearly left Ukraine early out of frustration, but he's glad he stayed because he loved the people and the country overall.

Another communism hangover is that arbitrary rules are posted everywhere. Fortunately, it's all in Cyrillic so you probably won't understand them, although I learned to spot their favorite phrase, "Strictly Forbidden!" Ukrainians probably ignored half of the rules under communism, but nowadays they seem to ignore all the rules.

> *The strictness of our laws is compensated for by their lack of enforcement. — Whispered Soviet saying*

Kyiv is an attractive city that delicately mixes splendid old architecture, glass skyscrapers, and crappy-looking commie buildings. Kyiv was the center of Kievan Rus', Europe's largest and most powerful medieval state. Its finest symbol is the Saint Sophia Cathedral and its nearby Cave Monastery, which together make up one UNESCO World Heritage Site. Thousands of worshipers kiss glass enclosures that cover a saint's tomb or icon. I hope they clean the glass often.

With 2.7 million residents, there's plenty to see and do in Kyiv. My favorite place is the cozy *Andriyivsky Uzviz* (Andrew's Descent). It's a descent down a charming cobblestoned street that takes you to the baroque-styled St. Andrew's Church. Nearby vendors promote a vast selection of *matryoshkas* (stacking dolls). Although Kyiv is a superb city, Ukraine is big and I wanted to see more, so I went to Odessa.

Ukraine's party town: Odessa

When I arrived in Odessa, I gladly let a taxi driver rip me off. We could hardly communicate, but he understood that I wanted to find an affordable hotel. At the first hotel, he asked the reception for the price. It was $60 per night. He said this was "*doroga*" ("expensive"). We drove to another place, where he liked the price ($15), so he demanded that we see the rooms. They were in poor condition and then he barked, "*Nyet garyachei vodi*!" ("No hot water!") We drove to a third place, which had hot water, a reasonable price ($25), and a decent location. He charged me an outrageous price for his taxi service ($20), but it was so amusing to see him run around and negotiate with all these hotels, I paid him.

Although Odessa has an unimaginative grid layout, it's a beautiful city with one million pretty people. In the summer, Odessa becomes a party town, where the young and good-looking show off the latest fashions, dance all night, and get utterly drunk. If you're a man, the endless stream of sexy Ukrainian women will make you turn your head so hard and often that you'll snap your neck.

French and Italian architects planned many of Odessa's elaborate buildings and infrastructure, yet it was an English engineer who designed its most iconic place: the Primorsky Stairs. Their Soviet name, Potemkin Stairs, is more popular. The stairs are fascinating for two reasons. First, they're wide and long. There are 192 steps with 10 large landings to give you a break. The top step is 12.5 meters (41 ft) wide, while the lowest step is 22 meters (71 ft) wide. These features create the second cool characteristic: twin optical illusions. One illusion is that from the bottom, you only see the staircase and no landings. From the top, you only see landings, no staircase! The narrowing of the staircase creates the other illusion: from the bottom it seems longer than it is, while from the top it seems shorter. It's a pity they didn't reverse that illusion.

From Odessa, I took an overnight train to visit the city where Churchill, Roosevelt, and Stalin had a famous conference in 1945. It's near Ukraine's southernmost point, in a peninsula called Crimea (Russians pronounce it *Crème,* as in the dessert *crème brûlée*). In 1786, Lady Elizabeth Craven told the locals of St. Petersburg that she was going to Crimea. They were horrified. They declared that "the air is unwholesome, the waters poisonous, and that I shall certainly die if I go there."[2]

The brave Lady Craven rolled her eyes and went anyway. The next year, in the cold winter of 1787, Catherine the Great of St. Petersburg wanted to check out Crimea. To travel there, she planned to go from the Baltic to the Black Sea. She wrote, "From every side people assured me that my march would be bristly with obstacles and annoyances. . . . People wanted to frighten me with the fatigues of the route, the aridity of the deserts, the insalubrity of the climate." People told me similar things whenever I ventured into the Hidden Europe. However, I agree with Catherine the Great, when she said, "To oppose me is to excite me."[3]

Going by train to Yalta

I love trains in Ukraine and Russia. Although they're slow, they act like teleportation machines. That's because you can close your eyes, fall asleep, and when you wake up, you're at your destination. I'd rather take a cheap, comfortable, overnight 10-hour train ride than a five-hour bus ride or two-hour plane flight. In comparison, the train is often cheaper and saves you from spending an extra night in a hotel. Although you miss out on the scenery in an overnight train, Ukraine and Russia have mostly flat, monotonous landscapes that will quickly put you to sleep anyway.

Trains have three classes: an open train car where there is little privacy, cabins that hold four passengers, and cabins that hold two. Toilets are basic. For a small fee, bedsheets and tea are provided. Most people bring their own food on board. Just like each hotel floor has someone on duty 24 hours a day, each train car has one person in charge. It's a great chance to meet locals, although few speak English. The train from Odessa crosses into Crimea and goes to Simferopol, where you can take a bus to Yalta.

When I arrived in Yalta, I preferred getting ripped off by the hotel than by the taxi driver. Therefore, I gave the taxi driver $5 and asked him to take me to a nice hotel. The hotel gave me an excellent room with high ceilings and a balcony for $70. Yalta is great. It's nice to stroll along the pleasant *Naberezhnaya* (Promenade) into the palm-tree lined Prymorsky Park and onto the *Ploscha Lenina,* the hub of activity. You can visit churches, palaces, or even a zoo. Yalta attracted two of Russia's greatest writers: Leo Tolstoy spent summers there and Anton Chekhov lived there full-time. Yalta has a much slower pace than Odessa. It attracts people who want to chill out rather than to rock out.

After tanning on a beach, you can visit several nearby places. Livadia Palace, for example, is where three guys who were hardly in Europe determined Europe's fate. Churchill and Stalin were both from Europe's periphery, while Roosevelt was from a different continent. The Yalta Conference drew the Iron Curtain a few months before the war was over. Ironically, Livadia Palace was once a mental institution.

From Livadia Palace, you can walk the Tsar's Path, a 6.4-kilometer (4-mile) relatively flat path, which cuts across the mountains to one of Europe's most picturesque castles, the *Lastochkino Gnizdo* (Swallow's Nest). A Baltic-German baron built this diminutive Neo-Gothic castle in 1912, which sits on a 40-meter high cliff that overlooks the Black Sea. It's an adorable fairy-tale castle with an Italian restaurant. You can also check out the Nikitsky botanical gardens. Lenin declared that Yalta was the perfect place for the tired proletariat to relax. At least he was right about something.

After Yalta, I headed to Russia. Along the way, I spent a day in Kharkiv, which is Ukraine's second biggest city. During the first 15 years of the Soviet Era, Kharkiv was Ukraine's capital. As a result, it became a powerful intellectual and industrial center. It has 13 universities. Although the capital moved to Kyiv in 1934, Kharkiv maintained its stature. Its most impressive feature is the *Maidan Svobody* (Freedom Square), which is Europe's sixth largest square. In 2012, it will be one of the host cities for the European Football Championship, which Ukraine and Poland are co-hosting. At that point, many Europeans will discover this hidden, attractive city.

Returning to Ukraine in 2004

Crossing the border between Moldova and Ukraine was as easy as I expected. That's right, it was a complete pain in the ass. The unpleasant Ukrainian border guards ordered everyone to get out of the bus to conduct a luggage inspection at 3:00 a.m. It was freezing outside. I stayed in the bus while my fellow passengers shivered. After ten minutes, the bus driver ratted me out, so I joined my trembling and tired comrades. I left my cocaine-filled handbag on my seat.

When I got off the bus, I placed my backpack filled with weapons of mass destruction at the end of the counter, pretending that it had already passed inspection. It worked. The customs agents ignored me and let us get back on board. They never checked any of the bags on the bus. At least there was no discrimination: I was the most Arabic-looking guy on the bus. Our bus continued to Odessa.

From Odessa, I traveled to the nearby Nerubayske to explore the *katakombi* (catacombs). Under Odessa is a labyrinth with over 1,000 kilometers (620 miles) of tunnels. The maze started when locals quarried the sandstone in the 1800s. Later, smugglers, revolutionaries, and WWII resistance fighters made the catacombs their home. The Museum of Partisan Glory explains how Ukrainians lived like rats to defend their country. Exploring the labyrinth with a flashlight helps you imagine what it was like to live underground. It feels like a human-sized version of an ant colony.

I returned to Odessa to stroll down the romantic, tree-lined *Prymorsky bulvar*. It's worth walking to the *vul Derybasivska,* which is a pleasant pedestrian shopping zone. Then there's the Pushkin Museum, which is ironic because Alexander Pushkin was kicked out of Odessa. He's now known as Russia's Shakespeare; he had gone to Odessa because the Tsar had thrown him out of Moscow 13 months earlier. Thus, no city wanted Pushkin while he was alive, but now every city wants to claim that he is theirs. To avoid spending a night at a hotel, I took an overnight bus to Chernivtsi.

What Ukrainians say about their country

When I arrived in Chernivtsi at 5:00 a.m. in mid-October 2004, I wanted to cry because it was so cold, but my tears would have frozen on my cheeks. I had six layers of clothing, one backpack on my back and another on my front, and I was walking uphill. And my teeth were still chattering. I know it was a cold spell, but I couldn't comprehend how all these people survive these winters. I couldn't even survive the fall!

That previous paragraph is what I wrote in my 2004 blog, which made Lena, a Ukrainian, write me an email saying, "You certainly have to update your site and information. It's almost 2007. Some of your comments about cold weather, poverty, and reproduction are inaccurate and somewhat inappropriate."

Sorry about that. So now as we enter 2012, Ukraine is, thanks to global warming, a tropical paradise. When you visit in the fall and winter, just bring shorts and a bikini. Most Ukrainians are rich. There is hardly any poverty. And Ukrainians have more babies than Albanians.

For those who prefer facts over fantasy, let's look at statistics. Ukraine's 2011 fertility rate is just 1.28, one of the world's lowest. Moreover, Ukraine's population growth rate is -0.62 percent, making Ukraine one of the top five fastest depopulating countries in the world. Regarding weather: there is no place in Ukraine where you can escape snow in the winter. Even places on the Black Sea get light snowfalls a couple of times a year. Yalta's average low temperature in January is two degrees Celsius (36 degrees F), whereas Odessa's is -3.5 degrees (26 degrees F). Kiev and Kharkiv both have average January lows of -8.5 degrees (17 degrees F). In short, Ukraine is warmer than Russia, but that's not saying much.

But let's forget the weather and reproduction! Lena also said that I was exaggerating the poverty level in 2004. Let's listen to what Ukrainians say about their nirvana. Looking at the Gallup's latest survey, Ukraine's picture is indeed different from how I depicted it in 2004. It's much worse.

Regarding poverty, Ukraine had the world's lowest score on Gallup's Personal Economy Index, which measures a respondent's economic situation and his/her community's economics. Although Ukraine is at the bottom of that index, most Eastern European countries are near the bottom to keep Ukraine company.[4] The CIA estimated that 35 percent of Ukrainians lived below the poverty line in 2009. Penelope Chamberlain, a British lady, told me, "Ukraine is one of the poorest countries I've been to. Especially the elderly. All pensions stopped and many were scavenging in rubbish bins at the rear of high-rise flats. We have many Ukrainians working in menial jobs in the UK. They are grossly over-qualified, but they are paid a pittance at home."

In 2010, Ukrainians were last in the world in being dissatisfied with their country's "efforts to increase the number and quality of jobs" with an eye-popping 99 percent being dissatisfied. The bottom 10 countries were all Eastern European. In 2011, the average Ukrainian made about $250 per month.

In 2010, Ukrainians were also last in the planet in being satisfied with their country's efforts to preserve the environment, with only nine percent feeling satisfied. The majority of all Eastern Europeans (except Belarusians and Finns) are dissatisfied about their country's environmental efforts.

Ukraine is the sickest country in Europe. In 2010, it ranked around 151 out of 155 countries in being satisfied with their personal health, according to Gallup. The east-west divide is well marked on this issue too, with all Western Europeans (except for Portugal) have satisfaction rates of 82% or more and all Eastern Europeans (except Macedonia and Turkey) being below 82%. Four in 10 Ukrainians agree that they have health problems that prevent them from doing some things that people their age would normally be able to do—that's the worst rate in Europe and the fifth worst on Earth.

Ukrainians hate their healthcare too. Only 18 percent were "satisfied with the availability of quality of healthcare." Only two African countries (Comoros and Congo) were less satisfied in 2010—all other African countries were more satisfied. Only 23 percent of Ukrainians have "confidence in their healthcare system," which helps them edge out the two countries which are at the bottom: Togo and Ethiopia. However, Zimbabwe is a bit more confident (27%).

When asked, "Are you satisfied with your standard of living, with all the things you can buy and do?", Ukrainians and Lithuanians were the least satisfied Europeans with less than a quarter being satisfied in 2010. That question illustrates yet another east-west European divide: all Eastern Europeans (except Finns) were below 72 percent, whereas all Western Europeans (except the Portuguese) were all above 72 percent.

In 2011, Ukraine ranked last in Europe in the World Bank's "Ease of Doing Business" survey. It was number 145 in the world, a few notches worse than Sierra Leone. Gallup's National Institutions Index aggregates many surveys to summarize people's confidence in the judicial system, military, government, and elections. Ukraine had the worst score in Europe and the fifth worst in the world, just above Chad.

What's really going on?

There's a paradox in these survey results. On the one hand, if you share them with Ukrainians, they'll probably say, "Yup, that's Ukraine." Indeed, when I talked with Ukrainians, they were often quite critical and pessimistic about their country. On the other hand, few sober Ukrainians would argue that life in Ukraine is as tough as it is in Zimbabwe, Togo, or Nigeria. During my travels throughout Ukraine, people had humble, but acceptable standards of living. There were a few beggars, but that's true even in the world's richest cities.

An American who has lived for over a decade in Ukraine told me, "The issue of wealth in Ukraine is a paradox. If you read the official statistics, you find that people are quite poor. But then you visit Kyiv, or other large cities in Ukraine, and you see all these fancy cars. It seems that there are even more of them than in most of the US. So people wonder: where are the poor people?"

I said "So how do you explain that paradox?"

He said, "Most Americans have a lot of expenses that most Ukrainians don't—like insurance, house payments, and very high utility bills. Most Ukrainians inherited apartments from the Soviet Union. They just privatized the apartments that they had been given for free at some point. So with utilities at a fairly low level, most of people's modest income is enough to live a decent life."

Although that helps explain why Ukraine's standard of living isn't as horrendous as the economic statistics suggest, it doesn't explain why Ukraine ends up at the bottom of several global surveys. Indeed, if a Martian only looked at opinion polls, the alien would conclude that life in Ukraine is similar to life in Sub-Saharan Africa. Everyone (including Ukrainians) agree that that's the wrong conclusion. So what's really going on? Are these surveys just cleverly manipulated propaganda tools that the wealthy elite use to serve their diabolical goals? Or is there something else?

The answer is that Ukraine represents the extreme of something that happens throughout Eastern Europe—there's a cultural tendency to complain, to view life pessimistically, and to play the victim. While Europeans tend to be a relatively cynical and crabby bunch, Eastern Europeans take the cake. Part of this tradition comes from the natural human tendency to compare yourself to others when trying to figure out if you're happy. Since Eastern Europeans tend to compare themselves with Western Europeans (instead of comparing themselves with Arabs or Africans), they end up feeling shortchanged. Moreover, the hopelessness of communism further encouraged this habit of whining about their existence.

Objective economic data (GDP per capita, the Human Development Index, unemployment rate, percentage who are starving, etc.) put Ukraine and most of Eastern Europe around or above the world average. Still, when you ask people to evaluate their lives, Eastern Europeans are often below the world average and, too often, among the world's worst. Instead of concluding that there is some sinister conspiracy behind these surveys, it's more reasonable to conclude that Eastern Europeans tend to see the glass as being half empty. Fyodor Dostoevsky must have been thinking about the East Slavic soul when he said, "Man only likes to count his troubles, but he does not count his joys."

Ukrainians (and Eastern Europeans) seem to bathe in their sorrows. In 2010, Gallup asked Europeans if they "learned or did something interesting yesterday." The majority of Western Europeans (except Italians) said *yes;* the majority of Eastern Europeans (except Finns) said *no*. Only three in 10 Ukrainians said *yes*—the lowest rate in Europe and in the world's bottom 10.

There are flowers everywhere for those who bother to look.
— *Henri Matisse*

You'd think that with all this depressing news, Ukrainians would be running for the exits. Nevertheless, only 15 percent would like to permanently move to another country, according to a 2011 Gallup survey. Although it's not easy for Ukrainians to emigrate, they certainly have more options now than during the *Holodomor*. Still, most Ukrainians seem to say: "I'd rather sit here and complain."

Beware of cold things in Eastern Europe

Although Ukrainians might sit and complain, you'll never find them sitting and complaining on a cold rock. That's because they, like most Eastern Europeans, believe that awful things happen when you sit on a cold rock. For example, when I was dining with 10 Estonians, I announced, "Raise your hand if you believe that it is extremely unhealthy to sit on a cold rock." All the hands went up. According to Eastern Europeans, sitting on a cold surface can lead to a urinary tract infection, kidney infections, ovary inflammation, and infertility. In Slovenia, the consequences can be even more serious. Slovenians warn their children, "*Če sediš na mrzlih ali vlažnih tleh, boš dobil volka v rit*" ("If you sit on cold or wet surface, you'll get a wolf in your butt").

During the winter, I loved to sit on a frozen surface and debate this issue with Eastern Europeans. They explained that the cold will create humidity around your anus. Counterarguments failed. You can say that butts, like armpits, are used to having humidity and bacteria around them without major problems. You can argue that ovaries are deep in a woman's body, which maintains a constant internal temperature regardless of outside conditions. You can say that cold doesn't cause inflammation, but rather decreases it. You can mention that infections and colds are usually caused by bacteria and viruses, which tend to thrive in warm places, not cold ones. You can try all these arguments in Eastern Europe, but only deaf ears will be listening.

Although the cold-seat theory is the most popular health myth in Eastern Europe, there are other cold-related perils to beware. For example, Maiu's Estonian doctor told her that she had a urinary tract infection because she didn't keep her feet and midsection warm. My young Serbian friends, Dijana and Marija, giggled when they shared the things they were taught: that walking barefoot will damage your ovaries and that a draft in the house will make you catch a cold. Marija laughed as she explained how her mother's house would feel like a sauna, but she would refuse to open a window for fear of creating a draft and catching a cold. If she sensed the tiniest of drafts, she would ask Marija to search around for the draft's source and plug it. Dijana also said that she was taught that girls should never leave the house with wet hair. You must wait at least six hours for it to dry, or else you might catch a cold. And, of course, if you go outside with wet hair, you'll get an ear infection.

It's unclear why Eastern Europeans cling to these kooky concepts. Yes, when you get chilly, your immune system weakens, thereby increasing your risk of getting sick. However, Eastern Europeans have taken this concept to an extreme. Perhaps Eastern Europe's brutal winters encouraged shamans to invent such harebrained theories. Or perhaps communist medical researchers were a bunch of quacks. Or maybe they know something we don't know. If so, keep your ass warm.

Visiting some of the Seven Wonders of Ukraine

In 2007, Ukraine selected its seven cultural wonders. In 2004, I unknowingly visited five of them. The Sofia Cathedral and adjoining cave are two of them. Chernivtsi has another—the Khotyn Fortress. Although it's a nice fort, I was more impressed with the city of Chernivtsi. It's graceful, cosmopolitan, and looks like a pretty Polish city. It helps that Poland ruled it long enough to build such Baroque buildings. The old town's elegant streets are covered with opulent vine-covered facades. Cafés, restaurants, and shops are plentiful in the tree-lined pedestrian avenues. The wooden balconies and covered staircases in the courtyards testify to the Turkish period. A delicately painted Armenian cathedral shows yet another side to the city. It's remarkable that most Europeans have never heard of this lovely city.

From Chernivtsi, I bused it to Kamianets-Podilskyi Castle, which is another one of Ukraine's Seven Wonders. It's a medieval fortified town that's on a sheer-walled rock island that was carved by a sharp loop in the Smotrych River. Its unique geography creates a near perfect moat. They probably would have filmed *The Lord of the Rings* here if they had only known it existed.

Nine stone towers overlook the superb castle that was built in the 1500s. There are two bridges into town. You'll feel heroic walking across the west one and entering the old town through the ancient gate. On its cobblestoned streets, near the Dominican Monastery, I asked a 16-year-old to take a picture of me. Surprisingly, he spoke excellent Spanish. His father, who is from St. Petersburg, now lives in Spain. Soon a dozen of his friends joined in. We toured the castle together. We were practically the only tourists that chilly mid-October day. In the end, they suggested I go to Ivano-Frankivsk, so I did.

After another long bus ride, I arrived in Ivano-Frankivsk. It has four plazas and is set at the base of the Carpathian mountain range. It lacks the dreary Soviet look that's so common in ex-USSR countries. Western Ukraine seems to have a monopoly on some of Ukraine's most stunning towns. After three regal towns, I went to western Ukraine's jewel: Lviv.

Lovely Lviv

Russians call it Lvov, but don't call it that in this patriotic city—it's Lviv. Just like St. Petersburg is Moscow's cultural and intellectual rival, Lviv is Kyiv's competitor. The city reminded me of the Prague I saw 20 years ago. With a bit of renovation, it will live up to its name: the Pearl of Europe. Until 1939, it had never been ruled from Moscow. Having escaped WWII's destruction, Lviv is a living museum of Western architecture from the Gothic to the present. Its 750-year-old town, which has many *Belle Époque* buildings and a neo-Renaissance opera house, is a UNESCO World Heritage Site. Although commie monstrosities exist, the charming narrow streets and dazzling historic center make it Ukraine's finest city and one of the best in Eastern Europe.

I arrived in Lviv early in the morning. To warm up, I climbed up to its highest point, the *Vysokyi Zamok* (High Castle). It's worth walking by Lviv's three impressive universities, its old town, and the Lychakiv Cemetery, which is Eastern Europe's most glorious necropolis. It's hard to imagine how great the cemetery was before 1975, when the Soviets finally stopped the vandalism of the Polish tombs that make up the bulk of the graves. At the *Ploshcha Rynok* (Market Square), near the *Ratusha* (Town Hall), I asked a tall lady with red hair to direct me to an Internet café. She gave me a good idea, so I thanked her and started to leave when she said, "Wait. Where are you from?"

I almost blurted out, "I am from the Russian Liberation Army and I am here to free you from your silly Ukrainian traditions." But instead I gave her an honest answer.

She replied, "Really? I thought you were Polish!"

That would have been a good guess 100 years ago, when 86 percent of Lviv spoke Polish. Even in 1931, only eight percent spoke Ukrainian—the rest spoke Polish or Yiddish. Even in 1944, when the Germans fled, two-thirds of the city were Poles. Even though Poland fought against the Germans, the Soviets gave the Poles a one-way ticket out of there. Today, less than one percent of Lviv is Polish.

This lady was an art student named Yuliya Hnylyukh. After chatting a couple of minutes in the chilly square, her friend, who was also named Yuliya, showed up. She had dirty blond hair and gray eyes. She was majoring in English. Next came Lena, a sweet brunette with glasses, a constant smile, and a limited English vocabulary. Finally, a boisterous, curvy blond named Evelina arrived. She spoke no English despite years of instruction. These four friends had agreed to meet at the *Ploshcha Rynok* at precisely the time I was passing through. I lamented my misfortune: I was stuck with four young, attractive Ukrainian women. I did my best to run away, but they insisted on going out for coffee before I took my night train to Kyiv. I reluctantly agreed and ended up learning much more about Ukraine.

Ukrainian language

When we arrived at the café, they told me to stop me from saying *spasiba* (thank you). "That's Russian," Yuliya said. "In Ukrainian, we say *dakuyu.*" (It sounds like *dya-koo-yoo*). Also, instead of *ya ne panimayu* (I don't understand), Ukrainians say something that sounds quite Balkanian: *ya ne rozumiyu.*

They estimated that Ukrainian has a 75-percent overlap with Russian. Among the three East Slavic languages, you have Russian on one extreme of the continuum, Ukrainian on the other, and Belarusian in the middle. They all use the Cyrillic alphabet, with minor differences. There is a high amount of mutual intelligibility between them, indicating that they are quite similar. Still, these students insisted that you should speak Ukrainian in Ukraine.

They understood Russian perfectly, but they said that Russians don't understand Ukrainian. Although this seems strange, we've seen this before when we compared two similar languages: Estonian and Finnish. There's a reason for the disconnect: the media flows in only one direction. Finns and Russians export their media to their southern, less populous neighbor, but they don't import any media in return. Thus, one group gets exposed; the other doesn't.

Ukraine's language dynamics are fascinating. During the Soviet period, Russian was the default language and dominated primary schools. After Ukraine's independence, Ukrainian had a major renaissance. Today, about 80 percent of primary schools teach in Ukrainian. Universities overwhelmingly use Ukrainian, although nearly everyone is bilingual. Ever since 2004, all Russian TV and movies must be either dubbed or subtitled in Ukrainian. Still, the adoption of Ukrainian is uneven.

In western and central Ukraine, Ukrainian is the main language, although Kyiv is a special case. In a 2003 survey, 75 percent of Kyiv's population said that Ukrainian was their "native language." They gave a different answer when asked, "What language do you use in everyday life?" Half said "mostly Russian," a third said 50/50, and only 20 percent said "mostly" or "exclusively" Ukrainian. Meanwhile, in eastern and southern Ukraine, Russian dominates.

After chatting for an hour, the ladies helped me buy train tickets to Kyiv. During our conversation, it was clear that they were tired of Russia's influence over Ukraine. They were angry that there's so much widespread corruption. During the 1990s, Ukraine suffered hyperinflation and lost 60 percent of its GDP. It was now 2004 and the pro-EU political candidate had just suffered dioxin poisoning. He looked like he aged 20 years in one week. They said his rival did it. Although he survived, he was disfigured and weakened. They were livid. The ladies said that Ukraine needed a revolution to westernize itself. About a month after I met them, their revolt began. It became known as the Orange Revolution.

When an orange looks good, but tastes rotten

In November 2004, a month after I left Ukraine, the Orange Revolution began when Ukrainians protested against the fraudulent election results that claimed that the pro-Russian party had won. After Czechia's Velvet Revolution and Georgia's Pink Revolution, Ukrainians dressed in orange colors and named their revolt the Orange Revolution. Its most passionate supporters were from the Lviv area. Yuliya sent me photos of her family protesting in Kyiv's *Maydan Nezalezhnosti* (Independence Square). Many of her friends spent weeks camping out in the freezing temperatures. Finally, Ukraine's Supreme Court ordered a re-vote, which the Orange team soon won.

When I returned to Ukraine in 2009, the optimistic Orange supporters were furious once again. This time they were angry at the people they helped put in power. Indeed, the Orange revolutionary leaders were just as rotten as the politicians they replaced. The Orange Revolution leader had the lowest political approval rating on Earth: 2.7 percent.

The Great Recession had battered Ukraine's economy, but it didn't excuse the continued corruption. The disillusioned revolutionaries stayed home during the 2010 election. Some votes were bought, some ballots were cast with vanishing ink, and one lucky polling station featured four strippers (that district had a high voter turnout). Despite these voting irregularities, most Western observers said that the voting was free and fair. This time, the pro-Russia party returned to power. Thus, Ukraine's current President is Viktor Yanukovych, a former convict. When he was 17, he was convicted of assault and robbery. When he was 20, he was thrown in jail again for another assault. He says more gaffes than George W. Bush. He speaks Russian better than Ukrainian. Still, most Ukrainians say, "At least he's not Orange."

Asian Americans in Dnipropetrovsk

One month before the 2004 Orange Revolution, my train arrived in Dnipropetrovsk, which was founded in 1776. With one million inhabitants, it's Ukraine's third biggest city. Like Kyiv, it's located on the Dnieper River. During the Soviet Era, tourists couldn't visit Dnipropetrovsk because it was manufacturing military, nuclear, and space-related hardware. Today, it's still an industrial city. While riding a *marshrutka* (minibus), an Asian man entered. I figured he was from eastern Russia, but he talked in English to his Ukrainian companion. When I asked him where he was from, he said, "LA."

I said, "Wow. What's the chance of two Californians sitting next to each other in a cramped *marshrutka* in Dnipropetrovsk? What are you doing here?"

His name was Ed and he was teaching English for the Peace Corps. His companion was called Nellie. They invited me to join them for lunch at a Mexican restaurant. When I asked Ed to compare Ukrainians with Americans, he said, "In some ways, Americans are more closed than Ukrainians. We hide our true feelings. We're outwardly happy, but inside we're sometimes struggling. Ukrainians don't hide their emotions."

In the evening, Nellie invited me to join her and Justin (another Asian Peace Corps member) for some drinks on the main boulevard: *Karla Marksa Prospekt*. At the end of the night, Justin, who was from Dallas, invited me to crash on his floor. I happily accepted. It's surprising how humble Peace Corps workers live. Maybe there's actually a US government program that is frugal. Justin crushed that hope when he said that the Ukrainian Peace Corps headquarters was lavish.

Dnipropetrovsk is functional, but not a tourist mecca, so I took a train to Kryvyi Rih. It's a great city if you love exploring a steel manufacturing center. The city serves the vast nearby ore deposits. About 40 percent of Ukraine's economy comes from aluminum and steel exports. Having been obliterated in WWII, Kryvyi Rih has wide boulevards, rows of unimaginative apartment blocks, and absolutely nothing interesting to see. It was time to return to Ukraine's vacation hotspot—Crimea.

Why Crimea doesn't feel completely Ukrainian

Imagine if the US Congress voted in 2014 to give New York's Long Island to Connecticut. New York State would grumble about losing an important tax base, but ultimately such a decision would have only minor significance since Long Island would still be part of America. However, now imagine that the US breaks up in 2051, whereby New York and Connecticut become independent countries. Would New York ask Connecticut to give Long Island back?

Welcome to Crimea's story. Look at a map and you'll see that Crimea's east side practically touches Russia almost as much as

Crimea's north side touches Ukraine. Ukrainians never dominated Crimea. For centuries, Russians and Tatars were the main ethnic groups. After WWII, Stalin inhumanely deported hundreds of thousands of Tatars to Central Asia. This ethnic cleansing transformed Crimea into a Russian peninsula with a Ukrainian minority. Nevertheless, in 1954, Soviet leader Nikita Khrushchev transferred Crimea to the Ukrainian Soviet Socialist Republic. It was a gift that seemed as meaningful as transferring New York's Long Island to Connecticut today. However, when the USSR broke up 37 years later, Ukraine walked away with Crimea and many Russians grumbled.

If a Ukrainian passed by, there would be nothing left for the Jew. — Russian saying

Today, ethnic Russians still make up 75% of Crimea. In 1991, 84% of Ukraine voted for independence, but only 56% of Crimeans supported it. When inflation was at an incomprehensible 10,000%, many Crimeans wanted either to go with Russia or to become their own country. That idea died out when Ukraine offered Crimea autonomy. Nevertheless, the story has one more twist.

Sevastopol, a Crimean port city, is home to Russia's Black Sea Navy Fleet. In order to get Russia to give up its claim over Crimea, Ukraine agreed to lease Sevastopol's best military port to Russia until 2017. In 2010, Ukraine extended the lease until 2042 in exchange for 30 percent cheaper Russian natural gas, which will save Ukraine tens of billions of dollars. Voting on the issue caused a brawl in Ukraine's parliament, but it passed. Because NATO controls the Black Sea's mouth at Istanbul, Crimea's port has limited military utility. Still, Ukrainian nationalists view the naval base like Cubans look at Guantanamo Bay—a foreign military is "occupying their land." The difference is that in the twenty-first century, Russia hasn't been torturing anybody there.

How Ukraine is like Canada

At first glance, Canada and Ukraine seem to have nothing in common except for cold winters. However, upon closer examination, there are parallels. For example, both are large countries that share a long border with a much stronger neighbor. The US and Russia dwarf their respective neighbors militarily, economically, and politically. For example, the GDP of America and Russia are both about 10 times bigger than their respective neighbors. Compared to Canada, the US spends 40 times more on the military, while Russia outspends Ukraine by 25 times. Because Canada and Ukraine have a big brother "protecting" them, both spend only about 1.2 percent of their GDP on defense, while the US and Russia each spend about four percent. Canadians often hate being confused with Americans, while many Ukrainians dislike being labeled as Russians. They say, "No, we're the *nice* guys."

Although Canada and Ukraine loathe to admit it, they are heavily dependent on their bigger brother. For example, 80% of Ukraine's gas and oil comes through Russia. Nuclear power, which supplies half of Ukraine's energy needs, comes mostly from Russia. Russia buys 21% of Ukraine's exports and 28% of Ukraine's imports come from Russia. Meanwhile, over half of Canada's imports come from the US and 75% of their exports go to the US. In addition, Canadians and Ukrainians are culturally so similar to their neighbor that few outsiders can see the difference, whereas anyone can easily see the cultural difference between the US and Mexico or Russia and neighboring Afghanistan. Finally, Americans and Russians generally have good or neutral feelings toward their neighbor, but Canadians and Ukrainians sometimes dislike and criticize their dominant brother.

Nevertheless, the parallelism eventually falls apart. Canadians may share many traits with Americans, but they feel that they are better at most things: they enjoy a higher standard of living, better schools, health care, skiing, nature, and hockey teams. According to Gallup's surveys, Canadians are right—they beat Americans on most metrics. In short, one can argue that Canada has taken the American model and improved it.

Ukraine, on the other hand, has taken Russia's post-communist model and screwed it up. Compared to Russia, Ukraine has more corruption, a lower standard of living, poorer health care, and a weaker ice hockey team. What's frustrating is that Ukraine has the potential to live better than Russia. It has plenty of resources, a rich agriculture, smart engineers, an enormous Black Sea coastline for tourism, the Carpathian mountains for skiing and hiking, and hot women. Canada, Switzerland, and Norway prove you don't have to be a political or military superpower to live well. Let other countries run the global rat race while you quietly live the good life.

Interestingly, the third highest number of Ukrainians (after Ukraine and Russia) is in Canada—they have 1.2 million ethnic Ukrainians. That may explain why Canada was the first country to recognize Ukraine's independence. Although Canada is colder than Ukraine, perhaps the Ukrainians there feel comfortable with the concept of living in a country that is overshadowed by a similar, but more powerful neighbor. At least in this case, they can brag that their adopted country has a superior standard of living and larger geographic size than its irksome neighbor.

An Englishman in Sevastopol

During the long bumpy bus ride to Sevastopol, I met David Watkins, a 40-year-old Englishman working for the British Council. He had a moderate build, thinning blond hair, and that sophisticated English accent that seemed out of place in the rough-around-the-edges Ukraine.

David had been living in Ukraine for three years. Brits have invaded Sevastopol before. Over lunch, David recounted the Siege of Sevastopol in the 1850s. To prevent the British and their allies from gaining easy access to the port, a Russian admiral purposefully sank his fleet at the mouth of the bay. The unusual tactic succeeded in impeding Russia's enemies from entering the bay. A century later, the Soviets impeded access in another way: like Dnepropetrovsk, they made Sevastopol a closed city (i.e., open only to local residents).

Today, Sevastopol lacks Odessa's youthful energy and Yalta's relaxing ambiance, but it's a fine city that was completely rebuilt after WWII flattened it. While we enjoyed the restaurant's view over the bay, David said that one thing Westerners can learn from Ukrainians is to "live for the day."

It's true. When you tour Ukraine, statistics don't seem to match what your eyes tell you. Like the Balkans, people always seem to find a way to eat well, drink hard, and goof off. David invited me to go clubbing with him that night to see some goofing off. It was Saturday night and it was my last night in Ukraine, so I agreed. At the club, David introduced me to his friend Inna. When I asked her what we can learn from Ukrainians, she echoed David's thoughts when she said, "Learning to be happy with little."

The nightclub was packed with eye candy. When young Ukrainian women go to the corner store, they dress like they're going to walk down a fashion runway. Thus, when they go clubbing, they blow you away with their perfectly placed makeup and their provocative outfits. It was a glorious way to end my last night in Ukraine. The next day, I took a boat to Istanbul.

Infected with materialism

Before I returned to Ukraine five years later, I met Rick DeLong. He was born in Minnesota, but he's obsessed with Eastern Europe. In 1994, when he was 17 years old, he spent a year in Slovakia. He said, "There were a lot of things about America that really didn't fit me entirely. I was drawn to cultures that were more people-oriented; a little less business-oriented or materialistic. I don't want to criticize the US. It's a wealthy country, and it's very economically organized. But I was interested in visiting a place that was a little wilder, and had an entirely different culture. I just felt like the Slavic cultures have something that I would really find interesting."

After his first year of college, in 1996, he went on a two-year Christian mission in St. Petersburg, Russia. Then, in 2000, he went to Kyiv.

He's lived there ever since. I said to Rick, "You were drawn to Eastern Europe because of the lack of materialism. However, between 1999 and 2004, I noticed an amazing change, not just in Kyiv, but in all of Eastern Europe. The culture of materialism has not just caught up to the West, but in some ways surpassed it. They're making such a big effort to catch up that they seem much more into brands and what kind of car you drive than Americans. Is that fair to say?"

"I would completely agree with you," Rick said. "Ukraine has changed significantly since I first visited it in 2000. I've noticed that Ukrainians are more focused on the latest cell phones than Americans and they're more focused on electronic gadgets and other things that I think Americans are a little bit calmer about because we have so many other belongings."

It's similar elsewhere in Eastern Europe. For example, my Hungarian friend, Zsuzsa, wrote, "I asked my brother why Hungarians always whine about how hard things are and then you drive around Budapest (the countryside is by far more normal, humble and unpretentious) and all you see is brand-new expensive cars everywhere. 'If things are so tough,' I asked, 'Why are there so many nice automobiles?' He said most of these automobiles are owned by the bank, not the person driving it. All these people who are trying to 'keep up with the Joneses' have taken on huge loans to pay for things they should not be owning. My brother said many people would rather starve than give up buying the newest phone. They live in a small hole in the wall, but they need to drive the flashy car. When a woman spends half her monthly earnings on a skirt, I call that a problem. And there are many such women out there."

"I saw such behavior in the Baltic too," I said.

She continued, "Eastern Europeans are used to living with less. What irks them is to see these *nouveau-riche* flaunting their money. The media encourages this fake celebrity culture, where your worth as a person is directly proportional to you net-worth. This creates a subculture of wannabes who, even though they cannot afford it, go to extreme lengths to try and pretend to belong to the 'Rich and Cool Club,' by buying all the 'in' cars, phones (the two items Hungarians seem to have picked as a measurement of wealth and coolness), clothes, jewelry, etc."

Nevertheless, Rick said, "No amount of iPads and automobiles can compensate for the underlying sensation of oppression and helplessness permeating Ukrainian society. By working hard and having the right connections one can jump up the corporate ladder, rise above the hardships of the common man, and physically separate oneself from the unpleasant elements of Ukrainian society and the innumerable 'tragedies of the commons,' but an enduring sense of security is always unattainable."

Good communist habits that didn't stick

Communism had noble ideals. It was about not giving into greedy capitalist materialism. It was about community, solidarity, and brotherhood—helping your fellow man. It was about equality—everyone had a similar standard of living and should be treated fairly. However, among Eastern Europeans, only Slovenians, Serbians, and Montenegrins had over 60 percent saying that their country was a "good place for racial or ethnic minorities to live." All Western Europeans (except Italy) had rates of 60 percent or more in 2010. Only a third of Ukrainians felt Ukraine was a good place for such minorities—that was the worst rate in Europe.

Communism was about developing the youth, like the fabled Soviet Pioneers. Gallup's 2010 Youth Development Index measures a community's focus on the welfare of the children, tracking issues like respect and development of youth, as well as the opinion of the education system. Fourth from the bottom of the world is Ukraine, which managed to only beat Ethiopia, Congo, and Haiti.

What do these results mean? Did communism truly instill people with these values and they just lost them during the capitalist transition? Or were these values never truly in people's hearts? Were they just pretending to support these ideals without actually believing them?

It's hard to know. Many Eastern Europeans told me that under communism people didn't just act differently, they thought differently. If so, then why did those values vanish so quickly? Why didn't Eastern Europeans keep their collectivized mindset and make a gradual transition to the Scandinavian socialist model? If people weren't materialistic and egocentric before, then why are they outdoing the symbol of excessive materialism and individualism, the United States? If capitalism is to blame, then why does the champion of capitalism, the US, do well on so many of these metrics?

Regardless what the answer is, it's clear that if communism taught Eastern Europeans anything noble, then they've forgotten it. If communism instilled values of equality, respect for minorities, community spirit, and non-materialistic pursuits, then Eastern Europe has abandoned those values.

Rick wrote, "After 15 years of visiting the former USSR, I can say that what is holding Ukrainians back most from a happy life is not a lack of money or economic development, but things like a lack of solidarity and community, a lack of trusting relations with their own government (the phrase even sounds comical), a sense of helplessness due to corruption in the law enforcement and judicial systems, the difficulty of legalizing one's activities and residence."

But other habits linger

Not all communist habits have vanished. Rick said, "The hardest thing about living in Ukraine is dealing with the poor organization of the economy, government, and laws. When you live here, you inevitably encounter these bureaucratic problems. There are so many questions that you can never get a straight answer to. It's extremely aggravating for Westerners who are used to transparent procedures for everything."

"How about legal contracts?" I asked.

"People are not writing the truth in the contract. They're changing the numbers that they're paying you, or they're changing the description of the task you did, so there's this endless mass of half-truths that you learn to live with. That's where the Western mentality can get in the way of just living and not worrying about it too much, because it isn't as big of an issue as it would be in the West."

"What about the older generation?"

"They only know how things are now and how they were in the Soviet Union. The consumer culture has become more and more internationalized and cosmopolitan, while politics is still dominated by people who began their careers in the Soviet Union and continue to gravitate to time-tested authoritarian and Soviet models of governance."

"So how much has changed?"

"Very little has changed in the operations of the government machine in the past 20 years. Dealing with these offices is like stepping back in time several generations. No one with any power has, as of yet, taken any decisive steps to transform the actual workings of the government machine."

Luba, a Ukrainian in San Francisco, told me, "There are tons of smart Ukrainians. Unfortunately, they either don't get to the top, or if they do, they get corrupted."

Ukrainians are dissatisfied. For example, Pew Global Research asked, "Do you approve of the change to the multiparty system?" In 1991, 72% of Ukrainians said *yes*. However, in 2009, only 30% approved. Thus, Ukraine is the only European country where less than half of the people approve of a multiparty democracy. When choosing because a "leader with a strong hand" and "democracy," only 20% preferred "democracy" in 2009—that's down from 57% in 1991.[5]

Ukrainians don't like capitalism either. In 1991, about half of Ukraine supported moving to capitalism. At that time, that was the lowest rate in Eastern Europe. In 2009, Ukraine's approval of capitalism sunk to just 36%. Now they're skeptical about anything Western.

For instance, 60% of Ukrainians don't want to join NATO and they're 50/50 about joining the EU. Meanwhile, few Ukrainians vote for the Communist Party, so everything sucks.

Ukraine is like the unfortunate child who inherits the worst traits of each parent, but none of the good traits. It's forgotten the noble ideas of communism (equality, community, non-materialistic pursuits), but kept its worst qualities (corruption, bureaucracy, and inefficiency). Meanwhile, it hasn't adopted the best qualities of free markets and democracy (efficiency, wealth generation, entrepreneurship, rule of law), but it's absorbed its worst qualities (greed, materialism, selfishness). Ukraine needs radical gene therapy. Fortunately, it's not all bad news.

Relationships matter

I asked Rick what he had learned after living in Ukraine for a decade that a tourist might not notice. He said, "Ukrainians are open. It's easy to make friends. People generally make time for their friends. They let others get close to them. It's an emotionally intimate culture."

I asked, "How does that compare to growing up in America?"

Rick said, "Ukraine is a lot more relationship-oriented than the US. In America, you're born in one state, you move to another, then maybe you move to another while you're in school, and then you head off to college to another state to get away from home, after college you move to another state to get that new job, and then you move a couple of more times. At each stage, you make new friends, but at the end of each stage, you break off, never to see most of those friends again. And that's one of the unfortunate things about the mobile, business-oriented culture in the US. In Ukraine, people put a lot more effort into maintaining childhood friendships and ties from their school and university days. It's easier here because people don't move around so much, and when they do, it's usually to the big cities where opportunities and wealth are concentrated."

Elena Wolter grew up in Odessa, married an American, and now lives in Phoenix, Arizona. When I asked her what she missed about Ukraine, she wrote, "I've been away from home for 11 years now and still one thing that I miss here in the US is genuine friendship. So many people are just too flaky and fake. And what does not help is that people just come and go. I want to have friendships when people can just drop in at your place or you can go to them without invitations, without worrying about being judged for what you have and how clean your house is. Perhaps it still exists here in the US, but not in a big city. That's what I miss."

Climbing on Ukraine's tallest mountain

After another five-year break from Ukraine, I returned in 2009 to climb its tallest mountain. Unlike my previous two visits, getting into Ukraine this time was painless—no expensive travel visa, no waiting in line, no need to explain where I will go and where I will stay. I just walked across the bridge from Siret, Moldova to Ukraine. The border guards simply stamped my passport and welcomed me into their country.

I arrived in Yaremche, an adorable gateway to Ukraine's Carpathian National Park. Aside from Crimea's southern tip, the Carpathians are the only mountainous region in Ukraine. You can feel the difference. Soviet relics are rare. The people are different too. Because they've been ruled by so many different countries in such a short period, their language and customs include bits of all of them. For example, many of the people in Yaremche are Hutsul people who came from Romania, which is just a few kilometers south of Mt. Hoverla. After eating *pyrizhky* (potato-filled buns baked in thickened cream and dill) at a restaurant, I slapped on my backpack, and walked to Mt. Hoverla.

It was still somewhat early in the hiking season (end of April) and the 10-kilometer road to Mt. Hoverla was deserted. Most national parks of similar quality in the West would see much more traffic. Here, only one car would pass every 10 minutes. A couple of horse-drawn carts went by. This will change if Ukraine wins its bid to host the 2022 Winter Olympics in the Carpathians. By the time I walked to the end of the road, only three hours of daylight remained. I relaxed at the enormous three-story mountain hostel, which had no customers. After sunset, I camped inside a mini-chapel to enjoy a bit of extra warmth on a cold night.

At dawn, I followed the trail up Mt. Hoverla, which is only 2,061 meters (6,762 ft) high. To increase the challenge, Ukrainians love to climb during the winter, which always leaves a few with frostbite. After passing streams and hiking through beech and spruce-forest cover for a couple of hours, the woods ended, thereby revealing Hoverla's smooth, snow-covered summit. The hike was easy, except for the last few steps to the summit. It was somewhat dodgy to kick-step my way up the last steep section because the icy snow was hard. However, it wasn't that scary. Falling wouldn't have been fatal, just disagreeable.

As soon as I clawed my way to the summit, a frigid blast of air slammed my body. I leaned into the cold wind and stumbled forward to the violently flapping flag. I was completely alone on Ukraine's tallest mountain. To the east, far below, was the main spring source to the Prut River that divides Romania and Moldova. After taking a few photos, the nonstop fierce freezing wind encouraged me to descend.

Ukrainians don't know much about us either

Most Europeans have always viewed Ukraine as a mysterious backwater country. For instance, when the king of Sweden, Charles XII, went to Ukraine to find some allies against the Russians, he confessed that he was "uncertain of his route." Sixty years later, in 1769, Joseph Marshall was also clueless: "[Ukraine's] being so extremely out of the way of all travelers, that not a person in a century goes to it, who takes notes of his observations with intention to lay them before the world."[6] Almost 250 years later, the country is still a mystery to most European tourists.

On the other hand, America is somewhat of a mystery to Ukraine too. After descending Mt. Hoverla, I hitchhiked to Rakhiv and then took a bus to Uzhorod. Along the way, at Khust, a college-educated woman named Ljudmila sat next to me. She said that she dreams of living in America and loves WWII history. So I tested her knowledge and said, "Did you know that the Soviet Union and America were allies in WWII?"

She looked at me, dumbfounded, and said, "Really?"

"Don't you know about the Yalta Conference?"

"What do you mean? What about Yalta?" she said.

I explained, "It's where Churchill, Roosevelt, and Stalin met to discuss how to divide Europe after the war. They agreed that the UK and USA would manage Western Europe and Russia would manage Eastern Europe."

She looked puzzled. "Have you heard about D-Day?" I asked, realizing that Ukrainians would call it something else. So I added, "It was June 6, 1944. Does that date ring a bell?"

"No," she replied.

"It's when 30,000 vehicles and 176,000 Allies crossed the English Channel and entered Europe. Over the next few months, millions of Americans pushed all the way to Germany."

"I never knew that so many Americans were in Europe during the war," she admitted. She thought the Soviets were the only reason the Nazis lost and that the other Allies played a meaningless role.

I told her, "I suppose they didn't teach you much about the part of WWII that happened in North Africa or around Japan."

She became frustrated, "I don't understand why we didn't get more education about this. Our professor seemed objective and knowledgeable—he was anti-Communist. We have new history books, not the old communist books."

Although re-writing history takes one day, having it permeate a society can take over a generation. It's been 20 years since Ukraine became an independent country, but this 20-year-old woman, who was an excellent student, was still ignorant of some basic facts about WWII. On the other hand, maybe a 20-year-old American might have trouble finding Europe on a world map.

Ignorance even thrives between neighbors. American Professor Neil Mitchell told me, "I will be teaching in Poland, less than 100 kilometers from the border with Ukraine. I asked my contact person about visiting Ukraine while we were in Poland. I might as well have asked about China! She seemed shocked that anyone staying in Poland would even think of visiting Ukraine."

Exiting at Uzhorod

After our bus spent the day rumbling through Khust, Berehove, and Mukacheve, we arrived at Uzhorod, a fine city on the Slovak border. The Uzh River splits Uzhhorod in two, separating the old and new towns. While waiting for a night bus to Slovakia, I met a beautiful, young Ukrainian couple. Their names were Milosh and Tanya. They offered to give me a quick tour of the old town in their car. We drove up a hill, parked, and walked around a well-maintained sixteenth-century castle. We walked to the Museum of Folk Architecture and Rural Life. It was closed, but Milosh bribed the guards to let us in. He said, "That's the way it works in Ukraine."

After touring through the outdoor museum that showed how Ukrainians lived centuries ago, we walked through the old town's pedestrian streets. We passed a gelateria that would be opening up in a month. The prices weren't posted yet, but they would be cheaper than Italy. In 2010, Ukraine had the world's cheapest Big Mac—just $1.84. Norway had the most expensive Big Mac—a fat $7.20. Milosh and Tanya had never tried gelato. I slipped Milosh some cash and told him to treat Tanya to a gelato when the store opens. They smiled and wished me good luck in Slovakia.

Ukraine's future

Ukraine's national anthem is called *"Sche ne vmerla Ukraina"* ("Ukraine Has Not Yet Perished"). It begins with the line, "The glory of Ukraine is not dead yet." It reminds me of the Polish anthem that also has the "we're not dead yet" idea. It's as if Poland and Ukraine subconsciously knew that there will be a time when greater powers will once again impose their will. They seem forever in an uneasy state of limbo, where at any moment their world can flip upside down just because their powerful neighbors sneeze.

In 2011, I reconnected with Rick DeLong, who was still in Kyiv, and asked him about Ukraine's future. He said, "Ukraine has been sort of in limbo for several centuries, and I expect that to continue. That's not necessarily a bad thing. It's determined by its geographic location, by the fact that it has the Russian and Ukrainian cultural identities. I think it will be a tug-of-war between the EU and Russia. Maybe in 10 years the EU will be less attractive. Who knows? It's unlikely that after these centuries of limbo, that Ukraine will make a clear choice, once and for all."

Indeed, Ukraine wants to be Eastern Europe's Switzerland—neutral, peaceful, and prosperous. Ukraine had the world's third largest nuclear arsenal when the USSR broke up. They gave it all to Russia for them to dispose of. Ukraine shrank their army's size in half. Although Ukraine was one of the three founding countries of the post-Soviet Commonwealth of Independent States (CIS), Ukraine recently left the organization. Ukraine, like Belarus, flirts with the EU to counterbalance Russia and vice versa. NATO wants Ukraine, but 60 percent of Ukrainians don't want NATO. Besides, in 2008, Putin threatened dismemberment if Ukraine tried to join NATO. That's political posturing, so don't expect any wars over this anytime soon, unless somebody drinks a bit too much vodka.

Elena Wolter met her Ukrainian mom in June 2011 and told me that her mom said that "the mood in Ukraine is somewhat negative now because of the new government. A lot of independent TV stations and newspapers have stopped or are heavily censored. . . . She is quite negative about a lot of things but that's her nature."

Ukraine continues its pattern of taking three steps forward and two steps back. What's clear to Rick is that "there's no going back to communism. That was clear about 10 years ago. I think the country will continue moving toward capitalism. Each year it stands more to lose if it doesn't. There are more and more investors waiting to get into Ukraine. It's practically inevitable that it becomes more capitalistic, but it will probably pursue a more European-style capitalism than an American one."

I asked, "What's positive about Ukraine now?"

He said, "Ukrainians are now better acquainted with the rest of the world. Many Ukrainians have been to Egypt, Turkey, Vienna, Poland, and Spain. Ukraine even got its first low-cost airline. Internet use is widespread among urban youth. Everyone is either using English, trying to learn English, or self-flagellating over not learning English."

In 2011, it felt like Ukraine had hit bottom. Relations with Russia and the EU are improving which means things can only get better—even if Ukrainians say otherwise.

What Ukraine Can Teach Us

- **Encourage marshrutkas (minibuses).** Minibuses are everywhere in Ukraine. They're a useful hybrid between a taxi and a bus. In the US, we rarely have nimble minivans as a public transportation option. It's sad to see immense buses consuming energy and polluting just to carry a couple of passengers. Transportation agencies should park the big bus for such unpopular routes and run a minivan instead. Ask your city leaders to make the change.
- **Have caller-pays-everything mobile phone plans.** America is one of the only countries in the world where it costs you money to receive calls or text messages on your mobile phone. Why should we pay money to talk with a fool? Sure, caller-ID helps you avoid cretins, but not always. Ukraine carried over the fixed-line-billing logic: the caller pays 100 percent; the receiver pays nothing. This is useful for parents who want to call their teenage kids. Even if the teenager has no money left in their account, they could still receive a call. Mobile phone companies, are you listening?
- **Cultivate and maintain profound friendships.** In the digital age, relationships have become more superficial and transient. Make an effort to meet your friends in person. Encourage your friends to drop by unannounced. Get rid of the mask and share your feelings.

Places I saw and recommend in Ukraine: Kyiv, Lviv, Yalta, and the Carpathian Mountains.

Travel deals and info: http://ftapon.com/ukraine

We've traveled from the Baltic to the Balkans. We've probed into Romania, Moldova, and Ukraine. We've seen 24 countries. The biggest one remains. Have we saved the best for last? Let's find out. It's finally time to go to Mother Russia.

25

Russia—Eastern Europe's motherland

Happy countries are all alike; every unhappy country is unhappy in its own way.

> *Russia is a riddle wrapped in a mystery inside an enigma.*
> — *Winston Churchill*

The biggest country on Earth

It's hard to grasp just how big Russia is. Numbers help only a little bit. Russia covers one-eighth of the earth's land. It spans nine time zones. It's 60 percent bigger than the world's second biggest country, Canada. It's nearly twice as big as the third biggest country, the US (even when you include Alaska). If the UK became 70 times bigger, it would still be smaller than Russia.

Russia is filled with extremes. It's the coldest country on Earth, with an average annual temperature of −5.5 Celsius (22 F). Russia has Europe's longest river and tallest mountain (Volga River and Mt. Elbrus at 5,633 m / 18,476 ft). It has the world's oldest, deepest, and most voluminous freshwater lake. It's the world's biggest oil producer. It has 40 percent of the planet's natural gas reserves. It has the greatest forest reserves and the second largest coal reserves. It has more tanks and nuclear weapons than anyone else. Most Eastern European countries have smaller populations than Moscow, Europe's biggest city.

When I conceived this book, I intended on leaving Russia out of it. I believed that Russians are not Eastern Europeans, they're *Russians*. They're unique. With a massive foot in Europe and a far larger one in Asia, Russia is in a class by itself. However, then I learned a curious fact: although roughly 75 percent of Russia's land is in Asia, about 75 percent of its population is in Europe. Thus, over 100 million Russians live in Europe, west of the Ural Mountains. Furthermore, how can one understand Eastern Europe without understanding the country that has influenced its development more than any other?

EU snobs sometimes act like Russia isn't in Europe. That's because they spend too much time looking at maps where Moscow is just peeking out of the right edge, omitting the vast land between Moscow and the Urals. Indeed, this book's color map is guilty of doing the same thing. So here's an eye-opening fact: 40 percent of the European continent is in Russia.

Russia wasn't always big. In 1156, Moscow was a small fort with a meek wooden wall around it. In 1238, Mongol invaders burned down the insignificant outpost and killed many inhabitants. Ironically, the beating did Moscow some good. About 100 years later, Russians cooperated with the Mongols, who helped Moscow defeat rival fiefdoms, consolidate power, develop their infrastructure, and improve their trade routes. Before the Mongols, the Slavic center was Kyiv. After sacking Kyiv, the Mongols helped shift the Slavic power base to Moscow. By the 1500s, Russians had kicked the Mongols out and began building the world's third biggest empire. Only the Mongolian and British empires were bigger.

Venice of the North

On June 21, 1999, I visited Russia for the first time. I took an overnight train from Kharkiv, Ukraine to St. Petersburg. I arrived just in time for White Nights—the celebration of the longest day of the year. Because St. Petersburg is so far north, the sun was still kissing the exquisite baroque buildings at 10:00 p.m. The city is filled with canals, which earned it the name Venice of the North. The graceful architecture, romantic atmosphere, and crisscrossing canals put St. Petersburg on my list of the top 10 most beautiful cities in the world.

It's a bit hard to imagine that St. Petersburg was once a mosquito-infested swamp. In 1703, Peter the Great forced 40,000 serfs per year to build the city under brutal conditions. It began with the *Petropavlovskaya Krepost* (Peter and Paul Fortress), which is built around a cluster of islands. After nine years of labor, Russia had a new, breathtaking capital.

Today, everywhere you look is a visual delight. St. Petersburg's heart is the Baroque *Zimniy Dvorets* (Winter Palace) and the *Dvortsovaya Ploshchad* (Palace Square). Nearby is one of the world's finest museums, the Hermitage. It's packed with works by Rodin, Picasso, Pissaro, Monet, Van Gogh, Cézanne, and Gauguin. It includes art from every era and style, including Egyptian art. Overlooking a canal is the ornate Church of the Savior on Blood, which got its name because it's where Tsar Alexander II was assassinated. During the communist era it was a potato warehouse. You can tour the Versailles-inspired Peterhof Palace, marvel at the neoclassical Marble Palace, or walk under the lime-colored Narva Triumphal Gate. Such a dignified city deserves another nickname: Eastern Europe's Paris.

In 1764, as St. Petersburg grew into one of Europe's greatest cities, Giacomo Casanova came to hook up with some babes. Casanova's autobiography has a boring title, *The History of My Life.* It might have sold more copies if he had called it *Banging Broads in the Baltic*. His book recounts how he saw "a peasant girl whose beauty was surprising" near St. Petersburg. He followed her into her family's hut. She cowered "in a corner of the room, like a rabbit afraid that the dogs it saw would devour it."[1] Clearly, this teenager was perceptive given that he was, after all, *Casanova.*

Casanova was a clever guy. He knew if he wanted to get lucky with girls all around the world, he couldn't just speak Italian. He was a polyglot. So speaking in Russian, he politely asked the girl's father if he could shag her. The father said, "But she's only 13 years old! And she's a virgin!" He wasn't about to give his lovely, innocent daughter so easily to a disease-carrying womanizer like Casanova, right? The proud Russian father thought deeply and finally said, "100 rubles." Yikes! With fathers like that, who needs pimps? Then they had this fascinating conversation:

> *"Suppose I were willing to give the hundred rubles?" Casanova asked.*
>
> *"Then you would have her in your service, and you would have the right to bed with her," her father replied.*
>
> *"And if she did not want it?"*
>
> *"Oh, that never happens. You would have the right to beat her."*
>
> *"Then suppose that she is willing. I ask you if, after enjoying her and finding her to my liking, I could go on keeping her."*
>
> *"You become her master, I tell you, and you can even have her arrested if she runs away, unless she gives you back the hundred rubles you paid for her."*
>
> *"And if I keep her with me, how much a month must I give her?"*
>
> *"Not a copper. Only food and drink, and letting her go to the bath every Saturday so that she can go to church on Sunday."*
>
> *"And when I leave Petersburg can I make her go with me?"*
>
> *"Not unless you obtain permission and give security. Though she has become your slave, she is still first of all the slave of the Empress."*
>
> *"Excellent. Arrange it for me. I will give the hundred rubles, and I will take her with me. . . ."*[2]

Wow. So you see, ladies, there is a deep truth to the saying, "You've come a long way, baby." Or not. For while I was looking at my St. Petersburg map, two skinny blond teenagers approached me and said, "You want fun tonight?"

I said, "No, I prefer to suffer."

They could barely speak English, but one said, "We can both give you a . . ." and then she pretended to thrust a banana in and out of her mouth, ". . . for 300 rubles."

That was $10. I raised one eyebrow. "Or," the other added, "You can . . ." she shoved her hips out, ". . . both of us for 600 rubles."

"No, thanks," I said, "Casanova said that the price was 100 rubles."

While Casanova was womanizing his way through Russia, Catherine the Great was doing real work. She was a German princess who married Peter III. After knocking off her husband, she reigned brilliantly for 34 years. If you add Empress Elizabeth's reign, women led Russia for most of the prosperous 1700s. Catherine the Great schmoozed with Voltaire and encouraged science. She funded artists who would eventually fill the Hermitage. Under Catherine, palaces were getting built faster than suburbs in America. While the monarchy continued to rule throughout the 1800s, the seeds for Russia's communist revolution were being planted in Germany.

Communism's parents: Marx and Engels

To find the source of communism, I traveled to Trier, a charming German city near the Luxembourg border. That's where Karl Marx, the guy who dreamed up communism, was born. His birthplace was surprisingly bourgeois. It's now a museum about Marx. Given his last name, I was surprised that he was Jewish. Turns out that Napoleon forced Jews to adopt non-Jewish names. Karl was kind of a loser. He wanted to go into academia, but failed. His father begged his son to control his spending habits. Nevertheless, foreshadowing of the fall of communism, Karl kept spending capital he didn't have.

In his mid-20s, Marx befriended a man who would change his life, Friedrich Engels. A high-school dropout, Engels worked for his rich dad who owned a cotton mill in Manchester. When Engels was 24, he was a profitable capitalist who wrote an anti-capitalist diatribe, "The Condition of the Working Class in England." Ironically, the wealth he generated from his capitalist endeavors funded a revolution against capitalism.

Meanwhile, in 1848, Marx was living in France because Prussia didn't want him—he was a troublemaker. When he was 27 years old, Prussia asked France to deport Marx to Brussels. Later, they revoked his Prussian passport, so he was stateless. Prussians tried to hunt him down, but he escaped. When he was 30, he wrote *The Communist Manifesto*. His next big idea was *Das Kapital,* but he only wrote one volume.

The other two volumes came out thanks to Engels. Marx was too lazy to finish them. Censors in Russia thought Marx's writings were so boring that they weren't worth banning.[3]

Marx tried to appear bourgeois. He married an aristocratic wife, had lavish parties, and seemed rich. However, like most communists, he was short on cash. His wife would beg Engels to give them money. For 20 years, Engels bankrolled Marx's ideas. Without Engels's financial support, communism would have never existed and Eastern Europe would have enjoyed the twentieth century a bit more.

Engels lived the good life: drinking champagne, romancing the girls, and doing it all thanks to the back-breaking labor of the proletariat who worked for him. Engels married a semi-literate Irish girl. When his wife died, he hooked up with her sister. He didn't marry her until she was on her deathbed. Although Engels had no children, he raised the illegitimate child that Marx produced with his housekeeper. Marx must have told her, "Baby, you gotta share the wealth and share the love."

You wouldn't want to be Marx's child. He conceived seven children with his wife, but four of them died early on. That left him with three daughters, who were all named after their mother, Jenny. The oldest died of cancer two months before Marx died. The youngest committed suicide in 1889. And the last daughter? In 1911, she also committed suicide.

> *Go on, get out! Last words are for fools who haven't said enough! — Karl Marx's last words, which he said while throwing his slipper at his housekeeper, who had just asked him if he had any last words to say*

In the 1880s, a Russian teenager named Vladimir Ilyich Ulyanov read Marx's works and got inspired. In his 20s, even though his brother was hung for trying to assassinate the Tsar, Ulyanov followed his brother's footsteps and also got caught. Instead of execution, he got solitary confinement and a free trip to Siberia. When he got out, he lived in Munich, London, and Geneva. He wrote revolutionary pieces using several pseudonyms. When he was 32, he settled on one name that was based on a Siberian river: Lenin.

During WWI, when Lenin was 47, Russia was experiencing what America had experienced 141 years before: a revolution against the monarchy. However, the revolutionary ideals were different: the main principle that American revolutionaries fought for was *liberty*, while Russians fought in the name of *equality*. After winning, Lenin moved Russia's capital from St. Petersburg to Moscow, which is where I went next.

Into the motherland's heart

When my overnight train to Moscow arrived, I felt small. The mega-city with over 10 million Muscovites is overwhelming. The city produces 24 percent of Russia's GDP. By 2012, they will have four giant transportation rings encircling the city. Moscow has the world's second busiest metro (after Tokyo) with 182 stations, 12 lines, and with escalators so long that you'll think you're descending to Hell.

Although we've all seen photos of Moscow's Red Square, I got goose bumps when I saw St. Basil's Cathedral. I entered Lenin's mausoleum, where his embalmed body rests for all to see. The Kremlin, which means *citadel,* has an armory, super-sized diamonds, regal tombs, sacred icons, and commie memorabilia. In the evening, I enjoyed a ballet in the Bolshoi Theater for $9. That was 1999. Today, expect to pay $100.

It's worth seeing Moscow's monument of Peter the Great because it was voted the world's ugliest statue. Supposedly, the statue was originally meant to represent Christopher Columbus and be placed in America. However, the US didn't want it, so the designer replaced Columbus's head with that of Peter the Great. It's not as ugly as people say.

Getting robbed twice

When I asked a foreigner who was living in Moscow what he will miss when he leaves, he said, "I will miss gypsy cabs. Hailing a gypsy cab is like hitchhiking. You put out your arm and random people who want to make some extra cash drive you wherever you want. It is easy, usually not super dangerous, as it is usually just ordinary people, and super cheap. You can get across the city for 300 rubles, which is like $10. I almost never use a real taxi, which is expensive."

I agree, although a gypsy cab driver once robbed me. I was an idiot. In 1999, a husky man drove me to a place where I needed to wait for a friend who never showed up. While we waited, he tried to pickpocket my wallet. I caught him in the act. He gave me my wallet back, but I stupidly didn't just run. Instead, I gave him some money for the fare, but not as much as he was asking (he was asking a lot). He followed me as I entered another cab and demanded that I give him more money. When I opened my wallet to give him a few more rubles, he reached his fingers into it, grabbed over $100, and ran.

The second time I was robbed in Moscow was also due to my stupidity. I was staying at the end of a long hallway in a large hotel. Moscow was experiencing a summer heatwave and at 8:00 a.m. my room already felt like a *banya* (sauna) even with the window open. I wanted to sleep more, so I cracked my door open to increase the airflow. Since I was at the end of the hallway, nobody would be walking by. However, when I woke up at 9:30 a.m., my wallet, which had been resting on the nightstand, was gone.

The next day, the hotel management "found" my wallet. Miraculously, my credit card and identification were still there. The money, of course, was not. Probably a cleaning lady entered my room while I was sleeping and got her monthly bonus. So far, even after visiting 75 countries, these were the only times in my life when I've been robbed.

An American in Moscow

In 2011, I was introduced to Lumina Resnick, an American who has lived in Moscow for five years. She's the personal assistant to a Russian mini-oligarch who wants his children to learn English. When I asked her what she will miss when she leaves, she said, "Snow is considered a blessing, Russians love it, and it doesn't impair their infrastructure at all. Even in a blizzard your plane will take off, the trains will run, and you can still drive anywhere. No worries. I heard that Moscow employs up to 30,000 people to move snow and clear the streets."

"What else?" I asked.

Lumina said, "The metro system here is *superb*. Trains come every 30 to 120 seconds, *and* your transfer train has often arrived before you even have time to walk to the other end of the platform. Also, hot water is *free*. It is state provided and never runs out. You can take an hour long shower and not worry. People dress up more here. They are less casual. And I like that. No one is running around in sweat suits. Of course that means you can't go out like a slob or people will think you are a mess, but I kind of prefer it."

"It's true that Russians take care of their appearances."

"And, you *can* get medical care for cheap, if you know where to go. I got a root canal at a dentist who spoke English well, in a modern facility, with modern equipment. I had three X-rays, two visits, a cleaning, and the whole thing cost me $150! Seriously. That would have cost over $1,000 in the USA, even with insurance."

"What things annoy you about Moscow?"

"They have very few drains on the street, so the streets are *dirty*. When it rains or the snow melts it gets really gross and messy. It ruins your shoes—if you don't clean them they can shrink due to the chemicals they use to melt the snow!"

When I asked her why she's been there for over five years, she alluded to the financial benefits. She said, "There is often a vast difference in the quality of life for an expat versus a local Russian. Expats are paid well for skills which are not readily available in the local population, like native fluency in a foreign language or experience in a particular business niche which is still under development in Russia. Hence, salaries for foreigners are very high. I recently read that half of the foreigners living in Moscow make over $200,000 a year. The other half are probably mostly teachers. Teachers working for language schools make between $20,000 and $35,000, while private teachers make between $60,000 to $150,000. The employer usually provides housing free of charge, including utilities. So despite the fact that Western food and goods are pricey, the cost of living is substantially lower for expats here than at home in the US, *and* most of your salary is saved."

"What other benefits are there?"

"Jobs tend to follow the European system, where employees get a month of paid holiday each year. In addition, Russia has many holidays which total up to another two weeks of time off. I personally get about two months off a year of paid holiday. As for working hours, I and other teachers work between 20 to 35 hours a week. Businessmen work much more than that, but I would say it is the same amount of hours as in the West."

I said, "In 2011, the average Muscovite wage is $1,500 per month. My friend Rick in Ukraine said that people can get by with much lower salaries because they have much lower fixed costs. Is the same true in Moscow?"

"Yes. Most people live in flats that were purchased cheaply when Russia was privatized. So they do not have housing costs. Utilities are very cheap, probably subsidized by the government. And if you don't buy western food, then food in general is cheaper than in the West. My Russian friend seems to be easily supporting his wife, child, and himself on his salary of $2,000 a month. They even have extra money to travel in Europe a couple times a year. My other Russian friend just had a baby and remodeled her flat, and also does not seem to have much financial trouble. Outside of Moscow, however, salaries drop to $450 per month for Russians and teachers alike. But costs of living also drop."

"How prevalent is violence?"

"I feel safer in Moscow than New York City. I rarely see fights. I did see somebody get beat up for trying to steal something on the metro yesterday, but that was well-deserved. I have heard violence is more prevalent here due to high alcohol consumption, but I have not experienced it personally. Domestic abuse is supposed to be pretty high due to alcohol. I read an article stating that it went both ways for men and women. About 50 percent of husbands beat their wives and 30 percent of wives beat their husbands. Beatings were for different reasons though between the genders: men wanting more sex, women wanting the husband to bring home more money (probably because the man was spending it on alcohol or a mistress)."

The carousing country

I'll confess: I wanted to disprove the stereotype of the drunk Russian. Despite my bias, it was impossible to ignore the mountain of evidence. A third of the male deaths and 18 percent of female deaths are alcohol-related. One study found that 21 percent of Siberian men between 1990 and 2004 had lethal or near-lethal ethanol blood concentrations.

During long-distance train rides, men often guzzled beer and vodka. You could smell the alcohol in their breath from far away. A few were obviously drunk: running around, causing a ruckus, and getting yelled at by the tough Russian train conductors. I sat next to a trash can for several hours (because there was a nearby power outlet for my computer) and I couldn't believe the number of beer and vodka bottles people were throwing away. I rarely saw any other beverage container being tossed.

I heard many stories during my visits to Russia. One woman told me that her father got drunk in the forest, passed out, and died from exposure. A woman from Porkhov lost both of her parents to alcohol abuse. A man from Moscow lost his grandfather because he was drunk and smoking in the bed. Another girl was drunk and sleeping on the grass when a drunk driver drove through and ran her over.

One man named "Sergey Cut" got his nickname because he got into a fight with another drunk man who had a knife. Sergey got sliced and now has a scar on his neck. Another alcoholic regularly begged a woman for cash. She normally gave him some, but one day she had enough and refused. He told her that he would kill himself, she said go ahead. So he did. He broke a bottle and shoved the broken end into his neck and died.

A grandmother's house was burned down for no apparent reason. She suspects it was some drunk hooligans. One guy hung himself because he was drunk and depressed. Another man told me how his father died of an alcohol overdose. I met a 28-year-old Russian in a wheelchair who told me that he had collapsed in a drunken stupor on railroad tracks. He woke up when the train sliced off his legs.

Wine we need for health, and health we need to drink vodka.
— Viktor Chernomyrdin, Russia's former Prime Minister

Here's what's shocking: I was not looking for stories of alcohol abuse. People told me these stories out of the blue. Clearly, if you wanted to write a book about alcoholism in Russia, you need only spend a week to get a mountain of anecdotes. Some Russians will refute the stereotype that Russians are heavy drinkers. Obviously, not everybody is an alcoholic. Still, a Russian denying that Russia has a drinking problem is like an American denying that Americans have a lot of guns.

Going nowhere or backwards

In 2011, there were nine countries whose life expectancy hadn't improved since 1970: six of them are in Africa; the other three are Ukraine, Belarus, and Russia. It's tempting to blame the move to capitalism. However, during the 1970s, most of the world saw its life expectancy increase by 3.5 years, but in the USSR, it *declined* by one year. Soviet statistics show that from 1965 to the early 1980s, Russian health was declining mostly due to smoking, poor diet, and, of course, drinking. Mikhail Gorbachev's 1985 anti-drinking campaign raised life expectancy by three years. Then life expectancy plummeted in the 1990s. Some blame the horrendous economic conditions. However, during that same period, the Balkans not only experienced economic depression, but also war, yet their life expectancy recovered far faster than in Russia. In 2011, Russian life expectancy was still below 1990 levels. Men were only expected to live 59.8 years.

In 2011, Russia's death rate was the fifth worst in the world, worse than Somalia's. That partly explains why Russia is depopulating at 0.47 percent per year. Many Russian deaths are preventable. About 15 percent of Russian deaths are tobacco-related because 37 percent smoke.[4] Russia's tuberculosis infection rate is 27 times worse than America's and only half of Bangladesh's. Russian male death rates are higher than levels in sub-Saharan Africa. As Niall Ferguson put it, Russia is "Nigeria with snow."[5]

There's one last metric to consider. In 1970, Russia's Human Development Index score was 0.71, while Saudi Arabia's was 0.45 and Oman's was 0.36. In 2011, Russia was 0.77, having gone effectively nowhere. Meanwhile, Saudi Arabia and Oman passed Russia with scores of nearly 0.8. It makes you wonder how Joseph Stalin would react to all these statistics.

Bank robber becomes a mass murderer

Lenin was perceptive. In his last testament, he wrote, "Stalin is too rude and this defect . . . becomes intolerable in a Secretary-General. . . . Think about a way of removing Stalin from that post and appointing another man in his stead who in all other respects differs from Comrade Stalin in having only one advantage, namely, that of being more tolerant, more loyal, more polite and more considerate to the comrades, less capricious, etc. This circumstance may appear to be a negligible detail. But . . . it is a detail which can assume decisive importance."

No kidding. When Stalin was young, he robbed banks and kidnapped people for ransom. He said, "Death solves all problems—no man, no problem." Stalin had lots of problems, so he killed far more innocent people than Hitler. As the Soviet leader, he engineered a famine that killed over six million of his own people. He deported over

14 million, with a high percentage dying along the way. About 2,000 writers and artists were sent to Gulag labor camps—most died.

Ideas are more powerful than guns. We would not let our enemies have guns, why should we let them have ideas?
— Joseph Stalin

Stalin's Great Purge was a nightmare. He removed or executed nearly all of his top 316 military officers, including three out of five of his top generals. Stalin was one of the six original members of Lenin's first Politburo. He executed the other five. In the next Politburo, only two out of seven survived. According to declassified Soviet archives, between 1937 and 1938, Stalin executed about 1,000 people a day. Most historians think it was much more, and that over a million were executed in all. Even the main guy coordinating the Great Purge got purged.

Some Russians have reasons to like Stalin anyway. He won the biggest war in history. He grew the Soviet Union by adding 14 republics and had Eastern Europe under his thumb. He turned Russia from an agricultural nation into an industrialized giant. He created socialist programs. Lastly, he gave Russia a nuclear arsenal, thereby making it a superpower. Despite these accomplishments, there is only one surviving painting of Stalin in Russia (I saw it in St. Petersburg's Museum of Russian Political History). The jury has voted.

Justice is like a train that is nearly always late.
— Yevgeny Yevtushenko, Russian poet

The Hidden Europe's most hidden part

Whenever you meet someone who claims he's been "everywhere" in Europe, ask him if he's been to Kaliningrad. There's a chance he may not have even heard about this unusual Russian territory. It's nestled in between Lithuania, Poland, and the Baltic Sea. On a map, Kaliningrad looks like a Soviet tumor that Eastern Europeans forgot to remove. It's as if the locals there didn't get the 1991 memo to overthrow their government and declare independence. It doesn't make sense, until you learn that the locals are not some bizarre, unknown Baltic ethnic group. They are nearly all Russians. That's weird. Ethnic Russians make up only six percent of neighboring Lithuania. How did that Kaliningrad get to be so Russian? On February 17, 2009, I left Lithuania and entered this mysterious land to find out the answer.

At sunset, our bus reached the Neman River that separates Kaliningrad from Lithuania. The entrance to Kaliningrad was dramatic. The Queen Louise Bridge that spanned the frozen river had a beautiful, old stone arch with two elegant towers. It implied that Kaliningrad wouldn't have a typical ex-Soviet look. Ironically, the first town we came to was called Sovetsk.

During the Soviet era, Kaliningrad was closed to foreigners because it was a military zone. Today, Russian border guards scan luggage with their X-ray machine. I left my big backpack on my seat. They never bothered searching the bus. Such sloppy security would never have happened in the USSR.

Sovetsk had gray, blocky communist-era buildings, but it also had some classy buildings that you might find in St. Petersburg. As we drove to Kaliningrad's capital, the landscape was flat and sparsely populated. We passed forests and fields. A few headlights on a black highway were our only company. In rare moments, we could see lights from the houses of farmers that were alone in the icy void.

How Kaliningrad became Russian

For most of recorded history, Kaliningrad has been German. For centuries, Germanic lands stretched across what today is Northern Poland. Furthermore, Kaliningrad wasn't some distant forgotten German outpost. In fact, the Germanic kingdom of Prussia had its capital in Kaliningrad (later they moved it to Berlin).

In the last century, everything changed. After WWI, Poland regained its sea access, which cut Kaliningrad off from the rest of Germany. The Nazis stormed through Poland and reattached Kaliningrad to Germany. After WWII, Germans were kicked out of most Eastern European countries. In most places that meant losing a minority of the population. In Kaliningrad's case, however, that meant losing practically everybody. After the war, the Soviets could have put up a big neon sign in Kaliningrad saying, "VACANCY."

To fill the empty German homes and land, Russians colonized it. Unlike other Baltic states, Kaliningrad became over 90 percent East Slavic. When Lenin's buddy, Mikhail Kalinin, died in 1946, the Soviets named Kaliningrad after him. What's confusing is that Russians called both the territory and its capital Kaliningrad. To avoid misunderstandings, we'll do what many locals do and call the capital *Koenig*, which is derived from its original German name, Königsberg.

Exploring Kaliningrad

After our bus arrived in Koenig, I took a city bus to get to the apartment of my couchsurfing host, Vadim Zangliger. He was a peaceful, bespectacled 40-year-old who spoke basic English. He was an engineer, a financial trader, and a single father. He shared his bedroom with his shy eight-year-old son, Artyom. Since the only other rooms were the kitchen and the bathroom, the three of us would be sleeping in the same room.

Vadim was the classic couchsurfing host: he was hungry to learn more about the world and meet foreigners. He was born in Belarus, but moved to Kaliningrad during the Cold War. Because Kaliningrad was closed to the world, he was eager to meet outsiders. We looked at maps as he described Kaliningrad's importance. It's the only ice-free Baltic port that Russia has, which is why they've stationed their Baltic Navy Fleet there. Vadim expects that at some point in this decade Russia will put missiles in Kaliningrad. NATO will whine about that, but it's just Russia's answer for NATO expanding into the Baltic, even though Bush Sr. had promised Gorbachev that NATO would never do that.

Imagine if the southern part of the US became a separate country, but that Florida stayed loyal to the US. Floridians would be isolated. To drive to the rest of the US, Floridians would have to transit through a foreign country. Similarly, Lithuania used to be a Soviet republic, but now it's a roadblock for those in Kaliningrad. Although Russians can get a transit visa through Lithuania, it's more complicated than before. As one Kaliningrad local told me, "Lithuanians and Polish people don't like Russians."

Thus, like Alaska, Kaliningrad has once again become an exclave—a disconnected piece of the mainland. Kaliningrad was once cut off from its motherland, Germany; this time, it is cut off from its new motherland, Russia. It seems that Kaliningrad is destined to be an orphan. Despite being disconnected, few locals want independence from mother Russia. Kaliningrad will continue being a hidden place. The day the world learns about Kaliningrad is the day Russians put missiles there.

Discovering Koenig

I interviewed Natasha Perreault for my WanderLearn Podcast. She was born and raised in Kaliningrad, but she married an American and lives in Washington, DC. She has a Belarusian father and a Ukrainian mother. She said, "Koenig doesn't look like a typical Russian town. It doesn't have all the Russian Orthodox churches that you normally see. It looks much more German."

She's right, yet it's remarkable that Koenig still has a German look. For four days, the British air force firebombed Koenig into oblivion. Three months of savage Nazi-Soviet battles demolished whatever was left. Today, ethnic Germans make up less than one percent of Kaliningrad. Natasha said, "Kaliningrad is a kind of melting pot. People from all over Russia came to Kaliningrad. In the 1950s, nobody was from there. Everyone came there to try to build a new life."

Natasha put me in contact with her 60-year-old uncle, Vladislav Fukalov, who lives in Koenig. He offered to give me a tour of the city. He wore an *ushanka* (a classic Russian fur hat) and had a hardened look: handsome wrinkles, a strong body, and piercing blue eyes. His behavior was the opposite of his looks: he was gentle, calm, and peaceful. He was born in a Russian village near Yekaterinburg, next to the Ural Mountains. He had traveled the world as a seaman and spoke decent English, which was unusual for a Russian of his generation.

Vladislav and I explored the best sites in Koenig. We took a bus to the *Korolevskie Vorota* (King's Gate), which is the best restored gate among the city's original entrances. It looks like a mini-castle made out of brick. Then we visited the Amber Museum, which has about 6,000 pieces of amber. About 90 percent of the world's extractable amber comes from Kaliningrad.

We walked on the snowy sidewalks to the *Tsentralny Ostrov* (Central Island). It has the handsome Gothic Königsberg Cathedral, which was first built in 1333. WWII destroyed it. Russians finally rebuilt it after the USSR died. Now it has a 38,000-pipe organ. Connected to the cathedral is the mausoleum of Immanuel Kant, the German philosopher, who was born and taught in Kaliningrad. We walked along the nearby Pregolya River, where there's a new, attractive Fish Village that has a Germanic theme. Communists ignored Kaliningrad's German heritage, today's Russians celebrate it.

For example, the majestic Königsberg Castle that was built in 1255 was damaged in WWII. Instead of restoring it, the Soviets idiotically demolished it in 1967. In its place, the USSR spent a decade building the repulsive *Dom Sovetov* (House of the Soviets). Natasha called it "the shame of the city and Soviet system." In addition to being butt-ugly, it's unusable. That's because the underground tunnels collapsed and made the building structurally weak. It's still empty. Vladislav gave me a wry smile and said, "It's the revenge of the Germans."

Russians are now considering rebuilding the German castle. It would be a welcome change. Most of what was built in the last 50 years is an eyesore. At night, Koenig has neon lights, flashy strobes, and tacky casinos. Car dealerships line the outskirts of the city. In 2006, they built one decent-looking building: the first Russian Orthodox church in Koenig—the Cathedral of Christ the Savior. "It is right behind the Lenin statue," Natasha told me, and then being amused by continued presence of Lenin remarked, "How funny! Can't help but laugh at how backward Russia is sometimes!"

Thoughts of Vladislav Fukalov

Yulia Tinyakova, who was born in Kaliningrad, told me, "Russia will get through everything, no matter what, as we have been doing for generations." Vladislav, who is 40 years older than Yulia, was less optimistic. He said, "Russia will keep falling more. It's a result of bad leadership. The government gave a few people who were well-connected big industries. The people got nothing. Today, I make $120 a month on my pension. That is not enough to live. I must work in a stadium, doing a simple job. But two months ago half the workers at the stadium lost their jobs. Those who kept their jobs had to take a 30 percent pay cut."

I asked, "What do you like about Russia?"

"The educational system used to be very good. Stalin was a cruel man, but he did bring the literacy rate up from 30 percent to 95 percent. Today, our education system is terrible. People do not know anything about World War II. People just care about money."

"What about China?"

"China is dangerous for Russia. Over 75 percent of Russians live west of the Urals. Many Chinese are moving to eastern Russia. One day they will make a referendum and say, 'This territory now belongs to China.'"

Ice fishing off the Curonian Spit

The next day, I went to Svetlogorsk, a sea resort overlooking the Baltic Sea. It has a long boardwalk, the remains of what was once a fashionable German beach and spa town. It has many attractive sculptures placed throughout the desolate beach. After freezing myself on its snowy beach, I went to Zelenogradsk to freeze my butt off at another beach.

Zelenogradsk was also a popular German tourist resort, but when Kaliningrad became a military outpost, tourism died. Today, it's back—at least for Russians. Rich Russians fill Kaliningrad's coast during the summer. Most Europeans continue to ignore it, mostly because Russia's expensive travel visa encourages them to visit other Baltic beaches instead. Still, the colorful wooden Germanic mansions and quiet beach make Zelenogradsk a special travel experience. Besides, it has Europe's largest sundial, even though the Baltic is known for its cloudy days.

My favorite Kaliningrad adventure was exploring the *Kurshkaya Kosa* (Curonian Spit). On a map, the spit looks like an artificial breakwater that separates the Baltic and the Curonian lagoon. It's just a few football fields wide. Nevertheless, this 98-kilometer (61-mile) long strip of beach is completely natural, which is why it's a UNESCO World Heritage Site. It has Europe's biggest sand dunes, which can be 60 meters (yards) high. Half of the spit belongs to Russia, the other half to Lithuania. In 2004, I explored the Lithuanian side in the summer. Five years later, I returned to explore the Russian side in the winter.

> *People don't notice whether it's winter or summer when they're happy. — Anton Chekhov, Russian writer*

South of Rybachiy, the bus driver dropped me off in what seemed like the middle of nowhere. I walked west through pine trees, then over sand dunes, and within two minutes I enjoyed a vast, empty Baltic Sea beach. After relishing the icy breeze, I returned to the road and walked east toward the lagoon. A frozen wooden sign indicated that something noteworthy was nearby. A few closed buildings greeted me. It seemed deserted, but then a friendly black cat walked through the snow to say hi. I gave her some cheese and then we came to the edge of the frozen lagoon. It seemed foolish to step on it without knowing its thickness, but it held the cat's weight, so I held my breath and stepped on the ice.

The ice crunched a bit, but it felt firm. I took another step. It felt solid. I walked slowly. Eventually, the cat felt I had gone far enough, so she returned to the shore. I kept walking over this immense white landscape. Even the clouds were steel white. After walking a few minutes, I spotted three humans almost a kilometer away. They were in the middle of the lagoon. I approached these lunatics.

They were Russian ice fishermen. They were in their 50s and had gold teeth to prove it. They were surprised that a California boy who speaks little Russian had found their favorite fishing spot. The holes that they had drilled showed that the ice was about as thick as a human leg. They sat on portable chairs behind a portable wall that blocked the frosty wind. Each had caught about 20 small fish. Although we could hardly communicate, we laughed as they offered me some of their snacks and vodka. Eventually, they were satisfied with their catch, so they packed up. These guys were tough—even though the 58-year-old was carrying a bunch of gear, I struggled to keep up with him as he walked briskly across the frozen lagoon. Russians are hardcore.

WWII beliefs

WWII helped shape Russia's rugged spirit. The Great Patriotic War, as they call it, defined Russia's unbreakable will. Still, as with all glorious national stories, there's a bit of myth-making. For example, a surprising number of Russians seem to believe that WWII was just a fight between the Nazis and Soviets. When I was in Porkov, a small town near Pskov, I met Ruslana, a young reporter. She said, "America was clever to get involved when WWII was over. Russia beat the Germans. The Americans talk about a 'second front.' Big deal. The Russians had already beaten the Germans by the time the Americans got involved."

There's some truth to this. In WWII, America "only" lost 418,500 people. The Soviets lost over 23,400,000. One of the deadliest WWII battles for the US was the Battle of the Bulge, where 19,000 Americans died. Compare that to the Battle of Stalingrad, where 518,741 Soviets died. American losses only account for 0.3 percent of all WWII deaths, whereas the USSR's share was 13.7 percent. Furthermore, of all the German deaths in WWII, the Red Army was responsible for over 75 percent of them. This is one way of measuring their credit: it would indicate that they should get about 75 percent of the credit for winning WWII.[6]

One death is a tragedy; one million is a statistic.
— Joseph Stalin

On the other hand, there's a reason the conflict is called World War II and not European War CXIII. In Africa, the Allies and Axis suffered over a million causalities. China and Japan lost roughly half as many people as the USSR and Germany, respectively. In six months, Japan took damage from air attack equivalent to what Germany sustained in the last three years of WWII. The USSR didn't participate in Africa and only entered the conflict in Asia after the US dropped an atomic bomb. Thus, when you consider all 4.35 million Axis soldiers who died, the Red Army was responsible for about 55 percent of them. After sharing such facts, Ruslana told me, "I don't want to hear more about your Japanese war."

In addition, the US contributed much of WWII's firepower. The US vastly outproduced the USSR in machine guns, military trucks, aircraft, naval ships, coal, oil, and iron ore.[7] Consider how many troops each country mobilized: Italy 4.5 million, the UK 4.6 million, Japan 7.4 million, the USA 11.5 million, Germany 17 million, and the USSR 29 million. The fact that the US was in third place is remarkable given that it had to cross either the Pacific or Atlantic Ocean to get near a battle.

John Keegan, a British WWII historian, wrote, "The Soviet war was limited to its own territory and contiguous areas, of which the most distant from the center was Manchuria. . . . But it was the United States that eventually achieved the widest global outreach. In 1944 it was conducting major land, sea, and air campaigns in western and southern Europe, in China, in Southeast Asia, and in the central and southern Pacific. The Second World War, at its apogee, was truly an American war."[8]

There was symbolism whenever the "Big Three" Allied leaders met—the American President always sat in the center. At the 1943 Tehran Conference, Roosevelt was seated in the middle with Stalin and Churchill at his sides. In Yalta, it was the same seating arrangement, even though Stalin could have argued to be in the center since he was hosting the event. The Chairman of the 1945 Potsdam Peace Conference was US President Truman, not Stalin. These symbols signal that perhaps the USSR didn't single-handedly win WWII, which is what many Russians (and other Eastern Europeans) told me.

Could the USSR have won WWII without its Western Allies?

A Russian who lives in America told me, "My father was a WWII expert, and I consider myself a good student of this subject. You say that millions of Americans entered Europe after D-Day. It was not millions, but a few hundred thousand." It's remarkable that even educated Russians underestimate the Western Allied effort. After I pointed her to a few sources, she admitted, "I was not aware of millions of American troops fighting on the Western Front."

I'm not suggesting that *most* Russians don't know that WWII was more than just a war between Germany and the USSR. In May 2011, the Moscow-based Levada Center asked Russians if the Soviets could have won the war without the help of their allies. The Levada Center wouldn't have asked that question if it didn't believe that most Russians know that the USSR wasn't alone in the fight. Still, the 2011 results were revealing: 60% said that the USSR would have won without any help, 32% said they would not have won, and 9% said it was too hard to answer. This is a significant change from 1997, when 71% said that the USSR could have won the war without Western Allied help.[9]

Few Russians have heard of (or place much importance on) America's Lend-Lease program, which gave military hardware to the Allies starting in March 1941. The US gave $31.4 billion to Britain, $11.3 billion to the USSR, and a couple of billion to France and China. That $50 billion would be worth nearly $1 trillion today. In WWII, the Soviets produced 92 locomotives; the US gave them 2,000 locomotives and 11,000 railcars. One in every five Soviet military planes were American gifts. Two-thirds of the Soviet trucks were made in America. The US also donated a significant amount of telecommunication technology, clothes, and food to the Soviets.

The Red Army nearly lost the titanic battles of Moscow, Leningrad, and Stalingrad. Just one small factor could have tipped those battles in Germany's favor. One could make a strong argument that Lend-Lease and the distracting battles in Western Europe and Africa gave just enough of a boost to turn a Soviet loss into a victory. Some historians say that the reason the Allies won is that "Britain supplied the time, America supplied the money, and the Soviet Union supplied the blood."

Most WWII monuments in the ex-USSR are engraved with the years "1941–1945." This was odd for me, because Westerners are taught that WWII was from 1939 to 1945. There are two reasons the Soviets emphasized the 1941 start date. First, it's when Germany attacked the USSR. Second, if the Soviets said it started in 1939, then they would get into the awkward position of explaining what it was doing between 1939 and 1941: collaborating with the Nazis, as well as attacking and conquering others. Apparently, that was neither war nor patriotic, which is why it's not included in their Great Patriotic War timeline.

Was the US a late-comer to WWII? It depends. WWII in Europe lasted 69 months. Since the USSR marks the beginning of the Great Patriotic War on June 22, 1941, they would say that they fought for 47 months. Americans started on December 7, 1941, so that's 41 months—a minor difference. On the other hand, American troops didn't land in Europe until September 1943, when they invaded Italy. Starting from that date, they fought in Europe for 20 months. That's because before that, they were fighting simultaneously in Asia and Northern Africa, a logistical challenge.

Russians minimize America's involvement in the European war just like Americans gloss over Russia's involvement in the Japanese war. Few Americans know that 1.6 million Russians pushed Japan out of Manchuria. The fight only lasted 11 days, but it was pivotal. Many Americans idiotically believe that the US was the main reason Germany lost. They're clueless that the vast majority of Europe's deadliest battles happened on the Eastern Front. Most Americans don't know that Poland and the USSR suffered and sacrificed by far the most.[10]

Every nation's view of history is biased. For nearly all of the Soviet era, Russians denied collaborating with the Nazis. They still hardly mention it. I went to a French school for 12 years and the teachers never talked about the French government collaborating with the Nazis. Russia's WWII viewpoint influenced much of Eastern Europe. For example, my young Polish friend, Emilia Łoś, wrote to me, "I hadn't realized that the US fought in WWII until last week, when I met a General from the United States, whose dad was fighting in Europe."

The proud Russian

Ruslana was born in 1976 and she acted as if the Cold War were still happening. She proudly said, "America can't beat Russia! Nobody in history has ever beaten Russia!" Ruslana's friend, Yuliya Trutko, was born in St. Petersburg, and she told me that people "are so proud of being Russian." In Russia, my Serbian friend Nenad Stojanović saw a T-shirt: "I'm Russian. Who the hell are you?"

While walking through Kaliningrad, Vladislav told me, "The new Russian man likes to puff himself up, make himself look bigger than he is. He wants people to think he has lots of money. He says, 'Look at my expensive clothes, my nice watch, my nice car, my nice phone.' He pretends to be big, but he is not. Before, the Russian man cared about others. Today, he only cares about himself."

Alina Lind, a Russian who lives in Estonia, tells her proud Russian friends, "What are you so damn proud about anyway? You're Russian because you were born one. Big deal. It's nothing you did or accomplished. It just as stupid as people who are proud of being a woman, of having blue eyes, or of being black or white. You were born that way. If you must be proud of something, be proud of something you achieved, not a characteristic that you were born with."

After meeting proud Ruslana, I mumbled, "Damn patriotic Russians." I sipped some tea and thought, "Americans aren't like that." Then, I put the cup down slowly and stared out into space as I said softly, "Holy shit. Actually, we are just like that."

12 negative things the USA and Russia have in common

I was born in 1970, so I grew up in the Cold War. My generation was taught that Russians and Americans are polar opposites. Thus, whenever a Russian habit or belief would annoy me, I attributed it to Russians being different from Americans. However, the more time I spent in Russia and the more I reflected, the more I came to the disquieting realization that many annoying Russian traits are also typical American traits. Here are 12 examples:

1. **We've got an ego that matches our size.** Texas prides itself on being big. Americans have huge homes and cars. Four of six of the biggest city squares in Europe are in Russia. Our motto is: bigger is better. And our egos correspond to it.
2. **We like guns and gangsters.** Russians love pistols and crime shows. The US and Russia are the world's biggest weapons manufacturers. About 20 percent of Russia's manufacturing jobs are related to the military. Our cultures are obsessed with violence, although America glorifies it the most.
3. **We're crass, vulgar, and unsophisticated.** We like kitschy art and tacky objects—think Las Vegas. Russian women often cross the fashion line between sexy and slutty, between classy and ostentatious, and between looking beautiful and looking like a tramp. They pose for photos as if they're trying to get on the cover of *Cosmopolitan*. Meanwhile, Americans are slobs who under-dress, wearing casual clothes to practically every occasion except maybe a funeral.
4. **Our health habits suck and we're fat to prove it.** In 1994, 20 percent of Russians were obese. In 2004, it rose to 28 percent.[11] Now, one-third is obese. That parallels the rise of obesity in America. The main difference is that young Russians are rarely overweight, while 20 percent of American teenagers are. We both consume an excessive amount of sugar, refined carbohydrates, and saturated fats. The most amount of exercise we do is picking up the TV's remote control.
5. **We're loud and obnoxious.** Several Eastern Europeans (including Russians) told me that when they pick a hotel, they ask if Russians go there often. If so, they prefer going else-

where because Russians are loud and rambunctious. Americans have the same rotten reputation. Stephanie Rexroth, an American who visited Siberia, said, "Americans have been arrogant and pretentious jerks when visiting other countries to the point that we've gained a crappy tourist stereotype." I told my Chinese roommate that Americans imitate Chinese speakers by making sounds like "Ching, chang, chong." I asked her what sounds Chinese make to imitate Americans. She said, "We don't make special sounds. We just talk in Chinese, but we talk *VERY LOUDLY.*"

6. **Most countries dislike our leadership.** According to Gallup's 2010 poll, 70 countries had a majority approving of America's leadership, while 82 countries had a majority disapproving (5 countries were split 50/50). Russia was even less popular: only 27 countries had a majority approving of Russia's leadership, while 123 countries had a majority disapproving it. In 2009, a Pew Research Center survey showed that Bulgarians and Ukrainians were the only Europeans who said that Russia had a positive influence on their country; elsewhere in Europe, people were more likely to say that Russia had a negative influence. In July 2011, only 4 out 22 diverse countries had a majority of the people holding a favorable view of Russia.[12]
7. **We're monolingual.** We expect everyone to speak our language and lose patience when someone doesn't speak it well. News programs dub over foreign languages. I never had heard Putin's voice until I heard him on Estonian TV. Russian national TV dubs over the voice of America's leaders (and vice versa). Russians dub foreign TV shows. Americans won't even bother showing foreign TV shows.
8. **When we expanded our nation, we were assholes.** In the 1800s, Americans drove west based on their Manifest Destiny and did countless evil acts against the Native Americans. In the 1600s, Russia drove east demanding that the natives pay *yasak* (tribute) to the Tsar. If the natives didn't pay, men would get hung on meat hooks while women and children were enslaved or raped. Both of us dislike talking about the dark side of our expansion.
9. **When we occupy a land, we think we're nice.** First of all, many of us don't even like to admit that we've ever "occupied" any land. "The Iraqis wanted us to move in," Americans say. "The Baltic countries welcomed the Soviets," Russians say. These myths have some truth to them. What's closer to the truth is that some people in these countries (not always the majority) wanted help overthrowing some jerk out of power, but they

usually didn't want us to stay, yet we often do. During that occupation period, we can be devils, but we don't admit it.

10. **We lead the world in incarcerations.** According to the International Center of Prison Studies, Germany has about 75 inmates per 100,000 people. America has 10 times more (748). Russia has 600 per 100,000. Most other countries are well behind Russia and the US: Brazil (240), Iran (220), Britain (150), China (120), Canada (115), France (98), and Japan (60).
11. **We humiliate tourists who want to visit us.** Perhaps the most annoying thing about visiting Russia is getting a travel visa. They may ask you: where you are staying, where you are going, what your latest bank statement is, what your job employment history is, and how much vodka you drink. Trying to visit America is also a degrading experience for most. We'll take your fingerprint and charge visa fees that will bankrupt most people in the world.
12. **We're blindly proud and patriotic.** Both of us have nationalism in our DNA, although Americans are even more flag-waving than Russians. In 2010, Pew Research Center revealed a survey that showed that 83 percent are "extremely" or "very proud" to be American. Six in 10 Americans displays a flag in their home, office, or car. It's hard to blame Russians for feeling proud when they hear their national anthem, which is the best in the world.

Being proud of one's country is different than being proud of yourself. In 2007, Gallup asked the world, "Were you proud of something you did yesterday?" Four in 10 Russians said *yes,* making them one of the least proud individuals in Europe. Only Belarusians, Bulgarians, and Albanians were less proud of themselves. Roughly 75 percent of those in the Americas and Australia were generally quite proud of something they did yesterday.

Communism's unintended consequences

Throughout this book, we've examined communism's impact on Eastern Europe. It's worth taking one last look at it since Russia was communism's chief cheerleader. Under communism, products were often sold for less than it cost to make them. Obviously, this is not sustainable, as any seven-year-old can tell you. Nevertheless, adults throughout the world adopted this ludicrous system.

Communism produced oddities. For example, to make basic food affordable, the state made bread so cheap that it cost less than the wheat needed to produce it. Thus, farmers sometimes fed their livestock bread rather than grain because bread was cheaper. Industries obtained fossil fuels at artificially low levels, which encouraged waste. The state made apartments a bargain in the name of social equity, but housing was constantly in short supply. Salt and matches were hard to find because the state didn't make enough of them. Shortages created a black economy that was made up a third of the GDP. In short, communism ignored customers, competition, and costs. Non-market based incentives resulted that shops were empty of stuff that people desired, while factories produced stuff of crappy quality.

A Spaniard that I met in Venice shared his story about visiting Moscow, St. Petersburg, and Kyiv in 1987. He had to make all his reservations through a state-controlled tourist board. He had to stay in state-approved hotels and have government tour guides most of the time around him. While we waited for a Venetian *vaporetto,* I asked him, "What was most shocking?"

"The lack of service," he said. "When we would go into stores, the clerks would walk away from you so they didn't have to work. They didn't care: they would be paid the same amount of money. Same goes for the restaurant. A nearly empty restaurant refused to seat us because we hadn't made a reservation. Any work, for the communists, was a chore to be avoided."

Communism took the idea of equality to extreme levels. The Soviets called owners of cars a *chastnik* (suspicious private person). In fact, the police ignored much of the vandalism against private cars in the early 1960s because they agreed with the vandals: the owners deserved it because nobody should be richer than his neighbor. In Estonia, I met a lady who had saved up money all her life so she could return to her native Russia. She bought a rustic cottage in the country and renovated it. Unlike most of her neighbors, she had a lawn. She planted many flowers on the lawn. However, after a few weeks, tractors plowed through the lawn. She understood the message: "Don't show off your wealth. Live like the rest of us."

> *The way I understand it, the Russians are sort of a combination of evil and incompetence. . . sort of like the Post Office with tanks. — Emo Philips, joking about the USSR*

Until 1972, the Soviet Union finally started making more private cars than trucks. People saw a double standard: the elite got cars; the rest didn't. If you saved up all your rubles, you might have been able to afford the Volga, whose interior was often filled up with noxious gas fumes. If you had bucks, you bought a new Lada. First, a mechanic would charge you to make it roadworthy. Next, you'd watch it rust. Need it fixed? Wait for weeks or even months, unless you can offer "personal favors" to get to the front of the line. After paying an arm and a leg, the mechanic might return it to you with certain parts missing.

Spare parts, like side mirrors and windshield wipers, were hard to get, so the mechanics would "borrow" them from their customers.[13]

> *How do you double a Lada's value? Answer: fill up the tank.*
> *— Soviet joke*

An American musician in Moscow in 1967

My friend Mimi Wallace told me of her first trip to Russia in 1967. She said, "Our singing group played music at the International Fashion Exhibit. Our playlist was highly restricted. We took an Aeroflot plane from Helsinki to Moscow. It was a Soviet transport plane converted to take regular passengers. The seats faced the sides, not the cockpit. The seats weren't even screwed down! The takeoff was very interesting!"

I said, "I can imagine you sliding around in your seats. Did they give you food?"

"Our stewardesses were dressed in Army skirts and shirts. We had to hold our food trays on our laps, picnic style. 'Here, eat,' the flight attendants said. It was probably the only English they knew. I looked at the mystery meat and said, 'Mmm, maybe not, but thanks.'"

"How was your hotel?"

"It was one of those 'modern' Russian buildings: totally lacking any style. While our guides were 'checking us in' (taking away our passports), I was wandering around the lobby. I didn't see this marble staircase in front of me, and I crashed into it, knocking me out cold. I was put on a lobby sofa and this very nice lady doctor came to see how I was. She called for 'vodka,' which was her cure for a concussion. I drank it right down and asked for a second hit as it was the first liquid I'd had since Finland. She also had a few pieces of chocolate in her pocket. Modern medicine at work!"

"Someday Americans will learn about the magical healing properties of vodka and chocolate."

"I did feel better after a bit. When I asked if there was anything I could give her in return for her kindness, she pointed to my issue of *Time* magazine that I had somehow managed to get past customs. 'Please,' she said, 'I would like that.' *Time* magazine! Oh sure, news from the outside. Who wouldn't consider that a great gift?"

"How were the rooms?"

"You didn't get a room key at the Rossiya Hotel. On every floor was a station where a *huge* Russian woman sat and watched over your every coming and going. She gave you your key (somewhat grudgingly) on your request. And you gave it back to her whenever you left the room. And that meant that whenever you would go across the hall to visit another band member, the *huge* Russian lady wrote it down and made a phone call! This went on for ten days."

I said, "I experienced tight hotel security in Russia and Ukraine 40 years after you. But your experience was much more extreme."

"Yes, we had two personal KGB officers with us most of the time," Mimi said. "We were told to never sell anything on the street. So what do rebellious New York rock and rollers do? We made a deal for our jeans. It was late at night and we'd been out (illegally) to visit musicians we had met earlier. This was also not allowed, but what the hell. We were alone. We took off our jeans, and then we wrapped our sweaters and jackets around our legs. Then, these two random KGB officers came out of nowhere! Caught naked in Moscow! Yikes!"

"Oh no! What happened next?"

"We made a deal. There were six of us, so we gave the KGB guys three jeans and the two buyers three jeans. Everyone went home happy! But try sneaking back into your hotel room past the *huge* Russian woman without your pants on! *Oy vey!*"

> *In Russia we only had two TV channels. Channel One was propaganda. Channel Two consisted of a KGB officer telling you: "Turn back at once to Channel One."*
> *— Yakov Smirnoff, Russian comedian*

When I asked Mimi about her general impressions of Russia under communism, she said, "Russia was totally grim and depressing. I remember on the street there was a trash can with a broom in it, so I borrowed the broom and posed with it in front of Tchaikovsky's house. A little *babushka* ran to me slashing her broom and yelling in Russian. I think during these times Russians were very paranoid, but also completely lacking in a sense of humor."

Although Mimi abandoned her music career, she dedicated the rest of her life to performing and teaching ballet in New York. I asked her, "So how did your trip end?"

"On the final day of our Moscow visit, I was trying to swat a fly in the bathroom and I stood up on the toilet seat to reach it better. *Oops!* I put a crack in the toilet seat cover. No big deal. I'll tell the front desk at checkout. Ha, ha, this is not America. The *huge* Russian woman reported it to front desk as we were getting ready to leave, and the KGB came to interview me to learn why the toilet seat broke. Really! After trying to explain, I finally got the US State Department to work things out, as Russians were not going to let me leave the country before I paid for the seat."

"So that's how it ended?"

"No. We wanted to give the two young KGB officers who had been 'escorting' us a gift from America. It was risky, but we gave them an old copy of *Dr. Zhivago* and a new copy of *Sgt. Pepper's Lonely Hearts Club Band,* which had just come out. We had smuggled them in our luggage. They were in tears with their thanks. It was a great final goodbye. But I don't recall giving the *huge* Russian woman anything. Not a single *kopek*!"

Seven wonders of communism

An anonymous Eastern European partially summarized the Seven Wonders of Communism:

1. Everyone had a job.
2. Despite everyone having a job, nobody worked.
3. Despite nobody working, the plan was 100% complete.
4. Despite the plan being 100% complete, nothing was in the shops.
5. Despite nothing being in the shops, everybody had everything.
6. Despite everybody having everything, everybody was stealing.
7. Despite everybody stealing, nobody lacked anything.

Indeed, communism had cradle-to-grave benefits. As a child, you never had to worry about your parents becoming unemployed or losing their house. You had a guaranteed good education. Crime rates were low, since the police was everywhere and justice was harsh. Parents didn't have to worry about their children getting hurt because Big Brother was always watching.

Teenagers didn't have to worry either. The government limited their university options. If the country needed more electric engineers, it would nudge you to get an engineering degree. There were no school loans to worry about since the state paid for everything. There was no job placement stress after graduating. The government would place you where you were needed. It would find you a place to live and subsidize your rent to make sure you could afford it. You didn't always have hot water in the summer, but neither did any of your neighbors, so you didn't feel poor. Your job was easy and secure. You rarely had to work very hard, few got fired, and you had plenty of free time to drink beer.

Although it was difficult and expensive to travel outside your country, you lived in the biggest country in the world, so you had plenty of places to visit. You didn't have a car, but public transportation was plentiful and cheap. The truly adventurous could go to exotic locations like East Germany, Hungary, and even Yugoslavia. After working for 40 years, the government would take care of your retirement. You would have free housing, medical care, and affordable food and vodka. When you died (usually before 60), the government would even help your family members with your burial.

Such a life appealed to many. Even today communism has fans, and not just *babushkas*. When I stayed with Artyom Panteleev, a 26-year-old Russian living in St. Petersburg, he told me that he would rather live in Belarus. "They live better there," he told me in 2009. He was dating a Belarusian and had gone to Minsk 15 times. He eventually broke up with his girlfriend when he saw her flirting with another man at a dance club. What Artyom doesn't realize is that communism is unsustainable. Belarus's economy only exists because of massive Russian support. The Soviet economy was also a fantasyland.

Pskov, Porkhov, and Polonoye

In November 2008, Yuliya Trutko invited me to join her and her Russian dad, Ivan, on a trip to Pskov, Porkhov, and Polonoe—all places in Western Russia that are somewhat near the Estonian border. They were going to visit Yuliya's grandparents. The Estonia-Russia border near Pskov had soft forested hills. Geographically, there was no obvious border. Nevertheless, once we made it across, there was one obvious difference: the roads. The Estonia highway was smooth and modern; the Russian highway was filled with potholes. Ivan laughed, "Welcome to Russia!"

We visited the Pskov Kremlin, a thirteenth-century medieval citadel with the splendid Trinity Cathedral. Across the river is the Mirozhsky Monastery, which is famous for its colorful frescoes. The city has a couple of nice government buildings and a statue of Lenin, but is otherwise average. We're not the only ones who decided to leave. During the last decade, the city's population has dropped over 10 percent, thereby returning it to the 203,300 population level it had in the USSR.

We drove an hour east to the small town of Porkov. It had a WWII monument in a grim, gray plaza. Decaying, antiquated buses rumbled around. Bundled-up old people were selling cranberries to supplement their meager pensions. It was the kind of town that the Soviets wouldn't let Westerners see. Then we went 10 kilometers east to visit Yuliya's grandparents' house, which is the kind of home that even the current Russian leadership wouldn't want Westerners to see.

Living like the 19th century in the 21st century

Yuliya's 81-year-old grandmother, Zoya Panteleeva, was born in Siberia, but lived most her life around the village of Polonoye. Lousy dirt roads were everywhere. The community *banya* (sauna) was in ruins. Zoya lived in a small one-story wooden house with a low wooden fence. When Zoya came out of the house, she was wearing a white long-sleeved shirt, a woolen vest, warm black tights, a simple headscarf, and gray *valenki* (felt boots). She was missing most of her teeth. She was thin, but like every Russian *babushka,* Zoya seemed supernaturally strong.

Zoya's 86-year-old husband, Alexandr, had stunning crystal blue eyes, a protruding belly, and a deep scar across the left side of his face. He would spend most of his time watching TV in his bedroom or smoking unfiltered cigarettes in the hallway. In the living room, there was a half-liter dark bottle of vodka that had 40 percent alcohol. The company that made the vodka has been around since 1884. The label had a photo of an old man with glasses and stethoscope. I read the bottle's label: "белый доктор" (*Belyi Doktor*, i.e., White Doctor). Yuliya giggled as she explained that it's a nineteenth-century tradition that when you have any pain, instead of going to a medical doctor, you have a swig of the "White Doctor" and everything will feel better.

> *Doctors are just the same as lawyers; the only difference is that lawyers merely rob you, whereas doctors rob you and kill you too. — Anton Chekhov*

Yuliya said, "My grandparents don't see doctors. They are afraid of them. Medicine is free, but horrible. They'll go maybe once every five years for absolute emergencies. For example, my grandmother had a broken hip a couple of months ago. The nearest hospital was in Porhov. The rooms were on the second floor. There was no elevator, so she had to stay home in bed. My uncle would feed her and make the house warm before going to work at 5:00 a.m. Kind of crazy. I wanted to send her an electric heater, but my mother said that Zoya will not use it because electricity is dangerous and expensive. Her house had an electrical fire a couple of years ago."

Although the house had electricity, it had no plumbing. At this point, they could connect to the municipality to get piped water, a flushing toilet, and a shower; nevertheless, Zoya had always lived without such luxuries and didn't think that having it now was worth it. Besides, her pension was just $50 per month. She would walk across the dirt road and fill up a bucket of water from the well. She had no gas for cooking. Instead, she had a ceramic wood stove that she would cook on and heat the house at the same time. The sink drained into a bucket, which she would empty out once or twice a day. During the night, Alexandr, who didn't like to go outside to pee, would pee in the sink.

Zoya was a teenager when the Nazis rolled through Polonoye. She said that life was somewhat normal during the German occupation. She milked the cows and tended the crops. The Nazis didn't even take food from her family. However, just 30 kilometers away (19 miles), Nazis ran inhumane prison camps, burned down the synagogue, and slaughtered Jews. There's an enormous concrete monument in Porkhov that commemorates the camp where the Nazis left thousands of prisoners to starve to death.

Zoya's niece, Valentina Ushakova, works at the Museum of Political History in St. Petersburg. She dropped by Zoya's home and told me what had happened when the Soviets forced the Nazis to retreat. With all the men at war, the 17-year-old Zoya and her mom hid in the forest. They dug a three-meter (10-foot) deep hole in the ground that was as big as a room. They covered it up to trap heat, provide camouflage, and protect against the rain and snow. They lived in this hole in the ground for months. Now you can understand why *babushkas* are so tough.

In the morning, I saw her holding the Bible in her trembling hands and reading aloud long passages. Although she was born in 1927, she not only lived as if she were in the nineteenth century, but she shared similar values. When I was quietly working on my computer, Zoya scolded her granddaughter, saying, "He has not eaten! You must *feed the man!*"

Russian cuisine and leaving Polonoye

With three men to feed, Zoya made a feast. She had three long strings of onions on the wall. She got all her ingredients within walking distance of her house. She made small boiled sausages, deep-fried chicken, sliced potatoes, pickled red peppers with tomatoes, rice in a tomato sauce, mashed potatoes, thick slices of ham, and buttered white bread with trout caviar. I drank tea, but the real men had whiskey.

Yuliya said, "Like most Russian countryside women, Zoya controls the alcohol in the family. She buys it and pours it. That was how she motivated her husband to work when he was younger: bring in wood—get a vodka shot; feed the pigs—get another shot. Now my uncle does the work my grandfather did. And so now my uncle gets the vodka shots," she laughed. She added, "Rewarding with vodka shots is typical in a village. Vodka is the currency in Russian villages."

During my voyages through Russia, I tried classic Russian cuisine such as *pelmeni* (beef dumplings topped with sour cream), *solyanka* (veggie soup), *ukha* (fish soup), and, of course, *borsch* (beet soup with cabbage and meat). Other common dishes include *goluptsy* (meat in cabbage leaves) and *vareniki* (boiled dumplings with mushrooms and potatoes). Russian cuisine is optimized for cold weather. Still, even when Russians move to warmer climates, it forever remains their comfort food.

Zoya and Alexandr were skeptical about the changes in Russia. Often senior citizens in Eastern Europe were less enthusiastic about democracy and free markets than young people. This difference was most obvious in Russia. In 2009, Pew Research's Global Attitudes Survey showed that while 65 percent of Russians under 30 years old supported the move to multiparty elections, only 27 percent of senior citizens agreed. A similar divide existed on the question of moving toward a market economy—the new generation gives it a thumbs up, the old gives it a thumbs down.

This impacts their satisfaction with life. In 1991, the Pew Research Center asked Russians to rate their lives on a one to 10 scale. Eight percent of Russians under 30 and only three percent of those over 65 rated it a seven or higher, indicating the misery during the Soviet Union collapse. By 2009, 41 percent of the youth were feeling very satisfied while only 25 percent of the senior citizens felt the same way. Nevertheless, Russian *babushkas* like Zoya are truly unflappable.

Leaving Polonoye

After stuffing ourselves, we visited Peter and Lidia Panteleev, a middle-aged couple who live in a humble apartment in Polonoye. Peter was Yuliya's uncle. They offered *chai* (tea) and cookies in their simple, clean living room. Peter, whose two gold front teeth shined when he spoke, said that Russia's recent economic boom had not touched their village. Given my French background, I was curious about what they thought of France. Lidia said, "Russians don't think about France. America is much more interesting for us. America is a big country; Russia is a big country. We have much in common. France is small and we don't really think about it."

Later, we walked around the village. An elderly lady with a wool coat and headscarf was gathering her garden's final harvest before the snowfall. While her German Shepherd looked at us, she said that most villagers had gardens where they grew potatoes, onions, and other plants. It lowered the cost of living. Then we met Yelena, a young Muscovite who had bought a home in Polonoye so that her child could enjoy fresh, clean air during the summer months. She rejoined her husband in Moscow for the rest of the year. Finally, we ran into Peter again. Earlier he was wearing a camouflage tank-top, now he had camouflaged pants. On the back of his blue raincoat was the word that hits every Russian soul: "отечество" ("Fatherland"). He was storing potatoes in an underground chamber with brick walls. He was a *real* Russian; he reminded me of *real* Americans.

It was sad to leave the tranquility of Polonoye. Yuliya remembers visiting the village 25 years ago. She said nothing has changed. Russia has many such villages. They quietly and stubbornly keep alive traditions and habits that urban Russia has abandoned. In mid-2011, Yuliya told me that both of her grandparents were doing well. Zoya was nearly 85 and Alexandr was nearly 90. That far exceeds standard Russian life expectancies. Alexandr still smokes like a chimney and still gets medical care from his reliable "White Doctor" bottle. Meanwhile, Yuliya said, "Grandmother finds her peace in reading the Bible daily."

The more refined one is, the more unhappy.
— Anton Chekhov

Big Brother becomes a Permissive Parent

Stalin sowed the seeds of the Soviet demise. In 1934, his thugs sent one of Gorbachev's grandfathers to Siberia to cut trees. In 1937, when Gorbachev was six years old, Stalin's secret police arrested Gorbachev's other grandfather because he was "an enemy of the people." Having both of his grandfathers suffer because of a repressive regime planted an idea in Gorbachev: Big Brother should become a Permissive Parent. That idea would doom the USSR.

Gorbachev was in his mid-20 when Stalin died and Nikita Khrushchev rose to power. Khrushchev dazzled the young Gorbachev by denouncing Stalin and making reforms. However, Leonid Brezhnev eventually muscled Khrushchev out of power and ruled sternly for 18 years. Two short-lived Soviet leaders followed, and then in 1985, Gorbachev sat in the driver's seat.

Around that time, I was a teenager, and I vividly remember a TV news report. A reporter was interviewing a Russian man at an American airport. He and his family were moving back to the USSR after having lived in the USA a few years. It seemed crazy. He basically said, "I tried American life, but I prefer life in the Soviet Union." In retrospect, it was probably the worst time to move to Russia. Not only did he suffer through the collapse of the USSR and Russia's depressing 1990s, but he also missed out on the booming 1990s in the US. His wife probably still nags him about it.

Gorbachev was Khrushchev on steroids. He didn't just reform the USSR—he revolutionized it. He established what became known as The Sinatra Doctrine: he told the 15 Soviet republics that they could all sing, "I Did It My Way." The revolution spiraled out of control. In 1989, the Berlin Wall collapsed and communist leaders fell throughout Eastern Europe. Gorbachev was like a parent who had given his teenaged daughter the taste of freedom and now feared that she would move away. He said, "Daughter, I promise I won't tell you what to buy when you go shopping, what to wear, where to go, where to work, how to live, or who to date! Sweetie, *just stay with the family!*"

To preserve the USSR, Gorbachev proposed the New Union Treaty. It would have transformed the USSR into something like Yugoslavia—a federation of independent republics with a common President, military, and foreign policy. It would have given each republic much more autonomy than under the USSR, but it would still have preserved the idea of a single country. Eight of the 15 republics agreed to it, a thin majority. On August 20, 1991, the Russian Republic was scheduled to sign this New Union Treaty. However, two days before the signing, a conspiracy changed everything.

USA to USSR: we're wiretapping your phones

Eight high-level Soviet leaders, known as the Gang of Eight, had enough of Gorbachev's permissive parenting. They wanted Big Brother back. On August 18, 1991, half of the gang flew to Crimea to visit Gorbachev who was relaxing in his *dacha* (vacation home). They demanded that Gorbachev declare a state of emergency so they could "restore order." Gorbachev refused. They asked him to resign. He refused. Therefore, they placed Gorbachev under house arrest.

The next day, the conspirators flew back to Moscow, rejoined the rest of the Gang of Eight, and staged a *coup d'état*. They shut down all independent media. They announced that Gorbachev was "ill." Tanks, infantry, and paratroopers took over Moscow's Red Square. Four important Russian reformers were detained, but not Boris Yeltsin, who was Russia's President and relaxing in his *dacha* near Moscow. Things seemed good for the Gang, but America's National Security Agency (NSA) had been covertly listening to conversations between Soviet military leaders. The juicy secret: the military was unenthusiastic about the coup.

US President George Bush Sr. faced a dilemma. On the one hand, he wanted to tell Boris Yeltsin that the pro-communist coup lacked deep military support. Armed with this information, Yeltsin could confidently resist the coup. On the other hand, spilling the beans would guarantee that the NSA wouldn't be overhearing future Russian conversations. The NSA begged Bush to shut up. Nevertheless, Bush called Yeltsin in his *dacha.* After hanging up the phone, Yeltsin raced to Moscow.

A confident Yeltsin came to the *Beliy Dom* (White House), which is Russia's Parliament building and is outside the Kremlin. With no media control, he spoke on top of a tank. He distributed thousands of leaflets. Citizens barricaded the streets with trolleybuses and street-cleaning machines. At 1:00 a.m., a column of tanks rolled toward the Parliament, which had thousands of protesters. As one of the Gang of Eight wrote later in his memoir, "From a purely military viewpoint, it did not require much effort to take this building. But a different thing was unclear: why the hell was it necessary to begin with?" After three civilians were killed and the other military groups didn't show up, the military retreated. The coup, like the USSR, had failed.

Gorbachev flew back to Moscow and discovered the coup's paradox: Gorbachev had won, but he had really lost. He had beaten the hardliners: the Gang of Eight were arrested for treason; two committed suicide. And yet, Gorbachev had lost to the radicals: Yeltsin wanted

Russia's complete independence, not just greater autonomy that the New Union Treaty promised. For his bravery and leadership during the coup, Yeltsin was Russia's new hero. Over the next few weeks, each Soviet Republic declared independence. On December 25, 1991, Gorbachev resigned and the USSR was terminated.

Why Russians dislike Gorbachev

Here's a fact that shocks many Westerners: for the last 20 years Gorbachev's approval rating among Russians has been less than five percent. When Gorbachev ran for the 1996 Presidential Election, he won only 0.5 percent of the vote. The Against-All-Candidates option got nearly 10 times more votes than Gorbachev.

Why do Russians dislike Gorbachev so much? You'd think that giving Russians freedom to say what they want, travel where they wish, and own private property would make them happy. Isn't ending the Cold War with practically no bloodshed worth something too? Apparently not. Russians dislike Gorbachev because he failed to do what the Chinese communists have so far managed to do: engineered a smooth transition to capitalism, while maintaining the country's unity.

> *In order to reform our country "the Chinese way," we would have had to have a different country—probably populated by the Chinese. — Mikhail Gorbachev*

China focused on economic reform first, and postponed political reform. Gorbachev did the opposite. He failed to abolish the monopolies, price controls, private property limitations, and nonconvertible currency. His excuse was, "In China, economic reforms faced no resistance from the party bureaucracy. In the Soviet Union, the *nomenklatura*—the party and economic bureaucracy—was extremely strong; they had stopped previous attempts at reform."[14]

Gorbachev had three great ideas, but you've probably only heard of the first two: *glasnost* (political openness), *perestroika* (political and economic restructuring), and *uskoreniye* (accelerated economic development). He needed to emphasize *uskoeniye,* not *glasnost.* In 1988, he allowed private businesses to exist, but it was too limited and too late. Eastern Europe's revolution was starting. Gorbachev caused, in the words of Vladimir Putin, "the largest geopolitical catastrophe of the century."

In the end, the Cold War "domino theory" was right; it just worked in the opposite direction. Eastern European revolutions toppled one communist regime after another. Communist dominoes fell in Latin America and Africa. Even communism in Belarus, China, and Vietnam softened so much that they're quasi-capitalists today. What's remarkable is that the dominoes fell relatively peacefully. For that, Gorbachev deserved five Nobel Peace Prizes. At least he got one.

The two most impactful humans in the last century were Russians: Lenin and Gorbachev. Although the two world wars certainly defined the last century, most of the century revolved around the worldwide communist experiment, whose epicenter was Russia. Lenin started it. Gorbachev ended it.

Most Russians lament the USSR's death. In 2009, a Pew Research Center survey showed that 58% of Russians agreed that it's a "great misfortune than the USSR no longer exists," 54% believed that "Russia should be for Russians" (up from 26% in 1991), and 47% agreed that "it is natural for Russia to have an empire."[15]

Defenders of communism say, "But life was great under communism. Everyone had a job, food, housing, education, security, and vodka." True, but it was based on an unsustainable system. There's a lesson for the West here. We're also living beyond our means. When the weight of debt and entitlements break our economic back, we'll be forced to downsize in the same draconian way that Eastern Europeans had to do in the 1990s. When we're forced to adopt a more austere way of life, people will complain, "But this new system sucks! Life was better before!" Of course it was. It always is when you're living beyond your means.

> *The United States needs its own* perestroika.
> *— Mikhail Gorbachev, said in 2011*

Kazan: capital of Tatarstan

One of my biggest dreams was to stand on the easternmost edge of Europe. Therefore, after revisiting St. Petersburg and Moscow, I took an overnight train heading east. Along the way, 800 kilometers (500 miles) east of Moscow, I stopped in the splendid capital of Tatarstan: Kazan. The city is located on the Volga River and has 1.1 million inhabitants, of which about half are Russians and the other half are Tatars. Russians mostly live in the city, whereas the Tatars dominate the suburbs. Tatars speak a Turkic language that uses the Cyrillic alphabet. They are mostly Muslims who often have tan skin and subtle Asiatic features. Tatarstan is another hidden part of Russia that few Westerners explore.

A few years before I visited, Kazan celebrated its 1,000-year anniversary. As a result, the city was still glowing from its the millennial celebration. Kazan's polished jewel is its white Kremlin, a UNESCO World Heritage Site filled with exquisite buildings. The most impressive is the new blue-roofed Qolşärif mosque, which is the largest mosque in Europe (if you don't consider Istanbul in Europe). Four white minarets surround the monolithic blue dome. Inside, there's an attractive museum about Islam. It may be Europe's prettiest mosque.

More people will discover Kazan when it hosts some of the World Cup soccer matches in 2018.

Kazan is filled with other fine architecture. The Qolşärif mosque is Kazan's newest religious building, while just a few steps away is Kazan's oldest: the sixteenth-century Annunciation Cathedral. The pure white cathedral has four blue cupolas surrounding a golden one. Kazan's symbol, the Söyembikä Tower, overlooks the citadel's entrance and a Soviet-styled proletariat statue. The city's downtown mixes classical structures like the Tatar State Library, and modern buildings like a large glass pyramid nightclub. In front of the elegant Kazan State University is a statue of Lenin that doesn't look like him. It depicts him as a young man because he studied law in Kazan. At night, I saw a circus where performers spun dogs and parrots in circles, made horses hop like kangaroos, and tossed snakes and alligators around. I'm sure the animals loved it.

The horrible 1990s

After Gorbachev left and winter set in, shops were empty. Russia had only two months worth of grain left. Farmers refused to sell grains at the money-losing fixed prices. Foreign debt was a back-breaking $72 billion. Foreign exchange reserves (i.e., the hard cash in the bank) were just $27 million—Russia was broke.

Yeltsin followed American advice and applied shock therapy. Russia revoked laws that prohibited companies from importing and exporting goods. Firms were allowed to acquire foreign currency and price controls were eliminated. In the mid-1990s, annual inflation was 1,500 percent, the ruble's value collapsed, two-thirds lived in poverty, life expectancies plummeted, the military had no paychecks or housing. By 1998, Russia's GDP had dropped nearly in half. To compare, America's GDP during the Great Depression fell 29 percent. In 2007, Russia's GDP finally returned to its 1990 level, reflecting just how lousy the 1990s was for them.

> *Any idiot can face a crisis—it's day-to-day living that wears you out. — Anton Chekhov, 1860–1904*

Russians often blame Yeltsin and his American economic advisers for the 1990s nightmare. It's easy to complain. Without a parallel universe, we'll never know if there was a better policy than shock therapy. It's probable that the transition from communism to capitalism would have been painful no matter what. All Eastern Europeans suffered as they transitioned. On one extreme was Estonia, which arguably endured the least, yet it still had a catastrophic banking crisis in 1992. On the other extreme was Yugoslavia, which suffered far more than Russia. Recall that when Russia transitioned from monarchy to communism in the 1920s, it endured much more than the 1990s: millions starved to death and a bloody civil war erupted. Major macroeconomic transitions are never pretty.

Nevertheless, Yeltsin made one hard-to-forgive error that still haunts Russia today: mismanaging the privatization process. Because of the boneheaded and corrupt privatization procedure, elite Russians gained state monopolies at bargain prices. This created Russia's Gilded Age. In the late 1880s, America's Gilded Age had oligarchs who controlled large monopolies: Rockefeller's Standard Oil, Andrew Carnegie's steel industry, JP Morgan's banks, Vanderbilt's railways, and so on. Russia's oligarchs are similar, although they got their wealthy empires practically overnight thanks to cronyism. This infuriates Russians partly because it unraveled 70 years of effort of pursuing economic equality.

> *We wanted the best, but it turned out as always.*
> *— Viktor Chernomyrdin, Russia's Prime Minister 1992–1998, referring to the sloppy reforms in the 1990s*

Communism did an excellent job at distributing income evenly. As we've seen, the Gini Coefficient Index is a 100-point scale based on wealth equality. Most communist countries scored between 20 and 25—indicating that they had some of the world's most equal distributions of wealth. However, in the 1990s, Eastern Europe's overall index rose from 25 to 35.[16] By 2009, Russia's index rating was 42, which was similar to the US and the not-so-communist China. Several Eastern European countries had fair privatization processes and were thereby able to preserve their relatively low Gini coefficients. Russia's poor privatization process, along with many other blunders, explains why Yeltsin's approval rating fell to *one percent*.

Why do Russians seem so damn grumpy?

On a short stop in Moscow, my Indian friend, Venkat Bhamidipati, told me that he was stunned by how savagely bad-mannered Russian customer service representatives can be. Yuliya Trutko admitted, "The service in Russia is rude." Nenad Stojanović, a well-traveled Serbian who spent weeks in Russia, told me, "Russians in the service industry were usually chilly. I've met some of the most unfriendly people in Russia."

Russians aren't the only Eastern Europeans who can be cold. When I was Ukraine, I was in a deserted place and I asked a young couple, *"Izvinite, vy govorite pa angliski?"* (Excuse me, do you speak English?") Without looking at me, the man mumbled, *"Shto?"* ("What?") They just kept walking without making a tiny effort to help, even though nobody else was around. Countless Russians yelled at me or treated me like dirt. At first, I thought it was because I was a foreigner. However, after observing how other Russian customers are handled, it's clear that everyone gets treated like shit.

Why is this? Russians aren't born this way. For example, children on overnight Russian trains smiled and giggled when they saw me. Yes, I was an American freak, but they laughed and smiled. At some point, this joyful habit is beaten out of the Russians (and most Eastern Europeans). Although the spiritless 1990s put on a frown on most Russian faces, you can't blame their bad-temper on that period since Russians were still grumpy in 2009. For instance, a Russian tour guide scolded someone who laughed at one of my stupid jokes. You shouldn't laugh. Life is serious. If you smile, you look like a moron. Elena Kogan, who grew up in Russia and lives in America, told me, "My mom scolds me if I laugh loudly—that's off limits. She feels it indicates that you're a 'loose woman,' or at least, a 'woman without manners.' She says smiling is OK, as long as it is not excessive."

To explain Eastern Europe's crankiness, I propose the Friendliness Between Strangers Theory (FBST). There are three factors that influence how friendly a nation's customer service will be (and it correlates with how we treat strangers on the street too):

1. **Population density:** people in villages tend to be more amicable than people in cities.
2. **Proximity to the Equator:** the closer, the friendlier people get.
3. **Communism:** ex-communist countries are less friendly than capitalist ones.

Let's expand on the last FBST point. Customer service is not valued in monopolies: why be nice if everyone *must* buy from you? Since monopolies are everywhere in communism, everyone was conditioned to be a jerk. Stephanie Rexroth, an American who spent one month in Russia, said, "American consumers believe we're the king. In Russia, it was strange not being catered to in customer-service settings. Russia's poor customer service comes from the lingering remains of the socialist era." Moreover, as we saw, the 1990s was dreadful for most ex-communist countries, which reinforced their sour and grouchy behavior.

After generations of grumpiness, it's hard to break the habit. For example, in preparation for the 2008 Beijing Olympics, China had to teach its citizens how to smile.[17] In 2010, Russian President Dmitry Medvedev admitted Russian crankiness when he said that they should learn how to face the world with "a smiling face," and that Russia should not "gnash its teeth at anyone, get angry, sulk or feel offended."

Most Eastern Europeans are cursed with being on the wrong side of the three FBST factors: they live in cities, are ex-communist, and are relatively far from the equator (their winters are atrocious). Therefore, your best hope to find a random congenial Eastern European is in a village. The FBST explains why southern Balkanians smile effortlessly (they're closer to the Equator than other Eastern Europeans) and why Finns have polite customer service (they were never communist). It also explains why the rest of the planet tends to be more cheery than Eastern Europe.

Of course, some Eastern Europeans will say that there are plenty of friendly people in Eastern Europe, that Western "friendliness" is phony, that you can't generalize, and that I'm an asshole. Inga Pažereckaitė, a Lithuanian who works in the government tourist office, wrote to me, "If Lithuanians do not smile it doesn't mean that they are angry or they are not kind. If they say 'Have a nice time,' or they just give a smile, then it is real; it's not a fake. It comes from the heart." True, but in customer service situations, I prefer a fake smile to a sincere scowl.

> *Comrades, this man has a nice smile, but he's got iron teeth.*
> *— Andrei A. Gromyko, Russian Cold War politician whose Western nickname was Mr. Nyet ("Mr. No")*

Of course, Russia being the land of extremes, it has plenty of helpful people. For example, at a Kaliningrad bus station, I asked a Russian if he spoke English. He shook his head, but said *"Padazhdite."* ("Wait.") He called an English-speaking friend on his mobile phone and passed me the phone. I told his friend that I wanted to know the bus schedule to Gdańsk. I passed the phone back to the Russian, who then communicated with the ticket vendor, wrote down all in the information, and then gave it to me.

Stephanie Rexroth said, "When I first met my chauffeur, he was the meanest guy, the worst driver, and an overall scary and intimidating person. When we met again a month later, he was the nicest, most compassionate man in all of Russia, the best/most cautious driver, and very jolly, friendly, personable." The bottom line is that Eastern Europeans are slow to warm up, but when they do, they're just as friendly and warm as an American pretends to be when he first meets you.

Totalitarianism Light

After 70 years of communism and 10 years of painful economic transition, Vladimir Putin walked on the Russia's stage at the dawn of the twenty-first century. Putin has effectively been in charge ever since then, even though Dmitry Medvedev has been the official President for four years. As I write this in July 2011, I predict that Putin will become Russia's President again in March 2012. If so, he will remain President until 2018 and, if he gets reelected, until 2024. By then, he'll be 72 and he'll probably retire to his *dacha.* Given the likelihood that he'll be Russia's top guy for a while, it's worth looking into his soul.

The Western media often portray Putin as a kinder, gentler, and cuddlier version of Stalin. There's some truth to that. Stalin watched Hollywood Westerns all night and forced his comrades to join him. There were no subtitles and he didn't understand English, but the message was inspiring: kill those you don't like, even if it means hunting them down. For instance, Stalin had his rival, Leon Trotsky, assassinated in Mexico. Putin's regime seems to continue the tradition. Many Russian journalists, businessmen, and politicians who have challenged Putin have been beaten, jailed, or assassinated. According to Reporters Without Borders, over 22 journalists have been murdered in Russia in the last 10 years. Thugs have beaten dozens of journalists, some to point of not being able to speak or type. The 2010 Press Freedom Index ranks Russia 140 out of 178 countries; only Belarus is worse for European journalists. Just 28 percent of Russians think their media coverage is objective.

Like Stalin, Putin's regime also distorts history. In June 2009, Russia's defense department's website claimed that Poland caused WWII by provoking Hitler. Later that year, Russian state TV argued that Poland conspired with the Nazis against the USSR. A historian who collected material about Germans who vanished in the Gulags was put under criminal investigation. Putin closed WWII archives and criminalized attempts to dispute Russia's version of history. If you try to draw parallels between Stalin and Hitler, you may go to jail. It's also prohibited to suggest that the USSR occupied Eastern Europe. In 2011, a renovated subway station in Moscow has a new sign carved in stone that says, "We were raised by Stalin; he inspired our faith in people, our labor and deeds."

These are compelling signs that Putin started a new period in Russian history that we'll call Totalitarianism Light. Putin sticks a heavy visible hand in Russia's economy and politics. For instance, instead of communist price fixing, he asked large retailers and food producers to enter a "voluntary" agreement that would fix low prices. If they didn't volunteer, they might get an intrusive tax inspection, arbitrary penalties, and a loss of business. The regime sometimes ignores private property rights. Vladimir Putin didn't call his political philosophy Totalitarianism Light, he did say, "Russia needs a strong state power and must have it. But I am not calling for totalitarianism."

> *Moscow bosses imitate imperial ambitions in the same way they imitate democracy. — Alexander Golts, Deputy Editor of the Yezhednevny Zhurnal*

Under totalitarianism, there were no elections. Nowadays, independent candidates simply aren't registered. Gorbachev called Russia's democratic institutions "fake" because the Kremlin blocked his efforts to start a new political party; eight other political parties have also been rejected for dubious reasons. In 2011, Gallup reported that only 23 percent of Russians have confidence in the honesty of the elections. In St. Petersburg, a man told me, "Russian politics follows Mark Twain's famous line."

> *Steal $5, you're a criminal. Steal $5,000, you're ready for political office. — Mark Twain*

Corruption is rife. If you want to get a project done, you must offer kickbacks to the local authorities and utilities. Mayors are often the main developer or financial beneficiary in urban projects. Many businesses must pay a *krysha* (roof): mafia "protection money." McKinsey Consulting determined that Russia's productivity is 26 percent of America, largely because of corruption and bureaucracy. In the US, it takes 40 days to get construction approval. In Russia, it takes 704 days, 17 times longer. According to a 2011 World Bank survey, Russia ranked 123 out of 183 countries for its ease of doing business, which put it right below Uganda. In Transparency International's 2010 Corruption Perceptions Index, Russia was ranked 154 out of 178 countries—by far the most corrupt in Europe.

What's in Vladimir Putin's soul?

Putin is crooked, but how many politicians aren't? The truth is that Putin isn't as bad as he's portrayed in the Western media. His patriotism is in his DNA. Vladimir Putin's grandfather cooked for Lenin and Stalin; he also worked for Lenin's wife. Lenin said, "Any cook should be able to run the country." Now the grandson of a cook is running Russia.

Like any patriot, Putin wants the best for his country—and that's what Russians elected him to do. In July 2011, according to the Levada Center, Putin's approval rating was 68%, while Medvedev's was 66%. In July 2011, Pew Research reported that 75% of Russians had confidence in Putin. That's because he's shrewd and pragmatic.

> *Anyone who doesn't regret the passing of the Soviet Union has no heart. Anyone who wants it restored has no brains. — Vladimir Putin*

The West criticizes Russia's corrupt justice system that imprisoned Mikhail Khodorkovsky, who was once Russia's wealthiest man. Yet earlier, the media was complaining about the unjust and corrupt privatization process that created oligarchs like Khodorkovsky. Putin was in a no-win situation: if he had done nothing, he would have been implicitly supporting the sleazy oligarchs; if he had tossed one in jail, he would have been unfair.

Russia's media is tightly controlled, political opposition parties are hampered, and elections are shady. Nevertheless, so far there has not been a situation where objective polls on Putin differ greatly from his election results. Russians see that life is better under Putin's strong arm than the chaotic "democratic" 1990s, which is why they support him.

Critics say that Russia's economy and politics are not free enough. However, according to the Pew Research Center's 2010 report, only half of Russians believe people are better under free markets, whereas roughly 70% of Britons and Americans feel the same way. (Ironically, communist China nearly tops the survey with 75%.) Pew Research asked Russians: what's better to solve Russia's problems, "a democratic form of government" or "a leader with a strong hand?" In 1991, 51% preferred democracy; in 2009, only 29% felt that way.[18] In short, Russians value multiparty elections, free media, and free speech less than any other European country.[19]

This doesn't mean that Russians have a Stalinism gene that compels them to love dictators. They just don't want to be a Western clone. In 2008, Gallup asked Russians what was ideal political system for Russia. The key answers (with the percentage supporting it): (1) a "Soviet system that is more democratic and market based" (40%), (2) "a Western-style democratic republic" (18%), (3) a pre-Gorbachev Soviet system (18%), (4) "a strong authoritarian system, which places order above freedom" (10%). In sum, two-thirds leaned toward democracy and one-third leaned toward authoritarianism.

We forget one of democracy's biggest flaws: unborn babies don't vote. We claim that we care about our children and grandchildren, but we don't vote that way. If people who will be born in 2020 (or 2120) could vote today, our elected politicians would dramatically slash social security, medicare, and military spending to avoid an irresponsible deficit and create a budget surplus for future generations. Such future-minded politicians would not just preserve the environment, but improve it by setting a steep carbon tax that doubles the price of gas; they would tax children to encourage depopulation so that people in 2120 would have more nature and resources per capita than people today. Enlightened and benevolent despots make wiser decisions than standard democracies, which only serve today's shortsighted voting public. Russians don't naively believe that Putin is a saint, but some hope that he's wiser than democracies that are directed by the myopic masses.

Russians are skeptical that the West knows best. In June 2011, the Levada Center reported two-thirds of Russians believe that "Western values" are "not suitable" for Russia.[20] Anatoly Chubais, who led Russia's privatization program, said, "I don't think Russia will follow the United States' way. I don't think Russia will follow the French way. I'm sure Russia will find its own way." We Americans believe that there's only one economic and democratic system that's right: ours. As Russian novelist Ivan Turgenev said, "Most people can't understand how others can blow their noses differently than they do."

Russia knows it's not perfect. In 2009, Dmitry Medvedev admitted that Russia suffers from "centuries of economic backwardness and corruption." He confessed that Russia has a "fragile democracy" and a "humiliating dependence on raw materials." He admitted, "Paternalistic attitudes are widespread in our society, such as the conviction that all problems should be resolved by the government, or by someone else, but never by the person who is actually there. The desire to make a career from scratch, to achieve personal success step by step is not one of our national habits."[21] Can Russia fix its problems overnight? Let's give them a chance. Besides, has the US looked in a mirror lately?

> *Whatever organization we try to create, it always ends up looking like the Communist Party. — Viktor Chernomyrdin, Russia's Prime Minister 1992–1998*

The West is frozen with its Cold War mentality. Russia is somewhat guilty too. We're like two kids who used to beat each other up in the playground, and now, at our 40-year reunion, we're reverting to our childhood roles. We recycle obsolete habits instead of viewing the world with fresh eyes. Russia has adopted a type of capitalism and democracy, so there's no meaningful reason why we must be so negative toward each other. The US is in bed with Saudi Arabia, a totalitarian regime that produced 15 of the 19 hijackers for September 11, yet we struggle to warm up to Russia. That's stupid. The ideological chasm between Russia and the US has shrunk dramatically, so let's grow up and act like adults.

> *Russia is a part of European culture. Therefore, it is with difficulty that I imagine NATO as an enemy.*
> *— Vladimir Putin*

Russia goes up and down with oil

In Kaliningrad, I asked Vladislav what he thought about Russia today. He said, "China has many factories, but in the last 20 years, Russia has not built any new factories. We have made no progress. If we had leaders like they did in China, and not have leaders like Gorbachev and Yeltsin, then we would still be a strong country. Instead, we destroyed everything. We have nothing today except gas and oil."

"Russia has a lot of trees," I dryly pointed out.

"Yes, but that brings little money," he said. "We used to have industry. It was not very good, but we made things. Today, we make nothing."

Oil and gas are Russia's lifeblood. Russia is the world's biggest oil producer. Yes, even bigger than Saudi Arabia. In 2010, it pumped out over 10 million barrels of oil per day. It's the second biggest natural gas producer, after the US. Russia has by far the highest proven natural gas reserves (47 trillion cubic meters vs. the US's 7 trillion). Oil accounts for about a quarter of the GDP, half of the government's revenues, and two-thirds of the exports. Russia's non-energy exports are smaller than Sweden's. Because their economy is built on oil and gas, interesting observations emerge.

When Lenin said, "Any cook should be able to run the country," he probably didn't realize just how accurate that was. Compare any Russian leader's approval rating with the price of oil and you'll see a remarkable correlation: the higher the oil price, the happier Russians are with their leader. Russia's well-being is so dependent on oil that if oil prices were high, you could put a monkey in charge and Russians would say that the monkey is a genius.

Unfortunately for Russia, it has practically no control over the oil price. It only controls 12 percent of the world's total oil supply. In *Armageddon Averted,* Stephen Kotkin demonstrated that the USSR would have ended in the 1970s if oil prices had not been high, or if Russia had not opened up the Siberian oil fields in the late 1960s. Expensive oil caused the world to consume less of it, knocking the price back down. Meanwhile, William Casey, the CIA Director during most the 1980s, took advantage of the Achilles' heel of Russia. He persuaded Saudi Arabia to dramatically increase oil production to make the price fall. By 1998, the real oil price was one fifth of what it was in 1980. That crushed the USSR. Putin took over right as the oil price soared for a decade, which explains why Russians love ~~the monkey~~ Putin.

In 2010, Pew Research asked Russians, "Do you agree or disagree that your success in life is determined by forces outside of your control?" Results: 60% agreed, 32% disagreed (8% don't know). Americans had nearly the opposite opinion, with only 29% agreeing and 68% disagreeing. Nevertheless, you can't blame oil for the results—Russian responses were in line with the rest of Europe. Nine out of 13 European countries surveyed (both in the east and west) feel they don't control their fate. Therefore, from a European perspective, Russia is not weird, it's America that's weird.

Since Putin's and Russia's success is mostly dependent on the oil price, let's briefly consider the *peak oil* argument, which claims that the world won't be able to produce enough oil to meet the rising demand. If so, this is good news for Russia in the short term and bad news in the long term. In August 2011, a barrel of oil cost about $85. Peak oil predicts that the price will quickly soar to hundreds of dollars per barrel. This will make Russia fabulously rich for several years. However, as the oil price rises, other energy sources become more attractive and energy innovations accelerate. Hence, over the long-term, oil will become just as appealing as an energy source as wood is today—and that's bad news for Russia.

An American professor in Izhevsk

From Kazan, our train went east toward the Urals. Along the way, we passed Izhevsk, a city famous for manufacturing the world's most popular assault rifle, the AK-47. Although I didn't visit Izhevsk, Professor Neil Mitchell told me about what it was like when he worked there in 2010. He said, "Izhevsk receives few foreign visitors. It is not even mentioned in the Lonely Planet guidebook. It was a city forbidden to foreigners during the time of the Soviet Union. Much of their military equipment was made there."

I asked him, "How did the fall of the USSR impact Izhevsk?"

"Many factories were shut down," he said. "As an aside, Russia is way ahead of its quota under the Kyoto Protocol to reduce greenhouse gas emissions, not because of renewable fuels, but because the entire economy contracted after 1990, which was the benchmark year for the global agreement. One of the cities most hurt was Izhevsk. When we first arrived we were taken on a tour of the city I complimented the guide on the fact that there was no pollution coming out of the smokestacks of Izhevsk. I thought this is a model environmental town. Then I realized that most of the factories were abandoned!"

"There's a silver lining in every polluted cloud."

He continued, "With Izhevsk's economy still suffering, I expected a fairly hostile reception from some of its citizens. Quite the opposite was true. We received such a warm reception that it made us want to fight the bureaucrats in Moscow for another visa to go back. We were showered with small gifts and Russian hospitality, all this from people who have little money, including the faculty of the university."

"Give me an example."

"The faculty was totally giving and appreciative of everything I did and the efforts of my wife. The students were struggling with English, but with a translator they responded from time to time, which was great. I concluded from my teaching experiences that the citizens of Izhevsk are prepared to do life one day at a time and do not expect the world at their doorstep."

"So, what have you learned?"

"The people of Izhevsk make do with what they have, crumbling buildings left over from Soviet times and no money to fix them. They work hard to slowly improve their lot and they remain cheerful. They have attracted an automobile assembly plant for one of their empty factories. They are believers that the slow and steady wins the race. This is a good message for North America where the consumer society and instant gratification seem to have taken hold. That is what I brought back from Izhevsk."

"When you returned to the US, you went through Moscow. What do you think of it?"

"About 10 percent of Russia's population lives around Moscow, which, along with St. Petersburg, has nearly half the nation's wealth. The rest of the country is poor by Western standards. Kazan was more prosperous than Izhevsk, but still not rich, in my opinion. One might call Russia a developing country in many ways."

"Do you feel it has shed its Soviet coat?"

"I have the impression that much of the government bureaucracy in Moscow is left over from the Soviet Union and that it serves little purpose now and that some of its employees are susceptible to bribes. Moscow is like any big city, the pace is fast, the transportation systems, both public and private, can be overloaded and tempers can flare. I would say that Moscow was not any more unfriendly than New York if one did not speak English, or Paris if one did not speak French."

Another American viewpoint on Russia

Scott Spires is an American who was born in India, raised in Argentina and the US, and is married to a Russian. They have been living in Moscow since 2005. Scott works as a legal translator and a part-time writer. When I asked him what Russians think about America, he said, "It is complicated. I have never met with hostility on a personal level due to my nationality. A lot of Russians however are in the habit of measuring themselves against America and wanting to challenge it, which is probably a hangover from Soviet times, when the government was always trying to 'catch up and overtake' the advanced capitalist countries. Vis-à-vis the US, Russia is neither weak enough to simply bow out of this rivalry, nor strong enough to win it, and I think that creates a certain tension in the relationship. There is also a paranoid fringe that sees American conspiracies in everything, but in that regard Russia is similar to most countries."

"How is life different than America?"

"Most people live in apartments rather than houses; they like to spend money, but do not live in a credit economy to the extent Americans do; small businesses and entrepreneurship are less prominent; people trust public authorities less (due to corruption and bureaucratic high-handedness); despite the ethnic diversity, it feels more homogeneous because the minorities tend to live in their historic homelands rather than being spread across the country. Meanwhile, there is a growing middle class that lives much as its counterparts in Europe and the US do."

Scott is right that most Russians live in apartments; however, according to Gallup, only 62 percent are satisfied with their current housing, making them the least satisfied Europeans on that issue in 2010. When I asked Scott what Americans can learn from Russians, he said, "How to survive in difficult circumstances; how to relax and get more value out of simple human relationships."

He's right about that too. In 2010, only one in 10 Russians said that they had "experienced stress" on the previous day, making them the least stressed out Europeans. In contrast, the US is the sixth-most stressed out country on the planet. Americans are so neurotic that nearly half said they were stressed the previous day. That's more stressed out than all the countries we've bombed.

A Russian from Perm who lives near Venice

After Izhevsk, the next major train stop was Perm—a city of one million residents with a large Tatar presence. When we arrived, I thought of Lena Akhmarova, a Russian from Perm who hosted me in Venice. She's a gate agent in Venice's airport. When she recalled living in Perm, she said, "We had to make an impossible choice. If we stuck with communism, we would have lots of money, but nothing to buy; if we became capitalists, we would have lots of things to buy, but no money."

I asked, "How were Russians and Tatars during the Soviet period?"

She said, "Russians were lazy. The Tatars are hard workers, but Russians aren't. They expect the government to give them everything on a plate: guaranteed education, job, home, and food. In the USSR, nobody could stand out. Even our schools emphasized equality. Teachers focused on helping the slowest students catch up to the rest. That bored the smart students. I still think that Russians need a strong dictator to rule them."

Lena and I got along well, but sometimes she seemed like one of those airport gate agents that you really don't want to piss off. Once you get to know her, however, she loosens up. Indeed, Lena was a classic Russian woman from the Urals: tough as nails, but with a soft heart. She acknowledged it when she said, "Russians are hard, but they have a good soul. If you cry for help, they will help you."

If you live in a Western metropolis and you go to the right places, you might conclude that Russian expatriates like Lena are everywhere. What's strange is that Russians rarely get out of the house. In 2009, only one in 100 Russians had a family member who, during the last five years, had moved to a foreign country. According to Gallup, that's the lowest rate in the world, demonstrating that Russians don't abandon *Rossiya-Matushka* (Mother Russia).

Igor and Liliana in Trieste

Two hours east of Venice is another Italian city on the Adriatic Sea: Trieste. On December 9, 2009, on my way to Slovenia, I stayed with a Russian couple, Igor and Liliana Chernova. They were in their early 30s. They spoke excellent Italian, English, French, and some Spanish too. Igor was a computer programmer and Liliana was studying languages. I asked Igor, "What was it like growing up in Russia?"

Igor said, "Russians who grew up in the 1990s are difficult people. Students either dropped out of school or didn't work hard. So it's an uneducated generation, but they're also quite strong because they had to find ways just to eat. Still, turmoil brings out the best and worst in people. Russia has had so many bad times that it has produced many great people, geniuses, and inventors."

I asked, "How do you think Russians view Americans?"

Igor said, "On a personal and economic level, the Russian and American relationship is good. Many big companies in Moscow are joint American-Russian companies. But on a political level, it's always been a problem. There are a lot of Russian nationalists. Francis, because of your dark looks, you might get beaten up in Russia." He looked at the ground and said, "It's the worst part of Russia."

Russians admit they have trouble tolerating other religions too. In 2007, only 42 percent of Russians and Lithuanians believed that their countries are a good place for religious minorities. That's the lowest rate in Europe, according to Gallup. I asked Igor, "So are you an Italian citizen now? You've lived in Italy for seven years."

He said, "No, I'm a proud Russian. I don't want Italian citizenship."

I asked Liliana, "So what's the difference between Italians and Russians?"

Liliana said, "Russians are crazy people. When they decide to do something, they do it. It doesn't matter the cost. They are stubborn. An Italian is adaptable. He will change his mind. A Russian is the opposite: he will stick to his principle."

Igor laughed, "We like to say that Italians are the comical copy of Russians and that Russians are the tragic copy of Italians."

Two Slovenians experiencing Russia

I crossed the old Iron Curtain that divided Trieste and Slovenia. In Ljubljana, I met two Slovenians who were getting university degrees in Russian. They spent three weeks in Moscow and four days in St. Petersburg. After their trip, I talked with Urša Vidrih and Ana Marinšek.

Ana said, "The things I admire about Russia are also things that I hate about it. At the beginning I thought that Russian men know how to behave. They open the door for you. They pay for you. On the other hand, the woman is still considered less than a man. They have well-developed manners, but their traditions limit you. They remind me of Serbians: they have a passion and a huge soul. I also learned that they don't rush and work like Slovenians."

I asked Ana what she learned from studying Russian for five years in the university. She said that she loved their dedication to the arts. Like T.S. Elliot is known for his epic *Wasteland* poem, poet Alexander Pushkin is best known for his mega-poem *Yevgeniy Onegin,* which is both fun and profound. Pushkin, at the age 38, learned that the pen may be mightier than the sword, but not mightier than the gun. He got into a macho duel and lost. Mikhail Lermontov, a literary genius who wrote *A Hero of Our Time,* suffered the same fate.

Urša Vidrih said, "I love Leo Tolstoy's poetic expression, his love for the people, land, and simple way of life. *War and Peace* is a masterpiece. I admire how Tolstoy looks at something from all possible perspectives so that the reader can't guess which is Tolstoy's viewpoint. Genius. Another genius is Fyodor Dostoyevsky, whose questioning of God in *The Brothers Karamazov* is magnificent."

Rick DeLong, an American who lived in St. Petersburg and has spent 10 years in Ukraine, said, "Culturally, there's a really deep appreciation for the arts in Russia and Ukraine. There are so many people who are honestly into poetry, especially in Russia. You can go to birthday party, and it's OK for someone to get up and recite some poetry."

Rick added, "Russian literature and art is very well taught in schools. Everyone knows what the classics are, they've read the books, they've read the poetry, they've memorized a lot of poems. They have a very clear sense of what their cultural heritage is in terms of the arts. That's definitely one thing that is lacking in the US. Try asking the average America, 'What are the American classics?' I think most people would have difficulty answering. They might mention Mark Twain. Someone might recall Hemingway, whether or not they've read *The Old Man and The Sea.* In the US, people don't really know who their classics are or who the great thinkers were. In Russia, there's a much clearer sense who the country's great writers and thinkers are."

When I asked Urša what part of Russia she wished she could import into Slovenia, she said, "I wish we could import some of their national pride. They have it too much. It would be nice to have some of it. We don't have it. I also wish we could import their metro system. It's so big that it would cover all of Slovenia!"

Stepping outside of Europe and into Yekaterinburg

Returning to Perm, our Trans-Siberian train creaked out of the station, heading toward Eastern Europe's edge—the Ural Mountains. After several hours, we sliced through the Urals and popped out in Yekaterinburg. With 1.4 million residents, Yekaterinburg is Russia's fourth largest city. As I got off the train, it hit me that I was now in Asia.

Yekaterinburg isn't a sexy city, but it has a few interesting places. The Gothic-styled Sevastyanov's House is nice and the city's *plotinka* (dam) creates a pleasant lake. On *Voznesenskaya Gorka* (Ascension Hill), there's a park with a grand yellow building with Corinthian columns. There's a statue of Alexander Stepanovich Popov, who studied in Yekaterinburg and invented the first modern radio in 1895. Locals were proud of their first skyscraper, a 30-story bank building. In fact, there were five cranes in the skyline indicating that the city is expanding. This expansion is deceptive.

Russia's growing cities hide the fact that the country has been shrinking ever since the USSR broke up. In 2010, Russia's population was 143 million. By the end of this century, it will have under 110 million, according to the UN. Meanwhile, Afghanistan will equal Russia's population in 2100, while Niger will exceed it. That's remarkable because today Afghanistan is a fifth of the Russia's size and Niger is a tenth.

In June 2011, Putin committed spending a staggering $54 billion to reverse this trend. Therefore, Russians will enjoy more festivities like Conception Day, which Ulyanovsk (a city south of Kazan) celebrates every September 12. Anyone who produces a baby on the following June 12 (Russia Day) wins a prize, which could be a refrigerator, $10,000 in cash, or even a four-wheel drive car. The city lets workers go home early that day and have sex.

Unfortunately, Yekaterinburg wasn't celebrating Conception Day when I visited. So instead, I had a less agreeable diversion: visiting the site of a brutal mass murder. The Church on the Blood commemorates the grizzly event. It happened on July 17, 1918, months after Tsar Nicolas II had fled St. Petersburg with his family. They were hiding from Lenin's revolutionary Bolsheviks. At 2:00 a.m., the Bolsheviks found them and ordered them to dress. The family stuffed their bodies with 1.3 kilograms (2.8 pounds) of diamonds and precious gems. The Tsar, his wife, children, and servants were taken to the basement. A firing squad entered the room. The four females survived the first hail of bullets because they bounced off the jewelry. The executioners used bayonets and head shots to finish them off.

The Bolsheviks didn't want the royal family's bodies to become a type of shrine. Therefore, in a nearby forest, they dug a deep hole, tossed the bodies in it, and burned them. To disintegrate the bones, they poured sulfuric acid on them. Although the bodies were well hidden, the house where they were executed became a pilgrimage site. Communists didn't like that. Therefore, in 1977, a young Boris Yeltsin, who was the communist party leader for the region, ordered the house demolished. Two years later, an amateur archaeologist found the royal remains in the forest. Fearing punishment, he didn't tell anyone about it until 1989. Eventually, DNA analysis confirmed they were the Tsar's family.

The royal burial site, the Ganina Yama, now has seven new wooden chapels—one for each royal family member. The chapels have green and gold decorations, which look lovely in the forest that surrounds the site. There's still a large hole where the royal family was buried. In 2007, they found two of the royal children's missing bodies. Our tour guide said that last Tsar tempted fate by not regularly wearing a cross. Ironically, in 1990, Yeltsin approved the construction of the church on the same site, and gave the family a proper burial in 1998. In 2008, Russia's Supreme Court announced that Nicholas II and his family were posthumously rehabilitated because they were victims of political repression. Now the question is, will Russia and the West rehabilitate their relationship?

Russia's future relationship with the West

It's easy to forget, but 70 years ago the US and Russia were pretty good friends. We weren't *best* friends, but we got along. Then came the Cold War. Luckily, nobody pushed the wrong button. When the USSR collapsed, the US didn't help Russia like the US helped Germany and Japan after WWII. Instead, in the 1990s, while Russia was in utter agony, the US picked its nose.

After September 11, 2001, Russia helped the US by supporting our UN resolutions and by giving military support. To thank Russia, America helped NATO expand into the Baltic, canceled the Anti-Ballistic Missile Treaty, planned putting up a missile shield, permanently set up military bases next to Russia, and attacked Serbia and Iraq without Russia's support. Clinton and Bush missed a great opportunity to create a friendship. Russia held out a hand, and we slapped it away.

Russians have buried old, negative attitudes. A July 2011 Pew Research survey showed that 56% of Russians view the US favorably and 63% view the American people favorably. Two-thirds of Russians have a favorable view of the EU, and 78% have a favorable view of Germany. Meanwhile, ever since Gorbachev, Americans have generally had a favorable view of Russia.[22] In July 2011, Pew Research reported that half of Americans have a favorable view and only 39% have an unfavorable view. The best news came in 2010, when Gallup showed that among Americans under 35 years old, 61% view Russia favorably—they aren't burdened with the rusty Cold War mentality. There's hope that the US will finally treat Russia more positively.

> *You can always count on Americans to do the right thing—after they've tried everything else. — Winston Churchill*

In the meantime, Russia is improving its relations with its neighbors. In July 2011, Belarus, Kazakhstan and Russia agreed to remove all customs borders in 2013. Russia's long-term goal would be to have a single currency for this vast region. Russia hopes to expand this free-trade zone, although only Kyrgyzstan and Tajikistan have shown interest. Ukraine seems more interested in joining the EU. After 17 years of having applied to the World Trade Organization, Russia may finally join it in 2012. Russia is placing another bet in the Shanghai Cooperation Organization, which may be Asia's answer to NATO and the EU. What's clear from all this is that Russia is back.

Russia's Return

In 2007, Yegor Gaidar, the architect behind Russia's economic shock therapy in the 1990s, wrote an excellent book called *Collapse of an Empire.* He warned of the "post-imperial syndrome." He saw parallels between Germany's post-WWI grievances and with Russia's current government. He worried that too many Russians blame America for conspiring to cause the collapse of the USSR instead of realizing that "the Soviet political and economic system was unstable by its very nature" and doomed to fail. Before he died, Gaidar warned, "We have to get through the next five to ten years and not start doing something stupid."

In 2011, the imprisoned oligarch Mikhail Khodorkovsky believes that Russia is doing stupid things. He said, "The Russian economy cannot be retooled under the current government system, which is inefficient, obsolete, and thoroughly corrupt. Russia, for a plethora of reasons, will be engulfed in yet another crisis around 2015." (He could be saying this because he hopes to get out of jail around then and run for political office.)

To predict Russia's future, you must predict the price of fossil fuels. If oil and gas prices rise, Russia's future is bright; otherwise, Khodorkovsky's prediction will be right. Given that fossil fuels are a limited and nonrenewable resource, I predict their price will generally rise since Asians will continue to demand more of it. Some forecast that Russia's known oil reserves will run out around 2030, but that assumes they will not discover new reserves, say, under the Arctic Ocean. Nevertheless, as the supply of fossil fuels inevitably diminishes, their price will rise so high that alternative energy and bioplastics will look like a bargain. That day will probably come before 2030. Russia is preparing itself before time runs out.

Despite all the complaints, Russia's 1990s shock therapy succeeded in cleaning up Russia's balance sheet. That, along with rising energy prices, helped Russia pay off its debts. In June 2011, Russia had $528 billion in foreign exchange reserves, which placed it after Japan and China. That's impressive for a country that was broke 20 years ago.

In 2010, McKinsey Consulting estimated the total debt as a percentage of GDP that major countries carry. This included not just government debt, but also non-financial business debt, financial debt, and household debt. Among 10 top industrial countries, total debt as a percentage of GDP increased from 200 percent to 300 percent from 1995 to 2008. Russia had by far the lowest total debt, just 71 percent.

Just looking at government debt, Russia's debt was only five percent of GDP in 2011. Most developed countries had percentages of over 50 percent—10 times higher.[23] In 2011, America's government debt was about 100 percent of GDP. The West is setting itself up to feel what Russia felt in the 1990s.

The spotlight will shine on Russia this decade. Investors have identified Russia as one of the fast emerging markets, which are called the BRICs (Brazil, Russia, India, and China). In 2014, Russia will host the Winter Olympics in Sochi. In 2018, Russia will host the World Cup. Even doomsday predictions of global warming make some Russians excited for the future. They'll have more Arctic resources to extract, more arable land for farming, and they might only have to wear three layers of clothing in the winter instead of five.

Russia 3.0

Russia 1.0 was communist Russia. Today, we have Russia 2.0, which transformed itself into a lightly authoritarian capitalist state whose lifeblood is fossil fuels. Commodities are 80 percent of Russia's exports—it is the world's largest energy-exporting country. To reach Russia 3.0, it must prove that it's a twenty-first century innovator and not just a bigger, colder version of oil-rich Venezuela.

That will be hard. In 2011, the percentage of GDP spent on research and development was as follows: Japan 3.3%, the USA 2.7%, the EU 1.7%, China 1.4%, and Russia 1.0% (which just beats out Belarus's 0.96%). Meanwhile, in June 2011, 21 percent of Russians would like to live abroad.[24] Most of those who have wanderlust are young, educated Russians—exactly the people Russia needs to keep. Until a couple of years ago, most Russians didn't know how to operate a computer—a higher percentage knew how to sew or how to fix a leaking faucet.[25]

This is why Russia is investing billions of dollars into the Skolkovo Innovation Center, which is located in Moscow's suburbs. Its nickname is *Inograd* (Innovation City). Dow Chemical and MIT are investing in Inograd, and IBM is seriously considering it. In 2014, the mini-city will be Russia's Silicon Valley. Will it create the next Facebook or iPad?

Perhaps. The challenge won't be conducting good research. Russia has an excellent scientific tradition (they were the first in space, after all). The challenge is getting their innovations adopted and diffused in their society and beyond. It has plenty of bright minds to do it. However, in this decade, Russia's most important innovations won't be a bunch of new nanotechnology products, sexy gadgets, or Twitter rivals. Instead, they might be more mundane innovations, like cutting out waste through clever management practices. That will ignite productivity, thereby accelerating Russia's creative power.

One foot in Asia, one in Europe

Although I was happy to get to Yekaterinburg, my dream was incomplete. I had dreamed of standing on Eastern Europe's edge—the spine of the Ural Mountains. The mountain range is one of the world's oldest (275 million years) and stretches 2,500 kilometers (1,550 miles) from north to south. Our train had just zoomed under it. Therefore, I took a bus that crossed the Urals and the driver made a special stop on the crest of mountain range. I jumped off the bus and I was surprised by what I saw.

I knew that the Urals were relatively low—the highest peak, Mount Narodnaya, is only 1,894 meters high (6,214 feet). Still, in my romantic vision, I pictured the spine of the Urals to be somewhat sharp and steep. Instead, where I stood, the grade was so soft and smooth that if you had drunk a bit too much vodka, you might think it's flat.

Nevertheless, there's a marble monument nearby that marks the continental border between Asia and Europe. In 2015, Russia plans to build a massive monument that will span the highway. When I went, the monument was less grand, but still memorable.

It had taken 18 hours on a train from Moscow to get here. Russia is simply enormous. As I walked up to the monument, I thought of what some Russians had told me when I said that I would be writing a chapter about their country. They quoted Fyodor Tyutchev:

> *Russia cannot be understood with the mind alone, no ordinary yardstick can span her greatness: she stands alone, unique—in Russia, one can only believe.*
> *— Fyodor Tyutchev, 1866*

Russia is indeed hard for the mind to digest. As much as I tried to understand her, she is unusually profound, mysterious, and complex. To fully comprehend her, you need several lifetimes. Nevertheless, I hope you feel like you've caught a glimpse of the soul of Eastern Europe.

What Russia Can Teach Us

- **Appreciate literature and art.** Russians are deeply in tune with their cultural heritage. They name airplanes after Russian writers. Do what many Russians do: discover classic literature, attend museums, and read poetry.
- **Play chess.** Russia produced more chess champions than any other country. It's a game that develops the mind and sharpens cognition. It beats watching mindless TV and video games.
- **Put busy street crossings underground.** The only way for a pedestrian to cross most busy city streets in Russia is to use an underground passageway. This offers several benefits. It lowers traffic congestion, thereby lowering pollution and saving gasoline. It forces foot traffic to get some extra exercise. It offers rain protection. It's a convenient place for kiosks and street musicians to make a little money.
- **Don't let the weather affect you.** Does the weather rule your mood? Russians seem impervious to weather changes. Sure, they like their warm summer days, but their brains and trains continue to function no matter what happens. Whether the world boils or becomes a frozen ball, Russia will keep going.
- **Institute a flat tax.** If the largest country in the world can implement a flat tax, so can the USA. Russia's flat income tax is just 13 percent. The low and simple tax rate encouraged high compliance, so Russia enjoyed a sharp boost in tax revenues. Flat taxes are the norm in Eastern Europe. It's time that the West catches up to the East.
- **Live in a high-rise.** In 2007, 68 percent of housing construction in Russia were high-rise apartment buildings, compared to 11 percent in the US. Living in a high-rise has a lower environmental impact than living in a single-family detached home. It also encourages community bonding and cultural development.
- **Don't stress.** Americans are babies—everything stresses us out. A Gallup poll showed that American are one of the most stressed out nations in the world; meanwhile, Russians are the least stressed country in Europe. Be a Russian: brush off imperfection.

- **Never surrender.** Reading Russian history is like watching a tennis ball bang around a washing machine. They've had many tough times. Unlike the US, Russia has had some serious invaders practically break them. Swedes, French, and Germans all tried to stab Russia's heart, Moscow. Russians endured history's deadliest siege (Leningrad), deadliest battle (Stalingrad), and deadliest invasion (Operation Barbarossa). They just don't give up. Moreover, they stay united even after civil wars and economic trauma. The two greatest virtues of Russians are loyalty and resolve. When you're facing tough times, think of Russia, stay strong, and keep going.

Places I saw and recommend in Western Russia: St. Petersburg, Kazan, Moscow, and any Russian village.

Travel deals and info: http://ftapon.com/russia

I jumped on the flat top of the monument that marks Europe's easternmost border. A thick white line cuts through the dark marble representing the Asian-European divide. I looked east, and failed to grasp the endlessness of Russia. I looked west, and all of Eastern Europe lay before me.

I put one foot in Europe and one foot in Asia. I was standing on the edge of Eastern Europe. I smiled. My dream was finally complete.

Conclusion—What Eastern Europeans Can Teach Us

Funny things would sometimes happen when I asked Eastern Europeans what they can teach us. Those who blurted out, "Lots of things!" often couldn't think of anything specific. Meanwhile, those who said, "Nothing!" eventually provided several insightful ideas. During the seven years that it took me to write this book, I've asked this question countless times. Although I've captured the best answers for each country, I've also wondered: what characteristics can you find in most Eastern European countries, but that are far less common in Western Europe (and other regions of the world)? In other words, what makes Eastern Europe unique and special? What, if anything, characterizes Eastern Europe?

This is a thorny question because, as we've seen, Eastern Europeans routinely deny that they are in Eastern Europe. Hence, they resist anyone who claims that there is a common thread throughout their region. They argue that the Iron Curtain was an arbitrary, artificial line and that we shouldn't use such an antiquated east-west division anymore. Nevertheless, while the Berlin Wall has been gone for nearly 25 years, its shadow still lingers. Surveys and anecdotal evidence reveal a clear east-west cultural divide. As soon as you step into Slovenia, Czechia, Hungary, or Poland, many survey results move away from the typical Western European answers. Although the gap between east and west tends to increase the further east you go, the mutual feelings among Eastern Europeans are undeniable. Some of these common bonds are positive, others are negative.

17 common negative Eastern European traits

Let's review some of the surveys we have looked at that indicate the negative themes that distinguish Eastern Europe from Western Europe.

1. **Eastern Europeans don't believe they live in a meritocracy, whereas Western Europeans do.** When Gallup asked 153 countries, "Can people in your country get ahead by working hard?" 22 out of the 29 countries on the bottom of the list were from Eastern Europe. In contrast, the Portugal was the only Western European country that didn't have a majority believing that hard work is rewarded.
2. **Eastern Europe is more corrupt than Western Europe.** Transparency International's 2010 Corruption Perceptions

Index ranks countries on a 10-point scale (10 means no corruption). All Western Europeans score above a six, except Italy (3.9). Meanwhile, all Eastern Europeans score below a five, except Poland (5.3), Estonia (6.5), and Finland (9.2). Countries with a high percentage of Russophones scored below three—Moldova, Ukraine, Belarus, and Russia.

3. **Eastern Europeans are highly dissatisfied with their country's efforts to deal with the poor.** In 2010, Gallup asked people if they were "satisfied" with their country's "efforts to deal with the poor." Among the 17 least satisfied countries in the world, 12 were from Eastern Europe. It reflects the letdown after enjoying years of equality under communism.
4. **When compared to Western Europeans, Eastern Europeans are less likely to donate money, volunteer time, or help strangers.** Finland, Kosovo, Poland, and Slovenia were the only Eastern European countries that had scores of 30 or more in Gallup's 2010 Civic Engagement Index, whereas all Western Europeans (except Italy and Portugal) had scores above 30. Despite their communist heritage, Eastern Europeans today are unlikely to help a random comrade.
5. **When compared to Western Europeans, Eastern Europeans are less accepting of religious, racial, and ethnic minorities.** Gallup's Diversity Index shows all Western Europeans (except Italians) scoring above 53 (on a 100-point scale) and all Eastern Europeans (except Finns and Serbians) scoring below 53.
6. **Eastern Europeans lead the world in alcohol consumption.** According to the World Health Organization, the top 10 countries based on per capita alcohol consumption are all from Eastern Europe.[1]
7. **Eastern Europeans are far more homophobic than Western Europeans.** When Gallup asked the world how good their community is at accepting gays and lesbians, 16 Eastern European countries were less accepting than Afghanistan. In contrast, most Western Europeans said gays are welcome. For homosexuals, the Iron Curtain has become the Gay Curtain.
8. **You're more likely to find an environmentalist in Western Europe than in Eastern Europe.** Western Europe's lowest recycling rate was in Germany: 77% recycle. All Eastern Europe countries had recycling rates below 60%. Turkey was the worst with just a 6% recycling rate (Russia and Ukraine were both 10%). Also, Gallup revealed that compared to Western Europeans, Eastern Europeans are less likely "to avoid certain products that harm the environment," to be active in an environmental group, and

to be satisfied with their country's "efforts to preserve the environment."

9. **Eastern European roads are worse than Western Europe.** At least 60 percent of Western Europeans (except the British and Italians) were satisfied with their roads in 2010, whereas no Eastern European country (aside from Finland, Croatia, and Turkey) had a satisfaction rate of over 60 percent.
10. **Eastern Europeans have generally two to 10 times lower real labor productivity compared to Western Europeans.** A 2011 World Bank report confirmed that communism's habits and bureaucracy linger.
11. **Eastern Europeans are less satisfied with their health and healthcare than Western Europeans.** When asked if they are satisfied with their health, all Western Europeans (except for Portugal) had satisfaction rates of 82 percent or higher. In 2010, all Eastern Europeans (except Macedonians and Turks) had satisfaction rates below 88 percent. There's also an east-west divide when Gallup surveys measure the confidence people have in their healthcare or what their opinion of its quality.
12. **Eastern Europeans are less satisfied with their standard of living than Western Europeans.** All Eastern Europeans (except Finns) had satisfaction rates below 72 percent, whereas all Western Europeans (except the Portuguese) were above 72 percent.
13. **Eastern Europe is not as great of a place for immigrants as Western Europe.** In 2010, Bosnia, Finland, Greece, and Serbia were the only Eastern European countries that were more accepting of immigrants than the least accepting Western European country, Austria.
14. **Eastern Europeans tend to be less happy than Western Europeans:** In June 2011, Gallup surveys showed that Eastern Europeans, especially elderly ones, are far less happy than Western Europeans.[2]
15. **Eastern Europeans are less stimulated than Western Europeans.** The majority of all Eastern Europeans (except Finns) did not "learn or do something interesting" the day before they were interviewed in 2010. Western Europeans (except Italians) were the opposite.
16. **Eastern Europeans smile and laugh less than Western Europeans.** Gallup asked the world, "Did you smile and laugh a lot yesterday?" Western European countries all have over 70 percent saying *yes*. Those in Eastern Europe all have scores below

70 percent (with the exception of Poland).

17. **Eastern Europeans are suckers for conspiracy theories:** I don't have a survey to prove it, but my experience indicates that, compared to Westerners, Eastern Europeans are much more likely to naively believe and place great importance in crazy conspiracy theories.

Some Eastern Europeans will reject this list, saying, "These are biased surveys that are just trying to reinforce an old, dead stereotype. The New Eastern Europe is nothing like this!" Perhaps. Obviously there are plenty of exceptions. Moreover, Eastern Europe is changing every day, mostly in a positive direction. Still, these survey results are based on the opinions given by people from each country. They are not the results of some guy with thick glasses in Switzerland who arbitrarily assigns a score for each country. These surveys are the voice of the people judging themselves. Survey questions and methodology are unbiased and usually have only three percent error margins. For the doubters: let's say that you find a reliable global survey which shows that, when compared to Europeans, Americans are far more likely to say that their fellow citizens are insincere and fake. And your anecdotal evidence confirms this. Would you deny the evidence or accept that it's generally true?

Six common positive traits

Eastern Europe shares common positive characteristics that not only distinguish it from Western Europe, but also from most of the world. During the twentieth century, few regions on the planet suffered as much as Eastern Europeans. They endured fascism, communism, corruption, economic chaos, invasion, occupation, famine, war, and genocide. Given that, it's amazing that Eastern Europeans aren't more screwed up. That brings us to their greatest trait: resilience.

1. **There's one characteristic that all Eastern Europeans share, from Finland to Macedonia, from Slovenia to Ukraine—it's *toughness*.** Eastern Europeans are a gritty, intense, and supernaturally sturdy people. Communism, wars, and winters have sculpted their tradition of getting by with little. They may whine and complain, but they'll endure any hardship and overcome any challenge with a stoic and grim determination.
2. **Eastern Europeans excel at having a simplified tax policy.** That's ironic because communist countries were known for their bureaucracy, while capitalist ones were known for their efficiency. However, today, Westerners are saddled with convoluted tax codes, while Eastern Europeans are champions of flat taxes. They've fulfilled a capitalist fantasy: simple, predictable taxes. Estonia led the revolution in 1994 and today has

a 23% flat tax. Lithuania (33% flat tax) and Latvia (25%) followed. Then, in 2001, Russia adopted a 13% flat tax. Next came Ukraine (15%), Slovakia (19%), Romania (16%), Serbia (14%), Czechia (12.5%), Macedonia (10%), Albania (10%), Montenegro (9%), Bosnia (10%), and Bulgaria (10%). Poland, Hungary, Croatia, Greece, and Slovenia are considering flat taxes. Meanwhile, Americans and Western Europeans are plagued with a Byzantine tax code.

3. **Eastern European cities have outstanding pedestrian zones.** Europe's six biggest squares are all in Eastern Europe. Although Western European cities have nice pedestrian zones, because Eastern Europeans don't have as many cars as Western Europeans, they're more likely to walk everywhere. In America, the only pedestrian zones are in our spiritless shopping malls. It's a pity we don't copy Eastern Europe and seal off vast areas in our city center for walkers.
4. **Eastern Europeans share a balanced work ethic.** Even with workaholic Slovenians on one extreme and relaxed Bosnians on the other, Eastern Europeans tend to balance work and play better than Americans. In this way, Eastern Europeans are similar to Western Europeans, although Eastern Europeans are one step more in the relaxed direction.
5. **Eastern Europeans are less stressed than Western Europeans.** When Gallup asked, "Did you experience stress yesterday?" Russians were the most chilled out Europeans, with just one in 10 answering *yes*. In general, Eastern Europeans are less stressed out than the West. Michael Derrer, a Swiss consultant and translator for Eastern Europe, told me, "Western perfectionism asks for improving situations, which of course is good in the long run, but Eastern Europeans can cope with situations that are not perfect, which is useful for the short-term individual well-being."
6. **Eastern Europe is depopulating faster than any other region.** People often describe a decreasing population as a "problem" or a "demographic crisis." However, a forever-increasing population is a doomed Ponzi scheme. Although Eastern Europeans haven't learned how to market their declining populations as a positive attribute, they can show the world the vast benefits of everyone getting more elbowroom.

Of course, there are other shared positive traits in Eastern Europe. For example, they maintain their traditions, focus on their families, are well-connected to their history, and are hospitable. However, these aren't just Eastern European traits; they are human traits. Moreover, Eastern Europe isn't the global leader on such issues (nor are they the laggard, either).

Michael Derrer observed another common bond that was neither negative nor positive. He said, "Eastern Europe has an untarnished relation to traditional European values. I do appreciate the liberalization in the western world during the past 40 years. But it is useful for us to see the old ideals still alive in the minds of Eastern Europeans. I am thinking of traditional values like progress towards higher well-being, family success, and traditional gender relations."

In conclusion, to claim that *Eastern Europe* is an antiquated or meaningless term because Eastern European nations have no longer anything in common is wrong. Of course, Eastern Europeans are a diverse bunch, as this book certainly proves. On the other hand, Western Europeans are also diverse (compare Portugal with Norway), yet that doesn't stop us from seeing their common traits. Indeed, Eastern Europeans routinely speak about "the West" (clumping the US and Western Europe) as if we're all the same. That's natural because there *are* common bonds, despite the diversity—the same goes for Eastern Europe. Although there is no longer a physical east-west barrier in Europe, there still exists a faint, but measurable, cultural and economic divide. Yes, it continues to fade, but it hasn't disappeared yet.

We're all at the crossroads

One common theme I heard in Eastern Europe was "our country is strategically located." For example, one author noted, "For Hungary does indeed occupy a most dangerous position in Europe, being situated at the point of intersection of the interests and strivings of the three great races—Latins, Teutons and Slavs."[3] A Bulgarian author wrote that Bulgaria's "territory is crossed by important international roads which connect Northern and Eastern Europe with the Mediterranean."[4] A Serbian lamented on a website, "Serbia had such bad luck to have been founded spot on the middle of the road. Exactly where everyone needs to thread to get from East to West and from North to South." Albanians, Romanians, and Belarusians all told me that they're located at a "crucial crossroad." Even Estonians think they are at the center of the universe.

Those who like to think that their country is special because it's at a "strategic crossroad" need to look at a globe. Not a two-dimensional map of the planet, but a spherical globe. Spin it and randomly point anywhere. Notice that whatever you're pointing at is at the crossroads of everything around it. And if you happen to live there, you'll find that everything around you is at least somewhat important in your little world. Even the Arctic is at a strategic juncture, as the recent international debates over its territory and oil have demonstrated. Western Europeans believe that the Balkans is in the periphery, but Balkanians think they're in the center and that France or Spain are "way out there."

Of course, Eastern Europeans aren't the only ones who believe their location is central and pivotal. All countries are guilty because, starting in grade school, we diligently examine two-dimensional maps where our country is in the center. No matter what the time period, we're always at the center. For example, a Moldovan studies his country's map and is struck by their good fortune of being located in the middle of the action between Romania and Ukraine, as well as having access to the vital Dniester River that empties into the nearby, priceless Black Sea. He concludes, "No wonder everyone wants a piece of our valuable, strategic territory!" Such beliefs are simply an extension of our own geocentric view: "I am the center of my world; thus, the country I live in is the center of everything important too."

It's stupid to talk about being at the intersection of things when you live on a big ball. Such an argument would make much more sense if our world were a two-dimensional rectangle or circle. If that were the case, then those who live near the center could legitimately claim to be at the vital junction between competing interests. Those who live near the edge would have trouble arguing that point. This brings up an ego-busting point: our galaxy (the Milky Way) *is* like a flat circle (think of a big Frisbee) and our solar system is located near the end of one of its spiral arms, far from the center. So when we finally join the Milky Way Galactic Federation, don't tell funny-looking aliens that our solar system is at the "crossroads" of anything important. The alien will laugh and say, "You stupid Earthling, you're just a lonely outpost in the hinterlands of the Milky Way. Go back to the boonies, farmer boy."

Answering the critics

To be objective, you must attack your own logic and conclusions. I like to do this, which is why I know what many critics will say about this book. For their benefit, here are my answers:

Some may say, "This book creates (or reinforces) stereotypes about Eastern Europe." Some people hate all generalizations, whether about race, gender, age, or nationality. A few will contort themselves more than a *Cirque du Soleil* acrobat just to avoid generalizing. For example, when I was in Barcelona, I asked Irina, my Russian friend who had been living in Spain for four years, to describe the difference between Russians and Spaniards. She said, "They're all types of people everywhere."

"Yes, I know," I said. "But are there any characteristics that Russians have more than Spaniards?"

"No."

"So you're saying that Spaniards and Russians are basically the same."

"Yes."

"Is there anyone on the planet that's different than Russians? Or are we all like them?"

Sensing that I had her in a corner, she dodged the issue and said, "I'm not sure."

You don't need to have traveled to Russia and Spain to know that her answers are bullheaded. Yes, of course, "people are people," but at the same time, we know that obvious differences appear as we move around the globe. I should have asked Irina to compare the people from Moscow with those of St. Petersburg (or those from Spain's Basque country with those of Spain's Andalusia region). Perhaps then she would have shouted, "Oh! They're *totally* different! You *can't* compare them!"

Eastern Europeans want an identity. They're tired of being viewed as one bloc. But what is an identity? It's a collection of generalities, both negative and positive. And like any stereotype, it obviously doesn't apply to everyone—there are plenty of exceptions. For example, I met friendly and polite Lithuanian bus station ticket sellers, poorly dressed Latvians, outgoing Estonians, Hungarians who couldn't care less about the Treaty of Trianon, lazy Slovenians, Montenegrins who love Albanians, Moldovans who don't drink alcohol, and Russians who can speak English. I've also met people from Texas who don't have a gun, polite New Yorkers who don't believe they live in the center of the universe, Iowans who know where Montenegro is, and Californians who have never smoked pot.

Still, when you seek to describe a nation, you look for the common threads that run through the society. It's those curious national habits which so many of us share that give us an identity beyond *Homo sapiens.* Denying that such common traits exist is as idiotic as denying that there are exceptions.

Moreover, it's fascinating to explore different levels of granularity. We can zoom in and ask how northern Serbians are different than southern Serbians. Do Poles in Warsaw have different cuisine than those in Wrocław? What do Moldovans on one side of the Dniester River say about Moldovans on the other side? Or we can zoom out and look for transnational bonds. How do Baltic traits compare to Balkan traits? Is there still common ground among the former Soviet Republics? Or, finally, zoom out a bit more and ask, "What are common characteristics throughout Eastern Europe?" Those who dislike generalizations prefer zooming out to the moon so that differences disappear, "See, humans and plants are basically the same—we're both living things!" Yawn.

Foreigners *are* different from your buddies back home, but just saying so isn't profound. Studying *what* those differences are and *how* we are different is. This WanderLearn Series seeks to answer that, along with capturing the collective wisdom and best practices of every place on this diverse planet.

> *There's very little difference between one man and another.*
> *But what little there is, is very important.*
> *— William James, quoting an unlearned carpenter*

Some may say, "It's not right to critique Eastern Europeans." Criticizing another country's culture is tricky. Alexander Pushkin said, "I despise my motherland, but it's disappointing for me, if a foreigner feels the same." Indeed, it's like dealing with the proud father who says, "*I* can call my daughter a slut, but don't *you* dare call her that."

Nevertheless, many Eastern Europeans will appreciate an outsider's perspective just as much as I love hearing the good and bad things that Eastern Europeans have to say after visiting America. Although my quest was to find Eastern Europe's best attributes, I didn't want to paint a rosy fantasyland. That means pointing out the less flattering parts. Fortunately, most Eastern Europeans will admit that their country has imperfections and they're tough enough to handle a fair critique. Wise ones will also understand that when you observe a blemish in another country, you're not necessarily claiming that your country is perfect.

> *Write books only if you are going to say in them the things*
> *you would never dare confide to anyone.*
> *— Emile M. Cioran, Romanian philosopher*

Some may say, "I jumped to the chapter on my country and it sucks!" Some Eastern Europeans will judge this book by reading the introduction, the chapter about their country, and the conclusion. Eastern Europeans are extremely sensitive about chapters that deal with their country, but can read other chapters more objectively. It's a thick book, but do try to read more than one chapter before you judge the whole book.

Some may say, "Who are you to give advice to my country? Yankee, go home!" Although I've occasionally offered solutions to a country's woes, my ideas aren't necessarily the best. I'm simply a curious outsider who may be wrong. If you don't like to hear an outsider's opinion, then ignore mine.

Some may say, "This book is America-centric or even pro-American." This book isn't about why America is great and why we do everything so fabulously. On the contrary: it's a cry that says, "America, we're not so great. Let's return to our tradition of learning from other countries and reinvent ourselves again before we crumble because of our hubris and complacency." Furthermore, the reason I've often compared

Eastern Europe with America is to help Americans (the main audience for this book) to understand Eastern Europe more clearly. Eastern Europeans no longer seem so incomprehensible once we realize that we do similar things (or would do similar things if we were put in the same situation). Also, comparing Eastern Europe with the US may help others learn a bit more about America and gain a new perspective.

Some may say, "This book is too basic for sophisticated, knowledgeable Europeans." I originally wrote this book for Americans and assumed they couldn't find Eastern Europe on a map. However, while I was writing the book, I learned that Western Europeans are surprisingly ignorant about Eastern Europe too. Few have traveled there or know much about it. Finally, I learned that Eastern Europeans hardly know Eastern Europe either! Slovaks didn't know anything about Moldova, Macedonians didn't have a clue where Latvia is, and Bulgarians had never heard of Kaliningrad. In short, the title of this book is unfortunately quite accurate: Eastern Europe is well-hidden . . . from everyone.

Some may say, "This book is too superficial." Yes, you can write a multi-volume tome on every country in this book; in fact, people have. On the other hand, you can also sum up a nation in a magazine article. Poets can do it in one sentence. Cramming 25 countries into a book involves compromise. If you don't like that, then read a multi-volume set on each country.

Some may say, "This book isn't scientific." That's right. This book isn't a formal ethnographic study—it's just my personal perspective based on three years in Eastern Europe. If you went on a similar journey, you'd have different conclusions. I don't pretend that my book has all the right answers or represents the absolute truth; indeed, despite all my efforts, I'm sure I've made errors. There may be factual errors or judgment errors. I will post errata on my website. Navigating the complex world of Eastern Europe is tricky.

On the other hand, before the book went to press, dozens of Eastern Europeans reviewed and commented on it, especially the chapter about their country. As a result of their input, I changed several details. The majority said that I "nailed it"—that I succeeded in capturing the spirit and reality of their country. Of course, the more who read it, the more dissenters appear since you can't please everyone. Some critics have legitimate issues, while others are being combative just to be a pain-in-the-ass.

> *The logic of worldly success rest on a fallacy: the strange error that our perfection depends on the thoughts and opinions and applause of other men. — Merton*

What I've learned

I've learned governments really can change the religion of a people. I've learned to use up all my currency before entering a new country. I've learned that the Cyrillic alphabet teases you into thinking that you can read something, but you really can't. I've learned 25 different ways to say *hello, thank you, excuse me,* and *where's the toilet.* I've learned that there are more men wearing white hats in Turkey than in Albania, and that most men don't wear any hat at all. I've learned to communicate with unfriendly and monolingual train ticket vendors. I've learned that America still has the ugliest currency in the world.

I've learned that it's smart to hold onto your camcorder very tightly when you're overlooking a cliff. I've learned to switch languages quickly so as not to offend the neighboring country (which often hates the neighboring language). I've learned that Baltic people can wear almost no clothes in freezing weather and not be cold. I've learned that Turkish people can wear lots of clothes in hot weather and not sweat. I've learned that Albania and Estonia really do exist. I've learned that most people who work for bus and train lines haven't traveled anywhere.

I've learned to make quick math calculations in my head when converting a dizzying number of currencies. I've learned that squatting toilets are as popular in parts of Eastern Europe as they are in Japan. I've learned that English has ludicrously simple grammar when compared to most Eastern European languages, but that spelling it is not phonetic. I've learned to carry toilet paper everywhere.

I've learned that people are fair, logical, and rational when judging distant conflicts, but that they lose those skills when judging conflicts in their backyard. I've learned that Baltic nations helped bring down the USSR by holding hands. I've learned that Central Europe has cities that look like Western Europe. I've learned that countries, like people, like to blame all their problems on "outside forces" rather than accepting responsibility. I've learned that the Black Sea isn't black. And I've learned that if you want to have fun and eat well, go to the Balkans.

Eastern Europe's most profound lesson

When Maiu and I visited Italy together, she saw an unnerving sight: a hammer and sickle on a red flag—the symbol of the Soviet Union—which was once all over her country, Estonia. We were in Bologna's main square and the flag was everywhere because Italy's Communist Party was having a rally. I wanted to hear their opinion, but it was hard to find a young Italian who could speak a foreign language (combined, Maiu and I were fluent in seven languages, but Italians are usually monoglots). Finally, I found two guys who spoke English well enough. One proudly proclaimed, "I'm a Stalinist."

Maiu cringed. Thanks to Stalin, Estonia was occupied for 45 years. Thanks to Stalin, millions of Eastern Europeans starved to death. Thanks to Stalin, Maiu's grandparents went to Siberia's labor camps. This clueless Italian was similar to the Americans and Western Europeans who championed communism throughout most of the twentieth century. Most of them were simply suffering from the grass-is-greener-over-the-hill syndrome—with little visibility of what was really going on behind the Iron Curtain, some believed that communism was a better system than capitalism. However, after the Iron Curtain collapsed, we learned that communism was closer to dystopia than utopia. Across the world, communist cheerleaders quietly put away their Styrofoam "We're #1" signs.

The failed communist experiment is, perhaps, the most important lesson we can learn from Eastern Europe. Although communism still has some nostalgic fans, when they take a break from their revelry and reflect, even these partisans usually admit that they don't want to return to that era. Eastern Europe teaches us that while authoritarian regimes may satisfy our basic needs, the downsides outweigh the benefits. Eastern Europe proved that a tightly controlled economy is not sustainable. Unfortunately, as the Italian communist rally indicates, some are already forgetting this lesson.

It's easy to criticize capitalism. Like nature, it's often brutal and merciless. However, free markets generally produce far better results than highly controlled markets. It was hard to find anyone under 60 years old who wanted to return to communism, even though they acknowledged that some things were better back then. To paraphrase Winston Churchill: free markets suck, but communism sucks more.[5]

Spreading Eastern European memes

Charles Darwin's *On the Origin of Species* introduced the concept of the survival of the fittest. Although Darwin focused on biological life, the same principle holds true for ideas. The biologist Richard Dawkins says ideas don't have genes, but *memes*. When ideas flow freely, the best memes often rise to the top. When you suppress these memes, a nation becomes less competitive and its standard of living decreases. America must welcome Eastern European memes (and genes) so that we stay vibrant. This book is filled with Eastern European memes—so please spread it around.

Throughout history, the strongest nations had the best technology. America's technology has been built on many Eastern European minds. Intel's founder is Hungarian and it's first investor was a Russian immigrant's son. Google's co-founder has Russian parents. An American of Bulgarian descent invented the digital watch. Four Estonians designed Skype. Several science Nobel Laureates are either Eastern European immigrants or their first-generation descendents. How many well-paid American jobs have these Eastern European immigrants created?

Eastern Europeans get great degrees from American universities, but then go back home because we don't give them a work visa. Foreigners get 40% of the science and engineering degrees and 65% of the computer science degrees. The story is more dramatic in graduate degrees: foreigners get half of all PhDs and 75% of the science PhDs. American immigrants file three times more patents than other Americans. However, only 85,000 visas a year are allocated to skilled workers. No country can get more than 10,000 visas, so that Russians, Ukrainians, and Poles have to wait for years just to *enter* the lottery. Meanwhile, one million immigrants are in line to become permanent residents.

Some of the lucky ones who get to stay have been gold mines. In 2000, immigrants founded about 25% of Silicon Valley's tech start-ups; by 2010, they founded over 50% of them. Immigrants are the CEO or CTO of roughly 25% of the tech start-ups, which end up generating $52 billion and employ 500,000 well-paid people. In 1998, immigrants submitted 7.6% of the patents; 10 years later, it was about 25%.[6] Goldman Sachs estimated that new migrants have added 0.5% to the US GDP each year for the last decade. We'd be fools to not encourage the brightest minds to come to the US.

Yet how many brilliant minds have we prevented from entering our country since September 11, 2001? Gallup's annual survey shows that the majority of Americans want to decrease immigration levels, about a third want to keep it the same, and only about one in six want to increase immigration. In the last paranoid decade, it's almost certain that we refused to give a visa to the future founders of the next Google. One day, when we'll all be using a Russian technology, its founder will tell Americans, "After getting my PhD from MIT, I couldn't get a work visa, so I created my company in Russia's Inograd technology park. We're a $10 billion company now, employing 12,000 Russians in high-paying jobs."

Open the Eastern European floodgates

An immigrant is the best deal in town. From birth to adulthood, humans are a drag. Children suck up years of time from two parents who teach them how to walk, behave, and crash the car. Children eat food, consume fuel, demand schooling, and yet the only thing they produce is an overpriced lemonade stand. From a purely economic perspective, children are parasites. They are an investment that takes 22 years to start producing anything. At that point, this investment generally continues to produce until it becomes an old fart. Then, like a child, it starts sucking resources again, although some continue giving back to society until they're dead. This is an unemotional way of analyzing human life, but that's how societies work economically.

Immigrants are magnificent because we get them when they're fully baked: they usually arrive as a young adult—fully educated and ready to work. Our society gets the benefit of harvesting a great fruit tree, but we never had to baby it from seed to maturity. Moreover, immigrants often burn with ambition and work like they have a fire under their ass. If they don't create companies and jobs, they work their butts off in companies. They produce a couple of children, who become typical Americans despite their parents' efforts. Their offspring often aren't even able to speak their parents' language. However, those children usually do inherit their parents' work ethic. Finally, what do many of these immigrants do when they retire? Go home. After paying taxes for years, they fulfill their dream of buying a mansion in their homeland, retiring there, and living like royalty. As a result, they diminish the cost of supporting them as senior citizens. If they decide to stick around, they are welcome—they've worked hard in America all their life and they've earned the measly retirement benefits that American society provides.

Unfortunately, many overestimate how many immigrants there are and want to limit them. *The Economist* reported that the average British citizen believes that immigrants make up 27% of the UK (it's really only 10%). When surveyed along with Canada and 6 western European countries, Brits and Americans were the most likely to believe that immigrants take jobs away from natives (52% of Brits and 42% of Americans agree). Also, 43% of Brits felt that legal immigrants should not have equal benefits as natives (only 22% of Americans agreed, fortunately putting them at bottom of the 9 country survey).[7] Too many people view immigrants with suspicion rather than realizing that they're a sweet deal.

> *If tyranny and oppression come to this land, it will be in the guise of fighting a foreign enemy. — James Madison*

Educated immigrants are such a splendid deal that we ought to follow a simple policy: if you have a technology or science degree, or any masters or doctorate degree, then you get an automatic USA work visa. Educated, entrepreneurial immigrants create more jobs than they take. If American xenophobes demand some restrictions, then at least make such a policy for Eastern Europeans. What the hell are we afraid of? How many Slavic terrorists have struck us? What percentage of Eastern European immigrants refuse to learn English? What percentage of them become criminals versus hard-working people who pay taxes? America's immigration policy is retarded. America has been strongest when we've been open to the world. Let's open our doors again.

Eastern Europe's future

Eastern Europe's communist ghost is fading. Ukraine and Russia now have enormous potential. The Baltic has picked up clever Nordic habits and investments. Balkan demons have retreated. Central Europe continues its healthy integration into the EU and the eurozone. The Adriatic Coast is becoming the new Côte D'Azure.

> *Europe has two lungs, it will never breathe easily until it uses both of them. — Pope John Paul II, referring to Eastern and Western Europe*

As Eastern Europe changes, so will the EU. In the last century, the EU was exclusively a Western European club. In 2011, 10 of its 27 members are Eastern European. When the EU invites the Balkans into the club, half of the EU members will be from Eastern Europe. NATO has already incorporated Albania, Croatia, and Turkey into Europe's defense. At some point, the term *European* will no longer just mean *Western European.* Speaking of terms, instead of dodging the *Eastern Europe* label, Eastern Europeans ought to embrace it. Hundreds of years ago, North America used to stand for *Home for European Rejects and Losers.* Instead of denying that they're in North American, Americans redefined their image. Now it's *Land of the Free, Home of the Fat.*

Likewise, Eastern Europeans should spend less time arguing that they're in Central, Northern, Southern, or Western Europe and just redefine what Eastern Europe means. It's part marketing, part real work. Given all the challenges that Eastern Europeans have overcome, this one is relatively easy. Eastern Europe is the most exciting, fastest changing region on the continent. Whereas Western Europe is getting old and gray, the east has Europe's youngest nation—Kosovo, where the average age is 26. Eastern European programmers are innovating in information technology faster than Western Europeans can boot up their computers. Few countries have outpaced Eastern Europe's economic growth in the last 20 years. Let's transform *Eastern Europe* from a pejorative connotation into a positive one. After all, Eastern Europe's future is brighter than ever.

Back home in San Francisco

Now, on the eve of 2012, after a three years of not touching American soil, I finally came back home. Readjusting to American life has been weird. For example, it's strange to be literate again. For years I've lived among 20 languages that I either hardly knew or just didn't know at all. It was rare to find someone who could speak English, French, or Spanish. However, whenever I did, they assured me that such speakers were plentiful. Now, back in America, I can no longer play dumb when the bus driver asks me why I haven't paid the correct fare.

It's also weird to have people talk to me in a normal voice. When Eastern Europeans were unable to communicate with me, they frequently resorted to screaming, thinking that it helps with my comprehension. For example, a Slovenian would say to me, *"Počisti wc, ko se poserješ."*

"I'm sorry, I don't understand," I would say.

"POČISTI WC, KO SE POSERJEŠ!!!!"

"Oh, OK, thanks for yelling. Now I understand completely."

Although I now understand the world around, sometimes it's hard to keep up with America's fast pace. The efficiency and helpful customer service is refreshing, but the go-go-go tempo leaves me breathless. It's also weird to have a phone again. For most of the last three years, I didn't have any phone. I enjoyed the uninterrupted life. I usually checked email about once a week. I didn't have a TV or radio. Few Eastern Europeans live such a primitive life, but it forced me to meet people face-to-face and to write without distractions. Now that I'm back in San Francisco, the phone cries and the Internet drug tempts.

I look strange when Californians talk about how hot it is and I say, "Yeah, it's must be 30 degrees!" It's annoying to convert from the glorious metric system to the confusing Imperial system. On the other hand, I'm happy to sit on American toilets again: it's nice not to have to clean the crapper after every poop. Still, there's one Eastern European toilet experience that will always make me smile: that time when I smashed out of a Finnish outhouse near the Arctic Circle.

I miss Eastern Europe. I miss Finnish bike lanes. I miss Maiu's soft Estonian voice. I miss mushrooming in Latvia. I miss drooling over Lithuania's pretty girls. I miss the adventure of exploring Belarus. I miss discussing history with the Poles. I miss eastern Germany's organization. I miss Czechia's romantic cities. I miss Slovakia's mountains. I miss debating with Hungarians. I miss my many Slovenian friends. I miss the magnificent view from the Croatian sea house where I wrote this book. I miss the Serbian sense of humor. I miss the Bosnian *burek*. I miss Kotor, Montenegro. I miss Albanian friendliness. I miss Kosovo's youthful optimism. I miss teaching students in Macedonia. I miss the four crazy housemates who hosted me in Thessaloniki, Greece. I miss Turkey's coastline. I miss the Bulgarian village of Turkinsha. I miss the Romanian language. I miss Moldova's humility. I miss Ukraine's Orthodox churches. And I miss Russia's vastness. I'd say that I miss Ana too, but she's right here next to me as I write these words.

> *He who returns from a journey is not the same as he who left. — Chinese Proverb*

A call to action

Anton Chekhov said, "Knowledge is of no value unless you put it into practice." As you reflect on this book, consider your own life. Too many people live life as if they're hypnotized. They act like robots, mindlessly copying whatever their peer group is doing. Some people live such a life because they sincerely and profoundly enjoy it. Bless them. However, others are asleep at the wheel.

> *Most people, even though they don't know it, are asleep. They're born asleep, they live asleep, they marry in their sleep, they breed children in their sleep, they die in their sleep without ever waking up.*
> *— Anthony de Mello, Jesuit Priest*

If you sense you're in such a pattern, then travel. In fact, whenever you're stuck anywhere in life, travel. Wandering to new places cracks open our mind, exposes us to new ideas, and creates new synapses. Embarking on a three-year journey is extreme, so if you're afraid, poor, or overcommitted, then start with a three-hour stroll around an unfamiliar place near your home. Interact with people, observe the surroundings, and ask yourself, "What can I learn from this new environment?"

> *People have a hard time letting go of their suffering. Out of a fear of the unknown, they prefer suffering that is familiar.*
> *— Thich Nhat Hanh*

And then the next time you need to reflect, travel longer and farther. Doing so may make perplexing puzzles in your life become understandable, and thorny dilemmas become solvable. Traveling will give you clarity and perspective unlike any other activity. Traveling is the best catalyst and university available. One voyage is worth one library.

> *The material world and your everyday needs distract you from living meaningfully.*
> *— Menachem Mendel Schneerson, Ukrainian Rabbi*

Others, however, may have a different challenge. They adore traveling, but can't figure out how to do more of it. If so, examine your way of life. Most of us own too much crap, spend money thoughtlessly, and become enslaved by toys we thought we needed.

> *There must be more to life than having everything.*
> *— Maurice Sendak*

Start living more simply and frugally. Chapter Two of my first book, *Hike Your Own Hike: 7 Life Lessons from Backpacking Across America,* provides ideas on how to do this. The good news is that it's free on my website.

I challenge you to travel more. Wander to exotic places that you would normally not consider. Learn a foreign language. Meet locals. I hope this book has inspired you to do this now.

Those who wander are not necessarily lost. — Kobi Yamada

What's next?

Within moments of returning to America my friends began asking, "Where will you go next?"

I said, "Can I first sit down for a few minutes and get myself a drink?"

Starting in 2012, I hope to begin a three-year trip exploring every country in Africa. My mom and friends are worried, but they know I love to wander. Although a risky life is dangerous, a life without risk is death. The third book of this WanderLearn Series will be based on that trip. Africa has more than twice as many countries as Eastern Europe and is 10 times bigger. This means I won't be able to sink my teeth into each country as deeply as I have for this book. Nevertheless, there are surely many things that Africans can teach us.

Travel Recommendations

Where to go in Eastern Europe

Although this isn't a guidebook, here are some quick recommendations to help you plan a trip to Eastern Europe. The top 15 places that most people would enjoy are: (1) Croatia's coastline; (2) Prague, Czechia; (3) St. Petersburg, Russia; (4) Krakow, Poland (with side trips to the Salt Mines and Auschwitz); (5) Kotor Bay, Montenegro; (6) Slovakia's High Tatra Mountains; (7) Baltic capitals (Vilnius, Rīga, and Tallinn); (8) Romania's medieval Germanic towns around the Transylvanian Alps; (9) Lviv and its nearby Carpathian Mountains, Ukraine; (10) Škocjan Caves, Slovenia; (11) most of Hungary's major cities; (12) Veliko Tarnovo, Bulgaria; (13) Metéora, Greece; (14) Kazan, Russia; (15) Albania's southern beaches.

If you are a bit nervous about exploring Eastern Europe, start with the westernmost part of Eastern Europe. You'll discover that Poland, Czechia, Slovakia, Hungary, and Slovenia feel like Western Europe with a twist. The Baltic is also quite tame and enjoyable. If you love to socialize and you want to meet Europe's friendliest people, then go to the Balkans. Outdoor lovers will enjoy the Carpathian mountains in Romania and Ukraine. If you enjoy going off the beaten track, but you prefer not to be kidnapped and chopped to pieces, then go to Belarus, Kaliningrad, Kosovo, and Moldova. They're all safe, yet they're Europe's four most hidden secrets.

Useful travel gear

Because products come and go, there's no point in giving specific recommendations in this book. Instead, I've created a special page on my website that summarizes my current favorite travel gadgets and gear: http://FrancisTapon.com/gear

Similarly, airline, hotel, and car rental deals change constantly. Therefore, follow this link to find the latest great travel deals that I recommend: http://FrancisTapon.com/traveldeals

ACKNOWLEDGMENTS

Thanks to all the anonymous and random Eastern Europeans I met during my journey. Some gave me valuable insight, yet I didn't have enough time to get their name.

Thanks to the Gallup Organization for giving me access to their rich database of global surveys.

Thanks to my Beta Readers. These were people who agreed to read drafts of this book. Some read just one chapter (often an Eastern European wanting to read about his country), but others read the whole book. János Molnar was remarkable not just in how much input he gave me on Hungary, but that by the end of the process he had the courage and logic to change some of his opinions as a result of our long debates. Thanks also to Nejc Trušnovec and Andrew Harrod, who were especially helpful and dedicated when reading my drafts. Nejc was superb at helping me research and translate ex-Yugoslav books and sources.

Melissa Finley, my editor, was great at giving me freedom to write, while only occasionally banging my head with the *Chicago Manual of Style*. My assistant editor, Andreja Nastasja Terbos of Slovenia, has a truly remarkable command of the English language. If only more Americans could know English as well as her.

Thanks to Anamarija Mišmaš. She's the graphic designer who laid out the book. More importantly, we went on some thrilling Balkan adventures together. We plan to travel together much more. I love her.

Thanks to my mom for putting up with my nonstop travel to places with scary names like Kosovo, Albania, and Moldova. She worries to death and is convinced that I'm making her age faster than if I just had a nice home, job, wife, kids, and dog.

Three donations

I'm donating 15 percent of my royalties to three nonprofits. First, I'm donating five percent of my book royalty to the Wiki Media Foundation, which runs Wikipedia as well as many other wiki sites. It's a way to thank the 100,000 volunteers who actively write and edit the Wikipedia's 20 million articles in 270 languages. Wikipedia is brilliant to find answers to questions like, "What's the name of that national park in Estonia?" For more controversial questions (e.g., "How many people died in WWII?" or "Who was Slobodan Milošević?") it was a great starting point that could lead me to other books and sources. Wikipedia isn't perfect, but no single information source is. Still, for a free source, there is no better one.

Second, I'm donating another five percent of my book royalty to Kiva.org. This non-profit facilitates micro-loans to individuals in developing nations. Please join my WanderLearn community on Kiva.org. We look for promising Eastern European and African entrepreneurs who need micro-loans. Invest as little as $25. When they pay back your micro-loan, you can either cash it in, lend it to someone else, or donate it to help cover Kiva's administrative costs. One theme in this book is taking personal responsibility for your fate as well as your nation's. Unlike a traditional donation, micro-financing doesn't just give people a fish—it teaches them how to fish. They take control of their destiny instead of just consuming a free handout.

Third, I use five percent of my royalty to send free copies of my book to official Eastern European nonprofits that have a good track record. They sell the copies I give them at fund-raising events or give it as a gift when someone makes a substantial donation to their charity.

Help spread the word

If you enjoyed this book, please spread the word by:

- Telling your social network.
- Giving copies of the book as a gift.
- Mentioning or discussing it on online forums.
- Asking your organization or media contacts to contact Francis for a talk.
- Writing a book review on your blog and other websites.
- Praising it on your megaphone.

MEET THE AUTHOR

Francis Tapon's mother is from Chile and his father was from France. Francis was born in San Francisco, California where he attended the French American International School for 12 years. Native French teachers convinced him that France is the coolest country in the universe. He is fluent in English, French, and Spanish. He struggles with Italian, Portuguese, Slovenian, and Russian. If you point a gun to his head, he'll start speaking other languages too.

He has a degree in religion from Amherst College and an MBA from Harvard Business School. After Harvard, he co-founded a robotic vision company in Silicon Valley. In 2001, he sold what little he had to hike the 3,000 km Appalachian Trail. That inspired him to write his first book, *Hike Your Own Hike: 7 Life Lessons from Backpacking Across America*.

He visited all 25 countries in Eastern Europe from June to November 2004. He consulted at Microsoft before hiking the 4,200 km Pacific Crest Trail in 2006. In 2007, he became the first person to do a round-trip on the Continental Divide Trail—a seven-month journey spanning 9,000 km.

In 2008–2011, he visited over 40 European countries, but focused on revisiting all the Eastern European ones. In 2009, he climbed up Mont Blanc and walked across Spain twice (once by traversing the Pyrenees and then by hiking El Camino Santiago). He's backpacked over 20,000 kilometers (12,500 miles) and traveled to over 75 countries. He has never owned a TV, chair, table, couch, bed, or rocket ship.

To learn more visit FrancisTapon.com. It has hundreds of articles and photos. Sign up for his bi-monthly newsletter to get the latest updates, exclusive content, and no spam. If you have questions or comments, visit the Forum to see if someone has had a similar thought. You also connect with him on Facebook or Twitter. He's also happy to receive hate mail—it makes him giggle.

If you want to meet Francis in person, visit his website's Events page, which shows where he will be next. If you want him to give a fun and informative speech or workshop for your organization, then contact him through his website. He also offers individual life coaching if you want to recalibrate your life. He hopes to inspire you to wander and learn more about yourself and the world. Or at least get out of the house.

Endnotes

If you're looking for an index, find it at http://francistapon.com/THEindex.

All Internet links were successfully retrieved on August 19, 2011.

Estonia

[1] http://www.who.int/substance_abuse/publications/global_alcohol_report World Health Organization, Global Status Report on Alcohol and Health (Switzerland: 2011), p. 274.
[2] http://francistapon.com/Travels/Eastern-Europe/Tallinn-Estonia-Tour-Bronze-Soldier-and-Old-Town for a video of the Bronze Soldier and Tallinn.
[3] http://francistapon.com/pct for videos and photos from our PCT trip.

Lithuania

[1] William Coxe, *Travels into Poland, Russia, Sweden and Denmark: Interspersed with Historical Relations and Political Inquiries* (London, 1785; reprinted New York: Arno Press and New York Times, 1971), pp. 142, 188, 201, 205.
[2] The names Arved and Aita share the same spelling as *arved* (invoices) and *aita* (help), but they are pronounced differently. Still, let's have fun with the idea.

Belarus

[1] Some claim up to 27,000 deaths, not 4,000. However, the higher number is disputed.

Poland

[1] John Keegan, *Atlas of World War II* (Smithsonian, HarperCollins, 2006), p. 70-71.
[2] John Ledyard, *John Ledyard's Journey Through Russian and Siberia 1787-1788: The Journal and Selected Letters*, ed. Stephen D. Watrous (Madison: Univ. of Wisconsin Press, 1966), p. 201-5.
[3] John Ledyard, p. 211.
[4] John Ledyard, p. 223.
[5] John Ledyard, p. 223.
[6] Louis de Jaucourt, "Pologne," *Encyclopédie: ou dictionnaire raisonné des sciences, des arts et des métiers*, nouvelle impression en facsimile de la première edition de 1751-1780 (Stuttgart: Friedrich Frommann Verlag, 1967), vol. XII, p. 930.
[7] Larry Wolff, *Inventing Eastern Europe* (Stanford: Stanford University Press, 1994), p. 342.
[8] Young people's Health in Context. Health Behaviour in School-aged Children (HBSC) study: international report from the 2001/2002 survey, eds. C. Curie et al., WHO Regional Office for Europe, WHO Policy Series: Health Policy for Children and Adolescents. No. 1, 2004.
[9] Zdrowie subiektywne, zadowolenie z życia i zachowania zdrowotne uczniów szkół ponadgimnazjalnych w Polsce w kontekście czynników psychospołecznych i ekonomicznych (red. A. Oblacińska i B. Woynarowska), 2006.

Eastern Germany

[1] For more info: Kristie Macrakis, *Seduced by Secrets: Inside the Stasi's Spy-Tech World* (Cambridge University Press).
[2] Andrew Curry, "Intel Inside," *Wired*, Feb 2008, pages 128, 148.
[3] Fyodor Dostoyevsky, *The Diary of a Writer*, Volume 2, page 1049.

Czech Republic

[1] http://www.who.int/substance_abuse/publications/global_alcohol_report World Health Organization, *Global Status Report on Alcohol and Health* (Switzerland: 2011), p. 274.
[2] http://en.wikipedia.org/wiki/List_of_countries_by_income_equality summarizes the sources, which are at http://hdrstats.undp.org/en/indicators/160.html top 10% vs. bottom 10%. See UN and CIA reports too.

Slovakia

[1] Emerson, J., D. C. Esty, M.A. Levy, C.H. Kim, V. Mara, A. de Sherbinin, and T. Srebotnjak. 2010. 2010 *Environmental Performance Index*. New Haven: Yale Center for Environmental Law and Policy. http://epi.yale.edu
[2] Wolchik, Sharon L. "Slovakia." *Microsoft® Encarta®* 2006 [DVD]. Redmond, WA: Microsoft Corporation, 2005.
[3] http://www.mkp.sk/eng/images/pdf/MINORITY%20REPORT%20-%20OCTOBER.pdf, which cites a phone interview on September 24, 2007.
[4] *Ibid*. Also, many of his statements have been documented on Wikipedia.org, just search for *Ján Slota*, who is the leader Slovak National Party (SNS).
[5] BBC News: http://news.bbc.co.uk/go/pr/fr/-/2/hi/europe/8248097.stm
[6] László Marácz, Hungarian Revival: Political Reflections on Central Europe (The Hague: Mikes International), p. 63.

Hungary

[1] http://gallup.com/poll/3742/new-poll-gauges-americans-general-knowledge-levels.aspx The poll didn't test Austrians, so we're using Germany as a proxy for Austria.
[2] When I asked five Hungarians to verify this fact, I got five different answers. Answers included: two ways, three ways, four ways, five ways, and even six ways of saying *you*! I let them all argue amongst each other, while I just picked four because I read it somewhere.
[3] More unorthodox views on Hungarian: Alfréd Tóth, *Etymological Dictionary of Hungarian* (The Hague: Mikes International, 2007), pp. 788.
[4] http://upload.wikimedia.org/wikipedia/commons/3/38/Europe_topography_map_en.png shows Serbia's Vojvodina autonomous province, which is in the Basin too and just south of Hungary. Another map is http://en.wikipedia.org/wiki/File:Carpathian-Basin.jpg
[5] Yves de Daruvar, The Tragic Fate of Hungary: *A Country Carved-up Alive at Trianon* (Nemzetor and Alpha Publications, Second Edition, 1970), p. 17.
[6] Charles-Marie, marquis de Salaberry d'Irumberry, *Voyage à Constantinople, en Italie, et aux îles de l'Archipel, par l'Allemagne et la Hongrie* (Paris: Imprimerie de Crapelet, 1799) pp. 65-66, 69.
[7] László Marácz, p. 15 and 54.
[8] Yves de Daruvar, p. 109.
[9] László Marácz, p. 4.
[10] Yves de Daruvar, p. 18.
[11] See Austria's land before the split: http://commons.wikimedia.org/wiki/File:Österreich-Ungarns_Ende.png
[12] Looking at Romania's industrial centers and land use is revealing also. Knowing that the Trianon areas lands lie in Romania's Northwest, you can see that there's not a whole lot of exciting industry going on there http://commons.wikimedia.org/wiki/File:Romania_Industrial_Centers_(1970).jpg and http://commons.wikimedia.org/wiki/File:Romania_land_use_(1970).jpg. Romania did have the precious metal mines and much of the timber. While important, those were hardly 90% of Hungary's resources.
[13] Yves de Daruvar, p. 31.
[14] László Marácz, p. 15.
[15] László Marácz, p. 62.
[16] The ethnographic map based on Hungary's 1890 census shows the percentage of Romanians in Greater Hungary. According to Hungary censuses, the percentages haven't changed dramatically for hundreds of years. This map has a red line to show the Trianon/present-day border: http://commons.wikimedia.org/wiki/File:Trianon-Romanians.jpg
[17] Given such a dramatic decline (70% to 35%), it's tempting to imagine a horrific bloodbath. However, this sharp drop doesn't mean Turks killed all those Hungarians (although they certainly killed many), but rather that Hungarians fled for their lives. The refugees settled elsewhere, assimilating into Austrian or Polish society. By the time

the Turks left 150 years later, the descendants of the original Hungarians were settled somewhere else, speaking other languages, and had nothing to go home to.
[18] Yves de Daruvar, p. 27.
[19] László Marácz, p. 83.
[20] http://en.wikipedia.org/wiki/File:Hungarians_in_Hungary_(1890).png 1890 Ethnographic map of Hungary
[21] 1880 census: http://en.wikipedia.org/wiki/File:Hungary-ethnic_groups.jpg 1890 census: http://upload.wikimedia.org/wikipedia/commons/0/05/Magyars_(Hungarians)_in_Hungary,_census_1890.jpg 1910 census: http://en.wikipedia.org/wiki/File:Austria_Hungary_ethnic.svg English version: http://commons.wikimedia.org/wiki/File:Austria-Hungary_(ethnic).JPG
[22] http://en.wikipedia.org/wiki/File:RomaniaBorderHistoryAnnimation_1859-2010.gif illustrates not only how the border has changed since 1859, but you can clearly see the corridor that pierces into Romania's core that gives the Hungarian population there access to the rest of Hungary.
[23] Modified http://en.wikipedia.org/wiki/File:Northern_Transylvania_yellow.png. Another map that shows the Vienna Awards: http://en.wikipedia.org/wiki/File:Hungary_map.png
[24] Compare Romania's pre-WWI ethno-map http://en.wikipedia.org/wiki/File:Romanians_before_WW1.jpg with its 2002 version http://en.wikipedia.org/wiki/File:Romania_harta_etnica_2002.PNG. Conclusion: not much has changed. Hungarians are still in eastern Transylvania as they've always been, and Romanians continue to surround them.
[25] László Marácz, p. 3.
[26] Yves de Daruvar, p. 187.
[27] Miklós Molnár, *A Concise History of Hungary* (Cambridge: Cambridge University Press, 2001) p. 263.
[28] László Marácz, p. 134.

SLOVENIA

[1] Knight Ridder News Service, June 22, 1999.
[2] Nikhil Swaminathan, "Use It or Lose It: Why Language Changes over Time, *Scientific American*. October 10, 2007 http://www.scientificamerican.com/article.cfm?id=use-it-or-lose-it-why-lan
[3] http://www.upenn.edu/pennnews/current/research/030410.html Easy languages spread faster and wider.
[4] John H. McWhorter, "What happened to English?" *Diachronica* 19:2 (John Benjamins Publishing Company, 2002), pp. 217—272. In his paper, he argues that "Overall, a comparison with its sisters reveals English to be significantly less *overspecified* semantically and less *complexified* syntactically. Some scholars, such as Lass (1987:317—332) or Hawkins (1985), recognize that English departs considerably from the Germanic template, but leave aside the question as to why, with the implication that the issue was a matter of chance." He concludes that "the evidence strongly suggests that extensive second-language acquisition by Scandinavians from the eighth century onwards simplified English grammar to a considerable extent."
[5] Daniel Coyle, "That Which Does Not Kill Me Makes Me Stranger," *The New York Times*, February 5, 2006.
[6] Bernadette McDonald, *Tomaž Humar* (Arrow Books, 2007), Forward by Reinhold Messner, p. xiv.
[7] Neven Borak, *Ekonomski vidiki delovanja in razpada Jugoslavije* "How the Yugoslav Economy Worked and How It Collapsed", (Znanstveno in publicistično središče, Ljubljana, 2002), p. 208, 16, 19, respectively.
[8] Pavle Sicherl, "Time-distance as a dynamic measure of disparities in social and economic development," *Kyklos* 26 (1973), pp. 559-75.
[9] Neven Borak, p. 211.
[10] Neven Borak, p. 236.

[11] Laura Silber and Allan Little, *Yugoslavia: The Death of a Nation.* Penguin Books, 1997, p. 157.
[12] Warren Zimmermann, "The Last Ambassador, A Memoir of the Collapse of Yugoslavia," *Foreign Affairs,* March/April 1995, p. 12
[13] Go to http://francistapon.com and search for "Piran Bay" for my analysis on this debate.

Croatia

[1] Alexander Kiossev, "The Dark Intimacy," *Balkan as Metaphor: Between Globalization and Fragmentation* (The MIT Press, Cambridge, Massachusetts, 2005), pp. 179-80.
[2] For more about how nobody wants to be part of the Balkans: Elena Zamfirescu, "The Flight from the Balkans," *Südosteuropa* 44, no. 1 (1995), pp. 51-62.
[3] This raises the question, "What is a language?" It's another murky affair that is way off the topic of this book, but I'll propose a simple, idealistic answer, while admitting that it's not perfect. A language must have less than 90% in common with another widespread and established tongue. Hence, Bolognese and Neapolitan would be classified as a language since they're not strongly related to Italian. If Bolognese and Neapolitan have over 90% in common with each other, then whichever tongue has more speakers is called the language, while the other becomes a dialect of that language. When two current widespread languages overlap over 90% (like Danish and Norwegian), then they ought to create a neutral name for their common language (like *Scandinavian*) and become official dialects of that shared language. On a language continuum (like Dutch-German), there will be a point when one dialect has less than 90% in common with German, but might begin to have 90% in common with Dutch—at that point of the continuum, that dialect switches from one language to the other. If the tongue dips below 90%, the orphan tongue joins up with other orphans to create an intermediary language group. If a tongue has more than 90% in common with two languages, then it becomes a dialect under the more popular language. Of course, there will be a myriad of questions and exceptional situations like why should it be a 90% threshold? How does one determine when you've crossed the threshold? Who decides? What about the written language? Experts can debate these details, I'm simply proposing a framework. Taxonomy of languages is a quagmire, but at least this solution is less arbitrary and random than the current haphazard methodology.
[4] Charles E. Gribble, "Serbo-Croatian." *Microsoft® Encarta®* 2006 [DVD]. Redmond, WA: Microsoft Corporation, 2005.
[5] http://wals.info/feature/129 Brown, Cecil H.. 2008. Hand and Arm. In: Haspelmath, Martin & Dryer, Matthew S. & Gil, David & Comrie, Bernard (eds.) The World Atlas of Language Structures Online. Munich: Max Planck Digital Library, chapter 129.
[6] John R. Lampe, *Yugoslavia as History: Twice there was a country* (Cambridge University Press, 1997) p. 204.
[7] Jozo Tomasevich, War and Revolution in Yugoslavia, 1941-1945 (Stanford University Press, 2001), p. 748.
[8] A Yugoslav Jew was 10 times more likely to die than a Serb. The Croatian and Serbian Republics lost about the same total number of people (272,000), while Bosnia lost a bit more. However, since each republic had ethnic minorities, these numbers hide the fact that a higher percentage of Serbs died than Croatians. Determining WWII casualties is an inexact science, so I used objective estimates instead of those by ex-Yugoslavs who often mix their political bias in their calculations.
[9] Rebecca West, *Black Lamb and Grey Falcon: A Journey Through Yugoslavia* (1941; London: Penguin Books, 1982), pp. 28-35.

Serbia

[1] Rebecca West, p. 208.
[2] Maria Todorova, Imagining the Balkans (Oxford: Oxford University Press, 1997), p. 14.
[3] http://shar.es/mOSIT and http://www.usaid.gov/locations/europe_eurasia/countries/rs/index.html
[4] Although the Memorandum is not a direct call for nationalism and it warns about the danger of its rise, it does encourage its politicians to be more forceful about the national needs: "Serbian politicians since the Second World War, who are always on the

defensive and always worried more about what others think of them and their timid overtures at raising the issue of Serbia's status than about the objective facts affecting the future of the nation whom they lead."

[5] http://www.trepca.net/english/2006/serbian_memorandum_1986/serbia_memorandum_1986.html 1986 Memorandum

[6] Slovenija 1968 kam? [Slovenia 1968, where to?] (Trieste, 1968; reprinted Ljubljana, 1990), pp. 10-12. Cited in Economic Change and the National Question in Twentieth Century Europe, edited by Alice Teichova et al, (Cambridge, 2000), p. 328.

[7] Jozo Tomasevich, p. 743.

[8] In 1992, Croatia claimed that tens of thousands of its women were raped. Bosnia said about 55,000 Bosnian women were raped. A few "patriotic" women's groups claimed Serbians raped 120,000 women in both countries. The European community's Investigative Mission reported about 20,000 raped women; the UN estimated over 12,000 rapes. The top four groups, in order of rapes: (1) Bosnian, (2) unidentified, (3) Bosnian Serb, and (4) Croatian. Source: M. Cherif, M. Bassiouni, and Marcia McCormick, "Sexual Violence: An Invisible Weapon of War in the Former Yugoslavia," Occasional Papers no. 1 (International Human Rights Law Institute, De Paul University College of Law, 1996), pp. 10, 11, 44.

[9] For example, the Memorandum makes half-baked arguments like: "There have been many cases in history of a confederation turning into a federation, but there is not one single example of the opposite occurring." Huh? There's one great example right under their noses: in 1868 when the Austrian Empire split into a confederacy of Austria and Hungary. And within it was the autonomous Croatia-Slavonia, another quasi-member of a confederacy. Or the Roman Empire splitting into an east-west confederacy. The debate between federation and confederation is simply another way of saying centralization versus decentralization—it's an old debate. Moreover, like fashion, countries (and businesses) sway from one side to the other. Sometimes the move is subtle, but other times it's revolutionary. Bottom line: it goes both ways. Had the Memorandum had the opportunity to be carefully reviewed by the Academy's peers, it would have been a stronger document. The leaked version sounded like a babbling academic.

[10] Kosta Mihailovic and Vasilije Krestic, "Answers to Criticisms," *Memorandum* (Belgrade: Serbian Academy of Sciences and Arts, 1995) p. 68. Available at http://www.rastko.rs/istorija/iii/memorandum.pdf

[11] *Ibid.*

[12] In 1950, the JNA was 60% of Serb and Montenegrin. In the mid-1980s, 68% of the JNA were either Serbians or Montenegrins; Croatians made up only 14%. By the late 1980s, Serbs had 75%. Source: John R. Lampe, p. 337.

[13] Oswald has his own doppelganger theory. *Khrushchev Killed Kennedy* claims that the Soviets replaced Oswald with a look-alike marksman named Alec. It's not clear how the Russian-Oswald imposter managed to speak English just like the American-raised Oswald, without any accent in an age when it was hard for a Russian to adopt the perfect American accent. I suppose I should read the book, but I prefer to keep believing that Elvis killed Kennedy.

[14] Laura Silber and Allan Little, p. 337.

[15] *Ibid.*, p. 201.

[16] John R. Lampe, p. 318.

[17] David Binder, "Yugoslavia Seen Breaking Up Soon," The New York Times, November 28, 1990.

[18] http://www-personal.umich.edu/~bnyhan/nyhan-reifler.pdf Brendan Nyhan et al, "When Corrections Fail: The persistence of political misperceptions," University of Michigan.

[19] If you think the CIA is clever, read: Peter Bergen, "Why US can't find Osama bin Laden," CNN, October 19, 2010. http://edition.cnn.com/2010/OPINION/10/19/bergen.finding.bin.laden

Bosnia and Herzegovina

[1] Niall Ferguson, *The War of the World* (Penguin, 2007), pp. 626–631. Also see, Marjanovic, D., et al, "The peopling of modern Bosnia-Herzegovina: Y-chromosome haplogroups

in the three main ethnic groups," *Annals of Human Genetics*, issue 69, 2005, pp. 757–763. http://www.blackwell-synergy.com/doi/abs/10.1111/j.1529-8817.2005.00190.x

[2] Ivo Andrić, *The Bridge on the Drina*, translated by Lovett F. Edwards (Beograd: Dereta, 2009), pp. 264-5.

[3] Stevan K. Pavlowitch, "Out of Context — The Yugoslav Government in London, 1941-1945," Journal of Contemporary History 16, 1981, p. 89-118.

[4] *Jugoslavija, 1918-1988, Statistički godišnjak*. Belgrade, Savezni zavod za statistiku, 1989, pp. 160-66. Also, "The National Composition of Yugoslavia's Population, 1991," *Yugoslav Survey 1*. 1992, pp. 3-24.

[5] Yves de Daruvar, p. 198.

[6] Giancarlo Besetti, *The Lesson of This Century: With Two Talks on Freedom and the Democratic State* (London: Routledge, 1997), p. 53.

[7] Sabrina P. Ramet, *Balkan Babel: Politics, Culture, and Religion in Yugoslavia*. Boulder, Colorado, Westview Press, 1992, pp. 133-39, 147-57.

[8] Compare to the USA: two-thirds of Americans said that religion is important and nearly half said they went to church the previous week. All the data in this paragraph comes from Gallup's 2010 worldwide survey.

[9] Čedomil Mijatović, *Servia of the Servians*, 2nd edition. London, 1911, p. 38. In the original text, he writes "Servians," which means "Serbians" in today's lexicon. I changed it for simplicity.

[10] Serbian Democratic Forum, Serbia, National consultation with human rights organizations, Fruška Gora, Serbia, October 10, 2008

[11] John R. Lampe, p. 273.

[12] Ivo Andrić, p. 426.

[13] Laura Silber and Allan Little, p. 373.

[14] National consultation with artists, Priština, Kosovo, May 10, 2009.

[15] Ivo Andrić, p. 353.

[16] Coalition for RECOM, *Report about the Consultative Process on Instruments of Truth-Seeking About War Crimes and Other Serious Violations of Human Rights in Post-Yugoslav Countries: May 2006-June 2009*. Humanitarian Law Center, Publikum, printed in Belgrade, Serbia, August 2009.

[17] Local consultation with civil society, Prijedor, BiH, May 13, 2009.

Montenegro

[1] Carlo Gozzi, *Memorie Inutili*, ed. Domenico Bulferetti, volume I, in *Collezione di Classici Italiani*, ed. Gustavo Balsamo-Crivelli (Turin: Unione Tipografico-Editrice Torinese, 1928), pp. 71-72.

[2] http://economist.com/blogs/newsbook/2010/05/montenegrin_murder Death in Montenegro.

Albania

[1] http://www.guardian.co.uk/environment/2004/mar/27/internationalnews.pollution1 Also based on a 2010 worldwide Gallup poll.

[2] Tomislav Z. Longinović, "Vampires Like Us," *Balkan as Metaphor: Between Globalization and Fragmentation* (The MIT Press, Cambridge, Massachusetts, 2005), p. 42.

[3] A. Dumont, *Le Balkan et l'Adriatique: les bulgares et les albanais; l'administration en Turquie; la vie des campagnes; le panslavisme et l'hellénisme*, 2nd edition. Paris, 1874, pp. 304-5.

[4] http://www.nber.org/papers/w14131 Naci H. Mocan, an Economist at Louisiana State University, published a paper on vengeance at the National Bureau of Economic Research

Kosovo

[1] Krzysztof Rębała et al., "Y-STR variation among Slavs: evidence for the Slavic homeland in the middle Dnieper basin," *Journal of Human Genetics*, Volume 52, Number 5 (Springer Japan: ISSN 1434-5161 (Print) 1435-232X (Online)) May, 2007.

[2] Oscar Lao et al, "Correlation between Genetic and Geographic Structure in Europe," Current Biology, Volume 18, Issue 16, 1241-1248, August 26, 2008. http://cell.com/current-biology/retrieve/pii/S0960982208009561

[3] Predrag Simic, *The Kosovo and Metohija Problem and Regional Security in the Balkans* (Institute of International Politics and Economics, Belgrade, 1995) p. 1.
[4] Noel Malcolm, *Kosovo: A Short History* (HarperPerennial edition, New York, 1999) p. 41.
[5] Krzysztof Piątkowski, "On the Kosovo Myth," *Cultural Identity and Ethnicity in Central Europe* (Jasiellonian University, Cracow) Editor Czelau Robotyck, pp. 85-95.
[6] Noel Malcolm, p. 57.
[7] All three maps are viewable online under the "Balkans" article in Wikipedia. In case the maps are no longer available, here is a description. In 1877, Edward Stanford, an Englishman, produced a map that shows Albanians dominating everything south of Pristina (with a smattering of Turks). Like an inverted pyramid, Serbs fan out just north Pristina towards the towns of Mitrovica and Leskovac. In 1877, a French geographer was also doing an ethnic map of the Balkans. In Kosovo, you'll see that four ethnicities lived there: Albanians, Turks, Serbs, and Bulgarians. Western Kosovo has more Albanians and Turks than Slavs; however, Serbs are clearly a minority also in Eastern Kosovo (where Bulgarians and Turks made up the majority). Like a big "C", Albanians concentrate around Pristina. A corridor of Albanians stretch from Pristina all the way to Niš. It's also interesting to note that Greeks dominated population in what is now southern Albania and that Albanians were still a major presence in Northwestern Macedonia like it is today. Ernst Georg Ravenstein, an English-German geographer, drew an ethnographical map of "Turkey in Europe" in 1880. It clearly shows how Albanians are the majority in Kosovo. It also shows how Albanians took over most of southern Albania, and it split its modern-day southern tip with Greeks.
[8] If you omit the non-Kosovo areas from their census and count 10,000 Gypsies as Muslims, then 72 percent of Kosovars are Muslims in the 1890s. Source: *Detailbeschreibung des Sandžaks Plevlje und des Vilajets Kosovo* (Vienna, 1899), pp. 80-1
[9] Serbian census noted in L. Rushiti, *Rrethanat politiko-shoquerore në Kosovë 1912-1918* (Pristina, 1981), p. 71. Russian report in S. Kolea, "Les Massacres serbes," AOBDIA, *2nd ser., no. 6* (Nov 25, 1918), p. 49.
[10] M. Larnaude, "Un village de colonisation en Serbie du sud," *Annales de geographie*, vol 39 (1930), pp. 320-4.
[11] Djordje Krstić, *Kolonizacija u Južnoj Srbiji* (Sarajevo, 1928), p. 81.
[12] M. Vučković and G. Nikolić, *Stanovništvo Kosova u razdoblju od 1918 do 1991* (Munich, 1996), p. 79.
[13] A. Baldacci, Studi Speciali Albanesi, vol. 1 (Rome, 1932-7), p. 273. N. Popp, "Minoritatea Româno-Albaneză din Jugoslavia," *Buletinul Societății Regale Române de Geografie*, vol. 50 (1931), p. 365.
[14] The rest was 1.3% Muslim and 3.6% Montenegrin. Source: *The 1918-1988, Statistical Summary of Yugoslavia* published in 1991 by government in Belgrade), p. 207. In 1981, Kosovo was 13.3% Serbian, 77.5% Albanian, 3.7% Muslim, 0.2% Montenegrin. J. Reuter, *Die Albaner in Jugoslwien* (Munich, 1982), pp. 54-70.
[15] "Albanians had made up nearly two-thirds of the province's population for the past 100 years, but jumped to 78 percent in 1981 and 90 percent in 1991." John R. Lampe, p. 332.
[16] M. Vučković and G. Nikolić, *Stanovništvo Kosova u razdoblju od 1918 do 1991* (Munich, 1996), p. 108. Albanians boycotted the 1991 census, but considering Albanians were about 90% of Kosovo in 1999, it's realistic to assume that they were over 80% in 1991.
[17] According to Yugoslavia's official government statistics, in 1961 two-thirds of Kosovo inhabitants were Albanians and 23.5% were Serbians. By 1981, it was 77.5% Albanian, 13.3% Serbian. By 1991, it was 80/20 and by 2001 it was 90/10. *Jugoslavija, 1918-1988, Statistički godišnjak.* Belgrade, Savezni zavod za statistiku, 1989, pp. 160-66. Also, "The National Composition of Yugoslavia's Population, 1991," *Yugoslav Survey 1.* 1992, pp. 3-24.
[18] The numbers changed to 29 in Kosovo, 18.5 in Macedonia, about 15.5 in Montenegro and Bosnia, and roughly 13 in the remaining republics.
[19] The source of the socio-economic indicators from 1953 to 1988 is Dijana Pleština, *Regional Development in Communist Yugoslavia: Success, Failure, and Consequences* (Boulder, CO, Westview Press, 1992) p. 1980-81.

[20] http://www.prb.org/Datafinder/Geography/Summary.aspx?region=214®ion_type=2 As of 2011, Kosovo still hasn't taken an official census. Current unofficial estimates for its fertility rate range from 2.5 to 2.9. Doubling Serbia's 1.39 rate gives us 2.78, which is in the middle of the estimates. Also consider birthrate estimates: Niger 51, Kosovo 21, Albania 15, Serbia 12. This also implies Kosovars produce almost twice as many babies as the depopulating Serbians.
[21] M. Roux, *Les Albanais en Yougoslavie: minorité nationale, territoire et développement* (Paris, 1992), pp. 151-3.
[22] Lidija Andolšek, ed. by Paul Sachdev, "Yugoslavia," *International Handbook on Abortion* (Greenwood Press, New York, 1988), pp. 495-504. Rada Drezgic, "The politics of abortion and contraception," *Sociologija*, 46(2), 2004, pp. 97-104. "Health Statistical Yearbook of Republic of Serbia 2008," Institute of Public Health of Serbia, 2009, http://www.batut.org.rs/uploads/pub2008.pdf. Good summary: http://www.johnstonsarchive.net/policy/abortion/ab-serbia.html
[23] http://www.johnstonsarchive.net/policy/abortion/mapyugoabrate.html Map of abortions percentages in ex-Yugoslavia.
[24] H. Islami, "Demografski problemi Kosova I njihovo tumačenje," in S. Gaber and T. Kuzmanić, eds., *Zbornik Kosovo — Srbija — Jugoslavia* (Ljubljana, 1989), pp. 39-66.
[25] R. Petrović and M. Blagojević, *The Migration of Serbs and Montenegrins from Kosovo and Metohija: Results of the Survey Conducted in 1985-1986* (Belgrade, 1992), pp. 110 and 179. The Serbian Academy of Sciences is the same outfit that produced the 1986 Memorandum, which is filled with misleading statements, which calls into question their 500-person survey.
[26] To learn more about post-WWII migrations read Ruža Petrović, *Migracije u Jugoslaviji i etnički aspekt* (Migration in Yugoslavia and the ethnic aspect). Belgrade, Istraživački izdavački centar, 1987. Also, Silva Meznarić, *Osvajanje prostora — prekrivanje vremena, migracije umjesto razvoja* (Conquering space and obscuring time: Migration in place of development). Zagreb: Socialoško društvo Hrvatske, 1991.
[27] John R. Lampe, p. 332.
[28] Neven Borak, Table 71, p. 258. Kosovo got 84 billion dinars, while Bosnia (45.5 billion), Montenegro (17 billion), and Macedonia (21 billion) got much less. On a per capita basis, that translates into these respective amounts: 42, 11, 28, and 10.
[29] Neven Borak, Table 67, p. 256. In 1988. Slovenia was producing 20% of Yugoslavia's output compared to Bosnia-Herzegovina 12%, Croatia 25%, Montenegro 2%, Kosovo 1.1%, Serbia 23%, Vojvodina 9.5% (Greater Serbia was about 33%).
[30] Neven Borak, p. 212. Unemployment 1952 Yugoslavia 0.4%, 1990 7.8%. In 1990, Kosovo 12.6%, Serbia 8.3%, Croatia 4.6%, Slovenia 2.2%
[31] Neven Borak, p. 212. GDP per capita in thousands of dinars based on the worth of the dinar in 1972, 1952 Kosovo 1.6, Serbia 3.4, Croatia 4.1, Slovenia 6.1. And then in 1990, Kosovo 3.35, Serbia 16.1, Croatia 19.4, Slovenia 30.8.
[32] Dijana Pleština, *Regional Development in Communist Yugoslavia: Success, Failure, and Consequences*. Boulder, CO, Westview Press, 1992, p. 1980-81.
[33] http://video.google.com/videoplay?docid=6312864596613878002 "Death of Yugoslavia," BBC. Watch the 15th minute of Part 1.
[34] Stjepan Gabriel Meštrović, *Genocide After Emotion: The Postemotional Balkan War* (Routledge, 1996) p. 95.
[35] Kosta Mihailovic and Vasilije Krestic, p. 11. Available at http://www.rastko.rs/istorija/iii/memorandum.pdf
[36] Edit Petrović, ed. Joel Martin Halpern, David A. Kideckel, "Ethnonationalism and the Dissolution of Yugoslavia," *Neighbors at War: anthropological perspectives on Yugoslav ethnicity, culture, and history* (Penn State Press, 2000) p. 170.
[37] Vesna Kesić, "Muslim Women, Croatian Women, Serbian Women, Albanian Women. . ." *Balkan as Metaphor: Between Globalization and Fragmentation* (The MIT Press, Cambridge, Massachusetts, 2005), p. 315.
[38] Naser Lajqi, Syri I Visionit Association, Kosovo, National consultation with students, Kosovo, Priština, April 15, 2009.

Macedonia

[1] Ivaylo Ditchev, "The Eros of Identity," *Balkan as Metaphor: Between Globalization and Fragmentation* (The MIT Press, Cambridge, Massachusetts, 2005), p. 237-8.
[2] Anthony D. Smith, *Nationalism and Modernism* (London: Routledge, 1998), p. 120.
[3] http://www.1911encyclopedia.org/Macedonia "Macedonia," *1911 Encyclopædia.* I've changed "Servians" to "Serbians" for modern clarity.

Greece

[1] Ivaylo Ditchev, p. 238.

Bulgaria

[1] Alexandre-Maurice Blanc de Lanautte, comte d'Hauterive, "Journal inedit d'un voyage: de Constantinople à Jassi, capital de la Moldavie dans l'hiver de 1785." In *Mémoire sur l'état ancient et actuel de la Moldavie: Présenté à S. A. S. le prince Alexandre Ypsilanti, Hospodar réganant, en 1787, par le comte d'Hauterive* (Bucharest: L'Institut d'arts graphiques Carol Göbl, 1902), pp. 311-13.
[2] Elizabeth Craven, *A Journey Through the Crimea to Constantinople: In a Series of Letters from the Right Honourable Elizabeth Lady Craven, to His Serene Highness the Margrave of Brandebourg, Anspach, and Bareith, Written in the Year MDCCLXXXVI* (Dublin, 1789; rpt. New York: Arno Press and New York Times, 1970), pp. 508-9. The original quote had "risques" not "risks." I changed it for modern clarity.
[3] Nadezhda Hristova, *Bulgaria: Geography, History, Culture* (Veliko Turnovo University Press, 2008) p. 56.
[4] Bochev, S. Фондация "Българска наука и ултура""Capitalism in Bulgaria," (1998) p. 253
[5] Genov, J. "Why Do We Manage So Little?" Хеликон (Sofia, 2004), p. 36, 166, 178.
[6] M. Semov, *The Virtues of the Bulgarian Person.* Center for Research of the Bulgarians, Bulgarian Foundation, (TANGRA TanNakRa: Sofia 1999), p. 701, 703, 704.
[7] Chavdarova, T., *The Informal Economics.* (ЛИК: Sofia, 2001), p. 35.
[8] http://siteresources.worldbank.org/ECAEXT/Resources/258598-1303157205578/RER23_April18_Rom.pdf Eurostat, World Bank staff estimates
[9] Ivaylo Ditchev, p. 235.
[10] Adrian Cioroianu, "The Impossible Escape: Romanians and the Balkans," *Balkan as Metaphor: Between Globalization and Fragmentation* (The MIT Press, Cambridge, Massachusetts, 2005), p. 219.
[11] http://appsso.eurostat.ec.europa.eu/nui/show.do?dataset=proj_10c2150p&lang=en Browse under "Statistics" and "Population" if this link is broken.
[12] http://www.stat.ee/29926 or find them at EuroStat: http://epp.eurostat.ec.europa.eu
[13] http://www.un.org/esa/population/publications/longrange2/WorldPop2300final.pdf United Nations Department of Economic and Social Affairs/Population Division, "World Population to 2300," (New York, 2004) p. 10.
[14] http://nature.com/nature/journal/v460/n7256/full/nature08230.html Mikko Myrskyla et al. from the University of Pennsylvania, *Nature,* 2009.
[15] "Fertility and living standards: the rich are different," *The Economist,* October 31, 2009, p. 32.
[16] Alexandru George, "Cei care n-au muncit, dar ne-au ţinut," Adevărul literar şi artistic, December 7, 1999.

Romania

[1] Adrian Cioroianu, p. 225.
[2] Nicolae Iorga, *Etudes Roumaines: Influences étrangères sur lea nation roumaine. Leçons faites à la Sorbonne* (Paris: Librairie universitaire, 1922), p. 10.
[3] Adrian Cioroianu, p. 210.
[4] *Ibid.,* p. 214.
[5] United Nations Development Programme, (UNDP), Human Development Report 2010 (New York: Palgrave Macmillan, November 2010) p. 75.
[6] Nicolas Spulber, "The Danube—Black Sea Canal and the Russian Control over the Danube," *Economic Geography,* vol. 30, no.3 (July 1954), pp. 236-245.
[7] Adrian Cioroianu, p. 209.

Moldova

[1] http://www.who.int/substance_abuse/publications/global_alcohol_report World Health Organization, *Global Status Report on Alcohol and Health* (Switzerland: 2011), p. 275.

Ukraine

[1] http://www.who.int/substance_abuse/publications/global_alcohol_report World Health Organization, Global Status Report on Alcohol and Health (Switzerland: 2011), p. 275.
[2] Elizabeth Craven, p. 184.
[3] Louis-Philippe, comte de Ségur, *Mémoires, souvenirs, et anecdotes, par le comte de Ségur,* vol. II, in *Bibliothèques des mémoires: relative à l'histoire de França: pendant le 18e siècle, vol. XX, ed. M. Fs. Barrière* (Paris: Librairie de Firmin Didot Frères, 1859), p. 87.
[4] http://www.gallup.com/poll/140963/Global-Economic-Crisis-Personal-Countries-Far-Wide See spreadsheet.
[5] http://pewresearch.org/pubs/1918/enthusiasm-for-democracy-in-egypt-tunisia-fragile-eastern-europe-experience-shows James Bell, "Will Enthusiasm for Democracy Endure in Egypt and Elsewhere?" Pew Research Center, March 8, 2011.
[6] Joseph Marshall, *Travels Through Germany, Russia, and Poland in the Years 1769 and 1770* (London, 1772; rpt. New York: Arno Press and New York Times, 1971), p. 179. The spelling of "travellers" is how he wrote it.

Russia

[1] Giacomo Casanova, *History of My Life,* trans. Willard Trask, Vol. 10 (London: Longman, 1971), pp. 110-12.
[2] Ibid., pp. 112-13.
[3] Archie Brown, *The Rise and Fall of Communism,* Ecco, 2010, pp. 736.
[4] http://www.levada.ru/press/2011071904.html 37% smoking statistic.
[5] Niall Ferguson, "The Year the World Really Changed," *Newsweek,* November 16, 2009, p. 34.
[6] John Keegan, p. 182-183.
[7] http://en.wikipedia.org/wiki/Military_production_during_World_War_II According to Paul Kennedy's *The Rise and Fall of Great Powers,* a breakdown of total global war-making potential in 1937 was United States 41.7%, Germany 14.4%, USSR 14.0%, UK 10.2%, France 4.2%, and Japan 3.5%.
[8] John Keegan, p. 185.
[9] http://www.levada.ru/press/2011061604.html retrieved 7/7/11.
[10] Poland loss over 16% of its pre-1939 population—the most of any nation. Belarus suffered the most (33%), but since it was part of the USSR, the Belarus statistic gets put in the USSR totals of 14%, which is the second biggest percentage loss after Poland. Recent research indicates that the USSR may have lost up to 16% of its population (26.6 million), but that would still put it slightly below Poland's percentage loss. Obviously in gross numbers the Soviets lost the most, with China being in second place.
[11] Sonya K. Huffman and Marian Rizov, "The Rise of Obesity in Transition Economies: Theory and Evidence from the Russian Longitudinal Monitoring Survey" *Centre for Institutions and Economic Performance* (Katholieke Universiteit Leuven, 2007), p. 4.
[12] http://pewglobal.org/files/2011/07/Pew-Global-Attitudes-Balance-of-Power-US-Image-2011-07-13.pdf p. 65. Global feelings for Russian/American people or the country of Russia/USA are more favorable.
[13] Lewis H. Siegelbaum, *Cars for Comrades: The Life of the Soviet Automobile* (Cornell University Press, 2008) pp. 309.
[14] http://www.theatlantic.com/international/archive/2011/06/mikhail-gorbachev-the-west-could-have-saved-the-russian-economy/240466/ Gorbachev interview.
[15] http://pewglobal.org/2009/11/02/end-of-communism-cheered-but-now-with-more-reservations "The Pulse of Europe 2009: 20 Years After the Fall of the Berlin Wall End of Communism Cheered but Now with More Reservations," November 2, 2009.
[16] Branko Milanovic, "Explaining the Increase in Inequality During the Transition," *Mimeo,* World Bank Policy Research Department (Washington: World Bank, 1999).
[17] http://www.asianoffbeat.com/default.asp?Display=1364 To find dozens of articles on the Internet about this, search for terms "China Beijing smile 2008 Olympics."

[18] http://pewresearch.org/pubs/1918/enthusiasm-for-democracy-in-egypt-tunisia-fragile-eastern-europe-experience-shows and http://pewresearch.org/pubs/1467/post-communist-millennial-generation-more-positive-democracy-free-market
[19] http://pewresearch.org/pubs/1554/hungary-economic-discontent-democracy-communism Richard Wike, "Hungary Dissatisfied with Democracy, but Not its Ideals," Pew Global Attitudes Project. April 7, 2010
[20] http://www.levada.ru/press/2011062304.html June 26, 2011 survey.
[21] http://www.russianembassy.org.za/bilateral/text/goRussia.html Dmitry Medvedev's speech.
[22] http://www.gallup.com/poll/126116/Canada-Places-First-Image-Contest-Iran-Last.aspx Don't confuse this with the unpopularity of Russia's and America's leadership. The pattern on both sides is: we like a country, its people, but not its politicians.
[23] Source: http://www.gfmag.com/tools/global-database/economic-data/10403-total-debt-to-gdp.html
[24] http://www.levada.ru/press/2011062101.html (in Russian).
[25] http://www.levada.ru/press/2011061601.html (in Russian).

CONCLUSION

[1] As explained in the Moldova chapter, Andorra is in the top 10, but we'll ignore it because its results get skewed from all the French/Spanish tourists who visit it.
[2] http://www.gallup.com/poll/148064/Europeans-Happiness-Doesn-Necessarily-Fade-Age.aspx When a source isn't mentioned in this list, it's a Gallup survey.
[3] Yves de Daruvar, p. 185.
[4] Nadezhda Hristova, p. 9.
[5] "Many forms of Government have been tried and will be tried in this world of sin and woe. No one pretends that democracy is perfect or all-wise. Indeed, it has been said that democracy is the worst form of government except all those other forms that have been tried from time to time." — Winston Churchill
[6] Fareed Zakaria, "The Future of America Power: How America Can Survive the Rise of the Rest," *Foreign Affairs*, May/June 2008.
[7] *Transatlantic Trends: Immigration*, German Marshall Fund et al 2009.

If you're looking for an index, find it at http://francistapon.com/THEindex.